DATE DUE

			PRINTED IN U.S.A.

CLASSICAL AND MEDIEVAL LITERATURE CRITICISM

Guide to Gale Literary Criticism Series

For criticism on	Consult these Gale series
Authors now living or who died after December 31, 1959	*CONTEMPORARY LITERARY CRITICISM (CLC)*
Authors who died between 1900 and 1959	*TWENTIETH-CENTURY LITERARY CRITICISM (TCLC)*
Authors who died between 1800 and 1899	*NINETEENTH-CENTURY LITERATURE CRITICISM (NCLC)*
Authors who died between 1400 and 1799	*LITERATURE CRITICISM FROM 1400 TO 1800 (LC)* *SHAKESPEAREAN CRITICISM (SC)*
Authors who died before 1400	*CLASSICAL AND MEDIEVAL LITERATURE CRITICISM (CMLC)*
Black writers of the past two hundred years	*BLACK LITERATURE CRITICISM (BLC)*
Authors of books for children and young adults	*CHILDREN'S LITERATURE REVIEW (CLR)*
Dramatists	*DRAMA CRITICISM (DC)*
Hispanic writers of the late nineteenth and twentieth centuries	*HISPANIC LITERATURE CRITICISM (HLC)*
Native North American writers and orators of the eighteenth, nineteenth, and twentieth centuries	*NATIVE NORTH AMERICAN LITERATURE (NNAL)*
Poets	*POETRY CRITICISM (PC)*
Short story writers	*SHORT STORY CRITICISM (SSC)*
Major authors from the Renaissance to the present	*WORLD LITERATURE CRITICISM, 1500 TO THE PRESENT (WLC)*

ISSN 0896-0011

Volume 24

CLASSICAL AND MEDIEVAL LITERATURE CRITICISM

Excerpts from Criticism of the Works of World
Authors from Classical Antiquity through the
Fourteenth Century, from the First Appraisals
to Current Evaluations

Daniel G. Marowski
Editor

Amy K. Crook
Associate Editor

GALE

DETROIT • NEW YORK • TORONTO • LONDON

STAFF

Daniel G. Marowski, *Editor*
Amy K. Crook, Michelle Lee, *Associate Editors*
Dana Barnes, Jelena Krstovic, *Contributing Editors*
Ira Mark Milne, *Assistant Editor*
Aarti D. Stephens, *Managing Editor*

Susan M. Trosky, *Permissions Manager*
Kimberly F. Smilay, *Permissions Specialist*
Sarah Chesney, Steve Cusack, Kelly A. Quin, *Permissions Associates*

Victoria B. Cariappa, *Research Manager*
Julia C. Daniel, Tamara C. Nott,
Tracie A. Richardson, Norma Sawaya, Cheryl L. Warnock, *Research Associates*

Mary Beth Trimper, *Production Director*
Deborah Milliken, *Production Assistant*

Pamela A. Reed, *Photography Coordinator*
Randy Bassett, *Image Database Supervisor*
Robert Duncan, Michael Logusz, *Imaging Specialists*
Gary Leach, *Macintosh Artist*

This book is printed on acid-free paper that meets the minimum requirements of American National Standard for Information Sciences—Permanence Paper for Printed Library Materials, ANSI Z39.48-1984.

Library of Congress Catalog Card Number 88-658021
ISBN 0-7876-1968-X
ISSN 0896-0011
Printed in the United States of America

10 9 8 7 6 5 4 3 2 1

Contents

Preface vii

Acknowledgments xi

Preface

Since its inception in 1988, *Classical and Medieval Literature Criticism* has been a valuable resource for students and librarians seeking critical commentary on the writers and works of these periods in world history. Major reviewing sources have assessed *CMLC* as "useful" and "extremely convenient," noting that it "adds to our understanding of the rich legacy left by the ancient period and the Middle Ages," and praising its "general excellence in the presentation of an inherently interesting subject." No other single reference source has surveyed the critical reaction to classical and medieval literature as thoroughly as *CMLC*.

Scope of the Series

CMLC is designed to serve as an introduction for students and advanced readers of the works and authors of antiquity through the fourteenth century. The great poets, prose writers, dramatists, and philosophers of this period form the basis of most humanities curricula, so that virtually every student will encounter many of these works during the course of a high school and college education. By organizing and reprinting an enormous amount of commentary written on classical and medieval authors and works, *CMLC* helps students develop valuable insight into literary history, promotes a better understanding of the texts, and sparks ideas for papers and assignments. Each entry in *CMLC* presents a comprehensive survey of an author's career, an individual work of literature, or a literary topic, and provides the user with a multiplicity of interpretations and assessments. Such variety allows students to pursue their own interests; furthermore, it fosters an awareness that literature is dynamic and responsive to many different opinions.

CMLC continues the survey of criticism of world literature begun by Gale's *Contemporary Literary Criticism (CLC)*, *Twentieth-Century Literary Criticism (TCLC)*, *Nineteenth-Century Literature Criticism (NCLC)*, *Literature Criticism from 1400 to 1800 (LC)*, and *Shakespearean Criticism (SC)*. For additional information about these and Gale's other criticism series, users should consult the Guide to Gale Literary Criticism Series preceding the title page in this volume.

Coverage

Each volume of *CMLC* is carefully compiled to present:

- criticism of authors and works which represent a variety of genres, time periods, and nationalities

- both major and lesser-known writers and works of the period (such as non-Western authors and literature, increasingly read by today's students)

- 4-6 authors or works per volume

- individual entries that survey the critical response to each author, work, or topic, including early criticism, later criticism (to represent any rise or decline in the author's reputation), and current retrospective analyses. The length of each author or work entry also indicates relative importance, reflecting the amount of critical attention the author, work, or topic has received from critics writing in English, and from foreign criticism in translation.

An author may appear more than once in the series if his or her writings have been the subject of a substantial amount of criticism; in these instances, specific works or groups of works by the author will be covered in separate entries. For example, Homer will be represented by three entries, one devoted to the *Iliad,* one to the *Odyssey,* and one to the Homeric Hymns.

Starting with Volume 10, *CMLC* will also occasionally include entries devoted to literary topics. For example, *CMLC-*10 focuses on Arthurian Legend and includes general criticism on that subject as well as individual entries on writers or works central to that topic—Chrétien de Troyes, Gottfried von Strassburg, Layamon, and the Alliterative *Morte Arthure.*

Organization of the Book

An author entry consists of the following elements: author heading, biographical and critical introduction, principal English translations or editions, excerpts of criticism (each preceded by a bibliographic citation and an annotation), and a bibliography of further reading.

- The **Author Heading** consists of the author's most commonly used name, followed by birth and death dates. If the entry is devoted to a work, the heading will consist of the most common form of the title in English translation (if applicable), and the original date of composition. Located at the beginning of the introduction are any name or title variations.

- A **Portrait** of the author is included when available. Many entries also feature illustrations of materials pertinent to the author or work, including manuscript pages, book illustrations, and representations of people, places, and events important to a study of the author or work.

- The **Biographical and Critical Introduction** contains background information that concisely introduces the reader to the author, work, or topic.

- The list of **Principal Works** and **English Translations** or **Editions** is chronological by date of first publication and is included as an aid to the student seeking translated versions or editions of these works for study. The list will focus primarily on twentieth-century translations, selecting those works most commonly considered the best by critics.

- **Criticism** is arranged chronologically in each entry to provide a useful perspective on changes in critical evaluation over the years. All titles by the author featured in the critical entry are printed in boldface type to enable the user to ascertain without difficulty the works being discussed. Also for purposes of easier identification, the critic's name and the publication date of the essay are given at the beginning of each piece of criticism. Anonymous criticism is preceded by the title of the journal in which it appeared. Publication information (such as publisher names and book prices) and parenthetical numerical references (such as footnotes or page and line references to specific editions of works) have been deleted at the editors' discretion to provide smoother reading of the text. Many critical entries in *CMLC* also contain translations to aid the users. Footnotes that appear with previously published pieces of criticism are reprinted at the end of each essay or excerpt. In the case of excerpted criticism, only those footnotes that pertain to the excerpted text are included.

- A complete **Bibliographic Citation** provides original publication information for each piece of criticism.

- Critical excerpts are also prefaced by **Annotations** providing the reader with information about both the critic and the criticism, the scope of the excerpt, the growth of critical controversy, or changes in critical trends regarding an author or work. In some cases, these notes include cross-references to excerpts by critics who discuss each other's commentary. Dates in parentheses within the annotation refer to a book publication date when they follow a book title, and to an essay date when they follow a critic's name.

- An annotated bibliography of **Further Reading** appears at the end of each entry and lists additional secondary sources on the author or work. In some cases it includes essays for which the editors could not obtain reprint rights.

When applicable, the Further Reading is followed by references to additional entries on the author in other literary reference series published by Gale.

Topic Entries are subdivided into several thematic rubrics in which criticism appears in order of descending scope.

Cumulative Indexes

Each volume of *CMLC* includes a cumulative **author index** listing all authors who have appeared in Gale's Literary Criticism Series, along with cross references to such biographical series as *Contemporary Authors* and *Dictionary of Literary Biography*. For readers' convenience, a complete list of Gale titles included appears on the page prior to the author index. Useful for locating an author within the various series, this index is particularly valuable for those authors who are identified with a certain period but who, because of their death date, are placed in another, or for those authors whose careers span two periods. For example, Geoffrey Chaucer, who is usually considered a medieval author, is found in *Literature Criticism from 1400 to 1800* because he died after 1399.

Beginning with the tenth volume, *CMLC* includes a cumulative index listing all topic entries that have appeared in the Gale Literary Criticism Series *Classical and Medieval Literature Criticism, Contemporary Literary Criticism, Literature Criticism from 1400 to 1800, Nineteenth-Century Literature Criticism,* and *Twentieth-Century Literary Criticism.*

Beginning with the second volume, *CMLC* also includes a cumulative nationality index. Authors and/or works are grouped by nationality, and the volume in which criticism on them may be found is indicated.

Title Index

Each volume of *CMLC* also includes an index listing the titles of all literary works discussed in the series. Foreign language titles that have been translated are followed by the titles of the translations—for example, *Slovo o polku Igorove (The Song of Igor's Campaign)*. Page numbers following these translated titles refer to all pages on which any form of the title, either foreign language or translated, appears. Titles of novels, dramas, nonfiction books, and poetry, short story, or essay collections are printed in italics, while those of all individual poems, short stories, and essays are printed in roman type within quotation marks. In cases where the same title is used by different authors, the author's name or surname is given in parentheses after the title, e.g. *Collected Poems* (Horace) and *Collected Poems* (Sappho).

Critic Index

An index to critics, which cumulates with the second volume, is another useful feature of *CMLC*. Under each critic's name are listed the authors and/or works on whom the critic has written and the volume and page number where criticism may be found.

A Note to the Reader

When writing papers, students who quote directly from any volume in the Literary Criticism Series may use the following general forms to footnote reprinted criticism. The first example pertains to material drawn from a periodical, the second to material reprinted from books.

Rollo May, "The Therapist and the Journey into Hell," *Michigan Quarterly Review*, XXV, No. 4 (Fall 1986), 629-41; excerpted and reprinted in *Classical and Medieval Literature Criticism*, Vol. 3, ed. Jelena O. Krstovic (Detroit: Gale Research, 1989), pp. 154-58.

Dana Ferrin Sutton, *Self and Society in Aristophanes* (University of Press of America, 1980); excerpted and reprinted in *Classical and Medieval Literature Criticism,* Vol. 4, ed. Jelena O. Krstovic (Detroit: Gale Research, 1990), pp. 162-69.

Suggestions Are Welcome

Readers who wish to make suggestions for future volumes, or who have other comments regarding the series, are cordially invited to write or call the editors (1-800-347-GALE; Fax: 313-961-6815).

Acknowledgments

The editors wish to thank the copyright holders of the excerpted criticism included in this volume and the permissions managers of many book and magazine publishing companies for assisting us in securing reproduction rights. We are also grateful to the staffs of the Detroit Public Library, the Library of Congress, the University of Detroit Mercy Library, Wayne State University Purdy/Kresge Library Complex, and the University of Michigan Libraries for making their resources available to us. Following is a list of the copyright holders who have granted us permission to reproduce material in this volume of *CMLC*. Every effort has been made to trace copyright, but if omissions have been made, please let us know.

COPYRIGHTED EXCERPTS IN *CMLC*, VOLUME 24, WERE REPRODUCED FROM THE FOLLOWING PERIODICALS:

American Journal of Philology, v. 115, Fall, 1995. Reproduced by permission of The Johns Hopkins University Press.—*Américas*, v. 18, October, 1966. Copyright © 1966 Américas. Reprinted by permission of Américas, a bimonthly magazine published by the General Secretariat of the Organization of American States in English and Spanish.—*Analecta Bollandiana: Revue Critique D'Hagiographie,* v. 103, 1985. Reproduced by permission.—*Children's Literature,* v. 12, 1982. Reproduced by permission.—*Children's Literature Association Quarterly,* v. 9, Summer, 1984. Reproduced by permission.—*Childrens Literature in Education,* v. 14, Spring, 1983 for "Aesop and Grimm: Contrast in Ethical Codes and Contemporary Values" by P. Gila Reinstein. Reprinted by permission of the Plenum Publishing Corporation and the author.—*China Reconstructs,* v. 4, July/ August, 1953.—*The Classical Journal,* v. 81, October-November, 1985. Reproduced by permission.—*Classical Quarterly,* v. 24, 1992. © Oxford University Press 1992. Reproduced by permission.—*English Literary History,* v. 43, Spring, 1976. Copyright © 1976 by The Johns Hopkins University Press. All rights reserved. Reproduced by permission.—*Greece & Rome,* v. XXXI, October, 1984. Reproduced by permission of Oxford University Press.—*Harvard Journal of Asiatic Studies,* v. 41, 1981 for "The Poet as Jurist: Po Chü-i and a Case of Conjugal Homicide" by Benjamin E. Wallacker. Reproduced by permission of the author.—*Hispania,* v. XLVII, December, 1964. Reproduced by permission.—*Tamkang Review,* v. XV, Autumn 1984 - Summer 1985. Reproduced by permission.

COPYRIGHTED EXCERPTS IN *CMLC*, VOLUME 24, WERE REPRODUCED FROM THE FOLLOWING BOOKS:

Aili, Hans. From *The Editing of Theological and Philosophical Texts from the Middle Ages.* Edited by Monika Asztalos. Almqvist & Wiksell International, 1984. © 1986 Monika Asztalos. Reproduced by permission.—Anderson, William S. From *Barbarian Play: Plautus' Roman Comedy.* University of Toronto Press, 1993. © University of Toronto Press Incorporated 1993. Reproduced by permission.—Blackham, H. J. From an introduction to *The Fable as Literature.* The Athlone Press, 1985. Copyright © 1985 H. J. Blackburn. Reproduced by permission.—Blount, Margaret. From *Animal Land: The Creatures of Children's Fiction.* William Morrow & Company, Inc., 1975. Copyright © 1974 by Margaret Ingle-Finch. All rights reserved. Reproduced by permission.—Cumming, William Patterson. From the introduction to *The Revelations of Saint*

Aesop

c. 620 B.C.-c. 564 B.C.

(Also transliterated as Aesopus, Hesopus, Esope, and Esop) Greek fabulist.

INTRODUCTION

Aesop is credited with developing the folklore fable during the ancient Greek period into a means of indirectly conveying a political message. Thereafter, Greek, Roman, and European fables have generally been attributed to Aesop, although some extant fables may be traced to sources predating Aesop in Sumer, Assyria, Babylonia, and Egypt; some to Indian folklore and literature; and some to such lesser-known writers after Aesop as Babrius, Phaedrus, Poggio Bracciolini, and Jean de la Fontaine. The collection of Aesopic fables is the nearest source for such common expressions as "sour grapes," "familiarity breeds contempt, and "a dog in a manger" as well as for references to characters in such fables as "The Hare and the Tortoise" and "The Boy Who Cried Wolf." The typical Aesopic fable, a short allegorical tale using animals to portray a moral, has come to define the genre of fable in popular thinking. Today, the Aesopic fable, which was developed in antiquity to teach political wisdom to adults, is commonly used to instruct children in practical wisdom and to entertain them with its fantasy world of talking animals.

Biographical Information

Aesop may have been born in Thrace to the northeast of Greece around 620 B.C., according to what the historian Herodotus says about him. Herodotus describes Aesop as a slave from Thrace who served under Iadmon of Samos at the same time as the female Thracian slave Rhodopis. Herodotus also mentions that Rhodopis was later ransomed from slavery in Egypt by the brother of the famous poetess Sappho, who was born around 612 B.C. A comparison of the possible ages of Aesop, Rhodopis, Sappho, and Sappho's brother suggests the date of birth for Aesop as 620 B.C. According to Aristotle in the *Constitution of the Samians*, Aesop served as the slave of a certain Xanthus, then served as the slave of a certain Iadmon (who later freed him,) and then went on to gain a strong reputation among the Samians by telling them the fable of "The Fox and the Hedgehog" as a defense for a politician on trial for embezzlement. In this fable, a hedgehog's offer to remove blood-sucking ticks from a fox is refused on the grounds that other unsated ticks will come to draw more blood. A controversial and romantic *Life of Aesop* written in the

first century A.D. relates that Aesop was then sent by the Samians to the court of Croesus in Sardis in order to persuade Croesus not to subjugate the Samian people. Croesus was so impressed with Aesop that he put aside his plans of conquest for Samos and gave Aesop a position at his court, which gave Aesop the leisure to write out his fables. Then, as part of Aesop's continuing service to Croesus, according to the biographer and essayist Plutarch, Aesop went on a diplomatic mission to Delphi, where his life was brought to an end. According to the *Life of Aesop*, Aesop had offended the priests of Apollo by suggesting that they had a great reputation abroad but lacked substance in person. In revenge the priests framed Aesop by putting a golden cup from the temple in his baggage, capturing him, and condemning him to death. In his defense, Aesop related two fables. The first, "The Frog and the Mouse," tells of a frog that was carried off by a bird of prey attracted by the thrashing of a mouse being gratuitously drowned by the frog; the second, "The Eagle and the Dung-Beetle," tells of the inexorable vengeance of a lowly dung-beetle on an eagle that had refused to heed the dung-beetle's request to spare the life of a rabbit. The Delphians refused to heed the morals of the fables and threw Aesop over the cliff. However, according to Herodotus, the Delphians in the third generation afterwards paid blood-money to the descendant of Iadmon to atone for the crime of their ancestors. According to the dating of the Christian chronographer and historian Eusebius, Aesop died in Delphi in 564 B.C.

Major Works

Aesop's fables are often defined on the basis of common internal characteristics. The Aesopic fable is generally an allegorical tale of a brief, fictitious action occurring in past time, usually between particular animals who act like humans, so that the actions suggest a moral, which may or may not be explicitly stated. Animal types in the Aesopic fable tend to represent types of human moral qualities: foxes represent cunning; asses represent stupidity; lambs represent helpless innocence; and wolves represent ruthlessness. The Aesopic fable often appears as a cautionary tale, revealing through humor or through cynicism and satire an amoral world that does not reward abstract virtue but rather a world that requires common sense and moderation for self-preservation. Aesop's fables are often defined by contrast with the literary genres of folktale, allegory, parable, and proverb. Fable, like folktale, has animals with lives similar to humans but, unlike folktale, has a short and simple narrative and usually gives an explicit moral. Although fable provides an allegory of the human situation in the actions of the animals, fable's use of animal characters and shorter narrative distinguish it from other forms of allegory. Fable differs from parable in its use of animal actors and its frequent humorous quality. Fable differs from proverb in its use of a brief narrative of the interaction of animals in addition to the brief moral statement common to proverb and fable. The Aesopic fable can also be defined by reference to its place in the development of the fable. The fable before Aesop seems to appear after the development of the Greek city-state during the Greek Dark Ages, perhaps because the new urban environment offered greater intellectual stimulation and thus a greater possibility of understanding and appreciating metaphor, the basic concept underlying the fable. The pre-Aesopic fable seems to be directed toward a particular individual in a specific context. For example, Hesiod's "The Hawk and the Nightingale" is directed toward Hesiod's brother, and Archilochus's "The Lion and the Fox" is directed toward Archilochus's former lover. Also, such pre-Aesopic fables appear in verse, are serious, and lack an explicitly stated moral. Aesop's fables, however, seem to have been prose compositions—either orally or in writing, depending on which details of the tradition one accepts—using animal stories for comic effect as well as for conveying a political message. It is probable that the fables that might reasonably be attributed to Aesop originally lacked an explicitly stated

moral. However, morals came to be attached to Aesopic fables as a result of the collection of fables attributed to Aesop compiled by Demetrius Phalerius around 300 B.C. According to Ben Edwin Perry, the addition of morals came about from moving the book-maker's heading, which summarized a fable for the purpose of indexing it according to its moral application, from its place at the beginning of the fable to the end, where it served to reinforce the moral.

Textual History

Four significant collections of Aesopic fables were published in classical antiquity. The first collection, no longer extant, was a work in Greek prose around 300 B.C. by Demetrius of Phalerum, probably for use as a reference book of fables for writers and public speakers. The second collection is the Augustana recension, or critical revision of the text, which may with good probability have been based on a first- or second-century A.D. compilation. The Augustana recension was the basis for three other recensions, which include the fourteenth-century edition of Maximus Planudes, which served as the vulgate version of the Greek text of *Aesop's Fables* until the Augustana recension proper was published in 1812. The third collection is the work of Phaedrus, who probably used Demetrius's collection as the basis for his Latin verse version of the fables produced before 55 A.D., the probable year of his death. Phaedrus both expanded the Aesopic material available to him and supplemented it with material from other sources and with material of his own invention. Phaedrus's collection was rendered in Latin prose as part of a fourth- or fifth-century A.D. collection attributed to Aesop. This Latin prose derivation of Phaedrus became the basis for three medieval Latin prose paraphrases referred to respectively as "Aesop of Ademar," "Aesop ad Rufum," and "Romulus," each of which modified the text by means of expansions, deletions, or additions. The fourth and last collection is the work of Babrius, who probably used Demetrius's prose fables of Aesop as the basis for his Greek verse version of the fables, produced perhaps in the late first or second century. Babrius may also have used the Augustana collection, and he seems to have supplemented his Aesopic sources with Near Eastern fables, such as the Assyrian fables of *Ahiqar* and the Babylonian fable of "The Gnat on the Bull's Horns." Babrius's collection was excerpted and put into Latin prose by Avianus around the beginning of the fifth century A.D. This collection of Avianus and the Latin prose paraphrases of Phaedrus were popular during the Middle Ages, and they inspired the verse imitations of Walter the Englishman and Alexander Neckham as well as the composition of original fables in verse by Odo of Cheriton. The Latin prose versions of Babrius/Avianus and Phaedrus continued to be influential in the Renaissance with Heinrich Steinhöwel's Latin-German edition (1476-77) of Romulus, Avianus, Petrus Alphonsus, the *Facetiae* of Poggio Bracciolini, and Rinuccio de Castiglione's Latin translation of some Greek prose adaptations of Babrius. First Steinhöwel's edition was translated into French by Julien Macho; then Macho's version was translated into English and published by William Caxton in 1484. Significant English versions of Aesop after Caxton include the versions of John Ogilby (1651), Sir Roger L'Estrange (1692), and Samuel Croxall (1722). Of these, L'Estrange's version is the only one to add significantly to the underlying text of Steinhöwel's edition with fables from the Greek Aesopic tradition that were published after Steinhöwel's edition. Modern critical work on Aesop dates from the writings of Neveletus on the Greek corpus in 1610 and that of Nilant on the Latin corpus in 1709. The scholars Richard Bentley (1662-1742) and Gotthold Ephraim Lessing (1729-1781) solved significant problems associated with the text. Modern critical editions, such as those of Émile Chambry (1925-26), August Hausrath (1940), and Ben Edwin Perry (1952), give first place to the earliest of the Augustana recensions and then add separately material from later Augustana recensions. The latter two editions put in last place material listed under sources other than Aesop.

Critical reception

Aesop's *Fables* have always had a mixed reception. The classical rhetorical educator Quintilian advised children at the beginning of their education to practice translating, paraphrasing, abbreviating, and elaborating the Aesopic fables. In rhetorical theory and practice, the fable seems to have been a rhetorical device for enhancing persuasiveness in public speaking. As such, the fable was expected to be adapted to different circumstances, and so the actual wording of the fable would change from one circumstance to the next. In this context, Demetrius's collection seems to have been made as a reference work listing fables for use in rhetorical exercises and public speaking. The situations just described show a regard for the content of the fables but little regard for their textual form. The situation of the works of Phaedrus and Babrius suggests another aspect of the reception of Aesop's fables. On the one hand, putting the fables into verse raised these productions to the level of literary art, and the text of their fables in certain textual traditions remained fixed and received critical but brief attention. On the other hand, the works of both authors in other textual traditions were put into prose and spread across Europe, serving as the basis for vernacular editions of Aesop's fables. Thus, the fables enjoyed popular acclaim partly as a school text, and inspired literary works, although they were not necessarily artful themselves—a fact underlined both by the anonymous or pseudonymous nature of the late classical and medieval Latin prose paraphrases and by the constantly changing text. Today, Aesop's fables continue to be considered useful as children's literature, and the process of adaptation

of the fables continues, primarily for this younger audience. Modern scholars also exhibit an ambivalent attitude toward Aesop's fables. Many tend not to critically analyze the literary aspects of relatively independent units of the corpus, such as the Augustana recension, or of groups of fables with a similar theme, or of the literary merit of individual fables. Such avoidance seems to result from a perception of a lack of literary sophistication in the Aesopic corpus and from the difficulty of proving something definitively from such an eclectic and non-homogenous text. Consequently modern scholars tend to discuss alternative aspects of the text, with some discussing the nature of the genre of fable and placing Aesop in that context. Robert Dodsley emphasizes the moral and also discusses the action, characters, and language appropriate for a fable. Ben Edwin Perry stresses the fictional, metaphorical, humorous, and satirical aspects of fable. Agnes Perkins, in comparing the Aesopic morals to the morals of the Buddhist *Jatakas*, proposes that Aesop's morals support action to one's personal advantage rather than action good in itself. H. J. Blackham analyzes fable according to Perry's definition as well as according to its use of images and its purpose. In addition, some scholars compare fable with other genres. Blackham compares fable with parable and allegory. Alternatively, both Margaret Blount and P. Gila Reinstein compare fable with folktale and fairy-tale. Blount suggests that folktale animals are closer to human and do not demonstrate a moral so explicitly as Aesop's animals, and Reinstein argues that Aesop's fables present a cynical and self-reliant philosophy, whereas Grimm's folktales present a belief in a moral order with the ultimate triumph of good over evil. Furthermore, other scholars discuss the sources of the fables. On the one hand, both Perry and Joseph Jacobs discuss the history of the ever-changing corpus of the written text. On the other hand, Louis Cons, J. H. Driberg, and Georgios A. Megas discuss the influence of the oral tradition. Cons suggests a neolithic source for a particlar fable; Driberg proposes African folktales as a source in general for Aesop; and Megas argues for a better preservation of the fables' internal relationships through oral transmission than through textual transmission. Finally, some scholars focus on the changes that individual authors make in their editions of Aesop's fables. Samuel Richardson, in addition to explaining his own changes, discusses those of Sir Roger L'Estrange and Samuel Croxall in their editions, especially in regard to the morals, in order to advance their own political viewpoint. Barbara Mirel discovers three methods of interpreting Aesop in various modern editions and shows how "The Fox and the Crow" is presented differently according to each. Mary-Agnes Taylor examines the changes made by various poets in favor of the ant in "The Grasshopper and the Ant." George Clark compares the fables of "The Cock and the Jewel" and "The Swallow and the Other Birds" in the versions of Aesop and Robert Henryson. In general, critics find fault with the lack of literary quality in the Aesopic corpus, with the political or religious bias of a previous collection of Aesop's works, and with the didacticism of the morals. However, critics commend the fables for their simplicity, humor, pointedness, and wisdom, and for the literary quality of particular productions.

PRINCIPAL WORKS

FABLES

"Androcles and the Lion"
"The Ant and the Fly"
"The Ant and the Grasshopper"
"The Ass in the Lion's Skin"
"The Bullfrog and the Bear"
"The Butterfly and the Wasp"
"The Cock and the Fox"
"The Cock and the Jewel"
"The Dog and the Meat"
"The Dog and the Wolf"
"The Dog in a Manger"
"The Eagle and the Beetle"
"The Eagle and the Vixen"
"The Farmer and the River"
"The Farmer and the Snake"
"The Father and His Sons"
"The Fir Tree and the Bramble"
"The Flies and the Honey-Pot"
"The Fox and the Cock"
"The Fox and the Crow"
"The Fox and the Grapes"
"The Gnat and the Bull"
"The Good Man and the Serpent"
"The Hare and the Tortoise"
"The Jackdaw and the Doves"
"The Lion and the Mouse"
"The Lion in Love with the Farmer's Daughter"
"The Lion, the Ass, and the Fox"
"The Miller, His Son, and Their Ass"
"The Milk-Woman and Her Pail"
"The Mouse and the Frog"
"The North Wind and the Sun"
"The Nurse and the Wolf"
"The Peacock and the Crane"
"The Snake and the Crab"
"The Stomach and the Feet"
"The Swallow and the Other Birds"
"The Town Mouse and the Country Mouse"; or "The Two Mice"
"Winter and Spring"
"The Wild Horse and the Stag"
"The Wolf and the Crane"
"The Wolf and the Lamb"
"The Wolf in Sheep's Clothing"
"The Wolves and the Dogs"
"The Woodcutter and Hermes"

PRINCIPAL ENGLISH TRANSLATIONS

Aesop's Fable (translated by Samuel Croxall [1722]; Limited Editions Club edition) 1933
The Fables of Aesop (translated by Joseph Jacobs [1894]) 1950
Fables (translated by S. A. Handford [1954]; Penguin Books edition) 1994
Aesop without Morals (translated by Lloyd W. Daly) 1961
Caxton's Aesop (translated by William Caxton [1484]) 1967
Aesop's Fables, 1740 (edited by Samuel Richardson [1740]) 1975
Fables from Aesop and Others (translated by Charles H. Bennett [1857]) 1978

CRITICISM

John Locke (essay date 1693)

SOURCE: John Locke, "Some Thoughts Concerning Education," in *The Educational Writings of John Locke*, edited by John William Adamson, Edward Arnold, 1912, pp. 21-180.

[*In the following excerpt, reprinted in 1912, Locke describes Aesop's fables as entertaining and containing useful moral instruction for the young.*]

[When a child] begins to be able to read, some easy, pleasant book, suited to his capacity, should be put into his hands, wherein the entertainment that he finds might draw him on, and reward his pains in reading; and yet not such as should fill his head with perfectly useless trumpery, or lay the principles of vice and folly. To this purpose I think *Æsop's Fables* the best, which being stories apt to delight and entertain a child, may yet afford useful reflections to a grown man; and if his memory retain them all his life after, he will not repent to find them there, amongst his manly thoughts and serious business. If his Æsop has pictures in it, it will entertain him much the better, and encourage him to read when it carries the increase of knowledge with it . . .

Samuel Richardson (essay date 1740)

SOURCE: Samuel Richardson, in a preface to *Aesop's Fables, 1740*, edited by Samuel Richardson, Garland Publishing, Inc., 1975, pp. i-xiv.

[*In the following excerpt, reprinted in 1975, Richardson discusses the reasons for editing Aesop that motivated Roger L'Estrange and S. Croxall and Richardson himself, especially in regard to the modification of the moral.*]

When there are so many editions of *Æsop's fables,* it will be expected, that some reasons should be given for the appearance of a new one; and we shall be as brief on this head, as the nature of the thing will admit. Of all the *English* editions, we shall consider only two as worthy of notice; to wit, that of the celebrated Sir *Roger L'Estrange,* and that which appears under the name of *S. Croxal,* subscribed to the dedication. And when we have given an account of what each says for his own performance, it will be our turn to offer some things to the reader with regard to our present undertaking.

> When first I put pen to paper upon this design, says Sir *Roger,* I had in my eye only the common school book, as it stands in the *Cambridge* and *Oxford* editions of it, under the title of *Æsopi Phrygis Fabulae; una cum nonnullis variorum auctorum fabulis adjectis:* propounding to myself, at that time, to follow the very course and series of that collection; and, in one word, to try what might be done by making the best of the whole, and adapting proper and useful doctrines to the several parts of it, toward the turning of an *excellent Latin manual* of morals and good counsels, into a *tolerable English one.* But, upon jumbling matters and thoughts together, and laying one thing by another, the very state and condition of the case before me, together with the nature and the reason of the thing, gave me to understand, that this way of proceeding would never answer my end: insomuch that, upon this consideration, I consulted other versions of the same fables, and made my best of the choice. Some that were *twice or thrice over,* and only the self-same thing in other words; these I struck out, and made one specimen serve for the rest. To say nothing of here and there a *trivial,* or a *loose conceit* in the medley, more than this; that such as they are, I was under some sort of obligation to take them in for company; and in short, *good, bad* and *indifferent,* one with another, to the number, in the total, of 383 fables. To these I have likewise subjoined a considerable addition of other select *Apologues,* out of the most celebrated authors that are extant upon that subject, towards the finishing of the work.

And a little farther,

> This *Rhapsody* of *Fables,* says he, is a book universally read, and taught in all our schools; but almost at such a rate as we teach *Pyes* and *Parrots,* that pronounce the words without so much as guessing at the meaning of them: or, to take it another way, the boys break their teeth upon the shells, without ever coming near the kernel. They learn fables by lessons, and the moral is the least part of our care in a child's institution: so that take both together, and the one is stark nonsense, without the application of the other; beside that, the doctrine itself, as we have it, even at the best, falls infinitely short of the vigour and spirit of the fable. To supply this defect now, we have had

several *English* paraphrases and essays upon *Esop,* and divers of the followers, both in prose and verse. The latter have perchance ventured a little too far from the precise scope of the author upon the privilege of a poetical licence: and for the other of antient date, the morals are so insipid and flat, and the style and diction of the fables so coarse and uncouth, that they are rather dangerous than profitable, as to the purpose they were principally intended for; and likely to do forty times more mischief by the one, than good by the other. An emblem without a key to it, is no more than a *Tale of a Tub;* and that tale sillily told too, is but one folly grafted upon another. Children are to be taught, in the first place, what they ought to do: 2dly, the manner of doing it: And, in the third place, they are to be inured by the force of instruction and good example, to the love and practice of doing their duty; whereas, on the contrary, one step out of the way in the institution, is enough to poison the peace and the reputation of a whole life. Whether I have in this attempt, adds Sir *Roger,* contributed or not, to the improvement of these fables, either in the wording, or the meaning of them, the book must stand or fall to itself: but this I shall adventure to pronounce upon the whole matter, that the text is *English,* and the morals, in some sort, accommodate to the *allegory;* which could hardly be said of all the translations or reflections before mentioned, which have served, in truth, (or at least some of them) rather to teach us what we should *not* do, than what we *should.* So that, in the publishing of these papers, I have done my best to obviate a common inconvenience, or, to speak plainly, the mortal error of pretending to erect a building upon a false foundation: leaving the whole world to take the same freedom with me, that I have done with others.

Thus far Sir *Roger L'Estrange.* Now we come to what the other gentleman has to say *for himself,* or rather, as he has managed the matter, what he has to say *against* Sir *Roger,* the depreciating of whose work, seems to be the cornerstone of his own building.

> Nothing of this nature, says he, has been done since *L'Estrange's* time worth mentioning; and we had nothing before, but what . . . was so *insipid and flat in the moral, and so coarse and uncouth in the style and diction, that they were rather dangerous than profitable, as to the purpose for which they were principally intended; and likely to do forty times more harm than good.* I shall therefore only observe to my reader the insufficiency of *L'Estrange's* own performance, as to the purpose for which he professes to have principally intended it; with some other circumstances, which will help to excuse, if not justify, what I have enterprized upon the same subject.

> Now this purpose for which he principally intended his book, as in his preface he spends a great many words to inform us, was for the use and instruction of children; who being, as it were, a mere *rasa*

tabula, or *blank paper, are ready indifferently for any opinions, good or bad, taking all upon credit; and that it is in the power of the first comer, to write saint or devil upon them, which he pleases.* This being truly and certainly the case, what devils, nay, what poor devils, would *L'Estrange* make of those children, who should be so unfortunate as to read his book, and imbibe his pernicious principles! Principles coined and suited to promote the growth, and serve the ends, of popery and arbitrary power. Though we had never been told he was a pensioner to a Popish prince, and that he himself professed the same unaccountable religion, yet his reflections upon *Aesop* would discover it to us: In every political touch, he shews himself to be the tool and hireling of the Popish faction: since even a slave, without some mercenary view, would not bring arguments to justify slavery, nor endeavour to establish arbitrary power upon the basis of right reason. What sort of children therefore are the *Blank Paper,* upon which such morality as this ought to be written? Not the children of *Britain,* I hope; for they are born with free blood in their veins, and suck in liberty with their very milk. This they should be taught to love and cherish above all things, and, upon occasion, to defend and vindicate it; as it is the glory of their country, the greatest blessing of their lives, and the peculiar happy privilege, in which they excel all the world besides. Let therefore *L'Estrange,* with his slavish doctrine, be banished to the barren deserts of *Arabia,* to the nurseries of *Turkey, Persia,* and *Morocco,* where all footsteps of liberty have long since been worn out, and the minds of the people, by a narrow way of thinking, contrasted and inured to fear poverty and miserable servitude. Let the children of *Italy, France, Spain,* and the rest of the Popish countries, *continue this tedious declaimer,* furnish him with blank paper for principles, of which free-born *Britons* are not capable. The earlier such notions are instilled into such minds as theirs indeed, the better it will be for them, as it will keep them from thinking of any other than the abject, servile condition to which they are born. But let the minds of our *British* youth be for ever educated and improved in that spirit of truth and liberty, for the support of which their ancestors have often bravely exhausted so much blood and treasure.

Thus we see the chief quarrel of the worthy gentleman is against the *Politicks* of Sir *Roger;* and we heartily join with him on this head. Sir *Roger* was certainly listed in a bad cause as to politicks, and his reflections have many of them a pernicious tendency. But the time in which he wrote, within view, in a manner, of the civil wars so lately concluded, and the anarchy introduced by them, to so great an extreme of one side, was so naturally productive of an extreme on the other, that many very great men of that time fell into the same error with Sir *Roger:* and perhaps a charitable mind, duly reflecting upon this, and not intent upon *partial* or *selfish* views, would have found something to have said, if not in *excuse,* yet in *extenuation,* of the fault.

The Doctor, for such I am told the gentleman is, proceeds to strengthen his own cause, by further observing,

> That *L'Estrange* (as he every where calls the deceased knight) made not fair reflections upon the fables in political points: that *Æsop,* though a slave, was a lover of liberty, and gives not one hint to favour *L'Estrange*'s insinuations: But that, on the contrary, he takes all occasions to recommend a love for liberty, and an abhorrence of tyranny, and all arbitrary proceedings: that *L'Estrange* (again!) notoriously perverts both the sense and meaning of several fables, particularly when any political instruction (*for this is still the burden of the Doctor's song*) is couched in the application;

and then gives an example in Sir *Roger*'s fable of the **"Dog and the Wolf";** and further objects against the Knight,

> that he has swelled his work, which was designed for the use of children, to a voluminous bulk; and by that means raised it to an exorbitant price, so as to make it unsuitable to the hand or pocket of the generality of children.

And here follows a very extraordinary conclusion of the Doctor, which we shall give *verbatim:*

> If I were, *says the good man,* to put constructions upon the ways of Providence, I should fancy this prolixity of his was ordered as a preservative against his noxious principles; for however his book may have been used by *Men,* I dare say, few *Children* have been conversant with it.

So that we see, at last, all the terrible apprehensions of the mischiefs of Sir *Roger*'s book, are merely the effects of the good Doctor's imagination, which, it is generally said, has run away with his judgment in more instances than the present.

If this then be the case, we presume to hope, that, even in the good Doctor's opinion, there will not be any necessity to banish poor *L'Estrange* to the barren deserts of *Arabia,* to the nurseries of *Turkey, Persia,* and *Morocco;* nor that he should be confined to the children of *Italy, France, Spain,* and the rest of the Popish countries; but, for the sake of the excellent sense contained in his other reflections, where politicks are not concerned; for the sake of the benefit which the *English* tongue has received from his masterly hand; for the sake of that fine humour, apposite language, accurate and lively manner, which will always render Sir *Roger* delightful, and which this severe Critick has in some places so wretchedly endeavoured to imitate: for all these sakes, I say, let him remain among us still, since our author thinks he can do no harm to *Children,* and *Men* may be supposed guarded by years and experience; and the rather, if it be only to shew the difference between a fine original, and a bungling imitation; and that no prating *Jays* may strut about in the beautiful plumage of the *Peacock*.

The Doctor proceeds, and fixes a stigma on the second Volume of Sir *Roger*'s Fables, and, in the main, I join with him in it; for, as a Book of Fables, it is truly unworthy of that celebrated hand; and for that reason we have made very little use of it in our present edition; though we cannot but apprehend, that he was put upon it rather by the importunity of booksellers, encouraged by the success of the first volume, than by his own choice ŏr judgment: and, after all, some allowance ought to be made for his circumstances, and his years, being, as he tells us, on the wrong side of fourscore when he wrote it.

It is but just to transcribe the concluding paragraph of the Doctor's preface.

> Whether, *says he,* I have mended the faults I find with him, in this, or any other respect, I, must leave to the judgment of the reader: professing (according to the principle on which the following applications are built) that I am a lover of liberty and truth; an enemy to tyranny, either in Church or State; and one who detests party-animosities, and factious divisions, as much as I wish the peace and prosperity of my country.

We greatly applaud this pompous declaration of the good Gentleman's principles: but though we might observe, that he has strained the natural import of some of the Fables, near as much one way, as Sir *Roger* has done the other, and may be censured for giving too frequently into political reflections, which had, on all occasions, if the book be meant for Children, better be avoided, where the moral will bear a more general and inoffensive turn; yet we shall only observe, that had this gentleman, who clothes himself in the skin of the departed knight, and, at first fight, makes so formidable an appearance in it, lived in the days of Sir *Roger,* and had Sir *Roger* lived in his, it is not impossible that the sentiments of both might have changed.

What I mean, is, the *Restoration* of Monarchy under King *Charles* II, made these now exploded doctrines as much the fashion then, as the glorious *Revolution* under King *William* III has made the Doctor's principles the fashion now. And for aught that appears from the *moderation* of the Doctor's principles, if we may judge of a Man's temper by his disposition, as shewn in several instances of his preface, had the Doctor lived when Sir *Roger* did, he might have been the *L'Estrange* of the *one Court;* as *L'Estrange,* had he been in the Doctor's place, might have taken orders, and become Chaplain in the *other.* If the living

Gentleman reflects, as he ought, upon the little mercy he has shewn to the dead, he will not think this too severe. And the comparison will appear the less invidious, to any one who considers, that Sir *Roger* suffered for his principles, bad as they were: and the Doctor, we hope, for the sake of the *publick,* as well as for his *own sake,* will never be called upon to such trials.

We have thus set the pretensions of the two gentlemen in a proper light: it remains for us, now to say something of our own undertaking.

The usefulness and benefit of such a work to children is allowed on all hands; and therefore we shall not insist upon a topick, which has been so much laboured by the gentlemen who have gone before us.

We have seen, that the only objections which a scrutinizing adversary, who had it in view to supplant the Knight, and thrust himself into his place, can find against him, are the *political* part, and the *bulk* and *price* of the performance: as to the rest, on comparing the works, we find a very great disparity between them: we therefore were assured, that we should do an acceptable service, if we could give the *exceptionable reflections* a more *general* and *useful* turn; and if we could reduce the work to such a size as should be fit for the *hands* and *pockets* for which it was principally designed; and at the same time preserve to Sir *Roger* the principal graces and beauties for which he is so justly admired: and this only, though we found afterwards, on a closer review, a necessity of going further, was our *first* intention.

We were the rather prevailed upon to take this liberty with Sir *Roger,* because he ingenuously declares, in what we have quoted from his preface, 'That he was under some sort of obligation to take into his medley, as he modestly calls it, here and there a trivial or a loose conceit, for company.' An obligation imposed upon him, we presume, by his unhappy circumstances (and which hardly those could excuse), in order to add to the bulk of his book, which he first published in folio.

This, with other proper alterations, &c. where the sense and poignance of the fable and reflections would best bear it, we thought would give us the opportunity of answering the objection about the *bulk* and *price*. And on looking closer into the subject, we found sufficient reason to justify our opinion.

Thus then, instead of banishing Sir *Roger* to the deserts of *Arabia,* we confess that it was our intention, everywhere, except in his *political reflections,* to keep that celebrated writer close in our eye: And in some places we have accordingly contented ourselves with the inferior glory of having only abridged him, where we could not, with *equal* beauty and propriety, give words and sentences different from his own; rather choosing to acknowledge our obligations to so great a master, than to arrogate to ourselves the praises due to another.

We have not, however, spared any of those conceits, as Sir *Roger* calls them, which we imagined capable only of a trivial, or liable to a loose construction. We have also presumed to alter, and put a stronger point to several of the fables themselves, which we thought capable of more forcible morals. And instead of the political reflections, we have every where substituted such as we hope will be found more general and instructive. For we think it in no wise excusable to inflame children's minds with distinctions, which they will imbibe fast enough from the attachments of parents, &c. and the warmth of their own imaginations. But nevertheless, we must add, that wherever the fable *compelled,* as we may say, a political turn, we have, in our reflections upon it, always given that preference to the principles of LIBERTY, which we hope will for ever be the distinguishing characteristic of a *Briton.*

If thus we have banished from Sir *Roger* all that his most partial enemy could except against him; and have preserved all that has gained him the approbation of the best judges: If we have avoided the faults of both gentlemen (and we think we could point out, if we were put upon it, where the one has been faulty as well as the other; and a thousand instances wherein he has infinitely fallen short of the author he aims to supplant): why should we not presume, that there may be room for this performance, which we now present to the publick? To whose judgment we therefore submit it; and are willing to stand or fall by its determination.

Robert Dodsley (essay date 1761)

SOURCE: Robert Dodsley, reprinted from "Select Fables of Esop and Other Fabulists," in *An Essay on Fable*, The Augustan Reprint Society, 1965, pp. lvii-lxxvii.

[*In the following essay, published in a second imprint in 1764 and reprinted in 1965, Dodsley describes the characteristics of the fable including its ability to convey moral truth without an offensive air of moral superiority.*]

Introduction

Whoever undertakes to compose a fable, whether of the sublimer and more complex kind, as the epick and dramatick; or of the lower and more simple, as what has been called the Esopean; should make it his principal intention to illustrate some one moral or prudential maxim. To this point the composition in all its parts must be directed; and this will lead him to de-

scribe some action proper to enforce the maxim he has chosen. In several respects therefore the greater fable and the less agree. It is the business of both to teach some particular moral, exemplified by an action, and this enlivened by natural incidents. Both alike must be supported by apposite and proper characters, and both be furnished with sentiments and language suitable to the character thus employed. I would by no means however infer, that, to produce one of these small pieces requires the same degree of genius, as to form an epick or dramatick Fable. All I would insinuate, is, that the apologue has a right to some share of our esteem, from the relation it bears to the poems before mentioned: as it is honourable to spring from a noble stem, although in ever so remote a branch. A perfect fable, even of this inferior kind, seems a much stronger proof of genius than the mere narrative of an event. The latter indeed requires *judgment:* the former, together with judgment, demands an effort of the *imagination.*

Having thus endeavoured to procure these little compositions as much regard as they may fairly claim, I proceed to treat of some particulars most essential to their character.

SECT I.

Of the Truth or Moral of a Fable.

'Tis the very essence of a Fable to convey some *Moral* or *useful* Truth, beneath the shadow of an *allegory.* It is this chiefly that distinguishes a *Fable* from a *Tale;* and indeed gives it the pre-eminence in point of use and dignity. A Tale may consist of an event either serious or comic; and, provided it be told agreeably, may be excellent in its *kind,* though it should imply no sort of Moral. But the action of a Fable is contrived on *purpose* to teach and to imprint some Truth; and should clearly and obviously include the illustration of it in the very catastrophe.

The *Truth* to be preferred on this occasion should neither be too obvious, nor trite, nor trivial. Such would ill deserve the pains employed in Fable to convey it. As little also should it be one that is very dubious, dark, or controverted. It should be of such a nature, as to challenge the assent of every ingenious and sober judgment; never a point of mere speculation; but tending to *inform* or *remind* the reader, of the proper means that lead to happiness, or at least, to the several duties, decorums, and proprieties of conduct, which each particular Fable endeavours to enforce.

The reason why Fable has been so much esteemed in all ages and in all countries; is perhaps owing to the *polite* manner in which its maxims are conveyed. The very article of giving instruction supposes at least, a superiority of wisdom in the adviser; a circumstance by no means favourable to the ready admission of advice. 'Tis the peculiar excellence of Fable to *wave* this air of superiority: it leavs the *reader* to collect the moral; who by thus discovering more than is shewn him, finds his principle of self-love *gratified,* instead of being *disgusted.* The attention is either taken off from the adviser; or, if otherwise, we are at least flattered by his humility and address.

Besides, instruction, as conveyed by Fable, does not only lay aside its lofty mien and supercilious aspect, but appears drest in all the smiles and graces which can strike the imagination, or engage the passions. It pleases in order to convince; and it imprints its moral so much the deeper, in proportion as it entertains; so that we may be said to *feel* our duties at the very instant we *comprehend* them.

I am very sensible with what difficulty a Fable is brought to a strict agreement with the foregoing account of it. This however ought to be the writer's *aim.* 'Tis the simple manner in which the Morals of Esop are interwoven with his Fables, that distinguishes him, and gives him the preference to all other mythologists. His Mountain delivered of a Mouse, produces the Moral of his Fable, in ridicule of pompous pretenders; and his Crow, when she drops her cheese, lets fall, as it were by accident, the strongest admonition against the power of flattery. There is no need of a separate sentence to explain it; no possibility of impressing it deeper, by that load we too often see of accumulated reflections. Indeed the Fable of the **"Cock and the Precious Stone"** is in *this* respect very exceptionable. The lesson it inculcates is so dark and ambiguous, that different expositors have given it quite *opposite* interpretations; some imputing the Cock's rejection of the Diamond to his *wisdom,* and others to his *ignorance.*

Strictly speaking then, one should render needless any *detached* or *explicit* moral. Esop, the father of this kind of writing, disclaimed any such assistance. 'Tis the province of Fable to give it birth in the mind of the person for whom it is intended: otherwise the precept is *direct,* which is contrary to the nature and end of *allegory.* However, in order to give all necessary assistance to young readers, an Index is added to this collection, containing the subject or moral of each Fable, to which the reader may occasionally apply.

After all, the *greatest fault* in any composition (for I can hardly allow that *name* to riddles) is *obscurity.* There can be *no* purpose answered by a work that is unintelligible. Annibal Caracci and Raphael himself, rather than risque so unpardonable a fault, have admitted *verbal explanations* into some of their best pictures. It must be confessed, that every story is not capable of telling its own Moral. In a case of this nature, and this only, it should be *expressly* introduced. Perhaps also, where the point is doubtful, we ought to shew *enough* for the less acute, even at the hazard of

shewing *too much* for the more sagacious; who, for this very reason, that they *are* more sagacious, will pardon a superfluity which is such to *them alone.*

But, on these occasions, it has been matter of dispute, whether the moral is better introduced at the end or beginning of a Fable. Esop, as I said before, universally rejected any separate Moral. Those we *now* find at the close of his Fables, were placed there by other hands. Among the ancients, Prædrus; and Gay, among the moderns, inserted theirs at the *beginning:* La Motte prefers them at the *conclusion;* and Fontaine disposes of them *indiscriminately,* at the beginning or end, as he sees convenient. If, amidst the authority of such great names, I might venture to mention my *own* opinion, I should rather *prefix* them as an *introduction,* than *add* them as an *appendage.* For I would neither pay my *reader* nor *myself* so bad a compliment, as to suppose, after he had read the Fable, that he was not able to discover its meaning. Besides, when the Moral of a Fable is not very prominent and striking, a leading thought at the beginning puts the reader in a proper track. He knows the game which he pursues: and, like a beagle on a warm scent, he follows the sport with alacrity, in proportion to his intelligence. On the other hand, if he has *no* previous intimation of the design, he is puzzled throughout the Fable; and cannot determine upon its merit without the trouble of a fresh perusal. A ray of light, imparted at first, may shew him the tendency and propriety of every expression as he goes along; but while he travels in the dark, no wonder if he stumble or mistake his way.

SECT. II.

Of the Action and Incidents proper for a Fable.

In chusing the action or allegory, three conditions are altogether expedient. I. It must be *clear:* that is, it ought to shew without equivocation, precisely and obviously, what we intend should be understood. II. It must be *one* and *entire.* That is, it must not be composed of separate and independent actions, but must tend in all its circumstances to the completion of one single event. III. It must be *natural:* that is, founded, if nor on Truth, at least, on Probability; on popular opinion; on that relation and analogy which things bear to one another, when we have gratuitously endowed them with the human faculties of speech and reason. And these conditions are taken from the nature of the human mind; which cannot endure to be embarrassed, to be bewildered, or to be deceived.

A Fable offends against *prespicuity,* when it leaves us doubtful *what* Truth the Fabulist intended to convey. We have a striking example of this in Dr. Croxall's Fable of the creaking wheel. "A coachman, says he, hearing one of his wheels creak, was surprised; but more especially, when he perceived that it was the worst wheel of the whole set, and which he thought had but little pretence to take such a liberty. But, upon his demanding the reason why it did so, the wheel replied, that it was natural for people who laboured under any affliction or calamity to complain." Who would imagine this Fable designed, as the author informs us, for an admonition to repress, or keep our complaints to *ourselves,* or if we must let our sorrows speak, to take care it be done in solitude and retirement. The story of this Fable is not well imagined: at least, if meant to support the Moral which the author has drawn from it.

A Fable is faulty in respect to unity, when the several circumstances point *different* ways, and do not center, like so many lines, in one distinct and unambiguous Moral. An example of this kind is furnished by *La Motte* in the observation he makes on Fontaine's two pigeons. "These pigeons had a reciprocal affection for each other. One of them shewing a desire to travel, was earnestly opposed by his companion, but in vain. The former sets out upon his rambles, and encounters a thousand unforeseen dangers; while the latter suffers almost as much at home, through his apprehensions for his roving friend. However, our traveller, after many hair-breadth escapes, returns at length in safety back, and the two pigeons are, once again, mutually happy in each other's company." Now the application of this Fable is utterly vague and uncertain, for want of circumstances to determine, whether the author designed principally to represent the *dangers* of the *Traveller:* his friend's *anxiety* during his *absence;* or their *mutual happiness* on his *return.* Whereas, had the travelling pigeon met with no disasters on his way, but only found all pleasures insiped for want of his friend's participation; and had he returned from no other motive, than a desire of seeing him again, the whole then had happily closed in this one conspicuous inference, that the presence of a real friend is the most desirable of all gratifications.

The last rule I have mentioned, that a Fable should be natural, may be violated several ways. 'Tis opposed, when we make creatures enter into unnatural associations. Thus the sheep or the goat must not be made to hunt with the lion; and it is yet *more* absurd, to represent the lion as falling in love with the forester's daughter. 'Tis infringed, by ascribing to them appetites and passions that are not consistent with their known characters; or else by employing them in such occupations, as are foreign and unsuitable to their respective natures. A fox should not be said to long for grapes; an hedgehog pretend to drive away flies; nor a partridge offer his service to delve in the vineyard. A ponderous iron and an earthen vase should not swim together down a river; and he that should make his goose lay golden eggs, would shew a luxuriant *fancy,* but very little *judgment.* In short, nothing besides the faculty of speech and reason, which Fable has been allowed to

confer even upon inanimates, must ever *contradict* the nature of things, or at least, the commonly received opinion concerning them.

Opinions indeed, although *erroneous,* if they either *are,* or *have* been universally received, may afford sufficient foundation for a Fable. The mandrake, *here,* may be made to utter groans; and the dying swan, to pour forth her elegy. The sphinx and the phœnix, the syren and the centaur, have all the existence that is requisite for Fable. Nay, the goblin, the fairy, and even the man in the moon, may have each his province allotted him, provided it be not an *improper* one. Here the notoriety of opinion supplies the place of fact, and in *this manner* truth may fairly be deduced from falsehood.

Concerning the incidents proper for Fable, it is a rule without exception, that they ought always to be *few;* it being foreign to the nature of this composition to admit of much variety. Yet a Fable with only *one* single incident may possibly appear too naked. If Esop and Phædrus are herein sometimes too sparing, Fontaine and La Motte are as often too profuse. In this, as in most other matters, a medium certainly is best. In a word, the incidents should not only be few, but short; and like those in the Fables of "the swallow and other birds," "the miller and his son," and "the court and country-mouse," they must naturally arise out of the subject, and serve to illustrate and enforce the Moral.

SECT. III.

Of the Persons, Characters, and Sentiments of Fable.

The race of animals *first* present themselves as the proper actors in this little drama. They are indeed a species that aproaches, in many respects, so near to our own, that we need only lend them *speech,* in order to produce a striking resemblance. It would however be unreasonable, to expect a strict and universal similitude. There is a certain *measure* and *degree* of analogy, with which the most discerning reader will rest contented: for instance, he will accept the *properties* of animals, although *necessary* and *invariable,* as the images of our *inclinations,* tho' never so *free.* To require *more* than this, were to sap the very foundations of allegory; and even to deprive ourselves of half the pleasure that flows from poetry in general.

Solomon sends us to the ant, to learn the wisdom of industry: and our inimitable ethic poet introduces nature herself as giving us a *similar* kind of counsel.

> *Thus then to Man the voice of Nature spake;*
> "*Go, from the* Creatures *thy instructions take—*
> "There *all the forms of social union find,*
> "*And* thence, *let reason late instruct mankind.*"

He supposes that animals in their *native* characters, *without* the advantages of speech and reason which are designed them by the Fabulists, may in regard to *Morals* as well as *Arts,* become examples to the human race. Indeed, I am afraid we have so far deviated into ascititious appetites and fantastic manners, as to find the expediency of copying from *them* that simplicity we ourselves have lost. If animals in themselves may be thus exemplary, how much more may they be made instructive, under the direction of an able Fabulist; who by conferring upon them the gift of language, contrives to make their instincts more intelligible and their examples more determinate!

But these are not his *only* actors. The Fabulist has one advantage above all other writers whatsoever; as all the works both of art and nature are more immediately at his disposal. He has, in this respect, a liberty not allowed to epick, or dramatick writers; who are undoubtedly more limited in the choice of persons to be employed. He has authority to press into his service every kind of existence under heaven: not only beasts, birds, insects, and all the animal creation; but flowers, shrubs, trees, and all the tribe of vegetables. Even mountains, fossils, minerals, and the inanimate works of nature, discourse articulately at his command, and act the part which he assigns them. The virtues, vices, and every *property* of beings, receive from him a *local habitation and a name*. In short he may personify, bestow life, speech and action, on whatever he thinks proper.

It is easy to imagine what a source of *novelty* and *variety* this must open, to a genius capable of receiving, and of employing, these ideal persons in a proper manner; what an opportunity it affords him to diversify his images, and to treat the fancy with change of *objects;* while he strengthens the understanding, or regulates the passions, by a succession of *Truths*. To raise beings like these into a state of action and intelligence, gives the Fabulist an undoubted claim to that *first* character of the poet, a *Creator*. I rank him not, as I said before, with the writers of epick or dramatick poems; but the maker of pins or needles is as much an artist, as an anchorsmith: and a painter in miniature may shew as much skill, as he who paints in the largest proportions.

When these persons are once raised, we must carefully injoin them proper talks; and assign them sentiments and language suitable to their several natures, and respective properties.

A raven should not be extolled for her voice, nor a bear be represented with an elegant shape. 'Twere a very obvious instance of absurdity, to paint an hare, cruel; or a wolf, compassionate. An ass were but ill qualified to be General of an army, though he may well enough serve perhaps for one of the trumpeters. But so long as popular opinion allows to the lion,

magnanimity; rage, to the tiger; strength, to the mule; cunning, to the fox; and buffoonery, to the monkey; why may not they support the characters of an Agamemnon, Achilles, Ajax, Ulysses and Thersites? The truth is, when Moral actions are with judgment attributed to the brute creation. we scarce *perceive* that nature is at all violated by the Fabulist. He appears, at *most,* to have only translated their language. His lions, wolves, and foxes, *behave* and *argue* as those creatures *would,* had they originally been endowed with the human faculties of speech and reason.

But greater art is yet required, whenever we personify *inanimate* beings. Here the copy so far deviates from the great lines of nature, that, without the nicest care, reason will revolt against the fiction. However, beings of *this* sort, managed ingeniously and with address, recommend the Fabulist's invention by the grace of novelty and of variety. Indeed the analogy between things natural and artificial, animate and inanimate, is often so very striking, that we can, with seeming propriety, give passions and sentiments to every individual part of existence. Appearance favours the deception. The vine may be *enamoured* of the elm; her embraces testify her passion. The swelling mountain may, naturally enough, be *delivered* of a mouse. The gourd may reproach the pine, and the sky-rocket insult the stars. The axe may sollicit a new handle of the forest; and the moon, in her *female* character, request a fashionable garment. Here is nothing incongruous; nothing that shocks the reader with impropriety. On the other hand, were the axe to desire a fine perriwig, and the moon petition for a new pair of boots, probability would *then* be violated, and the absurdity become too glaring.

Sect. IV.

On the Language of Fable.

The most beautiful Fables that ever were invented, may be disfigured by the *Language* in which they are clothed. Of this, poor Esop, in some of his English dresses, affords a melancholy proof. The ordinary style of Fable should be *familiar,* but it should also be *elegant*. Were I to instance any style that I should prefer on this occasion, it should be that of Mr. *Addison*'s little tales in the *Spectator*. That ease and simplicity, that conciseness and propriety, that subdued and decent humour he so remarkably discovers in those compositions, seem to have qualified him for a Fabulist, almost beyond any other writer. But to return.

The *Familiar,* says Mr. La Motte, to whose ingenious *Essay* I have often been obliged in this discourse, is the general tone or accent of Fable. It was thought sufficient, on its first appearance, to lend the animals our most common language. Nor indeed have they any extraordinary *pretensions* to the sublime; it being requisite they should *speak* with the same simplicity that they *behave*.

The *familiar* also is more proper for insinuation, than the *elevated;* this being the language of *reflection,* as the former is the voice of *sentiment.* We guard ourselves against the one, but lie open to the other; and instruction will always the most effectually sway us, when it appears least jealous of its rights and privileges.

The *familiar* style however that is here required, notwithstanding that appearance of *Ease* which is its character, is perhaps more difficult to write, than the *elevated* or *sublime.* A writer more readily perceives when he has risen above the common language; than he perceives, in speaking this language, whether he has made the choice that is most suitable to the occasion: and it is nevertheless, upon *this happy choice* that all the charm of the *familiar* depends. Moreover, the *elevated* style deceives and seduces, although it *be not* the best chosen; whereas the *familiar* can procure itself no sort of respect, if it be not easy, natural, just, delicate, and unaffected. A Fabulist must therefore bestow great attention upon his style: and even labour it so much the *more,* that it may appear to have cost him no pains at all.

The authority of *Fontaine* justifies this opinion in regard to style. His Fables are perhaps the best examples of the *genteel familiar,* as Sir Roger L'Estrange affords the grossest, of the *indelicate* and *low.* When we read that "while the frog and the mouse were disputing it at sword's point, down comes a kite *powdering* upon them in the *interim,* and *gobbets up* both together to part the fray." And where the fox reproaches "a bevy of jolly gossiping wenches making merry over a *disk of pullets,* that, if *he* but peeped into a hen-roost, they always made a bawling with *their dogs* and *their bastards;* while you yourselves, says he, can lie *stuffing your guts* with your hens and your capons, and not a *word of the pudding.*" This *may* be *familiar,* but is also *coarse* and *vulgar;* and cannot fail to disgust a reader that has the least degree of taste or delicacy.

The style of Fable then must be simple and familiar; and it must *likewise* be correct and elegant. By the former, I would advise that it should not be loaded with figure and metaphor; that the disposition of words be natural; the turn of sentences, easy; and their construction, unembarrassed. By elegance, I would exclude all coarse and provincial terms; all affected and puerile conceits; all obsolete and pedantick phrases. To this I would adjoin, as the word perhaps implies, a certain finishing polish, which gives a grace and spirit to the whole; and which, tho' it have always the *appearance* of nature, is almost ever the *effect* of art.

But, notwithstanding all that has been said, there are some occasions on which it is allowable, and even expedient to change the style. The language of a Fable must rise or fall in conformity to the subject. A *Lion,* when introduced in his regal capacity, must hold discourse in a strain somewhat more elevated than a *Country-Mouse.* The lioness then becomes his *Queen,* and the beasts of the forest are called his *Subjects:* a method that offers *at once* to the imagination, both the *animal* and the *person* he is designed to represent. Again, the buffoon-monkey should avoid that pomp of phrase, which the owl employs as her best pretence to wisdom. Unless the style be thus judiciously varied, it will be impossible to preserve a just distinction of character.

Descriptions, at once concise and pertinent, add a grace to Fable; but are *then* most happy, when included in the action: whereof the Fable of "Boreas and the Sun" affords us an example. An *epithet* well chosen is often a description in *itself;* and so much the more agreeable, as it the less retards us in our pursuit of the catastrophe.

I might enlarge much further on the subject, but perhaps I may appear to have been too diffuse already. Let it suffice to hint, that little *strokes of humour,* when arising naturally from the subject; and *incidental reflections,* when kept in due subordination to the principal, add a value to these compositions. These latter however should be employed very sparingly, and with great address; be very few and very short: It is scarcely enough that they naturally result from the subject: they should be such as may appear *necessary* and *essential* parts of the Fable. And when these embellishments, pleasing in *themselves,* tend to illustrate the *main action,* they then afford that nameless grace remarkable in Fontaine and some few others; and which persons of the best discernment will more easily *conceive,* than they can *explain.*

Joseph Jacobs (essay date 1894)

SOURCE: Joseph Jacobs, in *The Fables of Aesop: Edited, Told Anew and Their History,* by Joseph Jacobs, University Microfilms, Inc. 1964, 222 p.

[*In the following excerpt, reprinted in 1964, Jacobs discusses how the text of Aesop's fables has been preserved and changed as it passed through successive translators and publishers from antiquity to his day.*]

It is difficult to say what are and what are not the **Fables** of Aesop. Almost all the fables that have appeared in the Western world have been sheltered at one time or another under the shadow of that name. I could at any rate enumerate at least seven hundred which have appeared in English in various books entitled **Aesop's Fables.** L'Estrange's collection alone contains over five hundred. . . .

Aesop himself is so shadowy a figure that we might almost be forgiven if we held, with regard to him, the heresy of Mistress Elizabeth Prig. What we call his fables can in most cases be traced back to the fables of other people, notably of Phaedrus and Babrius. It is usual to regard the Greek Prose Collections, passing under the name of Aesop, as having greater claims to the eponymous title; but modern research has shown that these are but medieval prosings of Babrius's verse.

. . . . .

Most nations develop the Beast-Tale as part of their folk-lore, some go further and apply it to satiric purposes, and a few nations afford isolated examples of the shaping of the Beast-Tale to teach some moral truth by means of the Fable properly so called. But only two peoples independently made this a general practice. Both in Greece and in India we find in the earliest literature such casual and frequent mention of Fables as seems to imply a body of Folk-Fables current among the people. And in both countries special circumstances raised the Fable from folklore into literature. In Greece, during the epoch of the Tyrants, when free speech was dangerous, the Fable was largely used for political purposes. The inventor of this application or the most prominent user of it was one Aesop, a slave at Samos whose name has ever since been connected with the Fable. All that we know about him is contained in a few lines of Herodotus: that he flourished 550 B.C.; was killed in accordance with a Delphian oracle; and that *wergild* was claimed for him by the grandson of his master Iadmon. When free speech was established in the Greek democracies, the custom of using Fables in harangues was continued and encouraged by the rhetoricians, while the mirth-producing qualities of the Fable caused it to be regarded as fit subject of after-dinner conversation along with other jests of a broader kind ("Milesian," "Sybaritic"). This habit of regarding the Fable as a form of the Jest intensified the tendency to connect it with a well-known name. . . . About 300 B.C. Demetrius Phalereus, whilom tyrant of Athens and founder of the Alexandria Library, collected together all the Fables he could find under the title of *Assemblies of Aesopic Tales*. . . . This collection, running probably to some 200 Fables, after being interpolated and edited by the Alexandrine grammarians, was turned into neat Latin iambics by Phaedrus, a Greek freedman of Augustus in the early years of the Christian era. As the modern Aesop is mainly derived from Phaedrus, the answer to the question "Who wrote Aesop?" is simple: "Demetrius of Phaleron."

In India the great ethical reformer, Sakyamuni, the Buddha, initiated (or adopted from the Brahmins) the habit of using the Beast-Tale for moral purposes, or, in other words, transformed it into the Fable proper. A collection of these seems to have existed previously and independently, in which the Fables were associated with the name of a mythical sage, Kasyâpa. These were appropriated by the early Buddhists by the simple expedient of making Kasyâpa the immediately preceding incarnation of the Buddha. A number of his *itihâsas* or Tales were included in the sacred Buddhistic work containing the "Jātakas" or previous-births of the Buddha, in some of which the Bodisat (or future Buddha) appears as one of the Dramatis Personae of the Fables; the Crane, *e.g.,* in our **"Wolf and Crane"** being one of the incarnations of the Buddha. So, too, the Lamb of our **"Wolf and Lamb"** was once Buddha; it was therefore easy for him—so the Buddhists thought—to remember and tell these Fables as incidents of his former careers. It is obvious that the whole idea of a Fable as an anecdote about a man masquerading in the form of a beast could most easily arise and gain currency where the theory of transmigration was vividly credited.

The Fables of Kasyâpa, or rather the moral verses (*gathas*) which served as a *memoria technica* to them, were probably carried over to Ceylon in 241 B.C. along with the Jātakas. About 300 years later (say 50 A.D.) some 100 of these were brought by a Cingalese embassy to Alexandria, where they were translated under the title of "Libyan Fables" . . . , which has been earlier applied to similar stories that had percolated to Hellas from India; they were attributed to "Kybises." This collection seems to have introduced the habit of summing up the teaching of a Fable in the Moral, corresponding to the *gatha* of the Jātakas. About the end of the first century A.D. the Libyan Fables of "Kybises" became known to the Rabbinic school at Jabne, founded by R. Jochanan ben Saccai, and a number of the Fables translated into Aramaic which are still extant in the Talmud and Midrash.

In the Roman world the two collections of Demetrius and "Kybises" were brought together by Nicostratus, a rhetor attached to the court of Marcus Aurelius. In the earlier part of the next century (c. 230 A.D.) this *corpus* of the ancient fable, Aesopic and Libyan, amounting in all to some 300 members, was done into Greek verse with Latin accentuation (choliambics) by Valerius Babrius, tutor to the young son of Alexander Severus. Still later, towards the end of the fourth century, forty-two of these, mainly of the Libyan section, were translated into Latin verse by one Avian, with whom the ancient history of the Fable ends.

In the Middle Ages it was naturally the Latin Phaedrus that represented the Aesopic Fable to the learned world, but Phaedrus in a fuller form than has descended to us in verse. A selection of some eighty fables was turned into indifferent prose in the ninth century, probably at the Schools of Charles the Great. This was attributed to a fictitious Romulus. Another prose collection by Ademar of Chabannes was made before 1030, and still preserves some of the lines of the lost Fables of Phaedrus. The Fables became especially popular among the Normans. A number of them occur on the Bayeux

Tapestry, and in the twelfth century England, the head of the Angevin empire, became the home of the Fable, all the important adaptations and versions of Aesop being made in this country. One of these done into Latin verse by Walter the Englishman became the standard Aesop of medieval Christendom. The same history applies in large measure to the Fables of Avian, which were done into prose, transferred back into Latin verse, and sent forth through Europe from England.

Meanwhile Babrius had been suffering the same fate as Phaedrus. His scazons were turned into poor Greek prose, and selections of them pass to this day as the original Fables of Aesop. Some fifty of these were selected and, with the addition of a dozen Oriental fables, were attributed to an imaginary Persian sage, Syntipas; this collection was translated into Syriac, and thence into Arabic, where they passed under the name of the legendary Lôqman (probably a doublet of Balaam). A still larger collection of the Greek prose versions got into Arabic, where it was enriched by some sixty fables from the Arabic Bidpai and other sources, but still passed under the name of Aesop. This collection, containing 164 fables, was brought to England after the Third Crusade of Richard I, and translated into Latin by an Englishman named Alfred, with the aid of an Oxford Jew named Berachyah ha-Nakdan ("Benedictus le Puncteur" in the English Records), who, on his own account, translated a number of the fables into Hebrew rhymed prose, under the Talmudic title *Mishle Shu'alim (Fox Fables)*. Part of Alfred's Aesop was translated into English alliterative verse, and this again was translated about 1200 into French by Marie de France, who attributed the new fables to King Alfred. After her no important addition was made to the medieval Aesop.

With the invention of printing the European book of Aesop was compiled about 1480 by Heinrich Stainhöwel, who put together the Romulus with selections from Avian, some of the Greek prose versions of Babrius from Ranuzio's translation, and a few from Alfred's Aesop. To these he added the legendary life of Aesop and a selection of somewhat loose tales from Petrus Alphonsi and Poggio Bracciolini, corresponding to the Milesian and Sybaritic tales which were associated with the Fable in antiquity. Stainhöwel translated all this into German, and within twenty years his collection had been turned into French, English (by Caxton, in 1484), Italian, Dutch, and Spanish. Additions were made to it by Brandt and Waldis in Germany, by L'Estrange in England, and by La Fontaine in France; these were chiefly from the larger Greek collections published after Stainhöwel's day, and, in the case of La Fontaine, from Bidpai and other Oriental sources. But these additions have rarely taken hold, and the Aesop of modern Europe is in large measure Stainhöwel's, even to the present day. The first three-quarters of the present collection are Stainhöwel, mainly in Stainhöwel's order. Selections from it passed into spelling and reading books, and made the Fables part of modern European folk-lore.

We may conclude this history of Aesop with a similar account of the progress of Aesopic investigation. First came collection; the Greek Aesop was brought together by Neveletus in 1610, the Latin by Nilant in 1709. The main truth about the former was laid down by the master-hand of Bentley during a skirmish in the Battle of the Books; the equally great critic Lessing began to unravel the many knotty points connected with the medieval Latin Aesop. His investigations have been carried on and completed by three Frenchmen in the present century, Robert, Du Méril, and Hervieux; while three Germans, Crusius, Benfey, and Mall, have thrown much needed light on Babrius, on the Oriental Aesop, and on Marie de France. Lastly, I have myself brought together these various lines of inquiry, and by adding a few threads of my own, have been able to weave them all for the first time into a consistent pattern.

So much for the past of the Fable. Has it a future as a mode of literary expression? Scarcely; its method is at once too simple and too roundabout. Too roundabout; for the truths we have to tell we prefer to speak out directly and not by way of allegory. And the truths the Fable has to teach are too simple to correspond to the facts of our complex civilisation; its rude *graffiti* of human nature cannot reproduce the subtle gradations of modern life. But as we all pass through in our lives the various stages of ancestral culture, there comes a time when these rough sketches of life have their appeal to us as they had for our forefathers. The allegory gives us a pleasing and not too strenuous stimulation of the intellectual powers; the lesson is not too complicated for childlike minds. Indeed, in their grotesque grace, in their quaint humour, in their trust in the simpler virtues, in their insight into the cruder vices, in their innocence of the fact of sex, *Aesop's Fables* are as little children. They are as little children, and for that reason they will forever find a home in the heaven of little children's souls.

Guy Snavely (essay date 1908)

SOURCE: Guy Everett Snavely, "Latin Source of deVignay's Fables" in an introduction to *The Aesopic Fables in the "Mireoir Historical" of Jehan de Vignay*, edited by Guy Everett Snavely, J. H. Furst Company, 1908, pp. 31-36.

[*In the following excerpt, Snavely discusses how Jehan de Vignay translated Aesop's fables in a fairly literal manner from Latin prose versions into Old French.*]

While the ultimate source of the short collection of *Æsopic Fables* contained in Jehan de Vignay's *Mireoir*

Historial is probably to be found in Classical Greek literature,[1] it will be sufficient for the purposes of the present dissertation to investigate our author's immediate source. This latter is readily shown to be the same as that of the remainder of the work; namely, the *Speculum Historiale* of Vincentius Bellovacensis, which contains the same set of fables in a Latin prose form.

Vincentius Bellovacensis was a Dominican monk who lived from 1190 (?) to 1264, and who was on terms of intimacy with St. Louis (Louis IX, King of France, 1226-1270). Indeed it was he who assisted the King very largely in the formation of the newly-founded Royal Library at Paris, while at the same time the manuscripts of the King supplied him with the necessary materials for his own voluminous writings.[2]

The *Speculum Historiale,* the most popular of all his works, was written in Latin prose, by the order of his royal patron, St. Louis. In its manuscript form this is a massive work of four thick folio volumes divided into thirty-two books giving a general survey of the history of the world from the Creation to the beginning of the Thirteenth Century.

After a very brief account of the ancient nations of the East, the author proceeds to treat of the history of the Persians in Book IV. In enumerating the historic events of the reign of Cyrus the Great, he puts down as the most important occurrence in the first year of his reign the killing of Æsop by the people of Delphi, and proceeds to give a short account of his life and work in fable literature.

At this point our author gives by way of illustration a collection of twenty-nine *Æsopic Fables,* which he inserts bodily into his text. It seems likely that the general moral character of these fables recommended them to the attention of our author as being in close accord with the tone of all his own writings. In further support of this statement it is to be noted that especial emphasis is placed on the lives and deaths of the Christian martyrs, as would naturally be expected in a universal history written by a monk.[3]

If we turn our attention now to the text of the fables, we find that Jehan de Vignay has given a very close translation of his Latin original. Apparently he does not attempt to expand the text of his model, although he makes a few mistakes, as will be noted below.[4] We can not, however, make the same statement concerning all the translations by Jehan de Vignay. . . . [He] has shown originality in others of his works, and made many important additions to them.

To show how closely our author follows his Latin original in the fables under discussion, specimens of both the Latin and the French texts . . . will next be given. Let us compare first a few lines of the introduction to the fables:

VINCENTIUS BELLOVACENSIS.[6]

Anno regni primo Hesopus a Delphis interimitur.

Extant *Hesopi fabule* elegantes et famose quas Romulus quidam de Greco in Latinum transtulit et ad filium suum Tyberinum dirigit, ita scribens:

De civitate Attica Hesopus quidam homo grecus et ingeniosus famulos suos docet quid observare debeant homines. Et ut vitam hominum ostendat et mores, inducit aves et arbores bestiasque loquentes, probanda cuiuslibet fabula.

JEHAN DE VIGNAY.

En l'an du regne Cyre premier Esope est occis de Delphins.

L'Aucteur. *Les fables de Esope* sont nobles et renommees les queles Romulus, un Grec, estrait de Grec en Latin et les envoia a son filz, Tyberim, escrivant ainsi:

"De la cite de Atice Esope, un homme grec et engigneus enseigne ses sergens quel chose les hommes doivent garder. Et a fin que il devise et demonstre la vie des hommes et les meurs il amaine a ce arbres, oysiaus et bestes parlans a prouver chascune fable."

If we carefully compare these parallel passages, it is at once apparent that Jehan de Vignay closely imitates the style of Vincentius Bellovacensis. The former even, as it seems, places his words as near as possible in the same order as those in Latin. Thus in the first sentence he places the adjective "premier" after "Cyre," as if it modified that noun and not "an," as conveyed by the Latin "primo" in "anno regni Cyri primo."

This and similar examples tend to prove that Jehan de Vignay's translation is merely a mechanical rendering of the words without strict attention to the sense.

It is to be noted further that between the first and second sentences we have the words "L'Aucteur"[8] inserted in the French version. Although the interpolation exists in this form in all the manuscripts of the fables, the Latin text published by Hervieux,[10] as well as that of Inc. 1480 bis B, Bibl. de l'Arsenal, Paris,[11] contains the words: "Eusebius et actor." The same words appear again at the conclusion of the fables. They are written in red ink like all titles in all but the late manuscripts.

In the second sentence we find that our author again translates very literally. The only noticeable difference between the original and the translation is that the French has after "Romulus" the words "un grec," whereas "quidam" appears in the Latin original. This discrepancy and evident error (as Romulus sounds like a Roman name) may be explained by the proximity of the words "de greco" to "Romulus" in the Latin.

In the next sentence there is no variation at all from the Latin, and the translation is as literal as possible.

However, in the fourth sentence we find what might appear a slight attempt at originality of style; namely, the expansion of "ostendat" into "devise et demonstre." But as this is doubtless a common phrase in Old French and suits here very well our author readily adopted it. The remainder of the text is translated literally.

As a second specimen of Jehan de Vignay's methods of work we may cite a passage taken from about the middle of his fable collection, and compare it with the original:

VINCENTIUS BELLOVACENSIS.[13]

Item contra pauperum superbum. In prato quodam Rana uidit pascentem Bouem: putabat se posse fieri talem, si rugosam impleret pellem, et inflans se natos suos interrogauit. Sum ipsa quanta Bos? Dixerunt non.

JEHAN DE VIGNAY.

De rechief contre le povre orgueilleus. Une raine vit un buef pessant en un pre et cuidoit que ele peust estre faite icele se ele emploit sa piau froncie. Et ele enflant soy, demanda a ses filz se ele estoit ja aussi grant comme un buef, et il distrent que non.

Here, again, we notice the closeness in forms, order, and construction between the French text and its original. Jehan de Vignay, however, leaves his model in the last part of this passage, and changes the question and answer to the indirect form; that is, he has here preferred to keep to one style of narration, instead of changing to the direct form of address, as does his Latin original.

Another illustration, taken from toward the end of the collection, may now be finally given:

VINCENTIUS BELLOVACENSIS.[15]

Item contra pigros. Formica hyeme frumentum ex cauerna trahens siccabat quod estate colligens coagulauerat. Cycada autem eam rogabat esuriens ut daret aliquid illi de cibo, ut uiueret.

JEHAN DE VIGNAY.

De rechief contre les peresceus. Le formi el temps d'yver traioit le fourment de sa fosse hors et le sechoit, le quel fourment il avoit conqueilli en este. Le gresillon si le prioit que il li donnast aucune chose de viande pour vivre, car il mouroit de fain.

This, again, illustrates how closely our author followed Vincentius Bellovacensis in his translation. A few points may be commented upon, as his rendering of "hyeme," an ablative of time, by "el temps d'yver" instead of the more usual "en yver." This preposition "en" he employs a few lines below in the phrase "en este," as a translation for "estate." Moreover for the relative "quod" he gives in French both the relative and its antecedent, "le quel fourment." Again he condenses "colligens coagulauerat" into "avoit conqueilli." Finally de Vignay expands the participle "esuriens" into the clause "car il mouroit de fain."

But these changes, as well as those mentioned before, are of minor importance, and remembering that this same general closeness in forms and constructions prevails throughout the whole collection we may safely conclude that Jehan de Vignay translated as literally as possible.

[1] Cf. J. Jacobs, *History of the Æsopic Fable*, p. xx.

[2] Cf. L. Delisle, [*Le Cabinet des Manuscrits de la Bibliotheque Imperiale*, Vol. 1, Paris, 1868-81, p.8.]

[3] This fact was personally verified by an examination of MS. fr. 316 of the Bibl. Nationale, Paris, containing Jehan de Vignay's translation.

[4] See *infra*, pp. 33-36. . . .

[6] See L. Hervieux, *Les Fabulistes Latins, Phèdre*, Vol. II, 2nd ed., Paris, 1894, p. 234. . . .

[8] Cf. P. Meyer in *Romania* I, 364: *Spec. histor.*, XXIX, 108. *Author* (c'est-à-dire Vincent lui-même). . . .

[10] Cf. Hervieux, *op. cit.*, Vol. II, 2nd ed., pp. 234-245. The text here is taken from the second edition of Mentelin.

[11] A copy of the fables in this incunabulum was made by Dr. G. C. Keidel in 1897. . . .

[13] See Hervieux, *op. cit.*, Vol. II, 2nd ed., p. 240. . . .

[15] See Hervieux, *op. cit.*, Vol. II, 2nd ed., p. 245.

G. K. Chesterton (essay date 1912)

SOURCE: G. K. Chesterton, in an introduction to *Aesop's Fables*, translated by V. S. Vernon Jones, Doubleday Page & Co., 1912, pp. v-xi.

[*In the following excerpt, Chesterton describes each animal species in Aesop's fables as a symbol of a single fixed meaning, which enables the interaction of animal figures to convey its timeless message.*]

Æsop embodies an epigram not uncommon in human history; his fame is all the more deserved because he never deserved it. The firm foundations of common sense, the shrewd shots at uncommon sense, that characterise all the Fables, belong not to him but to humanity. In the earliest human history whatever is authentic is universal: and whatever is universal is anonymous. In such cases there is always some central man who had first the trouble of collecting them, and afterwards the fame of creating them. He had the fame; and, on the whole, he earned the fame. There must have been something great and human, something of the human future and the human past, in such a man: even if he only used it to rob the past or deceive the future.

The historical Æsop, in so far as he was historical, would seem to have been a Phrygian slave, or at least one not to be specially and symbolically adorned with the Phrygian cap of liberty. He lived, if he did live, about the sixth century before Christ, in the time of that Crœsus whose story we love and suspect like everything else in Herodotus. There are also stories of deformity of feature and a ready ribaldry of tongue: stories which (as the celebrated Cardinal said) explain, though they do not excuse, his having been hurled over a high precipice at Delphi. It is for those who read the Fables to judge whether he was really thrown over the cliff for being ugly and offensive, or rather for being highly moral and correct. But there is no kind of doubt that the general legend of him may justly rank him with a race too easily forgotten in our modern comparisons: the race of the great philosophic slaves. Æsop may have been a fiction like Uncle Remus: he was also, like Uncle Remus, a fact. It is a fact that slaves in the old world could be worshipped like Æsop, or loved like Uncle Remus. It is odd to note that both the great slaves told their best stories about beasts and birds.

But whatever be fairly due to Æsop, the human tradition called Fables is not due to him. This had gone on long before any sarcastic freedman from Phrygia had or had not been flung off a precipice; this has remained long after. It is to our advantage, indeed, to realise the distinction; because it makes Æsop more obviously effective than any other fabulist. *Grimm's Tales,* glorious as they are, were collected by two German students. And if we find it hard to be certain of a German student, at least we know more about him than we know about a Phrygian slave. The truth is, of course, that *Æsop's Fables* are not Æsop's fables, any more than *Grimm's Fairy Tales* were ever Grimm's fairy tales. But the fable and the fairy tale are things utterly distinct. There are many elements of difference; but the plainest is plain enough. There can be no good fable with human beings in it. There can be no good fairy tale without them.

Æsop, or Babrius (or whatever his name was), understood that, for a fable, all the persons must be impersonal. They must be like abstractions in algebra, or like pieces in chess. The lion must always be stronger than the wolf, just as four is always double of two. The fox in a fable must move crooked, as the knight in chess must move crooked. The sheep in a fable must march on, as the pawn in chess must march on. The fable must not allow for the crooked captures of the pawn; it must not allow for what Balzac called "the revolt of a sheep." The fairy tale, on the other hand, absolutely revolves on the pivot of human personality. If no hero were there to fight the dragons, we should not even know that they were dragons. If no adventurer were cast on the undiscovered island—it would remain undiscovered. . . . Fables repose upon quite the opposite idea; that everything is itself, and will in any case speak for itself. The wolf will be always wolfish; the fox will be always foxy. Something of the same sort may have been meant by the animal worship, in which Egyptian and Indian and many other great peoples have combined. Men do not, I think, love beetles or cats or crocodiles with a wholly personal love; they salute them as expressions of that abstract and anonymous energy in nature which to any one is awful, and to an atheist must be frightful. So in all the fables that are or are not Æsop's all the animal forces drive like inanimate forces, like great rivers or growing trees. It is the limit and the loss of all such things that they cannot be anything but themselves: it is their tragedy that they could not lose their souls.

This is the immortal justification of the Fable: that we could not teach the plainest truths so simply without turning men into chessmen. We cannot talk of such simple things without using animals that do not talk at all. Suppose, for a moment, that you turn the wolf into a wolfish baron, or the fox into a foxy diplomatist. You will at once remember that even barons are human, you will be unable to forget that even diplomatists are men. You will always be looking for that accidental good-humour that should go with the brutality of any brutal man; for that allowance for all delicate things, including virtue, that should exist in any good diplomatist. Once put a thing on two legs instead of four and pluck it of feathers and you cannot help asking for a human being, either heroic, as in the fairy tales, or unheroic, as in the modern novels.

But by using animals in this austere and arbitrary style as they are used on the shields of heraldry or the hieroglyphics of the ancients, men have really succeeded in handing down those tremendous truths that are called truisms. If the chivalric lion be red and rampant, it is rigidly red and rampant; if the sacred ibis stands anywhere on one leg, it stands on one leg for ever. In this language, like a large animal alphabet, are written some of the first philosophic certainties of men. As the child learns A for Ass or B for Bull or C for Cow, so man has learnt here to connect the simpler and stronger creatures with the simpler and stronger truths. That a flowing stream cannot befoul its own fountain, and that any one who says it does is a tyrant and a liar; that a mouse is too weak to fight a lion, but too strong for the cords that can hold a lion; that a fox who gets most out of a flat dish may easily get least out of a deep dish; that the crow whom the gods forbid to sing, the gods nevertheless provide with cheese; that when the goat insults from a mountain-top it is not the goat that insults, but the mountain: all these are deep truths deeply graven on the rocks wherever men have passed. It matters nothing how old they are, or how new; they are the alphabet of humanity, which like so many forms of primitive picture-writing employs any living symbol, in preference to man. These ancient and universal tales are all of animals; as the latest discoveries in the oldest prehistoric caverns are all of animals. Man, in his simpler states, always felt that he himself was something too mysterious to be drawn. But the legend he carved under these cruder symbols was everywhere the same; and whether fables began with Æsop or began with Adam, whether they were German and mediaeval as Reynard the Fox, or as French and Renaissance as La Fontaine, the upshot is everywhere essentially the same: that superiority is always insolent, because it is always accidental; that pride goes before a fall; and that there is such a thing as being too clever by half. You will not find any other legend but this written upon the rocks by any hand of man. There is every type and time of fable: but there is only one moral to the fable; because there is only one moral to everything. . . .

Louis Cons (essay date 1924)

SOURCE: Louis Cons, "A Neolithic Saying and an Aesop's Fable," in *American Journal of Archaeology*, Vol. XXVIII, No. 3, July-September, 1924, pp. 276-77.

[*In the following essay, Cons suggests that Aesop's fable of "The Farmer and the River" descends from a neolithic saying that comments on the infrequency of finding useable stone axe-heads in a river.*]

In Carl Halm's collection of *Aesop's Fables* (Leipzig, 1863) No. 308 . . . ["**A Woodcutter and Hermes**"] (No. 44 of Corais's collection) is the story of a woodcutter who, having dropped his axe into a river, refuses to accept the gold and silver ones that Hermes offers him in exchange. He asks only to have his own restored to him, and is rewarded for his honesty by the gift of the three axes. Other woodcutters having heard of this adventure, pretend to have lost their axes in the same river, and call for an axe of gold. Hermes indignant refuses to restore even their own. Then follows a moral to the effect that, in the eyes of the Divine, honesty is the best policy.

But in addition to this well-known version, there is another that in Halm's collection bears the number 308b, and the title . . . ["**A Farmer and a River**"]. In this variant, a peasant, walking by the river, let his axe or rather his axe-head . . . fall into the water. Hearing his lament, the River itself appears and there ensues the same scene of temptation, honest denial and reward as in the preceding version. Another man of the fields hearing of this, and wishing to enjoy the River's munificence, does what the others did. He jumps at the offer of the golden axe, and meets with a stern refusal. Then the honest peasant, seeing the disappointed schemer, tells him: . . . *"It is not every time that the River brings axes."*

Now on comparing these two versions, we are struck by several interesting facts that point to the more archaic character of the second. In the first place, the hero in 308b is no longer a "woodcutter," which smacks of a kind of professional specialization, but a plain man of the soil. In the second place, the lost tool is not an axe complete with its handle . . . , not the two-edged axe for felling trees, but . . . is properly an 'axe-head.' Thirdly, the divine agent is not Hermes but the River itself into which the axe was dropped. Finally—and this point seems to us to be the most striking and rich in conclusions—instead of the somewhat flat-footed and optimistic moral of the first version, we meet with a terse saying: *"It is not every time that the River brings axes."* It is especially in this connection that we may conjecture that we have to deal with a truly archaic form of the tale. Indeed if we give a little reflection to that last sentence, we realize that it is in all probability the whole nucleus, the original idea around which as it were, the tale gravitates, or better still around which it has crystallized. The situation strikes us as strangely plain and clear. Primitive man must have found sometimes in the river, axe-heads, evidently of stone, such as the fancy of the corrosive action of the streams will produce at times, and which are even today a source of confusion for the archaeologist and the anthropologist. Such lucky finds spared the neolithic man much work, and may we not surmise that a saying such as this one: *"It is not every time that the River brings axes"* represents a very natural generalization, and the most direct form of a proverb? In our variant, the object, . . . is precisely what we may expect in this hypothesis, what may naturally be found shaped in the bed of a river, an "axe-head"—not the more elaborate [complete axe] of the other version. But the axes of precious metals are probably accessories belonging to an ulterior stage of the tale, accretions added by ages in which the primeval [axe-head] of stone was no longer in use, by ages in which the primitive saying as it stood would have had no meaning. The story was elaborated in explanation of the saying.

If we are right we have here, represented by the version 308b of the Aesopic fables, a clear case of the way in which a tale grew out of a simple and immediate kernel: a prehistoric proverb. It would be too sweeping a statement to say that all fables must have grown that way. But it is at least worthy of mention to find one instance in which one fable did. We shall some day offer to the readers of the *American Journal of Archaeology* other such instances—if only the River brings us other axes to grind!

J. H. Driberg (essay date 1932)

SOURCE: J. H. Driberg, "Aesop," in *The Spectator*, Vol. 148, No. 5425, June 18, 1932, pp. 857-58.

[*In the following essay, Driberg discusses the possible influence of African folktales on Aesop's fables.*]

Little is known of Aesop till after he had won his freedom. Some say that he was a Phrygian slave—but that, perhaps, is because his master was Iadmon of Samos, who doubtless visited Phrygia from time to time. The more general view, however, is that he was an African, who, taken in slavery, drifted to Asia Minor and the Islands. His very name, Aesop, perverted from Acthiop, indicates his African origin. He visited the court of Croesus as a freed-man, and later met his death at Delphi, possibly (again accounts vary) for peculating trust funds—how could modern financiers survive such drastic treatment?—but more probably because, as was the way of Archilochus, his tongue was barbed with a greater degree of malice and sarcasm than the worthy Delphians could tolerate. That his fables early won him a reputation may be readily inferred, and it is remarkable that by Mohammed's time his reputation was so firmly established that the Prophet inscribed the thirty-first sura of the Koran to his name, Lokman as he was known to the Mohammedan world, the greatest fabulist then as now.

Caxton's translation from the French has now been worthily published by the Gregynog Press, a superb example of craftsmanship, beautifully and faithfully reproducing Caxton's delightful English and admirably decorated with engravings on wood by Agnes Miller Parker.[1] Such a volume reminds us of the debt which we owe to Aesop and which civilization owes to Africa. For many of the fables which the African slave wrote down for posterity in the country of his adoption are still current to-day in the country of his origin. Despite the transmutations they have suffered in their cultural migration their parenthood is still recognizable. They have acquired a new infection of morality: virtue is rewarded and wickedness punished: the evildoer does not "get away with it" as he so often does in Africa: the malicious joker falls into the snare which he sets for others, though we may perhaps see here the origin of the malice which was Aesop's own undoing. Certainly there is more than a trace of malice in many

of his stories, and in African folktales the hare, the father of mischief-makers, is compact of malice, cunning, falsehood, trickery and all the dubious elements which go to the making of a shady company-promoter.

How nearly he kept to his originals may be seen in his fable **"of the Wulf and of the Dogge,"** the moral of which, as Caxton remarked, is that "lyberte or freedome is a moche swete thynge," or in the fable **"of the Two Rats"** in which we learn that it "better worthe is to lyve in poverte surely than to lyve rychely beyng ever in daunger." What is this but the story of "the Dog and the Jackal," current to-day in the folk-repertoire of so many tribes? The dog having visited the jackal repays his hospitality by inviting him to a meal at his kind master's village. "Truly," cries the jackal, after seeing the dog soundly thrashed, "truly I, even if I live in the bush, am better off than you."

The crane, who was appointed their lord and master and ate up all the frogs, finds his prototype in many creatures as destructive of their subjects' lives. The fable **"of the Good Man and of the Serpente"** is reflected in the habitual kindness shown to snakes by many tribes: for snakes are the repositories of the souls of ancestors and they are cherished therefore and invited to live in the houses of men by daily gifts of milk. When the good man "was angry ageynste the serpent and took a grete staf and smote at hym . . . and felle ageyne in to grete poverte" as a result, his fate was what a good animist might have predicted for him. Frogs are still as arrogant as they were 2,400 years ago, when their ancestor puffed itself up to bovine proportions and burst: they never learn, it seems, but go on bursting themselves in the old way, and all because, just as Rostand's chantecleer brought in the sun, they bring in the rain—the proof of which lies in the fact that after a drought frogs croak with the first rains.

Less well known is the fable **"of the Foxe and of the Cocke."** Caught by a trick—for the cunning fox had flattered the cock into singing—the cock in his turn tricked the fox into speaking, whereon "the cok scaped fro the foxe mouthe and flough upon a tree"—of which the moral is that "over moche talkyng letteth: and to moche crowynge smarteth: therfore, kepe thy self fro over many wordes." Is this not one with the guineafowl, which, caught in a hunter's snare, kept first his daughter, then his son, then his wife and finally the hunter talking and arguing, and incidentally bragging, till with a sudden flutter of wings it flew out from the cooking pot, in which it had been placed alive, and (as the African tersely puts it) left the family and their friends to the joy of anticipation? "Words," it cried, as it flew away, "never cooked a guinea-fowl."

Then there is the Montayn whiche shoke, and all the people were "aferd and dredeful, and durst not wel come ne approche the hylle"—till they discovered that it was a mole which "caused this hylle shakynge," when "theyr doubte and drede were converted into Joye." There are hundreds of stories like this one in Africa, which tell of the fears and doubts of a people coming into a new country. The Lango, for example, coming to marshy lowlands from their old mountain homes were at first afraid to walk more than a cautious step at a time, lest the not too solid earth should engulf them, and their fears were only dissolved by the sight of an antelope running at full speed in front of them. But more often than not the modern fabulist reverses Aesop's order of things and tells how what is apparently harmless is found to be disconcerting or dangerous. In this class of stories is the enchanted stook of stubble, behind which two lovers lay in secluded contentment, till they were dragged back from their transports by the harsh voice of the stook—an uncompromising bachelor—telling them to be gone or he would turn them into slugs.

The Asse that frightened all the Beestes by his braying and would even have frightened the lion, if he had not been a party to the experiment, recalls the proverb which Aesop must have known that a roaring lion misses his prey. Even a cursory reading of his fables is enough to show how often Aesop embroidered this motif: for then, as now, the virtue of silence was well esteemed.

Assuredly, if Aesop was not an African, he ought to have been. For his fables, for all their gloss of an alien orthodoxy, have the fragrance of African forests, the malice of the hare that tricked the leopard to matricide, and the versatility of the chameleon who, sharing the cunning of the hare, possesses nevertheless an ambiguous morality which places it definitely on the side of the angels.

Notes

[1] *The Fables of Esope.* The Gregynog Press, Limited to 250 copies. . . .

Bateman Edwards (essay date 1942)

SOURCE: Bateman Edwards, "An Aesopic Allusion in the Roman D'Alexandre," in *Studies in Honor of Frederick W. Shipley, by His Colleagues*, Washington University Studies, 1942, pp. 95-100.

[*In the following essay, Edwards finds an allusion to Aesop in the "Roman d'Alexandre" that is not based on Phaedrus, Avianus, or any known French Translation, and so may be based on some undiscovered written source.*]

The study of fable transmission, with the enormous and complex amount of material of which much is still unknown or imperfectly studied, presents one of the most difficult problems in the history of medieval culture. The Middle Ages received their knowledge of the so-called Aesopic fable in general through the reworkings of Phaedrus and Avianus, which were themselves re-worked in numerous ways.[1] That these were not the sole sources of the medieval knowledge of fable material has, however, long been known, and various possibilities of diffusion have been suggested.[2] The following pages will show that, in twelfth- or thirteenth-century France, at least one Aesopic tale was known in a form which is similar to that of a Greek version, but which is not found in the usual Latin or French collections.

Three fables in the Greek Prose-Aesop present the jackdaw in a markedly similar light. In each he attempts to abandon his fellow daws for the company of other birds, and in each he is unsuccessful. In spite of these similarities, each fable represents a different type, with different motives, action, and moral.

1. Out of vanity the daw decks himself with feathers of various birds and presents himself at an assembly where he hopes to win the prize for beauty, but he is ignominiously stripped of his borrowed plumage by the birds he had laid under contribution. The moral teaches that those in possession of others' goods may appear to be what they are not, but that once stripped of their borrowed finery their true selves reappear.[3]

2. Out of vanity a large daw attempts to associate with the crows, but they refuse to accept him, and when he returns to his own kind he is likewise driven off. The moral is that those abandoning their own country are not looked on with favor in their new home and are shunned in their former one.[4]

3. Out of desire to share in the plenteous food of the doves, a daw whitens himself and attempts to pass himself off as a dove. When he utters a sound, however, he is recognized for what he is and driven off, and the daws, in their turn, refuse to allow him a share in their food. The moral is that we should be content with what we have, since avarice not only fails to gain the thing coveted but loses us what we have.[5]

Although in both 2 and 3 the daw finds himself cast out not only from the company of his choice but also from that of his kind, the motive of the desire for food is present only in 3, and only there is the moral directed against avarice. It is this motive and moral to which I find an allusion in a passage of the *Roman d'Alexandre.* In Branch IV, stanza 47,[6] Antiocus makes lament over Alexander's body, recalling his prowess and the great loss his death has brought to the world. Since Alexander was, for medieval times, the epitome of liberality, Antiocus finds occasion to commemorate what his dead master had once said to him in blame of illiberal, miserly rulers:

During rhetorical studies, fables were used to teach persuasiveness in public speaking.

Sire, vos me deïstes sor l'eaue de Dunoe
Qu'eschars rois pereceus tient l'usage a la
   choe
Qui quiert l'autrui viande et tous jors pert la
   soe.[7]

The antithetical expressions *l'autrui viande* and *la soe* can hardly refer to anything but the food which Aesop's daw sought unsuccessfully to obtain from the doves and that which his own kind subsequently denied him. In no other fable of the Prose-Aesop is the daw presented under similar circumstances. Likewise, the linking of the story with the moral directed against avarice appears in the French, and this fact constitutes additional proof of the latter's dependence upon the Aesopic fable.

Thus the connection between the Greek version and this medieval echo is evident, but what the intermediate links were by which the tradition entered western France cannot be determined. It is, at least, certain that the theme was not transmitted through Phaedrus or Avianus, since neither they nor their derivatives contain this fable.[8] Lacking any positive testimony, we can only speculate as to the way in which our French author acquired his knowledge of a theme whose meagre literary success is evidenced by the dearth of references to it. It is true that the Crusades offered opportunity for contact with Greek civilization, it is certain that the medieval period was not wholly ignorant of Greek, and it is likely that parts of the *Roman d'Alexandre* show first-hand knowledge of the Eastern countries. But such facts do not allow us to infer that our author is repeating a fable which he had heard told by voyagers returning from the East, or that he himself had made such a voyage. Oral tradition is certainly not an impossibility in the present case, but utilization of a written source is more strongly suggested by the fact that reference to the story is made in such a way as to emphasize the connection between the story and its moral. Now in both the Greek and the French the moral is a complex one. It is, as might be expected, a warning against greed, but more than that it brings out the point that excessive greed or avarice (. . . *escharseté*) defeats its own purpose and loses both the good possessed and that desired. This might well indicate that our French author knew the fable of **"the Jackdaw and the Doves"** in a written form which appended to the story proper the moral reflection usual in the Latin and French collections of his day.

So far, all attempts to find a contemporary version, either in Latin or French, have been unsuccessful. The earliest Latin version with which I am familiar occurs in the early printed collections of fables containing those translated by Lorenzo Valla in 1438 together with others translated by various Renaissance scholars. In the copy which I have examined, printed by Sebastian Gryphius in 1554[9] the fable reads as follows:

> Monedula, et Columbae.
>
> Monedula in columbario quodam columbis visis bene nutritis, dealbavit sese, ivitque, ut et ipsa eodem cibo impertiretur. Hae vero, donee tacebat, ratae cam esse columbam, admiserunt: sed cum aliquando oblita vocem emisisset, tunc eius cognita natura, expulerunt percutiendo: eaque privata eo cibo, rediit ad monedulas rursum: et illae ob colorem, cum ipsam non nossent, a suo cibo abergerunt, ut duorum appetens, neutro potiretur.
>
> Adfabulatio. Fabula significat, oportere e nos nostris contentos esse, consyderantes avaritiamm praeterquam quod nihil juvat, auferre saepe et quae adsunt bona.[10]

Although the fable is found in the only anonymous collection—*incerto interprete*—which the book in its present state contains, it would be rash to assume a date for the version sufficiently early for it to have served as source for the Old French allusion. If such were the case, this collection would be the only material in the book which is not due to Renaissance scholarship. Furthermore, the collection is dissimilar to the usual medieval productions because its extreme fidelity to the Greek amounts in the above fable, and in general throughout the seventy-seven others, almost in a word-for-word transposition.

Notes

[1] See Léopold Hervieux, *Les Fabulistes latins,* 2d ed., 5 vols., Paris, 1893-96; the article "Phaedrus" by August Hausrath in the Pauly-Wissowa *Real-Encyclopädie,* XIX (1938), cols. 1475-1505; Julia Bastin, *Recueil général des Isopets* (SATF), I (1929), pp. i-viii.

[2] George C. Keidel, "Problems in Mediaeval Fable Literature," *Studies in Honor of A. Marshall Elliott* (Baltimore, 1911), I, 281-303, especially pp. 284-286.

[3] Ed. K. Halm, *Fabulae Aesopicae Collectae* (Leipzig, 1901), No. 200[b]; ed. E. Chambry, *Ésope, Fables* (Paris: Les Belles Lettres, 1927), No. 162; ed. A. Hausrath, *Corpus Fabularum Aesopicarum* (Leipzig, 1940), No. 103. A variant of this type is given by Halm, No. 200. This theme has been exhaustively studied by Herbert D. Austin, "The Origin and Greek Versions of the Strange-feathers Fable," *Studies in Honor of A. Marshall Elliott* (Baltimore, 1911), I, 305-327, to whose article I am indebted for the present classification of types.

[4] Halm, No. 201; Chambry, No. 161; Hausrath, No. 125.

[5] Halm, No. 201[b]; Chambry, No. 163; Hausrath, No. 131. . . .

[6] *The Medieval French Roman d'Alexandre* (Elliott Monographs, Nos. 36 and 37), II (1937), 340.

[7] Branch IV, ll. 882-884.

[8] Phaedrus (I, 3) gives the story of the daw adorned with peacock feathers—a version related to type 1 above. Some manuscripts of the *Roman d'Alexandre* read *poe* for *choe,* probably in the attempt to connect the allusion to the Phaedrine fable of "Juno and the Peacock" (III, 18), but it is evident that the details of the two stories are incompatible.

[9] This copy is in the possession of the Library of Princeton University. A title-page, printed "apud haered. Seb. Gryphii," and giving the date of 1561, has been substituted for the original one, but the colophon furnishes the correct information. The Princeton copy is defective, lacking pp. 177-254 which contained the fables of Laurentius Abstemius. The Index Fabularum which follows (pp. 255-263) gives referecnces to fables on these lacking pages, although an attempt has been made to disguise the imperfect condition of the book by tearing off the page numbers of the Index and by cutting off that part of p. 255 which contained the final lines of the text. The fraud, however, is evident from the signature on pp. 257-263. The last signature preserved before the Index is *l,* while that on 257 is *r.* Thus all of *m, n, o, p,* and seven folios of *q* are lacking—a number which exactly makes up for the number of pages which, from the references in the Index, must have belonged in the complete book. One further peculiarity about the copy is the fact that the pagination of the Index Auctorum printed on the reverse of the substituted title-page does not agree with the paginatio of the book itself. It does, however, agree with that of an earlier Lyons edition, printed by I. Giunta in 1535. Of this last the British Museum possesses a copy which, like the Princeton volume, is incomplete, and lacks exactly the same material.

[10] P. 10.

Georgios A. Megas (essay date 1960)

SOURCE: Georgios A. Megas, "Some Oral Greek Parallels to Aesop's Fable's," in *Humaniora: Essays in Literature, Folklore, Bibliography,* edited by Wayland D. Hand and Gustave O. Arlt, J. J. Augustin Publisher, 1960, pp. 195-207.

[*In the following essay, Megas presents some oral Greek parallels to certain fables of Aesop in order to show how the oral tradition preserves the original relationships between animal actors and between action and moral better than the written tradition does.*]

It can be said concerning both folktales and fables that oral tradition preserves the original relationships more intact than does literary tradition.[1] This is especially true of Æsop's tales which, because of their shortness and their moral content, were used in the Schools of Rhetoric for centuries for the practice of students in writing correctly. They thus became linguistic essays whose main virtue was their concise form.[2] The "joy in relating" which is supposed to have attached to the old Æsopic fables, as Otto Keller[3] and Aug. Hausrath[4] rightly say, is not evident from the concise versions of the preserved collections. Of course, it is impossible for us to know how long these tales had survived in oral tradition before Demetrius Phalereus made the first collection of these tales in 316 B.C.

Thus, concerning both folktales and animal tales, the investigator should focus his attention particularly on oral traditions which present an integrity of relationships not found in versions in the literary tradition that have come down to us. I think that a few examples will suffice to prove this contention.

Let me take first the tale of the **"Snake and the Crab,"** Halm 346 = Chambry 291, Hausrath 211, Perry 196.

According to the ancient version, the crab advises the snake to improve its manners, and as the snake disregards his advice, the crab lurks while the snake is sleeping, seizes it by the neck with its claws and kills it. Seing now the snake lying straight as a rod in its hole, the crab said: "straight like this you should have been before; if you had been straight you would not have suffered this punishment."

Wienert explains the meaning of the tale thus: "die Schlange kann krotz allen Ermahnungen des Krebses von ihren krummen Wegen nicht lassen."[5] Similarly, Thompson's *Motif-Index* (J 1053) contains the reference: Snake disregards warnings to improve his manners: eaten by crab.[6] But the truth of the moral and practical way of living which underlies the last words of the crab is apparently different: One should be straight and sincere in one's manners; crookedness is punished. Besides, this is the meaning expressed in the

moral of the best version: "that those who approach their friends with evil intentions are harmed themselves." But no crookedness is evident on the snake's part against his friend the crab in the text of the tale. According to this, the snake's friend, the crab, kills the snake out of indignation, because the snake does not conform to his advice on morality!

But the story is different in the modern Greek versions of the tale. Here the killing of the snake is justified in the most natural and logical way: the two friends, after the entertainment that the snake received in the crab's nest, lie down to sleep; and then the snake, pretending that it is a habit of snakes to sleep coiled, coils around the crab and starts squeezing him little by little, intending to strangle him. So the crab's deed—killing the snake in his nest—is fully justified because of the necessity to defend himself against the sly intentions of his friend. Here is one of the popular versions of the tale that was written down in 1914, by a priest, Reverend P. Stampolas, in Megara, and published in *The Greek Tales,* 2nd ed. 1956, pp. 27-28, by G. A. Megas.

I. "The Crab and the Snake"

Once upon a time, a snake went down to the seashore and came across a crab and said to him: "My dear crab, I want one of you seafolks to be my pal that I may come down here now and then to eat some seafood, and if my pal wanted he could come over to my nest to eat some tender bits of grass. So what do you say? Do you want to be my pal?" And the crab, after having thought it over, replied: "Let it be so." Then they shook hands and sat down to eat right away.

The crab brought some seafood, shrimp and seaweeds for him. When they had finished the snake was in good humor and kept on saying to the poor crab, coiling around him in a way of embrace: "Cheer up friend, cheer up!"

His friend, the crab, was a little ashamed to say anything; yet he said to the snake: "You squeeze me too much, pal." "Yes, but I love you, pal!" answered the snake. And again after a while: "Cheer up, you friend, cheer up!" and the snake kept on squeezing him. "But you squeeze me too much, friend, and I'll blow up." And the snake that did it on purpose, said: "I can't help it, pal, I love you!"

"I love you too friend" answered the crab but he saw that things were going too badly. The snake kept on squeezing him all the more and did not loosen his hold at all.

After a while the snake squeezed him again, so much that the crab was desperate and turned around and stuck his claws in the snake's neck and then the snake let him loose at last and stretched out at full length in the crab's nest. Then the crab said to him: "There you are! That's all right now, nice and straight, friend, and not the other way, coiling around me as if you wanted to strangle me."

In some versions of the tale a cat sometimes replaces the crab. Published versions: I-2 of Peloponnesus. I. *Anecdotes, Tales, Proverbs,* by F. Chrysanthopoulos (Photakos), Mag. *Evdomas,* Vol. 3, 1886, p. 80 = *Historic Anthology* by Vlachoyannis, Athens, 1927, p. ιά. The crab pretends that he wants to tell a secret to the snake so that he will be saved from the snake's squeezing. The snake moves its head nearer the crab's mouth and so the crab sticks his claws in its neck and strangles it.[7] 2. Patras. Mag. *Laographia,* I (1909), 320: "The Crab and the Snake" = *Hellen. Laographia,* 1922, p. 255, by St. Kyriakides.[7a] After they have hunted together, they shared their prey in the evening. The snake wanted to eat the crab so that he might eat the crab's share too. But the crab said: "Why don't you lie straight friend?" And the snake answered "We snakes sleep this way" and after the snake had stretched, because of the pain it felt the crab said: "Now you are straight, pal." 3. Cyprus. Cypriot Fables by K. Hadjeioannou. Nicosia, 1948, p. 40, No. 10: "The Cat and the Viper Become Friends." The Viper crawled behind the cat which was walking one or two steps in front of her. The viper crawled now this way and then the other and tried to attack the cat. The cat turned around and said: "Why are you moving this way, friend?" "Mind your own business, friend," answered the viper. "There is nothing to worry about." But then, after a while, the viper started doing the same thing again. Then the cat turned around and struck the viper on the head with his claw and killed him. After he had killed him he started dragging him by the head; then he looked behind and saw that the viper was not going crookedly as before. "Now friend," he said, "you are going straight, but what's the use of having you now?"

Unpublished Versions:

4. Kyzikos, Asia Minor. Folklore Archives Mt. 276*, 1: "The Snake and the Crab". This is similar to the version from Megara. The Crab's words at the end are: "I want such a friend, a straight friend. I don't like such a crooked, cross-eyed friend." The antiquity of the tale is attested by its use in a couplet that is attributed to the poet Alcaeus (about 600 B.C.): . . .

The Crab said thus, having grabbed the snake with its claw; A friend should be straight and not think slyly.[8]

II. "The Farmer and the Snake"

We have two versions of this tale in Halm 96, which versions were also critically published by Chambry 81, Hausrath 51, I and III.[9] According to the first of these versions, the snake seems to have its hole in the farmer's field, and crawling out kills the farmer's boy without any reason at all. The farmer goes and lurks waiting for the moment the snake will crawl out of its hole so that he can strike it with his axe. But he misses the snake and strikes a stone nearby. According to the second version the snake has its hole under the farmer's threshold. Here also, the axe, having missed the snake, strikes at the opening of the hole and leaves its marks on a stone. In the first version, the attempt of the farmer to be reconciled with the snake is made simply by means of implorations out of fear, lest the snake kill him too. In the second version the farmer does not confine himself to words but puts a piece of bread and some salt by the snake's hole, bread and salt being the symbols of friendship among the modern Greeks in the same way as they are symbols of friendship among the ancient Greeks.[9a]

Both Chambry 81 and Hausrath 51 II carry in their critical edition a third version of the tale which had been already included in the edition by Koraes 1810 No. 141, p. 338. Here we have no explicit indication about the position of the snake's hole, and if we accept Bolte's correction, the farmer found the snake sunning itself. The main difference in this version from the previous versions lies in the fact that the farmer, having failed to strike the snake's head with his axe, cuts off only the end of the snake's tail, and then, in order to be reconciled to it, he puts some flour and honey by its hole, as flour and honey are usually offered in expiation to demons. That is why the snake's answer to the farmer's invitation refers here not to the marked stone, but to its cut-off tail. Two other versions, the third and the fifth in Chambry do not add anything new to the subject of our story.

Now, it should be noted that all three versions leave some obscure points as regards the subject of the Æsopian tale. There is no explanation (1) of exactly what the friendship between the farmer and the snake consists, so that the farmer wants to restore that friendship even after his boy's death, and (2) the reason the snake, which was so friendly, killed the boy. Concerning the food which the farmer puts by the snake's hole after the boy's death, there is a question whether this is offered only in expiation of the snake or as a symbol of friendship, or whether it represents merely a continuation of the daily offering of food to the snake. If the latter is true, what then was the snake giving in exchange to the farmer for this daily offering, since in folktales all over the world, animals are grateful to their benefactors? All that is obscure in the versions of the literary tradition is explained in the oral tradition of the Greek people in Thrace, Lesbos, Pontos, and the Peloponnesus. I give further the texts of the three popular versions, the first of which was written down in 1890 (it is included in the *Greek Tales* by G. A.

Megas 1957, p. 29, No. 7) in the village of Hadjigyrion, Kessanis County, in Eastern Thrace by a priest, Reverend Symeon Manasseides, and was published from a manuscript in the Folklore Archives of the Academy of Athens, Nr. 230, p. 132. The second version was written in the Pontian dialect in 1938 by Petros S. Petrides, a twelve-year-old student living in the village of Anatolikon, Ptolemais County, in Western Macedonia. This student heard the tale from his father who had come from Pontos (Folkl. Arch., Academy of Athens, No. 1202, p. 23). Finally, the third version written in 1938 by a fifteen-year-old girl student named Euphrosyne Eustathiou, comes from the village of Poulitsa, Corinthia County, in the Peloponnesus. She had not read any collection of tales, but she knew the tale, having heard it from her father (Folkl. Arch., No. 1182, p. 23).

III. "The Snake and the Shepherd"

1. Once upon a time there was a shepherd, and while he was milking his sheep he saw a snake crawling out of its hole and going about among his sheep. When the shepherd saw it, he poured some milk in a pot for the snake, and the snake drank it. The day after he poured some milk in the pot again, he put it near the snake's hole, and said: "My dear little snake, come out to drink some nice sweet milk," and the snake came out and drank it. When the shepherd went to get the pot he found a gold coin beside it, and he was very glad. At noon he put the pot of milk by its hole again and it came out and drank it, and it left another gold coin for him. And in the evening he poured some milk in the pot again, and he called it, and the snake came out and drank the milk. So the snake and the shepherd made friends, and he took some milk for the snake thrice a day, and it left three gold coins for him each day till the shepherd got very rich and decided to go to the Holy Grave, and he told his wife to give the milk to the snake every morning at dawn, every noon and every evening. Then he started out for the Holy Grave.

The shepherd's wife gave the snake its milk every day. The shepherd had also a little boy about five or six years old, and one day the boy was walking around among the sheep petting them and playing with them, but the snake was around too, crawling here and there. The boy did not see it and stepped on its tail, and the boy's pigskin shoes that had nails sticking out of their soles, cut off the snake's tail. Then the snake, hurt as it was, turned its head and bit the boy, and the boy was poisoned and died. And after the boy had died they buried him. At noon they put the pot of milk by the snake's hole, but the snake did not come out to drink it. In the evening they went to pour some more milk in the pot, but they saw that the milk they had poured at noon had not been drunk. So they did not put the pot of milk there any more, and the snake did not appear to crawl about in the fold any longer.

Six months went by; the shepherd came back from the Holy Grave and as he did not see his boy, he asked his wife: "Where's our boy?" "Our boy was bitten by the snake and died," said his wife. The shepherd did not say anything, he only poured some milk in the pot and he went to put it by the snake's hole and said to the snake: "My dear little snake, come out to drink some nice sweet milk!" But the snake shouted from inside: "Alas! Shepherd! As long as you remember your dead boy and I turn my head and see my tail cut off, what kind of friendship can exist between us?" So the friendship between the shepherd and the snake was broken.

. . . . .

2. In olden times there was a man who went to dig in his vineyard. His wife brought him a glass of milk. Then the husband said to her: "Leave it here, and go." When he went to drink the glass of milk he saw that a snake was drinking it. The man let the snake drink the milk and, in return for his kindness, the snake left a gold pound for him, and crawled back in its hole. Then the man took the pound and went home. This continued for two or three years. The man became rich, and one day he decided to go to the Holy Grave. So he took his son and went to the snake's hole and said to the boy: "Take this glass of milk, put it by the hole over there, and whistle for the snake. It will crawl out, drink the milk and will leave a gold pound for you." Then the man went home, and the next day he left for the Holy Grave. In the morning the boy went to the snake's hole, he left the glass of milk there and whistled. Then the snake crawled out, drank the milk and left a gold pound. The boy continued doing this thing for two or three days and then he got tired of it and said: "I'll kill the snake and I'll get all the pounds." In the morning the boy went there and put the glass of milk by the hole and the snake drank the milk and left a gold pound, and while it was crawling into its hole, the boy seized it by the tail, and the snake was pulling, and the boy was pulling at it till the snake's tail was cut off. The day after the boy went to the snake's hole, left the glass of milk, and whistled. The snake crawled out and while it was drinking the milk, it bit the boy and the boy died. When the boy's father came back, he asked where his son was. They said that the snake had bitten him and he died. The man got up in the morning and went to the snake's hole, and put the glass of milk there by its hole, and he whistled and the snake crawled out; it drank the milk, left a pound nearby and said to the man: "You are embittered about your boy, and I am embittered about my tail, and so there can be no friendship between you and me, and from now on you won't come any more; neither will I." So their friendship was broken.

. . . . .

3. Once upon a time there were a snake and a shepherd and the shepherd had many sheep; the

snake used to go and drink the milk secretly. But every time, before returning to its hole, it left behind a pound. As the snake used to go very often the shepherd saw it and hit it with his stick and cut off its tail. The snake went away and it was very angry; but it waited and found the opportunity it wanted; while one of the shepherd's little boys was sleeping, the snake went and bit him and the boy died. After some time, the shepherd who thought that he had lost both his little boy and the pounds, went to the snake's hole and shouted: "Hey! you snake, come out to talk with me." "O! my friend," said the snake "you miss your boy and I miss my tail, what sort of talk shall we have?"

Other versions of the tale:

Published versions:

4. Mytilene. *Zographios Agon* II, 1896, p. 23, No. 4.

> A poor old man who carried firewood on his back from the mountain, gave the meat he had roasted to the snake, which threw to him a pound with its tail. When the old man became rich, he left for the Holy Grave. His son got tired of taking meat to the mountain every day. He thought and planned to kill the snake and take all the pounds together. Having shot the snake, he managed to cut off only its tail, and it bit him and he died. Then the old man made an attempt to be reconciled to the snake by offering it some meat. But the snake said: "As long as I see my tail cut off, and as long as you remember your son, both of us will be sad and angry."

5. Audemion in Thrace. Mag. *Thrakika*, 10 (1938), 321, No. 206 = *Modern Greek Texts* by Loucatos, p. 53, No. 15.

> This is like the previous one, but the old woodcutter gives the snake milk instead of meat. His son, striking the snake with his axe, cuts off its tail and so it bites his arm, and his arm has to be cut off. Here the words of the snake are: "As long as you see your son's arm cut off, and as long as I see my tail cut off, we can't be friends any more."

Unpublished versions:

6. Adrianople. Folklore Archives, No. 285*: "The Man and the Snake."

> The snake, a big snake said to the man who was digging in his vineyard: "We snakes like milk. Bring me one oke of milk tomorrow." The snake said it would give him a reward of one gold coin a day. The same incident with the son of the vineyard owner: cutting off of the snake's tail and biting of the boy's leg. The snake's words and the moral are: "As long as I see my tail cut off, and as long as you see your son limping, there can be no friendship between us. . . ." The same is now with people:

"Once there is a dislike between two people, whatever you do to restore their friendship, you do it in vain."

As we can see in the above modern Greek versions, the connection of events is reasonable: the friendship between the man and the snake is based on the animal's gratitude for the offer of milk. It is a common belief that snakes like milk; and the killing of the farmer's son does not take place at the beginning of the tale, and without any reason, as in the ancient texts, but out of revenge toward the farmer's son for the avidity and ungratefulness he had shown toward the snake, which he had tried to kill during his father's absence so that he might gain its treasure. Thus, the man's attempt, after his return, to be reconciled to the snake again, is explained not by his fear "lest the snake kill him too," as is mentioned in some versions of the ancient tale, but by his wish not to be deprived of the reward that the snake used to give him before. This he does by offering the same kind of food that the snake liked from the very beginning—milk.

Offerings of the farmer to the snake are mentioned in the literary tradition also, and these offerings consist either of bread and salt, or of flour and honey. One might think that bread and salt are symbols of friendship, and indeed they have symbolized friendship in the customs and the language of Greece since ancient times. But it is more probable that bread and honey used to be offered to heroes and infernal Gods to calm them. Thus, the snake of the ancient tales falls into the class of these infernal Gods, and it should be thought of as the domestic snake, as is meant by a phrase in some versions: "a snake having its hole under a farmer's threshold." The description of the snake's living in a field should be taken only as a modification of that original form of the snake, so that the killing of the boy might be justified since the domestic snake was considered to be harmless.

My unforgettable teacher N. G. Politis who examined this Æsopian tale[10] considers its original to be a form of the tale that is preserved in the modern Greek tradition, and as taken down by Bernard Schmidt in Zante.[11]

> Eines Tages im Sommer kam eine Hausschlange hervor aus ihrer Wohnung und wand sich zischend an dem Herrn des Hauses, einem Landmann, vorüber, welcher eben mit Graben beschäftigt war. Dieser, nicht wissend, dass dieselbe der Schutzgeist seines Hauses sei, erhob sein Grabscheit und schlug damit auf sie los. Voll Unwillens floh die Schlange zurück in ihre Höhle. Tags darauf—es war ein Sonntag— da der Bauer mit seinem Weib zur Kirche gegangen war, kroch sie in das Haus, zerriss die besten von den Kleidungsstücken, die sie da vorfand, und nahm dann das kleine Kind, welches die Eltern in der Wohnung zurückgelassen, mit sich fort. Einige Frauen aus der Nachbarschaft hatten das mit

angesehen und berichteten es dem zurückkehrenden Vater. Da begab sich dieser, den Zorn der Schlange zu besänftigen, mit Brot versehen an den Eingang ihrer Wohnung und rief sie. Daraufhin kam denn auch die Schlange hervor samt dem geraubten Kinde, welches lebend und unversehrt war, und nahm das ihr dargebotene Brot an, sagte aber zugleich dem Bauer, dass er sich fortan hüten möge, sie zu misshandeln, da sie die Macht besitze, ihn und seine ganze Familie zu verderben.

Politis says that "in this legend we have a reasonable and independent account. The father struck the snake with his pick, having ignored the fact that it was the domestic snake. The snake in turn punished the sacrilegious man by tearing to pieces the best clothes in the house, and kidnapping his boy to its hole. The father, conscious of the snake's action, tried to appease it by offering it some bread. The snake accepted the offer which was a sign of favor, gave back the boy without harming him, and advised the host to respect it from then on because it had the power to ruin both him and his house."

According to Politis a later Latin adaptation of the Æsopian tale (Romulus II, II) is more similar to the popular tradition. Here is the translation from the Latin original:

> A snake used to come into a poor man's house under the table, and be fed upon crumbs. After a while the poor man became richer and, as he began feeling more and more angry with the snake, he hurt it one day with an axe. Some time after he was reduced to poverty again. He understood then that the lucky snake was the cause of what happened, and that it made him rich, before being wounded. He came to it to ask to be forgiven for his crime. The snake answered: "I will forgive you because of your repentance. But don't expect from me complete confidence, until my wound heals. We shall become good friends again on condition that I forget the perfidy of the axe. Suspected must be thus one who has hurt once somebody."[12]

As Marx assumed, as long as the snake frequented his house, the man was prosperous and happy. So the man understood that the snake was the cause of it.[13] It should be noticed that the relation in *Gesta Romanorum* C. 141[14] agrees with the tradition as well as the modern Greek version, Nr. 3, above, from Corinthia, because in this version the host of the house delivers the blow at the snake thoughtlessly. After that the snake takes revenge on him by going and biting his baby while he was sleeping. Evidently, as in the previous versions, it is the domestic snake here too. The shortcomings which this Æsopian tale presents are due, according to Politis, to the fact that "the man who adapted the tale, was not able to fit the elements which he received from the popular tradi-

tion to the purpose that the tale should serve and to its character." Also, the tradition from Zante in the writings of Schmidt, as well as the above modern Greek version, No. 3, from Corinthia, "indicates by what kind of changes the folk tales received sometimes the moral and didactic character which prevails in the collection of the Æsopian tales."

The tale of the farmer and the snake is found, as it is known, in the *Pantschatantra,* where it was inserted later. Here it has the same connection and sequence of events as in the modern Greek versions. Bolte and Polívka II 461f., who included the rest of foreign parallel versions (Kurdish, Serbocroatian, Syriac, Bulgarian, Turkish),[15] mention a version from the *Hist. Nat.,* (10,208), according to which a viper used to go every day to the table and take its food. Once, having its two young along, it happened that one of the little snakes killed the host's son. After that the viper killed its little one and did not go to the house any more. Pliny took the version from Phylarchos.[15] This same version we find in the redactions of the Latin tales absolutely unchanged. Therefore, owing to chronological reasons also, Bolte and Polívka[16] accept with Crusius, Marx, and Hausrath, that this tale which has so many versions, originated not in India as Benfey and Keller had asserted, but it is an original Greek tale.[17] At any rate, this tale, which, according to the oral tradition is a reasonable and independent version, and which, being widely diffused, as one can see in the parallel texts adduced by Bolte and Polívka, should be included in the *Types of the Folk-Tale,* by Aarne and Thompson, after Mt. 285.

It is true that all ancient tales do not survive nowadays in the oral tradition of the Greek people; however, those of the modern tales which correspond to ancient ones are more complete. They have a more logical connection of the details, and they do not depend mainly on the formulation of a moral, as is the case with the old tales that have come down to us. Therefore modern tales help us to restore the narrative aspects of the ancient tales. And not only that. There are cases where only hints of the existence of an ancient tale are found, and these hints are often preserved in one or two lines, or even in a proverb; in such a case the modern tales are able to fill the gaps of the ancient tradition. For example a mediaeval Greek proverb, which was preserved by Planoudis Nr. 275, says: . . . *Take me in your home so that I will drive you out of it* and in a more concise form Apostolis Nr. 676 . . . *The stranger drives out the tenant.* O. Crusius,[18] having in mind a sixteenth-century tale, narrated by Abraham a Santa Clara, which tells of hedgehog occupying a hare's den,[19] concludes that the Greek proverb had been derived from an ancient Greek tale.[19a] In reality, according to Bolte and Polßvka (II, 120), Archilochos, a poet of the 7th century, had in mind such a tale about a fox and a hedgehog. . . .

Plutarch refers to this verse as proverb. . . . [He observes that] the fox knows many things, but the hedgehog knows one important thing, that is, when the fox approaches him, as Ion (a poet of the 5th century) says, he curls up and makes a ball of spines out of his body so that the fox will not be able to harm him. The meaning of these verses is that he who is cunning will come across another person who is more cunning and will suffer some harm.[22]

The above meaning with a perfect justification of the details, is found in a modern Greek tale from Patras in Peloponnesus, published in the *Laographia,* I (1909), 322 = St. Kyriakides, *loc. cit.,* p. 255 = D. Loucatos *loc. cit.,* p. 6, No. 5.

"The Hedgehog and the Fox"

> Once upon a time when it was raining and hailing, a hedgehog found himself in a forest. He did not know where to find a hole so that he might be protected from the hail. After a while he found a fox hole and tried to enter it, but the fox which was inside would not let him. He begged her to let him put only his head in, as he did not mind about his body. After he had begged her very much, the fox let him put up his head in; but the hedgehog crawled in little by little and when he approached the fox he put up his spines and started pricking her. What could the fox do? She shrank into the corner as the hedgehog came further in. So little by little he threw the fox out of her hole and he remained the only master of it.

A version of this tale is published in *Laographia* 2 (1910), p. 692: "The Hedgehog and the Snake." This version also comes from Patras. The hedgehog who did not wish to make his den for the winter asked the snake to let him take the plan of his den. When he entered the snake's hole he prevented the snake from approaching by using his spines.

A second Greek version of the above tale, from Southern Italy, is published in G. Morosi's *Studi sui dialetti Greci della Terra d'Otranto,* Lecce, 1870, p. 76v = Em. Legrand, *Recueil de Contes Pop. Grecs,* Paris, 1881, p. 181: "La chèvre et le renard": The fox and the wolf are afraid of the horns of the goat, which is hiding in the fox's hole. The hedgehog throws her out.

The ancient tradition is completed perfectly by this modern Greek tale, but one more ancient tale can be added in the collection of Aesop's tales. This tale is similar in content to Aa-Th. 105: The cat's only trick (Motif-Index J1662—not 1661—), but it should be classified under an additional number between 105-110. The slyness of the hedgehog is seen in the fact that he enters the hole of the fox, and, pricking up his spines, throws out the fox little by little.[23]

Wienert in his notable study[24] recommends that we make a comparison between the ancient Greek tales and the fable literature of other peoples, as an appropriate method for the restoration of the narrative side of Aesop's tales to their old vividness.

I think it has been made clear by the examples given above, that this comparative research should have as a starting point the relations preserved in the oral tradition of the Greek people, because the Greek people of today have preserved along with their language, many customs of their ancestors and also the oral tradition, which, as it has been made clear already, has preserved the folktales purer than the literary tradition.[25]

Notes

[1] A. Aarne, *Leitfaden der vergleichenden Märchenforschung,* Hamina, 1913 (FFC 13), p. 8 and on.

[2] Bolte-Polívka, *Anmerkungen zu den Kinder- und Hausmärchen der Brüder Grimm,* IV 121. W. Wienert, *Die Typen der griechisch-römischen Fabel,* Helsinki, 1925 (FFC 56), pp. 26-28.

[3] Otto Keller, *Untersuchungen über die Geschichte der griechischen Fabel* (Jahrb. für klass. Phil. Suppl. 4 1862), p. 313.

[4] Aug. Hausrath, S.B. der Heidelberg.Ak.d. Wiss. phil.-hist.Kl. 9,2, p. 43 and 47 (1918). Cf. Wienert, *loc. cit.,* p. II.

[5] Wienert, *loc. cit.,* p. 89, ST. 13.

[6] This motif is not in the *Oral Tales of India* and it is missing from the *Types of the Folk-Tale* of Aarne-Thompson. In the Greek Catalog it was included under type No. 276.*

[7] It is mentioned that the hero of the Greek Revolution against the Turks, Theodore Kolocotronis told his men this tale at the beginning of the siege of Tripolis in 1821 in order to portray the crookedness of the Turks.

[7a] Also available for study in *Modern Greek Texts,* by D. Loucatos, Athens 1957, p. 52, No. 13.

[8] Ad. Koraes, *Collection of Aesop's Tales,* Paris, 1810, p. ιγ' and p. 315, note 6. See *Athenaeus,* XV p. 695A (Bergk *Poetae lyr. gr.* III 648,16). Cf. Hausrath, Pauly-Wissowa, RE VI,2 (1909), 1707.

[9] Unfortunately it was not possible for me to use the edition of B. E. Perry, *Aesopica,* Vol. I. Greek and Latin Texts, while writing this paper.

[9a] See Martin Nilsson, *Roman and Greek Domestic Cult,* p. 78, n. 1 (*Opuscula Romana* I in Acta Inst. Romani Sueciae XVIII 4° 1954).

[10] N. G. Politis, *Paradoseis,* Vol. 2, Athens, 1904, pp. 1096-97.

[11] *Das Volksleben der Neugriechen und das Hellenische Altertum,* Leipzig, 1871, p. 186.

[12] *Der Lateinische Äsop des Romulus und die Prosa-Fassungen des Phädrus.* Kritischer Text mit Kommentar und einleitenden Untersuchungen von Georg Thiele, Heidelberg, 1910, p. LIII, p. 118-120: "Der arme Mann und die Glücksschlange."

[13] A. Marx, *Griechische Märchen von dankbaren Tieren,* Stuttgart, 1889, p. 104.

[14] Bolte-Polívka, II 461.

[15] Two Turkish parallels should be added Eberhard-Boratav, Type 49, as well as the parallel in Tauschen, *Volksmärchen aus dem Jeyporeland,* No. 4 which is very different in meaning from the previous ones.

[15] Müller, *Fragmenta histor. Graec.* I, 340 fr. 27.

[16] *Loc. cit.,* p. 462.

[17] Cf. Hausrath, RE VI (1909), p. 1726.

[18] *Rhein. Museum f. Philologie,* Vol. 42, pp. 424-425.

[19] The following New Greek tale deals with the expulsion of the hare from its hole by the hedgehog. This tale comes from the village of Xiropigadon, near Naupactos, retold by an old woman. (Greek Folklore Archives, n. 1205 (M35), p. 33).

> Once upon a time there was a hare sleeping in his hole. There came a hedgehog and said to him: "Won't you let me sleep beside you, for daybreak has nearly overtaken me?" The hare drew himself aside and left a little place for the hedgehog to be too. And the hedgehog lay beside him and kept on getting closer to the hare so as to get warm. The hare, though unwilling, kept moving over, for the hedgehog with his big spines hurt him every little while. Thus it came about that the hare was thrown out of his den. Then the poor hare understood what had happened to him, and he swore, putting down a cross and seal, never to let anyone sleep in his den again.

[19a] N. G. Politis, *Laographia,* 1 (1909), 328.

[20] Bergk, *Poetae lyrici*[4] 2,418 fr. 118. Leutsch and Schneidewin, *Paroemiographi Graeci,* I, p. 147 (Zenob. V 68), 2,619,60. *Camerarius,* Fab. Aesopicae, 1570 p. 297.

[21] Plutarch, "Which of the animals is more prudent." 16, p. 971, and p. 1189,22.

[22] See the corresponding proverbs N. G. Politis, *Proverbs* Vol. I, p. 461, Nr. 37.

[23] The fable Hahn, *Griech. u. alban. Märchen* Nr. 91 is a version of the tale which I have classified under type No. 105**. Here the fox boasts that she has three sacks full of lies but the hedgehog, who is skilful in only one thing, that is to pretend that he is dead, manages to save her from a trap. See the foreign parallels Bolte-Polívka II 120.

[24] Wienert, *loc. cit.,* p. 27.

[25] See the last study by Karl Meuli, "Herkunft und Wesen der Fabel" Basel, 1954, Separatabdruck aus: *Schweizer. Archiv f. Volksk.* Bd. 50 (1954), p. 65f.

Spurgeon W. Baldwin, Jr. (essay date 1964)

SOURCE: Spurgeon W. Baldwin, Jr., "The Role of the Moral in 'La Vida del Ysopet con sus Fabulas Historiadas'," in *Hispania,* Vol. XLVII, No. 4, December, 1964, pp. 762-65.

[*In the following essay, Baldwin informs the reader that the moral in the fables of the Spanish Aesop under consideration is usually presented as a negative warning of punishment in a direct statement outside the story directed toward peasants more often than toward the aristocracy.*]

The first collection of fables to appear in Spain, made up primarily but not exclusively of fables attributed to Aesop, was printed at Zaragoza in 1489, and was given the title: *La Vida del Ysopet con sus fabulas historiadas.* This collection is available to us in a facsimile reproduction, with a prologue by Emilio Cotarelo y Mori, published by the Real Academia at Madrid in 1929. Although the Zaragoza edition is a translation of a volume printed in Germany, it occupies an important place in Spanish literary history for two reasons: first, it was probably one of the most widely read books of the time, judging from the large number of editions: second, it is the first known Spanish version of these fables, and served as model for a series of collections of Aesopic fables, having a popularity in Spain lasting almost down to the present time.

Cotarelo's valuable prologue is the lone twentieth-century study, and the only other detailed treatment is Alfred Morel-Fatio's "L'Isopo Castillan," which appeared in volume XXIII of *Romania* in 1894. The stories of the collection have been classified according to the Stith Thompson Motif Index by John E. Keller and James Johnson;[1] the most complete and up-to-date bibliographical work done on the volume appears in Michael Stern Pincus' *An Etymological Lexicon of the Ysopete historiado,* an unpublished doctoral dissertation of the University of North Carolina, 1961.

The fable bears stylistic resemblance to the most popular form of literary expression of the Middle Ages, the *exemplum,* a brief narration made for the purpose of illustrating in specific, concrete form the truth of an abstract moral expressed in more general terms. In like manner, the fable, an *exemplum* which usually employs animals as subjects rather than human beings, utilizes terse illustration to drive home the main point of an abstract principle (it should be understood that in stressing didacticism here we refer primarily to format, and intend no denial of the entertainment value of the fable).

There are two basic requirements for the successful fable: the physical events of the story must be based on characteristic traits and habits of the animals involved, and a logical connection must exist between those traits and some important abstract truth. In the common fable of the tortoise and the hare, for example, the traits are the slowness of the tortoise and the speed of the hare, and the facts of the narration have a clear relation with the abstract truth that persistent dedication to a cause can overcome the effects of unequal distribution of talent. The abstract truth must exist prior to the illustrative story, because the story is of interest only in that it illustrates the truth of the abstraction. On the other hand, the expression of the abstraction has no literary interest apart from its dramatic illustration by the facts of the story; the two are truly inseparable.

Most of the interesting traits and habits of the animal world had already been utilized in the most ancient of the Aesopic fables, composed by very astute observers of animal nature. Persistent efforts to invent different animal stories were made by the various composers of the 163 stories in the *Ysopet,* with the result that many of their fables were dull in subject matter, uninspired in plot, and tenuous in relation of story to moral (eventually their inventive efforts led them to extend the subject matter to include plants, inanimate objects, and human beings, just as writers of fables did in the Middle Ages and in antiquity).

Every story in this collection is told for the purpose of teaching the reader certain truths, with the possible exception of the well-known "Widow of Ephesus" story, which perhaps may be considered as lacking a moral, unless the antifeminism implicit in the tale (like such tales in the *Disciplina Clericalis* and the *Libro de los enganos* which attack the virtue of women) can be regarded as weakly moralistic. From the medieval collections of *exempla* down to Cervantes' *novelas,* the brief narration has no autonomous artistic exist-

ence; it always serves a larger purpose, to which the individual story is secondary in importance. In the italianate story, the larger purpose is fairly consistently to furnish entertainment during a period of time which otherwise promises to hold boredom for those present. In the medieval *exemplum,* the larger purpose is to illustrate a moral lesson; this tradition continues throughout the Middle Ages and early Renaissance, down to, and even through, the time of Cervantes. The morals of the *exempla* of Pedro Alfonso's *Disciplina Clericalis* are mostly not expressed, but they are clearly implied; many of the short stories of Cervantes carry the same kind of implicit moral (in the case of the stories in the text of the *Quijote,* the morals are explicit), and it was because of their didactic features, proceeding directly from the historical line of such stories, that Cervantes chose to call his short stories *novelas ejemplares.* The comments about the "larger purpose" refer to the general framework and format in which the stories are told. This does not mean that sober moralization pervades all of the stories; a story can be told ostensibly to illustrate a moral, while its real purpose is to entertain. It is now held by many scholars that the medieval *exempla* were didactic in form only, without any serious intent to teach, and that the tongue-in-cheek deference to didactic tradition constituted a part of the humorous appeal of the stories for the medieval audience. Scholars have traced this tongue-in-cheek tradition back from the medieval *exempla* to the tales related and written in Islam in the tradition of the Arabic *adab,* which can, in turn, be traced back to a similar tradition among the Persians and Hindus. It is not the purpose of this article to investigate the extent to which the stories in the *Ysopet* are soberly didactic or primarily recreational and entertaining, but further study along these lines is almost certain to yield interesting results.

Reasonable arguments can be made in support of the opinion that the *Ysopet* was directed toward the lower classes. Such an assertion is based in part on observation of the social level of the principal human characters in the fables; of the stories having as their subjects human beings, the overwhelming majority deals with peasants—farmers, shepherds, fishermen, charcoal makers, etc.

But the strongest supporting evidence lies within the morals themselves; even the most casual examination will reveal that the morals express truths of a type that would be of practical use to underlings, rather than to lords. Of the 163 stories, no less than thirty deal in some way with the admonition that one should accept his state in life and be satisfied with it. On the other hand, some nine or ten morals express the opinion that lords should always treat their inferiors with kindness and consideration. In the last section of the *Ysopet,* one story criticizes the wasteful recreation of the rich. Finally, there are many morals which preach the general theme that, if a person of low degree wishes to survive in a difficult world, he must be on guard against those who wish him evil and keep his wits about him.

The morals are without exception concerned with practical advice for getting along in life, often with overtones of stoicism highly appropriate and useful to those of low degree. Such morals express these opinions: reason is useless in the face of evil strength; don't fight when you can't win; endure suffering patiently; take the lesser of two evils; avoid evil company; always suspect a person who has done evil. The morals cited above have to do with defense against evil and represent an essentially negative point of view (the Golden Rule is expressed in negative form in several places, with words to the effect that one ought to refrain from doing evil to others, in order that others might likewise refrain from evil).

Since such morals as we have described above are concerned with precisely the same kind of subject matter treated in the proverbs of the people, and because glosses on proverbs in the form of illustrative stories were very popular later, it should be considered strange that the composers of the various morals should not have utilized that vast store of proverbs as a source of succinctly expressed practical morality. The still very popular Spanish proverb "Más vale pájaro en la mano que buitre volando" appears as the moral of one of the fables of Avianus,[2] but such an example, if not unique, is quite rare. We can also observe that the sort of homespun metaphor which is the very heart of the folk proverb is uniformly absent from the morals as they are expressed in the *Ysopet.*

In general, methods of expressing the moral are divided into two groups: direct statement outside of the story proper, and inclusion of the moral within the story, usually in the final speech of the character most concerned with the lesson. The latter alternative is by far the less satisfactory of the two alternatives, because it interferes with the unity of the action of the story.

There are many morals in the *Ysopet* illustrated by what are actually not stories at all, a feature shared by fabulistic lore of earlier ages, principally the Spanish Middle Ages. Number 11 of the first book (of the fables attributed to Aesop) can be completely summarized as follows: an ass made fun of a lion, but the lion declined to take vengeance, saying that he would not spoil his teeth on such "vana sangre"; there is really no story, and most of the narrative is devoted to the lion's statement of his refusal to take vengeance. A large number of other fables display a tenuous relation between the story and the illustrated moral: the normal story of the "dog in a manger" states as its moral that it is difficult to rid oneself of envy; another story tells of a man who both warms his hands and cools his

drink by blowing on them, and the pertinent lesson is said to be that one should beware of two-faced people. Both of these examples can be seen to have some vague connection with their respective stories, but they are dull and colorless. This feature supports the views of scholars who emphasize the entertainment value of such collections; the misfit moral may even have contributed to the humor for the fifteenth century audience. Furthermore, such tenuous relations between story and moral were widespread in medieval literature.

The most vivid example of a misfit moral is the one applied to the story of the man who caught a weasel along with a number of rats, and determined to kill them all. The weasel's valid protests that he actually helped, not hurt the man were rejected on the grounds that it had not been the weasel's *intention* to help him. The man then proceeds to kill the weasel, and the moral lesson is that motives behind acts are of great importance.

There are several instances in which the composer of the story has committed artistic error in the construction of his fable. Two stories in the collection are told to illustrate the moral that weak and small persons frequently have exalted opinions of themselves. These fables tell of flies that brazenly threaten to bite a bald man and a mule, respectively; in each case the story ends with a speech to the effect that the fly is wrong to have such an exalted opinion of his own importance. The moral lesson would be much more forcefully taught, and the artistic interests of the story served, if in each case the fly were in actual fact punished for his impertinence; to have him only warned lacks the force necessary to the artistic success of the fable. This same general criticism that the narrative does not fulfill its obligation to the moral holds truefor the fable of the man who catches a small fish: the fish protests to the man that he is too small to do him any good, and says that the man should throw him back until he grows up, at which time the fish will come back and be caught again by the fisherman. The fisherman states that he is too smart to be taken in by such a ruse, and the story ends; the lesson would be much more dramatically communicated if the story had as its end the mocking laughter of the fish as he swam away. Then the moral, that one ought not to give up that which is certain for that which is doubtful, would fit much more smoothly into the literary unity of the fable.

Briefly, these are the points stressed here: that the morals are concerned with practical advice for getting along in the world; that they are mostly directed toward lower class people, and are usually expressed from a negative point of view, stressing the prospect of punishment for imprudent acts: that the morals are stated either within the story proper or outside it, with the former alternative being the less desirable, artistically; that the story-moral format is frequently only traditional and that serious didactic purpose is therefore not an absolute requirement for the fable; that among the many fables presented in the *Ysopet* many fail to fulfill both basic requirements (presentation of characteristic traits of the animals, and relation of those traits to some important abstract truth) and exhibit shortcomings in the form of poor construction and of dull, tenuous, or completely inapplicable morals.

Aside from the implications one finds in Cotarelo's history (cited in the first paragraph), the impact of the *Ysopet* on the literature of the *Siglo de Oro* and subsequent times has not to date received the attention it deserves. Detailed study of the fabulistic material found in the various literary genres—short stories, plays, novels, etc.—would certainly produce enlightening and valuable results.

Notes

[1] *Southern Folklore Quarterly,* XXVIII, No. 2 (1954), 85-117.

[2] Latin poet of the 4th or 5th century A.D., author of 42 Aesopic fables.

Ben Edwin Perry (essay date 1965)

SOURCE: Ben Edward Perry, in an introduction to *Babrius and Phaedrus*, edited by Ben Edward Perry, Harvard University Press, 1965, pp. xi-cii.

[*In the following excerpt, Perry discusses the development of fable writing in Classical Greek and Roman literature, the transmission of the text of the fables, what constitutes a fable, and the influence of the ancient Near East on Greek fable lore.*]

1. *The Aesopic Fable in Antiquity*

In the long history of Aesopic fable, generically so called, the publication of a series of fables in verse meant to be read consecutively, each for its own interest and literary value, without a context or a specific application, is relatively late to appear. Phaedrus, in the time of Tiberius, is the first writer whom we know to have produced such a book, and his example was followed soon afterwards by Babrius, writing in Greek verse. The creations of these two poets mark a new epoch in the history of fable-writing and a midway point, as it were, in almost four thousand years of literary practice. Before Phaedrus, fables written in Greek prose were gathered into collections intended to serve primarily as repertoires of rhetorical materials, comparable to a collection of proverbs or apothegms of famous men, which would serve the needs of speakers or writers in quest of illustrations to be used within the context of an oration, a history, or an essay of

some kind. Such a fable-collection, written in prose, was informative in theory and purpose, rather than literary or artistic, although its author might, and usually did, take pains in the stylizing of it, so as to give it in reality a literary value apart from its ultilitarian *raison d'être*. The collection might be read in whole or in part for its own sake as entertainment, in case anyone chose to make that use of it, and some probably did; but it was not put forth by its author in the guise of literature or *belles lettres,* nor was it looked upon as such by the reading public.

Phaedrus and Babrius were the first writers to bring a disconnected series of Aesopic fables on to that avowedly artistic plane of literature, as an independent form of writing; but necessarily in verse, in order to sanction it as poetic composition. Only as such could it become, in theory, an independent form of literature in its own right, instead of a dictionary of metaphors. Told in verse a fable had the literary rating and recognition of poetry, by virtue of the form alone in which it was written, without regard to the subject matter; but a fable told in prose without a context, or a collection of such fables, was not literature, properly speaking, but raw material meant to be used in the making of literature, or orally. Archilochus in the seventh century B.C. had occasionally made use of beast fables written in iambic verse as a means of satirizing personal enemies, and Callimachus likewise includes a few Aesopic fables in his *Iambics,* just as he includes myths about gods and heroes; but in both cases it is the artistic verse that constitutes the literary form and the sanction for its publication apart from a context. A myth as such is not a literary form, but may be used as subject-matter in various kinds of poetry or prose, and the same is true of what we call fable. In the early period of Greek literature, and in the Alexandrian Age, fables might be the subject-matter of separate poems, but much more commonly they were used subordinately as illustrations in a larger context, whether of poetry as in Hesiod,[1] Aeschylus,[2] Sophocles,[3] and Aristophanes,[4] or in prose, as in Herodotus,[5] Xenophon,[6] Plato,[7] and Aristotle.[8]

It was not until late in the fourth century B.C. that the first collection of Aesopic fables in prose which we know to have been made was published by the orator and antiquarian scholar Demetrius of Phalerum as a handbook of materials intended primarily for the use of writers and speakers. This collection, entitled ***Aesopia*** and contained in one book-roll . . . , has not survived, but it was still extant at the beginning of the tenth century when Arethas had it copied, and it must have been one of the principal sources used by both Babrius and Phaedrus, as well as by such sophistic writers in late antiquity as Plutarch, Dio Chrysostom, Lucian, and Themistius in citing fables of Aesop.[9] There is no evidence that any book of Aesopic fables other than that of Demetrius, either in Greek or in Latin, was in existence before the time of Phaedrus; nor can we know to what extent, if any, the *Aesop* of Demetrius was altered or revised or incorporated in other collections in the course of its transmission throughout the Alexandrian Age. From the way in which Phaedrus speaks of his principal source as being a book of smaller compass than his own and as containing all the fables that he calls "Aesop's," we should infer that he knew only one book of Aesop and that that book was the official *Aesop* of Demetrius.[10]

Fragments of a collection of Greek fables in prose, in which each fable apparently was indexed with a promythium and ended with a gnomic sentence uttered by the last speaker in the fable, as in Phaedrus I 26 and IV 20, are preserved on the Rylands Papyrus No. 493, which was inscribed, according to its editor, C. H. Roberts, at some time in the first half of the first century after Christ.[11] This may well be a fragment of the book of Demetrius; but, whether it is really his text or not, it typifies, by its regular promythia and the absence of epimythia, the collection of Greek fables that must have served as the primary source for Phaedrus and the kind of fable-book that Demetrius himself had inaugurated.

The promythium, of which we have spoken, is a brief statement concerning the application of a fable made by the author before he begins the narrative, as in the Rylands Papyrus (lines 74 f.):

> *To a man who is rich, and also a scoundrel,*
> *the following fable applies.*

Or in Phaedrus III 5:

> *Success invites many to their ruin.*

The function of the promythium was to index the fable under the heading of its moral application for the convenience of a writer or speaker who would consult the fable-repertoire for the purpose of finding a fable that would illustrate an idea that he wished to express effectively; but since the promythium was also a summary of the fable's meaning, in other words its moral, it came to be added after the fable in the form of an epimythium, intended as an explanation . . . , when the original function of the promythium as an index had been forgotten or ignored,[12] as is the case in the first collection of Greek prose fables to be compiled after the time of Phaedrus, namely in the so-called Augustana collection, where we have epimythia throughout but no promythia. In Phaedrus epimythia appear for the first time along with promythia with increasing frequency; in his first book, where the formal influence of his Greek original is most conspicuous, the proportion of promythia to epimythia is 25 to 4, but in the fifth book it is 2 to 7. Babrius, writing in the last quarter of the first century, has some epimythia but no promythia.

The oldest and largest extant collection of prose fables ascribed to Aesop is that which is known as the Augustana, because the manuscript from which it was first published, now codex Monacensis 564, was once at Augsburg. This manuscript, with which the newly recovered tenth-century manuscript 397 in the Pierpont Morgan Library (cod. G) is very closely related, contains some 231 fables from the ancient collection and can be traced to an archetype of the fourth or fifth century. The original compilation was probably made in the second century, if not in the latter part of the first, but it was unknown to Phaedrus and uninfluenced by Babrius except for a few fables which may be later accretions.[13] The Augustana, known also as Recension I, is the parent stock on which three later editions of "Aesop's fables" were founded in large part, either directly or indirectly, namely Recensions Ia, II (known also as the Vindobonensis), and III (the Accursiana or the Planudean recension). Ia, consisting of some 143 fables, dates from late antiquity, probably the third or fourth century, and the same may be true, as I now think, also of Recension II,[14] which includes 130 fables in the best representative manuscript of its class, Vindobonensis 130. Some forty of the fables in this collection are in twelve-syllable verse and are derived indirectly from Babrius, but the others, in prose, are badly rewritten on the basis of I. Recension III, first printed by Bonus Accursius at Milan in 1474, hence known as the Accursiana, was made by Maximus Planudes near the beginning of the fourteenth century. It consists of 127 fables, of which 62 come from Recension II and are freely rewritten, the others mainly from the Augustana (I) with little or no alteration. In modern times this revised and abridged edition of the traditional fables was often printed as the vulgate Greek *Aesop* before the publication of the Augustana (I) by Schneider in 1812. The fables of Recensions I, II, and III are printed separately in the editions of Chambry[15] and of Hausrath,[16] and likewise such fables of Ia as are not found in I. What Chambry designates Class IV is the so-called Bodleian Paraphrase of Babrius, consisting of 148 fables briefly summarized in prose, introduced by promythia, and ascribed to Aesop by its unknown compiler. The Augustana fables of Class I and its derivatives are independent of the Babrian tradition, except that many of them are derived from an early source common to both I and Babrius, probably the *Aesop* of Demetrius. The entire corpus of Greek fables in prose, with the exception of fables depending on the citation of Greek authors other than fabulists, and of a few taken into the collections from unknown sources, is made up of Recensions I-IV, contained in upwards of one hundred MSS., all but three of which are of later date than the thirteenth century. Many of these manuscripts are of mixed contents, containing blocks of fables drawn from two or more of the recensions above mentioned, and in some of them there is much conflation of one textual form with another, and occasionally newly worded paraphrases of older forms.

With the exception of Aphthonius, the fourth-century rhetorician whose forty fables, written in a highly artificial style, are *not* ascribed to Aesop, all the authors of extant fable-collections in Greek or Latin prose are either anonymous, like the authors of Recensions I-IV, or else, like "Romulus," Pseudo-Dositheus, and "Syntipas," obviously pseudonymous. The real author of a collection such as the Augustana (I) does not put his own name on the book he has written, but lets it pass under the name of Aesop, because he is not literarily ambitious in what he is doing. He makes no bid for recognition as a writer. The substance of his fables is presumed to have been invented by Aesop, but the prose in which they are written can be anybody's text other than Aesop's and nobody was likely to claim it for himself. The fables of Babrius and Phaedrus were known and cited under their author's names so long as they remained in the original verse, but neither author's name survived on the prose paraphrases of his fables: Babrius became "Aesop," and Phaedrus "Romulus" translating "Aesop." Likewise in the medieval period we have many books of fables written in prose by unknown authors and a good number of fables in verse bearing the names of the authors who composed them: Avianus, Marie de France, Walter Anglicus, John of Schepey, Alexander Neckam.

The Arabic version of the so-called "Fables of Bidpai," known as *Kalilah wa Dimnah,* was translated into Greek by one Symeon Seth about A.D. 1080 and was widely circulated in many copies under the title *Stephanites and Ichnelates;* but this famous fable-book, derived from the Indian *Pañcatantra,* exerted thereafter, strange to say, not the slightest influence upon the traditional Greek *Aesop.* In the entire Greek tradition there is not, so far as I can see, a single fable that can be said to come either directly or indirectly from an Indian source; but many fables or fable-motifs which make their first appearance in Greek or Near Eastern literature are found later in the *Pañcatantra* and other Indian story-books, including the Buddhist *Jatakas.*

2. Nature and Origin of Fable

The rhetorician Theon in his *Progymnasmata* (ch. 3) defines fable in the Aesopic sense of the term . . . [as] a fictitious story picturing a truth. This is a perfect and complete definition provided we understand the range of what is included under the terms . . . [story] and . . . [truth]. The "story" may be contained in no more than a single short sentence, or it may be much longer, or include some dialogue; but it must be told in the past tense, as stories normally are, and it must purport to be a particular action or series of actions, or an utterance, that took place once upon a time through the agency of particular characters. . . . [Because] a fable "pictures" a truth it is, theoretically, only a metaphor in the form of a past narrative; and when it happens to be very short it is indistinguishable from what we call a prov-

erb, and what the ancient Semitic writers called a "likeness" (Aram. *mathla,* Heb. *mashal,* Ar. *mathal,* likewise Armen. *arak*). Proverbs are of several distinct kinds, according to the structural form in which they are cast, including precepts in the imperative mood, and generalities stated explicitly in the present tense; but the kind of metaphorical proverb which is identical with Aesopic fable, in respect to both its function as metaphor and its underlying structure as narrative of an event in the past, is peculiarly at home in western Asia and Greece throughout the ancient and medieval periods, in contrast with the various forms of proverb that have prevailed in western Europe, in ancient Egypt, and in the *Proverbs of Solomon;* which, by the way, betray their Egyptian background or inspiration by the very fact that they include no metaphorical proverbs of the Graeco-Semitic type of which we are speaking.[17]

Since fable as we have defined it amounts to nothing more than an indirect and inexplicit way of saying something, the truths that it pictures metaphorically can be, and are in practice, of many different kinds. Often the idea conveyed is a general proposition relating to the nature of things or to types of human or animal character or behaviour, with or without an implied moral exhortation; but often also it is a particular truth applying only to a particular person, thing, or situation. The general proposition implicit in the fable is not always a moral or ethical principle, as is sometimes supposed; on the contrary, the majority of fables in our collections, as W. Wienert in his study of *Sinntypen* has pointed out, do not teach moral truths, strictly speaking, but rather matters of worldly wisdom and shrewdness (*Lebensklugheiten*); and even the moral lessons are formulated more often than not on that basis.[18] The particular truth which a fable pictures is descriptive of some one thing and is often purely personal in its application. A fable of this kind may say in effect, for example: "You are (he is) the same kind of fool (or clever fellow) as the creature whose actions I have described," or, in the words of Nathan applying his fable about the unjust conduct of a certain man to King David (*2 Samuel* 12, 1-6), "Thou art the man." This is typical of many fables the primary aim of which is not instructive but satirical or in the nature of personal denunciation, and of those fables which consist mainly in a jest or a clever bit of repartee.

It will be seen from what we have been saying that fable, strictly defined according to its structure as fictional narrative in the past tense, and as metaphor, includes a very wide range of stories and brief statements which differ from each other multifariously, when we look at their narrative substance as such, at their brevity or extension, or at the many kinds of "truth" that they picture without stating it explicitly. Such is the theory of fable and the sanction for its inclusion, with all its varieties, in the wisdom books of the ancient Semitic Orient and in the collections of Greek and Latin fables. Considered from the point of view of its narrative substance, an Aesopic fable, which is a rhetorical device from the beginning, may be, at the same time, any one of the following types of story: a fairy tale (*Märchen*), an aetiological nature-myth, an animal story exhibiting the cleverness or the stupidity of this or that animal, or a series of amusing actions, a novella, like the story of the widow in Phaedrus (App. 15), a myth about the gods, a debate between two rivals (*Streitgedicht*), or an exposition of the circumstances in which a sententious or a witty remark was made. It is a mistake, often made in the past by literary historians, to look for the origin of fable in the narrative materials out of which fables are made. The history of those materials is something very different from the history of fable as a form of art, as a *façon de parler*. The latter has not originated until the peculiar purpose and metaphorical orientation which governs the material and shapes it, and thereby makes it fable, is in force. If we look for that rhetorical device in early literary history we shall find it and rightly call it the origin of fable; but if we look for the origin of fable in mere animal story or epic, as many have done, we shall never find it, because stories of that kind, not intended to teach anything by implication, have been told everywhere in the world from time immemorial.

Some of the materials contained in our ancient and medieval collections of fables ascribed to Aesop are not fables at all, but similes or allegorical descriptions of animal nature which fall outside the fundamental form-pattern of narrative in the past,[19] and, apart from the intrusion of such obviously alien forms, many of the stories which are made to look, at least faintly, like genuine fables in our sense of the term, by a *tour de force* on the part of the fabulist in his epimythium, are in reality nothing more than stories told for their own sake as amusement, with little or no concern for their metaphorical meaning or their application to anything. In their choice of stories to be told, the authors and compilers of fable-books throughout the ages have been guided at many points by motives other than what constitutes a "fable" in any strict sense of the word. They are naturally more concerned with the story itself as a means of entertaining the reader than they are with the matter of literary form, of which they take a very broad and, at times, somewhat dim view. They think of fable loosely as a story told for the purpose of communicating an idea or a truth of some kind dramatically and metaphorically; and, with that in mind, they usually, though not always, add a moral, even when the story itself does not invite one and the moral so given is plainly perfunctory or farfetched. So much they concede to theory. In practice, however, they are intent on entertaining or amusing their readers as much as possible with something interesting, witty, or dramatic; and in the pursuit of this more immediate purpose, they often choose a story for its own sake as

entertainment, with scant regard for its ethical or philosophic meaning, which may be anything or nothing and is not self-evident nor the real object for which the story was told.

A writer such as Phaedrus or Babrius seems to feel that his first duty is to be interesting, and that any story can be given a moral of some kind, if necessary, once the story is finished and the entertainment has been delivered. Any responsibility that he may feel for the metaphorical meaning of his story is, in the circumstances, vague and secondary. Because the fables in a collection can have no *specific* context to which they are subordinated as illustrations, which is the normal function of a Greek fable, but must be put forth as illustrations suitable for use only in *imagined* situations, accordingly the author is under no pressing obligation to choose a fable that would be effective in inculcating an idea metaphorically by its use. The idea pictured by the story that he brings in for its own interest may be obscure and hard to see in spite of the epimythium that he contrives, or his story may admit of two or more morals; whereas there could be only *one* moral, and that a very obvious one, to a fable used by a Menenius Agrippa in addressing a Roman crowd in a political crisis (Livy II 32, 9-12; *Aes.* no. 130), or by a writer such as Horace or Plutarch intent on bringing an idea forcefully to his reader's attention. Fables have a new orientation, and their aim swerves back and forth on the compass of the writer's artistic purpose, when they are brought into a collection and told one after another independently of any definite context. In that independent environment fables tend strongly to be told for their own interest as narratives, whether witty, clever, amusing, dramatic, satirical, sensational, sentimental, or wise. The story itself becomes the main thing, instead of the idea that it is supposed to convey implicitly.

Aetiological myths, of which many are included among the so-called fables of Aesop, are, as a type, ill suited for picturing a truth metaphorically, because they lead up to an *explicit* statement of how and why this or that reality came into being. Thus the long fable about the **"Eagle and the Beetle"** (*Aes.* 3 . . .), which Aesop is said to have told to the Delphians to persuade them not to violate the little shrine of the Muses at which he had taken refuge as a suppliant, was a nature-myth made up to explain aetiologically why eagles lay their eggs at a season of the year when no beetles are around; and it is only from one of several episodes in this myth, not from the sum of it, that the moral is drawn by Aesop in the *Life* (ch. 139), and a different moral by the author of the Augustana collection (=*Aes.* 3). The fable about the lark burying her father in her head, because there was not yet any earth, is ascribed to Aesop's telling by Aristophanes in the *Birds* (vss. 471 ff. = *Aes.* 477 = Halm 211), but it has no metaphorical meaning. For the speaker in Aristophanes it proved by explicit statement that the lark was older than the earth, but originally it was told to explain why the lark has a large crest on its head.

Another form of story that is alien by nature to Aesopic fable as we have defined it, although it is interspersed with Aesopic fables in literary texts from Sumerian times onward in the East, as well as in the Greek and Latin fable-books, is the literary debate between two rivals, each of whom claims to be superior in some way, or more useful to man, than the other, praising himself and belittling his opponent. The rivals may be seasons, trees, plants, animals, members of the body, material substances or implements, or human institutions. A familiar example is the contest between the laurel tree and the olive in the *Iambics* of Callimachus (*Aes.* 439), which the author, a studious antiquarian, attributes to the ancient Lydians. This is over 90 lines long. Other, much shorter, specimens of the same type which we find in the fable-collections are "**Stomach and Feet**" (*Aes.* 130), "**Winter and Spring**" (271), "**Peacock and Crane**" (294 = Babrius 65), "**Fir Tree and Bramble**" (304 = Babrius 64), "**Ant and Fly**" (521 = Phaedrus IV 25), "**Butterfly and Wasp**" (556 = Ph. App. 31), etc.[20]

Like attracts like, even when the likeness that brings things together is inherent in only one part or one aspect of a thing, rather than in the whole of it. Around a nucleus of proverbs and fables that picture a truth metaphorically, with the gnomic idea clearly outstanding, a large number of only partially and externally similar narratives, both short and long, have accumulated, by a kind of snowballing process, in the Greek and Latin fable-books, with the result that many fables, loosely so called, make their appeal to the reader primarily as something clever or amusing in itself, while the gnomic ideas or morals that they convey, if any, are not easily discernible.

Similar in many particulars is the heterogeneity of content which we find in the wisdom books of the ancient Semitic Orient, which books must claim our attention henceforth as the historical background of Greek fable. These Oriental wisdom-books, written in cuneiform script on clay tablets, belong in a continuous literary tradition that extends from Old Babylonian times down to the fall of the Assyrian empire, from around 1800 B.C., or earlier, to the end of the seventh century B.C., in Sumerian texts at first, then later in Akkadian, Assyrian, and Aramaic texts, including the *Book of Achiqar*. Most of the Akkadian wisdom-texts now known were published and interpreted by Orientalists before the year 1930; but since then, and indeed within the last decade, great advances have been made in the publication and interpretation of Sumerian literary texts of many kinds, and among these the proverbs and fables recently published and explained by Dr. Edmund Gordon have the closest bearing on the

early history of Aesopic fable in the Near East. In a long and very informative review-article written in 1960,[21] Dr. Gordon tells us that he "has now identified some 106 Sumerian fables and parables of 'Aesopic' type," so called with explicit reference to the definition of the type as we have given it. . . . "These include," he continues, "fifty-six fables containing quoted speeches (or even dialogues), twenty-five short fables without speeches, and twenty-five parables."[22] The clay tablets on which these fables and proverbs are written come mainly from Nippur and Ur, are dated by the Sumerologists to the eighteenth century B.C. or earlier, and are divided into upwards of twenty different collections of proverbs, which are designated by numbers, such as Collection One, Collection Two, etc.

The examples quoted below from the translations published by Kramer, Gordon, Ebeling, and others will serve to illustrate the nature of fable in the old Mesopotamian literature, and its fundamental similarity to Greek fable in the matter of form and sometimes even in substance. The following abbreviations are used to indicate the sources of our quotations:

> Kramer = S. N. Kramer's *From the Tablets of Sumer; Twenty-five Firsts in Man's Recorded History,* Indian Hills, Colorado (The Falcon's Press), 1956.

> Gordon (1958) = "Sumerian Animal Proverbs and Fables: Collection Five," by Edmund I. Gordon in the *Journal of Cuneiform Studies,* XII (1958), pp. 1-75.

> Gordon (1959) = Gordon's *Sumerian Proverbs, Glimpses of Everyday Life in Ancient Mesopotamia,* published by the University Museum, University of Pennsylvania, Philadelphia 1959. Contents described by Perry in *Am. Jour. Arch.,* 66, 205-207.

> Ebeling = E. Ebeling, *Die babylonische Fabel und ihre Bedeutung für die Literaturgeschichte* (= *Mitteilungen der altorientalischen Gesellschaft,* Bd. II, Heft 2), Leipzig, 1927.

> *Achiqar* = the Assyrian *Book of Achiqar* in the fragmentary Aramaic version edited and translated by A. Cowley in *Aramaic Papyri of the Fifth Century B.C.,* Oxford, 1923, pp. 222-226.

Kramer p. 157: "The smith's dog could not overturn the anvil; he therefore overturned the water pot instead." Ibid., p. 158: "Upon my escaping from the wild ox, the wild cow confronted me." Gordon (1959), p. 274: "The house built by the upright man was destroyed by the treacherous man." This metaphorical type of proverb, which is technically a fable in spite of its brevity, is common in Greek proverb lore, as was pointed out above. . . . Consider the following Greek specimens in comparison with the Sumerian in regard to form: Diogenian VIII 7, "The mountain laboured and gave birth to a mouse." We recognize this as a fable when Phaedrus (IV, 24) adds a few circumstantial details: "emitting tremendous groans, and the lands about were filled with the greatest expectations." Zenobius, V, 42, "Someone told a story to an ass and he wiggled his ears." *Iliad*, 17. 32: "The fool learned after the event." . . . Theognis, 329 f.: "The prudent man was slow-moving, but he overtook the swift-footed man in the pursuit, Kyrnos, by the righteous decree of the immortal gods." This is a fable as truly as the story of "**the Hare and the Tortoise**" (*Aes.* 226), which has the same meaning metaphorically. No. 105 in the medieval Greek proverbs ascribed to Aesop (*Aes.* pp. 261-291): "Even the sheep bit the man who was helpless"; cf. Phaedrus I 21, where an ass attacks a disabled lion.

Gordon (1959), p. 222: "The fox having urinated into the sea said, 'The whole of the sea is my urine.'" Compare Francis Bacon's summary of Abstemius 16 (= *Aes.* 724) in his essay *Of Vainglory*: "The fly sate upon the axle-tree of the chariot-wheel and said, 'What a dust do I raise!'" The identity of proverb and fable in such cases was recognized by Quintilian, who speaks of it as follows (*Inst. Or.* V 11, 21): παροιμίας *illud genus, quod est velut fabella brevior et per allegoriam accipitur: "Non nostrum, inquit, onus; bos clitellas."*

Gordon (1958) p. 69, no. 5. 116: "The dog went to a banquet, but when he looked at the bones (which they had for him to eat) there, he went away, saying, 'Where I am going now, I shall get more to eat than this.'" The point seems to be that it is foolish to let go the profit that one has in his hand in order to pursue a larger one that is not yet within reach; as in the fable of the dog with a piece of meat in his mouth going after his shadow in the water (Babrius 79, Phaedrus I 4).

Gordon (1958), p. 46, no. 55: "The lion had caught a helpless she-goat. 'Let me go, [said the she-goat and] I will give to you a ewe, a companion of mine.' . . . 'If I am to let you go [said the lion, first] tell me your name.' The she-goat [then] answered the lion: 'Do you not know my name? My name is You-are-Clever.' When the lion came to the sheep-fold he roared out: '[Now] that I have come to the sheep-fold, I am releasing you.' She [then] answered him from the other side [of the fence?]: '[So] you have released me! Were you [so] clever? Instead of (?) [giving you] the sheep [which I promised you] even I shall not stay [here].'" As Gordon observes, the she-goat seems to have out-witted the lion by flattering him, and the lion to have learned the familiar lesson that "a bird in the hand is worth two in the bush."

Ebeling, p. 42: "A mouse (?), fleeing from a . . . entered a snake's hole and said, 'The snake-charmer sent me here. Greetings!'"

Ebeling p. 50: "When the gnat had settled on the elephant he said, 'Brother, have I been a burden to you? [If so], I will go away, over there by the pond.' Said the elephant to the gnat, 'I was not aware that you had settled on me. What are you anyhow? And if you have left, well, I didn't notice your departure either.'" This is exactly the same fable as Babrius 84 . . . , except for the elephant in place of a bull. Note the reference to a pond in the Babylonian fable, corresponding to the river in Babrius. After quoting the Babrian fable Ebeling remarks that "here for the first time we can make out for sure that not only the substance of a Greek fable corresponds with that of a Babylonian fable but even the wording down to matters of detail. In this case one may almost speak of the translation of a Babylonian original into Greek or at least of a paraphrase." The fable of "**the Gnat and the Bull**" in the Augustana collection (*Aes.* 137) omits note-worthy details which Babrius has in common with the Babylonian version. The latter, according to its colophon, was "copied" in 716 B.C. "from an older original."—Gordon (1958), p. 1.

Achiqar (Cowley), p. 224: "The leopard met the goat and she was cold. The leopard answered and said to the goat, 'Come, and I will cover thee with my hide.' The goat answered and said to the leopard, 'What hast thou to do with me, my lord? Take not my skin from me.' For he does not salute the kid except to suck its blood."

Ibid., 226: " . . . one to the wild ass, 'Let me ride upon thee and I will feed thee' . . . '[keep for thyself] thy feeding and thy saddle, but I will not see thy riding.'" Here we have essentially the same story with the same moral as in the fable of "the [wild] horse and the stag," which Stesichorus, according to Aristotle in his *Rhetoric* (II 20 = *Aes.* 269a), told to the people of Himera.

Ibid., 225: "The bramble sent to the pomegranate saying, 'Bramble to Pomegranate, what is the good of thy many thorns to him who touches thy fruit?' . . . the pomegranate answered and said to the bramble, 'Thou art all thorns to him who touches thee.'"

Old Testament, 2 Kings 14. 9: "And Jehoash the king of Israel sent to Amaziah king of Judah, saying, 'The thistle that was in Lebanon sent to the cedar that was in Lebanon, saying, Give thy daughter to my son to wife'; and there passed by a wild beast that was in Lebanon, and trode down the thistle.'"

Aesopic fable in the sense in which we have defined it, as a rhetorical form of expression, was one of the cultural inheritances which the Greeks were bound to receive almost subconsciously from their western Asiatic neighbours; who, under the influence of the Sumerian-Babylonian-Assyrian literary tradition, had been morally minded and thoroughly literate for many centuries before the Greeks themselves had begun to write anything or to think philosophically. The narrative substance which came to the Greeks from the Babylonians and Assyrians is less significant for the history of fable than the traditional form-pattern which we have described; but it is noteworthy that form and substance have been transmitted together in some cases, as in the fable of the gnat and elephant quoted above, and that, regardless of form, the ideas implicit in the proverb-lore of the Babylonians ofter recur in Greek fables and proverbs. The story of the eagle and the vixen (= *Aes.* 1), for example, which was used in a fable by Archilochus, seems to be descended from the old Babylonian legend of Etana concerning the eagle and the serpent. . . . [23]

Notes

[1] *Works and Days,* 202-212, "Hawk and Nightingale" (*Aes.* 4a).

[2] In Fragment 139 from the *Myrmidons,* "Eagle shot by an Arrow winged with his own Feathers" (*Aes.* 276a); *Agamemnon* 716-736, Man who reared a Lion's Cub in his house, told to illustrate what Helen's coming to Troy meant for the Trojans.

[3] *Ajax,* 1142-1158, two short fables used by Menelaus and Teucer respectively in their altercation with each other.

[4] *Birds,* 474 ff. (*Aes.* 447), "Lark burying her Father" *Wasps,* 1401 ff., "Aesop and the Bitch" (*Aes.* 423); *ib.,* 1427 ff., "The Sybarite Man" (*Aes.* 428); *ib.,* 1435 ff., "Sybarite Woman" (*Aes.* 438).

[5] *History,* I, 141, "Fisherman pipes to the Fish" (*Aes.* 11a).

[6] *Mem.* II, 7. 11, "Sheep and Dog" (*Aes.* 356a).

[7] *Alcib.* 123a, "One-way Traffic into the Lion's Cave" *Aes.* 142, Babrius 103); *Phaedo* 60b, "Pleasure and Pain" (*Aes.* 445).

[8] *Rhetoric,* II, 20, "Horse and Stag" (*Aes.* 269a), said to have been told by Stesichorus; *ib.* "Fox and Hedgehog" (*Aes.* 427); *Meteor.* II 3, "Aesop at the Shipyards" (cf. *Aes.* 8); *Polit.* III 13.2, "Lions and Hares" (*Aes.* 450).

[9] See pages 288-290 and 304 ff. of my article "Demetrius of Phalerum and the *Aesopic Fables*" in *Transactions of the American Philological Association (TAPhA),* 93 (1962), 287-346.

[10] Cf. p. lxxxiv below in the section on Phaedrus.

[11] C. H. Roberts, *Catalogue of the Greek and Latin Papyri in the John Rylands Library,* Manchester, 1938, III, 119 ff.

[12] This is explained more fully in my article "The Origin of the Epimythium" in *TAPhA,* 71 (1940), 408-412, and in the article "Fable" in *Studium Generale,* XII (1959), 35.

[13] Concerning the dating of the original Augustana collection, see *TAPhA,* 93 (1962), 288 f., note 8, where the matter is discussed in detail.

[14] This recension, based primarily on I, has three interpolated episodes in the *Life* and many odd readings in both *Life* and *Fables* which cannot be Byzantine in origin, but must have been taken from an ancient and variant version of both texts. Because the manuscripts containing this Rec. II—what I have called SBP in the *Life*—are all later than the twelfth century, I had supposed that the interpolations that it contains were taken from an ancient text in the twelfth century; cf. *Aesopica,* I, pp. 22 and 308, note 30. Recently, however, a fragment of the *Life* in this recension has come to my attention written in an eleventh-century hand on a parchment leaf bound in a manuscript at Saloniki; and from this I infer that Rec. II with all its interpolated readings was made in late antiquity, in the fourth or fifth century.

[15] Aemilius Chambry, *Aesopi Fabulae,* Paris (Les Belles Lettres), 1925, 2 vols.

[16] A. Hausrath, *Corpus Fabularum Aesopicarum,* Vol. I, fasc. 1, Leipzig (Teubner), 1940; fasc. 2, *ib.* 1956; fasc. 2, second edition by H. Hunger, *ib.* 1958.

[17] Krumbacher (*Byz. Lit.*[2] 906 f.) states the matter truly, as follows: "Orientalisch ist . . . die Form: 'Einem schenkte man einen Esel und er schaute ihm auf die Zähne', occidentalisch die Form: 'Einem geschenkten Gaul schaut man nicht ins Maul.' Durch diese Eigentümlichkeit scheidet sich das byzantinisch-neugriechisch-südslavisch-orientalische Sprichwort prinzipiell von den abendländischen." This form of proverb is common in ancient Greek literature as well as in the Byzantine period. See the examples cited below on p. xxxi. Proverbs of this kind are common in Sumerian, Babylonian, and Assyrian literature, but I have looked in vain for examples in Erman's *Literature of the Ancient Egyptians* (English translation by Blackman, London, 1927), where, amid the numerous ethical and didactic writings of both the older period and that of the New Kingdom, one might expect to find them. For the literal dependence of a series of Solomon's proverbs in the Old Testament upon the Egyptian book of Amen-em-ope, see Erman in *Oriental. Literaturzeitung,* 1924, no. 5, and Gressmann in *Ztschr. für alttestam. Wiss.,* 42 (1924), 272 ff.

[18] W. Wienert, *Die Typen der griechisch-römischen Fabel,* Helsinki, 1925, p. 86.

[19] This is true, for example, of the statement about the way of the beaver in *Aes.* 118 (Augustana) and in Phaedrus App. 30; about the ape's twin offspring in Babrius 35; the description of the allegorical statue of Time in Phaedrus, V, 8; and how bears fish for crabs, *ib.,* App. 22.

[20] S. N. Kramer in his book *From the Tablets of Sumer . . .* p. 161 informs us that seven such "literary debates," all relatively long, are preserved wholly or in part on Sumerian tablets. Much shorter specimens of the same type also occur in the Sumerian and Neo-Babylonian proverb collections, and in; *Achiqar* for example, the contest between the elephant and the wren in No. 1 of Gordon's "Collection Five" . . . , which consists of one short speech by each of the characters, and that between the bramble and the pomegranate in *Achiqar*. The widespread use of this form in the medieval and early modern literature of Europe, and in Arabic and Hebrew texts, is described by M. Steinschneider in a monograph entitled "Rangstreit-Literature" in *Sitzungsb. d. Wien. Akad.,* 155 (1908). Many of these disputes are between plants or trees, and this type seems to be favoured more in the Orient, from the earliest times onward, than in the West; cf. A. Wünsche, *Die Pflanzenfabel in die Weltliteratur,* Leipzig, 1905. The Mesopotamian origin of this literary form, in relation to its Greek derivatives, was first pointed out by Hermann Diels in an article entitled "Altorientalische Fabeln in griechischen Gewande" in *Internationale Wochenschrift für Kunst und Wissenschaft,* IV (1910), 993-1002.

[21] "A New Look at the Wisdom of Sumer and Akkad" in *Bibliotheca Orientalis,* XVII, 122-152, Leiden, 1960. This study deals with the subject matter of J. J. A. van Dijk's important book entitled *La sagesse suméro-accadienne; Recherches sur les genres littéraires des textes sapientiaux avec Choix de textes,* Leiden, 1953. W. G. Lambert's *Babylonian Wisdom Literature,* which was still in press when Gordon wrote, is described as "a new and complete edition of all the Akkadian wisdom compositions, as well as the Sumero-Akkadian bilingual material." I have not yet seen this book, but it is bound to be one of great value for students of the history of fable in the ancient Near East.

[22] By parable Gordon understands what I should classify as a subdivision of fable, namely the kind in which "the action is possible, in contrast with fables in which the action is unreal."

[23] See R. J. Williams "The Literary History of a Mesopotamian Fable," in *Phoenix* 10 (Toronto, 1956), 70-77.

Kirby Congdon (essay date 1966)

SOURCE: Kirby Congdon, "Aesop Revisited," in *Américas,* Vol. 18, No. 10, October, 1966, pp. 1-2.

[*In the following essay, Congdon suggests that fables, using animals as abstract qualities, show individuals that they cannot control God but they can control themselves.*]

> Since there was probably never, at least in later times, any standard text of the fables, it was inevitable that both the range and their style of composition should change in accordance with the literary fashions of the day and the fancy of individual authors—Ben E. Perry. *Studies in the Text History of the Life and Fables of Aesop.* American Philological Association, 1936, (Philological Monographs, No. 7), p. 160.

The appeal of animal characters in fables lies in the fact that we, the reader, or listener, help create them in our minds. As with puppets and marionettes, we supply life to the disjointed action, expression to the immobile face, and finally meaning to the old and familiar roles of the animals. We clothe the minds and motivations of animal characters with the attire of human action or thought. The advantage is that they still remain removed from us, yet illustrative. If they were people, our tolerance, amusement and understanding would be short-lived because the satire or ironies would come too close to home and we would react in an emotional and subjective way instead of remembering the stories as classic and universal examples of common behavior.

Fables have the direct appeal of cartoons quickly told in words. But that simplicity can be misleading. Their dramas are so economically drawn that adults usually dismiss fables as children's literature. But behind the light mask of animal characters are eyes that do not blink. The flat tapestry is woven out of tough thread, and its depth is not so shallow as we may think. No trace of the original form of most of the well-known fables exists, but, however little we know of their original intent, we can still see in these works a power of vision and a philosophy grounded on solid earth. That earth is a pastoral one, but not romantic (let alone Disney-esque). It is a child's view of the world only in the sense that the child's frank eye sees all events without judging them, witnessing the bad with the same equanimity as it sees the good. Nor are these fables nostalgic reminiscences of the farmyard. The wildlife in them is wild. Whatever bucolic moments there are, these are times for the retraction of claws used for clawing, and for the folding of wings used for fleeing. Rest is for a drawing up of forces in reserve, a time of temporary safety between dangers.

This is Aesop's nature, La Fontaine's society and Krylov's politics. But fables reconcile the fierce and desperate side of nature with a firm belief in the humane. A fable "enforces some useful truth" and the need for the humane in a hard world is the essence of that truth.

As we see them in the fables, we see around us, too, the skills of selfishness, trickery, tyranny and ruthlessness practiced. The good do not always triumph. Fables tend to be amoral and realistic rather than lessons for proper behavior. The vision in fables is larger than moralizing, just as nature's reality, too, is beyond any of our systems of ethics. The authors seem to say that if we are to have any code of ethics or any other sense of humanity, we have to face the facts as they are before we can take them into our account. For, in fact, nature does not need us. We may say God's hand catches the sparrow, but the sparrow still falls. And, unless we believe that the sparrow falls, the hand is empty—if there is a hand. We may extend the idea of the hand, but the fabulists want us to be sure we see the sparrow first. The just outcome of our own conflicts, like those of the animals, is never secure. The last-act curtain never falls. Our personal dramas are disjointed and individual occurrences more than they ever are exemplifications of the good and meaningful life.

The plot lines subordinate the personal, or the psychologically interesting aspect of dramatic conflict as details which are incidental to the direct, visible and universal action itself on which fables depend, and in which real daily life, unanalyzed, exists and moves.

Yet, the actors are still ourselves, but once removed. They are animals—a dog, a cat, a fox. In those stories in which people do take a part, their identity, too, is abstracted and generalized into a farmer, a country maid, a traveler, a goatherd. The generalization of character focuses our attention on the action of the characters rather than on an analytical identification of a particular dog, cat, or person, and his individualized virtues. Lambs, as a breed, are helpless. Wolves by nature do eat lambs. There is no moral conflict here because these are facts, not plans or thought-out action. We see it happen. The moral connotations of innocence and experience which we may censor, or tack onto the action, calm us who may be lambs. But the Lamb is still dead. And the Wolf repententh not. We learn nothing new about either actor himself. What we learn is only how all wolves act and how all lambs act—or, in effect, how wolf-like and lamb-like people act.

Here, too, speaks the truth and the reality of the very ocean's roar: nature's indifference to, finally, our deaths and the irrevocability of that death. But this is a partial truth, because we are humans with egos, and, like all living things, wish or try to continue on and so defy that death. But the fabulists do not go that far. That is

philosophy and they are concerned with society—with the persistence of the human and humane spirit in contrast with the barbarian one of things and creatures in their wild state.

Now we learn that religious awe, which is the final and over-all moral in these amoral works, that comes not so much from hoping for things as they might or should be, but from comparing that hope with things as they are, without being destroyed or depressed by them. And that takes guts, and real morals, not moralizing.

The fabulists teach us that the realm of nature, or God, is whatever cannot be controlled. But man can reflect and can control his situation—to a degree. This degree, in proportion to the universe, is tiny, but to man himself, because it affects him most, it can take on a degree of greatness. In an age when man's own inventions, especially those motivated by an animal-like competition, a lust for private power and public acclaim, come close to controlling him, the fables are a precise picture of the moral disintegration and physical fears we ourselves, being human, can fall into, and also can, being human, wish to avoid.

The message of the fabulists, if we insist on a message, is that we cannot control God but we can control ourselves as a species and as individuals in it. We can try to maintain not mechanical and scientific progress, or big-brotherish rules of behavior, so much as human dignity in our private pleasures, the right to which and the need for which both our reasoning faculties and emotional sensibilities make apparent to us in fact and in fable.

Margaret Blount (essay date 1975)

SOURCE: Margaret Blount, "Folklore and Fable," in *Animal Land: The Creatures of Children's Fiction*, William Morrow & Company, Inc., 1975, pp. 23-41.

[*In the following excerpt, Blount compares the Aesopic fable to folktale and fairytale, and describes the effect that illustrating fables has on the interpretation of a fable.*]

'Long ago, when the animals could speak.' The golden age is somewhere in the past—perhaps in Eden or before the Flood, perhaps nearer, just beyond the memory of the oldest story teller; and in that time the gulf between animals and men had not been opened, the distinctions were not so sharp, magic was all about. As youthful things and creatures are always more alike than adult ones, as seeds are always more similar than plants and animals that grow more like themselves and so more different from each other every day, so in tales that belong to this youthful time animals and people were more alike, could communicate, have equal stature and often a similar moral life.

Folklore and myth bring animals nearer to men while fables and satire, while apparently doing the same thing, do the opposite; they are divisive and put animals in their place—further off.

The folklore story abounds in talking animals, clever animals that have an ambiguous or helpful role, or even appear to have private lives and families on the human model while co-existing with human masters, owners, or acquaintances. No one knows the origins of such stories, apart from the obvious racial strains which make a Japanese story different from an African, Danish, Scottish or English one. Talking animals seem to be as old as Man; and folklore tales read like Man's remote dreams, related by someone with dramatic and narrative flair but little imagination. Things are seldom described, they just *are* so, in a bright shadowless world just beyond the present where anything can happen and it may be any time at all. As large as life and quite as natural the animals come and go, changing their shapes and offering help—or vengeance—setting up home together like the Mouse, The Bird and The Sausage, working in the kitchen like Tittymouse and Tattymouse, usually on friendly terms with humans. Function and character can become delightfully, mysteriously, blurred. In such a story as 'All Gone' (*English Fairy Tales,* Joseph Jacobs collection, 1890) which concerns a friendship between a cat and a mouse, the cat uses as an excuse for its absence, 'I have a favourite cousin who has brought a small handsome son into the world, and I have been asked to be his godmother'; yet what the pair actually *do* is steal butter, which is animal and natural.

On the edge of life the animals are there. Reading these tales you feel that if you could go back far enough, you might have met a witch hare or a talking horse or cow; or joined the animals by being turned into one, or earned their help in impossible tasks imposed by kings or magicians such as picking up grains of sand, or choosing the right princess. Such animals are much nearer to the present climate than one imagines, from the pantomime *Puss in Boots* (who has changed his shape for the occasion) to Brer Rabbit, who is life-like in the same way as Paddington the bear, almost true, somewhere, as long as you don't look too closely. There is not always an obvious moral either, but usually a certain rough justice, plenty of cruelty, deaths, mutilations and revenge. The animals talk quite naturally, answering humans back and being accepted as semi-equals. The cunning ones, cats and foxes, often outwit humans and the more favoured ones, dogs and horses, are not usually as intelligent—perhaps because humans, who made the stories, feared them less. Sometimes the animal kingdom is allowed—as a sort of holiday—power over the human one and a turn at having the upper hand—a recurrent theme of animal vengeance, from 'The Travelling Musicians' to Hitchcock's *The Birds* (based on the Daphne du Maurier story), perhaps

prompted by something ever present in the human psyche; guilt at what Man has done to animals made deeper by the knowledge that animals can never 'win'. But such serious themes, leading in the end to the favourite satiric device that animals are morally superior to Man, as in Swift, or Erich Kästner's *The Animals' Conference* are not as common as simple comedy and magic transpositions. Until the Brothers Grimm made them respectable, folk tales were regarded, perhaps, as being rather on the level of comics—regretted by the Wife of Bath who blamed the clergy for suppressing them, compared unfavourably with Aesop and his obvious morals.

The classic 'fairy' tales are adult embellishment of folklore written in the late seventeenth century when the urbanity of the times allowed a greater toleration of fanciful tales with no particular moral uplift—though right is always rewarded and wrong punished. The *Contes de Perrault* are courtly romances, modified and embellished from their folklore origins, sometimes beautiful, like Madame de Villeneuve's *Beauty and the Beast,* or Madame d'Aulnoy's *The White Cat;* but often spoiled by complication. Animal help and the disguised human are favourite themes. The behaviour of the cat in *Puss in Boots* is that of a human in a cat's skin. He advances his master's fortune so that he wins the princess and the kingdom. He is the Clever Servant, and has all the initiative and all the ideas; he can order the peasants about, outwits the ogre and ends by enjoying his share of his master's good luck. The Beast, or the Frog Prince, are more obviously human—but, in his way, so is the Wolf in *Red Riding Hood.* Perrault makes this even more clear by his rhymed moral (A. E. Johnson's translation):

> *All wolves are not of the same sort;*
> *There is one kind with an amenable*
> * disposition*
> *Neither noisy, nor hateful, nor angry,*
> *But tame, obliging and gentle,*
> *Following the young maids*
> *In the streets, even into their homes.*
> *Alas! Who does not know that these gentle*
> * wolves*
> *Are of all creatures the most dangerous.*

The fairy tales of Hans Andersen are an even further development, with animal servants (*The Tinder Box*) and enchanted humans (*The Ugly Duckling*) given greater depth because their moral, and meaning, is not explicit.

A very old and rather different type of story based on animal folklore is the Beast Fable—the Animal Society theme where animals have taken the place of humans and act out human dramas. *Reynard the Fox* is the most famous, existing in many versions and printed by Caxton three years after *The Canterbury Tales* and before Aesop, Grimm's 'The Tomtit and the Bear' is a good example, dealing with an animal war in which a Fox is a valuable general. In *Reynard the Fox,* many strains and ideas have been developed into an animal epic in which animals are characters in a romance cycle, with plots, sub-plots, heroism, deception, trickery, humour, triumphs, victories, battles and death. In its time, the vogue for Reynard was enormous, but as entertainment for adults the style is quite dead however 'Dogland' 'Babar' and *Finn Family Moomintroll* are very-much-removed relations.

Aesop's Beast Fables, tongue-in-cheek human substitutions, have always been in favour. Perhaps from Caxton's time onwards, they have been regarded as the right books to give to children, recommended by educationists from Locke onwards. They are part of most people's early experience and are the very roots of that kind of humanisation which turns animals into facets of human character, and many writers have changed and revived them. Animals are here 'used' rather than presented and they point the way directly to those moral and satirical tales which were intended, from Swift to Orwell, to show the human race how it ought to behave.

The history of animal stories through these three strains—folklore, fable and romance—is one of growing seriousness; folklore animals are on the whole, a much gayer lot than those in later versions of Aesop. Perhaps the best folklore animal, and certainly the most famous, is Brer Rabbit. Though later in time than the *Reynard* cycle or Aesop, in treatment and essence he is earlier and more primitive and has the genuine amoral wily innocence that fairytale animals lack. Hans Andersen sometimes leaves one full of an odd, cold sadness, however delicate the allegory and beautiful the image; compared with this, Grimm's folklore tales are like tomato sauce out of a bottle, and Brer Rabbit comes out of the same jar, full of humour and rather undeserved retribution, of which Uncle Remus offers no explanation except that it *was* so, in the old days when the animals could talk. These African stories (*Uncle Remus,* Joel Chandler Harris, 1880) modified and translated into an American setting, have one or two Aesop themes such as '**The Tortoise and the Hare**', '**The Wolf and the Lamb**', '**The Dog and the Meat**', transformed and improved on, brought to life—the folklore version being a jollier one than the fable; in 'The Tortoise and the Hare' Brer Terrapin defeats Brer Rabbit, not because the rabbit does not try, but by posting various identical members of his own family along the route and at the winning post; and in the 'Bullfrog and the Bear' (Aesop's '**Wolf and Lamb**') the Bullfrog finally escapes, using a 'briar patch' ruse—the Lamb in Aesop is devoured. . . .

The moral: that is the sombre kernel for which the animals are a covering device. Aesop, the oldest and most influential animal story teller of all, used the attractive power of animals and narrative to get at his audience in a peculiar way, and the method has been seized on, enlarged, used and copied until, in the last century, the animal moral tale becomes almost wearisome. The genius of Aesop was to use the animal as a fixative, in an unforgettable way.

Prudence pays better than greed; or, it is better to keep what one possesses than to lose it while trying to gain the unattainable. This is easy to say but horribly cumbersome to *imagine*. 'A man's reach should not be greater than his grasp' is easier. Easier still is 'a bird in hand is worth two in the bush', which brings with it a Bewick picture of a man with a gun and two dogs and a pheasant; most brains supply pictures which fix abstractions. What Aesop did was to reverse the process so that the image comes first, and so no one forgets the dog dropping the bone to try to grasp the one that is only a reflection. Aesop well knew the power of a story and the graphic, simplified short cut that animals made towards human attention; if the same story began with a man crossing a bridge with a piece of meat in his hand all sorts of other considerations would enter, the least of which being why the man should be silly enough to mistake his reflection for reality. In pointing this sort of moral, human psychology is irrelevant. It is only later that one begins to be dubious and to consider that greed does not pay—not because generosity is better, but because, in a harsh world, prudence is best. The whole thing can be taken two stages further by an artist like Charles Bennet (*Aesop's Fables rendered into Human Nature,* 1866) who draws not only the animal agent but the moral too; a valet with a dog's head is shown rejecting a simple parlourmaid in order to yearn after 'The Quality' who are having a soirée in the next room.

Aesop's fables have none of the humour of folklore, none of the warm satisfaction of fairy tale—the sudden turn of fortune before the happy ending. They have surface justice or an amused shrug. They have a resemblance to folk tale in their short, plain, factual lack of light and shade, but there the likeness ends. Aesop's animals, behaving not like animals at all but as propositions in Euclid, or, as G. K. Chesterton suggests, pieces in games of chess, are interesting because they are the very beginning of that typecasting which animals have found so difficult to shake off since; but there is a flatness about the stories, a cynical assessment of human nature at its lowest, an acknowledgement that often the good and innocent are duped and that good works often pay, not because they are good, but because nature is sometimes arranged that way.

The people in Aesop are non-figures, the farmer, a man, a boy, an old widow; their interaction with the animals does not seem to belong to any golden age when the animals could speak and people understand, and even Mr McGregor, shadowy as he is, has more character. The people, like the animals, have to be ciphers. If they had any real, complex human attributes, all kinds of chemical reactions might set in and spoil the experiment. The tendency, on reading Aesop, has been to applaud, to remember, and lastly to add one's own moral, to decide perhaps that the Fox that lost the grapes was the most sensible beast ever. 'Some men, when they are too weak to achieve their purpose, blame the times,' says the Greek; but the story also tells one not to bother about what one cannot have. Roger l'Estrange's *Aesop*, 1692, pictures the Fox 'turning off his disappointment with a jest', a kindly interpretation, equally valid, and Samuel Croxall in 1722 was uneasy about the grapes for a different reason—grapes did not grow wild in England and foxes did not like them anyway.

L'Estrange was doubtful about Aesop's moral values, and thought that they might be 'more dangerous than profitable'; but Locke, in his essay on education, 1690, had no doubts at all. Aesop was the best book to offer to children to encourage them to read; because it 'may afford useful reflections to a grown man; and if his memory retain them all his life after, he will not repent to find them there, among his manly thoughts and serious business. If his Aesop has pictures in it, it will entertain him much the better.'

Although Robert Henryson in 1570 and La Fontaine in 1651 are Aesop's most notable interpreters, his illustrators have given the fables a certain depth and ambiguity. Croxall's *Aesop* has Bewick's beautiful woodcuts which are full of animation, the animals as natural as life, and perhaps the Fox, jumping to reach the grapes is unnatural. If you give the Fox a top hat and a cane the story becomes different, and that is what later illustrators have done, helping too to fix the animal prototypes by showing the Lion to be proud, the Fox devious and crafty. Robert Dodsley's Aesop, 1771, is interesting for its preface, which suggests this very thing—that the animals in the stories should act and speak according to their 'true' natures, perhaps thus applying the 'finishing polish, with the appearance of nature, the effect of art' which was his design in making the lion proud, the owl to speak with 'pomp of phrase', the monkey a buffoon. Literary animals have been doing this ever since, and finding it impossible to take character parts except by wrenching themselves somewhat unhappily and being a Reluctant Dragon, a Cowardly Lion (Frank L. Baum) or a Stupid Fox that is always failing to catch Clever Polly.

Walter Crane's Aesop—1887—with 'Portable Morals Pictorially Pointed' has rather violent streak—foxes and wolves have ferocious snarls, lolling tongues, and there are realistic gin traps. The fables are neatly versified in limerick form with an appended and not always obvious moral, i.e. '**the Cock and the Pearl**,' which is

about irony (as is much of Aesop), is interpreted as 'If he ask for bread will ye give him a stone', which is an ironic statement about something quite different.

Ernest Griset's Aesop—1869—again shows that violent streak in Victorian illustration to an unpleasant degree. These pictures are to a present-day eye, unhappy; they appear to belong to that black, sinister, ragged, rather dirty-looking world that one imagines the industrial revolution at its worst to have been happening in, a sort of de-urbanised Doré place, coal-tip countryside. The animals are beautifully drawn apart from the period convention that always makes elephants look pneumatic and lions like angry colonels. One oddity is that Griset dresses the evil animals—wolves and foxes, and seldom the others, and, as always, never birds; it is as if we see ourselves always to be guilty, never innocent or virtuous. Scenes of slaughter and death abound; in '**The Eagle and the Fox**' the Eagle is hideous, but equally so are its embryonic young fledglings. And Griset turns every *character* into an animal, i.e. in '**The Nurse and the Wolf**', Nurse and baby look and behave like monkeys and are gratuitously ugly *because* they are wearing clothes. Oddest of all, but pointing to an interesting sympathy of this period, is Griset's treatment of insects. '**The Ant and the Grasshopper**' have great charm. The Grasshopper has a mandoline slung at its back and it, and the Ants walk upright. The haymaking ants are as human as insects can be, leaning against the stack with their rakes, mopping their brows. Insects have not had much attention in more recent years. Perhaps Max Fleisher's *Mr Bug goes to Town* film cartoon, 1941[1] or Don Marquis' *Archy and Mehitabel* are the two most notable.

Far the most interesting illustrator of Aesop is Charles Bennet, whose *Fables of Aesop translated into Human Nature*, 1867, both dresses the animals completely and gives them a contemporary setting which is quite thought provoking, even now; though, in a sense, what he has done is to abolish the animal stereotype. The characters in Bennet are Victorian Londoners with animal heads on, i.e. in '**The Wolf and the Lamb**', the Wolf is a Bill Sykes with neckerchief and knobkerry, the Lamb is frock-coated and top-hatted and is garotted with his own gold-studded collar. There never was anything comic about this story, but perhaps there is in Bennet's '**Ass in the Lion's skin**'—the Ass is shown smoking in the Mess, pretending to be a Guards officer. Social observation is witty and exact and the applications unexpected. '**The Fox and the Crow**' story is given a new dimension when the Crow is a rich window, the Fox a philanderer, the Cheese not shown or mentioned; and in '**The Fox and the Grapes**' a vixen relates to her friend, a parrot, over the tea cups, the story of the man she did not marry. '**The Wolf in Sheep's Clothing**' is a policeman, taking supper in the basement with the cook—a sheep. They are dining, ominously, off a leg of lamb.

These animals have a sinister, stylish elegance in keeping with Aesop's message and its worldly application; an ox's horns curl upwards forming the brim of his smart top hat, a crocodile's hide is also his fur-collared, crocodile skin coat, ending in a tail; he is dressed and not dressed, the clothes a part of him. This *Aesop* is indeed sophisticated. The reader needs to know what Aesop wrote, what animals are like, what the London of the sixties was like, and what civilisation has done to human nature and human ethics since then. Yet this art form, seen here at its finest, is a sort of spiritual dead end. If animals have a message for us now, it is a completely different one.

The tendency to add a Christian moral to Aesop has been as irresistible as the view taken, in the Bestiaries, that animals were specially created for man's edification in symbolic form. While Robert Henryson's Aesop, 1570, written in the reign of James III of Scotland has verse only comparable with Chaucer in its delightful gaiety and wry charm, it is the moral that is important:

> *And als the caus that thay first began*
> *Wes to repreif the haill misleving*
> *Of man, be figure of ane uther thing.*

The Uplandis Mous and the Burges Mous (this is always the favourite fable for treatment; perhaps it owes its popularity to the enduring appeal of mice) converse formally, yet with natural human voices, in seven-line stanzas. The country Mouse has the sort of reality of any finicky adult justifying the delicacy of his appetite by blaming a weak stomach. After expressing disappointment and disgust in no uncertain terms

> *This burges Mous had lytill will to sing,*
> *Bot hevilie scho kest hir browis doun,*

looking, as well as feeling, glum. In the town, the Spencer interrupts their feasting; the country mouse is chased by the cat and swoons. One should be content 'with small possession', says Henryson. The moral is so obvious that this fable, were it new today, might be interpreted as a warning about changing one's environment too abruptly. But with '**The Rat and the Frog**' ('**The Paddock and the Mous**') though the charm of the expression is made greater by dialect, age, and gentle, mock-heroic humour, the moral is Henryson's and not Aesop's.

> *Ane lytill Mous came till ane river syde:*
> *Scho micht not waid, hir schankis wer sa*
>   *schort;*
> *Scho culd not swym, scho had na hors to*
>   *ryde.*

The Mous agrees to cross the river tied by the leg to the Paddock although greatly worried (and who would not be?) by the Frog's runkillit cheeks, hingand brows,

loggerand legs and harsky hyde; after the Mous has quoted some Latin and the Frog sworn to Jupiter, they set off, the Frog plunges down, the Mous begins to drown 'till at the last scho cryit for ane preist'. In the end, a hawk eats them both. Aesop's moral is the one about justice and the biter being bit, Henryson's are twofold: don't trust fair words, and another more complicated 'Whereby the beistis may be figurate.' The Frog is man's body, the Mouse his soul, the water is the world, and the hawk, death. The charm, and the parable, co-exist, and point directly to the animal didactic stories of the nineteenth century.

Notes

[1] This story is, in its way, about ecology, or the unhappy effect on a community of insects of the building of a new city block. It was drawn by the creator of Popeye and Betty Boop, both of whom displayed hard shells and a galvanic activity comparable with Hoppity the Cricket and Miss Honey Bee in the insect film; and many animal cartoon films have the harsh knock for knock automatism of the insect world.

George Clark (essay date 1976)

SOURCE: George Clark, "Henryson and Aesop: The Fable Transformed," in *English Literary History*, Vol. 43, No. 1, Spring, 1976, pp. 1-18.

[*In the following essay, Clark analyzes the significant differences between Robert Henryson's version and the more established version of Aesop's fables of "The Cock and the Jewel" and "The Swallow and the Other Birds."*]

Robert Henryson's *Morall Fabillis of Esope the Phrygian* have inspired his admirers to formulate radically differing explanations of the literary merit we recognize in these minor masterpieces. Older readings of these fables assumed that Henryson took up Aesop's plots but not his purposes, saw the excellence of the poems as the result of unAesopian "humor, realism, [and] compassion,"[2] and usually viewed the Aesopian moralizations as vestigial remnants of an earlier evolutionary stage.[3] Newer readings treat Henryson's *Fables* as emphatically Aesopian and moralizing and therefore good. One such critic writes that "The very intensity of Henryson's religious views accounts for the quality of personal involvement which makes his *Morall Fabillis* the finest Aesop of the Middle Ages,"[4] and complains that the older criticism dealt with agreeable aspects of Henryson's poems, but neglected them as literary wholes, particularly as perfect unions of story and moralization. In the most important exposition of this newer approach, Denton Fox[5] chooses two of the fables for extended analysis aimed at showing that the "*moralitas*, at least in these two cases, is an integral part of a completely unified whole" (p. 338).

As Henryson recreates them, his Aesopian stories outgrow the artistic and intellectual limitations of their traditional form; comparing one of Henryson's fables to its probable source, the difference seems essentially stylistic, but the development of the style produces narratives whose implications compel our attention and go beyond the explicit moralizations conventionally attached to Aesopian fables. The simplicity of the Latin or French original excludes complex moral judgments; a narrative paradigm matches a moralizing aphorism. Henryson's complexer style creates a world whose greater realism makes easy black and white evaluations inadequate, a facile assumption of individual responsibility unconvincing. The rhetoric of Henryson's fables and their real sense of a setting indicate the disparity of styles; traditional Aesopian fables give no impression of time or place, and their teller's personality hardly becomes an integral part of the narrative, but Henryson's stories have dimensions of space and time, and have a narrator who is not Aesop and whose characterization becomes part of the fable's art and meaning.

Beginning with the prologue, Henryson maintains a clear distinction between Aesop and the narrator:[6] "My author in his Fabillis" (43), "This Nobill Clerk, Esope, as I haif tauld. . . . And to begin, first of ane Cok he wrate" (57, 61); like the first, the second fable is labelled "Aesop's":

> Esope, myne Authour, makes mentioun
> Of twa myis, and thay wer Sisteris deir.
>
> (162-63)

The narrator becomes at least a hearsay witness to the aftermath of the narrative and obliquely suggests that we have the story on his authority rather than Aesop's. The narrator remarks that he does not *know* how the country mouse fared after her return home—"I can not tell how weill thairefter scho fure" (357),

> Bot I hard say scho passit to hir den,
> Als warme as woll, suppose it wes not greit,
> Fully beinly stuffit, baith but and ben,
> Off Beinis, and Nuttis, peis, Ry, and Quheit.
>
> (358-61)

Beginning the third fable, the story of "Chantecleer and the fox", the narrator announces his intention to report an interesting topical matter which he apparently knows at second hand:

> . . . as now I purpose ffor to wryte
> Ane cais I ffand, quhilk ffell this ather yeir,
> Betwix ane Foxe and ane gentill Chantecleir.
>
> (408-10)

The non-Aesopian "I" is not now a translator but a reporter whose subject is "Ane cais . . . quhilk ffell this ather yeir," and the contemporaneity of the story widens the separation between the ancient fabulist and the present narrator. In the sequel to the tale of Chantecleer, the storyteller's role grows from that of reporter to witness. The non-Aesopian "I" begins:

> Leif we this wedow glaid, I you assure,
> Off Chantecleir mair blyith than I can tell,
> And speik we off the subtell aventure
> And destenie that to this Foxe befell.
>
> (614-17)

Subsequently the narrator authenticates matter in his story when he comes in direct contact with its personae—"as Lowrence leirnit me" (634)—or becomes a direct observer:

> "Weill" (quod the Wolff), "sit doun upon thy kne."
> And he doun bairheid sat full humilly,
> And syne began with Benedicitie.
> Quhen I this saw, I drew ane lytill by.
>
> (691-94)

The story of "The Lion and the Mouse," together with its prologue and *moralitas,* makes the separation between Henryson's narrator and Aesop absolute by confronting the "I" of the *Fables* and the Phrygian himself. The narrator falls asleep under a hawthorn one fair day, "In the middis of June, that sweit seasoun" (1321), and dreams an encounter with Aesop. The narrator has been reporter, hearsay witness, or eyewitness to four of the preceding six fables, but he immediately welcomes Aesop as the author "that all thir Fabillis wrate" (1379) and begs to hear a fable from the master: "'I grant' (quod he), and thus begouth ane taill' (1404). The dreaming narrator had entered into a disciple-master relationship with Aesop—

> O Maister Esope, Poet Lawriate,
> God wait, ye ar full deir welcum to me—
>
> (1377-78)

and Aesop consistently refers to the narrator as "sone," but Aesop is the figure of the narrator's dream; hence the master-pupil relationship which Aesop dominates is also a creature-creator relationship. The dream encloses, encapsules, imprisons Aesop with the narrator's imagination. The meeting crystallizes the stylistic tension charging the prologue and the preceding tale; the form of the meeting, and its conclusion, reassert the narrator's presence, reality, and dominance. After the encounter and the fable of "The Lion and the Mouse," the narrator remains behind—

> And with that word he vanist, and I woke;
> Syne throw the Schow my Journey hamewart tuke—
>
> (1620-21)

and whatever way the dream figure of Aesop took, the audience remains with the narrator.

Denton Fox correctly notes that the *Prologue* identifies Aesop's stories as "feinyeit fabils" and that the Scots phrase commonly meant "tall story" or "lie." Fox rightly observes that Henryson's prologue raises the conventional question "how can fictional and apparently frivolous verse be justified?" and duly provides the conventional answer: poetry gives pleasure, and besides it has a moral purpose. A conventional defence of "fictional . . . verse" clashes with the rhetoric of poems presented as the narrator's exact knowledge of current and reliable report—like the Chantecleer story which is "Ane cais . . . quhilk ffell this ather yeir" ("cais" and "ffeinyeit fabil" are antithetical)—or given out, like the story of "The Swallow and the Other ‚Birds," as the narrator's report of his own direct observation.

The rhetoric of Henryson's *Prologue* sets up a contradiction running through the *Fables;* the narrator of this Aesopian collection is not Aesop; the poems are at once Aesop's "ffeinyeit fabils" and the narrator's truth, even his own experience. Moreover, the *Prologue* asserts general principles of interpretation for the fables which run counter to the common reader's view of them. The intention of the fables, their very origin—so far as the *Prologue* describes it—is simply, categorically, and exclusively to reprove man's depravity:

> And als the caus that thay first began
> Wes to repreif the haill misleving
> Off man be figure of ane uther thing.
>
> (5-7)

To accomplish this aim, the *Prologue* asserts, the animals of the fables simply represent man's "misleving"; Denton Fox remarks that the "whole basis of the fables" lies in the proposition that "mony men in operatioun / Ar like to beistis in conditioun" (48-49), a remark Fox renders "man often degrades himself to the level of animals" (pp. 339-41). The *Prologue* devotes a whole stanza to that process of degradation:

> Na mervell is, ane man be lyke ane Beist,
> Quhilk lufis ay carnall and foull delyte;
> That schame can not him renye, nor arreist,
> Bot takis all the lust and appetyte,
> And that throw custum, and daylie ryte,
> Syne in thair myndis sa fast is Radicate,
> That thay in brutal beistis ar transformate.
>
> (50-56)

Both men and mice might deplore the tenor of the *Prologue*'s dour identification of fabulistic animals as figures of man's corruption and—at least in the *Prologue*—nothing more, but few readers heretofore have indicated their acceptance of such a view. Even Fox, at the end of his essay, feels constrained to qualify the *Prologue*'s—and his own—apparently unqualified harshness: "Henryson refuses to oversimplify the natural world into an easy target for invective, he describes his short-lived and suffering animals from a sympathetic viewpoint; the *Fables* are filled, for instance, with pathetic and occasionally valiant sheep and mice" (p. 356). Most readers of the *Fables* would approve the latter statement and might even add that Henryson's animals truly represent the character and predicament of mankind, not merely human vice and folly, but neither the *Prologue* nor Fox's reading of his two representative fables give any hint of that sympathy for fabulistic animals—or mankind. Fox sums up on the cock of "The Cock and the Jewel" and the birds of "The Swallow and the other Birds" in terms entirely consistent with the *Prologue*'s darkest view of the animals: "The birds scratching busily in the dirt or chaff are powerful symbols for appetite, and ones which convey vividly its bestiality" (pp. 355-56).

Fox has taken the *Prologue*'s description of Aesop's fables as the program for Henryson's poems, but that introductory characterization becomes the contrastive base for Henryson's transformation of a genre usually sadly but wisely neglected. Whether he characterized "Aesop" fairly or not is beyond the scope of this paper, but Henryson's *Prologue* creates an image of Aesopian literature as harsh, almost misanthropic; his *Fables* transform that simplistic moralism into a deeper, more sympathetic, and finally more pessimistic view of the human condition. Henryson's *Fables* repeatedly suggest meanings quite inconsistent with their explicit moralizations; the meanings the stories suggest and the moralizations assert conflict, and the resolution of these contradictions completes Henryson's transformation of the fables; his animals do not simply represent a degraded mankind—the animals and their world become symbols for Henryson's view of man: more suffering than sinning, less a free agent with unambiguous moral choices than the victim of his inescapable environment.

I propose to deal with the same two fables, "The Cock and the Jewel" and "The Swallow and the other Birds," Fox treated, and in order to give a better indication of the meanings Henryson may have found in Aesop shall cite or characterize the probable sources of these two fables. As one might expect, the source stories take place in a suspended vacuum; one has no impression that the action occurs in real time or space, but Henryson has invested these fables with a sense of place ("The Cock and the Jewel") or time ("The Swallow and the other Birds") and these touches of reality open the way to a non-Aesopian reading of the fables. Awareness of real place in the cock's story sharpens our sense of the fable's hero as a real character, not a mere shadow of something else; in the story of the birds, the sense of time and its passing focusses our attention on the reality of the narrator's presence and his involvement in the events he relates.

The story of "The Cock and the Jewel" occupies eight lines in Walter of England, twenty-two in the *Isopet de Lyon,*[7] and sixty-three in Henryson. The Latin version runs:

> Dum rigido fodit ore fimum, dum quaeritat
> escam
> Dum stupet inventa jaspide Gallus, ait:
> "Res vili pretiosa loco natique decoris
> Hac in sorde jaces, nil mihi messis habes.
> Si tibi nunc esset qui debuit repertor,
> Quem limus sepelit, viveret arte nitor
> Nec tibi convenio, nec tu mihi; nec tibi
> prosum,
> Nec mihi tu prodes; plus amo cara minus."

The power of Walter's version lies in its barrenness; no realistic details weaken the intended comparison of cock and fool, jewel and wisdom; nothing in the narration directs the reader's attention to any consideration of cocks or jewels beyond the identifications the *moralitas* imposes:

> Tu Gallo stolidum, tu Jaspide dona sophiae
> Pulchra notes; stolido nil sapit ista seges.

Walter ignores the logical pitfalls inherent in argument by analogy and does not endow the cock with any character at all, much less one strikingly inconsistent with the moral pronouncement. We are not made to see that the cock is a barnyard feathered biped or the "jasp" is a precious stone. Perhaps a trace of mockery colors the narrator's otherwise neutral tone: the repetition of *Dum . . . dum . . . dum . . . ,* the *rigido ore,* and the *stupet* at the instant of discovery may briefly make the cock mechanically comic, but the fable hardly creates a sense of the narrator's attitude toward his subject. The *Isopet de Lyon* merely extends the cock's speech without adding any new dimensions to the narrative, but Henryson's additions give the cock a certain complexity of characterization, the action a real setting, and us an invitation to consider the cock and the "jasp" literally, that is as a real bird and a real jewel, not mere counters serving only to designate the *realia* under discussion.

Henryson's narrative concisely indicates the cock's physical, socio-economic, and moral reality and allows the bird a complex and sympathetic characterization. The cock has "feddram fresch & gay" (64) and his spirit appropriately matches his appearance for he is "Richt cant and crous, albeit he was bot pure" (65). The opposition between the cock's morale and status, his wholly commendable cheerfulness in the face of poverty, makes a favorable impression—if Chaucer's Pardoner who would not "Lyve in poverte wilfully" (VI, 441) and his "povre persoun" (I, 478) who would, and did, reliably indicate conventional medieval attitudes toward poverty. Indeed, the cock evidently agrees

with the narrator that "blyithnes in hart, with small possessioun" (388, 396) is truly the "Best thing in eird" (387). The apparently unnecessary explanation that jewels are occasionally swept out with the dust when young servant girls rush through their work— "Peradventure, sa wes the samin stone" (77)—adds more than social realism to the context of the fable. The cock's early rising and diligence, "To get his dennar set was al his cure" (67), contrast with the idleness and indifference of the hypothetical girls, and the juxtaposition of the busy cock and careless servants helps define the narrator's, and our, attitude toward the story's central character. Modesty and decorum dictate the cock's proposed diet, and a medieval audience could hardly choose but admire a prospective diner who announces "Had I dry breid, I compt not for na cukis" (105), mentions "draf, or corne" twice (91, 94) and "corne" once more (99). In contrast the widow's sustenance in the *Nun's Priest's Tale*—

> Milk and broun breed . . .
> Seynd bacoun, and somtyme an ey or tweye—
> (VII, 2844-45)

seems decidedly luxurious. Denton Fox believes that the cock's willingness to consume "small wormis, or snaillis" (94) would be "repulsive" to the audience,[8] but both commonsense and decorum will allow the diet, and if the "snaillis" are true snails, so will the *Larousse Gastronomique* which observes that this delicacy "was highly prized as food as far back as Roman times," adding gratefully that the "art of fattening snails is said to have been discovered by a Roman named Lupinus."[9] Lydgate's version of the fable too explicitly idealizes the cock, yet allows him to seek his dinner on a dunghill,[10] an indication that the medieval audience could stomach the idea of a cock's eating "small wormis, or snaillis" or whatever one finds in the midden.

Like his Aesopian predecessor, Henryson's cock rejects the jewel in the dungheap, but within the context of Henryson's story, he rightly rejects it and has in fact no other choice to make. The story has created a cock who is both sympathetic and real; sympathy with the character predisposes us to accept his decision, and a sense of the cock's reality in a real setting makes us view his decision as inevitable. In sober fact, a real cock who carried a precious stone into a jeweller's shop or kept it about his person would more likely be stuffed with sage than sagacity. When the narrator observes that his cock "Flew furth upon ane dunghill sone be day" (66), the local and temporal details assure us that our cock acts as literary authority and common experience agree he should, and give the narrative a ring of factualness alien to its presumed sources. The local setting further realizes the narrative: the jewel "Wes castin furth in sweeping of the hous" (70). The definite article in the phrase "of the hous" moves the narrative from the generality of "ane cok" (64) and "ane dunghill" (66) to an increasingly specific setting and thus individual reality, an impression strengthened by the distinction between lost jewelry in general and "the samin stone" (77) of this particular encounter. The careful distinction between this "real" event and the hypothetical servant girls similarly enhances the story's verisimilitude.

A pervasive sense of place strikingly distinguishes Henryson's story from the traditional fable of the cock and the jewel: Aesopian fables create no time or place, but the reality of Henryson's setting was apparent to his earliest publishers. Facing page five in H. Harvey Wood's edition (p. 7 in G. Gregory Smith, vol. II), we may see a reproduction of a drawing which, in the Harleian MS, introduces the text of the fable; the drawing also appears in Thomas Bassandyne's print. This illustration puts the cock, jasp, a small tree or shrub, dunghill, the farmer's house, hills and horizon in perspective. Henryson's references place the action of the fable in a social order ranging from the cock who is "bot pure" (65) to the "Damisellis" who are "wantoun and Insolent" (71)—they do not know their proper place—to "grit Lordis" (89) and "Lord or King" (81); the narrative establishes a hierarchy of places beginning "upon ane dunghill" (66) or "in this mydding" (82)—the cock's proper place—to "the flure" (74) "of the hous" (70, 73) and thence to "ane Royall Tour" (107). The cock rejects the jewel, not because of "false intellectual pride,"[11] but because he realizes that he occupies a given place in an ordered world, a place inconsistent with the possession of gemstones. The cock's peroration identifies the place the jewel should, because of its nature, occupy:

> "Quhar suld thow mak thy habitatioun?
> Quhar suld thow dwell, bot in ane Royall
>   Tour?
> Quhar suld thow sit, bot on ane Kingis Croun,
> Exaltit in worschip and in grit honour?
> Rise, gentill Jasp, off all stanis the flour,
> Out of this midding, and pas quhar thow suld
>   be;
> Thow ganis not for me, nor I for the."
>
>   (106-12)

The insistent reappearance of the verb "suld" in this stanza grounds the cock's rejection of the gem in his sense of propriety and place ("habitatioun," "dwell," "sit") and a realism which nicely complements the jaunty confidence attributed him from the first.

Like his fabulistic ancestors, Henryson's cock rejects the jasp, but the context of the action and the terms the rejection is stated in make immediate and concrete the disparity between the jewel and the bird, a disparity which calls attention to the logical fallacy in the traditional moralization, the misleading analogy. When

Henryson's cock turns his back on the useless gemstone, he does not behave foolishly, yet the *moralitas* asserts that the cock "may till ane fule be peir" (142), and when we impose the identifications of the *moralitas*—the cock as foolish man, the jewel as "science and cunning" (148)—on Henryson's story, Aesopian contempt for "fools," complacently identified as that distant mass of other men, gives way to a somberer meaning. To equate our cock with foolish mankind is to recognize that mankind's apparent freedom to choose wisdom or folly is mere illusion; to see wisdom in this gemstone is to admit that the world we live in makes wisdom—

> Quhilk makis men in honour for to Ring,
> Happie, and stark to wyn the victorie
> Of all vicis, and Spirituall enemie—
>
>   (131-33)

as inaccessible to mankind as a precious stone to a barnyard cock. The audience's awareness and anticipation of the traditional moralization, counterpointed against the developing apprehension of the fable's transformation, lends the story's essential pessimism enormous force. The traditional Aesopian tone, complacent, superior, sophomoric, scores fools off roundly in the *additio* to Walter of England's *moralitas:*

> Stultorum numerus infinitus solet esse;
> Stultus stultitiam monstrat ubique suam.

Henryson's involvement with the cock and with mankind gives his version of the fable a profounder and darker meaning than an expostulation against fools. If the cock does not reject the jewel out of arrogance or exclusive preoccupation with bestial appetite but because a real barnyard cock cannot pocket or possess a gemstone, the simplistic moral proposition that the free agent, man, wilfully disregards the wisdom that could secure him all the possible benefits of this and the next world gives place to a powerful impression that man, the prisoner of his inescapable limitations, has no plain and easy choice of wisdom and folly.

The birds of "The Swallow and the other Birds" illustrate still more darkly mankind's entrapment in a world where the supposedly obvious path to safety lies hidden in the gloom.

The text of "The Swallow and the other Birds" is defective in the *Isopet de Lyon,* but Walter's Latin will illustrate that Henryson's realism—a state of mind and sensitivity rather than a mere trick of style—transformed the complacent fable into an impressive, gloomy perception of the human condition:

> Ut linum pariat lini de semine semen
> Nutrit humus, sed Aves tangit Hirundo metu:
> "Hic ager, hoc semen nobis mala vincla
>   minatur,

Vellite pro nostris semina sparsa malis."
Turba fugit sanos monitus, vanosque timores
Arguit; exit humo semen et herba viret.
Rursus Hirundo monet instare pericula; rident
Rursus Aves; hominem placat Hirundo sibi,
Cumque viris habitans cantu blanditur amico
Nam praemissa minus laedere tela solent.
Jam linum metitur, jam fiunt retia, jam vir
Fallit Aves, jam se conscia culpat Avis.

Henryson suppresses one detail in the probable source: the swallow's defection to the fowler's party. He also adds a long philosophical prologue asserting the universal presence of a divine and beneficent order. The fable's prologue exhorts the hearer to remark the existence of this benevolent design, to embrace a philosophical optimism the fable disappoints. In "The Swallow and the other Birds" an ever-present sense of time becomes the chief instrument of pessimistic realism; as the seasons progress from spring to winter, the narrator seeks the benevolent order the prologue has described, but the fruit of his search is pain and sorrow, not that promised joy. The fable's action begins in spring or early summer with the narrator's out-of-doors walks, precisely the motifs which opened and closed the narrator's immediately preceding dream of Aesop. This seeming care to emphasize the juxtaposition of Aesop's fable within the dream and the narrator's direct experience highlights the contrast between the Aesopian stance and Henryson's. The fable itself re-echoes this conflict between the Aesopian vision and Henryson's: the events of the story appear inconsistently as Aesop's moralized fiction and the narrator's own experience. The onset of the *moralitas* demotes the narrator's truth to Aesop's yarning—unfavorably compared to his "mair autenik werk" (1890). As the story unfolds, it is insistently the record of the narrator's seeing, hearing, wondering, feeling, and finally sorrowing. The contradictions repeatedly built into the fable's authentication parallel the conflicting interpretations—tragic and moralizing—it generates.

The philosophical prologue asserts that man cannot perceive "God as he is, nor thingis Celestiall" (1632) but calls on mankind to see God's benevolence in visible nature: "Luke weill . . . Luke weill . . . Syne luke," and "As daylie by experience we may see" (1664, 1665, 1668, 1677). Denton Fox described the prologue as follows: "Structurally, there is a steady progression towards the natural world of the birds in the fable: the movement is from God to nature, from eternal stability to seasonal mutability, from abstract general philosophy to concrete specific experience. But throughout this whole introductory section there is the same view of the world. God is wise and generous, and the world that he has made is good both in its conceptual scheme and as man experiences it" (p. 350). The story proper begins with the narrator's response to spring and his determination to see and experience the joys of the season and its activities. The prologue admonishes us to look carefully and understand; the fable records what the narrator saw, unfolds his developing response, and discovers the difficulty in understanding a divine and benevolent order from experience. The fable begins with a search for direct experience of beauty and order:

> . . . in to ane soft morning
> Rycht blyth that bitter blastis wer ago,
> Into the wod, to se the flouris spring,
> And heir the Mavis sing and birdis mo,
> I passit ffurth . . .
>
>   (1713-17)

Renewed joy and optimism dominate the narrator's mood; the season's bustle inspires him with hope and happiness:

> Moving thusgait, grit myrth I tuke in mynd,
> Off lauboraris to se the besines,
>
>   . . . . .
>
> It wes grit Joy to him that luifit corne,
> To se thame laubour, baith at evin and morne.
>   (1720-21, 1725-26)

The first episode in the action of the story emphasizes the narrator's perception and feeling, two leading themes in a poem repeatedly characterized as the account of an engaged observer: "I passit ffurth, syne lukit to and fro, / To se the Soill . . ." (1717-18), "And as I baid . . . / In hart gritlie rejoicit of that sicht" (1717-28). The narrator's initial reaction to what he sees is exactly congruent with the tone of the fable's prologue, and as he looks and sees and responds, the narrator in the fable precisely follows the admonition laid down in the prologue. Denton Fox identifies the narrator as "a figure who has appeared in many earlier poems," a "stock figure" who allusively indicates that "an allegorical vision which will probably be connected, in some way, with the mysteries of spring" (p. 351) will follow, but Henryson's observer is also familiar from the preceding fables and a vital part of the narrative. As the narrator experiences the world he finds it includes evil, however benevolent its conceptual scheme, and his experience reveals that the problem of accounting for its evil cannot be satisfactorily solved by simply referring it back to the failures of bird or man.

The reality of Henryson's narrator and his emotions—his joy at spring, his wonder at the Swallow's preaching, his shock and sorrow at the death of the birds—and the reality of the world of his experience transform the discursive Aesopian paradigm into presentational narrative and create the tension between Henryson's and Aesop's fable. The pinched Latin text creates only a simple, uni-dimensional world for which a bare aphorism becomes an adequate analysis, but Henryson's poem reveals a world which an Aesopian aphorism cannot epitomize. A comparison of the representation of time in "The Swallow and the other Birds" and in its presumed sources will indicate the impression of a complex reality Henryson intends.

Steady emphasis on time connects the prologue and the narrative, but starkly contrasting characterizations of time oppose the prologue's philosophical optimism and the narrative's empirical pessimism. The prologue devotes five stanzas to a description of the seasons of the year; the movement is from summer to spring, but winter occupies two stanzas and thus outranks the other seasons even as it forebodes the outcome of the story to follow:

> Than [in winter] flouris fair faidit with froist
> man fall,
> And birdis blyith changit thair noitis sweit
> In styll murning, neir slane with snaw and
> sleit.
>
> (1696-98)

This darkly prophetic hint is swallowed up in the prologue's view of the order of nature as an illustration of God's benevolence. Denton Fox remarks that "Even Henryson's year runs from summer to spring, and not from spring to winter, from youth to death" (p. 350). But in the story proper, the progress of a specific year provides the time-scheme of the narrative and its most realistic details, and this year runs from a given spring to a given, fateful winter, from the foreboding of evil to its fulfilment. Henryson sharpens the conflict between optimistic dogma and tragic experience when he makes the abstract year end in spring and joy, his real one in winter, sorrow, and death.

To develop the Aesopian conception of the fable, that the evil which is visited upon the birds depends purely upon their obstinate refusal to heed the good advice of the Swallow, no specific description of the passage of time is required, and in the Latin of Walter of England only the sparest indications of real time appear; flax is sown and the seed grows, but the seasons are not mentioned at all. In place of Henryson's concrete vocabulary describing the passage of time and seasons, Walter relies simply on the adverb *rursus* to indicate the birds' repeated refusal to heed the Swallow: *Rursus Hirundo monent instare pericula; rident / Rursus aves,* and the colorless *jam,* not a detailed description of the season, marks the arrival of the catastrophe: *Jam linum metitur, jam fiunt retia, jam vir / Fallit Aves, jam se conscia culpat Avis.* Henryson, however, links every step in the unfolding tragedy to a specific moment in the progress of the year; the springtime plowing and sowing which assures the joyful narrator

of yet another life-giving harvest threatens the birds with death as the Swallow warns:

> Se ye yone Churll . . . Beyond yone pleuch,
> Fast sawand hemp, and gude linget seid?
> Yone lint will grow in lytill tyme in deid,
> And theiroff will yone Churll his Nettis mak,
> Under the quhilk he thinkis us to tak.
>
> (1743-47)

The narrator turns homeward, his original mood of satisfaction and joy converted to wonder and doubt:

> I tuke my club, and hamewart couth I carie,
> Swa ferliand, as I had sene ane farie.
>
> (1774-75)

What he has seen in fact, though not what he purposed to see, has challenged the validity of his initial response to experience. Time passes and the seed sown in the spring grows; the narrator returns and again he relishes, though less emphatically, the time of the year:

> Thus passit furth quhill June, that Jolie tyde,
> And seidis that wer sawin off beforne
> Wer growin hie, . . .
> I movit furth, betwix midday and morne,
> Unto the hedge under the Hawthorne grene,
> Quhair I befoir the said birdis had sene.
>
> (1776-78, 1780-82)

June, "that Jolie tyde" of promising growth, forebodes disaster as the Swallow cries:

> Luke to the Lint that growis on yone le;
> Yone is the thing I bad forsuith that we,
> Quhill it wes seid, suld rute furth off the eird;
> Now it is Lint, now is it hie on breird.
>
> (1793-96)

The Swallow's horror at the prospect of evil vividly contrasts with the narrator's reaction to spring and summer:

> My flesche growis, my bodie quaikis all,
> Thinkand on it I may not sleip in peis.
>
> (1799-80)

The flax is duly harvested, prepared, and converted into nets, but before the birds are netted, the year turns to winter whose harshness drives them irresistibly within reach of the fowler:

> The wynter come, the wickit wind can blaw,
> The woddis grene were wallowit with the
> weit,
> Baith firth and fell with froistys were maid
> faw,
> Sloniis and slaik maid slidderie with the sleit;

The foulis ffair ffor falt thay ffell off feit;
On bewis bair it wes na bute to byde,
But hyit unto housis thame to hyde.

(1832-38)

For a third time the birds do not heed the Swallow's prudent advice, and this time the unregarded warning goes unanswered as the starving birds flock to the fowler's net:

Thir small birdis ffor hunger famischit neir,
Full besie scraipand ffor to seik thair fude,
The counsall off the Swallow wald not heir.

(1867-69)

The birds have become birds only—the Swallow excepted—devoid of speech and totally at the mercy of the environment, victims of famine, winter, and death, in brief, subject to time; to claim that the "birds scratching busily in the . . . chaff are powerful symbols for appetite, and ones which convey vividly its bestiality"[12] is to ignore the real situation Henryson so carefully created and dismiss that grim and inescapable winter as window-dressing. The winter in which the birds suffer recalls the prologue's two somber stanzas describing winter as hostile to bird and beast:

And birdis blyith changit thair notis sweit
In styll murning, neir slane with snaw and sleit

. . . . .

All wyld beistis than ffrom the bentis bair
Drawis ffor dreid unto thair dennis deip,
Coucheand ffor cauld in coifis thame to keip.

(1697-98, 1703-05)

Time remains in the audience's mind throughout the narrative. The prologue's detailed and realistic set piece describes a year's progress season by season; seasons and seasonal activities, plowing, sowing, and reaping become the temporal context of the action; and until the catastrophe, the narrator's experiences come at a definite time of day. The narrator lives in time as do the birds themselves. Hence his first observation of the Swallow's preaching takes place in the morning—"in to ane soft morning" (1713)—but his second experience begins later in the day—"betwix midday and morne" (1780)—and ends with "it drew neir the none" (1824). The Latin version aims only at making clear the sequence and repetition of events; the representation of time is irrelevant to the Aesopian meaning of the story; only the fact, the birds' failure to heed the swallow's advice, and their stubborn persistence in unwisdom, is relevant.

When Henryson added the dimension of time to the fable he did more than embellish the plain tale or make a more interesting version of the story. To see the narrative, the birds, and the narrator himself in the constant flux of time, and to see time moving from spring to winter, from life to death, subverts the basic assumptions of the Aesopian fable: the real possibility of another outcome, the substantial freedom of the birds to choose wisely and avoid their fate, the exclusive origin of evil in the failure of the individual. The birds could indeed have picked up the seeds or rooted up the young flax-plants, but at the end it is winter which drives them in reach of the fowler's nets and famine which impells them to scratch vainly at the chaff set out as bait. In Henryson's poem, time becomes a symbol for fate, winter a token of unaccountable evil in the real world. This treatment of time and the pure grief of the narrator's response to the catastrophe—

Allace! It wes grit hart sair for to se
That bludie Bowcheour beit thay birdis doun,
And for till heir, quhen they wist weill to de,
Thair cairfull sang and lamentatioun

(1874-77)—

validates the tension between the Aesopian and the tragic conceptions of the fable. Taking the prologue and fable together, "The Swallow and the other Birds" includes competing impulses toward an Aesopian or moralistic reading based on philosophical optimism and a tragic interpretation rooted in philosophical pessimism; appropriately two voices respond to the catastrophe, but neither strikes the pure Aesopian note. The Aesopian attitude is almost cool and indifferent:

Utile consilium qui vitat, inutile sumit;
Qui nimis est tutus, retia jure subit.

Nothing unites the Aesopian narrator and the personae he casually dismisses; even the disapproval is unimpassioned. The Swallow begins with the Aesopian distance implied in "I told you so"—

Lo . . . thus it happinnis mony syis

. . . . .

This grit perrell I tauld thame mair than thryis—

(1882, 1885)

but her conclusion, "Now ar thay deid, and wo is me thairfoir" (1886), tempers the moralist's censure with compassion and unites the moralist and truant. Grief is the narrator's single response—"it wes grit hart sair for to se" (1874)—to his vision of the human condition in the real world. Though the *Prologue* asserted that Aesop's fables arose from a desire to reprove man's misbehavior, the *Morall Fabillis of Esope the Phrygian,* fables transformed, aim at fairly representing rather than harshly reproving mankind. Pity, not contempt, scorn and aloof disapproval, dominates Henryson's view of mortal man.

Notes

[1] Talks given at the Conference on Mediaeval Studies (Kalamazoo, 1968) and the Medieval Section of the MLA Conference (New York, 1968) included early versions of the matter presented in this paper.

[2] See Florence H. Ridley's review of John MacQueen's *Robert Henryson* (*JEGP*, 67 [1968], 299); cf. Denton Fox's remark that older criticism prized the fables because of "their detailed realism, their humor, and the slightly naive goodness that Henryson displays in them," ("Henryson's *Fables*," *ELH* 29 [1962], 337).

[3] Thus J. A. W. Bennett remarks that Henryson kept "'lust' and 'lore' formally distinct" (*The Parlement of Foules*, 2nd ed. [Oxford, 1965], p. 15) and G. Gregory Smith approves Henryson's segregation of moralization and story especially since it renders the moralization expendable: "If he [Henryson] is sometimes tedious in his 'moralizations,' he keeps these, as the Latin fabulists did, at the end and at the will of the reader, not mingling them with the story . . ." (*The Poems of Robert Henryson* [Edinburgh, 1914], I, xvi); Edwin Muir hints (*Essays on Literature and Society*, 2nd ed. [London, 1965], pp. 13-14) that on occasion at least the moralizations are deliberately and comically inappropriate, and Kurt Wittig observes with something like surprise that "The moralities of 'The Wolf and the Lamb' . . . or of 'The Sheip and the Doig' . . . are a certain exception in their close integration with the tale" (*The Scottish Tradition in Literature* [Edinburgh, 1958], p. 40).

[4] John Block Friedman, "Henryson, The Friars, and the *Confessio Reynardi*," *JEGP*, 66 (1967), 550.

[5] *ELH* (note 2 above), 337-56.

[6] H. Harvey Wood, ed., *The Poems and Fables of Robert Henryson*, 2nd ed. (Edinburgh, 1958) is cited throughout.

[7] John MacQueen has shown that these are Henryson's chief sources (*Robert Henryson: A Study of the Major Narrative Poems* [Oxford, 1967], pp. 96, 200-07); for the French and Latin texts see Julia Bastin, ed., *Recueil Générale des Isopets* (Paris, 1930), II.

[8] Fox, 345; MacQueen finds the cock's diet "repulsive" but "appropriate," p. 108.

[9] *Larousse Gastronomique*, edd. Nina Froud and Charlotte Turgeon (London, 1961), p. 882.

[10] *The Minor Poems of John Lydgate*, ed. Henry Noble MacCracken, II (London, 1934), "Isopes Fabules," ll. 106-09.

[11] MacQueen, p. 107.

[12] Fox, 356.

P. Gila Reinstein (essay date 1983)

SOURCE: P. Gila Reinstein, "Aesop and Grimm: Contrast in Ethical Codes and Contemporary Values," in *Children's Literature in Education*, Vol. 14, No. 1, Spring, 1983, pp. 44-53.

[*In the following essay, Reinstein shows that Aesop's fables, which reflect a non-idealistic and self-reliant approach to human interactions, were preferred by older, married, non-white, working-class students as a tool for educating the young, but that Grimm's fairy tales, which reflect an idealistic and self-sacrificing approach to human interactions, were preferred by young, single, white, middle-class students.*]

People often think of Aesop's fables and the folk tales of the brothers Grimm together, since both are collections of traditional folklore, classics of children's literature, and important sources of American popular culture. Both are retold in elementary school readers; both are regularly selected by artists for reinterpretation and reissue as picture books. Political cartoonists and advertising campaign designers take advantage of the public's familiarity with Aesop and Grimm for purposes of their own. Aesop and Grimm appear to have been adopted by and incorporated into our culture, to the degree that few children grow up today without somewhere along the way absorbing the plight of Cinderella and the fate of the tortoise and the hare. Sometimes these stories are first encountered in library books or school texts, but more often they are introduced through the popular culture, by way of animated cartoons, Sesame Street or Walt Disney adaptations, mass marketed books like those published by The Golden Press, and in the most traditional manner, by word of mouth.

Although the popular culture tends to link the stories of Aesop and Grimm together, actually the fables and folk tales are profoundly different and provoke very different responses from their readers. It is these differences in origin, in content, and in reader response which I propose to examine.

Neither fable nor folk tale originated as children's literature. Little is known of Aesop, himself, but legend has it, according to Perry, that he was a Greek slave of the 6th century B.C., and the fables attributed to him were originally designed as political criticism in an age of repression. The fables are not simplistic children's stories, but highly intellectual exercises which take abstract ideas and translate them into formalized dramatic encounters. Jakob and Wilhelm Grimm, in contrast, were nineteenth century philologists and students of German regional culture. They gathered the tales which bear their names from diverse sources, and their interest in the stories was not primarily child oriented; they were studying folklore and the history of words in the spoken German language.[1] Over the years, both Aesop's fables and the Grimm's folk tales became the property of all the people, not only intellectual orators, not only scholars of language and folk literature; and both have become the special property of children.

As early as the first century A.D., the Roman writer, Quintillian, recommended that children study the fables to help them develop skill in reading and writing.[2] Caxton produced an edition of Aesop in 1484, making it one of the first books ever printed in English. During the Renaissance, educators such as Sir Thomas Elyot, in his *Boke named the Governor* (1531) recommended that the fables be a child's first reading. Such notables as Sir Philip Sidney, Francis Bacon, and John Locke endorsed the teaching of Aesop to children. Since the first edition of Aesop that was designed specifically for children, in 1692, there have been many versions of the fables for children, with and without morals, illustrated and elaborated, almost without number.

The first collection of folk tales by the brothers Grimm was released in 1812, entitled *Kinder und Hausmarchen,* and although the Grimms intended the book to be read to children, they saw children only as a "secondary audience."[3] coming after adult scholars. The first English edition was published in 1823, and has been available ever since. There was some opposition to children's reading these fairy stories when they first appeared, because they violated the doctrines of rationalism, but Charles Dickens, Juliana H. Ewing, and others defended the folk tales as vehicles for the teaching of morality. In the October 1, 1853, edition of *Household Words,* Dickens wrote,

> It would be hard to estimate the amount of gentleness and mercy that has made its way among us [through fairy tales]. Forbearance, courtesy, consideration for the poor and aged, kind treatment of animals, the love of nature . . .

all are absorbed by young readers of these stories.

The fables and the fairy tales both convey values which our society respects. Each collection of Aesop's fables presents a fairly consistent world view, a philosophy, a prescription for right behavior. It is the same with the brothers Grimm. Despite Bruno Bettleheim's assertion in *The Uses of Enchantment* that the folk tales do not prescribe behavior, the Grimm stories present a rather clear ethical code based on an unstated philosophy that recommends certain behaviors and warns against others. It is perplexing that the ethical code of Aesop's fables is dramatically different from that of the Grimms' folk tales, and yet both are highly influential sources for the teaching of values to young people in our society. Each collection of folklore embodies a sense of what the world is like and how one must live to succeed in that world.

Some examples will help demonstrate their differences.

> A lion fell in love with a farmer's daughter and asked for her hand. The farmer couldn't bear to give his daughter to the beast, but since he was also too much afraid to refuse, he struck on this scheme. When the lion kept pressing his suit, the farmer said he found him quite worthy to marry his daughter, but that he couldn't give her to him unless he pulled out his teeth and cut off his claws, for his daughter was afraid of them. The lion was so much in love that he readily submitted to both, but the farmer was now contemptuous of him and chased him off with a club when he came back. [Lloyd W. Daly, trans., *Aesop without Morals,* p. 152]

This fable clearly suggests that love leads one to be foolish; one must, therefore, beware of it. Love produces weakness, not strength. The farmer's manipulative duplicity is rewarded, for this story takes place in a world in which the weak must use cleverness to survive when the strong seek to dominate them. The following fable further demonstrates that respect comes from power: surrender the means to power and you lose what you might otherwise have kept:

> A lion, an ass, and a fox reached an agreement with one another and went out to hunt. When they had made a big catch, the lion told the ass to divide it for them. When the ass divided it into three parts and told him to take his choice, the lion flew into a rage, jumped onto him, and ate him up. Then he told the fox to divide it. The fox left only a little for himself, put everything else in one portion, and urged the lion to take it. When the lion asked the fox who had taught him to divide things that way, he said, "The fate of the ass." [Daly, trans., *Aesop without Morals,* p. 155]

This fable teaches the reader to learn from the misfortunes of others, and if there is a lion in your midst, you had better respect his power. The clever but weak fox cannot hope for equality. Mercy is out of the question; justice is not to be expected. The fox is lucky to escape from the lion with his life. Another moral is illustrated here:

> A fox slipped in climbing a fence. To save himself from falling he clutched at a brier-bush. The thorns made his paws bleed, and in his pain he cried out: 'Oh dear! I turned to you for help and you have made me worse off than I was before.' 'Yes, my friend!' said the brier. 'You made a bad mistake when you tried to lay hold of me. I lay hold of everyone myself.' [S. A. Handford, trans., *Fables of Aesop,* p. 4]

Faithfulness and cooperation are meaningless here. In the world view presented by Aesop's fables, each individual must defend his own.

The familiar fable of "The Town Mouse and the Country Mouse," and the less widely known parallel story, "The Thorn Bush and the Oak Tree," teach the value of obscurity: safety comes before luxury or glory. Consider "The Grasshopper and the Ant" in all its variations: diligent toil is admired; the pleasure principle is a dangerous one to follow. The fable of "The Wayfarer and the Frozen Snake" suggests that a good deed is often not returned, and since some people are inherently evil, no kindness, no charity can change them.

Although there are some exceptions, taken all together, the fables teach pragmatic lessons: they recognize that the world is a dangerous place, full of exploiters, bullies, and false friends. Love counts for little; it exposes you and foolishly allows you to relax your defenses. The fables teach self-protection and the value of hard work. Goodness is rarely rewarded, but evil is often revenged. The fables recognize that in the real world, might does make its own right—unfair, perhaps, but true, nonetheless.

To put it mildly, Aesop's fables are not idealistic. They do not recognize miracles. The world is what it is: the enemies, the people in power, are tyrannical lions, tricky foxes, vindictive snakes; the victims, the little people, are vain crows, foolish donkeys, self-important rabbits, and ill-advised lambs. No one is perfect—neither oppressor nor oppressed—and no one can change who he is. The best you can do, according to the fables, is to stand up for yourself, selfishly, if need be, since you can expect no one else to stand up for you; trust only yourself; expect to be attacked and have the sense to lie low when threatened; and, if you are lucky, take your revenge when you get the chance.

The world of the folk tales collected by the Grimms recognizes enemies and dangers, but unlike the world of the fables, it also allows for perfect goodness and the possibility of coming through a trial unscathed, and resting on that one victory happily ever after. Aesop's fables present no ideal characters, no heroes, no heroines. The fairy tales, in contrast, offer many models of perfection. The perfect female is a Cinderella, a Snow White, a Rapunzel: young, beautiful, gentle, passive, and obedient. She must suffer patiently, until she is rescued by fate, usually in the form of a marriageable young man. The perfect male is young, handsome, kind, brave, generous, gentle, and lucky. He is the one who shares his crust with a fox who just happens to be endowed with magic powers, in "The Golden Bird"; he is the one who arrives, by good fortune, at the castle of the sleeping Briar Rose just when the one hundred years' spell is up. Often he is the simple, unsophisticated youngest son, mocked by his clever elder brothers. In the Grimms' world, intelligence and cunning are frequently signs of character weakness.[4] In their folk tales, forethought seems inferior to blind

action; common sense is less valued than simple faith. While Aesop's fables urge watchful cleverness, the fairy tales suggest trust and patience as the better way: after all, miracles can happen. Cinderella can go to the ball in a dress that rains down on her from a tree. Sleeping Beauty may have to wait for a century, but ultimately she awakens to love at first sight. Straw can be spun into gold; brothers can be turned into swans or ravens, and a sister's sacrifice can redeem them. And most significantly, what is dead can be made alive again.

According to the values promoted by the fairy tales, it is better to be self-sacrificing than to look out for your own interests. To go out and aggressively seek wealth and power pretty nearly guarantees a bad end: the gentle sister, in "The Three Little Men in the Wood," is sent to gather strawberries in the snow, clothed only in a paper dress. Her willing helpfulness to the three little old men wins her the dubious reward of having a golden coin fall from her mouth every time she speaks. When her assertive stepsister sensibly bundles up to go out and claim the same, she is cursed for her forwardness by having a toad jump from her mouth every time she opens it. And later, in the same tale, after the good sister has married a king, born him a son, and been transformed by her stepmother into a duck, she returns to care for her infant, not to seek vengeance against the stepsister who has taken her place in the royal bed. It is the evil stepmother who suggests her own awful punishment: "to be put into a cask with iron nails in it, and to be rolled in it down the hill into the water" [Lucy Crane, trans., *Household stories by the Brothers Grimm*, p. 81]. Once the wicked stepmother and the false queen are punished, the innocently murdered queen is restored to life and happiness.

The prevailing message of the folk tales reads: if you are happily poor, and neither complain nor take active steps to secure your fortune, you may be rewarded with wealth; if you are passively self-effacing and let others mock you, mistreat you, and enslave you, you may end up with both power and fame. Self-sacrifice becomes the prudent course of action. There is a puzzling irony here. The tales imply that it is wrong to set greater value on wealth than on goodness, yet material rewards are given to those who set the least store in them.

The Aesopic fables suggest that evil is commonplace. The Germanic folk tales present evil in more terrible guises, but also show that the virtuous victims are ultimately better off for having tangled with the evil.[5] Whatever curses or privations the innocent victims must endure, they are never embittered, never discouraged from their steadfast goodness. Cinderella doesn't whine to her stepmother about how unfair it is that she has to pick lentils from the ashes in order to win the right to attend the prince's ball; the girl in "Rumpelstiltskin" doesn't curse her father for putting her life on the line, saying she can spin rooms full of straw into gold when she hasn't got a notion how to do it. It is as if there is a shatterproof bubble around these characters, so that they are never tainted by their contact with evil, never permanently damaged. Even if they seem to die, like Red Riding Hood or the little brother in "The Juniper Tree," they are wonderfully restored to life. Magic helps them accomplish impossible tasks, and because of their flawless virtue, in the end, their burdens are lifted, their enemies are punished (brutally, as often as not), and they find themselves elevated to new planes of material success and emotional satisfaction.

Folklore does not exist apart from people; it rises from and expresses the beliefs, needs, and hopes of those people who created it and kept it alive. Aesop's and the Grimms' stories, although not native to America, have nonetheless been absorbed into the American folk and popular culture and can, therefore, be presumed to express ideas and values important to our culture. Because of the all-but-universal familiarity of American children with many of the fables and fairy tales, I have taught Aesop and Grimm to students in children's literature courses at two different colleges, to give them adult perspectives on material which they "have always known." The students in one group attended a four-year state college in New England; those in the other group were enrolled at a two-year community college, a branch of the City University of New York. Interesting as the differences between Aesop and Grimm are, almost as interesting are the different reactions of the students to the fables and the fairy tales.

Their response seems to vary with their own socioeconomic background. Students in children's literature classes at the New England college were predominantly young, single, white, and middle to lower-middle class. The students in comparable classes in New York City were predominantly older (30-60 years old), married and raising children, black or Hispanic, and working class or on welfare. The four-year college students were mostly straight out of high school, often idealistic, and relatively innocent of the ways of the world. The community college students, in contrast, had lived in the world—and a particularly rough, urban world.

Many of the state college students found Aesop's fables unpleasantly cynical and felt that they were inappropriate reading for small children, but made interesting intellectual exercises for children of 10 or older. These students believed that it was wrong to take from small children their sense of safety, their trust in loving adults who would shelter them from danger. On the other hand, these same students felt that the folk tales of Grimm fostered kindliness, loyalty, and love, qualities they highly prized. They felt that children should be exposed to the fairy tales early, stararting as young as 3 or 4 years old, to encourage imaginative and moral development, and they felt that the exposure should continue lifelong.

The community college students did not share these views at all. The city-wise older students discovered in Aesop much of the wisdom they felt their children needed to help them cope with the life of the streets, and they agreed among themselves that Aesop was the very book to read to small children of about 4 or 5 years old, before sending them out of the house alone to play or walk to school. As for the fairy tales of the Grimms, the City University of New York students enjoyed studying them, but reacted with cynical laughter to some of the Idealistic and, to them, totally unlikely behavior of the protagonists. These students felt that the Grimms' stories ignored reality and taught lessons appropriate for Sunday school but not for weekday use. Since most of them were churchgoers and believers, they felt uncomfortable about this inconsistency, but they couldn't avoid it: they did not want their children victimized. They could not afford to teach their children to be sweet, passive, and trusting when the world was so clearly Aesopic to them, so full of predatory lions, wolves, and foxes ready to swallow their children up, and once swallowed, chewed and digested, not magically restored to life unharmed. They saw themselves and their children as the lambs, the reeds, and the ants of Aesop's fables, the powerless creatures who must lie low, use their wits when threatened, and work hard the rest of the time. These students felt that the Grimms' idealized world was appropriate reading for older children of about 8 to 12, for by that time the children could distinguish reality from wishful thinking. Beyond this, they raised some angry sociopolitical questions reflecting their radicalized perception of the fairy tales as an attempt by the "power elite" to keep the masses passively hopeful, rather than rebellious over their lot. Among the more protected and upwardly mobile New England college students, these political issues did not arise.

And of course, the more you think about it, the more sense it makes. The fables and folk tales perform different functions. The former teach self-preservation, acknowledging the difficulties of life for ordinary people in the real world today—and, apparently, in every era of the past 25 centuries, if the continuous manuscript and publication history of Aesop's fables is any indication. Survival cannot be taken for granted; loved ones cannot always protect each other from harm. There are no apparent rewards for goodness, no assurances that justice will triumph. Fables are, and have always been, useful for the presentation of cautionary lessons to the underdogs in Western civilization. The folk tales also recognize that the world can be dangerous, but the rules governing existence are profoundly different. The folk tales create an overtly idealized world in which evil is confronted, fearful situations are mastered, wickedness is punished, and virtue is rewarded. Selflessness seems the sensible course, because it brings great rewards eventually. The lowly, if good

Aesop's fables are usually credited with spawning such phrases as "Slow and steady wins the race."

[4] Some of the stories run counter to this trend and urge a little self-help. Grettel must push the witch into the oven and slam the door; Rapunzel must jump from the tower to her beloved. Some of the stories, notably the animal tales such as "Cat and Mouse in Partnership," show the triumph of wit over simplicity. Other tales, including "Hans in Luck" and "Fred and Kate," mock stupidity. But in the main, the most memorable of the Grimms' tales focus on the passively good characters who stumble upon their rewards without any goal-directed behavior.

[5] Bruno Bettelheim has persuasively argued that satisfying psychological messages run beneath the surface of the folk tales. The protagonist's confrontation with danger and evil, most often emanating from mother and father figures, is necessary to the process of dealing symbolically with strongly felt, but unacknowledged emotions. See *The Uses of Enchantment* for amplification of these ideas.

References

Bettelheim, Bruno. *The Uses of Enchantment*. New York: Random House, 1976. Pp. 10, 27.

Crane, Lucy, trans. *Household Stories by the Brothers Grimm*. New York: Dover, 1963.

Daly, Lloyd W., ed. and trans. *Aesop Without Morals*. New York, 1961.

Handford, S. A., trans. *Fables of Aesop*. Baltimore: Penguin, 1954.

Perry, Ben Edwin, trans. *Babrius and Phaedrus*. Cambridge: Harvard University Press, 1965. P. xxxv.

enough, can, therefore, hope to be raised up. This is not the world we know, but the world we might wish to live in.

The students' reactions to Aesop and Grimm were strong and, I think, provocative. It is too often assumed that both fables and folk tales are interchangeably representative conveyers of the morality and values of our culture. Although both are examples of traditional folklore, still alive and meaningful, as well as entertaining and emotionally satisfying, they speak to different kinds of lives, reflect different needs, foster different dreams. Both are good and right, when they fit the lives, the needs, and the dreams of their readers.

Notes

[1] Eliot, Charles W., ed. *Folklore and Fable* (New York, 1909), p. 48.

[2] See Daly, *Aesop Without Morals,* p. 15.

[3] Peppard, Murray B. *Paths Through the Forest* (New York, 1971), p. 41.

Agnes Perkins (essay date 1984)

SOURCE: Agnes Perkins, in an introduction to "The Five Hundredth Anniversary of Aesop in English," in *Children's Literature Association Quarterly*, Vol. 9, No. 2, Summer, 1984, pp. 60-75.

[*In the following essay, Perkins argues that Aesop's fables do not promote the morality of kindness and generosity that the fables of the Indian "Jatakas" do, and that Aesop's fables present what is to one's personal advantage through a satiric representation of human-like foibles.*]

In 1484, William Caxton printed his translation of ***Aesop's Fables*** on the first English press. It has remained in print ever since; the book is still available in at least sixteen versions for children published in the United States alone. Five hundred years is a good long run for a book; it behooves us to try to understand its lasting quality.

When a current political figure proposed that the budget could be balanced by increasing defense spending and cutting taxes, and an opponent called it a scheme to bell the cat, he did not need to explain or add the "moral": "It is easy to propose impossible remedies." We are so familiar with Aesop's stories that we seldom look closely at just what they are saying and how they are saying it; as Aesop himself would say, "Familiarity breeds contempt." We may dismiss them as we do much of the didactic literature of the past as too moralistic for modern taste. But a rereading of Aesop convinces me that the fables are not so much lessons advocating moral goodness as sharply ironic, and often humorous, pictures of human foibles.

Aesop's fables are, of course, much older than five hundred years, having been in the oral tradition for perhaps twenty centuries before Caxton translated and printed them. We know little about Aesop the man. Tradition has it that he was deformed or crippled, a slave on Samos in the sixth century B.C. He is mentioned by several ancient writers, including Herodotus, Aristophanes, and Aristotle, and is pictured as using fables to plead various cases on trial. It is unlikely that he wrote down any fables, and unclear whether he composed those attributed to him or simply gathered those already known. The earliest collection was made by Demetrius Phalereus, founder of the Alexandrian library, about 320 B.C., but it has not survived. The Roman writer Phaedrus of the first century A.D. wrote at least five books of fables in Latin verse, which he called *Fabulae Aesophiae* and which were popular through the middle ages. It may well be that Phaedrus composed many of these himself, as in the seventeenth century Jean de La Fontaine wrote fables in French verse, some taken from earlier Aesop collections and some his own compositions. More important than speculation about Aesop as a person is that the Western body of fable from the oral and early written traditions has been assembled and known by his name.

By definition, a fable is a didactic story, usually a brief tale meant to teach a specific lesson. In distinguishing fables from novels, Mary McCarthy writes:

> Another class of prose fiction is the fable—from the Latin *fabula,* which in turn goes back to an ancient term *fari,* meaning simply "to speak"—the root, incidentally, of *fatum,* or "fate", i.e., "what has been spoken." . . .

> [Fables] did not go out with Aesop. The obvious contemporary example is *Animal Farm,* but I think *1984,* a cautionary tale, must be a fable too, and William Golding's *Lord of the Flies,* most of Golding, probably, also *Brave New World, A Clockwork Orange,* and quite a lot of science fiction.

Fables, with or without talking animals, are allegories—*allegoria,* the description of one thing under the image of another—and, whatever a novel may be, it is not an allegory.

Her definition would, I think, include as fables such books as *Jonathan Livingston Seagull, The Little Prince,* and *The Velveteen Rabbit,* all of which are, in my experience, more popular with pedogogically oriented adults than with children, who sense in them the lesson thinly veiled by story. Such books lack the saving irony of humor of Aesop. Even if one sticks to a more conventional definition of fable, one finds that most strongly contrast with Aesop's, particularly the *Jataka Tales,* the fables from India which ostensibly tell of the various incarnations of Buddha.

A comparison with *Jataka Tales* points up some of the non-moralistic qualities of Aesop's fables. A number of the Jatakas teach the moral value of self-sacrifice. The king of the Banyan Deer lays his head upon the butcher's block to save a pregnant doe, and is rewarded not only with his life, but with a promise that henceforth all the deer will be spared, or, in some versions, that the king and all his country will become vegetarians. The Spirit of the Sal tree pleads that, if the tree must be cut down, it be done painfully, little by little, so that the young trees nearby will not suffer in its crash, and the king promises that the tree shall be allowed to live on. The Hare, having nothing to offer a beggar except grass, which the man is unable to eat, willingly jumps into the fire so that his roasted flesh may feed the beggar, who turns out to be a god in disguise and saves the hare from the flame. The monkey leader saves his eighty thousand followers from the king's archers by making a bridge of vines from the mango tree where they are trapped, using his own body as the essential final link, and, though he dies as a result, he is honored by a magnificent funeral pyre and a shrine built on the site.

Other Jatakas are concerned with the value of kindness or good example. When the Brahmin bets that his ox can pull a hundred wagons and shouts at him, "Rascal!" and "Devil!", the ox plants his feet and will not move, and his master loses the bet. The next day, the ox having explained his grievance, the owner bets again and calls him "fine fellow" and "Great Joy," and the ox pulls willingly, winning great wealth for his master. The good-natured elephant is turned into a rogue when her kingly keeper is replaced by a stable hand who drinks, gambles, steals and quarrels; when his place is taken by wise counselors who are courteous and who discuss honesty, wisdom, and respect each night, the elephant again becomes gentle, good-natured and dependable.

Some Jatakas show how harmony is achieved when one works willingly for a weaker or less able friend.

An elephant, seeing that his owner, an old woman, is growing feeble, sets out to earn money and relieves the old woman of her burdens. A white elephant, grateful to some carpenters who pull a splinter from his foot, roots up the trees and does other labors for them until his good deeds catch the attention of the king, who takes him to live in the palace, presumably a more desirable fate than staying in the forest.

Except for **"Androcles and the Lion,"** which is sometimes included with Aesop's fables, it is hard to find an example in Aesop of this sort of idealistic philosophy. A direct comparison can be made between the Jataka tale, "Friends and Neighbors" and Aesop's **"The Wolf and the Crane."** In each a weaker animal aids one stronger and fiercer. In the Jataka, a jackal helps a lion who is stuck in the mud; in the Aesop, a crane with its long beak extracts a bone stuck in a wolf's throat. When each asks for a reward, the lion promises to be friend and to share with the jackal for life and even enforces this friendship, in later years, upon his mate. The wolf, however, tells the crane, "Ungrateful creature! It is reward enough to put your head into a Wolf's jaws, and take it out again alive!"

Even when the stories are similar, as many of them are, the ending of the Jataka tale is often kinder or more philosophical than that of the Aesop fable. In Aesop's **"The Flies and the Honey-pot"** and "The Jataka Sweet Tooth", creatures are attracted by love of honey into danger. In the Jataka tale, the king, having made his point, allows the rare Wind Antelope to return to the freedom of the forest. In Aesop, the flies bemoan their foolishness, which costs them their lives. One can imagine other Aesop tales with a more philosophical moral: the lion might let the mouse go, not because the mouse will return and free the lion from the net (i.e., even the least likely person may be of later use), but because compassion is a noble quality or because the strong have a moral obligation to aid the weak; the ant might welcome the grasshopper into its home to share in its winter stores so that they both can survive until spring; the crow or jackdaw which dresses in peacock feathers and is driven off by the offended birds might be welcomed back among his fellows with forgiveness, instead of being ostracized by his own kind as well. An Aesop fable, however, rarely promotes this sort of generosity or tells of reform in its characters.

What lessons, then, do Aesop's fables teach? A surprising number condemn, not evil intent, but foolishness. The frogs who want a king find themselves with a tyrant whose appetite they do not survive. The donkey who, seeking a lighter load, twice deliberately falls into the water so that the salt he is carrying will wash away, discovers how stupid his trick is when he is loaded with sponges. The frog who tries to blow himself up as big as the ox bursts in the attempt. The goat,

seeing a fox in the well, jumps in without considering how he will get out, and the fox, having climbed out with the aid of the goat's back, laughs at him. Often foolishness is combined with vanity. Chaucer's Nun's Priest's tale of Chanticleer is based on an Aesop's fable. **"The Fox and the Crow"** is a similar tale, in which the fox gets the crow's cheese by flattery. Others concern foolishness combined with greed. The man kills his goose which lays golden eggs in an attempt to achieve more wealth; the widow overfeeds her hen, hoping to get twice as many eggs, but instead makes the hen so fat that she stops laying entirely. The milkmaid, planning all the good things she will get when she sells the milk and raises chickens, stumbles and spills the milk and so has nothing. The boy, reaching into the jar and taking a fistful of nuts, finds he cannot get his hand out again because he has grabbed too many. Some teach that one should be content with his place in life. The donkey masquerading in the lion's skin is recognized and beaten for his pretentions; the ass who envies the war horse decides, on the day of the battle when the horse is killed, that its humble, hard-working life is better after all. A few of the fables promote cooperation. The old man teaches his sons that together they are strong, individually weak, when he shows them how easy it is to snap a single stick and how difficult to break a bundle. The great trees sacrifice their small neighbor, the ash, to the woodcutter who wants an axe handle, and soon find themselves victims of the axe.

This last is a good example of the negative presentation of the lesson, a method frequently found in Aesop; not "cooperate and you will save yourselves," but "fail to cooperate and you will be destroyed." In fact, the lesson itself is often not a moral in the sense of an exhortation to a virtuous act, but a cautionary anecdote followed by an application that would hardly be a desirable pattern to follow. When the fox invites the stork to dinner and serves its food on a flat plate and the stork returns the invitation with a dinner served in a narrow-necked jar, the "moral" that follows is, "One bad turn deserves another."

The lessons of Aesop's fables are less directions to righteousness or goodness than patterns of practical advantage; they are not about how to lead a good life but about how to get along in the world. They present practical "peasant wisdom" in a tone that is realistic, even callous. No sympathy is wasted on the boy who cries "Wolf!" and loses his sheep or, in some versions, his life. No tears are shed over the sick lion who is mistreated by his subjects or over the lion in love, who allows his claws to be trimmed and his teeth extracted until he becomes a laughing stock. No pity is extended to the man who lets his young wife pick out all his white hairs and his elder wife pluck out all the black ones, until he is bald. The characters' suffering is the way of the world and results from their own foolishness; it serves them right!

Most of us do not enjoy being preached at. Most moralistic literature is short-lived, and one might expect that, in the modern world at least, such tales would be relegated to those with a taste for the obscure or quaint. Instead, they are continually being revived in new collections or used as subjects for dramatizations and picture books. I suspect that their continued popularity is not because of any moral value they promote, in the sense of piety or virtue, but because they take a sharp, satiric view of the world and make us laugh ironically at the faults we recognize in our neighbors and, all too often, in ourselves.

References

Aesop's Fables for Modern Readers. Peter Pauper Press, 1941.

Aspinwall, Margaret. *Jataka Tales Out of Old India*. E. P. Dutton, 1920.

Babbitt, Ellen C. *Jataka Tales*. Century, 1912.

DeRoin, Nancy. *Jataka Tales*. Houghton Mifflin, 1975.

Gaer, Joseph. *The Fables of India*. Little Brown, 1955.

Jacobs, Joseph. *The Fables of Aesop*. 1894, rpr. Macmillan, 1964.

McCarthy, Mary. "Novel, Tale, Romance," *The New York Review of Books*, May 12, 1983.

Perry, Ben Edwin. "Aesop," *Encyclopaedia Brittanica* (1966), 1:220.

Barbara Mirel (essay date 1984)

SOURCE: Barbara Mirel, "Tradition and the Individual Retelling," in *Children's Literature Association Quarterly*, Vol. 9, No. 2, Summer, 1984, pp. 63-66.

[*In the following essay, Mirel analyzes the treatment given to the Aesopic fable of "The Fox and the Crow" by various authors representative of ways of interpreting Aesop labelled as the instructive approach, the empathetic approach, and contextualized-example approach.*]

In the past fifteen years, the noted children's authors Eric Carle, Jack Kent, Eve Rice, and Paul Galdone, and the less familiar writers Heidi Holder, Jack McFarland, Harold Jones and Ruth Spriggs have all published retellings of the ancient Works of Aesop. In addition, Joseph Jacobs' and Randolph Caldecott's collections have been republished. The existence of all these collections reaffirms that those writing and publishing for children still value these traditional fables; but as well as transmitting part of our cultural and literary heritage, each of these collections also engages readers in its own world view. Since readers get more from these collections than just a basic knowledge of some fables' storylines, any assessment of them must begin with an examination of the nature of an author's individual stamp on the retelling.

There seem to be three approaches to retelling Aesop. The first has traditionally occurred in a religious approach to fables. Even when stripped of religious overtones and set in a secular context, these instructive fables emphasize the authority of the "truth" shown in the fable's lesson. This approach uses our recognition of moral truth to direct our pursuit of individual betterment. The potential effect of such an approach is for readers to feel chastened, or at least cautioned, against foresaking "the straight and narrow," because of the consequences which the fable shows accompany moral failings.

A second type of retelling is lighter in tone. Fables using this approach convey the humorous side of human foibles. Instead of placing the focus on achieving moral betterment, such fables emphasize the shared nature of our human condition. Ideally, this type of retelling might move readers away from egocentricism, as they begin to feel a part of the larger human community in which we understand and accept our failings.

The third approach seems more akin to the classical Aristotelean vision of fables as they function in the context of "rhetorical argument." Here fables become examples which can clarify deliberations about larger social and political issues. When fables are presented in this manner, readers might be prompted toward an awareness of their own abilities to judge and act.

One qualification to make about dividing the retellings of fables along these lines is that humor is often present not just in the empathetic approach but in the other two also. But in the instructive group of retellings, humor often underscores the message of "just desserts," while in those with the contextualized-example approach it usually takes the form of social or political satire.

Holder, Rice, Spriggs and, to some extent, Jacobs fall into the "instructive" category. Kent, Jones, Lobel, Galdone and McFarland humourously highlight the human condition. As part of the third group of "contextualized" fables, Carle not only follows Caldecott's lead through suggestive illustrations, but also through a text that is somewhat more morally ambiguous than other retellings of fables.

Perhaps the most useful way to see how authors turn their literary choices to different ends is to examine the different treatments given to the same fable. **"The Fox and The Crow,"** included in almost all the books under consideration, is about a fox who uses flattery to trick a crow out of its cheese. The fox's goal is to get the crow to open its beak so that the cheese will drop down to where the fox stands.

In her rendition of this fable, Ruth Spriggs presents a very balanced interchange between the fox and the crow, told equally from both points of view. Beginning with a focus on the crow who has stolen the cheese, it then shifts to the fox who sees the crow, desires the cheese, and acts to get it. The focus continues to shift back and forth, first to the flattering words of the fox, then to the proud reactions of the crow. The shifting perspective stops once the crow opens her mouth to prove she can indeed sing. Then the cheese, itself, becomes the focal point, and we see it falling right into the fox's mouth. The victorious fox then parts with words of instruction. "You may have a voice, but no brains," he tells the crow.

Throughout the fable, the even-handed presentation of these characters make neither of them altogether guilty nor altogether innocent. Thus, we are left honestly wondering if the fox is really any less entitled to the cheese than the crow, who obtained it by illicit means. In fact, since our perspective has been so equally balanced all along, our judgement can be easily swayed by the last word at the end. This judgement is pronounced explicitly by the fox: the bird lacks brains. An active wit differentiates the fox from the crow. Both are prompted by desire to commit unscrupulous acts—thievery in the crow's case, false flattery in the fox's. Yet it is not the means which we are to judge, but the ultimate consequence, and here the crow comes up short. The reason for the crow's failure is that she has not put reason to work alongside desire. The fox, on the other hand, not only has done a masterful job of combining the two but, even more important, in doing so has somehow avoided any kind of sullied representation of his desire. Unlike other renditions such as Caldecott's or Jacobs' where the fox "pounces on" or "snaps up" the cheese, the fox in Spriggs' story displays no such ravenous or base instincts (with the cheese conveniently falling right into his mouth). In this type of simplified narrative where cause and effect are so evenly developed, no extraneous details leave readers wondering if perhaps there is more than one way to interpret events. The judgement clearly goes against the crow, and the lesson to be learned is obvious: "Vanity is expensive."

Jacobs' treatment of this tale does not paint such an even-handed picture of the fox and crow; it achieves the effect of moral certainty through a different tactic. The focus of the fable is predominantly on the fox, and his character colors our interpretations of the course of events. We readily blame the fox for being callously

desirous, scheming, and manipulative; at the hands of such a protagonist the fate of the crow's cheese is a foregone conclusion. So much is the focus on the fox that we never learn how the crow has gotten the cheese, and she is entirely passive until she "lifted up her head and began to caw her best." The fox snaps up the cheese and smugly imparts a bit of his "worldly wisdom" to the crow: "Don't trust flatterers." It little matters to him, or to readers, that implicit in his advice is a condemnation of himself. The fox knows the secret of all good con-men: his "sting" can only succeed if his "mark" suffers from a moral weakness like the crow's vanity. The lesson of the tale comes across through reference to the fox's point of view; we learn about the need to rectify our character flaws by means of our attention being drawn to the flatterer, not to our vanity.

Eve Rice also builds toward an irrefutable moral lesson: but she does so by tipping the initial balance between fox and crow to favor the fox. Rice effects this tilt in point of view when she writes, "Crow, of course, began to sing." In "of course" Rice subtly gears our interpretation of crow to accord with the fox's perspective. "Of course" enlists readers' tacit acknowledgements that, like fox, they knew all along that crow would inevitably fall for the ploy. Yet, more than just proving fox a crafty fellow, this "of course" affirms our right to judge crow harshly. Since no actual coercion is involved in fox's attempts to make crow sing, crow herself is responsible for the motives that result in her losing the cheese, and having to listen to the fox's words of mixed warning and advice. After the cheese falls directly into fox's jaws, he says, "Beware of those who flatter / and tell lies meant to please— / and be glad, you foolish bird, / you only lost your cheese." The con-man threatens danger. Thus, the shift to the fox's perspective not only functions to show that the crow's moral flaws and foolishness have given the fox control over the situation, but also to suggest that underneath this situation lies a more violent universe. Allusions to physical danger never occur before this endnote; apparently, Rice is not willing to rely solely upon the way the body of the fable is developed to convey the important lesson. To insure that there can be no misunderstanding about the moral's urgency, she creates an additional level of instruction at the end.

Comparing Caldecott's retelling to those in the "instructive" group reveals the dramatic divergences that can be caused by slight differences. Like Rice, Caldecott interjects "of course" into the narrative to evoke a sense of participation by the reader; he writes, "The Crow . . . began to caw vigorously, of course dropping the cheese." This "of course" enlists the reader's agreement, not in judging the crow foolish, but in recognizing the inevitability of the cheese falling. The first entails a subjective judgement of cause and effect, the second an objective judgement based on observable natural laws: with nothing to hold it, the cheese will fall. The instructive edge built in by Rice's use of "of course" is absent.

Caldecott tells the whole tale in four sentences, with consistent alternations in focus between fox and crow. By revealing the outline of the scenario in such a manner, Caldecott's narrative becomes a model framework in which fits a number of like situations, so that readers are able to translate the insights from this tale to other relevant circumstances in a direct way. Because the storytelling is so sparse, it is the few specific details that determine the meaning of the actions. The crow has stolen the cheese; the fox resorts to hyperbolic lies ("he went so far as to say that she had the best claims to be made Queen of the birds"); and the fox reveals the predatory nature of his desires as he "pounced" on the cheese. The last sentence of the tale, which is the only direct dialogue between the fox and crow, belongs to the fox, who says, "My good friend Crow, you have every good quality; now try to get some common sense." Such a critique of the crow's foolishness, and the story's implication that her foolishness is a function of her vanity, are a far cry from Rice's condemnation. Rather it is in the spirit of "fair play:" both fox and crow are thieves, crow able to come by her goods by her physical ability of flight, fox by his prowess of wit. He has earned the right to instruct her because he was more successful than she was.

Caldecott picks up on this somewhat open-ended message in his illustrations. Characteristic of his style are dual illustrations, on one page depicting the literal events of the story, on the next page showing how the tale relates to human society. His example here is a split frame set in a parlor which first shows a suitor in pursuit of a delicate looking woman while a heavy-set matron sits between the two, guarding the young woman from his advances. The suitor is directing his conversation to the matron, beckoning her to move to the piano, and we can imagine the flattering words with which he cajoles her to delight them with her musical talent. In the next frame, we see the chaperone thoroughly absorbed in her piano and song as the suitor, now placed on the couch next to the still demure young woman, kisses the hand of this object of his desires. In a word, the suitor's scheme is more "civilized"—and in the long run, more effective—than just resorting to grabbing what he wants, and perhaps this can be said of the fox also. Thus we begin to see the interchange between fox and crow in terms of the varying levels of sophistication that mark people's behavior rather than in terms of moral prescriptions.

Eric Carle's efforts to contextualize fables also depend on relatively open-ended presentations of the stories. His retelling of **"The Fox and The Crow"** is unique among all the collections. The crucial cues for effect are not found so much in sentence structure as they are in the apparent liberties he takes with the whole storyline and the twists he weaves into it. In his retelling, we do not discover how crow came by the food, we find him in a tree, beneath which sit Mrs. Fix and her son on a park bench. Young fox is hungry, and mother fox lights on the idea of feeding him by tricking the crow out of its food. The park bench, a human contrivance, has no direct relevance to the events of the story (as, say, the presence of equally human eating utensils do in fables like **"The Fox and the Stork"**). Rather it functions to create a setting outside the natural kingdom, one which has a number of social connotations attached to it. In fact, Carle plays on the association between park benches and the outcasts of the world in his illustration, which shows the two foxes somewhat huddled together on the bench, mother wrapped in a shawl, son dressed in clothes a bit too small for him. The angle of the drawing, looking from the crow in the tree down on the foxes, gives them a size strikingly smaller than the crow's, a large bird even more commanding by his apparel of tail-coat and tuxedo pants, and by the fine spread of sausages and wine which he has laid out before him. The foxes' neediness is reinforced as mother casts her eyes above to the feast and son fixes his gaze trustingly on his mother. As text combines with illustration, the connection between tale and social relevance is inescapable. The relevance is too colored by humor to seem heavy-handed; the tail-coat is an outgrowth of the crow's anatomy and the shawl a tattered version of fox-fur.

Carle also switches the conventionally assigned sexes of the characters for effect. Instead of the usually male fox who preys on the weakness of a female, his fox is a protective, nurturing mother who plays on the vanity of a prosperous male crow. Reversing the traditional expectations which permit us to see consistency in the notion of a female's vanity enhancing a male's power over her, Carle provides an equally consistent scenario of a female's resourcefulness outwitting a male's pride and sense of self-importance. Carle's reversal underscores the importance that social and political contexts have in shaping our interpretations, be they based on sex roles or some other criteria.

Carle also splits the fox persona into the two aspects of mother and son, with son serving as the personification of the motivating desire and mother as the craftiness which will satisfy that desire. Once she succeeds in getting crow to drop the food down next to the park bench, Mrs. Fox hands it to her son, saying, "Didn't I tell you that you'd have something good to eat?" Our sympathies rest with the foxes, as we see Mrs. Fox flattering crow not for her own benefit but for her son's. Method is separated from selfish appetite, and desire, in turn, is attributed to a youth too little to fend for himself. By showing the "want" and the "getting of it" as directly related but occurring between two distinct agents, Carle can build into the "fox character" more socially acceptable explanations for its conduct than when it is but a single actor.

The conventional focus on the need for the crow to mend its character is as present in Carle's retelling as it is in others. But in the tale's conclusion the crow is left singing, with the foxes quietly removing themselves from this irritating voice. Unlike other retellings, there is no direct instruction to the crow by the fox. Perhaps once the crow realizes his assumed audience is gone he will begin to question both the sincerity of the fox's words and his own wisdom in believing them. Then again, he might not. Thus, the reader's insights occur outside of the inner workings of the story.

Finally, Jack Kent's version of **"The Fox and The Crow"** represents the third group of "empathetic" retellings. Kent directly recounts just the essentials of the plot, favoring neither the fox nor the crow's point of view. His lightness of tone injects simplicity and humor into the course of events; the simplicity creates the effect that these events could happen to anyone and the humor works to take the edge off a moral rebuke. The fox's simple words of flattery give him no aura of being a master of words. In fact, he repeats his adjectives rather than building to a more and more powerful appeal to the crow's vanity: "What a beautiful bird!" said the fox, loud enough for the crow to hear. "Surely such a lovely bird has a lovely voice. How I long to hear her sing." Such commonplaces are obviously sufficient to entice the crow to open her mouth to sing. Yet Kent narrates this fateful move on the crow's part with a humorous turn as he writes, "But all that came out was a "caw" and the cheese." Kent's syntax sets up the expectation that the "all that came out" will lead to some expression about her singing capabilities, and there is a verbal delight in seeing juxtaposed to this comment on her voice a reference to the cheese also.

Kent's illustrations add to the humorous nature of the retelling. The characters are cartoon-like, the crow wearing a derby reminiscent of Heckle and Jeckle, the fox wearing Groucho Marx-like top-coat and-hat. The illustrations conjure up images of lovable rogues. The fox's motions with his hat first parody motions of sincerity (with hat held at breast as he speaks) and then reveal true intent (as he turns the hat upside down, extending it to catch the falling cheese). The crow's expressions, too, effect exaggeration. Her ludicrous attempt to belt out a song is highlighted by closed eyes and wide open beak with a big read "CAW" painted in. Also, after losing the cheese, the crow is shown leaning down from her branch over the fox as she watches the wide-eyed disbelief *him* eating *her* cheese. On the same page the text gives the fox's concluding instruction: "I see you do have a voice Madam Crow.

What you seem to be lacking is brains." Kent succeeds in cultivating readers' understanding attitude through the matter-of-fact and light-hearted nature of his presentation. We so readily find humor in the course of events not because we side with one character or the other, but in part because we too have experienced similar situations. Even if we have been on the losing end, we can see that there is a funny element in such situations. Not only Kent's illustrations show this comic element but his italicized moral at the end does too. Reinforcing the "practical joke" side of the circumstance, the tale tells us, "Don't be fooled by flattery." Thus, though there is a moral lesson which can be taken to heart about vanity, readers also come away learning not to lose their ability to laugh in the face of character lapses.

It should be clear from this analysis that there are particular world views in each of these retellings of a very simple story. In choosing versions of such stories we should be aware of the distinct nature of each one, and realize that young readers can be taught how to engage texts so that they see in them more than simple repetitions of the same story. The beauty of these works is that they have tremendous potential for use in refining young people's literary sensibilities. Beyond their traditional plots these tales offer young readers the opportunity to recognize such important literary aspects as detail, nuance, context, characterization, and writer's intent. None of these features in the fables are so subtle that children cannot begin to recognize them. By exploring the relation among such textual features children will begin to move toward a discovering of meaning through language. Treated in this way, fables can take on an exciting dimension well beyond the simple didactic messages usually associated with them.

References

Caldecott, Randolph. *The Caldecott Aesop.* Garden City, NY: Doubleday, 1978.

Carle, Eric. *Twelve Tales from Aesop.* New York: Philomel, 1980.

Galdone, Paul. *Three Aesop Fox Fables.* New York: Seabury, 1971.

Holder, Heidi. *Aesop's Fables.* New York: Viking, 1981.

Jacobs, Joseph. *The Fables of Aesop,* illus. Richard Heighway. New York: Schocken, 1966.

Jones, Harold. *Tales from Aesop.* London: Franklin Watts, 1981.

Kent, Jack. *Jack Kent's Fables of Aesop.* New York: Parents', 1972.

_____. *More Fables of Aesop.* New York: Parents', 1974.

McFarland, John. *The Exploding Frog,* illus. James Marshall. Boston: Little Brown, 1981.

Rice, Eve. *Once in a Wood: Ten Tales from Aesop.* New York: Greenwillow, 1979.

Spriggs, Ruth. *The Fables of Aesop.* New York: Rand McNally, 1975.

Anita C. Wilson (essay date 1984)

SOURCE: Anita C. Wilson, "To Instruct and To Amuse: Some Victorian Views of Aesop's Fables," in *Children's Literature Association Quarterly*, Vol. 9, No. 2, Summer, 1984, pp. 66-68.

[*In the following essay, Wilson surveys opinions of various Victorian writers regarding the explicit moral statements in Aesop's fables, showing that writers believed their readers wanted to be amused or instructed through an amusing story rather than through explicit moral statements.*]

During the Christmas season of 1847, the *Spectator* featured a notice of a new book entitled *A Selection of Aesop's Fables versified and set to Music,* "with Symphonies and Accompaniments for the Pianoforte" (11 December 1847). The appearance of such a work testifies to the popularity of Aesop's Fables during the Victorian era. Among numerous editions were the translations by Thomas James (1948; illustrated by Tenniel) and George Fyler Townsend (1867), and the illustrated editions by Charles Bennett (1857), who also wrote his own text; by Harrison Weir (1860); by Thomas Dalziel and others (1867); by Ernest Griset (1869); by Randolph Caldecott (1883); and by Walter Crane, whose version for the youngest children, *The Baby's Own Aesop,* appeared in 1887. The fable is, by definition, didactic. But the degree to which the lesson is thrust upon the reader may vary, and for that reason, Victorian attitudes to Aesop are particularly interesting. While the generalization that the Victorian period was a time of transition from instruction to amusement in children's books is over-simplified, questions about the balancing of didacticism and entertainment were certainly of great significance.

In the preface to his edition of *Aesop's Fables,* Thomas James set forth his intention to eliminate the sometimes elaborate morals which had been attached to the stories by previous translators: "an essential departure has been made from the common plan of the English Fabulists, who have generally smothered the original Fable under an overpowering weight of their own commentary." James did not reject the fables' didactic function; he merely wished to reinstate the use of brief and proverbial morals, instead of the lengthy ones in editions like Samuel Croxall's (1722), some of which are longer than the fables they accompany. In some cases, James incorporated the morals into the fables, and on occasion, "where the story seems to speak for itself, [the morals are] omitted altogether."

Some years earlier, Richard Scrafton Sharpe had taken a similar approach in his *Old Friends in a New Dress; or Familiar Fables in Verse.* In his preface to the fifth edition (1837), Sharpe observed that "children, whose minds are alive to the entertainment of an amusing story, too often turn from one fable to another, rather than peruse those less interesting lines that come under the term, 'application.'" To remedy this situation, Sharpe attempted to integrate the morals with the fables in a more cohesive fashion, "that the story shall not be obtained without the benefit arising from it; and that amusement and instruction may go hand in hand." Sharpe's endeavor was not entirely successful; in most cases he summed up the moral at the end of the fable, so that it could still easily be skipped. His version of **"The Lion and the Mouse,"** for example, concludes:

> Two lessons we from hence may learn,
>   "The lowly not to disregard;"
> And that "A kind and friendly turn
>   Will almost always meet reward."

Sharpe did not object to the idea of attaching separate morals to fables, but regretfully acknowledged that children would probably ignore them. Integrating story and message was as a practical concession motivated by anxiety that children might otherwise seize amusement without instruction; as a review of Sharpe's book in the *Monthly Mirror* warned, "the cake is eaten, and the task left undone" (August, 1807).

Forty years later, the *Examiner's* highly favorable review of James' edition, which it declared "must hereafter be *the* version of Aesop," displayed more faith in the intrinsic morality of the fable and was sharply critical of overly didactic versions:

> The present Edition is remarkable for the clearness and conciseness with which each tale is narrated; and the reader will not be slow to acknowledge his gratitude to Mr. James for having relieved the book from these tedious and unprofitable appendages called 'morals,' which used to obscure and disfigure the ancient editions of the work. A fable, if it be good, will inculcate its moral clearly; and it may safely be asserted that in all cases where it is necessary to extract the moral from the tale, and expand it into tedious prose, the fable itself must be intrinsically bad or defective, and had better be cast aside altogether (11 March, 1848).

This attitude reveals the gradual trend away from overt didacticism in mid-Victorian juvenile literature. An

1860 *London Quarterly Review* article on children's books reprinted in Lance Salway's *A Peculiar Gift* offers a typical response: "The great art of a story-writer, who wishes to make his book serve any moral, religious, or scientific purpose, is to secure that the principle to be taught is a genuine element in the story, and organically connected with it . . . (p. 316).

In "Books of Fiction for Children," which appeared in the *Quarterly Review* in 1967, Bennett Johns applied a similar philosophy to *Aesop's Fables*. Using James' version of **"The Wind and the Sun"** as an example of a fable which made its point through the story itself, without additional moralizing, Johns assumed that "there is a fair, wise moral hidden in sound, healthy fiction, which all may read who will." He was not discarding the role of didacticism, but was confident that if the moral were an integral part of the story and not the price exacted for pleasurable reading, children would naturally and effortlessly absorb the teaching: "The youngest reader who has any brains and takes an interest in what he reads—as every child does who is kindly taught—gets hold of the moral for himself without having it preached into him, and without even a reflection tagged on as an antidote to the fiction." The most effective lesson, then, is the least obvious and artificial one.

Yet it was also possible to argue that explicit and straightforward didacticism was preferable, since it at least let young readers know exactly what they were getting. The same *London Quarterly Review* essay which advocated an organic relationship between story and moral also praised the overt moralizing of the old-fashioned Aesops, because they allowed children to skip what they did not want. This anonymous critic took the role of didacticism in children's literature for granted ("it is impossible to overlook the necessity of teaching as well as delighting children") yet wryly observed that "at present so many ingenious devices have been discovered for insinuating moral or scientific truths into story-books, that children are never safe". Like Richard Sharpe, the essayist recognized that children were unlikely to acquire any moral lessons from stories unless the teaching was absorbed unconsciously through pleasurable reading. This behavior was not perceived, however, as regrettable, but as a natural and healthy characteristic of childhood: "It is a main requisite then of a child's book, that it should give pleasure. . . . In rejecting what we call the valuable information, and in readily assimilating what seems to us useless, the nature of the child is asserting for itself the real requirements of an age which perchance we have forgotten."

The manner in which Aesop was presented to Victorian children has been discussed primarily in terms of recreational reading, but the fables were also used in schools; James' edition was "undertaken with a view to remedy the deficiencies of the versions at present in use in schools." Although bringing Aesop into the classroom was hardly unique to the Victorian era, this was one of relatively few books of the time considered suitable for all social classes and types of schools. The publisher of James' version omitted no one from its projected audience, grandly offering "an amusing Handbook for All Ranks and Ages, and a Classbook for all seminaries, from the Royal Foundations to the Ragged Schools" (the latter of which provided basic education to the poorest of children). This comprehensive view was unusual; the criticism of children's books in major periodicals like *Fraser's,* the *Quarterly Review,* the *Examiner,* and the *Spectator* was directed to readers of middle-class or higher status, and took the concept of fixed class distinctions for granted. As Gillian Avery observes in *Nineteenth Century Children,* the "idea of the fixed social caste was a peculiarly Victorian one, so far as children's books went. No doubt it was precisely because people in real life were changing caste with such alarming rapidity . . . that writers hysterically resisted these encroachments" (194). The *Spectator's* review of Mary and Elizabeth Kirby's *The Discontented Children,* for example, matter-of-factly noted that the story inculcated the necessity "of doing our duty, and resting satisfied with our condition," whether humble or noble (11 November 1854). Similarly, Bennett Johns' *Quarterly Review* essay advised that "suppose we wish to teach that every one had better be content in his own place . . . what can tell it to a child more lightly and pleasantly than the following?" What follows is a poem describing how a mountain and a squirrel learn to appreciate each other's talents and position; it concludes, "Let both be content / With what is sent."

Although not questioning the concept of a fixed social structure, an 1865 essay in *Fraser's* called "On Lessening the Irksomeness of Elementary Instruction" displayed a markedly sympathetic attitude toward the largely working-class children in village schools. The essay asserts that school should be a pleasant and encouraging environment and that the purpose of school books is not primarily to teach the skill of reading, but to cause children to like reading and turn to it for enjoyment and recreation. A typical reading text, consisting of excerpts from stories and essays, is censured as "dismally repulsive." While the book is "highly irreproachable" in moral terms, the essay argues that it is unfair to burden lower-class children with reading that will not provide the interest and stimulation of books for more fortunate children; the writer sardonically questions whether this anthology is "the book that Miss Constantia and Master Reginald are learning to read out of at the Hall or at the Rectory?" Recommended are *Aesop's Fables, Robinson Crusoe, Sandford and Merton,* and Maria Edgeworth's tales, all of which (with the possible exception of *Sandford and Merton,* the most directly didactic of the group), were widely read at the time by children of higher social status also. The author voices the familiar objection to books displaying "too pedantic and elaborate a purpose of *direct* and immediate moral inculcation, simply because that very desirable end will not be promoted but defeated by such a course." The morals in Aesop should be omitted, since "few things have contributed more to the irksomeness of instruction than that obstinate traditionary notion that everything heard, seen, or read must have a hard-edged, definite, and ostentatious moral lesson appended to it. . . ." As is evident for other comments regarding Aesop and didacticism in children's literature, such an attitude was not unusual by the 1860's; less common, however, was the objection to moralizing in books intended specifically for children of the working class. In *The English Common Reader,* Richard Altick says that these children had little exposure to any recreational reading before the mid-nineteenth century; even in the 1860's, inspectors condemned the failure of most school books "to appeal to the child's imagination and emotions" (154).

Aesop crossed age as well as class lines; in 1851, James' version appeared in Murray's "Reading for the Rail," the publisher's series of books for train journeys. William Caldwell Roscoe, whose grandfather had written *The Butterfly's Ball* (1807) for the amusement of children, altogether rejected Aesop as children's literature, seeing the fables' only source of appeal in the accompanying illustrations:

> . . . though Aesop has been a good deal pressed upon the attention of 'the youth of the British isles,' we apprehend it has not been with much success: the pithy meaning in which the point of the story lies is lost upon him, and all that he cares for is any humour which may be embodied in the telling. Bewick's wonderful illustrations have charm indeed; but they swamp the fable, moral and all. . . . The tales gather an interest as elucidating the pictures; and that is all (27).

Roscoe's reaction was not typical, since most mid-Victorians considered Aesop mainly in terms of his appeal to a juvenile audience.

In the last decades of the Victorian age, the fables' status as children's literature was both affirmed and questioned. Aesop was not mentioned in Charlotte Yonge's *What Books to Lend and What to Give* (1887), although one year later Edward Salmon, in *Juvenile Literature As It is,* placed **Aesop's Fables** with the fairy tales of Grimm and Andersen as the most popular and universal works for younger children:

> Aesop's fame in the nursery is so great as to appear almost as fabulous, at least in its historic aspects, as the themes of which he treats. . . . Throughout the

ages, in the midst of ignorance and superstition, in the homes of rich and poor alike, Aesop has secured a place (47).

Since parents select a child's first books, Salmon assumed that the explicit didacticism of Aesop and the more implicit didacticism of fairy tales accounted for their presence in the nursery; he took for granted, however, that children themselves would skip the morals and enjoy the stories:

> The secret of this favour [among adults] is that fairy stories and fables are regarded practically as engines for the propulsion of all the virtues into the little mind in an agreeable and harmless form. Aesop is distinguished first by brevity; second, by the manner in which his moral is generally hung in an epigrammatic and easily-to-be-avoided form at the end of his narrative (47).

A decade later, the *Pall Mall Gazette* presented the results of a survey which asked children to list their favorite books. *Alice in Wonderland* came first on the list of twenty; *Through the Looking-Glass,* Andersen and the Grimms, Andrew Lang's fairy tale collections, a children's version of the *Arabian Nights,* and stories by Mrs. Molesworth also appeared. Aesop did not, presumable because of the morals: "Aesop's absence from the elect is perhaps to be attributed to the pernicious trick of printing morals that nobody wants along with the fables" ("What the Children Like," 1 July 1898). By the late nineteenth century, didacticism had relaxed considerably, and few critics worried if children ate the cake and left the task undone. Whether to eliminate the morals, however, or to leave them in precisely because children could then easily skip them, remained a point of contention. Victorian responses to Aesop—as a pleasure book, a school test, a work for all ages and social classes—reveal both the universality and enduring appeal of the fables, and the challenge of balancing instruction and amusement which helped determine the shape and context of much of Victorian children's literature.

References

Altick, Richard D. *The English Common Reader: A Social History of the Mass Reading Public, 1800-1900.* 1957; rpr. Chicago: Phoenix-University of Chicago Press, 1963.

Avery, Gillian, with Angela Bull. *Nineteenth Century Children: Heroes and Heroines in English Children's Stories 1780-1900.* London: Hodder and Stoughton, 1965.

"Books of Fiction for Children," *Quarterly Review* (American Edition) 121.243 (1867): 29-47.

"Children's Literature," *London Quarterly Review* 13 (1859-1860): 469-500; rpr. Salway, 299-331.

Darton, F. J. Harvey. *Children's Books in England: Five Centuries of Social Life,* rev. Brian Alderson. Cambridge: Cambridge University Press, 1982.

Houghton, Walter E. *Wellesley Index to Victorian Periodicals, 1824-1900.* Toronto: University of Toronto Press, 1966.

James, Reverend Thomas. *Aesop's Fables: A New Version, Chiefly from Original Sources.* London: John Murray, 1848.

"On Lessening the Irksomeness of Elementary Instruction," *Fraser's Magazine for Town and Country* 72 (1865): 328-334.

Roscoe, William Caldwell, "Fictions for Children," *Poems and Essays by the late William Caldwell Roscoe,* ed. Richard Holt Hutton. Chapman and Hall, 1860; rpr. Salway, 23-45.

Salmon, Edward. "Literature for the Little Ones," in Salway, 46-61.

Salway, Lance, ed. *A Peculiar Gift: Nineteenth Century Writings on Books for Children.* Harmondsworth, England: Kestrel-Penguin, 1976.

Sharpe, R. S. *Old Friends in a New Dress: or, Familiar Fables in Verse,* 6th ed. London: Grant and Griffith, 1849.

St. John, Judith. *The Osborne Collection of Early Children's Books, 1566-1910.* Toronto: Toronto Public Library, 1958, rev. 1966.

"What the Children Like," *Pall Mall Gazette* (July 1, 1898) 1-2.

Pat Pflieger (essay date 1984)

SOURCE: Pat Pflieger, "Fables into Picture Books," in *Children's Literature Association Quarterly,* Vol. 9, No. 2, Summer, 1984, pp. 73-80.

[*In the following essay, Pflieger discusses the effect that the use of illustrations has on the interpretation of individual fables.*]

With their minimal plots, fables seem a natural choice for picture books. The author and illustrator can embellish the tale and give it a personal touch. In picture books, the main characters in fables lose their anonymity and become more individual. These books stress the entertaining qualities of the tales, though without sacrificing the lessons, which are sometimes even strengthened by the text or the illustrations.

Most of the fables presented singly in picture books are those of Aesop or La Fontaine. Eighteen of the twenty-six picture books I investigated are based on tales from Aesop or on La Fontaine's version of them, two on a story in La Fontaine that does not appear in Aesop, and five on tales from Indian tradition, mostly from the Panchatantra. One picture book—*The Hare and the Tortoise and the Tortoise and the Hare,* by William Pène du Bois and Lee Po—retells and links together an Aesop fable and a tale similar to one found in the Panchatantra.

Many of these books are retellings of but a handful of fables. **"The Miller, His Son, and Their Ass,"** one of Aesop's fables, is retold in Katherine Evans' *The Man, the Boy, and the Donkey,* Roger Duvoisin's *The Miller, His Son, and Their Donkey,* Jean Showalter's *The Donkey Ride,* Brian Wildsmith's *The Miller, the Boy, and the Donkey,* and Mary Calhoun's *Old Man Whickutt's Donkey.* **'The Hare and the Tortoise"** appears as three works, illustrated by Brian Wildsmith, Paul Galdone, and William Pène du Bois. Aesop's version of **"The Lion and the Mouse"** has been illustrated by Ed Young and La Fontaine's version, "The Lion and the Rat," by Brian Wildsmith. **"The Town Mouse and the Country Mouse"** is retold in the book by the same name illustrated by Paul Galdone, and in a translation of Horace's version, *Two Roman Mice,* by Marilynne K. Roach. Katherine Evans, in *The Maid and Her Pail of Milk,* and Ingri and Edgar Parin D'Aulaire, in *Don't Count Your Chicks,* retell Aesop's **"The Milkwoman and Her Pail."** The tale of **"The Wind and the Sun"** is retold in both *The Wind and the Sun,* illustrated by Margaret Horder, and in *The North Wind and the Sun,* illustrated by Brian Wildsmith. La Fontaine's fable, "The Cobbler and the Financier," has been retold by Brian Wildsmith in *The Rich Man and the Shoemaker* and by Marcia Sewall in *The Cobbler's Song.* Two tales from the Panchatantra also appear in more than one version. "The Blue Jackal" has been retold by Marcia Brown and by Mehlli Gobhai. Shortened versions of "The Monkey and the Crocodile" appear as Paul Galdone's book by the same title and, with different characters, as the second story in *The Hare and the Tortoise and the Tortoise and the Hare* by William Pène du Bois and Lee Po.

A few fables seem to have appeared only once as picture books. Katherine Evans retells Aesop's fable, **"The Father and His Sons,"** in *A Bundle of Sticks,* his **"The Shepherd's Boy and the Wolf"** in *The Boy Who Cried Wolf,* and the Panchatantra tale "The Mice Who Ate Iron" in her book of the same title. Marcia Brown has retold and illustrated "The Mouse and the Hermit," from the Panchatantra, in *Once a Mouse . . . ;* Barbara Cooney has illustrated Geoffrey Chaucer's retelling of Aesop's **"The Cock and the Fox"** in *Chanticleer and the Fox.*

One fable has received attention of a very different kind from creators of picture books. Aesop's **"The Grasshopper and the Ant"** is the basis of two works which celebrate the grasshopper instead of the ant. In Leo Lionni's *Frederick,* the mouse who spends his days gathering sun rays, colors, and words instead of food uses these "supplies" to counteract his companions' winter doldrums. In John Ciardi's *John J. Plenty and Fiddler Dan,* the ant becomes so fearful of wasting food that he eats little of his hoard and grows weak with hunger, while the grasshopper survives the winter to fiddle again in the spring. Creative people, it seems, take issue against the dull, smug pragmatism the ant embodies.

Otherwise, picture book versions of fables stick very close to the basic plots of their originals. When there are differences in plot, they are usually for the sake of a happy ending. Thus, Aesop's short tale of the quarrelling brothers whose father shows them how brittle sticks can be unbreakable if bound together is lengthened in Evans' *A Bundle of Sticks* to show how the brothers learn to work together and thereby succeed in their endeavor. In the original version of "The Blue Jackal," the jackal who becomes king of the jungle animals when he is accidentally dyed blue is killed when the animals realize that he is not a special creature sent by the gods; in Brown's retelling, the jackal is merely chased away, as he is in Gobhai's version, where he wanders alone, probably to rejoin his jackal pack when the dye fades. Only Showalter follows Aesop's story of **"The Miller, His Son, and Their Ass,"** in which the man and his son lose their donkey in a stream by taking the advice of everyone they meet. Wildsmith follows La Fontaine's version of the story, in which no stream appears; in the other retellings, the animal either does not get dropped into the stream or is pulled out. The disappointing ending of Aesop's **"The Milk-woman and Her Pail"** is kept intact in Evans's version, but the old woman who drops her eggs in the retelling by the d'Aulaires goes home and realizes that she already has all she needs.

As the fables are translated into picture books, many are particularized. Though some books—for example, those by Wildsmith—have indistinct settings, others have settings that range from ancient Rome (*Two Roman Mice*) to Persia (*A Bundle of Sticks*) and the Australian bush (Horder's *The Wind and the Sun*). Elizabethan England is the setting of Galdone's *The Town Mouse and the Country Mouse,* and the Appalachian mountains are the background for Calhoun's *Old Man Whickutt's Donkey.* France seems to be the setting of most of Evans' works, though her *The Mice That Ate Iron* is set in Spain. Distinct as these settings are, they do not alter the basic plots of the works themselves; they merely provide backdrops for the actions of the characters.

Instead of being anonymous actors in a tale designed to teach, many of the characters in picture book fables are distinct individuals. Sometimes these characters are given names: all of Evans' characters have names, as do almost all the people who appear in Calhoun's *Old Man Whickutt's Donkey;* Roach's Roman town mouse and country mouse are appropriately named Urbanus and Rusticus. More often, the characters in the picture books are given motivations and personality traits which they do not have in the original fables. Peter, the shepherd boy in Evans' *The Boy Who Cried Wolf,* becomes lonely as he watches the villagers in the valley below go about their work and their play. In Horder's *The Wind and the Sun,* the sun is convinced that it is the stronger not merely in general principle, but because people look up to it, while the wind is sure it is the stronger because things bend before it; the wind is a sore loser, going off "in a huff" when the contest is done. The hare in du Bois' retelling of **"The Hare and the Tortoise"** is an obnoxious "crybaby-bully" who loses the race because he takes time out to insult everyone he meets, and because he is too fastidious to splash through puddles that dot the route. Galdone's country mouse takes his time deciding to visit the city, for he is as set in his ways as any rural stereotype, while the city mouse is one who looks out for his own best interest, quietly whisking into his hole at the first sign of trouble and leaving his country friend behind. Gobhai's blue jackal is timid on his own but unafraid when he is with the rest of the pack; he is pleased at the terror his blue coat inspires in the jungle animals. In Evans' retelling of **"The Milk-woman and Her Pail,"** Anna sees other girls in the market with fine clothes and boyfriends, and she longs to have these things, too, until her plans are spoiled when she spills her pail of milk. The father in Showalter's *The Donkey Ride,* based on **"The Miller, His Son, and Their Ass,"** is a man with "a comment for every occasion," and he and his son take to heart the comments others make about them. Though the boy cleverly figures out the motives behind the advice passersby give them, he is obedient and follows his father's sometimes-outrageous wishes. Old Man Whickutt, who owns the donkey in Calhoun's version of the fable, is a good-natured, if slow-thinking countryman glad to finally please the people he meets. This emphasis on character adds to the entertaining aspects of the fables, for it gives us characters to sympathise with.

But while the abstract, anonymous characters of the original fable allow us to focus on lessons rather than character, and while these reworkings have more character development, the lessons are still clear. Often the moral is worked into the story itself, either as a piece of advice one character gives another or as part of the plot. Although Brown's version of "The Blue Jackal" ends with a traditional quatrain about one's true identity, few adapters tack the moral of the fable onto its end. In Young's *The Lion and the Mouse,* the moral, which appears on the last page, seems to be spoken by the mouse itself. Wildsmith usually works the moral into the last paragraph of text, explaining, for example, that the sun in *The North Wind and the Sun* achieves by gentleness what the wind's brutality could not, or that the patient rat in *The Lion and the Rat* accomplished what the lion's strength was incapable of. More often, however, the moral of the fable is worked into conversation. The widow in *Chanticleer and the Fox* admonishes Chanticleer to ignore flattery after he and the fox have exchanged maxims at the end of their adventure. In both Galdone's and Roach's versions of **"The Town Mouse and the Country Mouse,"** the country mouse explains what it has learned to the city mouse before returning home. In Horder's *The Wind and the Sun,* the sun cheerfully calls the moral of the fable after the wind, which is rushing off. The men in all versions of **"The Miller, His Son, and Their Ass"** tell the moral to their companions in a kind of aside.

Details of the plot are also sometimes used to point up the lesson of the story. The cobbler in Sewall's *The Cobbler's Song* becomes so anxious about the gold he has received from a rich man seeking to trouble him that his happy home is almost broken up. Both picture book versions of **"The Town Mouse and the Country Mouse"** take care to stress the contrast between the rich, luxurious city food with the plain, simple food of the country, and to emphasize the terrors of the city life. In Horder's *The Wind and the Sun,* the wind goes overboard in its attempt to tear off the traveler's coat, not only blowing but trying the effect of a rainstorm. In *The North Wind and the Sun,* Wildsmith emphasizes the wind's destructiveness by describing how it sinks ships, blows the leaves off trees, and frightens animals; and he shows the sun's gentleness through the way it causes flowers to bloom and birds to sing and makes the animals go to sleep.

Rarely, the lesson of the fable is emphasized by what can be called positive reinforcement: that is, by applying the knowledge they have gained, the characters succeed in their endeavors. In a bit of didactic overkill, the quarrelling brothers in Evans' *A Bundle of Sticks,* having learned strength through unity from their father, apply this lesson to the weaving of a carpet which wins them a prize from a prince; he tells them that they have earned it by working together, and to remind them of the lesson, the brothers hang a bundle of sticks above their shop door, eagerly telling the moral of the fable to visitors (and—again—to the reader).

Half a picture book is illustration, and in some of these works the illustrations emphasize either the moral itself or those elements which are necessary for us to see the moral. In Wildsmith's *The Rich Man and the Shoe-maker,* the contrast between the happy shoe-maker and the miserable rich man is heightened by their appearances and their pets: the shoe-maker is a kindly-looking little old man dressed in bright clothes and accompanied by cuddly kittens, while the rich man looks hunted and haunted and resembles his Great Dane, which wears a large spiked collar. When the shoemaker receives his unexpected money from the rich man, his paranoia as he tries to hide it is emphasized as all the animals that live nearby seem to be watching him. In *Don't Count Your Chicks,* the old woman's growing pride in her imaginary possessions and herself is made clear in the fences that dominate the view of her future farm and in the way that she herself overshadows her future husband, looming in front of him in the doorway of their house. The objects she plots to gain follow her as she goes to market, appearing beside the road and in the shapes of the clouds, and, finally, formed as fleeing shapes in the yolks of the eggs she has dropped. As the old woman has learned her lesson, so has her cat, which loses a small mouse in its bid for a larger one. In *The Lion and the Mouse,* Young emphasizes the moral by emphasizing the relative sizes of the powerful lion and the puny mouse. The lion is at first only a furry landscape over which the mouse runs, and we see the entire lion only when it is in trouble; mostly we see bits and pieces of the lion from a mouse-eye-view. The incongruity of their sizes and their relationship becomes clear on the back cover of the book, where the mouse sleeps on the lion's tail, wrapping its own tail around that of its friend.

Such emphasis on individual rather than anonymous characters, and the working of the moral into the text or illustration, serve to make picture books recounting fables more entertaining than didactic. In some picture books, the lesson is lost: Galdone's *The Monkey and the Crocodile* and Po's "The Tortoise and the Hare" in *The Hare and the Tortoise and the Tortoise and the Hare* are more tales of a clever underdog defeating someone more powerful than lessons about giving away what one has gained. But most of these picture books retain the lesson and, in fact, reinforce it by a combination of text and illustration. Perhaps because fables are so strong on text, few of the books go much beyond a simply retelling of the fable, with illustrations. But all emphasize entertainment, with an ancient lesson thrown in for good measure.

Mary-Agnes Taylor (essay date 1984)

SOURCE: Mary-Agnes Taylor, "The Literary Transformation of a Sluggard," in *Children's Literature*, Vol. 12, 1984, pp. 92-104.

[*In the following essay, Taylor discusses how and why various poets change the moral of the "The Grasshopper and the Ant."*]

I cannot claim that I learned to read from *Dick and Jane;* I can, however, say that I remember quite well the first time that I was able to decipher *Baby Ray.* I can also remember that our class was not allowed to linger with such innocent reading matter. Rather quickly we moved to more substantial tales such as those found in a collection of Aesop's fables. From the very beginning we were made to understand that the selections were somewhat akin to our Sunday School lessons. But in spite of such exalted status, there was one story which particularly troubled my child mind: how could those miserly ants be so unkind to the grasshopper? Traditionally, from the fifteenth century to the present, adults have supported a utilitarian version of poetic justice: the frugal ant enjoys the fruits of his labor, while the shiftless grasshopper suffers the consequences of his indolence. However, happily for me, a few wise poets in the nineteenth and twentieth centuries have transformed the much maligned singer by giving value to his calling.

The first printed offering of the tale for English-speaking children came from William Caxton in 1484. Written in late middle English, the version is not comprehensible to the modern child. There is, however, a faithful adaptation that has been written by John J. McKendry for a publication by the Metropolitan Museum of Art. It reads:

> A grasshopper in the wintertime went and demanded of the ant some of her corn for to eat. And then the ant said to the grasshopper, "What hast thou done all the summer last past?" And the grasshopper answered, "I have sung." And after said the ant to her, "Of my corn shalt thou none have, and if thou hast sung all summer, dance now in the winter."

The epilogue, printed in red ink, leaves no doubt about the moral:

> There is one time for to do some labor and work, and one time for to have rest, for he that worketh not nor does no good shall have oft at his teeth great cold, and lack at his need.[1]

The Caxton cadence clearly reflects the rhythms of fifteenth century biblical translations. The initial "And" beginning new sentences; the "hast," the "shalt," and the "thou"; and the reverse word orders all follow those patterns. Furthermore, the epilogue is an obvious paraphrase from the third chapter of Ecclesiastes. Actually, Caxton's strong deprecation of idleness was not limited to his rendition of the fables. Many of the preface sheets of his voluminous output in other translations carried warnings about the evils of sloth. And he lived by his word, accomplishing most of his work with no skilled help. By example, Caxton has a personification of the fabled ant, and he held no truck with idle singers of song.

Although Caxton, by virtue of his early translations, holds a coveted "first" in the history of Western children's literature, he cannot, in a literary context, compete in charm with that seventeenth-century gentleman commonly referred to as *Le Fablier*—Jean de La Fontaine. In a critical analysis of La Fontaine's fables, Howard Hugo suggests that association of the pieces with children's literature "is more apparent than real," having grown primarily from La Fontaine's dedication of the first several books to the six-year-old son of Louis XIV. The appeal of the fables, he reminds us, goes far beyond the nursery, "perpetuating and renewing the classical tradition" for the whole of mankind. In a manner characteristic of the period of neoclassicism, La Fontaine employs a completely impersonal voice, revealing the fundamental natures of his subjects in a public rather than a private context.[2] His jocular, but objective, spirit is preserved in Marianne Moore's translation of **"The Grass-hopper and the Ant."**

> Until fall, a grasshopper
>   Chose to chirr;
> With starvation as foe,
> When northeasters would blow,
> And not even a gnat's residue
> Or caterpillar's to chew,
> She chirred recurrent chant
> Of want beside an ant,
> Begging it to rescue her
> With some seeds it could spare
> Till the following year's fall.
> "By August you shall have them all,
> Interest and principal."
> Share one's seeds? Now what is worse
> For any ant to do?
> Ours asked, "When fair, what brought you
>   through?"
> —"I sang for those who might pass by
>   chance,—
> Night and day, an't you please."
> —"Sang, you say? You have put me at ease.
> A singer! Excellent. Now dance."[3]

Here the fable ends without benefit of epilogue. La Fontaine's fable needs none. His mid-poem voice as third-party commentator has already performed the function of that traditional postscript. Initially, the grasshopper offers the ant a business proposition: she seeks a loan, not charity. But the third-party voice intrudes. "Share one's seeds? Now what is worse / For any ant to do?" La Fontaine's ant—whom he intimately calls "ours"—confirms the attitude behind the word "worse" by maintaining the established role of the self-righteous judge who chastises the singer. The refusal is managed with a chilling clarity of conscience. "Sang, you say? You have put me at ease. / A singer! Excellent. Now dance." The singer of songs remains a minstrel without champion.

Except for the third-party rhetorical question, it is difficult to find evidence that would classify La Fontaine as either ant or grasshopper in his sympathies. He leaves no clues such as those planted by Caxton. Nor is he the naturally clear-cut case of the Oliver Goldsmith and Thomas Bewick team.

Bewick, from the time of his impoverished childhood to the time of a solvent old age, exhibited antlike qualities. On the other hand, Goldsmith lived his entire life as an improvident grasshopper. Some brief biographical glimpses of the two lead to interesting speculation.

During a childhood spent on his father's modest Northumberland farm, Thomas Bewick developed two characteristics that were to shape his future: a love of drawing and a love of nature. His earliest works—mainly portraits of hunters, horses and hounds—adorned the walls of the homes of his rustic neighbors. Later, during an apprenticeship served from 1767 to 1774 at Newcastle, he received a number of commissions for woodcuts for children's books. Two of these—*New Lottery-Book of Birds and Beasts* and *Moral Instructions of a Father to His Son*—were tentative efforts that would become more sophisticated editions variously associated with Goldsmith.

As a young man, Oliver Goldsmith traveled over Europe on foot. In Flanders, Switzerland, and France he often played his flute for bed and board. Early exposure to an Irish schoolmaster, who preferred to teach tales and song rather then mathematics and letters, gave Goldsmith an inexhaustible supply of folklore. But the Italians did not care for Irish mirth, so Goldsmith there found himself at the gates of convents begging alms for food. Later, back in London, he turned to writing as a last resort. After publishing the epic *Traveller* in 1776, his fortunes, but not his wasteful ways, changed. Bewick became his illustrator for *Traveller,* and thus the two were brought together for other publications, among which was Bewick's *Aesopus, Select Fables of Aesop and Others,* for which Goldsmith wrote an introduction that included a biography of Aesop and an essay on the moral and aesthetic values of fable. Although some scholars had already begun to question the actual existence of Aesop, that possibility did not bother Goldsmith. His biography is filled with apocryphal details about Aesop's life and death.

How much of the rest of the text in *Select Fables* was actually composed by Goldsmith and how much by Bewick is a matter of question. According to the *Dictionary of National Biography,* both *Select Fables* and *Tommy Trip's History of Beasts and Birds* were "traditionally supposed to have been by Goldsmith, but the tradition is incapable of proof."[4] The *DNB* does state, however, that *Select Fables* grew from the earlier *Moral Instructions of a Father to His Son,* and

likewise that *Tommy Trip's History* was a reworking of *New-Lottery Birds and Beasts.* Some thirty years later, Bewick would again attempt yet another set of fables. If one compares the text of Bewick's third attempt—*Fables of Aesop* (1818)—with *Select Fables* (1784), enough differences emerge to lend credence to the belief that Goldsmith did indeed compose the melodramatic rhymes in *Select Fables.*

Modern editors have eschewed the Bewick fables and denounced them as some of the worst that ever were written for children. Not satisfied with the traditional epilogue to the fable of the grasshopper and the ant, Bewick, in his *Select Fables,* added a prologue that creates a ponderous overkill:

> O now, while health and vigour still remain.
> Toil, toil, my lads, to purchase honest gain!
> Shun idleness! shun pleasure's tempting snare!
> A youth of revels breeds an age of care.

The fable itself is handled in a traditional way, in neoclassical verse balancing terms and values. Like Caxton, in the epilogue the author borrows from the Bible; but instead of choosing from Ecclesiastes, he chooses from Proverbs (6:6) to support his advice that

> *Action and industry is the business of a wise and a good man, and nothing is so much to be despised as slothfulness.* Go to the Ant, thou sluggard, *says the Royal Preacher,* consider her ways and be wise; *which in a few words sums up the moral of this fable.*[5]

Although the moral in *Fables of Aesop* (1818) remains the same as that in *Select Fables* (1784), both the format and the style of writing are changed radically. The prologue is omitted, and the fable is recorded in a cumbersome single paragraph of only four sentences, which wind ponderously through a verbal maze. The opening scene depicts a "commonwealth of Ants" gathered in their "comfortable mansion" as they are approached by a lone grasshopper. One ant becomes spokesman for the group. Thus, in this particular version, the grasshopper suffers censure not only from an individual ant, but from a whole community of ants to expand the disapproval of the manner in which he has spent the summer.

Instead of an epilogue, Bewick attached an "Application" in this later edition, in which the prose remains as stilted as that in the fable. The appendage is fully as long as the primary text. In an extended metaphor, Bewick equates summer with youth and winter with old age. He began *Fables* after a long illness during his mid-sixties, a circumstance that no doubt contributed to the heavy tone. He preaches that youth and manhood are the times when one must lay "in such a stock as may suffice for helpless old age," but, he warns, there are many rational creatures, who squander away in a profuse prodigality, whatever they get in their younger days, as if the infirmity of age would require no supplies to support it, or at least would find themselves administered to in some miraculous way.

The second sentence—there are only two—restates the "admirable lesson" learned from the fable. The last part of this sentence I find of particular interest:

> for it should always be remembered, that "a youth of revels breeds an age of care," and that temperence in youth lays the foundation of health and comfort for old age.[6]

A question comes to mind. Why has "a youth of revels breeds an age of care" been placed in quotation marks? Certainly it is true that Bewick constantly borrowed from his own earlier works, and that many of his books for children represent a sequence of reworked materials. In light of this practice, it seems unlikely that he would, in an isolated case, put quotes around a phrase taken from an earlier work if that work had been his. The evidence is faint, but it does lend support to the belief that the rhymed verses in *Select Fables* are indeed the work of Goldsmith, and that Bewick, being the thoroughly honest man that he was, acknowledges it as such.

Caxton, La Fontaine, Bewick and Goldsmith are but a few of the many writers who have presented the grasshopper as a worthless character, but there have been some others who were not willing to vilify the long-legged singer. Somewhat parallel scenarios have been created by John Keats and John Ciardi. James Joyce has written an ironic adult parable that condemns the ant, while Leo Lionni, without chastising ants, has recast the grasshopper as a child reader's hero.

Keats's sonnet, titled "On the Grasshopper and Cricket," does not actually mention the ant, but habitual pairing admits allusion to the ant as a foil. Keats opens with the pronouncement that "The poetry of earth is never dead." This generalization is particularized in the octave through the observation that even when "all the birds are faint with the hot sun," a voice will be heard: it is the voice of the grasshopper. The sestet restates the opening line of the octave and then explains how the song is perpetuated:

> The poetry of earth is ceasing never:
>   On a lone winter evening, when the frost
>   Has wrought a silence, from the stove there shrills
> The Cricket's song, in warmth increasing ever,
>   And seems to one in drowsiness half lost,
>   The Grasshopper's among some grassy hills.[7]

The grasshopper's voice may be silenced by winter, but not song itself, for "from the stove there shrills / The Cricket's song" to effect a continuity, which is emphasized by the use of present tense and absolutes in the lines "The poetry of earth is never dead" and "The poetry of earth is ceasing never." Keats's respect for the singer contrasts sharply with that of Bewick's; and, in keeping with romantic sensibilities, it is his grasshopper-poet, not a pragmatist-ant, who reigns supreme regardless of season.

Ciardi, in a much longer verse, takes us full round literally to meet the grasshopper again next spring. He titles his rhymed melodrama *John J. Plenty and Fiddler Dan*. John J. was an ant workaholic. The summer birds sang as he packed his larder tighter and tighter. But a great sadness befell him—his beloved sister eloped with a grasshopper named Fiddler Dan. So magnetic were the fiddler's tunes that

> . . . all summer stirred to hear
> The voice of the music. Far and near
> The grasses swayed, and the sun and shade
> Danced to the love and music played.
>
> Dan played on for the world to turn,
> While his little wife lay on a fringe of fern.

John J. missed none of this. But he did pause long enough to warn that when winter came, the lovers could expect no help from him. Ciardi's winter, like that described by Keats, "wrought a silence" which assured John J. that the lovers were dead. He became so paranoid about the sufficiency of his larder that he ate only sparingly. Weakened by the self-imposed fast, he emerged in the spring. So surprised was he to hear the familiar sounds of Dan's fiddle that he fell on his face in the mud. Ciardi says he does not know where the fiddler and his wife hid during the winter. But he does "really know," just as Keats did, that you can

> . . . *Say what you like as you trudge along,*
> *The world won't turn without a song.*
> *And—Fiddlers grow thin and their hands turn*
>   *blue*
> *When winter comes, but they pull through.*
> *There's this about music—and, oh, it's true!—*
> *It never stays stopped.*[8]

Both Ciardi and Keats write in relatively simple, positive vein to affirm the eternal worth of the grasshopper, but James Joyce attacks the entire theme of the fable itself through a highly complex and satirical parable. His ploy is imbedded in *Finnegans Wake* as Shaun tells his brother Shem the "feeble" of the "Ondt" and the "Gracehoper." Whereas these three puns reveal the gist of the parable, they can in no way do justice to the depth and the sweep of the multiple puns and foreign-language references which are detailed in William Tindall's *A Reader's Guide to Finnegans Wake.* Tindall quotes his own earlier work on Joyce, noting that "the pun is mightier than the word."[9]

Feeble, we can see at once, attacks the total weakness of the parent fable's argument. *Ondt* is a Danish word meaning evil and thus doubly casts the original character. *Gracehoper* is likewise cast, being simultaneously the original sluggard and the poet in whom we observe grace and take hope. Shaun is the Ondt—the economically—and sexually powerful man of the world. Shem is the Gracehoper——the poet who, according to Shaun, is the offensive and ineffectual one. As Shaun relates the fable to his brother, instructing him in the worldly successes of the Ondt, it appears on the literal level that Joyce is praising the Ondt. But the whole tale is an extended example of the Irishman's superb verbal irony, for Joyce is unmistakably a grasshopper. He has the Gracehoper sing a mock apology to the Ondt for having offended him:

> I pick up your reproof, the horsegift of a
>   friend,
> For the prize of your save is the price of my
>   spend.
>
>   . . . . .
>
> Your feats end enormous, your volumes
>   immense,
> (May the Graces I hoped for sing your
>   Ondship sense!)
> Your genus its worldwide, your spacest
>   sublime!
> But Holy Salmartin, why can't you beat
>   time![10]

The Ondt responds in an epilogue which follows the apology. To pious folks his commentary may seem sacrilegeous because their eyes read, "In the name of the former and of the latter and of their holocaust. Allmen," while their ears hear, "In the name of the Father and of the Son and of the Holy Ghost. Amen."[11]

A possible objection in all of the fables discussed so far is that either the ant or the grasshopper is drawn as totally anti-heroic. One is rejected at the expense of the other. Their fixed incompatibility is synthesized by Joyce's Gracehoper: "The prize of your save is the price of my spend." Leo Lionni, however, in *Frederick* manages to present the two types in a harmonious way without belittling either. To do so, he resorts to a fundamental technique used by fablers of old. Just as they presented their humans in a disguised form—usually in feathers or fur—he takes Aesop's traditionally paired insects and recasts them as a family of mice.

From the beginning a warm tone is set: "Not far from the barn and in the granary, a chatty family of field mice had their home." "Chatty," "family," and "home" suggest compatibility—a pleasant bond. But the situation is not without conflict. The farmer had moved away, the granary was empty, and winter was approaching. The wise mice began to gather supplies. "They all worked day and night. All except Frederick." The story has scarcely begun, but the grasshopper syndrome is already apparent. The four working siblings asked Frederick why he did not work. Frederick replied, "I do work. . . . I gather sun rays for the cold winter days." Again they questioned his inactivity. He responded that he was gathering colors because winter was gray. A third time they reproached him more sternly. "Are you dreaming, Frederick?" His denial came quickly. "Oh no, I am gathering words." Lionni has set us up for the compleat artist, one who later starts his magic through the recall of sunlight and painted flowers. However, the other mice clamored for more than pictures; they wanted words. To accommodate them Frederick climbed up on a huge stone, a stage high above the others, and affecting a timid voice from the mount he asked,

> Who scatters snowflakes: Who melts the ice?
> Who spoils the weather? Who makes it nice?
> Who grows the four-leaf clovers in June?
> Who dims the daylight? Who lights the moon?
>
> Four little field mice who live in the sky.
> Four little field mice . . . like you and I.
>
> One is the Springmouse who turns on the
>   showers.
> Then comes the Summer who paints the
>   flowers.
> The Fallmouse is next with walnuts and
>   wheat.
> And Winter is last with little cold feet.
>
> Aren't we lucky the seasons are four?
> Think of a year with one less . . . or one
>   more!

When he finished, the others responded in gleeful surprise, "But Frederick, . . . you are a poet!" The vindicated bard "blushed, took a bow, and said shyly, 'I know it."[12]

In closing, one more epilogue is offered to make two points—one in the context of metaphor, and the other in a context of morality. Through early exposure to the Aesop collection, all of us have come to know some dog in the manger, some wolf in sheep's clothing, some joker who cries wolf. We know the loser who pleads sour grapes, and we know that it is almost impossible to find a brave soul to bell the cat. But we do not label anyone as lazy as a grasshopper, as worthless as a singer of songs. Admittedly, our society has never given poets unanimous support, but a few philosophers have always hailed them as the real seers of truth. To continue to cast the poets as worthless grasshoppers is to give credence to a misconception. Even though Keats, Ciardi, Joyce, and Lionni may all have been indulging in self-defense, they have at the same time defended the grasshopper, changing him from sluggard to bard. And in this time of poetry revival for children, I say unto you, "Go thou and do likewise."

Notes

1 *Aesop, Five Centuries of Illustrated Fables,* selected by John J. McKendry (New York: Metropolitan Museum of Art, 1964), p. 14.

2 Howard E. Hugo, introduction to "Masterpieces of Neoclassicism," *World Masterpieces,* 3rd ed. (New York: Norton, 1973), 2, 9.

3 From *The Fables of La Fontaine,* trans. Marianne Moore, copyright 1954 by Marianne Moore, copyright renewed 1982 by Lawrence E. Brinn and Louise Crane; reprinted by permission of Viking Penguin Inc.

4 *Dictionary of National Biography,* s.v. "Goldsmith, Oliver."

5 Thomas Bewick, *Treasury of Aesop's Fables illustrated by Thomas Bewick Together with the Life of Aesop, by Oliver Goldsmith* (New York: Avenel Books, Crown, 1973), pp. 56-57; rpt. from part 3 of *Aesopus, Select Fables of Aesop and Others* (Newcastle: J. Saint, 1784), commonly referred to as *Select Fables.*

6 Thomas Bewick, *Fables of Aesop,* ed. Michael Marqusee (New York: Paddington Press, 1975), pp. 307-08.

7 John Keats, *Selected Poems and Letters,* ed. Douglas Bush (New York: Houghton Mifflin, Riverside Edition, 1959), p. 19.

8 John Ciardi, *John J. Plenty and Fiddler Dan* (New York: Lippincott, 1963), unpaged.

9 William York Tindall, *A Reader's Guide to Finnegans Wake* (New York: Farrar, Straus, and Giroux, 1969), p. 7.

10 James Joyce, *Finnegans Wake* (1939; rpt. New York: Viking Compass, 1959), pp. 418-19.

11 Ibid., p. 419.

12 Leo Lionni, *Frederick* (New York: Pantheon, 1967), unpaged.

John F. Priest (essay date 1985)

SOURCE: John F. Priest, "The Dog in the Manger: In Quest of a Fable," in *The Classical Journal*, Vol. 81, No. 1, October-November, 1985, pp. 49-58.

[*In the following essay, Priest discovers the first appearance of "The Dog in the Manger" fable in the 1476/7 collection of Steinhöwel, traces the authority for its inclusion in this edition to the classical writers Lucian and Strato, and rules out known Near Eastern fables and proverbs as possible sources for the fable.*]

Locating the historical, cultural and geographical origins of gnomic sayings, is, at best, a precarious enterprise. Emerging as they do from the universals of human experience, proverb, maxim, and fable tend to be both cross cultural and trans-cultural. That "the burnt baby avoids the fire" was as true when fire was discovered or invented as it is today. Detailed folkloristic studies confirm the preceding generality.[1] Nevertheless, when a well-known saying is found in a most unexpected quarter, the curiosity cannot but be piqued and investigation pursued. The following note is the consequence of such a discovery.

The proverb, or fable,[2] of the dog in the manger is one of the best known in the Aesopic corpus.[3] Even those who are only vaguely aware of its connection with Aesop have no hesitance in describing some actions as being like those of the dog in the manger. "He can't or won't use something, but he sure won't let anyone else do so." The very pervasiveness of this story tends to divert the hearer or reader from critical inquiry. For if familiarity breeds contempt, it may also foster facile acceptance. Finding the saying in the Nag Hammadi Gospel of Thomas provoked me to turn to a detailed examination of the currency of the proverb in antiquity. Near the end of Thomas is the following logion:

> Jesus said, "Woe to the Pharisees, for they are like a dog sleeping in the manger of oxen, for neither does he eat nor does he let the oxen eat."[4]

This logion is clearly related to words ascribed to Jesus in Matt. 23:13, "But woe to you, scribes and Pharisees, hypocrites! because you shut the kingdom of heaven against men; for you neither enter yourselves nor allow those who would enter to go in." (The parallel passage in Luke 11:52 reads, "Woe to you lawyers! For you have taken away the key of knowledge; you did not enter yourselves, and you hindered those who were entering." It may be noted that another logion in Thomas, 39, follows the Lukan version even more closely: "Jesus said, 'The Pharisees and the scribes have taken the keys of Knowledge and hidden them. They themselves have not entered, nor have they allowed to enter those who wish to.'") The nature of the relationship between Thomas and the canonical gospels—i.e., is the former entirely dependent on the latter, or does it, in some instances at least, contain independent traditions which are as old as the sources behind the canonical texts?—remains a matter of dispute among specialists in the field. It would be presumptuous to enter that debate, nor is it necessary. It is the presence of the "Aesopic" saying which is our concern.

The dog in the manger, it turns out, has a somewhat mixed pedigree. The history of the development of the Aesopic collections and the text traditions of those collections is a fascinating chapter in critical scholarship, and a very brief summary of some of the pertinent details is in order. While fables are found in Greek literature before the time of Aesop (late seventh/early sixth century B.C.?)[5] it is with his name that the fable quickly became associated. Fables attributed to Aesop are cited in Greek authors from the fifth century B.C. onward,[6] but the first collection of Aesopic fables seems to have been compiled by Demetrius of Phalerum near the end of fourth or the beginning of the third century B.C.[7] His work is no longer extant but appears to have been known by the earliest collectors now available to us, Phaedrus (in Latin) in the middle of the first century after Christ and Babrius (in Greek) at the end of that century or early in the next.

Although Phaedrus relates twelve fables mentioning the dog (I. 4, 17, 18, 19, 20, 23, 25, 27; II. 3; III. 7, 15; IV. 19; V. 10 in the Loeb edition[8]), the dog in the manger is not included. Babrius utilizes the dog in fourteen fables (42, 69, 74, 79, 85, 87, 93, 95, 100, 104, 110, 113, 128, 129), but the dog in the manger is absent. What of other known Greek collections? European and American scholarship of the twentieth century has produced detailed critical analyses of the Aesopic manuscript tradition.[9] While there are considerable differences at some points, Perry's statement may be taken as a fair representation of their conclusions: "But in spite of the varying contents of the manuscripts, and of the mixing of sources, it is nevertheless easy to distinguish, among the fables themselves, at least four different recensions, upon one or more of which every known manuscript of any consequence either entire or in large part depends."[10] Since the fable of the dog in the manger is firmly a part of the Aesopic tradition as known in printed editions since the fifteenth century, it is an occasion of surprise that it does not seem to appear in any of the ancient collections and is consequently omitted in contemporary critical editions. It is included, however, in Halm's nineteenth-century collection, which was somewhat eclectic and non-critical in nature.[11] Whence its origin?

The Aesopic tradition in the Middle Ages depended primarily on Latin and not Greek sources. Indeed, it has been said that "Our *Aesop* is Phaedrus with trimmings."[12] The most extensive collection was the so-

called Romulus,[13] although collections attributed to Avianus and others supplemented the stock of fables in circulation. Though this note does not purport to set forth a summary of the history of fable collections, it is not inappropriate to mention briefly two additional ones which are of considerable interest to those of us in the English tradition and which bear, albeit indirectly, on the checkered history of the dog in the manger.

In the late twelfth century an Anglo-Norman writer, Marie de France, issued a collection of Aesopian fables. Though less well known than her Lais, the collection is a valuable witness to the spread of the Aesopic tradition in Western Europe. She included 102 fables,[14] most of which are drawn from the Romulus collections. She used other sources in addition, however, and a number of her fables are nowhere else attested. Her work is in Norman French, but she claimed that she was making a translation of an English collection which she attributed to Alfred the Great. She did not, among her independent fables, include the dog in the manger. Connected, directly or indirectly, with Marie de France was the Jewish fabulist Berechiah ha-Nakdam. Though a native of France, Berechiah apparently spent considerable time in England and his "Fox Fables," numbering 119 in the most recent critical edition,[15] show considerable dependence on Marie. Like her, he includes a considerable number of independent fables. Once again the dog in the manger is missing.

A brief summary is in order. The story of the dog in the manger is surprisingly missing from the major Greek manuscript traditions, from the standard Latin "Vulgate" (Romulus, Avianus and other miscellaneous Latin collections), and from the independent traditions upon which Marie de France and Berechiah ha-Nakdam drew. We may now turn to what is apparently its first appearance in an Aesopic *collection* of fables. Heinrich Steinhöwel, in 1476/7, published a comprehensive collection of Aesopic fables in Latin with a German translation. He utilized as his base the four books of the Romulus, which as we have seen do not include the dog in the manger, but he also included fables from a wide variety of other Latin sources.[16] One of those sources, consisting of seventeen fables, he entitled "Fabulae Extravagantes" since they were not found in any of the standard collections known to him.[17] The eleventh of the Extravagantes is the fable in question.[18] Steinhöwel's collection was an immediate success and became the basis of a French translation by Julien Mach in 1480 which, in turn, provided the material for Caxton's English translation in 1483/4. Caxton did not follow the scholarly caution of Steinhöwel, who had noted the extraneous nature of the Extravagantes, but simply included them as Book Five of *Aesop*. Thus, with Caxton, the dog in the manger became enshrined in the English Aesopic tradition.

One is led to ask whether we can account for the basis upon which this fable entered the tradition (even if it was seemingly by the back door). The answer is not difficult to find. Though they do not mention Aesop, at least two second-century authors, Lucian (*Adv. Indoctum* 30 and *Timon* 14) and Strato of Sardis (*Gk. Anth.* xii, 236), allude to the fable. Further, a four-teenth-century manuscript, Mosquensis 239, contains some so-called proverbs of Aesop, and in Krumbacher's edition of that manuscript the dog in the manger appears.[19] It seems appropriate to examine the forms in which the fable occurs in Lucian, Strato, and the Mosquensis.

Lucian: *Adv. Indoctum* 30 (Loeb translation)

But you never lent a book to anyone; you act like the dog in the manger, who neither eats the grain [barley] herself nor lets the horse eat it who can.

Timon 14 (Loeb translation)

. . . they were shutting out everyone else from a share in the enjoyment, like the dog in the manger that neither ate the barley herself nor permitted the hungry horse to eat it.

Strato: *Gk. Anth.* xii, 236 (Loeb translation)

A certain eunuch has good looking servant boys— for what use?—and he does them abominable injury. Truly, like the dog in the manger with the roses, and stupidly barking, he neither gives the good thing to himself nor to anyone else.

Mosquensis: 239 (My translation)

A dog lying in the manger does not eat nor does he permit the ass (to eat).

We may add the version found in Halm's edition, which cites Lucian, *Adv. Indoctum* 30, as the source. "A dog lying in the manger would neither eat of the barley herself nor permit the horse, who was able to eat, to do so" (my translation).

The essentials are constant in each version. The vari-ants, the shift of tenses . . . , and the substitution of ass for horse in Mosquensis, are inconsequential.[20] The Latin version, from the Extravagantes, is, as might be expected, expanded considerably. Two minor differ-ences may be noted, as one of them has some bearing on the form of the saying in Thomas. "A dog without conscience lay in a manger full of hay *(feno)*. When the cattle *(boves)* came to eat of the hay he would not let them, but showed his teeth in ugly mood. The oxen *(boves)* protested. . . ."[21] The change of food from barley to hay may be passed over, as no mention is made of grain in Thomas, but the presence of the cattle

(oxen) rather than the horse/ass in the Greek texts will require some discussion later in this note, since the specified animals in Thomas are also oxen.

We have thus far examined the fable tradition in its Greek and Latin forms, but even in antiquity there were divergent opinions concerning the culture which first produced fables. Libya, Egypt, Lydia, and Sybaris are mentioned.[22] Further, Babrius clearly states that "Fable, son of King Alexander, is the invention of the Syrians of old, who lived in the days of Ninus and Belus. The first to tell fables to the Hellenes, they say, was Aesop the wise; and to the Lybians Cybisses also told fables."[23] Although folklorists of the nineteenth century suggested a wide variety of cultures as the fountainhead of the fable, e.g. India, Arabia, North Africa, and Israel,[24] more recent archaeological dis-coveries have tended to support Babrius' comment. Fables and proverbs in the "Aesopic" form are found in Sumerian, Akkadian and Aramaic texts from the third millenium onward. While direct parallels in con-tent are rare, it seems established that the fable tradi-tion in Greece was derived from Mesopotamia, prob-ably through contacts in Asia Minor. Perry states the case succinctly:

In the Sumerian proverbs from Nippur, viewed in the light of their later tradition in the Semitic Orient, we have the final answer to the question that was often asked and variously resolved by philogogists and folklorists in the last century, namely, when and where did the Aesopic fable, as known to the Greeks, originate? As a form it did not originate with the Greeks themselves, and it did not come to them from the Hindus or the Hebrews or the Egyptians; it came to them by way of the neo-Babylonian and Assyrian wisdom literature.[25]

Although some scholars still minimize the "Assyrian" influence,[26] the weight of opinion supporting the view requires an examination of some of the evidence, par-ticularly as it may relate to the fable considered in this note.

The fable form was popular and pervasive throughout the ancient Near East. The collections alluded to by Perry in the quotation above provide striking confirmation of that observation, though the evidence is by no means limited to the material he was discussing. Kramer summarized the Sumerian material (as of 1959) in this way: "In the past several years Gordon has pieced together and trans-lated a total of 295 proverbs and fables relating to some 64 species of animal life: mammals, birds and mem-bers of the so-called lower species of animal life down to the insects."[27] There are approximately seventy ref-erences to the dog in the material published by Gor-don, but nothing resembling the dog in the manger has yet appeared. Thus, although the Sumerian material is of invaluable importance for tracing the history of the fable genre, it sheds no light on the saying in question.

Much closer to the time of Aesop is the well-known Aramaic tale of Ahikar. Embedded in the story are collections of proverbs clearly in the "Aesopic" tradition. According to Clement of Alexandria, there was a Greek translation which was known to the philosopher Democritus. According to Diogenes Laertius (V, 49-50), Theophrastus wrote one book on Democritus and another entitled "Achicar." Since Theophrastus was the teacher of Demetrius, who as we have seen is reputed to have been the first collector of Aesop, it is highly probable that the shape of the fable tradition in Greece was influenced by Ahikar and other similar Semitic collections.[28] The influence, as noted earlier, seems to have been more in form than content, although Perry called attention to some nine or ten fables in Babrius which he felt were derived from Ahikar.[29]

The dog is mentioned twelve times in the translations of the Syriac, Arabic and Armenian versions of Ahikar with an additional reference in an Ethiopic fragment.[30] One saying warrants special attention, as it has sometimes been stated that it constitutes at least a vague parallel to the dog in the manger.

> Syriac: My son, thou hast been to me like the dog that came to the potter's oven to warm himself, and after he was warm rose up to bark at them. (8:17)

> Arabic: O my son, thou hast been to me like the dog that was cold and it went into the potter's house to get warm. And when it had got warm, it began to bark at them, and they chased it out and beat it, that it might not bite them. (8:19)

> Armenian: Son, thou hast been to me like the dog which went into the oven of the potter. When he was warm, he began to bark at them. (8:19)

With these may be compared a Babylonian proverb which appears in a seventh-century-B.C. letter but which probably is older: "When the potter's dog enters the kiln it will bark at the potter."[31]

The exact point of the Babylonian proverb is not clear. It may indicate that "the dog inside the kiln is really in a very vulnerable position to bark at its master."[32] This interpretation is congruent with the additions in the Arabic version, but a general reference to ingratitude seems more likely. In any case, neither the saying in the versions of Ahikar nor the Babylonian proverb has a real link with the point of the dog in the manger.

Hebrew and Jewish literature in the Bible and in later rabbinic writings is a part of the cultural milieu being examined. The fable genre is not widespread in the Hebrew Bible, there being but two full-fledged examples.[33] Judg. 9:8-15 contains a somewhat lengthy fable about trees seeking a king to reign over them. The olive, pleading its fatness, the fig pleading its sweetness, and the vine calling attention to its role in making the wine which cheers gods and men, all declined. Then, the bramble accepted, with the warning that fire might ensue. The lesson was a warning to the inhabitants of Shechem who were choosing a potential firebrand to reign.[34] A much briefer fable is found in II Kings 14:9 = II Chronicles 25:18. "A thistle on Lebanon sent to a cedar on Lebanon, saying, 'Give your daughter to my son for a wife'; and a wild beast of Lebanon passed by and trampled down the thistle." Here the point is a warning against the inordinate pride of a Judean king, Amaziah, in comparison with his stronger counterpart, Jehoash of Israel. Solomon, the patron saint of Israelite wisdom, is reputed to "have uttered three thousand proverbs; and his songs were a thousand and five. He spoke of trees, from the cedar that is in Lebanon to the hyssop which grows out of the wall; he spoke also of beasts, and of birds, and of reptiles, and of fish." (I Kings 4:32 f. = Hebrews 5:12 f.) Some have inferred from this passage that there was an extensive fable tradition in Israel, but if such be the case it has left little mark in the extant biblical materials.

The collections of proverbial material attributed by tradition to Solomon mention animals in a number of sayings (6:6-11; 7:22 f.; 11:22; 14:4; 15:17; 17:12; 19:12; 20:2; 21:31; 22:13; 26:2 f.; 26:11, 13, 17; 27:8, 23, 26; 28:15; 30:15, 17-19, 24-31). Only three approximate the fable tradition. 6:6-11 is the famous "Go to the ant, thou sluggard . . . ," which is paralleled in the Aesopic traditions (fables 112 and 372 in Perry's edition).[35] 30:19 alludes to "the way of the eagle in the sky, the way of a serpent on a rock," suggesting an analogy from the animal world; and 30:24-31 may be cited in full to illustrate the difference between Israelite proverbs and "Aesopic" fables:

> Four things on earth are small,
>   but they are exceedingly wise;
> the ants are a people not strong,
>   yet they provide their food in the summer;
> the badgers are a people not mighty,
>   yet they make their homes in the rocks;
> the locusts have no king,
>   yet all of them march in rank;
> the lizard you can take in your hands,
>   yet it is in kings' palaces.
> Three things are stately in their tread;
>   four are stately in their stride:
> the lion, which is mightiest among beasts
>   and does not turn back before any;
> the strutting cock, the he-goat,
>   and a king striding before his people.

What is significantly lacking is the story form which is an essential ingredient of the fable. While timeless truths may be inferred from fables, they must be told as having occurred once at a specific time.[36]

Fables do appear in later Jewish materials, the Talmud and the Midrash, but even there they are comparatively rare.[37] There is a tradition that there was an extensive collection of Fox Fables, some three hundred in number, known to the late-second-century Rabbi Meir, but only two or three of them have survived. There is a note in the Mishnah, Sotah 9:15, that the making of fables ceased with Meir. None of the surviving fables sheds any light on the dog in the manger. Again a potential clue to the fable proves to be inutile, and our earlier summary of the omission of it in the Greek and Latin collections may be extended to the witnesses of Sumerian, Akkadian, Aramaic and Hebrew.

We have noted that the first appearance of the dog in the manger in a *collection* seems to be Steinhöwel's inclusion of the Extravagantes of unknown origin, but we have also noted that allusion to the fable is made by at least two authors in the second century, Lucian and Strato. To them we must return. Halm's edition, as noted above, cited Lucian as the source of the fable, and Chambry noted that the fable probably occurs for the first time in Lucian.[38] Strato should also be considered as a possibility. Our question is, do we know anything about either Lucian or Strato which might bear on the presence of the dog in the manger in Thomas?

The majority of Nag Hammadi specialists agree that the Gospel was written near the middle of the second century after Christ. There is less agreement to its geographical provenance, the most popular choices being between Greater Syria, which could include Palestine and western Mesopotamia, and Egypt.[39] The traditional dates for Lucian are c. 120-190 and for Strato in the reign of Hadrian (A.D. 117-135).[40] Lucian was born in Samosata, located on the upper Euphrates, occasionally refers to himself as a Syrian and implies that Greek was not his mother tongue. Further, contrary to advice he had given earlier, Lucian accepted a "bread and butter"[42] administrative post with the Roman government in Egypt. Biographical information about Strato is sparse indeed, but he was born at Sardis in Asia Minor, and all of his geographical allusions are to Asia Minor—with one exception. His epigram in *Gk. Anth.,* xi, 117 (Loeb edition) almost certainly refers to his presence in Alexandria.[43]

The similarities in date and place (broadly speaking) between the two classical authors from whom there is evidence for the saying and the Gospel of Thomas may be pure coincidence. Grant may be correct in saying that "The dog in the manger is, of course, proverbial, and it was proverbial in the second century, as we know from the Greek satirist Lucian (*Timon* 14; *Adv. Indoctum* 30). The story is told as a fable of Aesop (*Fab. Aesop.,* 228, page 111, Halm). Its presence in these literary or semi-literary sources does not

Modern scholars tend to discuss Aesop primarily with regard to the genre of fable.

mean that it was unknown outside them. Thomas could have picked it up anywhere."[44] It is true that one can hardly claim literary dependence on either side, and the use of "horse" in Lucian and "oxen" in Thomas almost certainly indicates that each drew upon a divergent form of the fable.[45] On the other hand, the similarities can be more than pure coincidence and provide us with some closing suggestions.

First, although argument from silence is dangerous, the earliest attested appearance of the proverb/fable in three second-century-authors supports the generally proposed date for Thomas. This is not new, but it is corroborative. Second, the reverse side of the coin is that additional support is given to the opinion that the first use of the proverb/fable by a classical author was by either Lucian or Strato. Again we have not new information but independent corroboration. Third, the presence of the saying in contemporary pagan and Jewish/Christian sources reminds us of the cultural interpenetrations of the late Hellenistic world. Religio-cultural isolationism is an impossibility.

There is a fable in Phaedrus which may seem applicable to this note. "A mountain, being in the pangs of labour, was emitting tremendous groans, and the lands about were filled with the greatest expectations. Then, behold that mountain gave birth to a mouse. This was written for you who threaten to do great things but fail to get anything done." (IV, 24 in the Loeb edition).[46] Obviously I would not agree, for though no "breakthrough" in scholarship has emerged from the study, careful re-evaluation of regnant theses in terms of new evidence can make a contribution to our understanding.

Notes

[1] The Stith Thompson *Motif Index of Folk Literature* (Bloomington 1932-36) is the classic example in English.

[2] Beginning with the formulation of Theon in his *Progymnasmata* (ch. 3) that a fable is . . . a ficticious story picturing a truth, I follow Perry's extended definition. "A fable must contain three features . . . it must be obviously and deliberately ficticious, whether possible or not . . . it must purport to be a particular action, series of actions, or an utterance that took place *once* in past time through the agency of particular characters . . . it must be told, at least ostensibly, not for its own sake as a story . . . but for the sake of a point that is moral, paranetic or personal." *Aesopica I* (Urbana 1952) p. ix. See also his extended discussion in *Studium Generale* 12 (1959) pp. 17-37 and his briefer summary in the Loeb edition of *Babrius and Phaedrus* (Cambridge 1965) pp. xix-xxxiv. This definition is, of course, not the only one in use. In this note the terms fable, proverb, saying and story are used interchangeably.

[3] Included in the corpus are both material collected under Aesop's name and material attributed to others but in the "Aesopic" style.

[4] Translation by Thomas Lambdin in *The Nag Hammadi Library,* ed. James M. Robinson (San Francisco 1981) p. 129. Other English translations include *The Gospel According to Thomas,* ed. Guillaumont, Puech, Quispel and al Masih (New York 1959), which includes the Coptic text, and *The Secret Sayings of Jesus,* ed. Robert M. Grant and David N. Freedman (Garden City 1960). The translation is by William R. Schoedel.

[5] For a discussion of Greek fables before Aesop, see Perry, *Babrius and Phaedrus,* p. xii, and Emile Chambry, *Esope* (Paris 1960) pp. xxii-xxiii.

[6] See the references in *Babrius and Phaedrus,* pp. xiii-xiv, and Chambry, pp. xxviii-xxxi.

[7] See B. E. Perry, "Demetrius of Phalerum and the Aesopic Fables" *TAPA* 93 (1962) pp. 287-346, for an extensive discussion.

[8] This includes Perotti's Appendix, pp. 373-417.

[9] Perhaps the most detailed are those of Chambry (French), Hausrath (German), and Perry (English).

[10] *Studies in the Text History of the Life and Fables of Aesop* (Haverford 1936) p. 73.

[11] Karl Halm, *Fabulae Aesopicae Collectae* (Leipzig 1868).

[12] Joseph Jacobs, *History of the Aesopic Fable* (New York 1970) p. 1. This was originally published in 1889.

[13] There was no "standard" Romulus, but rather "Romulean" collections. See Jacobs, *History,* pp. 1-15.

[14] This is the number cited in Mary L. Martin, *The Fables of Marie de France: A Critical Commentary with English Translation* (Ann Arbor 1979). This University of Texas dissertation is commended highly. See also Emanuel J. Mickel, Jr., *Marie de France* (New York 1974) for a good overview of the life and works of this remarkable woman.

[15] A. M. Haberman, *Mishle Shualim l'Rabbi Berekhyah ha-Naqdan* (Jerusalem 1945-46). An English translation, with introduction, is by Moses Hadas, *Fables of a Jewish Aesop* (New York 1967).

[16] For a succinct discussion of the Steinhöwel collection, see R. T. Lenaghan, *Caxton's Aesop* (Cambridge 1967) pp. 4-18.

[17] The source of the Extravagantes remains a mystery. Jacob's suggestion that they may represent the medieval Aesop of Alfred (*History,* p. 203) is dubious.

[18] The Latin text is in Perry, *Aesopica,* p. 696, and an English translation in *Babrius and Phaedrus,* p. 597.

[19] I have not had access to the Krumbacher edition and cite it from Perry, *Aesopica,* p. 276.

[20] Strato's obvious other interest in the fable probably led to the omission of the animal barred from the barley.

[21] Perry's translation in *Babrius and Phaedrus,* p. 597.

[22] See the brief discussion in *OCD*[2], p. 428.

[23] Loeb edition, pp. 138 f.

[24] See the interesting discussion in Jacobs, *History,* pp. 40-158.

[25] Perry, *AJA* 66 (1962) pp. 205-7. Cf. Moses Hadas, *History of Greek Literature* (New York 1950). "The fable constitutes the one genre in which the Greeks seem to have acted as intermediaries between the ancient East and ourselves" (p. 68).

[26] E.g. Chambry, p. xxv. Handford's comment represents well this position. "There is reason to believe that some Egyptian and Assyrian fables became known to the Greeks in classical times, but no evidence exists to suggest that the influences were early or important. As far as we can see, therefore, the fable was invented by the Greeks—it may well be the Greeks of Asia Minor, the country of the lion which appears so often in the stories, and the traditional birthplace of Aesop," *Fables of Aesop* (Hammandsworth 1964) p. xiv.

[27] S. N. Kramer, *History Begins at Sumer* (Garden City 1959) p. 127. The works of Gordon to which he refers have been designated Collections 1-5. Collection four was published in *JAOS* 77(1957) pp. 67-79, collection five in *JCS* 12 (1958) pp. 1-21, 43-75, and collections one and two in *Sumerian Proverbs* (Philadelphia 1959). Collection three, which Gordon noted was "the best preserved of all the proverb collections" (*BO* 17 [1960] p. 128) unfortunately has not yet been published because of the death of the editor. The editor of *JCS* has informed me by correspondence that it will soon appear in an edition being prepared by Dr. Robert Falkowitz.

[28] Perry, *Babrius and Phaedrus,* pp. lix-lx.

[29] *Ibid.,* p. lx.

[30] I have used the translations in *Apocrypha and Pseudepigrapha of the Old Testament,* ed. R. H. Charles (Oxford 1913) pp. 715-84.

[31] W. L. Lambert, *Babylonian Wisdom Literature* (Oxford 1960) p. 281. The proverb is translated quite differently by R. H. Pfeiffer, *Ancient Near Eastern Texts* (Princeton 1955) p. 426. Pfeiffer, however, gives an alternative translation close to Lambert's.

[32] Lambert, p. 281.

[33] Perry, *Studium Generale,* p. 23, includes three more, II Sam. 12:1-6; II Sam. 14:6-11 and I Kings 20:39-42. They seem to be problematical.

[34] This fable is found in Aesopic collections, 262 in Perry, and may indicate the work of a Jewish or Christian editor.

[35] It is interesting that the medieval Jewish fabulist, ha-Nakdam preserves this fable (Hadas, p. 38) and conflates it with Proverbs 22:13 and 26:13, "there is a lion in the streets."

[36] See the definition of fable in note 2 above.

[37] Most studies suggest that there are approximately thirty extant fables in the Talmudic and Midrashic material. See Jacobs, *History,* p. 110; Israel Abrahams, *Chapters on Jewish Literature* (Philadelphia 1899) p.

64; *Enc. Jud.* (Jerusalem 1972) vol. 6, col. 1128. Hayim Schwarzbaum, coll. 1128. Hayim Schwarzbaum, *Talmudic-Midrashic Affinities of Some Aesopic Fables* (Berlin 1965), does not refer to the fable under discussion.

[38] Chambry, *Aesope,* p. xxxiii.

[39] See the discussions in Hugh Montefiore and H. E. W. Turner, *Thomas and the Evangelists* (London 1962) pp. 12 f.; W. C. van Unnik, *Newly Discovered Gnostic Writings* (London 1960) p. 49; Helmut Koester, *The Nag Hammadi Library* (San Francisco 1981) p. 117; Hennecke-Schneemelcher, *New Testament Apocrypha I,* tr. R. L. McWilson (Philadelphia 1963) p. 306.

[40] Rudolf Keydell, "Bemurkungen zu Griechischen Epigrammen" *Hermes* 80 (1952) pp. 497-500, has argued that the epigram used to date Strato, *Gk. Anth.* xi, 117 (Loeb edition), is not to be ascribed to him. Keydell argues that a comparison of some epigrams in Strato and Martial demonstrates the priority of the former. He dates Strato in Nero's reign. In this note I continue to accept the traditional dating.

[41] *Bis accus.* 27 in Loeb, *Lucian* iii, pp. 136-37. See also *OCD²,* p. 621.

[42] Albin Lesky, *A History of Greek Literature,* tr. James Willis and Cornelis de Heer (London 1966) p. 841.

[43] Keydell's argument referred to in note 40 would remove Strato from Egypt. That would not affect the argument here, which is content to speak of a general eastern Mediterranean provenance.

[44] Grant, *Secret Sayings,* p. 190.

[45] A textual problem in Proverbs 14:4 is interesting in this respect. The received Hebrew text reads literally "Where there are no oxen, there is a manger of grain." This is usually emended to read "Where there are no oxen, there is no grain." The latter is probably correct, but the connection manger-grain-oxen in a variant reading might have some bearing on the shift in Thomas from horse to oxen.

[46] Cf. Horace, *AP* 139, "parturient montes, nascetur ridiculus mus."

H. J. Blackham (essay date 1985)

SOURCE: H. J. Blackham, in an introduction to *The Fable as Literature*, The Athlone Press, 1985, pp. xi-xxi.

[In the following excerpt, Blackham defines the fable through a discussion of its traditional definition, its relation to parable and allegory, its images, its purpose, and its sources.]

(*i*)

A reviewer who refers to a book as 'fable', casually or more intentionally, probably has in mind an eighteenth-century *'conte philosophique'*, described by Voltaire as a work which says more than it seems to say; he might indeed be thinking of *Candide*. Any non-literary person asked about fable would most likely think of Aesop. The two are not as far apart as they seem. *Aesop's Fables,* in one compilation or another, have an honourable lineage in literature and in education; they are fables, not nursery tales. In the early days of Greek and Latin fiction, when different forms were being tried out, comic fiction took the kind of liberties made familiar in Aesop and popular on the stage. Improbable but amusing stories were invented to provide, in a striking way, something to be thought about. It can be said that the embryo of the fable of which Aesop was one parent was fully formed in classical culture by the end of the second century AD, to be developed down the centuries in different cultural contexts by different applications and uses, to become a vehicle of literary expression with special resources.

If 'fable' is to be studied as a literary genre, the prevalent rather loose notion of it needs to be refined. Clearly, in this sense it is not merely a word for any fiction, nor a word specifically for the plot of an epic or a play, senses in which it has been used and may be used. Nor is it merely or mainly a story with animals for characters, nor a story with a moral. This last comes nearer, suggested by the dictionary word 'apologue', defined as 'a moral fable'. There are many stories with a moral, stories invented to bring home a moral, which are not fables at all. Improving stories for the young to show how those who do wrong come to a bad end will not be fables. They are too simplistic to require a fable to arrest and engage the mind. A fable gets past the garrison of resident assumptions, the mind's defences, to bring home its point or raise its questions: it is a tactical manoeuvre to prompt new thinking, Voltaire's story that says more than it seems to say—not a didactic story.

To start with, fable is narrative fiction in the past tense. A very early definition of the Aesopic fable was, 'a fictitious story picturing a truth'.[1] The 'picturing' implies a metaphorical representation of the 'truth'; so that a fable is basically a metaphor. Something in the mind is brought into the mind's eye by an image of its likeness. Thought and speech are steeped in metaphor. This was summed up long ago in the Epicurean dictum: Nature is its own standard; one thing throws light on another. Fable runs its metaphorical traffic on narrative rails: 'The mountain was in labour, and brought forth a mouse'. Brief, incongruous, effective: a miniature story representing graphically a familiar truth.

There are three elements, idea, image, expression. The idea is in the image, the image is its metaphorical expression; the metaphor is in the narrative, which is its formal expression.

Since a fable as a fictitious story is an imagined action, and is a metaphor, the action is used to portray something else which it resembles in some way, and this something else is in the mind, a 'truth'. A truth can be formulated as a general statement; that is what it is. If it is related as a fable, there should be some sufficient reason. This may simply be to make it graphic and memorable, for ready application: sour grapes, a leonine bargain, the lion's share, a wolf in sheep's clothing, an ass in a lion's skin. These metaphorical expressions are made available to apply to a variety of instances with the generality of a 'truth'. The particular story is put to general use as a truth, although not possibly true. A more ambitious fable will not merely express a truth graphically and memorably, but mainly will generate and store new meaning in the conception it represents, whereas a general statement relies mainly on established meanings. What *Animal Farm* says could be formulated, and may have to be for any evaluation of its 'truth'. But summary statements cannot resume all the meaning generated and stored in the images and events of the narrative. This may be true, with greater consequence, of *Brave New World*.

The metaphorical expressions which familiar fables have made current—a dog-in-the-manger attitude— make familiar also the nature and use of metaphor which they exemplify. No word or phrase is normally a metaphor in itself, since 'metaphor' implies transference of words from use in their proper contexts to use in an alien context. The word or phrase is borrowed for its descriptive power in the new application. In 'a stream of abuse', 'stream' is chosen as most appropriate to the occasion of use. Otherwise, it might have been, 'he fired abuse'. 'Abuse' is in general a verbal utterance, and can be a 'stream' or a 'volley' only in particular instances. A metaphor is chosen, and exists only in particular use. It may be a stereotype, 'a crushing bore', or specially chosen and fresh. The most successful become stale, and fail. We say, excusably, 'blood was literally streaming from the wound', and less excusably, 'killing time is literally killing life', or, 'things began literally to fall apart'. To say 'literally' of a metaphor is of course absurd, as though to say: 'This is no metaphor'—when it is solely as metaphor that the word serves. The addition of 'literally' betrays inarticulate anxiety. Thought and expression are primitively and permanently metaphoric in their fabric. The implied comparison—'a running sore', 'running with sweat'—does not in practice entail double reference: there is a compound reference which is grasped directly. In narrative form, the fable is an extended metaphor. There is a compound reference to the image presented and the conception represented.

This compound reference is read off, as it were, directly. The fox and the crow with a piece of cheese is wholly and solely about profit and loss in flattery, and does not otherwise refer to a transaction between a fox and a crow. The brevity and simplicity, and impossibility, of an Aesopic fable make this evident, so that it has become habitual to say what the fable is about in a title or moral. Thus a collection in Penguin Classics, selected and translated by S. A. Handford, gives a title to each which indicates an application, and a moral which explains it. However, this is only an editor's privilege; it is exemplary, not restrictive. A history of editions of the fables would show that. There is no definitive 'moral'. The metaphor is open; the comparison invites exploratory reflection.[2] One can see in the primitive Aesopic fable a potentiality for development as a mental artefact, which detains the thought that conceived it in the further reflection it prompts. Stripped and focused as it must always be, fable is then, like any work of art, dense enough to abide repeated examination, and to abound in stimulus. . . .

(ii)

Before saying more about that prospect, distinctions must be made between fable and other forms of allusive fiction with which it is liable to be confused, particularly parable and allegory. The books of the Bible are in general rich in imagery, and are studded with similitudes and allusive forms, allegories, dreams, visions, parables, and the like. Among them all, one is recognized as a fable. The trees at some time looked for a king among themselves, and asked first the olive, then the fig, then the vine. All refused because they had their own proper business to look after. Last, the bramble gave ironical consent upon an absurd condition that entailed a fearful penalty. This was Jotham's invention to bring home the realities of a situation to the perpetrators of it (Judges 9:8-15). In so far as it is a fable, it is so because it can stand on its own with a more general application—and there are Aesopic fables which it does resemble.

It used to be said that the only parable in the Old Testament was the story which Nathan told David (2 Samuel 12:1-7) to bring home to him his guilt in taking Bath-sheba: 'Thou art the man.' It is invented by Nathan for his purpose, and used and done with, which is what marks the parable; it is ancillary, brought in to explain or illustrate a particular point, dependent; not remaining as an independent statement in narrative form for general application, as a fable does—as in Kafka's *Metamorphosis,* in which a member of the family wakes up as a loathsome insect, with which all parties have to come to terms and live. A not uncommon occurrence is endowed with new meaning by these peculiar circumstances. This is fable using its daring metaphoric power in a transformation act of general significance, which the homely parable does not attempt. It might

be objected that Jotham's story was invented for the occasion and done with as much as Nathan's. That might be fair comment, for Jotham's story is not as self-contained as a fable should be. But it is in the mode of a fable, and it does scrape into the collections (Perry, p. 475).

For, though the point of separation holds between parable and fable, dependence and independence, the borderline may be blurred. "The Good Samaritan" is invented for an occasion, to answer the question, Who is my neighbour? Logically, however, it is a fable, in that the particular story is invented to represent a general pattern of behaviour, with the widest application. It is a conception, neighbour love, defined in a special narrative. Given some understanding of the relations between Samaritans and Jews in that cultural situation, it has an independence that takes it out of the main universe of discourse, about the kingdom of heaven, in which the other parables of Jesus have their occasion. The plainness of the story makes it uncharacteristic of fable. Surely, it is no more than a simple illustration of neighbour love, which is something anybody would immediately recognize and understand. So is the dog carrying a bone over a stream an illustration of greed, which is something everybody understands. In their originality, both broke new ground in ways familiarity now obscures. The difference between parable and fable is not between a story that might be real and one that could not be, as is sometimes supposed. The distinction is between independence and generality in the one case, dependence confined to the particular in the other. The parable of "the Prodigal Son" could not reasonably be said to be a fable, although indeed it can stand on its own as a story, and it does represent a general and familiar pattern of behaviour. As told by Jesus, it does belong intimately to the universe of discourse about the kingdom of heaven, and the point of its telling is in that. Its universality otherwise is trivial, merely the universality of what does happen more or less frequently, without any feature to make it significant. The same story is a different matter told in the *Gulistan* . . . or by Thurber, "The bat who got the hell out" Fable generates conceptual meanings, does not merely furnish an illustration in a particular instance.

An allegory in narrative form may seem close to fable. Again, the principal difference is that the allusion in allegory is to something particular, and in fable to something general. Rather, although both may embody general conceptions in particular forms, with roles in a particular action, fable will do this to focus attention on an illuminated patch exposed to thought, whereas allegory tends to explore labyrinthine manifestations with delight in the description. Allegory constructs a series of specific correspondences in two systems so that one translates into the other, either way. Bunyan's *The Pilgrim's Progress* represents the stages and vicissitudes of the Christian life, translating spiritual experiences into physical adventures, to give them imaginatively concrete reality. Personification has been largely used in allegories to give some abstraction, say Famine or Greed, a human appearance and a name, and a role in the action. Personification differs from an Aesopic image in a way that epitomizes the distinction. Personification describes an abstraction as a person who manifests in appearance and behaviour the name it bears, so that such agents may be used as characters in the argument of a plot, or paraded as figures in a pageant. The image of an Aesopic fable is a single action, in which the elements of meaning derived from the agents are integrated. In allegory, there is elaborate detail in detailed elaboration of the theme, heavily dependent of description of visual imagery. In fable, depiction jumps from particulars to the enactment. The ant and the grasshopper are not brought together because of what they are in nature. Popular beliefs are drawn on to construct an image of the carelessness of carefree enjoyment of life in humiliating confrontation with the righteousness of prudent foresight. Typically, allegory may represent human life as a voyage, in a sequence of images that recognizably correspond to features of life as lived. This is alien to the way of generalizing in fable, which would represent human life as lived by resuming it under a single aspect in an action imagined to bring home some part of human fate or folly.

(iii)

The images created by fables of the Aesopic type are deceptively homely: they have a quasi-mathematical abstractness and applicability. G. K. Chesterton likened the animals, in a Preface to a collection of Aesop's *Fables,* to an alphabet of humanity of which a language is made to write down and hand down the first philosophic certainties, and for this the figures had to be like abstractions in algebra or like the pieces in chess. This is roughly right, although the language of images is concrete and particular and picturesque. The virtue is that they can be and are used with the universality of abstractions. The essential theme of *Animal Farm* is anticipated in "**The Wolves and the Dogs**". The longer complex fables go beyond the simple images of the Aesopic fable, but simplify the abstractions they represent in a kind of model, as modern scientists build models of their invisible conceptual entities, based on measurements. Such models can be examined and questioned to give thought a firmer hold on experience. It is this power of fable not merely to represent but mainly to inform a conception that is its genius, beyond the scope of allegory. Anyone can write an allegory of sorts, or find an illustration. The invention of a fable is akin to that of the poet, as Plato recognized (*Phaedo,* 60-61)—in connection with Aesop Hazlitt had that insight, and it justified his enthusiasm: 'The invention of a fable is to me the most enviable exertion of human genius: it is the discovering a truth to which there is no clue, and which, when once found, can never be forgotten. I would rather have been the author of *Aesop's Fables,* than of *Euclid's Elements!'* ("On Wit and Humour"). This could hardly be said of parables or allegories. There is a recognized distinction. . . .

Formal definition is likely to be less than helpful if it has to say in general terms not only what fable is but also what fables do. The first part is straightforward, in that fable is not straightforward narrative but a device, and can be called a narrative device. What it does with that device varies with the fable, as does the device itself. This includes ways to move things around, bring together, take apart, switch contexts, shift perspectives, unsettle, reorganize; in short, imagination manipulates the environment, to take hold of things as they are taken to be in order to show the way they are. The play of fiction drops any pretence to play real life as it appears, in order to show seriousness that does not appear; and thus sharpen perception, or broaden understanding, or quicken passion. In each case the action represented forms a conceptual artefact fabricated for a special use. A formal definition might be: a narrative device, to provoke and aid concrete thinking, focused on some general matter of concern. That hardly hints at the incongruities or the ironic comparison or the baited bafflement or any of the temerities by means of which so many fables achieve their effects. . . . Meanwhile, there are some identifying general characteristics to be noticed here related to ways in which fable does its work.

(iv)

(1) Professor Perry has listed the following types of story as materials used in early fables:[3] a fairy-tale (*Märchen*), an aetiological nature-myth, an animal story, a series of amusing actions, a novella, a myth about the gods, a debate between two rivals, an account of the circumstances in which some aphoristic or witty remark was made. The point he is making is that the narrative material is indifferent; it neither makes nor excludes a fable. What makes a fable is the peculiar purpose and implied comparison that govern and shape the material. The type of story is not a criterion. The use made of it is. As fable developed and longer narratives were used, those in current vogue were often adopted and adapted, as voyages, travellers' tales, Eastern folk-tales or fantasies, and, latest, science fiction. These examples are of narratives which rather easily take human behaviour out of its normal contexts.

(2) The Aesopic fable established itself as a convention, and was its own excuse, however radically adapted. Longer fables had to make their own way in finding readers on their own terms. There were difficulties. The narrative is organized for the purposes of

the fable. In this sense and for this reason, it is not written for the reader, as the bulk of fiction is. The story may have to be read before it can be 'read', in order to recognize what it is that is said more than seems to be said. It has been said, 'each poem contains its own poetics'. Similarly, every fable has to justify itself in the telling. Cultural conditions may even forbid the attempt, when the conventional rules are too strict, or the climate of thought too uncongenial. But there are nigh-universal responses that help. This kind of serious fiction in which the writer must prevail, and prevail with the reader, has been regularly baited with the comic and the satirical. A reader's confidence, or interest, may be generated by tone of voice, encouraging, alluring, ironic, rapid. An author may banter and tease the reader with tricks, ploys, bluffs, a light buffet or two about the ears with the fool's bladder, to alert attention to the lurking intent. Above all, the reader is not tried too long. The story is simple enough and short enough to be memorable as well as telling. And since its main ostensible content is the plot, an action, it can often be translated without loss. People are not in the round, like Mr Pickwick or Mrs Poyser. It is not likely to matter what happened at the meeting in the wood, nor what passed between certain persons at yesterday's picnic. There is not the visual field of broad daylight. A spotlight is focused on an object, or a floodlight isolates a chosen area.

(3) Fable is a special form of literary composition, in the sense that it is occasioned, there is a reason for it. There must be cultural conditions not merely to make it possible, but mainly to make it expedient. Generally, these may be political or philosophical. Politically, opinions, a message may be cast in the form of a fable to baffle or deceive the official mind with meanings that cannot be literally construed as evidence, but get through plainly to those for whom they are intended. This is to use fable merely as a practical device; but it is legitimate, and when it is live its wit and bite are sharpened by incomparable excitement. Interaction between the two levels of meaning, literal and implied, is a different mechanism when the intention is philosophical, for the act of communication is at a different level, understanding or awareness, rather than praxis. Fable then has its proper generality and permanence.

(4) As a genre fable has a boundary, but every fable has its own neighbours, and its own affinities. One may be close to an allegory, another to a folk-tale, a third to what may be taken for an ordinary story. The boundary may sometimes be ill defined, but unless it is recognizably thereabouts at some point of distinction, there is no point in looking. What the neighbours are, however, is often relevant to what the fable is and does.

(5) Last, not least, the medium is the message. The message is not delivered—certainly not in the 'morals'

tagged to the Aesopic fables: it is embodied. It is in this sense that fable is a conceptual artefact, which remains to be used. Interplay continues between the thought provoked and the representation that provokes and aids it.

(*v*)

Enough has been said in a preliminary way about what fable is and does and how it differs from similar narrative forms. . . . A conspectus of [the history of the fable from its obscure beginnings to its maturity at the end of the eighteenth century] may help to establish the theme.

The sources of fable are found in the 'wisdom literature' characteristic of early civilization. Short pithy sayings and poetry spring spontaneously from the native soil, for later cultivation. The nucleus of the Book of Proverbs in the Old Testament was probably in oral currency at the time of the monarchy; and the later Wisdom literature of the Hebrews seems to have been in some sort of communication with Greek thought. The maxims with which this kind of literature is studded were useful in the instruction of children by their parents. The last chapter of Proverbs explicitly repeats what King Lemuel was taught by his mother. In the Apocrypha, these books go beyond moral instruction into the intellectual provinces of knowledge: 'To know the constitution of the world, and the operation of the elements . . . the diversity of plants and the virtues of roots' (Wisdom of Solomon: 7). The Indian fables were used to teach 'political science'. Fables abounded in the wisdom literature of India, but there were none in the Hebrew. However, in the old Mesopotamian literature, dating back to the eighteenth century BC and earlier, collections have been made of one-sentence fables of the Aesopic type, a clear anticipation. The developed Aesopic fable was useful material in the schools of rhetoric both as a linguistic discipline, in paraphrase, expansion, compression, and for apposite citation in the development of an argument. Rhetoric, the art of discourse, of persuasion and of thinking, was the main discipline in higher education throughout the classical period to the fall of Rome. It involved humanistic studies, as Cicero called them, including history, poetry and moral philosophy. The Aesopic fable was too useful to be forgotten in this context, if used sometimes half-apologetically. *Aesop's Fables* remained a school book in English grammar schools until the eighteenth century. When the fables were put into Latin verse of some accomplishment by Phaedrus and into Greek verse by Babrius, both in the first century AD, they found a lowly but secure place in polite literature, a status to be put beyond challenge by La Fontaine some sixteen hundred years later.

The philosophic background of fable in wisdom literature, and the loose connection of the developed Aesopic fable with the rhetorical discipline which had philosophic roots with the Sophist Isocrates (in opposition to Plato), had implied recognition when Lucian, the most famous rhetorician of his day throughout the Roman world in the second century AD, had it in mind to mate Socratic dialogue with the Aristophanic imaginative licence of the Old Comedy to produce a new kind of fiction that would use jest to put before the reader something to think about. With his *True History* he is said to have initiated a new genre of which *Gulliver's Travels* is a much later, and indebted, example.

The staple material of the Aesopic fable was destined to survive, and was found in the Latin inheritance of the European Middle Ages. The development achieved in classical culture was also destined to be re-enacted or paralleled, spontaneously. Marie de France and others put the fables into vernacular verse of some merit. They were available for use in homilies. In the great *Roman de Renart,* Aesopic material was worked up into a parody of courtly poetry that was so successful and continued so long that it left a lasting mark and a striking precedent, if it did not initiate a new genre, like Lucian. Although fable showed this manifest liveliness, it was not at home in a culture dominated by the Church, in which meaning was allegorical and predetermined. It had little independence; as parody or satire, it was parasitic. The Renaissance recovered Lucian, with lively appreciation on the part of such as More and Erasmus—particularly Erasmus, who imitated him in his Colloquies, and who incidentally produced a sustained independent and deadly Aesopic fable in one of the many revisions of his *Adages.* But it was in the eighteenth century, the Age of Reason, that fable achieved classical maturity, with books of accomplished modern fables in verse or prose (Gay, Lessing), with La Fontaine's sophisticated *comédie humaine* of these antique puppets, and with the new *conte philosophique,* whether of Lucian extraction—like *Gulliver's Travels*—or of Indian extraction, descending through the Persian versions that had become popular and had been in European circulation since the Middle Ages, a story type adopted and adapted by Voltaire or by Samuel Johnson in *Rasselas.* At this time, fable came of age and displayed the resources available to its purpose, uniquely serious in fiction.

However, the device was not to be used during the next century in England, save (almost accidentally) by the maverick Samuel Butler in *Erewhon* (1872), a notable exception. . . . [Reasons] for this void or avoidance . . . must be speculative. What is certain is that this was the period in which the novel established its dominion and became the dominant literary form; and one that opened ample scope to serious purpose. Since then, with most artistic forms, it has had its share of subversive movements; the anti-novel may be the most serious form of fiction. Experimental freedom

has left the fable as a device where it was at the end of the eighteenth century with the *conte philosophique,* outmoded because unnecessary. So it has been said. All the same, the protean fiction of the present time is rich in reputations made by productions that have the distinctive odour and inner logic of that philosophic fiction, whatever the class name they may get today. And Aesop survives in modern varieties that seem to conform more to Mendel's principles of transmission than to the legendary theory of Pythagoras.

Notes

[1] *Babrius and Phaedrus,* tr. Ben Edwin Perry (Loeb Classical Library, 1965).

[2] Take "The Wolf and the Lamb". The image is of helpless innocence as doomed victim of undeterrable inescapable power which closes in, as in one of Poe's tale. But that is not the moment of truth in this horror story. Rather, the action exposes the need of the agent to justify the unjustifiable. This may be taken as just a graphic illustration of a familiar truth, an arresting reminder. Or it might be taken as an insight into what goes on inside the indulgence in unjust practices. Aesop's fables and the truths they picture are long and early familiar. Some have corners of the truths they picture still unexposed.

[3] *Babrius and Phaedrus,* xxiii.

FURTHER READING

Biography

Adrados, Francisco R. "The 'Life of Aesop' and the Origins of Novel in Antiquity." *Quaderni urbinati di cultura classica,* n.s. I (1979): 93-112.

>   Discusses various incidents in the ancient "Life of Aesop" while arguing that the comic-realistic novel resulted from the merging of a Hellenic adaptation of the legend of *Ahikar* with the legend of a fable-telling Delphic *pharmakos,* or scapegoat.

Baker, Howard. "A Portrait of Aesop." *Sewanee Review* LXXVII, No. 4 (October-December 1969): 557-90.

>   Discusses various incidents in the "Life of Aesop" while arguing for the aptness of the traditional description of Aesop as ugly in the sense of a comic or Socratic figure.

Goldsmith, Oliver. "Life of Aesop." In *Bewick's Select Fables of Aesop,* pp. i-ix. New York: R. Ellis for Cheshire House, 1932.

>   Summarizes the major events of Aesop's life mentioned in the controversial "Life of Aesop" as well as commenting on Aesop's character, the invention of the fable, and various representations of Aesop.

Keller, John E., and L. Clark Keating, trans. "The Life of Aesop." In *Aesop's Fables, with a Life of Aesop*, pp. 7-51. Lexington: University Press of Kentucky, 1993.

> Provides a translation of the 1489 A.D. Spanish (via Latin) version of the ancient "Life of Aesop."

Smith, M. Ellwood. "Aesop: A Decayed Celebrity." *Publications of the Modern Language Association* XLVI (1931): 225-36.

> Traces the development in England of the ugly philosopher image of Aesop from the introduction of the "Life of Aesop" preserved by Maximus Planudes to the crushing criticism of that biography by Richard Bentley and finally to John Ogilby's collection of fables, which shows a rehabilitated attitude toward Aesop.

Criticism

Adolf, Helen. "The Ass and the Harp." *Speculum* XXV, No. 1 (January 1950): 49-57.

> Argues that the Aesopic fable of "The Ass and the Harp" represents a misunderstanding of the Babylonian representation of this combination.

Callahan, Virginia W. "Ramifications of the Nut-Tree Fable." *Acta conventus neo-Latini turonensis*, edited by Jean-Claude Margolin, Vol. I, pp. 197-204. Paris: Librairie philosophique J. Vrin, 1980.

> Investigates the interpretations and uses of the nut-tree fable by Erasmus and Andrea Alciati who was influenced by Erasmus.

Carnes, Pack. "Traditional Expectations in the Modern Fable." *Neohelicon* X, No. 2 (1983): 203-16.

> Examines the fables of James Thurber, Helmut Arntzen, and Wolfdietrich Schnurre in order to show how modern fables reflect or distort one's expectations for a traditional fable.

Dargan, E. P. "'Cock and Fox': A Critical Study of the History and Sources of the Mediaeval Fable." *Modern Philology* IV (1906): 1-27.

> Traces the development of "The Cock and the Fox" from classical to medieval literature in order to show that this fable is a composite of influences from Aesop or Phraedrus, from the folktale of the wolf adapted in England for clerical use, and from later popular use of the fable.

Dawson, Warren R. "The Mouse in Fable and Folklore." *Folklore* XXXVI, No. 1 (March 1925): 227-48.

> Compares the demotic Egyptian version of "The Lion and the Mouse" with the Greek version as well as summarizing certain Aesopic fables that contain the mouse.

Downs, Robert B. "Famed Fabulist." In *Famous Books: Ancient and Modern*, pp. 31-5. New York: Barnes & Noble, Inc., 1964.

> Gives a short biography of Aesop as well as a brief discussion of the nature of the fable and the influence of Aesop.

Dwyer, E. J. "'The Fowler and the Asp': Literary versus Generic Illustration in Roman Art." *American Journal of Archaeology* LXXXII (Summer 1978): 400-04.

> Suggests that generic representations of bird-catching in Greek art probably influenced the illustration of Aesop's fable, "The Fowler and the Asp" and that these two traditions then influenced the representations of bird-catching in Roman art.

Gopen, George D. Introduction to *The Moral Fables of Aesop: An Edition of the Middle Scots Text*, by Robert Henryson, pp. 1-32. Notre Dame: University of Notre Dame Press, 1987.

> Discusses Robert Henryson's fables in terms of the Aesopic tradition, the humor of the poems, and the seriousness of the work as evidenced by the imagery of morality, the structure of the book, and the function of the poems' *moralitates*.

Gordon, Edmund. I. "Sumerian Animal Proverbs and Fables: 'Collection Five.'" *Journal of Cuneiform Studies* XII, Nos. 1-2 (1958): 1-21, 43-75.

> Presents the often fragmentary text and translation of 125 Sumerian proverbs and fables, some of which resemble the Aesopic fable.

Hale, David G. "Aesop in Renaissance England." *The Library* XXVII, No. 2 (June 1972): 116-25.

> Traces the publication and use of Aesop's fables in England to demonstrate that English use of Aesop's text in Greek, Latin, or English represents for the most part an adoption of the results of continental scholarship and creativity.

Henderson, Arnold Clayton. "Medieval Bestiaries and Modern Cages: The Making of Meaning in Fables and Bestiaries." *Publications of the Modern Language Association* CXVII, No. 1 (January 1982): 40-9.

> Endeavors to discover a uniquely medieval viewpoint in period literature containing an explicit moral such as bestiaries and fables.

Jacobs, Joseph. *The Fables of Aesop, as First Printed by William Caxton in 1484, with Those of Avian, Alfonso, and Poggio*. 2 vols. London: D. Nutt, 1889.

> Gives a detailed analysis of possible influences on the text of Aesop from antiquity to the Renaissance in the first volume entitled *History of the Aesopic Fable*.

Jacobson, Eric. "The Fable Is Inverted; or, Donne's *Aesop*." *Classica et mediaevalia* XIII (1952): 1-37.

> Examines the question of the origin of the use of a stork instead of a water serpent in the fable of the frogs asking Jupiter for a king.

Larkin, Neil M. "Another Look at Dante's Frog and Mouse." *Modern Language Notes* LXXVII (1962): 94-9.

> Argues that Dante Alighieri's allusion to the fable of "The Frog and the Mouse" (*Inferno* XXIII, 4-9) was intended to illustrate the situation of Dante and Virgil, who needed help to cross the fifth boglia (hell) in the *Inferno*.

Malvern, Marjorie M. "'Who peyntede the leon, tel me who?': Rhetorical and Didactic Roles Played by an Aesopic Fable in the *Wife of Bath's Prologue*." *Studies in Philology* LXXX, No. 3 (Summer 1983): 238-52.

> Proposes that Geoffrey Chaucer's Wife of Bath, in satirizing the misogynistic writings of the clerks, is represented as the heroic lion who shows the proud man his folly in feeling superior to lions in the Aesopic fable of "A Lion and a Man."

Perry, Ben Edwin. "An Aesopic Fable in Photius." *Byzantische Zeitschrift* XLVI, No. 2 (1953): 308-13.

> Gives an example of the process of fable development and ascription to Aesop in classical antiquity.

————. "Fable." *Studium Generale* XII, No. 1 (1959): 17-37.

> Provides a definition of fable as well as a discussion of the origin of fable and its place in Graeco-Roman antiquity.

————. General Preface to *Aesopica: A Series of Texts Relating to Aesop, or Ascribed to Him, or Closely Connected with the Literary Tradition That Bears His Name*, edited by Ben Edwin Perry, Vol. I, pp. vii-xvii. Urbana: University of Illinois Press, 1952.

> Contains Perry's purpose and criteria for selecting fables for *Aesopica*.

————. *Studies in the Text History of the Life and Fables of Aesop*. Philological Monographs Published by the American Philological Association, No. 7. Haverford, Penn.: American Philological Association, 1936.

> Discusses the Pierpont Morgan Library manuscript in regard to its version of the "Life of Aesop" and the relationship of its version of the *Fables* to the authoritative Augustana recension as well as to aspects of other recensions dependent on the Augustana.

Van Doren, Mark. "Aesop and La Fontaine: Fables." In *The New Invitation to Learning*, edited by Mark Van Doren, pp. 135-49. New York: Random House, 1942.

> Presents Lin Yutang, Jacques Barzun, and Mark Van Doren in a conversation that raises such issues as the need for elaboration in modern versions of the fables, the use of fables under tyrannical political systems, the accretion of fables to the Aesopic corpus over time, the applicability of the fables to today's circumstances, and Aesop's world view.

Von Kreisler, Nicolai. "Satire in 'The Vox and the Wolf.'" *Journal of English and Germanic Philology* LXIX, No. 4 (October 1970): 650-58.

> Contends that the medieval English version of the fable, in which the Wolf raises the Fox out of a well by unthinkingly lowering himself in another bucket, satirizes the gullibility of parishioners through the Wolf as well as the corruption of the clergy through the Fox.

Waddell, W. G. "A Plea for Aesop in the Greek Classroom." *Classical Journal* XXXII, No. 3 (December 1936): 162-70.

> Introduces various fables to show such characteristics of Aesop's fables as morals about social virtues, humor, and etiological stories.

Additional coverage of Aesop's life and career is contained in the following sources published by Gale Research: *Children's Literature Review*, Vol. 14; *Something about the Author*, Vol. 64; and *Major Authors and Illustrators for Children and Young Adults*.

St. Birgitta of Sweden

c. 1303-1373

(Also Bridget, Birgit, Brigid) Swedish prophetic writer.

INTRODUCTION

The patron saint of Sweden, Birgitta was an influential figure in the religious and political life of fourteenth-century Europe. An outspoken proponent of reform within the Church, she is largely remembered for her prophetic visions later collected in the eight books of her *Revelationes* (c.1373; *The Revelations of Saint Bridget*). In this work, Birgitta called for the contrition of Christian society, which she believed had fallen away from the moral precepts of Christ as contained in the Bible. Many of her prophecies and visions evoke images of an *ira Dei*, the angry God of the Old Testament, as they denounce the sins of pride, avarice, and concupiscence to which Birgitta felt many Europeans had succumbed. She believed that Christians had strayed from the true path, and only through confession, purification, and penitence could they again achieve God's grace. Many of her later writings demonstrate her worldly goals, including the achievement of a reconciliation between the Church and the secular powers in Europe, the return of the Avignonese papacy to its traditional place in Rome, and an end to the long-standing and bloody conflict between the rulers of France and England known as the Hundred Years War. Among her other lasting accomplishments are the creation of the monastic order that bears her name and her critique of the Church in her *Revelations*, in which she foreshadowed many of the grievances that Martin Luther enumerated in the ensuing era of the Reformation.

Biographical Information

Birgitta was born in Sweden in about 1303, the daughter of Birger Person, then governor of the Uppland region. Her family was wealthy, politically influential, and strongly religious. In 1316 she conceded to her father's wishes and married prince Ulf Gudmarsson, with whom she had eight children, including a daughter who would become Saint Catherine of Sweden. In 1341 Birgitta, her husband, and a retinue of followers undertook a holy pilgrimage to Santiago de Compostela. In 1344, a few years after their return, Ulf's death prompted Birgitta to devote the remainder of her life to religious pursuits. She retreated to the Cistercian monastery at Alvastra for a while, immersing herself in prayer. Beginning in

this period, and for the rest of her life, Birgitta reportedly experienced a series of visions, mostly of Christ and the Virgin Mary. Many of these revelations urged Birgitta to undertake future tasks. Some of God's messages were of a political nature and were revealed before the court of King Magnus and Queen Blanche of Sweden. Others guided her in various pursuits, notably in the foundation of a devotional order in honor of the Virgin Mary. Another caused her to leave for Rome in late 1349 for the purpose of spreading God's word and to facilitate the return of the Papacy—residing at that time in "Babylonian Captivity" in Avignon, France—to the Italian capitol. While there, Birgitta formed an apostolate embraced by many Italians. Her assistance of the poor and homeless became legendary in the city and earned her the title of "The Angel of Rome." Yet another vision she experienced late in life prompted Birgitta to travel to the Holy Land in 1372. She returned to Rome from her well-publicized pilgrimage in 1373 and died on July 23 of that year. Her remains were transported to Sweden and buried at the site of the future monastery at Vadstena. Following her death, Birgitta's movement toward sainthood was relatively swift; Pope Boniface IX finished a process begun by Urban VI and canonized her on October 7, 1391. In 1396 she was named patron saint of her native Sweden. As for Birgitta's visions, nearly all were transcribed and eventually translated.

Major Works

Birgitta's literary works consist entirely of the many editions and translations of her *Revelations*. Comprising eight books in all—the last of which was added posthumously—the *Revelations* contain transcriptions of approximately seven hundred religious visions primarily featuring Christ and the Virgin Mary, as well as John the Baptist, God the Father, Saint Agnes, and others. Overall Birgitta's writings reflect a simplicity of style and rhetorical manner and evoke the author's pious obedience to the received word of God. The structure of the work, despite passing through countless editors and translators, has largely remained the same since the early fifteenth century. Books One and Two contain early revelations which Birgitta experienced in Sweden; their themes are mostly moral in nature. The next two books of the *Revelations* largely comprise Birgitta's visions of the Church in Rome. Book Five, generally known as the *Liber questionum*, or "Book of Questions," returns to the Swedish period. It features a monk on a ladder, who addresses questions to Jesus Christ on a variety of theological subjects, including the reasons for evil and suffering in this world. Book Six includes many biographical accounts from Birgitta's life as well as visions pertaining to a range of subjects, both secular and sacred. The topic of Book Seven is the years 1371 to 1373, including Birgitta's vision of and pilgrimage to the Holy Land. Book Eight, called the *Liber celestis imperatoris ad reges*, or "The Book of the Heavenly Emperor to the Kings," meditates on political themes and affairs. It includes portions drawn from the previous books of the *Revelations*. A final element of the work, made up of lost, discarded, or forgotten revelations and entitled the *Revelationes extravagantes*, was later added by editors. It contains revelations on a variety of topics, notably Birgitta's vision in 1345 on the subject of the Birgittine order, or the Ordo Sancti Salvatoris.

Textual History

Because Birgitta was unable to speak or write Latin, she dictated her *Revelationes* in Swedish to her confessors, who transcribed her words into the language of educated Europe. These manuscripts were later translated into Old Swedish, as well as German, English, and other European languages. Among her Latin confessors, one influential figure involved in the early

formation of the *Revelations* stands out. Alphonse de Jaén guided the editing process of Birgitta's writings near the end of her life and following her death. His manuscripts of the *Revelations* include the famous preface entitled *Epistola solitarii ad reges*—"The Letter of the Hermit to the Kings"—in which he defends Birgitta's writings from contemporary and future attacks on their authenticity, veracity, and divine authority. Later editors carried on Alphonse's work but often took liberties with the manuscript. One such editor, Nicolaus Orsini, greatly transformed the style of the visions that Birgitta dictated to her Latin translators by eliminating its unique form of address—that of Christ speaking directly to Birgitta as his bride. Modern critics see this act by Orsini as an attempt to deflect criticism of the *Revelations* from biased medieval observers who would refuse to accept that the word of God could be revealed through a woman. An English translation of the *Revelations* was produced between 1400 and 1415, while the first published edition of the *Revelations* appeared in Lübeck, Germany, in 1492. Another early edition of importance was sanctioned by the authority of Emperor Maximilian and undertaken at his request in 1500. Contemporary scholars have begun work on a modern Swedish critical edition of the *Revelations*, although the English standard remains the 1929 partial translation by William Patterson Cumming.

Critical Reception

Subsequent to her arrival in Rome in 1350, Birgitta experienced a period of immense popularity—to the level of cult adoration, according to some critics. This popularity grew following her canonization and the creation of her monastic order in Sweden in the late fourteenth century. In the meantime, other Birgittine monasteries appeared elsewhere in Europe, most notably in England at Sion. After the advent of the Reformation, however, Birgitta's *Revelations* were reviewed by the Council of Basel. Many passages were deemed dubious, and overall the popularity of the Birgittine order decreased. In the late sixteenth century, the convent at Vadstena that she had inspired was vacated. In the modern period, Birgitta's life and writings have elicited considerable interest among scholars. Some have discussed her *Revelations* as an example of medieval popular or mystical literature, by and large lacking in rhetorical refinement. Several have examined the question of prophetic legitimacy by investigating accounts of Birgitta as insane or falsely inspired. Roger Ellis has commented on her relation to Old Testament prophecy and the harsh judgment of a God enraged by lack of faith. Still others have seen Birgitta's work as a symbolic synthesis of the medieval desire for political and religious unity and as a powerful precursor of the ecclesiastical reform that took place in the sixteenth century.

PRINCIPAL WORKS

*Revelationes (spiritual revelations) c. 1373
†Revelationes extravagantes (spiritual revelations) c. 1380
†Liber celestis imperatoris ad reges (spiritual revelations) c. 1391

*The original manuscript of the *Revelationes* contains several earlier books of revelations, sermons, and prayers that Birgitta wrote between 1344 and 1373, including *Sermo angelicus*, *Quatuor oraciones*, *Liber questionum*, and *Liber celestis revelacionum*.
†Included with later editions of the *Revelationes*.

PRINCIPAL ENGLISH TRANSLATIONS

The Revelations of Saint Birgitta [translated by William Patterson Cumming] 1929

CRITICISM

William Patterson Cumming (essay date 1929)

SOURCE: An introduction to *The Revelations of Saint Birgitta*, edited by W. P. Cumming, Oxford University Press, 1929, pp. xxiii-xxix.

[*In the following excerpt, Cumming summarizes St. Birgitta's life and the literary merit of her* Revelations.]

A. *The Life of Saint Birgitta*[1]

In the year 1302 or 1303[2] Birgitta[3] was born at Finstad, a town a few miles from Upsala in the province of Upland. Her father was Birger, the lagman or governor of Upland.

Birgitta began to have visions at the age of seven;[4] in these visions an angel, the Blessed Virgin Mary, or Christ, usually appeared and talked to her. When she was 10 years of age she heard a sermon on the passion of Christ. That night Christ appeared to her as if he had just been crucified, and said, 'Thus am I tortured'. Birgitta, thinking that the wounds were fresh, asked, 'O Lord, who has done this to Thee?' Christ replied, 'Whoever despises Me and spurns My love does this to Me'. From that day on, the passion of Christ affected her so much that she seldom could think of it without tears.[5] It is a constantly recurring theme in her revelations.

At thirteen years of age her father, much against her wishes,[6] married her to the eighteen-year-old Ulf Gudmarson, a youth of noble family and fine personal character. They lived together continently for a year,[7] and Birgitta was especially fervent in her prayers and ascetic devotions. Ulf eventually became the lagman of the province of Nericia,[8] and Birgitta bore him four sons and four daughters.[9] St. Catherine, who later accompanied her mother on many of her journeys, was the most famous of her children.[10] During this period of Birgitta's life, the learned Matthias, canon of the cathedral of Lincöping, was her father confessor and constant adviser.[11] Ulf, her husband, died in 1344, after they had lived for some years in continence and pious study.[12]

A few days[13] after her husband had died, Christ appeared to Birgitta and told her that he had chosen her to be his bride.[14] From this time on Birgitta's life was changed; she turned over the management of her estate to others and devoted herself to a religious life. She greatly increased her self-discipline; she fasted often, dressed poorly, and underwent severe penances. In 1346 she received a revelation bidding her to go to Rome.[15] But it was no easy undertaking to leave her affairs and arrange for her children; two or three years elapsed before her journey began.[16] With a small retinue, including her two confessors, Peter, prior of Alvastra, and Peter Olafson, first confessor of the Vadstena monastery, she finally left Sweden, never more to return alive. On the way to Rome Peter of Alvastra began to teach her the use of Latin. However, she continued to write down her revelations in Swedish, and her confessors translated them into Latin.[17]

Long before leaving Sweden Birgitta had shown a fearless nature in her denunciations of the king and his court.[18] During the years of her stay in Rome she waged ceaseless war against the widespread corruptions in the Church. She unhesitatingly condemned the prelates, forced the abbots to improve the standard of living at their monasteries, and frequently sent letters of advice or denunciation to the pope himself.[19]

She was especially anxious that the papal seat, which had long been at Avignon, should be re-established at Rome. But the popes did not wish to leave the quiet of Avignon for the turmoil of a rebellious city. It was not until 1367 that Urban V brought the long absent court back to Rome. The conditions prevalent in Rome at that time were unendurable to the pope, and he decided to abandon Rome in 1370. This aroused in Birgitta great anger and grief; she warned him, upon penalty of God's severe displeasure and punishment, not to leave Rome.[20] This revelation was delivered to him by Alphonso,[21] one of Birgitta's devoted friends, but did not change the pope's decision. He left the city, and died the same year, in less than a month after returning to Avignon.

Another desire of Birgitta was to have her Order, the Order of St. Saviour or the Birgittine Order, officially approved. She firmly believed that she had received and had written down the rules of the Order exactly as they were given to her by the Mother of God. This Order, the founding of which is Birgitta's chief religious accomplishment, was to consist of sixty sisters and twenty-five monks. The monks and nuns were to live in separate houses, communicating with the church; the nuns' choir was to be placed above in such a position as to enable them to listen to the offices of the monks in the lower choir. The monastery was so arranged that the monks and nuns could not see each other, even at confession. Severe, chaste, and abstemious living were strictly prescribed.[22] After many years of command and entreaty by Birgitta, the Order was approved by Urban in 1370.[23] The monastery at Vadstena had been in existence for some time,[24] and after this date the Order rapidly expanded.[25]

In 1372, in obedience to the divine command,[26] Birgitta went to Jerusalem.[27] While in Palestine she had many visions revealing to her incidents in the life of Christ and the Blessed Virgin Mary; these revelations form the major part of Bk. VII. Birgitta returned to Rome the same year, very much enfeebled. On 23 July 1373, surrounded by a group of her followers, she died. Her bones were carried to Vadstena,[28] where they may still be seen.[29]

Her two confessors, and Catherine, her daughter, soon returned to Rome to inaugurate the proceedings for her canonization. Gregory XI appointed a commission to investigate the life and writings of Birgitta. The commission was headed by Cardinal Johannes de Turrecremata, who made a very careful study of the revelations. After some delay the canonization, performed by Boniface IX, took place with great pomp on 8 October 1391. On account of the great schism which had split the Church at that time, the validity of the canonization was questioned. The bull of canonization of Birgitta and her Order were confirmed by John XXIII in 1414; and after the schism had ceased, Martin V, after another investigation, signed a confirmation in 1419.[30]

B. *The Revelations of St. Birgitta*[31]

The works of many mystics show careful revision and study. Their writings are the result of a conscious reconstruction, caused either by the advice of a confessor or produced out of their own theological knowledge. Birgitta, on the other hand, immediately after beholding a vision, wrote down the revelation, or dictated it to an amanuensis if she were too ill to write it herself. She wrote in Swedish, and one of her confessors translated the revelation into Latin. This translation was then read to her that no word might be omitted or changed. The original was often destroyed, but Peter of Alvastra wrote the Latin in a book which developed into the **Revelationes Celestes**.[32]

It is this lack of supplementation and literary revision which differentiates Birgitta's visions from others of their type.[33] Her revelations were usually the result of some particular situation or occasion. A friend would inquire about the condition of a dead relative; shortly afterward, Birgitta would not only have a revelation which showed the condition of the soul of the dead person, but could also inform the anxious relative what alms or prayers would shorten the stay of the deceased in purgatory or alleviate his sufferings while there.[34] Or if the wickedness of a king or the worldliness of a prelate needed correction, Birgitta would receive a revelation in which Christ or the Mother of God denounced his sin in no uncertain words. After such a vision had been revealed and written down, a copy of it was made and immediately sent to the inquiring friend or offending sinner.[35] The lack of revision in the revelations shows itself in repetitions, useless elaboration, and frequent lack of cohesion and unity of thought.

If the revelations show lack of conscious literary style, they are strong in imaginative versatility. Birgitta had an unusually active imagination, and her descriptions of hell and purgatory, of Christ's crucifixion, and of incidents in the life of the Blessed Virgin Mary, stand out vividly. She prefers concrete representations to abstract theological discussions. She does not propound universal dogmas, as does Hildegard of Bingen; her visions are not rationally and consciously constructed as are those of Elizabeth of Schönau.[36] However, her fifth book (**Liber Questionum**) could (with very little rearrangement) be turned into a popular theological tract. These defects, however, do not obscure the positive literary qualities which the revelations possess. Through her visions Birgitta exercised a remarkable authority over the laity as well as over the kings and prelates of her time. The drastic strength of her warnings and the profuse wealth of images which her visions contain explain the popularity which they have enjoyed. The revelations are given a high place in Swedish literature of the Middle Ages by literary historians of the present day.

Notes

[1] The main authorities for the life of Birgitta are the *Vita Sanctae Birgittae* (edited in S.R.S. iii, pp. 185-206, by C. M. Annerstedt), which was written within four months after her death by her two confessors, Peter, prior of Alvastra, and Peter Olafson, the first confessor of Vadstena; and the later *Vita Sanctae Birgittae* (A.S., pp. 485-93), by Birger, archbishop of Upsala. The *Vita Abbreviata,* published in the first printed edition of her revelations, and also printed in Durantus's edition, uses the revelations themselves as a chief source. C. M. Annerstedt (S.R.S. iii, pp. 186-88) has a full list and critical discussion of the *Vitae.* Klemming (v, pp. 244-58) gives a list of manuscript lives and printed biographies up to 1884. The best

modern critical biographies are by Fr. Hammerich, *Den hellige Birgitta og Kirken i Norden,* Copenhagen, 1863; Comtesse de Flavigny, *Sainte Brigitte,* Paris, 1892; and K. Krogh-Tonnung, *Die heilige Birgitta, Sammlung illustrierter Heiligenleben,* Band v, Kempten and München, 1907.

[2] The earliest authorities differ (S.R.S. iii, p. 189, note *k*).

[3] Birgitta is her correct name, and not Brigitte, Brigida, or Bridget. Birgitta is probably from Brighitta (cf. A. Noreen, *Altschwedische Grammatik,* 339. 2), borrowed from Irish (Brighid), which is from (brigh), virtue, strength. . . . Cf. Fr. Stark, *Sitzungsber. d. Kais. Akad. v. Wissenschaften,* Phil.-hist. Classe, Wien, lix. 2. 196-7, 1868.

[4] S.R.S. iii, p. 190.

[5] Durantus, ii, p. 476 (*Vita Abbreviata*).

[6] S.R.S. iii, p. 225, *De Processu Canonizationis Birgittae,* depositio Katerinae filiae Birgittae, super quarto articulo.

[7] S.R.S. iii, pp. 191, 225. Their continency was probably due as much to their youth as to piety, which is the reason given by her biographers.

[8] The title 'Princess' of Nericia or Sweden was often given to Birgitta. C. M. Annerstedt has shown conclusively that she had no real claim to the title (S.R.S. iii, p. 188, notes *c, d, e*).

[9] S.R.S. iii, p. 209, *Chronicon de Genere et Nepotibus Sanctae Birgittae,* auctore Margareta Clausdotter, abbatissa Vadstenensi.

[10] Durantus, ii, pp. 530-53, *Vitae Divae Catherinae.*

[11] S.R.S. iii, pp. 191-2.

[12] S.R.S. iii, p. 193.

[13] A.S., p. 404, no. 151. Some of the early accounts say that it was a year or two after Ulf's death, but the weight of evidence seems to be that Christ chose her to be 'sponsa mea et canale meum' within a few days.

[14] S.R.S. iii, p. 194, note *k*. This revelation forms the first chapter of the Garrett MS.

[15] *Revelationes Extravagantes,* ch. 8: 'Christus loquitur Sponsae existenti in Monasterio Aluastri, dicens: Vade Romam, & manebis ibi, donec videas Papam, & Imperatorem, & illis loqueris ex parte mea verba, quae tibi dicturus sum. Venit igitur Sponsa Christi Romam, anno aetatis suae xxxxii, & mansit ibi iuxta diuinum praeceptum xv annis, antequam veniret Papa, videlicet Vrbanus V & Imperator Carolus Boemus. Quibus obtulit Reuelationes pro reformatione Ecclesiae, & Regulam.' Birgitta did not see Urban V until 1367, over twenty years later; see A.S., p. 444, nos. 317-18, for an attempt to explain this chronological discrepancy.

[16] S.R.S. iii, p. 202, notes *m, n, o.*

[17] A.S., p. 406, ch. xi.

[18] In *Revelationes Extravagantes,* chs. 74 and 77, Birgitta flays Magnus Erikson, the king of Sweden, and his court for their worldliness; she also visited and rebuked the king personally. Book VIII, called *Liber Celestis Imperatoris ad Reges,* has denunciatory revelations which were sent to many kings and queens. Although the revelations seemed to have but little effect on their lives, Birgitta must have instilled a wholesome fear in the hearts of those to whom she wrote, for she was received with the greatest consideration and respect wherever she went.

[19] See 5/20-6/12 of the text for an outspoken statement concerning the condition of the Church.

[20] Bk. IV, ch. 33.

[21] Alphonso the hermit, formerly bishop of Jaën, wrote the *Prologus* of Book VIII and edited Birgitta's revelations in 1377.

[22] Durantus, ii, pp. 351-70, *Regula Sancti Salvatoris.*

[23] A.S., p. 445, no. 322.

[24] S.R.S. i, pp. 1-224, *Diarium Wazstenense ab anno 1344 ad annum 1545,* edited by E. M. Fant.

[25] The monastery of Syon House, of the Birgittine Order, was founded by Henry V in the manor of Isleworth, in Middlesex, in 1414-16. It became one of the richest monasteries in England. See William Dugdale, *Monasticon Anglicanum,* London, 1830, pp. 540-4; G. J. Aungier, *History and Antiquities of Syon Monastery,* London, 1840; J. H. Blunt, the preface to *The Myroure of Oure Ladye,* E.E.T.S., E.S. xix, pp. xi-xix.

[26] Bk. VII, ch. 1.

[27] On the death of her son Charles at Naples see note on 117/37-118/1 of the text.

[28] Durantus, ii, p. 480; A.S., p. 462, no. 389.

[29] Sven Gronberger, *St. Bridget of Sweden, American Catholic Quarterly Review,* vol. xlii, 1917, p. 145.

[30] A.S., pp. 409-18, chs. xii-xiv.

[31] Birgitta's revelations reach a total of over 650.

[32] Klemming (iv, pp. 177-85) has edited the only two fragments of Birgitta's handwriting which have been preserved.

[33] In the *Sermo Angelicus* and the fifth book of the revelations (*Liber Questionum*) there is evidence of a re-ordering of the material.

[34] See note on 116/27.

[35] S.R.S. iii, pp. 196-7.

[36] Westman (pp. 151-259) compares Birgitta with the other mystics of her time. . . .

Roger Ellis (essay date 1982)

SOURCE: "A Note on the Spirituality of St. Bridget of Sweden," in *Analecta Cartusiana*, edited by Dr. James Hogg, Institut Für Anglistik Und Amerikanistik, 1982, pp. 157-66.

[*In the following essay, Ellis focuses on St. Birgitta's spirituality and the metaphorical nature of its exposition in her* Liber celestis.]

The present paper aims to describe the principal features of the spirituality of St. Bridget of Sweden, as revealed by her biographers and presented in the work which they collaborated with her in producing, the *Liber Celestis*.[1] Any discussion of Christian spirituality, it seems to me, rests upon assumptions like the following: (i) Christianity, the unity of man with God in and through Christ, by means of a single and perfect act, is as yet imperfectly realised. (ii) This partial realisation, which we call Christianity, is represented at any one time by the total Christian tradition then available, in relation to the particular perspectives on that tradition possessed by its followers. (iii) Such perspectives, however imperfectly, enact a man's sense of relationship with God, and presuppose their own communication. (iv) The individual perspective defines itself in relation to both the ideal and actual realisations of Christianity: in relation to the former, because it hopes to bring the realisation of the ideal closer; in relation to the latter, either by confirming its truths or by challenging its limitations. (v) Discussions of Christian spirituality therefore requires us to consider the interrelation between a person's experience, his articulation of that experience, and the deposit of tradition, as both he and his hearers/readers understand it.

The tradition within which St. Bridget operates, and which she faithfully presents to her readers, is that of a centralised (Latin) church under attack from without and betrayed from within: from without, by pagan practice (6.78A, 6.82A); by non-Christian religions (the most regularly cited is Judaism, eg 2.5, 4.61D, normally with reference to its historical rejection of Christ, and with explicit parallels to his rejection by most Christians, (eg 1.30A, 1.37); by schism (7.19F); and, from within, by heresy (7.7-8: of course, this category is capable of almost infinite extension);[2] by immorality and error among the faithful (references, for example, to the apostasy of the three estates, as at 1.56); and by a corresponding depravity among the leaders (the most potent symbol for this is the 'Babylonian captivity' of the Papacy at Avignon). Ranged against these enemies, as at 1.41, which so names pagans, Jews, the Pope, and evil Christians, we have the Saints, and God's few faithful friends on earth, a pattern echoed in 2.3, where the Pope is dropped from the list and an extra category created for those Jews and pagans willing to become Christians. The spirituality of St. Bridget is therefore, like that of the Old Testament prophets, one of crisis and judgement, whose central feature is a stark opposition of saved and damned, and whose central note a call to repentance and greater holiness of life.

This position has several important ramifications. St. Bridget understands her own relation to God, typically, in terms of what Riehle has called 'a spiritual sense perception':[3] that is, she encounters God with the immediacy of sense-perception, and can use metaphors of sensation to elucidate her experience of him (of course, insofar as they manifest themselves by physical signs, accessible even to independent observation, these experiences are metaphoric only in relation to God: though to say this is not to claim for all such references in the *Liber* the status of a literal experience.) Thus, God and good men may be encountered as a sweet smell, evil men as a foul smell (6.18C), or as sweet and bitter tastes respectively (*A et P* pp. 24 (art. 36), 96-7, 'De speciali signo spiritus'; and cf 1.54A). More importance attaches to St. Bridget's experience of God by way of her other spiritual senses, conveniently described for us in 2.18A, and many times repeated. There we learn that the Saint saw and heard God by way of physical images, and experienced him as a palpable motion in her breast. The *Liber,* a book of visions and revelations, is the record of the first two gifts, as Julian's book is of hers.[4] Occasionally the Saint declares her inability to comprehend or record what she saw and heard (4.50, 8.48, *Rev. Extrav.* 49) but the basic character of the message, like that of the third gift, is its absolute certainty (see below). Though there is little direct reference in the *Liber* to the third, it is regularly declared superior to the others, perhaps because God is operating no longer through images but directly upon the consciousness of the Saint. Elsewhere, this third motion is compared to the movement of a child within the womb (6.88: the accompanying revelation, given on Christmas Eve, urges a parallel with the Virginal conception of Christ). It is probably to be equated with the fire of love *(calor)* which St.

Bridget is recorded to have possessed, and whose seat similarly was the heart (7.4A and cf *A et P* p. 98 'ante lectum'). The motion, she is told, will last and increase according to the capacity of her heart to bear it (6.88).

These three gifts, a direct consequence of the Saint's total conversion to the spiritual life, as described in *A et P* pp. 80-81 (though earlier visions and revelations are recorded: *A et P* pp. 76-80), accompany, and are the principal effect of, that quietly wakeful and concentrated gaze on God described in the following from 7.27:

> vni persone in oracione vigilanti et contemplacioni vacanti, dum staret in raptu eleuacionis mentalis, apparuit Ihesus Christus (cf 6.52A).[5]

This ravishing *(raptus)* is itself manifested by physical signs, most notably the Saint's appearance as 'semi-mortua' (*A et P* p. 210); her failure to respond to a question, even though she could hear it as clearly as the words of the revelation then being given to her (p. 627: elsewhere, though, she is said to hear and see nothing going on around her, p. 15); lastly by hugging her arms to her breast (***Rev. Extrav.*** 116). Servants knew the signs well enough, it seems, to leave her alone when once she went into an ecstasy on horse-back (Prologue to Book 5: she received the whole Book in this ecstasy). Such gifts are not open to question. The revelations and visions are many times compared with those recorded in the Bible, including even the glorified humanity of the risen Christ (eg Zachariah 1.20D, prophet and Magi 1.32B, Moses 1.60, 2.10A, E, Christ 2.10E). They are declared the last, and most recent, in a series of spiritual benefits which began with the creation of man (2.17). They are not obscure like the words of the Apocalypse, nor to be hidden, like those seen by St. Paul in his own ravishing to the third heaven (1.56D, an image used elsewhere: see below). The grace of *calor* regularly appears in discussions on the discernment of spirits (eg 1.4, 1.54) as an infallible sign of the operation of the Spirit.

Of other spiritual graces recorded, the most notable is probably that of ecstatic prayer. Several such are declared inspired by the Saints (eg 3.29C, 4.21A, and most notably the **Quatuor Oraciones**), and their 'proof' is to be sought, *inter alia,* in a traditional but startling declaration of love, the so-called 'impossible supposition':[6] the Saint would choose not to be, or to live forever in Hell, rather than that the divine objects of her love should lose one point of their glory (7.1, ***Rev. Extrav.*** 63: Christ often uses a variant of this pattern to declare his abiding love for mankind eg 1.1c, 1.30A, 2.5B: 'si possibile esset . . . libenter adhuc semel morerer pro vobis').

These gifts can be considered as ends in themselves, in which case they talk about man's final unity with God as realised, and realisable, on earth, and advance a striking claim for the sanctity of the recipient; or they can be studied in relation to their end, in which case they speak to us of a process in which we are all involved. St. Bridget has much to say about this context of the gifts, but her teaching is not as clear or as single as her account of the gifts considered as ends in themselves. 6.14, for instance, charts the Saint's spiritual progress, by way of a double metaphor, from a little taste, and from childhood, through a greater appetite, to spousehood (and thence to the maturity, 'ad etatem', of adulthood, ie heaven), under three stages: (i) God seen in relation to the worldly goods given by him and used by the Saint; (ii) God, superior to worldly goods, now seen in relation to the Saint's own will (practices of abstinence, and attempts to do good works in the name of God); (iii) God seen as the only good (abandonment of the Saint's will to him). Elsewhere, though, similar patterns are used not to chart the progress of individuals but to describe an ideal social or religious state. In 4.2, for instance, we have three groups of men ('modica . . . minor . . . minima'). All three, as friends of God, offer their hearts to him. The first acknowledge their created state, and propose to use the world's goods 'ad sustentationem et refectionem carnis'. The second recognise the vanity and instability of the world, and give up their will to another (possibly by entering a religious order). The third declare their willingness to die for God. Presumably these three groups represent individuals at different stages of spiritual growth ('ever the higher the fewer' as the old phrase has it). We could therefore compare this revelation with 6.14, and identify the spiritual/physical martyrdom of the third group here with St. Bridget's abandoning of her will to God in the third stage of 6.14 (no very difficult conclusion to draw). But elsewhere, at 3.27, these stages of holiness are appropriated to an idealised account of the three estates; the text assigns positive, comparative and superlative degrees respectively, and in terms similar to those already seen, to marriage (laity), religious life, and knighthood ('carnem suam dederunt pro amore Dei').[7] Comparable elements also occur in 3.21, a revelation describing how St. Benedict's rule and order find place for three stages of men, simple monks, confessors and teachers, and martyrs: the first keep their monastic vows, the second give up love of worldly things and seek only the honour of God and the instruction and profit of others; the third desire to die for Christ. And there are other parallels which one could adduce (eg 4.85, ***Rev. Extrav.*** 40).

In other contexts this use of the one pattern both to map an individual's experiences and to depict an ideal society might point to a writer's conviction that the one set of experiences exemplifies and is exemplified by the other (hence readiness to die for the love of God, according to the context, is the defining property of knights, martyrs, and *perfecti:* and see further discussion of 1.18 below).[8] Here, though, the use in so many different contexts of the one pattern suggests that the content of the pattern, counts for less than the fact of the patterning itself. Spirituality, that is, is to be defined primarily in terms of the fundamental orientation, whether of an individual or of a society, towards God. The stages or states of the spiritual life, as an accidental consequence of that orientation, can be treated more casually, without too great a regard for consistency. We can put this another way: in treating the three degrees as, so to speak, the arbitrary creations of the human mind, the *Liber* democratises the spiritual life. The three groups of men in 4.2 may be at different stages of spiritual development, but, as far as they are able, they have all offered their hearts to God, and are all God's friends. Similarly, it is revealed in *Rev. Extrav.* 40 that the Brigittine order will contain those who seek to make God after their own image, with little interest in receiving the fullness of the divine sweetness. Yet, though they bring forth poor fruit (and, by a neat inversion of the metaphor, do not perfectly taste the will of their spouse), they remain one of the three fruits of the Order. In their degree, they will share in the benefits even now being experienced by those who, seeking only the sweetness of God, have abandoned themselves to him, and become 'sicut iumentum et non homo' (the third, and best, fruit of the Order).

A single felicitous image focusses this sense of the unity of the spiritual life with beautiful clarity. In 2.22A spirituality is compared to two different kinds of motion, linear and circular. At first we have the image of a laborious ascent of a high and cloud-topped mountain: the process is painful ('in via duricia lapidum . . . difficultas et preruptum est in ascensu'), but the end is that blessed glowing darkness spoken of in ch. 26 of *The Cloud of Unknowing* ('habebis quod exterius est tenebrosum sed intus fulgidum'). To this is added the image of circular movement:

> quasi circulus circumuoluitur, et adtrahet te sibi magis ac magis, dulciter et dulcius, donec leticia ab omni parte tempore suo perfundaris.

Beautiful though these two metaphors are, neither is adequate in isolation. The first, like that other traditional metaphor the ladder, invites consideration of the spiritual life as so many distinct stages: the second, like that other traditional metaphor the sea, describes endless process without progression. When the two motions are brought together, as in *The Consolation of Philosophy,* they serve typically only to contrast those who remain on the outer rim of the divine circle (hence subject to circular motion) where they acknowledge God's rule only partially and indirectly, with those journeying towards the centre (and thus the object of linear motion) and a fuller participation in the divine simplicity. St. Bridget brings the two motions together

into a kind of mystic spiral. This image, first used in ps.-Dionysius only as an alternative to the other sorts of motion, was not widely used in mystical writing, but it is extremely fruitful.[9] The logic of the spiral, as the conjunction of linear and circular motions, is that states and processes of spirituality cannot be spoken about except in relation to one another. And since Christ is himself the circle, process and end inevitably coalesce. A final complication of the metaphor is perhaps to be seen in the account of the soul, so to speak, drowned in joy ('perfundaris'): that is, ascent to God is also, as Dante discovered when he made the reverse journey in the *Inferno,* descent *into* God.

Prominent in several of the revelations so far discussed are other traditional metaphors for the spiritual life (particularly those of tasting and seeing, metaphors which, as earlier noted, St. Bridget's own spiritual experiences claim to have actualised and made literal). A most interesting one occurs in 4.81C, a revelation contrasting worldly and religious tears. The former spring from loss of worldly good and fear of the last things; the latter from mind of the love of God in Christ. The latter are compared to dew rising from, and returned as rain to fructify, the earth under the influence of the sun. The metaphor receives a very individual exposition: the dew is the soul's love for God (the earth) rising into the brain (the sky) and, warmed by the heat of God's love in the heart (the sun) returned as tears to the eyes, and producing the fruit of good works. The whole point of the metaphor is summed up in the closing words of the exposition:

> lacrime que ex diuina caritate funduntur claudunt deum in anima et deus animam in se trahit.

As so often in mystical writings, the exposition suddenly and dazzlingly threatens the stability of the metaphor. Agent and patient are so drawn together in the one loving act, whose rising and falling motion comprises an all-encompassing circle, that we can hardly distinguish them, or their respective actions, from one another (or, as Julian put it, 'in the soul is God and in God is all').[10]

But the Saint has other, less comforting, ways of describing the soul's relation with God. She presents herself not just as a visionary but also as a person liable to error, needing information about even basic points of doctrine, and bearing a weight of personal sin past and present from which she needs freeing. Hence she humbly requests enlightenment about a difficulty (3.18D-E). At other times we see a heavenly speaker anticipate a difficulty which she may be considering so as to answer it for her (1.26C, 1.47C), or question her so as to lead her to a new understanding (1.40A). Except when in the grip of an ecstatic utterance, the Saint reacts to the divine message with anxiety (1.4A) or bewilderment (2.15A, 2.18B). Sometimes, similarly, she will acknowledge her past sins; at other times a heavenly speaker will bring them to her notice in order to explain particular difficulties now besetting her (1.32B, 3.19A, 3.28A, 3.29A); at other times she is made aware of present sin, which will exact an inevitable penalty (1.12). Not the least of her sins, though not presented as that, is a tendency to judge a person by appearances (3.22: only a spiritual grace, like that of the sweet or bitter smell, enables her to judge a person's character truly). This sense of sin co-exists with heightened utterance, the necessary makeweight to everything St. Bridget wrote about the graces of the spiritual life. Practically every passage earlier considered in this essay occurs in a context of sin and judgement, whether of St. Bridget herself or of society at large, which receives as much attention. Frequently, indeed, such a passage will be placed at the beginning of a revelation, not so much for its own sake but rather as an authentication of the divine judgements which it introduces. Thus 3.29 begins with a prayer of adoration to the Virgin as the true 'templum Salomonis', in that she housed the true Solomon, Christ. But it ends with a plea for mercy, the only virtuous act of which the Saint is capable, because her own temple

> contrarium omnino tuo est. Est enim tenebrosum viciis, lutosum ex luxuria, corruptum ex cupiditatis vermibus, instabile ex superbia, labile ex vanitate mundanorum.

In context, this conventional picture sometimes seems little more than the religious equivalent of the modesty *topos* so beloved of medieval writers, a device to encourage faithful and faithless alike to seek for the mercy experienced by their representative, the Saint, in the moment of her ecstatic prayer. But the life of the Saint, as presented by her biographers, shows that it was no mere literary convention. We may characterise that whole life, indeed, as the co-existence of extraordinary graces and extreme physical rigours. Examples of the latter include the knotted cords she wore about her body (*A et P* p. 99: these, rotted with age, were kept by her disciples after her death and shared with others as a special favour, pp. 258, 450 'super x articulo'); the callouses on her knees as a result of her many kneelings (this detail we owe to the Bull of Canonization of 1391, which describes them, disarmingly, as like those of a camel); the wounds she inflicted on her body every Friday, as a memorial of the Passion, by dropping burning wax upon it (if such wounds healed, she scratched them open again, *A et P* p. 99); and the bitter herb she put into her mouth similarly every Friday, and whenever she spoke idly (*ibid*). These practices stand in a variable relation to the spiritual graces earlier described. Sometimes they mark a soul's distance from God, and need to atone for sin; sometimes they show a soul's identification with the crucified Christ; sometimes they are dispensed with altogether as irrelevant to the processes of unification with God

(thus, while St. Bridget, throughout her life, sought, and followed, spiritual direction, dispensations from rule and custom were granted occasionally on the grounds of God's being above all rule: *A et P* p. 81, 'Quomodo in principio'); at other times, they and the extraordinary graces are declared identical (cf ***Rev. Extrav.*** 63 on obedience to both St. Agnes and 'magistro tuo, qui ambo informant . . . de vno spiritu'). Traditionally, they are the means by which the soul comes to the graces of the spiritual life. Thus 1.15 explains that, when a man has accustomed himself to, and interiorised, the labours of ascesis, he will experience as spiritual grace what formerly he experienced, and outsiders still see, as pain and labour: 'sedent in sede que pungere videtur—quietissima tamen est' (1.15H).

All this leads to the conclusion, already insisted upon, that, however we define the stages of the spiritual life, we cannot usefully distinguish them from one another. At each such stage God calls upon us, whether directly by means of a heightened experience or utterance, or indirectly in cooperation with our preliminary labours of ascesis, to acknowledge him, and renounce sin, more wholly. A last indication of this can be seen in the obligation laid upon the mystic to act as prophet and preacher, and to participate not only in his own conversion but also that of others to the spiritual life.

The production and dissemination of the ***Liber*** is, of course, the primary fulfilment of this obligation (eg 1.52B-C), to which reference occurs many times in the work: at 4.128, where a hermit priest's question if he does well, from time to time, to come down from his solitude and contemplation to give counsel and encouragement to his neighbours, is answered decisively in the affirmative; in 2.14H, where Sts. Peter and Paul are made models for the practice (Paul's 'contemplation' is probably to be identified with his ravishing to the third heaven, Peter's with his participation at the Transfiguration);[11] and in 6.65I, where Martha's sister Mary, as a type for the contemplative, is urged to open her mouth ('os predicacionis sue') and generate spiritual sons for God. Elsewhere, preaching, normally understood as the action of speaking, occasionally open to the wider interpretation of witness through service, is declared the summit of the spiritual life (1.43B) and enjoined upon the Christian (1.22B, 1.26I: St. Bridget had a special devotion to such spiritual discourse, *A et P* p. 78, 'de lectura'). The generation of spiritual sons is many times declared the principal purpose of God's word to St. Bridget (eg 1.20D 'ego per te volo generare mioni multos filios . . . spirituales.'). This act of generation can be understood with particular reference to the conversion of individuals, or more generally: the two categories imply one another. A specific example of the former comes with St. Bridget's dealings with the young Eliacius of Sabrano, who came to ask her advice about his manner of living. She received him 'quasi in filium' (*A et P* p. 323) and transmitted a revelation to him (7.5). As a result, he was moved to change his life, and thereafter publicly called St. Bridget his spiritual mother (*A et P* pp. 524-5). An example of the latter, describing conversion in general terms, comes in 1.60, which presents three classes of men and predicts salvation for all of them: those who do not believe in God; those who believe in God, but doubt the message which the Saint claims to have transmitted from him; and those who believe in God and the message of his Saint.

The Saint is forgivably vague about the process whereby the first kind of men will become the sons of God (though, interestingly, she sees more hope in pious pagan and virtuous Jew than in a wicked Christian, eg 1.41, 1.59E, 2.3, 6.83, and she even forecasts Christ's abandonment of the latter to convert the former, 1.57, a prophecy which gives some point to her narrative of the conversion of a pagan woman, 6.50). But she knows of one way, at least, of carrying out this work. She will found a religious order, to whose members she will be, as she has continued to this day, their mother. Revelations predicting a general conversion may therefore also be prophesying, implicitly or explicitly, the creation of the new Order. In support of this claim, we may note (i) close verbal similarities between 1.60, already noted, and **Rev. Extrav**. 19, a revelation about the founding of the Order; (ii) the use of one revelation in two different places in the **Liber,** once to provide instruction about the foundation of the Order (**Rev. Extrav**. 30), once to give more general information about the requirements of the spiritual life (1.18: hence Peter of Alvastra could speak of the chapter as treating 'de vera humilitate', *A et P* p. 489). That is, the spread of the Order is a sign of, if not actually co-terminous with, a general conversion, and the graces which will characterise it ('vera humilitas') will be those of Christianity itself. A key image for this process is that of the Biblical Exodus. Its importance can be gauged from the prominence given in the **Liber** to those Saints who founded religious orders or were associated with the development of religious life (2.7 Anthony, 3.17 Dominic, 3.21 Benedict, 7.20 Francis).

A final word, by way of conclusion and, perhaps, of warning. The spirituality of St. Bridget, as revealed by the literary sources (the canonization documents and the **Liber Celestis**) is unlikely, for a number of cultural and historical reasons, to attract, or speak to the situation of, the modern reader. Its methods are those of medieval religious art, and the sermons for which the Saint had such affection; its perspective so strikingly medieval—even as we read, we feel the person disappearing into the Saint—that we find no easy entry into the experience of which it speaks. Yet it remains, a profoundly ambiguous witness, to remind the Christian that he is always living in the last days, that he has

an obligation to greater personal holiness, and that he must bring his neighbour with him into the Kingdom. The spirituality of St. Bridget is more attractively revealed elsewhere, in the Order which she founded but did not live long enough to enter.

Notes

[1] For biographical information, the primary witness is *Acta et Canonizacionis Beate Birgitte,* ed. I. Collijn, *SFSS* Ser. II, Bd. 1 (Uppsala, 1924-31), hereafter *A et P,* particularly a *Vita* (pp. 73-102), for discussion of which, see S. Ekwall, *Vàr äldsta Birgittavita, KVHAAH,* Hist. Ser. 12 (Stockholm, 1965). For such Books of the *Liber Celestis* as have appeared in critical editions (Books I, V, VII, the *Regula Salvatoris,* the *Sermo Angelicus,* and the *Reuelaciones Extrauagantes,* hereafter *Rev. Extrav.,* consult the bibliography in *St. Birgitta Revelaciones Book I,* ed. C. -G. Undhagen, *SFSS* Ser. II, Bd. VII:1 (Uppsala, 1978) Sub Bergh, Eklund, Hollman. For all other parts of the *Liber* (ie Books II-IV, VI, VIII, *Quatuor Oraciones*) and related texts, like the Bull of Canonization, consult the *editio princeps* by B. Ghotan (Lubeck, 1492). Reference to the *Liber* in the present essay is by book, chapter and letter subdivision of the Ghotan edition.

[2] On this general point, see G. Leff, *Heresy in the Later Middle Ages,* 2 vols. (Manchester, 1967).

[3] W. Riehle, *The Middle English Mystics,* trans. B. Standring (1981), ch. 8 (the quotation comes from the chapter title).

[4] Julian's work has a further point of connection with the *Liber.* With her threefold gift 'be bodily sight and by word formyd in my understondyng and be gostly sight' (*A Revelation of Love,* ed. M. Glasscoe (Exeter, 1976), ch. 9, p. 11) compare—and more appropriately, in my view, than the comparison usually offered with the teaching of St. Augustine—the following, from *Liber* 3.5B, a variant of the pattern in 2.18: 'placuit deo. . . . vocare te in spiritum sanctum ad videndum et audiendum et intelligendum spiritualiter.'

[5] I have discussed *Liber* 6.52 more fully in 'A Revelation and its Editors', *IRIS* 1 (forthcoming).

[6] This phrase comes from F. Vernet, *Medieval Spirituality* (1930): see pp. 184-8 for discussion.

[7] The placing of knighthood, instead of the religious life, at the summit of the spiritual life is a striking, occasional, feature of the *Liber.*

[8] One could adduce as a rough parallel the close connection between an individual's experience and the social forms that experience assumes, in the opening chapter of *The Cloud of Unknowing.*

[9] For ps.-Dionysius, see *Dionysius the Areopagite on the Divine Names and the Mystical Theology,* ed. and trans. C. E. Rolt (1920), *The Divine Names,* ch. 4, pp. 98-9. It is elaborated, and discussed, by St. Thomas (*STh* II[a] II[ae] q. 180 art. 6, the Commentary on the *Divine Names* IV.7, and the Commentary on the Sentences Lib. I, Dist. 37, q.4, art. i. This information I owe to the kindness of the late Fr. Gervase Matthew, O.P.

[10] For other images of mutuality in the *Liber,* see, eg, 3.20B (God as fire made by air and the breath of man), 4.2E (God as a pair of scales).

[11] On Peter at the Transfiguration as a type of the contemplative who must come down from the mountain, cf St. Augustine: 'Quid dicis, sancte Petre? Mundus perit, et tu secretum quaeris! Video tot gentes in unum convenire et tu quietem diligis' (source, *Ludolphus de Saxonia Vita Jesu Christi,* ed. L. M. Rigollot, 4 vols. (Paris, 1878), III.19b).

Hans Aili (essay date 1984)

SOURCE: "St. Birgitta and the Text of the *Revelationes.* A Survey of Some Influences Traceable to Translators and Editors," in *The Editing of Theological and Philosophical Texts from the Middle Ages,* edited by Monika Asztalos, Almqvist & Wiksell International, 1984, pp. 75-91.

[In the following essay, Aili studies the changes effected by Latin translators and by Alphonse of Jaén— the chief revisor of Birgitta's work—in the text of the Revelations.*]*

1. *Introduction.*

In recent scholarship on the Revelations of St. Birgitta of Sweden, the question has been raised, to what extent the surviving Latin version of the Revelations forms an older version of the text, as compared to the Old Swedish text, which has been retained in different versions in several manuscripts.[1] Moreover, in a recent paper, Jan Öberg[2] has raised the issue, whether the Revelations ought to be regarded as an authentic text or as an authorised version of the original text, as it was conceived by its author.

Both issues are vital in the Revelations: for, as is well known from various documents pertaining to Birgitta's canonisation[3], not only were the Revelations as we know them translated from Birgitta's original Old Swedish into Latin, but they were also revised by several persons, not wilfully but according to an expressly worded mandate[4]; in Birgitta's usual style, this mandate is couched in a revelation given to her from God. Moreover, the Revelations in their extant Old Swedish form are in many, probably even most instances, translated from the Latin text. As the latter was in all probability regarded as the authoritative version by Birgitta and her circle of friends, the originals were consequently lost or intermingled with those Revelations which were translated backwards, as it were, from Latin into Old Swedish.

In the greater part of the Birgitta corpus we thus face a situation where the original text, as written down by Birgitta herself in Old Swedish or dictated by her in that same language to her father-confessors, has been translated into Latin; this Latin text has later been re-translated into Old Swedish.

In a few isolated instances, however, we still possess the original Revelations text. This is the case in the two fragments belonging to Kungliga Biblioteket in Stockholm, which have been proven by Bertil Högman to be Birgitta's autographs.[5] Furthermore, there are also a few chapters among the ***Revelationes extravagantes,*** in the Prologue to Book I of the Revelations and in the final pages of Book IV[6], which in their Latin version represent a younger state of the text than does their Old Swedish counterpart. Finally, Sten Eklund has demonstrated in a recent paper that the extant Old Swedish text of the ***Quatuor oraciones*** represents an older stage of this text than does the Latin version; consequently, Eklund insists that the conclusion reached by Bergh in his edition of Book V of the ***Revelationes***[7], where the Latin text appears generally to have the priority, should not be considered a general rule for the entire Birgitta corpus. Each book—or even each chapter—must be considered separately.

This paper will deal with both issues mentioned above, first of all by presenting the text of one Revelation of Book IV, where in my opinion the Old Swedish text of the introductory paragraphs may represent an older stage in the history of the text than does the Latin one; this passage has not been discussed in this context before. Secondly, this paper will deal with one aspect of the issue of authenticity of the Revelations text, by illustrating the work performed by the foremost 14th Century editor and reviser of the Birgitta corpus; this man is the Spaniard, Alphonso Pecha de Vadaterra, formerly Bishop of Jaén, later Birgitta's father-confessor in Rome.

The common denominator of the two parts of this paper is the search for the original version of the Revelations text and the attempt to pinpoint, but certainly not delete[8], words or phrases which have been added to the text by Birgitta's translators and editors.

The text discussed in the first part of this paper is printed in its two extant versions, in Old Swedish and in Latin. In order to facilitate the investigation, both texts have been translated by myself into English. My translation is not intended or expected to have any literary value, but is only prepared as a service to those readers who do not read Old Swedish—the translation from the Latin is chiefly included in order to illustrate the similarities or dissimilarities of the texts.

2. *Latin and Old Swedish*

We now proceed to the examination of the text of that Revelation where I suspect the Latin version to represent a younger state of the text than that of the Old Swedish version. This Revelation is the 24th of Book IV, the text of which runs as follows in its Latin and Old Swedish versions.

Verba Virginis ad filiam, qui modus tenendus sit inter seruos Dei contra impacientes et qualiter superbia per dolium designatur. Capitulum XXIIII.

1 Mater loquitur: "Vbi dolium vini incalescit et intumescendo excrescit, ascendunt quedam exalaciones et spume, quandoque maiores quandoque minores, et subito iterum decrescunt. **2** Omnes autem circumstantes dolium considerant tales exalaciones cito detumescere et quod tales eleuaciones proueniunt ex fortitudine vini ad minuendum (K *tertia manus:* uniendum *codd.* innuendum *ed. princeps*) calorem eius. Ideo pacienter spectant finem et vini seu ceruisie perfeccionem. **3** Omnes autem circumstantes dolium, qui nimis applicant nares ad feruorem dolii, contingent eis duo: aut nimia sternutacio vel commocio aut cerebrum grauius pacietur.

4 Sic est eciam et spiritualiter. Nam contingit aliquando, quod quorundam corda intumescunt et ascendunt ex superbia mentis sue et impaciencia; quem ascensum viri virtutum attendentes considerant aut ex instabilitate animi aut motu carnalitatis procedere. **5** Ideo pacienter verba sustinent et attendunt finem scientes, quod post tempestatem fiet tranquillitas, et quia paciencia maior est expugnatore urbium, quia vincit hominem in se ipso quod difficillimum est. **6** Illi vero qui nimis impacientes sunt verbaque reddunt equipollencia non attendentes retribucionem gloriosam paciencie nec quam contemptibilis est fauor mundanus. **7** isti incurrunt infirmitatem mentis suis temptacionibus propter impacienciam, quia nimis appropinquant nares ad commocionem dolii, id est verba, que non sunt nisi aer, nimis apponunt cordi suo.

8 Ideo, quando videritis aliquos esse impacientes, ponite adiutorio Dei custodiam ori vestro, nec dimittatis bona incepta vestra propter verba impaciencie, sed dissimulate, in quantum iustum est, audita tamquam non audita, donec illi qui inuenire volunt occasionem exprimunt verbo quidquid notant corde."

Ed. H. Aili (forthcoming).

In my translation this runs:

1 The Mother speaks: "Whenever a jar of wine grows hot and rises and swells, some vapours and froth rise, sometimes larger sometimes smaller and suddenly decrease again. **2** And all those who stand around the jar consider that such vapours quickly subside and that such swellings are produced by the strength of the wine in order to lessen its heat. Therefore, they patiently await its end and the completion of the wine or ale. **3** But all those who, standing around the jar, put their noses too close to the heat of the jar, to them two things will happen: either a very strong sneeze or agitation or else the brain will suffer greatly.

4 It is also thus in a spiritual sense. For it sometimes happens that some men's hearts swell and rise with the arrogance and temptation of their minds; virtuous men, noticing this swelling, consider that it proceeds either from an instability of the mind or from a carnal impulse. **5** Therefore, they patiently endure words and consider the end, in the knowledge that there will be calm after the storm and that patience is greater than he who conquers cities, for it overcomes man in himself which is a most difficult thing. **6** But those who are too impatient and return words of the same meaning, without considering the glorious repayment of patience nor how contemptible is worldly favour, **7** these meet with feebleness of mind through their temptations, due to their impatience, for they put their noses too close to the agitation of the jar; that is, they take words, which are nothing but air, too much at heart.

8 Therefore, whenever you see somebody being impatient, with God's help put a guard over your mouth and do not desert the good you began for the sake of impatient words, but ignore, so far as is just, what you have heard as if you had not heard it, until those who wish to find an opportunity reveal by words whatever they mark in their hearts."

The Old Swedish text runs:

At hauande tholomodh xxiiij^m.

< **1** > GWZ modhir taladhe Huar ölkar görs ther ophöghir sik hwadhin bradhelica oc nidhirfallir sköt, < **2** > Ok the som när standa vitande at tholik oplyptilse vardhir aff ölsins makt bidha thy til at ölit är fulkomplica giort oc nidhirlagt < **3** > Än thom som näsana halla mykyt när til ölkarsins hita händir äntigia at the niusa hardhelica älla at hiärnin röris oc värkir hardhelica.

< **4** > Swa är oc andelica thy at stundom händir at somlica manna hiärta thrutma oc opfar aff sins hugx högfärdh oc otholomodh Än dygdha män vitande the höghfärdhinna framga aff hugxins ostadhoghet oc kötsins rörilsom < **5** > vmbära hardh ordh tholomodhelica akta ändalyktena vitande at lughn skal koma äptir storm Ok at tholomodhsins dygdh är meere

oc maktoghare än thän som vindir hallande hus thy hon vindir mannin j sik siäluom, hulkit som är vansamlicast. < **6** > Än the som äru mykyt otholuge vidh ordh oc atirgiälla jämpn ordh älla värre ey aktande ärofullo tholomodzins lön, oc ey huru smälikin värlzins thokke är < **7** > the koma j sins hugx ostadhughet oc frestilse oc nalkas ofnär til ölkarsins rörilsa thz är at the sätia ordhin som ey ära vtan som vädhir ofnär sino hiärta,

< **8** > thy nar j seen nakra vara othologha tha sätin gömo jdhrom mun mz gudz hiälp oc forlatin ey the godho gerning som j hauin byrghiat for otholamodz ordha skuld Vtan tholin ok vmbärin ordhin som j hördhin äptir thy skälikit är sua som j hafdhin ey hört thom Thil thäs the som vilia finna tilfälle mot jdhir oppinbara mz ordhom huat the mena j hiärtano.

Ed. G. E. Klemming: *Heliga Birgittas Uppenbarelser,* Stockholm 1860. (Paragraph numbers within brackets have been added by me.)

The Old Swedish text runs in my translation:

1 The Mother of God spoke: "Wherever a vat of ale is made, there froth rises suddenly and quickly subsides. **2** And those who stand close by and know that a rising of this kind is caused by the strength of the ale, thus wait until the ale is completely made and has settled. **3** But those who put their noses very close to the heat of the vat, to them either happens that they sneeze violently or else that the brain is agitated and aches strongly.

4 It is also thus in a spiritual sense. For it sometimes happens that some men's hearts swell and rise with the arrogance and impatience of their minds; virtuous men, noticing this swelling, consider that is proceeds either instability of the mind and the carnal impulse. **5** suffer hard words patiently and consider the end, knowing that a calm will come after a storm and that the virtue of patience is greater and more powerful than he who conquers strongholds, for it overcomes man in himself which is a most difficult thing. **6** Now those who are very intolerant of words and return equal words or worse, without considering the glorious repayment of patience nor how contemptible is the world's favour, **7** these fall into feebleness and temptation of their minds and approach too close to the motion of the vat of ale; that is, they take words, that are nothing but air, too much at heart.

8 Therefore, whenever you see somebody being impatient, put a guard over your mouth with God's help, and do not desert the good deed that you have begun for the sake of impatient words, but suffer and tolerate the words you heard, so far as is just, as if you had not heard them, until those who wish to find an opportunity against you reveal by words what they plan in their hearts."

We immediately notice that the first three paragraphs of the Old Swedish text gives a much shorter version than does the Latin text; the latter derives its greater length, not from a more ample subject-matter, but from sheer wordiness. The description this text offers of a rather commonplace household process, namely the brewing of ale, is so complicated and abstract that it is difficult at a first glance to decide what exactly it is that Birgitta is describing. In paragraph 1, *Vbi dolium vini incalescit et intumescendo excrescit* corresponds to the Old Swedish (in my translation) "When a vat of ale is made". In Latin, the process of brewing ale is described by a set of verbs that really indicate circumstances concomitant to the fermentation. Forthermore, "ale" in the Old Swedish corresponds to "wine" in the Latin, a difference which can be attributed to a desire to make the text conform to its future readers' experience.[9]

In paragraph 2, the Latin words *tales exalaciones cito detumescere* are a mere repetition from paragraph 1, and add no new information.[10] In the same paragraph, *Ideo pacienter spectant finem et vini seu ceruisie perfeccionem* corresponds to the Old Swedish "thus wait until the ale is completely made and has settled". The vacillation in the Latin text, giving both wine and ale as the subject-matter of the Revelation, is remarkable: in this case, it appears that the Latin translators added the words *vini seu* on their own accord, forgetting to leave out *ceruisie*. The Old Swedish text lacks a counterpart to the Latin *pacienter;* the absence of this word may indicate an error in the history of transmission of the Old Swedish version, as we note that the whole revelation is a treatise on the importance of being patient. *Finem* appears to correspond to a verbal phrase in the Old Swedish ("is completely made") in the same manner as *perfeccionem* corresponds to "has settled".

From this comparison of the three first paragraphs we may reasonably conclude that one of the two versions printed represents an editorial revision of the text; in my opinion, the differences between the versions, taken together, lend more support to the theory that the Latin version represents a more advanced stage of revision, and is therefore secondary, from the historical point of view, to the Old Swedish version. Repetition of phrases, circumlocutions instead of straightforward description, abstract nouns used in the place of more concrete verbal phrases all signify an attempt to polish a pithy, but stylistically fairly unsophisticated Old Swedish text into a more elaborate literary artifact.

The contrary hypothesis—the theory that the Old Swedish text has been translated from the Latin version—would presuppose a Swedish translator who permitted himself a great deal of freedom, achieving a translation which is close to being a paraphrase of the exemplar. A certain amount of paraphrasing and purging did occur in the Old Swedish re-translations, as Bergh demonstrates in his edition of Book V[11]; the general tendency of the Old Swedish re-translations is, however, to adhere as closely as possible to the Latin, giving a text which is, if anything, even more verbose than the Latin.[12] One typical feature of the translations is to construe abstract Latin words with two, nearly synonymous Swedish words. The passages discussed should have offered plenty of opportunity for this activity, but, as we can see, no such double renderings can be observed in the Old Swedish version of the first three paragraphs of this revelation.

Furthermore, if my theory of the priority of the Old Swedish version of these paragraphs over the Latin version can be accepted, it is fairly easy to understand why the Latin text should have been expanded in this fashion. Besides any possible stylistic considerations, the translators must have had in mind to remove the subject-matter from the brewing room of a provincial Swedish noble house, into an international context, readily intelligible to a Roman or French magnate of the Church—hence we notice the vacillation between wine and beer in the Latin. Moreover, the translators, being Swedes, would be much more familiar with the brewing of ale than with the fermentation of grapes, and their translation would suffer in precision accordingly.

"Brevior lectio potior" is a time-honoured dictum of textual criticism, which one might be tempted to introduce into this discussion, where the text considered to have the priority is so much shorter than that which is considered secondary; but this would not be entirely correct. For there are many instances in the Revelations, where it is the longer text which is to be considered to be older. Such is the case in many passages of Birgitta's autographs, discussed by Bertil Högman.[13] In either case, however, the elder version gives evidence of being thematically and stylistically less polished than the Latin one, irrespective of the relative lengths of the versions.

In the remaining five paragraphs of Rev. IV:24, the situation is rather different from that obtaining in those paragraphs discussed above. Linguistically, the Old Swedish text bears certain evidence of being, in fact, a retranslation from the Latin. This is indicated by such syntactic traits as the usage of the objectum cum infinitivo construction after the verb "vita" ("know") in paragraph 4: "vitande the högfärdhinna framga" ("knowing that this arrogance proceeds"). Furthermore, the use of the present participle as participium coniunctum also indicates an influence from a Latin exemplar; such instances are the use of "vitande" in paragraphs 2 (sic!), 4, 5 and of "ey aktande" ("without considering") in paragraph 6.[14] Finally, as Lennart Moberg demonstrates[15], the two Old Swedish conjunctions corresponding to the English "that": "at" and

"thet", are used indiscriminately in original Old Swedish texts, whereas "thet" almost never occurs in Old Swedish translations from the Latin. In the Old Swedish version of Rev. IV:24, there are no less than nine instances of "at" and none of "thet". The fact that one instance of "vitande" and four of "at" occur in the first three paragraphs may appear to contradict the theory introduced above, but I consider this evidence of lesser weight than that adduced for my theory, as neither usage appears to pertain exclusively to the translations from the Latin.

Finally, there is no indication, in the two versions of Rev. IV:24, that either text is to be regarded as the direct exemplar of the other; for there are a number of instances in both versions where the text is less complete than in the other version. The Old Swedish text thus lacks counterparts to the Latin words *ad minuendum calorem eius*[16] and *pacienter* of paragraph 2 and of *propter impacienciam* of paragraph 7. The Latin text on the other hand contains no words corresponding to the Old Swedish "hardh" < *dura* > of paragraph 5, "älla värre" < *vel grauiora* > of paragraph 6 or "mot jdhir" < *contra vos* > of paragraph 8.

Furthermore, in paragraph 7 the phrase *incurrunt infirmitatem mentis suis temptacionibus* corresponds to an Old Swedish phrase which, in Latin retranslation would run *incurrunt infirmitatem mentis sue et temptaciones.* More interesting, perhaps, is the reminiscence from the Vulgate, *Proverbs* 16,32: *expugnatore urbium* which in the Old Swedish has been rendered "som vindir hallande hus" ("who conquers strongholds"). It is impossible to tell whether the erroneous Swedish word for "stronghold" was introduced in the re-translation from the Latin of this part of the Revelation, or whether it existed already in the original Revelation and was corrected in the Latin version into conformity with the text of the Vulgate.

We may therefore assume that the first part of this Revelation, that is paragraphs 1 to 3, has descended in its two versions from a common exemplar, an Old Swedish text very close to Birgitta's original, whereas the second part, paragraphs 4 to 8, goes back in its Old Swedish version to a Latin exemplar not identical with that Latin text published above. The first part of the Revelation gives, as we have seen, a text which is probably closer, in its Old Swedish version, to the text of Birgitta's original. The second part is, on the other hand, probably a re-translation from a Latin exemplar.

The question then arises, why the Old Swedish editors should have chosen to use different exemplars for these two parts of the revelation. The answer in my opinion is to be found in the fact that the two parts also form the two main thematical units of the revelation, paragraphs 1 to 3 giving its *mise en scène,* as it were, whereas paragraphs 4 to 8 give the theological and spiritual interpretation of the rather commonplace process introduced.

It would hardly be remarkable, if the Old Swedish editors had found the Old Swedish version of the introduction far more useful as an effective introduction to the situation than the Latin version; on the other hand, the latter version had, as the editors must have known, passed through the hands of a number of learned editors who had been entrusted with the mandate of correcting the text from all errors on dogma. Small wonder, then, if the Old Swedish editors preferred this version in that part of the revelation where theology matters most.

In this connexion we may also ask whether the tendency observable in the three first paragraphs, where the Latin version describes a technical process in an abstract language full of circumlocutions, is an indication of a general policy adopted by the translators of this text, when confronted with a description of this kind. Much more research will be required to answer this question.

The most important conclusion to be drawn from the investigation above is the confirmation it offers of the results reached by Eklund, Öberg and other modern scholars on the Birgittine Revelations; consequently, the argument, that the text belonging to this corpus must be studied closely in order to identify any possible sections where the Old Swedish version represents an older stage of the text than does the Latin version, has gained considerably in force.

The main point in this connexion is the following: the revelation discussed above does not belong to any identifiable greater thematic unit of the Revelations, in a manner comparable to the other instances where the priority of the Old Swedish text has already been accepted. The revelation in this instance is instead embedded, as it were, in the middle of a mass of text where, so far as I have reason to believe, the Latin text has the priority. This means that we cannot assume that the Latin text of Book IV has generally a greater priority that the Old Swedish text, any more than we can assume that the Old Swedish text represents an older stage, generally speaking. We have no alternative but studying the Revelations separately and in detail.

The fact that there is no general rule for the relationship between the Old Swedish and Latin versions of Birgitta's text is best exemplified by Rev. IV:49, the text of which has reached us in no less than three main versions, first of all in Birgitta's own handwriting—this is the so-called A-autograph—secondly in the extant Latin version, which has been considerably revised as compared to the autograph, and thirdly in the Old Swedish re-translation of the Latin text.[17]

Why, we may reasonably ask, did not the Old Swedish editors of the 15th Century adopt the text of Birgitta's autograph, which was in all probability kept at their very place of work, the Library of Vadstena Cloister?[18] The explanation might be simple negligence on their part, but this is a rather unlikely explanation when we consider the methods of manuscript classification used at Vadstena Cloister.[19] A better explanation is that they may have decided against using the autograph and favoured instead the more polished Latin text. Due to the controversial nature of this Revelation, which is, in effect, a programme for abolishing a number of abusages within the Church, a rather rough and unfinished text, like that of the autograph, was more likely to give offence than that of the Latin version, which had passed the expertise of the ex-bishop Alphonso. Whatever the explanation, however, the implications remain the same: the Revelations must be studied in detail in their two versions, in order to establish in each individual case which version is closer to the original.

3. *Alterations made by Alphonso of Jaén*

We now turn to the second topic of this paper: the survey of influences due not to translators, but to one particular editor of the text of the Birgitta corpus, the ex-bishop and hermit Alphonso of Jaén, one of Birgitta's closest friends during her final years in Rome. It was to him the task was given to edit her Revelations, with the purpose of verifying their correctness from the dogmatical point of view, as well as polishing their Latin to the standard expected by the Roman Curia.

Alphonso's contribution to the literary form of the Revelations is most important: briefly, it was probably he who arranged the huge mass of Revelations, as yet only sporadically collected into coherent units, into seven books. He also excluded passages or even entire Revelations that he judged to be unsuitable in view of his expectation that Birgitta's Revelations were to be used as evidence in the process for her canonisation. He was probably also responsible for formulating the rubrics given to the various Revelations; this he did while editing the text of the seven Books of Revelations.[20]

Besides the seven Book of Revelations, the **Sermo angelicus** and the **Quatuor oraciones,** the original **Liber celestis revelacionum** in Alphonso's redaction also contained a collection of some fifty Revelations, whose contents was of such a nature that they could be regarded as Mirrors of Kings. These form a separate book, entitled **Liber celestis Imperatoris ad reges,** wholly arranged by Alphonso and provided with a preface written by him, the *Epistola Solitarii ad reges*. This book was later to be called Book VIII of the Revelations.

In the *Epistola,* Alphonso defends the notion of the heavenly origins and inspiration of the Revelations, providing definitions for separating such Revelations from visions inspired by the Devil. He also explains how he collected these potential Mirrors of Kings from among the other Revelations, and why. We can thus be sure that the Revelations contained in Book VIII have passed through Alphonso's hands. Since Alphonso had been given a fairly extensive mandate to revise the text of the Revelations. . . . it would be interesting for us to know to what extent he did use that mandate in this collection of Revelations.

Fortunately, the question can be answered. For within the **Liber Imperatoris ad reges,** that is Book VIII, no less than 26 Revelations were culled from the books already edited, namely Books II, III, IV, VI and VII. Ten of these Revelations were taken from the most voluminous book, the fourth.

We are thus in a position to study a few examples of the editorial changes which can be attributed to Alphonso. As far as I know, the relationship of those Revelations that occur both in Book VIII and in the earlier books, has as yet only been studied by Salomon Kraft[21], whose study on the Revelations text, when dealing with the present subject, treats mainly of Alphonso's technique in assembling the text of Rev. VIII:1 by utilising parts of Rev. VII:30, III:26, II:13 and II:7, as well as adding certain phrases of his own making. Kraft notes Alphonso's great liberties in rearranging the text to its new purpose. Latterly, the subject has also been discussed from another viewpoint by Jan Öberg.[22] The reason for this subject having been otherwise left aside is probably to be found in the way these double chapters—by which I mean chapters which belong both to Books II to VII and to Book VIII—have been copied in manuscripts and printed editions.

Even at a relatively early stage in the history of this text, the medieval copyists appear to have realised that the twenty-six Revelations mentioned occur twice in the corpus, and probably saw no reason to write down identical texts, as they most likely considered them, twice over. Therefore, one Revelation in each pair was generally disregarded by the scribes. The technique in this case was to write down the Rubric and Incipit of the Revelation in question; then a reference was given: *Require libro ad reges capitulo < tali >.* In the manuscripts belonging to the class which contains not only Alphonso's original redaction but also the supplementary material disregarded by him[23], Revelations are scrapped and references given with varying degrees of consistency: the problems connected with this system of referring the reader from one part of the work to another is a subject which I plan to deal with in another paper. It is, however, nearly always the case that the text is retained in Book VIII and left out in the earlier books.

In the *Editio princeps,* printed by B. Ghotan in Lübeck in 1492, the editors for some reason decided to adopt the opposite policy, printing each double Revelation the first time it occurred, that is in Book II to VII, giving only short references in Book VIII. Nonetheless, the text actually printed in Ghotan's edition is usually that edited by Alphonso for Book VIII: it was thus transported, as it were, from Book VIII into an earlier book.

But there still exists a group of manuscripts which contain only the text according to Alphonso's original redaction and lack all supplementary material. Among the manuscripts belonging to this group may be mentioned Ms. 225 of Balliol College, Oxford, and Ms. 498 of the Pierpont Morgan Library, New York. Their value as witnesses for the tradition of the text of the Revelations has only been established by the modern Birgitta editors, notably Bergh.[24] In this group of manuscripts, the double Revelations occur twice each: first in Book II to VII, then again in Book VIII. These manuscripts thus provide all available evidence for answering the question of how Alphonso's revisions of the Revelations of Book VIII affected their text.

The first example to be discussed here is from Rev. IV:48 which corresponds to Rev. VIII:7.

> Book IV:
> *Verba Filii ad sponsam de quodam rege . . .*
>   *Capitulum XLVIII.*
>
> 1 Filius loquitur: "Si iste velit me honorare, minuat primo dedecus meum et augeat honorem meum."
>
> Ed. H. Aili (forthcoming).

> Book VIII:
> *Christus imperator dicit regibus . . . VII.*
>
> < 1 > Filius Dei loquitur ad sponsam de quodam rege Swecie dicens: "Si iste rex velit me honorare, minuat primo dedecus meum et augeat honorem meum."
>
> Text according to *Codex Kalmarnensis,* at present in Lund University Library.

In this example we note two stages in Alphonso's revision of the text. While editing Book IV he added, as mentioned above, a rubric to the text; in this rubric he states explicitly that the Revelation deals with a king, a fact which is not apparent from the wording of the Revelation proper. The rubric thus gives . . . *de quodam rege;* the text only gives *iste.* In Book VIII there have been further revisions: a rubric has been written, and the text has been amplified by a new piece of information: *de quodam rege Swecie* and *iste rex.*

The reason for these modifications appears to be quite obvious: in a Mirror of Kings, the text must be shown to deal with kings, not with ordinary mortals.

I have assumed that it is, in fact, Book VIII which has been altered by Alphonso, not Book IV. It might be argued against this assumption that the text in Book VIII could represent the elder version, and that Alphonso may have expurgated or trivialised this text while editing Book IV. This activity would then have been carried out with the same purpose as when he excluded entire Revelations from the first seven Books. But in this case, why did he retain all these potentially damaging items in Book VIII? If all these pieces of information were dangerous, in the sense that they helped identify the persons involved, they would have been much more risky to include in Book VIII, which is of a rather restricted size; in the enormous bulk of Book IV, these snippets of personal information would be far less noticeable, and proportionally less dangerous.

It appears far simpler to assume that Alphonso, when editing his Mirror of Kings, added such words and phrases as would motivate the inclusion of the Revelations in question in this book. Such information Alphonso could easily find in his own, intimate knowledge of Birgitta's history and relations.

Alphonso's revisions have not been without consequences for modern scholarship; by adding information on his own initiative to the text he has, at least in one instance, given the text a doubtful value as a historical source. This passage is found in the following example.

Book IV:

Verba Dei ad sponsam de duobus spiritibus, scilicet bono et malo; et de mirabili et utili bello in mente cuiusdam domine orto ab inspiracionibus boni spiritus et a temptacionibus maligni spiritus; et quid in istis sit eligendum. Capitulum IIII.

1 Deus loquitur sponse: "A duobus spiritibus suggeruntur et infunduntur cogitaciones et infusiones in cordibus hominum, a bono spiritu scilicet et a malo. 2 Bonus nempe spiritus suadet homini celestia futura cogitare et temporalia non amare. Spiritus malus suadet diligere que videt, leuigat peccata, allegat infirmitates, proponit exempla infirmorum. 3 Ecce dico tibi exemplum, quomodo uterque spiritus inflammat cor illius domine tibi note."

Ed. H. Aili (forthcoming).

Book VIII:

Christus ostendit sponse cogitaciones suggestionum boni et mali spiritus, que in corde regine supra proximo dicte certabant inter se; et determinat Deus, quid ipsa de illis debeat eligere. XIII.

< 1 > Christus loquitur sponse dicens: "A duobus spiritibus suggeruntur et infunduntur cogitaciones

et infusiones in cordibus hominum, a bono spiritu et malo. < 2 > Bonus namque spiritus suadet homini futura celestia cogitare et temporalia non amare. Spiritus vero malus suadet homini diligere illa presencia que homo videt, leuigat peccata, allegat infirmitates et proponit exempla infirmorum. < 3 > Ecce dico tibi exemplum, quomodo uterque spiritus inflammat suggestionibus cor illius regine, de qua iam alias dixi tibi."

Text according to *Codex Kalmarnensis*.

In this context, the last few words of paragraph three are interesting. We note that whereas Book IV gives the words *cor illius domine tibi note* ("the heart of this lady, known to you"), Book VIII gives *cor illius regine, de qua iam alias dixi tibi* ("the heart of this queen, of whom I have already spoken to you elsewhere"). "Elsewhere", as we find in the rubric to this chapter, means in the preceding chapter (No. 12) of Book VIII. The rubric in Book IV is entirely neutral and does not mention that the lady was a queen, nor is this chapter preceded by another Revelation dealing with the same lady. As a matter of fact, Rev. VIII:12 does not correspond to the text of any other Revelation in the corpus, so far as I can find; it was therefore probably copied by Alphonso from some manuscript fragment now lost.

The two chapters in Book VIII, Nos. 12 and 13, have been taken to refer to Blanche of Namur, Queen of Sweden, the spouse of King Magnus Erikson.[25] But, as we have seen, all information leading to this conclusion is given by Alphonso; the older version of the Revelations text offers no such information at all. The historical source value of this Revelation in the version given in Book VIII and disseminated into the early printed editions, is therefore much reduced; for Alphonso is only a secondary source to the identity of the persons mentioned in the Revelations, whatever the scope of his personal knowledge.

Alphonso did not confine himself to adding political information of the kind just mentioned. The following example reveals his ambition to clarify obscure passages.

Book IV:74:

1 Filius Dei loquebatur sponse dicens: "Tu composuisti hodie, quod melius esset preuenire quam preueniri. Sic ego preueni te dulcedine gracie mee, ne Dyabolus dominaretur anime tue."

Ed. H. Aili (forthcoming).

Book VIII:34:

< 1 > Christus loquebatur sponse dicens: "Tu in gramatica composuisti hodie prouerbium, quod melius esset preuenire quam preueniri. Sic ego te

dulcedine gracie mee preueni, ne Dyabolus dominaretur anime tue."

Text according to *Codex Kalmarnensis.*

The text according to Book IV is direct and forceful as an opening to a conversation, but it does leave the ordinary reader wondering what had been going on: "You composed today that it were better to anticipate than to be anticipated." In Book VIII the text is far more explicit: it was in her daily *gramatica,* that is in her grammar or Latin lesson, Birgitta had composed this proverb, doubtless as an essay in using the Latin active and passive infinitives.

The text may be clearer, but we may well question whether Alphonso, in his eagerness to leave no detail unexplained, has not deprived the conversation of one of its outstanding characteristics: its air of being a private talk between two persons who knew each others' daily activities well enough to dispense with the formality of lengthy introductions.

A final example, taken from the middle of the same Revelation, shows another aspect of Alphonso's work: the elimination of doubtful dogma.

Rev. IV:74:

24 . . . Omnis quippe qui diligit proximum tenetur primum dolere, quod omnes qui sunt redempti sanguine Ihesu Christi non rependunt Deo dileccionem."

Ed. H. Aili (forthcoming).

Rev. VIII:34:

< **24** > . . . Omnis quippe homo qui diligit proximum tenetur primo dolere, quod omnes redempti sunt sanguine Christi, qui tamen omnes non rependunt Deo dileccionem" (non rependunt Deo dileccionem *in rasura per* K[2] *scriptum est*).

Text according to *Codex Kalmarnensis* (= K).

The text as given in Book IV suggests that not everybody has been redeemed by the blood of Christ: "Of all those who have been redeemed . . . not every one repays." Alphonso emends this doubtful statement economically, but not entirely effectively:[26] "Everybody has been redeemed . . . but not every one repays."

The full investigation into Alphonso's work as a reviser and emender of St. Birgitta's Revelations must await the publication of the modern editions of her text. In this paper I have only been able to give a few examples from those Revelations which coincide with my own sphere of work, namely Book IV. We may hope that a future examination of this kind will not only provide details on Alphonso's work on Book VIII, but will also yield clues that will help us identify his

handwriting, so to speak, even in other Revelations, where no material for comparison is at hand.

To sum up the discussion in this paper, I have tried to demonstrate how the Revelations text has been influenced by revisions from two different directions, from its translators and from its chief reviser, Alphonso. The result of the first part of my investigation is to underline again the necessity of studying the two versions in which the Revelations have been handed down to us, the Old Swedish and the Latin version. The primary aim of such a programme of study is to help produce reliable editions of the two versions; the ultimate aim is to reach beyond these versions and to attempt to reconstruct the lost original version of the Revelations text, when it had been formulated and revised by Birgitta herself and was not yet translated into Latin. Needless to say, the latter aim will never be but partly achieved; I hope, however, that this paper has demonstrated that the work will nonetheless be worth doing.

The second part of my investigation is a step into a land which is still largely unchartered, and deals with the marks left by Alphonso upon the text of Birgitta. In this area, too, we may confidently expect that future investigations will yield rich results.

Notes

[1] Cf. especially B. Högman, *Heliga Birgittas originaltexter,* Uppsala 1951; J. Liedgren, "Magister Matthias svenska kungörelse om Birgittas Första stora uppenbarelse. Ett förbisett dokument i Riksarkivet," *Meddelanden från Svenska Riksarkivet* för år 1958, Stockholm 1961, pp. 101-116; S. Eklund, "A Re-assessment of the Old Swedish Bridgettine Text Corpus," *Kungl. Humanistiska Vetenskaps-Samfundets i Uppsala Årsbok 1983-84,* Uppsala.

[2] Öberg, J.: "Authentischer oder autorisierter Text? Der Weg von Konzept zu moderner Edition an Beispielen von Petrus de Dacia und der Heilligen Birgitta." Published in the present volume, pp. 59-74.

[3] *Acta et processus canonizacionis beate Birgitte,* Ed. I. Collijn, Uppsala 1924-1931, pp. 3-11 (= SSFS: *Skrifter utgivna av Svenska Fornskriftsällskapet,* Ser. 2, Latinska skrifter I).

[4] St. Birgitta, *Reuelaciones extrauagantes,* Ch. 49, Ed. L. Hollman, Uppsala 1956 (= *SSFS,* Ser. 2, Latinska skrifter VI).

[5] Cf. note 1 above.

[6] The priority of the Old Swedish version of the Prologue to Rev. Book I was demonstrated by J. Liedgren (Cf. note 1, above); concerning Rev. Book IV, cf. K. B. Westman, *Birgitta-studier,* Uppsala 1911, p. 54.

[7] Bergh, B., Ed., St. Birgitta, *Reuelaciones* Book V, Uppsala 1971, p. 16-33 (= *SSFS*, ser. 2, latinska skrifter VII:5). Eklund (cf. note 1, above), following L. Moberg ("Heliga Birgittas första uppenbarelse i magister Mathias svenska version", *Studier i nordisk filologi* 62, Skrifter utgivna av svenska litteratursällskapet i Finland 490, Helsinki 1980, p. 193-211) maintains that the fact that the Old Swedish text is mainly a translation from the Latin need not imply that the Old Swedish translator used the Latin text as his only exemplar, as we cannot exclude the possibility that this translator also had access to an older, Old Swedish version. While true enough in itself, this argument does not refute Bergh's general conclusion as to the priority of the Latin text over the Old Swedish.

[8] It must be emphasised that the task of editing the Latin version of the Revelations is to be regarded as an endeavour parallel to that of editing the Old Swedish version; readings from one version may help elucidate problematical readings of the other one, but cannot justify extensive changes. As far as the Latin version of the Revelations is concerned, the original version to be reconstructed must be the so-called original of Alphonso. For the history of Alphonso's original, cf. C.-G. Undhagen, Ed., St. Birgitta, *Reuelaciones* Book I, Stockholm 1978, p. 14 ff. (= *SSFS*, ser. 2, Latinska skrifter VII:1).

[9] A striking instance of this desire is to be found in Rev. III:7, where the Latin word *testudo* ("tortoise") corresponds to the word "snighil" ("snail") in the Old Swedish version; the obvious reason for this change is the translator's desire to render the text intelligible to the medieval Swedish reader, who was not likely to know of tortoises. Since snails are not unknown in the Mediterranean countries, the revision is in this case not likely to have occurred when the text was first translated into Latin.

[10] *Eleuacio* is used here in a sense ("the rising of fluids") which I have only been able to find in two instances, in the *TLL*, both of which are considered to be allegorical expressions: Ambros. Iob 4, 5, 19 p. 280, 16 *ubi advertit David, quod elevationes fluctuum saecularium super se venirent,* and Hier. In Ion. 2, 4 p. 1153D: *quaerimus . . . quomodo omnes elevationes et gurgites et fluctus dei super salvatorem transierint.* Cf. *Thesaurus linguae Latinae* V. 359, 3-6.

[11] Bergh (cf. above, note 7) p. 24.

[12] Cf. Wollin, L., *Svensk latinöversättning*, I. Processen, 1981, II. Förlagan och produkten, 1983, Lund (= *SSFS*, Häfte 251-252), particularly part II, section 2.2 (summarized in English p. 162).

[13] Högman (cf. above, note 1) p. 35-37. In many passages, the Latin translation of the text corresponding to the autographs is more concise, rather than the opposite, as Högman notes on p. 51 ff. Quite correctly, he attributes both tendencies to a desire on the part of the Latin translator to achieve a more polished text.

[14] I owe this point to Dr. Lars Wollin of Lund, who has also pointed out to me that the Old Swedish edition by Klemming, being based on only one manuscript (Cod. Holmiensis A 5 a) gives a text that is in many respects inferior to that given by other Old Swedish Birgitta manuscripts, namely Cod. Holmiensis A 5 b, A 110 and Cod. Upsaliensis C 61. The latter manuscripts will therefore be a better basis for future comparisons between the Old Swedish and Latin versions. In the present instance, the difference between the edition of Klemming and the Old Swedish manuscripts named above is not great enough to change my conclusions concerning Rev. IV:24.

[15] Moberg (cf. above, note 7) p. 204 ff.

[16] All manuscripts collated for this edition read *uniendum,* which I can only construe as "in order to make it hot all through." Here, I have adopted the reading *minuendum,* which is the emendation suggested by manus tertia of *Codex Kalmarnensis,* as I consider this reading contextually superior and quite reasonable from the paleographical point of view.

[17] Högman (cf. above, note 1), p. 30 ff.

[18] Högman (cf. above, note 1), p. 18 ff.

[19] Cf. *Kulturhistoriskt lexikon för nordisk medeltid,* I, Malmö 1956, col. 523.

[20] Undhagen (cf. above, note 8), p. 14 ff. with further references.

[21] Kraft, S., "Textstudier till Birgittas Revelationer," *Kyrkohistorisk årskrift,* 29 (1929), p. 133-137.

[22] In his paper entitled "Kring Birgitta" (Kungl. Vitterhets Historie och Antikvitets Akademien, *Filologiskt arkiv* 13, Stockholm 1969) Öberg discusses a number of Revelations which show evidence of having been intended as letters to various politically important adresses: in some of these texts there exists an older version from which the letter was formulated. This is the case in Rev. III:10, which is an older version of a text that reappears in a shape which bears traces of having been adapted to an epistolary form, in Rev. IV:78.

For the present discussion, the relation between Rev. VII:18 and VIII:22, correctly established by Öberg, is most interesting, as in this instance it is the version in Book VIII that appears to represent an older stage of the text; VII:18, on the other hand, is clearly an epistolary redraft of the text, which contains instructions for the young King of Cyprus, Peter II, and his uncle, Jean de Lusignan, Prince of Antioch.

This observation clearly contradicts my own conclusions presented below; the solution to this dilemma probably lies in the fact that VII:18/VIII:22, just like III:10/IV:78 mentioned above, represent two stages in the drafting of a letter. When editing Book VII, Alphonso would have selected the most polished form of the text, whereas on the other hand a formulated letter would be less suitable for a Mirror of Kings.

[23] Undhagen (cf. above, note 8), p. 4 ff.

[24] Bergh, B., Ed. St. Birgitta, *Reuelaciones* Book VII, Stockholm 1967, p. 94 (= *SSFS*, ser. 2, Latinska skrifter VII:7) with further references.

[25] B. Klockars states this in her excellent treatise, *Birgitta och böckerna*, Stockholm 1966, p. 49 (= Kungl. Vitterhets Historie och Antikvitets Akademiens handlingar, Historiska serien 11), without, however, citing any external source for her theory.

[26] Several colleagues have pointed out that Alphonso's version of the text suffers from an ambiguity; for, whereas his main thought is clear, the words, *tenetur primo dolere, quod omnes redempti sunt,* yield the unfortunate impression that the redemption was the cause of the pain. A better expression would have been: *tenetur primo dolere, quod, cum omnes redempti sint . . . tamen omnes non rependunt.*

Barbara Obrist (essay date 1984)

SOURCE: "The Swedish Visionary: Saint Bridget," in *Medieval Women Writers*, edited by Katharina M. Wilson, The University of Georgia Press, 1984, pp. 227-39.

[*In the following essay, Obrist surveys St. Birgitta's life and influence, as well as the contents, style, and intent of her* Revelations.]

Bridget, the fourteenth-century Swedish mystic, left a canon of revelations widely read in the vernacular at the end of the Middle Ages, especially in the fifteenth century. She was an incult lay author, meaning that she did not Know Latin and thus wrote or dictated her revelations in Swedish. These were gradually translated into Latin by her confessors—Mathias, canon of Linköping cathedral; Petrus Olai of Skenninge; and Prior Petrus Olai of Alvastra. Only later were they retranslated into the vernacular. Despite these permutations, the specific features of what must have been Bridget's language seem preserved. These revelations, most very brief, consist of speeches addressed to her

by Christ and Mary or by Saints Agnes and John the Baptist, and of visions such as the torments of Christ and of human souls.

Bridget was born in 1303, the seventh child of one of the richest and most powerful families in Sweden. Her father, Birger Persson, was the lawman of the province of Uppland and resided in Finsta, close to Uppsala. We know little about Bridget's education, but she probably learned to read and write from the castle chaplain. She no doubt read mainly the lives of saints.[1] At the age of thirteen, she married Ulf Gudmarsson, before long the lawman of West Gotland (Närke); she bore eight children. By no means was her life to remain domestic, for she was summoned to the court at Stockholm (circa 1336) as a mistress in the royal household of young King Magnus and his bride, Blanche de Namur. In the beginning, Bridget seemed to have a great influence on the royal couple.[2]

In 1341, accompanied by others, Bridget and her husband undertook a pilgrimage to Santiago de Compostela. On their return, Ulf retired from his legal functions; he died in 1344 at the Cistercian abbey of Alvastra. After her husband's death, Bridget had her first revelations. The *Acta et processus canonizacionis* describes the visible signs of her conversion to spiritual life: she experienced convulsions of the heart, a sign that Christ had been born into it.[3] Among the early revelations are those concerning the foundation of a new order to be located in Vadstena; consequently, in 1347, Bridget moved to the court of Stockholm in order to obtain the approbation of the king and clergy for its foundation.

In her first years of widowhood, she encouraged King Magnus in his plans for war against Finland, and she seems to have been suspected as early as 1347 of wanting to push her son Karl onto the throne. Later, from Rome, she issued at least one prophecy supporting the insurrection of Swedish nobles against the king, predicting a new regent. Not surprisingly, this prophecy corresponds to a propaganda tract of the opposing party circulating in Sweden.[4]

Until her husband's death, Bridget had led the life of a Swedish nobleman, with its social duties. We have no undistorted view of this part of her life because of what she became as a widow: a visionary working miracles. As early as 1373, her confessors Petrus Olai of Skenninge and Petrus Olai of Alvastra supplied two *vitae* for use at the process of canonization (1377-1391).[5] Thus, her entire life was recast in the very strict forms of hagiography, since the criteria for canonization, in addition to working miracles, involve living a perfectly virtuous life. Bridget's early life was therefore stylized in the following manner. While still in the womb, she saved the ship her mother was on. At the age of seven (an important date in a saint's life), she had her first contact with Mary, who later helped her embroider a work of supernatural beauty. She entered into marriage as a duty but never forgot her spiritual goals. She frequently visited the poor and followed ascetic practices. Finally, after her husband's death, she gave away all her possessions.[6] However, there is evidence that she only complained of the burden of wealth and that as a widow she continued to be a landowner.[7] Such evidence raises problems about how we should evaluate the information that makes up the tradition of Saint Bridget.[8]

If she had not traveled to Rome, where she remained until her death in 1373, Bridget would most likely have become a saint of limited local importance in a peripheral country. But in Rome she became an influential supporter of Church politics. Her early vision of a new canonical order was realized after great difficulties in 1370. Ultimately she was canonized in 1391, for a combination of emotional, political, and even economical reasons. Less than fifty years later, grave doubts about the authenticity of her claims to sainthood diluted her importance in the official Church; but her native Sweden defended her as its patron saint (as she was named in 1396), and her revelations continued to be well known.

Bridget submitted her revelations to her confessors, who examined them for orthodoxy and who ultimately arranged them into seven books. The collection was probably completed shortly after her death in 1373. In 1391 an eighth book, the **Liber celestis imperatoris ad reges,** was added by the bishop-hermit Alfons de Jaen, who supervised the editing of Bridget's revelations during her last years. The **Extravagantes,** a collection of diverse revelations that for some reason were omitted, was added later.[9]

The division into eight books corresponds neither to a strictly chronological nor to a precisely thematic order. While books 1 and 2 contain early revelations in Sweden, marked by moral themes, books 3 and 4 depart from this locale with visions concerning the Church in Italy. Book 5 returns to the Swedish period with a dialogue on theological questions. Book 6 gathers revelations from all parts of Bridget's life and touches on a wide range of subjects. Book 7 contains the revelations from her pilgrimage to the Holy Land (1371-1373). As the title suggests, book 8 is a collection of revelations with a political content, partly drawn from the other books. Finally, the **Extravagantes** contains, among other things, revelations concerning her new order.

The first edition of Bridget's revelations appeared in Lübeck in 1492; it included prologues by her confessors and the rules of her order. A second edition followed in 1500 by Koberger in Nuremberg, at the request of Emperor Maximilian. Others followed.[10] A modern critical edition is in progress.[11]

An examination of the historical context of the midfourteenth century, along with Bridget's role in bolstering the Catholic Church—which had suffered serious blows to its authority—will permit an understanding of how such a controversial, uneducated woman attained international prominence. Because so much of her history is more fiction than fact, owing to the rudimentary state of analytical tools of studying documentation about saints,[12] these comments will be limited to information that has been carefully verified.

Bridget went to Rome in 1349 to attend the jubilee of 1350, an occasion she herself had pressed for in a delegation to Avignon which sought papal support for the new order.[13] But in a vision in 1348, between this mission and the jubilee, Christ told her to go to Rome and stay there until both emperor and pope had been to the city:

> Go to Rome where the avenues and the streets are made of gold and are red from the blood of saints, where a reduction [of sins] and a shortening of the way to heaven is made possible because of indulgences that have been gained by the saint pontiffs through their prayers. Stay there in Rome, until you have seen the highest pontiff and the emperor at the same time, and you will proclaim to them My words.[14]

According to the *Acta et processus canonizacionis,* people laughed at the notion of the pope's meeting with a king. Not only did the popes, who had been residing in Avignon since 1309, show no inclination to return to Rome, but the conflicts between Pope John XXII and the German Emperor Louis of Bavaria had caused unprecedented alienation. When Louis had come down to Rome in 1328 for his coronation as a Roman emperor, it was to incite insurrection and to elect a Franciscan antipope.[15] The brilliant state theoreticians who served Louis radically denied any divine origin of the pope's authority and affirmed that he could be deposed by the emperor. In truth, all of Italy was rising up against the pope. However, Bridget's revelation had some justification: it came to her two years after Charles IV's election in 1346, and it reflected the new monarch's intentions not to continue to divide the people's loyalty. He intended, on the contrary, to win the pope for the imperial side.

Actually, a short passage in one of Bridget's revelations concerning an ideal state of peace, symbolized by the reconciliation of the two swords in Rome, is repeatedly found in contemporary documents. Her prophecies expressed a yearning for a return of the glory of old Rome as well as hopes for Church reform. Thus, against the very background of a Rome reduced to a bloody battlefield, divided by the Colonna and the Orsini, and in a state of utter anarchy, Petrarch espoused the idea of reviving ancient Rome as the center of the empire.[16] His friend Cola di Rienzo dreamed equally of a unification of pope and emperor sealed in Rome and, through this unification, a restoration of the Age of Gold.[17] When Rienzo became tribune of the Roman people in 1347, the idea of ancient Rome found a new embodiment, but this hope collapsed in 1354 when the tribune, become a tyrant, was slain by the Romans in the capitol.[18]

The Church likewise envisioned a return to the golden age, with itself as the central power. As with the first jubilee in 1300, when Boniface VIII revived the cult of Constantine to show the subordination of imperial to papal power,[19] so the jubilee of 1350, permitting plenary absolution from sins, was designed to enhance the strength of the Church. Indeed, the Romans asked for such an event in 1342.[20] Thus Bridget's revelation in a way shows a synthesis of these wishes for political and religious unity. But the 1350 jubilee took place without the pope's presence in Rome; moreover, the tension between Charles IV and the Church proved to be so catastrophic that Legate Annibaldo de Ceccano barely escaped an assassination attempt during a procession. When he shortened the time for gaining indulgences, thus reducing the Romans' income, their anger rose dangerously.[21]

The Romans threatened not only the pope's representative with death but also Bridget. Her place was almost stormed, and she thought of fleeing.[22] Although no mention of the reasons for this animosity appears in the Latin versions of the revelations, we can easily assume that Bridget favored the pope's politics too openly. They attacked her as a sorceress to be burned, probably because she had made a name for herself by curing the Romans and by uttering the darkest threats against Rome in her prophecies.[23] The Romans considered that certain tribulations she predicted had come true too readily (such as the reduction of their income)—she very likely was suspected of making these prophecies come true. However, perhaps she was spared because of other prophecies she made that could not be deflected so easily. Her apocalyptic visions of Rome, of its depravity and state of utter desolation, coincided with constant battles within the city gates, the already abundant ruins from antiquity, the Black Death of 1348 which killed thousands, and the earthquakes in 1349.[24]

The entreaties for the popes' return to Rome, found so often during the fourteenth century, were of course linked not only to the desolate state of the abandoned bride, a common contemporary metaphor for Rome, but to the idea of a general reform of the Church. This comes out very clearly in Bridget's demand for their return. The popes' residence in Avignon had become the symbol of the Church's complete failure in its spiritual duties. As Petrarch points out, the curia was the Babylonian whore, a nest of treason, a temple of heresy, and hell upon earth.[25] And the Church acted openly as a purely political power. Being the big moneylender of the time, it not only used the all-powerful weapon of excommunication (as in the case against King Magnus, who defaulted), but it would also threaten subjugation by its mercenary army (as against Florence).[26]

Thus Bridget had visions both of Rome's decay and of the decay of the Church. Again, her revelations about the Church are by no means "miraculous," for much contemporary prophecy denigrated its authority. Others who cried out for Church reform were the Joachimites and the Franciscan spirituals—for them, the contemporary Church had simply become the embodiment of evil. In fact, a stream of Italian prophecies began in the second half of the thirteenth century, in a time of great economic depression. These prophecies were formulated by the followers of Joachim de Fiore, whose interpretation of history ends in an Age of Spirit when the carnal Church is no longer necessary. The Franciscans, partly adapting Joachimite views, developed an ideal of evangelical poverty, opposing the existing ecclesiastical wealth.[27] These prophecies predicted tribulations of the Church, sometimes in the form of a chastiser belonging to the imperial party, followed by ultimate purification. Expectations for a better future projected an angelical pope, unlike John XXII, whom they declared to be the Antichrist.[28]

Although Bridget was directly influenced by Joachimite prophecy, her prophecies about the Church share only the rebel tone without developing the specific themes.[29] Bridget shares with the Joachimites and Spirituals the claim to divine inspiration, the sharply eschatological outlook, the chastising of the Church for its corruption, and the prediction of punishments, ending in a final purification. But unlike these would-be reformers, several of whom were burned at the stake by John XXII,[30] Bridget did not favor either evangelical poverty or an Age of Spirit—she did not go so far as to attack the office of the priest or deny unworthy priests authority in presiding over sacraments. Thus Bridget, who might otherwise have been persecuted as a heretic,[31] ultimately served the Church by defending its hierarchy and its spiritual power over the empire. The meeting in Rome of the pope and the emperor was clearly for the recognition of the pope, not the emperor, as supreme; thus Bridget gained the sanction of the Church and even earned political influence within it.

Bridget was congenial to papal politics, as is evident in the delegation she sent to Avignon. As an influential Swedish princess, she was important to the Church in establishing good relations between Sweden and the holy see. When she arrived in Rome, the French brother of the pope offered her his palace, which acquired the function of an embassy. In the jubilee year, important Swedish pilgrims resided there, and shortly thereafter her confessor was named the confessor to the Swedish nation in Saint Peter's. Bridget knew the highest Roman nobility; the Orsini created contacts between her and the upper Church hierarchy. In 1354 the Papazzura offered her a palace.[32] Bridget also knew the Neapolitan nobility, including Queen Giovanna.[33]

As she stayed on past the year of the jubilee, Bridget gradually became a cult object to the Romans, for she seemed to work miracles and she was liberal toward the poor. Because of her popularity, the Church could not ignore her. But Bridget was constantly surrounded by controversies, reflecting the Church's own divided attitudes about prophetic phenomena. A real distrust of prophecy arose from the constant danger that rival sects might erode authority. Economic and political crises resulted in the flowering of various dissident groups within the Church (such as the Spirituals). And more or less uncontrolled lay movements, in which women could occasionally become important, added to the expanding competition with the Church.[34]

On the whole, Bridget served Church parties that favored the popes' return to Rome, for power groups even within the Church turned to those like her for propaganda. Their opposition, of course, would attack such exploitation by rational argument, although they too used the same kind of mystification. But Bridget was an especially easy target for their venom, for she was an uneducated lay person, ignorant of Latin, and above all a woman. For example, the French cardinals accused her of everything from merely acting out what had been made up for her by her supervisors, on the one extreme, to insanity on the other.[35] In the introductions to her revelations, her confessors refute these attacks in detail. Apart from lengthy arguments claiming her revelations authentic, Bridget herself insists that Christ in any event was free to accord divine inspiration to the poor, *idiotae,* and women.[36]

One of Bridget's revelations—reflecting these struggles among influential parties—is addressed to Pope Gregory XI. Christ tells Bridget that Gregory has to go to Rome. Bridget objects that others who claim to be divinely inspired advise the pope against this trip, but Christ assures her that what he is saying is true and that the other revelations are false.[37]

Bridget's role in the Church hierarchy came later and was finally less important than her popularity among the people—this fierce defender of the Church provided a key link between lay persons and ecclesiastical authorities. What made her revelations so successful? The answer is offered by Johannes Tortsch, who, about 1424, assembled what seemed to him the most important of Bridget's revelations.[38] His explicit purpose was to collect and explain her darkest predictions concerning the fate of humanity; he entitles the collection *Onus mundi, id est prophecia de malo futuro ipsi mundo superventuro.*[39]

Bridget's emphasis on an ever-angry God who at the same time offers help touched deep chords within the people; *ira Dei* is indeed a constant theme in her revelations. Because of the sins of humankind, Christ is no longer concerned with its well-being, and God is constantly on the verge of sending severe punishments. This important theme had surfaced in one of the first revelations about the sins of the Swedish people. An irate God about to inflict either three or seven plagues upon the world is fully developed in Bridget's revelations.[40] What makes the theme of wrath specifically relevant is the correlative theme of redemption. The gap between a sinful world and an angry God having become immense, special intermediaries (saints and prophets) must reestablish a connection so that souls can be saved. At this point Bridget becomes important: Mary, traditionally an intercessor for the sinful, chooses Bridget as a representative on earth, a channel for God's will.

As Tortsch points out, this special representative had to be a woman, in keeping with a repeated tradition that the world had been lost through a woman and would be saved by one.[41] Thus, God looked down to a simple laywoman, because, as Bridget says in a revelation addressed to the pope, the Church not only failed in guiding the pious, but it increasingly led them astray.[42] Of radical importance, then, Bridget represented for the lay person a direct point of contact with heaven: she could be asked for any kind of help, whether healing of the sick or political advice, for she was authorized to transmit these appeals to heaven. Moreover, the constant desire of Christ and Mary to speak to Bridget, and through her to humanity, showed that God's anger could be appeased.

Bridget was part of the enormously increasing multitude of saints at the end of the Middle Ages. The Church took advantage of this means of deepening its authority by unifying and institutionalizing the tendency for seers and prophets to make claims on the people's faith. In her revelations, Bridget constantly recommends action for the benefit of the Church. Above all, she is an eminent propagandist for indulgences. The creation of jubilee years and the expansion of this practice in the fourteenth century established indulgence business on a large scale.[43] As the papal see grew in political power, so the need for revenues increased. Bridget's role is interesting here because she pushed for indulgences for the dead. Many of her revelations are visions of purgatory; in one, her husband appears to her, and important themes about purgatory unfold: the soul's immediate judgment after death and its consequent dwelling in purgatory, even when almost sinless, before being transferred to a definite place. Most important, the soul asks for help from the living. Although Ulf's list of sins is short, he asks for masses to be read throughout the year in honor of those who are going to deliver him from purgatory. He also wants Bridget to give the Church his precious cups so that they may be transformed into chalices.[44]

In later purgatory visions, details of judgment appear as well as details of the torture of the soul, which sometimes takes place there in front of the judge. Bridget's revelations reinforce the whole system of damnation: the categories of sins, judgments of these and of their subdivisions, the deformation of every possible part of the body symbolizing the soul's sins, the consequent series of tortures, and finally the list of indulgences by which the soul can be delivered from its tortures.[45] Several times Mary stresses the fact that indulgences are the only way to buy the soul's salvation.

Since purgatory was the place where one could still have contact with the dead, anxious relatives consulted Bridget about their fate.[46] She would present the horrible picture of what the sinful soul looked like and the manner of its torture. Her vision of the soul of Neapolitan Nicolaus de Acciolis, whose death she had not been able to prevent but whose soul she proposed to deliver with the help of Mary and Saint Lawrence, depicts Lawrence dictating a list of good works that would save Acciolis' soul: thirteen chalices, thirty masses read by thirty priests, and thirty gifts of clothes and money to the poor.[47]

These visions of purgatory show that despite traditional doctrine, which claimed that the Church's jurisdiction did not go beyond the living,[48] what clearly characterized the Renaissance Church was already practiced in the fourteenth century: everything could be bought for the sake of the soul. Unlike the *quaestuarii* (seers consulted about the fate of the dead and paid for helping them), whom the Church condemned in 1312 for similar commerce,[49] Bridget was permitted, in the name of the Church, to draw in this money. Certainly, in spite of the profits they brought, these practices concerning the dead raised questions.[50] At the Council of Basel, Bridget's revelations were attacked; Johannes Nider would speak of women's visions of purgatory as "superstitious," induced by the demon.[51] At any rate, Bridget's revelations present a condensed form of all that Luther attacked which became a tinderbox for the Reformation—the ever-angry God who constantly had to be appeased by good works, the commerce in indulgences, the absurd proliferation of saints and their superadded altars and offices.

The revelations of 1345 about the founding of a new order, the Ordo Sancti Salvatoris, and the difficulties getting support from the popes again point up the clash between lay aspirations and the Church's attempt to bring them under control. In this struggle, Bridget was less influential in realizing the terms of her visions. She seems to have wanted a double convent emphasizing the authority of women. The functions of abbess would be analogous to those of Mary toward the apostles and disciples of Christ: the thirteen priests correspond to the twelve apostles plus Saint Paul, and the sixty nuns, four deacons, and eight lay brothers correspond to the seventy-two disciples of Christ.[52]

Bridget's first demand to Pope Innocent for approbation in 1347 was blankly rejected on the grounds that since the Lateran Council of 1215, founding new orders was forbidden. Then, Pope Urban V issued a bull with the decisions of the Council of Lyons, which required that every new monastical order had to accept the rules of an existing order. Thus the Brigittine rules were declared to be a supplement to the Augustinian rules.[53] On top of that, the rules were drastically changed—the Brigittine order now included two separate convents, and in later papal bulls, the role of men was increasingly that of supervising nuns, ostensibly to check the difficulties which the Church had with female congregations, such as the Beguines.[54] Bridget could not appeal to the revelations as documents for her order. Toward amending them to conform with accepted diction, Nicolaus Orsini transformed Bridget's confessors' Latin into chancellory prose. The hallmark of her style—the direct form of speech in which Christ addressed his bride—was completely stripped; only the current formula of divine inspiration remained.[55]

Coming at a time of schism after the pope's return to Rome in 1378, Bridget's canonization in 1391 did not end discussions about her, discussions which reflect the Church's problems. Councils that were supposed to clarify issues instead tried to limit the pope's authority, in order to reestablish a solid organization. A creation of this chaotic time of schism, Bridget became a special object of controversy not only at the Council of Constance (1414-1418) but also at the Council of Basel (1431-1439). At the former (which faced four popes in three years), Pope John XXII reaffirmed Bridget's canonization, brandishing her prophecies for his purpose.[56] On the other hand, eminent Church doctors Pierre d'Ailly and Jean Gerson fought against the increasing number who believed themselves inspired and who were used at random to claim papal power. Gerson goes so far as to quote the dying Gregory XI: had he not listened so much to the prophets, both female and male, the schism would not have occurred.[57]

Bridget's sainthood moved Gerson to write his treatise of 1415, *De probatione spirituum,* an attempt to give theologians both a theoretical framework and criteria for examining pretenders to inspiration. This treatise reflects the ambiguous position of the Church regarding such visionaries as Bridget. For Gerson, it is unworthy for the council to approve of these "false, illusionary, [and] frivolous visions," but, diplomatically, he states that they cannot be condemned either and that Bridget's canonization cannot be revoked, because the cult around her had grown so important that this would harm the Christian faith.[58] Then, he returns to the subject of false inspiration with biting remarks about fantasizing women like her—religious fervor can become suspect with adolescents and women, for it is "overheated, versatile, [and] unbridled."[59] Such women, under pretext of confession, vision, or any other story, give free rein to the urge of constant chat and should be scrutinized closely. "There is hardly any other calamity more apt to do harm or that is more incurable. If its only consequence were the immense loss of time, this would already be sufficient for the devil. But you must know that there is something else to it: the insatiable itch to see and to speak, not to mention . . . the itch to touch."[60] Gerson obviously feels what Luther stated over a hundred years later—Bridget had been crazy (*die tolle Brigit*) and had been deceived by the devil.[61]

Gerson's authority was insufficient to settle the controversies about Bridget. These matters, as well as problems about the Brigittine order, were reviewed at the Council of Basel, and a list of 123 doubtful passages in her revelations resulted.[62] The Reformation diminished the popularity of the Brigittine monasteries, and when Sweden adopted the Reformation the cult was abolished, and the mother convent, Vadstena, was closed toward the end of the sixteenth century.

Bridget's writings are not at all marked by speculative considerations, nor is her style full of mystical terminology. Rhetorical sophistication is absent, the short sentences sometimes approach spoken language, and her revelations are characterized by simplicity and directness. In both form and content, her revelations are more like the popular literature of this time. Christ and Mary address Bridget directly and familiarly, as if to an equal, when they speak of moral problems or give directives. Provocative and graphic depictions of judgments or scenes of torture, wherein she describes terribly deformed bodies, distinguish her works. Bridget sets forth in vivid, obsessive detail the agenda of monastic life, in accordance with the new order Christ has commanded her to found. This unique focus on the concrete in her writing is perhaps analogous to that of late medieval painting and sculpture, particularly in the northern countries. In any case, rhetorical simplicity and the sense of striking detail secured the success of her revelations.

Notes

[1] Johannes Jørgensson, *Saint Bridget of Sweden,* vol. 1, pp. 24 ff. For later readings, compare *Extravagantes* 96.

[2] Jørgensson, vol. 1, pp. 78 ff.

[3] *Acta et processus canonizacionis Beate Birgitte,* ed. Isac Collijn, pp. 81, 484, 500.

[4] Concerning Bridget's early ambitions, see ibid., p. 514. For Bridget and King Magnus and the later propaganda tract, see Ingvar Andersson, *Källstudier till Sveriges Historia 1230-1436,* pp. 108 ff., 151 ff., and *Extravagantes* 51. See also Toni Schmid, *Birgitta och hennes Uppenbarelser,* pp. 163 ff.

[5] *Acta et processus,* pp. 73-101, 614-664.

[6] Ibid., pp. 75 ff., 615-617; Alfons de Jaen, prologue to book 8, especially chap. 3.

[7] *Acta et processus,* p. 494; Jørgensson, vol. 1, p. 282, n. 5.

[8] An attempt to analyze the cult of female saints in the later Middle Ages has been made by Ortrud Reber, *Die Gestaltung des Kultes weiblicher Heiliger im Spätmittelater: Die Verehrung der Heiligen Elisabeth, Klara, Hedwig und Birgitta.* A more recent bibliography is *Europäisches Spätmittelalter,* ed. Willi Erzgräber, pp. 508 ff., 517 f.

[9] Knut B. Westman, *Birgitta Studier* pp. 10 ff.; Jørgensson, vol. 1, p. 300 f.

[10] On Maximilian's role, see Ulrich Montag, *Das Werk der heiligen Birgitta von Schweden in oberdeutscher Überlieferung,* pp. 103 ff. Early editions of Bridget's revelations are listed in Isac Collijn, *Sveriges bibliografi intill år 1600 I,* pp. 117 ff. In the present study, we are mainly using the 1500 Nuremberg edition.

[11] In *Samlinger utgivna av Svenska fornskriftsällskapet.*

[12] The pioneering and eminently important work of František Graus, *Volk, Herrscher und Heiliger im Reich der Merowinger: Studien zur Hagiographie der Merowingerzeit,* can be recommended as a model for an analysis of hagiography. Along with a general discussion of methodology, it offers an excellent survey of the research and includes an extensive bibliography. For a more recent bibliography, see Sofia Boesch-Gajano, *Agiografia altomedievale.*

[13] Jørgensson, vol. 1, pp. 183 ff., 198 f.

[14] *Acta et processus,* p. 94. Compare also *Extravagantes* 8, 41.

[15] *Storia di Roma,* vol. II: Eugenio Dupré-Theseider, *Roma dal Commune di Popolo alla Signoria Pontificia (1252-1377),* 464 ff.

[16] On Petrarch and Rome, see Dupré-Theseider, pp. 485 ff., and Karl Burdach and Paul Piur, *Briefwechsel des Cola de Rienzo,* pp. 46 ff., 118.

[17] Marjorie Reeves, *The Influence of Prophecy in the*

Later Middle Ages: A Study in Joachism, p. 421.

[18] Dupré-Theseider, p. 652.

[19] Compare Burdach and Piur, pp. 213 ff., 595 ff., 617 ff.

[20] Ibid., p. 615 f.; Dupré-Theseider, pp. 527 ff.

[21] Dupré-Theseider, pp. 619 ff.

[22] *Extravagantes* 8; Jørgensson, vol. 2, p. 81 f.; and *Acta Sanctorum,* Octobris tomus quartus, p. 241.

[23] According to Jørgensson, more information is in the Swedish *vita* of Petrus Olai of Skenninge; compare vol. 2, p. 316, n. 10. For revelations about Rome, see *Revelationes* 3. 27 and 4. 5, 10, 33, 57 and *Extravagantes* 8.

[24] Ferdinando Gregorovius, *Storia della Città di Roma,* vol. 6, p. 375 f. Gregorovius cites Petrarch. Even the important church of the Lateran seems to have been roofless.

[25] Petrarch, *Sonnets* 105-108.

[26] On Magnus and his sins against the pope, such as going to mass despite the interdict, see *Extravagantes* 43, 80. About Florence, see Richard R. Trexler, "Economic, Political and Religious Effects of the Papal Interdict on Florence 1376-1378," p. 23 f. Also see Edmund G. Gardner, *Saint Catherine of Siena,* p. 175 f.

[27] Compare Reeves, pp. 16 ff., 175 ff., 191 ff.

[28] Ibid., pp. 205, 401 ff.

[29] Ibid., p. 422.

[30] Ibid., p. 201.

[31] Compare *Revelationes* 1. 23 and 4. 41, 62, 132 ff., 136 ff.; *Acta Sanctorum,* pp. 249 ff.

[32] See the index to the *Acta et processus,* p. 657: Francisca Papazzura; Jørgensson, vol. 2, p. 84; Dupré-Theseider, p. 623.

[33] See *Extravagantes* 110.

[34] Reeves, pp. 248 ff. Reeves says that, in 1300 in Italy, at least two women inspired by Joachimites proposed to save the world on the grounds that it was ruined by a woman and was to be saved by a woman.

[35] *Acta Sanctorum* pp. 182 ff.

[36] *Revelationes* 4. 113; *Acta et processus,* pp. 532, 632; compare also Alfons de Jaen's prologue to book 8, chap. 2.

[37] *Revelationes* 4. 141. On the whole question of Bridget's revelations concerning the popes' return to Rome, see Eric Colledge, *"Epistola solitarii ad reges:* Alfons of Pecha as Organizer of Brigittine and Urbanist Propaganda," *Medieval Studies* 18 (1956): 19-49.

[38] Montag, pp. 71 ff., 151 ff. This collection was widely circulated in the fifteenth century.

[39] Johannes Tortsch's *Onus mundi* is edited by Montag, pp. 252-329; compare p. 252.

[40] The revelation concerning Sweden is included in the prologue to the revelations written by Mathias. In Tortsch, ed. Montag, see particularly chaps. 7, 12, 13, and 17. In fifteenth-century woodcuts, the *Pestbilder* shows how Christ holds three arrows which he is about to hurl down.

[41] Tortsch, ed. Montag, p. 260.

[42] *Revelationes* 4. 141.

[43] Augustin Fliche and Victor Martin, *Histoire de L'Eglise,* vol. 14, pp. 813 ff., and Henry Charles Lea, *A History of Auricular Confession and Indulgences in the Latin Church,* vol. 3, pp. 199 ff.

[44] *Extravagantes* 56.

[45] *Revelationes* 4. 7 ff., 51 f., 81 and 6. 10, 31, 52 ff.

[46] *Acta et processus,* p. 327.

[47] *Revelationes* 4. 7-10; *Acta et processus,* p. 329 f.; Jørgensson, vol. 2, pp. 185 ff.

[48] Lea, vol. 3, pp. 328, 337 ff., 346. Compare also Nikolaus Paulus, "Das Jubiläum vom Jahre 1320," *Theologie und Glaube* 5 (1913): 532-541, particularly p. 536. Paulus is a Catholic historian of indulgences.

[49] Lea, vol. 3, p. 339.

[50] Ibid., pp. 342 ff.

[51] Johannes Nider *Praeceptuorium legis* 1. 11.

[52] Tore Nyberg, *Birgittinische Klostergründungen des Mittelalters,* and *Regula sancti Salvatoris* 12.

[53] Nyberg, pp. 43 ff., and *Acta et processus,* p. 230 f.

[54] Montag, pp. 124 ff.

[55] Ibid., p. 126.

[56] Nyberg, pp. 82 ff.; *Acta Sanctorum,* p. 445; Colledge, p. 44.

[57] Jean Gerson, *De examinatione doctrinarum,* in *Oeuvres complètes,* vol. 9, p. 469 f.

[58] Jean Gerson, *De probatione spirituum,* in *Oeuvres complètes,* vol. 9, pp. 177 ff.; compare art. 5.

[59] Ibid., art. 7.

[60] Ibid., art. 11.

[61] Martin Luther, *Sämtliche Schriften,* vol. 2, p. 558 f., and vol. 17, p. 1406.

[62] See the *Epistola cardinalis de Turrecremata* in the Nuremberg edition of the *Revelationes.* The passages are printed in *Sacrorum conciliorum nova, et amplissima collectio . . . ,* ed. Giovanni D. Mansi, vol. 30, pp. 698 ff. See also Colledge, pp. 46 ff.

F. R. Johnston (essay date 1985)

SOURCE: "The English Cult of St. Bridget of Sweden," in *Analecta Bollandiana: Revue Critique D'Hagiographie,* Vol. 103, 1985, pp. 75-93.

[*In the following essay, Johnston investigates the influence of St. Birgitta's writings in England following her death and canonization.*]

The foundations of the *gloria postuma* of St Bridget[1] were laid by her *familia* immediately after her death in Rome in 1373[2]. Her daughter, St Katherine, arranged for the translation of her remains to Sweden where they were enshrined with great ceremony and reports of miracles at Vadstena, the mother house of her new order, the Order of the Savious[3]. Her confessors, Peter of Alvastra and Peter of Skänninge, composed an account of her life as a preliminary to petitioning for her canonisation[4]. In 1377 Alfonso of Jaen published her Revelations with a preface, *Epistola Solitarii ad Reges,* defending their authenticity[5]. Her supporters gained their objectives when Urban VI approved the Regula Salvatoris as constitutions for the Order of the Saviour and granted the order the privilege of the Vincula indulgence in 1378[6], and Boniface IX canonised her in 1391[7].

St Bridget's fame in the following century rested mainly on the spread both of her order and her writings. The Revelationes Celestes consisted of a series of visions, seven hundred in all, which she began to receive after her husband's death in 1344 and continued for the rest of her life[8]. The key passage is in Chapter XLVII of the Revelationes Extravagantes, which describes the manner of the reception of the visions and their purpose[9]:

> Transactis aliquibus diebus post mortem mariti, cum beata Birgitta solicita esset de statu suo, circumfudit eam spiritus Domini ipsam inflammans. Rapta in spiritu vidit nubem lucidam, et de nube audivit vocem dicentem sibi: 'Ego sum Deus tuus, qui tecum loqui volo . . . Noli timere. Ego sum omnium conditor, non deceptor. Scias, quia non loquor propter te solam sed propter salutem omnium Christianorum. Tu quippe eris sponsa mea et canale meum, audies et videbis spiritualia et secreta celestia, et spiritus meus remanebit tecum usque ad mortem.'

The contents of the Revelations, especially those contained in Book VII which concern St Bridget's pilgrimage to the Holy Land in 1372, are neatly summarised in the first English life of the saint[10]:

> Postea in Ierusalem in montem Calvarie eciam in sepulchro Christi . . . et in Bethlehem presepem Domini ostensum est ei per revelacionem Domini tota series nativitatis passionis et resurrectionis Christi de ascensione et adventu Spiritus sancti et multa occulta et mistica de ecclesia et apostolis et prophetis et de assumptione beate Marie Virginis et de reformatione Christianitatis et tocius mundi. De quibus Romam rediens plures libros mirabiliter scripsit et fidelibus commendavit.

She was however a prophetess rather than a mystic and had the moral purpose of the Old Testament prophets whose language she often recalls to us, often couching her warnings in lurid animal imagery and crude popular idiom[11]. Besides meditations on theological subjects, the Revelations consist of warning or encouraging messages to individuals or groups and visions describing the judgment of deceased (or sometimes still living) persons and their sufferings in Purgatory or Hell[12]. They became a standard textbook of devotion being well adapted to the fifteenth century taste for devotional rather than formal theological works, with particular emphasis on the Passion[13]. The influence of her writings on contemporary art is to be seen in paintings of the Nativity and the crucifixion[14]. At the Nativity Mary is depicted kneeling and adoring the Infant Jesus instead of in Childbed, whilst at the Crucifixion Christ is nailed to a previously raised cross and portrayed as the Man of Sorrows.

The foundation of the Bridgettine Order was due to another revelation received by St Bridget before she left Sweden[15]:

> Hanc igitur religionem ad honorem amantissime Matris mee per mulieres primum et principaliter statuere volo. Cuius ordinem et statuta ore meo proprio plenissime declarabo.

The order was in fact to be a double order with each monastery headed by the abbess and having 60 nuns, 13 priests, 4 deacons and 8 lay brothers[16]. The sisters were to sing a special office in honour of the Blessed Virgin with lessons known as the *Sermo Angelicus* which were revealed to St Bridget in Rome[17]. It differs from the traditional Lady Office in that instead of changing in accordance with the seasons, the texts vary each weekday, relating the life of Our Lady until her Assumption and defining her contribution to the work of our redemption. During the first half of the fifteenth century monasteries of the order were founded in lands which had supported the Roman pontiffs during the Great Schism and they naturally became centres of St Bridget's cult.

One of St Bridget's early revelations brought her to the notice of the English court[18]. It concerned the Hundred Years' War, comparing the Kings of France and England to two ravening beasts who were devastating France and causing the loss of souls, and ordered the kings to make peace through a marriage alliance. Though a mission to urge the pope to act as mediator failed[19], King Magnus sent a summary of St Bridget's message to England in 1348[20]. The revelation had no immediate effect, but it was quoted by Hoccleve[21] and mentioned frequently in English diplomatic memoranda in the following century[22].

Whilst in Rome (1349-73) St Bridget lived in the Campo dei Fiori[23] next door to the English Hospice, yet there are no records of her meeting any of the pilgrims there. The Two Englishmen who were greatly impressed by her sanctity were both expatriates who had no influence on her cult in England. William de Guellesis, *scutifer Anglie,* met her in Cyprus, joined in her pilgrimage to the Holy Land and later came to Italy to testify to the fulfilment of her prophecies of punishment for the sins of the Cypriots[24]. The Benedictine curial cardinal Adam Eston attributed his release from imprisonment to the prayers of St Bridget[25] rather than to the diplomatic intervention of Richard II[26] and wrote a Defense of her Rule[27], but did not include any of the saint's works among the books he gave to his brethren at Norwich[28].

Although there is no reference to England among the countries to which copies of the Revelations were sent immediately after their publication[29], there was at least one copy in England before the end of the century[30]. It is written in an English hand and includes in a different, but contemporary, hand an account of the saint's life which seems to have been composed by someone who knew her in Rome and which shows a refreshing independence of the standard Swedish lives—a characteristic of many of the lives written in England. This account includes one interesting detail not mentioned elsewhere, stating that St Bridget shortly before her

death was planning to visit St Catherine of Sienna and then return to Sweden to join the Vadstena community[31].

Early in the fifteenth century an English translation of the Revelations was made and again the text was accompanied by an account of her life[32]. The author of the life seems to have shared the interests of those who had rushed for copies in Rome and emphasises the saint's prophetical powers and her preaching of the need for church reform. He also gives some details of the Order of the Saviour and the foundation of Vadstena. Since he does not mention Syon it seems that the manuscript was written before 1415[33].

A second full English translation made in the same period[34] had two points of interest. The life which precedes the Revelations is an adaptation of the lessons in Birger's office for the saint's feastday[35]. However the manuscript is of northern provenance showing that interest in the saint's works had spread beyond London and Oxford. The scribe writes in a northern dialect[36] and the volume was in the collection of mainly northern manuscripts made by Sir Henry Savile[37]. It could well be that it originally belonged to Lord Scrope of Masham who mentioned a copy of the saint's works in his will, stating that he bought it at Beverley[38]. He was a kinsman and friend of Sir Henry FitzHugh who planned the introduction of the Bridgettines into England.

In the mid-fifteenth century Bridgettine studies in England were dominated by Thomas Gascoigne, Chancellor of Oxford. Unfortunately much of his work has been lost. For example, he tells us that he wrote a life in Latin which he later translated into the vernacular for the use of the sisters of Syon[39]. No trace of the vernacular life has been found. The Latin original may have been the item headed: 'Annotata quaedam de S. Birgitta et miraculis eius manu propria Thome Gascoigne' which was included in Cotton Ms. Otho A.xiv but has been destroyed by fire[40].

The chancellor certainly took a great deal of trouble in gathering his material. Not only was he familiar with Birger's Life and the Revelations themselves, as is shown by the annotations in his hand which occur in Balliol College Ms. ccxxv[41], but similar notes in Digby Ms. 172 which contains the lives of St Katherine of Sweden and Peter Olavus[42], show that his studies did not end with reading the ordinary sources. He also spent some time working in the library of Syon, where several members of the community were numbered among his friends[43]. It was there that he saw a copy of the Process of Canonisation of which he had a copy made for the use of the Augustinians of Osney[44] to whom he also gave a relic of the saint to encourage the community to celebrate her feast[45]. Some of his interest seems to have been passed on to his friends. John

Robert who was a witness of his will wrote a brief life of St Bridget on the flyleaf of a volume of Homiliae Dominicales[46] and may have been the author of a Defensorium used at Basel[47]. Another of his associates, Thomas Chaundler, is listed among the special benefactors of Syon[48].

Early in the sixteenth century a full life of St Bridget was included in Pynson's edition of the Nova Legenda Anglie and has been judged to be one of the best prose translations of the time[49]. It must rank with More's Richard III as one of the earliest major biographies in the vernacular. The work may well have been composed at Syon which would be the only place where the source material was available. It is a skilful blend of the original life by the Two Peters, relevant extracts from the Revelations and a life known as the 'Vita Abbreviata' which was included in printed editions of the Revelations, the first of which was published at Lübeck in 1492. Most significant of all, it seems that she had become English by adoption, as the prologue to the original version puts it[50]:

> tanto diligentiori studio perlegamus, eorum vivendi exemplo ad sacra conversationis studia pertrahamur, quanto maiori parte ex nostris sunt et patria et gente.

Pynson lays great stress on her widowhood, an unusual theme in mediaeval hagiography. It was an aspect of St Bridget's life which had been noted by Boniface IX when he took as his text for the canonisation sermon: 'Viduam eius benedicens benedicam'[51], and in England by the poet Audelay who, writing c. 1426, began his 'Salutatio Sancte Birgitte' with the words[52]:

> Hayle maydyn and wyfe, hayle wedow Brygytt.

Pynson lays even greater emphasis on this aspect of St Bridget's career[53]:

> St Bridget . . . a holy and blessed widow which life is right expedient for every manner of person to look upon most in especial for those that live in matrimony or in the state of widowhood that they may see what grace and virtue was in this blessed woman which lived in the same degree as they do and the rather to be encouraged to desire to have the like grace and virtue.

This literary interest in her married status links up with some of her most prominent admirers in England who were indeed of like status:—Margery Kempe and the two royal duchesses, Cecily of York and Margaret Beaufort[54]. The Swedish lives stress the influence the saint had over her husband especially in helping him in the study of law necessary for his work as a provincial governor and a royal councillor, and on the religious side teaching him to recite the Hours of the Blessed Virgin. Besides this she did much to care for the sick and poor around her home in the castle of Ulvåsa[55]. However as the lives were composed either to further the cause of her canonistion or for liturgical use afterwards they omit more awkward incidents such as Ulf's decision, for reasons of family aggrandisement, to marry their daughter, Martha, to a boorish knight, very much against his wife's wishes. She always referred to him as 'the Robber' and her judgement proved correct[56].

Turning back to the early years of the fifteenth century we find that English theologians were greatly involved in the controversies which centred round the Revelations and the Order of the Saviour. Though few of the works of the critics have survived, the Defensoria show the general lines of attack which they had to meet.

The first of these defences was composed by Adam Eston[57]. The attack was mainly directed against the Regula Salvatoris and the fact that a woman had been commissioned to found a new order. Eston pointed out the prominent role of women in the gospels as witnesses of the Resurrection and as receiving the Holy Spirit at Pentecost. Against a criticism of the style of the rule he argued that such documents should be in language suitable for their readers and literary style was a minor consideration. He went on to show that her teaching about the Blessed Virgin in the Sermo Angelicus was in accord with the church's doctrine and that the holiness of the saint's life was proof that her visions were genuine.

Ten years later a further defence was composed by Geoffrey, Abbot of Byland[58]. He had read a copy of the Revelations and was concerned to defend their orthodoxy. His work is divided into twenty-seven propositions, each concerned with a specific passage and the doctrine contained in it. In the fifth proposition, for example, Geoffrey pointed out the teaching of the Doctors on the doctrine of the Immaculate Conception was neutral, and that since the feast was celebrated in some parts of Christendom there was nothing unorthodox in the saint's assertion of it.

St Bridget caught the attention of the fathers assembled at the Council of Constance. In response to a petition from the King of Sweden her canonisation was confirmed with lengthy ceremonies, probably the last official act of John XXIII[59]. However there were virulent attacks on new religious orders[60] and an attack on revelations by the great French theologian, Gerson[61]. No details of the outcome of these onslaughts seem to be known, but it seems very probable that diplomatic pressure by King Eric and his wife, Philippa who was the sister of Henry V, was successful[62]. Certainly Henry went on with his plans for Syon Abbey and the new pope, Martin V, again confirmed the canonisation in 1419[63].

Opponents returned to the attack at the Council of Basel. Though specific attacks were made on one hundred and twenty three passages of the Revelations[64], the indulgences and the whole concept of double orders[65], these were only facets of more fundamental theological issues. The attacks may have been part of the continuing Thomist-Occamist disputes of the philosophers[66], but they were certainly at the centre of the debates about the powers of the pope. It is noteworthy that the leader of the critics was Matthias Doring, the author of the 'Confutatio Primatus Papae'[67], whilst the saint's chief defenders were the papal theologians Haimerich of Kempen and the Dominican, Turrecremata[68]. An English bishop, Reginald, took part in the controversy and wrote two short defensoria[69], in which he argued that prophecy was a gift of the Holy Ghost and did not end with the revelation of the New Testament. It had been possessed by many women and St Bridget's holy life was proof of the authenticity of her visions which contained nothing that was not either orthodox theology or at least the probable teaching of the church. He pointed out that such works were often couched in obscure language because our spiritual faculties need exercise as well as food. The outcome of the debate was that the Revelations were saved from condemnation, but the privileges and indulgences of the Order were curtailed[70].

The Defensoria show that English theologians were studying St Bridget's works carefully, a fact further demonstrated by the interest shown by the Carmelite Richard Lavenham, Confessor to Richard II[71], and the Dominican Thomas Stubbs[72], both Doctors of Divinity. These must be the type of men who used the full Latin texts of the saint's writings during the first half of the fifteenth century, whilst in the second half several Carthusian monasteries, including Shene and London, obtained copies[73]. Other learned writers early in the century knew her works well enough to quote relevant passages in their own treatises. The editor of the *Speculum Christiani,* a guide for parish clergy, chose a passage concerning our duty to consider our neighbour's spiritual welfare as well as our own[74]. Richard Ullerston, Chancellor of Salisbury, found a piece about the virtue of endowing new churches to support his case for the canonisation of St Osmund[75], whilst Gascoigne naturally quoted many sections which confirmed his gloomy view of the times:

> Sancta Birgitta, vidua et sponsa Christi, de regno Suecie, verba sancta et terribilia dixit contra peccatores[76].

St Bridget's writings were also of use to priests responsible for the spiritual direction of religious women whether within the cloister or outside. Two manuscripts containing lengthy extracts from the Revelations in the vernacular which discuss the virtues of the active and contemplative ways of life would have been suitable for this purpose[77]. Morevover about the year 1400 a local priest, Peter of Swine, gave a number of books including 'Liber S. Brigide' to the Cistercian nuns of that place[78]. But the most outstanding example of the influence of the Swedish saint was the way in which she affected the whole life and writing of Margery Kempe who came to regard herself as an English St Bridget and whose autobiography was composed about 1436[79]. Born at Lynn, the chief port for trade with Sweden, Margery probably heard people speaking of the saint almost from the time of her birth, and the influence must have been further strengthened by one of her principal confessors, the Carmelite friar Alan of Lynn, the composer of the 'tabulae' to the Revelations which is now Lincoln College, Oxford, Ms. lxix[80]. During a pilgrimage to Rome Margery talked to St Bridget's maid and visited the saint's house[81]. In her own autobiography Margery claimed that Christ would speak to her as he had to St Bridget and also that she had seen the sacrament in the priest's hands take the form of a dove and assure her of the truth of St Bridget's Revelations[82]. Her autobiography also sheds interesting light on the reactions of English prelates to such private revelations. Arundel, the Primate, and Repingdon, Bishop of Lincoln, appear to have been quite kindly disposed towards her, and even prelates who, like Bowet, did not view her with any great favour, took no stronger action than ordering her to leave their dioceses.

During the second half of the century several copies of the Revelations were owned by well-to-do widows, Elizabeth Sywardby[83], and Margaret Purdans of Norwich[84]. Such widows lived lives almost as nuns and were the most important readers of devotional works in the vernacular as they would not know Latin[85]. The most prominent of this class was Cecily, Duchess of York, who in 1495 bequeathed to her daughter Anne, Prioress of Syon, a book of the 'Revelations of Saint Burgitte'[86]. The survival of a document giving the routine of Cecily's household shows that her books were not merely ornamental, but were put to daily use[87]. Her day was arranged on monastic lines, very similar to St Bridget's routine in Rome, and included a 'lecture of holy matter' at dinner and a discussion of what had been read during supper.

Cecily's devotion to St Bridget impressed itself on her family. One of her daughters, Anne, became Prioress of Syon. Her son, Edward IV, not only chose the then very unusual name of Bridget for one of his daughters[88], but was regarded by the Syon community as their second founder because he restored much of the property they had lost through defective titles during the reign of Henry VI[89]. Another of Cecily's daughters, Margaret, married Charles of Burgundy, at whose court she would meet ladies whose piety equalled her mother's[90], and would find copies of the Revelations in the ducal libraries[91]. She herself seems to have been greatly interested in the Bridgettine house of Gouda where she was named as one of the trustees[92] and caused a history of the abbey to be written[93]. Her death is noted in the necrology of the monastery at Termonde[94]. This Yorkist interest may also be linked with the use of passages of the Revelations to support their claims to the throne as in the prophecies given in Cotton Vespasian Ms. E. VII and Ashmole Ms. 27, where passages relating to Sweden are adapted to English politics.

The interest of the continental printers in the saint's works was both earlier and greater than the English ones. Extracts of her writings first appeared in 1481 when Johannes Torsch's 'Onus Mundi', a book of prophecies taken largely from the Revelations, was printed in Nuremberg[95]. A full edition of her works was prepared at Vadstena and printed at Lübeck in 1492, to be followed by similar editions at Nuremberg in 1500 and 1517. Extracts were also issued in German and Dutch before the end of the century.

The first mention of St Bridget by English printers seems to be in the additional material added to the 1491 edition of Mirk's Festial in a sermon entitled 'Hamus Amoris' which may well have been composed by one of the Syon brethren[96]. However it was not until 1530 that Godfray issued a volume made up of the Epistle of St Bernard and Four Revelations of St Bridget[97]. A further selection of four revelations was edited by Richard Whytford, the Wretch of Syon, and published in 1531[98].

The use of the Revelations in English politics has been mentioned in connexion with the Hundred Years War and the Yorkist claims to the throne. Such use continued into the sixteenth century. The best known case is that of Elizabeth Barton, the Holy Maid of Kent. It has been claimed that her visions condemning Henry VIII's plan for divorce caused Wolsey and Warham to delay the proceedings[99]. Later she visited Syon and it was alleged when she was attained that the community of Syon 'daily rehearsed matter enough into her out of St Bridget and St Catherine of Senys revelations, to make up her fantasies and counterfeit visions'[100].

A further case occurs in a report on the state of Ireland in 1515. The writer quotes a passage in which St Bridget asked her good angel: 'Of what Christian lands were most souls damned?'. The angel showed her a land in the west part of the world, 'for there is most continual war, root of hate and envy . . . and without charity souls cannot be saved.' The writer concluded that it could not be denied by the very estimation of man, but that the angel did understand the land of Ireland[101].

The question remains as to what effect the activities of the Order of the Saviour had on the cult of their foundress. Even excluding Vadstena and Sweden where she was the national patron, devotion to the saint spread in districts where were monasteries of the order[102]. At Dantzig her cult was particularly popular[103]. After the foundation of an abbey at Cologne evidence of the development of the cult is seen in the dedication of new altars, windows and lights in honour of St Bridget and the inclusion of her name in German calendars[104]. All this was in addition to the literary activity of copying manuscripts and the growth of an apocryphal literature under her name[105]. Little of this type of activity is to be found connected with Syon apart from the production of texts. However there are several important features in its history which affect the cult[106].

The foundation of Syon Abbey was the work of a group of soldier statesmen. The idea was first put forward by Sir Henry FitzHugh when he visited Vadstena in 1406 when he was a member of the company escorting the Princess Philippa to Sweden for her marriage. At first the plan made little progress through lack of money. An endowment was finally provided from the property of the alien priories which had been sequestrated during the troubles with France. Henry V probably needed little prompting from FitzHugh since he was personally devoted to St Bridget, possessing a relic and naming her among the saints to whom he specially committed his soul in a will made before the invasion of France. As with the Yorkists there seems to have been some family interest. His sister, Philippa, was married to the Swedish king, visited Vadstena, became a member of the chapter and a benefactor, besides cooperating with her brother in defending Bridgettine interests at the Council of Constance.

The foundation charters shows that Syon was to be primarily a Lancastrian chantry; there is no mention of the famous incident of the penance for the murder of Archbishop Scrope, and throughout its history the monastery was visited by royalty until the last grim scene when Henry VIII's corpse lay there overnight and the coffin burst. The choice of site meant that Syon would always attract the attention of the rich and powerful, lying as it did midway between Westminster and Windsor with the river on one side and the main road on the other. The effect of this seems to be shown by the recruitment of the sisters from courtier and London merchant families, typical of the pattern in convents of recruiting from prosperous local families[107]. Yet despite the opportunities for worldly vanities all the references in contemporary accounts speak of the reputation of the community for austerity and learning.

One important attraction for visitors was the Pardon of Syon, the indulgences to be gained by pilgrims especially at Lammastide and the feast of St Peter's Chains, obtained by Henry V from the pope:

'devote visitantibus magnas indulgencias concedi a summo pontifice procuravit.'[108]

It was of course the indulgence that formed the main theme of Audelay's Salutation and surviving manuscripts show that both the general theology of indulgences and the special privileges granted to Syon were a frequent theme in the sermons of the brethren who were bound to preach in the vernacular on Sundays and feasts[109]. Odd references tell of pilgrims both high and low. The king, queen, Clarence and Gloucester went for the pardon in 1472[110], whilst Elizabeth, wife of John Lowe, visited the abbey in 1490[111].

Especially after the introduction of printing the brethren were able to promote the cult by their writings. Though Syon did not have its own press as some of the continental houses did, the brethren, particularly Richard Whytford, supplied material to the commercial printers. Apart from the extracts from the Revelations and the Life of St Bridget it was natural that their devotional writings should contain quotations from her works. Mention must also be made of the Jesus Psalter[112], a prayer very much in the Bridgettine spirit, which was edited by Whytford and remained a very popular devotion among Recusants during the sixteenth century[113].

The abbess was responsible for many appropriated churches and some evidence remain to show that work in this connexion promoted the cult. At Angmering in Sussex St Bridget appears on a new tympanum[114], at Mount St Michael's, Cornwall, there was a cloth with an image of the saint[115], whilst at Lancaster the whole church was rebuilt, earning the gratitude of at least one modern commentator[116]:

> 'We have reason to be profoundly grateful to these nuns of Syon for their zeal and munificence . . . under their hands the building arose in increased size and beauty, to be pride of many generations.'

The normal evidence of a cult is very slight in England. St Bridget's feast day, July 23rd[117], does not appear in the calendars of either Sarum or York. Nor are there any church[118] or chantry dedications or even stained-glass windows, wall-paintings or statues in her honour, with the possible exception of a marble statue still in the possession of the Syon community[119]. Artistic representations of the Swedish saint seem to be limited to several rood-screens in East Anglia and Devon[120].

Naturally St Bridget occurs in both liturgical and private prayer books connected with Syon Abbey[121], one rather unusual feature being a 'little office' in her honour in a Horae Sanctae Trinitatis[122]. Memoriae are found in a few private prayer books sometimes with a miniature, as in the late fifteenth century English Horae now in the FitzWilliam Museum[123].

One sign of the popularity of a writer is the appearance of apocryphal works. In St Bridget's case the most popular of the apocrypha was the devotion of the Fifteen Oes which is found in many manuscript Horae and came to be included in the printed editions[124]. The prayers also occur in some private prayer books such as the Preces Variae now at Stonyhurst College[125]. An interesting feature of the prayers is that their attribution to St Bridget is by no means universal. When attributions do occur they seem to take the form of an illumination showing the revelation of the prayers to the saint, or of a long introduction detailing the rewards to be gained by daily recitation of the prayers, mainly the release of souls from purgatory[126].

Two brief references must be made to the rosary. First there was the so-called Bridgettine Rosary of sixty three beads in honour of the sixty three years of the life of the Blessed Virgin[127]. An anonymous pamphlet printed in Bruges in 1834 entitled 'Oersprong des Rosenkreynkens onder den Naem van de H. Brigitta'[128] attributes the use of the devotion to Henry VII who asked for the prayers of the Bridgettines in times of difficulty. This may well link up with the special faculties for blessing rosaries granted to the brethren by the pope in 1500[129]. The second reference is to the sole surviving English pre-Reformation rosary. It is of gold and each side of each bead is engraved with the figure of a saint. The third decade is arranged to exhibit canonised women, including St Bridget portrayed as a crowned nun carrying a book[130].

Illuminations of the saint appear in a few manuscripts. The text of the Revelations in B. L. Cotton Claudius Ms. B.i contains several. At the beginning of Book III a miniature depicts the saint dressed in black with a white wimple, sitting writing in a book on her knee. To her left stands a bishop and above the drawing are the words 'Bryde and a byscop'[131]. At the beginning of Book VII she is again shown dressed in black with a white headdress, kneeling adoring the Holy Child. In the background the manger is shown with the ox and ass. To the left of the manger there is standing a lady with a halo, wearing a red dress with a blue mantle over it[132]. Both the miniatures illustrate the main topics of the books; Book III consists mainly of messages addressed to bishops and Book VII deals with the life of Christ with special emphasis on the Incarnation.

The early printers used several wood-cuts of the saint to illustrate books connected with her. The main theme is to show her receiving her Revelations with her pilgrim's staff, cap and purse included in the illustration. Each printer had his own variation on the theme. The earliest example seems to be Pynson's Calendar of the New Legend in 1516[133]. De Worde pictured her in his edition of the Horae in 1519 and Fawkes in the Mirror of Our Lady, Pepwell in the Dyetary of Ghostly Helthe and Treveris in his edition of Whytford's Werke for Householders[134].

This survey has not mentioned the many spiritual miscellanies which contain short passages from the saint's writings, nor has it attempted to solve such mysteries as to why a workman should have been given a 'Book of St Bridget' in payment for repairs to Warwick deanery[135]. However the evidence produced suggests that there was a widespread cult though mainly a literary one based on her writings, since even the artistic evidence is connected with books and would therefore influence the literate classes. It will be suitable to end by recalling the finest tribute of all to St Bridget from her followers, that when the crises came in 1539 and 1558 many of the community of Syon preferred to go into exile in order to continue living under her Rule rather than surrender to the Tudor Despotism[136].

Notes

[1] 'Birgitta quam vulgares Brigidam appellant' (Canonisation Bull in *Acta Sanctorum*, Oct., IV (1780), 624.

[2] Cf. P. Debongnie, *Ste Brigitte*, in *Dict. d'Hist. et de Géog. Ecclés.* (1938), VI, 719.

[3] R. Steffen, *Den Heliga Birgittas Uppenbarelser* (1909), xxx.

[4] Printed in I. Collijn, *Acta et Processus Canonizationis Beatae Birgittae* (1922).

[5] K. B. Westman, *Birgitta Studier* (1911), 44.

[6] H. M. Redpath, *God's Ambassadress* (1947), 154.

[7] Cf. I. Collijn, *Till 550-Årsminnet av Birgittas Kanonisation*, in *Fornvännen*, 1941.

[8] J. Wordsworth, *The National Church of Sweden* (1910), 127. The textual problems are discussed in B. Klockars, *Birgitta och Bökerna* (1973) and *Den Heliga Birgittas Revelationes Extravagantes*, ed. L. Hollman (1956).

[9] Hollman, 162.

[10] Written at the end of the fourteenth century and now Merton College, Oxford, Ms. ccxv, f. 238.

[11] W. A. Purdy, *Santa Brigida, la sua Epoca e la nostra*, in *Brigitta, Una Santa Svedese* (1974), 75.

[12] Klockars, *op. cit.*, 251.

[13] F. R. H. Du Boulay, *An Age of Ambition* (1970), 143; P. Janelle, *L'Angleterre Catholique à la veille du Grand Schisme* (1935), 15; E. F. Jacob, *Gerard Groote and the Beginning of the Devotio Moderna*, in *Journal of Eccles. Hist.* 1952; *Studies in Pastoral Theology*, ed. A. Murray (1961), 1, 87.

[14] *Revelationes Celestes*, Book VII, ed. B. Bergh (1967), Ch. xv and xxi; H. Cornell, *St Bridget, the Changing Ideas of her Time*, in *Brigitta, Una Santa Svedese;* cf. A. Wilmart, *Œuvres Spirituelles et Textes Dévots du Moyen Age* (1932), 62; M. D. Anderson, *The Imagery of British Churches* (1951), 101.

[15] A. Andersson, *Böken on Birgitta* (1977), 66; the growth of the order is described in T. Nyberg, *Birgittinische Klostergründungen des Mittelalters* (1965) and the legal and financial problems in H. Cnattingius, *Studies in the Order of St Bridget of Sweden* (1963).

[16] Andersson, *op. cit.*, 66.

[17] *Sermo Angelicus*, ed. S. Eklund (1972); H. J. Collins, *The Bridgettine Breviary of Syon Abbey* (1969); T. Lunden analyses the text in *Kyrkohistorisk Årsskrift* 1973.

[18] *Revelationes Celestes*, Book IV, Chaps. 103-5.

[19] Andersson, *op. cit.*, 52, 85.

[20] A copy is in Corpus Christi Col., Cambridge Ms. 404. A Swedish copy is mentioned in B. Klockars, *Birgittas Svenska Värld* (1976), 125.

[21] *The Regement of Princes*, ed. J. J. Furnival (1897), 194.

[22] Cf. J. H. Wylie, *The Reign of Henry V* (1914), I, 440; J. C. Dickinson, *The Congress of Arras* (1955); H. Nicholas, *Acts of the Privy Council* (1835), V, 352; *Letters and Papers Illustrative of the Wars of the English in France*, ed. J. Stephenson (1861), I, 1.

[23] In the Casa di S. Birgitta now the headquarters of the new branch of the order.

[24] *Acta et Processus*, VI, 432.

[25] In his letter to Vadstena in Bodley Ms. Hamilton 7, f. 248; cf. W. A. Pantin, *The Defensoria of Adam Eston*, in *Eng. Hist. Review* 1936, 779 et seq.

[26] The Diplomatic Correspondence of Richard II, ed. E. Perroy (1993), 63.

[27] *Infra.*

[28] *M. R. James and the Dean of Norwich, The Library of Norwich Cathedral*, in *Norfolk Archaeology* 1917, 67 et seq.

[29] The list by Magnus Petri, Confessor General of Vadstena, is in Lincoln Cath. Ms. 114, f. 16, and includes the Emperor, the King of France, the Queens of

Naples, Cyprus and Castille as well as the Teutonic Order and the University of Prague.

[30] Merton Coll., Oxford, Ms. ccxv (H. O. Coxe, *Cat. cod. Mss in Collegiis Aulisque Oxon.* (1852), I, 71).

[31] *Ibid.,* f. 238.

[32] B. L. Cotton Ms. Julius F.ii; cf. *Cat. of the Mss. in the Cottonian Library* (1802), 18. The life is printed in J. G. Aungier, *History and Antiquities of Syon Monastery* (1840), 19 et seq.

[33] Julius F.II. f. 254.

[34] Cotton Ms. B.i.; cf. *Cat. of the Cottonian Library,* 191. Details of the missing leaves are in W. P. Cumming, *The Revelations of St Birgitta* (1929), XVII.

[35] Printed in *Act. Sanct.,* Oct. IV.

[36] Cumming, *op. cit.,* XX.

[37] J. P. Gilson, *The Library of Sir Henry Savile of Banke,* in *T.B.S.,* IX, 135 et seq.

[38] C. L. Kingsford, *Two Forfeitures of the Year of Agincourt,* in *Archaeologia* (1918), 82.

[39] *Loci e Libro Veritatum,* ed. J. Thorold Rogers (1881), 139.

[40] W. A. Pronger, *Thomas Gascoigne,* in *Engl. Hist. Rev.* LIII (1938), 619, 625.

[41] Balliol Coll., Oxford, Ms. CCXXV, esp. fols. 173-6 and 191-217.

[42] W. D. Macray, *Cat. of Digby Manuscripts* (1883), Col. 180.

[43] Pronger, *op. cit.,* 625.

[44] *Loci e Libro Veritatum,* 169.

[45] *Martiloge of Syon,* Br. Libr. Add. Ms. 22, 285, flyleaf.

[46] J. Denucé, *Musaeum Plantin-Moretus.* Cat. des Mss. (1927), 112, and *Registrum Cancellarii Oxon.,* ed. H. E. Salter (1932), I, 406.

[47] Cf. *Act. Sanct.,* Oct. IV, 472. The texts are in Uppsala Ms. C. 518.

[48] *Martiloge,* f. 70.

[49] G. H. Gerould, *Saints' Legends* (1916), 288.

[50] *Nova Legenda Anglie,* ed. C. Horstman (1901), I, 3.

[51] Lincoln Cath. Ms. 114, f. 49.

[52] Printed in Cumming, *op. cit.,* xxxi et seq.

[53] Printed 1516 and reprinted without the conclusion in J. H. Blunt, *The Myroure of Oure Ladye* (1873), XLVII et seq.

[54] Cf. *infra.*

[55] The fullest account of her married life is in the office composed by Nicholas Hermansson who was tutor in her household before becoming Bishop of Linköping. It was printed by H. Schück in *Lund Universitäts Årsskrift,* Vol. 28.

[56] J. Wordsworth, *The National Church of Sweden* (1910), 126.

[57] There are texts in Bodley Ms. Hamilton 7 and B. L. Ms. Harley 612.

[58] Probably at Oxford in 1393 (*Snappe's Formulary,* ed. H. E. Salter (1924), 9); Abbot of Byland in 1397 (Cal. of Papal Regs., V, 329 and V. C. H., Yorks, III, 134.). His Defence is in B. L. Harley Ms. 612.

[59] Urich von Richtental, *Chronik des Konstanzer Conzils,* ed. M. R. Buck (1882), 53.

[60] H. Finke, *Acta Concilii Constanciensis* (1923), II, 597.

[61] H. von der Hardt, *Magnum Oecumenicum Constancie Concilium* (1700), III, 28.

[62] A. Lindblom, *Kult och Konst i Vadstena Kloster* (1965), 53.

[63] The bull 'Excellentium Principum' in *Acta Sanct., t. cit.,* 476.

[64] Wordsworth, 138.

[65] Concilium Basiliense, *Studien und Quellen zur Geschichte des Conzils von Basel* (1936), VIII, 126.

[66] Westman, 278.

[67] P. Albert, *Die Confutatio Primatus Papae,* Ihre Quelle und Ihre Verfasser, in *Hist. Jahrbuch,* 1890, 439 et seq.

[68] Their treatises are in Uppsala Ms. C. 518. Turrecremata's defence is in the printed editions of the Revelations.

[69] In B. L. Harley Ms. 612, Col. 777 et seq.

[70] Westman, 286.

[71] *D.N.B.*, XI, 652; J. Bale, *Index Britanniae Scriptores*, ed. R. L. Poole (1902), 354.

[72] *D.N.B.*, XIX, 121; Bale, 454.

[73] E. K. Thompson, *The Carthusian Order in England* (1930), 320, 326, 329.

[74] *Speculum Christiani*, ed. C. Holmstedt (1932), clxxx.

[75] A. R. Malden, *The Canonisation of St Osmund* (1901), 240.

[76] Quoted from Lincoln Coll. Ms. CXVII in N. D. Hurnard, *Studies in the Intellectual Life of England from the Middle of the Fifteenth Century till the Time of Colet* (unpublished Oxford D. Phil. thesis), 353.

[77] Garrett Ms. 145 was edited by Cumming, *op. cit.;* cf. also B. L. Ms. Arundel 197.

[78] M. R. James, *Cat. of the Mss. in the Library of King's College*, Cambr. (1895), 35.

[79] *The Book of Margery Kempe*, ed. W. Butler-Bowden (1936); *The Book of Margery Kempe*, ed. S. B. Meech and H. E. Allen, Vol. I (1940).

[80] Coxe, *op. cit.*, I, 38.

[81] The house and its associations with St Bridget are described in *Civiltà Cattolica* (1895), 471 et seq.

[82] Meech and Allen 47.

[83] *Testamenta Eboracensia*, ed. J. Raine (1864), III, 161.

[84] H. Harrod, *Extracts from Early Wills in the Norwich Registries* (1855), 336.

[85] A. I. Doyle, in *The Age of Chaucer* (1954), 99.

[86] *Wills from the Doctors Commons*, ed. Nichols and Bruce (1863), 3.

[87] M. Noble, *Some Observations upon the Life of Cecilly, Duchess of York*, in *Archaeologia* (1800), 7.

[88] In view of this paragraph I disagree with the view E. G. Withycombe, *Oxford Dict. of English Christian Names* (1977) that Edward meant St Bridget of Kildare.

[89] References to Syon are taken from the account of the abbey in V. C. H. Middlesex, I.

[90] F. Ingham, *Philippe-le-Bon* (1944), 183.

[91] Cf. *Bibl. Prototypographique . . . des Fils du Roi Jean* (1830), 165, 285.

[92] M. Van Hattum, *Nog eens het Brigittenklooster te Gouda*, in *Nederlandsch Archief voor Kerkgeschiedenis* (1945), 259.

[93] *Ibid.*, 258.

[94] A. De Vlaminck, *Nécrologie du Double Monastère de Ste Brigitte à Termonde*, in *Cercle Arch. de Termonde* (1901), 34.

[95] For printed editions cf. G. E. Klemming, *Heliga Birgittas Uppenbarelser* (1883), V; I. Collijn, *Katalog der Incunabeln der Kgl. Universitäts-Bibliothek zu Uppsala* (1907).

[96] Wordsworth and Littlehales, *The Old Service Books of the English Church* (1904), 144.

[97] Extracts are printed in J. E. G. De Montmorency, *Thomas a Kempis, His Age and Book* (1907), 10-12. The extracts are from Book VI and describe the judgment of certain souls. Cf. G. E. Klemming, *op. cit.*, 56.

[98] Klemming, *loc. cit.*

[99] E. J. Devereux, *Elizabeth Barton and Tudor Censorship*, in *Bull. of the John Rylands Library* (1966), 98.

[100] L. E. Whatmore, *Sermon against the Holy Maid*, in *Engl. Hist. Rev.* (1943), 469.

[101] C. Maxwell, *The Foundations of Modern Ireland* (1921), 18.

[102] T. Höjer, *Till Kännedomen om Vadstena Klosters Ställning såsom religiös Institut in Historiska Studier tillagnade Professor Harald Hjarne* (1908), 59 et seq.

[103] Cf. O. Gunther, *Die Handschriften der Kirchenbibliothek von S. Marien in Dantzig* (1921).

[104] Höjer, *op. cit.*, 78.

[105] Cf. C. Jungmark, *Eine Pseudo-Birgittische Christus-Passion* (1916).

[106] Unless otherwise stated references to Syon are based on the accounts in V. C. H. Middlesex, I. and T. Höjer, *Studier i Vadstena Klosters och Birgittinordens Hist.* (1905).

[107] H. T. Jacka, *The Dissolution of the English Nunneries* (London M. A. thesis, 1917), 120.

[108] Thomas De Elmham, *Vita et Gesta Henrici Quinti*, ed. T. Hearne (1727), 25.

[109] Simon Winter's sermon is in B. L. Harley Ms. 2321 and discussed in M. A. Hughes, *A Syon Pardon Sermon* (Liverpool M. A., 1959).

[110] Paston Letters (Everyman Ed.), II, 115.

[111] *Henrici VI Angliae Regis Miracula Postuma*, ed. P. Grosjean (1935), 57.

[112] The Jesus Psalter arranged by a monk of Ampleforth (1973).

[113] Cf. *An Elizabethan Recusant House*, ed. R. C. Southern (1952), 82.

[114] Black's Guide to Sussex (1886), 132.

[115] A. L. Rowse, *Tudor Cornwall* (1941), 186.

[116] Guide to Lancaster Priory and Cathedral Church, n. d., 16.

[117] Changes in her feast day are noted in *Acta Sanct., Propylaeum Decembris* (1940), 441.

[118] Dedications refer to St Bridget of Kildare, cf. F. Arnold Foster, *Studies in Church Dedications* (1899), II, 147.

[119] *A Royal Foundation, Syon Abbey Past and Present* (1946), 12.

[120] M. R. James, *Norfolk and Suffolk*, 97, 107, 152; C. Keyser, *On the Panel Paintings of Saints on Devonshire Screens*, in *Archaeologia* (1898), 197, 221.

[121] Full texts of the offices are in *Officia Propria Sanctorum . . . Ordinis Salvatoris* (16).

[122] A fifteenth century mss. in the possession of the Syon community.

[123] M. R. James *Cat. of the Mss. in the FitzWilliam Museum* (1895), 146.

[124] *The Prymer*, ed. H. Littlehales (1897), II, XLI; H. Thurston, *Uses that are really Superstitious*, in *The Month* 1919, 56; *The Fifteen Oes*, ed. S. Ayling (1869). Dr H. Toldberg studied the variant forms of the introductions and prayers but unfortunately his conclusions were never published.

[125] Stonyhurst College Ms. A. VII, 5, fol. 77 sq.

[126] Cf. M. R. James, *Cat. of the Western Mss. in the John Rylands Library*, II, pl. 175. For the introduction cf. B. L. Harley Ms. 172, fol. 3-5.

[127] H. Thurston, *The so-called Bridgettine Rosary*, in *The Month* (1902), 189et seq.

[128] A copy is said to be in the Bibliothèque des Bollandistes, Brussels.

[129] F. W. Nettelbla, *Nachricht von einigen Klöstern der h. Schwedischen Birgitte* (1764), 12.

[130] E. Maclagan and G. C. Oman, *An English Gold Rosary of about 1500*, in *Archaeologia* (1935), 1 et seq.

[131] f. 116.

[132] f. 269.

[133] E. Hodnet, *English Woodcuts 1480-1535* (1935), 323.

[134] *Ibid.*, 178, 447.

[135] J. Harvey Bloom, *Introduction to the Cartulary of St Mary's, Warwick*, in *Trans. of the Bristol and Gloucester Arch. Soc.* (1914), 88.

[136] The history of their exile is given in J. R. Fletcher, *The Story of the English Bridgettines* (1933).

Tore Nyberg (essay date 1990)

SOURCE: An introduction to *Birgitta of Sweden: Life and Selected Revelations*, edited by Marguerite Tjader Harris and translated by Albert Ryle Kezel, Paulist Press, 1990, pp. 13-51.

[*In the following introduction to* The Life of Birgitta of Sweden, *Nyberg examines the structure of Birgitta's* Revelations *and the theological doctrine it propounds.*]

Spiritual background and early life

Mystic union with God, redeeming words and deeds born out of a burning heart—all that we summarize under the heading "spirituality"—is not to be labelled male or female. It is both and at the same time either of them; seemingly a contradiction. In studying the mystics and the great men and women of spiritual life we find this contradiction dissolved into a kind of dynamic interaction between the level of the splendor of eternity, and the level of human relations in the sphere of creation. Many great spiritual men had the comfort of a female companion on their path. Catholic tradition shows that Francis of Sales had the countess Jeanne Françoise de Chantal, Francis of Assisi had St. Clare as an intimate associate, and the early story of Western monasticism offers the striking model for both of them and for many others: St. Benedict with his sister St. Scholastica.

The relationship of two such personalities was always one of deep interior affection and feeling of oneness, and yet at the same time restrained, demanding distance to a degree which sometimes seems incomprehensible to outsiders. Still more striking is this in the lives of women chosen to spiritual preeminence. Hildegard of Bingen, Elisabeth of Schönau, the two Mechtilds of the thirteenth century, Catherine of Siena, and many others had their confessors: men of high human and educational standards, dedicated to serving God, humbly impressed by God's work in a woman assigned to their spiritual direction and care, a woman in whom they often recognized higher gifts of grace than the ones to which they could pretend in their own lives. Such men saw that if theirs was the gift of discursive thinking and literary form, they would have to use these gifts to channel an overwhelming spiritual eruption, or the boundless richness of images and messages brought forth in a woman committed, under their care, to a higher vocation.[1]

Such, in short, was the situation of the three priests, theologians, and spiritual directors who play such an eminent role in the life and development of Birgitta of Sweden. First, there is the remarkable and learned theologian, Canon Matthias of Linköping, the first Swede known to have translated and ingeniously commented upon the Bible in the Old Swedish language and whose commentary on the Apocalypse of St. John has been copied in a number of manuscripts from all parts of Europe. Then there are the two Peters: the Cistercian prior Peter Olavsson from Alvastra, who practically gave up his monastic seclusion to be able to assist Birgitta during her many years abroad; and Magister Peter Olavsson from Skänninge, a gifted spiritual director, theologian, and musician. The two Peters are the authors of the *Life of St. Birgitta* which forms the first section of this volume.

A *Life,* a *Vita,* had been a fixed literary pattern for centuries,[2] and the two confessors in composing their work had to follow the reading habits of the 1370's and of the papal court, since such texts were meant to be used in the investigations leading up to a canonization. Ancestry, childhood, and early evidence of God's special calling would have to come first, followed by examples of heroic faith and action in the person's mature life. Attention is always paid to supernatural events in this kind of literature. The two confessors were not short of material in any respect. Their account became a sober document marked by humble confidence in God's prophetic call through Birgitta. Many things which the modern reader might have wished to know are lacking, e.g., her Christian life with her husband on the estate of Ulvåsa, her social attitude toward servants and beggars during that half of her life. Now, we only know of these aspects from witnesses during the canonization process.[3]

There are two main versions of the *Vita.*[4] The fullest account, well worked out stylistically as well as in regard to signs of Birgitta's holiness and divine election, is the one rendered in English here below. There has been, however, an important scholarly discussion on this version of the *Vita,* its origin and function. We find the text in its fully elaborated form among the acts of the process of canonization, and there its purpose is perfectly clear: to underline all characteristics of Birgitta which were most properly fitting to a saint of the Church, according to the standards of the late fourteenth century. As such, the *Vita* is a final evidence of attachment, affection, and awe among those who were able to follow her posthumous fame until the solemn declaration of her sanctity by Pope Boniface IX in 1391, only eighteen years after her death.

Although the canonization process was brought to its fulfillment by a pope who represented only a part of European Christendom—the Roman obedience in the Great Schism, as opposed to the Avignonese obedience to which, among others, France, Spain, and Scotland adhered—its juridical form was nevertheless lawful and traditional. Its validity was not questioned once the Great Schism was brought to an end at the Council of Constance by the election of Pope Martin V (1417). The so-called "Canonization of St. Birgitta at the Council of Constance," which took place on 2 February 1415, was nothing but a vain effort undertaken by the leader of the short-lived Pisan obedience, Baldassare Cossa, the antipope John XXIII, to vindicate, in the last minute, his authenticity as the only true bishop of Rome by invoking the prophetic voice of Birgitta. Yet this restating of the canonization may have worked as a preparation for the final solution of the Great Schism among his own adherents.[5] In all these events the *Vita Processus,* as it is called, was the authorized document making evident Birgitta's sanctity and divine election.[6]

There is, however, a shorter version of Birgitta's *Vita,* preserved in the MS C 15 of the University Library of Uppsala,[7] one of the numerous manuscripts from the medieval library of Vadstena Abbey happily saved and handed down to our days. As always in the case of two versions, the question was raised: is the *Vita Processus* the original version and the *Vita C 15* a shortened form of it, or is the *Vita C 15* the true original text which was later embellished and enriched upon? And if the second alternative is true, then were elements added to the *Vita Processus* which were not altogether authentic?[8]

The Swedish scholar Sara Ekwall, who studied this question carefully, brought forth in 1965 her conclusion: the *Vita C 15* must be the original one. Several characteristics led her to this view. The text shows a structure with chapters of basically equal length having each its own heading, whereas in the *Vita Processus* some chapters are unreasonably long (e.g., that on

Birgitta's stay in Alvastra, which contains a number of anecdotes on persons who experienced Birgitta's help and the strength of her prayer during this period: Gerekin, Bishop Hemming, a nun called Catherine, Master Matthias, and the Dominican master Algot). Another long passage without heading is devoted to some of Birgitta's mystical experiences of early years. This, says Sara Ekwall, cannot have been omitted in a shorter version produced out of a fuller one; but it may well have been added to a shorter version to make it more rich and attractive.

What is rendered in the addition should not be suspected of being untrue; it simply stems from another source, or it may have been added at some later point by the original authors, who thereby changed the original cast of the text. In same manner, the chapter on how the devil tempted Birgitta . . . brings forward short events which carry the mark of having been added later, says Sara Ekwall. Basically, the same may be true for the final portion of the *Vita* dealing with Birgitta's life in Rome and Italy. The passage on Naples and Jerusalem carries so strongly the character of a conclusion that the original *Vita* may have ended here. . . .

There are also a number of significant differences between the two versions pointed out by Sara Ekwall. In several passages the fuller version has a more correct Latin but also uses more literary and devotional formulas than the shorter one. In the shorter version Birgitta is often called "God's bride," but in the longer version the expression "Christ's bride" is much more common. The shorter version does not enter upon Birgitta's noble ancestry in the way the longer version does, where she is more often called "Lady Birgitta" (*domina Brigida* by the Italian form of the name). A number of persons are anonymous in the shorter version, while in the longer one their name and social status are given. The word *divinitus*, "divinely" revealed, which is common in the long version, is not used at all in the shorter one.

As decisive evidence, Sara Ekwall quotes a testimony of Prior Peter Olavsson and Master Peter Olavsson given in the canonization process. They recount how they wrote the *Vita* of St. Birgitta in Rome shortly after her death, but that they knew much more which they were not able to write down then because of their approaching departure from Rome in the fall of 1373 with Birgitta's earthly remains destined for Sweden.[10]

These arguments amount to a strong support of the view that the two confessors, shortly after Birgitta's death, wrote a concentrated *Vita* of her life without yet having an explicit purpose of convincing the judges of a canonization process about Birgitta's sanctity in canonical forms. Someone later worked the text over thoroughly and extended it with the canonization pro-

cess in sight. But if this was not done by the two confessors, who created the final version, the *Vita Processus* translated here below? Sara Ekwall is not in doubt. After stylistic and other comparisons with texts whose origin and author are secure, she reaches the conclusion that no one but Alphonsus Pecha, bishop of Jaen, is the author and redactor of the final, full version of the *Vita*.[11]

The question of who put the last finishing touch to the *Life of St. Birgitta,* then, enables us to arrive at a better understanding of the world of Birgitta as a spiritual writer. Four men guided her development successively: Master Matthias, Prior Peter Olavsson, Master Peter Olavsson, and Bishop Alphonsus Pecha. From their *Vita* and other sources, we can follow Birgitta's life in its main lines.

Born in the winter of 1302-03—probably around St. Sylvester, says Birgit Klockars, the able biographer of her childhood, youth, and married life in Sweden— Birgitta was surrounded by spiritual impulses preparing the way for her first confrontation with divine election: her first revelations in the period 1344-49.[12] She was guided by Master Matthias in interpreting them. Birgitta's religious experiences in childhood are faithfully recorded in the *Vita*. Nils Hermansson or Nicolaus Hermanni, a cleric born around 1326, prepared the way. He was perhaps the teacher of young Karl, Birgitta's eldest son, although probably of the same age as he. Later he was teacher to Birgitta's next son Birger. He became canon and bishop of Linköping and was one of Birgitta's faithful supporters in establishing Vadstena Abbey. He was a model for a cleric and a priest in Birgitta's eyes, serving God in daily prayer, pastoral care, and spiritual friendship. He died in 1391 and was venerated as a saint throughout the rest of the Middle Ages.[13]

Master Matthias's influence upon Birgitta has been studied by scholars like Bengt Strömberg, Hjalmar Sundén, and Anders Piltz.[14] Sundén, applying Jungian psychology to Birgitta's relationship to Master Matthias, based himself upon the image of Matthias as a theologian and a spiritual writer that Strömberg had created in 1944. Piltz has deepened our understanding of Matthias's theology considerably since then. "There is something anachronistic about him: he was a dedicated anti-dialectician some hundred or two hundred years behind his times. He would have been better off with John of Salisbury or Saint Bernard or Roger Bacon, and he echoes, as it were, their warnings against the perils of biblical studies detached from the biblical texts," says Piltz. He then quotes Matthias as saying: "A great corruption has prevailed in the Church for a long time, since theology is taught in a philosophical way and the philosophers are venerated instead of theologians."[15] This gives us an indication of how Matthias strove for a biblically centered theology and pastoral teaching.

Strömberg has demonstrated how Matthias found the model for his theological work among the Dominicans and the Franciscans, the preachers of those centuries. In his great theological treatise which starts *Homo conditus in omnibus bonis habundabat* (Created man overflowed in everything which is good) biblical quotations recur in every paragraph, whereas long philosophical deliberations are entirely lacking. Man's beauty according to God's creation is placed at the very beginning, man's corruption through sin and seduction constitutes the background for the full story of redemption, restitution, fullness of grace, and vision of God.

Faith, hope, charity are the healers of the sickness of the soul, which is sin. Suffering and Christ's God-willed passion reopen the path to the Father; the sacraments are the signs that communicate to us what Christ has won. Vices have their remedies in the virtues, the burden of which we impose upon ourselves. Christ in the gospel texts is our example and the saints guide our path in daily life through example and intercession.

Whereas *Homo conditus* probably was written for the use of parish priests, a more advanced and confidential teaching was presented in the same author's *Alphabetum distinctionum,* a selection of biblical passages in alphabetical order. Its commentaries often elaborate upon evils of the Church and of the clergy; the tone is not very different from what we often find in Birgitta's writings.[16]

It is not impossible that Master Matthias arranged Book I of Birgitta's **Revelations,** the first 60 spiritual texts which she apparently already received in Sweden. The famous introduction of Master Matthias to the **Revelations** called, after its first words, *Stupor et mirabilia* (Amazing and marvelous things are being heard on our earth) was meant to introduce the start of this new revelation of God's message through a woman. Birgitta was still living as a God-devoted widow in Sweden, planning the foundation of a monastery, writing letters to Pope Clement VI (1342-52) to have him act as a peace negotiator in the war between England and France.[17] There was not yet any prospect of her passage from Sweden to stay abroad for the rest of her life.

This changed with the Crusade which King Magnus Eriksson of Sweden and Norway launched against the city of Novgorod in 1347-48, and with the clash of opinions on how to carry out the Crusade—where apparently Matthias also entertained views of his own.[18] The situation was decisively altered when the great pestilence, the Black Death, started its ravaging tour across Europe. It is generally assumed that Master Matthias died in the great pestilence around 1350. He was buried in the Church of the Dominicans in Stockholm, but his body was later transferred to Vadstena, where he was venerated as a saint.[19]

Master Matthias, in his preface, presents the text of Birgitta's first recorded revelation, the text of which is given here in full:[20]

> The devil sinned in three ways: by pride, because I had created him good; by desire, to be not only similar to me, but superior to me; and by lust to enjoy so much my divinity that he willingly would have killed me, had he been able to, so that he might reign in my place. Because of this he fell from heaven, filled the earth with these three sins and so violated all mankind. Therefore I took on humanity and came into the world, to annihilate his pride by my humility, to destroy his desire by my poverty and simplicity. And I submitted to the most immense penance of the cross in order to annihilate his abominable lust and to open heaven, closed through his sins, to man by the blood of my heart and by my death—yet so far as he inserts his will to work for it, according to his ability. But now the men of Sweden, especially those who call themselves courtiers or knights, sin in the same manner as the devil did before them. They take pride in their well-shaped bodies, which I gave them. They surround themselves with fortunes which I did not give them. They overflow with their abominable lust to such a degree that they had rather killed me, were it possible for them, than abstained from their lusts or endured my frightful justice, which threatens them for their sins. Therefore their bodies, which they take pride in, shall be slain by sword, lance, and axe. These precious limbs, which they boast of, wild animals and birds shall devour them. Let strangers make spoil of all that they have drawn together against my will, and let them be wanting (Cf. Ps. 108:11). Because of their abominable lusts they offend my Father so that he does not hold them worthy of being admitted to see his face. And since they had rather killed me, if they could, they will be given over into the hands of the devil to be slain by him by eternal death. But I would have let this judgment pass over Sweden long before, if the prayers of my friends, who live in the midst of them, had not resisted; they moved me to mercy. Therefore, the time shall come when I shall draw these friends of mine to me, so that they shall not see the evil which I will make befall this country. Verily, some of my friends will live then, and they will see in the fullness of their merits. But now, since kings and princes and prelates do not want to recognize me in my good deed, and come to me, I will gather the poor, the wicked, the minors and the wretched, and with them I will fill up the place of the others, so that my army will not be weakened because of their absence.

The collaboration of the two, Master Matthias and Birgitta, grew into a procedure for cautious self-control. In his testimony at the canonization process Prior Peter Olavsson stated:

In case she was experiencing an illusion in these [revelations], she herself submitted all her visions and her way of experiencing them to the examination of Master Matthias, her aforementioned confessor, and of other masters in theology, and of men highly skilled in the knowledge and way of the spirit. She bowed totally to their decision, which was that . . . these ways of experiencing visions and of having visions were a gift of the Holy Spirit, taking into account the person seeing them, and the matter of the visions, and the ways they were seen.[21]

The first book of the *Revelations* contains themes and passages of great weight and impressiveness. In contrast to Books IV and VI, there is no mixture here of long and short, extravagant and straight, more and less important texts. Nothing seems to have been added or deleted—the number sixty indicates an original arrangement, just as the thirty revelations of Book II probably reproduce the very first plan for the arrangement of these texts. All the sixty chapters of Book I have been carefully worked out, each around its principal theme. They are often already in dialogue form, as later on in Birgitta's life, but here speeches or messages in direct form spoken by Christ or our Lady predominate. Sometimes there are additional teachings or explanations by angels (ch. 10), John the Baptist (ch. 31), St. Peter (ch. 41). Numerous quotations and allusions to the Old Testament make their mark upon Book I. The basic Jewish-Christian experience laid down in Exodus recurs often: Yahweh's witness to himself in the blazing of the bush is echoed in chapter 47; the staff of Moses in chapters 53 and 60; the plagues of Egypt in chapters 44 and 56; the Exodus from Egypt in chapters 26, 41, 49, and 60; the pillar of cloud in chapter 26; the march through the Red Sea in chapters 15, 45, 48-49, 53, and 60. The giving of the Law on Mount Sinai is referred to in six revelations: 10, 26, 45, 47-48, 53; the Golden Calf in three: 48, 53, 60. A similar amassing of references to the Exodus themes is not to be found in any other single book of the *Revelations*.[22]

One example from chapter 53 of Book I shows us how Birgitta interprets three great deeds performed by the staff of Moses. First, the staff is transformed into a serpent, to the fright of the enemies of Israel. Secondly, it divided the Red Sea in two halves to allow the people to walk safely in the middle to reach the other shore.

> Lastly, the rock gave out water by means of that staff. The rock is the hard parts of the people, for if they are struck with the fear of God and love, remorse and tears of repentance flow out. No one is so unworthy, no one is so evil that his tears do not flow from his eyes and all his limbs are quickened toward virtue if he turns to me interiorly, considers my suffering, realizes my power and thinks of the goodness which lets earth and trees bear fruit.

Here the stories from Exodus 4:2ff; 7:8ff; 14:16ff; 17:5ff have been drawn together and condensed into one single application containing three stages of God's action toward mankind. Very often this is the way Birgitta's meditation of Holy Scripture is echoed in her revelations.

The Monk on the Ladder

During her Swedish years as a widow, Birgitta's relationship to God and to his intermediary, Master Matthias, underwent a deep change. Recent scholarly work on this process seems to be unanimous in one respect: something like a "crisis" must have taken place.[23] There is no unanimity, though, concerning this crisis, or the deeper cause behind it. K. B. Westman (1911) and others understood it as the result of Birgitta's confrontation with God's calling to her after the death of Ulf, her husband—a "vocational" crisis, as it were, leading her under the guidance of Matthias straight to its logical historical scope. Sundén (1973) adhered to the idea that the crisis was due to the deterioration in Birgitta's relationship with the king because of the importance this relationship had for the future of the planned monastery for which the king had donated Vadstena royal castle. As Birgitta Fritz has shown recently (1985), however, this interpretation is open to doubt for chronological reasons. The more subtle problems of religious psychology have not yet been tackled in this regard.[24] But there seems to be one important agreement between scholars today: that Book V of the *Revelations* is a vestige of this crisis and thus constitutes a primary document of what really was at stake during this period of transition in Birgitta's life. Before entering upon other sections of the main bulk of the *Revelations* and the story of their redaction, then, we will have to halt for a moment and have a closer look at Book V, which makes up an important portion of the texts printed below.

Book V has been analyzed several times by scholars, primarily from the point of view of the texts and their authenticity,[25] and secondarily from the vantage point of C. G. Jung's school of psychoanalysis.[26] Some basic stages of research into this work, however, seem to have been forgotten. First of all, the sequence of questions which make up the basic pattern of this treatise conceived by Birgitta in the summer of 1349 has not yet been lucidly explained. The treatise consists of sixteen challenging interrogations directed to "the judge" by the "monk on the ladder, full of guile and devilish malice," who seemed, "in his most restless and unquiet bearing, to be more devil than humble monk." Each interrogation has five or seven questions and the corresponding answers of the judge. Thirteen longer or shorter messages and visions in the form of revelations have been irregularly inserted between the interrogations. One part of the scholarly discussion has been devoted to the problem of whether these revelations were put there by Birgitta herself or distributed in such manner by the redactors. Before entering upon this topic, let us follow the sequence of questions. This sequence is identical in the Latin text and the Old Swedish translation of the Latin text, whereas the insertion of revelations does not follow the same pattern in the two versions.

The first four interrogations, each consisting of five questions, belong so closely together that the Old Swedish text made one introductory chapter of the first three of them. A monk is seen standing on a ladder in front of Jesus Christ as judge; the judge is surrounded by all the heavenly host. The first questions are all modelled upon the questioner's individual needs: why, judge, did you give us senses and limbs, property, law, diversion, food, will, sex, vitality, if we may not use these things as we want? Why ought I feel pain when enjoying created things? Why should I suffer when the world is full of happiness and I myself, of noble birth, am meritorious, rich, and honorable and therefore deserve my reward? God's answers to these egotistic questions remain extremely short, never exceeding six lines in the critical Latin edition of the text. The common characteristics seem to make out of interrogations 1 to 4 (= chapters 1-2 in the Old Swedish text) a first separate entity of Book V.

With interrogation 5, the answers of the judge become fuller and more extensive. Even the pattern of questioning changes. Instead of questions like "Why did you give" and "Why should I," the monk now asks: "Why did you create . . . ?" "Why does N. N. suffer . . . ?" "Why did you make . . . ?" "Why did you not make . . . ?" This goes on from interrogations 5 to 8, with the exception of interrogation 7, which has six questions instead of five; they center again around the monk himself in his relationship to the created world. The answers of the judge show a similar shift: instead of the iterated "I have" in the answers to interrogations 1 to 4, we find at the opening of the first answer in interrogation 5 the decisive: "I created." This aspect is stressed again when it comes to the worship of idols in interrogation 8. The monk's questions insist upon created goods and their place in God's plan: How can you, judge, advocate being the originator of sickness, fear of death, bad judges, wild animals, and the well-being of evil men, all that which is a threat to happiness in this world? Why do you accept that many peoples adore idols, why don't you appear convincingly in your glory to all the world, why don't you show quite openly how detestable the demons are, so that all men avoid and detest them?

It has escaped scholars so far that there is a switch in the sequence after interrogation 8. Until now, Birgitta or her redactors have practically no comment in the form of a message, a revelation, in addition to the answers of the judge. After no. 8, commenting or con-comitant revelations are added to each single set of answers.

Then there is the switch of subject. By interrogation 9 the monk leaves the order of creation and moves into the order of salvation. He signifies it by addressing for the first time the judge as son of Mary. Why are the gifts of creation so unevenly distributed between angels, men, animals, and unspirited matter? Interrogation 10 enters deeper into the mystery of incarnation by accusing the judge, now precisely as Christ, for having submitted himself to these insulting human conditions without really being obliged to do so according to the plan of salvation. Christ ought to have followed another plan, as implicitly stated in interrogation 9. Number 11 elaborates on the same subject in that the monk is accusing Christ of having become subject to time instead of having revealed his glory and majesty in one second.

The set of interrogations proceeds according to a distorted salvation history. The basic plan of God's incarnation having been attacked by the monk, he now pursues his attack in detail: why did you not prove openly that Mary was a virgin, that you were God born to mankind? Why did you flee to Egypt letting the innocent children die for you—and how could you allow yourself to be so insulted during your passion? After this fulminating accusation in interrogation 12, there is an end to the sequence of subjects belonging to the order of salvation.

The last four interrogations (13 to 16) seemingly return to themes touched upon earlier. In fact, however, the uneven distribution of grace, which is the object of the monk's attacks in number 13, does not concern gifts of the creational order, but clearly belongs to the order of grace, connected to the working of the Holy Spirit. Why do you call men so differently with your grace, the monk asks? Some are called in their youth, some in old days; some receive a good understanding and some are as stupid as an ass. Some are always tempted, some are continually being consoled; the evil man gets a better life than the good man. The answers of the judge are now getting very discursive. This is also true for the answers of interrogation 14, where the monk turns to the injustice of children carrying their fathers' sins, of giving birth in pain, of fear for the unforeseen and of the good end of evil men, whereas the good sometimes are stricken unprepared by sudden death.

Central issues of faith are broken into pieces in the questions of the last two interrogations. Why do you not always listen to the prayers of the faithful? Why does the evil man not have your permission to go on being evil? Why do evil things happen to the good ones, and why does the devil stay for years with some and not with others? And finally: How can you find joy in separating the good from the evil on the day of judgment, the date of which you do not even know, although you are coequal with the Father? And why, at all, did you postpone your incarnation so long, if it really was so necessary? How can the gospels be so full of contradictions if the Holy Spirit spoke through the evangelists? And why did your word not yet reach out to all the world?

Interrogations 1 to 4 bring forward a set of questions concerning individual doubts of a single person only. For the other interrogations we arrive at this scheme:

- 4 interrogations (5, 6, 7, 8) move within the order of creation;
- 4 interrogations (9, 10, 11, 12) move within the order of salvation;
- 4 interrogations (13, 14, 15, 16) move within the order of sanctification.

Birgitta's treatment of human doubts is, then, fundamentally trinitarian in its set-up. Book V demonstrates her situation in the summer of the great European pestilence, the Black Death, when she was faced with the decision to leave Sweden or not for the sake of faith. We meet her here thoroughly imbued and animated by the revelation of the Triune God, Father, Son, and Holy Spirit. Book V is a sequence of doubts, growing out of the monk's personal discomfort, accelerating from his doubts about the reasonable purpose of creation, via his doubts about God's plan of salvation, to a challenging reproach to God for a number of allegedly false principles of spiritual life laid down in the Christian teaching of man's sanctification, of life in the unction of the Holy Spirit.

Understood according to this structure, Book V is evidently a challenge to any theologian acting as a confessor to the interpreter of such doubts, Lady Birgitta. The plotting out of revelations among interrogations 8 to 16 may well have seemed ephemeral to Birgitta herself, if hers was such a clear spiritual insight into trinitarian theology. In the first long revelation summing up interrogations 1 to 8 (or 5 to 8) the imagery of the doctor healing the sick is displayed. . . .

There is every reason to stress the importance of revelation 13 of Book V, as Hjalmar Sundén has done.[27] This message of the Father—only rarely does the Father and not Christ speak—appears as the solution to all sixteen sets of doubts laid down in strategical and trinitarian order in the sequence of interrogation. It is no wonder that Sundén found in this arrangement a confirmation of his Jungian interpretation of Book V as a testimony of the process of individuation which Birgitta allegedly went through prior to her departure for Italy. The monk is, according to Sundén, the *animus* of Birgitta; the doubts are but her own doubts projected upon the figure of the monk, who then takes

over all the negative elements, whereas Master Matthias, who might have given rise to many of these problems, is free from being accused in the last run.

Seen in the perspective of the literary form, the sixteen interrogations without regard to the series of revelations added to them are powerful enough to be evaluated even outside the key of Jungian psychology. If God's action is seen as a sequence, it does not necessarily mean that it is being understood as a sequence in time, either in Joachimite terms as ages of world history,[28] or in Jungian terms as stages in the history of a soul.[29] It could also refer to the different ways God turns his face to mankind: sometimes in his power over creation, sometimes in his message through human word and action, sometimes in the transformative, continuous stream of divine inner working. The symbolic arrangement of four times four interrogations evokes a pattern of limitless extension and expansion of God's power in all the four quarters of the world. For that reason, one might even imagine the set-up of Book V according to the geometrical pattern of the triangular pyramid, where one side is always at the bottom and the appearance from any side is a tripartite one, although it has four sides and four edges.

On the other hand, this does not ridicule a Jungian interpretation of the same text. One might rather see it as an explanation of how Sundén could arrive at his conclusions. For if God acts with man according to his different attitudes in a series of approaches, some points in time will inevitably become more important, more decisive than others to a person, since the human person is bound by the conditions of time and space. To the one person, God's action in the order of creation will be decisive, to the other, his action in the order of salvation. Most decisive to all, however, must be God's action in the order of sanctification, to which the gospel words on the unforgivable sins against the Holy Spirit have always been linked. The ultimative character of the order of sanctification certainly does not rest upon an arbitrary divine decision, but is based upon the internal order of things in themselves—for how can there be access to God if no attention is paid to the basic call of the Spirit to complete conversion and attachment to God through contrition, repentance, remission of sins, and the works of the Holy Spirit?

Sundén, therefore, is certainly right in focusing upon the process of Birgitta's identification and purification of self by and through the concepts about God's action which she brought forth in Book V. Only Sundén's assignment of Birgitta's crisis to a certain historical moment and a very specific situation in Birgitta's life may have been too much influenced by the doctrines inherent in Jung's psychology. Much of the process may have been far behind Birgitta in the summer of 1349. Her task was then to summarize all in the face of the imminent judgment of God—maybe also as a testament to her life in Sweden, to leave behind a document of the essence of her mystical relationship to God, as she had experienced it so far.

Salvation History

Birgitta's exodus from a Sweden overflowing with pride and concupiscence took place in late 1349. The prospects were good and bad at the same time. Master Matthias had supported her prophetic task and King Magnus Eriksson had been won over to the idea of transforming the castle of Vadstena ("Watz stena," the stone house on the water [of lake Vättern]) into a monastery (1346) and of proceeding in the form of a crusade against Novgorod east of Swedish Finland (1348). But then there was the expected "Egyptian Plague," the Black Death. The ravaging sickness, for which there was no known remedy, reached Norway's western coast by ship from England early in 1349, and rumors already spread fear and terror in advance. After having depopulated large stretches of Norway's cultivated valleys, it reached Sweden only in early 1350.[30] No doubt Birgitta fled as God's judgment approached. Birgitta must have felt like crossing the Red Sea with the chosen people of God, traversing Europe in the middle of death, protected as it were by the pillar of cloud through the desert. Her arrival in Rome, probably toward the opening of the Holy Year 1350, meant the end of Master Matthias's guidance in her life and the opening up of a new chapter, characterized by her two confessors by name of Peter Olavsson. From then on, they were her spiritual directors until she met the Spanish bishop Alphonsus Pecha, the "guardian angel" of her last years and of her spiritual heritage to future generations.

Prior Peter Olavsson, a Cistercian monk of Alvastra, joined Birgitta in Rome, but soon left again for Sweden. Because of his frequent travels, we cannot exactly follow his role in Birgitta's spiritual life during these first years abroad. Instead, Master Peter Olavsson from Skänninge must have been her most intimate guide during the early 1350's when she stayed in a flat at San Lorenzo in Damaso in Rome. He was a key person in the long process—over at least a year—when an angel regularly appeared to Birgitta, dictating to her a dogmatic treatise on salvation history known as "The Sermon of the Angel."[31] This treatise is best understood as a unit in itself, as one single revelation, yet received and written down during a long period of time. Its particular function in Birgitta's world is closely bound up with her hopes for the establishment of a monastic community. The *Sermo Angelicus,* divided into twenty-one long lessons, became the daily readings in the weekly Office of Our Lady of the nuns in the Order of the Holy Savior.[32]

The three times seven lessons assigned to seven days' matins (the night prayer office of monks, nuns, and other religious) treat seven stages in salvation history. Antiphons, responsories, prayers, and other liturgical items were written to match the main subject of each of the seven days and were repeated in identical manner every week through the year. The ordinary year of the Church from Advent to Christmas, Easter, Pentecost, and Last Judgment was present through the priestly office prayed by Prior Peter, Master Peter, and other priests and members of Birgitta's household. So it was a considerable advance for the spirituality of a female community when, instead of a simple Marian office prayed in the same way every day, the so-called *Officium parvum Beatae Mariae Virginis,* the nuns of the Order of the Holy Savior could pray and sing a "Great Marian Office" proper to their own order. Here the priest who must have been Birgitta's spiritual advisor during this period enters into the picture: it seems indisputable that Master Peter Olavsson actually wrote the liturgical texts of the Great Marian Office and even composed or adapted Gregorian chant to the texts, to fit the twenty-one lessons "dictated" to Birgitta by the angel.[33]

The Sunday texts were devoted to God's work of creating the world according to the most beautiful "model" for it, which was the Mother of God, the Virgin existing in God's consciousness and premeditation before all ages. The office proceeds on Monday to the angels, their beauty and fall; on Tuesday to Adam's fall, to the patriarchs and to the premeditated protection of the people of God through the Virgin, the Mother of God to come. Wednesday deals with the birth of the Virgin, her childhood and youth while chosen and elected with preeminence among all women. Thursday is devoted to the incarnation of the Word Divine, and Friday to the suffering and death of Christ in his manhood.

On Saturday, contrary to what one might expect, the meditation does not stay with Christ in his tomb, in expectation of the day of resurrection. Characteristically, it concentrates upon the theme of the Virgin's faith in Christ, in spite of all odds—her confidence during the first great Sabbath, when Christ went down to the nether world, that he would rise again, and, finally, her bodily assumption into God's presence. Nowhere is Birgitta's Mariology brought to a fuller expression.[34] And yet there is nothing entirely new compared to the revelations from her Swedish period collected in Book I. A good number of them start with the introductory: "I am the Queen of Heaven" or "I am Mary," if speaking to Birgitta, or referring to Birgitta as seeing her in a vision, or to the Mother as speaking to the Son. But whereas Mary in Book I is speaking and acting, the Sermon of the Angel is at face value a treatise on her role in salvation history—and therefore Mariology, not Marian piety. It is the doctrine of what she means in God's plan, not the story of her intervention in the present-day life of the Church. But on the other hand, being Mariology, and inasmuch as salvation history is present and working in any epoch of world history and in any stage of an individual's life, the Sermon of the Angel also tells of the daily, eternal story of Motherhood and Virginity interceding in any salvific events that surround us.

Master Peter's engagement in the shaping of the Marian Office for the nuns is revealing. It raises the question if, by chance, there was something in his religious outlook which helped bring Birgitta into a state of mind where this perspective on salvation history was close at hand. We cannot know this, since there are no distinct literary works known to be exclusively written by Master Peter. But considering the importance of confessors, the Sermon of the Angel may be taken as the fullest expression of Birgitta's first meeting with Rome, the city of martyrs, on the one hand, and the guidance of Master Peter on the other. In this situation the strict theological training of Master Matthias ceased to press its mark upon Birgitta, and the Italian milieu, perhaps also imbued with fresh experiences of Franciscan piety, made its impression upon her. As Toni Schmid has pointed out (1940), Birgitta's understanding of the Immaculate Conception of Mary is close to that of the Franciscans of the fourteenth century, more distant from that of the Dominican school, whereas for the assumption she deviates somewhat from the Franciscan view, absolutely stating against skeptics, however, the Virgin's bodily assumption (VI, 60).[35]

Psychologically and spiritually the Sermon of the Angel marks the end of crisis, Birgitta's arrival into the promised land in an even deeper sense. What used to be a perverted, chaotic world, an "inverse salvation history" presented by the monk on the ladder in his challenging God, has now turned into a cosmos, in which the essence of womanhood and motherhood has become the center toward which all doctrines and dogmas of faith are being oriented. In this case, as for the *Book of Questions,* the literary result of the process no doubt lags far behind the real event that made it possible. The moment Book V was conceived and written down, Birgitta must have overcome the crisis described in it and may already have arrived at a new cosmos, which was then activated and made productive in a literary sense by the apparition of the angel. God's answers to the monk's attacks may have paved the way for this new history of salvation.

Monastic Family

Two great revelations of Birgitta have been mentioned so far: Book V from the summer of 1349 and the Sermon of the Angel from 1352-53. These two texts give witness to Birgitta's transition from a life of a noble lady in Sweden to that of a noble guest and pilgrim in the holy city. She exchanged a life at home for that of a foreigner—a transition we encounter most dramatically in the Irish monks of the early Middle Ages taking lifelong exile as the most harsh form of penance, which it also certainly is in all ages of mankind. But the third great revelation of Birgitta, that of her vision of the Rule of the Holy Savior, has not yet been treated here, although it probably came first in time. There is a general assumption that Birgitta had this vision in Vadstena on one of the occasions when she stayed with King Magnus Eriksson and Queen Blanca in the royal palace, which was later to become the first monastery of the Order of the Holy Savior.[36]

The problem of the text is that we do not possess any original version to bring us back to the very moment of her vision.[37] What we have is an echo of the primary mystical experience she had, worked out to fit the exigencies of canon law, but framed by revelations retelling the circumstances surrounding her vision. If we remove the surrounding revelations, the division into chapters, the chapter headings, and a number of particular directives clearly intended at adjusting the text to the genre of a monastic rule, we become aware of three stages of mystical experience gradually broadening Birgitta's understanding of the task God wanted to entrust to her.

The first field of the vision is the young virgin chosen by Christ the Lord to lead a life of the elect in the sisterly community under the guidance of her mother abbess. In a solemn rite of transition she is taken out of the secular world, and removes her secular clothes, to be invested by Christ, here in the person of the bishop, in the gown of the chosen ones, and crowned with Christ's five marks of passion.

In the second field of the vision we meet the sisterly community of the elect in need of the complementary element of male assistance to represent the fullness of divine redemption. In a grand general view, the recruitment of this sister- and brotherhood of the elect is being sketched: how dowries and gifts are to be accumulated until a certain level of self-support has been attained, and how, thereafter, any surplus is to be distributed to the poor and needy.

The third field of the vision reveals the community's purpose: first, perpetual service of God in the love of a burning heart, where everything has to be directed towards this goal, on the human as well as on the material scale; second, ascetic practice, confession of sins, the preparation of the altars for the daily sacrifice of the mass, and the disciplinary supervision exerted by the bishop. In the final passage death is evoked: the daily rehearsal of the rite of *memento mori* is prescribed to prove that death is conquered by this perpetual, neverending praise of God, which lets individual death become nothing more than birth into a new life, making room for a new member to enter into the community of the elect.[38]

The Rule of the Holy Savior does not have its like in the history of monastic rules. Few other rules ever approved were composed of so few basic elements, and paid so little attention to all the practical needs of a monastic community. This perhaps explains the thorny path of this visionary text from its first version probably produced by the Swedish confessors in the 1340s, through its first presentation to the pope probably around 1367, its first summary approval by Pope Urban V in 1370, and the final approval of a revised version by Pope Urban VI in 1378, although formally only as constitutions to be added to the rule of St. Augustine.[39] But at that time Birgitta had already left the scene, and sons and daughters of her monastic family had to be content with this image of an original visionary impetus. And yet they found access to the fresh water in the vessel in which it was contained.

The Rule of the Holy Savior has been for hundreds of followers to the call the first acquaintance they ever had with Birgitta's visionary world. It is a text derived from the walk of her soul with Christ, her Lord and bridegroom, a walk in which he, with delicate care, introduces her to one secret after the other in stages of well-measured time. In like manner, new recruits to the Order of the Holy Savior met Christ taking their hands to introduce them with subtlety into the three stages of the community life of the elect: the personal decision and election; the human fullness of divine praise and its continuation through the generations; and the perfect sacrifice of the chosen people in spite of material limitations and individual death.

The Seven Books

There are, as we have seen, three great revelation texts in Birgitta's writings. Their relative sequence in time is: Monastic Rule, *Book of Questions,* Sermon of the Angel. But probably only the last-mentioned revelation got its final shape comparatively soon after it had been given. The *Book of Questions* was enriched by inserted revelations, the Rule was probably worked over again and again, so that the text, as we know it, is more recent than those of the other two great visions.

The bulk of Birgitta's writings consists of about six hundred longer or shorter texts stylized as sayings of God the Father, Christ, his Mother, or another saint.[40] Birgitta herself as the bride is often found speaking in the text, sometimes even opening it up by a question or by the retelling of something which happened to her. So many messages, spread out over a period of maybe thirty mature years, had to be arranged according to some external criteria. Scholars have discussed which one of Birgitta's confessors is to be credited for the arrangement of most of the texts in eight "books": one of the two Peters, or Bishop Alphonsus. The con-

clusion of Salomon Kraft (1929) was that the sequence is partly chronological, but on the basis of a scheme laid down by Bishop Alphonsus.[41] We can discern characteristic traces of the division in eight books. The first book, already treated above, contains sixty distinct revelations, all from Birgitta's time in Sweden. The second, third, and seventh books each contain thirty texts or a little more—30, 34, and 31, respectively. This is hardly accidental. The number of items joined into a unit was taken as a form to mirror a basic order inherent in matter. It seems to me very probable that an ideal number of 60, 30, 30, and 30 texts collected into four units may have been projected at a very early stage of the arrangement. This corresponds to the four different origin situations of the four groups:

Book I:	60 great revelations from Sweden
Book II:	30 other revelations from Sweden
Book III:	30(?) revelations from Italy
Book VII:	30(?) revelations from the Holy Land

An examination of Book III shows that among the 34 texts of the authorized version some are extremely short exhortations, of a type which can be found more often in Books IV and VI and among the *Extravagantes,* but is clearly exceptional here: chapters 9, 25, 32. Also chapters 22, 23, and 34 are comparatively short. It is easy to assume that four of these six texts have been added to an original number of 30 chapters. In Book VII, on the other hand, long and short texts have the same value inasfar as they each refer to a particular phase of Birgitta's journey to the Holy Land. Possibly chapter 9 is a later addition, a short promise to Birgitta increasing the total number from a planned 30 to 31 chapters; but this, of course, is a guess.

In any case, four books are arranged to give an approximate number of 150 revelations. To play a little with the numbers, one might also put it in another way: three opening books render a total of approximately 120 chapters. This is interesting, since Book IV at some stage seems to have consisted of 130 chapters, at the end of which the authorized version says: "This is the end of Book IV according to Alphonsus." What follows is an addition of special revelations addressed to popes and high prelates, raising the total number to 144 chapters. Of the first 130 chapters there are many rather short ones: 26-32; 35; 41-43; 56-57; 66; 73; 84; 91; 116-23. One might easily imagine ten of these texts to have been squeezed in among an original number of 120 chapters, which would bring a rather neat balance between Books I-III on the one hand, and Book IV on the other, as two units with 120 texts each.

One might even consider the 109 chapters of Book VI as a result of an increase from 90; adding Book VII to Book VI, then, would render a third great unit of roughly 120 chapters.

Whatever the plan might have been, it could not, however, not even with adjustments, comprise the total number of Birgitta's revelations. Some texts apparently unknown or discarded in the first run appeared again and again, as, e.g., when Prior Peter returned to Sweden in 1380.[42] It was, then, hopeless to try to force all the texts into the framework of the seven books which can be proved to have existed first. A Book VIII, containing political messages, was added; and yet there were still 116 revelations floating around that finally—after resultless efforts to arrange them in different series—were brought together and called the *Extravagantes*—texts outside the main collection (also inadequately called Book IX).

The story of the confessors trying to bring order into the mass of divine messages left behind by Birgitta is itself witness to the incredible span of inspiration in her mystical and literary heritage. Some texts are visions written down, with or without a summary, a goal indicating the inner tendency of the vision. Many texts are doctrinal, ascetic, or didactic treatises, in which an original visionary nucleus is surrounded by constructions such as applications to the moral life, often in a scholastic set-up. This fits perfectly well into the pattern worked out by Peter Dinzelbacher (1981),[43] who is able to identify a similar mixture of visionary and didactic elements in much female mystical writing of the fourteenth and fifteenth centuries.

No effort has been made yet among scholars to treat Books I, II, and III as a unit of some sort, the parts of which remain characteristically distinct. Is it merely accidental that *Book II* starts with the threefold temptation by the devil at Birgitta's calling? And that Book III initiates a sequence of personal messages to bishops and priests, some spoken by saints of Italian shrines—St. Ambrose (Milan), chapters 5-7; John the Baptist (St. John Lateran), chapter 11; St. Agnes (Rome), chapters 12 and 30; St. Dominic, chapters 17-18; St. Benedict, chapters 20-22—some directly addressing the moral corruption of the eternal city of Birgitta's years (chapter 27 ff.)? The common link between Books I, II, and III seems to be the transition in Birgitta's calling from the Swedish to the Italian scene, demonstrated in magisterial and solemn visionary texts, as if the redactor(s) wanted to collect in these first books the clearest, most outspoken, most predicative messages that Birgitta had received. One might easily imagine that in between she might have received many of the short glances of the divine will which we encounter so often in the many short texts of Books IV and VI, and among the *Extravagantes*. The proportion between great visions and short, didactically formulated insights in God's mysteries might have been about the same as that transmitted in Book VII, for the reasons stated above. This, then, makes Book VII, which is rendered in full in this translation, much more interesting.

First, however, what makes Book IV differ most from Books I, II, and III is probably the subject matter and the addressees of the revelations.[44] There is an opening sequence of revelations addressed to kings; there are visions of Rome, of the judgment; several times St. Agnes is speaking, once, John the Evangelist. The sequence in chapters 26-32 of several short messages by the Blessed Mother may indicate the end of a first section, for then, in chapter 33, a series of grand visions starts again: on Rome, on penitence, on the corruption of religious orders, on priests, on the government of the Church on earth: pope, bishops, priests. Chapters 64-66 constitute short, perhaps concluding messages of the Blessed Mother. New items are treated next: from chapter 67 onward great messages on obedience, temptation, and the passion of Christ are introduced, followed by the important messages on Christian knighthood and on "God's friends." *Amici Dei,* rendered "die Gottesfreunde" in German, was a special notion in Birgitta's time: a term used by groups of believers to designate themselves as Christians withdrawing from the world, cultivating an intimate, unpretentious friendship with God without immersing in worldly interests and desires, but also without formally joining a religious order.[45] Again, some very short texts are inserted here, e.g., chapters 83-85, 93-98. Somewhere around chapter 100 we meet still another type of text: the famous political messages to the kings of England and France; Birgitta's conversation with St. Denis, the patron saint of France; Christ's teaching on repentance, penitence, pride, humility, and good intention; and, in conclusion, a tremendous judgment vision on a bishop, as well as a mysterious vision of seven animals with strong symbolism (chapters 125-26). The unity of Book IV is indicated by the curious fact that the vision in chapter 2 is explained in chapter 129—the second last chapter in Book IV "according to Alphonsus."

Thus, Book IV is certainly more than a hodgepodge of everything which does not fit elsewhere. One might easily consider Books I, II, and III as a result of a first selection of solemn, magisterial revelations, those dealing with the most universal subjects of Christian faith. In Book IV, then, the redactor(s) may have undertaken a second selection, collecting texts directed to more specific categories of Christians and treating more specific matters of faith and morals. This very general attempt to explain the genesis of Books I, II, and III, in relation to Book IV is, of course, no more than a working hypothesis for further study; nevertheless, it may be worthwhile to try to see the texts in the light of such a hypothesis.

There is enough evidence to show that Books I, II, III, and IV were kept together as such at a very early stage of redactionary work and then generally followed by Book V, which by force of its extraordinary character may have been placed there as a kind of first conclusion to the preceding books. Westman and Kraft made the puzzling discovery that in the second earliest extant manuscript dated 1388, Book V is followed by Book VII, and only then comes what we afterward know as Book VI.[46] This seems to indicate that Book VI is indeed the arrangement of a number of remaining texts which probably did not reach the level of "great visions" and also were not, like Book VII, kept together by a common origin like the pilgrimage to Jerusalem. If the order of Books VI and VII can be reversed, it would be worthwhile to find out if Book VI also contains subgroups corresponding to units of some 30 revelations. Is this the case?

There are in fact some striking cuts in the sequence of the originally 109 (at present 122) texts of Book VI. How is it to be explained, for example, that chapter 34 starts out with a message of the value of the revelations in general and turns it into a message on the conflict between England and France—and that chapter 63 deals with the letter Birgitta was to send to Pope Clement concerning the same conflict? Between chapters 34 and 63 we find a number of texts testifying to the credibility of God's message: a knight at his judgment (ch. 39), sins of kings (ch. 41), purgatory (ch. 52), and the sequence of Marian texts on her Immaculate Conception, assumption, flight to Egypt, the birth and ascension of Christ, etc. (ch. 55-62). It seems reasonable to see chapters 34 and 63 as a kind of brackets, marking the beginning and end of the second section of Book VI. Chapter 65 is the opening of the third section: the very extensive revelation on Mary and Martha as symbols of the two vocations, the contemplative and the active. All the remaining texts, chapters 66-109, can be understood as illustrating both vocations: the contemplative way of priests and religious, the active way of men and women serving God in the world. Book VI, chapters 1-33, then, appears to concentrate on moral values, expanding upon impatience (ch. 6), pride (ch. 5, 15), luxury (ch. 19), temptation (ch. 6 and 17), repentance (ch. 20, 24), and conversion (ch. 26). Chapter 33, on the mutual love of bride and bridegroom—an old imagery with many symbolic implications—would be justly understood as the final summing up of such a first section of Book VI. Taking into account later additions to Book VI, we may assume an original plan of a third unit of 120 texts (90 for Book VI and 30 for Book VII) to balance Books I, II, and III on the one hand, and Book IV on the other.[47]

This allows us finally to turn to Book VII, in its entirety contained in the following translation.[48] There are 31 chapters, all dealing with the preparations and stages of Birgitta's pilgrimage to the Holy Land in 1372. This book was long regarded as the last of the whole collection, until Book VIII was added. Thematically Book VII starts with a prophecy from "after the year of the jubilee," that Birgitta was to go to Jerusalem and Bethlehem (ch. 1), a vision of the sorrows of Mary which Birgitta had in the church of Santa Maria Maggiore on 2 February (ch. 2, possibly in 1351, the first Lenten season Birgitta spent in Rome), and finally that very intimate experience she had of St. Francis on one of his feast days in the church dedicated to him in Trastevere (ch. 3). To share our Lady's sorrows and St. Francis's food and drink meant to enter on the narrow path to follow Christ on his earthly way from birth and childhood to manhood and death on the cross. This was prepared through Birgitta's visit to St. Thomas's relics in Ortona (ch. 4), her message to young Elziario of Ariano in Naples (ch. 5), and, finally, Christ's calling to her on 25 May 1371, to prepare herself for the pilgrimage to the Holy Sepulchre (ch. 6).

This is the signal for another series of six texts, chapters 7 to 12, dealing with subtle matters of conscience and spiritual distinctions, and basically located in Naples. A new series of six revelations starts with Birgitta's long-lasting doubts concerning the spiritual destiny of her own son Karl, who had a liaison with the queen of Naples (ch. 13). Expressedly, it is stated that her anxiety over the destiny of Karl followed her to the Holy Land. In such manner the scene is dramatically turned to Jerusalem, where Christ appears and talks to Birgitta on the grace of pilgrims (ch. 14), showing her the entire story of his passion and death (ch. 15) and the meaning of it (ch. 16). After this a short chapter on Birgitta's lodging (ch. 17) leads to the matter of Cyprus: first a letter she wrote to the king of Cyprus giving advice (ch. 18), then her confrontation with the actual situation there—apparently new to her—including the Greek Church and its representatives on Cyprus (ch. 19). Perhaps the letter in chapter 18 was added later, for there follows another sequence of six texts: the long chapter 20 dealing with the Franciscan Rule and the true followers of St. Francis, the four visionary texts from Bethlehem (ch. 21-24), and, finally, the speech of our Lady on humility (ch. 25). Then we reach the last section: Birgitta's last visits, which gave her the vision of the assumption of our Lady (ch. 26), the return to Italy by way of Naples (ch. 27 and 28), her letter to a bishop of Ancona (ch. 29), one of the great visions of the Judge (ch. 30), and, finally, Birgitta's last revelation five days before her death (ch. 31).

Regardless of the length of time which Birgitta spent in these different places, the redactor, doubtless Bishop Alphonsus, handed down to us in Book VII a wonderful piece of literary art, built up and held together by means of carefully selected texts and revelations. Much has been written on the profound devotion expressed in Birgitta's words when she describes Christ's and our Lady's appearances to her in the Holy Land.[49] But it ought not to be forgotten what a high degree of spiritual attachment has been laid down in the redactionary work found in this collection, so that each one of the great visions from the Holy Land stands out in its own force to convey the message of the divine meeting a chosen woman and revealing to her the secrets of heaven. No geographical or chronological affinity is comparable to this unity, stemming from the maturity of someone beholding God's mysteries after a long life of loving and suffering in God's presence.

Scholars agree that the first seven books of *Revelations* constitute the main corpus of God's message through Birgitta. But not everybody will consult such a huge collection of texts. The need for a digest was urgent already in the fourteenth century. Alphonsus himself took the first steps to comply with such wishes. He had three groups of addressees in mind:

1) kings and other civil authorities
2) pontiffs and bishops
3) the monastic family of the Order of the Holy Savior.

For each of these groups he produced a compilation in which texts already placed in one of the Seven Books were mixed with other texts of Birgitta which Alphonsus had either not known at the time he created the seven books, or which he had ruled out during the process.[50] The first compilation he called "The Book of the Heavenly Emperor to the Kings"; this has since that time been called "Book VIII" of the *Revelations,* although about half of the texts—there were originally 58 chapters, later 3 more were added—were already part of other books.[51]

The second collection, addressed to popes and bishops, *Ad pontifices,* has in fact not survived; it is found only in one manuscript. Its content is spread around at the end of Book IV and as sequences among the *Extravagantes.*[52]

The third collection, meant for the religious of the order, has been widely spread and studied under the name of *Celeste viridarium,* "The Heavenly Pasture," or, in the classical and renaissance sense of the word, "The Heavenly Garden." Book VIII has been adopted into the main collection probably partly because Alphonsus wrote his magnificent preface to it: "The Letter of the Hermit to the Kings," where he defends Birgitta against attacks which were bound to come, although at the time he wrote, in 1379, they were not yet as fierce as they became later on.[53]

Finally there are the extraordinary *Four Prayers* also translated and included in the present selection of texts.[54] The knowledge we have of these prayers and their origin is limited. They are extensive meditations in the form of prayers of praise to God for his blessings to mankind through the life on earth of our Lady and of Christ (first and second prayers), and through

the beauty of Christ in his manhood (third prayer), and of our Lady (fourth prayer). This type of prayer and meditation was widespread in the Middle Ages: Christ's head, face, lips, eyes, ears, tongue, shoulders, intestines, breast, arms, hands, legs, and feet are the objects of meditation for the part they play in the salvific action of God. Of all these devotions we have kept in our epoch only one: that to the Sacred Heart, which is also part of the third of Birgitta's four prayers. The same is true for the meditations on the limbs of our Lady in the fourth prayer.

The Doctrine

The doctrine of St. Birgitta is certainly, as can be derived from what has been said so far, most aptly understood as the result of a dialectical process partly between Birgitta and her confessors and spiritual advisors, partly between her own experiences and her mental and affective life.

The basic stages of spiritual development are all present in her life: purification from sin through contrition and acceptance of God's majesty, mercy, and care; illumination through steady progress in the virtues and through an ever greater understanding of and affection for God's salvific action towards his people by innumerable means; union of the soul with God as a bride is embraced by the bridegroom.[55] This spiritual development is decisively Christian in that Birgitta accepts God's grace in and through the Messenger, the Messiah, the Anointed One, Jesus Christ. With Christ the heavenly host is always present in dynamic activity and yet all-enduring peace and communion with God— Christ's Mother Mary, all the angels and saints. On the periphery the fallen angels, angry at not being allowed to participate in God's essence, are trying to disturb as much as possible the path of the human soul toward its goal.

Let us examine for a moment the teaching in Birgitta's revelations on the first steps of the path to heaven: contrition and repentance for sins, the return of the erring child to the caring love of its parents. "Come and rise quickly through penance and contrition, then I will forgive the sins and give you patience and strength to be able to withstand the plots of the devil" (VI, 30). It is Christ's program for the bride to proceed from the first to the second stage of spiritual life. There is "true" contrition if the person has a perfect intention of making good what was formerly destroyed, as in the parable of the goldsmith (II, 14), or, in a more subtle distinction, if the person has the firm intention of doing no more evil and of persevering in good deeds (VI, 24). If, as the words given to a Swedish lady in Rome show, contrition is not as deep as the lust in doing evil was great, God's special love is necessary to fill out the gap (VI, 102). As when two lovers meet in stages such as sending letters, talking together, and embracing, penance and contrition are like the second stage, the mutual talk between bride and bridegroom by which they become one heart and one soul, to proceed to the union of the naked human soul with God, which is pure love and heavenly desire (IV, 75).

Praying to God with contrition entitles one to be called God's friend precisely because of this contrition; and if contrition is firm, not only sin but also the penance for sin will be forgiven (III, 26). The symbols of a golden key, a silver vase, and a crown adorned with precious stones, all offered to God by an angel, denote the three stages of spiritual life. Here, the golden key is "pure" contrition for sins, by which the heart of God is being opened to let the sinner in (IV, 107). Two ways lead to the heart of God: the first is humility's true contrition leading man into spiritual discourse with God; the second way is meditation on Christ's passion, so that the hardness of man's heart is weakened and he runs with joy to the heart of God (IV, 101). All sorrow and tears of contrition are recalled in the scene when Birgitta suffers for her son Karl in Naples (VII, 13). Once contrition is likened to golden shoes which enable you to walk (III, 24), once to an undershirt which is closest to the body and therefore comes first when you dress (I, 7).

Contrition is like the point of a sword in the warrior's hand, since it kills the devil (IV, 89). Here, contrition hits and strikes; but on other occasions it also purges and Birgitta can place it in the intestines because this is where the cleaning process of the body takes place (IV, 115). Even the devil knows perfectly well the disastrous effects of contrition on his affairs. In a speech concerning a bad monk he characterizes it as a whirlwind which, if it leads to confession of sins and is strongly upheld, is the most secure path to peace with God—"and just from such heights," the devil declares, "I succeeded in pushing him down by his own desire to sin" (IV, 102).

Birgitta often returns to the theme of contrition immediately before death and its effect upon the eternal destiny of the soul, as, for example, when "for charity's sake" a contrition characterized as "divine" was given to a person shortly before his death; this contrition separated him from hell (IV, 9). Once the "Word" from the "Pulpit" told Birgitta that many who are guilty of numerous crimes receive the gift of full contrition before death, and that such contrition might even be so perfect that not only sins were forgiven, but also the punishment that ought to have been suffered after death (VIII, 48). But there is another side, as is clear from another passage: someone confessed his sins, but there was very little contrition in his confession, and so he was not saved—he did not deserve the kingdom of heaven. As the conclusion states: "If my friends want to be reconciled with my grace and friendship, they must needs make penitence and have contrition of all

their heart for having offended me, their Creator and Redemptor." The next step after contrition is confession of sins, the third is communion with the faithful, the Church (IV, 7, cf. below, VII, 27).

A person who had lived all his life without confession and communion in despair of salvation (such was possible even in the Middle Ages!) confessed his sins several times shortly before his death, so that the devil, with whom he had entered into a covenant and to whom he had given an oath of fidelity, fled. This was precisely because of his contrition. This contrition was given to him as a gift of God because the man had always felt some type of compassion with the Mother of God when he thought and heard of her, without, however, really loving her in his heart. But this was enough for a *compendium salutis suae,* as the text runs—an expression which might mean the "property" or the "area" of his salvation, but which could also mean "compendium of salvation" in the modern sense (VI, 97). The same expression is used for the bishop of Växjö, to whom contrition and confession are a *compendium* for life in this world (III, 12).

It is interesting to note that God's answers to the monk on the ladder in Book V do not enter upon contrition. It is as if God—being here the accused one—does not want to open his heart to the conversion of the monk, but rather marks the distance between what the monk propounds and what is in reality the true context of things. Contrition is a gift of God and a concept to denote a very intimate relationship between the soul and its Creator, as the likeness of the lovers tells us. The monk on the ladder has nothing that can serve as a vessel or a vehicle for the gift of contrition. Not the slightest compendium of salvation is present in him, only doubts and reasoning.

One explanation for this might be hinted at by another symbolic interpretation of the key. The only key to open and to close is the desire for God alone, so that man does not want anything but God, and him only because of his love. Only husband and wife, only God and the soul, can dispose of the key to their partner's intimate chamber, so that their common desire for each other is the only key to open it (II, 27). That contrition for sins can range among the meanings carried by the key indicates that it also has this character of intimate confidence which is peculiar to the act of opening and closing the door with the key.

The full doctrine of the spiritual life is again propounded in one of the revelations placed after Birgitta's journey to Jerusalem. The first stage is penance and contrition of heart because of the offense one has committed against the Creator and Redemptor. Confession of sins, humble and iterated, marks the beginning of the second stage which consists in making reparation for sins according to the advice of the confessor, so that God can approach and the devil withdraws from the person. The third stage, then, consists not only in the participation in the sacrament of the altar—our meaning of "communion"—but also in the "receiving of my body with a firm intention never to fall back into previous sins but to endure in good until the end" (VII, 27). "My Body" here obviously means the full communion and unity with the Church, Christ's mystical body.

Penance, characteristic of the second stage of spiritual life, may sometimes be only an empty gesture, as we saw in some examples above—penance without real and worthy contrition for sins. But generally Birgitta's teaching is that penance is a proof of the socialization of the person in that he or she starts to confess their sins regularly and to take the advice and submit to the guidance of their confessor. "While I abhorred penance I felt heavy as if in chains, but since I started to go to confession I feel so relieved and peaceful in my soul, that I don't care for honors nor if I suffer losses in my property," runs a personal comment added to a revelation (VI, 20). The grace of penance keeps a person in God's hands, even though he or she justly ought to have been handed over to the devil because of crimes (*Extravagantes* 89). Penance can wash clean what has become dirty (II, 26, and IV, 39), but this is true also for confession (VI, 16). The evil smell of a sinner, registered by Birgitta, can only be healed by penance, to evade God's wrath (*Extravagantes* 81). There will be no more account for those sins for which penance has been done; sins for which there was no penance done will have to be cleansed in other ways or remedied here and now (I, 36). In open words the Mother of God stated to Birgitta before she left for Jerusalem that God will never deny his grace to a sinner with a true contrition, a will to satisfy for sin, honest penance, and humble prayer with burning love to receive God's mercy (VII, 7).

But remedy for sins committed also implies hard efforts and training in acts of self-denial. To this and many other forms of mastering one's own will, feelings, thoughts, and abilities, Birgitta often uses the word *labor,* work, in more or less the modern sense of the word. "My friends should work diligently that justice be observed and upheld, that care be taken of society, that God's honor grow and that rebels and criminals be punished," says Christ to one of the kings (VIII, 18). This "work" is certainly understood as part of what in religious terms is called penance: "God's friends . . . ought to work in order that the evildoer improves and the good reaches perfection" (IV, 21). To preach and show others the way can be a "work" (I, 40), and by this same word ("before I started my work") Christ can refer to the beginning of his active three years of pronouncing the message (II, 15). We often have also the other meaning which the Latin word *laborare* can take: to suffer, to endure hardships. Mary

says about Jesus: "He worked with his hands" (VI, 58), and a mother's prayers and tears for her son can be called her "work" or "suffering" for him (VII, 13). There is intellectual work, as can be seen from a speech between two masters (II, 22), and the five senses can be said to have each their work to do (VI, 66). God's friends ought to work in order to save souls (VI, 47), and someone will have to work with the ground to earn his living (*Extravagantes* 83). Even the devil works, not against man's bodily existence, but against virtues, patience, and moderation in man (VI, 43), or to make him deaf and mute (IV, 107). But there is difference between work and work: some work only for material reasons and they receive no "crown," no eternal glory for that; but if this work is God's precept to them, then they serve him in their work (IV, 74). To attain true love we need humility, mercy, and the "work" or "suffering" of love, *labor caritatis* (III, 12, and IV, 126).

We get very close to Birgitta personally in her little dialogue with the Mother of God upon Birgitta's question: "Should I never work in order to earn my living?" The Blessed Mother gives her a question in reply: "What are you doing just now and every day?" Birgitta answers—in fact, the text reads, very exceptionally: "And I answered"—"I learn grammar and pray and write." Then the Blessed Mother said: "Don't give up such a work for physical work!" (IV, 46).

We reach another dimension, that of "good works" or "good deeds," when Christ speaks to Birgitta about Jacob who worked long to win Rachel as his wife. Love made his work easier, and this is true, then, for the spiritual life: "Many work in a manly way with prayers and good deeds in order to reach heaven, but when they think they have attained the peace of being with God, they get involved in temptations, their troubles increase, and just as they envisage themselves perfect, they discover that they are totally imperfect" (V, revelation 6).

It is in the nature of things that the third stage of spiritual life, called "the peace of contemplation," here rendered as "the peace of being with God," cannot be described in ordinary words, since it is a wordless union beyond letters and sentences—see the imagery of the lovers quoted above (IV, 75). If "communion" stands for this third stage, it is clear to us that this word cannot denote solely the act of receiving the Blessed Sacrament, the Body of Christ under the shape of the unleavened bread, and the Blood of Christ under the shape of wine mixed with a drop of water. Not even the "confession" of the second stage can be understood in Birgitta's writings as just the holy sacrament of penance. It means a more specific readiness to admit to all the fellowship that we are sinners, and that therefore we are called to appear in God's presence to be at his disposal in his salvific action towards all mankind. In like manner, the "communion" of the third stage must mean a permanent union with God's friends in whom God appears visibly to us and to our human eyes and understanding.

Taking this as basic to what Birgitta meant by "communion," we may have a closer look at some of her visions and messages belonging to this dimension.

Once in Italy on the first Sunday after Easter, Birgitta was inspired by 1 John 5, read on that day at mass. "There are three who give witness on earth: Spirit, Water, and Blood; and three who give witness in heaven: Father, Son, and Holy Spirit." The three are then linked to faith, baptism, and adoption in God, and Birgitta, as daughter of the Godhead, is told to receive the Body and Blood of Christ's manhood from the hands of the priest thereby to signify her readiness to do "our" will (says the Triune God) and in order that Christ testifies to her being his and belonging to him. In Christ, then, the Father and the Holy Spirit also testify to the same effect, that she belongs to all the three Persons by force of her true faith and her love (III, 23). No doubt "faith" here stands for the beginning, the first stage of spiritual life; "baptism" for the second stage, corresponding to contrition and confession in the texts quoted earlier. To be the daughter of God, adopted as it were, to be "his" without any further addition, then, must refer to the unitive stage of spiritual life; and precisely here Birgitta is told to receive the Body and Blood of Christ in the sacrament of the altar. Not the divinity of Christ, but the humanity of Christ is the way to union with God according to Birgitta's teaching here, for then the Godhead—Son, Father, Holy Spirit—testify to where their daughter belongs.

In like manner, the feast of Pentecost once revealed to Birgitta some of the most evanescent of God's expressions of love. During early morning mass, Birgitta saw a fire descend and surround the altar. In the fire she saw the priest with the Host in his hand, and in the Host she saw a lamb, and in the lamb "an inflaming face, like that of a man." The vision was interpreted to her by a voice telling her about the fire of Pentecost inflaming the hearts of the disciples. But the voice continued its message: "Through the word the bread becomes the Living Lamb, which is my Body, and the Face is in the Lamb, and the Lamb in the Face, for the Father is in the Son and the Son in the Father, and the Holy Spirit is in both." "And then," the text adds, "in the hand of the priest the bride saw, at the elevation of the eucharist, a young man of extraordinary beauty, who said: I bless you who believe; to those who don't believe I am a judge" (VI, 86). From what she saw first: an inflaming face like that of a man, Birgitta is carried on finally to stand face to face with Christ in the shape of a young man of extraordinary beauty. The transition is made pos-

sible by the fire from heaven and the final stage is closeness; but the intermediate stage is the short passing through doctrine and clarification of the Triune God before entering into the final union and communion, signalled by the elevation of the Host.

The last week of Birgitta's life sets forth an immemorial record of her union with the bridegroom. For a long time in June-July 1373 (the text does not say how long) Birgitta had felt the emptiness and desolation of her heavenly spouse not being with her—that feeling of night which other mystics have written more about. Sunday, the 17th of July, the fourth Sunday after Pentecost, she attended mass in her house. It may have been the Sunday named after its entrance verse: *Dominus illuminatio mea*—"The Lord is my Light and my Savior," and the gospel may then, as later, have been Luke 5:1-11, on the faith of St. Peter towards Jesus at the great fishing in the Lake Genesareth. Monday or Tuesday, Christ finally spoke to Birgitta, giving her relief with the words: "I was to you just like a spouse generally is, when he hides from his bride in order that she has greater desire for him. . . . So now after this probation proceed and be prepared, for now the time has come when that shall be fulfilled what I promised you, that . . . you shall be counted not only my bride, but also a nun and the mother in Vadstena" (VII, 31). On Friday, July 22, fell the feast of St. Mary Magdalene, and on Saturday, July 23, Birgitta died in her room which still exists at the Piazza Farnese in Rome.

The third stage of spiritual life, to her, was the indissoluble union with God, in which no element of mystical love was lacking.

Notes

[1] Recent publications with further references: *Temi e problemi nella mistica femminile trecentesca* (Todi, 1983), and Peter Dinzelbacher and Dieter R. Bauer, eds., *Frauenmystik im Mittelalter* (Ostfildern bei Stuttgart, 1985).

[2] Michael Goodich, *Vita perfecta: The Ideal of Sainthood in the Thirteenth Century* (Stuttgart, 1982, = Monographien zur Geschichte des Mittelalters, 25), pp. 48-68.

[3] Isak Collijn, ed., *Acta et processus canonizacionis beate Birgitte* (Uppsala, 1924-31, = Samlingar utgivna av Svenska Fornskriftsällskapet, Ser. 2: Latinska skrifter, I).

[4] Sara Ekwall, *Vår äldsta Birgittavita och dennas viktigaste varianter* [summary: La plus ancienne vie de sainte Brigitte et ses deux variations les plus importantes] (Lund, 1965, = Kungl. Vitterhets Historie och Antikvitets Akademiens Handlingar, Historiska Serien, 12).

[5] Karl Kup, "Ulrich von Richenthal's Chronicle of the Council of Constance," *Bulletin of The New York Public Library* (April, 1936). Eric Colledge, "Epistola solitarii ad reges: Alphonce of Pecha as Organizer of Birgittine and Urbanist Propaganda," *Medieval Studies* 18 (1956): 19-49, here pp. 44-45.

[6] Claes Annerstedt, ed., *Vita Sanctae Birgittae,* in *Scriptores Rerum Suecicarum medii aevi,* III, 2 (Upsaliae, 1876), pp. 188-206, and I. Collijn, ed. (*supra,* note 3), pp. 73-101. Another version of this text was published by I. Collijn, *ibid,* pp. 612-41, and by the same editor as facsimile in *Corpus Codicum Suecicorum Medii Aevi,* VII (Copenhagen, 1946).

[7] John E. Kruse, "Vita metrica s. Birgitte," *Acta Universitatis Lundensis* (Lund, 1891-92): 10-28.

[8] Ekwall, *op. cit.,* pp. 16-17.

[9] *Ibid,* pp. 62-63.

[10] *Ibid,* p. 70, from *Acta et processus.* (note 3), p. 73: et quod plura alia sciunt de vita dicte domine Brigide, sed propter eorum repentinum recessum ad partes Swecie ea scribere et testificari protunc non poterant.

[11] Ekwall, *passim.* Colledge (note 5) does not yet consider Alphonsus redactor of the *Vita.*

[12] Birgit Klockars, *Birgittas svenska värld* [The Swedish World of Birgitta] (Stockholm, 1976), pp. 32-33.

[13] *Ibid,* pp. 136, 152. Tryggve Lundén, ed., *Processus canonizacionis beati Nicolai Lincopensis* (Stockholm, 1963). *Idem, Nikolaus Hermansson, biskop av Linköping* (Lund, 1971), with summary in German, pp. 62-70, and edition of liturgical texts composed by Nikolaus, pp. 77-138.

[14] Bengt Strömberg, *Magister Mathias och fransk mendikantpredikan* [summary: Magister Mathias et la prédication des religieux mendiants français] (Lund, 1944). Hjalmar Sundén, "Den heliga Birgitta och hennes biktfar magister Mathias," *Kyrkohistorisk årsskrift 73* (1973): 15-39. Anders Piltz, *Prolegomena till en textkritisk edition av magister Mathias' Homo conditus* (Uppsala, 1974, = Acta Universitatis Upsaliensis, Studia Latina Upsaliensia 7).

[15] The quote is from Anders Piltz, "Magister Mathias of Sweden in his theological context. A preliminary survey," lecture given in Stockholm 1984, unprinted. Cf. *idem,* ed., *Magistri Mathiae canonici Lincopensis opus sub nomine Homo Conditus vulgatum* (Angered 1984, = Samlingar utgivna av Svenska Fornskriftsällskapet, Ser. 2: Latinska Skrifter, IX:1).

[16] *Idem,* "Mathias Ouidi," *Svenskt Biografiskt Lexikon,* 2nd ed. (Stockholm 1918-), 25: 248-51.

[17] Carl-Gustaf Undhagen, ed., *Sancta Birgitta Revelaciones Lib. I* (Uppsala, 1978, = Samlingar utgivna av Svenska Fornskriftsällskapet, Ser. 2: Latinska Skrifter, VII:1), pp. 229-40. Birgitta Fritz, "Den heliga Birgitta och hennes klosterplaner," *Festskrift til Thelma Jexlev* (Odense, 1985): 9-17.

[18] Anders Piltz, "Mathias Ouidi" (as in note 16). The crusade: J. L. I. Fennell, *The Emergence of Moscow 1304-1359* (London, 1968), pp. 265-67. *Idem,* "The Campaign of King Magnus Eriksson against Novgorod in 1348," *Jahrbücher für Geschichte Osteuropas,* 14 (1966): 1-9. John Lind, "The Russian Sources of King Magnus Eriksson's Campaign against Novgorod 1348-1351 Reconsidered," *Mediaeval Scandinavia* 12 (1986): pp. 248-72.

[19] Anders Piltz, "Mathias Ouidi" (as in note 16).

[20] Undhagen (note 17), pp. 237-38.

[21] Collijn, *Acta et processus,* p. 485, quoted from Birger Bergh, "A Saint in the Making: St. Bridget's Life in Sweden (1303-1349)," in Francis Cairns, ed., *Papers of the Liverpool Latin Seminar* 3 (1981): 371-84, here p. 378.

[22] As can be gathered from the excellent indices in Birgit Klockars, *Birgitta och böckerna. En undersökning av den Heliga Birgittas källor* (Lund, 1966, = Kungl. Vitterhets Historie och Antikvitets Akademiens Handlingar: Historiska Serien, 11). The observation of the Exodus theme has been made also by Roger Ellis, "A Note on the Spirituality of St. Bridget of Sweden," *Spiritualität heute und gestern,* ed. James Hogg (Salzburg, 1982, = Analecta Cartusiana, 35): 157-66, here p. 166.

[23] Birger Bergh (note 21) with further references.

[24] Knut B. Westman, *Birgitta-studier* (Uppsala, 1911), pp. 107-16. Hjalmar Sundén, *Den heliga Birgitta. Ormungens moder som blev Kristi brud* (Uddevalla, 1973), pp. 66-89. Birgitta Fritz (note 17).

[25] Birger Bergh, ed., *Sancta Birgitta Revelaciones Lib. V: Liber Questionum* (Uppsala, 1971, = Samlingar utgivna av Svenska Fornskriftsällskapet, Ser. 2: Latinska Skrifter, VII:5). Sundén (note 24). Bergh (note 21).

[26] Sundén (note 24). Bergh (note 21) and Fritz (note 17) do not basically challenge Sundén's position.

[27] Sundén (note 24), pp. 85-89.

[28] Recently, e.g., Robert E. Lerner, "Antichrists and

Antichrist in Joachim of Fiore," *Speculum* 60 (1985): 553-70, with further references.

[29] As in Sundén above.

[30] Yngvar Ustvedt, *Svartedauen* [The Black Death] (Oslo, 1985), pp. 82-92.

[31] A. Jefferies Collins, ed., *The Bridgettine Breviary of Syon Abbey* (Worcester, 1969, = Henry Bradshaw Society Vol. XCVI), pp. xvii-xxx. Tryggve Lundén, ed., *Den heliga Birgitta och den helige Petrus av Skänninge, Officium parvum beate Marie Virginis,* I-II (Lund, 1976, = Acta Universitatis Upsaliensis, Studio Historico-Ecclesiastica Upsaliensia, 27-28), pp. xi-xxxi (summary: The Lady-offices of Saint Bridget and Venerable Peter of Skänninge, pp. cv-cxii). Sten Eklund, ed., *Sancta Birgitta Opera Minora II: Sermo Angelicvs* (Uppsala, 1972, = Samlingar utgivna av Svenska Fornskriftsällskapet, Ser. 2: Latinska Skrifter, VIII:2).

[32] Lundén, *op. cit.,* and Dom Ernest Graf, *Revelations & Prayers of St. Bridget of Sweden* (London, 1928).

[33] Collins and Lundén, *op. cit.*

[34] Gabriele M. Roschini, *La Madonna nelle "Rivelazioni di S. Brigida" nel sesto centenario della sua morte (23 luglio 1373)* (Roma, 1973), pp. 69-86.

[35] Toni Schmid, *Birgitta och hennes uppenbarelser* [Birgitta and her Revelations] (Lund, 1940), pp. 94-98, 108-10.

[36] Sten Eklund, ed., *Sancta Birgitta Opera Minora I: Regvla Salvatoris* (Lund, 1975, = Samlingar utgivna av Svenska Fornskriftsällskapet, Ser. 2: Latinska Skrifter, VIII:1), pp. 21-23. Cf. Fritz (note 17).

[37] Eklund (note 36) uses a special letter for this unknown early version. Discussion of fragments in Old Swedish: Jostein Gussgard, *To fragmenter på svensk af den Hellige Birgittas skrifter* (Uppsala, 1961, = Samlingar utgivna av Svenska Fornskriftsällskapet, 230).

[38] Tore Nyberg, "Analyse der Klosterregel der Hl. Birgitta," *Festschrift Altomünster 1973,* ed. Toni Grad (Aichach, 1973), pp. 20-34.

[39] Eklund (note 36) and review of Eklund by Tore Nyberg in *Theologische Revue,* 77 (1981):221-24.

[40] Tore Nyberg, "Birgitta von Schweden—die aktive Gottesschau," *Frauenmystik im Mittelalter* (note 1), pp. 275-89, here p. 281.

[41] Salomon Kraft, *Textstudier till Birgittas revelationer* (Uppsala, 1929, also in: *Kyrkohistorisk årsskrift* 29 (1929): 1-196), pp. 52-69.

[42] Known through his witness in the canonization process, the socalled *Depositio copiosissima,* cf. Lennart Hollman, ed., *Sancta Birgitta Reuelaciones Extrauagantes* (Uppsala, 1956, = Samlingar utgivna av Svenska Fornskriftsällskapet, Ser. 2: Latinska Skrifter, V), pp. 85, 90-91.

[43] *Vision und Visionsliteratur im Mittelalter* (Stuttgart, 1981, = Monographien zur Geschichte des Mittelalters, 23).

[44] The critical edition of Book IV is being prepared by Hans Aili, Stockholm.

[45] Francis Rapp, "Gottesfreunde," *Theologische Realenzyklopedie* (Berlin, 1975-), 14:98-100.

[46] Westman (note 24), p. 264. Kraft (note 41), p. 68-69. Undhagen (note 17), p. 174-77. The ms. is W. 318 of Historisches Archiv der Stadt Köln.

[47] The critical edition of Book VI is being prepared by Birger Bergh, Lund.

[48] Birger Bergh, ed., *Sancta Birgitta Revelaciones Lib. VII* (Uppsala, 1967, = Samlingar utgivna av Svenska Fornskriftsällskapet, Ser. 2: Latinska Skrifter, VII:7).

[49] Karl Kup, "Bene veneris . . . filius meus. An Early Example of St. Birgitta's Influence on the Iconography of the Nativity," *Bulletin of the New York Public Library* 61 (1957): 583-89. Lottlisa Behling, "Symbole der Revelationes der Hl. Birgitta in Beziehung zum Isenheimer Altar des Matthias Grünewald, insbesondere für die Darstellung der knienden Maria im Goldtempel," *Festschrift Altomünster 1973* (note 38), pp. 138-62.

[50] Colledge (note 5), p. 33-34.

[51] Kraft (note 41), p. 71-72.

[52] Colledge (note 5), p. 33, correcting Westman. The MS is Harley 612 of the British Library, London.

[53] Colledge (note 5), pp. 40-42, with further references.

[54] See pp. 221-35.

[55] Adolphe Tanquerey, *The Spiritual Life,* 2nd ed. (Tournai, 1930).

Ingvar Fogelqvist (essay date 1993)

SOURCE: *Apostasy and Reform in the Revelations of St. Birgitta,* Almqvist & Wiksell International, 1993, 262 p.

[*In the following excerpt from his book discussing Birgitta's notion of the moral apostasy of her contemporaries, Fogelqvist outlines the first of many failings the Saint observed in her fellow Christians—a so-called "love of the world" reflected in the prevalent "sins of pride, covetousness, and carnal pleasure."*]

There are several revelations where St. Birgitta in general terms accuses the Christians of her time of having apostatised or fallen away. Of special interest in these revelations is how the Church relates to and is affected by sinful Christians. The relationship does not always appear immediately evident, as Birgitta uses different kinds of imagery when describing it.[1] Regarding her understanding of the Church, the distinction between *ecclesia congregata* and *ecclesia congregans* is helpful. We have here two aspects of the Church. The former views the Church in a passive sense, as the community of the congregated, consisting of people; the latter, seeing the Church in an active sense, emphasises the divine congregating and is the institutional aspect of the Church, the Church existing before its members and gathering them together.[2]

According to Hammerich, Birgitta understands the Church solely as the community of believers.[3] A closer examination, however, reveals that she often speaks of the Church as an institution.[4] This aspect is found in images where Birgitta distinguishes between the Church and the Christians belonging to it. For example, she compares the Church to an apiary, in which two kinds of bees live, i.e. good and bad Christians (II 19 E), or to a virgin having three children, signifying different kinds of good and bad Christians (III 24 C). Birgitta often speaks of the institutional Church with reverence, calling it "Holy Mother Church" (VII 18.13), and comparing it to a "noble castle" (I 5.1), a "blessed vineyard" (III 10 C; IV 78.22), and to a "magnificent and glorious house".[5] She writes that this Church was founded by Christ,[6] and contains the means by which he sanctifies man and enables him to attain eternal life. For example, she says of the Church that its "disposition is excellent in the faith, beautiful in the seven sacraments, praiseworthy in manners and virtue, amiable in its fruit, and shows the true way to eternity".[7] Thus, the Church being a divine institution, is beautiful and excellent, and therefore it can in no way be subject to any downfall.

Nonetheless, Birgitta also sees a difference between this beautiful Church and the visible Catholic Church of her own time. The Church, she writes, is not in an admirable condition (IV 74.25). The reason for this is the many apostate Christians in the Church. Traditional medieval theology speaks of them as belonging to the Church *numero non merito,* or *corpore non mente.*[8] Their membership is merely formal. This teaching constitutes the background to several of Birgitta's images showing the role of these Christians in the Church. In one image, they are described as perverted or ruined. For example, she compares Christ to a bridegroom, who wedded a beautiful and virtuous bride and led her into the bridal chamber. The bride, Birgitta says, signifies the Christians, inflamed with faith and charity, and the bridechamber means the Church. Now, however, she continues, the bride has become an adulteress, preferring the devil to Christ (VI 33.1-3). A similar image describing the Christians as corrupted or destroyed is given by Birgitta when she compares them to a city wall that has fallen down. She hears Christ speaking: "What is the wall of Jerusalem, that is of my Church, if not the bodies and souls of the Christians? Out of them my Church ought to be built. The wall of this Church has now fallen down".[9]

Another image of the fall of the Christians is Birgitta's description of the apostates as besiegers of the Church, which she compares to a strong castle containing the sacraments, the teaching, and the example of the saints. "This castle", she continues, "is now besieged by enemies, for inside Holy Church there are many, who proclaim my Son, but who are not in agreement with him as regards their behaviour." On the one hand, then, Birgitta explicitly says that these Christians are inside the Church, that is, inside the visible Catholic Church. On the other hand, the same Christians are described as being outside the Church, attacking it; they do not belong to it, since they lack the proper qualifications. Similarly, Birgitta compares the Church to a virgin, who has several children, one of whom made an attempt to rape her. That son signifies the evil Christians (III 24 B,D). Thus, from one point of view, the son belongs to the Church, from another, he is a brutal evildoer attacking it.

The assault on the Church is sometimes described by Birgitta not only as a siege; the evil Christians have also forced their way through and occupied it. This is the case in a revelation where she compares the Church to a castle, the foundation of which is the belief that Christ is a just and merciful judge. "Now, however, the foundation is undermined", for hardly anyone believes that he is a just judge (I 5.13). They have also occupied the Church, for Birgitta says that they oppress God's elect inside the castle (I 5.15). In other words, she says that many Christians inside the Church do not in reality belong there. A similar occupation is described in another revelation, where she writes of four sisters, who each had a seat and power in their patrimony. They represent four virtues found in the Church. These sisters, however, are now stripped of their patrimony and despised by everyone. Four illegitimate sisters have taken their place, signifying four vices: Lady Pride, Lady Delight of the Flesh, Lady Superfluity, and Lady Simony (IV 45.1-7). Thus, the Church, signified by the patrimony, is described as occupied by the vices of evil Christians, while the virtues are suppressed.

We have been dealing with Birgitta's understanding of the corruption of Christians, viewing the Church as *ecclesia congregans,* i.e. as an institution assembling the Christians. Sinful Christians belong physically to this institution, but not spiritually. Birgitta, however, also speaks of the Church as consisting of the community of the congregated, *ecclesia congregata:*

> God is disgusted by the fall and ruin of his holy Church, for its door bends down towards the earth . . . ; the hinges are straightened out as much as possible and in no way bent; the floor is completely dug up into deep holes without bottom; drops of burning and smoking sulphur are dripping from the roof; the walls are as revolting to look at as pus mingled with rotten blood.[10]

Birgitta, then, identifies this decaying edifice with the Church. Further down she writes that the Church is the "community of the Christians" (*kristna manna samføgil*). The door, she explains, represents the pope, the hinges signify the cardinals, the floor is the secular clergy in general; the roof is an image of the religious, and the walls signify the laity. Thereafter, an account follows of the vices of these categories of people.[11] Thus, the Church in decay refers to people, to the community of Christians.[12] The reason, according to Birgitta, as to why it is decaying is that they are not living as they should.

The Christians accused by Birgitta of having fallen away belong to all classes of society: "all grades have apostatised from their praiseworthy condition" (III 27 D). Often, however, within this general condition of apostasy Birgitta distinguishes between different classes.[13] According to medieval perception, each Christian must be as perfect as his state requires, though not every member of a more perfect state is necessarily more perfect than a member of a less perfect state.[14] Birgitta accuses the traditional three Christian orders of clerics, religious and lay people of having apostatised.[15] The distinction of these three orders is spiritual and based on religious anthropology. People of the Middle Ages also made a distinction based on social criteria, whereby they differentiated between clerics, warriors, and producers or labourers.[16] Birgitta also mentions these three groups of people and accuses them of having apostatised (I 55.14-19).

Not all are equally guilty in Birgitta's view. In particular, she accuses the two leading classes, the clergy and the knights, who also were the people with whom she had the closest contact, of having abandoned Christ. In a vision she sees an innumerable mass of people perishing in dangerous waves, because the steersmen constantly wish to steer the ship to places where—they think—there is greater profit to gain. These steersmen signify all those having secular and spiritual power in the world. The common people imitate their miserable deeds, and so the leaders cause both themselves and their subjects to perish (III 5 A-B). The guilt of the priests and the knights, then, is greater, for they have enticed the common people to sin. Birgitta also writes that of all the states of laity, the knights have apostatised more than others.[17] The clerics, however, are in Birgitta's view the worst of all, since more is expected of them in terms of sanctity. She says that Christ selected them before all angels, and gave to them alone the power to handle his body in the Eucharist (IV 133.9; IV 132.1). Now, however, they have become more troublesome to him than all the others (IV 134.2).

Finally, it can be noted that when describing the falling off of Christians, Birgitta often writes that it has taken place "now",[18] that is, in her own time. The apostasy is not understood by her as having more or less existed at all times in the history of the Church, nor is it to be regarded as a gradual process, but it has happened quite suddenly. She writes, for example, that the monastic fervour of the early Church continued "for a long time" (RS Prol. 3.26). The great change has occurred in her own time. In a vision she hears John the Baptist saying: "Not in a thousand years has God's anger at the world been so great" (IV 134.1). Thus, in Birgitta's view, the general defection in her own time is unparalleled in the history of the Church. In one revelation she speaks of the world as having three ages. The first age lasted from Adam to the Incarnation, the second lasted from the Incarnation and continued for a long time. The third age has just begun "now", in Birgitta's own time, and will last to the General Judgment. The special sign of the third age is widespread apostasy. Birgitta does not, however, identify this age with the time of the Antichrist; he will not be born until the end of the third age.[19]

In the following, I intend to examine how Birgitta understands the substance of apostasy. Three main defects can be distinguished: love of the world, contempt of Christ and contempt of neighbour.[20]

2.1. Love of the World

In an aforementioned parable Birgitta speaks of certain steersmen, who steer themselves and their passengers to places where the waves are seething horribly. An infinite number of the people perish in the waves. By the steersmen Birgitta understands those having secular and spiritual power in the world. "Many of them love their own will so much that they do not attend to what benefits their own souls or those of their subjects, by voluntarily entangling themselves in the fierce waves of the world, that is, of pride, covetousness and impurity" (III 5 B). In this passage, Birgitta mentions several causes of sin. We can note, to begin with, the significance of the disordered will; the Christians have "voluntarily" entangled themselves in sin. She often emphasises in the Revelations that people will to sin.[21]

According to traditional teaching, the proper principle of a sinful action is the will, since every sin is voluntary.[22] It can also be noted that Birgitta here is reflecting the voluntarism typical of twelfth century spirituality.[23]

As a result of man's having the will to sin, Birgitta says that the devil's power increases in him (I 32.9). She accuses the Christians of having put their faith in the devil and of obeying his will and suggestions (VII 30.6; I 1.5). She compares the devil to an adulterer whom the Christians have chosen instead of Christ, their bridegroom;[24] and to a vile robber, whom they have followed instead of Christ their true king, and who has carried them off by means of evil suggestions and false promises.[25] What is more, Birgitta says that the Christians obey the devil "with delight and gladness" (VII 27.12). He may incite men to sin by trying to impede them from performing good works, by presenting attractive objects to human appetite (VI 29.2-3) or by corrupting man's will and good desires (I 13.3). She emphasises, however, that the reason why the devil dominates in man is due to the inconstancy of human will.[26] In other words, the direct cause of sin cannot be the devil but man's own will alone.[27]

The passage in III 5 B above speaks of disordered self-love as a source of sin; the Christians love their own will. Birgitta repeatedly mentions this as an important characteristic of sinners.[28] She says that the way leading to love of the world is through self-will, which arises when man does not bother to resist his evil inclinations, but does everything that enters into his thoughts, whether licit or illicit (I 15.15). According to Thomas Aquinas, the fact that anyone desires a temporal good disorderedly, is due to the fact that he loves himself disorderedly.[29]

Another cause of sin mentioned in III 5 B is love of the world. The fierce waves at which the steersmen plunge the ship, and which cause so many people to perish, are identified by Birgitta with "the world". Here she uses the term "world" in a pejorative sense, referring to those aspects of the terrestrial order which are corrupt and transitory and to which man turns when sinning.[30] The sinner's will, Birgitta says in another revelation, is to please the world more than God (IV 52.16). She accuses the Christians of having abandoned the love of God and of taking delight in love of the world.[31] Their reason for doing so is that the world's promises seem more certain than Christ's (I 48.9). She compares the apostatised Christians' love of the world to that of the Israelites making and worshipping the golden calf in the desert (I 48.11).

The monk's love of the world is in particular serious, for he has formally renounced the world, that is, the world outside the monastery. Here Birgitta finds good reason for criticism. She accuses monks in Rome of having dwelling places in town: everyone has a house of his own (IV 33.17). Moreover, she is critical of the lax discipline apparent when the gates of nunneries in Rome are indiscriminately opened for both lay people and clerics, whomever it pleases the sisters to let in—even at night.[32] She also complains of how the worldliness of the monks is expressed in the laxity of the dress code and writes:

> It is now almost impossible to recognise a monk by his habit. The tunic, which formerly used to reach down to his feet, now hardly covers his knees. The sleeves, which formerly used to be honourably sewn and wide are now tight-fitting. A sword hangs from his side instead of style and slate. He hardly wears any garment by which a monk can be recognised, except for the scapular, which, however, is often hidden, as if it were a scandalous thing to wear a monk's clothing. Some monks are not even ashamed of carrying armour and weapons under their tunics, so that they can do what they please after nightfall.[33]

Here Birgitta describes a monk who dresses himself as a layman; he has conformed himself to the world outside the monastery. Similar complaints are found in Cistercian statutes from the fourteenth century.[34] Among other things, they mention monks carrying swords and knives.[35]

According to the passage from III 5 B, quoted at the beginning of this section, to love the world implies to fall prey to the three temptations of pride, covetousness and carnal pleasure.[36] For Birgitta, this triad forms the principal sins.[37] She repeatedly accuses the Christians in general of having yielded to these three vices.[38] The papal curia, prelates, the clergy and the religious have succumbed to them;[39] they abound in the kingdom of Sweden (Ex. 74.4; VI 23.6-7). Because of these three vices, she fears that few men will enter into her own monastery (Ex. 19.3). In addition, she says that the Greeks who refuse to submit to the Roman Church are affected by these sins (VII 19.34) and that they abound in Famagusta on Cyprus (VII 16.5).

In the medieval tradition, this triad of sin was often regarded as the cause and summation of all sins.[40] Another medieval categorisation of vice, quite different from the Three Vices, was that of the Seven Deadly Sins.[41] Birgitta mentions the concept occasionally,[42] but it is by no means as important in her teaching as the Three Vices. The familiar phrase "the devil, the world, and the flesh" is in the medieval tradition related to this triad as naming the sources of temptation.[43] In the Revelations, we also find the devil associated with pride, covetousness with the world, and pleasure with the flesh.[44]

Christian writers have traditionally seen the Fall of man in Genesis 3 as the beginning and pattern of all temptation, and they sought to associate avarice, sins of the flesh and pride with original sin. For example, the eating of fruit suggests gluttony, the wish to be like gods is vainglory, and the knowledge of good and evil, as well as the visual appeal of the luscious fruit illustrates avarice.[45] Similarly, Birgitta in her dramatic account of how the Christians of her time have defected (II 6 B) speaks of a new Fall. She does not explicitly mention Adam and Eve, but in her account the Christians have likewise given in to the devil's enticements and have succumbed to pride, avarice and carnal pleasure. This implies that Birgitta does not reproach the Christians of her day with having committed sins which are more or less found in every age. Instead, in her view, an especially great defection has taken place in her own time.

The relationship between the three sins in question can be explored further. We might in particular consider if any of them is regarded as the principal evil, in Birgitta's view. In the Christian tradition there was not complete freedom in singling out the most important vice, for the Bible indicated two as especially significant. Ecclus. 10:15 teaches that "Pride is the beginning of all sin". St. Paul, on the other hand, writes in 1 Tim. 6:10: "Covetousness is the root of all evil things." Most of the early medieval writers chose pride as the chief vice.[46] In the eleventh century, however, there began a shift of emphasis towards covetousness.[47] This was partly due to the change in economic values from agrarian to mercantile. During the period between 1000 and 1350 virtually all the basic structures of Europe's commercial economy developed. Alongside the new emphasis on covetousness, the older view of pride's predominance continued to have an influence.[48] Other writers maintained pride and covetousness on an even basis without letting the one take precedence over the other.[49]

A similar balancing of the leading vices is found in Birgitta's Revelations. In the main, she does not attach special emphasis to either covetousness or pride. It can be noted, however, that pride is in general the sin mentioned first by her in passages where the three sins are mentioned together.[50] Thus, it would seem that Birgitta regards pride, the desire to excel, as the principal vice from which all others emerge, and which motivates man to acquire temporal goods.

In the following, I intend to examine more closely how Birgitta understands the concept "love of the world", which we have seen consists of the three vices of pride, covetousness and carnal pleasure.

2.1.1. *Pride*

It is characteristic of pride *(superbia),* Birgitta writes, that it "raises a man . . . above himself *(supra se),* as if he were equal to God and righteous men" (IV 17.4). She agrees here with the traditional understanding of pride according to which a man is said to be proud because he wishes to appear above *(super)* what he really is; pride is the inordinate desire of one's own excellence.[51] Moreover, according to traditional teaching, the root of pride consists in man's not being subject to God and his rule.[52] Birgitta describes pride in a similar way when she says that the pride of Christians is so great that, if they could ascend above God, they would gladly do so.[53] There are several other aspects of pride found in the Revelations. I will in the following distinguish between inward and outward pride, a distinction also used by Birgitta (III 14 B).

2.1.1.1. *Inward Pride*

The first aspect of inward pride for us to consider is that of vainglory, the desire for empty or vain praise.[54] In the Revelations vainglory is closely related to man's hearing since it is through the hearing that the devil introduces into a man's heart the sounds of his own praise and thus puffs him up through pride in himself (VII 5.30). Birgitta accuses many of her contemporary Christians of having fallen prey to vainglory: "pride alone pleases their hearing" (I 57.3). According to her, they wish to hear their own praise and honour, by being called great and good by everyone (I 23.4; I 33.2). Characteristic of these people is that they do not refer the praise received to God. Birgitta writes of a person that his only aim concerned his own glory (III 4 A).

According to Birgitta, the desire for vainglory is a sin particularly affecting clerics. She mentions several ways by which they strive to win the praise of people: they seek to acquire a reputation of being learned (I 33.2; III 4 A), they give people money and benefices,[55] and they praise Christ for the sake of gaining their own praise. There are clerics, Birgitta says, who "lift up" Christ's praise to sublime heights, but with no other intention than to increase their temporal honour and fleeting benefit (VI 37.3). Vainglory, she says, often lies behind the eloquence of many priests.[56] An example given by her is of certain clerics who have the habit of singing Mass or the Divine Office in an affected way for the sake of vainglory (IV 102.20; VI 35.13,51). Finally, she is critical of clerics who treat people indulgently and ignore their faults in order to receive their appreciation. The priests, Birgitta writes, say what people like to hear in order to obtain applause.[57]

A second aspect of inward pride in the Revelations is ambition, the excessive desire for honour. Birgitta accuses the Christians of her time of desiring to be exalted in the world and be called great (II 8 B,D; VI 96.6). In a revelation she hears a cleric say: "I am called to honour. Therefore, I will strive to become honoured by men, for happiness consists in being great in the world." (Ex. 83.10). The knights' ambition is, according to Birgitta, focused on how they can extol their names and families, and how they are to raise their heirs and make them mighty to gain the honour of the world (VI 39.14). She also censures people for being eager to go to war and to give their lives in order to acquire honour (II 8 C) and of having married invalidly because of ambition: by marrying they seek only temporal glory, not God's honour (VIII 9).

The ambition of the religious is noticeable in their chief reason for entering the religious life, which according to Birgitta is the desire to be more honoured than others and to be able to hold places of honour (Ex. 83.11). She reproaches the clerics and the religious for striving to acquire honour by attaining the reputation of being learned,[58] or by acquiring ecclesiastical offices, in particular the office of bishop.[59] She accuses bishops, abbots and benefice-holders of having abandoned their flocks in order to receive other offices and positions of authority with the intention that in these offices they may be more honoured by people and raised to a higher status in the world (VII 29.5-6). Important in these passages is the reason why people seek higher honours. According to Birgitta, they do it "for the world's sake" (III 18 B), for their "personal freedom" and "bodily pleasure" (VII 20.23). In other words, they do not refer their desire of honour to God, nor do they seek it for the profit of others.[60] All this striving renders their desire for honour disordered.

A third aspect of inward pride is disobedience. Birgitta says that when living on earth Christ subjected himself to complete obedience, but the knights have followed the devil's advice not to allow anyone to be superior to them; they do not humbly bow their heads to anyone (II 8 B). Disobedience to God and their superiors characterises the Christians in general. According to Birgitta, they prefer to follow their own will, obeying only for the sake of worldly benefit.[61] She gives the example of the Franciscan Brother Adversary,[62] who intends to show himself so humble and obedient that all will reckon him a saint. However, when others are fasting and keeping silence, he will do the opposite: by eating and drinking and talking so secretly that none of the others will notice it.[63]

A fourth aspect of inward pride is anger, since "pride", as Birgitta writes, "often accompanies anger".[64] Also impatience, which traditionally denotes failure to bear up the evils that tend to make man sad and thus break his spirit,[65] is closely related to pride in the Revelations.[66] Why do worldly-minded people become so impatient when reproached, Birgitta asks. The answer is that they seek the praise of self rather than the praise of God (II 23 B). A man's impatience, then, is rooted in pride and vainglory. She reproaches her contemporary Christians for impatience with God's justice and design; they wish to obtain something else than he has

decided for them (IV 39.6; VI 52.51). They also get angry with him because his works are good and theirs are evil, and because he does not consent to their sins but sharply denounces them (VI 28.11-13, 15). Furthermore, Birgitta accuses the Christians of being impatient and angry with their neighbour (IV 17.27; VI 39.30), as when they cannot get hold of his goods (IV 17.27).

A fifth aspect of inward pride is mental pride. We are here not—as previously—concerned with man's will and affections but primarily with his intellect. Birgitta compares her contemporary Christians to a butterfly with broad wings and a small body, for their mind is inflated with pride like bellows filled with air (IV 112.3). One expression of this pride is the setting of oneself over others.[67] She censures them for considering no one to be their equal.[68] Either people take pride in their good life, which they consider to be better than that of others, or they pride themselves on their intelligence, thinking themselves wiser than others.[69]

Another kind of mental pride is when people think that what they have received from God comes from themselves. Thus, Birgitta reproaches the Christians for crediting themselves with the good things given by God (I 47.9; I 4.5), for example, their beautiful bodies, their possessions, servants, clothes, power and their noble descent.[70] According to Birgitta, many do not realise that they should thank Christ for giving them everything (I 19.5). A variation of this theme is when people think that they have received their good things because of their own merits. They say: "What I have gained is through my diligence, and I own it justly."[71] This pride extends also to spiritual matters. She accuses people of believing that they can obtain heaven through their own merits, and of believing that they can make satisfaction for their excesses by their own works (IV 20.9). She compares such people to the Israelites in the desert, who sinned because of pride when they, contrary to God's will, wanted to "ascend" to war.[72] Similarly, through their pride many Christians wish to ascend to heaven, having no confidence in Christ, but putting their trust in themselves and following their own will (I 53.10,17). As an example, Birgitta says of a certain brother that he refrained from eating altogether during Lent and also made other indiscreet fasts. He desired, she says, to obtain heaven through his abstinences, which, however, derived more from pride than from humility (VI 69.4-5).

2.1.1.2. Outward Pride

In Birgitta's Revelations, outward pride, that is the visible manifestation of pride, principally involves dress, speech, and actions.

First, we have Birgitta's criticism of people wearing ostentatious apparel (VIII 57 A; VI 15.5,8), Here, as often elsewhere, she is in continuity with a long Christian tradition of reproaching people for paying excessive attention to their outward appearance. Gregory the Great, to give only one example, says that there are some who think that attention to finery and costly dress is no sin. He argues against this, saying, surely, if this were no fault, the word of God would not say so expressly that the rich man who was tormented in hell had been clothed in fine linen and purple. No one, Gregory concludes, looks for costly apparel, such as exceeds his estate, except out of vainglory.[73]

Birgitta voices a similar criticism when she accuses people of wearing clothes that claim a status beyond their actual one. She says that friars and priests dress themselves like bishops (IV 33.25; IV 135.10). People can also be accused of exceeding their natural state, by using "unseemly forms of clothing." According to her, they do so because of pride and want their bodies to seem more beautiful and more lascivious than God created them. They also daub their faces with antimony and other extraneous colouring.[74]

In particular, Birgitta focuses on the deviations of the religious from their prescribed dress. She accuses them of being disgusted by coarse clothes (IV 127.11); they prefer soft and beautiful garments (VI 98.2-3), and use robes made of the same valuable material as those of rich bishops (IV 33.25). She is here commenting on a widespread relaxation of the monastic dress code. Similar accusations are found in the statutes of the Cistercian General chapter. For example, the General Chapter criticised a monastery where the monks had introduced the new custom of wearing woollen clothes contrary to the Rule.[75] The General Chapter also found it necessary to enforce repeatedly the prescription that costly dress should be abolished altogether.[76]

The statutes of the Cistercian General Chapter also criticised monks for wearing superfluous and irreligious clothes,[77] and excessively long robes.[78] Similarly, Birgitta accuses Benedictine monks of choosing clothes that appeal to people and excite carnal affections. She says that instead of a cowl, wear a cape so pleated, wide and long that they look more like proud boasters than humble monks. Instead of the regular scapular they wear a small piece of cloth in front and behind. On the head they wear a worldly hat, thus showing their pride and ostentation (IV 127.12-18).

A second manifestation of outward pride is proud speech. One kind is boasting.[79] Birgitta accuses especially the clerics of this sin (II 20 B; III 4 C). She writes of how bishops, abbots and other prelates boast about the offices and honours they have attained, although by gaining them they have abandoned their sheep and parishes (VII 29.6). Canonists boast that they know the Law of the Church, but in reality their knowledge aims at deceiving others (VI 15.10).

Birgitta tells of a certain proud monk who had visions and dreams to offer.[80] He claimed that St. Peter and St. Paul had told him that he would simultaneously become both pope and emperor, and that the archangel Michael had showed himself to him in the guise of a merchant (VI 68.3-4). There are also other religious topics for the proud to boast about. Of a certain bishop Birgitta says that he discusses continuously the passion of Christ and the miracles of the saints, in order to be called holy. In reality, however, these things are far away from his heart (III 14 B). Loquaciousness is yet another kind of proud speech (II 20 B), as well as scurrilous language, of which Birgitta repeatedly accuses her fellow Christians.[81]

Furthermore, proud speech is expressed in impatience and anger. Birgitta accuses her fellow Christians of impatient, disorderly and injurious speech against their neighbour.[82] She also accuses people of being guilty of blasphemy against God. In their anger, she says, they strive to hurt him by telling him how much they despise him, in particular because of his patience, goodness, his suffering, and death for mankind.[83]

Thirdly, there are the proud actions, one of which is hypocrisy. In the Revelations, the word "hypocrisy" is contrasted with "simplicity of religion" (VI 5.9). Characteristic, then, of hypocrites is that they lack sincerity or frankness: they have something to hide. In reality they are not so good or holy as they appear. There are people, Birgitta writes, who pretend to be good and yet find delight in sin. They sin secretly, when they can so that people will not notice them (VI 37.5). Birgitta accuses especially the clerics and the religious of hypocrisy. She writes, for example, of a certain Swedish Cistercian monk[84] that he got tired of keeping the Rule as he had vowed and instead thought of ways of pleasing people through simulated holiness in order to be able to indulge in gluttony in secret (IV 23.20). In this passage is also revealed what in Birgitta's view is the cause of hypocrisy, viz. vainglory.[85]

Birgitta mentions several kinds of hypocritical deeds of which the clerics and religious are in her view guilty. One example is of a bishop who appears to be humble in words and gestures, in dress and actions, but in reality he is proud and ambitious, considering himself holier than others (III 14 B). Another wishes it to appear that he owns nothing, yet he desires to own everything secretly (III 15 B; III 14 B). A religious pretends to fast and to keep silent. In secret, however, he delights in food, drink and talk. He, too, makes a show of poverty and fills his purse (VII 20.19-20).

According to Birgitta, the hypocrisy of the religious is sometimes seen in their desire to perform extraordinary deeds of various kinds. It is not enough for some to keep the common rule of the monastery and obey their superiors. For example, Birgitta says of a certain religious that he sought to be praised by men, rather than God, and therefore performed unusual and remarkable deeds.[86]

Not all proud actions, however, are hypocritical in character. Birgitta blames her contemporary Christians of living in extravagant luxury and pomp. According to her, the custom now prevails in the houses of bishops and lords of having an excess of gold and silver and of keeping large and expensive horses.[87] She accuses the Dominicans of erecting high and expensive churches (III 18 E). Her criticism, however, is not only directed against the religious orders and the priests, but also towards the laity who could indulge to a greater extent in extravagant luxury without opening themselves up to accusations of hypocrisy. The nobility imitates, she says, the proud manners of their parents; they like to sit among the first in rank and to have many servants (VI 52.16-17). She also accuses kings of burdening their subjects out of pride (IV 76.13). Pride also lies behind the rulers' killing and robbing of innocent people (VII 56 O).

2.1.2. Covetousness

The second of Birgitta's three major vices of the Christians of her time is *cupiditas,* "covetousness". A traditional definition of the term as unrestrained love of possessing is found in the *Summa Theologiae* of Thomas Aquinas. According to Thomas, in as much as the good consists in a certain measure, man is allowed to have external riches in so far as they are necessary for him to live in keeping with his condition of life, but it is a sin for him to exceed this measure by wishing to acquire or keep them excessively.[88] Birgitta, too, understands covetousness as the exceeding of an allotted measure. The covetousness of her fellow Christians, she complains, "exceeds all limit and measure",[89] and is "as insatiable as a sack with a hole in it" (VII 30.11).

It should be noted that, according to the traditional teaching, the word covetousness, understood as the unrestrained love of possessing, could in Birgitta's time be interpreted in both a general and a special sense. It is a general sin when defined as unrestrained love of possessing anything: goods, position, knowledge. Covetousness as a special sin is the disordered desire for money and possessions.[90] In Birgitta's Revelations, the term "covetousness" often occurs without her explicitly stating its specific meaning. In such cases the context may sometimes be of help to understand the sense. For example, the terms "pride and covetousness" in V rev. 3.6 correspond to "pride and ambition" in V rev. 3.7. Thus, covetousness here denotes primarily covetousness of honour. Another example is the "covetousness" mentioned in IV 126.105, which also refers to the desire for higher offices and honours.[91] Sometimes Birgitta expressly says that she is referring

to this meaning, as when speaking of "covetousness of worldly honours".[92] Thus, as these examples show, she can use covetousness in the general sense. This is also the case in passages where covetousness denotes a disordered desire for heaven (VI 39.13), or where the devil's covetousness denotes his desire to become mightier than God (I 34.22), as well as his desire to win as many souls as possible for hell (VI 31.14). Covetousness in the general sense also occurs in the Revelations where the term by Birgitta is contrasted with charity of God (III 27 D; II 19 E).

Birgitta, however, also uses covetousness in the special sense of denoting disordered desire for money and possessions. For example, covetousness in I 56.2 refers to the "sack of money" spoken of in I 56.1.[93] In some cases she explicitly mentions that she has in view covetousness in the special sense, for example when speaking of "covetousness of worldly possessions" (III 13 B), or of "covetousness of money".[94] In fact her use of covetousness in the Revelations suggests that it primarily is used in the special sense. For example, she accuses the Christians of being filled "with worldly ambition and covetousness".[95] Here covetousness cannot denote covetousness of honour, since ambition already refers to that sin. Instead, covetousness obviously stands for covetousness in the special sense, denoting greed.

With respect to the disordered desire for money and possessions, Birgitta is criticising developments which strained the social fabric of her time. The background to her criticism is the development of commerce and industry in the high Middle Ages, which is most markedly characterised by the widespread introduction of money into transactions where previously it had been virtually absent. By the fourteenth century, transactions involving money were an everyday occurrence. The rulers collected enormous sums of money through taxes, which enabled them to employ many officials. The increased circulation of money also enhanced people's interest in possessing money, and they tended to disregard the strict rules of the Church regulating how the Christian should handle it. During this time there is a shift of emphasis in devotional literature from pride as chief vice to covetousness.[96]

This increased emphasis on covetousness is reflected in Birgitta's message to Pope Clement VI, who is told that "covetousness and ambition" have flourished and increased during his pontificate (VI 63.6). Repeatedly she accuses the secular and spiritual leaders of society of having unrestrained desire for riches.[97] The priests have, she writes, received God's commandments and summarised them as: "stretch out your hand and pay!"[98] She emphasises the Christians' desire beyond measure for riches; these people are never satisfied although they already have more than enough (III 14 D; I 57.3).

She compares them to a bag without bottom and which can never be filled.[99] One effect of covetousness, she notes, is that it gives rise to restlessness by burdening man with excessive anxiety and care. She accuses the bishops of being excessively preoccupied acquiring things of the world; they are uneasy and disturbed because they never allow themselves any rest from worldly desire.[100]

So far we have analysed covetousness of riches in the sense of excess in the inner desire for riches. Covetousness is, however, also expressed in actions. First, it belongs to the vice of covetousness to exceed in retaining.[101] Birgitta asks if there are any kings who are prepared to restore what the Crown keeps unjustly (IV 76.13). Obviously, in her opinion, there are very few such kings in her time. Also the knights in general are accused by Birgitta of retaining their ill-gotten goods (IV 76.8; Ex. 75.14). Moreover, one nobleman is accused of not having paid his debts to the last farthing (VI 10.21), and another of not having given a widow complete satisfaction for the property he had bought from her (Ex. 56.3).

Another manifestation of excess in retaining is the refusal to give alms. For example, Birgitta tells of a religious whom she accuses of unlawfully taking for himself all those things that should be given to others out of compassion.[102] The covetous Christians give only with great reluctance. If one florin, she says, were to be levied from the knights, the religious and others, most of them would rather prefer not to tell the truth that they have the money than to admit it and so lose it (III 27 D; VI 39.23).

Secondly, the vice of covetousness entails to exceed in receiving. Birgitta accuses people of having acquired riches by unjust and illegal means. Simony she connects with covetousness (IV 45.7). More important is the connection of covetousness with theft and robbery. In particular, the secular rulers of society are accused of this vice. She accuses the knights in general of having followed the devil's advice to shed their neighbour's blood in order to acquire his possessions.[103] One example of this is Albrecht of Mecklenburg the younger, who, she says, was enticed by his mother to appropriate goods. He followed her advice and attacked poor people who could not defend themselves; he plundered their goods and killed them.[104] Another example is the behaviour of the two chief opponents in the Anglo-French conflict taking place at this time. Birgitta calls the kings of France and England "beasts", burning with the fire of anger and covetousness; they fight for gold and worldly riches and do not spare the blood of Christians (IV 104.8-9). A form of violence is also employed by those rich people, whom she accuses of forcing their labourers to work on feast days (IV 33.40). Obviously, the intention of the employees is to gain money.

The covetous man, in taking other people's goods, employs not only violence but also deceit. This is in particular prevalent among the religious who lack the power of the secular rulers to take goods by force. Thus, Birgitta accuses the clergy of accepting bribes to transmute the sentences of the courts; they extend their covetousness to all people and turn what is right into falsehood (I 55.14-16). The law of the Church, she says, is now read in the house of gamblers. For the small amount of justice which the canonists find in this law, they acquire a great sum of money. The law, she concludes, is no longer read to Christ's honour, but with the aim of getting hold of money (VI 15.4).

Another kind of excess in acquiring is to make money by disgraceful means, for example, the practice of usury.[105] According to Birgitta, usury is now flourishing in the City of Rome; the Christians practise it like the Jews and are even more covetous than they (IV 33.41).

The covetousness for riches among the religious is regarded by Birgitta as especially serious because of the violation of their vows of poverty. Sometimes it is individual poverty that is abandoned. For example, in the revelation concerning the Franciscan "Brother Adversary", Birgitta says that because he is aware that the Rule of St. Francis forbids him to touch money or possess gold or silver,[106] he will engage some special friend to keep his money and gold secretly on his behalf so that he may use it to his liking.[107] Sometimes the monastery as a whole is described as having fallen prey to greed. For example, when visiting a certain nunnery, Birgitta sees among the nuns a hideous "Ethiopian", also dressed as a nun. He is the "demon of covetousness", who advises the nuns to collect possessions, castles and great riches.[108] The mendicants in Rome have a reputation of being richer than people who consider themselves rich. Several of these own property, which, she points out, is against the rule (IV 33.23-24).

2.1.3. Carnal Pleasure

The third of Birgitta's three major vices of the Christians of her time is carnal pleasure. We can note, however, that she also uses other terms related to pleasure. In I 13.2 Birgitta compares the body of a certain Cistercian prior to a ship attacked by waves, which represents the devil's temptations. Just as the water broke into the ship through the keel, so, Birgitta writes, "pleasure" went into his body by the "delight" with which he rejoiced in his thoughts. Since he did not resist through penance or strengthened himself through the nails of abstinence, the "water of pleasure" increased daily. Then, when the ship was filled with "concupiscence", water flooded and overwhelmed the ship with "pleasure" so that it could not reach the port of salvation.

The vices mentioned in I 13.2 are all sins of the flesh.[109] The body is affected by pleasure *(voluptas),* a concept mentioned three times. The other terms used are delight *(delectatio)* and concupiscence *(concupiscentia).* In this text, the three terms appear to be used interchangeably. Since other revelations, however, make plain that there are certain differences between them, I intend to show how Birgitta understands them.

First, there is the passion of "concupiscence" *(concupiscentia).* Thomas Aquinas defines it as a craving for what is pleasant. Men and animals have certain strong and necessary desires—for life, food, drink, and propagation, which are forms of natural concupiscence. Among earthly creatures only man can desire things beyond natural needs, such as fame, promotion, entertainment, modish attire, etc. When strong or disordered, non-natural concupiscence is called covetousness.[110] Master Mathias also mentions these two kinds of concupiscence, but speaks of them solely as disordered.[111] In Birgitta's Revelations, too, concupiscence denotes an inordinate desire, an excessive appetite for what is pleasant. It is sometimes used to denote natural as well as non-natural sinful desire.[112] Mainly, however, it denotes natural concupiscence.

This is the case when Birgitta says that the Israelites sinned in the desert in craving meat *(concupierunt carnes),* which they had enjoyed in Egypt. Similarly, the Christians now sin through concupiscence of the flesh. She says that Christ gave man everything he needed to use honourably and moderately, but man wants to have everything immoderately and indiscriminately. If it were possible, she continues, the Christians would copulate without stop, drink without restraint and crave without measure, for as long as they could sin they would never stop (I 53.10, 14-15). Characteristic, then, of concupiscence of the flesh for Birgitta is that it is an excessive and uncontrolled craving for bodily pleasure. Two kinds of carnal concupiscence are mentioned by her: gluttony and sexual lust. Sometimes in the Revelations carnal concupiscence denotes solely sexual lust.[113]

Secondly, there is "delight" *(delectacio).* In the medieval tradition, concupiscence and delight are passions clearly distinguished from one another. While concupiscence, as we have seen, refers to the desire for what is pleasant, delight denotes the repose of the appetitive power in some loved good. There is a good delight, whereby the higher or lower appetite rests in what is in accord with reason, and an evil delight, whereby the appetite rests in what is discordant with reason and the law of God.[114] Birgitta, too, understands delight as a repose in some loved good. There is good as well as evil delight.[115] She accuses people of having yielded to "disordered delight".[116] Their delight has now become "irrational like that of animals" (Ex. 51.4). Thus, like Thomas, she mentions the irrational character of the disordered delight.

Characteristic of the disordered delight of many Christians, Birgitta writes, is that they have found it elsewhere than in God: "no one desires to have me as their delight", Christ complains to her.[117] She speaks of two kinds of disordered delights. First, there are "earthly delights" (VII 16.3) and "delights of the world", which please the sight of many Christians.[118] This is the temporal delight taken in possessions, honour, and the like. Secondly, there is the disordered delight directed at satisfying the body. Birgitta speaks here of "delight of the flesh".[119] The devil inspires man to fall prey to such delights (IV 23.12). They are described as "enemies" (VI 66.12) and "oppressive guests" (VI 65.39). In Birgitta's view, delight of the flesh is found in many Christians of her time. Instead of "Sister Abstinence", "Lady Delight in the flesh" now dominates in the Church.[120] The Christians, Birgitta says, take excessive delight in food and drink, in bodily comfort and in sexual lust.[121]

Thirdly, there is "pleasure" *(voluptas).* In the *Summa Theologiae* of Thomas Aquinas, "pleasure" is used interchangeably with "delight".[122] In particular, "pleasure" corresponds to "bodily delights".[123] Thus, important expressions of "pleasure" include sins of the flesh, like gluttony,[124] lust,[125] and effeminacy or softness, which is opposed to toil.[126] Also in Birgitta's Revelations, pleasure refers mainly to disordered bodily pleasures, pleasures of the flesh: "the flesh draws me to distorted pleasure", she hears a man saying.[127] The close relationship existing between pleasure and the flesh is seen in concepts such as *voluptas corporalis* (II 3 D), *voluptas corporis* (IV 7.46; VI 39.26), *voluptas carnis,*[128] and *carnalis voluptas.*[129]

Birgitta accuses her contemporary Christians of having succumbed to the "pleasure of the flesh".[130] Their carnal pleasure is so important to them, Birgitta says, that they would more gladly forfeit Christ than give up their disordered delight (VII 30.10). Birgitta emphasises the immoderate character of the Christians' pleasure; it causes them to exceed beyond every measure and laudable order (VI 27.14; III 13 B). Thus, carnal pleasure is a sin against the virtue of temperance.

Three sins, in particular, are included in Birgitta's concept of carnal pleasure: sloth, gluttony and lust (VI 39.26,32). They will be examined more closely in the following.

2.1.3.1. Sloth and Gluttony

Birgitta writes: "Since the body has a sense of feeling, it follows that it gladly feels pleasure and bodily rest" (II 23 D). In other words, there is a tendency of the body to enjoy pleasure by letting it rest from work. Birgitta accuses many of her contemporary Christians of having fallen a victim to the sin of sloth. For example, she says of a nobleman that he was lazy as regards doing good works to God's honour, wasting his time for the sake of bodily rest and holding bodily benefit and pleasure very dear.[131]

A weightier sin of unrestrained pleasure dealt with by Birgitta is gluttony, which traditionally denotes excess in eating and drinking. It is an uncontrolled indulgence in the delights of the palate.[132] She accuses many of her contemporary Christians of having fallen prey to this sin (IV 95.4). Not least the people of Sweden are singled out as being guilty of gluttony.[133] Just like a vessel open at both ends is never filled, even if the whole sea were poured into it, so, Birgitta says, the clerics are never satiated and their immoderate lasciviousness increases the sinfulness of their gluttony (VI 7.4).

More specifically, Birgitta blames people of simply eating too much: they eat "beyond measure".[134] She also accuses a Swedish nobleman of feeding himself too exquisitely, by preparing for himself too sumptuous courses, thereby gaining greater bodily delight.[135] A third aspect of gluttony occurs when Christians violate the prescriptions of the Church concerning fasting and abstinence. She complains that many healthy people in Rome eat meat during Lent, and very few are content with having only one meal a day during that time. Some of them abstain from meat during daytime, but at night they feast on meat at secret taverns. These abuses are practised by the clergy as well as by the laity in Rome. In doing so, Birgitta writes, they resemble the Saracens, who fast at daytime but satiate themselves with meat at night (IV 33.38-39).

A special problem is the gluttony she witnesses among many people belonging to the religious state, a gluttony which she believes to be contrary to the monastic ideal of frugality. She accuses individual monks and nuns of having made themselves guilty of overindulgence; they indulge themselves in unrestricted eating both as regards quantity and quality.[136] She also accuses the religious in general of having receded from the right road because of overindulgence (RS 28.273). This accusation includes the monks of Alvastra who are, she says, like serpents crawling on their belly of gluttony.[137] Furthermore, the religious are accused of having abandoned their special commitment to abstinence and fasting. For example, a certain Swedish Dominican was, Birgitta says, deceived by the "demon of gluttony" to eat and drink at forbidden times, even going to extremes and rejecting abstinence completely.[138]

2.1.3.2. Lust

Birgitta accuses her contemporary Christians of having yielded to lust,[139] the vice of indulging in unlawful sexual pleasures.[140] She calls the married people of her time "temporal married couples", and says that they indulge "in lust like cattle and worse than cattle"[141] It appears that she regards the sin as mortal (I 26.23). Her opinion comes close to that of Thomas Aquinas, saying that sexual intercourse inside the marriage is mortally sinful if man's sexual interest in his wife is so exclusively aimed at finding pleasure that he views her as only an object of lust, not as a wife.[142]

According to Thomas Aquinas, lust is present when a person tries to make himself attractive through clothing, appearance or speech in order to stimulate carnal desires and thus provoke sinful thoughts and actions. Thomas allows women to use means to please their husbands, if they do it soberly and moderately, but otherwise they cannot without sinning desire to give lustful pleasure to those men who see them because this is to incite them to sin.[143] Birgitta reproaches her contemporary Christians for this. The devil has, she writes, incited women in Sweden to wear indecent ornaments on their heads, feet and other parts of the body in order to provoke lust (VIII 57 A). She also accuses the inhabitants of Naples of being deformed from their natural state by the unseemly forms of clothing they are wearing. They do this so that those who see them may be more quickly provoked and inflamed towards carnal concupiscence. They also daub their faces with antimony and other extraneous colouring (VII 27.19-20). Another way of inciting people's lust, mentioned by Birgitta, is vulgar speech. A knight is accused of having—by his speech—induced not only his wife to a greater pitch of passion, but attracted also others to listen to him, and think about the scurrilous things he says.[144]

Furthermore, Birgitta accuses the lay people of committing adultery. She writes, for example, that, after a quarrel, many men in Rome desert their legitimate wives for as long as they wish without bothering about the ecclesiastical authorities. In place of their wives they take mistresses. Some men even keep a mistress together with the wife in the same house and are glad to see them simultaneously giving birth to children (IV 33.36-37). Birgitta also accuses wealthy people in Naples of keeping their female servants in their own houses as prostitutes both for themselves and for others.[145] It has been pointed out that one significant explanation of the existence of sexual licentiousness among the wealthier classes in the Middle Ages was the impact that the ideal of romantic love, proposed by some of the troubadours, had made on many of them. It was in effect an endorsement of romantic sexual activity separated from marriage and procreation.[146]

Lay people holding ecclesiastical property were not allowed to be married because of their canonical title. Birgitta accuses these laymen in Rome of keeping concubines in their house by day and in their beds by night. Despite this they say: "We are not allowed to be married, for we are canons" (IV 33.7-8). Another brand of impurity concerns a knight, who Birgitta says unduly and inordinately emitted his semen, for, although he was married and kept away from other women, he nevertheless ejaculated his semen through improper embraces, words and shameless gestures.[147]

Birgitta reproaches people for homosexual activities. According to her, in the kingdom of Sweden there is found a sin more abominable than the others,[148] for it incites man towards lust that is against nature itself (VI 80.4). She does not say which unnatural vice she has in mind,[149] but in her so called letter of revolt the unnatural vice is explicitly mentioned as homosexuality. She writes that—according to a widespread rumour—King Magnus has had sexual intercourse with men. In her view, the rumour is credible.[150] According to Gottfrid Carlsson, Birgitta's accusation is probably false.[151] Another scholar, Hans Furuhagen, is more hesitant.[152] Whether Birgitta's accusation is correct or not will not be discussed here. It can be noted, however, that the origin of the rumour on which Birgitta founded her accusation can—at least in part—be determined. The king had—against the law of the country—made his favourite, Bengt Algotsson, Duke of Finland.[153] Moreover, she mentions in VIII 11 that the king and queen had made a mutual agreement of continence. It is criticised by Birgitta, for, in her view, the king had made it out of new passion, indiscreet zeal and levity of mind. She also mentions the risk that the agreement may become an occasion of backbiting (VIII 11). What Birgitta here hints at is that the king's vow of continence gave rise to the rumour that he had homosexual relations.

As regards the clerics, Birgitta accuses them of keeping concubines, or as she puts it, "damned women", locating them in some safe place so that they can indulge their lust. They caress these women and take delight in them, while ignoring Christ (IV 132.14). The clerics in Rome are, she says, publicly happy when seeing their "harlots" with swelling bellies taking a walk together with other women. They do not even feel ashamed when someone tells them: "Look, sir, soon you will have a son or a daughter!" (IV 33.9-10). That the custom of keeping concubines was widespread in Birgitta's time is shown, for example, in the statutes of the diocese of Linköping in the 1350s.[154] In another statute from 1368, a provincial synod in Uppsala complains that priests hold concubines publicly and refuse to refrain from their "lustful pleasure".[155]

Finally, Birgitta accuses the religious of having abandoned their vow of chastity. For example, she writes that the monks in Rome gladly embrace their sons before the eyes of visiting friends, and say: "Look, this is my son!" (IV 33.17). The abbot of Farfa is accused of having several children (Ex. 105.1; III 22 A). Moreover, Benedictine monks are accused of dressing so as to excite lust (IV 127.11). As for the nuns, Birgitta compares the nunneries in Rome to brothels (IV 33.27).

Notes

[1] For an example of a scholar giving an inadequate interpretation in this matter, see below section 2.3.2.

[2] For these terms, see Henri de Lubac, *Méditation sur l'Église,* Paris 1953 (Théologie 27), pp. 87f.

[3] See above, section 1.1.

[4] See Klockars, *Birgitta och hennes värld,* p. 99, and her article "Borg och bigård: Om den heliga Birgittas syn på kyrkan", *Lumen: Katolsk teologisk tidskrift* 13 (1970), pp. 94-96; Ingvar Fogelqvist, "De kristna och kyrkan i Heliga Birgitta Uppenbarelser, in *Heliga Birgitta—Budskapet och förebilden,* pp. 146-148.

[5] IV 58.2. For the different images of the Church in Birgitta's Revelations, see Graziano Maioli, "Il volto della Chiesa nella visione di S. Brigida di Svezia: Spigolature in un campo dimenticato", *Ephemerides Carmeliticae* 17 (1966), pp. 191-198.

[6] I 55.12; I 5.1,12; II 19 E; III 10 C; IV 78.22.

[7] III 24 C. See also IV 18.15-17; IV 65.9; II 5 G; IV 116.5-6; IV 16.6-7.

[8] See Congar, *Die Lehre von der Kirche: Von Augustinus bis zum Abendländischen Schisma,* vol. III 3c of *Handbuch der Dogmengeschichte,* Freiburg im Breisgau 1971, p. 111, 141. The expression *numero, non merito* is used already by Augustine, *Ibid.,* p. 4.

[9] VI 26.2-3. See also III 27 E.

[10] Birgitta, *Originaltexter,* ed. Bertil Högman, *Heliga Birgittas originaltexter* (SSFS 205), Uppsala 1951, pp. 74f., ll. 16-23. A similar description of a building in a state in decay is found in III 10.

[11] Birgitta, *Originaltexter,* pp. 75-78.

[12] It can be noted that the identification between the Church in decay and the Christians is to a large degree subdued in the Latin version in IV 49.

[13] See Maioli, "Il volto della Chiesa", pp. 199-205.

[14] See, Morton W. Bloomfield, *Piers Plowman as a Fourteenth-century Apocalypse,* New Brunswick N.J. 1961, p. 49.

[15] Ex 83.7-12; VII 16.3. For the three traditional "orders" or classes existing in the Church, the *rectores* or *prælati* the bishops or prelates, the *continentes* or monks, and the *conjugati* or married, see Yves, Congar, "Les laïcs et l'ecclésiologie des 'ordines' chez les

théologiens des XIe et XIIe siècles", in *I laici nella "societas christiana" dei secoli XI e XII: Atti della terza Settimana internazionale di studio Mendola, 21-27 agosto 1965,* Milano 1968 (Miscellanea del centro di studi medioevali 5), pp. 86-88. For Birgitta's criticism of the religious, see Jarl Gallén, *La province de Dacie de l'Ordre des Frères Prêcheurs. I: Histoire générale jusqu' au Grande Schisme,* Helsingfors 1946 (Dissert. hist. 12), pp. 184-186.

[16] Congar, "Les laïcs et l'ecclesiologie", pp. 89-104. This distinction is known since the end of the 9th century. The three orders are mentioned by Thomas Aquinas in *Summa Theologiae,* cura fratrum eiusdem Ordinis, ed. Biblioteca de Autores Cristianos, 5 vols., Madrid 1951-1952, I, q. 108, a.2. (Hereafter referred to as STh). For quotations in English, I have used Thomas Aquinas, *Summa Theologica,* trl. English Dominicans, 5 vols., 1911, 1920, 1948; rpt. Westminister Maryland, 1981.

[17] VI 26.13. One individual is brought into particular focus by Birgitta: the Swedish king Magnus Eriksson. For Birgitta's relations with him, see Klockars, *Birgittas svenska värld,* pp. 118-133; Olle Ferm, "Heliga Birgittas program för uppror mot Magnus Eriksson: En studie i politisk argumentationskonst", in *Heliga Birgitta—budskapet och förebilden,* pp. 125-143.

[18] I 5.13; IV 45.4; VI 26.3; VI 33.3; RS Prol. 3.28.

[19] VI 67.2-11. Hjalmar Sundén, pp. 11-16, suggests that Birgitta's three ages are influenced by Joachim of Fiore's division of history into three "states" (*status*), respectively attributed to the Father, the Son and the Holy Spirit. For the opinion that Birgitta probably was acquainted with Joachim's ideas, see Johannes Jørgensen, *Den Hellige Birgitta af Vadstena,* II, København 1943, pp. 20-22; Carl-Gustaf Undhagen, in Birgitta, *Revelaciones,* Book I, p. 45, note 52; and Kjerstin Norén, "Själen är av långt bättre natur än kroppen: Om Birgitta av Vadstena," in *I Guds namn: 1000-1800,* ed. Elisabeth Møller Jensen, vol. I of *Nordisk kvinnolitteraturhistoria,* Höganäs 1993. There are, however, significant differences between Birgitta's and Joachim's concepts, which makes an influence little likely. As we have seen, Birgitta's third age is a time of apostasy at the end of which the Antichrist would be born. For the Abbot of Fiore, however, the defeat of the Antichirst occurs at the end of the second *status.* His defeat would usher a new stage of history, the *status* of the Holy Spirit, in which a renewed Church would reign in peace and contemplation. See Bernard McGinn, *Visions of the End: Apocalyptic Traditions in the Middle Ages,* New York 1979, pp.128f, 133f. Thus, for Joachim, the renewal of the Church, being a new eruption of the power of the Holy Spirit within history, was a renewal from the future rather than from the past, see Bernard McGinn, Introd., *Apocalyptic Spiri-*

tuality: Treatises and Letters of Lactantius, Adso of Montier-en-Der, Joachim Fiore, The Spiritual Franciscans, Savoranola, New York 1979 (The Classics of Western Spirituality), p. 108. Birgitta had another understanding. Her hopes centered on the ideal of the apostolic life and the early Church and was thus backward looking: she attempted to revive a golden past.

[20] Different aspects of these three vices are treated in I 23, where a bishop is criticized by Birgitta. In I 23.5 she writes of him: . . . *cogitacio eius tota est ad presencia et non ad eterna, tota, quomodo placeat hominibus et quid utilitas carnis requirit et non quomodo placeat michi et prosit animabus.* See also I 5.15. Often Birgitta deals with one of these vices at a time. The focus is on worldly delights in I 13.1-4, on the contempt of Christ in I 1.4-5, and on contempt of neighbour in I 41.10-17.

[21] II 6.14; I 30.3; I 32.10; I 37.6,9-10.

[22] See STh, I-II, q. 80, a. 1.

[23] See Constable, "Twelfth Century Spirituality", pp. 34f.

[24] VI 33.21. For this image, see Magister Mathias, *Homo conditus,* ed. Anders Piltz, *Magistri Mathiae canonici Lincopensis opus sub nomine Homo conditus vulgatum,* Uppsala 1984 (SSFS Ser 2, IX:1), 1.37,40-42. Hereafter this work will be referred to as HC followed by the chapter and paragraph number or numbers.

[25] I 1.4-6. For this image, see HC, 1.13.

[26] VI 3.8; IV 67.13; I 1.6.

[27] See STh, I-II, q. 80, a. 1.

[28] I 1.5, 16-17; I 37.23-25; III 26; V int. 13.9.

[29] STh, I-II q. 77, a. 4.

[30] See Donald R. Howard, *The Three Temptations: Medieval Man in Search of the World,* Princeton N. J. 1966, pp. 65f. According to Thomas Aquinas, every sinful act proceeds from inordinate desire for some temporal good, STh, I-II q. 77, a. 4.

[31] I 53.11-12; II 6 C; II 20 B; III 3 C-D; III 18 A; V int. 8.11; VI 33.5; VI 3548; I 13.3; I 48.9-11.

[32] IV 33.27. Since the late eleventh century, the respectability and the good reputation of a nunnery depended greatly on the rigid enforcement of enclosure, see Lekai, pp. 350f.

[33] IV 33.18-20. See also IV 127.13,17.

[34] *Statuta Capitulorum Generalium Ordinis Cisterciensis: Ab anno 1116 ad annum 1786,* ed. Josephus-Maria Canivez, 8 vols., Louvain 1933-1941 (Bibliothèque de la Revue d'histoire ecclésiastique 9-14 B), 1344.3, III (Bibl. 11), pp. 476f.; and 1360.5, III (Bibl. 11), p. 536.

[35] *Ibid.,* 1361.3, III (Bibl.), p. 537.

[36] Already in I John 2:16 the "world" is equated with lust of the flesh, lust of the eyes and pride of life.

[37] The Virgin Mary speaks in III 17 A: *Huic sancto* [St. Dominic] *inspirauit filius meus tria esse in mundo que displicebant eidem filio meo, superbiam, scilicet, et cupiditatem et concupiscentiam carnis.* Birgit Klockars has observed in *Birgitta och böckerna* p.173, that according to the Old Swedish legendary—a work to which Birgitta probably was acquainted—, St. Dominic once in a vision saw Christ inflamed with anger because of the three great sins of the world: "høgfærdh, giri ok oloflikin køzsins luste", *Ett Fornsvenskt legendarium,* ed. George Steffens, 3 vols., Stockholm 1847-1874 (SFSS 7), II, pp. 794f.

[38] VII 30.10-11,13; IV 79.4; IV 81.3; IV 116.7; III 5 B. The importance of this triad in Birgitta's teaching has been noted by Albert Nilsson, "Ära, rikedom och vällust", in his *Ur diktens värld,* Stockholm 1926, p. 26-27. See also Brilioth, *Medeltiden,* p. 153; Klockars, *Birgitta och böckerna,* p. 174, and Segelberg, *Kyrkotrohet och kyrkokritik,* pp. 11f.

[39] VII 12.4; III 10 C; III 22 A-B; VII 20.17; Birgitta, *Originaltexter,* p. 76, II. 52-54; p. 77, II. 63-64.

[40] For example, Master Mathias writes in HC, 4.114; *Verumtamen tercia impugnacio non minus grauis nobis cotidie imminet, temptaciones videlicet carnis, mundi et dyaboli. Caro nos temptat de luxuria et gula, mundus nos temptat de auaricia, sed dyabolus nos temptat de superbia. In hiis tribus simul conueniunt omnia peccata. Nam, vt dicit Iohannes, omne, quod est in mundo, aut est concupisceincia carnis aut concupiscencia oculorum aut superbia vite.* [1 John 2.15]. See also Bonaventure, *Breviloquium,* vol. I of *Obras de San Buenaventura; Edicion bilingüe,* ed. Leon Amoros et al, 2nd ed., Madrid 1955 (Biblioteca de autores cristianos 6) pars III, caput 9.1, p. 316; and STh, I-II, q. 77, a. 5.

[41] See Morton W. Bloomfield, *The Seven Deadly Sins. An Introduction to the History of a Religious Concept, with Special Reference to medieval English Literature,* East Lansing 1952 (Studies in Language and Literature); Bengt Ingmar Kilström, *Den kateketiska undervisningen i Sverige under medeltiden,* Lund 1958 (BTP 8), pp. 193-217.

[42] See, VI 54.6. In VI 39.10-37 seven chief sins are listed: *superbia, cupiditas, inuidia, auaricia, accidia, ira,* and *voluptas.* This list differs somewhat from the classical list of Gregory the Great, which includes *gula,* but not *cupiditas.* Moreover, Gregory speaks of *luxuria,* not *voluptas.* See *Moralia in Iob,* ed. Marcus Adriaen, 3 vols., Turnhout 1979 (CCSL 193), 31.45.87, p. 1610. See also Bloomfield, *The Seven Deadly Sins,* pp. 72-74. For another list of sins in Birgitta's Revelations, see III 13 B.

[43] See Howard, pp. 61f.

[44] See II 6 B: *Tandem vox diaboli, idest superbia, soniut in mundo, que ostendit mundi diuicias et carnalem voluptatem.* See also IV 135. 4-9.

[45] See Howard, pp. 47-53.

[46] The most influential of these were John Cassian, *De institutis coenobiorum,* ed. Michael Petschenig, Vindobonae 1888 (CSEL 17), 12, pp. 204-31, especially 12.7, p. 210, and Gregory the Great, *Moralia in Iob,* 31.45.87, p. 1610. For the concepts of pride and covetousness in the Middle Ages, see Lester K. Little, "Pride Goes before Avarice: Social Change and the Vices in Latin Christendom", *The American Historical Review* 76 (1971), pp. 16-49.

[47] See for example, Peter Damian, *Epistolae,* I.15, PL, 144, col. 234; John of Salisbury, Polycraticus, ed. Clemens. C.J. Webb, 2 vols., *Ioannis Saresberiensis Episcopi Carnotensis Policratici,* Oxonii 1909, 8.4, II p. 241.

[48] See Bernard of Clairvaux, *Liber de gradibus humilitatis et superbiae,* vol. 3 of *Sancti Bernardi opera,* eds. J. Leclercq, C. H. Talbot, and H. M. Rochais, Rome 1963, pp. 13-59; Bernard of Clairvaux, *Sermones de diversis,* vol. 6:1 of *Sancti Bernardi opera,* eds. J. Leclercq and H. M. Rochais, Romae 1970, Sermo 74, p. 312.

[49] See, for example, STh, I-II q. 84, aa. 1-2.

[50] For example, II 6 C; III 5 B; III 17 A; IV 49.16; IV 79.4; IV 81.3; IV 116.7; VII 19.22; VII 20.17; VII 30.10; Ex. 19.3; Ex. 74.4. See also I 40.7: *Hanc autem superfluitatem inuenit superbia, que nunc habetur et diligitur pro lege.*

[51] See STh, II-II q. 162, aa. 1-2.

[52] *Ibid.,* II-II q. 162, a. 5. See also Ecclus. 10:14: *Initium superbiae homimis apostare a Deo.*

[53] VII 30.10; II 8 B-C; II 9 C; VI 15.12. Having this desire, they resemble the devil, see VI 23.10; VII 27.7.

[54] See, for example, STh, II-II q. 132, a. 1. According to Gregory the Great, vainglory is an immediate off-spring of pride, *Moralia in Iob* 31.45.88, p. 1610. See also STh, II-II q. 132, a. 4.

[55] III 2 C; III 10 C; III 4 A; I 29.5.

[56] I 55.14; III 15 A; VI 35.51; I 48.19.

[57] I 55.14; III 2 D; III 15 A.

[58] I 33.2; VII 20.21; III 8 B-C.

[59] III 2 D; IV 126.104; Ex. 83.10-11; III 18 B; VII 20.23.

[60] See STh, II-II q. 13, a. 1.

[61] Ex. 43.1; Ex. 83.11; IV 102.18; IV 107.6,15-19; VI 35.11; VI 39.8; VI 43.6; VI 121.3.

[62] As regards the reason for this name, Birgitta is told by Christ, VII 20.17: . . . *iste frater meus. qui Aduersarius nominabitur ex eo, quod Francisci regule aduersarius erit, multos de ordine Francisci trahet de humilitate ad superbiam. . . .*

[63] VII 20.19; also III 33.3. Birgitta accuses the priests of a similar hypocrisy in I 48.24.

[64] VI 65.70. Anger and pride are mentioned together in IV 104.11. However, Birgitta can also occasionally relate anger to covetousness, for example in IV 104.8. It would seem that Master Mathias primarily relates anger to covetousness, see HC, 7.99.

[65] See STh, II-II q. 136, a. 1.

[66] IV 24.4; IV 17.26,28. Like anger, however, impatience can also be related to covetousness, IV 17.30.

[67] This vice is called *arrogantia* in STh, II-II q. 112, a 1; q. 162, a. 4 and 4.

[68] VI 23.7; VI 35; III 22.4-5; IV 17.28; IV 112.3.

[69] VI 39.10-11; I 48.34; IV 135; I 17.2.

[70] See Birgitta's revelation quoted by Master Mathias, *Prologus,* in Birgitta: *Revelaciones: Book I,* ed. Carl-Gustaf Undhagen, Uppsala 1978 (SFSS Ser. 2, 7:1), par. 35. Also 35; I 19.3.4; II 9.14; VI 39.11-12; IV 112.5; VI 52. A similar vice is mentioned in STh, II-II q. 162, a. 4.

[71] Ex 83.10. See also IV 112.3.

[72] See Num. 14:40-45.

[73] Gregory the Great, *Homiliae XL in Euangelia:* PL 76, col. 1305; See also Thomas Aquinas, *Summa Theologiae,* II-II q. 169, a. 1.

[74] VII 27.19-20; VII 16.27; VIII 57 A.

[75] *Statuta Capitulorum,* 1195.68, vol. I (Bibl. 9), p. 192.

[76] *Ibid.,* 1231.8, vol. II (Bibl. 10) p. 93; also *Ibid.,* 1270.1, vol. III (Bibl. 11), pp. 79f.; *Ibid.,* 1317.17, vol. III (Bibl. 11), p. 337.

[77] *Ibid.,* 1303.6, vol. III (Bibl. 11), p. 316.

[78] *Ibid.,* 1269.4, vol. III (Bibl. 11), p. 69.

[79] For the relation between boasting and pride in Christian tradition, see STh, II-II q. 112, a. 1, ad 2; II-II q. 162, a. 4 ad 3 and Bernard of Clairvaux, *De gradibus humilitatis et superbiae,* 13.41, pp. 47f.

[80] This is, according to Bernard of Clairvaux, typical of boasting *Ibid.,* 13 41, p. 48: *Quod si de religione agitur, statim visiones et somnia proferuntur.*

[81] VIII 10; IV 51.14; VI 39.28; VI 23; VI 15.6;VI 98.11. Vulgar words are in the Revelations mentioned together with pride in VI 52.61. See also Bernard of Clairvaux, *De gradibus humilitatis et superbiae,* 13.41, p. 48: *Dicas, si audias, rivum vanitatis, fluvium esse scurrlilitatis os eius . . .*

[82] IV 24.6; I 37.13; III 4 C; Ex. 75.7; VI 5.7; Ex. 75.6.

[83] I 5.17-18; I 30.2-3; V int. 12.40; I 58.5; I 18.3.

[84] He is called a hypocrite in the rubric of the chapter.

[85] Also VI 35.51. According to Gregory, hypocrisy is born of vainglory, *Moralia in Iob,* 31.45.88, p. 1610.

[86] VI 35.51. According to Birgitta, the devil often incites people to perform such singular acts, as excessive vigils, fastings, prayers, works, see IV 29; VII 5.38. Singularity is elaborated by Bernard of Clairvaux in the fifth step of pride, see *De gradibus humilitatis et superbiae,* 14.42, pp. 48f.

[87] VII 12.32-33. The allegorical figure of pride appears in medieval representations as a mighty person seated on a horse. See Little, p. 31.

[88] STh, II II q. 118, a. 1.

[89] I 56.2; also II 3 D; VIII 18 B; VI 31.12.

[90] See STh. II-II q. 118, aa. 1-2.

[91] In Birgitta, *Himmelska Uppenbarelser,* II, p. 215, Lundén translates, somewhat misleadingly, *cupiditas,* which occurs twice in this passage, with "vinningslystnad" and "girighet", terms which primarily denote disordered love of money. For another example where *cupiditas* seems primarily to denote covetousness for power, see VI 31.12-13.

[92] III 13 B. Another term for disordered desire for honours is *ambitio,* VII 16.5.

[93] See also I 16.7, where *cupiditas* should be related to *cupiditas pecunie* in I 16.2.

[94] I 16.2; also III 10 C; IV 140.14; VI 3.9. A term equivalent to *cupiditas* in the special sense, used by Birgitta, is *avaricia,* I 48.11.

[95] VI 36.9. See also VI 63.6.

[96] See Charles de la Ronciere, "Die Kirche und das Geld", in *Die Zeit der Zerreissproben (1274-1449),* ed. Michel Mollat du Jourdin, André Vauchez; German ed. Bernhard Schimmelpfennig, vol. 6 of *Die Geschichte des Christentums: Religion, Politik, Kultur,* Freiburg im Breisgau 1991, pp. 480-483; Little, pp. 20-31; Bloomfield, *Seven Deadly Sins,* p. 95.

[97] Master Mathias, *Prologus,* par. 35; VIII 47 G; I 56.8-9; Ex. 51.8; VI 96.5-6.

[98] I 56.9. A similar criticism of greedy priests is found in the villages of Ariège. See Emmanuel Le Roy Ladurie, *Montaillou: Cathars and Catholics in a French Village 1294-1324.* Harmondsworth 1980 (Penguin Books), p. 336: "Sybille Pierre reported what the Autiès had said in a house in Ax-les-Thermes (ii.404): The priests steal all men's possessions. . . . To say Mass, to do anything at all, they want money."

[99] I 56.1-2. The allegorical figure of covetousness that appears in medieval representations is closely connected with bags of money, see Little, p. 37; Kilström, *Den kateketiska undervisningen,* pp. 211, 213.

[100] II 10 B; III 6 C; IV 137.2. One of the daughters of covetousness is, according to Gregory the Great, restlessness. See *Moralia in Iob,* 31.45.88, p. 1610. Also STh, II-II q. 118, a. 8.

[101] See STh, II-II q. 118, a. 2.

[102] V int. 7.19. See also Ex. 75.7. According to Gregory the Great, one of the daughters of covetousness is insensibility to mercy, when a man's heart is not softened by mercy to assist the needy with his riches, *Moralia in Iob,* 31.45.88, p. 1610. Also STh, II-II q. 118, a. 8.

[103] II 8. See STh, II-II q. 66, a. 8, ad 1: *Quamvis possint in acceptione praedae iustum bellum habentes peccare per cupiditatem ex prava intentione, si scilicet non propter iustitiam, sed propter praedam principaliter pugnent: dicit Augustinus in libro De Verb. Dom., quod propter praedam militare peccatum est.*

[104] VI 32.22-23; VII 16.32-33; IV 1.6; Ex. 43.3; Ex. 74.6; VI 23.5. See STh, II-II q. 118, a. 2.

[105] On the traditional teaching on usury, see STh, II-II q. 118, a. 8 ad 4; II-II q. 78, a. 1. The practice of usury was widespread in Birgitta's time, see Charles de la Roncière, "Die Kirche und das Geld", pp. 475-478. For basic background reading on the theory and practice of usury in the Middle Ages, consult, Hans-Jörg Gilomen, "Wucher und Wirtschaft im Mittelalter", in *Historische Zeitschrift* 250 (1990), pp. 265-301.

[106] See Francis of Asissi, *Regula Bullata,* ed. Théophile Desbonnets et al., *Francois d' Assise: Écrits,* Paris 1981 (SChr 282), 4, p. 188.

[107] VII 20.20. See also VI 35.14.

[108] VI 99.3. See also Ex. 83.11.

[109] Also in other revelations Birgitta accuses her contemporary Christians of having fallen prey to carnal desires. See III 28 A; IV 122.9; Ex. 83.11; VI 52.41; III 27 E.

[110] STh. I-II q. 30. a. 3.

[111] HC, 6.98: *Sed qui voluerit non solum cauere mendacia ymmo eciam omne peccatum cauere, caueat matrem omnis mali concupiscenciam, que duplex est: concupiscencia scilicet carnis ad fruendum delectationibus mundi, et concupiscencia oculorum, que est cupiditas deliciarum mundi.* Also 6.105.

[112] In IV 126.85, for example, *concupiscentia* refers to *amor mundi* as well as to *amor carnis.*

[113] In particular the latter denotation is characteristic of carnal concupiscence. In I 26.10, for example carnal concupiscence is distinguished from hunger and thirst, and corresponds to *luxuria* in I 26.11. As for another example where concupiscence denotes sexual desire, see IV 53.5.

[114] See STh, I-II q. 34, a. 1.

[115] The good delight is described in IV 120.2,5: *Carnalis vel naturalis delectacio est, quando necessitate requirente refeccio sumitur. . . . Spiritualis delectacio est, quando anima delectatur in beneficiis Dei et temporalibus utitur et occupatur inuitus et ad solam necessitatem.* A similar good delight is *diuina delectacio*

in III 7.5. In Birgitta, *Himmelska uppenbarelser,* I, p. 293, Lundén translates this passage with "gudliga begärelser". See also VI 52.91; VI 65.3. As we have seen, however, *delectatiio* is not to be regarded as a desire for some loved good, but as a repose in it. Normally, Lundén translates *delectatio* with "lust", or "lusta".

[116] VII 30.10. See also VI 52.53.

[117] Ex. 51.3. See also IV 120.1.

[118] I 57.3; also Ex. 102.3; II 29 C; Ex. 19.3.

[119] I 26.10; VII 20.4; IV 4.4.

[120] IV 45.6. See also IV 49.16; IV 36.2; VI 35.39-40.

[121] In I 26.10-11, *delectacionem carnis* is expressly referring to *luxuria*.

[122] STh, I-II q. 58, a. 9.1; II-II q. 138, a. 1 ad 2; II-II q. 142, a. 3.

[123] *Ibid.,* I-II q. 2, a. 6: . . . *quia delectationes corporales pluribus notae sunt assumpserunt sibi nomen voluptatum.*

[124] *Ibid.,* II-II q. 148, a. 1.

[125] *Ibid.,* II-II q. 153, aa. 1, 3.

[126] *Ibid.,* II-II q. 138, a. 1.

[127] II 7 B. See also II 8 C-D. Occasionally, however, *voluptas* denotes a good pleasure. For example, II 11 B: *Veni, et repleberis diuina voluptate!* Also IV 133.21; 135.2; III 31 A. Normally, *delectatio* is used in such cases. In exceptional cases Birgitta speaks of *voluptatem mundi,* VI 35.42, which corresponds to the worldly delights mentioned above. Lundén sometimes incorrectly translates also *voluptas* with "begärelser", see Birgitta, *Himmelska uppenbarelser,* I, pp. 210, 293.

[128] II 1 C; II 23 D; III 10 B; III 27 C; IV 7.46; IV 32.3; IV 61.17; IV 62.4; IV 69.5; IV 95.5; IV 107.5,13,16; IV 108.16; IV 110.2; IV 111.13; IV 114.8; IV 123.6; VI 17.2; IV 55.1.

[129] II 6 B; IV 75.18; IV 81.10; VI 55.2.

[130] II 6 B; VI 5.10; IV 95.5. This is the case with the nobility, II 8 D-E; IV 7.46; IV 113.10; IV 122.3; VI 39.26,32,50; IV 81.3; VI 28.14; VI 56.11; VI 52.53,58,60,91, with the clerics, I 48.10; IV 132.14; 133.7; VI 7.7; III 7 A; IV 62.4, and with the religious, IV 102.20; VI 19.37; IV 23.19; IV 107.5.

[131] VI 39.25-26. See also IV 122.3; VII 13.42.

[132] See STh, II-II q. 148, a. 1.

[133] VI 80.4; Ex 74.4; VI 97.7.

[134] VI 10.6. See also VI 39.36; Ex. 56.12. See STh, II-II q. 148, a. 4.

[135] VI 39.35. See also VI 10.6; Ex. 75.6. See STh, II-II q. 148, a. 4.

[136] VI 98.4; IV 23.20; VI 19.3-4; VI 35.51.

[137] VI 14.15. See Klockars, *Birgitta och böckerna,* p. 192.

[138] VI 35.12. See also VII 20.19.

[139] I 26.20; I 57.3; IV 79.4; IV 95.4. I 16.2,7; VI 10.5; VI 81.3; VI 97.6; VI 56.10; IV 9.21; VI 32.21. The priests are often accused of this sin, I 59.20; IV 58.15; IV 132.13; IV 133.15,19; VI 15.10; IV 49.19; IV 142.7. Mainly, Birgitta uses the term *luxuria*. Other terms denoting this vice in the Revelations are *incontinencia*, I 4.5; I 59.20; VI 36.10; *impuritas*, IV 58.15; VI 56.11; VI 97.6; and *immundicia*, VI 56.10.

[140] For the traditional teaching on lust, see STh, II-II q. 153, aa. 1-2.

[141] I 26.27. See also I 26.18,20,22; V int. 23.6; VI 31.23.

[142] STh, Supplement, q. 49, a. 6.

[143] *Ibid.,* II-II q. 169, a. 2.

[144] VI 39.34. See also I 26.18.

[145] VII 28.13. For individuals of whom Birgitta mentions or hints at that they have committed adultery or fornication, see VI 10.5; VII 11.19; VI 80.5.

[146] See Ronald Lawler, Joseph M. Boyle, and William E. May, *Catholic Sexual Ethics. A Summary, explanation, & Defense,* Huntington, Ind., 1985, p. 43.

[147] VI 39.33: *Nam licet coniugatus erat et ab aliarum mulierum macula segregatus, tamen per amplexus et per verba inepta et eciam per gestus impudicos, effundebat semen suum modo indebito.* According to Gottfrid Carlsson, Birgitta in this text accuses the knight of homosexual acts. See his article "Heliga Birgittas upprorsprogram", in *Archivistica et mediaevistica: Ernesto Nygren oblata,* Stockholm 1956 (Samlingar och studier utgivna av svenskt arkivsamfund 1), p. 97. Whether the text actually is speaking of homosexual acts is, however, somewhat uncertain. Strictly speaking, the sin Birgitta describes is not the vice of sodomy but the vice of procuring pollution, without any copu-

lation, for the sake of sexual pleasure. See STh, II-II q. 154, a. 12. What arouses the suspicion about homosexuality are the words that he was *ab aliarum mulierum macula segregatus*. The words imply that he refrained from sexual activities with other women, but does not exclude that it was his wife who was the object of his sexual activites.

[148] Birgitta has previously in VI 80 mentioned gluttony and, it would seem, adultery.

[149] Thomas Aquinas mentions four types of unnatural vice: impurity, bestiality, sodomy and unnatural manner of copulation, see STh, II-II q. 154, a. 11.

[150] Birgitta, *Originaltexter,* p. 81. For Birgitta's accusation, see Olle Ferm, "Birgittas uppror mot Magnus Eriksson", p. 133. A similar accusation is found in the pamphlet *Libellus de Magno Erici rege,* ed. Claudius Annerstedt, in *Scriptores rerum Suecicarum medii aevi,* III:1, Upsala 1876, p. 14. The pamphlet, which is from the 1360s, was probably inspired by Birgitta, see Carlsson, pp. 96f. For Birgitta's influence on this pamphlet, see Ingvar Andersson, *Källstudier till Sveriges historia 1230-1436: Inhemska berättande källor jämte Libellus Magnippolensis,* Lund 1928, pp. 151-173.

[151] "Heliga Birgittas upprorsprogram", p. 99. In support of this, Carlsson writes that Birgitta had a certain tendency to accuse people she disliked of homosexual acts. His reference, however, to VI 39 is, as we have seen (note 147 above), an uncertain support in this respect.

[152] *Furstinnan av Närke som blev Heliga Birgitta,* p. 14f.

[153] See Kristin Drar, *Konungens herravälde såsom rättvisans, fridens och frihetens beskydd. Medeltidens fursteideal i svenskt hög- och senmedeltida källmaterial,* Stockholm 1980 (Bibliotheca Historico-Ecclesiastica Lundensis 10), p. 111.

[154] *Statuta synodalis veteris ecclesica Sveogothicae,* ed. H. Reuterdahl, Lund 1841, p. 45. Concerning the vice of incontinence, the synod says . . . *quod heu! in Sacerdotibus et Clericis nostri temporis inolevit, et honestatem inquinat clericalem.*

[155] *Ibid.,* p. 53.

Claire L. Sahlin (essay date 1996)

SOURCE: "Gender and Prophetic Authority in Birgitta of Sweden's Revelations," in *Gender and Text in The Later Middle Ages,* edited by Jane Chance, University Press of Florida, 1996, pp. 69-95.

[*In the following essay, Sahlin explores Birgitta's attempts to overcome the medieval bias against women by appealing to a prophetic authority sanctioned by God.*]

During her pilgrimage to the Holy Land and subsequent return to Rome in 1372, Birgitta of Sweden traveled through Cyprus, where she summoned rulers and nobility to hear God's words concerning the fate of the island. Birgitta, who was advanced in age and growing physically weak, claimed to speak to the Cypriots on behalf of God. She boldly announced on several occasions that God would soon destroy the kingdom, unless its leaders and people began to love Christ and carry out his will. In the city of Famagusta, Christ proclaimed his words of judgment through her: "This city is Gomorrah, burning with the fire of lust and of superfluity and of ambition. Therefore its structures shall fall, and it shall be desolated and diminished, and its inhabitants shall depart, and they shall groan in sorrow and tribulation, and they shall die out, and their shame shall be mentioned in many lands, because I am angered at them" (*Rev.* 7.16:5-6).[1]

These demands for reform received wide-ranging responses in Cyprus and became the occasion for both praise and ridicule of her activities as God's emissary, according to witnesses who testified in favor of her canonization.[2] Some members of her audience were simply astonished, apparently because of her claims to have received messages directly from God; others greatly revered her and asked her to pray for them. Still others disbelieved Birgitta altogether, and derided her. Simon, a Dominican theologian and astronomer, asserted that it would be foolish to believe her proclamations, since she obviously was demented (*una mente capta*) (*A et P,* 430). Several religious men, perhaps including Brother Simon, also discredited her by saying that it was "nearly impossible that God would speak with an ignorant little woman [*ignara muliercula*]" (*A et P,* 390). Presumably they could not believe that God would use a lowly woman, lacking theological training and expertise, as an instrument of revelation.[3]

Birgitta's mixed reception in Cyprus, extending from high accolades to disbelief and disparagement, typifies the reception she experienced throughout her thirty-year career as a visionary reformer. In Sweden, Italy, and throughout her travels to the Holy Land, Birgitta Birgersdotter (1302/3-1373) attracted numerous disciples and gathered a considerable entourage; she also was ridiculed, slandered, and threatened with physical harm. Many accepted and defended her assertions that God had revealed messages directly to her, but others questioned her motives, behavior, and sanity. Her sex made her especially vulnerable to criticism and rejection, as the episode in Cyprus illustrates. Repeatedly reminded that it was difficult for a woman to gain acceptance as a prophet, Birgitta and her followers were required to justify and authenticate her claims to be a channel of God's word.

All who claim to speak on behalf of God and pronounce judgment on the unrepentant face opposition,[4] but when the messenger is a woman, her gender amplifies the difficulties necessarily faced in gaining acceptance as a legitimate intermediary between God and humanity. In later medieval Europe such women encountered great resistance, even though influential theologians, who could not deny the presence of female prophets in the Bible, admitted the possibility of female prophecy. Prophecy, like visions and mystical experiences, was prominent in the lives of later medieval female saints, who gained a public hearing and assumed religious leadership by claiming to have been divinely inspired. Yet women who claimed this gift were often received with hostility, since they tended to violate gender conventions by interpreting scripture and advising political and ecclesiastical leaders. Widespread scientific and theological assumptions about women's intellectual weakness, spiritual instability, and vulnerability to delusion brought great suspicion upon female prophets.[5]

This essay examines some ways in which gender and prophetic authority are negotiated in Birgitta of Sweden's *Revelations,* an impressive record of divine communications that circulated widely throughout Europe in Latin and vernacular languages from the end of the fourteenth century until well into the sixteenth century. After providing a brief introduction to the *Revelations* themselves, I describe the nature of the authority claimed for Birgitta in this body of texts. Then, by discussing passages that reflect questions and tensions concerning her authority and gender, I identify methods by which the *Revelations* endeavor to defend, justify, and confirm her vocation. The *Revelations* counteract obstacles faced by Birgitta as a woman claiming to speak on behalf of God and simultaneously construct a picture of Birgitta as a holy woman endowed with the spirit of prophecy.

An Introduction to Birgitta's Revelations

Birgitta's *Revelations* comprise an enormous collection of over seven hundred visions and auditions of varying lengths from Christ, Mary, and numerous saints. Although she was reported to have received some revelations at a young age, the overwhelming majority of them were received after Birgitta was widowed—between 1346, when she received her prophetic call in Sweden, and 1373, when she died in Rome. Many motifs and themes in the *Revelations* reflect her life as the aristocratic mother of eight children and her activities in the Swedish court. Characterized both by memorable images and by obscure detail, the surviving record of her visions and auditions also discusses diverse topics of interest to later medieval Christians throughout

St. Birgitta is the Patron Saint of Sweden; the Patroness of Knights; and the Patroness of Pilgrims.

western Europe, such as the lives of Jesus and his mother, the Real Presence in the Eucharist, and the ages of the world. Her most famous revelations are a vivid description of the nativity (*Rev.* 7.21-22), exhortations to Avignonese popes to return to Rome (*Rev.* 4.136-44), and advice concerning a peaceful solution to the Hundred Years War (*Rev.* 4.103-5). In general, the *Revelations* attempt to effect the moral reform of the Church and society by proclaiming the will of God to the world.[6]

According to various passages in the *Revelations* and documents related to her process of canonization, Birgitta's confessors acted as amanuenses, translators, and editors of her visions. Birgitta recorded the revelations in her native language, Old Swedish, sometimes writing and rewriting until she adequately expressed the messages and visions that God had given her. She then handed her writings over to her confessors, Prior Petrus of Alvastra (d. 1390) and, to a lesser extent, Master Mathias of Linköping (d. 1350?) and Master Petrus of Skänninge (d. 1378), who translated them into Latin and read the translations aloud for her approval. In most cases her original writings appear to have been lost or discarded. Birgitta also dictated her revelations when she was feeling too weak to write. On those occasions the confessor immediately translated the words into Latin, and a scribe recorded them. Near the end of her life, Birgitta asked Alfonso (d. 1389), a Spanish hermit who was a former bishop of Jaén, to examine the orthodoxy of her revelations, polish their Latin, and prepare them for widespread circulation.[7] As a result of an extremely lengthy and complex process of editing by Alfonso, Prior Petrus, and members of the Birgittine monastery in Vadstena, Sweden, the *Revelations* were divided into eight books. These books were supplemented by the *Sermo angelicus* (lessons to be read at matins), *Quattuor oraciones* (Birgitta's prayers to Christ and the Virgin Mary), and the so-called *Reuelaciones extrauagantes* (a separate book of additional revelations), when they were published in Latin for the first time in 1492 by Bartholomaeus Ghotan of Lübeck.[8] Philologists in Sweden have been preparing modern critical editions of the Latin *Revelations* for the past forty years and have recently made great strides toward the completion of this project.[9]

Although most readers would agree that the extant *Revelations* embody Birgitta's strong voice and willful personality, the complicated history of the *Revelations* precludes accepting these texts as her exact words. The words that flowed directly from Birgitta's mouth or pen are refracted through several layers of translation and uneven editing. Her confessors polished, revised, and supplemented her descriptions of divine auditions and visions, sometimes apparently in consultation with her but also after her death. By comparing Latin revelations with the two remaining Old Swedish autographs and other Old Swedish versions, scholars have been able to demonstrate that some of these changes to the texts were made in the process of translation. (In most cases, the Old Swedish *Revelations* are retranslations from the Latin; portions of some Old Swedish texts, however, have been shown to be closer to Birgitta's own words than the Latin.) It is also well-known that Alfonso, who wished to advance the cause of Birgitta's canonization, added, excluded, corrected, and arranged various elements of the revelations, presumably in accordance with Birgitta's wishes (see *Extrav.* 49). To a lesser extent, Prior Petrus also arranged, revised, and added revelations, which were incorporated into Alfonso's version.[10] Thus, as Bridget Morris states, "there may be glimpses of Birgitta's original utterance in the extant corpus of texts, but in the end, . . . the visions cannot be separated from the recording of them by the confessors."[11] Because of the confessors' role in the production of the *Revelations,* I would like to point out that I am examining textual *representations* of issues concerning gender and authority in the Latin editions of the *Revelations* and not necessarily Birgitta's actual words.

Birgitta as Prophet in the **Revelations**

The *Revelations* claim for Birgitta a level of authority that few women of the late Middle Ages were able to match. She directs messages reportedly received from God to people of all social levels throughout much of western Europe—high-ranking clerics, kings, and judges, as well as aristocratic ladies and lowly female servants.[12] Birgitta gives detailed instructions to bishops and other clerics concerning their service to God and answers the religious doubts of a Franciscan friar and the archbishop of Naples.[13] She advises not only the king of Sweden and the queens of Naples and Cyprus, but also addresses Popes Innocent VI, Urban V, and Gregory XI.[14] Her authority to teach, direct, and rebuke these members of her society was based on her claims to be a prophet sent from God.[15]

In the *Revelations* Birgitta never explicitly applies the word *prophet* to herself, nor do her heavenly interlocutors ever call her a prophet directly. Perhaps Birgitta or her confessors thought it was too presumptuous for her to be called a prophet in her own *Revelations*. The title may also have been associated too closely with the Old Testament writers who predicted events in salvation history.[16] Nevertheless, this body of writings plainly portrays Birgitta as a divinely inspired prophet in both a very general and a more specific sense of the term.

First of all, Birgitta conforms to a broad definition of "prophet" adopted by Thomas Aquinas and other medieval theologians. In the *Revelations* she is a prophet in the sense that she is an individual who proclaims knowledge revealed from God concerning matters hidden from human knowledge.[17] Aquinas considered the prediction of a future event to be the highest form of prophecy since it is the furthest removed from human knowledge. However, like Gregory the Great and others, he believed that prophecy also consisted of knowledge about past and present realities.[18] He wrote: "All that comes under prophecy coincides in not being knowable by human beings except through divine revelation."[19] In this sense the entire collection of revelations can be (and was) understood as a record of Birgitta's prophecies. That is, the *Revelations* communicate the privileged knowledge concerning the past, present, and future that was given to Birgitta directly by God and other divine beings, in order that she might impart that knowledge for the edification of others. In the *Revelations* her knowledge of the past includes, for example, previously unknown details concerning biblical authorship, the life of Jesus, and Mary's preexistence before the creation of the world. Her knowledge of the present includes insights into the spiritual condition of numerous priests, kings, and common lay people. Moreover, her knowledge of the future includes her predictions concerning the imminent fate of individuals and political kingdoms. On the basis of

Birgitta's claims to have received such hidden knowledge through divine revelations, her fourteenth-century disciples maintained that she was endowed with the spirit of prophecy. According to the *Vita processus* written by her confessors Prior Petrus of Alvastra and Master Petrus of Skänninge, "she had from God the true spirit of prophecy and . . . intellectual vision had been divinely given to her. . . . Indeed, after this lady had been called into the Spirit of God, she prophesied not only about the future—as did the prophets—but also about the present and the past" (*A et P,* 86).[20]

Secondly, the *Revelations* present Birgitta as a prophet in a more specific, but obviously related, sense of the term. Like the Hebrew prophets, she uses her privileged knowledge of past, present, and future affairs to pronounce judgment on moral depravity and urge God's people to repent. Like Moses, Ezekiel, Jeremiah, and other biblical prophets, Birgitta receives a divine call to proclaim publicly God's grave displeasure with the spiritual condition of the people and to point out the way of salvation. This call to prophesy is described in the well-known passage from the *Extrauagantes,* which has been shown to exhibit stylistic similarities to biblical call narratives.[21] Birgitta hears God's terrifying voice speaking to her from a shining cloud, saying: "I am your God and I wish to speak with you. . . . Do not be afraid. For I am the creator of all and am not a deceiver. You should know that I do not speak to you for your sake alone, but for the sake of the salvation of all Christians. . . . You shall be my bride and my channel [*canale*], and you shall hear and see spiritual things and heavenly secrets, and my Spirit shall remain with you even to your death" (*Extrav.* 47:1-3). After receiving this commission, Birgitta speaks on behalf of God for the rest of her life and transmits the revelations she receives, so that those who have turned away from God will turn back. The *Revelations* are presented as the very words of God, like the words recorded in prophetic books of the Bible. Christ and the others who reveal messages speak in the grammatical first person in the *Revelations,* while Birgitta rarely speaks in the first person. Usually, the heavenly voices address her or the texts refer to her in the third person as Christ's spouse.[22] The *Revelations,* again like passages from the prophetic books of the Bible, use rather dramatic images and metaphors to describe God's wrath and incite others to convert. Startling analogies and harsh language, such as Birgitta's comparison of the city of Famagusta with Gomorrah, and terrifying messages akin to her predictions of imminent disaster on that city are not at all unusual in the *Revelations*. For these reasons, Birgitta can be seen as a prophet in the tradition of the Hebrew prophets. A social critic and religious reformer, she is called and compelled to announce to the world God's messages of judgment and repentance. "There are few," according to Johannes Lindblom, a scholar of biblical prophecy, "who have so great an affinity with the prophets of the Old Testament as Birgitta of Sweden."[23]

According to the *Revelations,* Birgitta, as a mediator of the word of God, fulfills a momentous role in the history of salvation that is analogous to the roles played by figures no less important than Noah, Abraham, Moses, and other significant individuals of the Bible. One passage (*Rev.* 2.17) represents the history of the world from the time of Adam to Birgitta as a struggle between God and the devil for human allegiance. When the devil assails human beings with various evils, God sends "remedies" through selected individuals, like the patriarchs and prophets of the Old Testament. Abraham and prophets of Christ's redemption brought hope where there was despair; Moses increased faith in the truth of God's words and activities where there was faithlessness. God now sends Birgitta to remind others of his mercy and justice, since people scorn Christ's words and forget his work of redemption (*Rev.* 2.17:44-46). Although some of her disciples claimed that she was similar to Deborah, Huldah, and the long row of female prophets from the Bible,[24] the *Revelations* associate her only with the male prophets of the Bible.[25] Of all the biblical prophets, the *Revelations* compare her most frequently to Moses, whom many, including Aquinas, considered to be the greatest of all prophets.[26] Christ identifies himself to Birgitta in several revelations as the voice that spoke to Moses from the burning bush. He says that he speaks in Birgitta's soul for the sake of his people, just as he spoke from the bush for the sake of the Israelites (see *Rev.* 1.60; 2.10; *Regula* 30).

Claims for Legitimacy and Signs of Authenticity in the Revelations

Birgitta's authority to speak out against moral laxity and to urge others to be mindful of divine retribution is based on her direct experiences with God, which both authorized her to speak and gave her a message to proclaim. The foundational sources of all prophetic authority, including Birgitta's, are divine revelatory experiences. However, as social theorists who are indebted to the writings of Max Weber have argued, a prophet's claims to have received messages directly from God are not sufficient for exercising authority. Prophetic authority, like all forms of authority, is established in and through social interactions. "Authority" refers to a social relationship in which subordinates attribute legitimacy to a superordinate's exercise of power. For a prophet to exercise authority, members of the prophet's audience must willingly accept the prophet as a legitimate channel of divine communication. There are two essential features of a prophet's authority, according to Thomas Overholt, who relies on sociological discussions of authority: "On the one hand, the prophet makes the claim that the deity has authorized the proclamation of a certain message. The basis of this claim is usually a religious experience that is private and therefore essentially intangible and unverifiable by the members of the audience. . . . Direct contact with a deity seems to be regarded as an absolutely crucial element in the constitution of a given occurrence of prophecy not only in ancient Israel but also in other cultures. On the other hand, prophets cannot be effective and cannot function as intermediaries unless the people acknowledge their claim to authority."[27]

Given this understanding of the social dimensions of prophetic authority, I shall turn now to the following questions: How do Birgitta's *Revelations* attempt to urge willing acceptance of her legitimacy? More specifically, what justification and evidence do the *Revelations* offer to encourage support for her authority as a female prophet? As has been observed already, Birgitta's gender increased her difficulties in gaining acceptance as an authentic prophet. The biblical injunction that women are not to teach or have authority over men (I Tim. 2:12) invited intense scrutiny of Birgitta and other visionary women who claimed divine sanction for speaking and writing.[28] Her lack of formal theological education and her unconventional behavior reportedly inspired some people to doubt her divine inspiration and urge her to terminate her prophetic activities. A statement by St. Agnes to Birgitta refers to one of these men: "He said to you abusively that he does not know by which spirit you were speaking, and that it would be more useful for you to spin in the manner of women than to examine scripture" (*Rev.* 4.124:2). Another person, a religious man "of great authority," reportedly did not find it credible or in agreement with scripture that God would show his secrets to "great women" (*magnificis feminis*) (*Rev.* 6.90:1-2). How, then, do the *Revelations* attempt to negotiate tensions between Birgitta's gender and her claims to prophetic authority, so that Birgitta will be received as a legitimate prophet?

The *Revelations* offer two commonplace verbal warrants for her prophetic vocation. They cite God's preference for using weak members of society to confound the strong, and they also elaborate images for Birgitta's role that stress her passivity and obedience to God. A chapter from the *Extrauagantes,* which recounts Christ's words to Petrus of Alvastra, employs the theological justification that recalls the words of St. Paul. When Petrus had difficulty accepting Christ's commission to record Birgitta's words in Latin and suspected that her revelations were demonic illusions, he heard Christ explain his choice of a female channel of prophecy: "You should know with great certainty that I want to do such a work through my words, which you write from the mouth of that woman, whence the powerful will be humbled and the wise silenced" (*Extrav.* 48:12). This paradox, used by Hildegard of Bingen (d. 1179) two centuries earlier to justify her own prophesying, recollects the apostle Paul's words to the Corinthians: "God chose those who are foolish in the world to shame the wise, and God chose the weak in the world to

shame the strong, and God chose those who are low and despised in the world, even those who are nothing, to bring to nothing those who are something" (I Cor. 1:27-28). As Barbara Newman points out in her discussion of Hildegard's use of the paradox of the weak shaming the strong, it is "doubly paradoxical" to claim that a privileged person born into a noble family is weak.[29] Although Birgitta came from one of the most powerful families of fourteenth-century Sweden, the passage from *Extrav.* 48 nevertheless applies St. Paul's words to Birgitta, recognizing that her status as a woman identifies her with the weak, low, and foolish of the world.[30] In another passage Birgitta herself questions why God would choose to bestow her with revelations: "O my Lord and son of the Virgin, why did you deem so worthless a widow worthy to be visited? For I am poor in all good works and have little understanding in knowledge" (*Rev.* 2.18:9). Christ responds to her with these words: " . . . I am able to make the poor rich, and the foolish one of little understanding sufficient [in understanding] and knowing" (*Rev.* 2.18:10). These words are a variation on the theme of God's preference for using the weak to shame the strong. When they are taken together with Christ's statement in *Extrav.* 48, the justification for Birgitta's prophetic vocation is clear: God desires to use a lowly, uneducated woman to bring the great men of the world to repentance, and he will supply her with the necessary strength and the wisdom to carry out the task.

The second prominent form of verbal justification for Birgitta's legitimacy as a female prophet is the *Revelations'* almost incessant use of images that accentuate her passivity and obedience. Many of these images are highly conventional, while others appear to be original. As a medium of God's word, Birgitta is not only a channel of the Holy Spirit (*Extrav.* 47:3; *Rev.* 3.30:8-9),[31] but also a musical instrument (*Rev.* 4.100; 7.31:5), a vessel of wine (*Rev.* 2.16), a servant carrying precious gold for the master (*Rev.* 2.14), and a daughter-in-law who carries out the wishes of her husband's aging parents (*Rev.* 6.88:6-7). Birgitta's *Revelations* delight in these images, sometimes embellishing them with extended descriptions. For example, in a revelation to the archbishop of Naples, Birgitta describes herself as a furnace (*caminus*): "My Lord, it sometimes happens that, from a black furnace, there goes forth a beautiful flame that is useful and quite necessary for fashioning works of beauty. But that does not mean that the furnace must then be praised for its black color. The praise and honor and thanks are owed to the artist and master of those works. It is a similar situation with me, who is unworthy, if you find something useful in my advice: for then you ought continually to show infinite thanks and willing service, not to me, but to God himself, who made and makes all things" (*Rev.* 7.12:7-9).[32] Implicitly, this striking image and many other images for Birgitta's role reinforce her claims to be speaking for God. They emphasize God's use of

Birgitta as an instrument of revelation by stressing that she does not act on her own behalf and does not claim the messages that she promulgates as her own. She is passive before God and is also steadfastly obedient, always ready and willing to be used as God desires. Birgitta did not take the initiative in becoming a messenger of God's words; rather, she was chosen because it was pleasing to God.

Supernatural signs of her authenticity, described in passages from the *Revelations* that recount moments of contested authority, are even more obvious, but equally important, justifications for Birgitta's authority. Dispersed rather haphazardly throughout the *Revelations* are several vignettes in which Birgitta's authority is challenged by doubters and detractors, only to be confirmed through supernatural verifications of her prophetic vocation. In these accounts one or more of Birgitta's contemporaries, usually religious men or political magnates, question or directly attack her. A jealous knight, for example, incites another man to denounce her revelations publicly as ridiculous illusions (*Rev.* 4.113:15-18). In another passage a member of the Swedish nobility, who was unhappy that the king listened to Birgitta's advice, pours water onto her from a high window while she is walking down a narrow Stockholm street (*Rev.* 4.122:7-10). Sometimes Birgitta responds in these stories with such extraordinary patience or humility that her opponent is converted into a follower. This is what happens in the account of the jealous knight. In other cases she displays supernatural knowledge or abilities that verify her visionary abilities. Knowledge from God enables her, for example, to predict accurately the imminent death of the nobleman who dumped water on her. In several anecdotes, the issue of Birgitta's gender is especially prominent and is resolved through supernatural confirmations of her authenticity. A close examination of some of these stories further illuminates how the *Revelations* negotiate the problem of gender and prophetic authority by constructing an image of Birgitta as a holy woman who was chosen by God to prophesy.

One passage, placed in the middle of the *declaracio* section of *Rev.* 6.30 in the *editio princeps* published by Ghotan, describes a prior who doubted that Birgitta's words came from God. No reason is provided in the text to explain why this friar—identified in the canonization process as Prior Kethilmundus of St. Olof's Dominican monastery in Skänninge[33]—distrusted her revelations. However, this passage reports that he became an ardent advocate of her revelations after receiving a supernatural confirmation of her divine inspiration:

> When the same brother had difficulty believing the grace given to the lady Birgitta, he saw in ecstasy the lady and a fire from heaven descending onto her. And when he, having been awakened, was astonished and was considering [it to be] an illusion, he fell asleep again and heard a voice clearly saying twice: 'No one can prevent that fire from going forth. For I, power itself, will send out that fire to the east and the west, to the north and the south, and it will inflame many.' After this the same brother became trustful of the revelations and a defender of them. (*Rev.* 6.30: *declaracio* 36-38)

This vision recollects the day of Pentecost described in Acts 2 when tongues resembling fire descended from heaven onto Christ's disciples. According to Acts, these tongues represented the arrival of the Holy Spirit and gave the early Christians the power to preach throughout the world.[34] Although the text does not state that Kethilmundus had difficulty believing that God would have inspired a woman to carry messages to the world, it is not insignificant that his vision recalls the day on which the apostle Peter preached from the words of the prophet Joel predicting that women as well as men would prophesy: "And in the last days it shall be, God says, that I will pour out my Spirit upon all flesh and your sons and your daughters shall prophesy . . . and indeed on my menservants and on my maidservants in those days I will pour out my Spirit; and they shall prophesy" (Acts 2:17-19).

By recollecting this biblical endorsement of women prophesying, Kethilmundus's vision justifies and promotes Birgitta's prophetic vocation. It reinforces her claims to be divinely inspired and lends support to her proclamation of her revelations. The Holy Spirit descends on Birgitta, like the women foreseen by Joel, and flows forth from her in prophecy.[35] This account of the prior's transformation from doubter to advocate of Birgitta's revelations is an obvious interpolation into the records of Birgitta's visions, presumably inserted by Prior Petrus. Prior Petrus seems to have used the original record of this vision during his testimony in Rome in support of Birgitta's canonization and later incorporated it into Alfonso's redaction of the *Revelations* after his return to Sweden in 1380.[36] This section from the *Revelations* is not one of Birgitta's texts at all, but functions to give independent warrant to Birgitta's role as God's spokeswoman.[37]

Similarly, a chapter from the *Extrauagantes* that describes revelations to a virtuous Cistercian lay brother, Gerekinus of Alvastra, offers justification for Birgitta's behavior that violated gender norms (*Extrav.* 55). This chapter, as it appears in the Ghotan edition, consists of two revelations concerning Birgitta: a celestial voice explaining her unusual presence at the male Cistercian monastery in Alvastra (*Extrav.* 55:1-2) and Gerekinus's vision of Birgitta elevated from the ground with water flowing from her mouth (*Extrav.* 55:4-5). The passages between and following the revelations describe signs of the monk's sanctity (*Extrav.* 55:3, 6-7).[38] Like the account of Kethilmundus's vision, this portion of the *Revelations* was not composed by Birgitta and does not recount any visions or auditions to her. Lennart Hollman believes that editors, who revised and assembled the revelations that came to form the *Extravagantes,* probably used records of Prior Petrus's deposition from the canonization process as their source for *Extrav.* 55:1-5. The editors of the Ghotan edition from 1492 gave *Extrav.* 55 its final form and inserted it among Birgitta's revelations.[39]

The passage discloses that Gerekinus, who was prompted by his zeal for the monastic rule, questioned the appropriateness of Birgitta's residence in buildings adjacent to the Alvastra monastery.[40] According to the passage, when she began living there, this virtuous man was deeply astonished and asked in his heart: "Why does that lady reside here in a monastery of monks against our rule, introducing a new custom?" (*Extrav.* 55:1). It is not surprising that monks of Alvastra would have objected to her physical presence among them, since Cistercian statutes explicitly prohibited women from entering the monastic enclosure and denied abbots the ability to grant special permission for their entrance. Although by Birgitta's time women were allowed to live on lands belonging to Cistercian monasteries (earlier statutes forbade this), women were still prohibited from entering the enclosure and their residence in close proximity to the monastery was highly irregular.[41] In spite of these statutes, Birgitta routinely listened to the singing of the offices and prayed in the church during the day and night. She also had close contacts with several brothers.[42]

While Gerekinus was experiencing doubts about Birgitta's close association with the monastery, he reportedly entered into a state of ecstasy and heard a voice telling him that "this woman is a friend of God and for this she came to the monastery, so that she may collect flowers under this mountain [Omberg, the mountain that overshadows Alvastra] from which all people, even beyond the sea and the ends of the world, will receive medicine" (*Extrav.* 55:2). This message identifies Birgitta as an ally of God and invokes her religious vocation as the rationale for her violation of monastic custom. The flowers that she collects at Alvastra apparently symbolize her divine revelations, which are to be dispersed throughout the world. Elsewhere in the *Revelations,* flowers explicitly represent the heavenly words given to Birgitta, which her confessors are to protect from harm: "Tell him [Alfonso] that he ought to be like one who carries the best flowers. These [flowers] are my [Mary's] words" (*Rev.* 7.16:19). The reference to medicine in the revelation to Gerekinus, moreover, recalls Christ's characterization of himself as a physician (Mark 2:17) as well as passages from the *Revelations* that represent Christ as a physical and spiritual healer and the words that he proclaims through Birgitta as medicine. For example, Christ states in *Extrav.* 48:10 that he is a physician (*"ego sum medicus"*), and *Rev.* 6.90:4-5 equates rejecting Birgitta's revelations with rejecting Christ, who himself is the medicine of the sick (*medicina infirmorum*). By making such allusions, the voice speaking to Gerekinus thus indicates that it is Birgitta's task to be a world-wide distributor of God's words of health and salvation. It also discloses that this mission, for which she is preparing herself at Alvastra, endows her with a privileged status that places her beyond gender norms and ordinary social conventions. It should be noted here that no demands are made for changing regulations to allow other women to associate closely with the daily life of a male monastery. Birgitta's residence at Alvastra is an exception; her uncommon vocation merely allows her to transcend the rules.[43]

The second revelation to Gerekinus in *Extrav.* 55 underscores Birgitta's special vocation by utilizing another image. Gerekinus saw her elevated from the earth with a stream of water flowing from her mouth. While praying, he heard a voice saying: "This is the woman who, coming from the ends of the earth, will give innumerable people wisdom to drink" (*Extrav.* 55:4).[44] This vision of water running out from Birgitta's mouth depicts her prophetic activity vividly. In biblical passages flowing water often symbolizes the Holy Spirit (e.g., John 7:38-39), and in other passages from the *Revelations* water represents the word of God. Christ, for example, tells Birgitta: "My words—which you hear from me frequently in spiritual vision—like the good drink, satisfy those who thirst for true charity" (*Rev.* 5.11:10;[45] see also *Rev.* 4.66:1; *Rev.* 8.47:1-4). By using the image of water, Gerekinus's vision portrays Birgitta as a vessel pouring forth the inspired word of God for the spiritual refreshment of others. By stressing the significance of her vocation in this manner, the passage reiterates the message of Gerekinus's previous revelation: Birgitta's divine commission places her beyond established rules prohibiting women's residence on the edge of a male monastery of the Cistercian Order.

Not only did men like Gerekinus and Kethilmundus quietly question her behavior or doubt the credibility of her visions, but some people openly derided and denounced her. The most extreme opposition to Birgitta's claims to prophecy was the threat of physical harm and even death. The *Revelations* (*Extrav.* 8) report that certain Romans, angered by Birgitta's sharp rebukes concerning the spiritual state of the Roman city and church (e.g., *Rev.* 3.27; 4.33), accused her of being a witch and threatened to burn her alive:

> During those fifteen years, in which she stayed in Rome before the arrival of the pope [Urban V] and the emperor [Charles IV], she had many revelations about the condition of the city, in which our lord

Jesus Christ denounced the trespasses and sins of the city's inhabitants with a grave threat of vengeance. When these revelations were brought to the notice of the Roman inhabitants, they directed a fomentation of deadly hatred against the blessed Birgitta. Whence, some of them threatened to burn her alive; others blasphemed her as being heretical and a pythoness [*phitonissam*]. (*Extrav.* 8:3-4)

By accusing her of being a "pythoness," a feminine title that corresponds roughly to "witch," "soothsayer," "sibyl," or "prophetess,"[46] the Romans were either suggesting that Birgitta was possessed by a spirit of divination that spoke through her or that she conjured such a spirit to foretell the future. The word *phitonissa,* derived from the Greek, is related to *pythia,* the name given to the priestesses of Apollo at Delphi who were renowned for inspired oracular speeches. In the Vulgate and medieval Christian writings the term is applied to the so-called witch of Endor, the medium who summoned the soul of Samuel to obtain oracular responses at the request of Saul (I Chron. 10:13; I Sam. 28:7-8). (See *Rev.* 5, interrogacio 13:13, where the ***Revelations*** follow the Vulgate and use this title for the woman whom Saul consulted.[47]) Filastrius, bishop of Brescia in the fourth century, asserts that it is a heresy to consult pythonesses or believe what they say; pythonesses are false prophets who deceive many by means of their visions and words.[48]

The Roman accusation that Birgitta's comminatory messages came from a deceptive spirit, instead of from God as she claimed, illustrates a phenomenon that scholars have observed across many cultures and traditions, including the Christian tradition. Women who challenge, subvert, or endeavor to assume legitimate power, that is, authority, are highly vulnerable to charges of witchcraft in patriarchal societies.[49] Not uncommonly in the history of Christianity, women who assumed spiritual power through prophecy were accused of being witches. As Rosemary Radford Ruether observes, "the line between seeing a woman as a prophet or as a witch was always fluid in Christianity."[50] Powerful behavior that was a reversal of ordinary, conventional behavior for women was perceived as illegitimate and labeled witchcraft.

Caroline Walker Bynum discusses manifestations of this phenomenon specifically in later medieval Europe.[51] She points out that from the early fourteenth century onward, male hostility toward religious women increased and manifested itself in witchcraft accusations, precisely when women's visions and prophecies came to be seen as sources of authority in contrast to the institutional authority conferred on men by virtue of their clerical offices. Bynum also remarks that "suspicion of prophetic women reflected the general fourteenth-century suspicion of popular religious movements and of mysticism. The period was one of deep hostility to visionary and mystical males as well. But the ambivalence of Church and authorities and theologians about women mystics also reflected a virulent misogyny—a misogyny that issued both in the actual witch accusations and in the witch-hunting theology of the fifteenth century."[52] In later medieval Christianity the line dividing female saints from witches was not drawn firmly. Not only Birgitta, but several other women who developed reputations for sanctity, including Catherine of Siena (d. 1380), Lidwina of Schiedam (d. 1433), and Columba of Rieta (d. 1501),[53] were accused of being witches or possessed by demons. Thus, the charges of witchcraft and threats of execution reported in *Extrav.* 8 exemplify the growing antipathy toward the authority of divine inspiration claimed by prophetic women of the late Middle Ages. Although they never materialized in formal proceedings against her, allegations that Birgitta was a pythoness were attempts to silence her harsh denunciations of Roman political and spiritual life by denying her claims to have received revelations from God.

In opposition to the accusations against her, *Extrav.* 8 offers evidence of Birgitta's uncommon patience, obedience to Christ, and divine protection as practical demonstrations of her legitimacy. This evidence is found in the chapter's brief comments concerning her biography and two revelations that promise immunity from harm. As Hollman argues, it is likely that the general confessor of the Vadstena Monastery, Ulpho Birgeri (d. 1433), was the redactor who constructed this chapter between 1427 and 1433 from revelations excluded by Alfonso's edition and from documents in support of her canonization.[54] Immediately following the statement concerning witchcraft accusations, the narrator describes Birgitta's patient endurance of abuse and her obedience to Christ's command to remain in the city:

> Truly the blessed Birgitta patiently suffered their threats and abusive words. But she feared that the members of her household and her other friends and relatives, who were staying with her in Rome, would abandon her, having been scandalized by these tribulations and abusive words. She considered for a while withdrawing from the furor of the malicious people and did not presume to depart for anywhere without Christ's special order. Throughout the twenty-eight years, after she left her home, at no time did she depart for some cities or provinces or other holy places without the command of Christ. (*Extrav.* 8:5-6)

This passage—a hagiographical tribute to Birgitta's virtues—represents the Roman threats of execution and charges of witchcraft as unjust persecutions successfully endured by a holy woman. While divulging her anxieties concerning the possible abandonment of her companions and disclosing her temptation to flee the tribulations of Rome, the passage stresses her submission to suffering, patient endurance of unjust afflictions, and continual compliance with the divine will throughout her entire career as God's mouthpiece.[55] Implicitly, these extraordinary behaviors are visible signs of Birgitta's divine calling and proof of the legitimacy of her vocation. Birgitta's two visions that directly follow in the chapter can also be seen as confirmations of her authenticity. In the first vision Christ acknowledges her allegiance to him, compares her persecution with his own suffering, and pledges to restrain those who plot her death from ever being able to harm her: "When you have me, you ought to fear no one.... Although my enemies crucified my humanity through my permission, nevertheless they will not at all prevail in harming or killing you" (*Extrav.* 8:8). In the second vision Mary verifies that Christ defends Birgitta against every "evil effort" and reveals that she will be Birgitta's "protective shield" (*scutum proteccionis*) against all enemies (*Extrav.* 8:9). These visions argue against accusations that Birgitta was a pythoness by suggesting that her exemption from all physical harm was the result of divine intervention. The protection that she probably received from her connections with powerful Italian families is not mentioned at all in this chapter.[56]

It is important here to note that Birgitta was also accused of being a witch while she was still living in Sweden. Although the *Revelations* make no mention of this, the testimony of Juliana Nilsdotter in favor of Birgitta's canonization reports that Swedish noblemen and their families, who were distressed that King Magnus was relying on Birgitta's counsel, charged that she was a witch (*sortilega*) (*A et P,* 66). The deposition of her daughter Katarina also describes the opposition of Swedish nobility against her, but without specifically mentioning witchcraft accusations. Katarina says that these people did not believe that she spoke on behalf of God and would have killed her had they not feared the retribution of her relatives (*A et P,* 313). With this knowledge in mind, it is possible to read chapters of the *Revelations* in which she rebukes those who place trust in pythonesses, fortune-tellers, diviners, and enchantresses as passages that deflect witchcraft accusations against Birgitta by distancing her from and asserting her superiority over others who claimed to have preternatural knowledge (*Rev.* 6.82, which dates from Birgitta's Swedish period; 7.28:18-24, which she received in Naples).[57] Likewise, passages from the *Revelations* that describe her ability to exorcise demons (an ability she shares with most saints) lend support to claims that she was divinely inspired. She does not consult unclean spirits and is not controlled by them; rather, she has divine powers over them (e.g., *Rev.* 1.60; 6.76).

Summary

Birgitta of Sweden's *Revelations,* which bear the indelible imprint of her confessors and friars from her order in Vadstena, are a remarkable testimony to this woman's struggles to assume religious authority in later medieval Europe. In this body of texts, we see how Birgitta's gender increased the vulnerability to hostility, derision, and physical harm that is faced by nearly all people who claim to be divinely ordained prophets. Her assertions that God had called her to proclaim words of judgment and mercy evoked denials that God would speak to an ignorant woman, criticisms of her unconventional behavior, and accusations of witchcraft. By examining passages that reflect tensions between Birgitta's gender and her claims to be a prophet, it has been possible to identify some of the verbal warrants and supernatural signs offered by the book of *Revelations* in support of Birgitta's authority: biblical justifications, elaborate metaphors, revelations to other individuals, displays of divine protection, along with Birgitta's own virtuous behavior, and her abilities to predict the future, discern the moral states of others, and exorcise demons. Theological justifications and visible verifications bolstered her claims to be speaking on God's behalf. By offering such evidence, the *Revelations* represent Birgitta Birgersdotter as a legitimate prophet whose divine calling and inspiration no one should dare to doubt.

Notes

[1] Birgitta of Sweden, *Birgitta of Sweden: Life and Selected Revelations,* ed. Harris, 191 (hereafter referred to as *Revelations,* ed. Harris). See Birgitta of Sweden, *Revelaciones, Book* 7, ed. Bergh, for the modern critical Latin edition. Parenthetical references in the text are to book, chapter, and sometimes verse numbers of the Latin *Revelaciones* (hereafter abbreviated in text citations as *Rev.*). For an account of the political situation between 1369 and 1374 that informed Birgitta's revelations concerning Cyprus, see Jönsson, *Alfonso of Jaén,* 99-103.

[2] See *Acta et processus canonizacionis beate Birgitte* (hereafter abbreviated *A et P*), ed. Collijn, 100, 266, 269, 326, 334, 372-73, 383, 390, 429-30, 431-32, 525, 544, and 636.

[3] Leclercq discusses the meanings of *muliercula* with reference to the writings of Bernard of Clairvaux, in *Women and Saint Bernard,* 169-71. As Leclercq points out, the diminutive *muliercula* was not necessarily used pejoratively by medieval Latin writers and could be used with overtones of affection. It was also used, however, to denote a weak woman, a feeble woman, or a lowborn woman. When religious men in Cyprus applied the term *muliercula* to Birgitta, it clearly assumed a pejorative sense. Its pairing with the adjective *ignara* accentuated Birgitta's low social status as a woman and lack of formal theological training. Dr. Beverly M. Kienzle kindly called my attention to Leclercq's discussion.

[4] Wojcik and Frontain, eds., suggest that the resistance of a prophet's audience is essential to the concept of prophecy itself, in "Introduction: The Prophet in the Poem," in *Poetic Prophecy,* 16.

[5] See Vauchez, "Jeanne d'Arc," 159-68; Bynum, *Holy Feast and Holy Fast,* esp. 20-23; Bullough, "Medieval Medical," 485-501; Maclean, *Renaissance Notion of Woman,* chaps. 2 and 3; and Allen, *Concept of Woman,* esp. chap. 4.

[6] Helpful introductions to various aspects of Birgitta's life and *Revelations* in non-Scandinavian languages include the following: Nyberg, "Birgitta von Schweden," 275-89; Nyberg's introduction in *Revelations,* ed. Harris, 13-51; Atkinson, *Oldest Vocation,* 170-84; Obrist, "Swedish Visionary," 227-51; and Fogelqvist, *Apostasy and Reform.* Jørgensen, *Saint Bridget of Sweden,* 2 vols., is the most comprehensive account of Birgitta's life in English, but should be used only with extreme caution. It is a romantic biography containing many inaccuracies.

[7] See especially the so-called Process Vita, *A et P,* 84; and Birgitta of Sweden, *Reuelaciones extrauagantes,* ed. Hollman, *Extrav.* 49. These two accounts of the process of composing and recording the revelations appear to be contradictory: the first portrays the *Revelations* as a literal record of God's very words to Birgitta, while the latter describes Birgitta's painful process of writing and rewriting and defends the editorial license of her confessors. Morris, in "Labyrinths of the Urtext," argues that these two accounts may be describing different stages in the production of the *Revelations* and may not be contradictory at all (23-33). Dr. Morris generously shared her essay with me prior to its publication.

[8] *Revelationes S. Birgitte* was printed in 1492 at the request of the Vadstena Monastery in honor of the centenary of Birgitta's canonization. It served as the basis for all Latin editions printed until 1680. For a comprehensive account of the history of the various redactions of the *Revelaciones,* see the general introduction to Birgitta of Sweden, *Revelaciones, Book I,* ed. Undhagen, 1-37.

[9] In addition to the *Reuelaciones extrauagantes, Revelaciones, Book I,* and *Revelaciones, Book 7,* which were cited above, the following critical editions of Birgitta of Sweden's works have been published to date: *Revelaciones, Book 4,* ed. Aili; *Revelaciones, Book 5, Liber questionum,* and *Revelaciones, Book 6,* ed. Bergh; *Opera minora,* vols. I (*Regula Saluatoris*), 2 (*Sermo angelicus*), and 3 (*Ouattuor oraciones*), ed. Eklund. Ann-Mari Jönsson's edition of *Revelaciones, Book 3* is expected to be published next.

[10] For discussions of the confessors' role in the production of the *Revelations,* see Morris, "Labyrinths of

the Urtext," 23-33; *Revelaciones, Book 1,* 4-37; Aili, "Att finna Birgitta i Birgitta," 14-39; Aili, "St. Birgitta and the Text," 75-91; and Kezel, "Translator's Foreword," in *Revelations,* ed. Harris, 59-66.

[11] Morris, "Labyrinths of the Urtext," 26.

[12] See *Rev.* 7.30:4-5, where Christ classifies his addresses into three groups: clerics, male political leaders, and women.

[13] See, for example, *Rev.* 3.1-3; 4.80; 4.126; 7.7; 7.12.

[14] See, for example, *Rev.* 8.2; 6.41; 7.11; 7.16: *addicio* 22-30; 4.136; 4.137-38; 4.139-44.

[15] Piltz has explored Birgitta's "self-understanding" as prophet in two recent articles: "Uppenbarelserna och uppenbarelsen," 477-69; and "Inspiration, vision, profetia," 67-88. I am grateful to Dr. Piltz for sharing the latter essay with me prior to its publication.

[16] See Piltz, "Vision, inspiration, profetia," 68.

[17] See, for example, Aquinas, *Summa theologiae,* ed. Blackfriars, 2a 2ae, questions 171-78; and *Life of Juliana of Mont Cornillon,* trans. Newman, 52-65. Kieckhefer surveys examples of prophecy from fourteenth-century *vitae* in *Unquiet Souls,* 161-65.

[18] See Gregory the Great, *Homiliae in Hiezechihelem Prophetam,* 1.1-3, ed. Adriaen, 5-7.

[19] Aquinas, *Summa theologiae,* ed. Blackfriars, 2a 2ae, question 171, article 3.

[20] *Revelations,* ed. Harris, 83.

[21] Costello, "Women's Mysticism and Reform," 91-95. See also Klockars, *Birgitta och bökerna,* 62-66.

[22] Birgitta of Sweden, *Liber Celestis of St. Bridget,* vol. I, ed. Ellis, xiv.

[23] Lindblom, *Prophecy in Ancient Israel,* 16. For further discussion of Birgitta's similarities to the Hebrew Bible prophets, see the articles by Piltz, "Vision, inspiration, profetia," "Uppenbarelserna och uppenbarelsen"; and Ellis, "Spirituality of St. Bridget," 157-66. I have also found Newman's discussion of Hildegard of Bingen's indebtedness to the biblical prophets to be stimulating for my own thinking about Birgitta. See her *Sister of Wisdom,* 25-34.

[24] See, for example, Alfonso of Jaén, *Epistola solitarii,* ed. Jönsson, chap. 1, paragraphs 23-26.

[25] This observation supports Bynum's belief that medieval religious women were not especially attracted to

positive female images. See Bynum, "'. . . And Woman His Humanity,'" 257-88. Birgitta, however, was zealously devoted to the Virgin Mary and her *Revelations* display evidence of *imitatio Mariae*. For further discussion of the significance of Mary to Birgitta's spirituality, see Børresen, "Birgittas teologi," 21-72; Koch, "Lignelses-, symbol- og billedsprog," 471-89; and Sahlin, "'His Heart Was My Heart,'" 213-27, and "'A Marvelous and Great Exultation of the Heart,'" 108-28.

[26] Aquinas, *Summa theologiae,* ed. Blackfriars, 2a 2ae, question 174, article 4.

[27] Overholt, *Channels of Prophecy,* 70. Hopenwasser also finds Overholt's study of prophecy helpful for illuminating Birgitta's role as prophet. See her essay "Human Burden of the Prophet." For discussion of the social dimensions of prophetic authority, see also Long, "Prophetic Authority as Social Reality," 3-20. For a helpful discussion of the concept of authority, see Holmberg, *Paul and Power,* 124-61.

[28] See Newman, *Sister of Wisdom,* 34-41; and Bynum, *Holy Feast and Holy Fast,* 22-23.

[29] Newman, "Divine Power," 103.

[30] See Newman, "Divine Power," 103-4; and Maclean, *Renaissance Notion of Woman,* 21-22.

[31] See Piltz's discussion of Birgitta as *canale,* in "Uppenbarelserna och uppenbarelsen," 451-52.

[32] *Revelations,* ed. Harris, 177-78.

[33] See *A et P,* 503, 628, 667. I have found no reason to identify the prior of *Rev.* 6.30 with Ragnvald of Alvastra, as Tryggve Lundén and many others have done.

[34] Christ's revelation to Birgitta in *Rev.* 6.36 discusses the day of Pentecost directly and states that the Holy Spirit came upon his apostles and disciples as a torrent, a fire, and tongues. Elsewhere in the *Revelations* the words of the Holy Spirit that are given to Birgitta are described as fire: "Truly, that fire is my Spirit, which exists and speaks in you," *Rev.* 5, *revelacio* 12:7; *Revelations,* 153.

[35] Prior Petrus's testimony at the canonization process and the so-called Panisperna-*vita* provide an additional detail that reinforces Birgitta's prophetic vocation: Kethilmundus saw what appeared to be the divine fire leaving Birgitta's mouth and inflaming many people who were surrounding her (*A et P,* 503, 628).

[36] See Undhagen's introduction to *Book I,* 26-30, 114, for discussion of Prior Petrus's role in supplementing

Alfonso's redaction with the *declaraciones* and *addiciones.* See also Bergh's introduction to *Book 6,* 11-12, 18-20, for an analysis of the supplementary material in *Rev. 6.*

[37] A striking fifteenth-century painting of Kethilmundus's vision (see frontispiece) is on the outside door of a reredos from the Appuna Church in the Swedish province of Östergötland. It is now in the Museum of National Antiquities in Stockholm. The most recent discussions of the Appuna reredos are the following: Lindgren, *Bilden av Birgitta,* 26-27, 112-16; and von Bonsdorff and Kempff, "Vadstena kloster," 262.

[38] *Extrav.* 55:3 states that Gerekinus never went outside of the monastery for forty years, was absorbed in prayer both day and night, beheld nine choirs of angels when he was praying, and saw Christ in the form of a child when the eucharistic host was elevated. *Extrav.* 55:6-7 recounts how the Virgin Mary miraculously enabled Gerekinus to pray when he was supposed to be working in the monastery's bakery.

[39] See Birgitta of Sweden, *Reuelaciones extrauagantes,* 28-45, and 85-94, esp. 91, for discussion of the textual history of *Extrav.* 55, and analysis of the various editions of the supplementary material that forms the basis for Hollman's edition of the *Extrauagantes.* Parallels to *Extrav.* 55:1-3 are found in the *Vita processus* and the Panisperna-*vita* (*A et P,* 82, 619). However, on the basis of a passage in MS. C 631 in the Uppsala University Library, Hollman shows that *Extrav.* 55:1-3 was probably not taken from the *vita,* but was based instead on a copy of Prior Petrus's deposition that is not extant. See *Reuelaciones extrauagantes,* 91. Parallels to *Extrav.* 55:4-5 are found in the *Vita processus,* the Panisperna-*vita,* and the depositions of Magnus Petri and Prior Petrus (*A et P,* 82, 620, 275, 545).

[40] Prior Petrus's testimony states that she received a divine command to live in buildings contiguous to the monastery (*in domibus contiguis monasterii sancte Marie de Aluastro monachorum ordinis Cisterciensis*), *A et P,* 509. Ortved, *Cistercieordenen og dens klostre i norden,* vol. 2, 93, states that she lived in a small house outside the church's northeast corner. For a study of Birgitta's presence and reforming activity at Alvastra, see McGuire, "Spiritual Life and Material Life," 300-310.

[41] Ortved, *Cistercieordenen og dens klostre i norden,* vol. 1, 60-61; vol. 2, 93-94. See Lucet, *Les codifications cisterciennes,* 321-22. McGuire, "Spiritual Life and Material Life," 301-4, provides a helpful discussion of Birgitta's residence at Alvastra. See also Klockars, *Birgitta och bökerna,* 191. Note that when Birgitta wanted to stay at a male Benedictine monastery at Farfa, the monks refused to allow it, saying that it was not their custom to cohabitate with women (*Extrav.* 97; *A et P,* 491).

[42] *A et P,* 65, describes Birgitta's prayers, vigils, and manual labor while living at Alvastra.

[43] This is also the message of a passage from the *Vita processus,* which has no exact parallel in the *Extrauagantes* or other books of the *Revelations.* This passage reports that God commanded Birgitta to stay in Alvastra, thus removing all responsibility from Birgitta for violating the Cistercian rule. It also says that God spoke to Birgitta in a vision telling her that he does not intend to change the rule: "I, God of all, who am above all rules, permit you to reside at the present time near the monastery, not so that I may abolish the rule or introduce a new custom, but rather so that my wonderful work may be displayed in a holy place" (*A et P,* 82; also Panisperna-*vita, A et P,* 619). For discussion of biblical claims for the prophet Jeremiah's privileged social status, see Long, "Prophetic Authority as Social Reality," 6-13.

[44] This voice continues by informing Gerekinus that Birgitta will accurately predict his death, which will take place sometime before certain evils (probably the plague) fall on Alvastra (*Extrav.* 55:5).

[45] *Revelations,* ed. Harris, 148.

[46] Birgitta of Sweden, *Reuelaciones extrauagantes,* ed. Hollman, 243; *Revelaciones, Book 5,* ed. Bergh, 178; *Revelaciones, Book 6,* ed. Bergh, 284. Russell cites "pythonissa" as one of the numerous names for a witch or a sorcerer in the Middle Ages and translates *pythonissa* as "prophetess," *Witchcraft in the Middle Ages,* 16.

[47] See *Revelations,* ed. Harris, 264-65, n. 310.

[48] Filastrius of Brescia, *Diversarum hereseon liber,* 26.1-7, 226-28.

[49] Brain, "Anthropological Perspective on the Witchcraze," 15-16; Rosaldo, "Women, Culture, and Society," 34. Rosaldo writes that "societies that define women as lacking legitimate authority have no way of acknowledging the reality of female power. This difference between rule and reality is reflected in our own society where we speak of powerful women as 'bitches'; elsewhere in the world, the powerful woman is often considered a witch." Interestingly, Piltz believes that Birgitta is dismissed by Swedes today as a *satkärring* (bitch); see his article "Birgitta—profet och provokatör."

[50] Ruether, "Prophets and Humanists," 9. See also Mack, "Women as Prophets," 19-45, esp. 31-33, where the relationship between the categories of female prophet and witch in the seventeenth century is analyzed.

[51] Bynum, *Holy Feast and Holy Fast,* 20-23.

[52] Ibid., 23.

[53] Ibid., 316 n. 46.

[54] Birgitta of Sweden, *Reuelaciones extrauagantes,* ed. Hollman, 40-44, 90.

[55] Kieckhefer, in *Unquiet Souls,* observes that Birgitta's patience was mentioned more frequently in the canonization process than any other of her virtues, 51-52.

[56] The Orsini family in Rome probably helped protect Birgitta from harm. See Andersson, *Saint Bridget of Sweden,* 88.

[57] Wilson writes that "the witchcraft accusation . . . is a two-edged sword. It can be used by societies that want to repress difficult minority groups, but it can also be used in various ways by minority groups and individuals," *Prophecy and Society in Ancient Israel,* 75.

FURTHER READING

Blunt, John Henry. Introduction to *The Myroure of Oure Ladye,* edited by John Henry Blunt, pp. vii-xlvii. New York: N. Trübner & Co., 1873.
> Contains a historical account of the Birgittine monastery at Sion and a summary of the life of St. Birgitta.

Butkovich, Anthony. *Iconography: St. Birgitta of Sweden.* Los Angeles: Ecumenical Foundation of America, 1969, 102 p.
> Includes a collection of images of St. Birgitta accompanied by brief biographical and historical anecdotes.

———. *Revelations: Saint Birgitta of Sweden.* Los Angeles: Ecumenical Foundation of America, 1972, 110 p.
> Recounts the life of St. Birgitta, paying particular attention to her role in political decisions of courts and the Church.

Cnattingius, Hans. *Studies in the Order of St. Bridget of Sweden I: The Crisis of the 1420's.* Uppsala: Almqvist & Wiksell, 1963, 181 p.
> Examines the characteristics and early history of the monasteries of the Birgittine order.

Hogg, James. "St. Birgitta's *Revelations* Reduced to a Book of Pious Instruction." In *Vox Mystica: Essays on Medieval Mysticism,* edited by Anne Clark Bartlett, pp. 201-29. Cambridge: D. S. Brewer, 1995.
> Explores the history of St. Birgitta's *Revelations* and offers summaries of the various books that make up this collective work.

Plautus

c. 254 B.C.-184 B.C.

Roman dramatist.

INTRODUCTION

Plautus is considered to be one of ancient Rome's most popular and successful comic playwrights. For nearly a century after his death, more than 130 plays were attributed to Plautus; it has been speculated that many of these plays were the work of lesser dramatists who used Plautus's name to bolster attendance. Scholars have since determined that Plautus penned at least twenty-one comedies, of which twenty are complete and comprise the largest existing collection of classical dramatic literature. The plots of Plautus's plays are Romanized versions of earlier Greek models written by Menander, Philemon, Diphlus, and Alexis. Described as New Comedy, Plautus's plays, like those of his Greek predecessors, focus on the personal relationships of ordinary people and the opposition to such relationships posed by financial, social, or parental obstacles.

Biographical Information

Little is known about Plautus's life. Born to poor parents in the village of Sarsina in Umbria, Plautus is believed to have traveled to Rome at an early age to work in the theater. He may have worked as a laborer or merchant before or concurrent with the writing of his early comedies, although this has been disputed by modern scholars. It has also been speculated that Plautus lost the profits from his younger years in an unsuccessful shipping venture, after which he turned—or, perhaps, returned—to writing plays as his sole source of income.

Major Works

Although Plautus has been faulted by some critics for the similarity of plot in his plays, others have argued that the plays differ significantly from one another while making use of similar elements and thematic devices. For example, a number of Plautus's plays rely on mistaken identity to create humor and conflict. *Rudens* has been identified as the Plautine play that most approaches the spirit of romantic comedy. It features mistaken identities and recognition, a shipwreck, and

a rare, on stage dalliance between lovers. The story of *Poenulus* is that of an old Carthaginian seeking his long-lost daughters, whose mistaken identities are eventually revealed. *Epidicus* complicates a basic plot—a young man in love needs money to win a woman—with a series of mistaken identities. The plot of *Menaechmi* is concerned with the mistaken identities of identical twins with the same name who are unaware of the other's presence. Shakespeare's *Comedy of Errors* is an elaboration of this Plautine plot.

It has been noted by some critics that Plautus's plots do not tend to guide love along the path to marriage. In several plays, while love does lead to marriage, Plautus manages to direct the audience's primary interest to other dimensions of the play, de-emphasizing the value of marital love. In other plays, the prospect of marriage becomes either impossible or is simply irrelevant. While a happy marriage is featured at the end of *Aulularia*, the misfortunes of a miser take center stage. In *Cistellaria*, the love plot is upstaged by the activities of other characters; in *Curculio* the love plot is presented from the outset as ridiculous. *Truculentus* focuses on the exploits of a courtesan to achieve material success at the expense and ruin of her would-be lovers. Like *Truculentus,* several other plays, including *Persa, Pseudolus,* and *Bacchides* subvert such traditional values such as the social relevancy of marriage. *Bacchides* centers on the difficulties encountered in the pursuit of love by two young men as well as two courtesans, the sisters Bacchides, who are willing to do anything for money. At one point in the play, the sisters seduce the fathers of the two young men. Several of Plautus's plays include the stock character of the *senex amator,* or the lecherous old man who falls for a young girl. In at least three plays—Asinaria, Casina, and Mercater— this character and his motivation serve as a primary focus of the play. Other works which include an appearance by this stock character include *Bacchides* (the two seduced fathers); *Cistellaria,* in which the *senex amator* interprets everything spoken by the object of his desire as an expression of love until he discovers that she is the woman who is corrupting his son; and *Stichus,* in which an old man relates to his sons-in-law the story of a friend whose own sons-in-law provided him with a female "companion." The old man leaves the scene wrongly believing that his sons-in-law will do the same for him.

Critical Reception

While Plautus's work was immensely popular among his audiences, he has long been taken to task by scholars. The Roman poet and satirist Horace (65 B.C.-8 B.C.) chastized Plautus for valuing the financial success of his plays over adherence to rules of dramatic construction. One of the most heavily debated issues surrounding Plautus's work is the question of originality. It has always been known, thanks to original Latin texts, that Plautus and such Roman dramatists as Terence (185 B.C.-159 B.C.) wrote plays that were adaptations of earlier Greek works. In the nineteenth century, questions arose primarily among German Romantic scholars regarding the extent of Plautus's adaptation of Greek models. These critics allowed that Plautus inserted Roman allusions and Latin puns into his playsand debated whether Plautus's Romanization of Greek texts included borrowing the structure of the Greek originals. These critics were reluctant to credit Plautus with much skill or creativity and often suggested, when confronted with great divergence between Plautus's plays and Greek models, that Plautus must have combined several Greek plays into one.

Many twentieth-century critics, while acknowledging Plautus's indebtedness to the Greeks, have defended his originality, approaching his texts from several different avenues. Roland Kent examines the divergences of Plautus's plays from what he maintains is believed to be the "typical" Plautine plot. Kent shows that none of the plays contain all the elements of this so-called typical plot and that even those that contain many typical elements are remarkably different from one another. Furthermore, Kent also groups the works according to the roles of the heroines within the plays and the plays' outcomes, further emphasizing the individuality of Plautus's plays. Erich Segal (1968) highlights the uniquely and thoroughly Roman flavor of Plautus's plays, demonstrating how connected they are to the concept of the Roman holiday. During Roman holidays, Segal explains, the rules and social conventions of everyday life were not only ignored but flamboyantly broken. Segal goes on to argue that this holiday mentality is reflected in Plautus's plays, in which the rules of the Forum are contrasted with holiday festivity and freedom from those rules, making the comedies uniquely appealing to Roman audiences. K. C. Ryder (1984) takes another approach in asserting Plautus's originality by analyzing the stock character of the *senex amator* in Plautus's plays. Ryder maintains that despite Plautus's frequent use of this character, the *senex amator* is portrayed differently in each work. This variety, Ryder urges, suggests a higher level of "subtlety of approach and execution than [Plautus] is usually credited with." Other critics have looked to specific aspects of particular plays to argue in favor of Plautus's originality. J. C. B. Lowe (1992), for example, compares Plautus's *Asinaria* with its Greek model. Lowe examines specific inconsistencies in the plot and the appearance of the character Philaenium in order to demonstrate the possibility of Plautine innovations. Similarly, William M. Owens (1994) analyzes a specific event in *Bacchides,* a play heavily concerned with deception. While the Greek model for the play (Menander's *Dis Exapaton*) contains two incidents of deception, *Bacchides* contains three deceptions. It was believed by earlier critics that this aspect of the play was introduced by Plautus through the process of *contaminatio* (the use of another, unidentified play as a source). Owens demonstrates the possibility that this third deception is Plautine in origin and is used to depict the antithesis between Roman trust, or *fides,* and Greek deception. Despite varying degrees of confidence in Plautus's originality, critics agree that the characters and plot situations popularized by Plautus have influenced and inspired countless works throughout the world of drama.

---

*PRINCIPAL WORKS

Amphitruo [*Amphitryon*] c. 186 B.C.
Asinaria [*Comedy of Asses*]
Aulularia [*Pot of Gold*]
Bacchides [*Two Bacchides*]
Captivi [*Captives*]

Casina
Cistellaria [*The Casket Comedy*] c. 201 B.C.
Curculio [*The Weevil*]
Epidicus
Menaechmi [*Twin Menaechmi*]
Mercator [*Merchant*]
Miles Gloriosus [*Braggart Warrior*] c. 211 B.C.
Mostellaria [*Haunted House*]
Persa [*Persian*]
Poenulus [*Carthaginian*]
Pseudolus 191 B.C.
Rudens [*Rope*]
Stichus 200 B.C.
Trinummus [*Three Bob Day*]
Truculentus [*Truculent Man*]
†*Vidularia*

*As the dates of most of Plautus' plays are unknown, his works are listed here in alphabetical order. Dates are provided when they are known or conjectured.
†This work survives only in a fragment of about 100 lines.

PRINCIPAL ENGLISH TRANSLATIONS

Plautus, 5 vols., translated by P. Nixon [complete works] 1916-38
Roman Drama, 2 vols., edited by G. E. Duckworth [complete works] 1942
The Rope and Other Plays, translated by E. F. Watling [*Amphitryon, Mostellaria, Rudens, Trinummus*] 1964
The Pot of Gold and Other Plays, translated by E. F. Watling [*Aulularia, Captivi, Menaechmi, Miles Gloriosus, Pseudolus*] 1965
Roman Drama, translated by F. O. Copley and Moses Hadas, [*Menaechmi, Mostellaria, Rudens*] 1965
Plautus; Three Comedies, translated by Erich Segal [*Menaechmi, Miles Gloriosus, Mostellaria*] 1969
Plautus: The Darker Comedies, translated by James Tatum [*Bacchides, Casina, Truculentus*] 1983

CRITICISM

Roland G. Kent (essay date 1923)

SOURCE: Roland G. Kent, "Variety and Monotony in Plautine Plots, in *Philological Quarterly,* Vol. II, No. 3, July, 1923, pp. 164-72.

[*In the following essay, Kent outlines what is often said to be the "typical" Plautine plot and identifies the ways in which Plautus's plays vary from this stereotype.*]

The amusing comedies of Plautus, despite their great influence on the comedy of later times,[1] have suffered diminished favor with the readers of Latin, to some extent, perhaps, because they are regarded as a low form of literature,[2] even apart from the indecencies of language and of situation in which certain of the plays abound, but even more, I suspect, because the several plays are believed to be only minor variations on one typical plot.

This plot would be summarized about as follows:[3] An unmarried young man of good family, often during the absence of his father, has fallen in love with a slave-girl of dubious or more than dubious character, whom he desires to purchase from her owner and keep as his mistress. He is aided in his attempt to get the necessary funds, by a rascally slave; but his father, returning home (if indeed he had been away), detects the son and the slave in their schemes, and seeks to thwart them, though sometimes he remembers his own not impeccable youth and helps his son. In either instance, the young man's mother opposes the aims of her own husband. There is usually a rival for the girl's favors, not infrequently in the character of a *miles gloriosus* or braggart soldier. The play ends with the victory of the young man, while the young woman is often found to be of free birth and wrongly held in slavery, and her character is then redeemed by marriage to her lover. The scene of the action is usually Athens.

There are twenty plays of Plautus which have come down to us complete or so nearly complete that their plots may be analyzed with certainty. Let us examine them in the light of our typical plot:

1. An unmarried young man of good family: not true of the **Amphitruo,** the **Casina** (so far as the play itself is concerned), the **Menaechmi,** the **Persa** (where the hero is a slave), the **Stichus** (which has two young men, with their wives).

2. Often in the absence of the father: true only of the **Mostellaria** and of the **Trinummus** (here only the father of the secondary young man has been away). There are other absences: of the husband of the heroine, in the **Amphitruo;** of the young hero, in the **Epidicus** and in the **Captivi;** of the young man who is ultimately to marry the heroine, though that is not part of the story itself, in the **Casina;** of the slave-hero's master, in the **Persa;** of the husbands of the two heroines, in the **Stichus.**

3. Has fallen in love with a slave-girl of dubious or more than, dubious character: true of the **Asinaria,** the **Bacchides,** the **Epidicus,** the **Miles,** the **Mostellaria,** the **Pseudolus,** the **Truculentus;** and with qualifications, of the **Menaechmi** and the **Persa.** In the **Casina** and in the **Mercator,** the heroine is a slave-girl in a private family. In the **Cistellaria,** the **Curculio,** the **Poenulus,** and the **Rudens,** the heroine is a prospective *meretrix* who proves to be of free birth.

4. Whom he desires to purchase from her owner and keep as his mistress; not true of the *Amphitruo,* the *Aulularia,* the *Captivi,* the *Casina,* the *Menaechmi,* the *Mercator,* the *Stichus,* the *Trinummus.*

5. He is aided by a rascally slave: the hero always does have the assistance of a slave, though his energies are not always directed along dishonest channels.

6. In an attempt to get the necessary funds: true of the *Asinaria,* the *Bacchides,* the *Curculio,* the *Epidicus,* the *Mostellaria,* the *Persa,* the *Pseudolus.*

7. The father detects the son and the slave in their schemes: the father is not a character in the *Amphitruo,* the *Aulularia,* the *Captivi,* the *Curculio,* the *Menaechmi,* the *Miles,* the *Persa,* the *Poenulus,* the *Rudens,* the *Stichus,* the *Truculentus.*

8. And seeks to thwart them: true of the *Cistellaria,* the *Epidicus,* the *Mostellaria,* the *Pseudolus.* The father is opponent and rival in the *Bacchides,* the *Casina,* the *Mercator.*

9. Though sometimes he remembers his own not impeccable youth: true of the *Asinaria,* the *Bacchides,* the *Casina,* the *Cistellaria,* the *Epidicus,* the *Mercator,* the *Mostellaria.*

10. And helps his son: true only of the *Asinaria,* where the father is rival also, and of the *Trinummus,* which is a play of honorable love.

11. In either instance, the young man's mother opposes the aims of her husband: this feature is found only in the *Asinaria* and in the *Casina,* while a slight variation of it occurs in the *Mercator.*

12. There is usually a rival for the girl's favor: this is not the case in the *Captivi* (where there is no love-story), the *Cistellaria,* the *Menaechmi* (with a qualification), the *Mostellaria,* the *Persa,* the *Rudens.*

13. Not infrequently in the character of a *miles gloriosus* or braggart soldier: such is the case in the *Bacchides,* the *Curculio,* the *Epidicus,* the *Miles,* the *Poenulus,* the *Pseudolus,* the *Truculentus,* though the soldier sometimes plays a very unimportant part in the action, or even does not come upon the scene at all. Other rivalries are found on the part of the young man's father, or of another youth; less often of the young man's uncle, of the heroine's husband, of a fellow-slave.

14. The play ends with the victory of the young man: for various reasons, this can be called true only in part, or not at all, of the *Amphitruo,* the *Bacchides,* the *Captivi,* the *Menaechmi,* the *Stichus,* the *Truculentus.*

15. While the young woman is often found to be of free birth and wrongly held in slavery, and her character is then redeemed by marriage to her lover: this is true of the *Casina,* the *Cistellaria,* the *Curculio,* the *Epidicus,* the *Poenulus,* the *Rudens.*

16. The scene of the action is usually Athens: so in twelve of the twenty plays. The *Amphitruo* is laid at Thebes; the *Captivi* in Aetolia, which seems to be a city; the *Cistellaria* at Sicyon; the *Curculio* at Epidaurus; the *Menaechmi* at Epidamnus; the *Miles* at Ephesus; the *Poenulus* at Calydon; the *Rudens* at Cyrene.

Possibly the variations from our typical plot become clearer if we see how many points the plays score, out of the total sixteen; the highest possible score is fifteen, since points eight and ten are mutually exclusive. The *Asinaria* and the *Epidicus* each score thirteen, having eleven points in common; yet they are very unlike, for the *Asinaria* centers about the father's assistance to his son in cheating the rich mother out of the necessary sum of money and the discovery of the father by the *uxor dotata* at an unrestrained banquet with the girl, which was the price of his assistance to his son, and the *Epidicus* deals with a young man with two girls on his hands, a twofold swindling of the father, and a series of mistaken identities. The *Mostellaria* scores eleven, the *Bacchides* ten, the *Pseudolus* nine. A number of the plays score eight, but it is hardly worth while to list them, for not infrequently a play will show a feature in such a way that it is hard to say whether it is to be counted. Thus in the *Epidicus* the youth is freed of the one girl by finding that she is his own long lost half-sister, and he is free to keep the other as his mistress, she being frankly a *meretrix,* while the half-sister was a war-captive.

The plays may also be grouped by the heroines and the outcomes, in a way which will bring out the differences even more effectively.

I. The heroines are professional *meretrices,* held by a *leno* or by a *lena: Asin., Epid., Miles, Most., Persa, Pseud.*

a. She is sought and won by an *adulescens* of good family. In the *Most.,* the youth purchases her in his father's absence, and has his difficulties when the father returns. In the *Pseud.,* the girl is secured by an impersonation and some borrowed money, afterward repaid by the father as the result of a sporting bet that he would repay any money which the tricky slave might that day secure by his swindling. In the *Epid.,* as we have said, the young man gets two girls on his hands, but when he finds that his war-captive is his own half-sister, he returns to his mistress, whom his slave had purchased for him in his absence on the campaign. In the *Miles,* the youth follows the girl to Ephesus, whither she has been taken by a *miles,* and with the assistance of a jolly old bachelor secures her without loss of money. In the **Asin.,** the youth buys the girl for one year, with the assistance of his father, who bargains for a share of her favors, but is haled away just in time by his justly enraged wife.

b. She is bought and freed by a slave: **Persa**. The slave-hero swindles the *leno* himself out of the sum which he has taken temporarily from his own master's funds, which were to be spent fcr the purchase of cattle.

II. The heroines are free professional *meretrices:* **Bac., Men., Truc.** In the **Bac.,** there are two sisters, loved by two youths; but the sisters lure also the fathers of the young men into rivalry with them. In the **Men.,** the *meretrix* is finally deserted not only by her lover, but by his twin brother, whom none had been able to distinguish from one another. In the **Truc.,** the *meretrix* has three lovers, none of whom she is willing to relinquish, though the hero of the play has become betrothed to the girl whom he has wronged, and the *miles* who had been her lover is evidently eager to escape from her blackmailing.

III. The heroine is a slave in the household of her master: **Cas., Merc.**

a. She retains her slave status in the **Merc.,** where she was purchased by the hero from a friend of his father, who was his host while he was traveling as a trader. On his return, the father tries to get the girl for himself, but after some merry misunderstandings he withdraws his claims.

b. She is sought by father and by son, in the **Cas.,** as wife for a personal slave, which would then give the slave-husband's owner special claims upon her; but she is later found to be of free birth, and becomes the wife of the son.

IV. The heroine is a prospective *meretrix,* held by a *leno* or by a *lena,* but is really of free birth, as is later discovered: **Cist., Curc., Poen., Rud.** In the **Cist.,** the girl is proved to be free by some *crepundia,* and is restored to her parents; she has already been living with her lover, but had run away from him because his father had wished to betroth him to a daughter of a friend. In the **Rud.,** her freedom is proved by the same means, and she is similarly restored to her parents; but she had previously been quite inaccessible to the youth. In the **Poen.,** the *leno's* slave betrays the truth about her origin, and her father comes in search of her. In the **Curc.,** she recognizes a ring now belonging to a *miles* who desires to purchase her, as her own father's ring. In all these cases, the play ends with a prospect of legal marriage.

In the **Epid.,** a similar discovery is made, but as the girl proves to be the young man's half-sister, the revelation merely sends him back to his first love.

V. The heroine is a free girl who has been wronged by the hero of the play and has born him a baby; when the facts are established, he marries her: **Aul.** In this play the hero's elderly bachelor uncle seeks to marry the girl, but withdraws in favor of his nephew. There is a similar situation in the **Truc.,** where the hero is infatuated with a *meretrix,* but leaves her to marry the mother of his child, which had been stolen and used by the *meretrix* in an attempt to get money from one of her former lovers, a *miles.*

VI. The heroine is a free girl, sought by an honorable lover, and there is no problem but that of dower: **Trin.**

VII. The heroines are two sisters, young wives, faithful to their long absent husbands; there is a secondary story of the loves of two slaves for their fellow-slave Stephanium: **Stichus.**

VIII. The heroine is a wife, deceived by Jupiter's assumption of her husband's appearance: **Amph.**

IX. There is no love-story in the play: **Capt.**

Even this division does not bring out fully the diversity of the plots of the Plautine plays; and a survey of the chief features of each play will be a fitting supplement to what has been said.[4] In the first place, there are four plays which are not only very different from all the other plays but also from each other. The **Amphitruo** is a travesty on the story of Jupiter and Alcmena, and finds its interest in the confusion of Jupiter and Amphitruo, and of their respective attendants, Mercury and Sosia; a confusion which is intensified by the ability of the god to divine the story of the mortal husband and to perform miracles of theft without breaking seals. A satisfactory conclusion is effected by the god's intervention in propria persona. The **Menaechmi,** with the twin brothers of identical appearance, is similar only in this point; for neither brother suspects the presence of the other, while Jupiter is aware of the doings of Amphitruo, and the Menaechmus of Epidamnus has both wife and mistress, both of whom he leaves at the close of the play, while Amphitruo has only a wife, with whom he becomes reconciled.

The third of these special plays is the **Captivi,** which has no love-story at all, but is a comedy of war-captivity and ransom, complicated by the exchange of characters by a free youth and his devoted slave, who had fallen together into the hands of the foe. The fourth is the **Stichus,** where two young wives remain faithful to their long absent husbands, despite their father's urgent pleadings that they remarry. There is also the comedy of the loves of two slaves for their fellow-slave-woman; but the plot is extremely slight, and perhaps centers more about the persistent failure of the *parasitus* to secure even a suggestion of an invitation to a dinner.

The *Trinummus* distinguishes itself by being a play of reasonably polite circles, as it contains no disreputable characters, except the brother of the heroine; but his profligacy is brought in only as the explanation of his inability to dower his sister properly when a very suitable proposal for her hand is made. The play resolves itself into a study in the problem of dower: the attitude of the lover, that of the lover's father, that of the girl's brother, that of the girl's father's friend, and finally that of the girl's father himself, who returns from abroad just in time to set matters aright. The *Aulularia* also has a problem of dower, but its interest centers about the terrors of the old miser, the girl's father, lest he lose his precious *aula* of money.

The *Rudens* stands out by itself for its seaside atmosphere, with its fishermen and its shipwreck, the casting ashore of the girls in the storm and their seeking refuge in the temple from which their owner seeks to tear them. The recognition of the heroine's freedom by her *crepundia* suggests, it is true, the *Cistellaria;* but this play is very different, for the heroine has been living with her lover and has deserted him when she hears that his father has betrothed him to the daughter of a friend; and the series of events which results in the discovery that she is really a half-sister of the other girl is very different from the events of the *Rudens*.

The *Casina* also stands by itself, with the sham marriage in which the husky young Chalinus is substituted for the fair young Casina, to the confusion of the bridegroom Olympio and of Olympio's master; though it ends in one of the conventional ways, with a discovery of her free birth and her marriage to the youth who loves her. The *Poenulus* is distinguished by the character of the old Carthaginian Hanno, seeking his lost daughters, and talking Punic to the amusement of his audience. The *Miles* is a study in the character of the braggart soldier, who believes himself irresistible in love, and allows himself to be deceived at every turn, even to the losing of his mistress and to his being caught in an amour with one whom he supposed to be his neighbor's wife.

The *Curculio* is distinguished by the nocturnal visit of the youth to the house where the girl is living, and the enticing forth of the drunken *ianitrix* Leaena by the fumes of the wine poured on the doorsill; by the deception of the *miles* and the discovery that the *miles* is the girl's brother, and the final requirement that the *leno* must refund the money paid for the girl. The *Pseudolus* is in certain points similar to the *Curculio,* but centers around the *leno* Ballio and his school of courtesans, and the promise of the youth's father to repay any sums which his son's slave might secure by trickery that day, a promise which he felt sure he would never have to make good. The *Mostellaria* is built around the concealment of the youth and his friend and their mistresses in a house which is locked and apparently unoccupied, under pretense of its being haunted, and the reputed purchase of the neighbor's house, which leads to many amusing contretemps. The *Epidicus* is a drama of a youth with two young women on his hands, and a series of mistaken identities. The *Mercator* represents the youth as bringing home from his business voyage an attractive young slave girl, whom his father desires for himself, and places in the home of his own aged comrade, where that comrade's wife, suddenly returning from the country, suspects her husband of misconduct.

The *Persa* is, as has often been remarked, a play without a single respectable character: a play in which a slave purchases and sets free his mistress, "borrowing" some of his absent master's money for the purpose until he replaces it by selling to the *leno* the daughter of a *parasitus* as a foreign war-captive of unguaranteed slave-status, who is then reclaimed as free, while the *leno* apparently must bear the loss without possibility of redress. The *Truculentus* is a drama of a free *meretrix* with three lovers whom she strives more or less successfully to keep entangled in her toils. The *Bacchides* is a play of the wiles of two sisters, *meretrices,* who by a mistaken identity cause their lovers to quarrel with each other, and then finally entice their lovers' fathers into rivalry with their sons. Finally, the *Asinaria* shows a dissolute father with a rich wife, helping his son to cheat his wife and to secure his mistress in return for a first share in her favors, in which he is thwarted by his wife's appearance on the scene.

In these plays we certainly find as great diversity of plot as in an equal number of plays or novels of the present time, analyzed in the same way, if allowance be made for the conditions of society and of scenic production. Both of these factors restricted choice and the treatment of the themes; but the infrequency of production of the plays made certain kinds of similarities less objectionable to audiences. Further, the rapidity of the spoken dialogue is commonly forgotten by us moderns, who spread the reading of a Plautine play over days or weeks, while the ancient audience heard the complete play in two hours or less. When we read a whole play at a sitting, we do not feel the dragging of the movement nor the monotony of certain portions nor the use of similar devices; we get a keen impression of a witty dialogue, abounding in unexpected turns, which we enjoy quite in proportion to our ability to understand it quickly. Latin becomes then a truly living language, with natural turns of expression, and the apparatus for conveying all the ordinary ideas and thoughts of normal life of any time of the world's history. Plautus's plays are, therefore, deserving of much more attention from readers of Latin than they normally receive; and if they suffer from a reputation for similarity to one another, as I think they do, they suffer this wrongly.

Terence normally has two love-stories in every play; in the *Hecyra,* where alone this is lacking, the young man has two love-affairs, one with his wife, whom he had wronged before marriage without knowledge of her identity, and the other with a *meretrix,* who at the end is quite willing to bring about a reconciliation between him and his wife. This, then, is a combination of our Types I and V, with the same *adulescentes* in both. The *Andria* has loves of Types V and VI; the *Eunuchus,* of Types II and V (nearly); the *Heauton Timorumenos,* of Types IV and I, in the latter of which the youth abandons the *meretrix* for an honest marriage to a girl not previously mentioned. The *Phormio* has Types I and VI, the marriage taking place before the beginning of the play; the *Adelphoe* has Types I and V.

But these stories may be classified, or rather described, by some central theme. The *Andria* shows the youth consenting to an undesired marriage because he does not expect it to be acceptable to his future father-in-law when certain facts become known. The *Heauton Timorumenos* shows the stern father repenting his sternness toward his son, which has driven that son away from home, and finally for this reason consenting to all manner of extravagance and irregularity: The *Eunuchus* shows a young lover disguised as a slave-eunuch, that he may gain access to his love. The *Phormio* presents a marriage based on a fraudulent application of the nearest-of-kin law, which turns out to be a true application. The *Hecyra* gives a separation between a newly married couple, for which the mother-in-law is wrongly blamed. The *Adelphoe* shows the outcome of strictness and of laissez-faire in the education of youth. The differences are truly impressive.

In the plays of Menander of which we have sufficient portions for the restoration of the plots, mainly through the happy discovery of papyrus copies in recent years, we find that in all cases the young woman is the mistress or the victim of the young man who later marries her. The *Epitrepontes* gives a situation much like that of Terence's *Hecyra.* The *Samia* presents the amour of a youth and a free girl, with their marriage after the facts about their baby have become known to the youth's adoptive father; the adoptive father himself has a housekeeper-mistress of supposedly foreign origin, who probably is found to be of Attic descent and therefore eligible to the position of legal wife. The *Epiceiromene* is the story of a poor girl, the mistress of a *miles,* who became jealous at seeing the advances of another youth who turns out to be her brother; and the *miles* marries her when her parentage is established. The *Hero* is the story of a foundling girl, who with her brother is working as a slave to pay off certain debts; she has been wronged by a youth of good birth and is sought in marriage by a fellow-slave, willing to overlook the matter, but when she and her brother are found to be the children of the master for whom they

are working, a legal marriage with her free lover is in prospect. The *Georgos,* though somewhat more fragmentary, gives us a poor girl who has been wronged, but is later regularly betrothed to the young man.

In all three authors, it should be insisted, the variety is essentially in the treatment of the theme rather than in the theme itself; and yet the themes or plots have their own essential differences. In these plots, Plautus shows greater variety than either Terence or Menander: we speak of necessity on the basis of plays extant entire or in sufficient amount for the formation of a judgment. The two Roman dramatists were drawing from a large stock of Greek plays, and the greater variety in the Plautine plays may indicate that Plautus showed better judgment in the selection of his sources, than did the more polished, but less lively Terence.

In championing the reading of Plautus, of Terence and of Menander, perhaps one should speak of the moral tendencies or otherwise of the plays.[5] Fairly rough and unrestrained they may be, but they represent at least the best morality of their time.

Notes

[1] Cf. for example Fowler's edition of the *Menaechmi,* pp. 26-8, with references to previous literature, and especially Karl von Reinhardstoettner, *Plautus, Spätere Bearbeitungen plautinischer Lustspiele,* 1886.

[2] Cf. W. W. Blancké, *The Dramatic Values in Plautus,* 1918.

[3] Cf. for example the introductions of E. P. Morris to the *Pseudolus,* p. ii, and to the *Mostellaria,* pp. xiv-xix.

[4] A detailed consideration is to be found in G. Michaut, *Histoire de la comédie romaine,* Vol. II, pp. 98-159.

[5] Cf. Lamarre, *Histoire de la littérature latine,* Vol. II, pp. 473-488.

Philip Whaley Harsh (essay date 1944)

SOURCE: "Plautus," in *A Handbook of Classical Drama,* Stanford University Press, 1944, pp. 333-74.

[*In the following excerpt, Harsh offers an overview of Plautus's major plays, commenting on the source materials, plots, and the influence of the plays on later works.*]

The twenty extant plays of Plautus constitute an astonishingly varied collection of good, bad, and indifferent comedies. Even the worst, however, usually have one or more effective scenes, and most of the indifferent ones doubtless were successful in his theater. For modern dramatists, good and bad alike have served as a continually plundered storehouse of interesting comic characters and amusing situations. The structure of the *Amphitryon*, for instance, is not well proportioned, to say the least; but the play's situation is so infallibly amusing that it has attracted innumerable adapters. Nor have imitators been frightened away from the *Twin Menaechmi* merely because its basic situation is fantastically improbable. The *Braggart Warrior* is very poorly constructed, but its title character remains eternally popular. The widely adapted *Pot of Gold*, however, calls for no apology on any score, for it is a masterpiece. These four plays, the most influential ones, well illustrate the variety of Plautus' work.

It is obviously difficult to determine the personal contributions of a dramatist all of whose plays are adaptations of Greek plays now lost. Still this can be done for Terence with comparative clarity, for his literary prologues and the ancient commentaries give much detailed information. Besides, his plays themselves are remarkably consistent in subject matter, structure, and various other features of dramatic technique, some of which are known not to have been characteristic of Greek comedy. But for Plautus the situation is quite different. He has no literary prologues, and no commentaries have been preserved. We are thrown back, therefore, upon the plays themselves; and, except in style, these show great variation.

In meter the variation is great but consistent and significant: Plautus began his career using little or no lyric measure and gradually increased its use as time went on. The *Braggart Warrior,* for instance, is dated by its reference to the imprisonment of Naevius (lines 209-12) about 205 B.C. It has no elaborate lyric and, except for a single passage in anapests, it is confined to iambic and trochaic lines of six or seven and one-half feet. This is the simplest metrical structure of any Plautine play. The *Stichus,* produced in 200 B.C., opens with an elaborate lyric, has two passages in anapests, and one passage in lyric iambic measure of eight feet, as well as a few lyric lines at the end of the play. The *Pseudolus,* dated 191 B.C., is literally filled with lyric and anapestic measures. These are the only plays which can be dated with certainty, and with these three as a framework modern scholars have arranged the other plays in the order of their metrical elaborateness and have assumed that this was more or less the order of their composition. This assumption must not be pressed too closely, however, for presumably a serious comedy of character like the *Pot of Gold* admits fewer true lyrics and requires more restrained dialogue than an extravagent farce like the *Casina*. It is hardly necessary to add that in Plautine comedy, as in Greek tragedy and Aristophanes, the meters are skillfully adapted to the subject matter. Changes in meter emphasize changes in tone and are especially effective in a melodramatic play like the *Rope*.

In subject matter, Plautus seems to run the gamut of New Comedy and perhaps to reach into that of Middle Comedy; nor has any clear and significant development in this regard been observed. The mythological travesty of the *Amphitryon* is certainly the oldest material, but the elaborate meter of this play places it in the period of Plautus' maturity. The *Captives,* usually assigned to this same period, is an extraordinary play concerning the exchange of prisoners of war. The majority of Plautus' plays, however, like most of those of New Comedy, concern the gay life of the gilded youth of Athens, their eternal need of money with which to purchase sweethearts, and the frequent recognition of these sweethearts as Attic citizens.

The dramatist's attitude toward his material shows equal variety. Thus the *Pot of Gold* is a serious comedy of character, the *Haunted House* a farce, and the *Two Bacchides* a comedy of character and intrigue. These are all from the mature or late periods, and Plautus seems to have undergone no development in this regard, although comedies of intrigue are the most frequent from the beginning of his career to the end. Thus the *Comedy of Asses* presumably comes near the beginning and the *Pseudolus* near the end; the intrigue of the one is very similar to that of the other, although the *Pseudolus* is in every way vastly superior.

In dramatic structure, also, the plays vary tremendously. The *Braggart Warrior,* the *Comedy of Asses,* and the *Merchant,* all having simple metrical structure, are usually classed together as the earliest plays. But of these three, the *Merchant* is constructed excellently, the other two miserably. The *Stichus,* slightly later, has practically no plot at all—not, of course, necessarily a fault. Among the later plays, however, it is not so easy to point to such indisputable contrasts, and it may be that Plautus improved somewhat in this regard. Still, certain of the late plays, such as the *Persian,* are surely not distinguished in structure or in their general technique.

Another item of remarkable variation is found in the total length of the different comedies. The longest are the early *Braggart Warrior* (1,437 lines), the *Carthaginian* (1,422), and the middle or late *Rope* (1,423) and *Pseudolus* (1,334). The shortest are the *Curculio* (729), the *Epidicus* (733), the *Stichus* (775), and the *Persian* (858). These plays are from the early, middle, and late periods.

This astonishing variation of the plays, in the opinion of the present writer, seems to indicate that Plautus took his plays without much critical discrimination from a wide variety of authors and that these authors are responsible for the main features of the plays. It is conceivable, of course, that the actual manuscripts available to Plautus at Rome may have been limited. If he used any criterion consistently, it was that of theatrical effectiveness. Horace was not wholly unjustified in saying that Plautus rushed over the stage in loose "socks" and cared only for popular success. Many modern critics, however, assume that Plautus so mauled the original Greek comedies that he himself is responsible for most of the faults of his plays. Perhaps these critics would have a higher opinion of Plautus' intellect if they set their hands to translating the delightfully delicate ironies and the brilliant wit of the **Amphitryon**. Certainly all but the very keenest modern translators have fallen far short of Plautus' attainment.

That Plautus had no slavish respect for the Greek originals is obvious from the plays themselves. As he changes the meters to suit himself, so he introduces various Roman allusions. References to Greek places or customs or events that would be obscure to a Roman audience are usually eliminated. Greek gods are changed to Roman. This, of course, is mere expert translation, and even Terence regularly followed this practice. But Plautus has the habit of mixing Greek and Roman in a way offensive to the modern reader, though it doubtless seemed natural enough to his original audience. It is now disconcerting, for instance, to have the Greek atmosphere broken by a reference to the Praetor. Even more disconcerting is a reference to a particular place in the city of Rome or—for comic effect—to the country town Praeneste or Plautus' own Sarsina. Terence was careful to avoid all such confusion.

Plautus sometimes combined two Greek plays into one Roman or omitted a scene from the original, and in general he adapted with considerable freedom. So says Terence in defense of his own practice. Modern scholars have expended a huge amount of energy in attempting to analyze the comedies and determine the innovations of Plautus; but most of these studies have been made without sufficient literary background and consist, as someone has said, of a comparison of the known with the unknown. To assume that the very prolific Greek writers of New Comedy made no blunders or allowed no inconsistencies to creep in is obviously fallacious. In short, a detailed reconstruction of the original plays from the plays of Plautus is quite impossible.

In matters of style, the personality of Plautus, greatly influenced by the conventions of his day, is observable throughout his works. His dialogue is vigorous and rapid and filled with delightful humor. In general, however, his style, like that of his contemporaries, is far more exuberant than the chaste elegance of Greek New Comedy. Plautus' Latin abounds in alliteration, redundancy, puns, and word play. This exuberance is seen in its most extreme manifestation in his anapestic and lyric passages, an English prose translation of which often sounds utterly ridiculous. Such passages

should, of course, be translated into the idiom of modern popular songs. Ancient critics such as Cicero give Plautus credit for an admirable mastery of colloquial Latin. He is very bold in his word coinages, which are often made for comic effect, such as in the awkward "loan translation" of a Greek compound, *turpilucricupidus* ("filthy-lucre-grabber"). Occasionally a bit of Greek or local dialect is admitted for the same effect. But very few cases of merely bad translation are found.

In certain respects Plautus distantly resembles Aristophanes. Certainly his sense of humor is robust and all-inclusive. He is fond of comedy based on physical effects, such as the pouring of slops on Amphitryon near the end of that play, the vomiting of Labrax in the **Rope,** and the drunken belching of Pseudolus. He likes indecent jests; but these usually seem a little prim in comparison with those of Aristophanes or those of Naevius. His language and his meters are similarly exuberant. His use of interminable lists, as in the **Pot of Gold** (508-19), and his employment of a dinning repetition line after line, as in the **Rope** (1212-24), also strike Aristophanic notes. He is similarly informal. So the property manager in the **Curculio** interrupts the play to give a discourse on the various quarters of Rome. More frequently, the dramatic illusion is broken by direct address to the audience or by directly insulting the audience. So Euclio in the **Pot of Gold** (718) declares that many of those in the audience, as he well knows, are thieves. We need not assume that any of these characteristics of Old Comedy had wholly died out in the Greek tradition, but possibly they are somewhat more frequent in Plautus than in his originals. The contrast with the dignified and formal Terence, at least, is again most striking. Nor need we assume that Plautus is consciously following the Aristophanic tradition—it is merely that he has a strain of the immortal comic spirit.

Amphitryon

Though constructed with something of the careless nonchalance of Old Comedy, the **Amphitryon** is so filled with delightful irony and irrepressible low comedy and tells such an immortal story that it is one of the most interesting plays of Plautus.

About three hundred verses, it is usually assumed, are missing from the text after line 1034.

LEGEND.—The legend concerning the twin birth of Heracles and Iphicles, like that of the triple birth of Helen, Castor, and Pollux, finds its eventual origin in the old popular superstition which attributed multiple births to supernatural causes. Thus the strong twin, Heracles, was thought to be the son of a divinity and only the weaker Iphicles the true son of the mortal Amphitryon.

The most striking features of the legend of Heracles' birth were the disguise of Jupiter, the long night which was necessary for the conception of this mighty child, the divine manifestations at his birth, and the miracles wrought by him in infancy. Obviously there should be at least seven months between the long night and the birth, and some months more between the birth and the miracles. But if Aristophanes in the *Acharnians* could have Amphitheus go to Sparta, arrange truces there, and return to Athens all within the space of fifty lines, his contemporaries, if they so chose, could doubtless combine the long night—transformed, as in Plautus' play, perhaps from the night of generation to a night of incidental dalliance—the birth, and the miracles all into one comedy.

SOURCE.—No subject material has held the boards so long and successfully as the story of Alcmena and Amphitryon. Only the story of Oedipus and possibly that of Medea and a few others were more frequently dramatized by the Greek poets. Aeschylus wrote an *Alcmene.* So did Euripides and each of at least three minor poets of the fifth and fourth centuries. Other plays entitled *Amphitryon,* which may have dealt with entirely different phases of the story, were written by Sophocles, an Alexandrine poet, and the Roman Accius.

This subject would seem naturally to lend itself readily to parody; and the comic writers, as usual, doubtless centered their attention on the version of Euripides. A reference at the opening of Plautus' **Rope** (86) amusingly recalls the realistic stage effects which were employed at the climax of Euripides' play. Two contemporaries of Aristophanes essayed the subject—one, Archippus, calling his play the *Amphitryon;* the other, Plato "Comicus," calling his the *Long Night (Nux Makra).* Philemon also wrote a *Night,* and Rhinthon, a Greek of southern Italy writing burlesque, was the author of an *Amphitryon.* Almost nothing is known of these plays.

It is usually assumed that the immediate original of the Latin play was a comedy of the Middle or New period. This may be correct. But the **Amphitryon,** though in some ways typical of New Comedy, exhibits more technical characteristics of early comedy than any other play of Plautus. One can hardly doubt that such writers as Archippus and Plato "Comicus," perhaps Rhinthon also, have left their marks upon the play. Informality is its most striking feature. The scene at one time seems to be laid before the house of Amphitryon, at another somewhere near the harbor. Such variation was not unnatural on the long Roman stage, however, and less striking examples are found in other plays. The very fact that Thebes is placed near the sea is a bold distortion, like the coast of Bohemia in Shakespeare. The utter contempt for the dramatic illusion, also, is reminiscent of Old Comedy. So are the various effects of low comedy: the beating of Sosia and Mercury's pour-

ing ashes and slops down on Amphitryon. Time is boldly telescoped. There is something too of the inimitable spirit and verve of Old Comedy.

INFLUENCE.—There are vast numbers of modern adaptations of Plautus' **Amphitryon.** One of the most famous of these is Molière's *Amphitryon.* (1668), which has been translated into many languages and frequently reproduced. Especially noteworthy in his version is the introduction of Sosia's wife. Sosia's "girl friend" is given only a brief reference in the play of Plautus (659). Well known also are the version of Rotrou (*Les Sosies,* 1638), which had considerable influence on Molière, that of John Dryden (1690), and that of von Kleist (1807). In the *Comedy of Errors* Shakespeare adopted certain motives from the **Amphitryon.**

Most interesting of all, however, is the brilliant contemporary production of Jean Giraudoux, *Amphitryon 38.* This is an astonishingly original reworking of material so often dramatized before, and it has very little in common with the play of Plautus. Indeed the story has been made into delightfully high comedy. In a bedroom scene filled with subtle irony Jupiter praises the night just past in the most effusive terms, but for his every adjective Alcmène insists upon recalling a night (with Amphitryon, of course) that was much superior. Thus the comedy is mainly at the expense not of Amphitryon but of the god himself! Alcmène also pays her generous share, for she mistakes the real Amphitryon for the god and, thinking that she is playing a clever deception upon him, sends him in to the bed of Jupiter's former playfellow, Leda. The comedy closes with a gift of forgetfulness—a faint reminiscence perhaps of Molière's ending. An English adaptation of this play was produced in America with great success.

DISCUSSION.—Except for the *Plutus* of Aristophanes, the **Amphitryon** is the only example of mythological travesty that has been preserved. This genre, though occasionally written at Athens during the fifth century, came into great popularity during the first half of the fourth century and to some extent prepared the way for the development of intimate social comedy.

The basic plot of the **Amphitryon,** a wife's adultery and the duping of a husband, was one which convention usually forbade comedy. The cruel irony of the situation, difficult for any husband to enjoy wholly without misgivings, is well exploited, however, even in the *Iliad* (3. 369-454), where Menelaus still toils on the field of battle while Paris, rescued from him by Aphrodite, has taken Helen to bed. The situation is softened in the comedy of Plautus because a well-known myth is being parodied and because Alcmena is morally innocent. Here the duping of the husband is played up into a comedy of errors and, to make confusion worse confounded, Mercury is introduced in the disguise of Sosia.

The opening of the *Amphitryon* is remarkably recitational and farcical. Here is the best example of the proverbially long-winded god of the prologue. Almost a hundred lines of clever foolery have gone by before Mercury finally begins with the argument of the play. Another fifty lines are used for explaining the situation. Since this is a comedy of errors, the poet is careful here and throughout the play to instruct the audience with painful explicitness before every new development. Incidentally Mercury reminds us that some Roman actors, being slaves, might be whipped for a poor performance, and he makes interesting revelations concerning *claqueurs* in the ancient theater.

The entrance of Sosia does not begin the action but leads to another prologue! Now we hear in detail the story of Amphitryon's campaign, and the mortal is no more concise—and no less clever—than the immortal has been. Practically nothing in this long monody, occasionally punctuated by a remark of Mercury, has any structural significance except the reference to the gold cup of Pterela (260). No normal dramatic conversation develops until almost three hundred fifty verses have been spoken in these two prologues. Still, this opening, though static, is far from dull.

After the amusing low comedy between Sosia and Mercury, the slave departs, and the god speaks another prologue! We are now told the complications that are about to take place, and even precisely how everything will be made right in the end.

The two scenes between Jupiter and Alcmena are among the best of the play and prove that, after all, ancient dramatists could write scenes of sentimental dalliance. The exchanges here, of course, are pervaded by a delicate irony. Alcmena can well say, "Gracious me! I am discovering how much regard you have for your wife (508)." And Mercury can be quite sure that he is telling the truth when he says to Alcmena: ". . . . I don't believe there's a mortal man alive loves his own wife (*glancing slyly at Jupiter*) so madly as the mad way he dotes on you." Incidentally in this scene Jupiter gives Alcmena the gold cup which, as we have heard before (260, 419-21), Amphitryon has received as his special reward, and which is to play such an important role in the subsequent action.

The comedy of errors now continues with the introduction of Amphitryon; and the structural function of the earlier mystification of the slave, it now appears, is to furnish the first step in the gradual mystification and maddening of the master. The second step quickly follows with the strangely cold reception which Amphitryon receives from Alcmena. Her production of the gold cup adds a third. Meanwhile the irony continues, but it is not always as delicate as it is in the very proper oath of Alcmena (831-34): "By the realm of our Ruler above and by Juno, mother and wife, whom I should most reverence and fear, I swear that no mortal man save you alone has touched my body with his to take my shame away."

When Amphitryon, convinced of his wife's infidelity, has rushed off to find her kinsman, Jupiter returns for another session of dalliance and to set the stage for the supreme humiliation of Amphitryon. He also foretells the coming action and solution, repeating in part what Mercury has said previously. Later Mercury reappears as the "running slave," and carefully explains how he will mock Amphitryon.

Failure to locate the kinsman of Alcmena aggravates Amphitryon's ill humor, and when he returns to find the house closed to him his frustration knows no bounds. But this is only the beginning of his grief. He must be taunted unmercifully by the divine lackey and finally have ashes dumped upon him and slops poured over him—a scene which doubtless brought down the house, be it Greek or Roman. All this time Jupiter is taking his pleasure of Alcmena inside. Finally Jupiter himself comes forth and tows the conquering hero Amphitryon about the stage by the nape of his neck. There is not a scene even in Aristophanes that carries low comedy quite so far as this.

When Amphitryon finally regains his feet, now stark mad, he resolves to rush into the house and slay everyone whom he meets. But at this crucial moment come thunder and lightning, and he is struck down before his house. There can be no vacant stage here, and doubtless Bromia quickly enters, though her subsequent account reveals that a great deal of time is supposed to have elapsed. Amphitryon, recognizing the unmistakable signs of divinity, is thoroughly placated. He considers it an honor to have had his wife adulterated by Jupiter. Nevertheless, the play must end in true tragic fashion with an appearance of Jupiter as the god from the machine. The last line of all, reminiscent of the humor of Mercury in the prologue, is perhaps the best of the play (Nixon's translation): "Now, spectators, for the sake of Jove almighty, give us some loud applause."

. . . . .

Pot of Gold (Aulularia)

The **Pot of Gold** is a delightful comedy of character with an abundance of dramatic action. Unfortunately the final scene has been lost, but fragments and the arguments of the play indicate the main features of the solution.

It is thought that Menander was the author of the original—a very attractive but unproved assumption. The miser was a favorite type with Menander, as may be seen in his *Arbitration,* where also a cook is used for a scene of low comedy.

SIGNIFICANT NAMES.—The name Staphyla ("bunch of grapes") suggests that this character, like so many of the old women of comedy, is addicted to winebibbing, and certain of her lines confirm this (354-55). The cooks, too, are picturesquely named Congrio (*gongros*, "eel") and Anthrax ("a coal"). From the point of view of American slang, however, the most aptly named character is that of the young man who has violated Euclio's daughter—Lyconides ("wolfling").

INFLUENCE.—The ***Pot of Gold*** has been a very influential play. Ben Jonson's *The Case Is Altered* is an adaptation of this and of the ***Captives***. But by far the most famous adaptation is Molière's *L'Avare* (1668), which itself inspired various imitations, including comedies entitled *The Miser* by Shadwell (1672) and by Fielding (1732).

A comparison of the play of Molière with that of Plautus is a profitable study; but only a few points can here be noted. Molière, like Plautus, employs significant names. Among these Harpagon ("grappling hook," "snatcher") is a Greek-Latin formation and was doubtless suggested by the cognate verb which occurs in the ***Pot of Gold*** (201), or by the name Harpax in the ***Pseudolus*** (esp. 654). Molière has enriched the plot by adding a son and his love affair, in which Harpagon himself is involved. Several passages closely follow Plautus. Harpagon rages at the loss of his gold much as Euclio does and even descends to making similar remarks directly to the audience (IV, vii). The scene where Valère confesses to Harpagon also follows Plautus very closely in its elaborate irony. The Menandrean humanity of Euclio, however, has been wholly lost in the grossly exaggerated Harpagon.

DISCUSSION.—The main plot of the ***Pot of Gold*** is an unusual one. A miser, Euclio, through excess of caution, is made to lose his recently discovered treasure. By the good offices of a young man who has violated his daughter, however, he recovers the treasure. Meanwhile he has learned a lesson; and so he apparently gives the money to his daughter as a dowry and is happy to be relieved of the task of guarding it. Thus this comedy, like the *Brothers* of Terence, has a serious theme. The minor plot concerning the daughter and her violation is trite, but skill is shown in combining it very closely with the main plot. Indeed it is employed almost wholly to bring out the character of Euclio and facilitate the main action.

The play opens with an omniscient prologue by the patron divinity of the household. Noteworthy here is the explanation that the proposal of the old man, Megadorus, is merely a device of the divinity for uniting the girl to the father of her child. Surely a modern playwright would have preferred to dispense with the prologue altogether and to reserve Megadorus' proposal for an exciting complication. But the ancient

dramatist has some justification for rejecting this method. He is anxious in no way to detract from the emphasis on Euclio's character. Even in the prologue, the primary concern is to show that the miserliness of Euclio has been inherited for generations. Indeed the proposal of Megadorus itself is primarily designed to bring out the point, essential to the plot, that the present Euclio will not even give a dowry to his daughter though she must inevitably lose social status if she marries a wealthy man without one. So the very liberal character of Megadorus is designed by contrast to display the niggardliness of Euclio.

The scenes between Euclio and Staphyla, also, serve to illustrate the character of the miser. Incidentally, preparation for his subsequent distrust of the very bland Megadorus is contained in his complaint that all his fellow citizens, seeming to know that he has found a treasure, now greet him more cordially.

Eunomia and Megadorus are introduced with an elaborate duet in which it is brought out that an old brother is being forced to do his duty to society by an old sister who has already done hers. Since Eunomia must have a role later in the play, the dramatist has done well to introduce her here, and she is very nicely drawn. Her slightly archaic Latin perhaps suggests that she belongs to that class of staid matrons whom attention to the home has caused to lose contact with the latest developments of a changing world—a type of old-fashioned womanhood well known and admired by Cicero.

The cooks furnish low comic relief in this very serious play but are also necessary in the machinery of the plot. Significantly emphatic are the repeated references to the notorious thievery of cooks, especially the slave's monologue devoted exclusively to this subject immediately before the re-entrance of Euclio (363-70). The distinctly lower atmosphere of these menials is subtly suggested also by a few indecent jests.

So Euclio is brought to the fatal mistake of removing his hoarded gold and burying it elsewhere. Megadorus' genial threat to make him drunk merely adds to his uneasiness, though he has been pleased with Megadorus' disgust of rich wives and their extravagance.

The action which leads the slave of Lyconides to steal Euclio's treasure is well motivated; but the technique of eavesdropping is awkward in the extreme, for misers, however old or fond of talking to themselves, are careful not to talk of their treasures aloud. To present their thoughts in soliloquies may be permissible, but to have another discover the secret by overhearing such a soliloquy violates all probability.

The best scene of the play, perhaps, is that in which Lyconides confesses one sin but Euclio thinks that he is confessing another. The ambiguity here is more easily maintained in Latin or French than in English. Highly amusing, too, is the later effort of Lyconides' slave to withdraw his confession of having stolen the treasure.

Doubtless little of importance has been lost at the end except Euclio's final speech of reformation.

Two Bacchides (Bacchides)

. . . The **Two Bacchides,** somewhat like the *Self-Tormentor* of Terence, opens as a splendid Menandrean comedy of character but soon hastens off into the usual stereotyped play of intrigue. Noteworthy is the rapid shift in the fortunes of the various individuals. Mnesilochus now has an abundance of money, now none, and soon an abundance again. The fortunes of his father change even more rapidly and, of course, end at a humiliatingly low level.

An undetermined number of verses have been lost from the opening, but the play is essentially intact.

SOURCE.—The source of Plautus' play is revealed by verses 816-17, which translate one of Menander's most famous lines, "Whom the gods love dies young." Menander's play was called the *Double Deceiver (Dis Exapaton)*. From the title it is obvious that Menander's play also centered about the intrigue to secure money. Some modern scholars, however, have insisted that Plautus has added one deception—the second letter. Chrysalus does cite three deceptions (953-78). That later Nicobulus (1090) and one of the sisters (1128) count only two has been taken to indicate that Plautus here reverts to the original text of Menander. But it is ridiculous for modern scholars to assume that Plautus could become confused on such a simple score. The inconsistency is only apparent. Indeed, Bacchis clearly says that Nicobulus has been "trimmed" twice; and this certainly, as presumably the earlier phrase of Nicobulus and the Greek title, can only refer to actual financial losses. In short, there is no evidence that Plautus has changed the plot, though we can feel certain that he has greatly elaborated the simple meters of the original.

INFLUENCE.—More important than the few adaptations in modern times has been the influence of certain of the play's many types of characters, especially the strait-laced pedagogue and the deceiving servant. Chrysalus' wild tale of the sloop (279-305) eventually, perhaps, turns up in Molière's *Les Fourberies de Scapin* (1671; II, xi) after appearing in various intermediary plays, including Cyrano de Bergerac's *Le Pédant Joué* (possibly 1654).

DISCUSSION.—The **Two Bacchides** exhibits an embryonic double plot, for it contains two young men and their difficulties in love. The best of the play is doubtless found in the opening scenes between the naïvely innocent Pistoclerus and the more than competent Bacchis. Both are delightfully characterized, and Bacchis shows great skill in ensnaring him as she and her sister are later to ensnare the fathers of both young men. Very amusing is the reaction of Pistoclerus' pedagogue, Lydus, who cannot realize that his ward is no longer a child and whose moral code, in comparison with that of his masters, is ridiculously high.

From the first, Pistoclerus has been acting as the agent of Mnesilochus, and with the return of this second young man, the need of money to save his love from the soldier becomes the chief concern of the action. Pistoclerus practically disappears after he has caused the minor complication of Mnesilochus' returning all the money brought from Ephesus to his father. Part of this money must now be recovered through the usual type of intrigue engineered by the usual clever slave. The victim is forewarned repeatedly, as in the **Pseudolus,** and yet repeatedly deceived. As in the **Pseudolus,** also, return of part of the money is promised to the victim at the end of the play. The intrigue itself and especially the elaborate comparison which Chrysalus draws between himself and Ulysses are clever and amusing, though of course the whole depends upon the mechanically pat entrance of the soldier. As a comic character, however, Chrysalus falls far below the level of the colorful Pseudolus.

In general the portrayal of characters is masterly. But contrast of characters, except for the indirect contrast between the strait-laced Lydus and the unscrupulous Chrysalus, is not here employed as effectively as in the *Brothers* of Terence and in other Menandrean plays. This shortcoming is all the more striking because the cast includes two young men, two old men, and two courtesans.

The final scene wherein the sister courtesans take in the old men has often been criticized on moral grounds. Though amusing, it is undeniably crude. Satire is often so. There is not the slightest ground, however, for thinking that either crudity or satire is not Menandrean. The Greeks saw life whole and honestly recorded what they saw.

Captives

The **Captives** is a quiet comedy of delightful humor and somewhat melodramatic pathos. Lessing considered it the finest comedy ever produced because, in his opinion, it best fulfills the purpose of comedy and because it is richly endowed with other good qualities. The opinion of Lessing, however, was attacked in his own day, and the merit of the **Captives** is still a matter of debate and violent disagreement. This arises in part from differences of opinion concerning the purpose of comedy and from attempts to compare incomparables.

Various types of comedy naturally have various appeals, and the *Captives* is admittedly lacking in the robust gaiety and occasional frank indecencies of the *Pseudolus* as it is lacking also in the verve and activity and romance of the *Rope*. It is nevertheless a very successful play.

Nothing is known concerning the Greek original.

INFLUENCE.—Among comedies indebted to the *Captives* may be mentioned the following: Ariosto's *I Suppositi* (about 1502, adapted into English by George Gascoigne [1566]), Ben Jonson's *The Case Is Altered* (about 1598, combining the *Captives* and the *Pot of Gold*), and Rotrou's *Les Captifs* (1638).

SIGNIFICANT NAMES.—The significance of the name Ergasilus ("working for a living," but here, as elsewhere, with the connotation of "courtesan") is explained by the parasite himself in his opening lines. The name Hegio ("leading citizen") obviously suggests a gentleman. The names Philocrates ("lover of mastery"), Aristophontes ("best-slayer"), and Philopolemus ("lover of war") all suggest mighty warriors, and there is more than a shade of irony in the fact that all these men have been captured in war. Stalagmus ("drop") is a derisive name applied to a slave of diminutive stature. The name Tyndarus is apparently taken from the legendary Tyndareos, father of Helen, and is obviously a slave's name.

STRUCTURE.—The *Captives,* like most of the plays of Plautus was probably presented without intermission or interlude; but the traditional "acts," which date from the Renaissance, here divide the play into well-defined chapters of action. It is not unlikely, therefore, that these divisions are the same as those of the original Greek play, which probably had five sections marked off by four choral interludes.

The first section (126 lines) is designed to put the audience into a pleasant mood, characterize Hegio, and repeat the essential facts of the exposition (for the play is a unit practically independent of the prologue). The second section (266 lines) again explains the confusion of identity and successfully launches the intrigue by which Hegio is made to send away the gentleman, Philocrates, rather than the servant, Tyndarus. The third section (307 lines) presents Hegio's discovery of the ruse and the downfall of Tyndarus. The fourth (154 lines) announces the return of Hegio's captive son and is mainly concerned with the foolery of the parasite Ergasilus. The fifth (107 lines) contains the actual arrival of Philocrates, Philopolemus, and the wicked slave Stalagmus. Most important of all, Tyndarus is here recognized as the long-lost son of Hegio.

DISCUSSION.—An intrigue by which two enslaved captives cheat their purchaser furnishes subject matter

refreshingly different from that of most later Greek comedies. But the *Captives* still has many conventional features. The parasite is the usual stereotyped character, and to eliminate him would be to sacrifice the most amusing character of the play. Stock incidents, too, are found in the confusion of identities and in the use of intrigue and recognition. The appearance of Stalagmus, also, is too happy a coincidence for serious drama. No proper explanation is given for his return, although some preparation for this and for the recognition is made by Hegio's account of his earlier loss of a son (760). Nor is it true, as the speaker of the prologue alleges, that the play contains no indecent lines, although moral purity has contributed more than its share to the popularity of this play in modern times. In order to be fair to the poet, however, we must admit that even the conventional features are handled with unusual skill and freshness. The indecent jests are few and are employed almost exclusively to emphasize Ergasilus' irrepressible exuberance when he is bringing the good news to Hegio (867, 888). The confusion of identities is here entirely credible—although this has been disputed—and bears no resemblance to the implausibly maintained confusion in the *Twin Menaechmi*. The actors may well commend this play, therefore, for its effort to break away from the stereotyped characters and the stock incidents of New Comedy.

Unique in New Comedy is the appearance of two actors along with the speaker of the prologue in order that the audience may understand the true identity of Philocrates and Tyndarus beyond all doubt. The prologue also reveals that Tyndarus is the son of Hegio, although Tyndarus and Philocrates do not know this during the subsequent scenes. This inconsistency should hardly be considered a fault, for it is here assumed that the play has not yet begun.

Although most of the information given in the prologue is as usual repeated in the following scenes, a prologue was absolutely essential in this play, for without the knowledge that Tyndarus is Hegio's son the audience would fail to appreciate much of the dramatic irony which pervades the whole action and constitutes perhaps the chief virtue of the play.

Dramatic irony and suspense tend to be mutually exclusive, since the one often depends upon the superior knowledge of the audience and the other upon its ignorance; yet the *Captives* combines both to a remarkable extent and with unusual subtlety. The suspense concerns the return of Philocrates, of course, and it is built up primarily by means of the irony of Philocrates' lines and the earnest anxiety of Tyndarus in their scene of farewell.

The dramatic irony of the play begins when Hegio first addresses his two captives. Philocrates plays the role of the confidential slave with consummate skill especially in his assured self-reliance and in his impudent boldness, whereas Tyndarus assumes the modest restraint of a gentleman. Many of these speeches obviously have one meaning for Hegio but another, truer, meaning for the captives and the audience. This humorous irony is very materially aided in Latin by the usual omission of articles and pronouns. Thus when Tyndarus, posing as the gentleman, speaks of sending the "slave" Philocrates *"ad patrem,"* the reference is amusingly ambiguous.

The dramatic irony reaches its greatest height, however, in the scene of farewell. When the supposed master recites at great length the virtues of the slave, he is really praising himself; and when the supposed slave recites the virtues of the master, he, too, is really praising himself. But the poor naïve Hegio is so taken in by the deception that he is greatly impressed with what he thinks to be the sincere mutual praise of master and slave (418-21). The effect here is primarily comic; but there is real pathos in the true Tyndarus' fear of being abandoned, a fear which Hegio cannot understand but which the audience fully appreciates. The high point of this aspect of the dramatic irony comes when the "slave" who is being sent home gives an oath to Hegio and to his former "master" that he will never be false to Philocrates. Such an oath reassures Hegio, but it can only disquiet the true Tyndarus.

The most serious and pathetic irony in these scenes, however, is contained in those speeches in which the truth can be appreciated only by the audience. The true Tyndarus in his first conversation with Hegio, for instance, says that he was formerly just as much a free man as Hegio's own son and that his father misses him just as much as Hegio misses his own son. Whereas Tyndarus here intends to lie and Hegio thinks that Tyndarus is Philocrates and is telling the truth, the audience know that Tyndarus is really saying what is true because he is the son of Hegio.

Another scene of pathetic irony is that in which Hegio undertakes to punish Tyndarus, really his own son. When Tyndarus boldly insists that his action has been commendable and proper, Hegio himself is forced to admit that he would have been very grateful indeed if a slave had performed such an action for a son of his. This is precisely what Tyndarus has done, for by securing the release of Philocrates he has really made possible the return of his own brother, the captured son of Hegio.

Indirectly, of course, Tyndarus has also made his own recognition possible. Yet Hegio thinks that this action of Tyndarus has made him lose his second and last son. Although this scene is not without its touches of humor, the tone is on the whole very serious, and the solemn simplicity of the iambic meter here, as Lindsay

points out, is reminiscent of tragedy and offers a very strong contrast with the bustling comedy of the preceding scene.

Hegio is not the stupid old man characteristic of comedy, although his figure has its amusing aspects; nor is he the stereotyped kindly old gentleman. He is thoroughly an individual. Before his entrance he is described briefly by Ergasilus as a man of the old school whose present business of trading in captives is most alien to his character. Thus we are prepared for Hegio's being taken in by the clever ruse of the captives. Undeniably amusing is his meticulous but naïve and wholly ineffectual caution in handling the captives. This caution is brought out both in his directions to the Guard and in his first conversation with the "slave" Philocrates. Amusing also is the manner in which Tyndarus and Philocrates talk to each other in their scene of farewell with an irony which wholly deceives the old man.

Sudden changes in the emotional tone of the play are emphasized by the figure of Ergasilus. Besides enlivening this unusually serious play with the usual low comedy, Ergasilus serves as an emotional foil for Hegio. At the beginning of the play both Hegio and Ergasilus are worried and not too optimistic. But as the play progresses and arrangements are made for sending the "slave" to Elis, Hegio becomes elated at the prospect of securing the return of his captured son. Just at this point, Ergasilus appears and, in strong contrast to Hegio's elation, pours forth his woeful tale of hopeless failure to discover a patron in the forum or even to raise a laugh. He would gladly dig the eyes out of this day that has made him so hateful to everyone. Immediately after this depressing monologue and the exit of Ergasilus, Hegio reappears in a state of elation greater than before, relating how he has been congratulated by everyone for successfully arranging the return of his son. The irony of his situation again presents the old man in a somewhat humorous light.

After the deception of the captives has been discovered, Hegio himself falls into a dreadfully depressed state and presents a figure of almost tragic pathos. But Ergasilus now appears in a state of ecstatic elation over the good news which he has for Hegio. The day which before was so hateful to him he now recognizes as his greatest benefactor. Ergasilus has time for only a few lines, however, before Hegio reappears. In a brief song, very different in tone from his earlier song of self-congratulation, Hegio now bitterly complains of his disappointment and chagrin, anticipating the scorn of everyone when they learn of the way in which he has been taken in. Here the irony of Hegio's depressed state fuses the pathos and the humor of his figure to make him the most appealing character of the play. A final brief song by Hegio, in the same meter, opens the last section of the play and expresses Hegio's solemn gratitude for the return of his captive son.

Tyndarus and Philocrates, like Hegio, are entirely admirable characters, and their virtues are fittingly rewarded as we should expect in a comedy. Still, they do not become saccharine in their goodness. Tyndarus is more than willing, for instance, to see Stalagmus punished. Sentimentality, which might have run rampant in the final scene, has been avoided by maintaining the usual classic restraint and honesty.

Casina

Like much of Aristophanes, this spirited musical farce is grossly indecent and irresistibly amusing. Its popularity is well-attested in the prologue, part of which, at least, was written for a reproduction some time after Plautus' death. The text in the broad scenes near the end of the play is only partially preserved. The play as a whole is the most lyric of Plautus' comedies, and many a delightfully extravagant line of the original falls very flat in translation.

The *Casina* has had some unimportant modern adaptations, but the resemblance of its plot to the *Mariage de Figaro* of Beaumarchais is thought to be fortuitous.

The original Greek version of this play, like that of the *Rope,* was written by Diphilus, who called his comedy the *Lot-Drawers (Kleroumenoi).* Modern scholars often assume that Plautus has revamped the whole play and introduced much of its grossness. Diphilus, however, was distinguished among the poets of New Comedy for his frankness, and it is not easy to imagine how this material could be handled very differently from the way in which Plautus has handled it. It is obvious from Diphilus' title that his play too centered about a contest, and it is likely that this contest was the rivalry of two slaves, reflecting, as in Plautus, the rivalry of father and son. Certainly if the father was involved, the subject was a scandalous one and fitted only for broad farce.

If Plautus is responsible for the suppression of the nauseatingly frequent motive of recognition, he is to be heartily congratulated; but there is no trustworthy evidence on this point. Certainly the play is skillfully constructed, and the tone is consistent throughout. Quite in keeping with this tone is the burlesque of tragedy when Pardalisca first comes rushing upon the stage in pretended mortal terror (621). Similar is Palaestra's song of more genuine terror in the *Rope* (664). But to discuss at length a play which makes its simple point—uproarious laughter—so obviously and so adequately would be mere pedantry.

. . . . .

Epidicus

The *Epidicus* is another play of intrigue and recognition. Though not as gay and spirited as the *Pseudolus,* it is interesting from several points of view. The intrigue is extraordinarily complicated, although the action as a whole, lacking any elaboration of the love affair or of the involved past of Periphanes, is too slight. This play and the *Curculio* are the shortest ancient comedies.

The crafty slave Epidicus, who dominates the action from the beginning to the end, has played an important role in the formation of modern counterparts such as Scapin, Scaramouche, and Figaro.

The plot begins as the usual one of a young man in love and desperately needing money to secure his sweetheart. The situation here, however, is somewhat complicated; for Epidicus has previously secured a slave girl, Acropolistis, of whom the young Stratippocles has until recently been enamored. This girl is already within the house at the opening of the play, and the father is convinced that she is his natural daughter. But now Stratippocles returns from the wars with his newer sweetheart, who is hardly his own until he pays the banker her purchase price. The stress placed upon the virtue of this second girl foreshadows her recognition, but we may well be astounded when by this recognition the girl turns out to be Stratippocles' half-sister. Nowhere in New Comedy, perhaps, is there a more startling surprise. This has been made possible by the absence of an omniscient prologue and—even more strikingly—by the failure to elaborate the story of Periphanes' illegitimate daughter, references to whom are enigmatically brief, though the matter is subtly maintained before the minds of the audience by Periphanes' references to his past indiscretions (382-92, 431-32).

Many scholars think that Plautus is responsible for the omission of a prologue. If so, it would seem that he is deliberately striving for suspense and surprise and is thus anticipating the regular practice of Terence. Similar to Terentian technique also is the excellent scene of dramatic exposition and the employment of a protatic character to facilitate it. But the original existence of a prologue is at least doubtful. Though it is customary to inform the audience in plays where recognition occurs, the *Epidicus* gives no opportunity for effective dramatic irony on this score. It should be noted also that the whole emphasis of the piece is upon the machinations of Epidicus and not upon the love of Stratippocles. Indeed it is obvious that this infatuation is only a few days old. Its frustration in the end, therefore, is a matter of little consequence, especially since his former sweetheart, as Epidicus himself points out (653), has already been secured for him.

The play has been criticized, also, for the nature of its ending, which leaves various incidental matters unsettled. But perhaps the playwright is superior to his critics here again; for Epidicus must remain the center of attention, and his affairs certainly are beautifully concluded in the amusing final scene. He is saved by a highly improbable coincidence—Stratippocles' buying his own sister—but this, of course, is typical of New Comedy.

The comic ironies are noteworthy. Epidicus feigns great modesty before the old men, and they praise the cleverness of his scheme. With less truth but with equal comic effectiveness Epidicus praises the shrewdness of Apoecides. Epidicus convinces the old men that he has bought the flute player, who is actually only hired; he also convinces them that the girl herself has been deceived into thinking she is only hired. Thus, when the ruse is discovered, the girl proves to be hired as she has claimed to be from the start. This phase of the humor reaches its high point when Apoecides says that he too pretended that the girl was only hired and assumed an expression of dullness and stupidity. Then he proceeds to illustrate this expression for Periphanes and the audience; in production, we can be sure, his actor did not make the slightest change in his expression to illustrate dullness and stupidity on the face of Apoecides (420).

Twin Menaechmi (Menaechmi)

This skillfully constructed farce is very spirited and amusing. It has fared unusually well at the hands of English translators, furthermore, and it is said to be the Latin comedy most frequently reproduced in American schools and colleges.

Nothing is known of the Greek original, although Athenaeus, an ancient scholar who had read more than eight hundred plays of Middle Comedy alone and whose interest was centered in cooks and foods, says that slave cooks can be found only in the plays of Poseidippus. Cylindrus in this play, of course, is a household slave. Except for the elaboration of monologues into cantica, the Latin version presumably follows the Greek original.

SIGNIFICANT NAMES.—Especially noteworthy among the names used in the play is that of the parasite, whose Latin name, Peniculus, means "Sponge," perhaps the most apt name for a parasite that occurs in Plautus. Erotium, "Lovey," is an effective but not uncommon name for a courtesan, and her cook is well-named Cylindrus, "Roller."

INFLUENCE.—Along with the *Amphitryon,* the *Pot of Gold,* and the *Braggart Warrior,* the *Twin Menaechmi* has been one of the most influential plays of Plautus. Various adaptations have appeared, including those of Trissino (1547, *Simillimi*), Rotrou (1636), Regnard (1705), and Goldoni (*I Due Gemelli Veneziani*). But Shakespeare's adaptation (1594 or earlier), of course, is by far the most famous.

The Comedy of Errors takes certain motives from the *Amphitryon,* especially the twin slaves and the exclusion of Antipholus from his own house while his twin is inside; but it is primarily an elaboration of the *Twin Menaechmi.* Here we may observe Shakespeare at work and may analyze that fusion of the classical and romantic traditions which characterized Elizabethan drama. From the romantic come its abundance of incident and its utter disregard of plausibility, its plethora of youthful emotional appeal, its insistence upon a romantic love affair, its melodramatic suspense, its vacillation between the comic and the tragic—both sentimentalized—and its grand finale where almost everyone shares in the general happiness. From the classic tradition come its elaborate plot, its observation of the essential unities, and its fundamentally realistic dramatic outlook.

DISCUSSION.—Basically the plot of the *Twin Menaechmi* is one of recognition. A great deal of complication, however, is built up about the somewhat involved personal relations of the Epidamnian Menaechmus. The similarity of the appearance of the twins naturally leads to a comedy of errors. This was a favorite motive, and no less than eight Greek comedies are known to have been given the title or subtitle "Twins." Indeed this motive plays an important role in several other comedies of Plautus himself, including the *Amphitryon,* the *Two Bacchides,* and the *Braggart Warrior.*

In a comedy of errors, the ancient playwright thinks it essential to explain the real situation very carefully beforehand to the audience, and the *Twin Menaechmi* opens with a long omniscient prologue. This is followed by another long monologue when Sponge enters. Two such speeches make for a slow opening. But with the amusing song of the Epidamnian Menaechmus the play assumes that rapid pace which is necessary for successful farce.

The scene between this sporty gentleman and Erotium finishes in the details of the setting and with the theft of the wife's mantle initiates the dramatic action. As gentleman, parasite, and courtesan withdraw, the Syracusan Menaechmus, accompanied by his slave Messenio, steps into the situation which has been nicely elaborated for them.

The weary Messenio warns his master that here in Epidamnus the world finds its greatest voluptuaries and drinkers; it is full of sycophants and flattering parasites; the courtesans are the most seductive on earth, and the city is so named because almost no one stops here without his purse's suffering damnation. The amusing reaction of his master is to demand the purse in order to avoid at least one risk in Epidamnus! The cook Cylindrus immediately appears and seems to prove the accuracy of Messenio's description beyond all question. Indeed, Messenio is taken in by his own cleverness, as we should expect in a comedy of errors; and, instead of realizing at once that his master is being mistaken for his lost twin brother, Messenio feels certain that they are being attacked by the pirate courtesans of this Barbary coast. His worst fears seem quite justified when the seductive Erotium appears. Thus the dramatist creates a very amusing situation while he is furnishing some plausibility for the long continuation of the comedy of errors.

There now follows a series of scenes wherein one person after another mistakes the Syracusan for the Epidamnian. After Cylindrus and Erotium comes Sponge, and then a servant of Erotium. In these episodes the twins are shown to resemble each other as closely in their dishonesty as in their appearance. The Syracusan is also mistaken by the wife of the Epidamnian Menaechmus and finally by the father-in-law as well. All the complications which these errors involve are skillfully manipulated. Especially noteworthy is the way in which the parasite, usually an unessential figure, is worked into the mechanism of the plot to become the link between the double lives which the Epidamnian Menaechmus is living.

The best of the episodes of error, however, is that with the physician. Of all the galaxy of comic characters none perhaps surpasses the medical quack in age. He is listed in accounts of early Greek improvisations. Though this passage is the only one in Roman comedy where he has survived, he must have been a stock figure. His most striking characteristics in any age are here well brought out—his technical jargon, his endless number of impertinent questions, his extravagant claims, and of course his utterly incorrect diagnosis. Characteristic too of quack or expert in all ages is his prescription of the most expensive treatment possible.

Only near the end of the play does Messenio meet the Epidamnian Menaechmus and mistake him for his master. This error quickly leads to the climax, where no one except the slave, apparently, has enough sense to bring about the solution. If the gentlemen had been given more, the play could not have continued so long!

Very different is the ending of Plautus from that of Shakespeare. Far from arranging a reconciliation between the Epidamnian Menaechmus and his wife—to say nothing of Sponge—the cold cynicism of the author remains to the last lines, where along with the other chattel to be offered at auction is included the wife—if anyone is so foolish as to wish to buy her.

. . . . .

Braggart Warrior (Miles Gloriosus)

The **Braggart Warrior,** usually assumed to be one of the earliest extant plays of Plautus, is interesting for several reasons. Of all ancient comedies it presents the most complete portrait of the immortal braggart soldier, and it has therefore been very influential. The two plots of the play, also, are immortal. Its characters are vividly drawn, and the final scenes are uproariously funny. But the whole play is very crude farce, and the deception of Sceledrus in the opening sections has little to do with the later entrapment of the soldier.

SIGNIFICANT NAMES.—Pyrgopolinices is an elaborate Greek compound meaning "victor of fortresses and cities." The name Artotrogus signifies "bread-chewer," Acroteleutium "tip-top," Philocomasium "fond of drinking bouts," Sceledrus "dirt," and Palaestrio "wrestler," or "trickster."

SOURCE.—The title of the Greek play is given in the internal prologue, the *Braggart* (*Alazon*); but nothing is known of the Greek author. Most scholars assume that two plays have here been combined by Plautus; and this may well be so, but any Greek dramatist who would stoop to the crudity of such farce might also fail to appreciate the niceties of plot construction.

The literary motive of the secret passageway is very old. In an age when lack of transportation and the need of protection necessitated extreme conservation of space within cities, common walls between houses were the rule, and secret passageways must not have been such very rare exceptions.

The second plot also is a very ancient one. A man, usually husband or lover, is persuaded to send away a girl with another man and even to give them gifts or the means of escape. The deception is threatened by various complications in its final stages; but all comes out well, and pursuit or revenge is prevented by some device. This plot is used by Euripides in the *Iphigenia in Tauris* and especially in the *Helen*. The scene of departure in the *Helen* is notably similar to that in the **Braggart Warrior;** comic irony plays a major role in both. Palaestrio's grief in this comedy, furthermore, shows more than a tinge of Oriental deception, resembling the grief of an Egyptian prince taking leave of Caesar during his Alexandrine campaign.

The motive of the secret passageway is found combined with this second plot of deception not only in Plautus. In a fascinating Albanian tale, a priest is duped into marrying his own pretty wife to a merchant next door. At the ensuing wedding banquet, the priest is made drunk, his beard is shaved off, and he is disguised as a robber and left by the side of the road. When he awakes in the morning he actually joins a band of robbers. But here, although the secret passageway is used precisely as in Plautus, the person deceived by it is the main character, and the two plots are closely and effectively joined.

INFLUENCE.—The professional soldier of fortune was a very common figure on the streets of Athens during the period of New Comedy, and nowhere was he more popular than on the comic stage. This is evidenced by many plays of New Comedy, including Menander's *Shearing of Glycera* (*Perikeiromene*), Terence's *Eunuch,* and various other plays of Plautus, especially the **Two Bacchides,** the **Carthaginian,** and the **Truculentus**. This type is exploited in innumerable modern plays and finally results in such masterpieces as Falstaff. Indeed, Pyrgopolinices' boast that his children live for a thousand years (1079), as has been pointed out, is a gross understatement.

Many comedies have been directly influenced by the **Braggart Warrior**. Among the most notable may be mentioned Nicholas Udall's *Ralph Roister Doister* (before 1553; indebted also to the *Eumuch* of Terence), Dolce's *Il Capitano* (published 1560), Baïf's *Le Brave* (1567), Mareschal's *Le Capitan Fanfaron* (published 1640), and Holberg's *Jacob von Tyboe*.

DISCUSSION.—The **Braggart Warrior** is very clumsily constructed, for only a feeble effort has been made to connect its two actions. The soldier, the main character of the second action, is well characterized and his propensity for the fairer sex is given significant emphasis at the opening of the play. Thus the minor plot, which follows immediately, is suspended within the major. Several incidental references are made to the twin sister, an important element of the first action, during the latter part of the play. Sceledrus, too, is there mentioned and may reappear at the very end. Both actions, furthermore, are engineered by Palaestrio, and both are crude and farcical. But the first makes no real contribution to the second. The long episode with the genial old Periplectomenus has little to do with either. Incidentally annoying are the innumerable asides used to elaborate obvious jests. At times Palaestrio's handling of the soldier, however, shows real cleverness.

Haunted House (Mostellaria)

Like the **Three Bob Day** (**Trinummus**), the **Haunted House** begins with a series of excellent scenes presenting situation and characters but soon hastens off into the most obvious farce. Here, however, the farce is as good as farce can be.

The Greek original seems to have been entitled the *Ghost* (*Phasma*). Records of three such comedies have been preserved, and it is usually assumed that the original of this play was the one written by Philemon. This assumption, even though no sound evidence for it exists, is attractive because of the play's structural similarity to the **Three Bob Day,** which was certainly written by Philemon. The tendency of high comedy to degenerate into farce, however, is observable in other plays such as the **Two Bacchides**.

The **Haunted House** has been very influential. Among adaptations may be mentioned Thomas Heywood's *The English Traveller* (printed 1633), Regnard's *Le Retour Imprévu* (1700) and its adaptation by Fielding, *The Intriguing Chambermaid* (1733), and Holberg's *Huus-Spögelse* or *Abracadabra*. The names Tranio and Grumio, furthermore, are used for servants in *The Taming of the Shrew,* in which perhaps certain motives also are taken from Plautus.

The **Haunted House** has very little plot. A young Athenian gentleman, Philolaches, has been living a gay life in the absence of his father. Upon the father's unexpected return, Philolaches is surprised in a very embarrassing daytime carousal. The clever slave Tranio, therefore, undertakes to prevent the father from entering the house until the members of the party have sobered and dispersed. Constantly threatened with exposure, Tranio constantly becomes involved in more and more elaborate deceptions. Finally, after his ruses are all discovered, he is rescued by the boon companion of Philolaches, who smoothes things over with the ease of a *deus ex machina*. All the activity of Tranio, of course, has really been much ado about nothing, for at best he could hope to deceive the old man for only a few hours. The initial pretext, however, is not implausible at first glance, and the rapidity of the action allows us no time for cogitation.

Although the whole play is amusing, the opening scenes are by far the best. Their primary function, of course, is to create the atmosphere of gay living. Various characters also are brilliantly presented here. But both creation of atmosphere and portrayal of character are carried far beyond the length justified by their importance in the main action. Obviously the dramatist intends these scenes to be enjoyed for their intrinsic charm.

In all New Comedy, no better scene of exposition is found than that of Grumio and Tranio. Not only is the situation most vividly presented but an effective warning of a day of reckoning is sounded, and the brazen Tranio is thoroughly individualized by contrast with the honest Grumio. The one fault of the scene is that Grumio, who is characterized even more interestingly than Tranio, does not reappear in the play.

The scenes presenting Philolaches and his companions also are delightful. The humor of Philolaches' remarks as he watches his love Philematium ("Little Kiss") complete her toilet and the masterly portrait of this delightfully naïve girl more than justify the theatrical awkwardness of the staging. The carousal too is skillfully presented. The drunken man, of course, is almost infallible low comedy; but Callidamates, with all the seriousness and moral callousness of inebriation, plays the role so entertainingly that we forget the triteness of the motive. Indeed this whole group of characters is so interesting that we, somewhat like Philolaches, may well regret the return of father Theopropides; for he is merely the stereotyped old man of comedy, conservative to—and beyond—the point of stupidity, so cautious where there is no need of caution and elsewhere so rash. He forms the perfect dupe for the wily Tranio, and these two monopolize the stage for the remainder of the play.

Persian (Persa)

The **Persian** is a thin but amusing little farce of "high life below stairs." It is unique, however, in certain respects. The original Greek play is thought by some scholars to have been written before the conquests of Alexander (line 506, very doubtful evidence) and therefore to have belonged to Middle Comedy. A free girl who is a virgin takes an active role in the play; and the whole seems more closely to approach comic opera than any other play of Plautus.

The simple plot concerns the intrigue of a slave, Toxilus, who in the absence of his master is living the life of a king (31), which of course includes being in love with a strumpet and keeping a parasite. Toxilus, like any young gentleman, wishes to free his sweetheart. With the aid of a friend and of the parasite's daughter he succeeds in doing so and in thoroughly humiliating the slave dealer. Perhaps it is unfortunate that this material has not been more effectively employed as a burlesque of the life of Athenian gilded youth.

The comic opera elements are many, of which lyricism is the first and most important. External formalism also is noteworthy. The first lines between Toxilus and Sagaristio constitute the only certain case of metrical responsion in Plautus. Balanced speeches are the rule throughout this first scene and frequently occur elsewhere in the play, especially in the scene of pert repartee between Sophoclidisca and Paegnium. The very admission of such a scene is suggestive of comic opera, for it is obviously inserted merely for its quaint buffoonery. Below the ordinary level of New Comedy, furthermore, is much of the stage action, especially the "planting" of the girl and Sagaristio to come in just at the right moment, and later the similar "planting" of Saturio. The extravagant implausibility of the intrigue, the use of disguises, and the way in which the intrigue is made a mere joke in the final scene—these, too, are proper to comic opera or burlesque. The saucy Paegnium ("play-thing"), though far from the harmless innocent of the modern stage, belongs to this same sphere. Perhaps the daughter of the parasite might here be included. The reversal of nature by which daughter lectures father on honesty and reputation is ridiculously incongruous with the girl's lowly position in life, as with her unenviable role in the intrigue—incongruous, indeed, with the whole atmosphere of this comedy of low life. Last of all may be mentioned

the exotic costumes and the carefully identified dances in the very gay final scene. While some of these features may well be due to Plautine originality, they would not be unnatural developments of the lyricism and extravagance of Old Comedy. Certainly the Persian's four-line name (702-5) and the drunken revel (*komos*) of the final scene are reminiscent of Aristophanes.

. . . . .

Rope (Rudens)

The **Rope** more nearly approaches the spirit of romantic comedy than any other ancient play. It contains more important characters and more dramatic action than almost any other, and it is among the longest (1,423 lines). It is noteworthy not only for its romantic atmosphere but also for its unsurpassed vivacity, its irrepressible and sometimes sardonic humor, its dramatic irony, and its melodramatic pulsation of emotions.

SOURCE AND INFLUENCE.—The god of the prologue intimates that the author of the Greek original was Diphilus, but the name of that play is not given. It has been argued that Plautus made many important alterations in the play, but these arguments seem unconvincing.

Among adaptations, which have not been numerous, may be mentioned Thomas Heywood's *The Captives* (1624).

DISCUSSION.—The **Rope** is primarily a play of discovery in which, somewhat as in Menander's *Arbitration,* a father unwittingly adjudicates the fate of his own lost daughter. Various exciting complications are furnished by the daughter's shipwreck, the quarrel between her lover and the slave dealer who is attempting to recover her, and the contest of the two slaves over the trunk. That honesty is the best policy is the obvious moral to be drawn from the action.

The locale of this comedy is as picturesque and striking as it is unusual: the desolate seashore near the North African city of Cyrene, an ancient Brighton or Deauville.

Since the play is to contain concealed identities and a recognition, the author has considered an omniscient prologue essential in order that the irony of the action may be fully appreciated. Perhaps such a prologue is also the simplest method of revealing the complicated exposition of the play—the soundest justification for the Euripidean prologue, which seems to have been used regularly by Diphilus. Not much of the coming action, however, is here foreshadowed in the prologue.

Very unusual is the scene in which Sceparnio pretends to look off and sight the shipwrecked men and the two girls in a lifeboat. Action that could not be presented "on stage" frequently occurs in tragedy, where it is usually described in a messenger's speech. In comedy, such action is rare, and the method of describing it here employed, though informal, is very effective.

As soon as the stage is cleared—the exit of Daemones is dramatically necessary but surely somewhat forced and implausible—Palaestra, like a tragic heroine, appears singing her monody of complaint against Heaven and her cruel fate. The pathos of this is more significant for the audience, since they know that she is actually standing very close to the house of her long-lost parents. After Ampelisca has entered with a few plaintive lines we have a charming duet with the tragic cretic meter beautifully adapted to the scene (esp. lines 235-37). Indeed, this whole episode is one of the most charming in Plautus. As poetry, however, it is hardly superior to the "chorus" of fishermen who appear soon afterward. Here we have a passage of real beauty such as is common in Aristophanes but rare in New Comedy and apparently unknown in Menander. This chorus is usually considered a vestige of the old comic chorus, and their introduction here is certainly very felicitous. With their reed poles and, doubtless, fishermen's hats, they add a delightful bit of local color—obviously an artistic addition rather than an interruption like the ordinary interlude chorus. Their quaint humor forms a winsomely comic relief for the tragic tone of the two girls in distress.

Lovers' dalliance on stage is rare in ancient comedy, but slaves are allowed more liberty of action in certain situations than ladies and gentlemen, and we find an amusing if somewhat risqué example of love-making in the scene between the slaves, Ampelisca and Sceparnio. We may assume that Ampelisca starts this flirtation by ogling Sceparnio and caressing her words in a manner most likely to win over a stranger from whom she wishes to ask a favor. Sceparnio, however, is won over even more effectively than she wished, and it is all the girl can do to keep the situation in hand. With the aid of feminine tact and deceit, however, she succeeds in gaining her request by mere promises. While Sceparnio is gone to fetch the water, she is put to flight by the approach of the slave dealer. When Sceparnio returns with his high hopes of an easy conquest, he presents a figure whose ridiculousness can hardly be appreciated without actually seeing him as he carries the jug and searches eagerly about the stage for the vanished girl. His fear now of being caught as a thief and, finally, his utter disgust at having done some real work for nothing form a very amusing contrast with his high spirits at the opening of the scene.

Various scenes of low comedy occur throughout the play which set off and relieve the more serious episodes. Amusing is the scene wherein the slave dealer

Labrax and his friend Charmides first emerge from their shipwreck. They come on stage with their garments drenched, shivering and, as the meter apparently indicates, chattering from cold. They curse their fortune and each other. They run the gamut of low comedy from miserable puns to vomiting.

The influence of melodramatic tragedy is evident in many scenes of the *Rope*, but most of all in the scene where the girls flee from the temple of Venus to the altar. Palaestra's monody here is remarkably similar to a fragmentary monody from a tragedy of Plautus' contemporary, Ennius, wherein a woman, Andromache, is seeking refuge. Both songs are in part written in cretic meter, characterized by elaborate alliteration and assonance, the use of synonyms and various artificialities of high style. The grouping about the altar, furthermore, is remarkably similar to that of a scene from an unknown tragedy represented on a Greek vase. The whole scene here, then, may be a parody of a definite tragedy.

The amusing Sceparnio does not appear in the second half of the play; but a counterpart for him is found in the fisherman, Gripus, the slave of Daemones, who is not mentioned in the prologue and of whom we hear nothing until Daemones comes on stage to deliver a short monologue and then returns into the house (892-905). Obviously this somewhat awkward speech is designed solely to introduce Gripus, who enters immediately after Daemones makes his exit. The emotions of Gripus, like those of Sceparnio, shift very rapidly: he enters in the greatest elation over his discovery of the wicker trunk, and in an amusing monody he daydreams aloud on becoming a millionaire, a tycoon in the world of trade, and on founding a city to commemorate his fame. The humorous irony of these lines may easily be overlooked in reading the play; but it could not be lost in the theater, for we may be sure that during his monody, as he walks slowly toward the center of the stage, his spying adversary, Trachalio, is already on stage behind him.

One of the most delightful scenes of the play is the ensuing one between Gripus and Trachalio with their mock juristic arguments. It is easy to understand why Plautus chose to name the play after this scene and the tug of war of the two slaves over the trunk. Especially delightful is the naïve way in which the slaves, when their casuistry runs short, resort to barefaced lies and elaborate threats of violence which reveal that each is actually very much afraid of the other.

The scene in which both slaves appeal to Daemones is a continuation of this argument, in which Gripus is at least more consistent than Trachalio, who at one time renounces all personal claims (1077) and at another demands half of the booty (1123). The zeal of Gripus increases as the apparent justice of his case fades away, and he does not fail to anticipate every possible device of his opponents.

Comedies usually come to a close very shortly after the solution of the plot, but the **Rope** continues for some time after the main complication has been solved with Palaestra's restoration to her parents. Still, there are minor threads of the plot that must be neatly finished off. The play does not, therefore, appear to be unduly extended, especially since the final scenes are so gay and amusing; throughout this comedy, gaiety and amusement are more important than the progression of the plot.

The romantic pulsation of emotions, already noted in the earlier parts of the play, continues to the very end and is nicely emphasized by appropriate metrical variation. Trachalio and Daemones are in high spirits, Trachalio and Plesidippus in even higher spirits—especially Plesidippus, who is ecstatic over the good fortune of Palaestra and their coming marriage. These scenes, of course, are in the gay trochaic meter which was probably accompanied by music. But between these scenes with Trachalio, wherein the author runs riot in word play in a manner more characteristic of Aristophanes or Rabelais than of New Comedy, the ill-humored Gripus in prosaic iambics continues his haggling argument with his master over the ownership of the trunk. This ill-humor is even more amusing, of course, than the gaiety of the other characters.

The ironic humor, also, with an occasional thrust of real satire, is maintained to the last line, where the audience, if they will applaud loudly, are invited to a drinking party—all, that is, under sixteen years of age. Sixteen was the usual age for the assumption of a man's dress and status at Rome, and from this passage it has been concluded that minors were not allowed in the Roman theater.

. . . . .

Three Bob Day (Trinummus)

Lessing considered this play second only to the **Captives** among Plautus' comedies, but such a high rating seems hardly justified. There are certainly some excellent scenes of high comedy, especially in the first part of the play; but the climax falls off disappointingly into obvious farce.

The Greek original, as we are plainly told, was the *Treasure* of Philemon (*Thesauros*). Probably some monologues of the original have been elaborated into monodies, but otherwise perhaps few if any changes have been made.

No female role is found in the **Three Bob Day**. This feature, so entirely natural in a play like the **Captives**,

is here somewhat unfortunate from the modern point of view, in that this unusual plot seems ideally suited for intimate romantic comedy. Such development, however, was left for a Frenchman, Néricault Destouches, whose adaptation, *Le Trésor Caché,* brought to life the two girls that are to be married to the young men at the end of Plautus' play. Another adaptation, Lessing's *Der Schatz* (1750), is well-known.

DISCUSSION—Precisely to define the plot of the **Three Bob Day** is difficult, and this very fact marks the play out as extraordinary in New Comedy, where the plots are usually all too stereotyped. The main problem, however, concerns the honor of Lesbonicus, a young man who in the absence of his father has so dissipated his property that he finds himself greatly embarrassed over the prospect of his sister's being forced to marry without a dowry. The modern reader may easily underestimate the seriousness of this situation. According to the Athenian moral code, this young man's first duty in life was to look to the honor and decent marriage of his sister. For her to marry without a dowry and thus to sacrifice all social prestige naturally meant utter disgrace for him. A minor problem of the play is centered about the honor of Callicles, an old friend whom the father of Lesbonicus has charged with something of the family interests during his absence. Both these problems are excellent dramatic material.

After a quaint prelude which well strikes the moral tone of the play and also serves as a literary prologue, the play opens with a very delightful scene between Callicles and a friend, Megaronides, who has come to castigate him for his apparent breach of faith. Both are nicely characterized as old men by their jests on wives and marriage, their use of proverbs, and their complaints of the moral degeneration of the times. Their main function, of course, is to give the exposition; and this they succeed in doing in a most natural fashion. Megaronides is not, as we might expect, a protatic character but has been skillfully worked into the subsequent action. One fault, however, may be found with this scene: no immediate dramatic action or complication is suggested. The mention of Lesbonicus' sister has been too brief, and nothing has been said that might suggest her marrying in the near future.

When this episode is ended, Lysiteles, a young man of whom we have heard nothing, appears with a charming monody, the length of which, if nothing else, indicates the importance of the speaker. His problem is a serious one: to be or not to be—in love. Seeing only too clearly that love is a waster of property and a corrupter of good morals, this strange young man decides that he will not be. He wishes, as we later discover, to marry instead!

When Lysiteles has reached this very virtuous decision, his father, Philto, opportunely comes on, and the ensuing scene is even more delightful high comedy than that between Callicles and Megaronides. Philto lectures his son in a moral fashion that qualifies him to rank as an ancestor of Polonius. But Lysiteles is somewhat cleverer than Laertes. He actually encourages his father; indeed he anticipates Philto in reaching the extreme limit of virtue and suggests a definite virtuous action—marrying a girl without a dowry. Any translation of virtuous words into action would doubtless have been disconcerting enough for Philto; and this particular action carries virtue far beyond the limits which he had envisaged even in his most abstract cogitations. But the receptiveness and docility of Lysiteles have been so great that the father is now embarrassed to refuse. Never in New Comedy is a father thrown for a neater and less-expected fall than this. The whole scene is a masterpiece.

Philto agrees to his son's marrying the sister of Lesbonicus without a dowry. This initiates the dramatic action at last, and it also sets the stage for the entrance of Lesbonicus, whose efforts to trace down the rapid flight of his funds are very amusing. Philto, as if he had not learned his lesson, continues with philosophizing, and his subsequent interview with Lesbonicus nicely points up the dilemma of this young man. Indeed, Lesbonicus becomes so desperate that he actually longs for the return of his father! Stasimus, his impudent slave, furnishes the low comedy of the scene. This reduces the level of the play's humor somewhat, although, in his not very successful efforts to deceive Philto, Stasimus is made the butt rather than the author of the humor.

Lesbonicus has been unable to settle the problem of the dowry with Philto, and so goes off to find Lysiteles. Meanwhile Callicles reappears and makes known his intention of somehow providing for the dowry. Lesbonicus knows nothing of this, however, and he is still desperate when he returns with Lysiteles and they debate the matter at great length. This scene might be called the climax of the play, for here the complication reaches its point of highest tension.

The play now degenerates rapidly. Megaronides' plan to provide the dowry from the secret treasure of Charmides is too much the usual comic intrigue. With the timely arrival of Charmides, furthermore, the working out of this plan becomes obvious farce. The stage technique, also, especially the continual use of asides, is somewhat awkward.

The farce in these later sections of the play can hardly be said to strike an inharmonious note, for the tone of the play has been charmingly light throughout. But it seems unfortunate that the serious moral dilemma of the young men is not exploited in a more satisfactory manner. The solution adopted, of course, is purely external. Another fault of the play is its failure at an early point to focus upon a single character and to maintain him as the center of interest. Unfortunate also is the continual harping on the moral degeneration of the times. This theme, a commonplace in New Comedy, is put to real service where Philto is concerned, and possibly the play as a whole would have been more effective if it had been reserved for him alone.

Truculentus

The ***Truculentus*** is a remarkable but not an amusing play. Like the novel *Sapho* of Alphonse Daudet, it is written for the enlightenment of a young man on youth's eternal problem. Vice would flourish less, says Diniarchus in his "prologue" (57-63), if the experience of one generation could be passed on to the next. The play, then, is very serious. We might be tempted to call its outcome tragic. Certainly few tragedies are so depressing. But Aristotle (*Poetics*) says that the spectacle of the evil prospering is the most untragic of all. Phronesium is certainly evil, and she certainly prospers. An amazing detachment is maintained by the dramatist throughout, and he coldly refuses to display the slightest sympathy with his characters. Indeed, this play is one of the most remarkable pieces of stark realism in classical drama. Its ending is similar to that of the ***Two Bacchides*** and the *Eunuchus;* but those plays seem very light and gay compared to this.

The ***Truculentus*** has been somewhat neglected by modern scholars because the text tradition is deplorably bad—the worst of all the plays of Plautus, though there are no lengthy lacunae.

The author of the Greek original is unknown.

DISCUSSION.—The play has almost no plot. It is merely the spectacle of a very real Circe turning men into swine. Four men are chosen for purposes of illustration. They are all typical, and properly so, for the author wishes to include all mankind; but they are treated in a far from typical manner. The various episodes dealing with these four are adeptly interwoven, though there is no artificial complexity about the play. The young Athenian gentleman, Diniarchus, is the first to be taken up and the only one whose case history is given in some detail. He has long since been a lover of courtesan and of courtesan's maid alike and, now bankrupt, he still is their lover. After he has been introduced and retires into Phronesium's house, the truculent slave comes on. He is the most picturesque character of the play. From his first line he is most aptly characterized as a bumpkin. His metaphors are rustic, and he swears by the hoe. Such referential swearing, though common in Aristophanes, is not frequent in Roman comedy. He is also characterized by his quaint perversity in the use of language, something like Antipho's use of riddles in the ***Stichus***. Though this slave shows some signs of human frailty to the courtesan's maid, we naturally expect him to remain truculent throughout the play; and when he leaves the stage with the declaration that he will inform his old master of the young master's goings on, we anticipate the appearance of the old man. Such action would recall that of Lydus in the *Two Bacchides*.

Diniarchus now returns to the stage, and after the splendid fanfare of the early scenes, Phronesium makes her entrance and works her magic spell upon him. Much of this scene is concerned incidentally with the story of the soldier and the supposititious child, thus anticipating the appearance of the next victim and preparing for the discovery of the child's true identity. When Diniarchus has gone off to scrape up gifts, the stage is carefully set and the preparations perhaps include a seductive negligee. As the soldier enters he informs the audience by direct address not to expect the usual foolery of the braggart soldier from him; and indeed this soldier does not strut in the ordinary comic fashion, though a few mild jokes are admitted. The theme of Diniarchus is now fused with that of the soldier upon the entrance of the young gentleman's slaves bearing his gifts to Phronesium under the very eyes of the soldier. Nothing could better portray the soldier's enslavement; and after this scene has passed, we put little faith in his wrathful decision to remain aloof for a few days in order to bring Phronesium to her knees. At this point Strabax, the rustic young master of the truculent slave, comes on with money which he has purloined from his father for the woman whom he loves more than his mother (662). He is taken in with little ado, and immediately his slave reappears, no longer truculent and not with his old master, as we expected, but actually with his savings and a determination to take a fling at the type of life which is so attractive to his betters. Thus free and servile, weak and strong, all are here enslaved.

Diniarchus returns in the greatest elation over Phronesium's reception of his gifts and her invitation to rejoin her. The unexpected appearance of Strabax with far more money, however, has already changed Phronesium's situation and given her an actor for the role of the soldier's rival. So the maid keeps Diniarchus outside the house and regales him with a description of Strabax' enjoying the provisions which Diniarchus himself has lately furnished. Diniarchus is bitterly disillusioned. His futile protests before the house are interrupted by the episode with Callicles. No hint of Diniarchus' violation of Callicles' daughter has been given previously. But the dramatist here, as in the sudden change of the truculent slave, is not striving for surprise; he merely wishes to repress the minor phases of the play and maintain an effective unity. This incident with Callicles is designed merely to illustrate the utter ruin of Diniarchus. After he learns that his lack of restraint has cost him so dearly, he is still unable to

master his passions and to demand the child—discovered to be that of Callicles' daughter and himself—from Phronesium, who now comes on mildly intoxicated but still having far more self-mastery than her lovers, drunk or sober. With a view to securing her favors after his marriage, Diniarchus weakly allows her temporarily to retain the child in order to swindle the soldier. After this moral nihilism, the baseness of the soldier and Strabax in their final agreement to share Phronesium seems almost an anticlimax.

John Arthur Hanson (essay date 1965)

SOURCE: John Arthur Hanson, "The Glorious Military," in *Roman Drama*, Basic Books, Inc., 1965, pp. 51-86.

[*In the following essay, Hanson studies Plautus's use and development of the stock character the* miles gloriosus, *or braggart soldier, maintaining that this character was used by Plautus as a commentary on Roman military ideals of his time. Hanson goes on to survey the appearance of this character in the works of later dramatists, including William Shakespeare.*]

A stock character is a scholar's delight. He may be traced backward and forward in time, across national boundaries from writer to writer, engendering Quellenforschungen and appreciations of our debt to classical culture. With a figure as frequent as the *miles gloriosus,* the mere tabulation of his occurrences in Western literature might exhaust a learned lifetime. Such a catalogue would have to follow the intrepid soldier through Greek Comedy, Old, Middle, and New, across the Adriatic to Republican Roman Comedy and around the Mediterranean through various forms of prose fiction, then up through Italy in the Commedia dell' Arte and across the spread of the Renaissance stage in Europe; thence multifariously through each nation's dramatic and fictional literature to the present moment.[1]

The present essay will not attempt to review this military parade in detail, from Lamachus to Sergeant Bilko, although the mere names on the roll call have their entertainment value: Therapontigonus Platagidorus, Horribilicribrifax, Ralph Roister Doister, Matamore, Chateaufort, Parolles, Bobadill, Bluffe, Bloody Five. . . .

The presence of a literary ancestor for a fictional character is of course in some measure critically significant: in so far as the author and audience can also be presumed to be aware of the ancestry, it is a contributing factor to the understanding of the character in his own environment. Thus Evelyn Waugh can make use of the classical education of his readers and add a Plautine reminiscence to the already anachronistic self-glory of Apthorpe in *Men at Arms* by entitling a chapter 'Apthorpe Gloriosus'. Thus Plautus himself can make use of his hearers' expectations embodied in the stock traits of the *miles gloriosus* by comically disappointing these expectations: in the ***Truculentus*** he lets Stratophanes, named and dressed for a conventional entrance of boasting and threatening, tease the audience with his first line, 'Ne expectetis, spectatores, meas pugnas dum praedicem' (***Truc.*** 482).

Yet in his quest for ancestral traits and family similarities, the literary historian may unconsciously obscure other critical questions which are raised by the iteration itself, by the very repetitiveness of the stock character. One must try to answer, both for the *miles gloriosus* as a type and for any specific embodiment of that type, questions of both motive and means. What attracts a playwright to the braggart warrior, and, once he has adopted him, how does he fit him into the formal and thematic structure of his play? What relation, if any, does he bear to the extra-literary world? Specifically, given the fact that Pyrgopolinices in Plautus's ***Miles Gloriosus*** is probably a copy in many essentials of a Menandrean military braggart, what values does he have in Plautus's play in Plautus's Rome? If the starting-point for this essay were Shakespeare instead of Plautus, there would be little need to insist on the primacy of these questions. Yet the sight of Latin sometimes tends to obfuscate the critically obvious and the prejudices which shape the directions of literary studies among classical scholars have been especially strong in the case of Roman Comedy. Critical opinion has in general valued Greek literature higher than Latin and deprecated the latter as derivative. Since in addition scholars manifest an unconquerable desire to reconstruct the non-existent from the extant, the chief use to which Plautus and Terence were put until 1958 was as a tool for the hypothetical reconstruction of Greek New Comedy. In that year the publication of Menander's *Dyskolos* ensured the world at least one genuine example of a Greek New Comedy, and lifted from Plautus and Terence the unreasonable burden of simultaneously permitting their critics both to divine their sources and measure their departure from those same sources.[2]

One may not of course ignore completely the problem raised by the derivative nature of Roman Comedy, since both Plautus and Terence freely admit, even proudly advertize the fact that they have 'translated' Greek originals. Terence in the prologue to his *Eunuchus* first cites his model as Menander's *Eunuchus,* then counters the charge that he has stolen his soldier and parasite from Plautus and Naevius.

> si id est peccatum, peccatum imprudentiast
> poetae, non quo furtum facere studuerit.
> id ita esse vos iam iudicare poteritis.
> Colax Menandrist: in east parasitus Colax
> et miles gloriosus: eas se hic non negat
> personas transtulisse in Eunuchum suam
> ex Graeca.
>
>   (27-33)

But that he 'transferred' the character of the soldier Thraso from Menander does not prevent Terence from translating him into Roman terms, at least in details of military terminology, as in the following dialogue during the siege of Thais's house:

> *Thraso:* ubi centuriost Sanga et manipulus
>   furum? *Sanga:* eccum adest.
> *Thraso:* quid ignave? peniculon pugnare, qui
>   istum huc portes, cogitas?
> *Sanga:* egon? imperatoris virtutem noveram et
>   vim militum; sine sanguine hoc non posse
>   fieri: qui abstergerem volnera.
> *Thraso:* ubi alii? *Sanga:* qui malum 'alii'
>   solus Sannio servat domi.
> *Thraso:* ti hosce instrue; ego ero hic post
>   principia: inde omnibus signum dabo.
> *Gnatho:* illuc est sapere: ut hosce instruxit,
>   ipse sibi cavit loco.
> *Thraso:* idem hoc iam Pyrrhus factitavit.
>
>   (776-783)

Thus even Terence, agreed by all to be more faithful to the tone of his Greek originals than Plautus to his, has Romanized the scene with technical words like *centurio, manipulus, imperator,* and *principia,* and with the appropriate historical example of Pyrrhus. Such relatively minor adaptation of detail, found even more abundantly though less consistently in Plautus, along with the ebullient linguistic expansion that is so characteristic of Plautus's style, is usually what is meant by the 'originality' of Roman comedy, but this is hardly sufficient to establish its own validity in its Roman cultural milieu, and hardly consonant with what we know of other Roman adaptations of Greek forms, where individualization permeates far below surface translation.

There are numerous theories about the fundamental characteristics of good comedy and the causes of laughter. Central to many of these theories, and axiomatic in the rest, is the notion of familiarity. From the paradigmatic vaudeville joke—'Why does a chicken cross the road? To get to the other side'—to the fantasy of Aristophanes' *Birds,* the comic involves the rhetorical figure of *para prosdokian,* the cheating of expectations. As in reading an old issue of *Punch* or the *New Yorker,* much of our difficulty in properly understanding Plautus results from our failure to 'get the point', that is, our failure to recognize the expected in such a way that we may appreciate the unexpected.

Comedy always alludes in some degree to its environment, but the allusiveness of Plautus, since it does not name names in Aristophanic style, is difficult to prove. We have little contemporary material for comparison: the *senatus consultum de Bacchanalibus* and a handful of other inscriptions of meagre content. Our view of the social and ideological history of the period is based almost entirely on two writers: Polybius, writing analytically a generation later of Rome's and the Scipios' rise to imperial glory, and Livy, who had Cato and Ennius, Augustus and Virgil between himself and the realities of the early second century B.C.

Although it is now generally conceded that in small things Plautus is Plautine and Terence even Terentian, the view is still often held that the larger world of Roman drama, including the moral, philosophical, and psychological framework within which the characters act and speak, is foreign. Yet when Plautus's characters issue pronouncements such as 'alii, Lyde, nunc sunt mores' (**Bacch.** [**Bacchides**] 437) and 'haec huius saecli mores in se possidet' (**Truc.** 13), he cannot have expected his audience to hear the words *nunc* and *huius saecli* in terms of the Athens of a century before. If so, Plautus should have continued working as a stage hand. If so, then the Roman audience was indeed a collection of strange bumpkins who would keep coming back to laugh at what was incomprehensible and not pertinent to their own experiences. In this light the stock soldier, a borrowed character who intrinsically need have no allusive relation to the life around him, forms an interesting test case. The aspects of real life which he embodies, the military and the glorious, are an important phase of Roman ideology, treated with the utmost seriousness by Romans and Roman historians. It thus matters greatly in our evaluation of Plautus as a comic playwright whether the repeated portrayal of military glory in his plays is to be taken as an academic allusion to the mercenary armies of Alexander and the Diadochoi or as a commentary on the military ideals of his own time.

The *miles* appears in seven of the twenty preserved plays of Plautus, with his fullest development in the **Curculio, Truculentus,** and **Miles Gloriosus.**[3] His function is that of the young hero's rival for a girl, a role which could be filled as well by several other occupational types, as long as they were rich enough to contrast to the young hero's lack of ready cash. It is not the rivalry itself and the personal confrontation of the two suitors that makes up the stage intrigue. Most often it is the necessity for the young man to obtain money, usually from his father, with the help of a clever slave. Once he gets the money, the girl is effectively his, and the rival *miles* seldom need appear on stage. Far from being an unavoidable necessity of the plot, then, the role of the braggart soldier was a flexible element which could be expanded or contracted as Plautus chose; the very frequency of its appearance must itself be regarded as a deliberate preference of Plautus, not an accident of his sources.

Plautus's *miles gloriosus* had seen new and exotic-sounding lands in the Greek East, had conquered many of them with incredible rapidity, and had been courted by their kings. He had come back laden with riches and extravagant honors, nor was he reticent about his miraculous feats. On his return men might find him vain, hard to approach, ready to threaten instead of reason, yet they might also flatter him, even to the point of finding a reason for his success in some special relationship to the gods. All this can be said as well of Rome's historic heroes of Plautus's time, who had taken Rome up from the disastrous trough of Cannae through the battles of Zama and Cynoscephalae into the Seleucid Empire.[4] This fantastic series of successes brought with it an extravaganza of wealth and glory which the historian glimpses largely through the tradition of Cato's stern censorship. Both historian and literary critic should profit by a more detailed examination of the Plautine soldier to discover whether the parallelism between stage and contemporary reality that is clear in its broad outlines may be confirmed in particulars as well.

The soldiers' names, Greek or pseudo-Greek according to the conventions of the Roman stage, are Cleomachus, Stratophanes, Antamoenides, Pyrgopolinices, Polymachaeroplagides, and Therapontigonus Platagidorus. Pyrgopolinices also names an opponent, Bumbomachides Clutomestoridysarchides. In addition to a Rabelaisian relishing of the name itself, Plautus underscores the point of its length in the **Curculio** by having the banker Lyco say of Therapontigonus Platagidorus:

> novi edepol nomen, nam mihi istoc nomine,
> dum scribo, explevi totas ceras quattuor.

(*Curc.* 409-10)

One may well see an allusion here to the extra heroic military cognomina which accrued to Roman generals in Plautus's time, like Cunctator and Africanus; or perhaps even the specific occasion in 188 when the younger brother of Africanus, not to be left behind in a contest of name length, took the cognomen Asiagenus. That Plautus is not afraid of an even more pointed allusion to a name is clear from the joke in the **Miles Gloriosus** at the expense of the easily satirized cognomen of the Claudii. The maid greets Pyrgopolinices, 'Pulcher, salve', to which he confidently replies, 'meum cognomentum commemoravit' (1037-38).

The polysyllabic Therapontigonus Platagidorus is introduced to us largely through the imaginary description of the parasite Curculio, who has acquired the soldier's seal and must now draw a sufficiently boastful picture of the soldier to convince the banker that he is his *bona fide* representative. Asked why the *miles* was not there in person to retrieve his money, Curculio answers that he had just arrived in Caria from India, and there

nunc statuam volt dare auream
solidam faciundam ex auro Philippo, quae
    siet
septempedalis, factis monumentum suis.

                    (*Curc.* 439-41)

This passage gains point in the light of contemporary phenomena such as the honors paid Flamininus in Greece after the liberation proclamation, which, if they did not include seven-foot solid gold statues, did include his portrait on gold coinage. One of Cato's censorial speeches was entitled 'De signis et tabulis' and dealt with the violation of propriety in the proliferation of statuary in Rome, and Plautus gains a touch of the prophetic in view of the fact that the first gilded statue of a human was set up by Acilius Glabrio to himself in the temple of Pietas in 181. Plautus might well be less than prophetic, since this temple was dedicated by Acilius after the battle of Thermopylae and the routing of Antiochus in 191, and plans for the gilt statue 'made from Philip's money' might well have been known soon thereafter, before the traditional date of Plautus's death in 184.

Lyco the banker then asks Curculio why the general needs a commemorative statue. The answer:

        quia enim Persas, Paphlagonas,
Sinopas, Arabes, Caras, Cretonas, Syros,
Rhodiam atque Lyciam, Perediam et
    Perbibesiam,
Centauromachiam et Classem Unomammiam,
Libyamque oram omnem, omnem
    Conterobromniam,
dimidiam partem nationum usque omnium
subegit solus intra viginti dies.

                    (*Curc.* 442-48)

Despite attempts to date the Greek original by explaining this geographical buffoonery in terms of Alexandrian conquests or the career of Demetrius Poliorcetes, the best formal parallels are Roman honorific inscriptions. Although the sepulchral *elogia* of the great Scipios of Plautus's time are not among the famous inscriptions found in the Tomb of the Scipios, the family style can be demonstrated even from the *factis monumentum suis* of the earlier Lucius Cornelius Scipio Barbatus, despite his limited geographical range:

    Taurasiam Cisauriam Samniom cepit,
    subegit omnem Loucanam opsidesque
      abdoucit.

Even the farcical counting scene at the beginning of the **Miles Gloriosus,** where the parasite Artotrogus stands with a tablet and stylus doing the sums of the enemy soldiers killed by Pyrgopolinices on various battlefields:

in Cilicia	150
in Scytholatronia	100
Sards	30
Macedonians	60
	———
total	7000

has its somewhat embarrassing analogy in the marked desire for numerical precision of official Roman monuments of conquest, from the *Res Gestae Divi Augusti* to the *Columna Rostrata,* where Duilius about 260 B.C. described his feats in part as follows:

> . . . and all the Carthaginian hosts and their most mighty chief after nine days fled in broad daylight from their camp; and he took their town Macela by storm. And in the same command he as consul performed an exploit in ships at sea, the first Roman to do so; . . . and by main force he captured ships with their crews, to wit: one septireme, 30 quinqueremes and triremes; 13 he sank. Gold taken: 3,600 pieces; silver: 100,000; total in sestertii: 2,100,000.

Such reckoning of the commander's victims continues both in official and popular tradition. In Vopiscus's life of Aurelian we find this account:

> Aurelian alone with three hundred guardsmen smashed the Sarmatians as they were breaking out in Illyricum. Theoclius, a writer of imperial times, states that in the Sarmatian war Aurelian by his own hand on one day killed forty-eight, and more than nine hundred and fifty on various other days. The result was that boys made up verses and ditties for Aurelian which they used to dance to on holidays:

> mille mille mille decollavimus
> unus homo mille decollavimus
> mille bibat quisquis mille occidit
> tantum vini nemo habet quantum fudit
>   sanguinis.

             (S.H.A., *Vita Aureliani,* 6-7)

Another theme of the soldier's ditty, the so-called *versus Fescennini* which were a traditional part of triumphal processions of famous generals, was the sexual prowess of the commander. Julius Caesar's troops chanted

> urbani, servate uxores: moechum calvum
>   adducimus;
> aurum in Gallia effutuisti, hic sumpsisti
>   mutuum.

                (Suet. *Iul.* 51)

Although Plautus's braggart soldiers are not usually taunted about their love-making, except in so far as they end up as the unsuccessful rival for the girl, Pyrgopolinices in the *Miles Gloriosus* is the butt of teasing about his amorousness: he is *inpudens, plenus adulterii* (90), *magnus moechus mulierum* (755), *moechus unguentatus* (924), has long curly locks (64, 923), thinks himself handsomer than Alexander (777), is a 'skilled stud horse for the mares, both male and female' (1112-3), and is tricked in the finale and threatened with the standard penalty for adultery because of his belief in his own irresistibility.

> ipsus illic sese iam impedivit in plagas;
> paratae insidiae sunt: in statu stat senes,
> ut adoriatur moechum, qui formast ferox,
> qui omnis se amare credit, quaeque aspexerit
> mulier: eum oderunt qua viri qua mulieres.
>
> > (1388-92)

The hero believes himself both bold and handsome, and his double vanity, military and amatory, accounts for much of his comic appeal. The underscoring of Pyrgopolinices' double pride—in great deeds and good looks—seems almost formulaic:

> fortem atque fortunatum et forma regia. (10)
> virtute et forma et factis invictissumis. (57)
> cum hac forma et factis. (1021)
> formam et facies et virtutes. (1027)
> hominem tam pulchrum et praeclarum virtute
> et forma, factis. (1042)
> saltem id volup est quom ex virtute formai
> evenit tibi. (1211)
> forma huius, mores, virtus. (1327)

The pairing of *virtus* and *forma,* seemingly un-Roman, can best be paralleled in the epitaph of Scipio Barbatus, whose 'forma virtutei parisuma fuit'.

Beauty aside—since few military heroes might legitimately boast of such an endowment—Plautus's soldiers are normally labelled with epigrammatic tags of civic *virtus:*

> virtute belli armatus promerui ut mihi
> omnis mortalis agere deceat gratias.
>
> > (*Epid.* 442-42)

Stratophanes in the *Truculentus,* refusing to tell tall stories, philosophizes instead about the sufficiency of *virtus:*

> facile sibi facunditatem virtus argutam invenit,
> sine virtuti argutum civem mini habeam pro
> praefica,
> quae alios conlaudat, eapse sese vero non
> potest.
>
> > (494-96)

But his boasting comes a few lines later in his pride for the baby whom he thinks is his new-born son. He is told that immediately after birth the infant reached for sword and shield, and expresses wonder that the child is not now away in battle winning booty: He congratulates Phronesium for adding to the glory of his name.

> gratulor, quom mihi tibique magnum perperisti
> decus. (517)
> filium peperisti, qui aedis spoliis opplebit tuas.
> (522)

This parallels the projected progeny of Pyrgopolinices:

> PALAESTRIO: meri bellatores gignuntur, quas hic praegnatis fecit, et pueri annos octingentos vivunt.
> MILPHIDIPPA: vae tibi, nugator!
>
> PYRGOPOLINICES: quin mille annorum perpetuo vivunt ab saeclo ad saeclum.
>
> > (*Mil.* 1077-79)

One thinks too of Hercules, the other miraculous babe in Plautus, of whom Jupiter tells Amphitryon, 'suis factis te inmortali adficiet gloria' (*Am.* [*Amphitruo*] 1140), and again of the epitaphs of the Scipios:

> facile faceteis superases gloriam maiorum.
> virtutes generis mieis moribus accumulavi,
> progeniem genui, facta patris petiei.
> maiorum optenui laudem, ut sibei me esse
> creatum
> laetentur; stirpem nobilitavit honor.

The divine aura which formed around Scipio Africanus and which Polybius was at such pains to rationalize is also drawn around Stratophanes and Pyrgopolinices. The latter is a self-styled *nepos Veneris* (1265), comically turned into *Venerius nepotulus* (1413, 1421) after his ill-fated attempt to seduce the supposed wife of Pleusicles. The best statement of his divinity occurs in an earlier exchange between Milphidippa and Palaestrio:

> MILPHIDIPPA: ecastor hau mirum si te habes carum, hominem tam pulchrum et praeclarum virtute et forma, factis. deus dignior fuit quisquam homo qui esset?
> PALAESTRIO: non hercle humanust ergo—
> nam volturio plus humani credo est. (1041-4)

All the Scipionic parallels adduced up to this point are not meant to create a picture of Plautus as a political pamphleteer opposing the Scipionic faction in government. The modern critic is at the mercy of his sources, which are disproportionately concentrated on the Scipios—accidentally in the case of the inscriptional evidence and deliberately in the case of historians. Although to his contemporaries Africanus probably was a leading symbol of Rome's new heroism, the effects of the rapid military and diplomatic success of the period not only were visible in the other ruling families, but also permeated other social levels. The typical Roman soldier of the early second century was not the yeoman leaving his plough for an occasional short campaigning season, but a professionalized military man who saw nearly regular service in several theatres of war. One can see the pride of such a campaign veteran in Livy's version of a speech by Spurius Ligustinus, a centurion of Sabine origin, who in the period from 200 to 171 B.C. had served twenty-two years in the army, been *primus pilus* four times, had been rewarded thirty-four times by various generals *virtutis causa,* and had won six civic crowns (Livy, xlii. 34).

The impact of the returning hero, whether general, centurion, or common soldier, on Roman society is clearly revealed in Plautus. There is no reason to doubt the realism of his description in the *Epidicus* (208-15) of the streets full of soldiers carrying their weapons and leading their pack-animals, and being met by fathers looking for their own sons and by crowds of prostitutes, all dressed for the occasion. Nor is there any reason to doubt the justice of one of his few explicit criticisms of war greed at the beginning of the same play, where the slave Thesprio, returning well-fed from an overseas campaign, remarks that the wars have converted him from a sneak thief to an open robber (*Epid.* 10-12).

Plautus's *miles gloriosus,* then, is relevant to his own society. If originally he reflected the early Hellenistic mercenary captain, his traits as we meet him in Plautine comedy have become thoroughly congruent with the native Roman general turned world conqueror in Plautus's time.

Artistically, however, one must further question the relevance of the *miles* to the play or plays within which he occurs. Although satirizing society by stringing together a number of socially recognizable characters may be interesting in itself and provide good fun, great comic drama is more than this. The critic demands—and finds—unifying elements of structure, whether they be formal or thematic, imagistic or psychological. On the other hand, the usual critical *comparanda* of Plautus are vaudeville and Gilbert and Sullivan: his plots are thin, his construction loose, he will do anything for a laugh. Yet some understanding of the coherence of Plautine comedy may be gained by studying the role of the *miles gloriosus* in its dramatic context.

This coherence is not primarily a factor of the plot as such. The soldier is neither a prime mover of the action, nor is he, except in the case of Pyrgopolinices in the *Miles Gloriosus,* an important antagonist who must be met and overcome. In the *Curculio,* Thera-

pontigonus is deceived *in absentiâ* by the eponymous hero in order to deceive the banker to pay the *leno* to get the girl who turns out to be Therapontigonus's sister anyway. The soldier meanwhile returns and rages ineffectually at both banker and *leno,* but all ends happily when he is invited to dinner, getting neither girl nor retribution. In the *Epidicus,* the soldier enters only after the father has been deceived, is incidentally discomfited in a brief scene, and leaves the stage never to be mentioned again. In both *Poenulus* and *Bacchides,* the soldier, although an absent rival for the hand of the heroine, is not the effective enemy of the hero and arrives on stage only after the battle is essentially over. He struts and threatens for a time, and in the *Poenulus* returns at the happy ending to help gloat over the *leno.* In the *Pseudolus,* the Macedonian *miles* never appears in person, being replaced by his slave Harpax. Even in the *Truculentus,* a love-story without a hero in the usual sense, Stratophanes is merely one of Phronesium's three fools, whose deception by her leads to no *peripeteia,* but who is instead given a half share of the booty at the end.

Clearly, then, whatever organic quality the *miles* may have in Plautus does not depend on the dramatic exigencies of plot. It depends rather upon the parallelism of roles, the thematic repetition in other characters of the traits of the braggart warrior. In the *Bacchides,* for example, the role of Cleomachus seems perhaps more nearly fortuitous than that of any Plautine soldier. He appears in one short scene in which he is merely a tool used by the slave Chrysalus to defraud the old man Nicobulus. But the soldier's appearance is framed by the character of Chrysalus, who dominates the stage for a long period both before and after the brief apparition of the professional swaggerer with his identifying sword and shield. Chrysalus's entrance in this portion of the play is highly revealing. The young man Mnesilochus has just sung a monologue of utter despair. Although his friend Pistoclerus tries to console him, he only makes matters worse by mentioning the recent arrival of a parasite from Cleomachus to demand either the soldier's money or his girl.

PISTOCLERUS: tace modo: deus respiciet nos aliquis. MNESILOCHUS: nugae!

PISTOCLERUS: mane. MNESILOCHUS: quid est? PISTOCLERUS: tuam copiam eccam Chrysalum video.

CHRYSALUS: hunc hominem decet auro expendi, huic decet statuam statui ex auro; nam duplex facinus feci hodie, duplicibus spoliis sum adfectus.

(638-41)

Pistoclerus's assurance that some god will help them is answered immediately by the appearance of Chrysalus, who begins with a claim that his glory warrants him a golden statue, like Therapontigonus in the ***Curculio***, and clearly identifies himself with the military profession in the next line by a reference to his 'double-dealing spoils'. In heroic style he tells of the splendid wealth—'regias copias aureasque optuli' (647)—gained through his bravery—'mea virtute parta' (647). When he discovers that Mnesilochus has given the money back to his father in a sentimental rage because of a foolish misunderstanding, the slave becomes the commander in earnest to devise a new strategy, scheming in military metaphor:

> de ducentis nummis primum intendam
>   ballistam in senem;
> ea ballista si pervortam turrim et
>   propugnacula,
> recta porta invadam extemplo in oppidum
>   antiquom et vetus:
> si id capso, geritote amicis vostris aurum
>   corbibus,
> sicut animus sperat.
>
>   (709-13)

He tells the young men not to rise from their banquet until he gives the battle cry, to which Pistoclerus replies, 'o imperatorem probum' (758-9). After his preliminary skirmish with the conventional soldier Cleomachus, Chrysalus produces a truly epic piece of self-glorification, comparing his past and future exploits to those of the Greek heroes at Troy.

> Atridae duo fratres cluent fecisse facinus
>   maxumum,
> quom Priami patriam Pergamum divina
>   moenitum manu
> armis, equis, exercitu atque eximiis
>   bellatoribus
> milli cum numero navium decumo anno post
>   subegerunt.
> non pedibus termento fuit praeut ego erum
>   expugnabo meum
> sine classe sineque exercitu et tanto numero
>   militum.
> cepi, expugnavi amanti erili filio aurum ab
>   suo patre . . .
> ego sum Ulixes, quoiius consilio haec gerunt . . .
> poste cum magnifico milite, urbis verbis qui
>   inermus capit,
> conflixi atque hominem reppuli; dein pugnam
>   conserui seni:
> eum ego adeo uno mendacio devici, uno ictu
>   extemplo cepi spolia . . .
> sed Priamus hic multo illi praestat: non
>   quinquaginta modo,
> quadringentos filios habet atque equidem
>   omnis lectos sine probro:
> eos ego hodie omnis contruncabo duobus solis
>   ictibus.
>
>   (925-75)

After the besieged old man gives the slave money for the second time, Chrysalus-Ulysses comments:

> hoc est incepta efficere pulchre: veluti mi
> evenit ut ovans praeda onustus cederem;
> salute nostra atque urbe capta per dolum
> domum redduco iam integrum omnem
>   exercitum.
> sed, spectatores, vos nunc ne miremini
> quod non triumpho: pervolgatum est, nil
>   moror;
> verum tamen accipientur mulso milites.
>
>   (1068-744)

Thus exists the slave, at once more boastful and more military than the *miles gloriosus* whom he has overcome. The physical caricature of resplendent militarism momentarily introduced on to the stage in Cleomachus is only one statement of a theme which is repeated more fully in the extravagant language of the slave-hero. Artistically Cleomachus and Chrysalus reinforce one another, the soldier being a literal embodiment of the figurative language and behaviour of the slave, and the slave generalizing the specific humorous traits of the soldier.

In the ***Miles Gloriosus***, where Pyrgopolinices' role is the most extensive of all Plautus's soldiers and would not seem to need reinforcement from outside, the slave Palaestrio again acts as his counterpart in mock heroism. When he learns that his fellow-servant Sceledrus has seen Philocomasium kissing Pleusicles, he first calls a council with himself to plot his strategy:

> paullisper tace,
> dum ego mihi consilia in animum convoco et
>   dum consulo
> quid agam, quem dolum doloso contra
>   conservo parem.
>
>   (196-98)

After much painful thought accompanied by tragic gesture, he devises a plan and is warned by his young master of the dangers in the enemy forces:

> viden hostis tibi adesse tuoque tergo
>   opsidium? consule,
> arripe opem auxiliumque ad hanc rem: propere
>   hoc, non placide decet.
> anteveni aliqua, aliquo saltu circumduce
>   exercitum,
> coge in opsidium perduellis, nostris praesidium
>   para;
> interclude inimicis commeatum, tibi muni
>   viam
> qua cibatus commeatusque ad te et legiones
>   tuas
> tuto possit pervenire.
>
>   (219-25)

Palaestrio accepts his *imperium* and storms Sceledrus with siege machines:

> si invenio qui vidit, ad eum vineam
>   pluteosque agam:
> res paratast, vi pugnandoque hominem
>   caperest certa res.
>
>   (266-67)

Next he throws him from the bastions:

> meus illic homo est. deturbabo iam ego illum
>   de pugnaculis.
>
>   (334)

Then after a new council of war (597 ff) Palaestrio leads his maniples against Pyrgopolinices:

> quantas res turbo, quantas moveo machinas!
> eripiam ego hodie concubinam militi,
> si centuriati bene sunt manuplares mei.
>
>   (813-5)

Although he is viewed momentarily as a shipbuilder laying the hull of a fine trick (915 ff), when the time for launching comes he returns to his proper métier of imperator:

> PLEUSICLES: oppidum quodvis videtur posse
>   expugnari dolis. date modo operam.
> ACROTELEUTIUM: id nos ad te, si quid velles,
>   venimus.
> PALAESTRIO: lepide facitis. nucn hanc tibi ego
>   impero provinciam.
> ACROTELEUTIUM: impetrabis, imperator, quod
>   ego potero, quod voles.
>
>   (1157-60)

Of all the speeches of these slave generalissimos, perhaps the most effective is that of Pseudolus just before he meets Harpax, the slave of Polymachaeroplagides.

> nam ego in meo pectore prius ita paravi
>   copias,
> duplicis, triplicis dolos, perfidias, ut,
>   ubiquomque hostibus congrediar
> (maiorum meum fretus virtute dicam, mea
>   industria etmalitia fraudulenta),
> facile ut vincam, facile ut spoliem meos
>   perduellis meis perfidiis.
> nunc inimicum ego hunc communem meum
>   atque vostrorum omnium
> Ballionem exballistabo lepide: date operam
>   modo;
> hoc ego oppidum admoenire ut hodie capiatur
>   volo.
> atque hoc meas legiones adducam; si hoc
>   expugno facilem hanc rem meis civibus
>   faciam,

> post ad oppidum hoc vetus continuo meum
>   exercitum protinus obducam:
> ind' me et simul participes omnis meos praeda
>   onerabo atque opplebo,
> metum et fugam perduellibus meis me ut
>   sciant natum.
> eo sum genere gnatus: magna me facinora
>   decet ecficere
> quae post mihi clara et diu clueant.
> sed hunc quem video quis hic est qui oculis
>   meis obviam ignobilis obicitur?
> lubet scire quid hic venit cum macchaera et
>   huic quam rem agat hinc dabo insidias.
>
>   (579-92)

Military activities are here combined with more serious attributes of the Roman nobility: dependence upon the *virtus* of one's ancestors and confidence in one's future fame, as well as high-minded concern for the citizenry (although 'vostrorum omnium' and 'meis civibus' become merely 'participes meos' when it comes to sharing the boodle). The *para presdokian* in the first lines is biting, with the long heroic phrases culminating in *dolos, malitia, perfidiis,* and *Ballionem.* Such in general is this Plautine heroic type, who with legions of perfidious machinations besieges the stronghold of an old man or pimp for the booty of a prostitute which he brings home in triumph to a dissolute and spendthrift young man. Boaster of his talents, he is clearly one of Plautus's most popular creations, on whom the playwright lavished his verbal imagination to a high degree. If one includes his parasite counterpart Curculio, he appears in nine plays, and it is significant that all but one of the plays in which a *miles gloriosus* appears also boasts a *servus gloriosus.* The exception is the ***Truculentus,*** and in this play the meretricious Phronesium and her maid Astaphium play the role usually afforded a Pseudolus or Palaestrio, devising the tricks and managing the action. They are in fact called *gloriosae* (157). The *militia* which forms a pendant to the stage soldiery of Stratophanes is here the *militia amoris.*

> ASTAPHIUM: amator similest oppidi hostilis.
> DINIARCHUS: quo argumento?
>
> ASTAPHIUM: quam primum expugnari potis, tam id optumum est amicae.
>
>   (170-71)

> ASTAPHIUM: numquam amatoris meretricem oportet caussam noscere, quin, ubi det, pro infrequente eum mittat militia domum.
>
>   (229-30)

As in the elegiac poets of Augustan times, where love is the preferred soldiery and foreign service is deprecated because it detracts from the service of one's mistress, so Plautus' young men may occasionally express their passion in military metaphor. The ***Curculio*** opens with the following dialogue between the young Phaedromus and his slave Palinurus:

> PALINURUS: quo ted hoc noctu dicam proficisci foras cum istoc ornatu cumque hac pompa, Phaedrome?

> PHAEDROMUS: quo Venus Cupidoque imperat, suadetque Amor: si media nox est sive est prima vespera, si status, condictus cum hoste intercedit dies, tamen est eundum quo imperant ingratiis.

(1-6)

If it is not quite true in Plautus that 'militat omnis amans', it is still the conquest of hearts or of money that motivates most of the heroism. *Virtus* is presented full-blown upon the stage. Whether it wins or loses is irrelevant: it usually does both. Palaestrio conquers, Pyrgopolinices falls; Chrysalus defeats Cleomachus; Phronesium cheats Stratophanes of his money but Stratophanes still gets his spoils of the girl. Both hero and dupe are *gloriosus,* and on both sides the *gloria* is perverted. (Falstaff and Hotspur lie side by side on the battlefield.) In Plautine comedy—and probably in all comedy—glory can only appear as vainglory. The tall tales of the hyperbolic stage soldier, as well as the pronouncements of slaves and mooning lovers, are equally incongruous settings for the language of official military dispatches. Critics have varied in interpreting Sosia's long announcement of victory in the ***Amphitruo***. It has been considered both a serious ode of victory addressed by Plautus to his fellow-Romans and a comic parody of Ennius. It is both: a lavish pronouncement of official *res gestae* delivered in epic style through the mask of a cowardly slave who was drunk in his master's tent during the entire battle. Such is the mask of military glory in Plautine comedy, a mask assumed by other characters as well as the *miles gloriosus* himself.

The comic playwright deals as extensively with *hybris* as the writer of tragedy. Man boasts, and the hollowness of the boast brings terror or laughter, but is never allowed to stand unanswered. The mighty shall fall, whether they be mighty in wealth, manners, learning, or war. The sentimental shell is cracked, and what is left is that 'A man's a man'. In warfare the gap between the sentimental slogan and the reality behind it is enormous. The Roman legionnaire as well as the modern infantryman exists for the messy business of shedding blood and letting blood. Although there have been revolutions in the technique and even the sociology of warfare, this fundamental gap has never narrowed. War may still give rise to heroic sentiment and men may glory in a machine gun as much as in a *machaera,* may count the victims of an automatic rifle as proudly as those of a sword.

When lunchtime arrived on the front lines on Guam, a Marine automatic rifleman, picking off Japs caught in a pocket, mixed business with pleasure.

With precise rhythm, he fired, rolled over, took a mouthful of rations, rolled back, fired, rolled to the food, ate, and so on, until simultaneously both rations and Japs gave out.

Before we started it was great fun. We grinned and chortled. . . . I recalled Major Mill's instructions: 'We don't intend to neutralize the island. We don't intend to destroy it. We will annihilate it'. . . . At dawn our planes came in. We could see them disappear into the smoke and flame. We could hear the sputter of their machine guns. We could see the debris raised by their bombs. It was wonderful.[5]

One might have supposed that the trench warfare of World War I killed the romanticism of combat, but a new generation became aces with new weapons, and unfortunately there is no intrinsic reason to suppose that a button pusher might not boast of his expertize in some future atomic conflagration. If war appears on the comic stage, it appears perforce as *alazonia,* and the great soldier cannot be drawn otherwise than as the great boaster, the *miles gloriosus*. There may indeed be times in which war is not a subject for comedy. A defeated nation may be too depressed and a militant government too jealous.[6] But there have been surprisingly few periods in the national literatures of Europe when the *miles* has been long absent from the stage, although, for example, Abraham Cowley felt it necessary in 1658 to append the following defence to the preface to *Cutter of Coleman Street*. This play was a revised version of *The Guardian* which he had produced in 1641; the years between had clearly been difficult ones for the spirit of comedy.

> And it has been the perpetual privilege of Satyre and Comedy to pluck their vices and follies though not their persons out of the Sanctuary of any Title. A Cowardly ranting Souldier, an Ignorant Charlatanical Doctor, a foolish Cheating Lawyer, a silly Pedantical Scholar, have alwayes been, and still are the Principal Subjects of all Comedy, without any scandal given to those Honourable Professions, or ever taken by their severest Professors; And, if any good Physician or Divine should be offended with me here for inveighing against a Quack, or for finding Deacon *Soaker* too often in the Butteryes, my respect and reverence to their callings would make me troubled at their displeasure, but I could not abstain from taking them for very Cholerique and Quarrelsome persons. What does this therefore amount to, if it were true which is objected? But it is far from being so; for the representation of two Sharks about the Town (fellows merry and Ingenious enough, and therefore admitted into better companyes than they deserve, yet withall too very scoundrels,

which is no unfrequent character at *London*) the representation I say of these as Pretended Officers of the Royal Army, was made for no other purpose but to show the World, that the vices and extravagancies imputed vulgarly to the Cavaliers, were really committed by Aliens who only usurped that name, and endeavoured to cover the reproach of their Indigency or Infamy of their Actions with so honourable a Title. So that the business here was not to correct or cut off any natural branches, though never so corrupted or Luxuriant, but to separate and cast away that vermine which by sticking so close to them had done great and considerable prejudice both to the Beauty and Fertility of the Tree.

Cowley further fitted action to his words by changing the description of Cutter in the *personae* from 'a sharking souldier' in *The Guardian* to a 'merry, sharking fellow about the town, pretending to have been a Colonel in the King's Army'. Such an elaborate protestation of innocence does far more than any citation of parallels to prove the relevance of stage soldier to his contemporary counterparts in real life. Although the best comic playwright does not explictly moralize, the comic vision is *per se* pacifistic. Shaw the essayist, however, annotates Shaw the dramatist. In the preface to the four 'pleasant plays' of *Plays: Pleasant and Unpleasant,* he writes thus of *Arms and the Man,* with its ironic Vergilian title:

> In spite of a Liberal Revolution or two, I can no longer be satisfied with fictitious morals and fictitious good conduct, shedding fictitious glory on over-crowding, disease, crime, drink, war, cruelty, infant mortality, and all the other commonplaces of civilization which drive men to the theatre to make foolish pretences that these things are progress, science, morals, religion, patriotism, imperial supremacy, national greatness and all the other names the newspapers call them.

Neither Plautus nor Shakespeare wrote explanatory prefaces, and of all the alleged literary descendants of Pyrgopolinices none has perhaps raised more critical problems than Falstaff. To begin with, there is little agreement as to whether he is properly to be called a *miles gloriosus.* While the majority of literary historians would view him as a version, albeit a distinctive one, of the conventional *miles,* most critics feel that the appellation limits and lightens the more complex character of Sir John. They follow in part the lead of Maurice Morgann's *Essay on the Dramatic Character of Sir John Falstaff,* written in 1777 to vindicate his courage and deny the propriety of calling him a *miles gloriosus.* The particular arguments, however, which Morgann adduces indicate a misunderstanding, not of Falstaff, but of the Plautine *miles.* 'If Falstaff had been intended for the character of a *Miles gloriosus,* his behaviour ought and therefore would have been com-

mented upon by others.' But except for the asides of the parasite Artotrogus which characterize Pyrgopolinices as a liar—a fact which the audience does not need to be told and which serves to characterize the parasite more than the *miles*—Plautus does not make use of other characters to point up the falsity of his soldier's boasted *virtus.* Further, Morgann feels that Falstaff's character is not that of a real braggart, because his lies are 'too extravagant for practised imposition', a description certainly equally apt for the Plautine feats of scattering legions with a breath (*Mil.* 16-18), breaking elephants arms with a fist (*Mil.* 25-30), bringing down 60,000 flying troops by shooting bird-lime at them with slingshots (*Poen.* 470-87). Finally, the critic examines Falstaff's battle experience to show that it does not prove his cowardice. Yet none of Plautus's *milites gloriosi* are convicted of cowardice on the stage. The worst one can say is that they show Falstaffian 'discretion', like Terence's Thraso in his siege of Thais' house:

> omnia prius experiri quam armis sapientem
>   decet.
> qui scis an quae iubeam sine vi faciat?
>   (*Eun.* 789-90)

In a scene which would have given a natural opportunity for a portrayal of real cowardice, the confrontation between the cook Cyamus and the soldier Stratophanes in the *Truculentus,* the soldier ought to have run off in fright at the sight of the cook's butcher knife, but he actually drives off the cook with his longer sword. Although Pyrgopolinices gets a beating at the end of the *Miles Gloriosus,* it is not a coward's but a lecher's punishment, and he is held by a group of slaves while he takes his blows. Despite the fact that the sensitivity of Roman audiences was not shocked by watching a good stage beating, there is nothing in Roman comedy to correspond to the cringing cudgelling in English Comedy of Bessus or Bluffe or Bobadill.

Although in his polemic Morgann takes too narrow a view of the dramatic values of the *miles gloriosus* before Shakespeare's time, he understands that Falstaff must be understood, if at all, in terms of the incongruities of his character and his relations with other roles in the play.

> To this end, Falstaff must no longer be considered as a single independent character, but grouped, as we find him shewn to us in the play;—his ability must be disgraced by buffoonery, and his courage by circumstances of imputation; and those qualities be thereupon reduced into subjects of mirth and laughter:—his vices must be concealed at each end from vicious design and evil effect, and must thereupon be turned into incongruities, and assume the name of humour only;—his insolence must be repressed by the superior tone of Hal and Poins, and take the softer name of

spirit only, or alacrity of mind; . . . he must thrive best, and flatter most, by being extravagantly incongruous; and his own tendency, impelled by so much activity, will carry him with perfect ease and freedom to all the necessary excesses.

What else is this but a definition of the comic *alazon* at his best, a definition which would fit Plautus's Pyrgopolinices or Shaw's Sergius equally well? Coward and no-coward, Falstaff is an embodiment of military glory who raises the question of cowardice. On his lips, 'the better part of valour is discretion; in the which latter part I have saved my life', may be a comic proposition, but it has a serious relevance to the corpse beside him. 'Zounds, I am afraid of this gunpowder Percy, though he be dead; how if he should counterfeit too, and rise? I am afraid he would prove the better counterfeit.' In a play which begins and ends with plans for war, Hotspur is the example which King Henry wished Prince Hal to follow:

> He doth fill fields with harness in the realm;
> Turns head against the lion's armed jaws;
> And, being no more in debt to years than
>   thou,
> Leads ancient lords and reverend bishops
>   on
> To bloody battles and to burning arms. . . .
> Thrice hath this Hotspur Mars in swathing-
>   clothes,
> This infant warrior in his enterprise
> Discomfited great Douglas.

Hotspur's first appearance in the play is in a short scene framed between the two parts of Falstaff's inglorious robbery, between the deed at Gadshill and the boast at Eastcheap. He enters reading a letter and reviling the cowardice of his correspondent: 'You are a shallow, cowardly hind, and you lie . . . What a frosty-spirited rogue is this. . . . O, I could divide myself, and go to buffets, for moving such a dish of skimmed milk with so honourable an iron.' Lady Percy reveals that even in his sleep he thinks of the heroics of war:

> In thy faint slumbers I by thee have
>   watched,
> And heard thee murmur tales of iron wars;
> Speak terms of manage to thy bounding
>   steed;
> Cry, Courage!—to the field!—And thou hast
>   talked
> Of sallies and retires, of trenches, tents,
> Of palisadoes, frontiers, parapets,
> Of basilisks, of cannon, culverin,
> Of prisoners' ransom, and of soldiers slain,
> And all the currents of a heady fight.

At the tavern, while they await Falstaff's return, Prince Henry thus characterizes Hotspur:

I am not yet of Percy's mind, the Hotspur of the North; he that kills me some six or seven dozen Scots at a breakfast, washes his hands, and says to his wife, 'Fie upon this quiet life! I want work'. 'O my sweet Harry', says she, 'how many hast thou killed today?' 'Give my roan horse a drench', says he; and answers, 'Some fourteen', an hour after, '—a trifle, a trifle', I pr'ythee, call in Falstaff: I'll play Percy, and that damned brawn shall play Dame Mortimer his wife.

Enter Falstaff with 'A plague of all cowards'. The valorous boast of the comic *miles*—'Why, thou knowest I am as valiant as Hercules: but beware instinct; the lion will not touch the true prince'—illumines the valorous boast of the historic *miles*. Which of the two glories is the vainer is decided on the battlefield: '. . . for worms, brave Percy'.

> who lined himself with hope,
> Eating the air on promise of supply,
> Flattering himself with project of a power
> Much smaller than the smallest of his
>   thoughts:
> And so, with great imagination,
> Proper to madmen, led his powers to death,
> And, winking, leaped into destruction.

As Falstaff illumines Percy in Part I, so Pistol illumines Falstaff in Part II. Pistol, with his name, his military title—'Captain! thou abominable damned cheater, art thou not ashamed to be called captain?'—his learnedly heroic language—'shall packhorses, and hollowed pampered jades of Asia, which cannot go but thirty miles a day, compare with Caesars, and with Cannibals, and Trojan Greeks? nay, rather damn them with King Cerberus'—is the more obvious swaggerer, whose swaggering is both called and proved hollow by Sir John:

> He's no swaggerer, hostess; a tame cheater, i'
> faith; you may stroke him as gently as a puppy
> greyhound: he will not swagger with a barbary
> hen, if her feathers turn back in any show of
> resistance.

Falstaff rises above his own vanity, as it were, to become the touchstone of the vanity of others. Yet the same extravagant mythology that was a part of Pistol's boast is turned immediately upon Falstaff in Doll's congratulations on his bravery in driving off Pistol:

> ah, rogue! i' faith, I love thee. Thou art as valorous
> as Hector of Troy, worth five of Agamemnon, and
> ten times better than the nine worthies: ah villain!

Caveat lector. Again it is Falstaff who 'see's the bottom of Justice Shallow'. He is *alazonia* looking at itself. Like the *milites gloriosi* of Plautus, he remains detached from the central action of the play, yet concentrates in his own character the theme of the vanity of honour and military glory which is crucially relevant to the central action and reiterated in other characters. His range is wider than that of any Plautine *miles,* and in this he is rather more like the Plautine slave. That he is a greater figure than either is in part simply due to the fact that his creator is Shakespeare, but in part because his context is not comedy. The heroes with whom he shares the stage are Hotspur and Prince Henry, not the *adulescentuli* of the Roman stage.

Much of the same dramatic use, if less subtle, is made of the *miles gloriosus* in Beaumont and Fletcher's melodramatic treatment of incest between brother and sister, *A King and No King.* Bessus, 'valiant enough upon a retreat', opens the play by boasting of his accomplishments at a place now called 'Bessus' Desperate Redemption'. Mardonius, King Arbaces' friend and counsellor, informs the audience of Bessus' cowardice:

> Thou knowest, and so do I, thou meanedst to flie, and thy fear making thee mistake, thou ranst upon the enemy, and a hot charge thou gavst, as I'll do thee right, thou art furious in running away, and I think, we owe thy fear for our victory; if I were the King, and were sure thou wouldst mistake always and run away upon the enemy, thou shouldst be general by this light.

His comic boasting continues to be displayed and convicted throughout the play. When the king twits him on his cowardice, he shows his sword and maintains: 'If I do not make my back-biters eat it to a knife within this week, say I am not valiant.' When he is later disgracefully beaten by Bacurius and has his sword taken from him, he begs at least for his knife back, so that he can show it to the king and assert that this was all that was left uneaten of his sword. When the king's sister asks for news of the king, he talks only of himself:

> *Panthea:* And is he well again?
>
> *Bessus:* Well again, an't please your grace: why I was run twice through the body, and shot i'th'head with a cross-arrow, and yet am well again.
>
> *Panthea:* I do not care how thou do'st, is he well?
>
> *Bessus:* Not care how I do? Let a man out of the mightiness of his spirit, fructifie Foreign Countries with his blood for the good of his own, and thus shall he be answered; why I may live to relieve with spear and shield, such a lady as you distressed.

Now styled a hero, he must defend his honour in duels, and all those whom he has boorishly insulted before the war come to challenge him. He joyfully proclaims in a monologue that he is really a coward and then escapes another duel by telling the challenger's second that he is already engaged

> . . . 'upon my faith Sir, to two hundred and twelve, and I have a spent body, too much bruised in Battail, so that I cannot fight, I must be plain, above three combats a day: All the kindness I can shew him, is to set him resolvedly in my rowle, the two hundred and thirteenth man, which is something, for I tell you, I think there will be more after him, than before him, I think so; pray you commend me to him, and tell him this'.

After he has been kicked and cudgelled by Bacurius, two sophistical teachers of swordmanship attempt to prove by argument that he was really brave in being beaten, as long as he laughed enough to show that he contemned the beating:

> If he be sure he has been kicked enough.
> For that brave sufference you speak of
>   brother,
> Consists not in a beating and away,
> But in a cudgelled body, from eighteen
> To eight and thirty; in a head rebuked
> With pots of all size, degrees, stools, and
>   bed-staves,
> This shows a valiant man.
>
> *Bessus:* Then I am valiant, as valiant as the
>   proudest,
> For these are all familiar things to me;
> Familiar as my sleep, or want of money,
> All my whole body's but one bruise with
>   beating,
> I think I have been cudgelled with all
>   nations,
> And almost all Religions.

Through all this beating, the braggart buffoon learns no lesson, remains undaunted, since, as he himself remarks, 'A base spirit has this vantage of a brave one, it keeps always at a stay, nothing brings it down, not beating'. But King Arbaces, Bessus' heroic counterpart, does not 'have this vantage'. In him, because he *is* a brave man, the exaggeration of military boastfulness is no comic folly, but a tragic distortion.

> *Bessus:* Come, our King's a brave fellow.
>
> *Mardonius:* He is so, Bessus, I wonder how thou camst to know it. But if thou wert a man of understanding I would tell thee, he is vainglorious, and humble, and angry, and patient, and merry, and dull, and joyful and sorrowful in extremity in an hour. . . . Here he is with his prey in his foot.

Arbaces enters, glorying over the fallen Tigranes:

> Be you my witness earth, need I to brag,
> Doth not this captive prince speak
> Me sufficiently, and all the acts
> That I have wrought upon his suffering land;
> Should I then boast! where lies that foot of
>   ground
> Within his whole realm, that I have not past,
> Fighting and conquering; far then from me
> Be ostentation. I could tell the world
> How I have laid his kingdom desolate
> By this sole arm propt by divinity,
> Stript him out of his glories, and have sent
> The pride of all his youth to people graves,
> And made his virgins languish for their loves,
> If I would brag, should I that have the power
> To teach the neighbour world humility,
> Mix with vain-glory? . . .
>
> *Mardonius:* 'Tis pity that valour should be
>   thus drunk.

Then Beaumont and Fletcher repeatedly display the braggart coward and braggart king together, with the effect of making the one more ludicrous, the other more pitiable. At first, the experience of seeing himself caricatured does not abate Arbaces' boastfulness. To Mardonius in defence of his earlier speech:

> There I would make you know 'twas this sole
>   arm.
> I grant you were my instruments, and did
> As I commanded you, but 'twas this arm
> Moved you like wheels, it mov'd you as it
>   pleased.

After promising not to insult the captive king Tigranes any further, he delivers another self-laudatory speech at his own triumphal procession. Yet as the drama is about to become tragic, as his vanity is about to ruin him irrevocably by making him flaunt moral law and make love to his sister, he once more confronts Bessus, whom he has asked to play the pander for him. Bessus' eagerness to be of service is expressed in what is perhaps the most shocking sentence in English drama: '. . . and when this is dispatched, if you have a mind to your mother, tell me, and you shall see I'le set it hard'. The king recoils at this incredibly vulgar image of himself, and the play begins to move toward the comic conclusion implicit in its title.

Falstaff and Bessus are unusual *milites gloriosi* in that the effect of their comic military boasting is enhanced by being set in the dramatic context of serious military heroism. Their *alazonia* finds both contrast and tragic counterpart within the play itself. More frequently the *miles gloriosus* in Western literature is less ambiguously comic in his setting. His military analogies lie in

real life and epic literature, but his stage world is a world of pure comic bluster. His heroism need never be matched against heroism of another level of value, but only against other follies as comic as itself: flattery, pedantry, social pretentiousness, romantic sentimentality. Thus, for example, appear Bobadill in Jonson's *Every Man in his Humor,* Don Armado in Shakespeare's *Love's Labour's Lost,* Cutter in Cowley's *The Guardian,* Bluffe in Congreve's *The Old Bachelor,* Matamore in Corneille's *L'Illusion Comique.* They keep pace with the times in their weapons, their fashions in dueling, their historical allusions. Like the Plautine soldiers, they raise laughter with their incredible feats, their inaccurate arithmetic, their unfulfilled threats, their epic comparisons. Like Pyrgopolinices, they are perhaps most amusing when they combine military vanity with vanity in the amorous sphere.

Every reader will have his favourite exponent of such 'un-in-one-breath-utter-able skill'. Jacob von Tyboe, a creation of the eighteenth-century Danish playwright and scholar Ludvig Holberg, may serve as an example. In an explanatory prologue, Jesper Oldfux, a combination of counsellor, confidant, and spy, reveals that his young friend Leonard, currently penniless and in love with Lucilia, has two rivals for her hand.

> The first one's name is Jacob von Tyboe, a man with a screw loose in his head, as far as I can tell. He says he's done service overseas, but can't show service papers or an honourable discharge. The other officers here in town put on a good face with him, and call him Captain, or Major, or even General, depending on his pretensions. When he talks about his campaigns, they pretend to listen with astonishment; when he gets in trouble with the law, they go to court for him; and when he needs some soldiers, they lend him some of their own and order them to treat him with respect and reverence. *En somme,* he is a *divertissement* for the whole garrison.

In encouraging Leonard not to lose hope, Jesper assures him that von Tyboe

> is so stark raving mad that I can easily convince him that he has fought far greater campaigns than Alexander the Great, that Prince Absalom was no comparison for him in beauty, and that every time he hears the church bells ringing it's to bury some woman who has died of unrequited love of him.

The other rival is the Magister Tychonius, and the stage is superbly set for the confrontation of the braggart pedant and the braggart warrior by a debate between their respective servants, Jens and Peer, on the relative merits of the suffix '-us' and the prefix 'von' in ennobling Tycho and Tyboe. The real obstacle in the way of Lucilia, explains Tychonius, is her chambermaid Pernille, who is 'the outwork that must be stormed before one can reach the fortress, and this can only be accomplished *aureis et argentis armis, id est* with gold and coin'. Jesper, much as a Plautine slave might do, devises a trick to get each of the *gloriosi* in trouble with Lucilia. Since von Tyboe cannot read or write, but wishes to send his love a name-day verse in Latin, Jesper arranges to have an obscenely insulting verse written for him by a certain Petronius posing as a poet; Tychonius is cleverly disposed of by turning the *aurea et argenta arma* with which his servant is trying to bribe Pernille into copper pennies, the distinction of the deceit lying in the fact that Tychonius' servant himself is made to trade the sack of silver which he is carrying with the larger sack of worthless coins carried by von Tyboe's man Christoff, who pretends to be in a drunken stupor. Meanwhile the *miles* boasts in accordance with our expectations and assisted by Jesper:

> *Tyboe:* Yes I guess they do know me all over Holland, what with the siege and the great engagement near Amsterdam, where I singlehandedly slew over six hundred.
>
> *Jesper:* Oh, you must add another zero.
>
> *Tyboe:* Let someone else do it. I've never been concerned about the count. In those days another hundred more or less didn't matter to Jacob von Tyboe. What I can't understand is how my broadsword held out so long.
>
> *Jesper:* Oh, you could cut people in half with a penpoint. It isn't the sword that matters, but the hand of the man who wields it. I was reading in an old history book about Alexander the Great who could cut the head off the biggest English bull with one stroke. Alexander was Nebuchadnezzar's field-marshal at the time, and when he heard about this he wanted Alexander to lend him his sabre so that he could try it too. But Nebuchadnezzar missed and got mad and said, 'Das ist nicht die rechtet Sabel, Herr General', to which Alexander replied: 'I lent your Imperial Majesty my sabre, not my arm'.

Of the two braggarts, the maid Pernille prefers the military one, because she likes red clothes and the plumes in his hat send chills up and down her spine. His language of courtship follows the best heroic traditions:

> I am no longer the invincible hero and lion-hearted von Tyboe of a moment ago. The cannons of your eyes have shot such a breach into the fortress of my heart that I am forced to surrender at discretion. I lay at your feet that sword with which I have brought a million men to their grave. If the King of Holland should see me in this posture, he would say, 'Where is your former

courage, your Herculean bravery, Wohlgebohrener Herr von Tyboe'? And I would answer him that even Hercules, who had subjected the five zones of the world, had to have his Delilah to trick him.

The climax is reached in a stichomythy in which Tycho follows Tyboe boast for boast:

> *Tyboe:* Perhaps you have not met Herr von Tyboe?
>
> *Tycho:* Perhaps you have not met Herr Magister Tychonius?
>
> *Tyboe:* I have won more than twenty battles.
>
> *Tycho:* I have disputed *absque praesidio* more than twenty times.
>
> *Tyboe:* Everyone knows me in Holland and Brabant.
>
> *Tycho:* All *literati* know me in Rostock, Helmstad and Wittenberg.
>
> *Tyboe:* I have laid the strongest heroes low with my bare hand.
>
> *Tycho:* I have laid the strongest *opponentes* low with my bare mouth.
>
> *Tyboe:* In half a second I can set a man like you on your rump.
>
> *Tycho:* With half a syllogism I can reduce a whole army *ad absurdum*.

At the end, *miles* and *magister* line up on opposite sides of the stage with four soldiers each. Since neither wants to fight, Jesper easily arranges a truce, while preserving the pride of each. They decide to unite forces and storm Lucilia's house, but both armies are driven off by one pistol shot in the air from Leonard, who himself collects the booty.

Holberg's comedy was written in a period when Denmark was trying to disentangle herself from military alliances and simultaneously assert her cultural independence. He alone contributed much to both these goals through his *History of Denmark* and numerous other works, both serious and satirical. His comedies, although derivative in the same sense that Plautus's were, are not without relevance to these same goals. Holberg especially liked to ridicule the German orientated culture of the bourgeois, as is apparent in von Tyboe. The satire of soldiery will have had a specific timeliness for his audience since Jacob von Tyboe was produced in 1723, only three years after the Treaty of Copenhagen had ended, ingloriously for Denmark, a series of political involvements with the Netherlands that had sent Danish troops into battle throughout northern Europe.

It is only natural that Shaw, who wrote, 'Idealism, which is only a flattering name for romance in politics and morals, is as obnoxious to me as romance in ethics or religion', should make use of the *miles gloriosus* in his 'general onslaught on idealism'.[7] Sergius, in *Arms and the Man,* led a magnificent cavalry charge, which, like Bessus', succeeded by a lucky accident. As his fiancée's mother tells it:

> You can't guess how splendid it is. A cavalry charge—think of that! He defied our Russian commanders—acted without orders—led a charge on his own responsibility—headed it himself—was the first man to sweep through their guns. Can't you see it, Raina; our gallant splendid Bulgarians with their swords and eyes flashing, thundering down like an avalanche and scattering the wretched Servian dandies like chaff.

As his less romantic opponents see it:

> He did it like an operatic tenor—a regular handsome fellow, with flashing eyes and lovely moustache, shouting a war-cry and charging like Don Quixote at the windmills. We nearly burst with laughter at him; but when the sergeant ran up as white as a sheet, and told us they'd sent us the wrong cartridges, and that we couldn't fire a shot for the next ten minutes, we laughed at the other side of our mouths.

Shaw then confronts Sergius with his 'realistic' counterpart, and the stage directions define the contrast: The chest of drawers in Raina's bedroom 'is covered by a variegated native cloth, and on it there is a pile of paper backed novels, a box of chocolate creams, and a miniature easel, on which is a large photograph of an extremely handsome officer, whose lofty bearing and magnetic glance can be felt even from the portrait'. Into this room walks a man whose unromantic name, Shaw later informs us, is Bluntschli:

> A man of about 35, in a deplorable plight, bespattered with mud and blood and snow, his belt and the strap of his revolver case keeping together the torn ruins of the blue coat of a Servian artillery officer. As far as the candlelight and his unwashed, unkempt condition make it possible to judge, he is a man of middling stature and undistinguished appearance, with strong neck and shoulders, a roundish, obstinate looking head covered with short crisp bronze curls, clear quick blue eyes and good brows and mouth, a hopelessly prosaic nose like that of a strong-minded baby. . . .

With this, the 'chocolate cream soldier', the son of a Swiss hotel owner, begins to win the novel-reading Raina, while Sergius, true to his stage character and therefore convinced of his own intense attractiveness to women, wins the vulgarly practical maid Louka for his wife. Each deserves his match, and, with typical Shavian irony, the play ends as romantically as it had begun.

Shaw permits Bluntschli speeches of realistic bitterness relatively untempered by comic distance.

> *Bluntschli:* You never saw a cavalry charge, did you?
>
> *Raina:* How could I?
>
> *Bluntschli:* Ah, perhaps not—of course. Well, it's a funny sight. It's like slinging a handful of peas against a window pane: first one comes; then two or three close behind him; and then all the rest in a lump.
>
> *Raina* (her eyes dilating as she raises her clasped hands ecstatically): Yes, first One!—the bravest of the brave!
>
> *Bluntschli* (prosaically): Hm! you should see the poor devil pulling at his horse.
>
> *Raina:* Why should he pull at his horse?
>
> *Bluntschli* (impatient of so stupid a question): It's running away with him, of course: do you suppose the fellow wants to get there before the others and be killed? Then they all come. You can tell the young ones by their wildness and their slashing. The old ones come bunched up under the number one guard: they know that they are mere projectiles, and that it's no use trying to fight. The wounds are mostly broken knees, from the horses cannoning together.

The fact that soldiers are 'mere projectiles' and *a fortiori* incapable of individual heroism, although it probably underlies any great comic vision of war since Aristophanes, has been more often implicit than explicit until modern times. An exception is Goldoni, whose *La Guerra* is perhaps the bitterest indictment of military glory possible within the framework of comedy. Here, a disillusioned courtesan and ruthless profiteer form the background against which romantic young braggart warriors fight duels and speak of the honour of war. The comedy was not successful, audiences having preferred the more gallant and less shocking *L'Amante Militare.* Yet the realistic tone of parts of *La Guerra* accurately predicts the way in which war has most often appeared in the twentieth century.

Bertolt Brecht's *Mother Courage* has this same collocation of the boast of glory and the sordidness of reality. Eilif, the 'brave son' of the titular heroine, is as truly a *miles gloriosus* in his swagger as any Plautine soldier. Yet his *alazonia* is immediately negated on the stage, not by the impossibility of the boast, but by its frightful truthfulness. His great feat was the theft of cattle from peasants.

> *Eilif:* The rest was a snap. Only the peasants had clubs—and outnumbered us three to one. They made a murderous attack on us. Four of them drove me into a clump of trees, knocked my sword from my hand, and screamed: Surrender! What now? I said to myself, they'll make mincemeat of me.
>
> *Commander:* So what did you do?
>
> *Eilif:* I laughed.
>
> *Commander:* You what?
>
> *Eilif:* I laughed. And so we got to talking. I came right down to business and said: 'Twenty guilders an ox is too much, I bid fifteen'. Like I wanted to buy. That foxed 'em. So while they were scratching their heads, I reached for my good sword and cut 'em to ribbons. Necessity knows no law, huh?

Mother Courage, while taking inventory of her provision wagon, disposes of the *alazonia* of another of the play's representatives of military glory.

> Pity about the Chief—twenty-two pairs, socks— getting killed that way. They say it was an accident. There was a fog over the fields that morning, and the fog was to blame. He'd been telling his men to fight to the death, and was just riding back to safety when he lost his way in the fog, went forward instead of back, found himself in the thick of the battle, and ran right smack into a bullet. . . . I feel sorry for a commander like that—when maybe he had something big in mind, something they'd talk about in times to come, something they'd raise a statue to him for, the conquest of the whole world for example—Lord, the worms have got into these biscuits. . . .

In Brecht's *A Man's a Man,* 'Nothing is sacred any more unless it's identity cards.' The porter Galy Gay has the makings of a *miles gloriosus* with his 'famous self-conceit'. 'So big and fat on the outside, you'd never guess he had an inside like a raw egg,' says Mrs. Gay. The transformation is easy, requiring only a uniform and a new identity card: 'A man like that does the turning all on his own. Throw him into a puddle and he'll grow webs between his fingers in two days.' And the transformation is complete: he accepts the identity of Jeraiah Jip, the attentions of the widow Begbick, his comrades' rations, and the crushing of the Sir el Dchowr fortress as his due. 'Then you're the greatest man the army has, Jeraiah Jip! The human fighting machine'.

In a close structural relationship, reminiscent of the relation between slave and soldier in Plautus, Galy Gay's counterpart, Bloody Five, goes through precisely the opposite process, losing his identity, and then his literal manhood, because he loses his uniform. Early in the play, after he recounts the story of his heroics against the Sikhs, his men chorus, 'What a great soldier you are, Bloody! You give off sparks! Thrilling! The strength of those loins must be terrific too'! But after he is tied up and thrown on the transport train in civilian clothes, his powers are transferred to Galy Gay, and Bloody Five can only threaten and boast and worry about his name:

> The eyes of the whole country are upon me. I was a big wheel. A cannon wheel. My name is Bloody Five. A name that is to be found three times over all through the pages of history! . . .
>
> *Galy Gay:* On account of his name, this gentleman did something very bloody to himself. He shot his sex away. I was very fortunate to see it, for now I see where pigheadedness leads, and what a bloody thing it is for a man to be dissatisfied with himself and make such a fuss about his name!

The self-inflicted castration of Bloody Five, which might strike the reader as shockingly modern, is a literary reiteration of the threatened punishment of Pyrgopolinices, in the last scene of the ***Miles Gloriosus***.

Brecht is enjoying enormous posthumous success in our generation, although we might seem to be living in a period when it is difficult to obtain a comic perspective on war. It is interesting to observe that in *A Man's a Man,* which has been produced several times in recent years, the figure of the *miles gloriosus* is still remarkably close to his Plautine ancestors. Eric Bentley has remarked that 'Brecht's final attitude would be vehemently antitragic. The newfangled notion of Epic Theatre can be construed as a synonym for traditional comedy'.[8] Bloody Five and Galy Gay are not only 'synonyms' of the stock braggart warrior, but they are simultaneously a commentary on the possibility of this stock figure maintaining itself in the twentieth century, concerned as it is with the problem of preserving individual identity in the face of mass numbers and mechanization.

Notes

[1] One may refer, with gratitude, to several excellent studies which have laid the historical groundwork for this and any treatment of the *miles gloriosus*. Otto Ribbeck, *Alazon—Ein Beitrag zur antiken Ethologie* (Leipzig, 1882), collects the Greek material illustrating the various forms of *alazonia,* enabling one to see the predominance of the braggart warrior over other brag-

garts: doctor, cook, soothsayer, etc. Karl von Reinhardstoettner, Plautus, *Spätere Bearbeitungen plautinischer Lustspiele* (Leipzig, 1886), collects and liberally quotes from later adaptations of the *Miles gloriosus,* as of all the Plautine plays, showing incidentally the relative popularity of this particular comedy, second only to the *Amphitruo* and perhaps the *Menaechmi.* Daniel C. Boughner, *The Braggart in Renaissance Comedy, A study in Comparative Drama from Aristophanes to Shakespeare* (Minneapolis, 1954), although perhaps over-ambitious in its sub-title, discusses with critical insight the vast number of *milites gloriosi* who appear in Renaissance comedy in Italy, Spain, France, and England; the reader who is troubled by the jump in this present essay from Plautus to Jonson and Shakespeare will read Boughner with pleasure and illumination. The best guide through the morass of scholarly literature on Plautus is George E. Duckworth, *The Nature of Roman Comedy* (Princeton, 1952), with its extensive bibliography. Of critical works published subsequently Raffaele Perna, *L'originalita di Plauto* (Bari, 1955), is excellent. My own views on the subject of Plautine originality are discussed in detail in 'Plautus as a Source-Book for Roman Religion', *TAPA [Transactions and Proceedings of the American Philological Association],* XC (1959), pp. 48-60. D. C. Earl, in two recent articles, 'Political Terminology in Plautus', *Historia,* IX (1960), pp. 234-43, and 'Terence and Roman Politics', *Historia,* XI (1962), pp. 469-85, has had the courage to use Roman comedy to illustrate Roman political concepts, and I owe much to his example.

² The state of Plautine criticism previous to 1958 may perhaps best be described by imagining what Virgilian criticism would be if only a few scattered fragments of Homer and Apollonius of Rhodes were extant. It is still too soon (in 1963) to measure fully the impact of the *Dyskolos,* and in the light of announcements that more Menander is forthcoming it would show *alazonia* indeed to attempt in this essay a re-evaluation of the role of the braggart in Menander. Although there are a half-dozen passages in our fragments referring to a *miles,* this is scarcely enough on which to base any valid critical judgment.

³ The other four are *Bacchides, Epidicus, Poenulus,* and *Pseudolus.*

⁴ Twenty-three triumphs and ovations are known from the period 200-184 B.C.

⁵ Taken from *Semper Fidelis: The U.S. Marines in the Pacific*—1942-1945, edit. by Patrick O'sheel, USMCR, and Staff Sgt. Gene Cook, USMCR (New York, 1947), pp. 62 and 30.

⁶ The following sample may give one pause. In 1878 the German scholar J. Thummel wrote in an essay on the *miles gloriosus:* 'After the recent wars, which have clearly revealed to the people the seriousness of the situation and the significance of the army, we no longer have any taste for this sort of witless absurdity.'

⁷ In the preface to Volume II of *Plays, Pleasant and Unpleasant.*

⁸ *Seven Plays by Bertolt Brecht,* edit. by Eric Bentley (New York, 1961), p. xvii.

Erich Segal (essay date 1968)

SOURCE: Erich Segal, in *Roman Laughter,* Harvard University Press, 1968, 229 p.

[*In the following excerpts from his book-length study of Plautus's comedies, Segal sketches Plautus's career as a professional playwright popular with Roman audiences and explores the relationship between Plautine Roman comedy and the Roman holiday mentality.*]

Introduction

Of all the Greek and Roman playwrights, Titus Maccius Plautus is the least admired and the most imitated. "Serious" scholars find him insignificant, while serious writers find him indispensable. He deserves our careful attention, not merely because his twenty complete comedies constitute the largest extant corpus of classical dramatic literature (more plays than Euripides, nearly twice as many comedies as Aristophanes, more than three times as many as Terence), but because, without any doubt, Plautus was the most *successful* comic poet in the ancient world. We know of no setback in his artistic career comparable to Aristophanes' frustrations with the *Clouds,* or to Terence's inability to hold his audiences in the face of competition from gross athletic shows. What is more, Plautus is the first known professional playwright. Like Shakespeare and Molière (to name two who found him indispensable), Plautus depended upon the theater for his livelihood. Terence could afford to have the *Hecyra* fail twice. Subsidized by the aristocrats of the so-called Scipionic circle, he had merely to satisfy his patrons. Plautus the professional had to satisfy his public.

It was primarily his economic motives which put Plautus into disrepute with the "classicists." Horace threw one of the first stones when he taxed the Roman comedian for seeking only to make money, and therefore ignoring all the rules for proper dramatic construction.¹ But it was easy for Horace to criticize, doubtless in the comfort of the Sabine farm given him by the eponymous Maecenas, far away from the *profanum vulgus* to whom Plautus had to cater—in order to eat. For, if such an attitude be a fault, Plautus must share Boileau's objection to Molière, that of being "trop ami du peuple." Terence could afford to call the Roman audience *populus stupidus* (*Hecyra* 4), but Plautus knew only too well that those "who live to please must please to live." Even the characters within his plays keep an eye on the mood of the spectators. "Be brief," says one of them as the plot nears its conclusion, "the theatergoers are thirsty."[2]

One of the few indisputable statements which can be made about Plautus the man is that he enjoyed great popular success. The ancient biography states that he twice amassed a fortune in the theater. Having lost his first profits in a disastrous shipping venture, he bailed himself out of a Roman version of debtors' prison by writing once more for the comic stage.[3] Thereafter, he entertained no further business schemes; he merely entertained the Romans.

Plautus' popularity reached such phenomenal proportions that his very name acquired a magic aura. It seems that the mere words "I bring you Plautus" were enough to captivate a huge, unruly—and probably drunken—crowd.[4] In contrast, the prologues of Terence, which work feverishly for the spectators' attention, never once mention their author's name, although they refer to *Plautus* three times. And it is well known that unscrupulous producers would put Plautus' name on plays by others to enhance their market value. A century after the playwright's death, there were in circulation over 130 comedies of allegedly Plautine authorship. It had long since become a scholarly enterprise to determine the authenticity of these plays.[5] And Varro's diligent triple cataloguing of definitely-, probably-, and probably-not-Plautus was by no means the final word. Several centuries thereafter, Aulus Gellius is found passing judgments on Plautinity, as is Macrobius still later, on the threshold of the Dark Ages.

The tribute of such prolific plagiarism and forgery is unique in the annals of literature. One never hears of any Aristophanic apocrypha, of pseudo-Menander or pseudo-Terence. The only valid analogy would seem to be with the Spanish Golden Age, when Lope de Vega's name was forged on dramatic manuscripts to increase their commercial value. Even the Shakespearean apocrypha cannot be considered in this regard, since the counterfeits were never so numerous, nor did they entice vast audiences into the theater, as the names of Plautus and Lope obviously did.

No less amazing than the strength of Plautus' name is the durability of his comedy. This phenomenon of vitality is evident not only on the pages of works like Karl von Reinhardtstoettner's exhaustive chronicle of *Spätere Bearbeitungen,*[6] but on the stages wherever comedy has flourished. The Roman playwright is still very much alive in our own day. As recently as 1962, an unabashed *contaminatio* of the **Pseudolus, Casina,**

and **Mostellaria** entitled *A Funny Thing Happened on the Way to the Forum* delighted Broadway audiences for almost a thousand performances, repeated its triumph throughout the world, and was transformed into a motion picture. Horace might boast that he created a *monumentum aere perennius,* but Plautus created a perennial gold mine.

And yet few scholars of the last century have been willing to examine Plautus for what he undeniably was—a theatrical phenomenon. While the ancient professors like Varro (*diligentissimus,* as Cicero praised him for his research methods) concerned themselves with giving Plautus his due credit by rescuing his name from inferior Latin comedies, the modern approach has shifted from integrity to disintegration. Plautine comedy has become the child in the Judgment of Solomon. From Friedrich Ritschl in the mid-nineteenth century to T. B. L. Webster in the mid-twentieth, a possessive family of scholars have stressed the Roman playwright's "echt-attisches" parentage, considering the value of Plautus to consist solely in what may be discerned of his Greek models which lie beneath an exterior defaced by jokes, puns, songs, and anachronisms.[7] Webster states his views in temperate terms, and a few sentences from his *Studies in Later Greek Comedy* may serve to epitomize the attitude of the Hellenists toward Roman comedy in general. He begins by stating that "the Roman copyists . . . are known quantities," and continues:

> Plautus may elaborate the particular scene to the detriment of the play as a whole; he remodels his text to produce song and dance where there was plain dialogue before; he substitutes elaborate metaphor and mythological allusion for the plain and "ethical" language of the original. But this colouring and distortion is a recognizable quality for which allowances can be made.[8]

And Webster is far more objective than was Gilbert Norwood, who argued:

> When the plays are strongly suffused by Plautus' own personality and interests, they are mostly deplorable . . . The result is that we find only one rational principle for discussing his work. The genuinely Greek passages should be distinguished from the far larger bulk where the original has been smothered by barbarous clownery, intolerable verbosity, and an almost complete indifference to dramatic structure.[9]

Norwood's views have not gone out of fashion. And, although recent discoveries of Menander have done little to strengthen the myth of "the perfection of New Comedy," many scholars still attribute everything that sparkles in Plautus to his models, and everything that falters to his fault.[10]

But the case for Roman artistry has not lacked partisans. Eduard Fraenkel's monumental *Plautinisches im Plautus* demonstrated, even to the satisfaction of the Hellenists, that certain turns of phrase, rhetoric, and imagery are uniquely Plautine—and praiseworthy.[11] Indeed, Webster himself acknowledges a debt to Fraenkel's perceptive work.[12] Moreover, in recent years, sound and persuasive studies, particularly by D. C. Earl, Gordon Williams, and John Arthur Hanson, have pointed out the dramatic purpose of many seemingly random Roman references in the comedies, thereby directing Plautine studies into the area which the present writer considers the most vital: the playwright's relation to his public.[13] And yet the Greco-Roman tug of war still occasions extreme arguments on both sides. Thus, in passionate defense of his countryman's art, Raffaele Perna can loose Plautus entirely from his Greek moorings and eulogize "l'originalità di Plauto."[14]

But what exactly is the "originality" being debated? The "fresh new jokes" which Aristophanes keeps boasting of? That "novel something" which Boccaccio presents in each of his hundred tales? If innovation alone were a standard of excellence, King Ubu would take the palm from King Lear. Clearly this is a notion both unclassical and unsound. Ancient theories of art were based on mimesis within traditional genres: an imitation of life. To this Platonic-Aristotelian concept, Roman aesthetics added a second mimetic principle: imitation of the Greeks. Horace in the *Ars Poetica* states it as the first rule of artistic composition. But this had been Roman practice long before it became Horatian precept. One thinks of Catullus and Sappho, or (more to Horace's liking) Virgil and Homer or, for that matter, the odes of Horace himself. Conscious emulation of Greek models was the tradition in Rome from the very beginning.

And for us Plautus *is* the beginning, the very earliest surviving Latin author. After all, Livius Andronicus is some lines and a legend; Plautus is a literature. There is nothing which distinguishes his treatment of Greek models from that of later Roman artists. The *Ars Poetica* enjoins the poet: *exemplaria Graeca . . . versate manu* (lines 268-269). Plautus frequently describes his technique of composition in a similar manner, e.g. (***Trinummus*** 19):

> Philemo scripsit: Plautus vortit barbare.

> Philemon wrote it: Plautus made the "barbarian" version.

What a paradox that Horatian *versare* is a praiseworthy practice and Plautine *vortere* (the same root, after all) is looked upon as a reverse alchemy which transmutes the gold of Athens into Roman dross.[15] The problem is not eliminated even when a scholar of Fraenkel's stature sets out to redeem the Plautine

vortere,[16] for this merely aggravates the general tendency to anatomize the playwright, to separate "Plautinisches" and "Attisches." But the real Plautus only exists as the sum of his parts—whatever these parts be: *invenies etiam disiecti membra poetae.*

We cannot deny the value of studying a playwright's sources. It is interesting, for example, to know that Shakespeare took Enobarbus' colorful description of Cleopatra on the barge directly from North's Plutarch. The bard copied it almost word for word, altering it chiefly to turn (*vortere?*) prose into pentameter.[17] But are these lines, once in the play, any less Shakespearean? Did it matter to the groundlings who wrote them first? Surely the Roman audience did not care whether what they heard was copied or concocted, as long as it made them laugh. Like Shakespeare and Molière, Plautus begs, borrows, and steals from every conceivable source—including himself.[18] But we must acknowledge that once the play begins, everything becomes "Plautus" just as Plutarch becomes "Shakespeare."

Another circumstance cannot be left unnoticed: Shakespeare's sources fill several well-edited volumes, but there is not a single Greek original to which a Plautine version may be directly compared. There is not even a scene or a speech [See now E. W. Handley, "Menander and Plautus: A Study in Comparison" (London 1968)] that we might contrast with its Latin counterpart in the way Gellius is able to compare Menander and Caecilius.[19] But we do have twenty-one thousand lines of Plautus, twenty Latin plays which share many common elements, regardless of origin. Of course our view of Roman popular comedy, like that of Old Attic comedy, is somewhat distorted, since the work of only one of its many authors is extant. What will be said of Plautus in the succeeding pages may well have been true of the comedy of Naevius and Caecilius.[20] Terence, of course, represents an entirely different tradition: drama for an aristocratic coterie.[21] The Elizabethans who paid their penny at the Globe would not have stood for the theatricals composed in the polite circle of the Countess of Pembroke any more than the Roman groundlings put up with the *fabulae statariae* of Terence.

Even if he disagrees with some of the conclusions put forth on the pages that follow, the reader should not view this study as yet another round in the *agon* between "Plautinisches" and "Attisches." For whether we insist upon calling Plautus' comedy Greek, or dissect it so minutely that we can term it "Greco-osco-etrusco-latin,"[22] there is one undeniable fact to be faced: Plautus made them laugh. And the laughter was Roman.

It is impossible to understand Plautine comedy without appreciating the context in which it was presented; for Roman drama from the earliest times is inextricably connected with Roman holidays. Livy (7.2) associates the beginning of theatrical activity with the *ludi Romani* in 364 B.C., when Etruscan *ludiones* were imported to perform for the populace. At this same September holiday in 240 B.C., Livius Andronicus introduced the first (Greek-into-Latin) "play with a plot." But there is evidence that some kind of performance took place at this harvest festival long before Livy's traditional dates, in the *lusus iuvenum,* which Varro regarded as the true ancestor of Roman dramatic art.[23] Horace describes the "rustic banter" that delighted the farmers during September holidays of a bygone age (*Epist.* 2.1.145-148):

> Fescennina per hunc inventa licentia morem
> versibus alternis opprobria rustica fudit,
> libertasque recurrentis accepta per annos
> lusit amabiliter . . . [24]

> From this tradition [of primitive holidays] the Fescennine, verses developed, and rustic abuse poured forth in dialogue-verse. This freedom, playing happily along, was welcomed year after year . . .

What characterized these festive occasions (and we need not discuss the precise nature of the "entertainment") was *licentia* (line 145) and *libertas* (line 147), attitudes which also describe the *ludi* in the poet's own day (*Ars Poetica* 211ff), as well as the "libertà e licensiozità carnevalesca" of later Italian festivals.[25] Sir James Frazer found this phenomenon in various cultures throughout the world:

> Many people observe an annual period of license— when the customary restraints of law and morality are thrown aside [for] extravagant mirth and jollity. Though these festivals commonly occur at the end of the year, they are frequently associated with one or another of the agricultural seasons, especially the time of sowing and harvest.[26]

The best known of such festivals is, of course, the Roman Saturnalia held in December.[27] There is a strong possibility that this holiday may have originally taken place in September, that is, at the time of the *ludi Romani.* Many scholars even see in the name Saturnus the suggestion of an agricultural deity.[28] Fowler cites the frequent incorporation of winter "saturnalian" customs into harvest holidays—like the *ludi Romani.*[29]

But I am not arguing for the direct influence of specific holiday customs on Roman comedy. The important connection is the fact that "the holiday occasion and the comedy are parallel manifestations of the same pattern of culture."[30] With this principle as his point of departure, C. L. Barber has provided brilliant new insights into Shakespearean comedy. But if Barber's premise is at all valid for Elizabethan drama (which was basically a year-round activity), how much more so would it be for ancient Rome, when the holiday

occasion and the comedy are not merely "parallel manifestations" but simultaneous occurrences. All Plautus is literally "festive comedy," since the various *ludi* were the only occasions for dramatic presentations, a condition which prevailed even as late as Juvenal's day.[31]

The festive feeling, as Freud described it, is "the liberty to do what as a rule is prohibited,"[32] a temporary excess which implies everyday restraint. Comedy, likewise, involves a limited license, a momentary breaking of society's rules. Man's inner urge to "misbehave," the psychological tension between restraint and release, is not a concept new with Freud. Plato long ago recognized this unconscious desire as one of the prime appeals of comedy.[33] Moreover, if there is truth in Max Beerbohm's statement that "laughter rejoices in bonds,"[34] that the joy of the release is in direct proportion to the severity of the restraint, then Roman comedy must have given rise to a laughter of liberation which even the art of Aristophanes (albeit *fecundissimae libertatis,* according to Quintilian)[35] could not equal.

For the "bonds" in Plautus' day were literary as well as social. Greek Old Comedy was distinguished for its παρρησίᾳ that celebrated freedom of speech which licensed even the most brutal personal attacks on individuals of high rank. But the Roman Twelve Tables (those antique *tabulae vetantes,* as Horace calls them)[36] forbade the merest mention of an individual by name— even to praise him. Cicero mentions this in the *De Republica* (4.10): *veteribus displicuisse Romanis vel laudari quemquam in scaena virum, vel vituperari,* "the ancient Romans looked askance if a particular person was either praised or criticized on the stage."[37] "Censorship" is, after all, a Roman invention and originally involved much more than jurisdiction over words. The Roman censor was essentially a guardian of behavior.

We must constantly bear in mind that the age of Plautus was also the age of Cato the Elder. In fact, when he wishes to describe the historical period of the late third century B.C., Aulus Gellius links the names of comic author and authoritarian censor in what at first glance seems a most curious tandem (*N.A.* 17.21.46):

> Ac deinde annis fere post quindecim bellum adversum Poenos sumptum est . . . M. Cato orator in civitate, et Plautus poeta in scaena floruerunt.

> And then, almost fifteen years after the beginning of the Punic War, the men of prominence were Marcus Cato the orator in the state, and Plautus the poet on the stage.

The atmosphere in Rome of this era is constantly described by scholars as "spartan" or "puritanical," and it was, without question, conservative in the extreme.

Early Roman society was distinguished for its "thou shalt not" attitude which was embodied in a unique series of restrictive, moralistic ordinances, about which Crane Brinton comments in *A History of Western Morals:*

> We here encounter clearly for the first time another persistent theme in the moral history of the West, and one that confronts the sociological historian with some difficult problems: sumptuary, prohibitory, "blue law" legislation accompanied by official or semi-official educational propaganda toward a return to "primitive" virtues.[38]

Plautus was just beginning his theatrical career when the first of these laws, the *Lex Oppia,* was enacted in 215 B.C. And the date traditionally given for Plautus' death—184 B.C.—was the famous year in which Cato and Valerius Flaccus assumed the censorship, to wield their power with a reactionary rigor that became a legend. Plutarch reports that they expelled one man from the senate for kissing his wife in public.[39] What actual effect these "blue laws" had on the Romans does not bear upon our arguments.[40] Whether or not they were strictly adhered to is less important than the fact that the rules were promulgated; they were there. And to appreciate what Plautus' characters are doing, we must be aware of what his contemporary Romans were not supposed to do.

Of course conservatism by definition yearns for the good old days, and Byron's wry observation is quite true: "all days when old, are good." Yet in Rome the conservative conscience was very special. For the Romans had created an impossible ideal and transferred it to the past, making myths out of the men who were their forefathers. The Roman obsession with the greatness of their ancestors is epitomized in Cicero's well-known apostrophe (*Tusc. Disp.* 1.1):

> Quae enim tanta gravitas, quae tanta constantia, magnitudo animi, probitas, fides, quae tam excellens in omni genere virtus in ullis fuit ut sit cum maioribus nostris comparanda?

> What people ever had such dignity, such stoutheartedness, greatness of spirit, uprightness, loyalty, such shining qualities of every kind that they could possibly compare with our ancestors?

The guiding principle for behavior was *mos maiorum,* our forefathers' precedent. But which forefathers? Cicero lavished praise on Cato's day, and Cato himself evokes the precedent of still earlier *maiores nostri.*[41] No Roman of any age could fulfill the dictates of *mos maiorum* any more than Sisyphus could push his rock to the summit. Roman *gravitas* (at least as it is celebrated in literature), was more than seriousness and avoidance of frivolity. It was a pervasive melancholy

nurtured by a vague sense of guilt and personal unworthiness. The final lines of Horace's Roman Odes express this (*Carm.* 3.6.46-49):

> Damnosa quid non imminuit dies?
> aetas parentum, peior avis, tulit
>   nos nequiores, mox daturos
>   progeniem vitiosiorem.

> What has ruinous Time not tainted?
> Our parents' age, worse than their ancestors',
>   Bore us, less worthy, soon to bear
>   Children still unworthier.[42]

We find this sentiment everywhere. Cicero begins Book Five of *De Republica* with the same thoughts. The Roman mentality was suffused with guilt feelings analogous to Christian original sin. In the ode quoted above we hear of *delicta nondum expiata.*[43] In Virgil's *Aeneid* it is voiced even more strongly; the sins being purged in Elysium are described as *vetera mala, scelus infectum, concreta labes* (6.735-746).[44] The fact that these are poetic references to the recent civil wars, as well as to the mythical sin of Romulus, does not adequately explain the omnipresence of this motif. It was more than Adam's transgression which caused the medieval loathing for the flesh. In both societies, the guilt is even more psychological than historical. *Gravitas* may describe a paragon of behavior, but it may also reveal a pathology.

A Freudian psychologist would describe the early Romans as a people with an overdeveloped superego. The superego, as A. A. Brill defined it, is

> a precipitate of all the prohibitions and inhibitions, all the rules which are impressed upon the child by his parents and parental substitutes. The feeling of *conscience* depends altogether on the superego.[45]

These very same words serve as a precise definition of *mos maiorum,* the rules imposed upon the Romans by various parental figures, not the least of whom was *pater* Aeneas! Every Roman institution was a sacred patriarchy, every family the state in miniature. But Aeneas was a myth, and the ideal he embodied an impossibility. It is small wonder that *mos maiorum* is linked with *gravitas.*[46] The superego is the father of melancholy.

But comedy has been described by the psychiatrist Ernst Kris as a "holiday for the superego,"[47] and Plautus, reflecting as he does the festive spirit, banishes Roman melancholy, turning everyday attitudes and everyday values completely upside down. To a society with a fantastic compulsion for hierarchies, order, and obedience, he presents a saturnalian chaos.[48] To a people who regarded a parent's authority with religious awe and could punish any infringement with death, Plautus presents an audacious irreverence for all elders. The atmosphere of his comedy is like that of the medieval Feast of Fools (product of another highly restrictive society), which some see as "providing a safety valve for repressed sentiments which otherwise might have broken their bonds more violently."[49] But we need not stress the cathartic value of Plautine comedy; we need only appreciate the fascination which a flouting of the rules would have had for people so bound by them in everyday life. This very appeal to what Shakespeare called "holiday humor" accounts in large measure for the unequaled success of Plautus.

If we are to understand the whole tradition of popular comedy, we must see Plautus in the proper perspective, and acknowledge that his work is a significant milestone.[50] If it seem bold to compare him with Aristophanes, let us not forget that Cicero did so.[51] Nor should we hesitate to compare to Molière a writer who had also mastered "le grand art de plaire." The most passionate partisan would never place Plautus' achievement on a par with Shakespeare's, but no reasonable man should deny that Plautus was like Noah: great in his age. His art does not give rise to "thoughtful laughter," but Meredith may not be correct in seeing this as the aim of True Comedy. For True Comedy should banish *all* thought—of mortality and morality. It should evoke a laughter which temporarily lifts from us the weight of the world, whether we call it "das Unbehagen," loathèd melancholy, or *gravitas*.

Plautus is our only example of popular Roman entertainment, comedy "as they liked it." His twenty plays show us what delighted a nation on the verge of world domination, in the only age when its theater lived and flourished. Rome went on to build much that remains vital and viable in our own day. The most obvious monuments to her craftsmanship are the aqueducts which still carry water, the bridges and highways which can still be traveled. But when Zero Mostel as Pseudolus trod nightly on his way to the Broadway forum, he was walking another Roman road of astounding durability.

. . . . .

From Forum to Festival

The primary characteristic of "holiday" is its distinct separation from "every day." Ordinary activities cease, the agenda completely changes. In a mood of sincere admiration (not, as so often, sarcastically) Horace praises the ideal "Roman day" (*Epist.* 2.1.103-107):

> Romae dulce diu fuit et sollemne reclusa
> mane domo vigilare, clienti promere iura
> cautos nominibus rectis expendere nummos,
> maiores audire, minori dicere per quae
> crescere res posset, minui damnosa libido.

At Rome it was a pleasure and a practice of long standing to be up and about in the early morning, with the house doors open, giving legal aid to clients, carefully investing money with good-risk creditors, heeding one's elders and teaching the younger generation how to increase their wealth and decrease the ruinous urge to be profligate.

. . . [I]t is interesting to note that Horace is here comparing the responsible Romans with the fun-loving Greeks (whom he has just described in lines 93-102). The latter, he intimates, are a "holiday race," whose everyday activities are play, not work. Such noble practices as *clienti promere iura* are contrasted to a Greek agenda filled with games and levity. Horace describes Greek behavior as *nugari* (line 93) and *ludere* (line 99), words which always had pejorative connotations to the Roman.[1]

Horace's "Roman day" also stands in direct opposition to the activities of a "Plautine day." . . . [T]he people of Plautus do the precise opposite of "heeding one's elders." Such an attitude was a prime characteristic of *pietas,* and this virtue is turned topsy-turvy by the comic playwright. Unlike the economical, obedient sons whom Horace eulogizes, the younger generation in Plautus is always in passionate pursuit of *damnosa libido*. And if Horace epitomizes as *ludere* all activities that contrast with the duties of a "Roman day," it is understandable that the Roman festivals were all called *ludi*.[2]

The **Menaechmi** illustrates in dramatic terms the longing of an ordinary citizen for temporary escape from his everyday agenda. The two houses on stage represent the conflicting forces in the comedy. They are not unlike the statues of Artemis and Aphrodite which frame the setting of Euripides' *Hippolytus*. In both plays, the action takes place in a magnetic field between personifications of restraint and release. It is no mere coincidence that the house of Menaechmus I stands at the exit nearer the forum. The Epidamnian twin is bound by innumerable ties, legal, financial, and social obligations, not to mention his marital bond to a shrewish wife who is constantly "on the job." Menaechmus describes his wife's behavior as excessive *industria* (line 123), a term which almost gives allegorical overtones to the action of the comedy.

Across the stage, and nearer the harbor whence visitors come, dwells a lady of pleasure aptly named Erotium. (Menaechmus' spouse has no name at all, she is merely called *matrona*. Shakespeare reverses this situation in the *Comedy of Errors,* creating a nameless "courtesan.") Menaechmus always seems to have *le mot juste,* for he refers to his mistress as *voluptas,* which is not only an endearment, but the most appropriate description of the atmosphere at Erotium's house, one which contrasts diametrically with the *industria* across the stage. In going from one side to the other,

Menaechmus is "acting out" the inner direction of the comic spirit. The comedy itself presents the conflict of *industria* and *voluptas,* holiday versus everyday, or, as Freud would describe it, the reality principle versus the pleasure principle.

As the parasite Peniculus remarks, today's celebration is much overdue, there has been a long "intermission" (*intervallum iam hos dies multos fuit,* line 104). But when Menaechmus gives a party it is almost a national holiday. His parasite, who must be regarded an expert in these matters, says as much (lines 100-101):

> Ita est adulescens: ipsus escae maxumae
> Cerialis cenas dat . . .

> That young chap is like this: the greatest of
>   all eaters,
> The feasts he gives are festivals of Ceres . .

To Peniculus, his patron's entertainments are like those gala Roman occasions when banquets were served in the Circus; this will be quite a day indeed.

We first meet Menaechmus battling soldier-like against domestic oppression.[3] To him, the precondition for holiday is the absence of his wife (line 152):

> Clam uxoremst ubi pulchre habeamus atque
>   hunc comburamus diem.

> Hidden from my wife, we'll live it up and
>   burn this day to ashes.[4]

He describes her restrictive behavior in no uncertain terms (lines 114-118):

> Nam quotiens foras ire volo,
>   me retines, revocas, rogitas,
> quo ego eam, quam rem agam, quid negoti
>   geram,
> quid petam, quid feram, quid foris
>   egerim.
> portitorem domum duxi, ita omnem mihi
> rem necesse eloqui est, quidquid egi atque
>   ago.

> However often I try to go out, you detain
>   me, delay me,
>   demand such details as:
> Where I'm going, what I'm doing, what's
>   my business all about,
> Deals I'm making, undertaking, what I did
>   when I was out.
> I don't have a wife—I've wed a customs
>   office bureaucrat,
> For I must declare the things I've done,
>   I'm doing, and all that!

His wife is the antithesis of the holiday spirit; she is both rule book and conscience, always questioning his behavior. Her *industria* has driven Menaechmus to seek festive release, as he himself tells her (lines 122-124):

> Malo cavebis si sapis,
>   virum observare desines.
> atque adeo, ne me nequiquam serves, *ob eam
>   industriam*
> hodie ducam scortum ad cenam atque aliquo
>   condicam foras.

> Watch out for trouble, if you're wise,
>   A husband hates a wife who spies.
> But so you won't have watched in vain, for
>   all your diligence and care,
> Today I've asked a wench to dinner, and
>   we're eating out somewhere.

The playwright himself understood the psychological motivations for his hero's behavior, as indicated by the remarks of Menaechmus' father-in-law later in the play. When his wife sends for him to complain about her husband's antics, the *senex* blames her, not Menaechmus (lines 788-791):

> SENEX: . . . Quotiens monstravi tibi viro ut
>   morem geras,
>   quid ille faciat, ne id observes, quo eat,
>   quid rerum gerat.
> MATRONA: At enim ille hinc amat meretricem
>   ex proxumo.
> SENEX: Sane sapit,
>   atque *ob istanc industriam* etiam faxo
>   amabit amplius.

> OLD MAN: . . . How often have I warned you
>   to behave yourself with him.
>   Don't watch where he's going, what he's
>   doing, what his business is.
> WIFE: But he loves a fancy woman next door.
> OLD MAN: He's very wise!
>   And I tell you thanks to all your diligence,
>   he'll love her more!

The old man echoes Menaechmus' opening tirade almost verbatim (especially lines 115 and 122). He excuses the husband's desire to revel, seeing it as the natural result of the wife's excessive vigilance: *ob eam industriam* (Menaechmus, line 123), *ob istanc industriam* (Old Man, line 791).[5]

In contrast to the wife's *industria,* the mistress represents its polar opposite, pleasure personified. When he first spies her, his explanation emphasizes this antithesis, counterpoising as it does *uxor* and *voluptas,* withholding the verb, and hence the entire meaning of the outcry until the last possible moment (line 189):

Ut ego uxorem, mea voluptas, ubi te aspicio,
   odi male!

Oh my wife, my joy, when I look at *you*, how
   I hate *her!*

Wife and mistress dwell at the antipodes of human experience; Plautus states this in no uncertain terms. To visit Erotium is *pulchre habere* (line 152), whereas life with his wife is a perpetual atmosphere of *male habere* (line 569). This contrast—the essential conflict of the *Menaechmi*—goes even further. Just as Erotium is nothing at all like Menaechmus' wife, so too the day which will be devoted to her will differ totally from an ordinary day. Even the banquet which the wayward husband orders would underscore for the Roman audience in a very specific way that the usual rules would be set aside (lines 208-213, 215):

Iube igitur tribus nobis apud te prandium
   accurarier,
atque aliquid scitamentorum de foro
   opsonarier,
glandionidam suillam, laridum pernonidam,
aut sincipitamenta porcina aut aliquid ad eum
   modum,
madida quae mi adposita in mensa miluinam
   suggerant;
atque actutum . . . propera modo.

Please arrange a feast at your house, have it
   cooked for three of us.
Also have some very special party foods
   bought in the forum.
Glandiose, whole-hog, and a descendant of the
   lardly ham.
Or perhaps some pork chopettes, or anything
   along these lines.
Let whatever's served be "stewed," to make
   me hungry as a hawk.
Quickly too . . . and hurry up.

In many ways Menaechmus' menu resembles the slave's request for festive food in the ***Casina***. . . . His desire for something "stewed" echoes Olympio's call for a "drunken dinner," and in both instances there is an emphasis on "holiday haste."[6] Most important, each celebrant rejects ordinary Roman fare. For Olympio, this merely meant "something fine and fancy" as opposed to "bland barbarian beans." But the delicacies which Menaechmus orders and all food "along those lines" were specifically forbidden to Romans by the current sumptuary laws. These, according to Pliny, forbade the eating of *abdomina, glandia, testiculi, vulvae, sincipita verrina*.[7] Not only do these outlawed items figure prominently on Menaechmus' bill of fare, but Plautus plays with them verbally, concocting dishes like *sincipitamenta,* and the comic patronymics *glandionida* and *pernonida*. Apparently Menaechmus is sa-

voring his words in anticipation of the breaking-of-the-rules banquet.

According to Pliny, Cato's orations constantly inveighed against gastronomic luxury, especially eating certain cuts of pork.[8] In spite of this (perhaps because of this), Plautine gourmets went whole hog, and so, it appears, did the characters of Naevius. Just as the fragments of Plautus' comic predecessor reveal traces of *pietas* abused, so too they mention some of the unlawful delicacies.[9] Once again we discover a Plautine characteristic which may well have been common to the general *palliata* tradition: a holiday from the rules (here dietary), further emphasized when the playwright calls attention to the very prohibition being violated.[10]

After ordering his un-Roman banquet, Menaechmus leaves for the forum. A split second later, his long-lost twin enters from the harbor. And by artful coincidence, the visiting brother's very first word upon arrival in Epidamnus is *voluptas* (line 226). He is little aware of the reverberations that word will have for him and how apt a description it is for the whole way of life in this place. For with the exception of his twin brother's house, this is the ultimate in "party towns." When the slave Messenio describes it to his master, he uses only superlatives (lines 258-264):

Nam ita est haec hominum natio: in
   Epidamnieis
voluptarii atque potatores maxumi;
tum sycophantae et palpatores plurumi
in urbe hac habitant; tum meretrices mulieres
nusquam perhibentur blandiores gentium.
propterea huic urbi nomen Epidamno
   inditumst,
quia nemo ferme huc sine damno devortitur.

Now here's the race of men you'll find in
   Epidamnus:
The greatest libertines, the greatest drinkers
   too,
The most bamboozlers and charming flatterers
Live in this city. And as for wanton women,
   well—
Nowhere in the world, I'm told, are they
   more dazzling.
Because of this, they call the city Epidamnus,
For no one leaves unscathed, "undamaged," as
   it were.

The visiting twin does indeed encounter "voluptuaries," especially the dazzling Erotium, but unlike an ordinary tourist on an ordinary day he will suffer no damage (*damnum* literally means financial ruin). This boy from Syracuse belongs to a great comic tradition: a lowly stranger who arrives in town, is mistaken for someone of greater importance, and fulfills the comic dream: everything for nothing, or more specifically, food, sex, and money. Xanthias in the *Frogs* is the first of such types in surviving ancient comedy, and true to this tradition is Khlestakov, Gogol's humble government clerk who is mistaken for the Inspector General and treated accordingly. Like Gogol's hero, the traveling Menaechmus has come to town virtually penniless. What ensues seems too good to be true. A lovely courtesan calls him by name and invites him to a lavish feast of all the senses . . . at no cost. What Menaechmus II receives is the precise opposite of *damnum*. In fact he profits in every imaginable way. Having reveled to the fullest and been given an expensive dress (supposedly to be taken to the embroiderer for improvements), he emerges from Erotium's house drunk, garlanded and euphoric; no man, he says, has ever received more favors in just a single day (lines 473-477).

But someone has to pay the bill. And here the local twin suffers a double *damnum,* physical as well as fiscal, for the significant reason that he has gone to work on a holiday. Acting "the good Roman," Menaechmus I has gone to the forum and ended up defending a client in court. According to Horace, *clienti promere iura* was one of the primary duties of the ideal Roman day. . . . The fate of Menaechmus I emphatically demonstrates how inimical this activity is to the festive agenda. He finally reenters with a barrage-in-song against the patronage system (lines 571ff).[11] It is a bothersome thing to have clients (lines 588-589):

> Sicut me hodie nimis sollicitum cliens quidam
>   habuit, neque quod volui
> agere aut quicum licitumst, ita med attinuit,
>   ita detinuit.

> I was just now delayed, forced to give legal
>   aid,
>   no evading this client of mine who had
>   found me.
> Though I wanted to do you know what—and
>   with who—
>   he just bound me and tied ropes around me.

Fulfilling one's civic obligations is a form of restraint, it "tied up" Menaechmus (*ita med attinuit, ita detinuit*) and prevented him from following his instinct (*quod volui agere*).[12] In the famous *canticum* which follows, the twin of Epidamnus realizes that his great error was even thinking of business on a holiday. It is as much his fault as his client's (lines 596-599):

> Di illum omnes perdant, ita mihi
> hunc hodie corrupit diem,
> meque adeo, qui hodie forum
> umquam oculis inspexi meis.
> diem corrupi optimum.
> iussi adparari prandium,

> amica exspectat me, scio.
> ubi primum est licitum, ilico
> properavi abire de foro.

> By all the heavens, cursed be he
> Who just destroyed this day for me.
> And curse me too, a fool today,
> For ever heading forum's way.
> The greatest day of all destroyed,
> The feast prepared, but not enjoyed.
> My love awaits, I know. Indeed,
> The very moment I was freed
> I left the forum with great speed.

Plautus stresses the haste with which Menaechmus rushes away from the commercial center (*ubi primum . . . ilico / properavi*). From business in the forum, he dashes to pleasure at its polar opposite: across the stage, at the house of Erotium. The antipodes of the Plautine world are *industria* and *voluptas,* forum and festivity. At Rome, the first step in a holiday direction was always (as quickly as possible) *abire de foro.*

Forum and festivity are also specifically counterpoised in the **Casina**. Like young Menaechmus, old Lysidamus has set this day aside for merrymaking (*ego cum Casina faciam nuptias!* line 486), and has ordered a luxurious banquet. But again like Menaechmus, Lysidamus has been detained by a lawsuit in the forum. He finally reenters, having learned his lesson (lines 563-568):

> Stultitia magna est, mea quidem sententia,
> hominem amatorem ullum ad forum procedere,
> in eum diem quoi quod amet in mundo siet;
> sicut ego feci stultus. contrivi diem,
> dum asto advocatus cuidam cognato meo;
> quem hercle ego litem adeo perdidisse
>   gaudeo.

> It's folly, that's what I would call it, total
>   folly,
> For any man in love just to approach the
>   forum,
> The very day his love awaits, all fancied up.
> That's what I've done, fool that I am. I've
>   ruined the day,
> While acting as attorney for a relative.
> By Hercules, I'm overjoyed we lost the
>   case!

Ad forum procedere has destroyed Lysidamus' festive plans (*contrivi diem*) just as a similar journey had spoiled Menaechmus' day (*diem corrupi optimum, Menaechmi* 598a). Again, like the twin of Epidamnus, Lysidamus has been defeated in court.[13] Totally devoid of professional pride, Lysidamus is happy to have failed. These lawyers' laments prove conclusively that funny things happen only on the way *from* the forum.[14]

The prologue to the *Casina* affirms this interpretation of the festive rule.[15] It demonstrates that the lesson which Menaechmus and Lysidamus learn the hard way is actually the first principle of Roman holiday. The prologue's appeal to the public is very specific (lines 23-26):

> Eicite ex animo curam atque alienum aes,
> ne quis formidet flagitatorem suom.
> ludi sunt, ludus datus est argentariis;
> tranquillum est, Alcedonia sunt circum
>   forum.

> Just kick out all your cares, and as for debts,
>   ignore 'em.
> Let no one fear fierce creditors will sue.
> It's holiday for everyone—for bankers too.[16]
> All's calm, a halcyon quiet floats around the
>   forum.

The prologue speaks not merely of the play, but of the day as well. The *ludi* are on, here in Rome, and there is an unusual silence even in the very center of business. So unequivocal is this statement that all commerce has ceased that each of the lines quoted contains a financial or business reference: to debts, creditors, bankers, and the banking district. During the *ludi* all ordinary activity came to an absolute standstill, a practice which Cicero, in the heat of prosecuting Verres, vehemently objects to, but could do nothing to change.[17] On a Roman holiday there was simply no business—but show business. The forum was empty because the theater was packed. The sons of Aeneas, longing like Menaechmus to loose their everyday ties, to travel from the regions of *industria* to the realm of *voluptas,* had all beaten a path to that festive place which may best be described as being as far as possible from the forum.

The Roman may have flatteringly pictured himself as a paragon of *pietas,* but an objective view sees him as more pragmatic than pious. His materialistic attitude is evident even in Horace's idealized "Roman day," where the poet lauds the noble practice of heeding one's elders. The parents he pictures are not imparting to their children *mos maiorum* in the spiritual sense but are rather lecturing them on sound investment policy: *per quae / crescere res posset (Epist.* 2.1.106-107). And *this* was in fact considered a Roman virtue. In the oft-quoted eulogy by Quintus Metellus at his father's funeral (221 B.C.), the son claims that his father achieved the ten greatest things (*decem maximas res optimasque*) which wise men strive for, and these include not only being first in war and first in peace, but being first in finance as well: *pecuniam magnam bono modo invenire.*[18] It is well attested that the Romans were extremely fond of money and would pass up no opportunity for financial gain.[19] Horace's picture of the Roman father teaching his son to enlarge his patrimony serves well to de-

scribe Cato the Elder, who, according to Plutarch, considered a man who increased the capital he inherited to be "marvelous and godlike." . . .[20]

Polybius, like Terence, was a protégé of Scipio Aemilianus and could hardly be praised for writing *sine ira et studio;* yet in his Universal History he punctuates what is essentially a panegyric celebrating the superiority of Roman qualities to Greek with the candid observation that the Roman was extremely difficult, in fact a stickler when it came to financial matters. As Polybius sees it, this quality is not unpraiseworthy; it suggests that the Romans were hyperefficient and kept a good house. He states in no uncertain terms that at Rome you get nothing for nothing (31.26.9): . . .

> Absolutely no one gives anyone *anything* he
> possesses of his own free will.

Polybius' emphatic language demonstrates how antithetical the typical Roman outlook was to the comic spirit. Max Eastman observes that in comedy it is "the *too* much—always and absolutely—not the *much* that is funny."[21] But according to Polybius "too much" is a completely un-Roman concept. In the pragmatic "nothing-for-nothing" atmosphere of workaday Rome, there could be none of the laughter which Freud saw as inspired by the aspect of "an excessive expenditure of energy."[22] The Romans had a violent aversion to spending anything, as Polybius notes further: "their punctiliousness about expenditures is as intense as their compulsion to turn every second of time into profit" (31.27.11). One of Plautus' most brilliant characters, Euclio the miser, reflects this trait, caricatured to absurdity. He would not only refuse to expend the energy for laughter, but he is parsimonious even with his ordinary breath (*Aulularia* 302-303):

> PYTHODICUS: Quin cum it dormitum, follem
>   obstringit ob gulam.
> ANTHRAX: Cur?
> PYTHODICUS: Ne quid animae forte amittat
>   dormiens.

> PYTHODICUS: Why when he sleeps he strings
>   a bag around his gullet.
> ANTHRAX: What for?
> PYTHODICUS: So he won't lose a bit of
>   breath while sleeping.

Euclio is also madly possessive about his bath water (line 308), his hunger (line 311), and his fingernails (lines 312-313). When he is viewed with Polybius' description in mind, Euclio seems very much a "Roman parody." . . . The Romans were notoriously stingy (we need not paint the lily by calling them "economical"). Plautus even mocks their well-known miserliness in one of his prologues. . . . [T]he *Truculentus* opens with an invitation to the audience to make room in their imaginations so that Plautus can deliver Athens to Rome (lines 1-3). The prologue then muses light-heartedly about what would happen if Plautus would ask the spectators to *pay* for this delivery. He quickly concludes that Romans would refuse to hand over any cash whatever, noting further that the spectators would be following in the footsteps of their forefathers (line 7):

> Eu hercle in vobis resident mores pristini!

> By Hercules, the great traditions live in you![25]

Although in the "Roman day" which we have been discussing he lauds the pursuit of wealth, Horace the moralist more often deplores the Roman predilection for material gain at the expense of spiritual enrichment.[26] But whether we believe the poet when he is admiring or critical, we are none the less presented with a Roman society imbued with the doctrine of acquisition. And "doctrine" it was. This attitude seems to have been characteristic of the Romans from the earliest times, and at least one scholar sees it as an implicit aspect of *mos maiorum*.[27]

Moreover, while the Roman praised profit-making by noble means, as in the elder Metellus' accumulation of wealth *bono modo* (see above), in point of fact he gathered his lucre *quocumque modo,* by means fair or foul. Witness Horace's deprecation of a current maxim (*Epist.* 1.1.65-66):

> . . . rem facias rem
> si possis, recte, si non quocumque modo,
>   rem.

These are the very lines that Ben Jonson renders in describing the materialistic atmosphere of his contemporary London (*Every Man in His Humour* II v 49-51):

> The rule, "get money"; still, "get money, boy,
> No matter by what means; money will do
> More, boy, than my lord's letter."

Thus while the Romans may have extolled *virtus* in word, in deed they placed money before morality, *virtus post nummos.* Horace imagines this as a phrase which echoes and reechoes from one end of the forum to the other.[28] Even Cato, for all his celebrated asceticism, chased huge profits in the most disreputable manner.[29] Ironically, Livy praises him as a *contemptor . . . divitiarum* (39.40.11), an ambiguous compliment, suggesting that he had no regard whatever for wealth, in the very manner Virgil described his ideal hero Aeneas, who responded nobly to King Evander's request, *aude, hospes, contemnere opes.*[30] But Livy surely means that Cato was unawed by the riches of others, probably

because he had gathered so much for himself, and *quocumque modo,* at that.

In direct contrast to Horace's picture of the forum resounding noisily with shouts of *quaerenda pecunia,* we may have the situation described by the **Casina** prologue, *tranquillum est, Alcedonia sunt circum forum* (line 26). This atypical calm, this empty business district, characterizes a Roman holiday, the only occasion on which the city did not echo with the cry, "get money."

The characters of Plautus display an attitude diametrically opposed to the markedly Roman regard for profit. His comedies almost always involve money matters, but never the pursuit of wealth for its own sake. The typical Plautine youth may be *amans et egens,* but he only seeks money enough to win his beloved. Quite unlike Balzac in his *Comédie Humaine,* Plautus never presents a scheming protagonist in search of "une femme et une fortune." His young men are lunatic-lovers who scorn material things. Phaedromus in the **Curculio** (*verum totum insanum amare,* line 177) provides a ready example: *sibi sua habeant regna reges, sibi divitias divites* (line 178), "let kings have kingdoms, rich men have their riches." This is, of course, a cliché, a romantic outburst that in most contexts would be taken with a grain of salt (although it specifically reminds the student of Latin poetry of that unRoman poet Tibullus).[31] But these Plautine lovers live up to their word; they want the girl, not the gold.

Nowhere in Plautus do we find an ambitious young man like Balzac's Eugène de Rastignac. Though there are several marriages in the plays, the affluence of the girl's family is never a motivating factor.[32] Yet this affects even Shakespeare's suitors from time to time, as, for example, Fenton in *The Merry Wives of Windsor* (III iv 13-16):

> Albeit I will confess thy father's wealth
> Was the first motive that I wooed thee, Anne,
> Yet wooing thee, I found thee of more value
> Than stamps of gold, or sums in sealèd bags.[33]

The attitude of Plautus' lovers toward dowries stands in sharp distinction to what actually went on in Roman society at the time, where the size of the bridal portion greatly influenced most marriages. Polybius makes this point, describing very complicated dowry arrangements, the payments to be made in three precise installments, and so forth.[34] Not only does the behavior of the Plautine hero differ from the practices of the audience, but it contrasts with the outlook of almost all comic heroes, perhaps typified by Beaumarchais's scheming barber, of whom the countess remarks, "Figaro n'est pas homme à laisser échapper une dot." In fact Figaro is after *two* dowries and ends up with *three,* a triumph celebrated in the final song,

Triple dot, femme superbe
Que de biens pour un époux![35]

Even if a dowry is mentioned in Plautus (which is seldom), it is dismissed with a shrug or rejected without regret. Thus Megadorus in the **Aulularia** is not only willing, but anxious, to take Euclio's daughter *sans dot,* a condition which became a famous *mot de caractère* in Molière's adaptation.[36] The plot of the **Trinummus** involves arranging a dowry for a young man who wants none at all. Lysiteles tells his father that he would marry into his best friend's family (lines 374-375, 378):

> LYSITELES: Soror illi est adulta virgo grandis:
>   eam cupio, pater,
>   ducere uxorem sine dote.
> PHILTO: Sine dote uxorem?
> LYSITELES: Ita.
>
>   . . . . .
>
> PHILTO: Egone indotatam te uxorem ut patiar?

> LYSITELES: Sir, his sister is a grown-up girl,
>   and she's the one I'd like to
>   Take to wife without a dowry.
> PHILTO *(choking)*:   Without a dowry?
>   Wife?
> LYSITELES: That's right.
>
>   . . . . .
>
> PHILTO: Can I really bear to let you wed a
>   wife without a dowry?[37]

The sire is far from pleased, but the son convinces him.[38] Even when the girl's father arrives unexpectedly from abroad and offers a marriage portion, Lysiteles insists, *dotem nil moror* (line 1158). He finally relents, but the subject is dismissed forever three lines later. In the **Cistellaria,** young Alcesimarchus rejects great riches and a huge dowry for his true love Silenium. His father is distraught and beseeches his son to abandon a sweetheart who "keeps you from great wealth, a dowry both fat and plentiful," *prohibet divitiis maximis, dote altili atque opima* (line 305), but not even the most passionate pleas can impress upon the Plautine lover the (everyday) value of money.[39]

If a dowry is suddenly reduced, as in the **Truculentus,** because the young man has been too forward with his fiancée, the youth cares little (lines 844-846):

> CALLICLES: . . . verum hoc ego te multabo
>   bolo:
>   sex talenta magna dotis demam pro ista
>   inscitia.
> DINIARCHUS: Bene agis mecum.

> CALLICLES: . . . you'll be fined a pile for this:
>   Six whole talents from her dowry for your
>   little indiscretion.
> DINIARCHUS: Oh, you're very kind to me.

And the situation in this play differs vastly from that of the **Cistellaria.** Here young Diniarchus is not a rhapsodic Romeo willing to give all for love and the world well lost. When the above-quoted conversation takes place, he has already ravished Callicles' daughter, given her a child, and then broken the engagement. From a pragmatic point of view, he has a very strong bargaining point, since the old man is anxious to give his grandchild legitimacy. Yet here again, and this time without strong motivation, a Plautine lover pays no attention to the practical matters that concerned his audience almost to the point of obsession.

Scholars have called attention to the multitude of commercial references in Plautus, to the countless mentions of contracts, debts, lawsuits, business trips, and so forth. But few have noted that this is rarely "business as usual." The only meaningful transactions are those which bring the youth the girl he longs for. In almost every instance, the sum of money for which the clever slave is scheming turns out to be just enough to buy his master's sweetheart and nothing more. Profit for its own sake is never a factor; gold is merely the means to an end. Here again Plautine and Balzacian worlds stand in direct contrast. At the end of *Eugénie Grandet,* for example, Judge de Bonfons marries the heroine for her fortune, but agrees to forgo all conjugal rights. In Plautus the situation is just the reverse: *connubium* always takes precedence over *commercium.*[40] As one of his typical *adulescentes* expresses it (*Poenulus* 328):

> Namque edepol lucrum amare nullum
>   amatorem addecet.

> A lover should love love, by Pollux, not love
>   lucre.

Plautus presents a world where *ludi sunt argentariis,* whereas in Balzac, as old Grandet tells his daughter, "la vie est une affaire."

In Plautus, money is meaningless, coins are merely tokens to be redeemed for pleasure. It is more than coincidence that in the **Asinaria** the amount needed to purchase the girl Philaenium is precisely the sum being delivered as payment for the asses: twenty *minae.* This price is mentioned no less than eighteen times during the play, but its "value" lies only in what it represents, a yearlong holiday with a beautiful courtesan (*Asinaria* 636-637):

> ARGYRIPPUS: Videtin viginti minae quid
>   pollent quidve possunt?

ille qui illas perdit salvos est, ego qui non
perdo, pereo.

ARGYRIPPUS: You see what power and
potential twenty *minae* have?
To spend them is to save myself; with none
to spend, I'm spent![41]

The aim is to gain the money with a view toward "losing
it" again. The sum they are after is just enough; but to
the Plautine lover, "just enough" is *satis superque.*

An even stranger phenomenon is that the prime mover
in the plots, the clever slave, is never after profit for
himself.[42] This is especially odd considering that slaves
in Plautus' day were not only permitted, but encouraged, to amass their own *peculium* (personal savings).
Bondsmen who did not try to save toward their ultimate
freedom were looked upon with disdain and suspicion.[43]
Yet Plautine slaves do not care for cash. Epidicus ex-
ecutes his particular scheme so well that he obtains
more money than his master needs. Triumphantly, he
hands the sack of gold over to his young *patronus,*
asking for no financial reward (*Epidicus* 345-347):

EPIDICUS: . . . accipe hoc sis.
STRATIPPOCLES: Quantum hic inest?
EPIDICUS: Quantum sat est, et plus
satis: superfit.
decem minis plus attuli quam tu danistae
debes.

EPIDICUS: . . . now take this please.
STRATIPPOCLES: How much is here?
EPIDICUS: Enough and more—an extra
overflow.
I've even brought you ten more *minae* than
you owe the broker.

How would the Roman audience react to this? Polybius
claimed that absolutely no one in Rome would refuse
any opportunity for any sort of profit, yet here a slave
rejects an ideal occasion to add to his *peculium.* For
Plautine slaves, however, the playing's the thing. Toxilus
in the *Persa* best expresses this attitude when he
shouts, *iam nolo argentum!* (line 127).[44] Like Epidicus
and other slaves with like esprit, the only profit he
seeks is nonmaterial.

The *Poenulus* presents an interesting variation on this
theme. Here the young lover is not *egens,* but *affluens.*
His riches could easily buy the lovely Adelphasium from
the pimp. But his clever slave Milphio would never
permit such an ordinary procedure (lines 163-169):

MILPHIO: . . . Vin tu illam hodie sine
dispendio
tuo tuam libertam facere?

AGORASTOCLES: Cupio, Milphio.
MILPHIO: Ego faciam ut facias. sunt tibi intus
aurei
trecenti nummi Philippi?
AGORASTOCLES: Sescenti quoque.
MILPHIO: Satis sunt trecenti.
AGORASTOCLES: Quid iis facturu's?
MILPHIO:
Tace.
totum lenonem tibi cum tota familia
dabo hodie dono.

MILPHIO: . . . How would you like, today,
To free her at no cost to you?
AGORASTOCLES: I'd really love to.
MILPHIO: I'll see to it you will. Do you have
gold inside—Three hundred *nummi?*
AGORASTOCLES: I could give you *double* that.
MILPHIO: Three hundred is enough.
AGORASTOCLES: What will you do?
MILPHIO: Just wait.
Today I'll take that pimp with his entire
household
And give him to you as a gift.

From a practical point of view, all the trickery in the
Poenulus is absolutely superfluous. Agorastocles can
afford to purchase whatever he desires. But one of the
prime characteristics of "holiday" is its sharp distinction from the ordinary. Thus Milphio, who insists upon
extraordinary, *un*businesslike methods, will have his
way. Like Epidicus, Milphio uses cash merely as a
stage prop in his merry masquerade. In fact, later in
the *Poenulus,* Plautus has one of the lawyers whom
Milphio has hired for his trickery step forward and
break the dramatic illusion to emphasize, paradoxi-
cally, that "it is all illusion" (lines 597-599):

Aurum est profecto hoc, spectatores,
comicum
macerato hoc pingues fiunt auro in barbaria
boves;
verum ad hanc rem agundam Philippum est:
ita nos adsimulabimus.

Folks, this money here is strictly "player's
gold."
When the stuff's dissolved, it's used by
foreigners to fatten bulls.
But, to act this whole thing out, we'll just
pretend King Philip coined it.[45]

This is quite in the spirit of the prologue to the *Casina,*
which reminded the audience that all businesses were
closed, while at the same time referring to many commercial activities. Here too, at the very moment the
actor is assuring the audience that all is "play," he also
alludes to Roman ("barbarian") husbandry, noting that
the lupine seeds being used on stage as money were

ordinarily soaked and fed to fatten oxen. Today is a holiday for *farmers* too.

But we still have not explained why Milphio has cooked up this theatrical scheme, this game with *aurum comicum,* when his young master Agorastocles could have solved all problems—that is, purchased the lovely Adelphasium—in a normal businesslike manner. Indeed, there has been much critical discussion on this matter. Why does the playwright present such "psychological improbabilities"? This is a question posed by Legrand, who then adds: "Occasionally the devices and tricks by the actors have no *raison d'être,* or else there is no possibility for their resulting in any good."[46] What Legrand here objects to is precisely what Johann Huizinga in *Homo Ludens* defines as "play," an activity with no *raison d'être,* "and no profit can be gained by it."[47] We are near the very fountainhead of comedy, which developed, as Freud saw it, from "play."[48] The profitless trickery which Plautus presents reflects a levity quite the opposite of *gravitas:* the spirit of holiday, and especially that of the Roman *ludi.*

Plautus' heroes go even further than ignoring monetary gain. They rush with holiday haste toward financial disaster. Prodigality replaces pragmatism as the order of the day. As mentioned earlier, good business sense was an implicit aspect of *mos maiorum.* A fine Roman son will increase his patrimony, *bono modo* if he is a noble Metellus being praised posthumously, but *quocumque modo* if he is anything but dead. In the *Mostellaria,* Plautus uses the verb *patrissare* to suggest this "business tradition." When old Theopropides returns from abroad, he is told that his son has purchased a house. Overjoyed at the youth's sound judgment, he exclaims (line 639):

> Patrissat! iam homo in mercatura vortitur.

> Taking after father! Now the boy's become
> a businessman.

The truth, of course, is that his son has turned in precisely the opposite direction. The verb which best describes young Philolaches' behavior is not *patrissare,* but *pergraecari* (line 960), as well as *potare* (lines 946 and 964) and *perpotare* (line 977). In a phrase, instead of taking after father, he is taking *from* him: *suom patrem . . . perdidit* (line 979), a contrast which Plautus drives home with abundant alliteration.[49]

In reality, *mos maiorum* was more mercantile than moral. Young Charinus in the *Mercator* acknowledges as much. His father had set a shining precedent, investing his own patrimony in *mercatura* and acquiring prodigious wealth (lines 73-78). Charinus realizes that his sire expects him to turn to commerce as well: *me idem decere, si ut deceret me forem* (line 79). And much to his parent's delight, the boy embarks on a commercial voyage. At first he seems his father's son (lines 93-97):

> Rhodum venimus ubi quas merces vexeram
> omnis ut volui vendidi ex sententia.
> lucrum ingens facio praeterquam mihi meus
>   pater
> dedit aestimatas merces: ita peculium
> conficio grande.

> We came to Rhodes, where all the goods I
>   brought along
> I sold—and just the way I wanted to. I made
> A great enormous profit, far above the price
> That father specified. So for myself I gained
> A lot of extra money.

The youth's spectacular success has realized a double reward, *lucrum ingens* for his father, and *peculium grande* for him. But the subsequent fate of this money exemplifies what happens to all income in Plautus (lines 98-99):

> Hospes me quidam adgnovit, ad cenam vocat.
> venio, decumbo acceptus hilare atque
>   ampliter.

> An old friend spied me and invited me to
>   dinner.
> I came, relaxed, received a lush and lovely
>   welcome.

The initial intent to *patrissare* is overcome by the irresistible urge to *pergraecari.*[50] The youth succumbs to the holiday spirit *hilare atque ampliter,* and by the morning, *lucrum* has been sped to its polar opposite, *damnum.* The Mercator's son has surrendered to the same *damnosa libido* against which the elders in Horace's "Roman day" have preached. He has squandered all his earnings on a girl whose very name, Pasicompsa ("Omni-pleasant"), suggests that she is pleasure personified. Since it is not unlikely that Plautus invented her name,[51] the metamorphosis of *peculium* into *pasicompsa* would then be a conscious echo of the *industria* to *voluptas* theme in the *Menaechmi,* another victory of the pleasure principle over the reality principle.

The voyage of Charinus, the Mercator's son, typifies the behavior of innumerable other Plautine characters toward matters pecuniary. Moreover, they are reckless with *pecunia* in its most literal sense: *pecus,* farm animals.[52] Very often in Plautus we find the un-Roman tendency to forsake livestock in pursuit of liveliness. One thinks of three ready examples which would have made the author of *De Agri Cultura* shudder, if he couldn't laugh. Asses in the *Asinaria,* oxen in the *Persa,* and sheep in the *Truculentus* all become debit items to pay for pleasure.[53] In the first play, as mentioned earlier, the asses have been sold for the magic sum of twenty *minae.* This payment is en route to Demaenetus' wife and the plot revolves around a masquerade to have the right price fall into the wrong hands. In the *Persa,* the slave Sagaristio has been given money by his master to purchase *domitos boves* (line 259), but these funds will serve bachelorhood, not husbandry (lines 262-264):

> SAGARISTIO: nam hoc argentum alibi abutar:
>   boves quos emerem, non erant;
>   nunc et amico prosperabo et genio meo
>   multa bona faciam,
>   diu quo bene erit, die uno absolvam . . .

> SAGARISTIO: Yes, I'll waste this money
>   somewhere else. The oxen won't exist.
>   Now I'll help a friend and do myself a few
>   good turns. We'll *live!*
>   In a single day we'll burn it all . . .

Sagaristio fully realizes he is putting good money to bad uses, *argentum abutar,* but proper business procedure will be ignored for one splendid day of pleasure.[54]

In the *Truculentus,* the sheep represent earnings from a deal which Strabax' farmer-father has negotiated. But here again, profit is quickly reversed to loss. Forgetting the frugal ways his parent has taught him, Strabax hastens from country simplicity to city luxury, in passionate pursuit of "joy" (he states his desire to *gaudere* three times in lines 922-924). His own account bears quoting in full, since he displays many of the (disgraceful) characteristics we have previously noted in Plautus' young men (lines 645-657, 660-661):

> Rus mane dudum hinc ire me iussit *pater,*
> ut bubus glandem prandio depromerem.
> post illoc quam veni, advenit, si dis placet,
> ad villam argentum meo qui debebat *patri,*
> qui ovis Tarentinas erat mercatus de *patre.*
> quaerit *patrem.* dico esse in urbe. interrogo
> quid eum velit.
> homo cruminam sibi de collo detrahit,
> minas viginti mihi dat. accipio libens,
> condo in cruminam. ille abit. ego propere
>   minas
> ovis in crumina hac in urbem detuli.
> fuit edepol Mars meo periratus *patri,*
> nam oves illius hau longe absunt a lupis.

> . . . . .

> eradicarest certum cumprimis *patrem,*
> post id locorum matrem . . .

> This morning early father sent me to the
>   country,

He ordered me to give the cows some nuts
  for breakfast.
But when I reached the farm, a man came—
  praise the gods!
A man who owed a sum of money to my
  father,
Because he'd bought some sheep a while ago
  from father.
He asks where father is. I say he's in the city.
I ask him what he wants.
He takes a leather wallet from around his
  neck,
He gives me twenty *minae.* I accept. Why
  not?
I put them in my wallet. Then he goes. I rush.
I bring the wallet with the sheep-cash to the
  city.
By Pollux, Mars was surely angry with my
  father,
These sheep of his are not far from "the house
  of wolves."

. . . . .

My plan is this: I'll first completely wipe out
  father
And then I'll wipe out mother . . .

No son could be more aware of his filial obligations. Strabax mentions his father four times in the first six lines. Like young Charinus in the *Mercator* (line 79), he fully realizes that he should be taking after father, not taking from him. But he suddenly receives the magic sum of twenty *minae,* which is precisely the cost of the girl (and the asses) in the *Asinaria* and the same amount which Pseudolus must swindle to win his master's sweetheart. And in young Strabax we note once again the holiday haste (line 654) toward merriment reminiscent of Menaechmus, Olympio, and so many others. In but a few seconds, pragmatic provincial becomes prodigal parricide,[55] as Strabax throws his father's sheep-money "to the wolves."

To state the comic paradox succinctly: pound-foolishness in Plautus is as common as penny-pinching was in the Rome of his day. And the Latin poet is not merely presenting an extravagant revel, for this is at the heart of every comedy. Yet Aristophanes can present a *komos* without mentioning who is paying the bill. In Plautus, however, part of the pleasure seems to be that *someone else's money is being wasted.* To explain why this appealed to his audience we may invoke Freud or *Schadenfreude:* the stingy Roman enjoys a vicarious prodigality similar to the secret pleasure he derived from seeing *pietas* abused. For the parsimonious, *industria*-bound spectator, Plautus provides an imaginary excursion to a land of *voluptarii maxumi* much like the place where Menaechmus lives, there to succumb to what might be termed *Epidamnosa libido.* But prodigality of the imagination involves no real loss; on holidays, joy comes *sine damno.* In fact, since these revels are paid for in *aurum comicum,* they bring dividends of laughter.

Notes

Introduction

[1] Cf. Horace *Epistles* 2.1.175-176:

> Gestit enim nummum in loculos demittere, post hoc
> securus cadat an recto stet fabula talo.

> The man only gets excited about adding a coin to his money box. After he does, he couldn't care less whether the structure of his play stands straight or falls flat.

Being a true man of the theater—as well as a classicist—the Spaniard Lope de Vega understood, as Horace could not, that good rules do not necessarily make good (i.e., successful) plays. Quite the contrary, says Lope in his *Arte nuevo de hacer comedias,* if one wishes to enjoy public favor, one must completely ignore the classical precepts. The Spaniard began his own playwrighting process as follows: "encierro los preceptos con seis llaves" ("I lock up the rules with six keys"). And, after all, Horace's *Ars Poetica* virtually ignores the greatest theatrical skill, for, according to Molière, "le grand art est de plaire."

[2] *In pauca confer: sitiunt qui sedent* (*Poenulus* 1224). Among many similar examples, we might cite *Casina* 1006 and *Pseudolus* 720-721, wherein Plautus' characters express concern about keeping the audience attentive and content. Of course this attitude is not a Plautine innovation, as witness Aristophanes *Ecclesiazusae* 581ff.

[3] Gellius *Noctes Atticae* 3.3.14. Perhaps there is all fancy and no fact in this *vita*; it may describe the plays and not the playwright. Leo (*P.F.*[2], [Friedrich Leo, *Plautinische Forschungen,* 2nd ed., Berlin, 1912] pp. 63-86) demonstrates how the famous story of Naevius' imprisonment could have been based on the poet's *Hariolus.* And there is a suspicious similarity between both Plautus' and Naevius' writing plays while incarcerated. Many scholars regard the tale of Plautus' being sent *in pistrinum* to be a reflection of the countless references to such punishment in his comedies. Still, Gellius insists that his authority is the great Varro *et plerique alii.*

The strongest evidence for Plautus' unique success is statements like those added to the prologue of the *Casina* for a revival performance (lines 11-13, 17-18):

> Nos postquam populi rumore intelleximus
> *studiose* expetere vos Plautinas fabulas,
> antiquam eius edimus comoediam.

> . . . . .

> haec cum primum acta est, vicit omnis fabulas.
> ea tempestate flos poetarum fuit . . .

> After the uproar of the people let us know
> You're all *so very anxious* to see Plautine plays,
> We've re-produced this ancient comedy of his.

> . . . . .

> When first presented, this play beat all other plays.
> Those were the days when greatness flourished on the stage.

[4] *Apporto vobis Plautum—lingua non manu,* "I bring you Plautus—not in person, just his play," *Menaechmi* 3. On the rowdy, intoxicated audience, cf. Horace *Ars Poetica* 225.

[5] The playwright Accius (c. 170-c. 86) is the first known scholar of Plautinity; it seems reasonable to assume that the "authenticity question" became a live issue right after the poet's death. See Paratore [Ettore Paratore, *La Storia del Teatro Latino,* Milano, 1957], p. 80.

[6] Karl von Reinhardtstoettner, *Plautus: Spätere Bearbeitungen plautinischer Lustspiele* (Leipzig 1886).

[7] Friedrich W. Ritschl, *Parerga zu Plautus und Terenz* (Leipzig 1845) (rep. Amsterdam 1965); T. B. L. Webster, *Studies in Later Greek Comedy* (Manchester 1953). Other major works which stress Plautus as a "spoiler" of his models include Legrand, *The New Greek Comedy,* and Gunther Jachmann, *Plautinisches und Attisches* (Berlin 1931) [= *Problemata,* Heft 3].

[8] Webster (above, n. 7) 2-3. With these principles set forth, Webster can then discuss such Greek plays as "Diphilos' *Rudens*" (p. 7).

[9] Gilbert Norwood, *Plautus and Terence* (New York 1932) 27-28.

[10] Studying a complete comedy by Menander enables L. A. Post to dissociate the Greek playwright "from the frivolous inconsequence of Plautus and Terence" ("Some Subtleties in Menander's *Dyscolus,*" AJP [*American Journal of Philology*] 84 [1963] 37). Plautus is defended in the next issue by Robert B. Lloyd, "Two Prologues: Menander and Plautus," AJP 84 (1963) 146-161.

[11] Fraenkel, *Elementi Plautini in Plauto*. [Eduard Fraenkel, *Elementi Plautini in Plauto,* rev. ed. of *Plantinisches im Plautus* (Berlin 1922), translated into Italian by Franco Munari (Florence 1960)]. The discovery of *Dyskolos* has called some of Fraenkel's conclusions into question. For example, Walter R. Chalmers observes that Menander's mythological passage in lines 153ff is, by Fraenkel's criteria, "Plautine" ("Plautus and His Audience," *Roman Drama,* p. 48 n. 22). Several scholars have pointed out the similarity between the boisterous finales of the *Dyskolos* and the *Pseudolus.*

[12] Webster (above, n. 7) 98.

[13] D. C. Earl, "Political Terminology in Plautus," *Historia* 9 (1960) 234-243. (Earl studied these same elements in a subsequent article on Terence, with less rewarding results: *Historia* 11 [1962] 469-485.)

John A. Hanson, "Plautus as a Source-Book for Roman Religion," *TAPA* [*Transactions and Proceedings of the American Philological Association*] 90 (1959) 48-60, hereafter cited as "Religion in Plautus."

————"The Glorious Military," *Roman Drama,* [ed. T. A. Dorey and Donald R. Dudley (New York 1965)], pp. 51-85.

Gordon Williams, "Some Problems in the Construction of Plautus' *Pseudolus, Hermes* 84 (1956) 424-455.

————"Evidence for Plautus' Workmanship in the *Miles Gloriosus,*" *Hermes* 86 (1958) 79-105.

————"Some Aspects of Roman Marriage Ceremonies and Ideals," *Journal of Roman Studies* 48 (1958) 16-29.

[14] See, for example, Perna's discussion of the *Amphitruo, L'originalità,* p. 91. For a recent survey of the "Plautinisches-Attisches" debate, see Perna [Raffaele Perna, *L'originalità di Planto* (Bari 1955)], pp. 10-37 (although the author's critical bias must be borne in mind).

A fine general introduction to the contemporary view of Plautus may be found in Chalmers (above, n. 11) 21-50. Chalmers' essay appeared just after the first draft of this book was completed; certain similarities in our observations are coincidental and would seem to indicate the present trend in Plautine scholarship. Invaluable to the specialist is John A. Hanson's "Scholarship on Plautus since 1950," Parts I and II, *Classical World* 59 (1965-1966) 101ff, 141ff.

[15] These critics of Roman Comedy say precisely what Terence's literary enemies said of him: he made good Greek plays into bad Latin ones, *ex Graecis bonis Latinas fecit non bonas* (*Eunuchus* 8).

[16] Fraenkel, p. 6.

[17] *Antony and Cleopatra* II ii 191ff.

[18] Cf., for example, Gordon Williams, "Pseudolus" (see above, n. 11) 448ff.

[19] Gellius *N.A.* 2.23. This early exercise in comparative literature concludes with the scholar's unhappy observation that the Latin poet *nescio quae mimica inculcavit,* "he stuck in some farcical stuff," a criticism echoed by Boileau when he complained that Molière in *Les Fourberies de Scapin* "à Térence a allié Tabarin."

[20] Fraenkel makes this same point, p. 324. Many scholars believe that Naevius influenced Plautus (e.g., Duckworth [George E. Duckworth, *The Nature of Roman Comedy* (Princeton 1952)], p. 394), and some of the fragments suggest as much. I have tried to incorporate these fragments into my discussion.

[21] On the two traditions of dramatic literature evident even from the earliest times, see Paratore, p. 64.

[22] *Ibid.,* p. 18.

[23] See J. H. Waszink, "Varro, Livy and Tertullian on the History of Roman Dramatic Art," *Vigiliae Christianae* 2 (1948) 229.

[24] Cf. Virgil *Georgics* 2.38off. Horace's account describes how the *libertas* of fescennine jesting grew bolder and bolder, hence the strict Roman law against libel on the Twelve Tables. See my discussion on pp. 9-10.

[25] The "saturnalian" tradition in Italy has been studied in depth by Paolo Toschi of the University of Rome (*Le Origini del Teatro Italiano* [Torino 1955]). It is Toschi's thesis that Italian popular comedy from the very first (and who is to say where Roman ends and Italian begins?) reflects the atmosphere of Carnevale, the Italian festival celebrated at the same time as the Saturnalia and without question a descendant of the Roman event (p. 112). Carnevale, says Toschi, is a "frenesia gioiosa . . . un momentaneo allentamento nei vincoli di una rigida morale" (p. 9), which could be an equally apt description of the holiday being enjoyed by Horace's *agricolae prisci.*

[26] Sir James Frazer, *The Golden Bough* (one vol. abr. ed., New York 1951) 675.

[27] There was never any drama associated with the Saturnalia in classical times (perhaps because of the weather), although it was the occasion for the revival of Roman comedies during the Renaissance.

[28] G. Wissowa connects Saturnus with *sero-satus*, assuming him to have originally been a god of sowing; *Religion und Kultus der Römer* (2d ed., Munich 1912) 204. This etymology is questionable because of the difference in vowel quantity: *Sāturnus-sătus*. Its origin may be Etruscan. See H. J. Rose, *Religion in Greece and Rome* (New York 1959) 225.

[29] W. Warde Fowler, *The Roman Festivals* (London 1925) 177.

[30] Barber, [C. L. Barber, *Shakespeare's Festive Comedy* (Cleveland and New York 1963)] p. 78. I have already acknowledged how deeply this entire study is indebted to Barber's work.

[31] Cf. Juvenal *Sat.* 6.67-69:

> . . . aulaea recondita cessant
> et vacuo clusoque sonant fora sola
>   theatro
> atque a Plebeis longe Megalesia . . .

[female theater fans have nothing to watch] when the stage curtains lie quietly stored away, when the theater is empty and closed—only the forum's now alive with noise—and it will be a long time between the Megalensian Games and the Plebeian.

In Plautus' day, in addition to the *ludi Romani,* the *ludi Plebeii* (November), *ludi Apollinares* (July), and *ludi Megalenses* (April) were occasions for theatrical entertainment. See Lily Ross Taylor, "The Opportunities for Dramatic Performances in the Time of Plautus and Terence," *TAPA* 68 (1937) 284ff. Or, more briefly, Duckworth, pp. 76ff.

[32] Freud, [*The Complete Psychological Works of Sigmund Freud,* ed. James Strachey, Anna Freud, Alix Strachey and Alan Tyson, 24 vols. (London 1953———)] XIII, p. 140, in "Totem and Taboo."

[33] Plato *Republic* 10.605a-b. It is interesting to note that both Plato and Freud see comedy as affecting man's inner desire to "break rules." But while the Greek philosopher objects to comedy because it may lead its spectators to *enact* the disgraceful things they see on stage, the psychoanalytic view is the exact opposite! Drama to Freud affords man the opportunity to "act out" (inwardly) the potential aberration, thereby serving a useful social function.

[34] Max Beerbohm, "Laughter," in *And Even Now* (New York 1921) 308: "[for great laughter] nothing is more propitious than gravity. To have good reason for not laughing is one of the surest aids. Laughter rejoices in bonds."

[35] *Inst. Orat.* 10.1.65.

[36] *Epist.* 2.1.23.

[37] On the very strict laws against libel, see Harold B. Mattingly, "Naevius and the Metelli," *Historia* 9 (1960) 416. Some scholars have discerned covert allusions to proper names in Plautus (e.g., R. W. Reynolds, "Criticism of Individuals in Roman Popular Comedy," *Classical Quarterly* 37 [1943] 37-45), but this is unlikely. Mattingly argues that even the famous story of Naevius' imprisonment for slandering the Metelli is fictitious (p. 423); in fact *metelli* may not have been a family name at this early time.

[38] Crane Brinton, *A History of Western Morals* (New York 1959) 111.

[39] Plutarch *Cato Maior* 17.7. Here as elsewhere the Roman moral outlook is like that of the Middle Ages. One may compare Cato's attitude toward the "kissing senator" to Peter Lombard's argument that to have great love for one's wife was, in effect, a grave sin: *omnis ardentior amator propriae uxoris adulter est.* This morbid severity contrasts sharply with Oscar Wilde's ironic description of the very same situation: "The amount of women in London who flirt with their husbands is scandalous. It looks so bad. It is simply washing one's clean linen in public" (*The Importance of Being Earnest,* Act I).

[40] In fact Pliny (*N.H.* 8.78.209), in discussing the Sumptuary Laws, mentions that Publilius Syrus, composer of mimes, was notorious for his flagrant infringement of the dietary prohibitions. Yet Publilius does not appear ever to have suffered for his "crimes."

[41] For example, Cato's famous speech on the status of women (195 B.C.), as quoted by Livy 34.2.11.

[42] The verses quoted follow an evocation by Horace of "the good old days," which, from the poet's standpoint, are the days of Cato and the Punic Wars.

[43] Cf. also *Epode* 7.

[44] In *Eclogue* 4, Virgil predicts that Pollio's consulship will restore the Golden Age, purging mankind of its old "traces of sin" (lines 13-14):

> Te duce si qua manent sceleris vestigia
>   nostri,
> inrita perpetua solvent formidine terras.

John Dryden's rendering of these lines is interesting:

> The father banished virtue shall restore;
> And crimes shall threat the guilty world no
>   more.

[45] A. A. Brill (ed.), Introduction to *The Basic Writings of Sigmund Freud* (New York 1938) 12.

[46] Of course it is impossible to state with certainty that the average Roman was *gravis*. But the fact that the Romans constantly praised and preached *gravitas* is clear beyond doubt, and it is this fact which is important for our discussion. After all, the precondition for French Boulevard Comedy (or any bedroom farce, for that matter) is merely an awareness among the audience that the Seventh Commandment *exists*.

[47] Ernst Kris, *Psychoanalytic Explorations in Art* (New York 1952) 182.

[48] If the Roman obsession with order and precision needs any documentation at all, one might cite Fabius Pictor's mission to Delphi in 216 B.C., when he carried an itemized list of the gods and goddesses, the exact manner in which each was to be addressed, etc. (Livy 23.1-6).

[49] Allardyce Nicoll, *Masks, Mimes, and Miracles* (London 1931) 19.

[50] It is distortion enough when Gilbert Norwood prefaces a discussion of Plautus by calling him "the worst of all writers who have ever won permanent repute" (*Plautus and Terence*, p. 4), but Albert Cook goes still further, entirely omitting any consideration of Plautus (or Terence) from his study of the comic tradition because "only the accident that Western Europe had nothing in the genre for a long time could have imparted such an undeserved reputation to works so devoid of ideas" (*The Dark Voyage and the Golden Mean* [Cambridge, Mass. 1949] p. i).

[51] *De Officiis* 1.29.104: *Duplex omnino est iocandi genus, unum illiberale, petulans, flagitiosum, obscenum, alterum elegans, urbanum, ingeniosum, facetum. Quo genere non modo Plautus noster et Atticorum antiqua comoedia, sed etiam philosophorum Socraticorum libri referti sunt,* "There are two completely different categories of wit: the first coarse, wanton, shameful, and foul, the other graceful, civilized, inventive, and charming. This second category includes not only our own Plautus and Attic Old Comedy, but it abounds as well in the books of the Socratic philosophers."

. . . . .

From Forum to Festival

[1] Catullus provides a ready example. He depreciates his own poetry as *nugae* (1.4) and refers to the writing of verse as trifling *ludere*. E.g., *multum lusimus in meis tabellis* (50.2) and his famous renunciation of poetry, *multa satis lusi* (68.17).

[2] Johann Huizinga comments on the appropriateness of the term *ludi* to describe Roman holidays in his fascinating study of "play" as a cultural phenomenon,

Homo Ludens: A Study of the Play Element in Culture (English trans., Boston 1950) 174.

[3] Menaechmus' use of hostile military language has already been discussed in Chap. I, p. 24.

[4] As stated earlier (Chap. I n. 33), I am aware that *pulchre habeamus* is not the favored reading for *Menaechmi* 152.

[5] Williams comments on the significance of *morem gerere* as an important virtue for Roman wives, "Some Aspects . . . ," pp. 28-29 (see above, Introduction n. 13). As usual in Plautus, the wives behave in a manner which is precisely the opposite of the ideal. Ironically, Menaechmus refers to Erotium as *morigera* (line 202).

[6] Fraenkel (p. 394) sees "das Properare" as a quality extremely Plautine. Elsewhere (p. 296), he interprets the *Casina* as a conflict between speed (Lysidamus and Olympio) and delays (the wives). This serves equally well as a description of the fate of Menaechmus I, whose experience in the forum is like those of Molière's protagonist in *Les Fâcheux*, who is constantly stopped on his way to an amorous rendezvous. It is perhaps significant that one critic sees this as a theme of Molière's comedy in general (Alfred Simon, *Molière par lui-même* [Paris 1957]).

[7] Pliny *N.H.* 8.78.209. Pliny admits, however, that the censors' strictures had little real effect on the eating habits of the populace. But here again the mere fact that there were such prohibitions provides the basis for comedy (see Introduction, p. 11).

[8] Pliny *N.H.* 8.78.210. Cf. such portions of proscribed cuts of pork in Plautus as *Pseudolus* 165-167 and *Curculio* 323.

[9] Naevius, frags. 22-24, mentions *volvula madida*, which recalls Menaechmus' menu not only because of the forbidden meat but because it seems to be another "drunken dinner" (cf. *Menaechmi* 212). Naevius presents another such bill of fare in frag. 104.

[10] Long catalogues of food were already a familiar comic motif in the days of Aristophanes. Cf. the antiphonal offers of delicacies made by the Paphlagonian and the Sausageseller to Demos in *Knights* 1162ff, not to mention *Ecclesiazusae* 1167ff, a menu for which Aristophanes concocted a seventy-nine-syllable dainty (lines 1169-1175), a bit of verbal audacity which makes a Plautine coinage like *glandionida* seem tame indeed. And yet, in content if not in expression, Menaechmus' menu is a more daring comic utterance, containing, as it does, a list of *forbidden* delights. Also of significance is Fraenkel's argument (pp. 238ff and 408ff) that the references to pork are peculiarly Roman and most probably Plautine additions.

[11] The special "Roman-ness" of *Menaechmi* 571-601 has often been remarked upon. Fraenkel (pp. 152ff) believes that when Menaechmus says *hoc utimur maxime more* (line 571) he is saying "we Romans." This is supported by Earl's conclusions on the significance of *mos* and *mores* to the ears of Plautus' public ("Political Terminology . . . ," p. 237; see above, Introduction n. 13). But we need not go so far as some scholars who believe that Plautus is alluding in this passage to the Lex Cintia regarding the relationship between *clientes* and *patroni* (see Perna, p. 291 n. 1). In fact, even if we conceive of Menaechmus as heading off to the *agora,* the polarity between *industria* and *voluptas* remains the same.

[12] Plautus stresses the "tenacity" of the many ties which bind Menaechmus by using three variations of *tenere.* First *retinere* (line 114) in reference to Menaechmus' wife, then *attinere* and *detinere* (line 589) to describe his clinging client.

[13] Cf. *Menaechmi* 591-595. To his credit, Menaechmus has performed well; the suit has been lost because of his client.

[14] This view may be further substantiated by examining an instance of the same phenomenon in the opposite direction. Simo, the next-door neighbor in the *Mostellaria,* has been dining at home. His wife has been especially lavish in her preparations, providing him a *prandium perbonum* (line 692). But Simo realizes that this festive meal is "to get him in the festive mood," as it were. He slips out of the house, however, explaining to the audience that he wishes to avoid the sensual experience and will head in the opposite direction (lines 696, 698, 707):

> Voluit in cubiculum abducere me anus
>
> . . . . .
>
> clanculum ex aedibus me edidi foras
>
> . . . . .
>
> potius hinc *ad forum* quam domi cubem.

> My ancient wife tried to entice me to the
> bedroom
>
> . . . . .
>
> But secretly I sneaked outside the house
> unseen
>
> . . . . .
>
> I'd rather go to business in the forum than
> to bed at home.

Simo would gladly have traded clients with Menaechmus. Earl ("Political Terminology . . . ," p. 236; see above, Introduction n. 13) sees what I have described as the forum-festivity polarity in *Trinummus* 259ff and especially *Trinummus* 651: *in foro operam amicis da, ne in lecto amicae,* "Go serve your friends in court, not court your friend in bed." He considers the references to be Plautus' articulation of a Roman aristocratic ideal, concern with one's *clientela.*

[15] Some of the prologue to the *Casina* is obviously post-Plautine, but the later interpolations are obvious enough and bear no relation to our argument. Friedrich Leo, who was, if anything, overzealous in distinguishing non-Plautine lines, considers the passage under discussion to be authentic: "in fact, if we disregard the specific revisions, that is, remove verses 5-20, we can consider the entire prologue as Plautine" (*P.F.*², p. 207 n. 2). Leo's view has found almost universal support. For a list of recent scholarship on this question, see Perna, p. 250 n. 3.

[16] Even though *ludum dare* is the conventional way of saying "to give a holiday to someone," there may well be, as Mason Hammond suggested to me, a subtle insinuation of *ludificatio* in the Prologue's speech, inasmuch as so many Plautine comedies involve the bamboozlement of "banking" types.

[17] In his first oration against Verres, Cicero complains that the opposition is stalling until the *ludi* begin, during which there can be no business. Hence the trial will be suspended and the force of Cicero's argument will, by the passage of time, be *defessa ac refrigerata* (*In Verrem* 1.10.31).

[18] Pliny *N.H.* 7.139ff.

[19] Leffingwell, p. 132 (see above, Chap. I n. 5).

[20] Plutarch *Cato Maior* 21.8.

[21] Max Eastman, *The Enjoyment of Laughter* (New York 1936) 150.

[22] Freud, VIII, p. 187, in "Jokes and Their Relation to the Unconscious." Barber, p. 99, writes, "festivity in wit is language which gives you *something for nothing*" (italics mine). . . .

[25] In evaluating these remarks, we must once again refer to Earl's observations on the term *mores* in Plautus (see above, n. 11).

[26] Cf. Horace's disappointment that Roman education spends too much time on bookkeeping instead of books (*Ars Poetica* 325-326):

> Romani pueri longis rationibus assem
> discunt in partis centum diducere . . .

Roman schoolboys, by long calculation, learn how to divide a single penny into a hundred parts.

Horace criticizes this curriculum aimed to teach a youngster *rem [posse] servare tuam* (line 329); he decries the Roman *cura peculi* (line 330). Yet in the "Roman day," he had nothing but praise for those elders who taught their sons not merely to guard their assets, but how to have them increase, *per quae / crescere res posset . . .* (*Epist.* 2.1.106-107).

[27] "This businesslike disposition, this primeval inheritance, survived through the ages," J. Wight Duff, *A Literary History of Rome* (3rd ed. rev., London 1960) 33.

[28] *Epist.* 1.1.53-56:

> "O cives, cives, quaerenda pecunia primum
>   est;
> virtus post nummos." haec Ianus summus ab
>   imo
> prodocet, haec recinunt iuvenes dictata
>   senesque.

> "O citizens, citizens, get money, first of all, get money. Be worth a lot—then afterwards be worthy." These words great Janus, banking deity, proclaims across the forum, and these same dictates are echoed by the young and by the old.

[29] Plutarch *Cato Maior* 21.5-8. In view of this statement that even the good Cato was profit-mad, it is interesting to note that Brutus, Shakespeare's "noblest Roman of them all," was, at least to Cicero, more Shylock than saint. The orator accuses him of the most exorbitant usury in *ad Att.* 6.2.

[30] Evander's famous remarks to Aeneas (8.364) became proverbial in Rome. Juvenal mocks them ironically in *Sat.* 11.60, and Seneca quotes them with what he would have his reader believe is moral fervor (*Epist.* 18.12). But it is hard to imagine that this millionaire-philosopher was really a *contemptor divitiarum* except in the sense Livy used the term to praise Cato.

[31] Tibullus 1.1 is a locus classicus: *divitias alius fulvo sibi congerat auro*, "Let someone else pile up a wealth of shining gold." On a grander scale we have the most un-Roman remarks of Shakespeare's Antony, who forsakes duty for Cleopatra's arms (I i 33-37):

> Let Rome in Tiber melt and the wide arch
> Of the rang'd empire fall! Here is my
>   space.
> Kingdoms are clay; our dungy earth alike
> Feeds beast as man. The nobleness of life
> Is to do thus (*embraces Cleopatra*) . . .

[32] Legrand, [Philippe Legrand, *The New Greek Comedy,* trans. James Loeb (London and New York 1917)] p. 48, calls attention to this phenomenon.

[33] Claudio in *Much Ado About Nothing* is another "money-minded" Shakespearean lover. Cf. Act I i, esp. 262ff.

[34] Polybius 32.13. Cf. also Leffingwell (above, Chap. I n. 5) 46.

[35] The countess' remark is from *Le Marriage de Figaro* IV iii, the song from the *premier couplet* in V xix.

[36] Cf. Molière, *L'Avare* I v. To keep the record straight, Megadorus in the *Aulularia* is neither an *adulescens* nor impoverished like the young Plautine lovers in the rest of this discussion.

[37] Strangely enough, Ernout [Alfred Ernout, *Plaute, Comedies, Texte et Traduction,* 7 vols. (Paris 1932-1940)] (vol. VII, p. 14) believes it was *this* dialogue which inspired the "sans dot" of Molière's miser.

[38] In Menander's *Dyskolos* young Sostratus protests that he wants Knemon's daughter "sans dot," but he gets one all the same; the *dyskolos* is not really a pauper. And even the soldier Polemon in Menander's *Shearing of Glykera* receives a dowry of three talents (cf. frag. 720 Kock).

[39] True enough, Selenium is finally "recognized," in typical New Comedy fashion, and Alcesimarchus ends up with love and money. It is equally true, however, that the young man's actions are never motivated by gain. As Lejay rightly observes (above, Chap. I n. 71), p. 129, "nulle part il n'y est question d'argent." Of interest may be Paratore's opinion (p. 123) that the *Cistellaria* is the most Menandrian of Plautus' comedies. See also the preceding note.

[40] But the Plautine hero, unlike both the Terentian and the Balzacian protagonist, does not look to get *married* under any circumstances. He longs for a *gamos* without "benefit of clergy," a desire shared by both Plautine and Aristophanic heroes.

[41] The terms of Diabolus' "contract" specify what the twenty *minae* are buying (*Asinaria* 751-754):

> Diabolus Glauci filius Clearetae
> lenae dedit dono argenti viginti minas,
> Philaenium ut secum esset noctes et dies
> hunc annum totum.

> Diabolus transfers to Cleareta, bawd,
> The sum of twenty *minae*, all in cash. This
>   deal

Makes Philaenium stay with him both day
  and night
This next entire year . . .

[42] It is true that Pseudolus ends up with an extra
twenty *minae* as a result of the spectacular success
of his trickery, but all indications are that the money
Simo gives him will be passed on to his master
Calidorus, or so Pseudolus states (lines 485-488).
The wily slave is really unconcerned with cash; he
even offers to refund half to the bamboozled old man
(line 1329). In the *Bacchides,* Chrysalus successfully
obtains the 200 *nummi* needed to save his master and
does set about getting more, but for a special reason
(lines 971-972):

  Nunc alteris etiam ducentis usus est, qui
    dispensentur
  Ilio capto, ut sit mulsum qui triumphent
    milites.

  Now we need two hundred *nummi* more that
    we can spread around when
  Troy is taken, so there'll be sweet wine to
    toast the soldiers' triumph.

Chrysalus wants to double the stakes, so that all can
have a party. And yet he insists that it is not his party:
*non triumpho . . . nil moror / verum tamen accipientur
mulso milites* (lines 1073-1074), "For me no triumph's
needed . . . I don't care / I only hope the troops will
get their sweetened wine." The others can revel; for
Chrysalus, playing the game was sufficient. And he
turns every bit of the extra money over to his master:
nunc hanc praedam omnem iam ad quaestorem deferam
(line 1075), "I'll now transfer all of this conquered
booty to the quartermaster." Surely Chrysalus and
Pseudolus are in the best tradition of the unmaterialistic
Plautine slaves who, like Toxilus, cry: *iam nolo argentum,* "I don't *want* money!" (*Persa* 127). Indeed, they
love the game and not the prize.

[43] Leffingwell (above, Chap. I n. 5), p. 79. Moreover,
a slave gathering his own *peculium* enhanced his own
value on the market; his ambition would show him to
be a willing worker. Cf. *Digesta Iustiniani* 21.1.18.
There is no reason to believe that this situation did not
prevail even in the earliest times.

[44] This rejection of money contrasts diametrically with
the desires of the "agelast," a character to be discussed in the next chapter. Unlike Toxilus and other
merry Plautine slaves, this anticomic figure wants *only*
money.

[45] Euanthius (*De Fabula* 3.8) calls this practice of
addressing the audience out of character *vitium Plauti
frequentissimum.* But such instances are found even in
Menander, not to mention Aristophanes.

[46] Legrand, p. 317.

[47] Huizinga (above, n. 2) p. 13.

[48] Freud (VIII, pp. 128ff) discusses the psychogenesis
of comedy from "play" in "Jokes and Their Relation to
the Unconscious." It is remarkable that the author of
Homo Ludens never read a word of Freud. On this
phenomenon, see R. L. Colie, "Johann Huizinga and
Cultural History," *American Historical Review* 69, 3
(April 1964) 626.

[49] Cf. *Mostellaria* 976-977:

  Et, *postquam eius hinc* pater
  sit *profectus peregre, perpotasse assiduo* . . .

  And following his father's faring forth
  For foreign parts, the fellow fell to full-time
    drinking.

[50] These two verbs from the *Mostellaria* do not appear
in the *Mercator.* They are used here merely to illustrate my argument.

[51] The question of whether Plautus himself coined the
redende Namen of his characters has long been debated. Duckworth, for example (pp. 347-350), believes
Plautus took the names right from his Greek originals,
as does Legrand, pp. 842ff. The problem is really part
of a larger question, i.e., how much Greek did Plautus'
audience know? This is impossible to determine with
certainty. Leo's argument (*P.F.*[2], 107ff) that Plautus'
Greek names are coined in exactly the same manner as
his Latin ones still seems convincing. Fraenkel (p.
141) considers Plautus to be the inventor of the girls'
names. It may also be pointed out that in contrast to
the infinite variety of intriguing female appellations in
Plautus, Terence seems content to present "Pamphila"
in play after play. But even if our poet did not coin the
names, I believe that his audience would still have
understood enough Greek to appreciate something like
"Pasicompsa," if not "Pyrgopolynices." There is perhaps an analogy with the French which Shakespeare
scatters now and then in his plays. His audience certainly appreciated the humor of King Henry V masquerading as "Harry Le Roy" (IV i 48ff).

[52] On the deeper connotations of *pecunia,* specifically
the "cattle-money" in Homer, see B. Laum, *Heiliges
Geld* (Tübingen 1924) 8ff.

[53] The *Bacchides* provides another ready example. Here
Chrysalus (somewhat like Strabax in the *Truculentus*)
has been given money by a debtor in Ephesus to be
delivered to Chrysalus' master, old Nicobulus. But the
cash will never reach its rightful owner, and tricky
Chrysalus, like Sagaristio in the *Persa,* will transfer these
funds to a "pleasure account" (*Bacchides* 230-233):

Mille et ducentos Philippum attulimus aureos
Epheso, quos hospes debuit nostro seni.
inde ego hodie aliquam machinabor machinam
unde aurum efficiam amanti erili filio.

From Ephesus, we brought twelve hundred
   golden Philips,
A sum indebted by our host to our old master,
A sum for which today I'll schematize a
   scheme
To transfer all this gold to master's lover-son.

[54] This very common behavior of Plautine slaves, risking everything for a single day of pleasure (such is Epidicus' attitude in the scene discussed on p. 62) will be fully discussed in Chap. V.

[55] Cf. my discussion, in the preceding chapter (p. 17), of the "anti-*pietas*" comedy in these lines.

James Tatum (essay date 1983)

SOURCE: James Tatum, in an introduction to *Plautus: The Darker Comedies*, translated by James Tatum, The Johns Hopkins University Press, 1983, pp. 1-13.

[*In the following excerpt, Tatum explains that three of Plautus's comedies—*Bacchides, Casina, *and* Truculentus—*are less familiar today than his others because of their unconvential use of the family and love. Tatum briefly discusses the more cynical aspects of each play and comments on the problems related to the translation and production of these plays.*]

The Playwright and His World

Our knowledge of the literary history of Greece and Rome often depends on little evidence.[1] In the case of Titus Maccius Plautus that evidence is particularly meager, anecdotal, and suspect. He seems to have stood still scarcely long enough to write down the lines of his comedies. Like one of his own harried characters, he ran across the stage of Roman life and literature, from some point in the latter half of the third century B.C. until perhaps 183 B.C. After many years of intensive research, we know less than we would like to know about him and the conventions of his theater: less, for example, than we know about the stagecraft of Aeschylus, Sophocles, Euripides, or Aristophanes.[2]

Plautus based his comedies on Greek New Comedy of the fourth and third centuries B.C.—"new," that is, in relation to the Old Comedy of the fifth century B.C. The greatest poet of all was Menander of Athens (ca. 342-291 B.C.). He and others wrote for a city transformed from the democracy of Thucydides and Aristophanes. Unhappily, save for his only complete play, *Dyskolos* (*The Grouch*), or a long fragment like *Samia*

(*The Woman from Samos*), Greek New Comedy survives only in fragments.[3] Enough remains to show that we would search through them in vain for echoes of the kind of momentous political and social upheavals so vividly reflected in comedies like Aristophanes' *Clouds* or *Lysistrata*. Menander was celebrated in antiquity for being an unrivaled student of the human comedy. As the saying went, "O Menander and Life, which of you imitated the other?" His subjects were the politics of the family, the desires and the intrigues of fathers, sons, mothers, daughters, slaves, and courtesans, not genuine political figures of the magnitude of Pericles.[4] For us today New Comedy may seem tame compared with the liberal imagination and fantasy of Aristophanic comedy. But in antiquity, when he existed in his entirety rather than in his parts, Menander was regarded as a poet equal to Homer and superior to Aristophanes himself.[5]

In Plautus's hands this already politically discrete theater became doubly removed from the arena of public politics and controversy. His plays are never set in Rome, but rather in some Greek city, often, as with **Bacchides, Casina,** and **Truculentus,** in Athens itself. With the exception of a few characters who have Latin names, such as Truculentus, the casts are made up of persons at least nominally Greek. There are occasionally topical allusions, as when a supposedly Greek slave makes fun of the city of Praeneste outside Rome (**Truculentus** III.2), but these local in jokes are rare and funny precisely because they break the dramatic illusion of a play set in Greece. What results on the stage is a free, vaguely Greek world which is at the same time thoroughly Roman in its outlook and, of course, Latin-speaking. Together with Terence (ca. 195-159 B.C.), his only successor at Rome, Plautus exercised enormous influence on theater in the West. Lope de Vega, Shakespeare, Jonson, Molière, Dryden, Kleist, and Giraudoux all reveal Plautus's influence in their comedies, either by direct imitation of a particular play or, sometimes, by adapting Plautus's dramatic techniques for their own purposes.

Since the kind of open theater which Euripides or Aristophanes enjoyed was never welcome at Rome, even the most assiduous reading between the lines of Plautus has yielded frustratingly little new information about the political situation of his day.[6] The plays also reveal little about Plautus himself. One of our few "facts" is that he made a living out of his comedies, probably as much by being an actor and director of his *grex* (herd or troupe of actors) as by being a playwright. Hence the prologue's hope in **Casina** for our well-being and our entertainment. These are more than conventional pleasantries: they are there because Plautus depended on audiences for his livelihood.

Serene as they are about serious matters of national politics, Plautus's comedies provided popular entertainment for a generation of Romans who were themselves anything but serene. His lifetime spanned an age in which Rome fought one bitter war after another with Greeks, Carthaginians, and any other nation that stood in the way of what came to be seen, in hindsight, as an inevitable rise to mastery of the Mediterranean world. The devastation caused by the Second Punic War with Hannibal was the greatest threat Rome ever faced, and it was for a nation locked in such life-and-death struggles that Plautus wrote his comedies.[7] His plays were designed for performance on those festival days which afforded the leisure (*otium*) for relaxation from the Romans' usual regimen of hard work and business, that daily routine they interestingly termed *negotium,* "not leisure time."[8] The Hellenophile Simone Weil, no friend of Roman civilization, has suggested that Plautus's mordant, cynical comedy appealed to a well-developed national taste for cruelty, whether on the stage or in real life.[9]

Of all Rome's neighbors, the Greeks nonetheless resisted with the most ingenuity, and not in the way a Roman general or statesman could have anticipated. As Horace was later to put it, the rude conquerors became themselves captives of the Greece they had conquered. While the Italians had their own native poetic and dramatic forms, such as the *fabulae Atellanae* (popular farce) and *fabula togata* (comedy in native dress), such indigenous literary efforts counted as nothing in the face of the overwhelming influence of the Greeks. Latin literature was completely transformed by the Greeks, and this transformation was well under way during Plautus's lifetime.

The process of adapting Greek literature to the Latin language and Roman ways was complex. From the first it was far more than simple translation, though that task in itself was difficult enough. Plautus and other Roman authors in effect added a new chapter to the history of every literary genre the Greeks had invented.

We do not know how many plays Plautus wrote and produced. By the end of the first century B.C. over 130 were attributed to him. At that point the Augustan scholar Varro attempted to establish an authentic canon of Plautine comedy; he arrived at a list of twenty-one plays. The same number of comedies survived the vicissitudes to which all ancient texts were subject. Possibly but not certainly the plays we have are the same ones Varro approved.

Bacchides, Casina, and Truculentus

Anyone familiar with Plautus's most popular plays might wonder what to expect of a collection of his "darker comedies." By this title I mean to suggest that this is not a random collection. The three comedies are unconventional in plot and in morals. They are uncom-

promisingly derisive of the family and of the conventional uses of love. Their endings offer no redemption and no return to an easy social order. They were probably all produced late in Plautus's career. Each of them suffered considerable damage in the transmission of texts from the ancient world.

While many of Plautus's comedies depict a comic inversion of society, with slaves the masters and masters the slaves, *Bacchides, Casina,* and *Truculentus* go well beyond our usual expectations of Roman comedy. The cheerful resolution of *Miles Gloriosus* or *Menaechmi* seems all apple-cheeked innocence by comparison. In *Truculentus* the courtesan Phronesium and her maid Astaphium snare all four of the men they set out to catch, and take all their money in the bargain. In the finale of *Bacchides* the sisters Bacchis succeed in persuading two fathers to join their own sons in the same bed. The cast of characters in *Casina* is more domestic, but the play is not more respectable. Unambiguous scenes of transvestism and homosexuality offended at least one member of every audience to which the comedy was played, and sometimes many more than one. Everywhere there is an acid tone to the humor: there is not one pair of amiable young lovers, no courtesan with a heart of gold, no old man of decent or kindly disposition. *Bacchides* and *Truculentus* do not conform to the conventions of New Comedy which Northrop Frye speaks of in *The Anatomy of Criticism:*

> The plot structure of Greek New Comedy as transmitted by Plautus and Terence, in itself less a form than a formula, has become the basis for most comedy especially in its more highly conventionalized dramatic form, down to our own day. . . . What normally happens is that a young man wants a young woman, that his desire is resisted by some opposition, usually paternal, and that near the end of the play some twist in the plot enables the hero to have his will. In this simple pattern there are several complex elements. In the first place, the movement of comedy is usually a movement from one kind of society to another. At the beginning of the play the obstructing characters are in charge of the play's society, and the audience recognizes that they are usurpers. At the end of the play the device in the plot that brings hero and heroine together causes a new society to crystallize around the hero, and the moment when this crystallization occurs is the point of resolution in the action, the comic discovery, *anagnoresis* or *cognitio.*[10]

There are no heroines or heroes to be seen in *Bacchides* or *Truculentus,* at least none in the ordinary sense of those words. *Casina* comes the closest of the three to resembling the "barrier comedy" which Frye describes, since the old man Lysidamus does try to steal his son's bride on her wedding day. In the end, he is thwarted by his wife Cleostrata. But Plautus is more interested in Lysidamus and his humiliation than in young love.

The hero and heroine (Casina and Euthynicus), traditionally the center of the plot of New Comedy, never even appear on the stage. Plautus's more familiar comedies are better known in no small part because they are more conventional in their plot and in their resolution. A comedy like **Miles Gloriosus** could serve as a text for secondary school, for example, and so it has for a very long time. It is still hard to imagine **Casina, Bacchides,** or **Truculentus** serving in the same capacity.

The Original Text

Aside from the cynical morals and unconventional plots, the most serious obstacle to a wider audience has undoubtedly been the condition of the Latin text. The special problem of textual criticism does not require much comment here, but by way of a more objective balance to the above remarks about these three comedies, it should at least be mentioned in passing.

The transmission of any text from the ancient world was always a precarious business, and of no author was this truer than of Plautus. Even his most popular comedies, the ones which survived intact in manuscripts, present the scholar with hundreds of puzzling constructions, possible interpolations, spurious readings, or just plain nonsense. Many of these textual problems are not yet solved, and may never be. These three plays very nearly did not survive at all. The opening of **Bacchides** is almost entirely lost, as is much of the closing scene of **Casina. Truculentus** has problems everywhere; it is the most damaged of all the complete comedies which survive, with fully one-third of the text from its manuscripts lost or muddled beyond repair. Only the labors of many textual critics and other translators made it possible to think of attempting new translations and productions.[11] More detailed comments about each play's text will be found below, in the notes to each translation.

The Translations

Although much in each English play is close to the original Latin, these versions were never conceived as line-by-line translations to the letter. They are memoirs of performances, production scripts designed to give the reader a sense of the actual theatrical experience of Plautus's comedies. . . .

Translating for actors poses special problems.[12] While footnotes work well enough in a text that is only to be read, they cannot dance across the stage during a performance. Plautus's exuberant language is a constant flow of puns, parodies, and other kinds of wordplay, above all alliteration. Actors need equivalent effects in the lines they speak as much as they need the sense of the original. One feature peculiar to Plautine comedy requires special comment. **Bacchides, Casina,** and **Truculentus** are plays in which the spoken dialogue frequently alternates with passages in elaborately varied rhythms, originally for what was probably chanted song or recitative. Such a passage is traditionally called the *canticum* (in the plural *cantica*). In general, directors and actors will find that the *cantica* vary the pace of action and heighten important moments in a play. Because of the *cantica,* Plautus has often been compared to Gilbert and Sullivan or Rogers and Hammerstein, as if he were a writer of musical comedy. The analogy is in fact misleading.[13] We know very little about how the *cantica* were performed in Plautus's day, save that there was at least a flute player on stage with the actors. We know even less about Roman music itself, although it is clear that the instruments at hand would have been simpler than any combination in use in a modern theater. One point must be stressed: *cantica* are not show tunes like "You coax the blues right out of the horn, Mame. / You charm the husk right off of the corn, Mame" or patter songs like "When I was a lad I served a term / as office boy to an attorney's firm." Unlike the strophe and antistrophe of choruses in Greek tragedies, they do not unfold in regular stanzas, but in sequences in which the verse can change meter from one line to the next.[14] Nor is their language the language of lyric poetry. They are immensely varied; by turns parodic, explosively alliterative, they always raise ordinary dialogue to a more rhetorical and artificial level.

For a modern production, a balance has to be struck between two extremes. The *cantica* should not be rendered as normal speech, since this would result in a flatter and blander script than Plautus intended. Neither should they invariably be turned into something which I think would be alien to the nature of many *cantica,* the show tune of a Broadway musical. My solution was to translate the *cantica* to give actors and directors an opportunity for a variety of theatrical effects. Some seemed to work best as passages to be sung, with or without musical accompaniment; others were blocked out as dance or mime; still others only as soliloquy. The aim of this heuristic approach was to construct theatrical events. This is what the *cantica* must be: spectacular scenes.

A word of warning is also in order about the lines. They will not always seem natural or easy to speak. They are not easy to read in Plautus's Latin. The mellifluous elegance which a poet of the later Republic or the Augustan age favored was not always Plautus's concern; nor is this to his discredit. Actors or readers must be ready to deliver bombastic speeches like the orations of the braggart warrior Stratophanes (**Truculentus** II.6), the stuttering, alliterative lines of the slave Chrysalus when he is confronted with the soldier Cleomachus (**Bacchides** IV.8), or the "mad scene" of Pardalisca (**Casina** III.5) as if they were the most normal way in the world for one human being to speak to another. The exuberant language reflects the enormous energy of the comedy itself.

Production

When Plautus is produced today, much will depend on the resources at hand. To re-create an authentic performance in the style of his original productions remains an ideal beyond our reach.[15] Whatever those first performances were like, they took place in a setting far more modest than anything an archaeological ruin of an ancient theater might suggest. Plautus rarely had such monuments to perform in. His theater was more likely a cleared space with a narrow stage. Modern production of his comedies can succeed with comparatively simple sets, costumes, and technical support. Some care must be given to the choice of theater. Small, intimate halls and theaters in the round should be avoided. Such spaces tend to restrict the movement of the cast and to bring audience and actor too close together. Unless the audience sits at some distance from the stage, and at a higher sight line, a director will have great difficulty in establishing effective blocking for asides, mime, and dance. With stage right an exit to the forum and stage left an exit to the country (or the harbor, or the market), the actors need a long, shallow playing area for most scenes. As a general principle, the stage design should underscore visually the nonillusory nature of the plays: bright, primary colors for sets and costumes, exaggerated clown make-up for the actors' faces. (Masks should not be attempted, both because the present scripts are written for actors who use their faces, and because the authenticity of masks for Plautus remains an open question.) In sum, the way a production looks should complement the way the characters speak and act upon the stage.

The important principle to keep in mind is that Plautus must *not* be performed in a realistic style. The broader the style of acting, the better. He is closer to the Marx Brothers than to Molière. His plays have nothing whatever to do with psychological plausibility or the orderly development of a plot. His works are farces which must be played with no effort at creating a realistic illusion. Just as his language is self-conscious, and constantly calling our attention to that fact, so too the style of acting that he demands must be self-conscious, very much on the surface of things. His is a theater always conscious of its own theatrical nature, one which always reminds the audience that they are watching a play.[16] An aside such as this one from *Casina* requires the performer to deliver not only the lines but also a commentary on those lines:

> LYSIDAMUS [*falls on his knees*]
>   But, wife, grant pardon to your husband.
>
> [*Turns to Myrrhina*]
>
>   Myrrhina, plead with Cleostrata for me.

> [*To company and audience*]
>
> If I ever fall in love with Casina after this, or if I ever begin to—not to speak of making love—if I ever hereafter do anything of the sort
>
> [*To Cleostrata*]
>
> you'll have every right, my wife, to string me up by my thumbs and give me a sound lashing.
>
> MYRRHINA [*eagerly*]: Oh, I think *this* pardon ought to be granted!
> CLEOSTRATA [*grimly*]: I'll do as you say.
>
> [*Turns to audience, brightly*]
>
> And the main reason I shall grant this pardon now, and with less reluctance, is to avoid making a long play even longer than it already is.

One suggestion may be offered about the actual performance itself. Plautus is a calculating playwright who builds his comic effects by means of a surprisingly economical number of scenes. There should never be an intermission in the performance of Plautine comedy. The longest of these three plays is ***Bacchides,*** and it runs a little under two hours. To break the action at any point can easily destroy a comedy's dynamics. If the audience knows there will be no break, and if the director sets a properly fast pace to the action, crowding one scene on another, the comic energies inherent in Plautus's text will easily sustain the performance in a single continuum.

Notes

[1] Only criticism available in English will be cited here. The standard handbook to consult is George E. Duckworth, *The Nature of Roman Comedy* (Princeton, 1952); see also W. Beare, *The Roman Stage,* 3d ed. (London, 1964). For comprehensive surveys of later Plautine scholarship see John A. Hanson, "Scholarship on Plautus since 1950," pts. 1 and 2, *The Classical World* 59 (1964): 101-29 and 60 (1966): 141-48; and Erich Segal, "Scholarship on Plautus since 1966," ibid., 74 (1981): 353-433. More detailed remarks about each of the plays can be found in the essays introducing each translation.

[2] See Duckworth, *The Nature of Roman Comedy,* pp. 49-51, for a concise summary of the evidence.

[3] For a readable and performable translation of Menander's only complete comedy see Carrol Moulton, *The Dyskolos of Menander* (New York, 1977).

[4] For a sociological reading of a Plautine comedy see David Konstan, "Plautus' *Captivi* and the Ideology of the Ancient City State," *Ramus* 5 (1976): 76-91.

[5] An excellent and sympathetic study of Menander's dramatic art is now available in Sander M. Goldberg, *The Making of Menander's Comedy* (Berkeley and Los Angeles, 1980).

[6] For an analysis of possible parallels between Scipio the Elder and the characters Jupiter and Amphitryon see G. K. Galinsky, "Scipionic Themes in Plautus' *Amphitruo*," *Transactions and Proceedings of the American Philological Association* 97 (1966): 203-35. Typical of the delicacy of the relationship between poet and politician is the often cited transgression of Plautus's contemporary Naevius: A verse in one of his plays (*Fato Metelli Romae fiunt consules*, "By Fate the Metelli are made consuls of Rome") was ambiguous; *fato* could mean "by Fate" or "to the misfortune of Rome." Metellus (consul in 206 B.C.) was said to have replied, *Dabunt malum Metelli Naevio poetae*, "The Metelli will cause the poet Naevius a lot of trouble." Naevius was subsequently thrown into prison.

[7] For an ancient account of the wars with Hannibal (and a good indication of how deep an impression those wars still made on the Roman psyche two centuries later) see Livy *A History of Rome (Ab Urbe Condita)*, bks. 21-30; for a modern historian's account see H. H. Scullard, *A History of the Roman World from 753 to 146 B.C.*, 3d ed. (London, 1961), pp. 133-331.

[8] For Plautine comedy's mockery of such Roman virtues as *gravitas* (seriousness of character) and *pietas* (sense of duty) see Erich Segal, *Roman Laughter* (Cambridge, Mass., 1968). Segal's theory owes much to C. L. Barber, *Shakespeare's Festive Comedy* (Princeton, 1959).

[9] " . . . Plautus, whose work is among the most sombre in the world's literature, though that is not its reputation" (Simone Weil, "The Great Beast: Some Reflections on the Origins of Hitlerism," in *Selected Essays, 1934-1943*, selected and translated by Richard Rees [Oxford, London, and Toronto, 1962], p. 121).

[10] Northrop Frye, *The Anatomy of Criticism* (Princeton, 1957), p. 167.

[11] No translations of *Bacchides* and *Truculentus* have appeared since George E. Duckworth's *The Complete Roman Drama* (New York, 1942). Paul Nixon's translations from 1916 to 1938 in the Loeb edition are in fact more durable; see Paul Nixon, *Plautus*, 5 vols. (Cambridge, Mass., and London, 1979).

[12] See Robert W. Corrigan, "Translating for Actors," in *The Craft and Context of Translation*, ed. William Arrowsmith and Roger Shattuck (Austin, 1961), pp. 95-106.

[13] There is an astringent but helpful discussion of the subject in Beare, *Roman Stage*, pp. 219-32.

[14] Consider the entrance of Cleostrata in act II of *Casina*. In a passage of some fifty lines, she and her confidant Myrrhina speak in over twenty different meters. To give an idea of the complexity, a partial list of the meters . . . would include the anapaestic octonarius . . . , the cretic tetrameter . . . , the anapaestic tetrameter . . . , iambic dimeter . . . , the bacchiac dimeter and tetrameter . . . , the trochaic tetrameter . . . , the choriambic dimeter . . . , and the glyconic. . . . Such asymmetry in versification has no parallel in English prosody. To attempt to reproduce the meters of the *cantica* exactly line by line would yield something quite alien to our ears.

[15] But for a recent investigation of the tradition of performance in Plautus's day see Bruno Gentili, *Theatrical Performances in the Ancient World: Hellenistic and Early Roman Theater* (Amsterdam, 1979).

[16] This critical perspective, new to the study of Plautus, is brilliantly developed in Niall W. Slater's "The Theatre of the Mind: Metatheatre in Plautus" (Ph.D. diss., Princeton University, 1981).

K. C. Ryder (essay date 1984)

SOURCE: K. C. Ryder, "The *Senex Amator* in Plautus," in *Greece & Rome*, Vol. XXXI, No. 2, October, 1984, pp. 181-89.

[*In the following essay, Ryder discusses Plautus's use of the stock character the* senex amator, *asserting that Plautus's handling of the lecherous old man who falls for a young girl differs in each of the six plays in which the character appears.*]

Of the twenty-nine *senes* in the Plautine corpus, seven may legitimately be called *senex amator*—that is, an old man who for some reason contracts a passion for a young girl and who, in varying degrees, attempts to satisfy this passion. They are Demaenetus (*Asinaria*), Philoxenus and Nicobulus (*Bacchides*), Demipho (*Cistellaria*), Lysidamus (*Casina*), Demipho (*Mercator*), and Antipho (*Stichus*). Two others—Periplectomenos (*Miles*) and Daemones (*Rudens*)—still, perhaps, feel the sap rising, but they keep their instincts within acceptable limits, and both are regarded as *senes lepidi*, a description which usually denotes approval of a character.

I

What is interesting is that Plautus' handling of the *senex amator* always differs. In the *Asinaria* the characterization and behaviour of Demaenetus are carefully and methodically orchestrated so that each stage of the play (corresponding with the Act divisions, as it happens) represents a different stage of his debauch. Very early we have established for us his relations with his wife—he dreads her, he wishes her dead, he finds her difficult to get on with, and she keeps him powerless.[1] The rest of the first scene exists to open up the idea that Demaenetus should arrange for his slave Libanus to swindle him out of the money which will eventually buy the girl that his son is after[2]—the girl that in due course Demaenetus himself will fall for.

The only way that Demaenetus can get his hands on this money without his wife's knowledge is by tricking the Merchant who has come to buy the two asses (hence the play's title) into paying the money direct to him, or a slave acting on his behalf, rather than to his wife.[3] It is this subterfuge which forms the second part of the play. It is only later (735ff.) that his own desires towards the girl are revealed for the first time, when we learn that he expects a night with the girl as reward for helping his son. His expectations are so far advanced, in fact, that he has already entered the house where she is, undetected by his son—or his wife's servants:

> Angiporto
> illac per hortum circum iit clam, ne quis se
>   videret
> huc ire familiarium: ne uxor resciscat metuit.
>
> (741-3)

In 812ff. we are given the first of several insights by the playwright into how he expects an old fool to behave with a young girl:

> apud amicam munus adulescentuli
> fungare, uxori excuses te et dicas senem?
> praeripias scortum amanti atque argentum
>   obicias
> lenae? suppiles clam domi uxorem tuam?
>
> . . . . .
>
> cum suo sibi gnato unam ad amicam de die
> potare, illam expilare.

Finally, and predictably, his wife finds out, but not before we ourselves have seen him in action. It is quite a shock to her—she had thought him 'frugi . . . siccum, frugi, continentem, amantem uxoris maxume', but now she knows him to be 'ante omnes minimi mortalem pretii, madidum, nihili, incontinentem atque osorem uxoris suae'. (Incidentally, those who complain that Plautus is unsubtle, and little more than a peddlar of slapstick and farce, should note how finely poised these two opinions on Demaenetus are, each element balanced and cancelled out by another.)[4]

Like anyone else wise after the event, she puts two and two together and makes sense of previous odd behaviour on his part, which he has always excused on the grounds of appointments with business colleagues, all of whom are remembered and recited more or less alphabetically by his wife[5]—how many times has she been over this list in her mind before, we wonder?

The focus of our attention now switches back to the old man and his antics with the girl—his embrace with her has been a long one, much too long for his son's comfort!

> Quid modi, pater, amplexando facies?
>
> (882)

He is totally besotted with her, nothing would persuade him, he says, *not* to steal his wife's *palla* for the girl. Not surprisingly, the girl does not think much of his amatory talents: he is 'osculator carnufex, capuli decus' (895), and he has almost killed her with boredom (921). Her final insult to him comes when, Demaenetus having been confronted by his wife, the girl throws in his face three times his promise concerning the *palla* (930, 939, 940). His riposte is most ungallant—'I in crucem!'

Before this Artemona (the wife) has burst in on the scene, and he expresses fear (921), shame (933), and embarrassment (939). For him, quite plainly there is to be no forgiveness as he is tersely ordered: 'Surge amator! I domum!' (921), and again in 940. All in all, we cannot help feeling a little sorry for him—he is not a nasty man, merely rather pathetic; and his wife *is* something of a dragon.

II

In the **Bacchides** the situation is totally different. For a start the amatory behaviour only becomes an issue in the final 95 lines of the play, when Nicobulus and Philoxenus go to the two Sisters to complain about the influence that the sisters are exerting over their sons (1118ff.). As soon as they see the old men, the two women begin a series of oblique insults round the idea that the old men are 'oves . . . balitantes', maintained until 1149. The men themselves join in in this in the end, proclaiming that they will prove a pair of rams if their sons are not returned safely to them (1147-8).

Events take a new turn when the Sisters decide to try to placate the old men by flirting with them:

> senem illum tibi dedo ulteriorem, lepide ut
>   lenitum reddas;
> ego ad hunc iratum ingrediar.
>
> (1150ff.)

They will take one each. The suggestion is not received with enthusiasm by the other Sister—'quam odiosum est mortem amplexari'—but immediately Philoxenus is hooked, though at first he is ashamed to admit it (1155a). A few lines later, when he does admit it, Nicobulus' immediate reaction is one of shock—'flagitium est'—though he himself recognizes that they are 'perlecebrae et persuasitrices' (1167). The attraction becomes even stronger for him a few lines later—'ut blandiloquast!', but he still fears to give in.

Philoxenus, meanwhile, is enjoying himself. He is described as 'magis tranquillus' (1174), and begs to be taken inside by his particular Sister. Nicobulus stoutly resists and continues to disapprove:

> Vidi ego nequam homines, verum te neminem
> deteriorem
>
> (1180)

and Philoxenus is quite pleased and proud to acknowledge this—'Ita sum!'

At last the blandishments of the Sisters prove too much for even stout-hearted Nicobulus—'caput prurit, perii, vix negito' (1193); he wants to succumb, but is still afraid (1196), until suddenly he collapses (1199-1200), recognizing that through their efforts he has become a wicked man. The play closes with Nicobulus abandoning himself completely to the will of the Sisters, becoming their abject slave:

> Ducite nos quo lubet tamquam quidem
> addictos.[6]

In the two plays examined so far we see similar patterns and attitudes—the sense of shame, the feeling of wrong, the contempt of the young woman for the old man—but the way in which the situation is created, its whole motivation, is different; and in the case of one old man (Nicobulus) the blame for his 'fall' lies squarely with the woman and her corrupting influence.[7] Is there a hint here of a stronger moralizing purpose than Plautus is usually credited with?

III

The *senex* in the **Cistellaria** provides us with a cameo picture of lechery in old age, difficult to decipher exactly on account of the corruption of the text. What we are able to deduce from the seventy or so lines that he is on stage is interesting. As soon as he spots Gymnasium at the moment of his entry he is fascinated by her:

> mulierculam exornatulam. quidem hercle scita
>
> (306)

He proceeds to declare his desire for her as if he were a horse:

> quamquam vetus cantherius sum, etiam
> nunc. . . .
>
> adhinnire equolam possum ego hanc, si
> detur sola soli.

The extent of his desire, and of his absurdity, is shown clearly in 310-15 by the way in which he listens in to her remarks, and interprets everything she says almost as an invitation to love. When she says that there is not a woman alive who loathes being alone more than she does, his response is 'me vocat' (310). When she comments on the attractiveness of the house, his riposte is that the house is bound to be lovely if Venus herself is there (311-12). And so on.

As soon as he realizes, though, that she is the woman who is corrupting his son (316-17), his reaction is the usual bluster and abuse. He first addresses her as 'mali damnique inlecebra' (321), then accuses her of driving him and his family to rack and ruin (365-6). Shortly afterwards he leaves, and the episode closes with Gymnasium's gloss on one aspect of the usual behaviour of old men in love:

> 'datores
> negotioli belissumi senices soletis esse'
>
> (373-4).

IV

Lysidamus, in the **Casina,** is—with Demaenetus from the **Asinaria**—the leading exponent of the *ars amatoria* by a *senex*. Forehand[8] and Cody[9] have both published useful and interesting expositions of the part played by Lysidamus. The former draws attention to the degree of his lechery, and the stupidity this involves him in; the latter talks at length about the three homosexual encounters in the play. Plautus himself tells us early in the play what is going to happen: we are to see a father in opposition to his son (another new aspect of the type), commissioning his bailiff not only to act on his behalf but also to marry the girl, in order to ensure access for him, the old man (48ff.). His wife finds out, so determines to act in support of the son.

The role of the wife is another new development: when she has found out, she does not immediately wade in, punishing her husband with her tongue, or with financial or sexual restraints. Instead she enlists the help of another slave to work against the old man and promote the interests of her son. Gross deception is practised on the old man—'gross' in degree and in nature—which he falls for completely. Indeed, he will stop at nothing to achieve his ends—he bribes his bailiff, borrows his neighbour's house, and is prepared to submit entirely to the whims and wishes of the bailiff, Olympio. At 567 we are told that Lysidamus stands 'advocatus cui cognato meo', so that presumably he is invested with a certain measure of dignity and authority; and yet at 733ff. we have a revolting picture of him grovelling, with not a scrap of pride, to Olympio: 'servos sum tuos' (738) . . . 'Opsecro te . . . mi pater, mi patrone' (738-9) . . . 'Tuos sum equidem' (740a). Once he finds he has been fooled, he experiences confusion and shame (937ff.), is abject in front of his wife (1000ff.) and is finally forgiven by her (1005).

The portrait is interesting too for the description it includes of the *behaviour* of a *senex* in love. At 217ff. he gives foolish expression to his love: he is unable to think of anything which has 'plus salis plusque leporis'; 'fel quod amarumst, id mel faciet'; 'magis niteo, munditiis munditiam antideo'. At 226 and again at 228 we find references to the use of perfumes. At 467 the portrayal takes a grotesque turn as he pictures himself making love to Casina:

> ut ego hodie Casinam deosculabor, ut mihi
> bona multa faciam clam meam uxorem.

There are also two drooling instances of the language of the doting lover—at 836 'meum corculum, melculum, verculum', and at 854 'belle belliatula'. If there are any genuinely unpleasant *senes* in Plautus, Lysidamus is surely the unpleasantest, a characteristic also noted by Forehand.[10] It is difficult to find even a hint of a saving grace in him, and we are bound to conclude that for his wife to forgive him (as she does) is itself unforgivable. Perhaps in the end she has realized that nothing is going to change this lecherous old fool, and she may as well make the best of a bad job and follow the sort of liberal course recommended by her friend Myrrhina in 204ff.:

> noli sis tu illi advorsari,
> sine amet, sine quod libet id faciat, quando
>   tibi nil domi
> delicuom est.

V

Demipho in the **Mercator** is an example of the old man who falls for a girl after a chance encounter, with the added complication this time that he does not realize that it is his son's mistress he has fallen for; nor is the son willing to release the information for fear of his father's reaction to how he has spent the money entrusted to him to do business with abroad. As a further complication, the old man tries to house the girl with his next-door neighbour, with the result that the neighbour's wife thinks the girl has been installed for *her* husband's benefit. The novel aspect this time is the lengths the old man goes to to dissuade his son from having the girl enter their house (385ff.), and in fact to hide from his son any inkling of his own involvement.

At 203ff. we come across another gloss on the behaviour of the lecherous old man—as soon as Demipho has seen

the girl on board his son's ship, 'subigitare coepit'. We can hardly believe Lewis and Short here, incidentally, where we find that the verb means 'to lie with illicitly'—not even an old lecher like Demaenetus would get down to it so quickly, and on board a strange ship! Presumably the meaning that Plautus would have us understand here is[11] 'to excite sexually by fondling; to coax and cajole',[11] a meaning supported by **Miles** 652 and 1402, and **Casina** 964. The word is rendered quite clear by *Heauton* 567, when Clitipho is reproved by his father on the grounds that it is outrageous to invite your friend to stay and then 'subigitare amicam'. The 'clue' occurs 4 lines earlier, when the old man claims to have seen his son 'manum in sinum . . . ingerere'.

A detail of the *senex amator's* behaviour that we find nowhere else in the canon is to be found at **Mercator** 692ff., where we learn that Demipho is seeking to impress the object of his attentions, and lure her, with lavish preparations of food. His neighbour Lysimachus is amazed:

> decem si vocasset summos ad cenam viros,
>   nimium obsonavit.

Earlier there have been other examples of the language of the *senex* in love. At 262ff. Demipho declares that what he has experienced has immediately driven him to distraction:

> quam ego postquam aspexi, non ita amo ut
>   sani solent,
> sed eodem pacto ut insani solent

and five lines later he repeats the idea. At 292 he describes himself as a 'puer . . . septuennis', again to his neighbour's bewilderment, and at 304ff. continues in the silly, love-conundrum way that lovers have:

> Hodie ire in ludum occepi litterarium . . .
> ternas scio iam.
>   Quid ternas?
>   A-M-O.

Lysimachus' response is savagely dismissive: 'Tun capite cano amas, senex nequissime?'

The final display of lovers' language occurs at 547ff. when Demipho, with an outlook that would please Horace, asserts 'breve iam relicuom vitae spatiumst: quin ego voluptate, vino et amore delectavero,' further maintaining that old age is the fit time to have your fling, when you are no longer tied up with business and money-making, and that you should devote yourself to leisure and love while you can.

Another point of interest, similar in nature to the sheep imagery noted in the **Bacchides,** is the repetition of the 'goat' motif, which first occurs in Demipho's account of his dream at 225ff., recurring at 575. (The 'sheep' idea is used in fact at 567, when Lysimachus describes him as *vervex*.) Plautus has also made comic capital out of the goat imagery at 272ff. Lysimachus enters speaking to an off-stage farm-slave, saying that he wants the *hircus* that is such a nuisance castrated—Demipho, overhearing, woefully sees this as what his wife's reaction will be if she catches him, Demipho, carrying on with the girl.

VI

The last *senex* in this category is different again, and rather pathetic: Antipho, in the **Stichus**. The situation arises at one isolated point, 540ff., and continues for only 30 lines. Meeting his two sons-in-law on their return from abroad, he cooks up a tale of a 'friend' he once had who was in a similar situation to his now—old and lonely—and whose sons-in-law provided him with a flute-girl for having furnished them with wives. Moreover, if one was not going to be enough, they had been willing to offer two more, and two more on top of that. Antipho considers that his 'friend's' request had been a fair one, and leaves the stage a few lines later, happy in the belief that he is to receive the same sort of kindness himself.

Once he has gone, the young men are cruelly, but realistically, dismissive of him: they will send him a girl—to sing to him in bed!

> edepol aliud quidem illi quid amica opus sit
> nescio!
>
> (573)

I have looked in detail at the *senex amator* in the belief that it will have thrown considerable light on the range of variation which can be applied to a seemingly stock character in a stock situation. It is true that all seven of the *senes* examined have fallen for a young girl, and that certain patterns have emerged—the ridicule with which their attempts are viewed; the imagery which suggests that they are motivated largely by animal passion; the childish behaviour and the reversion to the love-language of their youth. The fact remains though that all their cases are different. At the very sketchiest level we have one who desires his son's mistress through having helped the son to her in the first place, behind his wife's back; one who desires a girl as soon as he has seen her, though he went there in the first place to complain against her; one who accompanies him and is at first scandalized, but himself eventually and reluctantly succumbs when the girl turns on her charms specifically to placate him; there is a little picture of an old man who pathetically turns everything he hears from the lips of the girl he desires into what he wants to hear, before turning round and abusing her; there is an old man who will stop at

nothing, and is prepared to degrade himself to any lengths, to encompass his desires, and underlines for us just how unsavoury his passion is by seemingly enjoying making sexual attempts at his slave (male), in the belief that this will induce his slave to help him; another *senex* sets himself up as rival to his son, without either of them being aware of the other's sexual intentions; and finally one who seeks to cure his loneliness and lust by indicating that he expects others to find women for him, as a reward for favours he claims he has done.

All seven in the end share one desire. All seven arrive at the situation by different routes, and attempt to fulfil their desires by different methods. It is the variety achieved within one basic situation which makes this such a fascinating study, suggesting as it does that in Plautus there is far more subtlety of approach and execution than that playwright is usually credited with.[12]

Notes

References to the text are from OCT[9] (Oxford, 1959).

[1] *Asin.* 15ff., 42ff., 62ff., 85ff.

[2] *Asin.* 88ff.

[3] *Asin.* 333ff.

[4] The Prologue tells us that Demophilus wrote the original of this play (*Onagos*), and of course it is possible that Plautus here has merely translated what he found before him; even if that is the case, the fact that he has kept what he found (we know from elsewhere that he was quite capable of changing his source material) argues an appreciation of the balance anyway.

[5] *Asin.* 864ff.

[6] Lewis & Short: '*Addictus:* one who has been given up or made over as servant to his creditor.'

[7] One enjoys the irony of course, as it is this very corrupting influence that the old man has gone there to complain about in the first place.

[8] Walter E. Forehand, 'Plautus' Casina: an Explication', *Arethusa* 6 (1973), 233-56.

[9] Jane M. Cody, 'The *senex amator* in Plautus' *Casina'*, *Hermes* 104 (1976), 453-76.

[10] Op. cit., *passim:* Lysidamus is 'only concerned with encompassing his plans for his lechery' (238). 'This old fool develops no qualities or explanations to win even a small measure of our sympathy' (242). 'The old man is a lecher, pure and simple, without redeeming

virtues' (244). 'He is a lecher to the manner born' (245). ' . . . the old man remains a thoroughly objectionable character from beginning to end' (253).

[11] *Oxford Latin Dictionary* (1983).

[12] Much has been written concerning morality in general, and adultery in particular, in Ancient Athens, and one has to conclude that the dice were very heavily stacked against the woman. Two very readable and authoritative accounts appear in W. K. Lacey, *The Family in Classical Greece* (London, 1968), and A. R. W. Harrison, *The Law of Athens* (Oxford, 1968). There seems not to be available the same quantity of authoritative information concerning Rome, and what there is mostly covers the late Republic and after. Presumably, though, adultery in old men must have been a recognizable and fairly commonplace feature of Roman life in Plautus' own day for the situations created in the plays to have had any comic point.

J. C. B. Lowe (essay date 1992)

SOURCE: J. C. B. Lowe, "Aspects of Plautus' Originality in the *Asinaria*," in *Classical Quarterly*, Vol. 42, No. 1, 1992, pp. 152-75.

[*In the following essay, Lowe compares Plautus's* Asinaria *to its Greek model* Onagos *and identifies several aspects of Plautus's comedy which are perhaps Plautine innovations rather than further derivations from Greek materials.*]

Introduction

The problem of Plautus' originality

That the *palliatae* of Plautus and Terence, besides purporting to depict Greek life, were in general adaptations of Greek plays has always been known. Statements in the prologues of the Latin plays and by other ancient authors left no room for doubt about this, while allowing the possibility of some exceptions.[1] The question of the relationship of the Latin plays to their Greek models was first seriously addressed in the nineteenth century, mainly by German scholars, under the stimulus of Romantic criticism which attached paramount importance to originality in art.[2] Since then the question has been constantly debated, often with acrimony, and to this day very different answers to it continue to be given. Yet the question is obviously important, both for those who would measure the artistic achievement of the Latin dramatists and for these who would use the plays to document aspects of Greek or Roman life. It is not disputed that Plautus' plays contain many Roman allusions and Latin puns which cannot have been derived from any Greek model and must be attributed to the Roman adapter.[3] What is disputed is

whether this overt Romanization is merely a superficial veneer overlaid on fundamentally Greek structures or whether Plautus made more radical changes to the structure as well as the spirit of his models.

In the earlier part of the nineteenth century it was the originality of the Latin dramatists that was emphasized, in response to the charge that they were no more than slavish translators.[4] Attention was drawn to the obvious Roman allusions in Plautus and to the great difference between his comedies and those of Terence. Whereas Terence was held to have followed his Greek models relatively faithfully, it was argued that Plautus must have treated his with considerable freedom. Confirmation of this was found in Terence's reference to the *neglegentia* of Naevius, Plautus and Ennius as a precedent for the liberties he took with his Greek models (*And.* 15-21). Terence admits incorporating into three of his plays material from a second Greek model (*And.* 9-14, *H.T.* 16-21, *Eun.* 30-3, *Ad.* 6-11), and makes clear that his critics objected to this on the ground that *contaminari non decere fabulas*. From these passages it was inferred that what Terence did was not new but had already been practised by earlier writers of *palliatae,* and that *contaminare* did not here have its normal sense of 'spoil' but a technical sense of 'combine'. If Plautus treated his models more freely than Terence, it seemed likely that he would have practised 'contamination' even more than Terence. 'Contamination' was seen as a mark of the Latin dramatists' originality; and the possibility was acknowledged that Plautus' *neglegentia* might also have included other kinds of change to his Greek model.

Throughout the rest of the nineteenth and into the twentieth century Plautus' plays were subjected to increasingly intensive analysis, pioneered by Ladewig, with the aim of discovering how Plautus 'contaminated'. Many inconsistencies were found in the plays and seen as indications of 'contamination', when they were not attributed to post-Plautine *retractatio.*[5] At the same time there developed a tendency to emphasize the Greek element in Plautus and correspondingly to devalue his originality, no doubt under the continuing influence of Romantic philhellenism. Before the first papyrus discoveries brought to light substantial fragments of Menander's plays, parallels were collected from extant Greek literature for many aspects of Plautus' subject matter, thought and dramatic technique, notably by F. Leo in the masterly chapter on 'Piautus und seine Originale' in *Plautinische Forschungen.*[6] Leo recognized that not all apparently Greek elements in Plautus were necessarily derived from his Greek model (*P.F.*[2] p. 103), but in practice he was rather too ready to assume that they were. Like other German scholars of this period, Leo was grudging in his estimate of Plautus' ability to invent new dramatic action, although he paid generous tribute to his creative genius in the sphere of language and metre; he described him as essentially a translator, even if a very free translator, and his plays as inferior to their Greek models.[7] He supposed that Plautus cut much from his models and sometimes drastically truncated a Greek plot, as in the case of the *Casina* (*P.F.*[2] pp. 167f.). He also attributed to Plautus the invention of numerous short passages and some rather longer ones, such as Ergasilus' auction of his *logi* in **Stich.** [*Stichus*] 193-235 (*P.F.*[2] p. 169). He supposed that Plautus sometimes drastically restructured his main model but only by 'contamination', now seen in a negative light as a practice adopted by playwrights incapable of original invention.[8]

Plautine scholarship became obsessed with 'contamination'; the result was a mass of theories but little agreement.[9] It was easy to criticize many of the theories as based on flimsy arguments. Many of the supposed flaws in Plautus' plays used as arguments for 'contamination' were trivial or conventional features of ancient drama or could be shown to have some dramatic purpose. Moreover the nineteenth-century interpretation of *contaminare* in Terence's prologues as meaning 'combine' was refuted and the inference that Plautus had done exactly the same as Terence was questioned.[10] Inevitably a reaction set in against the excesses of structural analysis and the associated 'contamination' theories, but this took different forms. Many scholars rejected the analytical method more or less entirely, regarding it as fundamentally flawed. As usual the pendulum swung too far. Almost any explanation of an inconsistency in Plautus was preferred to that of dual authorship. 'Psychological' explanations were put forward which confused drama with real life. Moreover the unitarians divided into those who saw Plautus' plots as largely his creation and those who saw them as largely taken over from the Greek originals.

One party is inclined to believe that, although Plautus drew most of his material from Greek comedy, he used it with great freedom to produce plots which bore little resemblance to any Greek play.[11] This approach has flourished particularly outside Germany, in reaction to the low estimation of Plautus' originality by the German analysts. Its proponents can only support it, however, with general and inconclusive arguments, and tend to concentrate on denouncing and sometimes misrepresenting the 'contaminationists'.[12] Although they pay lip-service to the known fact that Plautus adapted Greek plays, they often ignore it in practice. The other party regards Plautus as usually faithful to his Greek models at least in the structure of his plays, and in general tends to regard as Greek anything in the Latin plays which is not obviously Roman, especially if something remotely similar can be found in Greek literature. This party naturally includes Hellenists whose primary concern is with Greek drama, but also others.[13] They attribute the differences between Plautus and Terence to a large extent to their use of different Greek models. They hold that many of the inconsistencies in Plautus were already present in the Greek originals, some resulting from a sort of 'contamination' practised by the Greek dramatists themselves, that is the combination of heterogeneous motifs from earlier plays to make new plots.

Others, more fruitfully, have continued the analytical tradition but attempted to improve on the methods of their predecessors. A major advance was made by E. Fraenkel.[14] Consciously reacting against his teacher Leo, Fraenkel set out to show that the Roman element in Plautus' plays was substantially greater than Leo had allowed.[15] He started by collecting a number of figures of thought and style which he showed to be characteristic of Plautus, such as the grotesque comparison of a slave with a hero of myth or history (e.g. **Bacch**. [*Bacchides*] 925ff.) or the comic personification of an inanimate object (e.g. **Stich**. 191 *eo . . . verbo lumbos diffractos velim*). By a comparison of the Plautine plays known to be based on Menandrian models (**Bacch., Cist.** [*Cistellaria*], **Stich.**) with Terence's Menandrian adaptations and the newly discovered papyrus texts of Menander Fraenkel established a strong probability that most, at least, of these Plautine figures were his invention and not taken from his Greek models, even if there was room for argument about individual cases. In some cases supporting evidence of various kinds could be used to identify with probability the limits of a short Plautine addition, e.g. a repeated phrase at the beginning and end of the insertion.[16] Whereas demonstrably Roman subject matter had previously seemed the only reliable criterion of Plautine authorship, Fraenkel was able to expand the range of criteria to include many characteristically Plautine features of thought and style. In particular he showed that many more apparently Greek motifs than Leo had supposed were probably in fact Plautus' invention, including comic allusions to Greek myth. Fraenkel further showed that these characteristically Plautine motifs were particularly associated with certain characters, especially the scheming slave, and convincingly argued that by such superficial changes, together with his metrical innovations, Plautus could substantially modify the characterization, and thus the whole emphasis of a play. Most scholars have accepted these positive conclusions of Fraenkel as largely right, even if not his interpretation of every individual passage.[17] With regard to the possibility that Plautus made structural alterations to his Greek models, however, Fraenkel came to negative conclusions; he moved beyond Leo, but not very far. He supposed less 'contamination', and practically dispensed with the hypothesis of major 'contamination' involving the intricate fusion of two or more Greek plots. He showed that the inconsistencies which had given rise to theories of 'contamination' could often be explained by supposing numerous small Plautine alterations; for the rest he posited for certain plays minor 'contamination' as practised by Terence, namely the insertion of relatively limited material from another Greek play into the plot of his main model. Although, however, he credited Plautus with the invention of some new visual effects in his small-scale insertions as well as purely verbal ones,[18] he denied that Plautus was capable of 'true dramatic invention and the creation of dialogue which advances the action'.[19]

Since Fraenkel the trend amongst analysts has been against the hypothesis of 'contamination' and towards that of more extensive Plautine invention, bringing them closer to the position of those who wish to maximize Plautus' originality. Already G. Jachmann[20] and Drexler[21] supposed for the **Rudens** considerable structural changes by Plautus which did not involve a second Greek model. W. E. J. Kuiper[22] and E. Lefevre[23] have argued for massive Plautus invention in the restructuring of some of his plots, even if many of their arguments have convinced few. Very recently a detailed analysis of the **Menaechmi** has led E. Stärk to the conclusion that the plot is entirely Plautus' invention.[24] In most at least of the places where Fraenkel supposed 'contamination' others now find Plautine invention more likely.[25] A. S. Gratwick supposes 'contamination' in the **Poenulus** in a very different sense from the traditional one, involving the borrowing from another Greek play of no more than the basic idea for an insertion.[26] Analysts are still prone, it is true, to going beyond the evidence and indulging in unsupported speculation of the kind that leads opponents of the method impatiently to dismiss their arguments out of hand. The discovery, however, since 1958 of the first complete play of Menander, substantial fragments of others and in particular fragments of the *Dis Exapaton,* the original of the **Bacchides,** has introduced a major new factor into the debate.

This new material has taught us a great deal about Menander's dramatic technique and provided reliable information on Plautus' methods of work. It justifies and greatly facilitates the attempt to separate Greek and Roman elements in the Latin plays. So far as they go, the *Dis Exapaton* fragments show Plautus treating the details of his Greek model with great freedom, but on the other hand following the Greek plot and sometimes translating very closely.[27] Better understanding of Menander's use of the conventions of five-act structure and the three-speaker rule provides us with a standard against which to measure the dramatic technique of the Latin plays and more objective criteria for identifying Roman originality than were previously available.[28] In recent years it has been possible to recognize ever more clearly certain types of change made by Plautus (and Terence) that go beyond what Fraenkel was willing to allow. Leo established the principle that it is necessary to collect groups of similar phenomena.[29] Fraenkel achieved this at the level of language and style, but it is now possible to progress to the level of dramatic structure and identify with considerable probability certain types of structural change made

by the Latin adapters to their Greek models. One change is now well established, that Plautus and Terence, having no singing and dancing chorus at their disposal, sometimes bridged the act-divisions of their models; in itself this was a minor change, but it could involve altering characters' movements and could be linked to other changes. The *Dis Exapaton* fragments now document a case in which the omission of a choral *entr'acte* by Plautus was connected with the omission of the two flanking scenes and hence inconsistencies in Nicobulus' offstage movements.

The researches of several scholars, including the present writer, have shown it to be probable that both Plautus and Terence not infrequently inserted an extra character into a pre-existing scene of his Greek model, in Terence's case sometimes a character borrowed from another Greek play, traditionally 'contamination', but also sometimes an invented character,[30] sometimes a character who appeared in other scenes of the Greek original;[31] in many cases this must be regarded as the probable explanation of the involvement of more than three speaking characters in a scene of the Latin play, contrary to Menander's practice and to Horace's dictum *nec quarta loqui persona laboret* (*AP* 192). The greater part of this article will seek to demonstrate further instances of this technique from the **Asinaria,** arguing that whereas Philaenium's first appearance in III 1 derives from Plautus' Greek model, her subsequent appearances in III 3 and V 2 were added by Plautus.

The Asinaria *and its critics*

The **Asinaria** has been subjected to harsh criticism, though not usually as extreme as F. Ritschl's description of it as 'devoid of any artistic merit'.[32] Apart from objections to the play on moral grounds, it has been criticized especially for incoherence of plot and inconsistencies of action and characterization; and various theories have been put forward to explain these features. The play can serve as a not untypical example to illustrate some past trends in Plautine scholarship and to point the way to future progress.

The plot in outline is simple enough. An impecunious young man, Argyrippus, is in love with a *meretrix,* Philaenium, who returns his love (542). Their relationship is threatened when Philaenium's mercenary mother, the *lena* Cleareta, tired of mere promises (524-34), delivers an ultimatum; unless Argyrippus can at once produce 20 *minae* as the price of Philaenium's exclusive services for a year, she will find someone else who can (229-31). In the opening scene, a dialogue between Argyrippus' father Demaenetus and his slave Libanus, Demaenetus reveals that Argyrippus has sought his help and that he would like to give it but has no money of his own, being dependent on his well dowered and domineering wife Artemona, who keeps a tight control over all domestic expenditure through her steward Saurea. He therefore encourages Libanus to obtain the money for Argyrippus through some trick. The opportunity for such a trick is provided by a chance encounter of Libanus' fellow-slave Leonida with a stranger bringing 20 *minae* from a merchant of Pella to Saurea as payment for some Arcadian asses (333-7). Leonida impersonates Saurea and, not without difficulty, succeeds in obtaining the money from the stranger with Demaenetus' help (579-84). Meanwhile Argyrippus is in despair, having learnt that a rival, Diabolus, has promised to pay Cleareta 20 *minae* that very day (633-5), when the slaves bring him the money. The lovers celebrate with a party in Cleareta's house, joined by Demaenetus, who claims the right to share Philaenium with Argyrippus for one night as a reward for his help. Diabolus arrives, accompanied by his parasite, all prepared to sign a contract with Cleareta, but finds that he is too late. In his anger he sends the parasite to inform Artemona that Demaenetus is in the *lena*'s house; and this leads to a farcical finale in which Artemona bursts in on the party and drags Demaenetus home in disgrace.

It is obvious that this plot contains numerous stock motifs, which can easily be paralleled from other plays of Greek New Comedy or its Latin adaptations, the love of a young man for a *meretrix,* his inability to pay the money demanded by a *lena,* the opposition of a parent, the rival, the slave's scheme to raise the money by a trick, the deception of a stranger by impersonation, the henpecked husband who attempts to indulge himself but is punished by his *uxor dotata.* More often the obstacle to a young man's amours is an unsympathetic, tightfisted father, who has to be tricked by a wily slave into providing the necessary cash; in this case the stock theme is varied in that it is the *uxor dotata* who is the unwilling source of funds for her son. The plot fits comfortably in the context of Greek New Comedy. It is more than adequate as the basis of a comedy and no more implausible than many other plots of Plautus, Terence and Menander. So far as the main framework of the plot is concerned there is no incoherence but a neatly integrated combination of traditional motifs. When the prologue informs us that the Latin play is adapted from Demophilus' *Onagos* (10f.), we are justified in taking it to be highly probable that Plautus took over from his Greek model at least the basic framework of the plot. The title *Onagos,* 'The ass-driver', if it presents certain problems, fits the plot well enough.[33]

Many inconsistencies and loose ends have been noted in the play. They are more or less superficial, however, and do not destroy the essential unity of the plot, although they sometimes obscure it. Critics speak of the play as consisting of a series of loosely connected scenes. Yet every scene serves in some way to advance the plot; none is dispensable. A truer judgement is that there are inconsistencies in the connexions be-

tween scenes, or at least a lack of clarity about the action supposed to have taken place off stage, and that certain scenes are developed into comic set-pieces which retard the main action and by their disproportionate length tend to obscure the underlying plot. Various theories have been proposed to explain these inconsistencies, broadly speaking divided into those which find the explanation in Plautus' changes to his Greek model and those which find it in post-Plautine alterations to the text. Most often inconsistencies have been noted between I 2-3 and other scenes, and to explain these it was suggested by G. Goetz and G. Loewe that I 2-3 were 'contaminated' from another Greek play;[34] this theory gained the support of Leo,[35] but has had no recent adherents. L. Havet on the other hand argued that the cause of the inconsistencies was an error in the transmitted text of I 2-3; whereas the MSS. identify the lover who appears in these scenes as Argyrippus, Havet reattributed the rôle to Diabolus, and this change has won widespread support.[36] Havet also supposed the loss in transmission of a scene from the Latin play, but this theory has been generally ignored.[37] More extensive 'contamination' involving other scenes as well as I 2-3 has been supposed by M. Brasse,[38] and more recently by J. N. Hough[39] and G. Rambelli;[40] these theories have gained little support and their improbability has been argued by P. Ahrens,[41] Munari[42] and Bertini.[43] Finally, the omission by Plautus of a scene of his Greek model has been supposed by Webster.[44] The fact that all these theories have been advanced suggests that the inconsistencies are sufficiently serious to require some explanation and that they should not be brushed aside as trivial. I shall argue that, with the benefit of our increased knowledge, it is now possible to put forward a theory which explains them more satisfactorily than any previous one. I suppose substantial Plautine rewriting in I 2-3, where I believe L. Gestri was on the right lines but did not go far enough;[45] in III 3, where Fraenkel and others have recognized Plautine expansion,[46] I go farther and argue that Plautus introduced Philaenium to the scene, altering the action of his model. Again in the final scene of the play there are certain inconsistencies in connexion with the *cena* which takes place partly in and partly outside Cleareta's house. The solution of O. Ribbeck was to suppose the loss from Plautus' text of a scene before 828;[47] other scholars have found the solution to the problem in the deletion of two lines of text, 828f.[48] I shall argue that the difficulty results from a substantial rewriting of the scene by Plautus, and that, although it is impossible to identify all the changes Plautus made, these include the introduction of Philaenium once again and the transfer of the drinking party on stage from behind the scene.

Argyrippus and The Lena in I 2-3

Of the various theories advanced to account for inconsistencies between I 2-3 and other parts of the play, that of Havet at present holds the critical field. I concentrate on refuting it. Ahrens attempted a comprehensive refutation but, although he made some good points, not all of his arguments were sound.[49] I do not discuss the 'contamination' theories in detail but only note objections to them in passing. Instead I offer different explanations of the inconsistencies.

According to the MSS. the young man (133) who delivers a monologue (I 2) and then takes part in a dialogue with Cleareta (I 3) is Argyrippus, although he is not named in the text. Havet argued that the lover of these scenes is really Argyrippus' rival, Diabolus, who appears later in IV 1-2.[50] As a few scholars have recognized, however, Havet's theory is open to fatal objections. After I 1, of which the principal theme is Argyrippus' predicament, an audience would inevitably assume that the unnamed, impoverished lover of I 2-3 was Argyrippus.[51] Furthermore the theory itself leads to new difficulties. The lover of I 2-3 has no money now, even if it is suggested that he did have in the past. Yet later in the play Diabolus appears to have no lack of funds; he is able and willing to enter into a contract that very day. Finally, the lover of I 2-3 is highly emotional; yet, unlike Argyrippus, Diabolus in IV 1-2 shows little sign of being emotionally involved with Philaenium.[52]

Havet's case rests essentially on certain inconsistencies in the text, some more serious than others. He demands, however, a higher standard of consistency than is to be expected of Plautus. At least some of the inconsistencies are such as we should not expect to find in Menander, but that Plautus was tolerant of inconsistency to a high degree should be beyond dispute.[53] The inconsistencies in this case are of two kinds; some are structural, in that they concern the central action of the play, others are more superficial. The former relate to Argyrippus' next appearance in III 3. The lover who is banished by Cleareta in I 2-3 makes his exit at 245 towards the forum, whereas Argyrippus is described by Libanus as *intus* at 329, at his next appearance comes out of Cleareta's house together with Philaenium and says nothing of having been ejected before. These inconsistencies, however, can be explained satisfactorily by the hypothesis which I shall put forward of Plautine changes in III 3 without either invoking Havet's theory or postulating 'contamination'. I discuss them in detail below.

The superficial inconsistencies on the other hand can plausibly be explained by the hypothesis of Plautine rewriting in I 2-3. Whereas it is often stated or implied in these scenes that the lover has spent a lot of money on Philaenium, in III 1 Cleareta states that Argyrippus has never given anything except promises. To some extent the discrepancy could be attributed to exaggeration on both sides.[54] Still, Cleareta's statements in 524-31, and in particular the clear implication that Argyrippus

has promised to pay when his mother dies (529), agree with the situation revealed in I 1: Argyrippus' mother Artemona holds the purse-strings and neither Argyrippus nor his father have any resources of their own. We may accept that Argyrippus' claims in I 2-3 are inconsistent with this situation;[55] and we might well be reluctant to attribute this inconsistency to a Greek dramatist. It can be explained, however, by supposing minor Plautine additions and modifications such as were a normal part of the process of *vortere*. So far as the development of the plot is concerned, the essential point is that the lover has no money now, when Cleareta has lost patience and issued an ultimatum (cf. 534); on this these scenes are in full accord with Argyrippus' situation. They depict in fact a stock situation, that in which a lover has spent all his money on an insatiable *lena,* who now turns him away; Argyrippus' situation differed from this in that he never had any money to give, but only promises. It is not difficult to believe that Plautus has here distorted a sentimental picture of a young man's relationship with a *hetaera* by the introduction of conventional motifs associated with the stock figures of the mercenary *lena* and *meretrix* (cf. Ter. *H.T.* 39, *Eun.* 37). There is little doubt that he did similar things elsewhere, for example in *Poen.* I 2, where Adelphasium and Anterastilis are depicted as experienced *meretrices,* although this is inconsistent with their subsequent rôle in the plot.[56]

There are other grounds for supposing Plautine rewriting in these scenes. I 2 consists of a 26-line entrance monologue, a *canticum* in which the speaker's emotional excitement is reflected in the metres, first cretics, then trochaic *septenarii;* Plautine expansion is as likely here as anywhere.[57] The reference to Roman *tresviri* in 131 (cf. **Truc. [Truculentus]** 761) is obviously Plautine, and most, if not all, of this verbose tirade against *lena* and *meretrix* could well be Plautine invention. There is a small inconsistency between 151 *atque eccam inlecebra exit tandem,* implying that Cleareta has not previously been on stage, and 153-5, which suggest that she has heard everything the lover said; it is a plausible guess that in the *Onagos* lover and *lena* entered at the same time in conversation.

In I 3 also there are indications of substantial Plautine rewriting. In a detailed study of this scene Gestri showed that the characterization of Cleareta in the scene has two contrasting aspects.[58] At times she is presented as giving a reasoned defence of her behaviour: she is running a business (186) and must look after her own interests (177), Argyrippus unreasonably expects something for nothing and resorts to abuse only because he has no money (188f.), she needs money for her own expenses and, like any other tradesman, expects payment for goods supplied (198-201), and her profession has special expenses which she must in the end recoup (215-18). At other times she is presented as a conventionally rapacious *lena:* like Ballio in the ***Pseudolus,*** she positively delights in being abused (153-5) and in living up to the bad reputation of her profession (173-5). Even if not all Gestri's subtle arguments command assent, he has made a persuasive case for supposing that Plautus transformed a more reasonable *lena* of the *Onagos* into a typical *improba lena* (Ov. *Am.* 1.15.17), as part of an extensive reworking of the scene.[59] The necessary corollary of depicting Cleareta as rapacious was that Argyrippus had spent a lot of money on her. In support of this hypothesis Gestri drew attention to abrupt transitions of thought in the dialogue (e.g. 156, 178, 186) and passages in characteristically Plautine 'cantante' style, in which rhythm and sound effects predominate over logic (179-85, 204-14). A clear example of Plautine expansion is the extended comparison with fowling in 215-25. The first part of the simile, 215-18, probably derives from the *Onagos;* it neatly makes the point that the *lena* legitimately expects a return on her professional investment. In the development of the simile in 219-25, however, this point, which coheres with Cleareta's other arguments justifying her treatment of Argyrippus, is dropped in favour of a characteristically Plautine list of particular points of comparison between the professions of *lena* and fowler and picturesque details of how the *lena* catches her prey.[60] The extended comparison with fishing in *Truc.* 35-45 is similar, one of a number of similarities, in both thought and language, in the depiction of the *quaestus meretricius* in these two plays;[61] these led Leo to posit a connexion between the Greek models of the two plays, but they are better ascribed to the common Latin adapter.

A similar answer can be given to Havet's assertion that the violent threats and lack of any expressions of tender feeling for Philaenium in I 2-3 are inappropriate to the Argyrippus described by Cleareta as *largus lacrumarum* (533) and depicted in 585ff. Even when allowance is made for the speaker's anger,[62] the fierceness of his invective, and particularly his outburst against Philaenium as well as Cleareta in 131f. *ibo ego ad trisviros vostraque ibi nomina faxo erunt, capiti te perdam ego et filiam,* no doubt go beyond realism.[63] That is not a sufficient reason, however, to deny that Plautus could have put this diatribe in the mouth of Argyrippus. The lover of I 2-3 is depicted as emotional, no less than Argyrippus is later; in both cases strong emotion is expressed in exaggerated language. We should not expect a greater consistency of characterization from Plautus than that; he was concerned above all to make his audience laugh and for this purpose stereotypes were more useful than subtly drawn characters.[64] Argyrippus' threats and abuse cohere with the conception of Cleareta and Philaenium as *pessumae* in this scene and will equally be Plautine additions, as is confirmed by the Roman allusion in 131; Gestri has pointed to traces in the scene of a humbler Argyrippus (190, 229).

Havet's other arguments are nugatory and can be briefly answered. Taking 135a *in mari repperi* to imply that the speaker had engaged in profitable commerce, which Argyrippus could not have done,[65] he presses too hard the logical implications of a piece of Plautine rhetoric. The comparison of the women with the sea coheres with the conception of the voracious *lena* swallowing the lover's wealth, which dominates I 2-3 (cf. ***Truc.*** 568f.). It culminates in 135b *hic elavi bonis,* which plays with the idiomatic meaning of the verb, 'to be cleaned out'.[66] The idea of the sea as a source of wealth in 135a provides a convenient antithesis; it should not be accorded a significance extending beyond its immediate context. That Diabolus later brings a draft *syngraphus* in 746ff. is no reason to suppose Cleareta's words in 238 *syngraphum facito adferas* addressed to him rather than to Argyrippus. Cleareta was evidently willing to enter into a contract with anyone, provided he could produce 20 *minae* (230f.). It is no real inconsistency that, whereas in 89 Demaenetus knows about Argyrippus' need for 20 *minae,* Argyrippus should ask in 229f. *dic, quid me aequom censes pro illa tibi dare, annum hunc ne cum quiquam alio sit?* and receive Cleareta's answer *viginti minas.* Argyrippus must be supposed to have heard Cleareta's terms before, but it is natural enough that he should seek final confirmation, if only as a delaying tactic (cf. *mane, mane*); this leads to a last desperate claim to be able to raise the money somehow (233f.).[67] Nor is it surprising that Argyrippus should in 245-8 announce his intention of trying to borrow money from his friends and say nothing of the possibility of enlisting his father's help; the opening scene made it clear that he had already approached him (74f.) but could have little hope in that quarter.[68] Finally, it is not significant that in III 1 Cleareta does not mention to Philaenium that Argyrippus still hoped to produce the money demanded (234); she had heard such expressions of hope before and was not now disposed to believe them.[69]

Havet's change is therefore definitely to be rejected. Rather we should recognize that substantial Plautine rewriting has in these scenes depicted Argyrippus' relationship with Philaenium in a way that is inconsistent with what is implied elsewhere in the play.

Philaenium and The Horseplay Of III 3

Anomalies explained if Philaenium added by Plautus

Philaenium first appears in III 1 with her mother Cleareta. In this short scene she is depicted in an attractive light. She shows herself genuinely fond of Argyrippus and eager to continue a relationship with him, although he has no money. Her romantic attitude is contrasted with the hard-headed realism of her mother. There is no reason to doubt that in essentials this scene goes back to the *Onagos.* Its tone is serious and it follows naturally from I 3, in which Cleareta banishes Argyrippus from her house unless he can produce 20 *minae* (228-30 ~ 532f.).[70] Philaenium laments the loss of her lover (515 *illo quem amo prohibeor*) and Cleareta lectures her on her filial duties.

The scene in which Philaenium next appears, however, III 3, shows a number of features suggesting modifications by Plautus to his Greek model. First, the scene involves four speaking characters. There is now very substantial evidence that this was at least not normal in Greek New Comedy; and in many of the scenes of Plautus and Terence which involve more than three speaking characters there is cause to believe that one or more of these were added by the Latin adapter.[71]

Secondly, as already noted, it is anomalous that at 591 Argyrippus enters with Philaenium from Cleareta's house, whereas his last exit was in the direction of the forum (245 *pergam ad forum*).[72] It is usual in Plautus and Terence, regular in the extant Menander and probably a general rule of New Comedy, that a character who makes an exit in the direction of some place supposed to be situated off stage, whether into the interior of a house visible on stage or towards marketplace, harbour or country, on his next appearance enters as if returning from that place.[73] That it was a regular convention of New Comedy is supported by the fact that exceptions to it are occasionally explained in the text by a statement that a character will move from one place to another off stage by a 'back street' or 'garden' out of sight of the audience (e.g. 741-3).[74] Other exceptions without such an explanation can plausibly be attributed to the Latin adapter,[75] and one case is certainly due to Plautus; we now know that inconsistencies in the movements of Nicobulus in the **Bacchides** result from Plautus' omission of scenes of Menander's *Dis Exapaton*.[76] In the **Asinaria** it is nowhere explained how Argyrippus returned to Cleareta's house.

It is true there are some indications that as early as II 2 Argyrippus is again in Cleareta's house, but they do not stand up to critical examination; they look less like Greek dramatic technique than makeshift attempts by Plautus to cover up an inconsistency of his own making. When in II 2 in response to Leonida's inquiry in 328 *ubinam est erus?* Libanus replies *maior apud forumst, minor hic est intus,* an uncritical spectator might take this at face value and thereby be prepared for Argyrippus' next entrance from Cleareta's house. But how does Libanus have this information? If he is relying on knowledge that when he himself left for the forum at 117 (cf. 108), Argyrippus was still in Cleareta's house, he is wrong; and although he could have learnt of Argyrippus' ejection and subsequent return if the two met in the forum, it is nowhere stated that they did.[77] A more critical spectator might well hesitate to accept Libanus' statement as true, when it conflicted with the evidence of his own eyes. Again in III 1 it seems likely that Cleareta's words in 533 *ille*

. . . *trudetur . . . foras,* whether or not in their context they necessarily imply it, are intended to suggest that Argyrippus is at that moment in Cleareta's house. This is contradicted, however, by the whole tenor of the scene, which strongly suggests that Argyrippus is not now there.[78] Is it likely that the two women would come out leaving him inside? Should the dialogue not have run differently if they had? When Cleareta says to Philaenium in 532f. *nisi mi huc argenti adfert viginti minas, ne ille ecastor hinc trudetur . . . foras,* this is hardly compatible with her having allowed Argyrippus to return empty-handed after she gave him his marching orders in 228-31. Rather she seems to be merely reaffirming her earlier ultimatum, 'Unless he brings 20 *minae,* he will be thrown out (if he succeeds in entering the house)'. Only the phrase *trudetur foras,* rather than *excludetur,* suggests that Argyrippus is at present in the house; the sentence as a whole suggests the opposite.

Thirdly, after Argyrippus has been thrown out of the house by Cleareta at 127 (161 *eicis domo;* cf. 152) and told to return only if he brings 20 *minae* (228-31), it is improbable that he should have attempted to enter the house again without any money (631) and that, if he did so, he should have been allowed to get as far as seeing Philaenium.[79] In fact Argyrippus' pathetic emergence from the house in III 3, as if only now finally ejected by Cleareta (cf. 596, 632), can be seen as an unneccessary and unrealistic duplication of his earlier ejection.

All these anomalies can be economically explained by the hypothesis that in the *Onagos* Argyrippus here entered alone from the direction of the market-place, no doubt expressing despondency about his situation in an entrance monologue, and that it was Plautus who made him come from Cleareta's house together with Philaenium in order to exploit the dramatic potential of the resulting situation. Philaenium's participation in the scene is not essential and serves primarily to enhance its comic effect. The phrases in 329 and 533 suggesting that Argyrippus is again in Cleareta's house will on this hypothesis be consequential Plautine additions preparing for III 3. A detailed analysis of the scene will provide further support for the hypothesis.

The slaves' delaying tactics suggest Plautine expansion

The scene contains a kernel of dramatic action which is essential to the development of the plot. The two slaves hand over to Argyrippus the money obtained through Leonida's impersonation of Saurea, in order that Argyrippus may have the means of continuing his relationship with Philaenium. Thus is fulfilled the task enjoined upon Libanus by Demaenetus in the opening scene of the play. Whereas in real life, however, the slaves might have been expected to hand over the money as soon as Argyrippus appeared, Leonida and Libanus deliberately delay doing so for a considerable time, so that the actual hand-over does not take place until 732ff., 140 lines after Argyrippus' entrance. Their delaying tactics make possible a variety of comic effects, and that is obviously their dramatic function. In this long scene, which delays the progress of the plot for the sake of comic effects, at least some Plautine expansion is intrinsically very likely.

The eavesdropping episode, 591-618

The first delaying device consists of an eavesdropping episode, 591-618, in which the slaves Libanus and Leonida, on stage from the previous scene, listen to and comment on the dialogue of the new entrants, Argyrippus and Philaenium. This eavesdropping is prepared by the end of the previous scene, 585-90, where the slaves observe the entrance of Argyrippus and Philaenium and stand back with the intention of eavesdropping. Now the eavesdropping convention, and the withdrawal which prepares for it, undoubtedly originate in Greek dramatic technique.[80] That does not mean, however, that in every case where these conventional devices are used by a Roman dramatist they must derive directly from his Greek model. In fact there is good reason to believe that Plautus developed the eavesdropping convention, as also other conventions of New Comedy, and used it in insertions of his own invention.[81] In particular the technique whereby two characters eavesdrop on the dialogue of two others and themselves carry on an aside dialogue, necessarily involving four speaking characters, has no known Greek parallels and seems a Roman development.[82] This eavesdropping episode and its preparation show a number of characteristically Plautine features. In 585-90 the assonance of 587 *lacrumantem lacinia tenet lacrumans* deserves mention; but much more significant is the way in which the idea of the eavesdroppers' silence (586 *opprime os*, 588b *taciti auscultemus*) is developed into a brilliant conceit, in riddle form, in which the money derived from the sale of some asses is identified with the asses themselves, who in the world of Plautine fantasy come to life and threaten to betray the eavesdroppers by their braying.[83] As to the eavesdropping itself, we may first note that it does not serve to advance the action by giving the eavesdroppers any new information; its dramatic justification lies in the momentary effect of the lovers' lamentations and in the sardonic comments of the slaves in the background. From the beginning the word-play on *vale* and *salve* in 592f. prevents us from taking seriously the pathos of the lovers' farewell.[84] Their extreme sentimentality, culminating in reciprocal threats of suicide, is surely meant to seem exaggerated and ridiculous. The slaves' comments and 'mocking presence in the background' also serve to undercut any pathos.[85] Libanus' verdict (616f.) is that an unhappy lover is a great deal more fortunate than a flogged slave! In 588-605 the slaves' aside exchanges extend to an unrealistic length characteristic of Plautus but not Menander or Terence; and these asides are prompted by Argyrippus' words in 597 *nox, si voles, manebo,* which are totally inappropriate to the dramatic situation but make possible the comic conceit of the nocturnal profligate and day-time 'Solon', which Fraenkel recognized as Plautine.[86] Both the form and most of the content of this eavesdropping episode can very plausibly be attributed to Plautus, although he may have derived one or two ideas for it from somewhere in the *Onagos*.

The meeting and preliminary skirmishing, 619-28

After the eavesdropping comes the meeting of the pair of slaves with the pair of lovers. Again the slaves are in no hurry to impart their good news. Instead, there follows a passage of badinage, in which conventional greetings are mixed with jokes and verbal skirmishing, before the dialogue turns to the business in hand (619-28). The eavesdropping is brought to an end with unnaturalistic stage movements in keeping with the rollicking iambic *septenarii* in which the whole scene is written; as the lovers embrace (615, 619), the slaves approach them from opposite sides (618 *circumsistamus, alter hinc, hinc alter appellemus*). This stage business, which we have to imagine as best we can, is clearly connected with a certain symmetry in the following lines, in which first one slave addresses Argyrippus (619), then the other addresses Philaenium (623).[87] One is reminded of the antiphonal jesting of the *Fescennina iocatio* (Catull, 61.120) traditional at Roman weddings, amongst other occasions.[88] Argyrippus' tears prompt a typically Plautine joke, in which Philaenium is comically identified, in the form of a riddle, with smoke (619f.)[89] Then Leonida indulges in a rather feeble equivocation on the meaning of *perdere* (621f.). Libanus' greeting addressed to Philaenium receives a conventional reply, *dabunt di quae velitis vobis;*[90] whereupon Libanus, taking literally the stereotyped phrase, a common Plautine device,[91] makes the grossly impertinent retort *noctem tuam et vini cadum . . .* (623f.). Argyrippus threatens Libanus, Libanus corrects himself[92] and switches to a gratuitous attack on Leonida, so that the passage ends with the two slaves exchanging abuse on the theme of *verberare*. All this is typical Plautine slave-talk. Philaenium's rôle in the passage is to provoke a joke from one slave and an obscene suggestion from the other.

Argyrippus in despair, 629-38

629-38 contain a more serious piece of dialogue between Argyrippus and Libanus, in which Argyrippus laments the situation which drives him to contemplate suicide, his lack of money and ejection by Cleareta. The change of tone from the preceding passage suggests that Plautus is here following his Greek model more closely. This receives some confirmation in the fact that 633-5 introduce a crucial aspect of Argyrippus' situation, the existence of a rival, Diabolus, who has actually promised to pay 20 *minae* for Philaenium's services for a year. It is true that Cleareta had already offered a contract for this sum to Argyrippus (229-40) and hinted at the *possibility* of a rival by her statement that she was willing to accept 20 *minae* from the first comer (231; cf. 195). The first mention of a definite rival, however, and of Diabolus' name, is in 634. It is possible that Plautus cut some earlier reference to him, but the natural presumption is that Argyrippus only learnt of Diabolus' offer when he went to the market-place at 248, although Plautus does not make this explicit.[93] 633-7 then mark a new development in the action, which is likely to derive from the *Onagos*.[94] Libanus' response in 638 is significant; he inquires whether Diabolus has already given Cleareta the money, and on being told that he has not, encourages Argyrippus not to worry. The audience, knowing that the slaves have obtained money for Argyrippus' benefit, would expect them now to reveal the fact; but this expectation is disappointed.

The ludificatio *planned in an aside dialogue, 639-48*

Leonida suddenly draws Libanus aside and the two slaves must be imagined as putting their heads together in a conspiratorial huddle (639). For Argyrippus suggests that they might as well embrace while talking, a sally not at all in keeping with his present situation and mood (640). Libanus (or Leonida) replies that they do not fancy each other and makes the counter-suggestion that the lovers should embrace (641-4); this they willingly do and are thus kept occupied while the slaves, in a brief aside dialogue, plot to make fun of Argyrippus (645-8). Thus 639-48 explicitly prepare for a *ludificatio* of the lovers,[95] of which 619-28 provided a mild foretaste[96] but which will turn into slapstick farce and extend to 731. Leonida gives it as his specific aim to get Philaenium to embrace him in the presence of her lover (647); and this foreshadows the major rôle which Philaenium plays, as we shall see, in the actual *ludificatio*. Now there are indications that this little episode, clearly defined by the movement of the slaves away from the lovers (639 *secede huc*, 646 *concedite istuc*) and back again (648 *sequere hac*), is a Plautine insertion.[97] It is a self-contained episode which abruptly cuts short the dialogue between Argyrippus and Libanus in 629-38[98] and separates Libanus' reassuring words in 638 from their natural continuation, the revelation that Leonida has obtained the 20 *minae* Argyrippus needs, which in fact follows in 649-56;[99] and it is unrealistic in the circumstances that Argyrippus should be so tolerant of the delay. Moreover the dramatic device of withdrawal in order to devise a scheme out of hearing of the intended victim, a specialized development of the aside convention, is

one which occurs elsewhere in Plautus in a context where there is reason to suspect Plautine originality. In *Pers.* 833-43, in the boisterous finale of the play, involving five speaking characters, Toxilus persuades a reluctant Lemniselenis, in an unrealistically long aside dialogue, to *ludificare* Dordalus (833, 843), causing Dordalus to comment *certo illi homines mihi nescioquid mali consulunt* (844); the inconsistency of Toxilus' crude bullying of Lemniseienis with his love for her and the extended play with the idea of *clientela* there suggest the hand of Plautus.[100] In both passages the planning is rather belated, serving merely to make explicit a *ludificatio* which is in fact already in progress; and this explicitness is characteristic of the stagecraft of Plautus in contrast to the greater naturalism of Menander and Terence.[101] Finally, the withdrawal itself gives rise to the joke about embracing slaves, which, with its connotation of homosexuality, is very Plautine.[102]

The slaves deliver their good news, 649-56

It seems probable that in the *Onagos* the slaves proceeded to impart their good news to Argyrippus without delay, in other words that 649-56 represent the original continuation of the exchanges between Argyrippus and Libanus in 638. Even here allowance must be made for the distortion of Plautine *vortere* and we cannot hope to reconstruct the Greek dialogue. Leonida's claim to be rewarded with his freedom (649-52) could, in embryo, derive from the *Onagos;* but when he caps Argyrippus' *libertos* with *non patronos?* (652), the reversal of real-life rôles, whereby the resourceful slave is conceived as *patronus*, the helpless lover as *libertus* is characteristically Plautine.[103]

The ludificatio, *657-731*

In 657-731 massive Plautine expansion has been suspected before.[104] In this passage occurs the slaves' prolonged *ludificatio* of the lovers. That this is at least in large part the work of Plautus is likely on general grounds. The *ludificatio* delays the progress of the main action of the play very considerably, to great comic effect but at the cost of any pretensions to realism. That the preparation for it in 639-48 has been shown to be a probable Plautine insertion reinforces the case for supposing the *ludificatio* itself at least largely Plautine. Analysis of the whole passage provides further arguments in support of the hypothesis. It is possible to distinguish four sections: (a) 657-61, (b) 662-97, (c) 698-710, (d) 711-31. With these sections are associated three leading themes. (a) and (c) revolve around the idea of carrying, whether the purse full of money or Libanus; we may label this the 'burden' motif. (b) contains an *exoratio* directed by the lovers first at Leonida, then at Libanus. In (d) the slaves in turn demand that they should be addressed as gods, Salus and Fortuna respectively.

For the present argument (b) is the most important. Only in this section does Philaenium play a major and essential rôle, a rôle which was foreshadowed in 647 in the planning of the *ludificatio;* each slave in turn duly demands an embrace from her as well as verbal endearments.[105] There are grounds for supposing this section entirely Plautine invention. That it separates (a) and (c), which are thematically linked by the 'burden' motif, is at least suggestive. Then the parallelism, whereby the *exoratio* of Leonida balances that of Libanus (662-79 ~ 680-97), looks Roman.[106] Finally, the slaves' grotesque parody of lovers' endearments (666-8 ~ 693f.) is very Plautine and paralleled by **Poen.** [*Poenulus*] 355-96, another *exoratio* which is most probably Plautine invention.[107]

It is probable that (d) also is purely Plautine. The identification of Libanus and Leonida with Salus and Fortuna and their implied deification takes the exaltation of the salve to its ultimate extreme. This is characteristic of Plautus but not very likely in Greek New Comedy.[108]

Only in (a) and (c) is it likely that something derives from the *Onagos*. How much, can hardly be determined. It is at least not unlikely that the 'burden' motif itself, as introduced in (a) in a relatively sober form, derives from the Greek (cf. Ar. *Frogs* 1-32). Less likely, but not impossible, is that the farcical development of the motif in (c) also had some counterpart there (cf. Men. *Dysk.* 890ff.). Typically Plautine, one the other hand, is the humiliation of the free citizen at the hands of his slave (702 *sic istic solent superbi subdomari*),[109] as well as the reference to pederasty in 703 *asta igitur, ut consuetus es puer olim.*[110]

Conclusion

To sum up, it can hardly be doubted that Plautus greatly expanded III 3. There are substantial grounds for regarding all the parts of the scene which involve Philaenium as Plautine additions.[111] This supports the hypothesis that Philaenium was not present in the corresponding scene of the *Onagos,* a hypothesis which explains inconsistencies between this and earlier scenes. The convergence of a number of arguments is sufficient to give the hypothesis a high degree of probability.

Philaenium and The Cena of V 1-2

Finale with five speaking characters

Philaenium last appears in V 1-2, the final scenes of the play. That five speaking characters are involved in these scenes is alone sufficient reason for supposing some Plautine alterations to his model. 880-910 form an eavesdropping episode, in which, as in 591-618, a pair of eavesdroppers carries on a dialogue commenting on another dialogue; here the parasite and Artemona eavesdrop on a dialogue between Argyrippus, Demaenetus and Philaenium. The only dramatic purpose of the eavesdropping is the comic effect of Artemona's indignant reactions to Demaenetus' crude remarks about her. In 920-41, after the exit of the parasite, the remaining four characters converse together. There is no known Greek parallel for this dramatic technique. On the other hand there is evidence that especially in the finale of a play the Latin adapters not infrequently increased the number of speaking characters.[112]

Characterization of Philaenium

Furthermore, as has often been noticed, Philaenium behaves in V 2 with a pertness which is inconsistent with her characterization in III 1.[113] The hypothesis that her rôle in this scene is a Plautine addition provides a good explanation of this inconsistency. That Plautus should here depict her as a typical *meretrix* and use her for momentary comic effects is entirely characteristic and in keeping with his treatment of her in III 3 and of Cleareta in I 3. This hypothesis is supported by other features of these scenes.

Drinking parties on stage introduced by Plautus

It is abnormal that a drinking party actually takes place on stage. Although New Comedy plots often involve some sort of feast, especially at the end of the play, this normally takes place behind the scene.[114] Only in four plays of Plautus does eating or drinking definitely take place on stage. In all the scenes in question there is at least some reason to believe that Plautus has transferred on to the stage a party which in the Greek original took place behind the scene. Gaiser has very plausibly suggested that this was the case in **Most.** [*Mostellaria*] 308ff., another scene involving five speaking characters, one purpose of the change being to bridge the act-division of the Greek play.[115] In **Pers.** [*Persa*] 753ff., another five-speaker finale and an elaborate polymetric *canticum,* substantial Plautine rewriting is probable, for reasons which cannot be discussed in detail here.[116] That Plautus created this on-stage symposium is suggested by the fact that it is introduced in 757 as the traditional feast with which a Roman general entertained his victorious troops,[117] and that an important rôle is played in it by the *puer delicatus* Paegnium (as cupbearer and as dancing *cinaedus*), a probably wholly Plautine character.[118] Although it is now generally held that a nucleus of the **Stichus** finale derives from Plautus' model,[119] some Plautine rewriting is nevertheless probable, and it is at least not unlikely, though difficult to prove, that Plautus is responsible for the scenario of reclining slaves (696, 703, 750, 752) drinking on stage in a parody of a symposium; the *cena* behind the scene (662-5, 678-81) no doubt goes back to Menander's *Adelphoi* I, but its finale could have presented merely some postprandial merriment similar to that at the end of the *Dyskolos.*

Peculiarities of the Asinaria *drinking party*

Asinaria V 1-2 display several peculiar features which do not look like Greek dramatic technique and for which a good explanation is provided by the hypothesis that Plautus brought on stage a drinking party which in the *Onagos* took place behind the scene.[120] Of course the theatrical conventions of ancient Greece and Rome required that many activities had to be depicted as taking place out of doors which in real life would more naturally have taken place indoors.[121] Nevertheless the situation in **Asinaria** V 1-2 is particularly unrealistic. When Demaenetus, Argyrippus and Philaenium, garlanded (879), come out of the house at 829 and recline (829, 831f., 878, 921-5), presumably on couches, beside a *mensa* brought out by slaves (829), to take part in a symposium, they are transferring into the street an activity which Diabolus had already witnessed taking place in the house (825f. *cum suo sibi gnato unam ad amicam de die potare;* cf. 851).[122]

Moreover this drinking scene on stage involves some dramatic awkwardness. Artemona enters with the parasite at 851 but not until 880 does she become aware of the party taking place on stage; on the other hand the dialogue of Demaenetus and Argyrippus is suspended during the 30-line dialogue of the parasite and Artemona, of which they take no notice. Granted that it was an established Greek convention that two characters could be on stage together but unaware of each other's presence, one may well feel that the convention is here stretched more than a Greek dramatist would have allowed.[123] This awkwardness can plausibly be explained as the result of Plautus' having brought the symposium on stage in V 1; and the nature of V 1 itself supports this hypothesis. The dialogue between Demaenetus and Argyrippus in V 1 does not advance the plot but elaborates and presents dramatically an idea already adumbrated in 738f., Argyrippus' feelings of jealousy at watching his father fondle Philaenium.[124] The theme is developed amusingly with Argyrippus' forced attempts to put on a smiling face (837-41). Philaenium is silent throughout this scene but has an important visual rôle as the object of Demaenetus' lascivious attentions; and the very fact that she makes no protest at having to play this rôle is hardly in keeping with the way she is depicted in III 1, although consistent with her behaviour in V 2. It is a plausible hypothesis that at most the basic idea of V 1 derives from the *Onagos* and that its scenic realization is the work of Plautus.[125]

876-80 would be more appropriate as preparation for the revelation of a scene inside the house, the parasite's instruction in 876 *sequere hac me modo, iam faxo ipsum hominem manufesto opprimas* serving to bring Artemona towards the door of the house, as is the situation in **Bacch.** 831 *sequere hac me, faxo iam scies.* In Plautus this manoeuvre further underlines the artificiality of Artemona's slowness in observing the symposium taking place on stage. If in the *Onagos* the drinking party remained inside the house, something of Demaenetus' behaviour and perhaps of his conversation could have been indicated indirectly through the comments of the onlookers, as in **Bacch.** 834ff. Artemona would naturally watch for a few moments before bursting in. The nature of the eavesdropping episode, 880-910, however, suggests that it is largely Plautine invention.[126]

Perhaps the strongest argument, however, for supposing that in the *Onagos* the drinking party took place behind the scene, not on stage, is to be found in the parasite's monologue, 911-19. The parasite's exit, motivated by such an exit monologue, is natural enough, now that he is no longer needed. His exit monologue, however, awkwardly interrupts the meeting between Artemona and the revellers, which is already taking place. The preceding dialogue has prepared the audience well for a confrontation between Artemona and her husband. In 909f. Artemona, her patience exhausted and encouraged by the parasite, addresses a threat directly at Demaenetus, loudly enough to draw attention to her presence; in 911 Argyrippus greets her *mater, salve* and she replies curtly *sat salutis.* At this point she must be supposed to be at least starting to move towards the revellers and the centre of the audience's attention. Yet at this critical moment the audience is expected to switch its attention to the parasite. This is strange dramaturgy. The peculiarity is explicable, however, if the parasite's monologue is a relic of the situation in the *Onagos;* it would have been well suited to fill the gap while Artemona fetched Demaenetus from the house.

Conclusion

In this article a few scenes of one play of Plautus have been analysed in detail; but analysis of other plays would produce similar results. The picture of Plautus' practice which emerges is of free adaptation but within the framework of the original Greek plot. Whether Plautus is to be accorded the title of 'dramatist' or 'poet' is in part a matter of terminology. Certainly his drama is very different from that of Menander; in spirit it is probably closer to the improvised popular farces which existed in Italy before the introduction of the *palliata.* Plautus shows himself more concerned with the dramatic effectiveness of the individual scene than with the overall structure of the play. Moreover he is more dependent on his models than were Shakespeare or Molière. It is right to recognize the limits of his dramatic invention. There is no disputing his originality however. To call him a 'translator' is, to say the least, misleading, given the present-day implications of the word. Very few have ever denied that in his highly individual style he was a creative artist of a kind. His originality went beyond that, however, and beyond what Fraenkel was willing to allow. Fraenkel's isolation of discrete Plautine insertions was a necessary step in the discovery of the true extent of Plautus' originality, but it must be recognized that there are scenes, such as *Asinaria* I 3, which Plautus has rewritten so thoroughly that a neat separation of his additions from original Greek material is impossible.[127] Such rewriting can lead to inconsistencies with other parts of the play, especially in characterization; in particular we have noted a tendency to depict certain characters in brighter colours and to substitute comically exaggerated stereotypes, such as the greedy *meretrix,* for realistic characterization. Furthermore it must be recognized that Plautus has made structural changes and substantive additions to his Greek models which are clearly in some sense 'dramatic'. We have found reason to see him as a master of stagecraft in the creation of new action, if on a relatively limited scale, as well as new verbal comedy, in the addition of an extra character in *Asinaria* III 3 and the introduction of a symposium on stage in V 1-2, in the development of the Greek eavesdropping and aside conventions for novel effects. This fits well with the tradition that he came to playwriting from practical experience of the theatre.[128]

Any attempt to separate by analysis Greek and Roman elements in his plays must take into account this enlarged conception of Plautus' capabilities. One important consequence of crediting Plautus with greater inventive capabilities is that there is less need to postulate 'contamination'; indeed the hypothesis of 'contamination' is rendered rather implausible, at least in its traditional sense of the more or less mechanical stitching together of material from different Greek models. It cannot be ruled out a priori but in fact it has nowhere been demonstrated beyond dispute. Even if it could be demonstrated, from the point of view of the modern critic it would not differ in principle from other modifications by Plautus to his principal model which did not involve borrowing from a second Greek play. It has sometimes been suggested that the scope of the word 'contamination' should be widened to include all such Plautine changes.[129] Better rather to reduce to the minimum the use of a word with an unhappy history and to define it in a narrow sense. It is indeed very probable that when he made changes to his primary model Plautus often used traditional Greek motifs and sometimes had a particular Greek play in mind; but it is not helpful to use a crude general term without discrimination to cover varying degrees of Greek influence, if it can be established, or none.

If this picture of Plautus as a free adapter of his Greek models is in general correct, it has implications for historians. The Hellenist needs to exercise extreme caution in using Plautus' plays as evidence for New Comedy. Greek thought and dramatic technique are undoubtedly embedded in the Latin plays but have often

been given a new twist by Plautus. Where an aspect of social life or law forms an integral part of the basic plot, the Greek historian may with some confidence take it as reflecting Greek life in the New Comedy period, but he must be constantly aware of the possibility of Plautine distortion in detail and will be wise to look for confirmation from other sources. The Roman historian on the other hand may be encouraged to see reflections of contemporary Roman society in passages which structural analysis shows to be probably Plautine insertions. He may legitimately look for possible political factors behind Plautus' changes; and in any case he is entitled to see topical significance in what Plautus deliberately left unchanged. The problem in using Plautus' plays as evidence for Roman life is a different one, namely that they do not purport to depict Roman but Greek life;[130] and in fact the unashamed insertion of Roman allusions into plays with a Greek setting, together with Plautus' penchant for grotesque exaggeration, creates a Saturnalian fantasy world, an anti-Rome, which to a considerable extent turns the real world upside down.[131] To use such texts as historical evidence requires nice judgement. Finally Plautus provides a case-study of the reception of Greek culture in Rome at the beginning of the second century. Master of racy Latin, although by birth an Umbrian from Sarsina, if we believe tradition, he is evidently thoroughly familiar with Greek New Comedy and its conventions but confidently adapts his Greek models to produce a very different kind of drama, one which proved a great success with Roman audiences. He is no fumbling imitator. He may lack the sophistication of the Augustan poets, but in his plays we can see already the characteristic Roman ability to transform borrowed Greek goods.

Notes

[1] E. g. *Asin.* 10f., *Cas.* 32 4; *Merc.* 9f., *Trin.* 18f., Ter. *Ad.* 6f., Gell. *NA* 2.23; cf. G. Michaut, *Histoire de la comédie romaine: Plaute,* ii (Paris. 1920), pp. 204-8. R. Perna, *L'originalità di Plauto* (Bari. 1955), pp. 6f.

[2] According to A. W. Schlegel. *Vorlesungen über dramatische Kunst und Litcratur,* ed. G. V. Amoretti, i (Leipzig, 1923), pp. 171f. Plautus and Terence could not be regarded as creative artists. He allowed that the Latin adapters made some changes to their Greek models, but only for the worse. See M. Barchiesi, *Maia* 9 (1957), 201-3, B. A. Kes, *Die Rezeption der Komödien des Plautus und Terenz im 19. Jahrhundert* (Amsterdam, 1988), pp. 59-65.

[3] Michaut, *Plaute,* ii. 223-38.

[4] W. H. Grauert, *Historische und philologische Analekten* (Münster, 1833). pp. 116-207 'Über das Contaminiren der Lateinischen Komiker', W. A. Becker, *De comicis Romanorum fabulis maxime Plautinis quaes-*

tiones (Leipzig, 1937), Th. Ladewig, *Über den Kanon des Volcatius Sedigitus* (Neustrelitz, 1842), id. in A. Pauly, *Real-Encyclopädie der Altertumswissenschaft* (Stuttgart, 1848), v. 1728-39, G. Boissier, *Quomodo graecos poetas Plautus transtulerit?* (Paris, 1857).

[5] O. Zwierlein, *Zur Kritik und Exegese des Plautus,* I: *Poenulus und Curculio* (Abh. Ak. Mainz 1990/4, Stuttgart, 1990), again sees *retractatio* as a major cause of inconsistencies, but unconvincingly.

[6] 2nd edn. Berlin, 1912, pp. 87-187.

[7] *P.F.*[2] p. 87 'Seine Komödien sind nicht sein, und sie waren schöner und besser ehe er sie zu eigen machte', p. 185 'Plautus hat, neben einer so hoch gesteigerten Kunst des stilmässigen Ausdrucks, die eigentliche dramatische Fähigkeit . . . nicht entwickeln können'; cf. Th. Mommsen, *Römische Geschichte*[11], i (Berlin, 1912), p. 906 'Ohne Zweifel hat der Bearbeiter auch hierin mehr das Gelungene der Originale festgehalten als selbständig geschaffen'. According to A. Kiessling and his pupils Plautus often reproduced mechanically what he found in his Greek models without regard to whether his audience could understand it (Perna, *L'orig. di Pl.* pp. 11f.).

[8] *Geschichte der römischen Literatur,* i (Berlin, 1913), pp. 125-32.

[9] Michaut, *Plaute* ii. 239-80.

[10] K. Dziatzko and R. Kauer, *Ausgewählte Komödien des P. Terentius Afer,* II: *Adelphoe* (Leipzig, 1903), pp. 7f., W. Schwering, *Neue Jahrb.* 19 (1916), 167-85, A. Körte, *Berl. phil. Woch.* 36 (1916), 981, *Gött. gel. Anz.* 195 (1933), 355-61, W. Beare. *The Roman Stage*[3] (London, 1964), pp. 310-13. For a brief history of the theory of Plautine 'contamination' see L. Schaaf, *Der Miles Gloriosus des Plautus und sein griechisches Original* (Munich, 1977), pp. 11-14; on the meaning of *contaminare* see now G. Guastella, *La contaminazione e il parassita* (Pisa, 1988), pp. 11-80.

[11] E.g. P. Lejay, *Plaute* (Paris, 1925), p. 216 'A raisonner seulement d'après les vraisemblances, à en juger d'après le tempérament vif et le faire rapide du poète, on peut supposer que Plaute a traitè les modèles grecs très librement, cousant à une intrigue une scène prise ici et une scène prise là, poursuivant une idée comique qu'il a saisie dans quelques vers d'une troisième pièce, dèveloppant, raccourcissant, mèlant, et partout y mettant du sien'; cf. G. E. Duckworth, *The Nature of Roman Comedy* (Princeton, 1952), p. 385, Perna, *L'orig. di Pl.* p. 471, B.-A. Taladoire, *Essai sur le comique de Plaute* (Monaco, 1956), pp. 62f., E. Paratore, *Storia del teatro latino* (Milan, 1957), p. 168.

[12] Frequently repeated slogans are that the analytic method rests on the assumption that Greek New Com-

edy was perfect and without flaw, that its practitioners attribute anything good in the Latin play to the Greek original, any faults to the Latin adapter, and that they are interested only in reconstructing lost Greek plays—not entirely without truth but gross exaggerations. Since the analytic method was from the start closely associated with the theory of 'contamination', the two things have understandably not always been as clearly distinguished as they should be. For a vigorous defence of the method see H. Drexler, *Gnomon* 18 (1942), 28-30.

[13] E.g. Ph. E. Legrand, *The New Greek Comedy* (London and New York, 1917), p. 43 'I do not believe that a single essential element of a plot, a single important feature of a character in the plays of Plautus is fundamentally, necessarily, undeniably Roman', p. 283 'I think that, as a rule, he and his rivals were content to be mere transcribers', p. 285 'It appears to me that the activity of the Latin transcribers was almost restricted to making omissions and to practising contamination', F. Marx, *Plautus Rudens* (Abh. Sächs. Akad. Wiss., phil.-hist. Kl. 38/5, Leipzig, 1928) Vorwort, 'Das mir vorschwebende Ziel war, bei jedem Vers des Plautus den Wortlaut des griechischen Vorbilds möglichst feststellen zu können'; cf. B. Prehn, *Quaestiones Plautinae* (Breslau, 1916), p. 4, W. H. Friedrich, *Euripides und Diphilos* (Zetemata 5, Munich, 1953), pp. 259-61, T. B. L. Webster, *Studies in Later Greek Comedy* (Manchester, 1953), pp. 2f., Beare, *Rom. Stage*[3]. pp. 63-6, Zwierlein (n. 5), 5.

[14] *Plautinisches im Plautus* (Philol. Untersuch. 28, Berlin, 1922), Italian translation with Addenda *Elementi plautini in Plauto* (Florence, 1960).

[15] *P. im P.* pp. 3-5 = *El. Pl.* pp. 3f.

[16] E.g. *Rud.* 515 ~ 540; cf. *P. im P.* pp. 112f. = *El. Pl.* pp. 106f.

[17] W. G. Arnott, *Menander, Plautus, Terence* (Oxford, 1975), pp. 34-6. Sceptics include J. J. Tierney, *Proc. R. lr. Acad* 50/c (1945), 21-61, H. W. Prescott, *TAPA* 63 (1952), 103-25, E. Csapo, *CQ* 39 (1989), 148-63.

[18] *P. im P.* pp. 391f. = *El. Pl.* pp. 370f.

[19] *P. im P.* p. 406; cf. pp. 282, 320 = *El. Pl.* p. 384; cf. pp. 271, 306.

[20] *Plautinisches und Attisches* (Problemata 5, Berlin, 1931), pp. 3-104; cf. S. Prete. *A. e R.* 2 (1952), 145f.

[21] *Die Komposition von Terenz' Adelphen und Plautus' Rudens* (Philologus Supp. 26, 2, Leipzig, 1934).

[22] E.g. *The Greek Aulularia* (Mnemosyne Supp. 2, Leyden, 1940).

[23] E.g. *Hermes* 112 (1984), 30-53 on *Miles Gloriosus.*

[24] *Die Menaechmi des Plautus und kein griechisches Original* (ScriptOralia 11, Tübingen, 1989).

[25] See. for example, *Phoenix* 39 (1985), 19f. on *Most.* 690-713, *BICS* 35 (1988), 101-10 on *Poen.* I 2, H.-W. Nörenberg, *Rh. Mus.* 118 (1975), 285-310 on *M.G.* III 2, Gratwick, *Mnem.* 34 [1981], 331-5 on *Trin.* IV 3, A. Primmer, *Handlungsgliederung in Nea und Palliata: Dis Exapaton und Bacchides* (Öst. Ak. Wiss., phil.-hist. Kl., Sitzungsber. 441, Vienna, 1984), pp. 84-8 on *Bacch.* IV 9.

[26] *Cambridge History of Classical Literature,* ed. P. E. Easterling and E. J. Kenney, ii (Cambridge, 1982), pp. 99-103.

[27] E. W. Handley, *Menander and Plautus. A Study in Comparison* (London, 1968). For subsequent discussion see Arnott (n. 17), 38-40 with n. 49, J. A. Barsby, *Plautus Bacchides* (Warminster, 1986), pp. 139-45.

[28] On the five-act convention see *Hermes* III (1983), 442-4, on the three-speaker rule references in n. 71 below.

[29] *P.F.*[2] p. 110; cf. Barchiesi (n. 2), 185 n. 50.

[30] E.g. the cook in *Curc.* 251-370, a doublet of Palinurus (*C. Ant.* 4 [1985], 95-9), Pinacium in *Most.* 858-903; a doublet of Phaniscus (I. Weide, *Hermes* 89 [1961], 198-203). Dorias in Ter. *Eun,* 615-726, a doublet of Pythias (Webster, *Studies in Menander* [Manchester, 1950], p. 73); cf. *Rh. Mus.* 133 (1990), 292 n. 62.

[31] E.g. Milphio and Agorastocles in *Poen.* 210-409 (*BICS* 35 [1988], 101-10), Palaestra and Ampelisca in *Rud.* 664-882, 1045-1128 (K. Gaiser, *ANRW* I. 2 [1972], 1075f., Antipho in Ter. *Pho.* 465-566, 606-712 (K. Büchner, *Das Theater des Terenz* [Heideiberg, 1974], pp. 330-5, 338-41, 347-50, 454-7, 482); cf. *CQ* 33 (1983), 428-44, 39 (1989), 390-9, *Hermes* III (1983), 431-52.

[32] F. Bertini, *Plauti Asinaria* (Genoa, 1968), pp. 27-43, conveniently summarizes the judgements of earlier scholars.

[33] Cf. F. Della Corte, *Dioniso* 35 (1961), 38-41 = *Da Sarsina a Roma*[2] (Florence, 1967), pp. 299-304.

[34] *T. Macci Plauti comoediae, Asinaria* (Leipzig, 1881), praef. p. xxiv.

[35] *Plauti comoediae,* i (Berlin, 1885), on 127.

[36] *Rev. Phil.* 29 (1905), 94-7. His suggestion has been accepted in the editions of A. Ernout, *Plaute,* i (Paris, 1932), and Bertini, by Legrand, *N.G.C.* pp. 422f., G.

Burckhardt, *Gnomon* 7 (1931), 421f., F. Munari, *SIFC* 22(1947), 16-18, Della Corte, *Da Sarsina*[2], p. 30, A. Traina, *Par. Pass.* 9 (1954), 202, Fraenkel, *El. Pl.* p. 434, R. L. Hunter, *Mus. Helv.* 37 (1980), 221 with n. 29, D. Konstan, *Roman Comedy* (Ithaca and London, 1983), p. 55 n. 7.

[37] Op. cit. (n. 36), 99; see below nn. 51, 93. So already A. Spengel, *Die Akteinteilung der Komödien des Plautus* (Munich, 1877), p. 47; cf. Bertini (n. 32), 48.

[38] *Quatenus in fabulis Plautinis et loci et temporis unitatibus species veritatis neglegatur* (Diss. Breslau, 1914), pp. 80-2.

[39] *AJP* 58 (1937), 19-37.

[40] *Dioniso* 19 (1956), 46-57.

[41] *De Plauti Asinaria* (Diss. Jena, 1907), pp. 29-36.

[42] Op. cit. (n. 36), 10-16.

[43] Op. cit. (n. 32), 51-3.

[44] *S.L.G.C.* p. 235; see below n. 75.

[45] *SIFC* 17 (1940), 181-214.

[46] *P. im P.* p. 275 n. 1 = *El. Pl.* p. 265 n. 1, Hough (n. 39), 32 n. 30. Webster, *S.L.G.C.* p. 236.

[47] *Rh. Mus.* 37 (1882), 579.

[48] C. H. Weise, *M. Accii Plauti comoediae*[2], i (Leipzig, 1847), J. L. Ussing, *T. Maccii Plauti comoediae,* i (Copenhagen 1875), Leo *ad loc.* See n. 122 below.

[49] Op. cit. (n. 41), 13-23.

[50] Loc. cit. (n. 36).

[51] Hough (n. 39), 24-6, Webster, *S.L.G.C.* p. 235. Munari (n. 36), 18 n. 1, following Burckhardt (n. 36), 422, supposes the loss of a reference to Diabolus from the prologue 'senza di che lo spettatore non poteva capire chi fosse l'adulescens di I, 2-3'. Hunter (n. 36), 221 admits 'any audience might, however, be forgiven for believing this young man to be Argyrippus in the light of the opening scene between the *senex* and his slave'. Hough (n. 39), 29 and Rambelli (n. 40), 53f. suppose for the *Onagos* an appearance of Argyrippus earlier than 585. Havet [n. 36], 99f., supposes for Plautus' play a lost Argyrippus/Cleareta scene.

[52] Ahrens (n. 41), 21; cf. Munari (n. 36), 18 n. 1.

[53] There are collections of Plautine inconsistencies in P. Langen, *Plautinische Studien* (Berliner Studien 5,

Berlin, 1886) and H. Marti, *Untersuchungen zur drama-tischen Technik bei Plautus und Terenz* (Diss. Zurich, 1959).

[54] Ahrens (n. 41), 16f., Hough (n. 39), 25 n. 13.

[55] Cf. Hough (n. 39), 25, Rambelli (n. 40), 46-8, Della Corte, *Da Sarsina*[2], p. 299.

[56] *BICS* 35 (1988), 101-10; cf. Fraenkel, *P. im P.* pp. 147-52, 277f. = *El. Pl.* pp. 140-5, 267, Gaiser (n. 31), 1083, Gratwick, *C.H.C.L.* ii. 105-10. I am not per-suaded by the attempt of Zwierlein (n. 5), 149f., to explain away the inconsistency; and he himself admits (152) the possibility that Plautus here exaggerated the 'Hetären-Züge'.

[57] Cf. Fraenkel, *P. im P.* pp. 142-206 = *El. Pl.* pp. 135-95.

[58] Op. cit. (n. 45).

[59] Gestri probably underestimates the extent of Plautus' rewriting. He does not address the inconsistency with III 1 of the references to Argyrippus' gifts in this scene. His attempt to reconstruct an outline of how the dialogue went in the *Onagos* is perhaps over-optimistic.

[60] Cf. Fraenkel, *P. im P.* p. 178 = *El. Pl.* p. 169. Gestri (n. 45), 185-91 shows that the fish simile of 178-85 has probably been similarly expanded by Plautus; it is significant that in the development of the simile the lover's gifts are emphasized (181f.).

[61] Leo on 127, *P.F.*[2] p. 149, Munari (n. 36), 25 n. 1, Webster, *S.L.G.C.* p. 235.

[62] Ahrens (n. 41), 17f., Hough (n. 39), 25 n. 13.

[63] Langen, *Pl. Stud.* pp. 99f., Della Corte, *Da Sarsina*[2], p. 299, Hunter (n. 36), 221 n. 29. In 209-14 also Argyrippus implies that Philaenium's attitude to him has changed and he addresses her and Cleareta as *pessumae;* cf. Gestri (n. 45), 201f.

[64] The monologue of Mnesilochus, *Bacch.* 500-25, in comparison with the corresponding monologues of Sostratos in Menander's *Dis Exapaton,* well illustrates how differently the two dramatists depict the emotions of a lover; cf. Handley, *Men. and Pl.* pp. 14f., Barsby *ad loc.*

[65] Cf. Della Corte, *Da Sarsina*[2], p. 299. Havet and A. Freté, *Pseudo-Plaute, Le prix des ânes* (Paris, 1925), p. 7, followed by Rambelli (n. 40), 50, unconvincingly take 191 *aetatis atque honoris . . . tui,* in conjunction with 135, as suggesting a middle-aged merchant (cf. Havet [n. 36], 102).

[66] Cf. Ussing *ad loc., Rud.* 579.

[67] Ribbeck (n. 47), 55, Ahrens (n. 41), 14-16.

[68] Ahrens (n. 41), 18f.

[69] Ahrens (n. 41), 20, makes too much of the fact that Cleareta did not hear Argyrippus' soliloquy, 243-8.

[70] The theory of Rambelli (n. 40), 57-78, that III 1 and 3 are from a second Greek play rests on unconvincing arguments and is very improbable.

[71] Diomedes, *Gramm. Lat.* i. 490, Σad Aesch. *Choeph.* 899, Gaiser (n. 31), 1037f., 1073-9, F. H. Sandbach in *Le monde grec—hommages à Claire Préaux,* ed. J. Bingen, G. Cambier and G. Nachtergael (Brussels, 1975), pp. 197-204, K. B. Frost, *Exits and Entrances in Menander* (Oxford, 1988), pp. 2-5. We need not here concern ourselves with the question whether a three-*actor* rule in the strict sense was valid for New Comedy.

[72] Spengel, *Akteinteilung,* p. 47, Goetz-Loewe (n. 34), xxiv, Havet (n. 36), 96, Hough (n. 39), 25, Munari (n. 36), 18f., 21, Rambelli (n. 40), 50f.

[73] Duckworth, *N.R.C.* pp. 118-21. This was one of the ways the dramatist could control off-stage space, time and action so as to avoid glaring inconsistencies which might distract the audience; cf. Handley, *Entretiens Hardt* 16 (1970), 9f.

[74] M. Johnston, *Exits and Entrances in Roman Comedy* (Geneva, N.Y., 1933), pp. 137-43, Duckworth, *N.R.C.* p. 119 with n. 43, Beare, *Rom. Stage*[3], p. 181.

[75] E.g. in Ter. *Phormio* it seems probable that Terentian changes are responsible for the inconsistent exit and re-entry of Phaedria at 310 and 484 (*Hermes* 111 [1983], 450) and of Demipho at 314 and 348 (Lefevre, *Der 'Phormio' des Terenz und der 'Epidikazomenos' des Apollodor von Karystos* [Munich, 1978], p. 17). The hypothesis of Webster, *S.L.G.C.* p. 235, that Plautus omitted a scene in which Argyrippus was seen to return, would explain this anomaly but not the oth-ers; Rambelli (n. 40), 53f, also supposes the omission of such a scene as part of an unconvincing complex of changes.

[76] Handley, *Men. and Pl.* p. 20 n. 11.

[77] Cf. Hough (n. 39), 26f, with n. 17. It is somewhat awkward that both Libanus and Demaenetus go to the forum, their exits being separated only by Demaenetus' short monologue (618-26), and Libanus' trip achieves nothing (Langen. *Pl. Stud.* p. 99, Hough [n. 39], 23f., Rambelli [n. 40], 52). There is little to commend Hough's theory that in the *Onagos* Libanus remained

on stage for a scene which Plautus cut; more likely is Rambelli's suggestion that he went into Demaenetus' house (coming out again in the next act—the rest of Rambelli's reconstruction of his movements in the *Onagos* is unconvincing).

[78] Hough (n. 39), 31.

[79] Goetz-Loewe (n. 34), xxiv, Hough (n. 39), 25 n. 12, Perna, *L'orig, di Pl.* p. 245 n. 4, Rambelli (n. 40), 53.

[80] Cf. Men. *Sam.* 368 . . . , Leo, *Der Monolog im Drama* (Abh. Gött. Ges. Wiss., phil.-hist. Kl. N.F. 10, 5, Berlin, 1908), p. 68, Fraenkel, *Beobachtungen zu Aristophanes* (Rome, 1962), pp. 22-6.

[81] On *Most.* 687-717 (687 *huc concessero*), introducing a *flagitatio,* see *Phoenix* 39 (1985), 20f.; on *Pseud.* 410-44 (414 *huc concedam*), bridging a Greek act-division, ibid. 20, n. 45; on *Poen.* 203-329 *BICS* 35 (1988), 105-9; on *Pers.* 548-74 (548 *tacill contemplemus*) *CQ* 39 (1989), 396f.; on *Cas.* 424-503 (434 *concedam huc*) Lefevre, *Hermes* 107 (1979), 321f.; on *Trin.* 516-68 (517 *huc concede*) G. Jahn, *Hermes* 60 (1925), 33-49 (wrongly supposing a transposition from later in the play; cf. Jachmann, *Pl. und Att.* pp. 230f.); on *Trin.* 1008-23 (1007 *huc concessero*), a *servus currens* entrance, Gratwick, *Mnem.* 34 (1981), 331-5; on *Men.* 571-601 (570 *huc concedamus*) Stärk, *Menaechmi* pp. 91f.; cf. Barsby on *Bacch.* 404.

[82] Cf. Barsby on *Bacch.* 1149-65. In Ter. *Eun.* 1053-60 the aside dialogue is between Thraso and Gnatho, the two characters introduced by Terence, on his own admission (30-3), into his main Greek model; cf. B. Denzler, *Der Monolog bei Terenz* (Zurich, 1968), pp. 53-5. Zwierlein (n. 5), 153, asserts that the similarity of technique in a 'doppelter Zweierdialog' in *Poenulus* I 2 and V 4 'kann nicht auf Plautus zurückgehen'. Why not? Zwierlein does not discuss the other Latin parallels which suggest that it does.

[83] Plautus used variants of the same idea on several other occasions: *Pers.* 265 *hominibus* (*bobus* Ritschl, *alii alia*) *domitis . . . ex crumina,* 317 *boves . . . in crumina, Truc.* 654f. *minas ovis in crumina,* 956 *pecua . . . in crumina.* On Plautine riddles see Fraenkel, *P. im P.* pp. 48-50 = *El. Pl.* pp. 45f., on *Belebung des Unbelebten P. im P.* pp. 101-10 = *El. Pl.* pp. 95-104.

[84] Traina, *Par. Pass.* 9 (1954), 187 'la beffa dell'amor patetico', *Comoedia—antologia della palliata*[2] (Padua, 1966), p. 66, P. Flury, *Liebe und Liebessprache bei Menander, Plautus und Terenz* (Heidelberg, 1968), pp. 84f., 91f.; *contra* Munari (n. 36), 13f., Perna, *L'orig. di Pl.* p. 207. There is probably also a Roman joke in 594; *mater supremam mihi tua dixit, domum ire iussit* (*suppremum* codd.: corr. Turnebus) can be taken as referring to Argyrippus' impending death, but Fraenkel recognized an allusion to the praetor's formula for announcing the end of the day's session in the *comitium* (*P. im P.* p. 43 n. 4 = *El. Pl.* p. 40 n. 4). The use of juridical terminology in an amatory context is characteristic of Plautus (cf. 131f., 607, N. Zagagi, *Tradition and Originality in Plautus* [Hypomnemata 62, Göttingen, 1982], pp. 106-31).

[85] N. W. Slater, *Plautus in Performance* (Princeton, 1985), p. 63.

[86] Fraenkel, *P. im P.* pp. 215-17 = *El. Pl.* pp. 206-8; cf. Jachmann, *Pl. und Att.* pp. 35-7.

[87] I follow the distribution of speakers printed by recent editors, although this is not entirely in accordance with the evidence of the MSS, and is open to dispute (cf. Bertini's apparatus criticus). It is hardly possible to differentiate the characters of the two slaves or their roles in this scene so as to assign each speech to one or the other with confidence. This uncertainty does not affect my argument.

[88] Cf. Liv. 7.2.7, Hor. *Ep.* 2.1.145f., J. Blänsdorf in E. Lefevre, ed., *Das römische Drama* (Darmstadt, 1978), p. 96 with n. 14, Stärk, *Menaechmi,* p. 73 with n. 324. See Fraenkel, *P. im P.* pp. 401f. = *El. Pl.* pp. 379f. on Plautine *altercationes.* With 618 *circumsistamus* compare *Pseud.* 357 *adsiste altrim secus* introducing a Roman *flagitatio;* cf. H. Usrer, *Rh. Mus.* 56 (1901), 1-28 = *Kl. Schr.* iv.356-82.

[89] Fraenkel, *P. im P.* p. 49 = *El. Pl.* pp. 45f.

[90] Cf. 45, *M.G.* 1038, *Stich.* 469, *Trin.* 436f., 1152, Hor. *S.* 2.8.75f.

[91] Cf. 592f., P. J. Enk, *Plauti Truculentus* (Leyden, 1953), on *Truc.* 126, 259, Hough, *AJP* 66 (1945), 282-302.

[92] Cf. 43, *M.G.* 1039f.

[93] Havet (n. 36), 99, implausibly supposes that Argyrippus learnt of Diabolus' offer in a lost Argyrippus/*lena* scene.

[94] Cf. Munari (n. 36), 15, against Hough (n. 39), 21f. This does not exclude the possibility of some superficial Plautine additions; the play with *perdo/pereo* may well be one (~ 243f.; cf. the play with *perire* in *Truc.* 45-50, 707, Flury, *Liebe,* pp. 81, 84f.), although it is not inconceivable that there was something similar in the Greek.

[95] Cf. 677 *delusisti,* 679 *delude,* 711 *delusistis,* 730 *ludatis,* 731 *satî iam delusum.*

[96] Cf. Bertini on 618.

[97] Rambelli (n. 40), 76 supposed this passage a Plautine insertion, but for inadequate reasons.

[98] Havet-Freté suppose a lacuna after 638.

[99] 648c *ecquid est salutis?* would follow well after 638 *ne formida.* In its Plautine context the phrase makes sense if Argyrippus supposes the purpose of the slaves to be to devise a scheme for his benefit (Ussing on 639, Havet-Freté on 638).

[100] Cf. *Men.* 571-87, Fraenkel, *P. im P.* pp. 159-62 = *El. Pl.* pp. 152-4, Stärk, *Menaechmi,* pp. 90f., S. J. Rosivach, *Maia* 35 (1983), 86f. with n. 11. Another scheming aside dialogue is *Bacch.* 1149-54, in a four-speaker finale (cf. Barsby *ad loc.*).

[101] Cf. Handley, *Men. and Pl.* pp. 14, 17.

[102] Cf. S. Lilja, *Arctos* 16 (1982), 57-64, D. Hughes, *Rh. Mus.* 127 (1984), 51 n. 8. Bertini is wrong to follow the MSS. in distributing 643 between Argyrippus and Leonida, and in rejecting Pylades' correction of *haec* to *hic.* After 641 *non omnia eadem aeque omnibus . . . suavia,* 643 *ego* forms the necessary antithesis to 642 *vobis* and must be spoken by the same speaker; and in the context of Argyrippus' suggestion that the slaves embrace *each other* a reference to Philaenium is out of place.

[103] Cf. 689f., *Cas.* 739, *Most.* 406-8, *Rud.* 1265f., 1280, E. Segal, *Roman Laughter* (Harv. stud. in comp. lit. 29, Cambridge, Mass., 1968), p. 106 et passim.

[104] See references in n. 46 above.

[105] The view of Rambelli (n. 40), 63f., that Philaenium does not actually kiss Leonida seems refuted by 679 *age sis tu in partem . . . amplexare hanc.*

[106] Cf. p. 16 above with n. 88, Segal, *Rom. Laughter,* p. 105, *Pers.* 1-6 ~ 7-12 (Fraenkel, *P. im P.* pp. 227f. = *El. Pl.* pp. 218f.), 168-82 ~ 183-99 (Hughes, [n. 102], 54f.).

[107] *BICS* 35 (1988), 104f., Gratwick *C.H.C.L.* ii.110 n. 2; cf. Fraenkel, loc. cit. (n. 46). Amatory language is similarly parodied in *Pseud.* 64-73 (cf. 1259-61, *Cas.* 134-8, 837, Jachmann, *Philologus* 88 [1933], 451). See Perna, *L'orig. di Pl.* ch. 7 on 'la parodia dell'amore' in general. Another *exoratio* of a slave by a free man is *Epid.* 728-31 (cf. Segal, *Rom. Laughter,* pp. 109f., 122f., E. Fantham, *Pap. Liv. Lat. Sem.* 3[1981], 22f.).

[108] Fraenkel, *P. im P.* p. 116 = *El. Pl.* p. 110; cf. Segal, *Rom. Laughter,* pp. 108f.

[109] Cf. 670f., *Epid.* 728f., *Pseud.* 1285ff., Segal, *Rom. Laughter,* ch. 4.

[110] Cf. *Aul.* 637, *Capt.* 867, *Poen.* 612, *Rud.* 1074, C. J. Mendelsohn, *Studies in the Word-Play in Plautus* (Univ. of Pennsylvania, Ser. in Phil. and Lit. XII. 2, Philadelphia, 1907), p. 84, W. Stockert, *T. Maccius Plautus Aulularia* (Stuttgart, 1983), on *Aul.* 637 and references in n. 102 above. I am not persuaded by suggestions that there are other obscene allusions in the passage (cf. Bertini on 702-10. Segal, *Rom. Laughter,* p. 203 n. 20. Mendelsohn, op. cit. 26, sees play with Argyrippus' name in the action of this scene; but, if the horseplay was in the *Onagos,* this could have inspired the Plautine character's name (cf. Ussing [n. 48], i.349).

[111] Rambelli (n. 40), 76f., noted that there is no sign of Philaenium's presence during the actual handing over of the money; but in a short passage this fact would by itself not necessarily be significant.

[112] See above p. 17 on *Pers.* 777ff., *BICS* 32 (1985), 83f. on *M.G.* 1394ff., *Rh. Mus.* 133 (1990), 287 on *Poen.* 1120ff., Barsby on *Bacch.* 1120ff., Sandbach (n. 71), 199-204 on Ter. *And.* 904ff., *H.T.* 1045ff., *Eun.* 1025ff., *Ad.* 958ff.; cf. *Cas.* 963ff., *Curc.* 599ff., *Trin.* 1125ff., *Truc.* 893ff.

[113] Munari (n. 36), 20, Rambelli (n. 40), 64, and references in Bertini on 930.

[114] Johnston, *Exits,* p. 144. It would be very rash to assume that drinking scenes on stage never occurred in Greek New Comedy, but those supposed by Webster, *Stud. Men.* p. 112 n. 1, are quite uncertain.

[115] Op. cit. (n. 31), 1074f.

[116] See above p. 17. 767 *in summo* (cf. 771ᵃ) suggests the seating arrangements of a Roman *triclinium* (E. Woytek, *T. Maccius Plautus Persa* [Öst. Ak. Wiss., phil.-hist. Kl., Sitzungsber. 385, Vienna, 1982], *ad loc.*).

[117] Cf. *Bacch.* 1074, *R-E* vii.510 s.v. *triumphus.* Fraenkel, *P. im P.* pp. 234-40 = *El. Pl.* pp. 226-31, showed that in 753-7 Toxilus uses the traditional language of Roman triumphs.

[118] Hughes (n. 102), 46-57.

[119] Gaiser (n. 31), 1084; but cf. Fraenkel, *El. Pl.* p. 443.

[120] Weise on 828f., K. Kunst, *Studien zur griechisch-römischen Komödie* (Vienna, 1919), p. 156 and Webster, *S.L.G.C.* p. 237, amongst others, suppose Plautus' scene played with the banqueters off stage and seen through a partly opened door, but nothing in the text justifies this interpretation (Johnston, *Exits* p. 144, Beare, *Rom. Stage³* p. 179).

[121] R. C. Flickinger, *The Greek Theater and its Drama*[4] (Chicago, 1936), pp. 237-43.

[122] Cf. Ussing on 821, Brasse (n. 38), 81, A. Thierfelder, *De rationibus interpolationum Plautinarum* (Leipzig, 1929), pp. 129f., Perna, *L'orig. di Pl.* p. 245 n. 4. Ussing and Leo follow Weise in deleting 828f., but this would not change the basic situation; moreover there are significant verbal parallels between these lines, *Most.* 308f. *age accumbe igitur. cedo aquam manibus, puere, appone hic mensulam* and *Pers.* 768-9[a] *hoc age, accumbe . . . date aquam manibus, apponite mensam.*

[123] D. Bain, *Actors and Audience* (Oxford, 1977), pp. 162-71.

[124] There are also other echoes of earlier parts of the play: 834 *merito tuo facere possum* ~ 737 *meritissumo eiius quae volet faciemus*, 835f. *nolo ego metui, amari mavolo, mi gnate, me aps te* ~ 67 *volo amari a meis* (cf. 77).

[125] It seems not unlikely that the terms demanded by Demaenetus in return for handing over the 20 *minae* to Argyrippus, the enjoyment of Philaenium for one night, are a Plautine invention. This motif is introduced suddenly in 735f. and not prepared in I 1 (Langen, *Pl. Stud.* p. 104, Hough [n. 39], 22f., Munari [n. 36], 23, Webster, *S.L.G.C.* p. 234, Perna, *L'orig, di Pl.* p. 247). The fact that Demaenetus had aided and abetted the trick to misappropriate Artemona's money (cf. 814f.), aggravated by his participation with Argyrippus and Philaenium in a drinking party in Cleareta's house, would be a sufficient cause for Artemona to take revenge on him. That Artemona's revenge probably does derive from the *Onagos* (if not the *Prügelmotif* of 936 and 946; cf. E. Schuhmann, *Philologus* 121 [1977], 62f.) is implicit in my arguments above. After the scheme, which forms the main strand of the plot, has been brought to a successful conclusion and the young lovers have been reunited, the revenge of Diabolus and Artemona at Demaenetus' expense provides an amusing ending to the play; similarly in Terence's *Phormio* the parasite Phormio takes his revenge on Chremes by reporting him to his wife (Kunst [n. 120], 154, Webster, *S.L.G.C.* p. 237). It is appropriate that Demaenetus should be made to pay for his part in the deception of his wife; and it is well prepared by the characterization of Artemona in I 1.

[126] Schuhmann (n. 125), 55-64, observes that the expression by a husband of his distaste for sexual relations with his aging *uxor dotata* (894f.; cf. 872-4) and of his wish for her early death (901, 905; cf. 909) are motifs found elsewhere in Plautus (e.g. *Most* 703-7, *Trin.* 41, 51) but not in Menander or Terence, and shows that the characterization of the Plautine *uxor dotata* is in large measure to be attributed to the Latin adapter. Stärk, *Menaechmi*, pp. 31-6, 47-59, plausibly

sees the influence of the pre-literary Atellan farces in the crude comedy which Plautus regularly attaches to the figures of the *senex amator* and *uxor dotata*, noting that their typically Plautine features can more easily be paralleled in the literary Atellana than in Greek New Comedy; but some allowance must be made for the influence of the *palliata* on the literary *Atellana*. Gratwick (n. 81), 341 n. 4, believes the adventitious use of the *palla* motif in 884-6 (cf. 929f.) a Plautine borrowing from the *Menaechmi*, where the motif plays a central rôle in the plot (cf. E. Fantham, *C. Ph.* 63 [1963], 176f.); and he may be right. It seems likely, however, that the motif was a stock one in New Comedy (*pace* Stärk, *Menaechmi*, pp. 14f.), even if it is not actually attested in the Greek fragments; Plautus could have used it without having a specific model. The verbal similarities which Gratwick sees between this scene and the *Menaechmi* are hardly sufficient to prove the priority of the *Menaechmi*.

[127] Gestri (n. 45), 205; cf. Jachmann, *Pl. und Att.* p. 69.

[128] Gell. *NA* 3.3, Duckworth, *N.R.C.* pp. 50f.

[129] Grauert (n. 4), 205, Körte, *Berl. phil. Woch.* 36 (1916), 981, Schaaf, *Miles*, pp. 378-80.

[130] *Men.* 7-9, *Stich.* 446-8.

[131] Leo, *P.F.*[2] p. 111, Fraenkel, *P. im P.* pp. 400f. = *El. Pl.* pp. 378f., G. Williams, *JRS* 48 (1958), 18, P. P. Spranger, *Historische Untersuchungen zu den Sklavenfiguren des Plautus und Terenz*[2] (Stuttgart, 1985), p. 117, Segal, *Rom. Laughter* passim, Gaiser (n. 31), 1079, 1107.

William S. Anderson (essay date 1993)

SOURCE: Willam S. Anderson, in *Barbarian Play: Plautus' Roman Comedy*, University of Toronto Press, 1993, 179 p.

[In the following two chapters from his book-length analysis of Plautus's work, Anderson first examines the way in which Plautus subverts the conventional love plot in order to transform Greek romantic comedy into Roman comedy. Next, Anderson traces the development of the concept of "heroic badness"—the immoral tendencies shared by humanity and acted on by Plautus's "heroic rogues"—throughout Plautus's comedies.]

Plautus' Plotting: The Lover Upstaged

When classical scholars began to develop an interest in New Comedy, then to pursue that interest with fervour under the stimulus of the new papyrus finds of this century, they themselves were living in a period of sentimentality. Tastes in the Anglo-American cultures agreed with the romantic ideals of Victorian society, and parallel romanticism affected the judgment of other European classicists. Thus, it is common to find in general comments on New Comedy that the plot focused on love: 'The central theme was usually the course of true love, and the action depicted the efforts of a youth to obtain possession of his mistress, often in the face of the determined opposition of a parent or guardian, and with the assistance of a tricky slave.'[1] Even the diction of this sentence by Ashmore, which dates from 1910, sounds Victorian. Once it became conventional to treat New Comedy as romantic comedy, it also became easy to see how it anticipated the romantic plots of Renaissance, Italian, and Shakespearean comedy[2] and how it has continued to exert its influence on the romantic scenarios of Hollywood (especially of the 1930s and 1940s) and of the various so-called situation comedies (sitcoms) of postwar television.

Although I am suggesting that classical scholars, children of their own sentimental age, were predisposed to find and value romantic love plots in Greek New Comedy and to minimize the significance of exceptions, I hasten to add that earlier ages, also sentimentally inclined, made the same generalizations. It was a commonplace, for instance, that love was the 'breath of life' in Menander's plays. Ovid said it in the first decade of the first century AD (as he defended his own use of love topics in his poetry): *fabula iucundi nulla est sine amore Menandri* ('No play of delightful Menander exists without love'). Later, in the same century, Plutarch, a great admirer of the Greek playwright, declared that in every play of Menander the breath of life comes from love. The sententious and sentimental Stobaeus cited Plutarch's comments with full approval in the sixth century.[3] Plutarch also commented with great admiration on the propriety of Menander's love plots. Menander always left his audiences with a good feeling about love, an optimism about marriage and the commitments of mutual affection.[4]

Plautus did not agree with Menander on this point, as on so many others, and in this chapter I review the ways in which he sabotaged the love plot and its amatory themes and upstaged the lover, determined not to write romantic comedy but Roman comedy with an emphasis on humour derived from intrigue, roguery, wit, and outright romantic parody. We can watch him taking the Menandrian originals, which centred their attention on the positive worth of love, and warping them into a new anti-romantic theme. The changes which he introduced in *The Double-Deceiver,* as he adapted it into the **Bacchides,** involved, among other things, denying the fathers the authority to control their sons' irresponsible love and instead subjecting them to the same irresponsible urges as their immature progeny. Plautus' final scene does not point towards responsible domestic love, but towards sexual promiscuity.[5]

The two fathers, Nicobulus and Philoxenus, storm up to the house of the courtesans where their two sons, they now know, are royally entertaining themselves with the money fraudulently gained from Nicobulus. When the two Bacchides open the door at their loud pounding, angry Nicobulus faces one, and the other makes Philoxenus, a milder and more impressionable old man, her target. As the women seductively tease the men, Philoxenus begins to melt. Here is the conversation of the two greybeards: Philoxenus: 'Do you see that one?' Nicobulus: 'Yes.' Philoxenus: 'That's a woman who's not bad.' Nicobulus: 'Damn it, she *is* bad, and you're a scoundrel.' Philoxenus: 'Why waste words? I love her.' Nicobulus: 'You in love?' Philoxenus: 'Certainly' (spoken in ostentatious Greek, like French *mais oui*). Nicobulus: 'You decrepit human being, do you dare to become a lover at your age?' Philoxenus: 'Why not?' Plautus has let these characters bandy around the word for love—*amare*—as their theme, but the context makes a joke of Philoxenus' foolish infatuation. In the two different connotations of the word *mala* ('bad,' lines 1161-2), he produces a clever comic assessment of this love. Whereas Philoxenus ignores entirely the ethical nature of the courtesan and sees only her physical attractions and her pleasing manner, Nicobulus insists on her essential badness. But . . . a woman's badness *(malitia)* has special positive value in Plautus' world, and so, although Philoxenus is weak and ridiculous in 'loving' his Bacchis, he also strikes the Roman audience as thoroughly in line with the comic 'virtues' supported by Plautus: not romantic love, but sensual love that can be gratified by old and young alike.

Did Greek New Comedy Always Feature Romantic Love?

Before I examine the ways in which Plautus lets the lover be upstaged, it would be well to modify somewhat the seemingly stark opposition between what I have called the romantic love of Menander (and, by implication, of all Greek New Comedy) and the anti-romantic, Roman enjoyment of sensual love in Plautus. Although it may be convenient to attribute to the Greek writers of comedy a single sentimental attitude towards love, even our fragmentary acquaintance with Menander's main rivals obliges us to admit that they treated love differently. Whereas Menander built up plots where love meant a serious commitment and ultimately found deserved success in marriage and family, love breathed a different life in Philemon's and Diphilos' comedies.

Charinus of Philemon's *Emporos* (Plautus' **Merchant**) does not win the sympathy and interest of the audience in the way that Menander's lovers do.[6] He seems so helpless and so full of histrionic, 'tragical' self-pity, and his love, for a courtesan whom he has rashly bought, has no possibility of depth or long duration. In his opening soliloquy, he talks at length of all the faults *(vitia)* that accompany love (lines 18 ff). But this interminable and one-sided list is introduced by the statement that Charinus fell in love with a woman of outstanding loveliness while trading on Rhodes. Thus, his words about love's faults seem inconsistent with his confession of love: evidently, he does not really accept the fact that love amounts to a catalogue of negative qualities. But he has nothing very cogent to say about love on the positive side, and the woman he has suddenly become enamored with cannot offer him a lasting relationship such as those developed by Menander. Charinus will never be able to marry her, a foreigner and experienced prostitute. Nor does the love become any more valid when his foolish father suddenly abandons his strict principles and becomes Charinus' unknown rival. Philemon plots this love so as to create tensions between father and son, and between the two friends, and those tensions and resolutions constitute his primary interest: love is, in certain respects, only a comic gimmick.

Love occupies a still smaller part in the plot of Philemon's *Treasure* (Plautus' **Trinummus**), subordinate to the confusions of friendship between the two young men and the bumbling but well-meaning efforts of the older generation. Lesbonicus is no lover at all, and his friend Lysiteles seems to want to marry Lesbonicus' sister more out of friendship for Lesbonicus than for any affection for the girl (who is not allowed to appear on stage and impress the audience with the reality of this future wife). Like Charinus in *Emporos*, Lysiteles produces a soliloquy about love on his first entrance (lines 223 ff), and it also lays out the destructive, costly features of love. Lysiteles debates whether to commit his life to love or to practical advantage. As he slants it, there is no contest: Plautus makes him pun and say that love produces bitterness (*Amor amara dat tamen*, line 260), and that it will be no 'friend' of his (*Amor, mihi amicus ne fuas umquam*, line 267). Then, with an inconsequence that Plautus probably exaggerated, this same serious, practical, and reasonable young man suddenly proposes to his father (presumably the source of such wisdom on love) that he marry the dowerless sister of his chum Lesbonicus, merely as an act of friendship! We might think of this self-contradictory soliloquy on love's disadvantages, spoken by a young man who is taking on those admitted disadvantages, as a hallmark of Philemon and an indication of his special comic diminution of love and irrational lovers.[7]

Plautus . . . preserves the main lines of two comedies of Diphilos in his **Rudens** and **Casina**.[8] Neither makes significant use of romantic love. In the first, young

Plesidippus does love the pseudo meretrix Palaestra, who eventually proves to be the long-lost daughter of Daemones and therefore marriageable. How little love contributes to plot and theme emerges clearly from the petty role of Plesidippus, the total lack of contact between the 'lovers' on stage, the absence of any words of love from either, and the careful attention devoted to other delightful details—namely, the wild behaviour and punishment of the pimp; the somewhat parodic Recognition; and all the comic excitement generated by the trunk, the rope, and the conflict of Gripus first with his fellow slave, then with the infamous pimp. If love is the breath of life for Menandrian comedy, for Diphilos it is a momentary gasp.

In the **Casina** (Diphilos' *Lot-Drawers*), young love has been removed from the play, so that the comedy can concentrate with raucous laughter on the crude lust of elderly Lysidamus, the witty obstruction and punishment contrived by the 'heroic' wife Cleustrata, and the rivalry between the slaves which Diphilos hilariously dramatizes in his inimitable scene of drawing lots. The Latin play now carries the name of the young girl who is the object of Lysidamus' lust (and supposedly of the honourable love of the absent son), but she never appears, and the title—which may replace Plautus' title, *Sortientes,* a translation of the Greek (line 32)—might well remind us of how far Diphilos has allowed himself to stray from the conventional romantic love-and-recognition plot. In short, Greek New Comedy does not present a standard attitude towards love: Menander tends to emphasize its humane qualities, both bad and good, and to plot his plays so that the lover earns a loving relationship by learning responsibility and commitment to family; Philemon isolates certain sententious views about love's disadvantages, then plays with somewhat foolish young and older lovers who nevertheless fall in love and cause complications that increasingly interest him; Diphilos rather quickly marginalizes love, in order to free himself to use his broader sense of comedy on more obviously funny situations, especially the brawling of slaves, the beating of pimps, and even the physical humiliation of wayward masters.

Plautus and Love that Eventuates in Marriage

The standard romantic plot, of which Menander made himself supreme master and which Terence regularly employed after Plautus, takes marriage seriously and channels love towards that recognized social institution. Usually, an impetuous and irresponsible lover, in the course of the drama, comes to recognize his personal and social duties so that the love, which seemed doomed by his choice of female partner—courtesan (who in fact will locate her father and so become a legitimate choice for wife), virginal victim of his sexual assault, or virgin daughter in a family of slight financial means—becomes earned and worthy of ratification in marriage. We know of a few plots, too, that involve a young couple in their first year of marriage—such as Menander's *Arbitrants* and Terence's *Mother-in-Law* (adapted from an original by Apollodoros)—and in which an act of rape before marriage, which results in an early pregnancy after marriage, has to be dealt with. (The rape occurred under amazing conditions—drunkenness and darkness—so that neither rapist nor victim can recognize the other afterwards; and by sheer coincidence the rapist and his victim have married each other, in ignorant good faith on both parts. Since being married for these few months has brought genuine love, the plot works to preserve marriage, love, and the family, i.e., the new baby.)

Plautus does not favour plots that channel love into marriage, and even those that he adapts from his Greek sources he alters so that neither love nor marriage becomes the true goal of the action or the romantic end that his Roman audience desires. Only five of his twenty comedies proceed towards marriage (*Aulularia, Cistellaria, Curculio, Poenulus,* and *Rudens*).[9] Of these, only *Aulularia* involves a virgin who has been raped; the others portray the complications of a love that has been initiated with a courtesan who later proves to be the long-lost daughter of an Athenian, either kidnapped or abandoned as an infant, and, when 'recognized' during the play, capable of reintegration into legitimate society, and thus of happy marriage. Let us see what Plautus does with both these plot types and the ways in which he upstages the lover.

The Pregnant Virgin: Aulularia

In comedies where the initial complication is rape by an impetuous lover, the girl never appears, and her voice is heard only once: when she cries out with labour pains (e.g., *Aulularia,* lines 691-2).[10] What love emerges, therefore, depends on the words and character of the young man and on the indirect description of others. Menander employed a significant device in *The Samian Woman* to introduce the lover and the serious quality of his commitment from the beginning: he had Moschion speak the prologue, explain the background, admit his rape, and sketch out the difficulties that were interfering with his determination to marry the girl and assume the role of father. In the *Aulularia,* a Household God delivers the prologue, and he concentrates on the miserly tradition of Euclio's family background. Euclio has a daughter who has proved to be a striking exception to the family's avarice: she has been reverent towards the god and has won his favor. Out of concern for her, the god has started the chain of circumstances that will lead to her happy marriage, one of love and financial security. The girl has been raped at a nighttime festival of Ceres, and, although the god does not admit that as part of his plan, he exploits the crime for her benefit. What he does insist is his doing is: a / Euclio's discovering a treasure

buried by his grandfather; b / a rich older man, the uncle of the rapist, asking to marry the pious and seemingly virginal daughter. The girl has not recognized her assailant in the night, but the rapist, Lyconides, does know her identity and will (by the god's plan) marry her. What is lacking in this prologue is any clear indication of the young man's feelings and intentions.

Plautus might have remedied that lack and placed the theme of serious love in a key position in the play, had he desired to, by bringing Lyconides on early to declare his feelings in soliloquy or to indicate them in a scene with one of the principal characters.[11] But Plautus does not wish to distract himself or the audience with what he regards as insignificant and negligible amatory issues. He refuses to equalize the roles of the miser Euclio and the lover Lyconides so as to bring about a reasonable reconciliation of these two antagonistic irresponsibilities. Because the miser plays into his own comic sensibilities, whereas the lover leaves him largely alienated, Plautus lets Euclio upstage Lyconides, and he turns the play into a lively, hilarious comedy about a mad miser.

Lyconides first appears on stage after the mid-point of the plot development (lines 682 ff). In a short scene, which omits all mention of love and feelings (and, I assume, has been radically cut by Plautus), the 'lover' indicates that he has just confessed all to his mother and urged her to intercede with his uncle so that the older man will abandon his marriage plans. At precisely this critical point, the girl goes into labour, and the urgency of Lyconides' request becomes even more obvious. In fewer than twenty lines, he has departed, with no convincing words about the girl; his last five lines refer to his anxiety about his slave, and represent a bridge to the slave's entrance. (The slave has managed to steal Euclio's pot of gold and is carrying it off to his master.)

Lyconides does have one important scene before the manuscript became damaged and so deprived us of the final act. Euclio rushes on stage first, shrieking bloody murder and performing a wonderful routine with the lyric metres and language Plautus has invented for him. When Lyconides hears him howling outside his home, he comes out to see what is the matter, and the key scene (lines 731-807) begins. Up to this point, Euclio has hardly noticed his daughter and, incredibly but most significantly, he does not know that she has been raped or that she has become pregnant or that now she has given birth. For him, the loss of his gold alone counts. In contrast, Lyconides knows nothing about the treasure yet, and he concentrates exclusively on the marriage he desires. Thus, Plautus creates here the finest ancient example of comic cross-purposes and incomprehension (which so fascinated Molière and his admirer, the comic theorist

Bergson).[12] Since Lyconides assumes that Euclio exclaims 'tragically' over the birth of his grandchild, he quickly confesses to the crime (*facinus,* line 733). But Euclio focuses on a different 'crime' and knows nothing of his domestic crisis. So the naïve honesty of Lyconides serves mainly to expose the weird extremism of a miser who has entirely ignored his daughter, who has cherished his pot of gold and tried to conceal it but never noticed the growing pregnancy of the girl—what we might call a more precious 'treasure.'[13] In the course of his misunderstood confession, Lyconides declares that he acted under the force of love and wine (line 745), but Euclio angrily rejects such an excuse.

Having dismissed all discussion of love, Euclio soon breaks the comic framework of incomprehension by charging Lyconides with outright theft (line 759). Hereupon, Lyconides asserts himself for the first time in the play, and Euclio yields centre stage to a man of higher social status and wealth, not to a lover. Lyconides reveals to the miser two more disasters to climax the 'tragedy' of his lost treasure: namely, the decision of his uncle to break off marriage arrangements (line 783) and then the details of the rape nine months earlier (lines 790 ff). Assuming complete command of the wailing, seemingly broken old man, Lyconides sends him indoors to talk to his daughter and check on the details of his story. Although the comic extremism of the miser has been brought under some control at the end, Plautus has not balanced it with any convincing emphasis on Lyconides' love. The pot of gold, not the baby, remains the dominant symbol and interest of the comedy. As the manuscript fails, we find Lyconides talking with his slave and learning about the theft. How much Plautus elaborated this situation is unclear; but the slave tries to extort his freedom and is in the process of defying Lyconides when the Latin text ends. Two ancient plot summaries indicate that eventually Lyconides did resume possession of the pot and restored it to the overjoyed Euclio, who then happily assented to the marriage of his daughter.[14] Thus, the comedy ends with the prospect of happy marriage, but Plautus has given Euclio and his avarice the dominant role, a role of such lyric and comic energy that no audience can pay much attention to Lyconides and his love.

The Kidnapped Or Foundling Maiden: Cistellaria *and* Curculio

The other plot type that led to marriage, when the girl has been kidnapped or abandoned and trapped into the world of prostitution (from which Recognition will rescue her during the play), had an advantage the dramatists quickly appreciated: the girl, not confined by family proprieties, but allowed the 'freedom' and the 'free speech' of the courtesan, could both move and speak in public and thus be shown in situations of dramatic action and dialogue to reveal her personality. Moreover, instead of making the father and family the obstacle to love, this type had the monstrous pimp (or bawd) as a much more unappealing killjoy, and the father became the saviour, the loving parent who searched out the daughter and finally rescued and restored her to happiness. Of the four such plays that Plautus has left us, one, the **Rudens,** derives from Diphilos; it dealt with a kidnapped girl. I have already sufficiently described the way Diphilos (and Plautus after him) diminished the love element by keeping the lovers apart and eliminating amatory language and themes. A second, the **Cistellaria,** seems to be a relatively early adaptation from Menander, completed during the Punic War before 200. In its presentation of a very sympathetic foundling, it reveals the anti-romantic Plautus confidently at work, even at that date.[15]

In the opening scene, which gave Menander's play its title (*The Women Breakfasting Together*), Selenium has invited two women to her house, and they chat about life as courtesans before coming to the business at hand, namely, Selenium's misery. Having fallen in love with the first man who hired her services, she has prevailed upon her mother to be allowed to 'live with him' rather than to seek many lovers/customers. For he swears he loves her and will marry her (line 97). This love idyll has lasted a while, but now it has been shattered by the necessity, imposed by his father, that Alcesimarchus, the ardent lover, face reality and marry a very eligible, rich young lady. Selenium is brokenhearted; her companions remark that women are supposed to be heartless (line 66). She laments the bitterness of being in love (line 68), using the same pun as in **Trinummus,** line 260: *eho an amare occipere amarum est, opsecro?* At the end of the scene, she goes off, bedraggled and in tears, leaving her courtesan-friend Gymnasium to face the faithless Alcesimarchus. And Gymnasium's mother, a hardened bawd, comments: 'Now that's why I keep pounding it into your ears, never love any man' (lines 116-17). With only a slight touch of cynical realism, Plautus has allowed the love of Selenium to be sympathetically presented, in contrast to the practical courtesans' denial of love and all feeling.

After the chatty details of a verbose delayed prologue, Plautus introduces us to the lover, Alcesimarchus, who has hurried back, he trusts, to Selenium after being kept for six frustratingly tedious days in the country at his father's manor. In an entrance soliloquy, to which Plautus gives his special emphasis by shaping it as a lyric monody, the young man declares at length how wretched he feels. Love, he asserts, must have been the inventor of torture, to judge from his own pains. He exceeds the agonies of all the men in the world (lines 203 ff). By the overstatement, where five Latin verbs replace one Greek, where repetition and alliteration invite us to savour sound more than meaning, and by the rollicking anapaestic metre, Plautus starts the process of undermining Alcesimarchus. From the fragmentary state of the text, it still is possible to infer that, when he found that Selenium had left him, he went momentarily wild in despair (again, comically exaggerated by Plautus), then charged after her to her mother's house.

Finding Selenium there, he tries in vain to explain the situation, but neither she nor her mother wants to listen to his 'lies.' Selenium goes indoors, and Alcesimarchus spends a long time pleading with her mother, Melaenis, to give him a chance to prove that he won't marry the girl his father has chosen for him, that he will remain loyal to Selenium. He launches into a long, incoherent oath, sworn by a series of gods whose relationships he gets wrong, forcing Melaenis to interrupt repeatedly to correct him. 'You're bewitching me, and that's why I am making these mistakes,' he claims (line 517). When she remains unmoved, his oaths turn into threats, which Plautus also sabotages by Alcesimarchus' own admission of confusion (*quid dicam nescio,* line 520) and by the comic intrusions he adds. Here are his sworn threats: 'May all the gods, large, small, and even those of the platter [an irreverent reference to the Lares], deny me the chance while alive to kiss the living Selenium, if I don't butcher you both today, you and your daughter [i.e., Selenium!], then if I don't slaughter you both tomorrow at dawn's first light, and finally, by god, if I don't strike you dead in a third assault—unless you send her back to me. There, I've said what I wanted,' (lines 522-7). Anyone who desires to may try to figure out the logic of all that incoherence, all those repeated murders over a kiss, but it is clear that Plautus aims to make the audience laugh at this lover.

Alcesimarchus stalked away and returned to his empty house, full of anger, self-pity, and despair. Soon after, Plautus turns his attention to the process of getting Selenium recognized. Melaenis, who is not after all the natural mother of Selenium, overhears a conversation which enables her to identify the real mother and realize that she cannot hold on to the girl. 'Now,' she says, 'I must be good against my nature, even though I don't want to be' (lines 626-7), and she decides to restore Selenium to her true parents. Therefore, as she and the girl are walking down the street to the home of those parents, they pass Alcesimarchus' house. Without seeing them at first—though perhaps Plautus used some broad pantomime here to indicate otherwise—the desolate lover prepares to commit suicide there in public. As he loudly invokes Death, 'friend and well-wisher' (line 640), Selenium of course notices him and the sword he histrionically brandishes, in this parody of a tragic suicide (such as that of Ajax). She rushes to stop him; he welcomes her as his salvation; he picks her up and hurries back inside his home and orders his slaves to bar the doors. Thus, on the verge of the recognition, love has impetuously and comically asserted itself. This is the last we see of the two lovers.

The remainder of the play focuses on the melodramatic action which accounts for the Plautine title, *Cistellaria*. In the confusion caused by Alcesimarchus' violent removal of Selenium, the old servant who was carrying the identifying trinkets of the girl in a small casket (*cistella*) dropped it in the street. Plautus pokes fun at the sentimental stages which lead up to the moment of recognition: the old woman is bumbling; the true mother is tearfully anxious; and the servant is roguish, witty, and ribald. But having got us to this big moment of family reunion, Plautus sends everybody indoors, except the caustic slave Lampadio. He is there to greet the last interested character, the long-lost father of Selenium, who wants to know what is happening. Plautus makes sure we take this scene with suitable amusement. In answer to his master's question, the slave pompously declaims: 'I am delighted to inform you that by my efforts you have acquired more children.' 'That does not please me,' the master grumbles. 'I don't like to have more children created for me by another's effort,' (lines 776-8). And with that mild ribaldry Plautus brings down the curtain in another three lines. Menander's delicate love situation has been mocked; the family reunion has been turned into a ridiculous scene over a casket of trinkets; and finally comes a joke about illegitimate children (from the father who was the original sire of Selenium out of wedlock, as they say). And the lovers are ignored by Plautus for the final 125 lines of the comedy, which prefers to plot out of the play their amatory happiness, saccharine and silly to the playwright and his audience, and instead concentrate on foolery. The lover Alcesimarchus has been upstaged by the impudent slave, the pathetic Selenium by the bumbling old Halisca, and Plautus' new comic emphasis has earned Menander's comedy a new title.

In the *Curculio* (*The Weevil*), a play of Plautus' maturity, the love plot and the lover are presented as ridiculous from the opening scene. Again, the girl has been kidnapped as a baby, under the confusion of a storm (lines 644 ff.). In this standardized situation, young Phaedromus and his brash slave Palinurus approach the house of a pimp at night. By the dialogue outside, Phaedromus acquaints his cynical slave and us with his silly feelings about love and with the trite details of his infatuation with a young courtesan who, he insists to the incredulous Palinurus, still retains her chastity and has awakened true love in him. Palinurus has no sympathy with such love and mocks all romantic sentiment. Knocking at the door, Phaedromus bribes a bibulous bawd with a jug of wine to let him talk with his beloved Planesium ('The Wandering Girl'). That should have been a brief and incidental bridge scene, but Plautus builds it up into a wonderfully animated comic routine, using his lyric genius to render the rhapsodies of the old soak with her wine and the equally foolish rhapsodies of the lover addressing the closed door. As the one personifies lovingly her wine and the other the bolts of the door, in operatic strains, Plautus and his audience laugh at their folly, the lover's no less than the crone's.

The old bawd leads Planesium anxiously out, trying to avoid any sound for her master the pimp to hear. She puts some water on the door hinges to prevent their creaking, and that provokes the sardonic Palinurus to sneer at her 'medical treatment,': 'She has learned to drink her wine straight, but she gives the doors water to imbibe' (lines 160-1). After that comic crack, Plautus gives Planesium her first lines—florid, alliterative, and artificial. The Latin might be partially captured with the following: 'Where are you who have summoned me to appear at the court sessions of sex?' (*ubi tu's qui me convadatu's Veneriis vadimoniis?* line 162). Phaedromus responds to her in the same high-blown diction, and the only realistic language during this scene of overacted passion comes from Palinurus, who is tired, bored, disgusted, and utterly disenchanted by these lovers. When he tries to break up their embraces and get his master to go home, he earns for himself a beating, which only increases his alienation at this 'crazy' pair. Eventually, Planesium has to go back indoors. The scene ends, then, with a nice contrast between lover and slave. Phaedromus moans emotionally: 'What a beautiful way I have died'; but Palinurus corrects him: 'Not I, who am dead with your beating and sleepiness' (lines 214-15). Down-to-earth reality puts the lover's verbiage in perspective. Although Palinurus may not exactly upstage his master, he prepares the audience to make light of the lover and his amatory plot, so that, when the parasite Curculio appears, he can indeed take over the lead.[16]

Unlike the slave, Curculio acts in a free and enterprising manner and owes no allegiance or advice to Phaedromus: he serves for the food he can get. Thus, he has no interest whatsoever in love for itself, only for what meals it can produce for him. He has a fine impudent entry, in which he assumes the officious airs of a noble, to whom all wayfarers should yield passage (lines 280 ff). And, indeed, all other characters let themselves be upstaged by this energetic and picturesque person. Though he has failed to borrow the money Phaedromus sent him to Caria to get, he has returned confidently with a stolen ring and the means of intrigue, the kind of plot that appeals to Plautus. Donning disguise and employing false documents sealed with this ring's signet, Curculio bilks the loanshark and then the pimp of Planesium. The entire centre of the play features his intrepid activities, and Phaedromus has only a bit part, Planesium none at the same time. Love and lovers have yielded, in Plautus' biased plotting, to intrigue and parasite.

To wind up the plot, it is necessary to make the courtesan an eligible virgin, that is, to have her recognized as a member of a suitable family and become marriageable. All this works itself out with considerable economy. The man whom Curculio defrauded in Caria of ring and access to the girl, a braggart soldier who typically serves as victim of the lover's henchman, enters furiously and grabs Curculio, who extricates himself neatly when the stolen ring identifies the soldier as brother of Planesium. The recognition, perfunctorily completed in twenty-five lines (635-58), gives the opportunistic and masterful Curculio the cue to stage his final triumph. He urges the soldier to celebrate the recovery of his sister at a banquet today, and Phaedromus to hold an engagement party tomorrow (lines 660-1). And he then presides over the official words of engagement, throwing in his own quixotic 'dowry,' that he will let the groom feed him as long as he lives (line 664)! Curculio has taken over from Palinurus and carried out Plautus' purpose in the plot, to upstage the lover in the most flagrant and impudent manner. The crazy seriousness of the lover cannot hold its own, in Plautus' theatre, with the witty realism of down-to-earth rogues like Curculio the weevil.

Love where Marriage is Impossible and Irrelevant

In Graeco-Roman society, middle-class and upper-class families could not cope with unions that endangered the family's cohesion and economic well-being. Since the family constituted the recognized heart of society, New Comedy tended to contrive plots that enacted the justification and preservation of the family against such centrifugal forces as selfish passion, of young and old alike, and selfish extravagance. An ideal comic myth or scenario developed in which a young man (or, occasionally, a father of the family) fell in love with a courtesan, spent large sums of the family finances on her and even worked to buy her freedom, against the will or without the knowledge of the rest of the family—above all, that of the authority figure (father or wife). The problem of the plot then became to bring this irresponsible love under some control, so that the lover either abandoned it (having come to his senses) or continued it temporarily on a reduced and more practical basis. If he abandoned the courtesan in the play, he probably replaced her with a fiancée;[17] if he was allowed to carry on for a while, it is implicit that eventually he will make the decision to opt for a marriage that benefits family and society. Among the Menandrian comedies that Terence chose for adaptation were several in which the playwright represented both types of irresponsible love, that which carelessly pursued a girl who could eventually be married (though of modest means, pregnant, or incorrectly thought to be a mere prostitute) and that which also carelessly but more dangerously involved itself with a girl who was unquestionably a prostitute with no possibility of change.

In the various antitheses that these paired loves permitted, Terence (and Menander before him) threw a carefully angled light on the criteria of legitimate marriage.

Now, imagine a comic artist who perceives in this material, suitably manipulated, a richly comic vein of irreverence and a challenge to traditional romanticism—perhaps, too, to the exclusive dramatic concern with the family lives of the upper classes (of Greece more than of Rome?). He decides to make a mockery of the family and what he can present as its corrupt prejudices, so as to deny its traditional validity in comedy as the criterion and goal of all action. To replace it, he adopts its old enemy, namely, irresponsible love. Not that he views such love with benevolence and generosity, free of the social bias of fourth- and third-century Greek writers. On the contrary, it is the fact that it manifests irresponsibility rather than love that wins his enthusiastic assent, that it opens an avenue to a view of a comic world where the family has little validity, but pleasure earned by witty intrigue of social outcasts constitutes a valid and admirable goal, recognizable by everyone in the audience. Such a comic artist, or even comic genius, I suggest, is Plautus.

A Slave's Intrigue for His Own Prostitute: Persa

In one comedy, Plautus almost entirely eliminates the criterion of the family, and thus he simplifies the conflict to one between the roguish lover and the infamous pimp. He accomplishes this feat by making the lover a slave and confining his social range to the lowest level: slaves, pimp, parasite, and prostitute. Toxilus proclaims himself a typical lover in a brief opening lyric, and his companion, another slave, remarks with surprise: 'Do slaves now fall in love here?' (*iam servi hic amant?* line 27). Thus, Plautus deliberately calls attention to the way the slave apes the folly of the typical spoiled young Athenian. And Toxilus faces the usual crisis: he needs to buy his girlfriend's freedom from the pimp who owns her. To do this, since of course he lacks money (like the typical *adulescens*), he must resort to intrigue. As a rogue-slave, Toxilus finds intrigue easy enough, but he is a rare beneficiary of intrigue (which most frequently serves the helpless young master).[18]

The plot falls into two phases. First, his slave-friend from another household temporarily 'borrows' money he was supposed to spend on some cattle, and lends it to Toxilus, who then surprises the pimp by paying good cold cash for the girl. Having disarmed the pimp, Toxilus then can develop a plot against him, luring him into purchasing for the same sum a beautiful young girl in exotic dress, who is introduced to him by a pompously masquerading slave as a valuable Arabian captive. In fact, this girl is the freeborn daughter of a parasite, who has willingly cooperated in the plot, in order to earn a good meal. It is of course illegal to purchase a freeborn Athenian, and the purchaser loses both his purchase and the money he paid, once the identity of the girl can be established. Toxilus can then repay his loan, the other slave can buy the oxen, and all can celebrate their victory over the comic villain, the pimp.

The heroic slave Toxilus acts in a context that ignores his normal subservient position: for the duration of the play, his master is away (line 32), and he has the run of the house. His love hurts nobody and no family priorities. It is significant, I think, that his intrigue involves exploiting harmlessly the family situation of the parasite and his daughter. Her appearance as the beauteous 'Arabian' is a mark of her father's enslavement to food, and her typical female cleverness (*malitia*), a quality of all women in Plautus, slave or free. As a lover, Toxilus is a superb intriguer; but he never becomes the silly, helpless, self-pitying character we usually encounter among the free young lovers. And his energetic invention and participation in the deception of the pimp occupies Plautus' attention and dominates the audience's interest. After the first brief, lyric lover's effusion, the rogue starts to take over. Before the Act I has ended, he has set his companion slave to work and devised a plan that will make use of the parasite, as he confidently announces: 'I have worked out the entire plot, how the pimp with his own money will make her [i.e., his slave] today his freedwoman,' (lines 81-2). There is no further reference to love, amid the spectacularly developing intrigue, and only in the final celebration of victory does the love receive some attention again. Toxilus emerges with a lyric speech of victory, full of pompous Roman language that implies his free heroic status on a par with that of the great Roman generals of the century. No words about love there, as he elaborates the nature of his victory celebration (lines 756 ff). Feeling ignored, the girlfriend, who was ostensibly the reason for all this energetic scheming, asks why she and he are not doing something together (line 763). At that, Toxilus launches himself into an enthusiastic mix of love, drinking, and hilarity, which Plautus enlivens by more lyric. But after thirteen lines of that, the pimp emerges from his house, tragically emoting over his financial loss, and the remainder of the play abandons the love theme in order to exult over the pimp's misery. That comic situation merits almost one hundred lines of Plautine excitement, and the final word of the slave is from the triumphant intriguer, not the gratified lover: *leno perit* (line 857)—'The pimp is dead!' In a significant way, then, Toxilus the lover has been upstaged by Toxilus the rogue.

Gratifying Foolish Young Love: Pseudolus

The initial situation of **Curculio** and **Persa,** the desperate desire of the impecunious lover to buy free the beloved courtesan owned by the pimp, recurs frequently in the plays of Plautus where marriage is irrelevant. Buying free a woman whom one can never marry constitutes the height of romantic folly. Yet in Plautine comedy after comedy, the woman does get her freedom at great expense. However, that freedom proves to be less a tribute to the beauty and desirability of the woman than a means to assert Plautus' theme—that sensual pleasure achieved by unscrupulous roguery merits our applause, at least on the stage. In some plays, like **Mercator** and **Mostellaria,** the young lover has bought the beloved free before the dramatized action starts, and that unwise purchase provides an initial complication. In others, finding the money to free the girl provides an opening for the intrepidity of the slave or parasite. I shall consider **Pseudolus** in this light.

Pseudolus has no more respect for the romantic love of his young master, Calidorus, than does Palinurus for that of Phaedromus in **Curculio**. When Calidorus gets hysterical with helplessness and tries to borrow a drachma from Pseudolus so as to buy a rope and hang himself, the slave delights us by his practical question: 'Who will pay me back the drachma if I give it to you? Do you intend to hang yourself deliberately so as to cheat me?' (lines 91-3). Nevertheless, realizing how useless Calidorus is, Pseudolus promises to get him the needed money somewhere, somehow. And with the brashness born of years of successful roguery, he publicly proclaims to all his friends and acquaintances to beware today, not to trust him in any way, or else they will be bilked (lines 124 ff).

Plautus makes clear his concentration on Pseudolus, the ironic facilitator of love, but even more the master-trickster (as his name implies), by giving no speaking part to Phoenicium, the prostitute so passionately desired by the young fool. After Calidorus fails to make any impression on the arch-villain Ballio the pimp, Pseudolus sends him off to find a clever man who will be able to get things done (line 393). In other words, Calidorus must locate a man who can do for him what he, in his ineptitude, cannot do for himself. Left to his own resourceful devices, Pseudolus improvises in several encounters, and actually has a workable plan by the time Calidorus returns with a friend who will provide the trusted helper (line 693). Calidorus has subordinated himself to Pseudolus, and at the end of this scene (line 758) he disappears from the comedy. Although the play is hardly half-finished, Plautus insists on so upstaging the lover as to remove him from the stage, so that the intrigue can have his and the audience's undivided attention.

When Calidorus vanishes from the play, Plautus makes it clear that the lines of thematic opposition do not focus on the family and pit father against son. Rather, they focus on money, on the stern father who wants to hold on to his wealth and his dubious ally, the pimp, who wants to make as much money from his exploited prostitutes as possible. This pair hopes to keep Pseudolus the trickster in check. As Pseudolus celebrates his triumph in Act V, he drunkenly describes the scene of sexual revelry in which Calidorus has participated, and Pseudolus, too. The slave has earned his pleasures, and it is appropriate that he be the one to report them. But his supreme pleasure involves his 'victory' over his cheerless and angry old master, Simo: to that Plautus devotes the finale of the play. Thus, not only does the young lover yield the stage to the slave, but the old master has to act out Pseudolus' superiority.[19]

Guilty Elderly Love Balked: Asinaria

The old man in love (*senex amator*) was a ridiculous figure, pursuing an activity which, by comic definition, was reserved for young men. To ensure our bias, the dramatist regularly insisted that this untimely lover was already married and thus had primary responsibility to his wife and household. We have already seen how Demipho in the **Mercator** unwittingly competed with his own son over a courtesan and finally was disgraced and shamed, though it was agreed that his wife would not know anything. In the early **Asinaria,** the father, Demaenetus, plays the role of a rather black-hearted rogue who cheats his wife out of money to buy a prostitute free for his son, then turns around and tries to exploit the situation so as to enjoy the girl before his son can. Theoretically, Plautus could have emphasized romantic love quite easily in such a situation, by contrasting the real affection of the son with the sleazy lust of the father. But the playwright shows his concern to ridicule both lovers and subject them and their warped passion to humiliation.

The son, Argyrippus, loves the courtesan Philaenium, but has no money to keep up the relation; and her greedy mother insists on a sizeable sum to guarantee Philaenium's exclusive services for a year. Although Philaenium seems to be an unwilling victim of her mother and, despite her cruel situation, eager to respond to Argyrippus' love, Plautus interrupts their single scene of romance (lines 590 ff) with a raucous series of pranks by a pair of slaves, who humiliate both lovers and show how much they will compromise their love for money. Argyrippus stands helplessly aside while Philaenium all but makes love to the slaves, as the price of the stolen money, then allows the slaves to ride him as a donkey, acting out the reversed roles in the household. Thus, young love is first upstaged, in preparation for the upstaging of older love and for the final feeling in the audience that love in general has yielded to something realer and better: roguish humour and wit.

When Demaenetus introduces himself and his purposes, he says nothing about his pursuit of prostitutes in his old age. Instead, he declares himself to be an unusual father, in that he expresses full support for his son's affair with Philaenium, the prostitute in the house next door (line 53). He sides with the son against his wife, who has full control of the money in the household—presumably, it all comes from her family—and keeps a tight rein on the son's sexual extravagances. (It also emerges later, but not here, that she has been cramping the style of Demaenetus as a would-be old lover.) With no sense of financial responsibility, then, well practised in cheating his wife to finance his own illicit pleasures, the father happily encourages the boy's loyal slaves to engage in any malpractice, with his full cooperation, to swindle the wife of the necessary money for Philaenium. 'I want to be loved by my family,' he grandly claims (line 67); but, since he doesn't include his hated wife, he really means: 'I want my son to love me, his father' (line 77). At first sight, then, if we ignore the culpable attitude towards the rich wife, it might seem that Demaenetus is one of those endearing contrasts to the stern and angry father: he seems like the kindly, supportive, and tolerant father (*lepidus pater, senex*). And, indeed, it is he in person, we are told, who acted decisively to ensure that the slaves' trickery actually succeeded. So the slaves admit as they praise his congenial nature (line 580).

In fact, Demaenetus is a hypocritical old reprobate, but Plautus has minimized the full facts about him so as to spring them on us suddenly at the end of the comedy. Family love means little to this father, much less than the lust he pursues at every opportunity, and notably here, in the case of Philaenium, whom he boldly tries to exploit at this opportunity. After Argyrippus has been forced to submit to humiliation from the slaves, he learns that he has more humiliation to accept. His good old dad has made the money available, the slaves are to report, on condition that Argyrippus allow his father to enjoy a dinner and night of sex with Philaenium (lines 735-6). Argyrippus' craven character cooperates, as Demaenetus knew he would, with his own baseness: he agrees to his father's terms. The servants, having had their fun and delivered their heartless but grotesquely amusing message, prepare to leave, and the young lover bids them farewell (*valete*). They reply, also using the plural: 'And you, too, love well' (*et vos amate,* line 745). That plural may apply only to Argyrippus and Philaenium, who stand there rather forlornly on stage: or it may include also Demaenetus (soon to appear). At any rate, the irony of the final remark is unmistakable and would no doubt have been emphasized by the roguish speaker.[20]

The stage is set here for the reappearance of the father, now revealed as hypocritical old lover (*senex amator*) rather than a kindly and indulgent paternal figure. But, before his entrance, Plautus introduces us to the angry young man who will bring about his

punishment. Of about the same age as Argyrippus, but with the money to satisfy his own passions, this character shows the spunk absent in the son. He intends to inform Demaenetus' wife, Artemona, and thus humble the old lover for his robberies. In the finale, then, as Demaenetus starts to enjoy his pleasure in front of the pained but compliant Argyrippus, Artemona secretly enters, to watch and overhear with indignation her husband's outrages. He promises to steal a robe from Artemona for Philaenium, he kisses her lustily and comments on the sweet breath she has, which is so wonderful after his wife's halitosis; he wishes that the wife may be destroyed 'with interest,' so that he won't be interrupted while kissing; and finally, he invokes Venus to grant to him Philaenium and to his wife, death. At that, Artemona no longer restrains herself, but bursts into the corrupt celebration and commands Demaenetus: 'Get up, lover, and go home!' (*surge, amator, i domum,* line 921). He slinks off, totally humbled and terrified, awaiting the judgment that will be meted out to him at home (line 937). Enjoying their moment, Argyrippus and Philaenium taunt him and his promises. Not much can be said for romantic love after this comedy; and, indeed, the final comments of the assembled troupe to the audience urge the amoral moral, that anyone, if he had the chance, would act like Demaenetus and pursue his own satisfactions (lines 944-5). Plautus does not use untimely old love as a way of validating young love, but rather as a way of utterly discrediting romantic love: all love, young and old, is a prime target for his comedy.

The Courtesan Mocks the Lover: Truculentus

In the comedies we have been using as examples in this section, the impecunious young man—helpless, ridiculous, and far less interesting to Plautus than the rogues and scamps that both help and interfere with the course of his love—eventually gets to take his courtesan-friend to bed, for a while. The lover and his love have proved to be of minimal comic sympathy and regularly replaceable with characters and qualities that make a mockery of romance and rather validate an energetic, resourceful engagement with a more ordinary reality that thumbs its nose at feckless feelings. The audience's attitude can also be affected by the manner in which the courtesan behaves. We have seen Philaenium of the **Asinaria** play the naïve affectionate girl, at the start of the play, until she gets caught up in the tricks of the libidinous slaves and old father. Her natural innocence helps to put in the desired satirical perspective the hypocritical lust of the males, father and son. In the **Pseudolus,** Phoenicium never says a word and appears only once, to be led silently weeping and unknowing from the house of the pimp Ballio to reunion with Calidorus. Both she and her lover are suppressed, upstaged by the trickster slave. In the **Bacchides,** the courtesan sisters are delightfully seductive, but definitely not ruled by their affections.

They seduce Pistoclerus at the opening, to escape an unwelcome debt to a soldier; throughout the play their seductiveness determines the efforts of Mnesilochus and his slave Chrysalus; and in the finale they complete their victorious campaign by seducing the two fathers. Therefore, although we can say that the young lovers, after being upstaged, have gotten their satisfaction at the end, Plautus' emphasis rests on the triumphant courtesans, who celebrate not love but their successful manipulation of men in the interests of security. In the **Truculentus,** which is a work of Plautus' old age, the satisfaction of young lovers and the sensual pleasures of all disappear from the comic plot: with a strong satiric tone, the comedy focuses on the materialistic success of the courtesan, gained at the expense of stupid would-be lovers. The lover has been conclusively upstaged, and deservedly so, by the totally self-serving Phronesium, the woman of ruthless intelligence. An independent operator, like the Bacchides, she owes nothing to any pimp, but works exclusively for her own advantage.

There are three lovers, and none of them gets to take Phronesium to bed, but each pays extravagantly for the vain hope that he will get his money's worth. The yokel Strabax comes to Athens from the country, shaggy, unkempt, and boorish, the last person in the world that anyone could love. But he serves Phronesium's purposes well: he is easily controlled by her, and his very unlikely nature can whet the jealousy of other potential lovers. When he appears from the farm, naïvely carrying money which belongs to his father (lines 653-5), the eyes of Phronesium's smart female slave fall on the money, and she invites Strabax indoors. An hour or so later, he emerges and complains that he is exhausted from having waited for his 'friend' inside, lying in the bed (lines 915-16). But that arrival plays into the hands of Phronesium, who is talking to the soldier Stratophanes and wheedling him out of money by lies about a supposed child of his that she has borne while he was absent on campaign. Stratophanes gets angrily jealous and plunges into a 'war' of rival gifts, which the courtesan, of course, brilliantly directs. Although the two go together into the courtesan's house then, promising themselves sexual satisfaction, we are not convinced, especially since Phronesium stays behind to exult before the audience on the success of her 'hunt' for silly bird-victims (lines 964-5).

The yokel and the soldier are two typical losers in the love plots of New Comedy, and we are not surprised to see them cancel each other out, even if Phronesium's materialistic exploitation seems unusually overstressed. But the third lover comes from the most respectable level of Athenian society. He has had a long, expensive relationship with the courtesan in the past, but been forced out when Phronesium got her hooks into the more extravagant Stratophanes. Just back from a minor diplomatic trip, he starts the play off with a soliloquy on the crippling cost of courtesan-love and the ruinous greed of pimps and prostitutes. On his return, he has incredulously heard that Phronesium has had a baby (lines 85-6); it does not seem likely to him that so clever a courtesan would ever permit herself to get pregnant and ruin her business. So it must be a trick to control the soldier, he thinks. And he is jealous and eager to become her lover again. Promising to bankrupt his estates, he gets himself admitted to the house (lines 175 ff). But he, too, is disappointed after a long wait: Phronesium is taking an interminable bath (lines 320 ff). He does eventually get to talk with her, and her friendliness (activated by her not too subtle greed) sends him off cheerily to pawn his property and buy her a lavish gift (lines 425-6).

Evidently, Diniarchus, the affluent young diplomat, is as much a fool for love as the rustic and the soldier. However, he emerges soon as more contemptible than laughable, a young man whose status has encouraged him into irresponsible and reprehensible self-indulgence. The baby, which Phronesium has confessed to him is not hers, much to his delight, and which he then laughs to see being used against the gullible soldier, turns out to be his, Diniarchus'. He had had an illegitimate affair with a respectable Athenian girl; she became pregnant and gave birth during his absence, and she abandoned or exposed the baby to avoid embarrassment. Thus, the baby proves to embarrass Diniarchus more than anybody, and, just after he has lavished presents on Phronesium, it obliges him to confess his paternity and accept marriage to the girl. Then, to emphasize how low Diniarchus has sunk, Plautus shows this new 'father' happily conspiring with Phronesium to lend her his baby so that she can complete her scam of the foolish soldier (and later, Diniarchus hopes, reward Diniarchus with a night or two of 'love').

Male love, accordingly, is totally discredited in the characterization of these two fools and of the scoundrel Diniarchus. Now, consider the object of their love in Plautus' satiric representation. Phronesium, whose name has nothing to do with love or physical attraction, the usual source of courtesan's names in Plautus, is the thinker or calculator. She herself never feels love—never expresses genuine affection for anyone, male or female—but easily manipulates the language of love in order to gain material profit. The fact that she has pretended to have given birth to a son, which we know from the prologue (line 18), symbolizes clearly her calculating exploitation of words, acts, and feelings of love. Indirectly introduced by the words of Diniarchus about his subjection to her and by the impudent remarks of her maid Astaphium (= Raisin), who has a lyric solo about the ruthless 'philosophy' of prostitutes (lines 209 ff), Phronesium finally makes her first entrance at line 352. She immediately starts her act, using calculated amatory language to enthral the easily duped Diniarchus. He has waited endlessly, remember, for her to finish her so-called bath, and he feels grouchy. 'Do you think my doorway will bite you, tell me, that you are afraid to enter, my sweetheart?' (lines 352-3). 'Why are you so grumpy on your return from Lemnos as not to give your girlfriend a kiss?' (lines 355-6). By the end of the scene, sullen Diniarchus has become putty in her artful hands. He calls her 'Sweetheart' at the very moment he happily succumbs to her wiles and declares it a 'profit' to himself when she asks him for a gift (*lucrum hercle videor facere mihi, voluptas mea, ubi quippiam me poscis,* lines 426-7). And he gullibly misconstrues, as she intended, her confession about the fake baby as utter proof of her deepest, most reliable love (lines 434 ff.).[21]

The women of this comedy, Phronesium the heroine and her bawd-maid Astaphium, encourage the three foolish male lovers in their folly and deliberately exploit them and the trappings of love for personal material profit. Their real thinking assumes a hostile world and militant behaviour against lovers. 'A lover is like an enemy city,' says Astaphium. 'As soon as he can be taken, he is great for his girlfriend' (lines 170-1). 'A proper bawd should have good teeth,' reflects Phronesium, 'so that she can laugh and smoothly speak to every visitor, plotting evil in her heart, but speaking good with her tongue' (lines 224-7). 'The good lover,' she adds, 'is the man who abandons all his possessions and destroys his estate.' The women measure and value men for their money: the men throw away money in pursuit of their false conception of love, which they ludicrously identify with these mercenary women. It is not unusual or disturbing that the men get what they clearly deserve: no love and heavy losses. What is unusual is the total success of the unromantic and antihedonistic courtesans. There is no celebration at the end of this comedy, because, although Phronesium has scored a complete victory and, as she exults, had a wonderful 'hunt' (line 964), her grasping, insensitive nature does not open up to sensual indulgence and careless spending of any kind. Plautus has exposed the ways of love in the most uncompromising satire, making love, not the 'breath of life' in the comedy, but the touch of death. The courtesan sucks the wealth of the stupid lover (like Diniarchus) and considers him 'dead' when he has no more to give (lines 164-5). Her house resembles Acheron (the home of Death): once it receives anything, it refuses to disgorge it again to Life (lines 749-50).

Heroic Badness (malitia): Plautus' Characters and Themes

If you can remember your own childhood, or if you have watched and listened to children as they were playing, you perhaps have observed how very impor-

tant to them are those simple moral terms 'bad' and 'good.' Not, I hasten to say, that children are entirely innocent, naïve, and narrowly puritanical about their use of such terms. Along with the powerful word 'No!,' they have been hearing parents, grandparents, and siblings smiling-and-cooing at them 'Good' and growling, shrieking, and roaring at them 'Bad,' often with gestures and various movements, including pats, spanks, and blows, that ought to have made the meaning of 'bad' and 'good' amply clear—that ought to have aligned them solidly and safely on the side of Good against Bad. Why is it, then, that the little imps get the message twisted and somehow, at an early age, show that they have a sneaking admiration of Bad, that they even want to play at being bad? Let us dismiss with contempt the child who has, alas, gotten the official message too well and says to his or her unruly playmate: 'You're bad; what you're doing is naughty; I'm going to tell Daddy or Mama, and you're going to get it.' There's a future supporter of Law and Order with the character of a skunk. No, the children I refer you to are those we overhear in a conversation like this: A (with a note of admiration): 'Mother said that was naughty. How can you hope to get away with it?' B (with bravado): 'I dunno, but it's fun being naughty.' These are children whom I think we all know (recalling our own behaviour in childhood) and probably rather like, for their humanity if not for their obedience. In this chapter I shall be considering how Plautus explored this fundamental 'immoral' tendency in all of us, children and adults, and gave it comic form as Heroic Badness, which is one of the great achievements of Roman and comic literature.

As parents know, the tendency in children to go astray over the words 'No!' and 'Bad!' starts somewhat before they reach the age of two. When my son approached that age, with his boyish energy and gusto he revealed just how stubbornly the human soul cherishes the simple idea of Bad. It did not matter to him whether what we called Bad was Dangerous, Hot, Cruel, Messy, Dirty, Tiresome, or What-have-you: if we said it was bad, then it had to have something interesting, pleasurable, and hence 'good,' about it. It had to be tried. And the threat and experience of spanking only increased the challenge. I think that, if my son had had a younger brother, the irrepressible way he went about playing with matches, climbing and falling from trees, opening and crawling out windows, etc., would have made him a 'hero' to his younger sibling at the same time that he was driving his parents and sisters to distraction. I am no psychologist and do not intend to explore the psychological motivations for this Original Sin in all human beings, but I am interested in the way, as Milton's Lucifer willed it, evil becomes good in comedy as well as in tragedy and epic, but with a very different plot and audience reception, above all, in Plautus. Among some teenagers today, one can hear exactly the words and note that the Roman poet long ago struck: admiration for what is called Badness. I wish to go back to Plautine Rome to see how he elicited that admiration in his comedies.

The particular kind of badness which I call 'heroic' turns up in the favourite form of Plautine comedy, that of intrigue, where a character or characters use various means of deception to swindle money or the possession of a slave-prostitute from the rightful owners. The deceivers, like the slave Chrysalus and the Bacchis-sisters of the play I reviewed in chapter 1, come from the lower ranks of the social order and can be declared 'bad' in social terms by those above them, their victims. But what is more important, for Plautus' presentation, is that social inferiority goes hand-in-hand with (and, to some extent, stimulates) a striking indifference to strict ethical tenets; an adaptability to conditions; an energetic curiosity; basic cunning and enjoyment of deception; a combative, anarchic attitude towards life; and total indifference to such ordinary things as property rights, duty, responsibility, truth, or authority—in other words, social badness merely covers a much more interesting and universal ethical quality, which might be labelled 'Badness' and praised or punished in the course of a comedy, but is, in fact, a compound of bad and good, as the most attractive comic qualities usually prove to be. It is an obvious fact that Plautus aligns his audiences on the side of the deceivers, for all their badness, against the people who usually control Law and Order, fathers, mothers, rich men, and property-owners (nicely symbolized by the frequent victim, the pimp, the slave-owner of certain desirable prostitutes).

If Plautus' main concern were the sociopolitical hostility between the deprived and the rich, between slaves and slave-owners, as some modern theorists have argued, who have read into Plautus contemporary political antagonisms, then the comic nature of Badness would have no function and not appear.[1] As it is, however, what dominates audience interest and made the plays of Plautus successful at all levels of society—and still does—is the way Badness represents the personal response of every member of the audience, the will to explore, experience, and enjoy what our parents and all authority figures brand as Bad, that is, what often looks to us as perhaps dangerous, but mighty Good. It follows that, if a bad goal appeals to our imaginations as somehow good, then the so-called bad man or woman who pursues and achieves it, even if briefly, appears not only good but heroic, a kind of paradigm of our pipedreams.

The basic scheme from which the plot started was the need of a young man for money to pursue a love affair, in Plautus regularly an affair that has to be 'illicit' and temporary and stupidly wasteful ('bad' from the viewpoint of parents and greybeards), but understandably appealing precisely because it is a reckless move

towards sensual pleasure. Since the young man lacks worldly experience and street skills, he desperately turns to the domestic slave, who is usually five or ten years older than he, and centuries older in practical experience. This slave has defied his owner, the boy's father, before and is regarded as a typical 'bad slave,' often declared to be 'worse than any other slave' or simply 'the worst slave in existence' (*servus pessimus*).[2] To the young master, however, many aspects of this badness look hopeful and useful, and he implores and finally persuades this 'bad slave' to do what has become for the love-addled young man a definite good. In their conversation, Plautus rather typically has master and slave articulate this inversion not only of good and bad, but also of their own social roles.

The boy ends up by hailing the slave as his 'patron' as he himself assumes the subordinate role of needy 'client.'[3] Then, the slave assumes masterful airs: he talks about his civil and military authority (Latin *imperium*), and he calls his companions into a senatorial session, to take counsel and plan their strategy. In other words, this base slave (whom we can imagine as originally foreign, non-italian, reduced to slavery as a result of military defeat) arrogates to himself the status of the highest political position in Rome, the consul, and treats himself as an official in wartime, about to lead his troops forth on a critical campaign on behalf of his country.[4] The goals of this expedition, however, fall comically short of the level of nobility. To be consonant, after all, with the purposes of the deception, this

Plautus's 20 complete plays comprise the largest existing collection of classical dramatic literature.

commander must come away with a considerable amount of money in the form of 'booty' or 'plunder' (Latin *praeda*). So there is no question about saving the country or avenging some defeat or some other misdeed of the enemy: this special army seeks booty.[5] In due course, the deception achieves its end: the enemy-father or pimp is swindled out of the necessary money, which the slave-general triumphantly carries off as plunder to his anxiously waiting young master. Then, it remains to be seen whether reality catches up with this fantastic slave, whether he plunges back down from his improbably and tenuously won Good to his proper role as 'bad slave,' at the mercy of his humiliated and irate master.

In the great comedies of Plautus' maturity, the playwright managed to twist the plot so that, with full audience approval, reality was pleasantly deflected or excluded. I shall come back to that, but, for the present, it suffices to sketch out the Plautine pattern. To put it briefly, as soon as the tricky bad slave takes on the Mission Impossible of helping out his young master in a quest for money for love, he becomes 'good,' surrounded with symbols of freedom and Roman dignity and authority, admired by his friends and feared by his intended victims for the very same qualities—trickiness, deceptivity, plausibility, adaptability, and restless energy. His 'goodness' is merely 'badness' seen from a new viewpoint. Or, in the Latin terms Plautus employs to epitomize his comic ethical paradox, the clever intriguing slave, whose character can be summarized by the word *malitia* (badness), aims at a goal which in conventional Roman terms is the proud one of military conquest of a despised enemy, the highest achievement of manliness (*virtus*). Since *virtus* extends its meaning in Latin then to cover what we call 'virtue' and what the Romans meant by 'goodness,' the Plautine representation of intrigue is one of badness becoming, with our enthusiastic approval, goodness.[6]

The Plautine intriguer, as is obvious, falls into the class of wonderful comic characters that we recognize as rogues. There seem to be no rogues in Menander; I am not sure that there were any in either of the other masters of Greek New Comedy, Philemon or Diphilos.[7] It looks, at any rate, as though this special rogue, who makes a virtue of his badness (*malitia*), is Plautus' contribution not only to New Comedy in Rome, but to the comic genre. Granted that Aristophanes had worked out the designs of a delightful rogue in the late fifth century, but that was an Athenian rogue, a free man or woman with a different manner of operation and a quite different ethical stance.[8] So, even if Plautus did have some knowledge of Aristophanes—which remains doubtful to many scholars—his Roman rogue emerges as a strikingly new creation. It is the express emphasis on the dialogue between good and bad within the rogue, the focus on his Roman *virtus,* his 'heroic'

military enterprise and success, that defines the comic invention of Plautus.

I think that I can make the nature of Plautus' heroic rogue somewhat clearer by turning to another marvellous rogue in his moment of roguish heroism. I refer to Shakespeare's Falstaff and his role during the Battle of Shrewsbury, in Act V of *Henry the Fourth, Part I.* Just before the battle starts, Shakespeare lets us assess the combatants in their respective camps. In Scene 1, we survey the King and his supporters, his princely sons Hal and John, and Falstaff. One by one, they leave the stage, solemnly prepared to do their best to fight bravely, and Hal, before departing, recommends to Falstaff, the last man, to say his prayers and farewell, to face the fact that he owes God a death. It is his simple heroic responsibility to be a man.

This, however, is no metaphorical battle of swindling, and Falstaff feels notably uncomfortable and out of his natural element. Alone, then, he delivers his famous soliloquy, a superb comic speech in the best Shakespearean vein: "Tis not due yet [i.e., the death mentioned by Prince Hal]: I would be loath to pay him [i.e., God] before his day. What need I be so forward with him that calls not on me? Well, 'tis no matter; honour pricks me on. Yea, but how if honour pricks me off when I come on? How then? Can honour set to a leg? No. Or an arm? No. Or take away the grief of a wound? No. Honour hath no skill in surgery then? No. What is honour? A word. What is that word, honour? Air. A trim reckoning! Who hath it? He that died o' Wednesday. Doth he feel it? No. Doth he hear it? No. Is it insensible, then? Yea, to the dead. But will it not live with the living? No. Why? Detraction will not suffer it. Therefore I'll none of it: honour is a mere scutcheon. And so ends my catechism.'[9]

There is much common as well as comic sense in what Falstaff has said here. This battle is not simply a question of honour; the political values being contested are ambiguous; and the most obvious embodiment of honour, Hotspur, is ridiculed as a fool by his own closest, so-called friends. So when Falstaff rejects honour and advocates the traditional creed of the practical rogue—'he who fights and runs away, lives to fight another day'—the audience sympathizes.[10] But when the battle ensues, and other men fight, and some die for their partly honourable goals—including loyal Blount on behalf of the king and the enthusiast Hotspur for his personal glory—when Hal risks his life to defend his father, then Falstaff's words and roguish behaviour cannot withstand inspection, cannot continue to command approval. During the battle, although he finally engages in combat with Douglas, he suddenly falls down motionless and pretends to be dead, thus saving his life. Almost at the same moment, Hotspur, who has challenged Hal for supreme honour, falls to the ground mortally wounded and really dies.

The pejorative effect on our impression of Falstaff is obvious. But Shakespeare has worse to show about this rogue. As soon as Hal goes off to continue fighting, Falstaff gets up, easily and confidently, smoothly mouths his 'heroic' creed, that the better part of valour is discretion,[11] and then gets his supreme idea of roguish heroism: he stabs the corpse of Hotspur with his sword and starts to lug the body off, to claim it as *his* honour that the enemy is dead, to claim a reward for *his* 'valour.' It is a fraud that has to strike us as grotesquely ignoble and unfunny, especially since Prince Hal, who knows the truth, makes no effort to reclaim his own credit as hero; he shows his undoubted and well-earned moral superiority by dismissing the whole situation as the act of 'the strangest fellow' and allowing Falstaff to pose as noble and worthy of reward. We may have some questions about honour still, but Shakespeare leaves no doubt about what manliness has required here.[12]

Whereas Shakespeare drags the reluctant rogue on to the real battlefield and, by juxtaposing him with genuine warriors who accept war's creed, shows him up as a coward and rat, Plautus lets his rogue-plotter celebrate his success, the result of his witty deception over others' folly and avarice, and we recognize him as the 'best' person in the play. All the others, those who have been his victims and those who have shared in his intrigue, have been inferior to him. So the metaphorical language which has been building up during the comedy—that the master-plotter is like a consul at war, commander of an army on campaign against a powerful and rich enemy—properly soars to a climax at the moment of success, in a triumphant speech, typically in flamboyant lyric metre (clear proof that it is a Plautine production, not just a translation of the Greek).

The greatest of these triumphant effusions is spoken by the slave Chrysalus in **The Bacchis-Sisters**. It occupies more than fifty lines (925-78) and is a rollicking performance, an actor's dream and the audience's delight. Chrysalus is so full of himself that he compares himself favourably with the best heroes of the Trojan War, not only with Agamemnon who commanded the expedition, but also with his brother Menelaus (husband of Helen) and with Ulysses who, known by Chrysalus to have been 'bold and bad' (*audacem et malum,* line 949), provides the perfect heroic paradigm for his claim to heroism. But Chrysalus' monody is but the extreme example of a typical Plautine context. Accordingly, a short section of an anapaestic triumph-song from one of the less-well-known comedies, **The Persian,** will illustrate the general type: 'The enemy are beaten, the citizens are safe, the situation's calm, total peace is achieved, / The war's at an end, the campaign was well waged, without loss to the troops, without hurt to the camp. / Lord Jupiter, since it was by your kind help and the other gods mighty in heaven, / I feel and give thanks to you all in this hymn, that I fitly took vengeance this day on my foe. / For that reason now, to all who shared in the fight, I'll give shares of the plunder, division of the spoil' (*hostibus victis, civibu' salvis, re placida, pacibus perfectis, / bello exstincto, re bene gesta, integro exercito et praesidiis, / quom bene nos, Iuppiter, iuvisti, dique alii omnes caelipotentes, / eas vobis gratis habeo atque ago, quia probe sum ultus meum inimicum. / nunc ob eam rem inter participes dividam praedam et participabo* [**Persa,** lines 753-7]).[13]

The speaker is the slave Toxilus who has engineered a scam against a pimp he hates, in order to cheat him out of a large sum of money, the purchase price of a prostitute. The scam has been a total success, and in these lines Toxilus, acting like a victorious Roman commander, proclaims verbosely his achievements— total, bloodless victory no less—gives thanks to the gods, and then proceeds to the final phase of a triumph—the sharing of the booty with the soldiers and the large-scale public celebration, with much food, wine, and love, of the war's happy conclusion.

This victory of Toxilus and the wild celebration that follows are wonderful comic action for Plautus' audience, and they enjoy without reserve the wild performance of this 'heroic' slave. That a slave should be the cleverest person in the comedy, that he should be able to make comic sense by posing as the supreme commander of the free Roman population, that he could wage a heroic campaign against a pimp and convincingly heroize what is nothing but fraud, is entirely acceptable to the audience of free Romans as a fantasy in which they can imaginatively participate: the ability of the little man to succeed by native wit. Let Dordalus the pimp enter raging against Toxilus as the worst of scoundrels (*pessimus corruptor,* line 779): we watch the slave and his fellow conspirators enjoy their physical well-being and even go on to tease unmercifully the helpless, furious Dordalus. The theme of war, triumph, and the honour of military success does not function as a corrective, to expose the base roguery of this slave, but rather to ratify his grandeur, to guarantee that we fall in with his wild fantasy. The lowest and 'worst' member of the population has earned the right, by his sheer energetic use of street wisdom, to be regarded as the best of all: a true Roman hero. Thus, Plautus' comic part for Toxilus differs radically from that designed for Falstaff. Falstaff had to be isolated, exposed as a basically bad man, and then dismissed from the final scene of victory; but Toxilus has, indeed, been the cause of this metaphorical 'victory,' and so becomes the very centre of triumphant celebration.[14]

This conception of 'heroic badness,' we may be pretty certain, did not come to Plautus from his Greek originals, nor was it fully developed in Plautus' imagination at the time he began his career as comic playwright—which, in turn, means that it did not come from his Roman predecessors, such as Naevius and Livius Andronicus, nor directly from some parallel native Italian form of farce. It is worth while, I believe, sketching out a line of development for this key theme, and I shall suggest that *The Bacchis-Sisters,* with which we are quite familiar by now, occupies a pivotal position in my proposed scheme.

One intrigue play has survived from Greek New Comedy in sufficient fullness (namely, in three acts) so that we know how the deceiver operated, and we can observe that, in accordance with expectations, he is neither bad nor a heroic rogue. Menander's comedy *The Shield,* which has been known for less than twenty years, since its lucky recovery from Egypt, depicts the efforts of an entire family to thwart the greedy scheme of a selfish uncle to claim money left by his supposedly dead nephew, a very successful mercenary soldier, and (since that is the legal condition on which he can get the money) to claim also the hand of his young niece. The uncle is the first surviving example of a Menandrian villain, and his villainy, whose symptoms are avarice and violation of the natural order of love, consists essentially in disruption of the integrity and good order of the family. The deceiver proves to be a slave, who indeed devises a very clever scheme and enjoys himself immensely in the process, but he functions as a loyal slave, devoted to his dead master and the welfare of the family. His deception is not anarchic at all, not designed to encourage the wasteful, unwise passion of an irresponsible young master, but it promotes the best interests of the household and frustrates the anarchic intentions of the bad uncle.[15] It is only appropriate, then, that a good older member of the family (in fact, another uncle, the antitype of the villain) participates in the deception. We don't have the final two acts of the comedy and cannot assert exactly how the slave was handled at the end, but it seems pretty clear to me that he would not have stood out as a figure of 'grandiose badness,' or even as a very important character, once he had served his function in the intrigue. For the intrigue was only one thread in a complicated romantic plot which eventually brought the supposedly dead nephew back to Athens and then, we assume, climaxed in a betrothal of two young couples, thus ensuring the future happiness of the family. In those developments, the slave would play no significant part; it appears that he had the pleasure of welcoming his beloved master home in Act IV, but thereafter yielded to other family members.[16]

If we had more of *The Double-Deceiver,* the Menandrian comedy Plautus adapted for his *Bacchis-Sisters,* we might have a more useful example of the limits imposed by Greek comedy on the rogue. The prototype of the flamboyant Chrysalus, who runs verbal riot in the centre of Plautus' comedy and plays repeatedly on the various possibilities of his name, had the ordinary name Syros in Menander; that is, he came originally from Syria. We know that he told a story to the father that resembled the tale Chrysalus spins for Nicobulus on his arrival in port. But no evidence survives to prove how the 'second deception' went, or what then happened for an ending. I have conjectured . . . that Plautus has suppressed Menander's final act and replaced it with his own creation, that emphasizes the anarchic, irresponsible, anti-family qualities which I consider patently non-Menandrian. Menander, I believe, would have made a more sympathetic and valid authority figure in his father, who was able at the end, with the Greek audience's full assent, to reassert his authority over the anarchic son and his slave and to reunite the family. Syros would have had no magnificent speech of triumph—not in lyrics, of course, but not in iambics either—because Menander's thematic goal and structural plan had no place for such emphasis on the defiance of legitimate paternal concern for the family. The slave would have been brought up short in his deception, but the main focus of Menander would have been on the wayward son Sostratos. Although I believe that is a reasonable conjectural account of the way Menander would have restrained the operation of Syros as rogue, it cannot now be proved. Let us, then, go on to the early intrigue-comedies of Plautus, to see how he started off.

Two very early Plautine plays, which operate with intrigue, can serve as useful examples of the beginnings of 'heroic badness.' They are the *Ass Comedy* and *Braggart Soldier*. In the first, a young man needs money for a prostitute—the basic situation—and two household slaves take part in a plot of deception that swindles the mistress of money owed her for an ass. Once the swindles has succeeded, they control the finances for a while and are given a long scene in which they act out their exulation triumphantly, in order to demonstrate dramatically for the Roman audience their superiority.[17] However, Plautus allows them to play no part in the dénouement of the comedy, and it is evident that he devised the slaves' moment of triumph as an episodic comic effect, not as a central thematic statement. In fact, the slaves did not really make the decision to help the young lover, or even carry through the plan of deception themselves: it was the idea of the father, who ordered them to proceed, and it was the father who performed the decisive deception that got the money. So when Plautus abandons his momentary delight with the impudent slaves, he comes back to the father, the arch-deceiver. *The Ass Comedy,* then, shows a basically subordinate role for slave-rogues, in conformance with the Greek original, I think, and with the general reality of Roman social practices. They are not heroes, though bad enough, and they occupy a distinctly inferior role (except for a promising sequence) in the total comic structure.

The Braggart Soldier is generally considered to have been composed a few years after the ***Ass Comedy,*** and it shows further development of the promise for a rogue of heroic badness. The problem is once again the love of a helpness young man for a courtesan, and again the slave helps him gain his girl by ingenious deception. Plautus certainly expands the role of this slave, Palinurus, by contrast with the previous play, and shows *him* plotting and carrying out his tricks. However, the target of the deception is a fool and knave, the braggart soldier, who combines within him all the relevant negative values for Plautus and his audience: he is a boastful coward, he is rich, he has kidnapped the prostitute, and he has become the illegitimate second master of Palinurus. When Palinurus disobeys and deceives this master in the interests of his original master, the young lover, to recover the kidnapped girl, his actions are not anarchic, but contribute to restoration of order and love.

Morever, the slave does not act without authority and numerous allies. His young master, like all such young lovers, is utterly helpless, but an older friend, at whose house he secretly is staying, proves energetic and supportive. He keeps urging Palinurus on, and he shares in the illegal moves of the deceptions, at his own risk, with an enthusiasm that delights us. Thus, with his cooperation, a common wall between his and the soldier's house is secretly opened up to allow clandestine meetings between the prostitute and her lover, his guest. Later, he offers his house as the place where the soldier will be trapped in supposed adultery (a hoax, since the woman who pretends to be a rich and dissatisfied wife is really a clever and compliant prostitute-friend of his, always ready for some fun). It is the witty old man who playfully attributes senatorial and military dignity to Palinurus.[18] The slave himself makes no such claims, and he has no scene of triumph and plays no part in the final humiliation of the soldier: that, again, is the amusing task of the old man. In short, Plautus does not yet develop the opportunity for the comic transvaluation of the 'bad slave' into the heroic, central character; Palinurus functions as but one of the majority who are dedicated to punishing the knavish soldier and restoring legitimate order. It is true that, as the slave leaves the soldier and the play, Plautus has the foolish man aptly climax his folly with these words: 'Before this happened, I always used to think he was the worst of slaves [*servum pessumum*]; now, I realize that he is entirely loyal to me,' (line 1374). But that is a momentary ironic joke. Acting, as he does, on the side of the angels, Palinurus cannot really be designated as either a person of exemplary badness (*malitia*) or one of heroic Roman manliness. It turns out, indeed, that Plautus displaces *malitia* in this comedy to the characters who really show wonderful verve as actors in the plots to dupe the soldier. The courtesans each get credit as an exemplar of clever badness that elicits the admiration of Palinurus and the old man

and helps out the weak young lover (cf. lines 188 and 887). Indeed, their action against the soldier becomes a competition of female badness (*conlatio malitiarum,* line 942).

A decade later, Plautus, at mid-career, had developed many possibilities of heroic badness. In ***The Haunted House,*** the slave Tranio clearly functions as the central character throughout the play, and the wonderfully improvised deceptions that he contrives to get money for his young master from the father are anarchic and like the heroic badness quite literally explored in later comedies. He is allowed to boast of his achievements as on a par with those of Alexander the Great (three iambic lines, 775-7), and he calls a 'senatorial session' of his supporters, but just as the plot is about to collapse, to make its ending more comic, not to magnify its beginning (line 1049). And, indeed, the plot fails, as we know from the start it must: Tranio takes refuge on the altar from his older master, who is furiously intent on punishing him, and only the intervention of an outsider buys the old man off from his fury and leaves Tranio for another day. Thus, the would-be hero is reduced to his proper role, and the father, though mocked and cheated, regains his authority.

The next step for Plautus is to allow the slave's badness complete success and to leave him heroically in power in the final scene. Examples of that fantastic scheme are two comedies composed in the late 190s, ***Pseudolus*** and ***Epidicus.*** For many readers today, Pseudolus is the quintessence of Plautine comic invention, and I would certainly want to view him as an exemplar of heroic badness.[19] He is the most self-conscious of any clever Plautine slave, so he constantly calls attention, with impudent pride, to his badness, to the incredible way he undertakes superhuman tasks and then accomplishes them. He humiliates his older master, Simo (though he does not actually defraud him), and he cheats a pimp of the price of a prostitute, who of course is desperately desired by the young master. The finale of the comedy has been composed as a lyric scene of drunken triumph, in which Pseudolus rubs his victory, impudently and with impunity, into the face of old Simo. The slave reels around the stage, burps familiarly at Simo, good-humouredly recites to him the victor's creed—'woe to the defeated' (*vae victis* 1317)—and confidently styles himself as *vir malus,* smiling as the frustrated Simo calls him *pessumus homo* (line 1310). Admittedly, Plautus presents it as a moment of temporary victory, but it is total in the special comic representation.

Epidicus similarly scores a triumph over his outraged master, and he has the pleasure of turning the tables on angry Periphanes in the finale, so as to outwit his fury and to convert it into such total compliance and abject gratitude that the old man frees him on the spot. Thus,

Epidicus' wits have enabled him to escape permanently from his slave role as 'worst of men.' The epilogue puts it all in a nutshell: 'Here is a man who has gained his liberty by his badness,' (*hic is homo est qui libertatem malitia invenit sua,* line 732). The slave has been able to nullify his master's anger because, in the course of supporting his young master's double love affair and of cheating Periphanes out of the price of two girls, he has accidentally bought to freedom a long-lost daughter of the old man. Learning of his lucky work before Periphanes does, he can then pose as having planned this noble deed and piously claim the reward of freedom: that is true heroic badness![20]

Some five years later, Plautus staged **The Bacchis-Sisters,** which builds the slave Chrysalus up into a superlative epic hero of badness and gives him the perfect triumph song. Up to that point late in Act IV, we might have expected that Plautus was taking the slave of Menander's *Double-Deceiver* and turning him into another Pseudolus or Epidicus. But he deliberately stops short, abandons Chrysalus to his celebrations off stage, and refocuses his and the audience's attention on the courtesan sisters. Chrysalus has, it seems, gone as far as he can on his own, and he faces inevitable and painful reality—his master's rightful anger—unless someone can intercede for him (as for Tranio). As I said earlier, I believe that Menander did let the father restore order and authority in his threatened home, bringing Sostratos and slave Syros to heel. Plautus, however, lets the Bacchis-sisters take over the play, which thereby changes its title aptly, and the forces of badness, domestic irresponsibility, social anarchy, and sensual pleasure completely prevail, to the humiliation of paternal respect and family honour.[21]

The changes that Plautus made to Menander's play and to his own highly successful characterization of the heroic rogue-slave, by shifting the emphasis and title from the slave-deceiver to the artful courtesans, suggest that the line of development of heroic badness has still not reached its conclusion in Plautine comedy. The triumphant slave is but a phase in a longer, more ingenious scheme. As I noted in the case of **The Braggart Soldier,** Palinurus the slave cannot work his schemes without the help of an energetic older man and a pair of witty, enterprising courtesans; and Plautus applies to them what is for him a praise-worthy term, *malitia.* Similarly, Chrysalus may exult in his reputation as 'a bad one' (line 783), but it is Bacchis who talks of her *malitia* (line 54) at the beginning of the play and accordingly seems to prepare us for Plautus' new emphasis.[22]

In Menander, if it is thematically necessary for the impudent slave to submit at the end to the older master's wise authority so that the home and family may operate under an intelligible hierarchy, it is even more necessary for the prostitute to yield to the interests of the family. Her erotic attractions and the money she demands of young lovers threaten the family, for she diverts the young master from taking a responsible role as husband of a suitable woman, father of the next generation, and careful steward of the family fortune. But Plautus does not treat the family as the essential measure of value for his comedy, and so, though he recognizes the stereotype of the 'bad prostitute' (*mala meretrix:* **Captivi,** line 57), he tends to change her character from that of negative menace to one of positive appeal: her 'badness' becomes the basis for her superiority to the male characters who share the stage with her. The Bacchis-sisters seduce the two young men; then, when the fathers of the young men storm over to the sisters' house to drag away the boys and Chrysalus, the sisters seduce the ridiculous old men. In Plautus' comic world, the appeal of sex, wine, and food is infinitely preferable to that of domesticity, and the Bacchis-sisters must dominate the old men and implicitly emerge as 'heroic.'

Among Plautus' last comedies are the **Truculent Man** and **Casina.** The former takes the theme of the masterful courtesan to a point where the comedy turns—for Plautus—unusually satiric.[23] The woman, suggestively named Phronesium (perhaps best translated as 'Prudence'), juggles with great skill and profit to herself, as I described in chapter 3, three simultaneous affairs. Not one of the three men earns our respect. However, the character of Phronesium herself causes problems for readers of Plautus, for, while she is manifestly superior in wit and *malitia* to her three victims, she acts only from selfish motives and does not exhibit the usual Plautine roguish qualities of verbal wit, physical energy, and good-humoured self-importance that combine to win over the audience.

Plautus assigns her one lyric monody early in the play (lines 448 ff), but does not let her bewitch us by the performance. Phronesium lacks the flamboyance and fantastic attractions of the rogue-slave, and her imagery does not move her into the world of Roman politics or heroic myth: she is a predatory creature. She has no senate, no army of supporters, no enemy to defeat for the public good; instead, her lover becomes metaphorically like an enemy city, full of plunder (line 170). In the inflexible world of Plautine Rome, a prostitute could not hope to escape her cruel conditions and become rich enough to settle down in dignity and be socially eligible, because of wealth, for respectability and even marriage. So Plautus could not fantasize very far with the success of Phronesium. She remains a somewhat depressing example of a certain kind of *malitia,* no heroine, but demonstrably better than all three men with whom she is involved.

For a more appealing portrait of woman's badness (*muliebris malitia*), we need to turn to the last surviving Plautine comedy, **Casina.** As Plautus organizes the plot, there are no prostitutes and no young lovers; he uses two slaves, who appear strictly subordinate to their owners, one to the husband and the other to the wife.[24] The husband, Lysidamus, starts off as the would-be rogue: he has a plot to fool his wife and, by using the cover of his servant's marriage with an attractive housemaid, to sleep with the maid himself the first night. Cleustrata, the wife, instinctively opposes the marriage, because she claims it as her right to dispose of the maid from her area of domestic responsibility. As we saw, Diphilos and Plautus solved this marital dispute dramatically by the brilliant scene of the lot drawing, which gave Diphilos' (and, perhaps originally, Plautus') comedy its title. Cleustrata loses, and her roguish husband seems to have scored a complete victory. Then, when she discovers the real purpose and the extent of her husband's perfidy, she sets out energetically and maliciously (if you want) to frustrate his plans and to humiliate him so openly that he will have to crawl back home and behave in the future. She now preempts the role of rogue, and the victory with it. In this scheme, the wife stands on the side of good sense and marital fidelity, whereas the husband behaves like an adolescent, and his dishonesty and false acting are both ridiculous and highly punishable. In his frustration, the husband and his caretaker accuse Cleustrata and her supporters of being 'bad stuff' (*mala res,* line 228), 'bad merchandise' (*mala merces,* line 754), and the worst kind of trickster (line 645). They mean what they say as pejorative, but Plautus invites us to take the terms otherwise, because he has inclined us to view the women's side as 'better.'

Cleustrata, then, develops a clever series of frustrating devices by which her husband is fooled and the audience entertained. In this respect, she removes herself far away from the merely mercenary tricks of Phronesium. She does not even resemble the usual angry wife (e.g., in *The Ass Comedy*), who is concerned to protect her property as well as to punish her husband; Cleustrata does not have a large dowry, and her interest is in reordering the wayward household with the greatest number of laughs at her guilty husband. The key word for her activity is the Latin *ludi,* which refers to games, play, and stage performances. She 'plays games' (*ludificem,* line 560; *ludi ludificabiles,* line 761) with her husband, and she 'stages plays' (*ludos nuptialis,* line 856) for the audience. First, she acts the innocent herself and interferes with plans to make an empty house available for her husband's 'first night.' Then, she sends out a clever servant, Pardalisca, to act out a scene from tragedy, to terrify her husband with the story that Casina, like the operatic Lucia di Lammermoor, has gone crazy and is wielding a murderous sword and looking for him (lines 620 ff). And, finally, she organizes a comic performance, at which she as well as we are a laughing audience, where her husband goes to bed with her brawny slave (who is disguised as the bride Casina, of all things) and gets

a bad beating for his lust, then rushes out in a state of considerable disrepair and publicly admits his disgrace. This is a special kind of triumph, and Cleustrata's 'badness' is also special. Neither a senator nor a victorious general in metaphorical terms (positions about which Plautus entertains some ambiguity), she is a creative artist, a veritable 'poet' (line 861), and that is probably the highest accolade that the poet Plautus can award to anyone.

In this chapter, I have attempted to describe the principal features of a special Plautine character, on whom he concentrates his comic attention: a rogue, male or female. Tracing Plautus' development of the rogue, I have shown how he starts tentatively with an uppity slave (*servus malus*) and, in successive plays, expands him into a superlative type, the worst of slaves (*servus pessimus*), a pyrotechnical scamp who can wrest freedom as well as gold from his angry, avaricious master. The Plautine rogue can also be female. She shows up supporting deception as a kind of 'wicked witch' or 'blasted bitch' (*mala meretrix*) among the courtesans of the early comedies, then develops to become the title character of *The Bacchis-Sisters* and almost the demonic principal of *The Truculent Man*. In his last play, *Casina,* Plautus heroizes the wittily independent wife Cleustrata (whom her scoundrel-husband considers *mala mulier* because she frustrates his infidelity).

Notes

Plautus' Plotting: The Lover Upstaged

[1] S. G. Ashmore, *The Comedies of Terence, edited with introduction and notes* (Oxford: Oxford University Press, 1910), 5.

[2] See Leo Salingar, *Shakespeare and the Traditions of Comedy* (Cambridge: Cambridge University Press, 1974), and Karen Newman, *Shakespeare's Rhetoric of Comic Character. Dramatic Convention in Classical and Renaissance Comedy* (New York: Methuen, 1985).

[3] Ovid, *Tristia,* 2.369: Plutarch, *Amatorius* (*Moralia* 763b), cited by Stobaeus, 4.20.34, who, however, says more than our present text of Plutarch. He seems to attribute to his source this statement: 'One thing there is that gives birth to all the plays of Menander alike: love, which acts like a breath of life in common to them.' He then goes on to argue against the irrationality of love, citing the same passage of Menander that Plutarch does, but giving eight lines where Plutarch provides only two.

[4] Plutarch, *Moralia* 777f, which I have discussed in 'Love Plots in Menander and His Roman Adapters,' *Ramus* 13 (1984), 124-34.

[5] See chapter 1, 26. For Plautus' treatment of love in general, see P. Grimal, *L'Amour à Rome* (Paris: Hachette, 1963) [= *Love in Ancient Rome,* tr. A. Train, Jr (New York: Crown 1967; University of Oklahoma Press, 1986)], especially chapters 3 and 4, on love and marriage and courtesans.

[6] See chapter 2, 40.

[7] The similar lyrical soliloquy by the young lover at the opening of the anonymous *Mostellaria* is one of several reasons that lead some scholars to assign it to Philemon.

[8] See chapter 2, 46.

[9] Marriages do result from the developments in *Trinummus* and *Casina;* however, neither their Greek writers, Philemon and Diphilos, nor Plautus, their adapter, makes matrimony the essential goal of either plot.

[10] Cf. Terence, *Adelphoe,* line 486. At line 473 in *Andria,* Glycerium (who has not been raped, but is pregnant) delivers her one line, which is so formulaic that suspicious old Simo assumes that she is faking a birth.

[11] At the start of the *Dyskolos,* Menander, who has used a god in the prologue, as is done in *Aulularia,* then introduces the young lover Sostratos and favourably characterizes his love.

[12] Molière borrowed and developed this comic scene in Act V of *L'Avare.* Bergson, in his admirable essay, 'Laughter,' described this device as one of 'reciprocal interference.'

[13] It is Molière who expands the mutual incomprehension by letting each character use, in different ways, the word 'treasure,' the miser quite literally, the lover metaphorically.

[14] One of these summaries states that Euclio (apparently having at last realized the negligible value of riches) gave the money (a kind of dowry?) as well as his daughter to Lyconides. I consider that ending (at least, as it is simplistically understood) unlikely. Molière may come closer to the intention of Plautus with his version, where Harpagon the miser, true to his 'idée fixe,' ignores all his family as he happily clutches his recovered wealth. Konstan (*Roman Comedy* [Ithaca, NY: Cornell University Press, 1983]), in his chapter on the *Aulularia* (pp. 33 ff), studies the miser's alienation from his community and the city-state.

[15] For useful studies of this comedy, see W. Süss, 'Zur Cistellaria des Plautus,' *RM* [*Rheinisches Museum für Philologie*] 84 (1935), 161-87; W. Ludwig, 'Die plautinische Cistellaria und das Verhältnis von Gott und Handlung bei Menander,' *Ménandre: sept exposés* (Geneva: Fondation Hardt, 1970), 43-110; G. Thamm, 'Zur Cistellaria des Plautus,' (Dissertation, University of Freiburg, 1971); and Konstan, *Roman Comedy,* 96 ff.

[16] Palinurus drops from the play after line 321; Curculio has just appeared, forty lines earlier, at 280, and rapidly taken over the chief role of comic energy.

[17] I refer to the young man here. The old lover always had to give up his foolish love and return to his marriage.

[18] For the basic anthropological formulation of Plautine plots, see M. Bettini, 'Verso un' antropologia dell' intreccio,' *MD* [*Materiali e discussioni per l'analisi dei testi classici*] 7 (1982), 39-101. Slater's analysis of Toxilus as lover and rogue (*Plautus in Performance: The Theatre of the Mind* [Princeton, NJ: Princeton University Press, 1985], 55 ff) is useful.

[19] On Pseudolus' diverse qualities as a rogue, see chapters 4 and 6.

[20] On the incipient rogues of the *Asinaria,* see chapter 4.

[21] On Phronesium as a 'flawed rogue' in a satiric comedy, see chapter 4 and 6.

Heroic Badness (malitia): Plautus' Characters and Themes

[1] I particularly think of P. S. Dunkin, *Post-Aristophanic Comedy: Studies in the Social Outlook of Middle and New Comedy at Both Athens and Rome* (Urbana: University of Illinois Press, 1946) [= *Illinois Studies in Language and Literature,* Vol. 31, nos. 3-4].

[2] This is the soldier's description of the slave Palaestrio in *Miles* (line 1374). Pseudolus, in his final triumph, is called *pessimus* by his master Simo at lines 1285 and 1310, and he has the effrontery to call himself *vir malus* as he sardonically hails his master with the phrase *viro optimo* (line 1293). Pseudolus, in his turn, hails his ally Simia as a man who could not be worse (*peiorem*) or 'more deviously bad' (lines 1017-18). In the opinion of the pimp Dordalus, who has been victimized by him, Toxilus the slave is *pessumus corruptor* (Persa, lines 779). Lyconides rails angrily at his slave in *Aulularia* (line 825) as *scelerum cumulatissume.* The rogue, for Plautus, is superlative in badness.

[3] E. Segal has carefully followed out this theme in *Roman Laughter* (Cambridge, MA: Harvard University Press, 1968), Ch. IV, 'From Slavery to Freedom,' 99 ff.

[4] Military *imperium* and a campaign against 'enemies' constitute a key symbol in the intrigues of *Bacchides*

(especially lines 925 ff), *Miles, Persa* (especially lines 753 ff), and *Pseudolus*. On the militant theme in Plautine comedy in general, see J. A. S. Hanson, 'The Glorious Military,' in *Roman Drama*, (ed. by T. A. Dorey and D. R. Dudley), 51-85. London: Routledge and Kegan Paul, 1965.

[5] Cf. *Bacchides,* lines 1058, 1069, and 1075; *Persa,* line 757; and *Pseudolus,* line 588.

[6] Pseudolus links *virtus* with his *malitia* at line 581; the slave Libanus boasts of the success achieved by himself and his fellow-slave and represents it as a total victory earned by their heroism (*virtute, Asinaria,* line 556). In later plays, when Plautus casts this 'victory speech' as a lyric hymn, the format itself, no doubt parallel to that of Roman victory announcements and inscriptions, implies the presence of *virtus* even in the absence of the word.

[7] Menander's slaves regularly possess more experience and practical wisdom than their masters, and we have a fair number of sententious fragments in which it seems likely that slaves are lecturing their young masters. However, their actions appear to have been circumscribed. It is unfortunate that we lack the Greek passages that followed out the trickery of Syros, the inspiration for Chrysalus in *Bacchides*. But, as I argue below, the role of Daos in *Aspis* shows how a trickster in Menander is a loyal slave working *for* the family, not what Plautus would have made him: a rogue challenging the family structure and supporting anarchy and dissipation.

[8] What I call the Aristophanic rogue has been ably analysed by C. H. Whitman in *Aristophanes and the Comic Hero* (Cambridge, MA: Harvard University Press, 1964).

[9] Lines 128 ff. Note how Shakespeare abandons heroic verse as soon as the king leaves the stage; Falstaff speaks in unheroic prose.

[10] The saying about 'he who fights and runs away' is not Shakespearean. In the thirteenth Centennial edition of *Bartlett's Quotations* (Boston and Toronto: Little, Brown, 1955), 69a, the first definite form of the expression is credited to Tertullian; but Menander may have used it four hundred years earlier. At the end of Scene 3, just before leaving, Falstaff declares: 'Give me life; which if I can save, so; if not, honour comes unlooked for, and there's an end.'

[11] Scene 4: 'The better part of valour is discretion; in the which better part, I have saved my life.'

[12] It is significant that Shakespeare excludes Falstaff from the final scene (5), which he casts in heroic verse and uses to bring the battle to a dignified conclusion.

[13] My translation

[14] Similarly, Pseudolus is the heroic force in the play named after him, and so the 'victory celebrations' of the finale centre on him.

[15] Soon after the *Aspis* was first published, I wrote an article in which I suggested that Daos, in lines 399-420, performs in his role as trickster like the *servus currens* of Plautus. See *Phoenix* 24 (1970), 229-36. Although I still believe that the excited and overacted running of Daos, as he mouths tragic lines from Euripides and other dramatists, anticipates the histrionic running entrance of the Plautine slave, I must agree with others now who argue that Menander himself was thinking back to the stereotype of the 'tragic messenger.'

[16] In the tattered remains of Act IV, at lines 506 ff, the editors assume that the soldier knocks at the house-door, which Daos opens and thus becomes the first to greet his returned master.

[17] *Asinaria,* lines 267 ff. Leonida moves briefly into military metaphors at lines 269-71. For recent studies of this play, see D. Konstan, *Roman Comedy* (Ithaca, NY: Cornell University Press, 1983), 47 ff, and N. Slater, *Plautus in Performance: The Theatre of the Mind* (Princeton, NJ: Princeton University Press, 1985), 55 ff.

[18] *Miles,* lines 219 ff

[19] See John Wright, 'The Transformations of Pseudolus,' *TAPA* [*Transactions of the American Philological Association*] 105 (1975), 403-16, and Slater's chapter (*Plautus in Performance,* pp. 118 ff) that develops and modifies the invaluable groundwork of Wright.

[20] In the light of Sander Goldberg's recent article on this play, 'Plautus' *Epidicus* and the Case of the Missing Original,' *TAPA* 108 (1978), 81-92, in which he argues the possibility that Plautus may have composed it without any specific Greek source (apart from the general conventions of New Comedy), the unique ending, freedom for the rogue-slave, makes sense as Plautus' invention. Slater (*Plautus in Performance,* 19 ff), in his chapter on this play, argues that it celebrates in the slave Epidicus 'the powers of self-creation.'

[21] Nicobulus continues to demand vengeance against Chrysalus up to line 1187, after which he collapses under the seduction of Bacchis. In his analysis of the comedy, Slater (*Plautus in Performance*) emphasizes Chrysalus, and he explains the slave's departure as one of significant choice that defines the total superiority of his role. As he reads lines 1072-3 (pp. 112-13), Chrysalus declares his refusal to continue in his

role. I prefer to think that Plautus himself is preparing us for the abandonment of the clever slave and his final stress on the courtesans.

[22] Cf. the epithets (*pessumae, mala*) applied to the courtesans in *Bacchides,* lines 1122 and 1162, and the comic alliterative terms of line 1167, *probriperlecebrae et persuastrices.*

[23] Konstan (*Roman Comedy*), in his chapter on this play (pp. 142 ff), rightly calls it 'satiric comedy.' See also Cynthia Dessen, 'Plautus' Satiric Comedy: The *Truculentus,' Philol. Quarterly* 56 (1977), 146-58. See also P. Grimal, 'A propos du Truculentus. L'anti-féminisme de Plaute,' *Mélanges Marcel Durry* (Paris: Belles Letters 1970), 85-98.

[24] On Chalinus, the slave who poses as Casina and thus promotes the disgrace of the husband, yet, in my opinion, plays a subordinate role, unlike the typical Plautine rogue, see my article, 'Chalinus *armiger* in Plautus' *Casina,' ICS [Illinois Classical Studies]* 8 (1983), 11-21. Slater (*Plautus in Performance*), in his chapter on this play, ably traces the way Cleustrata seizes control of the plot in the second half (pp. 84 ff).

Bibliography

Anderson, W. S. 'A New Menandrian Prototype for the *Servus currens* of Roman Comedy.' *Phoenix* 24 (1970), 229-36

———'Chalinus *armiger* in Plautus' *Casina.' ICS* 8 (1983), 11-21

———'Love Plots in Menander and His Roman Adapters.' *Ramus* 13 (1984), 124-34

Ashmore, S. G. *The Comedies of Terence.* Oxford: Oxford University Press, 1910

Bettini, M. 'Verso un antropologia dell' intreccio: Le strutture semplici della trama nelle commedie di Plauto.' *MD* 7 (1982), 39-101

Dessen, C. S. 'Plautus' Satiric Comedy: The *Truculentus.' Philol. Quarterly* 56 (1977), 145-68

Dunkin, P. S. *Post-Aristophanic Comedy: Studies in the Social Outlook of Middle and New Comedy at both Athens and Rome.* (Urbana: University of Illinois Press, 1946

Goldberg, S. 'Plautus' *Epidicus* and the Case of the Missing Original.' *TAPA* 108 (1978), 81-92

Grimal, P. *L'Amour à Rome.* Paris: Hachette, 1963 [=*Love in Ancient Rome,* tr. A. Train, Jr. New York: Crown Publishers, 1967]

———'A propos du Truculentus: L'antiféminisme de Plaute.' *Mélanges Marcel Durry,* 85-98. Paris: Belles Lettres, 1970

Hanson, J. A. S. 'The Glorious Military.' In *Roman Drama,* ed. by T. A. Dorey and D. E. Dudley, 51-85. London: Routledge and P. Kegan, 1965

Konstan, D. *Roman Comedy.* Ithaca, NY: Cornell University Press, 1983

Ludwig, W. 'Die plautinische Cistellaria und das Verhältnis von Gott und Handlung bei Menander.' In *Ménandre: sept exposés,* 43-96. Geneva: Fondation Hardt, 1970

Newman, K. *Shakespeare's Rhetoric of Comic Character: Dramatic Convention in Classical and Renaissance Comedy.* New York: Methuen, 1985

Salingar, L. *Shakespeare and the Traditions of Comedy.* Cambridge: Cambridge University Press, 1974

Segal, E. *Roman Laughter.* Cambridge, MA: Harvard University Press, 1968

Slater, N. W. *Plautus in Performance: The Theatre of the Mind.* Princeton, NJ: Princeton University Press, 1985

Süss, W. 'Zur Cistellaria des Plautus.' *RM* 84 (1935), 161-87

Thamm, G. 'Zur Cistellaria des Plautus.' Dissertation, University of Freiburg, 1971

Whitman, C. H. *Aristophanes and the Comic Hero.* Cambridge, MA: Harvard University Press, 1964

Wright, J. 'The Transformations of Pseudolus.' *TAPA* 105 (1975), 403-16

William M. Owens (essay date 1994)

SOURCE: William M. Owens, "The Third Deception in *Bacchides*," in *American Journal of Philology,* Vol. 115, Fall, 1994, pp. 381-407.

[*In the following essay, Owens compares Plautus's* Bacchides *to the Greek play on which it was based (Menander's* Dis Exapaton) *and demonstrates that several aspects of the play's plot and themes are Plautine in origin.*]

Chrysalus is one of Plautus' most clever slaves. In the course of ***Bacchides*** he deceives his master three times. But the model for ***Bacchides*** was Menander's *Dis Exapaton,* "The Man Deceiving Twice," whose title implies only two deceptions. This difference in arithmetic was the seed of a scholarly controversy which germinated in 1912 with the publication of Eduard Fraenkel's dissertation, *De Media et Nova Comoedia Quaestiones Selectae*. Fraenkel suggested that Plautus added the final deception in *Bacchides* through the process of *contaminatio,* using another, unidentified Attic comedy for his model. The response to this hypothesis was mixed; eventually Fraenkel himself abandoned it in response to the critique of Gordon Williams.[1] Nonetheless, the notion that the third deception is a Plautine addition, if not an example of *contaminatio,* has persisted, most recently in the work of Eckard Lefèvre and Adolf Primmer.[2]

Fraenkel's original hypothesis, its reception by Williams and other critics, and the recent work of Lefèvre and Primmer belong to the tradition of Plautine source criticism, or *Quellenforschung,* which seeks to analyze the text into those parts which are Roman, created by Plautus himself, and those parts which are Greek, adapted by Plautus from his models, which themselves are largely lost to posterity. In the effort to sort out the Roman from the Greek, the text of Plautus has been minutely analyzed in all of its poetic, dramatic, and cultural aspects. But since, apart from fragments, the texts of Plautus' models are lost to us, such *Quellenforschung* is a kind of philological shadowboxing in which the text of Plautus is matched against the text of a play which no longer exists. Small wonder that consensus is often difficult to achieve on the questions traditional Plautine source criticism addresses.

The present essay takes a different approach to the problem of the third deception (a difference which may not at first be apparent, when I conduct a necessary review of Fraenkel's original hypothesis and Williams's critique),[3] through a close reading of *Bacchides* as a dramatic unity. I argue that the play is about trust and deception, a thematic antithesis which Plautus has characterized in ethnic terms: on the one hand, trust is romanized as *fides;* on the other, deception is characterized as Greek. This is relevant to the third deception because the ethical expectations of *fides* help shape the action and the behavior of the characters at several key points. Plautus' nominally Greek characters at times seem rather Roman in their attitude towards *fides.* I suggest that the third deception works only because the *senex* Nicobulus, like a good Roman, has regard for *fides.* This may not prove that the third deception is Plautine in origin; the theme of "trustworthiness" could have been present in Menander's play, now garbed by Plautus in Roman dress as *fides* to appeal to the sensibilities and ethical preoccupations of his audience. However, I show that where a direct comparison between *Dis Exapaton* and *Bacchides* is possible, it is clear that Plautus has introduced *fides* independently of his model. This suggests that *fides* is not merely the Romanization of a theme already present

in *Dis Exapaton*. Ultimately I suggest that the characterization of *fides* as Roman and deception as Greek may be understood in the broader context of Plautus' society and its encounter with Greek culture. *Bacchides* enables us to see this Roman bias function in the context of an organic and unified work of literature. While we must be careful not to confuse Roman comedy with the Roman social reality, *Bacchides* both permits us to examine the tensions within the antithesis and helps reveal some of the complexity of the Roman response to Hellenism.

Fraenkel's Theory of Contaminatio

Before reviewing Fraenkel's *contaminatio* theory and Williams's critique, it is useful to review the three deceptions in *Bacchides*. The first deception is a straightforward lie. Before the action of the play begins, Nicobulus has sent his slave, Chrysalus, and his son, Mnesilochus, to Ephesus so they may collect money deposited with a guest-friend. However, the two have decided to keep the money for themselves, to help further the young man's romance with a courtesan, Bacchis of Samos. Chrysalus cobbles together a tall tale in which a treacherous guest-friend, pirates, and a narrow escape have forced him and Mnesilochus to leave the money behind in Ephesus. But this deception is as easily undone as it had been accomplished. Back in Athens, Mnesilochus wrongly suspects his friend Pistoclerus of having stolen Bacchis from him. In fact, Pistoclerus has fallen in love with Bacchis' twin, Bacchis of Athens. At any rate, in his distress Mnesilochus tells his father the truth and returns the money. But Mnesilochus soon learns that his friends are true and that his intemperate honesty has created the need for a second deception. Chrysalus has Mnesilochus compose a letter to his father, warning him that Chrysalus is planning to deceive him again and that Nicobulus ought to keep the slave under guard. As the old man has Chrysalus bound up, the slave adroitly seizes an opportunity to impose Bacchis of Samos on Nicobulus as the wife of Cleomachus, an outraged and bloodthirsty soldier, who is now on the verge of catching his "wife" and Mnesilochus *in flagrante,* but who may, nonetheless, be mollified by an appropriate cash payment. Mnesilochus appears to have his Bacchis, but Chrysalus deems that some extra money is necessary, so that the victorious troops may have proper drink to celebrate their triumph (972-72[a]). Thus we have a third deception in *Bacchides:* Chrysalus has Mnesilochus write a second letter in which he confesses to his father that he has promised to pay Bacchis of Samos, who Nicobulus still thinks is the soldier's wife, 200 gold philips; unless Nicobulus pays this amount, Mnesilochus will have perjured himself. So that his son may avoid that shame, Nicobulus pays up again.

Fraenkel's hypothesis that the third deception in *Bacchides* was not in Menander's *Dis Exapaton* was based on both the title of Menander's play and Chrysalus' reference in the great *canticum* to the legendary *tria fata* auguring the fall of Troy.[4] Chrysalus draws an explicit connection between these *tria fata* and the three deceptions he has contrived against his master (953-56). The passage is generally recognized to be Plautine in origin. Fraenkel also suggests that the third deception is a case of *contaminatio;* it was derived from another, unidentified Greek play. Like the second deception, this deception too was based on a letter. For Fraenkel (*Quaestiones* 102-3) its polished style suggested Attic origins.

Even skillful surgeons leave a scar. Plautus' insertion of material from another play into his adaptation of *Dis Exapaton* created some confusion for the action of *Bacchides*. Fraenkel discerned the Plautine suture marks at 920-24, that is, immediately before the *canticum*. Nicobulus has already promised to pay 200 gold philips to the soldier; however, before he fulfills his promise Plautus has him indulge renewed suspicion about his slave. He resolves first to speak again with his son before paying the money (920-22), but suddenly changes his mind and decides to reread his son's letter: *uerum lubet etiam mi has perlegere denuo; / aequomst tabellis consignatis credere* (923-24). These last two lines give no indication of Nicobulus' subsequent movements.[5] This vagueness would have been unlikely in Plautus' model, for Greek New Comedy was generally careful in accounting for the exits and entrances and the movements of characters on and off stage. As is frequent in Plautine *Quellenforschung,* the Roman dramatist is faulted for his failure to meet the aesthetic standards of his Greek model. For Fraenkel the perceived ineptness of 923-24 was partial proof of their Plautinity. Fraenkel implies that in Menander's play the old man would have gone somewhere where he would learn the truth: perhaps to see his son at the courtesans' house, an intention suggested by 920-22; or perhaps to the forum to pay the soldier, from whom he would learn all, which of course is what eventually happened in *Bacchides*. At any rate, Plautus defers the moment when Nicobulus learns what is going on, and creates a space in which the third deception may unfold.[6]

Williams raised three objections which persuaded Fraenkel to abandon this hypothesis. First, the evident tampering at 923-24 may be attributed to the need to create dramatic space for the *canticum* at 925-78, not an additional deception. In *Dis Exapaton* there would have been no such *canticum*.[7] Second, to square his view that there were three deceptions in the Greek play with Menander's title implying only two, Williams develops a suggestion of Ritschl's that the title simply ignores the first, frustrated deception;[8] thus there were three deceptions in *Dis Exapaton,* but the title refers only to the second and third, the two accomplished by letter.[9] Third, Williams argues that it was improbable that Plautus found an episode in another Greek play whose many details readily fit the action of *Bacchides*. This final objection was perhaps the most persuasive for Fraenkel, who resisted the idea that Plautus could create dramatic action without relying on a model.[10]

It is worth examining Williams's arguments in some detail.[11] The first point, that lines 923-24 may be adequately motivated by Plautus' insertion of the *canticum* which follows, cannot be resolved. The *canticum* and the third deception are so closely connected that it is difficult to know whether the obscurity raised by 923-24 creates dramatic space for the *canticum* alone or both the *canticum* and the deception it introduces. Williams's apparently simpler solution is not necessarily the correct one. Second, in his effort to discount the first deception Williams argues that only a moralist interested in the process of deception itself would have counted three deceptions in Menander's play. In his view only the actual extraction of the money would have mattered to Menander's audience—the proof of the perjury was in the payment. Thus when Mnesilochus returned the money to his father, the first deception was no longer a deception. Hence Williams argues ("Construction of *Pseudolus*" 453-54) that only a moralist would have been tempted to call Menander's play *Tris Exapaton*. This is surely special pleading. In the first deception Chrysalus successfully deceived his master because Nicobulus believed his lie. That deceit occurs when a lie is believed is not a view peculiar to moralists. But if we wish to accept Williams's argument to the contrary, we should remember that the money acquired through the third deception is also returned (cf. 1184). In that case we should have expected Menander to have called his play *Hapax Exapaton*.

Williams also objects that Fraenkel's theory of *contaminatio* asks us to accept the improbable idea that Plautus had at his disposal another Greek play containing an episode neatly fitting the details of *Bacchides* and ready to be grafted onto the main plot. This was a serious objection for Fraenkel, in whose view Plautus did not compose dramatic action which furthered the plot independently of a Greek model. But it is not a serious objection for us. Recent scholarship in the tradition of Plautine *Quellenforschung* has established a more generous appreciation of Plautine originality, one that acknowledges the Roman dramatist's ability to compose original dramatic action.[12] In particular, Primmer, in his reconstruction of *Dis Exapaton* from close analysis of *Bacchides,* argues that the third deception is Plautine, on the basis of the probable structure of Menander's play.[13]

The argument advanced here for the Plautinity of the third deception differs from that of Primmer and others writing in the tradition of Plautine source criticism in that it emphasizes the dependence of the third deception on the main dramatic idea of the play, the antithesis between Roman *fides* and Greek deception, a theme which is Plautine in origin. The third deception works only because Nicobulus, like a good Roman, has regard for *fides*. The antithesis between the Roman ethic and its Greek opposite accommodated **Bacchides** to the biases of its original audience and provides us with some of the social logic behind Plautus' alteration of his Greek original.

Fides *in* Bacchides

Before discussing the importance of *fides* in **Bacchides,** it is useful to review the importance of the ethic in the lives of the play's audience.[14] Plautus' audience would have recognized an important aspect of *fides* in the "reliability" or "trustworthiness' of the individual. This aspect of *fides* was concerned with the honoring of contracts and obligations of all sorts, personal, political, and commercial. Here *fides* worked as a social ethic, regulating the various ties which bound society together. This concern with social ethics is related closely to another aspect of *fides* concerned with personal morality. For the audience of **Bacchides,** as much as for its characters, *fides* was the guarantor of oaths and solemn promises such as *stipulatio*. To break one's word was an offense against *fides*. The ethic was associated with a particular pair of reciprocal promises: first, the promise of protection made by the strong to the weak; then, the promise of loyalty and subservience made by the weak in return for the protection the strong afford. In this regard Romans closely associated *fides* with the distribution of power and the social order.

This last aspect would have addressed the concerns of the aristocrats in the audience. The reciprocity of *fides* moderated the relationship between people of unequal rank, such as master and slave or patron and client. Thus while *fides* provided for some measure of protection for the weaker, it also recognized and legitimated the privileges of the stronger. For the aristocrats in the audience, in whom the personal and the political were inextricably bound, *fides* pertained to political as much as to personal conduct. The aristocrat's desire to maintain his *fides* was motivated not just by a concern for ethics and consideration for the weak. One's reputation for *fides* was also an index of one's power. The patron who failed to protect his client suffered injury not only to his ethical reputation but also to the public perception of his power—hence the practice in Roman politics of attacking a man through his clients. Correspondingly, the act of affirming one's *fides* could serve as a demonstration of one's power as much as it could serve as proof of ethical probity.

Finally, many in the audience, some more than others, were aware that the Romans had exported *fides,* the domestic ethic which regulated unequal relationships within Roman society, and used it as a principle in Rome's dealings with subordinate foreign powers. Foreign states which submitted themselves to the will of Rome and expected protection in return were said to be in the *fides* of the Roman people. The Romans themselves advertised their *fides* to other states as a guarantee of Roman reliability and fairness, but also as a reminder of Roman power.[15] This principle of conduct had been given concrete expression in the temple to the goddess Fides on the Capitoline, which was constructed in the 250s and served for the reception of foreign embassies.

Thus, in the ideal if not the reality, *fides* was an ethic that played a role in almost every aspect of a Roman's life, both public and private. Plautus' audience were both well prepared to recognize situations in **Bacchides** where *fides* was at issue and well conditioned to judge a character's moral worth in relation to his *fides*. Such a situation occurs at 526-62, a point when Mnesilochus has already undone Chrysalus' first deception, told his father the truth, and returned the money. He now confronts his friend Pistoclerus, who, Mnesilochus erroneously thinks, has betrayed him by falling in love with his girlfriend. We are fortunate that discovery of a papyrus from Oxyrhynchus containing fragments of *Dis Exapaton* permits us to compare this episode from **Bacchides** directly with its model.[16] In the corresponding passage of *Dis Exapaton* the young lover, named Sostratos, soliloquizes on the relative guilt of his girlfriend, Bacchis, and his friend, whom Menander called Moschos. Direct comparison shows clearly how Plautus has reformulated the ethical aspect of the action, which in Menander turns on a notion of *dikē*, into terms of the Roman concept of obligation, *fides*.

In Menander the first part of 108-10, in which Sostratos tells Moschos of his grievance, is badly mutilated, but in light of Moschos' response in 111 the essence of Sostratos' charge appears distilled in the word *ēdikēkas* (110): Moschos has committed an injustice.[17] From this passage and Sostratos' soliloquy, where he notes the *adikēma* (101) committed against him, it is clear that Menander has dramatized the situation in terms of justice, *dikē*. Moreover, Sostratos charges Bacchis with the chief responsibility for the *adikēma*. Moschos, to whom he has given a sensitive trust involving the young woman, is not as harshly judged (100-102). In Plautus, Mnesilochus' judgment on Pistoclerus is not as forgiving.

In Menander, directness and economy characterize the exchange between Sostratos and Moschos. On the other hand, Plautus draws out this scene by having Mnesilochus baffle Pistoclerus, his imagined betrayer. Mnesilochus is wearing a long face and leaves it to Pistoclerus to discover what is wrong. Pistoclerus asks a series of questions and from the other's answers learns that a false friend, yet unnamed, has wronged Mnesilochus. In response to this partial revelation Pistoclerus inveighs against such false friends, ignorant that it is he himself who stands accused:

multi more isto atque exemplo uiuont, quos
    quom censeas
esse amicos, reperiuntur falsi falsimoniis,
lingua factiosi, inertes opera, sublesta fide.

(540-42)

There are many men like that. You think
    they're your friends,
they turn out to be perfidious perjurers,
all talk, no show; *fides* means nothing to
    them.

Lines 540-42 are the Plautine rendering of what Menander distills in one word.[18] But the difference between Plautus and Menander lies not only in the more extravagant rhetoric of the Roman poet. Plautus has reinterpreted the Greek idea, based on *dikē*, into a Roman one, based on *fides:* the *fides* of such men is *sublesta,* "of no consequence." The ethical terms in which Plautus has dramatized the conflict are reflected in the new name he has found for his unjustly accused protagonist: Pistoclerus. Built on Greek *pistis,* this name echoes in Greek the new Roman theme and underscores Pistoclerus' true innocence.

This Romanization of the ethical terms that frame the action affects the characterization of the two young men, who seem Roman in their attitude towards *fides.* In Menander, Sostratos expresses pity for the foolishness of his friend (99) and reserves the harsher judgment for Bacchus; in Plautus, the emphasis is on Mnesilochus' anger at his friend and Pistoclerus' guilt. Pistoclerus himself unknowingly articulates the nature of the charge: he has betrayed the *fides* placed in him. Recast in these Roman ethical terms, Pistoclerus' supposed betrayal of his friend represented, dramatically and ethically, a more serious matter for the audience of *Bacchides* than alleged betrayal in *Dis Exapaton* represented for its audience. Like the good Romans in the audience, both Mnesilochus and Pistoclerus have little sympathy for a betrayal of *fides.*

Plautus takes the Romanization of the young men a step further, intimating an aspect of *fides* associated with Roman political life, when Pistoclerus condemns friends who are *lingua factiosi. Factiosi* is a word closely associated with Roman politics and means something like "busily active on behalf of one's political faction." It thus implies a political aspect of *fides,* which could guarantee political as well as personal *amicitiae.*[19] This reference to politics, while relevant to *fides,* seems unconnected with the action, which concerns an imagined betrayal of a personal friendship—the success the young men seek is sexual, not electoral. So it is tempting to fault Plautus for lack of artistry. However, there is a rationale for this apparent infelicity, which, as I argue later, affected how the audience perceived the "Romanness" of Mnesilochus and Pistoclerus.

In the second deception Chrysalus gulls Nicobulus into believing that Cleomachus is Bacchis' husband, about to catch his "wife" in bed with Mnesilochus, her adulterous lover: *iam manufesto hominem opprimet* (858).[20] The wily slave heads the soldier off, getting Nicobulus to promise payment to him as compensation for the outrage (842-924). The key event in this scene reflects circumstances in both Menander's Athens and Plautus' Rome, where a husband who caught his wife and her lover in the act had the right to kill the adulterer. At the same time, the arrangement in which the adulterer is able to make amends to the injured husband with a payment of money seems peculiarly Greek. Thus the second deception, while depicting a legal situation common to both Athens and Rome, is likely to be Greek in origin.[21]

Though basically Greek in its legal background, the second deception turns on the Roman contractual practice of *stipulatio,* an institution which depends on *fides.*[22] At 865-66 as Cleomachus blusters about, threatening to kill Bacchis and her lover, Chrysalus urges his master to "come to terms" with the soldier through a payment of money: *pacisci cum illo paullula pecunia / potes* (865). It is a suggestion Nicobulus desperately adopts (cf. 866), especially after Cleomachus' bloodthirsty threat at 868-69: *nunc nisi ducenti Philippi redduntur mihi, / iam illorum ego animam amborum exsorbebo oppido.* The ambiguity of *redduntur* reflects the misunderstanding: the soldier intends that something which belongs to him be returned; Nicobulus, who believes Bacchis is his wife, understands *redduntur* in reference to the meeting of an obligation, namely, the payment of the debt incurred for the violation of the man's marriage.[23] He urges Chrysalus again and again to "come to terms" with the soldier (*pacisce,* 870, 871). Chrysalus steps forward and orchestrates a formal promise between the two men:

> CH. roga hunc tu, tu promitte huic. NI.
>   promitto, roga.
> CL. ducentos nummos aureos Philippos
>   probos
> dabin? CH. "dabuntur" inque. responde. NI.
>   dabo.

(881-83)

> CH. You! Ask him for the money. You,
>   promise him. NI. I promise—ask for it!
> CL. Will you give me 200 good gold philips?
> CH. Say, "They shall be given,"—answer! NI. I
>   shall give them.

In *stipulatio,* "the substance of the answer had to correspond to the question and the verb used in reply had to be the same as that of the question." The prime guarantor of such a contract was the *fides* of the promiser (cf. 878, *uerbum sat est*); no writing or witnesses were required, although "no one possessing ordinary caution would fail to avail himself of one of these modes of proof."[24] This dramatization of the *stipulatio* indicates that Nicobulus' promise is a legal and formal one, one which he was obligated to fulfill according to the oldest and most deeply felt principles of Roman morality.

Here again Plautus' introduction of Roman practices and ethical standards has helped to Romanize his Greek characters. Chrysalus and Nicobulus, though nominal Greeks, were as familiar with the conventions of *stipulatio* as the audience of **Bacchides**. Nicobulus eagerly asks Chrysalus when he should make his formal pledge: *quam mox dico "dabo"?* (880). In other words, Plautus characterizes them in some way as Romans. On the other hand, the soldier, who would likely have been a foreign mercenary in Menander's play, is still depicted as a foreigner but, here, one who is unfamiliar with *Roman* practices. Thus Chrysalus and Nicobulus instruct him in what he must say in the *stipulatio* (881). We note that later, when misinforming Cleomachus about the whereabouts of Bacchis, Chrysalus supplies the kind of details that might interest a foreigner and tourist: *Illa autem in arcem abiuit aedem uisere / Mineruae. nunc apertast* (900-901).[25]

In Nicobulus' *stipulatio* to Cleomachus, Plautus again has associated a public or political aspect of *fides* with a private arrangement. This is accomplished through the emphasis on Nicobulus' "Romanness" and the "non-Romanness" of the Greek soldier Cleomachus. As Gruen notes (*"Pistis* and *Fides"* 54-55), in their dealings with foreigners at this time Romans placed particular emphasis on the *fides* of the Roman people as a guarantee of Roman reliability, protection, and fairness. Characterized ethnically, as a promise made by a Roman to a Greek soldier, Nicobulus' *stipulatio* suggests an allusion to Rome's tendency to advertise its *fides* in its dealings with other nations.[26] Here again, Plautus appears to have suggested a political aspect of *fides* which seems inappropriate to the action. The high-minded allusion to Roman foreign conduct does not fit the circumstances of Nicobulus' *stipulatio,* which is a desperate promise to save his son from a disgraceful death in a tawdry affair. As with the reference to Roman politics implied by *factiosi,* I argue below that this apparent infelicity was intended to adjust the audience's perception of the characters' "Romanness."

Nicobulus' "Romanness" is confirmed by the unswerving determination he exhibits through the rest of the play to keep his promise. Both slave and master emphasize the connection between the promise and the certainty that Nicobulus will pay. This is the basis for Chrysalus' confidence at 968-70:

> is nunc ducentos
> nummos Philippos militi, quos
> dare se promisit, dabit.

The 200 philips he promised—now he'll give them to the soldier.

Nicobulus himself refers to his promise at 920 and 1051. At 1096-98, after he has learned the true relationship between the woman and the soldier, Nicobulus pays nonetheless, because of his promise:

> ita miles memorat meretricem esse eam quam
>   ille uxorem esse aiebat,
> omniaque ut quidque actum est memorauit,
>   eam sibi hunc annum conductam,
> relicuom id auri factum quod ego ei
>   stultissumus homo *promisissem* . . .

> The soldier told me that the woman Chrysalus
>   said was his "wife" is a "working girl."
> He told me all the details, that he'd hired her
>   for the year,
> and finally the truth about the money, which
>   I, like an idiot, *promised to pay.*

Promised to pay . . . and therefore had to. Of course, in real life Nicobulus would have been relieved of his obligation under such circumstances. But real life matters less here than the comic reality and the social assumptions behind it. The fulfillment of the second deception makes a kind of comic sense because it plays on the Roman ideal, if not practice, according to which one's *stipulatio* was strictly observed, as well as the Roman awareness of the moral obligation implied by *stipulatio.* Plautus' audience could have seen in Nicobulus a Roman fantasy of comic exaggeration, an extreme version of themselves. We do not know what was in Plautus' model at this point; however, there was no Greek equivalent to *stipulatio.* Nor does it seem likely that Menander would sacrifice social verisimilitude to the distorted demands of comic logic as Plautus has here.[27]

The Third Deception and the Case for Plautine Invention

The *stipulatio* and the emphasis on Nicobulus' *fides* we have just seen in the second deception anticipate the theme of the third deception. However, in contrast to the second deception, which appears to reflect Greek practices and realities regarding adultery, the third deception is thoroughly Roman in its preoccupations and motivation. This Roman tenor is signaled by the words Nicobulus speaks at the controversial lines 923-24. While the soldier is gone, Nicobulus orders Chrysalus to go into the house of the Bacchis sisters to read young Mnesilochus the riot act. Nicobulus himself wavers. First he resolves to confer again with his son before paying, because Chrysalus cannot be trusted (920-22). But then he abruptly changes his mind:

> uerum lubet etiam mi has pellegere denuo:
> aequomst tabellis consignatis credere.

But just the same, I'd like to read this letter
again.
You can depend on a document that's
signed and sealed.

The vagueness of these lines about Nicobulus' subsequent movements led Fraenkel rightly to suspect that Plautus ceased to follow *Dis Exapaton* at this point. However, while these lines sacrifice Menandrian clarity, they add thematic relevance to the coming deception. Fraenkel notes ("*Fides*") that *fides* may also be the quality which makes a person or thing worthy of trust or belief. The issue here is the *fides* of the letter, which Nicobulus foolishly takes for granted.[28] This neatly anticipates the manner in which he is about to be deceived again.[29] Not only is Nicobulus comically foolish in maintaining his own *fides,* he is incapable of estimating the *fides* of others. Thus the Roman motif of the third deception is introduced at the suspected point of Plautine insertion.

Chrysalus has been planning a third deception, a scheme to procure money for a wild party with the Bacchis sisters. He reenters bearing tablets which contain a second letter from Mnesilochus to his father, a second letter which, in fact, he has dictated to the boy. His entrance monologue is a triumphant Plautine *canticum* built around a grandiose, polyvalent metaphor comparing the mulcting of his master to the sack of Troy (925-78).

Nicobulus encounters Chrysalus after the Iliadic song. The slave falsely affirms that he has chastised Mnesilochus and presents his master with a letter from the boy. Fraenkel argues that the charm of this letter pointed to its Attic origins, that Plautus borrowed it from another Greek model.[30] The key moral issue, however, is Roman. After groveling apologies and expressions of shame (1007-9, 1013-16), Mnesilochus entreats his father for a second 200 gold philips:

> NI. (reading) "ego ius iurandum uerbis
>   conceptis dedi,
> daturum id me hodie mulieri ante uesperum,
> priu' quam a me abiret. nunc, pater, ne
>   peiierem
> cura atque abduce me hinc ab hac quantum
>   potest,
> quam propter tantum damni feci et flagiti."
>   (1028-32)

> "I gave my most solemn word of honor
> that I would give the woman the money today
>   before evening.
> before she left me. Now, father, arrange it
>   so that I won't have broken my word
> and take me away from here, as far as
>   possible from this woman,
> because of whom I have committed so much
>   outrage and suffered so much loss."

Mnesilochus pretends to need the additional money because he has promised it to the soldier's wife; if he cannot pay, he will have perjured himself. The formulae *ius iurandum* and *uerbis conceptis* characterize Mnesilochus' supposed promise as solemn and binding. The Roman solemnity of this promise echoes that of the earlier *stipulatio.* However, whereas that promise to pay reflects an actual Athenian law providing that an adulterer compensate the outraged husband, Mnesilochus' promise here has no such legal point of reference. We may be dealing with Plautine burlesque of Athenian law—in this case, it is the woman who is offered money. It seems less likely that such a travesty of Athenian law would be in Menander.

Nicobulus asks Chrysalus for his advice. The slave knows his master's attitude toward promises and slyly replies that he himself would rather pay the money than permit a situation to come about in which the boy would have committed perjury:

> dem potius aurum quam illum corrumpi sinam.
> duae condiciones sunt: utram tu accipias
>   uide:
> uel ut aurum perdas uel ut amator peiieret.

> I would rather pay the money than allow him
>   to be compromised morally.
> You have two choices; you be the judge:
> either you lose the money or lover-boy is a
>   liar.

Nicobulus realizes he must pay again; Chrysalus helps him rationalize the expense with the observation that the loss of more money is preferable to a public airing of *that* disgrace—that his son is a perjurer:

> si plus perdundum sit, perisse suauiust
> quam illud flagitium uolgo dispalescere.

> If more money must be lost, it is better to
>   lose it
> than to have that shameful deed aired in
>   public.

Thus Chrysalus pries even more money away from the old man. Nicobulus fears the disgrace Mnesilochus would incur by reneging on a solemn promise. In *flagitium uolgo dispalescere* there may be an allusion to the Roman practice of *flagitatio,* a right which allowed an offended party to expose and shame publicly a person who had failed to maintain his *fides.* Thus, the aspect of *fides* at issue here concerned the question of one's public reputation for trustworthiness.

The third deception succeeds only because Plautus has endowed Nicobulus, nominally a Greek, with a Roman sense of scrupulosity for *fides* which the old man carries to the point of farcical obsession. It matters not that he thinks the woman to whom Mnesilochus made his promise was herself an adulterous wife. Nor does it occur to Nicobulus that the *flagitium* his son may incur for breaking his word to such a woman may pale in comparison to the *flagitium* he has already admitted as an adulterer. I sense that Plautus' Roman audience had little difficulty recognizing a caricature of themselves in Nicobulus' obsession. Both this social caricature and the deception itself make "sense," albeit comic sense, in terms of Roman society only, which held *fides* as a core value. This, I suggest, points to the Plautine and Roman origins of the third deception.

The Social Context

It is now time to go beyond the parameters of this old problem in Plautine source criticism and to consider the antithesis between trust and deception in *Bacchides* in its social context. We have seen that the audience would have recognized many aspects of the wide nexus of conducts and behaviors implied by *fides,* both social and moral, public and personal, in the behavior and attitudes of Pistoclerus, Mnesilochus, and Nicobulus. But there is more to this play than a dramatic anatomy of *fides* in all its parts. The Plautine treatment of *fides* in *Bacchides* depicts a state of moral disorder, for Nicobulus is deceived repeatedly, not only despite his *fides* but in fact because of it. It is tempting to see Plautus here as a social critic—one who, for example, might mock the Roman value through Nicobulus' foolish gullibility. But Plautus was a comic playwright, not a social commentator; the implications of his treatment of *fides* are not so straightforward.

Bacchides is a play about deception as well as trust. Nicobulus' credulity and his comic concern to preserve his *fides* are the foils which show off the brilliant deceptions of his slave Chrysalus, who is as ready to deceive as his master is to be honest. Moreover, while Nicobulus' honesty is dramatized in the context of Roman *fides,* Chrysalus' talent for deceit is characterized as Greek. The social "message" of *Bacchides* needs to be considered in the context of the ethnic antithesis Plautus draws between these values.

Plautus emphasizes the "Greekness" of Chrysalus' deceptions through the use of Greek words. At 240 Chrysalus puns in Greek just before embarking on the first deception: *opus est chryso Chrysalo.* In the letter prepared for the second deception Chrysalus uses a Greek word (*sycophantias,* 740) to characterize the intrigue he plans. The same letter states that Chrysalus hopes his intriguing will enable Mnesilochus to "party like a Greek" (*congraecem,* 743).

Moreover, the contrast between Greek deceit and Roman honesty is implied in the *canticum* at 925-78. The *canticum* contains a fantastically elaborated metaphor in which Chrysalus compares his deceit of Nicobulus to the exploits of the Greeks at Troy: the *tabellae* on which the second letter has been written are the Trojan Horse; the letters in the *tabellae* are the Argive soldiers; Pistoclerus is Epius; Mnesilochus is Sino at one point, Paris at another; Cleomachus is Menelaus. Chrysalus' three deceptions are the *tria fata* which presaged the fall of Troy: the theft of the Palladion, the death of Troilus, and the razing of the Phrygian Gate. Chrysalus himself is Agamemnon; but above all, he is Ulysses, who, like the slave, was "bold and bad" (*audacem et malum,* 949).[31] Thus, Chrysalus' exploits are set in the context of one of the most famous events in Greek literature; the slave himself is compared to Ulysses, the cleverest and most deceitful of Greek heroes. Chrysalus' target is Nicobulus, who is compared to Troy and Priam, an allusion to Rome through Rome's Trojan ancestors. This contrast between Greek and Roman is further emphasized in the episode which immediately follows, the third deception, in which Chrysalus exploits his master's zeal to honor the Roman obligations of *fides.*

This ethnic antithesis between Roman *fides* and Greek deception appears to reflect a similar distinction made by the comic poet's society: Romans had *fides;* Greeks were dishonest.[32] This stereotype is reflected in the reason Polybius adduces for the difference between the Greek and Roman procedures of auditing public officials. The Greeks assumed corruption and ruthlessly audited their officials. For the Romans, the *fides* of the official was sufficient to guarantee proper conduct (6.56.14). Even when, *mirabile dictu,* a Roman was deceiving a Greek, as was the case when Q. Marcius Philippus deceived Perseus regarding Roman intentions prior to the Third Macedonian War, the stereotype prevailed. Certain senators, adding insult to injury, implied that Philippus' sharp practice had more in common with Greek *calliditas* than Roman *virtus* or *religio* (Livy 42.47.7). While this attack on Philippus was politically motivated, it nonetheless presupposes the existence of a Roman bias to which Philippus' opponents could appeal. The stereotype is reflected in anecdotes such as Cato's assertion that the Greeks speak with their lips, the Romans with their hearts (Plut. *Cato* 12.5), and in the proverbial oxymoron *fides Graeca.*[33] Plautus generously catered to the prejudices of his audience. His words for deception and trickery, such as *sycophantia, machinae,* and *techina,* are generally of Greek origin.[34] The point here is not the fairness or historical reliability of the antithesis; we are dealing with a self-serving myth. We should note that although the Greeks had no form of oral contract such as the *stipulatio,* they valued honesty, the maintenance of oaths, and the fulfillment of obligations nonetheless. No single nation, not even the Romans, has ever had a monopoly on these virtues.[35] In other contexts Romans themselves were ready to acknowledge their own corruptibility, which they were disposed to blame on the pernicious influence of Greek mores.[36] The Romans trumpeted their *fides* the loudest when they wished to distinguish themselves from other peoples, and from the Greeks in particular.

The construction of this stereotypical antithesis may be connected with two events: Rome's acquisition of an overseas empire and its first extensive confrontation with the achievements of Greek culture. Both events contributed to a crisis in traditional Roman values: on the one hand, empire furnished immense wealth and temptation; on the other, the Greek achievement in literature, philosophy, science, and art presented an intimidating standard. The Romans reexamined their traditions, but now in relation to Greek culture. There evolved a tendency for the Romans to think of themselves and the Greeks stereotypically and antithetically. The antitheses they constructed allowed the Romans to rationalize the achievements of Greek culture and reassure themselves regarding the superiority of their own. The concern here is Greek dishonesty and Roman *fides;* other antitheses from this period include those between Greek extravagance and Roman parsimony, Greek lasciviousness and Roman sexual restraint, Greek *levitas* and Roman *gravitas,* the Greek love of theoretical discussion and Roman pragmatism.[37]

This antithesis between Roman *fides* and Greek deceit is not historically fair or accurate. Nonetheless, it helps suggest the complexity of the Roman reaction towards Hellenism. In particular, *Bacchides* offers us the opportunity to consider the complex and contradictory aspects of the reaction in the context of an organic literary work.[38] We must make allowances for the genre: the aim of Roman comedy was laughter, not the accurate reflection of Roman social attitudes. Still, it is possible to infer from the exaggerations and distortions required by the comic genre how Plautus' audience may have actually felt about the Greeks.

At the center of *Bacchides* is the audacious and brilliant Chrysalus. Not only does he deceive Nicobulus three times, but after the first deception he warns his master to be on guard against more trickery (742-44). The slave even predicts the conditions under which Nicobulus will be deceived; he will not need to filch the money, for the old man will surrender it of his own accord (824-25). This audacity is based on Chrysalus' confidence that he knows how to manipulate his master; the melodramatic events that Chrysalus narrates in the first deception blind Nicobulus to the improbability of the story; in the second and third deceptions Chrysalus appeals to his master's reflexive and unthinking concern to protect his son and preserve his *fides.* Thus Chrysalus' Greek deceitfulness is served by his facility for persuasive talk, a talent which the Romans particularly associated with the Greeks.[39]

Of course the Romans were keen practitioners of rhetoric themselves, perhaps no less than the Greeks. But this reality did not stop them from constructing a stereotype of "Greek" rhetorical cleverness. On hearing a Greek speaker, many a Roman would have tempered his enjoyment with caution. In 155, for example, Romans thrilled to the public philosophical lectures of Carneades, Diogenes, and Critolaus, who were present in Rome as ambassadors representing Athens. Carneades in particular enthralled his audience on one day arguing in favor of the notion that justice exists in nature; on the next day he argued brilliantly against it. Cato was scandalized. The censor urged the Senate to decide the issue on which the philosophers had come as ambassadors and send them on their way, because, according to Pliny, *illo viro argumentante quid veri esset haut facile discerni posset (NH* 7.112).[40] Similarly, in *Bacchides* Chrysalus' brilliance also excites and enthralls a Roman audience; at the same time it encodes a Roman caution regarding the slave's Greek rhetorical cleverness. For Plautus has characterized the stock New Comic situation in which a clever slave deceives his foolish master in ethnic terms: the clever *Greek* slave deceives the trustworthy and overly trusting *Roman* master; Greek Ulixes dupes Roman Priam. Thus Chrysalus symbolizes an aspect of Greek accomplishment which fascinated the Romans but potentially caused them uneasiness. Perhaps we may speak more generally: Chrysalus' facile manipulation of Nicobulus might reflect an underlying Roman uneasiness regarding the superiority of Greek culture in general, in literature, philosophy, science, art, and architecture.

Plautus would not have amused his audience by suggesting they were inferior and leaving it at that. His humor worked by raising a matter of the Roman concern and then rendering it harmless. The acknowledgment of Greek superiority implicit in Chrysalus' triumph is mitigated by several strategies. First, Nicobulus' regard for his *fides* represents both the clearest suggestion of his Romanness and at the same time the reason why he is deceived. Thus, for all his foolishness, there is something admirable about the old man in defeat: he is the only character in the play who upholds a principle, even when it causes him material loss. Second, Nicobulus' adherence to the higher morality of *fides* also helps to rationalize his defeat. It is not an even contest when one antagonist cleaves to a demanding code of behavior and the other can do whatever it takes to win.

Next, the ethnic symbolism of Chrysalus' triumph is blunted because Nicobulus, for all that he kept his *fides,* is not really a Roman but a Greek character in a *fabula palliata.* His eagerness to guarantee his son's reputation for good faith ignores Mnesilochus' confessed (falsely, no less!) disgrace as an adulterer. Nicobulus observes the punctilio of *fides* rather than its true spirit. Thus, Plautus simultaneously suggests Nicobulus'

Romanness, through his concern for *fides,* and denies it, through Nicobulus' inability to get it right. Nicobulus' moral deficiency is also apparent at the end of **Bacchides.** After an initial show of resistance, Nicobulus finally succumbs to the seductions of Bacchis of Athens when she offers to return half the money cheated from him. With Philoxenus, the other *senex* and Pistoclerus' father, he joins the Bacchis sisters and the two young men in their revels. Thus, the old man's delinquency results from a combination of prurience and greed. Plautus provides an ethnic rationale for this fall from grace which goes beyond the previous depiction of Nicobulus as a Roman manqué. For Nicobulus surrenders to temptation because he is a Greek. He will participate in the same revelry condemned earlier as *congraecari* (743). Plautus further suggests the Greekness of this sort of celebration early in the final scene itself. While he is still in an attitude of resistance, Nicobulus asks Philoxenus if he is "in love," that is, if he intends to join the party. *"Nai gar!"* exclaims Philoxenus in Greek (1162). Like his deficient Romanness, Nicobulus' Greekness provided Plautus' audience with an assuaging ethnic rationale for the old man's delinquency.

Two other episodes suggesting the Romanness of characters in **Bacchides** are undercut. When Mnesilochus wrongly suspects his friend Pistoclerus of betrayal, the imagined wrong is dramatized as a breach of *fides,* and both young men seem rather Roman in their regard for the ethic. However, when Pistoclerus condemns those false friends who are *lingua factiosi . . . sublesta fide,* he describes his relationship to Mnesilochus in the language of Roman politics, with no apparent relevance to the action. The inappropriate reference to an aspect of *fides* associated with Roman politics helped remind Plautus' audience that despite their concern for the Roman ethic, these young men were not really Romans after all. In the second episode Plautus depicts Nicobulus' *stipulatio* to Cleomachus in ethnic terms, as an arrangement between a Roman and a foreigner; this ethnic contrast alludes to the conduct of Roman foreign policy, in which *fides* served as a guarantee of Roman fairness to subject states. But Nicobulus is promising to save his son from a disgraceful death, and this high-minded allusion does not fit the circumstances of his *stipulatio* and undercuts the suggestion of Nicobulus' Romanness. Thus these references to Roman society, far from being incidental Plautine infelicities, were essential to the Roman poet's subtle presentation of the "ethnicity" of his characters.

Finally, the apparent superiority of Greek Chrysalus over the "Roman" characters he manipulates is further undercut by the fact that the clever slave, for all his cleverness, is still a slave, and wishes to remain one. After the reversal of the first deception, when he warns his master to expect more trickery, Chrysalus predicts that Nicobulus will offer him his freedom and he will refuse it (828-29). Thus, Chrysalus' *calliditas* reassuringly presents no threat to the existing order of things and may be dismissed as a trivial and servile sort of cleverness.

Final Remarks

In the contrast between Roman *fides* and Greek deceit in **Bacchides** we may discern some aspects of the Roman response to the Greeks and Hellenism. Chrysalus' manipulation of the "Roman" characters suggests anxiety at Greek intellectual superiority. However, Plautus renders this superiority harmless and allows his audience to dismiss it. He accomplishes this through a subtle modulation of the ethnic characterization of his "Roman" characters that simultaneously suggests and undercuts their Romanness; Nicobulus, Mnesilochus, and Pistoclerus are not really Romans, but Greeks. Chrysalus, for all his cleverness, is a slave and knows his place. Whatever the trivial advantages of Greek *calliditas,* the Romans possess *fides.*

Bacchides itself may represent an assertion of Roman superiority. With the addition of a third deception, Plautus in a sense surpassed his model—a likely ambition in any artist, perhaps more so when the artist was Roman and the master Greek. Plautus himself may allude to this achievement in the course of **Bacchides** itself, when Chrysalus boasts:

> non mihi isti placent Parmenones, Syri,
> qui duas aut tris minas auferunt eris.
>
> (649-50)

> I don't like those Parmenos and Syruses
> who steal two or three measly minae from
> their masters.

Syrus was the slave in Menander's play. In Chrysalus' declaration of superiority over Syrus may be Plautus' claim for the superiority of his **Bacchides,** with three deceptions, over Menander's *Dis Exapaton,* with two.[41]

Notes

[1] Fraenkel's hypothesis, originally presented in *Quaestiones* 100-104, was further developed in *Elementi* 57-58 and n. 2. Williams's response is included in the appendix to his article "Construction of *Pseudolus*" 446-55. Fraenkel's retraction is noted in the supplementary notes to *Elementi* 403. For a bibliography of the response to Fraenkel see Lefèvre, "Plautus-Studien II" 520-21. To the critics I would add Finette, "Fourberies." To Fraenkel's supporters add Thierfelder, "Generi in Plauto."

[2] Lefèvre, "Plautus-Studien II." Primmer, *Handlungsgliederung.*

[3] This first step is useful because however we may feel about his theory of *contaminatio*, Fraenkel has noted important clues that Plautus significantly altered his original; on the other hand, Williams's response, while the most cogent defense of the idea that all three deceptions were originally in Menander, is nonetheless flawed.

[4] Fraenkel, *Quaestiones* 100-102 and *Elementi* 57-58 and n. 2.

[5] The following summary of Fraenkel's views regarding the significance of 923-24 (with some of my own amplification) is drawn from his *Elementi* 57-58 n. 2.

[6] Skutsch, "Notes," has argued that Nicobulus' presence onstage at 923 may be explained simply: Plautus wanted him to be onstage but not to notice the arrival of Chrysalus, thus creating space for the *canticum*. Skutsch further observes that Nicobulus would have also provided an amusing visual counterpoint to Chrysalus.

[7] Williams, "Construction of *Pseudolus*" 452, argues that the Nicobulus character may have waited onstage for his slave to return, covering his absence with a monologue, and acknowledged the slave directly on his reentrance. Primmer, *Handlungsgliederung* 84-94, argues that Nicobulus exited at 920 to the forum, clearing the stage for the end of the fourth act.

[8] In Ritschl's *Opuscula Philologica* II 365, quoted by Williams, "Construction of *Pseudolus*" 453.

[9] I concur with Williams, "Construction of *Pseudolus*" 453 n. 1, in rejecting an alternative accounting which regards the two letter deceptions as a single one. The two letter deceptions share a method, but are two distinct acts of deception. For the bibliography on this question see Lefèvre, "Plautus-Studien II" 520-21.

[10] Fraenkel, *Elementi* 383-84: "Essi [sc. Plautus' models] debbono fornirgli la materia prima per le sue produzioni ciò che egli non sa creare di suo, la vera e propria invenzione drammatica e la condotta di un dialogo che promuova l'avanzare dell'azione."

[11] Apart from the arguments which follow, it should be noted that Williams's interest in the problem is connected with his thought-provoking but problematic attempt to determine the relative dating of *Bacchides* and *Pseudolus*. The general consensus since Ritschl has been that *Pseudolus* came first. Williams reaches the opposite conclusion in an analysis which compares motifs common to both plays. He argues that in *Bacchides* these common motifs are used consistently with the plot and thus derive from the Greek original; on the other hand, in *Pseudolus* the same motifs can be shown to be Plautine additions or reworkings of the model. Williams implies that this more independent use of the motifs in *Pseudolus* indicates Plautus' poetic development; therefore *Bacchides,* not *Pseudolus,* is the earlier play. The third deception involves one of the motifs in question, where the master himself insists the slave take some money (cf. 825 and 1059-66). According to Williams, *Bacchides,* the earlier play, was here following its Greek model. On the other hand, if the view is adopted that Plautus has added a third deception on his own initiative, Williams's earlier date for *Bacchides* would be undermined. See Questa, *Parerga* 15-22, for a review of the various approaches to the question of the date of *Bacchides*. Questa himself endorses the traditional view that *Pseudolus* came first.

[12] See the concise and helpful summary of this scholarship in Lowe, "Originality."

[13] Primmer, *Handlungsgliederung*. Earlier Büchner, *Literaturgeschichte* 92-96, had suggested without arguments that the third deception was a free creation by Plautus. Lefèvre, "Plautus-Studien II" 520-21, also argues that Plautus has added the third deception, in a complex reconstruction that distinguishes what is Plautine and what is Menandrian—but in greater detail than the sources allow. According to Lefèvre, Plautus created two letter deceptions from what was a single deception by letter in Menander. Plautus retained the circumstances of the Menandrian deception in his first letter deception, but composed a new letter for it, the one in which Chrysalus warns Nicobulus to be on his guard. The original Menandrian letter, with appropriate modification, was transposed to the second letter deception, Plautine in origin, in which Mnesilochus asks for a second 200 philips to give to Bacchis. Lefèvre's reconstruction has been endorsed by Barsby, *Bacchides* 170.

[14] It is neither possible nor necessary here to determine the "original" meaning of *fides*. Fraenkel, *"Fides,"* sees the original sense in the protection offered the weak by the strong, which he argues is less a moral and more a practical or social commitment. On the other hand, Heinze, *"Fides,"* stresses the moral compulsion implied by *fides,* a quality clearly present in Plautus. The related connection between *fides* and power is emphasized by Piganiol, *"Venire in fidem,"* who sees *fides* as a quality akin to *imperium,* inspiring confidence in the authority of the leader. Hellegouarc'h *Vocabulaire* 23-40, emphasizes the social importance of *fides*. A useful summary of theoretical views on *fides* is found in Dahlheim, *Struktur und Entwicklung* 26-31.

[15] See Gruen, *"Pistis* and *Fides."*

[16] Following the lead of Handley, *Comparison,* much has been written about these passages. In particular, I

cite Gaiser, "*Bacchides* und *Dis Exapaton*"; Questa, *Parerga* 46-54; Bain, *"Plautus uortit barbare"*; Schönbeck, *Beiträge* 91-130; Arnott, *Menander, Plautus, Terence* 38-40. For bibliography up to 1975 see Fogazza, "Plauto 1935-1975"; up to 1976, Segal, "Scholarship."

[17] The line references to Menander are those of Sandbach, *Menandri Reliquiae Selectae*.

[18] Controversy surrounds 540-42, which are part of a passage (540-51) omitted by the Ambrosian manuscript. The passage was defended by Leo, *Forschungen* 131, who says that the description of the false friend is certainly derived from Menander. Tränkle, "Zwei Stellen," led the attack on Plautinity of the lines. His arguments were endorsed by Schönbeck, *Beiträge* 115-18, and Bain, *"Plautus uortit barbare."* Tränkle's attack on the passage is comprehensive but unconvincing. Most surprising among advantages he sees with the removal of the lines is that the scene would have more *Zielstrebigkeit*. However, readers of Plautus would be surprised if the poet himself had held such "purposiveness" as an aesthetic desideratum. Indeed, the passage seems a fairly characteristic example of Plautine expansion, transforming the Greek material in accordance with a Roman theme. More significantly, a key phrase, *sublesta fide,* is echoed at *Persa* 348 (*fides sublestior*), a scene in which *fides* has similar thematic importance. Handley, *Comparison* 17, may well be right, that the passage was omitted initially to shorten the scene in production and that this abridgement was eventually adopted by editors who observed the passage was inorganic and had no parallel in Menander. See also Questa, *Parerga* 49-54.

[19] Plautus frequently colors the language of personal relationships with the language of Roman politics. See Earl, "Terminology in Plautus" and the first chapter of his *Tradition* 11-43.

[20] For a detailed analysis of this scene see Schönbeck, *Beiträge* 131-59.

[21] See Barsby, *Bacchides* 164, who notes that *manufestus* is Roman legalese. On Roman legal usage see Corbett, *Marriage* 127-46. Roman law provided for compensation of the outraged husband, but from the offending woman's dowry. On the situation under Athenian law see Harrison, *Law* 32-38, and Harris, "Seduction."

[22] On the importance of the *stipulatio* in *Pseudolus* see Williams, "Construction of *Pseudolus*" 424-46.

[23] On *reddere* see Williams, "Construction of *Pseudolus*" 445-46.

[24] Watson, *Private Law* 117.

[25] It is interesting to note that the soldier uses some odd and extravagant expressions which perhaps may suggest his foreignness: *nam neque Bellona mi umquam neque Mars creduat, / ni illum exanimalem faxo, si conuenero, / niue exheredem fecero uitae suae* (847-49). Chrysalus, in fact, may even be mocking Cleomachus' manner of speech when he threatens to make the soldier (approximately) "more full of holes than a dirge for a dormouse"—*te faciam, si tu me inritaueris, / confossiorem* (888-89)—gibberish which Cleomachus, in his ignorance of the local patois, mistakes for some awful form of retaliation. For a survey of earlier views on these lines see Schönbeck, *Beiträge* 148-49.

[26] If MacMullen, "Hellenizing," is correct and Plautus' audience consisted of the Roman elite, they would have recognized this allusion without great difficulty. However, it seems likely that even the Roman hoi polloi were acquainted with the rhetoric which promoted Rome's image abroad by advertising its *fides*.

[27] The father may well have paid the money then and there, completing the second of the two deceptions in *Dis Exapaton*. Williams, "Construction of *Pseudolus*" 426-27, suggests that the *stipulatio* at *Pseudolus* 115-16 replaces a simple promise in the Greek play. According to Primmer, *Handlungsgliederung* 74-80, the Nicobulus character followed the soldier to the forum to pay the money at the conclusion of this scene.

[28] It is possible that this reference contains a topicality that is lost to us. Public records in Rome, *tabellae,* were not always carefully maintained, as Cicero indicates in *Pro Archia* (9), noting that in the case of a particular practor *calamitas omnem tabularum fidem resignasset*. A similar scandal may have been behind Nicobulus' naive remark at 924.

[29] Questa, *Parerga* 63-64 n. 51, notes Gian Biagio Conte's view *per litteras,* that these lines are ironically relevant in that Nicobulus, warned not to trust Chrysalus, falls victim to deceit by not trusting him.

[30] Fraenkel, *Quaestiones* 102-3: "Quam actionem nulla Graeca fabula adhibita Plautum libere finxisse ut parum uerisimile est, plane refutatur eximia epistulae uenustate. Talia Attici poetae stilum redolent." Lefèvre, "Plautus-Studien II" 522-25, and Primmer, *Handlungsgliederung* 65-70, 84-88, have argued that the second letter derives mainly from *Dis Exapaton*.

[31] Jocelyn, "Chrysalus," argues that this *canticum* has been subjected to extensive post-Plautine interpolation. However, I accept its essential Plautinity and the view expressed by Slater, *Performance* 111 n. 26, that "Jocelyn has done a real service in minutely describing the shifts within the monologue, but all or nearly all are in the imaginative range of one poet and the performance powers of one actor." See Lefèvre, "Plautus-

Studien V," for a more detailed defense of the Plautinity of the metaphorical twists and turns in the *canticum*.

[32] On the Roman contrast between Greek deceit and Roman honesty see Petrochilos, *Attitudes* 43-45.

[33] Plautus refers to *fides Graeca* at *Asinaria* 199.

[34] For other examples of Greek terms for deception in Plautus see Brotherton, *Intrigue*.

[35] Certain aspects of *fides* and *pistis* may be closer than the common view has allowed. Gruen, *"Pistis and Fides"* 64-66, has argued that *pistis* played a role similar to *fides* in the conduct of relations between Greek states, including the regulation of arrangements between stronger and weaker powers. However, he does not address the question whether *pistis*, like *fides*, regulated the relationship between stronger and weaker individuals.

[36] For a discussion of Roman perceptions of Roman moral corruption see Lintott, "Moral Decline."

[37] Most of the evidence for these stereotypes is from the late Republic. However, as Gruen suggests, *Hellenistic World* 260-66, it appears that the late Republican stereotypes had their roots in Plautus' period. For other discussions of the Roman stereotype of the Greek see Petrochilos, *Attitudes* 35-53, and Balsdon, *Romans and Aliens* 30-40.

[38] Petrochilos, *Attitudes,* examines the complexity and contradictions in the Roman response to Hellenism. His work is useful as a collection of evidence for Roman attitudes; however, much of the evidence he has assembled is post-Plautine and taken out of the context in which it originally appears. Gruen, *Studies,* sees a tension between Rome's private embrace of Greek culture and a public effort to distance the state from Hellenism and assert what is distinctly Roman; such tensions were at play in Rome's reception of the cult of Cybele in 201, the suppression of the Bacchus cult in 186, the burning of the Pythagorean books in 181, and periodic expulsions of Greek philosophers and rhetoricians. He perceives a similar ambivalence to Greek culture in Plautus, for all that the poet worked in a Greek genre. MacMullen, "Hellenizing," discusses the motivation behind Roman Hellenism, which was self-promotional as well as aesthetic. He distinguishes between aspects of Greek culture which received acceptance, such as literature and architecture, and aspects rejected, such as homosexuality and luxury.

[39] On the Roman stereotype of the Greek as a clever talker see Petrochilos, *Attitudes* 35-45, and Balsdon, *Romans and Aliens* 32-33.

[40] On Cato and the embassy see Astin, *Cato* 174-77. Plutarch's account of the incident (*Cato Maior* 22-

23.1) stresses that Cato was hostile to Greek philosophy in general.

[41] I thank W. Geoffrey Arnott, Sander Goldberg, Niall Slater, and my colleagues at Ohio University, James Andrews and Stephen Hays, for their helpful criticism on earlier versions of this paper.

Bibliography

Arnott, W. Geoffrey, *Menander, Plautus, Terence.* Oxford: Clarendon Press, 1975.

Astin, A. E. *Cato the Censor.* Oxford: Clarendon Press, 1978.

Bain, David. *"Plautus uortit barbare:* Plautus, *Bacchides* 526 and Menander, *Dis exapaton* 102-12." In *Creative Imitation and Latin Literature,* edited by David West and Tony Woodman, 17-34. Cambridge: Cambridge University Press, 1979.

Balsdon, J. P. V. D. *Romans and Aliens.* Chapel Hill: University of North Carolina Press, 1979.

Barsby, John. *Plautus Bacchides.* Oak Park, Ill.: Aris & Phillips, 1986.

Brotherton, Blanche. *The Vocabulary of Intrigue in Roman Comedy.* Menasha, Wis.: George Banta, 1926.

Büchner, Karl. *Römische Literaturgeschichte.* 4th ed. Stuttgart: A. Kröner, 1968.

Corbett, P. E. *The Roman Law of Marriage.* Oxford: Clarendon Press, 1930.

Dahlheim, Werner. *Struktur und Entwicklung des römischen Völkerrechts im dritten und zweiten Jahrhundert v. Chr.* Munich: C. H. Beck, 1968.

Earl, D.C. *The Moral and Political Tradition of Rome.* Ithaca: Cornell University Press, 1967.

———. "Political Terminology in Plautus." *Historia* 9 (1960) 234-43.

Finette, Lucien. "Le *Dis Exapaton* et les *Bacchides:* deux ou trois fourberies?" *Cahiers des Etudes Anciennes* 15 (1983) 47-60.

Fogazza, Donatella. "Plauto 1935-1975." *Lustrum* 19 (1976) 232-37.

Fraenkel, Eduard. *De Media et Nova Comoedia Quaestiones Selectae.* Dissertation, Göttingen (Officina Academica Dieterichiana), 1912.

———. "Zur Geschichte des Wortes *Fides*." *RhM* 7 (1916) 187-99.

————. *Elementi Plautini in Plauto*. Translated by Franco Munari. Florence: "La Nuova Italia," 1960.

Gaiser, Konrad. "Die plautinischen *Bacchides* und Menanders *Dis Exapaton*." *Philologus* 114 (1970) 51-87.

Gruen, Erich. "Greek *Pistis* and Roman *Fides*." *Athenaeum* 60 (1982) 50-68.

————. *The Hellenistic World and the Coming of Rome*. Berkeley and Los Angeles: University of California Press, 1984.

————. *Studies in Greek Culture and Roman Policy*. Leiden: Brill, 1990.

Handley, E. W. *Plautus and Menander: A Study in Comparison*. London: University College, 1968.

Harris, E. M. "Did the Athenians Regard Seduction as a Worse Crime than Rape?" *CQ* 40 (1990) 370-77.

Harrison, A. R. W. *The Law of Athens: The Family and Property*. Oxford: Clarendon Press, 1968.

Heinze, Richard. "*Fides*." *Hermes* 64 (1929) 140-66.

Hellegouarc'h, Joseph. *Le vocabulaire latin des relations et des partis politiques sous la République*. Paris: Les Belles Lettres. 1963.

Jocelyn, H. D. "Chrysalus and the Fall of Troy (Plautus, *Bacchides* 925-978)." *HSCP* 73 (1969) 135-52.

Lefèvre, Eckard. "Plautus-Studien II: Die Brief-Intrige in Menanders *Dis exapaton* und ihre Verdoppelung in den *Bacchides*." *Hermes* 106 (1978) 518-38.

————. "Plautus-Studien V: Plautus' Iliupersis (*Bacchides* 925-77)." *Hermes* 116 (1988) 209-27.

Leo, Friedrich. *Plautinische Forschungen*. 2d ed. Berlin: Weidmann, 1912.

Lintott, A. W. "Imperial Expansion and Moral Decline in the Roman Republic." *Historia* 21 (1972) 626-38.

Lowe, J. C. B. "Aspects of Plautus' Originality in the *Asinaria*." *CQ* 41 (1992) 152-75.

MacMullen, Ramsey. "Hellenizing the Romans (2d Century B.C.)." *Historia* 40 (1991) 419-38.

Petrochilos, Nicholas. *Roman Attitudes to the Greeks*. Athens: National and Capodistrian University of Athens, Faculty of Arts, 1974.

Piganiol, André. "*Venire in fidem*." *RIDA* 5 (1950) 339-47.

Primmer, Adolf. *Handlungsgliederung in Nea und Palliata: Dis Exapaton und Bacchides*. Sitzungsberichte der Österreichische Akademie der Wissenschaft, Phil.-hist. Klasse, 441. Vienna, 1984.

Questa, Cesare. *Parerga Plautina*. Urbino: Università degli Studi di Urbino, 1985.

Sandbach, F. H. *Menandri Reliquiae Selectae*. Oxford: Clarendon Press, 1972.

Schönbeck, H. P. *Beiträge zur Interpretation der plautinischen Bacchides*. Düsseldorf: Mannold, 1981.

Segal, Erich. "Scholarship on Plautus 1965-1976." *CW* 74, no. 7 (April-May 1981) 353-433.

Skutsch, Otto. "Notes on Plautus' *Bacchides*." *HSCP* 86 (1982) 79-80.

Slater, Niall W. *Plautus in Performance: The Theatre of the Mind*. Princeton: Princeton University Press, 1985.

Thierfelder, Andreas. "Su alcuni generi particolari del comico in Plauto." *Dioniso* 46 (1975) 89-109.

Tränkle, Hermann. "Zu zwei umstrittenen Stellen der plautinischen *Bacchides*." *Museum Helveticum* 32 (1975) 115-23.

Watson, Alan. *Roman Private Law around 200 B.C.* Edinburgh: Edinburgh University Press, 1971.

Williams, Gordon. "Some Problems in the Construction of Plautus' *Pseudolus*." *Hermes* 84 (1956) 424-55.

FURTHER READING

Bruster, Douglas. "Comedy and Control: Shakespeare and the Plautine *Poeta*." *Comparative Drama* 24, No. 3 (Fall 1990): 217-31.

    Argues that a character common in Shakespeare's works—the "controlling playwright figure"—is a derivation of Plautus's *poeta*, or clever slave.

Forehand, Walter E. "Irony in Plautus' *Amphitruo*." *American Journal of Philology* XCII, No. 4 (October 1971): 633-51.

    Analyzes *Amphitruo* in terms of ironies of language and plot and comments on "the implications of these ironies for our view of the play as a whole."

Goldberg, Sander M. "Act to Action in Plautus' *Bacchides*." *Classical Philology* 85, No. 3 (July 1990): 191-201.

Compares *Bacchides* to its Greek model, Menander's *Dis Exapaton* and argues that the primary difference between the two works is a matter of "fundamental changes in the idea of comic theater."

Handley, E. W. *Menander and Plautus: A Study in Comparison.* London: H. K. Lewis & Co., Ltd., 1968, 23 p.
Offers an assessment of Plautus's literary debt to Menander, his Greek forerunner.

Levin, Harry. "Two Comedies of Errors." In *Refractions, Essays in Comparative Literature*, pp. 128-50. New York: Oxford University Press, 1966.
Examines the comic techniques used by Plautus in *Menaechmi* and the ways in which these techniques influenced Shakespeare and other dramatists.

Lowe, J. C. B. "The *Virgo Callida* of Plautus, *Persa*." *Classical Quarterly* 39, No. 2 (1989): 390-99.
Examines the theme of trickery and deception in *Persa*.

————. "Prisoners, Guards, and Chains in Plautus, *Captivi*." *American Journal of Philology* 112, No. 1 (Spring 1991): 29-44.
Explores staging issues in *Captivi* and identifies contradictory evidence of Plautus's intentions as to how it should be performed.

O'Bryhim, Shawn. "The Originality of Plautus' *Casina*." *American Journal of Philology* 110, No. 1 (Spring 1989): 81-103.
Argues that Plautus used two comedies as a basis for *Casina*, made changes within portions of each comedy, and blended these portions with his own material in order to create a "coherent, tightly constructed plot."

Prescott, Henry W. "The 'Amphitruo' of Plautus." *Classical Philology* VIII, No. 1 (January 1913): 14-22.
Dissects F. Leo's 1911 critical analysis of the play and argues that *Amphitruo* "is the most important document . . . for reconstructing the antecedents of the New Comedy of Hellenistic Athens."

Slater, Niall W. *Plautus in Performance: The Theatre of the Mind.* Princeton, N.J.: Princeton University Press, 1985, 190 p.
Attempts to reconstruct both the initial performances and original audiences of Plautus's plays.

Zagagi, Netta. "Tradition and Originality in Plautus: Studies of the Amatory Motifs in Plautine Comedy." *Hypomnemata* 62 (1980): 15-159.
Analyzes Plautus's debt to his Greek predecessors for the depiction of love in his plays.

Additional coverage of Plautus's life and career is contained in the following source published by Gale Research: *Drama Criticism*, Vol. 6.

Po Chü-i

772-846

(Also known as Pai Chü-i) Chinese poet and political writer.

INTRODUCTION

One of the most prolific of the T'ang poets, Po Chü-i was among the most popular and widely read writers of his time. Po devoted most of his life to political service, and his work profoundly influenced the course of Eastern literature—particularly in China and Japan—reconfiguring the relationship between a government and its people.

Biographical Information

Po Chü-i was born in Hsincheng, Honan Province, in 772. His father and grandfather were minor bureaucrats in the local government, and Po was raised in relative poverty and an unstable political climate. Rebellion continued for almost thirty years after the uprisings led by An Lu-shan and Shih Ssu-ming in 756, and the empire's lands and revenues had significantly decreased. The taxation necessary to sustain China's armies—which often pillaged the towns of its own countrymen—put a burden on Po's family that he would remember throughout his life; from personal experience he developed an acute understanding of China's social problems. When Po's father died in 794, it precluded the possibility that Po would study for the provincial exams to gain government service, and he began to wander Hupeh, Kiangsu, and Chekiang looking for work. Although his faith in government was faltering, he studied independently and passed the difficult examinations for Advanced Scholar in 800.

Po and the other members of his class became good friends and formed an intellectual force in the court of Emperor Te-tsung. Although the group faced resistance by other political factions, Po was named Imperial Library Collator. When Te-tsung died in 805, followed shortly by his son Shun-tsung, Hsien-tsung came to the throne and appointed Po clerical supervisor at Chou-chih District. Po became a renowned advisor in the region, so much so that Emperor Hsien-tsung named him an official critic of his court in 808. The emperor was open to scholarly criticism of his administrative policies, and Po composed written and oral remonstrations that secured the emperor's respect and trust.

Po's mother and daughter died in 811, and after a period of mourning, Po was assigned to be advisor to the Crown Prince. In that position, however, he was too outspoken on political matters and was shortly demoted to marshal in Chiang-chou, where his duties were minimal. There he read the poetry of T'ao Yüan-ming, Hsieh Ling-yün, Li Po, Tu Fu, and Wei Ying-wu, and he composed poems and conversed with Zen monks in the local monastery. His poetic treatment of the troop rebellion in the Huai River area garnered him many friends and supporters, and he became governor of Chung-chou in 818.

After Hsien-tsung's death in 820, Po returned to Ch'ang-an, where he once again became a court official, this time for Emperor Mu-tsung. Mu-tsung was not as open to Po's criticism as his predecessor had been, and Po was soon transferred from the capital. Declining health made him eager to retire, but the death of Mu-tsung in 824 and the instatement in 826 of Wen-tsung, who was sympathetic to the positions of Po and his colleagues, brought Po to Ch'ang-an to head the Palace Library. There he continued his study of the poetry of his forefathers. Further health problems forced him to take a part-time post with the Crown Prince in Loyang, where he stayed until retiring from public life in 842. Po died in 846 and was buried, by his request, at a Buddhist settlement by the Lung-men Mountains of Loyang.

Major Works

In 815, Po Chü-i wrote in a letter to his friend Yüan Chen that poetry should serve the state and society; an acute understanding of the plight of the poor inform many of the 3,840 pieces in his *Collected Works* and has earned Po the appellation "The People's Poet." Some of his more widely read poems, written in the New Music Bureau Style, attempted to restore Confucianism in order to strengthen the moral fabric of the society and insure a better life for the poor. Others, such as "The Imperial Collector of Poetry," encourage his emperor to be attentive to the needs of the people. But the didacticism of Po's poetry should not be overstated; his lyrical prowess in such frequently anthologized poems as "Lament Everlasting" and "Lute Song" and his many songs in praise of drinking, friendship, and nature contributed just as significantly to his renown.

Critical Reception

Unlike the poetry of Li Po and Tu Fu, a large part of whose work has been lost, more than 2,800 of Po Chü-i's poems have survived, mostly because of the meticulous work of Po himself to preserve them. Although he produced a number of short collections of songs, such as the ten *Songs of Chin* and, in 810, fifty *New Songs*, his full book did not appear until 824, when Yüan Chen edited a fifty-chapter collection called *Ch'ang Ch'ing Chi*. Po followed by editing two more collections, of twenty and five chapters, respectively. He later collected all three of these works, along with seventeen chapters exchanged between Po and Yüan, five chapters exchanged with Liu Yü-hsi, and ten chapters about Po's experiences in Lo-yang, into his *Collected Works* of 845. Po considered the *Collected Works* to be definitive and complete. Copies were given to five Chinese temples, where they were copied and transmitted throughout the Eastern world, especially in China, Japan, and Korea. Contemporary scholars generally rely on the so-called Naba and Ma texts copied by Japanese scholars Naba Doen in 1618 and Ma Yüan-tiao in 1604; unfortunately, the sources on which these texts were based remain unknown.

Critical Reception

Po was a popular poet and politician in China, and his poetry was eagerly sought and translated by Japanese and Korean travelers to T'ang China. In the preface to *Ch'ang Ch'ing Chi*, Yüan Chen writes, "Po's poems were found on the walls of palace buildings, monasteries, temples, and post stations; they were frequently on the lips of cow-herds and grooms as well as the nobles and womenfolk." Critics find in Po Chü-i a poet whose relevance to his contemporaries cannot be overestimated and whose mark has been indelibly left on Eastern literature. Several recent essays and books written in Chinese, Japanese, and English discuss his poems, prose writings, political career, and life, as well as his influence on Chinese and Japanese literature.

PRINCIPAL WORKS

Ch'ang Ch'ing Chi (poetry) 824
Po's Collected Works (poetry) 845
Po shih ch'ang ch'ing chi, 71 chüan (poetry) 1606

PRINCIPAL ENGLISH TRANSLATIONS

Po Chü-i as a Censor: His Memorials Presented to Emperor Hsien-Tsung during the Years 808-810 (translated by Eugene Feifel) 1961
Translations from Po Chü-i's Collected Works, 4 vols. (translated by Howard S. Levy) 1971-78

CRITICISM

Kwei Chen (essay date 1953)

SOURCE: Kwei Chen, "Po Chu-i: People's Poet," in *China Reconstructs*, Vol. 4, July/August, 1953, pp. 31-5.

[*In the following essay, Chen expounds on the social criticism found in Po Chu-i's poetry.*]

Popular, bitter and lyrical, the poet Po Chu-i (772-846 A.D.) is no stranger to people outside China. For over a thousand years, his name has been inseparably connected with Chinese poetry, which is of course an integral element of Chinese civilization. But today Po has a fresh significance for Chinese poetry lovers and for the people of the world. The new, correct interpretation of Chinese history strengthens our appreciation of his contribution to the humanitarian mainstream of world literature, and to the "people first" tradition which was at times obscured but never extinguished in the five-thousand-year development of Chinese culture.

Fearless Social Critic

Po Chu-i is now admired and studied in China chiefly as a man who was at once poet and fearless social critic. This should not be construed as negligence or indifference on our part to his extraordinary lyrical quality as shown in the well-known *Song of the Lute* or the *Song of Unending Sorrow*, both of which have been translated time and again into nearly all modern languages. Now that our people are liberated and know more of the joys of life, they have greater reason than ever to appreciate the beauty of lyrical poetry. But it is on Po Chu-i the humanist, the ardent lover of the people and valiant champion of their cause that attention is centred today. In his own time, Po Chu-i was universally appreciated by the people. Since the liberation, his poetry is once again treasured by the people as their own. We are paying this great poet the high tribute of gratitude and affection that has long been his due, but has been so long delayed by historic circumstances.

Po Chu-i stood resolutely and persistently for the union of poetry with the social and political life of the people. True to this principle, he carried out in practice what he firmly believed in theory. No matter what might be the consequences, he spoke for the inarticulate millions of China whose lot, at that time, was not much better than that of the Russian serfs in the time of Nekrassov. The 174 satires he wrote during the first decade of the ninth century offended those in power to such an extent that his enemies, who were also the enemies of the people, conspired to silence him by banishing him, in the year 815, to Kiukiang (then called Hsunyang) in Kiangsi province, about a thousand miles overland from Changan, the capital of China at that time.

Po's theory and practice as a poet place him in the main current of the Chinese literary tradition which can be traced as far back as the *Book of Odes* edited by Confucius. But in his lifetime very few literary men shared his stubbornly held views. Misunderstood and extremely lonely he confided to his intimate poet friend, Yuan Chen: "Today the world can only appreciate such of my poems as the *Song of Unending Sorrow*. I set no store by what the world values. My satires are expressions of my indignant, challenging and agitating ideas in plain, outspoken language . . . Of my contemporaries you alone understand and love them. Who knows, a thousand years hence, perhaps some one like you will be born who will also understand and love my satires?"

It is 1,107 years since Po Chu-i died. A whole people, almost 500 million strong, have now awakened to the value of his poetry. Never has it been more true that "a poet is a prophet".

Life and Views

Po Chu-i was born in Hsincheng, Honan province, a few years after the death of Li Po and Tu Fu, the two other members of the great triumvirate of Tang poets. His father was poor and often in difficulties. In his youth he wandered about Hupeh, Kiangsu and Chekiang provinces seeking a living. At twenty-eight he passed the state examinations in the capital and started on an official career, the one and only opening for a Chinese scholar at that time.

The poet was conscientious and took his work seriously. "Since entering his majesty's service," he wrote, "I have grown older and gained experience by degrees. Talking with people I often ask about current events; studying history and literature I seek for the ways of reason. I have begun to realize that the work of literature must truthfully reflect the life of the people."

Political Poetry

Well versed in state affairs, Po was no courtier. He was too honest to win official approbation at that time. Court poems are not the important part of his work. Believing earnestly that poetry should be used as a political weapon, he used it to satirize the misrulers high and low. In his poem, *The Imperial Collector of Poetry* he reminded the emperor that the ancient sage kings had acquainted themselves with the people's joys and sorrows by paying close attention to songs and satirical poems composed for or by the people and had even maintained a special office for that purpose.

> The Imperial Collector of Poetry
> Collected poems and listened to songs,

> The true voice of the people, true criticism;
> The criticizers were not to blame.
> The criticized should heed warning!
> When criticism from below reached up to
> The Most High, all was well.

> Unfortunately, for over a thousand years,
> There has been no office of Collector of
>   Poetry.
> Now all the Emperor hears are songs in his
>   praise—
> Hymns sung for ancestor worship in the
>   Imperial Temple
> Or Songs thrilling the banqueters with
>   pleasure. . .

> Bold are the corrupt officials, oppressing
>   and fleecing the people.
> Bolder are the State Ministers, deceiving His
>   Majesty.

This poem leaves no room for doubt that poetry has an important political function in ancient China. Applying this criterion to the poetry of his predecessors, Po Chu-i found little to admire after the Chin dynasty (265-419 A.D.) and "mourned that poetry had deteriorated and decayed." For nearly four hundred years, he complained, the poets simply ignored or neglected the political role of poetry. They merely tossed around such words as wind, snow, flowers and grass, but did not use them as metaphors to satirize political wrongs and social follies.

Historical Setting

And political wrongs and social follies were not wanting in Po's day. The endless civil wars and the taxes levied to pay for them, not to mention the material devastation they left in their wake, all meant untold suffering for the people. In addition, the people were the main sufferers from the rapacity and extortions of the hosts of officials of all ranks whose promotion depended on the amount of tribute they paid to the court. Because the historical conditions for basic change were not yet present, Po Chu-i could not realize that the feudal suffering was in itself a bad thing. The only struggle he could conceive was to attempt to improve the lot of the common people within the existing framework of society. His poems burn with scathing social criticism devoted to this purpose.

People's Sufferings Sung

The satirical poems of Po Chu-i expose two things: the grinding exploitation of the peasants and the rapacity and lust of the officials. With a bitterness which resembles Nekrassov's in *Who Can Be Happy and Free in Russia*, Po wrote his ten plaintive *Songs of Chin* (Chin, a powerful kingdom in ancient China, was located in what today is Shensi province). When the bigwigs and their favourites heard these songs, they lost countenance.

The Heavy Taxes, one of this group, reads in part as follows:

> The rapacious official heedlessly follows
> bad practices. . .
> He fleeces me to woo the favour of his
> superior,
> Always demanding, extorting, first in spring
> and then in winter. . . .
> Weaving silk taffeta, not even enough to
> make a bolt,
> Spinning silk thread, not even weighing a
> pound,
> I am forced to give the village tax collector
> all;
> At once, with not a single moment's delay!. . . .
> Oh you wretched official!
> You have stripped the warmth from my back
> To buy favours for yourself!

How can one ever forget this picture of the unbearable sufferings of the oppressed! Let us turn to another word picture of the peasant's hard life which the poet painted in ***Watching a Wheat Harvest***.

> The summer earth burns the toilers' bare
> feet,
> Rays of the flaming sun scorch their naked
> backs. . . .
> Exhausted with work they no longer feel the
> heat,
> Toiling on, making full use of the long
> daylight. . . .
> By their side stands a woman in threadbare
> clothes,
> Holding her infant son close to her breast;
> Her right hand gleans the fallen ears of
> grain,
> On her left arm hangs a broken basket. . . .
> "All we reap has to go in taxes," she says,
> "I glean the fallen grain to pacify our
> hunger. . . ."

Frequent crop failures brought additional calamities to the already hard-pressed peasants. Po Chu-i always stood up for them and was always ready to proclaim their grievances. The bitter irony of ***The Herb Gatherer*** leaves a lasting impression on the reader's mind:

> Roaming in the fields all day I dig up wild
> herbs
> Which I hope to exchange for some coarse
> dry food.
> In the early morning I go out with my hoe,
> seeking. . . .

> But by nightfall my basket is still unfilled. . . .
> I carry it to the door of the big mansion,
> And sell it to the gentleman with the plump
> cheeks
> To feed his strong, stout horses that will
> grow
> Coats so sleek, they will reflect the light.
> I exchange my herbs for some fodder left
> after his horses have eaten
> To relieve me from the sharp pains of
> hunger. . . .

In the year 809, when Po was 37 years old, he was appointed Counsellor to Emperor Hsien Tsung. He immediately reminded this ruler of the importance of listening to the voice of the people through the Imperial Counsellor, whose duty it was to speak for the people instead of flattering the emperor. He often argued with the other courtiers and the emperor himself about tax acts, famine relief measures, conscription and the imposing of various penalties. In 810 he published fifty ***New Songs***, in the preface of which he wrote:

> . . . My language is simple and direct, intelligible to all who can read; my meaning is plain and exact, unmistakable to those who will take the warning; my exposures are all based on facts, credible to anyone who cares to collect them; my style is easy and modulated, adaptable to music for popular singing. In a word, my poems are composed for the people, contain facts and are meant to be perused by the state ministers and scrutinized by His Majesty. I do not make poetry for poetry's sake.

Attack on Oppressors

One of the fifty songs, ***The Old Man with the Broken Arm***, a satire against militarism, was widely publicized after the first World War. It relates how an old peasant deliberately broke his arm in order to escape conscription. Another song in the same series is the ***Old Peasant of Tu Lin***, from which the following is an extract:

> The rain expected in the third month never
> came,
> Instead a dry wind rose . . .
> My wheat sprouts had not yet grown into
> ears but turned yellow and died. . .
> Suddenly the autumn became unusually
> cold,
> In the ninth month unseasonable heavy
> frosts fell,
> My rice withered in the ear, while still green
> and unripe. . .
>
> The official knew all, but took no heed,
> made no report!

Taxes were urgently demanded . . . taxes
   were forcibly collected . . .
To win his own promotion was all he cared
   and hoped for!

For the taxes I mortgaged my mulberry trees,
   sold my land.
Whence will come my food and clothes
   before next harvest?
From my body, Official, you have stripped
   the clothes,
From my mouth you have taken away the
   food. . . .
Every beast that preys on man is a wolf—
It need not have hooked nails or bloody
   teeth,
Just the same it devours human flesh!

In his exposure of the criminal and evil deeds of the official class, Po Chu-i used his masterful pen to depict striking contrasts—both sides of the social contradiction. While on the one hand the poor peasants were bled white by heavy taxes, on the other hand, the high officials lived amid luxury and lust. The building of private parks and sumptuous houses was in great fashion among them. With his *Lament Over a Big Mansion*, one of the ten **Songs of Chin**, the poet sounded the trumpet of warning. Like an oracle, he predicted the inevitable unhappy fate of the ill-starred mansions and their owners, notwithstanding their apparent and temporary prosperity.

Who owns this big mansion, this stately
   house
With its scarlet gates opening on the wide
   street?
Six or seven halls stand side by side,
The roofs are of glittering green tiles,
And a high wall surrounds all.
A single hall must have cost a million *cash*!
The owner living in it has now for ten years
Held important posts in the government.
In his overstocked larder, the meat is rotting,
In his treasury, copper coins corrode with
   rust. . .

Let him take warning from the questions i
   ask:
Have you not poor relations near in blood?
can you bear to leave them hungry and
   cold?
Do you care for yourself only, disregarding
   all others?
can you enjoy your good fortune a
   thousand years?

The fine buildings owned by the Ma family
Have been confiscated and are now the
   Feng Chen Park. . .

It was for standing up for the people, disregarding the risk of offending the emperor and his flatterers that Po Chu-i was disgraced or dismissed many times. His critical verses made enemies for him right and left. His friends were anxious about him but not sympathetic. "I made a name in the world by poetry," he remarked ironically. "It is really fit that I should have earned my penalty with poetry!" Disgusted by the underhand dealings of the court lackeys, he was glad to leave the capital to become Prefect of Hangchow, Chekiang province. The most notable thing he did there was the building of the dykes and locks around the Chientang lake, saving thousands of acres of farmland from drought.

Loved by People

The Tang dynasty was the Golden Age of Chinese poetry. The number of works produced was tremendous. Po Chu-i alone wrote 3,840 poems. And he was as popular as he was prolific. He deliberately chose the simple language of the people as the medium for his poetic expression and succeeded so well in his use of it that his poems were intelligible even to illiterate old peasant women. Over a period of years, in Changan, the capital, his poems were copied on the walls of temples and post stations. They were also known in many provinces.

"From Changan to Kiangsi," Po wrote to his friend, "I travelled a distance of three thousand *li*. I frequently saw my poems on the walls of country schools, hotels, Buddhist temples and even in the cabins of boats. And just as frequently I heard them being recited by Buddhist monks, learned scholars, illiterate women and young girls."

Outside China, in Korea, Japan and other neighbouring countries Po's poems were also read and valued during his lifetime. Whenever merchants from Korea came to trade in Changan they bought copies of his new poems. They said they would make a big profit by selling them in their own country.

Memory Treasured

Po Chu-i's greatness is shown by the fact that while his poems were universally appreciated by the common people, they were bitterly hated by the rich and powerful. It is of great significance that he drew a demarcation line between the oppressors and the oppressed, which, as we now see, illuminated the irreconcilability of the contradictions between the feudal rulers and the people. Herein lie his merit and the reason we cherish the memory of this great poet today.

Po Chu-i was above all a humanist who, like Leonardo da Vinci and Victor Hugo, used his art to criticize men and affairs from the viewpoint of the people. He spoke for the Chinese people and for all people. And that is why all people will treasure his work.

Howard S. Levy (essay date 1970)

SOURCE: Howard S. Levy, in *Translations from Po Chü-i's Collected Works,* translated and described by Howard S. Levy, Paragon Book Reprint Corp., 1970, 181 p.

[*In the following excerpt, Levy surveys several groups of Po Chü-i's poetry—including those of social criticism, in praise of pleasure and drinking, and lamenting aging and death—and explores their influence on Japanese literature.*]

Chapter 3

The Poems of Social Criticism and Class Consciousness

. . . Po Chü-i had a great sympathy for the weak and the exploited, and he scorned those who oppressed the multitudes and profited at their expense. In his didactic poems, as an ally of the weak he frequently made appeals to the throne to relieve their sufferings. These are the poems of early maturity, written in his late thirties while he was serving at court as an imperial critic. They embody an early conviction that the poetic mission should be to reveal the situation of the masses and to suggest to the ruler ways and means to improve the general welfare. There are 172 poems in his collection under the didactic category; he assembled fifty of them in poetic forms based mainly on T'ang folksong patterns and referred to them as "New Music Bureau Poems". Yüan Chen also wrote fifteen poems in this style, which was probably initiated by the compositions no longer extant, of Li Shen (775-846). Po probably composed his New Music Bureau Poems in 809, though in some instances there is evidence of later revision. Chinese critic Ch'en Yin-k'o stated that Po's poems in this style were superior to those of Yüan Chen and that Po restricted himself to one subject in a poem, while Yüan Chen tended to be diffuse and unclear.[1] Many later poets imitated Po, but none achieved his social and literary effect. The "newness" of these poems in the New Music Bureau style was in their avoiding the use of stereotypes, restoring the cadences of folksongs, and combining didactic themes with a non-conventional outlook. One Chinese scholar has referred to them as pseudo-folksongs.[2]

Po Chü-i deplored the tendency of T'ang poets to flatter the sovereign in verse and to avoid words of remonstrance, saying that remonstrative words could not be found among the thousands of compositions submitted to the throne. To Po the result was tragic, for the Emperor's ears only heard words from his court—his eyes didn't see things which were happening in front of his gate: greedy officials remorselessly harmed the people, and rapacious ministers brazenly hid facts from him.[3]

A generation before, Tu Fu had reflected that those who wrote poems in the Music Bureau style should preserve the original intent of this genre, namely to enable one to reflect on customs and to discern the weighty from the trivial. Those in a superior position could use the poems to indoctrinate those below, while those in an inferior position could use them to criticize their superiors. Po, who admired Tu Fu, was also impressed by the poems in the Old Music Bureau style of Chang Chi (c. 765-830), a contemporary who had lived in poverty near Ch'ang-an for fifty years. He lamented the fact that Chang had been ignored by the court. Po stated in verse that Chang had worked on his Music Bureau poems for more than thirty years, reducing the volume of other writings as a consequence. Chang followed the principle of the *Book of Odes,* as did Po, and never wrote empty verse. His poems warned profligate sovereigns, condemned greedy ministers, expressed compassion for lowly prostitutes, and encouraged the downtrodden. Po noted that the sovereign who read Chang's poems could learn how to help the people and improve his own conduct. Chang worked on these poems day and night. Po regretted the failure of the T'ang to imitate the ancient Chou dynasty by appointing an official to select poems from throughout the empire to be used as guides on how to govern. Writing as if Chang were with him, Po sadly remarked that Chang's poems had been ignored and stated his fear that they would be unheard of after his death. Po wanted them to be collected and preserved for posterity, since to his way of thinking words were buds coming forth from the will, actions the roots of words. T'ang Ch'ü (fl. early ninth century), another of Po Chü-i's friends, was still poor at fifty; at his death he left only a thousand poems. Po stated in one poetic stanza that T'ang wept easily over disloyal behavior but that he, Po, couldn't weep. Therefore, he had composed the New Music Bureau poems to let the Emperor know of the people's sufferings. Each of Po's poems in this style is devoted to a single theme, described in a preceding sentence or phrase. As the poet makes clear in a general preface, his ambition in writing the poems was to emulate the didacticism of the *Book of Odes,* and his primary concern was with content rather than form. Despite his assertion that poetic form was of little concern, he tended to adhere to a seven-character line, with three-character lines often used to set the theme. Three-, five-, nine-, ten-, and eleven-character lines were interspersed, with each poem tending to number about forty or fifty lines, and with end-rhyme falling on the even lines.

Po Chü-i, then serving as a court critic, composed his didactic poems as a device to get the Emperor to listen to his opinions. He wanted him to discover the things concealed by fawning bureaucrats and to understand the feelings of the people. Po tried to clear the way of communication, a way blocked by greedy officials and rapacious ministers. He made known to the Emperor the impoverishment of the masses and suggested specific remedies.

For Po Chü-i to set himself against the central administration was an act of daring that could not be tolerated by those in influence. As the poet states in a letter to Yüan Chen, when the critical poems in the New Music Bureau collection became known, "Those close to the mighty and eminent looked at one another and lost color; those controlling the government clenched their fists in anger; and those in military power gnashed their teeth."[4] Having incurred the hatred of those in authority, when he returned from mourning he came under attack and criticism, and in 815 was transferred from court and demoted in rank to be marshal of Chiang-chou. The ostensible cause was his filial disrespect, the real cause the enmities he had incurred through expressing frank opinions in poetry and prose.

The fifty poems in the New Music Bureau style vary greatly in readability and in the extent to which they still communicate ideas. A few of the poems concern history; these have so many allusions to past persons and events that they need lengthy annotation to be understood. These poems were intended for the Emperor and an intellectual court elite, and their circulation must have been restricted to a literate few. Most of them, however, focus on people or on things commonly encountered, and here the imaginative genius of the poet is such that he enters into the psyche of the person, conjures up the feeling of the inanimate, and proceeds from the concrete situation to the abstract generalization and the fitting conclusion. The seventh poem in the collection, entitled **"White-Haired Person of Shang-yang"**,[5] is a good example of Po's poetic imagination at work, and I have therefore selected it for discussion and translation.

The intent of the poet was to criticize the centuries-old custom of incarcerating thousands of women, in the prime of life, so that they wasted away in the solitude of the harem, bereft of love, family, and mate. He made his points by criticizing, not his own times, but events in the reign of T'ang Hsüan-tsung that had occurred more than half a century before. Towards the end of Hsüan-tsung's reign, Precious Consort Yang monopolized the imperial favor, and after 748, potential harem rivals were relegated to secondary imperial harems such as Shang-yang in Loyang, the eastern capital subsidiary to Ch'ang-an. The effect of the poem is enhanced by a fictional elaboration of the theme, and the reader is moved to empathize with the forlorn harem occupant. By focusing on the sufferings of one, the poet achieves his objective of depicting the sufferings of all. Other poems on associated subjects make clear the poet's concern for the plight of woman in T'ang male-oriented society and his wish to improve her welfare. There are forty-one lines in this poem about a harem lady. The seven-character line dominates, varied by a few three-character lines, while two ten-character lines conclude. The seven-character lines are almost all divisible into two syntactical units, the first of four and the second of three characters. In my translation, these syntactical units are rendered by individual lines. The reference to the T'ien-pao era (742-55) is to the latter part of Hsüan-tsung's reign, which culminated in the rebellion of An Lu-shan and was followed by a decade of civil war. In writing about this harem occupant, Po includes terms commonly used in the palace. The title of "Documents Supervisor" was known prior to the T'ang, as early as the Three Kingdoms period. The *fu* poem by Lu Hsiang, erroneously attributed to Lu Shang, was written by a literatus who served Hsüan-tsung in an official capacity. Lu Hsiang wrote the poem to criticize the Emperor because he had recruited beauties for his harem from everywhere in the empire.[6]

A White-Haired Person of Shang-yang (Lamenting her Unwed Solitude)

A person of Shang-yang,
a person of Shang-yang,
rose face aging unawares,
white hairs renewed.
Green-clothed eunuch overseers
guard the harem gates;
once locked behind me,
how many springs?
In Hsüan-tsung's closing years
I was first selected;
I entered at sixteen—today I am sixty!
Over a hundred, selected with me;
years dreary and desolate,
this body withered.

Remembering the past, holding back tears,
parting from my family.
They helped me into the carriage,
not letting me cry.
"Once you enter the palace
you'll enjoy His Lord's favor."
My face like the lotus,
my bosom like jade;
before it was permissible
that His Lord see me,
I was glared at askance
by Consort Yang,
who jealously ordered my secret transfer
to Shang-yang Palace.

My whole life there,
facing an empty room;
living in an empty room
autumn nights are long,
long and sleepless,
unbrightened by dawn.
Withered candle flickering,
shadowy wall reflection;
lonely sighing hidden rain
beating a window sound.
So long the spring days,
long the day, sitting lone,
so hard for day to darken.
Sweet songs of palace orioles,
in melancholy, I loathe to hear.
Swallows on the cross-beams paired,
jealousy stilled through old age.
Orioles returned, swallows departed;
forever was I grieved and bereft.
Spring left, autumn came;
I can't remember the years.
I only faced the harem depths,
looked towards the bright moon;
it returned in fullness
east-west hundreds of times.

In the harem today
I'm the oldest.
His Highness bestowed on me
the title of Documents Supervisor.
My shoes are pointed,
my dress tight-fitting,
my eyebrows sombre colored,
slender and elongated.
Outsiders don't see me—
if they did, they'd surely laugh,
for these were the fashions
at the end of T'ien-pao.

A person of Shang-yang,
distressed most of all;
distressed in youth,
distressed in old age,
this lifelong distress,
comparable to what?
Haren't you seen Lu Shang's
poem of old about the beauties?
Now won't you look at my song,
about a white-haired one of Shang-yang?

Yüan Chen also wrote about harem ladies. One of his most famous poems, written in a nostalgic vein, describes aging harem residents and indirectly shows the close relationship between the poetic themes of Yüan Chen and Po Chü-i:

Fallen-desolate the old provisional palace;
palace flowers red in loneliness.
White-haired palace ladies
idly sit and talk of Hsüan-tsung.[7]

The poems by Po Chü-i in the New Music Bureau style cover a multitude of themes. The poet was concerned by the tendency in T'ang China to prefer everything foreign, and in several poems he criticized the influx of non-Chinese songs, dances, and cosmetic fashions. Po Chü-i and Yüan Chen extolled ancient music and scorned modern music, calling for a return to the old ways in order to pacify the people. Po had a personal view of dynastic history; he felt that the introduction of foreign elements into the national consciousness had weakened the body politic and prepared the way for rebellion by the non-Chinese An Lu-shan and an aftermath of civil chaos and unrest. Some of his older acquaintances had lived through the rebellion, and the reaction against "barbarians" still persisted. In his own times, Po cautioned against treating greedy barbarians too lavishly when they appeared at court. Po Chü-i was radical in his condemnation of corruption and his compassion for the mute suffering of the masses, but his Confucian-oriented radicalism looked back to past ages and benevolent rulers for solutions. In seeking to restore effective government and humane rule, he was oriented towards reverence of Confucian classics and orthodox interpretations of such classics. Saddened by the neglect of ancient music and the decline of the ancient tunes, Po argued that the spirits above would never be moved by the poor musical productions of his own era and that the tunes now heard failed to stir the people to patriotic reflection.

He was a nationalist but not a jingoist and was vehemently against the waging of wars in foreign lands, knowing it was the people who paid for military adventures. He launched a poetic attack against the foreign aggressions of Chinese armies, developing his argument out of an incident involving an old man who had broken one arm deliberately to avoid conscription and service abroad, thereby escaping the holocausts of war. He also underscored the profiteering of frontier military officials and stated that generals were overbearing and proud in the royal presence, while great civil officials suffered the indignity of being virtually ignored and dismissed after brief and cursory audiences. In one of his poems he castigated frontier officials who did nothing constructive and submitted false claims of victory. He also criticized the tendency of militarists to feast, frolic, and spend lavishly. Po wrote with the anger of the direct participant and the immediate observer.

Po revealed in these poems philosophic interests in Buddhism and Taoism but shared Yüan Chen's disdain for the ways in which these religions expanded their holdings. In one poem he criticized the increase of Buddhist temples at the expense of dwellings for the masses; in another he ridiculed the Taoist religion for encouraging a futile search for longevity not propounded in the writings of Lao-t   He involved himself in the human equation. When he looked at a luxurious rug, he thought of the hardships of the weaver and concluded that it was best to use the thousands of silken stands to clothe the poor in the locale in which the rug was made. When he looked at silks, he likewise thought of the labor that had gone into the making of the finished product. His compassion extended to the animal as well as to the human world; a poor ox which spilt its blood in toil so that a chief minister might enjoy the privileges of a special private roadway was vividly described. He cited the case of a charcoal seller to criticize the terrible exactions made of the poor by buyers sent out from the palace, and was distressed by the poverty of the peasants, heavily taxed in times of drought and devoid of food or clothing for the year to come. He advised the sovereign to follow precedent by listening to the humble and by regarding them as mirrors reflecting the true state of the empire. He requested in verse that the wall between the Emperor and his subjects be cleaved through, just as a famous ancient sword could cleave through to the sun and the Heavens.

Objects in nature served his poetic-ideological purposes. He gave a fictional account of a rock, relating how on it were inscribed the names of those loyal to the throne in times of peril. He used the writing brush as a symbol to castigate those in high office who misused it by being dishonest in their writings. And in his final poem, he exhorted the Emperor to welcome poems of criticism like his own in order to find out how people really felt, and reminded his sovereign that in antiquity the critical poet-official was not incriminated by his didactic poems and that everyone read and reflected on his social comments.

The second poem in the New Music Bureau style which I have selected for translation, the thirtieth in the collection, describes the plight of the peasant in times of natural disaster and is entitled **"An Old Man of Tu-ling"**. Tu-ling, an area in the southern suburbs beyond Ch'ang-an, suffered from famine in the late spring of 809. The poem contains twenty-three lines, all seven characters in length, except for two three-character lines, two five-character lines, and one nine-character line.

An Old Man of Tu-ling

An old man of Tu-ling,
living at Tu-ling,
yearly cultivating
a dozen acres of barren ground.
The third month rainless,
a drought arose;
the young wheat grew not,
mostly yellowed and died.
Frost fell in the ninth month,
autumn soon got cold;

before the ears of corn ripened,
they greened and withered.

The official in charge clearly knew
but didn't report it.
He hurriedly taxed, forcibly exacted,
seeking a good showing for himself.
To get the tax
I pawned the mulberries,
sold the land; next year
what will I do for food and clothing?
Stripping the clothes from my body,
snatching the rice from my mouth.
Oppressors of men and despoilers of things
are ravenous wolves;
why must hooklike claws and sawlike teeth
eat human flesh?

Who it was I don't know,
but someone reported to the Emperor.
His heart was moved with compassion;
he learned of man's corruption.
On white hemp paper
virtuous words resounded,
and all fields by the capital
were freed from this year's taxes.

Yesterday a village clerk
came to my door
holding the royal wooden tally
to be displayed in the hamlets.
But of every ten households to be taxed,
nine have already paid;
so in emptiness they receive
Their Lord's tax remission.

Po officially recommended to the Emperor that taxes be reduced and harem expenditures curtailed. These recommendations were followed and, in true Confucian fashion, the rains came.

The fifty didactic poems in the New Music Bureau style are the best known. Next in fame is a cluster of ten poems completed earlier by Po Chü-i in 807 and entitled **"Songs of Ch'in"**. As the poet explained in a brief foreword to the poems, they were written about things which saddened him when he was in Ch'ang-an in the late eighth and early ninth centuries. In one poem he revealed that when he first wrote the **"Songs of Ch'in"**, his friend T'ang Ch'ü alone appreciated them and wept as he read them a second time. T'ang sent him thirty of his own poems, and after T'ang's death he opened the case to look at them, only to find that they were moth-eaten. Po and poetic friends like T'ang Ch'ü carried on a friendly rivalry, and were not professionally petty or jealous about one another's writings.

The **"Songs of Ch'in"** are in the five-character old poetic style line, with end rhyming of the even-numbered lines. They vary in length from sixteen to thirty lines. The poems are permeated with the poet's class consciousness and keen awareness of the contrast between poverty and wealth, and there is in them an admirable insistence on clear thinking and forthright expression. The impact of the poems at court must have been considerable, for the poet reveals that powerful and aristocratic groups there paled when they heard them.

He begins the **"Songs of Ch'in"** series with a discussion of marriage, contrasting the ease with which rich girls get married with the hardships endured by poor and virtuous maidens when they want to wed. He next stresses the superior qualifications of the maiden reared in poverty. For dramatic effect, the poet creates an imaginary conversation, in which he addressed himself to a prospective groom and a wedding party:

Discussing Marriage[8]

There is no absolute musical standard in the
   world,
for each enjoys that which pleases his ears.
There is no absolute beauty standard among
   men,
for each enjoys that which pleases his eyes.
Beauty is only a matter of slight degree,
but rich and poor are clearly distinguished!
The poor are always cast aside,
but everyone flocks to the rich.

A girl of a rich family, in a vermillion
   mansion,
wears a jacket of embroidered silk, spun
   with golden threads,
doesn't draw hands back into sleeves upon
   seeing a man,
and at early sixteen is womanly but
   ignorant.
Mother and elder brother haven't begun to
   talk about it
when she is married in an instant.
A girl of a poor family, within green
   windows,
passes the age of twenty in lonely solitude.
Her thorn hairpins are worthless,
and no pearls embellish her dress;
she is on the verge of betrothal several
   times,
but prospective bridegrooms falter as the
   day approaches.

The groom-to-be assembles go-between,
filling wine to overflowing in a jade pot:
"Everyone seated, don't drink yet,
but listen to me sing of the two ways.
The girl of a rich family easily weds,
weds early and slights her husband;

the girl of a poor family finds it hard to
   wed,
weds later and is filial to her mother-in-law.
Hearing that you wish to take a wife,
may I ask what your intentions are?"

Po Chü-i next contrasted the wealth of the tax collector and the goods turning to dust in the imperial warehouse with the poverty of the oppressed peasants. He described an official who lived in a splendid mansion with so much food in his kitchen that it rotted. Pointedly, he asked the official in verse if he didn't have any hungry relatives to feed and reminded him that wealth didn't last forever, citing the case of a mansion which had been converted into a government park.[9] The poet was grieved by the fickleness of friendship; a scholar with whom he had been very close when they both were poor achieved eminence, and now when they met in the street the scholar passed him by as if they had never met. The fifth poem in the Ch'in series, concerning government service, could apply with equal validity to Chiang Kai-shek and Mao Tse-tung, for in it Po deplored the way in which old men ignored the instruction in one of the classics to resign from office by the age of seventy and instead clung to their jobs to the very end. There were men of his time of eighty and ninety, half-blind and half-toothless, who had such greed for profit that they refused to retire. Po Chü-i scorned the custom of setting up monuments to the worthless, composing empty words to them as if in life they had had the virtues of Confucius. He contrasted this hypocrisy with the example of a beloved village official, poor and honest, who died with no monument raised to him but who was still remembered in the hearts of the villagers.

He castigated court officials for their pride and self-satisfaction. To illustrate the differences in outlook between the ruling and the ruled, the last two lines of the seventh of the songs of Ch'in contrasted the abundance of food and drink on official tables with a recent drought in Kiangnan that had led to cannibalism among the starving. In a poem evoking winter scenes, a warden and a judge were described as they dined in warmth and luxury in a splendid mansion while, unbeknownst to the warden, his prisoners were freezing to death from the cold. In Po's final poem of the series, lamenting the gap between rich and poor, a villager sees a cluster of beautiful flowers on sale and sighs because with the sales price being asked, the taxes of ten average households could be paid. One verse laments the preference for new music, a favorite subject of Po Chü-i's; elsewhere he achieves a dramatic variation on this plaint by telling the story of a discarded lute. The lute was dusty and for a long time had been unheard. Its sounds were mournful. It wanted to play for the sovereign but he didn't want to hear it, preferring barbarian instruments instead. Apart from these wistful looks towards a Chinese musical past, the ten **"Songs of Ch'in"** concerned themselves with unmasking the abuses committed by authorities who were either oblivious to the suffering about them, or who aggravated such suffering because of their rapaciousness and irresponsibility.

The poems in the Music Bureau style and the **"Songs of Ch'in"** make up over one third of the first part of the collection of poems of social criticism. The other 112 poems, mostly written in a five-character line, old poetic style, similarly propound the values of truth, friendship, integrity, loyalty, and sympathy for the oppressed. The first poem in the collection, praising Emperor Hsien-tsung, was written when Po was thirty-six years old, just after a time when no rain had fallen from winter to the following spring. The Emperor was worried at this sign of Heaven's displeasure and he confessed his guilt in an imperial proclamation. He lightened criminal sentences, released women from his harem, and reduced the number of horses in the imperial stables. He also ordered that the starving be fed, and in general delighted the underprivileged with his behavior. A week later, it rained for three days and the grains turned green. The poet realized that the ruler in his heart shared the joys and griefs of his subjects, congratulated him on such an auspicious beginning, and hoped that he would some day enjoy an equally auspicious ending. The advice by implication was that the Emperor should stave off disaster by identifying his needs with the needs of the masses. There was then a belief current that droughts could be caused by the excess of female (*yin*) over male (*yang*) elements, evidenced by a profusion of woman in the imperial harem. The poet described famine conditions, when people tried to barter land for food, and during a summer drought he asked Heaven why it was that rain hadn't fallen for such a long time. Writing about village poverty in winter, he felt ashamed of being well fed and clothed. He contrasted the toil of the peasants with his own affluence; unlike the toilers, he got his wheat without having to drudge for it:

> Thinking of this,
> secretly I felt ashamed,
> and all day
> couldn't put it out of my mind.

To avoid the heat on a stifling, hot day, he escaped to a Buddhist pagoda beyond the city gates and reflected that while he could do so, the withered crops could not. He seemed to enjoy religious sites because they gave him a chance to "get away from it all" and to meditate at leisure, but he looked askance at fanatics, such as the Taoist adept who cherished the thought that through religion he could have eternal life on earth. He reiterated that those who sought the longevity of Immortals did so in vain and related what happened to someone who based his foolish behavior on the import of a dream. He was told in the dream that immortality

could be gained in fifteen years, and he waited for thirty before finally reverting to the earth like a pile of dung. Immortality was something beyond the human potential, and to waste a lifetime on the search was absurd:

> How pitiful!
> To dream of an Immortal,
> and for one dream
> to ruin a life.

Po, rich in compassion, wept for those who met with a tragic fate. He was a friend in deed and he composed many elegy-like remembrances in verse for fellow scholars of worth who had died obscure and unsung. It was his general observation that Confucian scholars of the times studied hard but in poverty, while the sons of the rich were ignorant, profligate, and influential. There seemed to be no way out of this paradox either in T'ang or in antiquity. He praised one scholar for being poor and hungry but content and another scholar for looking upon gold as if it were dirt. While in Ch'ang-an in 810, he heard that K'ung Kan (retired 807) had died in Loyang, and he wept at the news. He portrayed K'ung as one who was upright and unwavering in the Way, serving with rare competence. When K'ung went to Loyang, everyone thought that he should be employed in a high position, but sadly he spent his life in obscurity and never came before the imperial presence. He died like any ordinary man, his steadfastness reverting emptily to earth. Po asked rhetorically: "If Heaven doesn't love the people, why does it produce benevolent ones like K'ung? If Heaven does love the people, why does it take his life so abruptly? Heaven's ways are hard to grasp, but who holds the key to fate?"

His poems of social import include detailed exchanges with Yüan Chen, in which he responds to poems by Yüan; these are generally much more difficult to read and understand. Po also comments in verse on historical situations, referring to events which occurred in former dynastic eras and assigning praise or blame to the participants in accord with his moral-didactic views. Since he possessed a vivid imagination, everything in the universe was subject to his poetic touch. He based many of his poetic arguments and criticisms on similies and used ordinary objects, either natural or man-made, to expand his themes. These provided the base and the points of departure for him to launch general observations from particular instances. It was in the closing lines of a poem that he might reveal a truth he felt about the human condition:

> Heaven-cold, no sun's light;
> T'ai-hsing Peak is vast.
> I've heard of its dangers,
> and now I go alone.
> The horse's hooves, cold and slippery.
> It winds like a sheep's intestines,

it can't be climbed.
But if you compare it to life's difficulties,
    it seems more level than the palm of one's
    hand.

Similes were everywhere and at his poetic service. When sons of two friends failed official examinations, he comforted his friends by likening the failure to the solitary lute and the virtuous pine, which remained aloof from the throng. He advocated filial piety. In commenting poetically about a man who had left his parents, he drew an analogy from nature to show that even swallows grieved when their young left the nest; this should make one aware, he concluded, of the feelings of one's parents. And he complained that, while the bird cried for its lost mother, people were not even as filial as birds. He compared an autumnal scene to the evanescence of fame sought by shallow officials, the dismissal of a friend from office to a tree in the courtyard killed by frost. Just as the homely jujube tree could be used in making carriage wheels, so were men who were upright and firm better than officials who were attractive but treacherous. Po described a tree which, like him, should be at court but instead was isolated on a mountain. The talented went their ways unappreciated, like unseen beauties of nature. He wished to send white temple lotuses to Ch'ang-an but feared that once the lotuses left the mountains they would perish in the mortal realm below. Broken pines were like distressed scholars. He envied birds and fishes travelling in groups, for he was alone. Other similes in this first section are:

> The wistaria looks pretty, but it enfolds itself around a tree like a snake and kills the tree. This is like treacherous ministers and evil wives, so Emperors, take heed.

> Lotuses are transplanted to a dirt pond where they can't emit fragrance, like men forced to serve in unsatisfactory posts.

> An enlightened ruler should use his ministers as one uses the falcon to catch birds, neither overfeeding or underfeeding.

> The *t'ung* tree stands alone, fragrant in spring but unappreciated by passersby. (This is probably an indirect reference to his being ignored by the ruler.)

> Everyone ignores the white peony, preferring red and purple to white, but beauty or ugliness is not in the thing itself but in the heart of the observer. (Among T'ang poets the peony was a common metaphor. It was a symbol of the *yang* principle and represented masculinity, brightness, good luck, and distinction.)[10]

> A certain tree is beautiful, but its fruits are so fragrant that one can't bear to eat them. Many things in the world are like this; truth and falsehood are hard to distinguish. There are hidden thorns in beauty, and bitter taste and injuriousness may be concealed.

> The pine tree is like the heart of Yüan Chen, straight and unyielding. (The pine symbolized constancy in adversity.)[11]

> The tree stands alone like jade, as a man should stand.

> A sharp sword may be compared to talent and good jade to virtue, but virtue is superior to talent. A sword melts in the furnace but jade does not.

> There is a sword, broken through reasons unknown, which is now left in the ground and ignored. The poet preferred hardness to softness; (it is) better to be a straight broken sword than a curved hook.

> The crane is virtuous and flies alone. Those who flurry about for wealth and fame are to be criticized.

> It is hard to see one's fate, which is like the division of the flowers and the trees. Heaven doesn't grant more than one good attribute to each. The lichee is sweet but not pretty, the peony pretty but not sweet.

In one poem Po noted the uncertainty of riches and in another said that age, good fortune, influence, and position were taken from us like thieves in the night. He was aware of the then popular belief that certain houses in Ch'ang-an were haunted because of the calamities that befell previous owners, but he refuted the belief. What happened in a house depended on its residents, he said, and the house itself had nothing to do with it. Everyone feared calamity, he continued, but the reasons for calamity were predictable. Those in power easily fell out of power, especially if they were proud and haughty. He stated his viewpoint in still another way, noting that one could not get to be rich and influential merely by living on a site of good fortune. He concluded that the Chou dynasty lasted for eight hundred years but the Ch'in dynasty only three generations because of governing principles rather than fortuitous circumstance. Glory and fortune changed overnight; it was hard to stay in power, easy to be expelled.

Po chü-i was an earnest advocate of his political and moral convictions, but his earnestness was tempered by the realization that fame and influence were transient. He was attracted by the joys of life that accorded with one's personal tastes and philosophical interests. This ability to enjoy life as a man apart, as well as a bureaucrat within, stood him in good stead during his official service in the capital and his transfers to points beyond. It moved him to create poems in a harmonious and non-rebellious mood, the poems of quiet pleasures to be discussed in the next chapter.

Chapter 4

The Poetry of Pleasure: In Praise of Drinking

As we have seen, Po Chü-i's first advocacy was that poetry should contribute to the advancement of politics. He also proposed that one seek happiness in private life by cultivating frugality, reasonableness, and the enjoyment of pleasure in suitable propositions. His second advocacy differed from the first (in which he strived to achieve happiness for the masses) in that here he was proposing one's right to a personal pursuit of happiness. He wrote 186 poems on this theme, calling them poems of quiet pleasures, and placed them in the second section of his collection.

Please bear in mind that these poems were composed from 803 to 823, while he was in government service. They do not follow his didactic poems chronologically, as some Japanese scholars have implied, but parallel most of them in time. Slightly more than half were written prior to his demotion as marshal of Chiang-chou in 815, while the remainder were composed during his next eight years of service, which culminated in his appointment as governor of Hangchou. The concurrent composition of didactic and poetry of personal pleasure suggests that Po Chü-i was a split personality, embodying within himself at the same time the Confucian man of duty and the Buddhist-Taoist recluse. A desire to withdraw from the mundane world and the struggles of the market place, noticeable in his youth, heightened when he was demoted to Chiang-chou in 815, at the age of forty-three. And this sense of alienation became an integral part of Po's world outlook in the years that followed. Several critics stressed his Buddhist and Taoist leanings and exalted him as one who had the characteristics of an Immortal or a Buddhist adept. But such interpretations dealt only with the philosophic aspect of Po's writings.[1]

As he wrote to his friend Yüan Chen, Po's so-called poems of quiet pleasure were composed when he withdrew from public life and lived alone; when he lived quietly under the pretext of illness; and when he sang of love.[2] (The love referred to here must have been a love for nature and for predecessor and contemporaries.) These poems describe the joys of private life—the life apart from public involvement—in which his companions are song, lute, and wine, probably in that order. Such pleasures were to be enjoyed quietly and in peaceful contemplation of surrounding nature, with the poet striving philosophically not to counterbalance his involvement with society but rather to blot out memories of its very existence. There is not the overt display of vigor in these poems that we have seen in the didactic poetry, for as the poet himself stated in a letter to Yüan Chen, the features common to all were light thought and meandering expression.[3] The poet stressed again and again in these poems his contempt for and indifference to, worldly gain. This avowed indifference may have been a reflection of how he reacted to the political fluctuations and uncertainties of his times, for while he later occupied much higher posts than that of imperial critic in Ch'ang-an (808-10), never again did he take such an active role in policy formulation or show such direct concern with political events at the court. His work shifted from political involvement with the central bureaucracy towards consideration of less urgent administrative and office routine.[4]

With one minor exception, Po Chü-i wrote his poems of quiet pleasure in the five-character line, old-poetry style. There was rhyming of the even lines but no fixed internal tonal arrangements, and the poet expressed himself freely. The poems, varying in length from four to 260 lines, generally total sixteen to twenty lines. He derived thematic inspiration from T'ao Yüan-ming and Wei Ying-wu. T'ao was the poet-drinker-recluse of earlier centuries who finally spurned officialdom in favor of rustic retirement, while Wei was an older T'ang contemporary who likewise preferred the quiet life. Po expressed his admiration for T'ao and Wei in a verse written in 815, which he inscribed on the wall of a terrace. He referred to T'ao as "T'ao P'eng-tse" because T'ao had once served as magistrate of P'eng-tse County. Wei was called "Wei Chiang-chou" in the poem because, like Po, he had been sent to Chiang-chou in demotion. Wei, who had been governor of Suchow, was usually referred to as "Wei Suchow" rather than "Wei Chiang-chou". The places named in the poem were located in the vicinity of Hsün-yang; the "Great River" referred to the Yangtze. Po concluded the poem by modestly confessing to a feeling of shame at having had the audacity to compose a poem in the area formerly graced by T'ao and Wei, two of China's Poet-Immortals:

> I am always fond of P'eng-tse;
> literary thoughts so elevated and profound!
> I also marvel at Wei Chiang-chou;
> poetic feelings likewise pure and quiet.
> This morning I climb this terrace
> and know why they were as they were;
> the Great River is cold and one sees to its
>   depths,
> the Lu Mountains are green and lean
>   against Heaven.
> Deep night—the moon at P'en River;

usual dawn—the smoke at Lu Peak.
Clear brilliance and spirit vapors
day and night supply poetic matter.
I lack the talent of the two men,
so what can I do on coming here?
Because of the elevation
perchance I compose a poem,
but look up and down,
feeling ashamed (before) river and mountain.

Po was in Suchow in 786 during his youth, while Wei Ying-wu was serving there as governor. Wei achieved literary fame in his lifetime and was called a Poet-Immortal. Wei liked the simple and the quiet; he would burn incense, sweep his quarters clean, and sit in meditation. Wei's poems were quiet and tranquil, brief but deep in underlying meaning. In his lifetime Wei was compared to T'ao Yüan-ming, and when conversing, people coupled their names. Po Chü-i emulated Wei and T'ao by trying to adopt a frugal and quiet way of life unrelated to worldly gain and to describe this with directness and effect. He revealed that he intended to make Wei's poetic attitudes his own and praised his predecessor for the purity and elegance of his lines and the lofty sentiments and quiet candor of his poems.

When his mother died in 811, Po withdrew from official life to observe the mourning period and remained in retirement until 814. While living north of the Wei River, he wrote sixteen drinking poems in emulation of twenty poems about the pleasures of wine which T'ao Yüan-ming had composed more than four centuries before. T'ao was famous for two things—being a recluse and drinking wine. It was not until about a hundred years after T'ao's death that a complete collection of his works was compiled. T'ao once said that there was wine in one poem after another of his, and it was this poet-to-wine relationship that primarily interested later researchers, Lu Hsün included.[5] So in general, when one speaks of T'ao Yüan-ming one thinks of wine. The wine theme is found in about half of the 130 poems in T'ao's extant collection. Twenty are entitled, "Drinking Wine", and these are the twenty which set the theme for Po Chü-i. Like Po, T'ao failed to achieve his social objectives; wine-imbibing by both men helped them to relax and forget the outside world. T'ao realized deeply the inevitability of death and regretted only that because of poverty he hadn't drunk enough wine in his life. T'ao's official rank was low and he was always poor, a member of the small landowner class. When he died in 427, at the age of sixty-two, people gave him the posthumous name of "Mr. Quiet and Chaste".

T'ao and Po wrote prefaces to their drinking poems. T'ao explained that he was living in withdrawal from society, drinking night after night. In a tipsy state, he composed some lines to amuse himself, in no particular order, and had an old friend write them down for him. T'ao concluded with the hope that his compositions might amuse the reader.[6] Po stated in his preface that during a prolonged rainy season he closed the gates of his home and stayed inside. Having no other way to amuse himself, he warmed and drank home-made wine, often getting tipsy and sleeping away the daylight hours. Po felt lazy and did as he wished, taking up one thing and forgetting another. He chanted T'ao's poetry aloud and found that it accorded with his mood. He then wrote sixteen poems in imitation, using the same five-character old-style form. When Po sobered up, he laughed at the wild words he had written but saw no reason to conceal them from his friends. Po may have been moved to emulate T'ao in such verse because he revered him for having left official service to return to his native village and till the soil and for refusing to return. A study of Po Chü-i's poetic themes reveals a recurring mood of yearning to withdraw permanently from the bureaucracy. Po's poems on drinking are more subjective than T'ao's compositions on the same theme, for he tends to write about how he feels while T'ao tends to write impersonally about the nature of man. Po writes about the "I" of man, T'ao about the "non-I" of nature. Po used scattered words and phrases from T'ao and had far more descriptive and connective words than T'ao. He therefore is less cryptic and easier to understand.

Po's first poem in the series contrasts the brevity and uncertainty of life with the permanence and inevitability of death, which spares not even the sage. (T'ao's first poem stressed the constant change in human fortunes as evinced by glory and decay.)

The unmoving—thick earth;
the unresting—high heaven.
The immeasurable—sun and moon;
the long existing—mountains and rivers.
Pines and cypresses, turtles and cranes,
all live a thousand years.
Alas! Among all beings
Only man is not so.
He goes out early to court and market
and by night has reverted to the nether
　springs.
One's shape-substance and life-fate
are as imperilled as wisps of smoke.
Yao and Shun, Chou and K'ung,[7]
anciently proclaimed Sages and Worthies—
but if you ask where they are today,
they went once and did not return.
I don't have the herb of no death.
All things shift in accord with change;
what is not definitely known
is the brevity or duration of the interval.
Lucky when we have a healthy day,
we should sing before the wine cup.
Why wait for someone to persuade me?
I think of this for my own amusement.

Po's second poem evokes a mood of solitary communion with sombre Nature: "Cloud piled on cloud for more than a month; Heaven lowering, daily rains. When I raise the screen and look at Heaven's colorings, the yellow cloud formations are as dark as earth. Accumulations of rainwater destroy the fence; swift winds damage the roof. Common weeds grow in the courtyard; the fields are lost in mud. The village depths are cut off from visitors; the windows are dark and companionless."

> All day I don't leave my bed;
> leaping frogs occasionally enter my door.
> Leaving the gates, there's no place to go.
> Entering the room, I return to my lonely
>   place.
> If I don't amuse myself with wine,
> who can I talk to in my aloneness?

Po's next poem describes how he amused himself in the rain. In the morning he drank a cup of wine to attune his spirit with the universe. Like an unthinking oaf, he still lay in bed with the sun on high. He read at night, and it was as if the ancients were saying fine words to him. He was as pleased as if he had met them. He sat alone in the depths of night, with his lute at hand, and had more than enough time to press down on the strings. He composed poems with mad rapidity, and could not put down the writing brush. With three or four things (books, wine, lute, and poems), he passed days and nights. Therefore, while it rained he didn't leave his cottage for a ten-day period.

> First do I realize that one who lives alone
> with a peaceful heart can also pass the time.

The poet compassionately considered the plight in which his neighbors had been placed by the incessant rains, describing how a woman who gathered silkworms to the west tilled the soil but sorrowed because the beans she had planted sprouted prematurely because of the rains.

> But I alone, how happy,
> warming wine just as I please.

When the rainy spell coincided with the new brewing of a wine, he opened the bottle and filled the cup, a goblet of liquid jade and gold. Holding the wine cup was a pleasure and tasting the wine a delight. With one drink color came to his face; with a second drink melancholy disappeared. Four or five glasses, and tipsiness diffused every limb.

> Suddenly I forget
> the distinction
> between myself and others.
> Who is to distinguish
> the right and the wrong?

"The rains continue night after night, and I am helplessly drunk and oblivious. My heart is so topsy-turvy that I am laughed at by my (rain-)worried neighbors."

The fifth poem in the series might be dedicated to drinkers and the art of drinking:

> Morning—alone in drunken song;
> night—alone in drunken sleep.
> One jug of wine not yet emptied,
> already drunk three times alone.
> I don't mind drinking too little,
> but delight in the good
> that little quickly brings.
> One cup and then another—
> three or four at the most.
> I then am pleased at heart,
> external things all forgotten.
> Forcing another drink on myself,
> in exuberance I leave every entanglement.
> He who drinks at once a vast amount
> merely considers quantity as precious;
> but when he gets helplessly drunk,
> he's no different from me.
> So laughingly I tell heavy drinkers,
> "Why foolishly waste wine money?"

This drinking poem gives evidence that Po Chü-i was not a heavy drinker, but one who could feel the effects of three or four cupfuls. He regarded wine as a stimulant which weakened the bonds of the vexatious world, but in this poem he expressed a preference for moderation. Here Po also depicts the way of the poor, who cannot afford to drink excessively. To the man in straitened circumstances, drinking to excess by another may seem a form of unparalleled gluttony. Po's poor-man philosophy on drinking contrasts with that once expressed in verse by T'ao, who said he regretted only that he hadn't drunk enough wine in his life. Po Chü-i drank in the surroundings of his home, but unlike Li Po, for example, was not a carouser.[8]

The weather finally cleared: "It is an autumn day, not a cloud in the sky, not a dust speck on quiet earth. Round-round the new moon, a white disc arising beyond the forest. I remember yesterday's darkness and rain; it has rained continuously by now for thirty or forty days. I entrust myself to homemade wine and am unaware of time's passage. I say to myself that I can stop drinking when the rains stop, but

> When I face the color of the new moon,
> unless I drink it saddens me.

What remains of the wine jug by the head of the bed has an especially good aroma; I take it beneath the southern eaves and raise it to drink with diligence. Its sparkling clarity enters the cup and (I drink until) the white dew arises on my clothes. Then I know that,

day or night, how can I do without Mr. Wine? I have
poems in the Music Bureau style, composed but not as
yet made known:

> This morning I was drunkenly elated
> and wildly sang, startling the neighbors.
> Alone I enjoy (the moon) again and again—
> how much better together with friends!

To Po Chü-i the moon symbolized homesickness and
thoughts of home, for everyone shared the view of the
moon, no matter where: "Mid-autumn festival, the fifteenth night; bright moon at the front eaves. I approach the wine goblet but suddenly don't drink, remembering ordinary life pleasures. I have like-hearted
persons, the far-far Ts'ui and Ch'ien; I have van-
ished-trace friends, the distant-distant Li and Yüan.
Maybe they have soared to clouds of high officialdom,
maybe they have fallen twixt rivers and lakes. You
haven't seen me now for three or four years and I've
no ground-shrinking magic. And you aren't wine-fly-
ing Immortals. How can I get all four to come and
talk under the bright moon? It is hard to find such a
good night, but destiny precludes our meeting. The
bright moon won't remain and it gradually descends to
the southwest. How can there fail to be other meetings for us? Regretfully (I stand) before this scene!

"Ts'ui" refers to Po's friend Ts'ui Hsüan-liang (772-
833), "Ch'ien" to Ch'ien Hui (755-829), "Li" to Li Chien
(764-821), and "Yüan" to Yüan Chen. By the time the
poem was written, Yüan Chen had been sent to Chiang-
ling in demotion.[9] The eighth poem in the collection
adopts several words and phrases from T'ao Yüan-
ming's poems on drinking and other themes.[10] "Double-
Nine" was a festival held on the ninth day and ninth
month of the lunar calendar, a day on which special
foods were prepared and eaten. One also climbed hills
and on hilltops drank chrysanthemum wine to ward off
malevolent influences.[11] The introductory theme for Po's
poems seems to have been taken from the ninth poem
in T'ao's wine series, in which he describes a knock on
the door and a visit by an old villager with a wine jug.
Here is Po's eighth poem:

> Homemade wine all drunk up,
> no wine on credit in the village.
> Seated in melancholy, sober tonight,
> what to do about autumnal feelings?
> A guest suddenly knocks on my gate;
> how fine his words are!
> "I'm an old man of South Village,
> coming to call with a jug of wine."
> Delighted that the jug isn't dry,
> how can I ask how much is in it?
> Though Double-Nine has passed,
> there are chrysanthemums remaining by the
>   eaves.
> I am delighted, but distressed by day's brevity;

> before we realize it, night falls.
> Don't go back so hastily, old man;
> wait for the new moon's splendor.
> The guest leaves but interest remains—
> all day I drink and sing alone.

Po next likened himself to Yüan Hsien and Yen Hui,
two of Confucius' poor disciples; he was cold and
hungry, but the little he had sufficed, and he enjoyed
mental tranquillity and lived in leisure near the pure
waters of the Wei River. There were more than a
hundred willow trees and a dozen huts nearby:

> Cold, I depend on the sun neath the eaves;
> hot, I wash my body in the stream.

When the sun comes out I don't get up, but when it
sets I'm again asleep. A western breeze fills the villages and lanes; (there are) the clearness and coolness
of an autumn day. There are only the sounds of birds
and dogs; one doesn't hear the noise of horse and
carriage. At times I tilt a jug of wine, while seated and
looking towards the mountains in the southeast. My
little niece is just learning to walk; she tugs at my
clothes and plays before me. One can delight in this,
almost as (Confucian disciples) Yen Hui and Yüan
Hsien once did."

In his tenth poem, Po extols wine's unsung merits,
using a series of classical allusions which I have rendered in paraphrase:[12] "Darkly sparkling, the wine in
the cup; it has merit but it doesn't boast. If it doesn't
boast, men are unaware (of it), so I'll now speak for
it. Good generals approaching a great enemy urge forth
troops of a thousand, ten thousand, make wine and
food offerings to the river spirits, and go to their
deaths with hearts as one. Brave warriors sharpen
their short swords stirred with courage and a spirit of
anger, but, once drunk, they forget revenge and their
limbs seem boneless. The killing of a filial wife in Han
times was followed by more than a year of drought,
but one libation poured to her spirit brought on rains
unending through the night. The prison air of the Ch'in
(dynastic capital of) Hsien-yang—such wrongdoing and
pain that it produced a demon. For a thousand years
it was unwilling to leave, but it vanished through one
outpouring of wine. How much more so the lamentations of women and children and other illnesses of
solitude and grief! Pleasurable drinking will always
disperse these, like frost getting to a spring day. Then
I know that the spirit of the liquor-fermenting yeast
among the myriad things is unparalleled."

The eleventh poems in the wine theme series of Po
Chü-i and T'ao Yüan-ming consider the problem of
life and death and reach melancholy conclusions. T'ao
notes that the virtuous Confucian disciple Yen Hui still
died prematurely, praised by posterity but having had
to endure a life of hardship. After death there is no

consciousness, argues T'ao, so enjoy life while you can. That the body is worth a thousand gold can only be said of the living and not of the corpse.[13] Here is how Po comments poetically on the quest for longevity: "Smoke and clouds obstruct the Immortal's dwelling; wind and waves restrict the Immortal's mountain—how could I not wish to go there? The great sea route hinders and is distant. Gods and Immortal—though I have heard talk of them, the spirit herbs can't be sought; those who don't attain long life stay in the world like ephemeral ants. One who has passed on returns not again; why be pained and cherish a hundred griefs? Thinking of this, suddenly my inner organs are warmed; seated, I see that a white hair has been produced. I raise my wine cup and turn to drink alone; looking back to my shadow, I invite it (to join me) in vain. My heart and mouth make a pact: We won't say stop till we're drunk.

> If this morn I don't drink to the utmost,
> do I know if there will be a tomorrow?

Don't you see beyond the suburb gates pile after pile of grave mounds and hills? The moon's brightness saddens man utterly, worthless weeds blow mournfully in the wind. If the dead had awareness, they'd repent not having lit candles to frolic (while they lived).

Po's next poem is in praise of T'ao Yüan-ming, describing him in these terms:

> I've heard that at Hsün-yang Commandery
> there was formerly learned Gentleman T'ao.
> He loved wine, not fame;
> grieved at being sober, not poor.
> He was once P'eng-tse magistrate
> but only served for eighty days.
> He lamented and, suddenly displeased,
> hung his seal on office gates.
> He hummed his poem of returning home,
> on his head a wine-filtered turban.
> Officials couldn't get him to stay.
> He went right into old mountain clouds.
> Returning, under his five willows[14]
> he again cultivated truth through wine.
> Glory and profit among men
> fall away like mud and dust.
> Already gone a long time,
> he left behind writings.
> One after another urge me to drink;
> besides this, there's nothing said.
> Since I've gotten old
> I secretly yearn to be as he was;
> I can't come up to him in other respects,
> So I imitate his intoxicated muddledness.

The thirteenth poems of T'ao and Po deal with the same subject, the different pattern of behavior in two men. One was always drunk, states T'ao, and the other always sober, and they were always together. But somehow to T'ao the straitlaced one seemed stupid and inferior to the drunkard. Po amplifies the theme somewhat, with historical personages cited to make the same point: "The Prince of Ch'u doubted a loyal official and released Ch'u Yüan to Chiang-nan; the Chin dynasty slighted an elevated scholar and abandoned Liu Ling below the forest. One man was constantly drunk and alone, the other constantly sober and alone. The sober one had many unattained ambitions, the drunk one many pleasurable feelings. Pleasurable feelings can be trusted for personal goodness, but what do unattained ambitions finally achieve? (Liu Ling) proudly lay down among the wine jugs while (Ch'u Yüan), emaciated and decayed, walked about the marsh banks:

> One worried and the other enjoyed,
> the reasons are exceedingly clear!
> I hope you'll drink wine.
> Think not of posthumous fame.

Po Chü-i was fond of using the storyteller's technique, resorting to fiction to dramatize content and make a more effective general observation from a particular instance. Here is the story he told in the fourteenth poem, probably referring obliquely to personal circumstances: "There was a scholar from the Yen-Chao region, whose words and looks were wondrous and rare; day after day he went to the wine houses, pawning his clothes for a few cupfuls (of wine). I asked, 'How were your spirits thwarted?', and he replied, 'I was begotten in lowly weeds. The land was cold and my fate was bleak; my talents for assisting the sovereign were of no use. How could I be without a plan for saving the age? (But) a good go-between was lacking at His Lordship's gates. I presented proposals time after time but they went unreported; slowly I returned, with empty hands.

"'There was also a classmate of mine who first ascended the ladder to the blue clouds (of high officialdom); the road (we were travelling) was severed by his eminence and my humbleness, and though I knocked on his vermillion gates he failed to open them. When I went back (to my village) I planted crops, but for three years drought caused disaster. I entered the mountains to burn herbs of immortality, but one day they turned to ashes. Stumbling along for more than fifty years, my whole life has been distress unending. Everywhere unable to set forth, I have thus reverted to the midst of wine.'"

The next-to-last poem in Po's series emulating T'ao's poetic style and thought again stresses the meaninglessness of fame:

> There is a man of eminence in South Lane,
> in a high-topped carriage drawn by four horses.

I ask, "What distresses you so
that at forty your beard is white?"
"You don't know," he replies,
"but high rank means many worries."
There is a poor scholar in North Quarter;
broken jars for windows, ropes for doors.
He goes out supporting a mulberry cane;
he enters to lie in a snail's shed.
He is lowly and useless and without a care,
heart at ease and body comforted.
There is a rich old man in East
   Neighborhood,
with goods piled up in five cities.
He collects grains and silks in the Eastern
   Capital,
sells gold and pearls in (Ch'ang-an's) West
   Market.
He toils by day and plans by night,
day or night lives untranquilly.
There is a poor person in West Cottage,
lowly wife mated to lowly male.
Cotton-clothed, she is hired to beat the rice;
short-garmented, he is hired as a scribe.
Through this they seek food to eat;
once satiated, are overjoyed.
The eminent and humble, the poor and rich:
Though there is a difference in their
   stations,
worry and joy, profit and loss
are not far from one another.
Thus, in the view of all-persuasive man,
the myriad things are as one.
But we still do not know life and death—
which is victory, which defeat?
Slowly doubting and unknowing,
let's enjoy ourselves with wine.

The last poem in the series describes the arbitrariness of the universe to nature and to man, an arbitrariness which is unfathomable. Drink and be unaffected, the poet seems to say, for life is without discernible rhyme or reason: "The Ch'i River is clear and pure, the Yellow River muddy and yellow. As communication (systems), they are enumerated among the four great rivers; clearness or muddiness does not harm the one or the other. (In the Chou dynasty) the Grand Duke battled in the fields (in support of the Martial Prince), but Po-i (refused to assist the Prince) and starved at Shou-yang (instead). At the same time both were called Worthies and Sages, so advance or withdrawal did not prevent one or the other (from being so honored)."

The poet then poses unanswerable questions: "If you say that Heaven doesn't love the people, why does it bring the grains to life? If you say that Heaven really loves the people, why does it bring jackals and wolves to life? If you say that the gods give blessings to the good, Confucius the Sage after all flurried and bustled (his whole life). If you say that the gods send disaster to the evil, (why did) the tyrannical First Emperor of Ch'in rule over all? What crimes did worthies Yen Hui and Huang Hsien commit that they died so young? The principles of things are unfathomable; the ways of the gods are also hard to figure. I raise my head to look up and question Heaven, but Heaven's color is but a blue-blue."

One should merely
plant more millet,
be drunk all day,
wine goblet in hand.

In a Sung compilation, literatus Huang Shan-ku once commented that while Po Chü-i and Liu Tsung-yüan (773-819) composed poems in imitation of T'ao Yüanming, Liu's compositions were closer to the originals.[15] Wang Li-ming, in considering Huang's statement, opined that Liu Tsung-yüan was close in words but not in spirit, Po Chü-i close in doctrine but not in words. Wang believed, therefore, that each T'ang poet attained one aspect of T'ao's writings.[16]

Po Chü-i was demoted in 815 and sent south to Chiang-chou. In 816 he visited T'ao's former residence nearby and composed a preface and poem in remembrance. He explains in the preface that because he admired T'ao as a person he had earlier composed the sixteen poems in imitation (translated above). Chancing to pass by two areas where T'ao had lived when he quit his magistrate's job at forty and retired, Po Chü-i thought of him, visited his former home, and had to write a poem in praise. Po, who was then in his early forties, must have been in low spirits about his bleak prospects. To paraphrase the poem: "The world of dust and dirt," Po remarks, "doesn't blemish jade, and similarly the holy phoenix doesn't partake of offensive-smelling flesh. Ah, Mr. T'ao Quiet and Chaste!"[17] Born between the Chin and Sung (dynasties), there was something he truly protected in his heart though he finally was unable to utter what it was. T'ao admired the ancient Sage who concealed himself in the mountains and starved to death rather than serve a ruler he considered improper. Certain ancients were not at all distressed by hunger and poverty because they were single, but T'ao had five sons and with them shared hunger and cold:"

The food in his belly not full,
the clothes on his body not complete.
Often summoned, he didn't arise—
such can be called a true Worthy.

Po states he was born five hundred years (it was actually four hundred years) after T'ao and that every time he read T'ao's autobiography, *The Biography of Mr. Five Willows,* he was filled with thoughts of him and felt a yearning in his heart. He had already sung of the essence bequeathed by T'ao in sixteen poems;

now when he came to visit T'ao's house of old there was a stillness, as if the ancient was before his eyes. Po didn't envy the fact there was wine in T'ao's goblet or that his lute was not strung. (T'ao, not caring for music, carried around a stringless lute; the "wine in the goblet" referred to one of T'ao's poetic lines).[18] But he did envy the way in which T'ao abandoned honor and profit in order to age and die by his hill and garden. Oh, the old village, the old mountain stream where he had lived! Po didn't see the chrysanthemums under the eaves which T'ao had mentioned in one drinking poem, but there was still the mist in the village, the mist which T'ao had poetically described. T'ao's descendants were unknown but his clan still hadn't moved from the locale. Everytime Po met someone with the T'ao surname, he was overcome by a feeling of yearning.

Chapter 5

The Quieter Pleasures

The drinking poems written in emulation of T'ao Yüan-ming differ markedly from the poems of tranquillity and sobriety which dominate that part of Po's poetry collection devoted to the quiet pleasures. The poet evokes a mood of yielding resignation to time and events, coupled with a realization that social action and involvement create traps for the unwary. He expresses this sentiment in poem after poem, seeking to meditate, to identify with Nature, and to lose his consciousness of ego in a world of competition and strife. He wants to surmount the confines of birth, death, and rebirth by mentally transcending the cycle of life and death. He knew a mountain-dweller named Wang who was trying to lengthen his life, but he reminded him that everything was relative, including the duration of the time interval:

> I hear you reduce sleep and food,
> listen daily to talks of God and Immortals.
> You secretly await Adepts extraordinary,
> covertly seek longevity's mystery.
> Long is long in relation to short—
> you can't leave the life death track.
> Even if you attain longevity,
> it's merely better than dying young.
> The pine withers in a thousand years,
> the hibiscus perishes in but a day.
> Finally both join the void.

Why should one boast about one's years? There is a natural difference between living to be as old as a Methuselah[1] or dying in childhood, but there's no (real) difference between life and death:

> It's best to study non-life;
> non-life is non-annihilation.

Po Chü-i was almost forty when he clarified in verse what he meant by being at ease: "Body at ease, I forget arms and legs; heart at ease, I forget right and wrong. At ease, I forget ease as well and (attain a state where) I don't know who I am. My limbs are like rotten wood, and I sit upright and unaware. My heart is like dead ashes, and I am silent and unthinking. Today comes and tomorrow follows; heart and body suddenly leave. At thirty-nine, I am in the twilight of my years. (Mencius said that) at forty his heart was immovable,[2] and now I've almost reached the same level of awareness."

He was pessimistic about life, which to him was unsubstantial and devoid of lasting significance, and he transformed this pessimism into one of his major poetic themes. One night in autumn he and a friend were viewing the bright moon and the early dew. Po was fifty at the time, and he urged his friend to listen to the words of his song about life: "After fifty, man deteriorates; before twenty, he's a fool. Since night and day divide (even the thirty intervening years) in half, how little time there really is! Before birth, one doesn't delight and enjoy, and after death there is an excess of accumulations. But how can one use pearl bed coverlets and jade ornament cases in the yellow springs of the netherworld?"

The poet stressed mind over matter. In 811, while in mourning, he went fishing on the Wei River. The river, the color of glass, held carp and bream. Po usually suspended a bamboo rod into the stream. A slight breeze blew the long fishing line here and there and, though Po sat facing the fish, his heart was in the realm of egolessness. He commented on the story about a white-haired old man of ancient times who also went fishing north of the Wei River. The old man didn't go there to get fish but rather to seek the friendship of the Cultured King of the Chou dynasty. But Po lacked even the old man's motivation, for he was interested in neither man nor fish and wasn't skilled enough to catch either. He was amused by the sparkle of the autumnal waters and, stimulated, returned home and drank wine.

Tipsiness was a subordinate theme in the descriptions of pleasurable experiences, for Po sometimes reached a state which rendered even the wine cup superfluous. As he wrote in one poem: "Newly-bathed limbs extended, I sleep alone with my heart at peace. Moreover, having sat upright till the depths of night, I sleep till the sun is high. The spring coverlet is thin but warm, the room I sleep in secluded and quiet. I forget about the matters of men, and seem to have become a Pillowed Immortal. Utterly at ease, I have dreamless thoughts and I enjoy a harmony difficult to describe. It is indeed better than the drunkenness of T'ao Yüanming,[3] and can rival the meditations of a renowned Liang dynasty temple priest (who lived three centuries ago).[4] What beckons me to awake? The cry of the shrike. When I do, wife and children laugh; life in spring is unbounded."

Po was proud of being lazy and claimed that he was even lazier than Hsi Shu-yeh, a literatus of the Three Kingdoms' State of Wei cited in my translation of the next poem.[5] **"Singing of Indolence"** was probably written in 814, when the mourning period for Po's mother came to a close.

Singing of Indolence

> There is officialdom but, indolent, I don't
>   choose it;
> there are fields but, indolent, I don't till
>   them.
> There is a hole in the roof but, indolent, I
>   don't repair it;
> my clothes are torn but, indolent, I don't
>   sew them.
> There is wine but, indolent, I don't drink it;
> it would be the same if the cask had long
>   been empty.
> There is a lute but, indolent, I don't play it;
> it would be the same if it were stringless.
> My family tells me the rice is gone;
> I want to cook but, indolent, don't pound
>   the grain.
> Relatives and friends send me letters;
> I want to read them but am (too) indolent to
>   open the seals.
> I have heard of Hsi Shu-yeh,
> who spent his life in indolence.
> He played the lute and forged iron;
> compared to me, he wasn't indolent.

Po Chü-i's "indolence" was a reaction of withdrawal from the harshness of bureaucracy and the vagaries of the human condition. As he once commented: "Yesterday there was wailing at a neighbor's home south of mine; how painful those wailing sounds! They say it's a wife wailing for her husband, twenty-five (when he died). This morning there is wailing at a north ward; they say it's a mother wailing for her child, (deceased) at seventeen. With all the neighborhoods like this, there is much premature death; one realizes that men of this floating world rarely get to be white-haired. I am now past forty and, remembering the early deaths of others, pleased (at still being alive). From now on I won't mind seeing reflected in this bright mirror a snowlike head (of hair)."

There are several poems written between 816 and 818, after the poet left Ch'ang-an to serve in the south, in which he stresses meditation and release: His noon nap in the rear pavilion sufficing, he arises and sits, confronting the evening spring scene. Aware that his eyes are still muddled, unthinking his heart true resides:

> Serenely I return to my oneness nature,
> emptily quiet leave ten thousand thoughts.

To the poet, there was nothing comparable to this realization:

> It is originally the Village of Non-Being,
> also called the Place of Non-Usefulness;
> practising meditation and sitting forgetfully,
> returning together on the same road.

He once spent the day seated under a pine tree, occasionally strolling along the banks of a pond. Strolling or standing, sitting or lying, at heart he was indifferent and inactive:

> Unaware of the swift passing of the years,
> letting white hairs grow as they may.
> If I weren't slighted by the world,
> how could I pursue feelings of leisure?

The poet, skilled in self-revelation, sang of his thoughts in another poem: "I often hear the words of Chuang-tzu, stating that the clever toil and the wise are grieved and saddened. They are not equal to those of no talent who eat their fill and ramble about for pleasure. Having spent a year at Chiang-chou in the south in demotion, I now approach this doctrine. I don't differentiate things as black or white but immerse myself in and float with time. The morning meal and the evening sleep are the sum of personal planning; apart from these I relax and let go, at times seeking the solitude of mountain and stream. I ramble to a famed Chin dynasty temple site in spring and to an equally famous Chin dynasty terrace in autumn:

> I may hum a verse of poetry;
> I may drink a bowl of tea.
> Heart and body unencumbered,
> vast-vast like an empty boat.
> Wealth and eminence also have distress,
> distress in the heart's peril and grief.
> Poverty and humbleness also have pleasure,
> pleasure in the body's freedom.

The poet advised himself to conquer adversity by adhering to simplicity and by remembering that all paths high or low led to the grave. He once napped after a meal and on waking rose and drank two bowls of tea. Then he looked up at the sun, about to set:

> People in joy regret the quickness of the sun;
> people in grief detest the distance of the
>   years.
> Those with no joy and no grief
> entrust to life, long or short.

Po, who inclined towards Taoism, wrote two poems based on a passage in the *Chuang-tzu*[6] on the oneness of things: "The green pines are a hundred feet high," he remarked, "the green orchids but a few inches low. Since both are born in the great universe, long or short are destined. The long cannot withdraw, the short cannot advance. If one makes use of the principle (of relativity), failure and success are both griefless." He contrasted a long-lived tree cited by Chuang-tzu, which survived eight thousand springs,[7] with a type of hibiscus whose blossoms failed to last the night. There was among the plants the gradually maturing lone bamboo. Its body aged in three years but it was green throughout the four seasons. It had to cede to Chuang-tzu's long lived tree for age, but it was still superior to the hibiscus.

He needed to live just a little longer in order not to be a ghost by the age of fifty. He knew his destiny and was satisfied; he entrusted to fate and was at peace with himself. Therefore, though he had known days of failure and withdrawal, his face showed no grief. He formerly served in a period of worldly honor. Now he no longer planned to exert physical effort but rather to elevate his heart and purify his aspirations. Failure and success did not depend on oneself; pleasure and distress did not depend on Heaven. Heaven's mandate was something one could do nothing about, but one could get one's heart to be at peace. One should strive to be self-reliant, and it was not difficult to look inward:

> Don't question Heaven's mandate;
> Heaven is high and hard to talk with.

Po returned to the theme of man and fate in two poems which he entitled **"Arriving at Principles"**: "What thing is robust and does not age? When is there failure and not (later) success? This is like music and regulation being transposed into the first of the five musical notes:

> My fate alone is so hapless!
> Much sadness and little splendor.
> In the vigorous years prematurely
>   deteriorated;
> brief tranquillity, and return to long
>   impoverishment.
> There is nothing I can do about fate;
> I entrust to the Natural and await my end.
> My fate can't do anything about me;
> my heart is like emptiness and void.

Befuddled, he was one with transformation; confused, he was one with the world. Did one who could sit amidst distress have to be hurt by it? The implication of the concluding lines is that one who frees his heart from striving is emancipated from the cycle of failure and distress.

The second poem about arriving at principles cites miracles described in revered ancient works: One ancient's daughter changed into a stream; a certain man sickened and on the seventh day of his sickness turned into a tiger. A willow was produced from someone's left elbow, a man changed into a woman. The classics-oriented Po Chü-i cited miracles as if they were precise truths and went on to say they showed how birds, beasts, water, and wood differed from man. They produced changes and did not await death to revert to earth. Then he referred to the human cycle:

> All my bones are my own,
> but I still can't master them.
> How much more so, other times and fates!
> What's the sense of counting blessings and
>   disasters?
> When the time comes, one can't hold back;
> when life goes, how can one arrest it?
> One should only cultivate boundlessness.
> I have heard the words of the all-pervasive
>   ones.

In 822, when Po was riding to Hangchow to become governor, he dozed on his horse and on waking composed the following poem:

> A long journey—started for some time;
> the forward residence still not reached.
> My body is tired, my eyes befuddled—
> tired and napping, I finally doze off.
> My right sleeve still dangles a whip,
> my left hand gradually relaxes the reins.
> Suddenly I wake and ask my servant:
> We've only travelled a hundred paces.
> The division between body and spirit
> is in this time distinction;
> time specified on horseback
> but events unlimited in dreams.
> How true! Words of the all-pervasive ones—
> a hundred years is the same as a single
>   sleep.

The poet sang of butterflies and flowers, to reinforce his thesis about the futility of competition. The crane of longevity remained aloof in the lofty pine, away from the disturbing noise and bustle of contention:

> Autumn blossoms—purple flourishing;
> autumn butterflies—yellow scattering.
> Under the flowers, butterflies new and small
> fly and play, flocking east and west.
> Day and night a cool wind comes;
> confused-disorderly, flowers fall in clusters.
> The night is deep, the white dew cold;
> butterflies have died among the clusters.
> Born by day, to die together by night;
> each follows its own order of species.
> Don't you see the thousand-year cranes,
> mostly nesting in the hundred-foot pines?

He wrote another poem about nature in a different mood, praising the mountain pheasant which lived unfettered and in natural harmony. Better it is, he seems to say, to be poor and free than to be well fed but marked for slaughter in the world of master and mastered: "Five paces, a mouthful of grass; ten paces, a drink of water. The mountain pheasant follows life in accord with its nature. Above the rafters (of the bridge nearby) there is neither net nor arrow, and below there is neither kite nor hawk. (That is why) cocks, hens, and fledglings get to finish the years (allotted to them by) Heaven. Alas! There is the chicken under the eaves and the goose within the pond. Since they receive the favor of rice and grains (from their owners), they inevitably have the worry of being sacrificed."

Even on becoming governor of Hangchow, Po indicated in verse that his philosophy was unaffected and that he still tried to see into the spirit rather than the outer frame. In singing of his feelings, he mentioned that formerly he was an official in the Secretariat at Ch'ang-an, while now he was governor of Hangchow (referred to literally as "two thousand piculs", which was a governor's annual rice allowance). Comparing the two periods of official service, he felt that the past was inferior to the present, but others said the opposite:

> In the past, though I lived in proximity to
>   the throne,
> all day many were the worries and cares.
> There were poems I dared not sing,
> there was wine I dared not drink.
> Now though I live far away,
> to the year's end I am unencumbered by
>   service.
> I eat my fill, sit all day,
> sing long songs, am drunk all night.
> Human life is within a hundred years;
> it speeds by like a passing rift.
> Strive first for a body tranquil and at ease;
> next wish for the heart to enjoy pleasure.
> Getting things is a loss,
> but losing things is a gain.
> Therefore, men who see the Way
> see the heart and don't see traces.

Chinese tradition placed a limit of a hundred years on human existence and throughout the centuries used "a hundred years" as an expression synonymous with life. There are many references to this phrase to be found in literary works from the Han dynasty onwards.[8]

There are series of poems in this section, written from 805 to 823 (with a gap from 819 to 821), in which the poet indicates what he enjoyed. The pleasures he writes about are pleasures of the mind. He looked for quiet circumstances and scenic elegance. When confined by busy office routine in Ch'ang-an, he sought to escape mentally from the restriction of city surroundings by visualising mountain scenes and temple stillness. There were many temples and monasteries in Ch'ang-an, and he once stayed in one of them in the bothersome heat of midsummer. It was a day of lonely wind and rain, and at night cicadas cried. The Ward of Auspiciousness Everlasting (just east of the imperial city) was still, Hua-yang Monastery was in solitude. No horses or carriages reached here, and cassia blooms of autumn portent filled the earth. Time passed and worldly things were distant. Why did one have to wait for deterioration and old age to first become aware of buoyancy and rest? How long distant true seclusion was! The way of completeness was attainable through closed eyes: "Though my body is in the world, my heart wanders with the empty none. Morn hungry, there is a simple meal; night cold, there is a cloth coverlet. Luckily, I avoid cold and starvation; besides this, what is there to seek? Having few desires, even with small ills I enjoy Heaven's (way) and my heart doesn't grieve. How do I clarify my intentions? With a copy of the Book of Changes at the head of my bed." (*The Book of Changes* was an ancient guide for telling one's fortune.)

Po Chü-i was a student par excellence. Early one morning in 805, when he was thirty-three, he said farewell to friends scheduled to take additional official examinations. Here is how he describes the scene: "Early in the morning I ride in my carriage to send off the Elevated Persons; the east has still not lightened. 'I have gotten up too early,' I say to myself, but already there are horses and carriages about. The torches of cavalrymen cast shadows high and low; street drums (announcing the dawn) can be heard far and near. The pitiable early morning (test candidates) look at one another and their spirits rise:

> The dust flies when the sun comes out;
> everyone is active scheme-scheming;
> scheme-scheming, what do they seek?
> Nothing else but profit and fame.

But I often get up late and live emptily in Ch'ang-an City. Spring is in its depths and my official term of service has been fulfilled; daily I have that return-to-the-mountains feeling."

In 807 he received a few days of sick leave and went to South Pavilion. While enjoying the view from its heights, he composed the following: "Inclining on my pillow and not seeing things, the bolt of my gate has been closed for two days. I first realize that the body of an official doesn't get any rest till he gets sick. My pleasurable intent is not in the remote, but in a small pavilion ten-feet square. Above the bamboo tops by the western eaves I sit looking at T'ai-po Mountain, and feel ashamed that the clouds above the distant peaks confront this face of mine in the realm of dust." (There were many mountains called T'ai-po, but the mountain Po Chü-i refers to here could be seen from Ch'ang-an.)

He spent a night alone at the Temple to Which Immortals Wander: "A sand crane ascends the steps (of the pond) and stands; moon reflecting on the water's edge, I open the gates. These hold me here for lodging, and for two nights I cannot go back. Fortunate in meeting with a quiet scene, I rejoice in not having companions with me to urge me to return. Since I have had this lone excursion, I do not propose to come (here) with others any longer."

He described an autumn scene in his front courtyard:

Dew falls on bamboo mats, color like jade;
wind on screens, shadows like waves.
Sitting in melancholy, tree leaves fall.
Central courtyard bright-moon filled.

Po enjoyed reading the poetry of contemporaries and earlier poets, and he described this enjoyment in a poem. He was seated in a small official pavilion, leisurely looking outward: "Windblown bamboos scatter echoes of purity, and smoke-trailing cassias affix their green figures. The sun is high, people and officials have left, and I sit tranquilly in a thatched hut. With coarse clothes I ward off heat, with simple food I appease morning hunger. I trust in these to satisfy myself and mentally and physically do little. When my lone singing above the pavilion stops, there is nothing before my eyes. The snow on T'ai-po Mountain peaks, a volume of T'ao Yüan-ming's poems. People like different things and this is what I like. To be sure, those who crave fame will laugh at me, but I'll willingly let them.

Wu-t'ung tree by the well, cool leaves move.
The neighbor's pestle, autumn sounds
  starting.
Alone I sleep beneath the eaves,
feeling half my bed moon-occupied.

He derived quiet pleasure from seeing and communing with nature, and wrote about the sounds of the pines: "Fine moon, I like to sit alone, twin pines before the balustrade. A slight wind comes from the southwest to enter secretly the branches and leaves. Before the bright moon in the depths of night, lonely and desolate are the sounds emitted (by the pines), (like) the soughing of rain on a cold mountain or the cold notes of a lute in autumn. Hearing it once, the fierce heat is washed away; hearing it twice, muddled care is broken through. I don't sleep all night (because of it) and my mind and body are clarified. Horses and carriages move from the street to the south, songs and music resound from my neighbors to the west, but who is

aware that under the eaves no noise fills my ears?" Even while on duty in the palace, he was pleased by quietude:

Gates majestic, ninefold of silence.
Windows forlorn, a roomful of tranquillity.
It seems like a place to rectify one's heart;
why must one be in the deep mountains?

We are able to achieve a state of "have-not" tranquillity, needing little and wanting less: "Few guests before the gates, many pines and bamboos neath the steps. Autumn scene descends the west wall and a cool breeze:

There is a lute but, indolent, I don't play,
there are books but, tranquil, I don't read.
In my heart throughout the day
tranquillity and non-desire.

The poet then asks himself: "Why must one have extensive quarters? I don't need many accumulations. A ten-foot hut can accomodate my body, a peck of stored grain can fill my stomach. Moreover, I lack the art of ruling and, doing nothing, receive official rewards. I don't plant a single mulberry tree or hoe a single crop, but all day I am filled with food to eat and all year I am abundantly clothed. Aware of my heart of shame, it is naturally easy for me to be satisfied. . . ." The poet during his struggles with bureaucracy was pursued by these thoughts of withdrawal, longing for rusticity: "If the iron is soft, it doesn't become a sword; if the wood is crooked, it doesn't become a carriage. I am now like these, dull-stupid, not getting (even) to the gates. I willingly turn away from profit and fame, obliterate my traces, and revert to the hills. I sit and lie in a thatched hut, facing lute and wine goblet. My body leaves the world of complexity and care, my ears deny the din of the market place. Blissful and non-doing, I read the five thousand words (of Lao-tzu), on a griefless and joyful plane, with few desires and a cleansed heart."

Once while working in the palace, Po dreamed of visiting the Temple to Which Immortals Frolic: "By the western balustrade I have drafted the edict and am free; the pines and bamboos are deep and still. The moon appears and a clean breeze comes. Of a sudden it resembles a night in the mountains. I then have a dream of (the mountain) to the southwest and in the dream become a guest of frolicking Immortals:

When I wake and hear the palace water
  clock,
I still say it's the dripping of the mountain
  stream.

He was a mountain-climbing enthusiast: "Long sick and remiss in appreciation in the heart; this morning I climb the mountain. The mountain is autumnal and the touch of clouds is cold; these accord with my clear and emaciated features. I lie and can be pillowed on white rocks, stroll and can climb on green grasses. In my mind it is as if I've obtained, and all day I don't want to return:

> Human life is but an instant,
> life sent twixt Heaven and Earth.
> The heart has a thousand years of grief,
> the body lacks a simple day of leisure.
> When can I release this Web of Dust?
> Coming here, I'll close the gates behind.

The lute, one of the companions of the Chinese literatus, also afforded joy to Po Chü-i, the joy of music clear and controlled which blended with a meditative mood. The lute was a respected musical instrument, considered representative of the music of the ancients, and lute-playing was considered one way to enlightenment.[9] Po described in verse the joy of playing the lute on a clear night:

> The moon appears, the nest is birdless;
> I sit in solitude in an empty forest.
> This time my heart's bounds are tranquil,
> and I can play the plain wood lute.
> Cool, clear sounds come from the wood
>   nature.
> whose peacefulness accords with the human
>   heart.
> The heart heaps up harmonious vapors,
> the wood responds with old orthodox
>   sound.
> Echoes from the movement of things are at
>   rest;
> the song ends—autumn night is deep.
> I feel the origin of orthodox sound,
> Heaven and Earth pure, deep profound.

While in mourning at Wei Village from 811 to 814, the poet recaptured and redefined the mood of the recluse. He expressed his feelings poetically soon after arrival, saying: "The lodging heart is in the body and the lodging nature is in the heart. This body is an external thing; how can it be worth paining with grief and love? There are, moreover, leftover adornments, embellished hairpins, and lofty carriage covers. (But) these are removed from the body, externals added to externals. How worried in accumulating them, how saddened by losing them! One then knows that name and fame are injurious, whether gained or lost. The scholar who lives in poverty and utter ease has the fragrant grasses for his turban and sash. Since I have secured this Way, my body is impoverished but my mind peaceful."

It was also at Wei Village in 811 that he described quiet living:

> Stomach empty—one bowl of rice;
> starved for food—there's an excess of taste.
> Lying half a day under south eaves,
> warmly reclining, I went to sleep.
> A cotton robe covered two knees,
> a bamboo armrest supported twin wrists.
> From dawn right to dusk
> mind and body at one in non-happenings.
> Heart satisfied is then wealthy,
> body quiet then equals eminence.
> Wealth and eminence being in this,
> why must one occupy high position?
> Look at Minister P'ei:
> His gold-printed damasks illumined the
>   ground,
> but his heart was distressed daily
> and he died at only forty-four.
> Then one realizes riders in lofty carriages
> are there mostly in worry and fear.

Po, who was keenly aware of aging, asserted in his late thirties and early forties that he felt the onset of age and had no worldly ambitions. The pleasures of temple dwelling remained a preferred poetic topic, and in 812 he wrote: "Famous official—I'm aging, (too) indolent to seek (to be one), so I retire and take my body's ease in the fields. Home and gardens—I'm sick and (too) lazy to return, so I dwell in a monastery.[10] Rustic clothes in exchange for official garments, a goosefoot (cane) in place of horse and carriage:

> In my goings and stoppings I'm free,
> and feel utterly unencumbered in body;
> at dawn; I frolic above a southern mound,
> at night I rest under an eastern retreat.
> The thousand, ten thousand human world
>   things
> do not concern my heart at all.

Po had none of the intellectual's disdain for the untutored peasant. On the contrary, he was drawn to the scene of the toilers in the fields and felt compassion for their labor and its meager rewards. He returns in poem after poem to the theme of self-shame, saying he consumes but doesn't produce. He anticipated the views of the Communists in China more than a millenium later, who were to insist that intellectuals spend time working in the countryside alongside the peasants. Here is how the poet described an autumn harvest: "The labors of the world do not attract me; I am usually happy and tranquil. Nights, I go to look at the fields and quietly walk alongside village hamlets. The harvest is piled in the fields, flocks of sparrows chirp in flight. How can the year's bounties be only for man? The sounds of birds and beasts are also joyous.

"An old man of the fields meets me and is pleased; he silently gets up and arranges the wine cups. Hands reverently drawn in sleeves, he invites me to partake of wine remaining from the autumn sacrifices. Embarrassed by his diligence and reverence, my goosefoot walking stick is tarried-calmed. His words and actions are natural and truthful and I am unaware of (any) evils of farmers. I stop drinking to ask him about ordinary things; he tills the field and his wife and children harvest. Their muscular vigors are harassed by toil, their clothing and food are often simple and poor:

> I feel ashamed that salaried officials
> never toil in the fields.
> Filling themselves without toiling;
> how does this differ from the man of Wei's
>   cranes?

The last line refers to a story in the *Tso-chuan* (Tso's comments on the *Spring and Autumn Annals* attributed to Confucius). Towards the close of the second year of Duke Min's reign, a certain marquis was so fond of cranes that he had them carried around in official carriages. This wasteful extravagance made such an adverse impression that when the time came to repulse invasion, everyone said that the cranes should fight the enemy instead of the people.[11]

In 815 Po Chü-i inscribed a poem on a wall of the Temple of Jade Springs:

> Placid-placid, the color of jade springs;
> far-far, the bodies of floating clouds.
> Heart at ease, I face the settled waters.
> Clear and clean, we both lack worldly dust.
> In my hand grasping a green bamboo cane,
> on my head wearing a white silk turban.
> Having enjoyed myself fully, I descend the
>   mountain,
> not even knowing who I am.

He once withdrew from court on an autumn day and amused himself south of Ch'ang-an. The poem he wrote about this experience is the last in the series of pleasure poems composed prior to his demotion in 815 to marshal of Chiang-chou: "Withdrawing from court, my horse is not yet fatigued; early autumn, the days are still long. I turn the reins and go south of the city, the fields in the suburbs just then clean and cool. Water and bamboo straddle the paths, which wind through hills and streams. Looking up, I see the evening color of the mountains; looking down, I enjoy the illumination from the autumn springs. Tying up my horse by the green pines, the white rocks become my bed. The hairpins of officialdom which usually encumber me are on this day forgotten, as is my body. At dawn, I line up in official rank like phoenix and egret; at night I play alongside seagull and crane. The heart of deceit is thus extinguished, and neither (as official nor as recluse) do I go astray. Who can know my heart and its traces? It is neither journeying nor withdrawn."

After the poet reached Chiang-chou, he had a small pond built by his official quarters: "Beneath the eaves I open a small pond; water fills it to overflow. White sand is spread along the bottom, green stones piled up in the four corners. Don't say it's not deep and wide, but consider that it pleases the solitary man. The water ripples from a slight rain at morn, looks pure under the bright moon at eve. How it lacks the great river's waters, with whiteness of waves extending to the Heavens! (But even an ocean) can't compare with this ten-foot square pond, little more than a foot in depth. Pure and shallow—(in play) one can drag one's hands in it, and all troubles and vexations can be washed away:

> What I love the best is dawn and dusk,
> when it's a flake of jade of an autumn day.

He mentioned a Taoist monastery where he took lodging, bringing to life inanimate objects of nature: "White clouds are still stationed on the cliff and red leaves in the forest scatter for the first time. The autumn light induces me to stroll leisurely, and I don't know if I have journeyed near or far. At night I lodge in a Taoist monastery and, on lying down, sense that my common-dust heart is extinguished. Fame and profit my heart has forgotten, and the dream of Ch'ang-an is also at an end. If things are like this after coming here for the moment, how much more so if I spend a life in concealment! How shall I control the evening hunger? With a spoonful of the Immortal's flour called 'mother-of-the-clouds'."[12]

His free time as the Chiang-chou governor's nominal assistant in 816 is briefly referred to in a poem entitled **"A Pact With My Heart"** ("green robes" refers to his official dress):

> Black locks—white hairs invade;
> green robes—common dust eddies.
> Steady unmoving and swift soaring,
> at Chiang City I ascend to assistant.
> Mornings, I go to my lofty study,
> harmoniously basking, lying in the sun;
> nights, I go down before my small pond
> and tranquilly sit facing the water.
> I've already made a pact with body and
>   heart
> always to pass my days as I did today.

It was early spring in Chiang-chou, and the poet was alone:

> The snow thaws and the ice also melts,
> the scene harmonizes and the wind again warms;
> courtyard and fields are moist filled,
> tiny buds sprout at the base of the wall.
> My official residence—quiet without incident;
> the sun slopes westward, covering my door.

If I don't read Chuang-tzu and Lao-tzu,
with whom can I wish to talk?

He was entranced by the first warmth of spring and, approaching his middle forties, reflected on the spring of youth and the spring of now: "From where has spring's warmth come? A slight harmony arises in the blood. My breath and bones are exhilarated, and I sleep confusedly by the eastern window. It is the last day of the first lunar month; I am free, with no official business. Sleeping deeply, I can't put a stop to it, and sleep from noon to two in the afternoon. Thinking far back to the days of youth and health, (when) I slept quickly and was often joyous:

But once deterioration and illness set in,
this kind of flavor the pillow lacks.

No pleasure derived from contemplation of or absorption in nature was too slight to escape Po Chü-i. Here he describes the delights of eating the bamboo shoots abounding in Chiang-chou, saying that in this regard the southern prefecture excelled either Ch'ang-an or Loyang:

The area being Bamboo Hamlet,
spring shoots fill mountains and valleys.
Mountain peasants break them off, carry
   bundlefuls,
carry them early into the city for sale.
Things which are numerous being cheap,
for two cash one can buy a bundle,
I place them in a rice steamer,
cooking them together with the rice.
The purple bark is peeled off (like) old silk,
the white flesh broken open (like) new jade.
I then add it daily to my food,
for ten days don't think of meat.
I have been long a guest of Ch'ang-an and
   Loyang,
where this taste was often insufficient;
now I eat them without indecision.
The southern breeze blows and makes
   bamboo.

The appeal of food to the starved is described by Po Chü-i in another poem about the simple joys: "Reclining yesterday without supper, today I rise and am morning-starved. What is there in my poor kitchen? I cook rice and steam (the vegetable called) autumn mallow. The red rice grains are fragrant and soft, the green leaves (of the mallow) glistening and fat. When starvation comes, it is stopped by filling up; but after filling up what thoughts are there? I remember days past when I met with glory; now it is the time of impoverishment and withdrawal. Now I don't suffer hunger and cold; in the past I also had no excess of resources (but enough to provide the bare necessities). My mouth has food undiminished, my body has

clothing undiminished. I comfort my heart and secretly ask myself, 'What is glory or decline? Don't study the feelings of ordinary men, for they make distinctions of right and wrong'." (The poet implies his contemporaries erred in contrasting glory and right with decline and wrong.)

During his Chiang-chou tour, a small pond near a pavilion comforted him:

At noon, wearied by the heat in my front
   study,
at night, loving the purity of a small pond.
When the forest-reflected remnant sun goes
   down,
a tiny coolness arises near its waters.
Seated, I hold my fan of rushes and palms,
idly humming two or three poems.

At forty-five, Po wrote about closing his gates to the world and described a child of his about to talk: "My heart has long forgotten the world; the world also is not involved with me. For me it is therefore a matter of nothingness and that is why my gates long are closed. How long have my gates been closed? Without realizing it, two or three years. My writings already overflow the bookcases, and a child has been born who is about able to speak:

I first realize that the body easily ages;
am saddened anew by the many hardships
   in the world.
Looking at those who flurry about with the
   times,
they toil-toil in the dusty realm.
At the end of their years what do they get?
It is better to be tranquil and at leisure.

The 817-18 period was marked by rebellion and civil disorder. Po refers in verse to the troop movements and makes it clear that he prefers not to be involved in military planning. The poem was written from a lofty terrace overlooking the river: "A hundred-foot terrace along the river bank, before the terrace a thousand-li road.[13] I depend on its height to look over the plain—it suffices to soothe my feelings. On the station road, travel unending, defending the grasslike passes. In coming here, on a day of such busyness, I particularly feel how good it is to be a man of leisure. My years are past those of 'not being deluded' (a reference to Po's being past forty, since Confucius was quoted as having said that when he was forty, he was not deluded.) For me to withdraw in retirement is really not early. Henceforth, I shall brush the dust (of the world) from my clothes and return to the mountains not yet old."

Po compares his sense of isolation and of lateness in rearing a family with the dilemma of the sparrow who builds a nest for its young when it is too late in the season, when it should be returning southward with the other birds: "All the birds have finished producing young but autumn swallow alone stumble-slips. The fifth day of autumn already nears, (when it should fly south with the rest). What is its intent in holding mud in its mouth (to build a nest for the young)? Unaware that time and season are late, it vainly uses its labors to excess. Things in the world of man are also like this. It is not only the swallow that makes a nest (too late and in vain)."

From 819 to 821 there is a three-year hiatus in the poetic record of quiet pleasures. In a poem written in 822 Po Chü-i asserted that he had forgotten the scenic splendors which enhanced court and palace. However, he still remembered the simple and unpretentious bamboo which grew before his window when he was serving at Hsin-ch'ang, a district in Chekiang:

> I don't recall the pines of West Office,
> I don't recall the chrysanthemums of South
>   Palace;—
> I only recall the courtyard at Hsin-ch'ang,
> the bamboos sough-soughing by north
>   window.
> By the window, pillow and bamboo mat—
> who lodged there after me?

The plight of a withered mulberry tree is likened to the plight of a man consumed by anxiety:

> An old withered tree by the road—
> it got withered but not in one morning.
> Its bark is yellow, externally it is still alive,
> but its heart is black, its innards first got
>   scorched.
> It is like the people who worry a great deal,
> not because a fire is burning outside
> (but because they are on fire within).

In 823 Po wrote poetically about his life in Hangchow as governor, comparing it to his past life at Ch'ang-an: "Vast-vast the tides are level for the first time, mild-mild the spring sun arrives. Distant rivers and mountains, empty vast; clear and bright the good weather from Heaven. Beyond, there are things to accord with one's feelings and nothing within to encumber the heart. Several songs are sung to the bamboos, a wine cup drunk as I look towards the clouds. I stroll along, supporting myself with a cane, lie down, read, and take my sleep. Long cultivating a sick frame, I am deeply versed in the flavor of leisure. My distant thoughts of the capital, where there is confused-disturbed flurrying for fame and profit. This morning is an odd-numbered day and for court visits there will be many horses and carriages. (On the odd-numbered days the Emperor held court.) Those in favor guard against the censure of others, those in power cherish worries and fears. Those who are rewarded with riding in lofty carriages do not, I fear, have true wealth and eminence."

Chapter 6

On Friends and Friendship

Po Chü-i shared with his friends the quest for quiet pleasure removed from strife. They would exchange visits, go on excursions to temples and famous scenic sites, and correspond in verse. He and his friends shared the enthusiasm of Ch'ang-an's residents for flower viewing, usually at famous temples and monasteries which were known for the beauty of their peonies or of their peach, lotus, and apricot blossoms. There were many strolling groups and couples, and the botanical diversity of the Serpentine made it suitable for pleasure strolls in any of the four seasons. In his poems, Po urged friends to stay the night with him in quiet surroundings, and when this couldn't be done he sang of his heartfelt disappointment and sadness. His intellectual and emotional involvements were with fellow scholars and poets, and the outpouring of emotion for Yüan Chen, Liu Yü-hsi, and other men was a dominant theme in the intimate dialogues which concerned and moved him.

The first poem in the section on quiet pleasures was sent in the spring of 803 to eight friends, among them Yüan Chen, after they had passed official exams. Po was then working as a library collator and living in northeast Ch'ang-an, near the imperial palace area.[1] This first of his many poems written to friends about enjoyments shared include human interest comments on living conditions. Wrote the poet: "The imperial capital is a fame-and-profit place; after the cock crows there's no quiet living. There is only the lazy one, who still hasn't combed his hair when the sun is high. Skill and clumsiness differ in nature, as do clues to advancement and withdrawal. Fortunately, I have encountered an age of peace and a Son of Heaven[2] who likes literary scholars. Since I have little talent, it is hard to use me in a high (capacity) so I am (just) a collator in the library. I enter there twenty out of thirty days a month, and therefore am able to cultivate my foolish and heedless person. I have a four- or five-room thatched hut, one horse, and two servants; a (monthly) salary of 16,000 cash gives me a monthly surplus.

"I don't have the encumbrances of (worrying about) my daily livelihood and am little involved in bothersome human events. That is why my youthful heart is always tranquil. Don't say that I have no friends, for I have active acquaintances and quiet ones. There are seven or eight in the library with whom I go out. When we have been prevented from chatting and laughing together for a ten-day period, I look for their carriages day and night. Who can (take a rest from) collation duties to unloosen his sash and recline in my hut? There are bamboos playing before my window and a wine seller outside my gates. How can I wait on you gentlemen? With a few bamboos and a jug of wine."

He wrote the next poem in this collection to his friend Yüan Tsüng-chien, an elder cousin of Yüan Chen's who died in 803. He was responding to one of Yüan's poems about a stroll they had taken to the Serpentine, a stream in beautiful surroundings located in extreme southeast Ch'ang-an. This poem to Yüan Tsung-chien, typical of the way in which Po Chü-i responds to poems by contemporaries, recalls a trip they had once made: "There are thousands and ten thousands in Ch'ang-an, all busily leaving their gates on respective endeavors. Only you and I trusted to our horses to go far along. When we got to the head of the Serpentine, the late sun's reflection was bright on grass and trees. South Mountain had a fine look and this sick journeyer felt mental lucidity. The water birds fluttered white feathers and the lotuses bent stalks before the breeze. Why did we have to go (like) Mencius[3] to the River of the Vagabond to wash our turban tassels, since we could do it here?

"That fine scene won't come twice; it will be hard to again enjoy such things together. I sit in melancholy in the red dust; the evening drum has a rat-a-tat sound. Passing one night after the return, mundane thoughts again gradually arose (in me). But when I heard your beautiful jade song (in verse), I was able to recleanse myself of the dust on my garments."

Moon-viewing was one of Po's favorite pastimes. In the summer of 803 the thirty-one-year-old poet went together with other collators to enjoy the sight of the moon at K'ai-yüan Monastery and to spend the night there. Here is how he described the scene: "A few friends and I have our names written in the official registers at the capital, but our posts are insignificant, with no responsibilities of note, and we've more leisure than if we were visitors. Deep-deep within the Taoist monastery is where the expectation for my heart's enjoyment resides. Getting to the gate, we turn back our horses and carriages and enter the monastery courtyard with turbans and canes. It is the start of the pure and harmonious (fourth lunar) month, and the trees are just now resplendent with blossoms. The wind is pure and the new leaves are shadowed by it; the birds yearn after the remaining blossoms on the branches. Towards evening the heavens clear; haze unveils from the southeast.

"We arrange wine below the western corridor and await the moon, leisurely lining up the wine cups. In a little while its golden spirit arrives, as if it has a date with us. The moon glow is resplendent, and once it

sheds its radiance the different heights of a complex of buildings are revealed:

> Before the pure scene, through the night
> we laugh, sing, and know no fatigue.
> In Ch'ang-an, fame-and-profit place,
> how many know these pleasures?

Po became an administrator at Chou-chih District in 806 and invited his friend Wang Chih-fu to visit him. **"Lament Everlasting"** was written that year at Wang's suggestion:

> You have washed your feet (of the world),
> a guest of clouds and rivers;
> I must bend my waist,
> hairpin and official scepter adorned.
> Our footsteps contrast tumult and quiet;
> a few miles apart, but long the days.
> If you suddenly go on a pleasure journey,
> don't regret you are visiting noise and dust;
> I have especially planted bamboos before
>   the window,
> and they will be your hosts.

Mountain-viewing with Wang Chih-fu one other time was commemorated with a six-line, three-rhyme verse. He also responded in kind to the poem of a friend about their once viewing an old grass chapel in the mountains. Po described the chapel as being removed from the dusty world, amidst scenic splendors. It was glorious to wear embroidered silks and imposing to uphold official duties, but his pleasure was not in these society-markers: "I look in vain towards the skies of that grass chapel." Po wrote poetry to and harmonized poems with fellow-official Ch'ien Hui (755-829); the first poem describes how they shared lodgings one winter's night inside the palace:

> Night deep—the memorial draft finished;
> mist and moon intense piercing cold.
> About to lie down, I warm the remnant last
>   of the wine;
> we face before the lamp and drink.
> Drawing up the green silk coverlets,
> placing our pillows side by side;
> like spending more than a hundred nights,
> to sleep together with you here.

He wrote a poem in response to one shown him by Ch'ien Hui, in which his friend described how the palace looked at dawn. Po used the occasion to comment on how he felt, hemmed in by bureaucracy:

> The window whitens—a star galaxy;
> the window warms—remnant of lamp light.
> Seated, you roll up the coverlet of red,
> watch me seal the purplish-inked writing.[4]
> Far-far water clock leaks away,

rise-rise rose-ray scene.
The towered terrace—red glow illuminates
pines and bamboos in green luxuriance.
You love this season's fineness,
turn and say especially to me,
"I didn't know the pure realm of majesty
in dawn scene was so incomparable."

Po was close to a censor named Hsiao in mood and emotion, and he lamented Hsiao's absence from the palace one summer night as he slept alone: "Your Censorate is a place for legal matters, my Hanlin Academy an office for clear petitions. (You are like) a hawk majestically seeking a bird of the fields, (I am like) a swift steed in goodness seeking the mountains. Though we differ in our searches, we both revert to what is unsuitable. This is why in our hearts we're lost and secretly think of one another. Going to sleep alone on a summer's day, the day is long—what to do? Placid in mind and without reflection, my teacher is emptiness and quietude. My outer form has the encumbrance of events, but my heart has an appointment with eventlessness. Once there's an in-heart expansion, external trouble seems left behind. My rank is eminent but I am personally oblivious; intent on quiet, the realm comes as a consequence. I face pine and bamboo as I do when in the mountains. How can these thoughts not be for you? Most of the others would never understand."

Po wrote a poem to his Taoist friend Wu Tan (744-825), admiring the way in which Wu had resigned an important post near the throne: "Clever ones are forceful in painful labors, wise ones mindful of painful griefs. You, my beloved sir, lack cleverness and wisdom; throughout the year you are quiet, remote. You once ascended to the Censorate and assisted the nobles of the east. Drafting memoranda by hand to reprove human transgressions, your heart met with the fortunes of complete victory. The way of officialdom is like wind and waves, but your heart was like an empty boat.[5] Drifting along and not possessing, gaining freedom from (the unpredictability of) advance and withdrawal. Now you have come to doff the hat trimmed with sable, though at times you attend at the Dragon Palace.[6] Your official functions match your heart's quiescence, and your dwelling accords with solitude's traces. In winter you are sustained by the sun of the southern eaves, your limbs warm and soft in the extreme; in summer you lie in the breeze of the northern window, pillow and mat like cool autumn. South Mountain enters below your cottage, the wine jug is at the head of your bed. There are areas of quietude in the human realm; why must one be concealed by forest and hill? Looking at myself, I am stupid and dim, stirring all my life and utterly unrested. My once having entered the golden (Hanlin Academy), gates, stars, and mist have made three or four (yearly) revolutions. His Lordship's favor and trust are hard to repay; for

long I have merely stayed close by. In the end I should request an idle post, withdraw, and go frolicking with you.

Lying alone in the palace, Po described the scene and thought of Diarist Wang:[7]

Slow-slow drips away the palace water
　clock,
anxious-anxious cries the darkness crow.
Cassia flowers fell in last night's rain;
slight coolness as I lay by northern eaves.
Dawn, remnants of lamps not yet
　extinguished,
the screen quietly turning over, (shaken by)
　wind.
Everytime I secure a quiet circumstance,
I think of talking with my old friend.

In a longer poem written to Li Chien (764-821), a Confucian vegetarian, he recalled a visit to Li's home: "External matters bother my body and external things bequile my emotions. Long after parting from Mr. Li, pettiness and stinginess arise within me. I recall that when I visited you I would dismount and knock on the brushwood and thorn (gates of your poor home). Sometimes you hadn't gotten up yet; your children would happily precede you in welcome. (Or) they would stand alongside you and laughingly appear at the gates, you with clothes turned about or hat awry. Sweeping the steps, there were the green patterns of the moss; brushing the porch, there was the pureness of the wistaria's shade. The homemade wine warmed with the coming of spring, the garden vegetables, cooked with the dew. We looked to the mountains, seated at the east pavilion, awaited the moon, and strolled by the southern plain. There was quiet at the gate, with only the talk of birds; the market was distant and (hour-announcing) drum sounds few. We faced one another and talked the whole day, never about profit and fame. We separated, but when will we come together? The bright moon has already been full three or four times. When we parted, the remaining flowers fell, but by now new cicadas cry. Spring's fragrance is suddenly waning, and the remorse in my heart at parting is still unpacified. How can I not think of ordering my carriage? But official duties bind me to my seat. You formerly made a promise to visit me and come to the mountain city (with me). My heart of appreciation has long been blocked; promised words should not be disregarded. Fortunately, we are not distantly separated, a one-day journey on horse."

Po wrote a poem of praise to Yüan Tzu, a Minister on the Right who was governing Hua Prefecture in 805 when Po made a trip there.[8] The poem gives us an idea of Po's concept of the good official. This was an infrequent poetic theme up to this time (the year 805), when he was thirty-three, and perhaps he was deliberately trying to flatter an important superior in the hierarchy. He refers to him in the last line of the poem as "Duke Yüan": "Wei River green full-full; Hua Mountains blue-green, lofty-aloft. How beautiful these mountains and rivers! And you are right in their midst. Your talents are fitting for the world, and things in it are moved to accord with your sincerity. The Star of Fortune[9] sends down blessings for mankind, the timely rains assist the yearly outcome. Changes are carried out and there are no complaints; the jails have been emptied for a thousand days. Governing is suitable and the atmosphere harmonious; the crops have been abundant for three years. I have come from the capital, urging on my horse to get east of the passes. I love the people of this commandery, for it is like seeing the ways of great antiquity. The heart of the current Son of Heaven worries about the people and is caring-anxious.[10] How can all under the Heavens be protected? Let all things be obtained by (ruling) like Duke Yüan."

He received a poem in 806 from Yang Hung-chen, a scholar in Ch'ang-an who was ill, and characteristically admired Yang for cherishing virtue and for being oblivious to wealth:

> Pillow concealed, you're lonely-lone;
> bending my waist, I strive and strive.
> I sigh at the passage of time;
> we're but a night's lodging apart.
> When was it? That other day, strolling
>   hand-in-hand,
> the spring waters at K'un-ming Pond[11] were
>   placid.
> How many days since we left the
>   commandery?
> Summer clouds have arisen on T'ai-po
>   Mountain.
> You have not yet gained your intent,
> poor and sick, a guest in the capital.
> Poverty strengthens the chasteness of the
>   determined,
> sickness prolongs the feelings of the
>   elevated.
> You recline on a bench, undisturbed,
> close your gates—no welcomes or partings.
> The dragon reclines, heart-awaiting,
> the crane is emaciated, pure in looks.
> The purity came forth in the writings
> you gave to me like resplendent jade.
> How can I comfort your hunger and thirst?
> I offer you this, a poetic strain.

To the Chinese poet, the pine symbolized longevity, elevation above the throng, and purity held steadfast; it was to the pine that Po Chü-i likened his friend Neng Lun, lamenting the fact that his talents were ignored: "The pines by the mountain torrent are lofty a hundred measurefold, cold high soaring through the four seasons. On confronting the breeze there is purity's sound; they face the sun without crookedness or shadow. How is it that the common man of the times only appreciates forests of peach and plum? How is he unaware of the virtue of steadfastness? The fragrant and scented seduce his heart. Mr. Neng studied writings; his spirit is elevated and his merits deep. In his hands a hundred verses, phrase after phrase revealing gold in sand. He has been distressed and chaste for twenty years, with no one assisting his sunken state. Now I am still poor and humble, so I can merely be your friend (but can't financially relieve your distress)."

At West Pavilion, Po inscribed a poem to Yang Ying-shih which was impersonal in tenor, concluding that one does not have to enter the realm of Immortals in order to renounce the world. Yang Ying-shih was possibly one of his wife's relatives:

> Quiet obtains in the area above the pavilion,
> its distance matching traces beyond the
>   dust.
> Leaning on the balustrade, looking
>   southeast,
> birds extinguished, mountain upon mountain.
> Bamboo dew is cold to human vexations;
> blowing cryptomerias purify sick faces.
> High-spirited, to true interests suited,
> way and heart have a meeting.
> Since here one can leave the world behind,
> why does it have to be a peak of
>   Immortals?[12]

He sent a poem to Taoist Adept Cheng, who had left retirement to serve in the Secretariat, only to sicken and revert to the reclusive life. Po reveals how living in nature appealed to the T'ang Confucian oppressed by work: "Sir Cheng got The Natural, so that emptiness arose in heart and bosom. He inhaled the vapors of smoky mist and congealed into a form (like that) of eternal snow. His Grand Lordship (the Emperor in 785) at the start of the era of Virtue Primordial, sought worthies and achieved peace. In a small chariot (Cheng) entered the blue-green of the hills and, welcomed, descended T'ien-tai Peak. At Red City Mountain (nearby) he took leave of Immortals and at terraced palaces associated with worthy officials. Time and again he received official advancement, but with reposed countenance he resigned at the palace gates. The cage-leaving crane fluttered, the forest-returning phoenix cried. In the fire one distinguishes the good jade, and passing through the mist one recognizes the virtuous pine. For his new dwelling he depended on the Ch'u Mountains, the mountains jade green and the ravines deep. The cinnabar ovens fired, smoke was dispersed; the yellow-essence (grasses) bloomed, an abundant profusion. A bed curtain of fragrant grasses, the night lute clear; a cassia (colored) wine goblet, the spring wine warmed. The men of the times didn't go to his place, the moss on the rocks had no evidences of dust. What am I doing now? I am scurrying about society in a body of senility. If I don't visit you in the direction of those forest ravines, there is no way for me to meet you in the city's streets. I finally must shed the entanglement of dust, get a place (for retirement) through divination, and wander with you . . .". The expression in the last line, literally "to divine a dwelling", referred to the practice of selecting through divination an auspicious site on which to build a home. There was an age-old Chinese belief that men should be instructed in how to erect buildings so that the dead, the gods, and the living could all be located within the auspicious influences of nature.[13]

He described a visit by a fellow scholar named Ch'ü,[14] who likewise preferred quietude:

> The west study is silent, it is already dark.
> A knock on the gate with a rap-rap sound.
> I know that you are coming to stay,
> brush off the dust mats myself.
> What is there in a village home?
> Tea and fruit to welcome the guest.
> Poor and quiet like a monk's dwelling,
> a bamboo forest leaning on four walls.
> The kitchen lamp casts a shadow aslant,
> the sound of rain drips against the eaves.
> If you were not a quiet-loving man,
> would you be willing to share this night?

In 812, while in mourning by the Wei River, he wrote a poem in sympathy to someone identified only as Yü the Seventh, on learning of Yü's demotion. He consoled Yü with the reminder that while fame was uncertain, the mind, conscious of the arbitrariness of good or ill, triumphed over adversity.

> I am sick, reclining north of the Wei River,
> you are old and exiled east of Pa.
> We pity one another with a long sigh;
> my thin fate is the same as yours.
> Having sighed, I go back to laughing;
> neither laughing or sighing are yet ended.
> My later heart mocks my former intent—
> how deluding dull what one sees!
> Human life between Heaven and Earth,
> like a great bird feather in the wind;
> it may soar above the blue clouds,
> it may fall into mud and mire.
> In court robes assisting the empire,
> it comes about but I know not why.
> In cloth garments trusting to the fields,
> a chance going not of my own efforts.
> External things cannot always be;
> one should cherish personal emptiness.
> Don't let grief and melancholy
> lodge themselves in heart and bosom.

Po states that his poems were poorly regarded technically and thematically by contemporaries, but conjectures that admired predecessors like T'ao Yüanming and Wei Ying-wu would have appreciated them. He felt that only Yüan Chen esteemed his efforts, but Yüan lived far from him: "Lazy and sick, I always have much leisure, but when leisure comes, what to do? Still unable to abandon pen and ink, I occasionally compose a poem. The poem is done, insipid and flavorless, and is largely laughed at by the crowd. Above, they are criticized for dropping the tones and final rhymes; below, they are disliked for their stupid words and phrases. At times I hum them to myself, and when the humming ends I have my thoughts. Wei Ying-wu and T'ao Yüan-ming were of different times than mine, but apart from them who would be fond (of my poetry)? There is only Yüan Chen. He was exiled to Chiang-ling Prefecture and for three years has been an official there. We are two thousand *li* apart; the poem is done but he is distant and unaware (of it).

Strolling along in autumn by the banks of the Serpentine in Ch'ang-an, which coursed by the Garden of Hibiscus, Po addressed the distant Yüan Chen in a mood of reminiscence;

> Lonely and desolate, the banks of the slope;
> walking alone, my thoughts in excess.
> The autumn lotus, on sick leaves
> has white dew large as pearls.
> I suddenly recall we two enjoyed the area,
> the north-south corner of the Serpentine.
> The pond in autumn has few visitors,
> there were only you and I together.
> Crying crickets hidden in red luxuriance,
> emaciated horses stepping on green
>   wasteland.
> That time and this day,
> both the start of late autumn—
> the season so very similar,
> but that time and scene no longer.
> There are only men who scatter;
> year after year I get no letter.

Po happened to meet Li the Third, a fellow scholar (perhaps Li Chien, 764-821), and he insisted that Li spend the night: "In life we soon become wandering officials, but don't say we lack intimate friendships. Like my heart and yours—there must be reasons for their having gotten acquainted. We parted before the Gate of Spring's Clarity (in Ch'ang-an) and met on Golden Slope. Two or three cups of village wine, detaining us through the cold day's eve. Don't despise the insipidness of village wine; we can trust to it for discussing the plain truth in our hearts. Please be less indecisive; bind your horse to the tree before my gate. Next year, if I'm in health, I am thinking of going to the rivers and lakes. If we think of one another some other day, the one I know won't be able to search me out. Our later meetings are uncertain, so stay tonight."

The unexpected visit of an old friend supplied Po with a brief poetic theme on the dispelling of loneliness:

A Friend Visits at Night

Bamboo mat, with pure breeze between the
    eaves;
wine cup, with a bright moon under the
    pines.
My solitary intent was just like this
and then my old friend came!

A long poem to Yüan Chen written in 815, before Po's demotion and transfer from Ch'ang-an, describes how Po Chü-i enjoyed leisure while at the capital. (Bright Nation Ward was located in southeast Ch'ang-an, near the Serpentine.) "I proceed into (the royal enclosure) and do obeisance before the palace gates, and then withdraw and eat breakfast below the corridor. I return to (my home at) Bright Nation Ward; the man lies down, the horse is relieved of its saddle. Then I sleep till noon, and on arising and sitting up, my heart is boundless. How much more so in the fine season, a day clear and harmonious after the rain! The green shade of the persimmon trees is fitting and the gardens and pavilions of the royal family are extensive. Hu County wine in the jug, Chung-nan Mountains above the wall. I sleep alone and then I sit alone, opening my robes before the breeze. The Zen priest and the poet-stranger gradually regard one another. If one wants to talk all-night talk, one must sleep an all-day sleep. Outside of my official calls at court I have nothing else to obstruct me:

Though my years are lengthy, my body is
    strong;
my rank is poor and my heart much at ease.
Luckily, I've no sudden sickness and ache,
haven't reached painful starvation and cold.
From now on I trust in quiet pleasures
with which externals cannot interfere.
I only trust those who are quiet;
it is hard to speak for the active.
Attendant-Worthy Yüan in the Censorate,
sooner or later you will be a higher official,
but until you are,
you lack leisure to accompany me.

Wu Tan sent him a poem in Ch'ang-an and he responded in kind, likening his Taoist friend to an Immortal sentenced to live in the world below. In the first line, Po refers to himself in the third person: "The Serpentine has a sick guest, one whose gates are mostly closed. Recently, since my horse died, I do not go out and am even more idle. Still, I hear someone has sent a letter and get up and go to the door to look. A white

envelope with red characters written on it, inside a jadelike poem. I hum it with my mouth, listen to it with my ears, and the heat suddenly flies away. It is like rinsing the mouth with a water of cold jade, like hearing the strains of an autumn wind. The opening lines sigh at the seasons, the closing phrases (make me) think of laughing and talking with you. Slack and lazy, I don't visit others; a street apart is like a mountain apart. I once heard T'ao Yüan-ming's words that, heart remote, he was inclined towards his own area. You live in Peaceful Village Ward (just below the East Market), with tumult from carriages right and left. Bamboos and herbs enclosed in a deep courtyard, lute and wine cup opening on a small veranda. Who realizes that a southern section of the city has been converted (by you) into a world beyond? You were originally an Immortal, with your name (inscribed) in the Stone Dwelling (of Immortals). I don't know what fault you committed, to be exiled to be an Immortal in the human realm. I often fear that when your years come to fullness you will return like a breeze-wisp to Purple Smoke (Immortal realm). Don't forget that in the ephemeral world of ants, there is this Advanced Scholar who passed examinations with you in the same year."

Po expressed delight at the unexpected visit of a Mr. Ch'en, referring to him as his "elder brother", a term of deference still used today among Chinese friends:

Rejoicing at Elder Brother Ch'en's Arrival

The yellow bird's cries about to cease,
the green plum clusters half-ripened;
I sit and pity the extinction of spring things,
arise and enter the east garden for a stroll.
I take along a goblet and lazily pour wine;
suddenly I hear a door-knock sound.
When a man of leisure comes, I still rejoice,
but how much more so for Elder Brother
    Ch'en!
We talk away the day naturally and easily,
the prolix speech of grown men of feeling.
Don't slight a glass of wine—
(through it) one can speak a lifetime.

A poetic presentation to his friend Li Chien contains Po's philosophy of life on reaching the early forties: "The ways of the world are to esteem salary and rank, (but) Confucius fluster-flurried without them. The feeling of mankind is to love age and longevity, (but) Yen Yüan (a disciple of Confucius) died early. What were these two men like? They could do nothing about Fate and Heaven. I now believe I have much good fortune, comfort myself, and feel ashamed (to face those two) former worthies. I am already forty-four and have become a fifth-rank official. Moreover, besides satiety I have tranquillity. In early years, through personal experience I went directly to the Taoist chronicle of the blissful state; in recent years, my heart has turned towards the sect of southern Zen.[15] Outwardly, I obey the ways of the world; inwardly, I leave the causation of the world. Proceeding without caring into busy streets, withdrawing without caring from the human realm. Since I've reached this mindfulness, I move about with nothing but peace. My body is at leisure without message, my mind at ease without (having to be) among rivers and lakes. High-spirited, I may drink wine; with nothing to do, I mostly close my gates. Solitary and quiet, I sit till the depths of night, tranquil steady sleep till the sun is high. In autumn I am not pained by the long nights, in spring I don't regret the flowing years. I entrust myself beyond youth and old age, forget to have cherishings between life and death. Yesterday I spoke with you, and with me you were heart-to-back.[16] This is the Way (of the Tao) that can't be expressed, but for you I have forced myself to talk about it."

The next poem in Po's collection is addressed to Chang the Eighteenth, perhaps Chang Chi (765-830), urging him to stay the night:

Stopping hunger—a basket of food.
Stopping thirst—a jar of broth.
For going and coming—just one horse.
For sleeping and waking—just one bed.
Apart from these I have nothing else;
to me, having is like not having.
Why is not satiety known?
For fame and profit, hearts toil-moil.
Thinking of this; I get lazier and more lax,
piling up habits till they're commonplace.
For ten days I don't leave my gates,
all day don't go down to the yard.
Mr. Chang, who shares my sickness,
lives poorly and simply at Extended Peace
   Ward.
In my indolence I often think of you,
these thoughts which cannot be forgotten.
The far-far street lined with green cassias,
apart from me by eight or nine wards.
Autumn comes, I still haven't seen you;
you probably have some new poems.
Quickly, come and stay with me;
the weather turns clear and cool.

In 816, after Po had been demoted and sent south to Chiang-chou, he received a poem of comfort from a friend and expressed his gratitude in verse: "Opposite the wine an old friend sighs, sighs at my being at the end of the world. He saw my honorable treatment in former times, he thinks of me now stumbling about. He questions me about being marshal; what does the office mean? In reply I say, 'Don't sigh, listen to my song for you. I was originally a man of the hovels, more rustic and humble than mud and sand. My book-reading was less than a hundred volumes, and I relied on making verbal fun of "wind-and-flowers" (verse).

After first starting official service, I received imperial mandates six times, and three times passed examinations. Looking upon my embarrassingly empty and inferior self, I really attained a great deal. Free and easy duties suffice to obscure my person, a meagre salary can supply my household. I look at my fate and am ashamed of myself (for having received such a good post); how could I consider it unseemly? I have troubled you, opposite your glass of wine, to emit a sigh for me. . . .'"

In this poem and many others, Po holds back his self-pity and stresses mind over matter in surmounting obstacles. The statement that he is still a salaried bureaucrat shows that even while demoted he received his salary, a salary on which he and family relations depended. In describing his position at Chiang-chou, he modestly refers to it as one which allowed him maximum leisure because the governor there recognized his incompetence and let him go about as he pleased. It was at Chiang-chou that he once visited a Mr. Li, describing the visit in a poem: "The duck-weeds are small and the rush leaves short, and the spring waters of the southern lake increase. You live near the lakeside, in quiet circumstances matching your elevated feelings. I am the marshal of (Chiang-chou) Commandery, scatterbrained and stupid, with nothing to manage. The Governor (in charge) knows that I am rustic-natured, and he (lets me) withdraw from official duties and idly stroll. In my strolls I take along a small jug of wine; encountering the flowers, I incline towards them alone. Half-drunk, I go to your home, dismount and knock on (your gates of) brushwood and thorns. How can I hold back my steps? Those myriad bamboo paths winding about the eaves! How can I sober up from the wine? That single sound being hummed in (Mr. Li's) Wu accent![17] In an instant he offers the food of the fields, the food being rice (along with which) are eaten celery beauties. White plates and green bamboo chopsticks, simple and clean, no rank meat or fish odors. About to leave, I hesitate again and again; the evening crows are already aloft and crying. When can I come here again to frolic? I'll await you when the lake waters are tranquil."

He invited a neighbor east of him to spend the night:

Small jug—two liters of wine;
new matting—six feet of rest.
Can you come tonight and talk?
The pondside verges on autumn coolness.

The first two lines contain an exact parallelism in word order, setting forth a rustic scene. The last line may convey the poet's mood at the passage of time. The second and fourth lines rhyme.

His frustrations were intensified when he thought of colleagues who, out of contempt for society, were living as recluses. He wanted to join them but he had to work to support his family. Here is a poem written for Yüan the Eighteenth in 817,[18] inscribed on the wall of a mountain pavilion: "I marvel at you for not rejoicing in work and for rambling about in smoke and rosy hue. Today I go to your lonely place and become clearly aware of your reasons. You dwell at the stone mountain stream pavilion; the sound of the flowing stream fills your ears. For drink, your wine is in cowry shell cups; drunk, you lie down and cannot rise. I see you at the (loftiest peak of Mount Lu, the) Peak of the Five Ancients, and repent exceedingly that I live in the city. I love your three sons, and for the first time sigh that I am childless. Below Lu Peak I am about to put together a house and become a recluse. North of the mountain and east of the mountain; my goings and comings will start from this time."

Po wrote a letter in reply to letters from Ts'ui Ch'un and Ch'ien Hui comforting him on his having been demoted to Chiang-chou, and followed this up with a poem in which he made it clear that he accepted fate. He compared himself to a fish in a muddy stream and his friends to phoenixes soaring above. The phoenix usually symbolized either the Emperor or matters pertaining to him, such as service in his court: "Day and night—twice vegetables and food, during the day a leisurely sleep. This then completes one day; it has already been like this for three years. My heart doesn't select the pleasures of the times, my feet don't seek the tranquillity of the locale. Success or failure, far or near, are one coherency without two extremes. I often see the men of the present, whose hearts are not this way. In toil they think of rest, in a place of quiet they think of noise. If one uses heart and body like this, there is no way not to injure and despoil oneself. Seated—if grief and worry enter how can (such persons) get a wholeness of form and spirit?

"I have two friends of the Way, splendid—resplendent Ts'ui and Ch'en. Together they soar above the green-cloud path (of high promotion); alone I fall into the muddy yellow springs (of demotion). At year end all things change, but unchanging their old feelings (towards me)! They have the same hearts as always and share the same stream with me. The imperial hamlet (of Ch'ang-an) is farther than the sun, the Man of Beauty (on the throne) is high in the heavens. Who says that ten thousand *li* separate us? It is often as if you are before my eyes. The fish enjoys the muddy stream; the phoenix rambles along the path of clouds. Don't say the clouds and mud differ, for in bliss transcendent they are the same. Therefore, because you asked about my feelings (on being demoted), after writing a letter I later by chance composed this poem. I caution you not to speak to others, for people will mostly laugh at these words."

"Empty Boat" Kuo, an alchemist friend,[19] paid a call on a cold night in 818 and the visit was remembered in verse. "Empty Boat" was probably a Taoist appelation, implying that Mr. Kuo had achieved a state of perfect quietude:

> Morning warm, we go to the southern eaves;
> evening cold, we return to the rear room.
> At dark we drink one or two cups of wine,
> at night play two or three games of chess.
> Cold ashes bury the obscure light,
> dawn's glow focuses on the remnant candle.
> He doesn't mind, this man of poverty and cold,
> and at times spends the night with me.

After a lapse of three years in the poetry collection (819-21), Po wrote a poem in 822 to describe how he was moved by the sight of an old hat given him by one now deceased:

> Formerly, your black gauze hat
> you presented me, the white-haired old man.
> The hat is now atop my head,
> but you've returned to the (netherworld)
>   springs.
> A thing old can still bear use;
> a man gone cannot be met.
> The Ch'i Mountains—this night's moon.
> Grave trees—just then an autumn breeze.

In the last poem concerning friends and friendship to be cited from his section on the quiet pleasures, which he wrote at fifty, he reverted to his favorite topic of the meaninglessness of life and the emptiness of things. Laughing at life as Chuang-tzu advised was the alternative to meditation:

> South-soughing wind, warning of the cold,
> dark-darkening sun, concealing its brilliance.
> I urge you to drink the murky brew,
> listen to me sing in clear melody (style).
> The fragrant season changes to
>   impoverished shadow,
> the morning light becomes the evening glow.
> I was born in this world with you.
> Not meeting, we've increased the fewness of
>   our years.
> This morning allowing ourselves this frolic,
> how can we plan on a tomorrow?
> If we don't sit in cross-legged meditation,
> we should open our mouths and laugh.

Chapter 7

Autobiographical Poems

The last series of poems about quiet pleasures are autobiographical. In these poems the poet looks at personal and family situations, comments on life, and remarks on aging. The poems, presented in chronological order, date from 800 to 822, or when the poet was twenty-eight to fifty. They cover the periods of early service in the capital, mourning for his mother, demotion to the south, and assignment as governor of Suchou. The first poem, written in 800 after Po Chü-i passed the exams for Advanced Scholar, describes how he left his friends and got ready to return home: "Ten-years constant hard study; one elevation, fallaciously making a name. Getting chosen isn't yet being eminent; there will first be honor when I congratulate my parents. Six or seven of my fellow examinees send me forth from the imperial city. Horses and carriage about to move, the music of leave-taking resounds. Self-satisfaction reduces the remorse of parting, and half-drunk I look lightly upon the distant journey. Flutter-flutter, the swiftness of the horses' hoofs; the spring day reverts to feelings of home."

When Po Chü-i was thirty-four, he wrote a poetic reflection on the passage of time, an oft-echoed later theme: "Mornings, I see the sun ascend the heavens; evenings, I see the sun enter the earth. Before I have realized it, in the bright mirror suddenly my years are thirty-four. Don't say my body still isn't old, for age quickly is about to come. Though white hairs still have not grown, my rose face has already deteriorated in advance. What is human life like? It's like being in the world as an overnight guest. Though there is a seventy-year period, not one or two out of ten (achieve it). Now I am still not enlightened and often feel dissatisfied. Why don't I store up a spirit of boundlessness in my heart? Poverty and humbleness—there is no one who doesn't hate them, but the way is there and it is not worth (trying to) avoid. Wealth and eminence—there is no one who doesn't love them, but when the time comes they arrive of themselves. Therefore, the heart of an all-pervasive man can't be bothered by externals. One should only drink fine wine, be happy-jolly drunk all day. Such words are superior to gold and jade; respect them, don't let them fall away."

Three years later, as a Hanlin Academician, Po commented in verse on his philosophy of tranquillity: "I am not old and I am not young; my years exceed thirty-six. I am not humble and I am not eminent, and at court I have first risen by command. My talents are small and my destiny easily suffices; my heart is extensive and my body is always in comfort. Whatever fills my intestines is fine food; anything which accommodates my knees affords easy living. Moreover, below this Pine Tree Study are one lute and several books. The books— I don't seek detailed understanding; the lute—I depend on for self-amusement. Some nights I sleep within His Lordship's gates; (other) nights I return (home) and recline in my hut. My body entrusts itself to natural movements, my heart is committed to emptiness and void. Holding to these I am about to pass my days— in naturalness there is much tranquil pleasure. I am muddled and silent, not wise and not foolish."

In 810, at thirty-eight, Po wrote a poem to express pleasure at having gotten an administrative post near Ch'ang-an. He was delighted with the salary increase that his parents and relatives could now share: "By imperial mandate I have been appointed administrative officer; I uphold the mandate and thank my Lordship for his favor. Thanking him for his favor is not for myself; the emoluments (of the new position) extend to my parents. My brothers wear official adornments; their brides strictly (regulate) dress and kerchief (to pay a formal visit to their in-laws). They arrive below the lofty hall (of my parents), and splendid—resplendent offer congratulations. My state salary is forty-fifty thousand cash monthly; I can supply (our needs) day and night. My food income is two hundred piculs, so all year my rice storehouse can overflow. Noisily the horses and carriages come; congratulatory guests fill our gates. They don't consider me greedy, knowing my family's poverty. We give a banquet, inviting the congratulatory guests, and guest after guest delights and enjoys. They laugh and say; 'From now on you won't have to worry again about an empty wine goblet.' I reply, saying: 'It is as you say; please wait a bit (for my words). I have an ambition in life, and after getting tipsy will set it forth for you. Human life is a hundred-year period, but how many get to be seventy? Drifting honor and empty rank; the body's (temporary) guests. Only food and clothing are coarsely related to the body's (essential needs). If one merely avoids hunger and cold, other things are one and all (as insubstantial as) the floating clouds'."

Po also served as a Hanlin Academician, and in 810, while in service, he inscribed this poem on a portrait of himself done by portraitist Li Fang. He was thirty-eight: "My looks I myself don't recognize; Li Fang draws my likeness. Quietly looking at its spirit and bones, it is just like a man in the mountains. The river willow by its nature easily decays, (out) the heart of the deer is hard to train. How did I come to serve in the red(-lacquered) palace courtyard, for five years a (Hanlin) official in attendance? With such a firm but timid nature, moreover, it is hard for me to be in harmony with others in the world. I am not only not an official of eminence, but I fear I will beget disaster. I should quit soon and consign my body to clouds and stream."

He wrote two poems about leisure at forty, reiterating that officialdom was suited to the crooked but not to the straight:

Heart At Ease (I)

I have been a traveller for ten years,
constantly grieved by cold and hunger.
For three years I was a censor,
covered by the shame of total inability.
There was wine but no time to drink;

there were mountains but I couldn't frolic.
How could I lack ambition in life?
I was hemmed in and unfree.
One morn I returned to above the Wei
    River,
drifting about like an untied boat.
I place my heart outside worldly things,
without joy, and without grief.
All day one coarse meal,
all year one cloth garment.
Cold comes—I am especially lazy and
    unrestrained,
several days combing my hair but once.
Mornings, I sleep enough and then first
    wake;
evenings, I get drunk on wine and then rest.
The human heart is nothing more than
    ease—
beyond ease what is there to seek?

Heart At Ease (II)

In early years I travelled everywhere,
extremely familiar with the world's ways;
in middle age I added official ranks,
fully seeing into matters of court.
To be a journeyer is truly difficult,
to be an official is especially not easy.
Moreover, I was just then timid and
    cautious,
and what I did often caused opposition.
The straight way accelerated my calamities;
the fawning encounter was not my ambition.
In my bosom for ten years,
boundless vigor entirely dissipated.
Since returning to the (Wei) farmlands,
suddenly I feel a lack of grief and shame.
(This) twisted tree is hard to use for doing;
the floating clouds easily pursue the heart.
Anxiety on anxiety, one's body and world;
from here on I will abandon both.

At thirty-nine, he wrote a poem at the start of summer to celebrate his having been cured of illness: "How long since I've been born? Fourteen thousand days. When I reflect on that interval, if I wasn't worried, then I was sick. As age goes, my thoughts gradually settle; as the years advance, my sickness is first cured. Suddenly I rejoice that heart and body are at peace and without pain. Moreover, this early summer moon is pure and harmonious and of the fine season. A slight breeze blows my garments; I am neither hot nor cold. I move my pillow under the shadow of the trees. Throughout the day what do I do? I may drink a bowl of tea, I may hum a couple of poems. Inwardly, I'm not oppressed by grief or care; outwardly, I'm not fettered by official duties. If this day I don't please myself, what time is the time of pleasure?"

In late spring he went to buy wine and wrote of how it brought on obliteration of the senses: The hundred flowers fall like snow; the hair on both temple (sides) suspends a silken (white). Spring goes and comes again, but I age and have no (second) time of youth. Humans in life await wealth and eminence and for pleasures are often distressed and slowed. Days of poverty and humbleness are better, for then melancholy is dispelled as destiny decrees. I sell the horse I am riding, pawn my old court clothes, use everything to buy wine to drink, walk in drunkenness, and am about to return. My given name and surname daily more obscure, my physical form daily deteriorating. I lie down drunk in Mr. Huang's wineshop; does anyone there know who I am?

Po at forty replied in verse to a fortune-teller, stating why he didn't need to have his fortune told:

Sick eyes, muddled like night;
failing hair, blowing like autumn.
Except for essential food and clothes,
I desist from all things in life.
I know you are a skilled seer;
you ask if I've decided to have my fortune
    told.
If I don't, there is no other reason
than that among humans nothing do I seek.

In 812, while in mourning at Wei Village, Po wrote three poems on the joys of farm labor. The title of the poetic trilogy was **"Returning to the Fields":**

The First Poem

What desires are there in human life? What is desired is only the two extremes. Ordinary men love wealth and eminence, elevated scholars envy Gods and Immortals. But Gods and Immortals must have a (religious) registration; wealth and eminence likewise depend on Heaven. Don't love the ways of the capital, don't seek mountains of Immortals. The dust of the western capital is vast, the waves of the eastern sea are boundless. The golden gate (where scholars await the imperial mandate) cannot be (easily) entered, and how can the jade trees (on the mountains of Immortals) be climbed? Better to return beneath the mountains, to till spring fields as prescribed.

The Second Poem

I have already resolved to till the fields. How have I resolved to do it? I'll sell my horse and buy calves to use, and go back on foot to my thatched hut in the fields. Welcoming spring, I put farm implements in order; awaiting rain, I open barren fields to cultivation. Leaning on my cane, I stand at the head of the fields, personally instructing my servants. I hear the words of an old peasant: "In farming take precautions at the start. Don't be careless in whatever you do and your reward will always be abundance. Above, seek to offer up the king's taxes; below, hope to supply your household stocks. How can you let yourself be lazy and indolent, folding hands and dragging along the garment hem?" Studying farming is not being plebeian; friends, don't laugh at me. Wait till after next year; you yourselves will determine the plow and grasp the hoe.

The Third Poem

At thirty, I was an official close (to the Throne), at my waist a girdle of tinkling jade. At forty, I am a peasant, studying how to rake in grain in the field. How can one say that in ten years a change could be as swift as this? This way is definitely the usual one; success and failure are interdependent. For fish there is the deep water, for birds there are the high trees. Why must one guard (only) one corner (of life); in distress one hems oneself in. Changing my feet to a horse's (hoofs), I would therefore be able to travel the land. Changing my hands to pellets (to fire at birds), I would therefore be able to seek flesh (for my food). My external form is a strange thing but, entrusting to what is accorded, my heart is still satisfied. Fortunately, I was able to revert to farming; how does one know that this isn't good fortune? Furthermore, I am about to get old, gradually dimming like a candle before the breeze. Who can even for an instant take his heart and bind it to (concepts of) glory and shame?

He described how he strolled about the fields in the autumn of 812, just before a large harvest was due. He conversed with the peasants and was well received: "The seventh (lunar) month is already half gone; there is an early coolness and the weather is clear. On a morn I rise, comb and dress, slowly walking beyond my (gate of) brushwood and thorn. There is dew on the walking cane and the bamboo is cold; the wind blows my garment and the Annam banana cloth is light. I go quietly hand in hand with my younger brothers and their children, going up together in autumn for a stroll to the fields. The new jujubes are not yet entirely red, the late melons have an excess of aroma. With these fruits, a dependable old peasant welcomes us. Since I have gone to this village, my white hairs often appear. (But in) the village I have old acquaintances, and young and old all have feelings (about me). We stop (here and there) and towards evening I turn homewards. Tree after tree—wind and cicadas crying. The new rain suffices at this time, and grains on both sides of the road are green. Seeing this causes men complete satisfaction; why must one await the autumn harvest?"

Later that autumn, during the festival of Double Nine, Po Chü-i ascended West Plain with his brothers to feast and look around. He described the next poem as a joint compilation by him and his brothers: "Sick, I love the coolness of pillow and mat; the sun is high but my sleep still hasn't ended. My brothers call me to rise—today is the festival of Double Nine.[2] I rise, climb West Plain and look around, cherishing the thought that we share the diversion as one. We change our places and go to a chrysanthemum grove, lining up before the rice cakes and the wine. Though there are no string or reed instruments, we sing and laugh as we please. The bright sun has not yet declined, (but) our faces are flushed with wine and our ears are hot. Wine-intoxicated, we look in the four directions; how empty and vast the six points of the universe! Heaven and Earth are long and old of themselves, but how long will this man live? Please look at the village beneath the plains; the villagers die unceasingly. Forty families in one village, weepings and burials month after month. Pointing to this, we each encourage the other; on the good occasions delight and take pleasure."

Po Chü-i, ill in 812, wrote about the inevitability of illness in a poem sent to comfort a sick friend: "At thirty-two, white hairs came to life, the chronic ailment of early deterioration. At forty, I was a seventh-rank official, (so low in rank) only because of my stupidity. My facial features decline and wither daily, my fate becomes daily more hapless. How can I alone be like this? Even sages and worthies cannot avoid it. When I look around at intimates and old friends, I lift up my eyes and sigh excessively (at their fates). Some die in old age, sunken in humbleness like mud and sand; others in initial robustness are scattered suddenly like flowers to the wind. In impoverished hunger and early death many are worse off than I. Because of this, on the contrary I comfort myself and often make my heart at peace and in harmony. So I say to the one who joins me in illness, 'Cause your sighs to turn into song'."

At forty, Po was keenly aware that youth had vanished and that the worst was before him. He entitled his poem **"Playfully Enjoying the Chrysanthemums at East Garden"**: "My youth was already gone the other day, my fragrant years are also finished. With such a lonely feeling I come again to this cool barren garden. In the garden I long stand alone; the sun('s rays) are shallow, the wind and dew cold. The autumn vegetables are completely overgrown with weeds, the good trees are likewise withered with frost. There are only a few clusters of chrysanthemums, newly opening their blossoms by the fence. Holding a wine goblet in hand, depend on it for drinking and for dawdling before the flowers:

> I remember the small days of my youth,
>   when it was easy to be drawn into
>   enjoyment.

I saw wine and drank without season—
I was happy (even) without drinking.
Now that I have recently gotten older,
I gradually feel it is hard for me to enjoy.
I often fear this getting feebler and older
and force my drinking, but without pleasure.
I turn about and say to you
   chrysanthemums,
"So late—why are you alone still fresh?
I really know it is not for me,
but for a bit you've resolved my
   melancholy."

Po is most engaging when he writes about himself, for here he succeeds in removing barriers between poet and reader; whatever he feels is fully revealed, without rationalization or artifice. This is a poem about his own stupidity:

What is received (from Heaven) are
   cleverness and stupidity;
what one cannot change is one's nature.
What is (likewise) bestowed are the cordial
   and the thin;
what one cannot remove is one's fate.
My nature is stupid and clumsy,
my fate is thin and difficult.
If you ask me how I know,
I have good reasons for knowing.
I also once raised my two feet,
imitated mankind's trodding on the red dust.
From this I knew my nature was stupid
for I could not understand (why men)
   revolved like a cart's wheels.
I also once flurried my wing feathers,
flying aloft the green clouds (of officialdom).
From this I knew my fate was thin,
for my wings withered and I soon fell to
   earth.
I envy the eminent and loathe the humble,
enjoy riches and hate poverty.
In this all are the same twixt Heaven and
   Earth—
how am I any different from (other) men?
If my nature and fate are like this,
by opposing them I produce bitterness and
   pain.
Therefore, I am tranquil with my fate,
though impoverished, always happy and
   cheerful.
Repairing sedge to make my hut,
plaiting weeds to make my door.
I weave cloth to produce my outer robe,
plant grains to fill my food bowl,
quietly read the books of the ancients,
leisurely fish by the clear Wei River's
   banks.
Self-satisfied and in frolic
I'll trust to these to end my days.

In 814, mourning ended, Po spent a lonely winter's night. His usually buoyant mood changed to one of despondency at being isolated:

House poor, loved ones scattered;
body sick, social intercourse ceased.
Not a person before my eyes,
alone I lie, concealed from the village.
Lonely and cold, the lantern light is dark;
apart and revealed, screens and curtains are
   broken.
Falling-falling before window and door
I hear the new snow coming down.
As I get older I gradually sleep less,
in night depths I rise and sit erect.
I do not study sitting with a vacant heart—
how can I spend my loneliness?
Solemn seated, my body is world-entrusted,
but my boundless heart is change-entrusted.
Like this for four years,
one thousand three hundred nights.

Po Chü-i appreciated the scenery in the Mount Lu area, and in the autumn of 816 he decided to build a grass chapel on the side of a peak there close by a Buddhist temple. The chapel was completed the following spring, constructed from choice building materials. The mountain could be seen above, the running stream heard below. A tea-and-fruit reception was held there on the ninth day of the fourth lunar month, the day after the Buddha's birthday, attended by twenty-two local temple priests and friends.[3] Po had then been living in the chapel for thirteen days. Here is a poem he inscribed on a rock about his feelings on having built the chapel:

North side (of Mount Lu)—Fragrant Hearth
   Peak;
West side—the Temple of Love Bequeathed.
White rocks, how fresh and bright!
Clear streams with flowing sounds.
There are several tens of pine trees,
there are over a thousand bamboos.

The pines extend a cover of green
   umbrellas,
the bamboos lean against reddish jade.
There is no one living below them.
How remote! So many years.
Sometimes monkeys and birds are
   assembled,
throughout the day empty smoke and
   breeze.
At the time there is a foolish one
surnamed Po, given name Lo-t'ien.
He ordinarily has no likes,
but seeing this his heart yearns.
It is if he has gotten his year-ending land
and suddenly he forgets to return.

Peak supported, he builds a thatched hut,
makes a moat and opens a tea garden.
How shall I wash my ears?
With the falling stream flying above my
    roof.
How shall I wash my eyes?
With white lotuses rising neath stone steps.
In my left hand I hold a single jug,
in my right hand grasp a five-stringed lute.
Proud and self-satisfied in intent
I sit with legs extended into the (scenic)
    midst.
Intoxicated with interest, I look to Heaven
    and sing,
in the song depend on words to convey
    (what I feel).
Say I am fundamentally a man of the fields,
mistakenly drawn into the net of the world.
Formerly, I served the Sun (of the Heavens);
old, I now return to the mountains.
The weary bird gets to the thick tree
    foliage,
the stranded fish returns to the clear stream.
Rejecting this (area) where could I go?
So many dangers and difficulties in the
    world of men.

In another poem about scenic beauty, written when he was forty-five, Po asserted the best time to enjoy leisure was between forty and fifty:

At thirty, one's vigor is most imposing,
in one's bosom much right and wrong.
At sixty, one's body is too old,
the four limbs do not support it.
From forty to fifty
is just the time for withdrawal and leisure.
Getting older, I recognize my destiny;
heart indolent, I want to manage little.
Seeing wine, the excitement's still there;
climbing mountains, my strength still hasn't
    decayed.
My years happily reaching these,
I'll soon make a date with the white clouds.

He was also forty-five when he wrote a poem about playing with his niece and daughter, who exerted on him a this-world attraction and prevented a this-life abandonment:

"I have a niece just six years old, called A-kuei; I have a daughter three years old—her name is Lo-erh. One first learns how to laugh and talk, one can sing songs and poems. In the morning they pillow my clothes. How late you've been born! My years are already going towards decay. Human feelings—one can think for the small; human intent—as one gets older compassion increases. Wine is beautiful but it must finally spoil; the moon is round but in the end something is lacking. It is like the affinity of favor and love, the source of worry and affliction. Looking at the world, it is all in these bonds, but how can I leave it?"

There were rebellions in 817 and 818. In a poem written during this period, Po commented on his military inability and cautioned himself against getting involved. The poem was inscribed on a corner of his chair: "My hands are not entrusted with a spear, my shoulders cannot bear a plow. I evaluate my strength and estimate its use, and it isn't even equal to that of one man. Luckily, because of the merit of pen and ink, I got to climb the path of scholarly advance. I had five or six successive official posts, my emoluments sufficing for wife and child. I have a few servants left and right, a one-rider carriage for going in and out. Though what I receive is not substantial, still I don't come to starvation and distress.

"If one reaches this point, what is it like from a bystander's view? (The bystander will envy him.) Though one is a worthy, he's lucky (to have good fortune;) how much more so a rustic and fool like myself! Po-i was an ancient worthy (but) starvation in the mountains was his sentence. The times! With no help for it, all are changed into death from starvation. Remembering others, I feel more and more ashamed and do not dare to forget this even for an instant. My ordinary honor-and-profit heart has been broken through and destroyed; nothing of it remains. I still fear that delusions of the (realm of) dust will arise, and (therefore) inscribe this poem on the corner of my chair."

In his middle forties, Po Chü-i looked at the portrait done by Li Fang ten years earlier and wrote a poetic commentary:

In the past when I was thirty-six,
face drawn in cinnabar and green.
I am now forty-six,
old, decrepit, recumbent in Chiang City.
How was I limited to ten years of aging?
I have taken on all manner of distress.
I contrast the old portrait (with my present
    looks),
but never will my former looks reappear.
Form and reflection silently look at one
    another
like a younger brother facing an elder
    brother.
How much more so letting others look;
how can it not obscure the usual me?

The Sun's charioteer whips the sun to run, and for me it won't stop even a little. Form and skeleton are subordinate to sun and moon; what suffices to startle one about getting old? What I am remorseful about is that in the Pavilion of Lofty Mist I did not get to (have my portrait) painted (as one of the officials with) a meritorious name.[4]

Po Chü-i wrote a poem during these times (817-18) about living in withdrawal, incidentally the same theme that had induced T'ao Yüan-ming to compose his twenty drinking poems. But Po's poem was in a sober, spartan mood:

> Lungs sick, I do not drink wine;
> eyes dimmed, I do not read books.
> Sitting erectly with nothing to do,
> mind and body have an excess of leisure.
> Birds go to roost, darkness falls by the
>   bamboo fence;
> snow reflects on trees of a sparsely wooded
>   forest.
> Solitude and loneliness already at extremes,
> why does one have to live in the
>   mountains?

In 818 he spent time with younger brother Po Hsing-chien (c. 774-826), a renowned Advanced Scholar and prose writer. He showed Hsing-chien the following poem, which includes family details: "This morning one jug of wine—how we delight and enjoy! This joy comes from within; how can others know of it? We are only the two brothers, with distant separation always paining and saddening. This spring, you returned tranquilly ten thousand *li* from the Szechwan gorges. There are also two adolescent younger sisters, at the age of putting up the hair (at fifteen) but not yet contracted for; the other day their weddings were completed and their good men can both be depended on. Grief and anxiety disperse and are resolved, like a knife cutting through a rope which binds. My body light and my heart unfettered, suddenly I want to soar above the Heavens. If troubles accumulate in human life, (even) eating meat is often like (suffering from) starvation. Since my heart is without distress, (by merely) drinking water I can get fattened. Hsing-chien, I urge wine for you. Hold your cup and listen to my words. I do not sigh at the distance of (your) hamlet (from home), I do not detest the trifling official emoluments, but I wish that you and I to the end of our days will never be separated."

In 822 the fifty-year old Po journeyed towards Hangchow to take up the post of governor. En route he lodged at Clear Stream Temple, a site in Shensi where he had been years before on his way to demotion at Chiang-chou. Here are his poetic reflections: "In the past, when I was banished to Hsün-yang (in Chiang-chou), I rested at night in Circular Rim Valley (in Shensi). Now on a journey to Hangchow, again I pass by and lodge at this temple. How many years has it been? The valley grasses have turned green sixteen times. I don't see the old monk of the house; green are the newly-planted trees. In the empty heavens run

sun and moon, and in the world, mountain changes to valley. I was born and lodged in the midst; who can escape (the cycle of) blessings and misfortunes? In accord with affinity I again go south, to live well (if destiny so decrees) among the bamboos of the eastern verandas." ("Sun and Moon" sometimes allude to Emperor and Empress.)

The next poem, composed on horseback, contains his thoughts on the vicissitudes of fortune which he experienced prior to the Hangchow appointment. It too was written when he was fifty: "In getting through life I have not been unlucky; honors to my person have been excessive. In honors I became Grand Pillar of the State, in enfeoffment a Grand Minister of the Court. I ask myself what talent I have, to twice enter a residence for attending officials. I also ask what political talent I have, to ride again in a red-wheeled carriage (for the eminent). Moreover, I am a man of the eastern mountains, one who himself is merely simple and crude. I play the lute and again have wine, but I envy (the famed Three Kingdom inebriates) Hsi (K'ang) and Juan (Chi). I secretly was pushed forward by my village and mistakenly ascended to the writing ability of a worthy. Once registered as a court official, I consequently became entangled in the net of the world. Above, there was the worry from the nets (set by evildoers); below, there were the pitfalls (to be avoided). I always felt the universe was narrow and never experienced comfort of mind and body. I took false steps for twenty years, and below my jaw there sprouted a white beard. Why say I was sent out in demotion? I still was able to reside as a local official. Hangchow—five thousand *li* (beyond); I go there like a fish tossed into the water's depths. Though I still have not rid myself of official duties, I nevertheless come to drift along rivers and lakes. There are many poets in the Wu (region where Hangchow is situated) and also quite a few wine sellers. They hum their poetry in high voices, laugh aloud, and the wine cups fly. At fifty, I am not yet completely old and can still delight and enjoy. I use this (poetry and wine) to send off the sun and moon; what do you gentlemen think of it? The autumn breeze starts up on the river, the bright sun falls by a corner of the road. I turn my head and speak to my governor's horses; go on (to Hangchow), don't be undecided."

Singing Alone in the Mountains (818)

> Men all have one bad habit;
> my bad habit is poetic forms.
> All my common affinities have disappeared,
> leaving only this won't-go-away (poetry)
>   sickness.
> Everytime I encounter beautiful scenery
> or confront good relatives and friends,
> in high voice I sing a stanza,
> transported as if I've met with the gods.

Since becoming a traveller at Chiang,
I've lived in the mountains half the time.
Sometimes new poems are produced;
alone I ascend the east cliff road.
My body leans on a precipice of white
    rocks,
my hands grasp a green cassia tree.
My wild singing startles forest and stream—
monkeys and birds all peek at me.
Fearing I will be laughed at by the world,
I therefore go to places unpeopled.

Po Chü-i's feelings of compassion extended to all things and beings; here is a poem he wrote in 817 or 818 about releasing birds from captivity: "On a clear dawn I approach the river and look; birds on the river are just then noisily clamoring. The ducks and geese and the seagulls and egrets flurry their wings, swim about, and play in the blazing sun of morn. Just then a chicken peddler happens by, grasping roosters; he comes from a distant village. Flying and crying about for those (river birds), what pleasures! (But) for these (roosters) that have been bound—what remorse! Cackling, beating their fourteen wings, bound together in the same bird cage. Their feet are injured, their golden claws shrivel; their heads are ruffled up, their crowns misshapen. For two nights, all out of food and drink. When the sun is high they will call on the butcher's gate. Turning about in the cage but not yet dead, so hungry and thirsty they wish to swallow down (food and drink) together.

"I have often yearned for the ways of the ancients; trust and benevolence, extending (even) to pigs and fish. Seeing this, my feelings of compassion arise, and I buy and release them at Twin Forest Garden. When I open the cage and untie the ropes, all of you roosters listen to my words: 'I gave three hundred cash for you, a small favor not worth talking about. Don't imitate that ring-holding sparrow who put himself into difficulties in order to repay a kindness'." (The reference to a "ring-holding sparrow" is to a story in the Later Han about a young boy who rescued a sparrow from the clutches of another bird. In return, the sparrow gave the boy four white rings and told him his descendants would be as pure white as the rings.)[5]

Po was fundamentally a man of peace, wishing to live removed from bustle, confusion, and disorder, a man who preferred roaming temples to military exploit. In 816 he once enjoyed himself by West Forest Temple at Mount Lu; after describing the grandeur of early spring in the first lines of his poem, he referred to a troop rebellion that started in 815 and was pacified two years later:

This year the Huai bandits arose,
everywhere there's the impetus of warfare.

Wise scholars labor in thinking up
    strategies,
military officials are pained (trying) to
    subjugate.
There is only the me of no talent,
mountain-playing with streams and rocks.

Po composed a long poem in the autumn of 814, 260 lines in all, about the pleasures of roaming temples and in it revealed his poetic versatility in conjuring up scenic splendors and in sustaining a mood of wonder at the majestic sights beheld. He deliberately chose rare words to convey impressions of rare scenic beauty. Here is convincing evidence that Po Chü-i usually wrote verse which is simple and easy to comprehend through choice rather than necessity. He could, if he wanted, exhaust the lexicon in his search for the precise phase. The allegation of a Sung writer that Po first read his poetic compositions to an old woman to ensure that she understood is persuasive for much of Po Chü-i's poetry but implausible for poems like the one translated below. Po's poems could be as easy or difficult to read as he wished, for his range of competence was extensive and varied. This poem, entitled **"Frolicking to the Temple of Truth Realized"**, illuminates another side of Po's nature, that of the Buddhist devotee who accepted the popular faith unquestioningly and believed in its miracles. The poem first depicts his entering the mountains and next describes how he enters the temple, leaving behind the ordinary world and sensing that he has reached a realm of Immortals. He visits famed temple sites and stays the night. On the following day he climbs the highest of the adjacent mountain peaks and then visits the Shrine of Immortals and the Temple of the Painted Dragon; in the temple he sees a painting by Wu Tao-tzu and calligraphy by Ch'u Sui-liang. Wu Tao-tzu (c. 700-60) was the most renowned painter of his age, noted for wall paintings in temples and mountains. Ch'u Sui-liang (596-658), who became a prominent official during the reign of T'ang T'ai-tsung, was especially famed for his mastery of old styles of calligraphy.

The poem has 130 rhymes, restricted to the so-called ancient-level tone; in terms of contemporary Peking speech, all rhymes end in either first or second tones. One Chinese critic has described the effect as being like a succession of detailed statements which abound in splendor and contain no superfluous or weak words.[6] Many of the phrases coined by Po in this poem have remained in Chinese, still listed in dictionaries in their line contexts. But despite its literary merits and refined elegance, **"Frolicking to the Temple of Truth Realized"** is relatively unknown. It lacks the enthralling narrative qualities of **"Lament Everlasting"** and **"Lute Song"** and requires more intellectual effort by the reader. It was composed in 814, when the forty-two-year-old poet was probably concluding the prescribed mourning for his mother:

Frolicking to the Temple of Truth Realized

Autumn—ninth year of Original Harmony;[7]
the eighth month, its first quarter moon.
I frolic to the Temple of Truth Realized,
the temple in the Mountain of Royal
    Accord.
Leaving the mountain four or five li
one first hears the flowing current sounds.
From here, abandoning horse and carriage,
one first fords the bend of Blue Ravine,
hand supporting a green bamboo staff,
feet trodding white stones of the rapids.
I gradually marvel at the remissness of my
    senses,
not hearing the clamor of the human world.
Below the mountain, I look up at it
and suspect at first it can't be climbed;
who knows there is a road in its midst,
crooked, winding peak to peak?
I rest beneath a flagstaff,
rest again beside a stone niche,
the niche interval more than ten feet long,
with its doors boltless.
Looking down and peeking I see no one;
rocks ferns suspended like braids of hair.
Startled exiting white bats
flying paired like overturned snow.
Turning around to view temple gates,
blue cliffs straddling red eaves,
like breaking open the mountain's belly
to place a temple in its midst.

Entering the gates, there's no level area,
the land narrow, the sky void unconfined;
rooms and corridors, terraces and halls,
highs and low according with peaks and
    ridges.
Cliff and precipice handfuls of earth,
the trees mostly lean and sturdy.
Roots and stumps stone-wrapped and long,
crooked and bending (like) coiled insects
    and snakes.
Pines and cassias chaotic and disordered,
all four seasons densely luxuriant.
Fragile branch tips blowing pure,
sounding like musical strings in the wind.
The sun-moon rays don't penetrate,
greenness and shadow interchange and
    protract;
a solitary bird—then one sound;
hearing it it's like a cold cicada.

At first I rest at Guest Status Pavilion,
going to a seat, not yet tranquil.
In a moment I open the north door
to ten thousand li of bright openness;
brushing away the eaves, rainbow formation,
coiling round pillars, clouds encircling.

White shower between red sun,
cloudy and clear sharing lone stream,
field greenery crowding grasses and trees,
the eye's world swallowing capital fields.
The Wei River—tiny, unseen;
The Han Tombs[8]—smaller than one's fist.
When I look back at the road I came,
winding about, reflecting red balustrades,
a clear order of mountain ascenders
distantly can be seen, one by one.

In front I face Many-Treasured Pagoda,
wind bells crying in its four corners;
cornice—supporting corbels, doors, and
    windows,
with harmonious gold-jade muchness.
It is said in antiquity Kasyapa Buddha[9]
on this ground sat in nirvana.
To this day His iron almsbowl exists,
the bottom bearing His hand-shape.
West I open the Hall of Jade Images,
white Buddhas crudely back-to-back;
I shake and sift dust-laden garments,
worship before the eternal snow visages.
Piled-up hoarfrost becomes the kasaya
    robe,[10]
threaded hailstones become the hair
    adornment;
looking closely, one suspects supernatural
    merit—
its traces aren't dug and carved outwardly.
Next I ascend to the Hall of Kuan-yin;[11]
before arriving smell sandalwood fragrance.
I climb the stairs, removing both sandals,
reverent steps ascending to a mat
    immaculate.
Six great pillars displaying jade mirrors,
four sides spreading gold and inlays.
Black night naturally glows bright
without awaiting lamp or candlelight.
All treasures reciprocally low or lofty,
ornaments of greenish jade, girdle gems,
    coral.
The wind-coming seems like Heaven's
    music,
sound impinging on tinkling sound;
white pearls hanging down, congealed,
red pearls dripping blood-colored.
Adornments on the Buddha's headdress,
joining in a crown of seven treasures.[12]
Twin vases of white porcelain,
color like coldness of autumn waters;
separated from the vases, I see holy bones
turning round like a golden elixir.
A jade flute, of dynasty unknown:
A man of Heaven bestowed it on Jetavana.[13]
Blown like the sound of a crane in autumn,
one could thereby send down spirits and
    Immortals.

The time is just mid-autumn,
fifteenth-day moon perfect round.
Treasure Hall—opening three gates,
the moon's gold disc is before me.
Moon and treasure dazzle one another,
bright glows compete for freshness and
    elegance.
Illuminating man, heart and bones cold,
all night I don't want to sleep.
At dawn seeking the southern pagoda route,
disorderly bamboos bending with beauty
    and charm.
Forest solitude, not encountering men,
cold butterflies, quick-quick flight.
Mountain fruits—I don't know their names
flourishingly drooping down both road sides
suffice to cure hunger and fatigue;
picking and tasting, flavor sweet-sour.

South of the road, the God of Indigo
    Ravine:[14]
Purple rain protector, white paper money;
if the year has flood or drought,
duckweed-mugwort offerings by royal
    command.
Because the ground was pure and clean,
sacrificial offerings lacked rank-flesh smells.
Perilous rocks piled up four and five,
lofty one on the other, leaning and pared.
The creator of Things—what intent
heaping these on the cliff's eastern incline?
Cold-slippery, no human traces,
moss-dotted like flowered notepaper.
I come and climb to the peak top,
look down on an unfathomable abyss.
Eyes giddy, hands-feet trembling,
not daring to lower my head and look.
Winds arise from beneath the rocks,
pressing humans and striking upwards;
my clothes resemble bird feathers,
opening-extending, about to fly aloft.
Soaring-soaring, peaks on three sides—
pointed peaks, a series of single and double
    edged swords;
oft-oft white clouds passing,
opening rifts to reveal azure skies.

When the sun falls in the northwest
the evening glow is round, round red.
A thousand li beyond a green folding
    screen
a downward-running pellet of cinnabar
    sands.
When the moon rises in the southeast,
the evening air is clear unending.
Hundreds of feet to the base of jade-green
    lake,
a sketched-out yellow plate of gold.
River's color indigo-like,

day and night, long flow-flow,
turning round, revolving about the
    mountain.
Looking down, it is like a blue-green ring;
sometimes it spreads as a lenient flow,
sometimes is roused as a rushing torrent.
Clear profound in the deepest places,
outward flowing scaly dragon saliva.
Inclining my body to enter its midst,
suspended stone bridge, most dangerous
    and difficult.
Grasping creepers, trodding down-crooked
    branches;
going down I drive away stream-drinking
    gibbons,
snow-speckled rising white herons,
brocade-fluttering startled red carp.
Setting to rest, I then wash hands, rinse
    mouth,
cleanse out the fatigue in my limbs.
Deep or shallow, both can be seen through;
it can illuminate brain and liver.
I only want clearly to see its depths,
want to seek but do not know the source.

East Cliff abounds in rocks unusual
(like) piled-up tiles, jade like stones,
warm moist appearing on the outside,
hoarding within their beautiful gems.
Pien Ho (the jade discover) dead so long,
good jade is mostly cast aside;
at times it divulges a brightness and
    sparkle,
which at night links it with moon and stars.
On the highest peak of the central slope,
heaven-supporting bamboos of green jade.
Brindled rats can't ascend,
so how can I climb and scale it?
Above, there is a pond of white lotuses,
white corollas covering pure waves.
I hear its name but cannot reach it,
for the place is not in the realm of Man.

Moreover, there is one rock
large as a square-foot tile
inserted above a half cliff,
below it suspended measureless sheer walls.
It is said there was once a teacher,
who sitting here got the non-life realization.
It was called Heart-Settling Rock;
monk-elders transmitted to disciples for
    generations.
Withdrawing, I ascend and visit the Shrine
    of Immortals,
creeping grasses spreading endlessly.
Anciently, I hear, a Prince Immortal[15]
ascended wing-converted to Heaven.
West of it, the Terrace of Drying Herbs
still facing fields of fungi and thistle.

In time again a night of bright moon.
Hearing above the (Immortal-ridden) yellow
    crane's voice,
I turn and seek the Hall of Painted Dragons.
Two old men, spotted beards and hair;
thinking they see and hear the Holy
    Doctrine,
gladdened-joyed they make obeisance at the
    altar.
Again I return beneath a cave of streams,
converted into a dragon wriggling tortuous,
before the steps there is a stone hole;
about to rain, white smoke arises.

There was once a sutra-writing priest,
body quiet, heart fine and concentrated.
Affected by him were pigeons beyond the
    clouds,
flying in with a thousand flutterings.
They come to add to the inkstone water,
going to suck up a neath-cliff stream.
One day thrice back and forth,
little deviation from the appointed time.
The sutra completed, he was called the Holy
    Monk
and his disciples were named Difficulty-
    Raisers.
Chanting this Hymn of the Lotus Blossom,
so replete in number (of words) as to be
    countless.
His body spoiled but his mouth unspoiled,
the root of his tongue like a red lotus;
today his skull is not to be seen,
but a stone case (with his bones) exists.
On a white wall there is Wu (Tao-tzu's)
    painting,
brush strokes and color with the freshness
    of old.
On a white screen there is Ch'u (Sui-liang's)
    calligraphy,
black color as if it has newly dried.
The spirit realm and its rare traces;
looking everywhere, with nothing
    unexplored.

One excursion—five days and nights,
about to return but still lingering.
I am originally a man of the mountains,
mistakenly dragged in by the net of the
    times.
Dragged in and directed, caused to read,
pushed and pulled, ordered to imitate
    officials.
I had already passed the written tests,
and further disgraced as Admonitioner.
Stupid and direct, I didn't fit in with the times;
of no benefit, like a parasitic consumer.
Because of this, ashamed and apprehensive,
worried-worried, often pleasure-stinted,

non-achieving, heart and vigor exhausted,
not yet old, form and bones decayed.

Now I remove official hairpins and girdle,
first feel I have left grief and melancholy.
Getting to ramble about mountain and river,
finally able to be remiss and useless as I
    please.
The wild deer breaks the confining fetters,
walking and running without restraining ties;
the fish in the pond is released to the ocean;—
once gone, when will it return?
My body wears the dress of the recluse,
my hand grasps a volume of the Chuang-tzu.[16]
Finally coming to this mountain to live,
rejecting forever mundane world causation.
I am now more than forty,
withdrawn hereon till my body ends.
If I hope for seventy,
I can still have thirty years.

Chapter 8

Seasonal Poems: The Autumnal Mood

There are more than two hundred poems in the "moved-to-sorrow" category and, except for twenty-eight selections composed in accord with New Music Bureau forms, all are written in the old five-character poem form. Someone once made the discerning comment that Po Chü-i was a poet of autumn;[1] the autumnal mood certainly dominates these poems, so tinged with melancholy. The poet never forgets that the sum of being is illness, old age, and death; in his view, autumn symbolizes the decay and withering away of man and Nature before Time's silent onslaught. The flower killed in autumn will revive next spring, but where are the friends of yesteryear? In the early evening, at the beginning of autumn of 807, he rode along the banks of the Serpentine in Ch'ang-an's southeast corner:

Early coolness clearness after-coming,
remnant heat, darkness comes and scatters.
About to rejoice that the fiery heat is
    consumed,
again sighing at the change of the seasons.
I am thirty-six in years,
have newly passed half of seventy.
You should still face the wine and laugh;
don't give way to sighs at the approaching
    breeze.

He was living in Ch'ang-an at the time, lodged in the Forbidden Palace:

The wind turns over red-lined curtains,
the cold rain penetrates officially-provided
    pillows.

Restless, my back to the sloping lantern;
my bed in autumn, sleeping alone.

He returned to the Serpentine in early autumn a year later, again to reflect poetically on the contrast between the easy diminishment and decline of youth and the inexhaustibility of the sun's rays:

Man's longevity is not mountain-like;
the illumination of his years is swifter than
a river.

He was working at the Hanlin Academy in 808 when the sounds of the cicadas in the palace area reminded him of seasonal change:

The palace cassias have autumn intent;
evening breeze, flowers scattered in
disorder.

He thought of his close friend Wang Chih-fu, who was then living away from the capital in the Mountain to Which Immortals Frolic:

There is only recluse Wang
who knows I remember the white clouds;
what day to the Temple to Which Immortals
Frolic,
to see you in autumn before the lake?

In autumn he felt a communion with the decaying, soon-to-be-forgotten red peonies:

A late grove, white dew at eve;
decayed leaves, cool breeze at morn.
Its red beauty long has faded,
its green fragrance now also gone.
The man of solitude sits facing them,
at heart sharing their lone desolation.

He returned to the Serpentine in the autumn of 810, there to reveal his seasonal thoughts as had the ancient P'an Yüeh in an ode called "Autumn's Flourishing".[2] Here is how he expressed himself at the Serpentine, moved by autumn:

Land of sandy grasses in the new rain,
willow branches by the bank in the cool
wind.
Three years moved by autumn thoughts,
all at the pond of the Serpentine.
Early, the cicadas already cried; late, the
lotuses again scattered.
Thoughts of the two past autumns
arise at this time, one after the other.
The ancient (Po Yüeh) at thirty-two
already spoke of sadness in "Autumn's
Flourishing".
I am now about to be forty;

my autumn thoughts can also be known.
Years and months aren't set in vain;
this body decays with the days.
Secretly aging, personally unaware (of it);
proceeding directly to produce white hair.

His reaction to an autumn day a year later, in 811, makes it clear that on reaching the forties (by Chinese reckoning) he felt that the spring of life had ended and that he was at the threshold of old age:

Autumn Day

The pond a water remnant scattered lost,
beneath a window the sun about to set.
Waving-waving, muchness of the autumn
breeze,
cassia blossoms half-producing seeds.
Below there's a man who stands alone,
his years coming to forty-one.

On a journey, the melancholy of autumn was intensified by thoughts of home. Even under thirty he was poignantly aware of the aging process:

I already feel the sudden quickness of the
years,
again hurt by the faded fallenness of things.
Who can not be pained and saddened?
Heaven's time pulls at man's emotions.

He directed his poetic inquiry to a Buddhist disciple:

I venture to ask a Disciple of the Empty
Gate
which dharma is easy to cultivate and
practise,
to cause me to forget my heart,
not to cause feelings of vexation to arise.

He was travelling in the late autumn of 800, returning home:

Beneath the bright travelling lamp
I grieve much and seldom sleep.
Village thoughts, treasuring an early start,
setting out before the cock's cry.
In the ninth month grass and trees fall,
level fields are linked with distant
mountains.
Autumn's shade harmonizes with dawn's
light,
trees ten thousand are green-green.

Last autumn I wandered eastward,
but this autumn I journey westwards (home).
My horse is emaciated, my clothes torn,
separated from my family for two years.
Thinking of returning, returning sadly,

returning without a cent in my purse.
Though my heart lacks orchid fragrance,
how can I not be at ease?

"Orchid fragrance" alludes to the disappearance of orchids with the cooler weather. In a poem written about the same time, called **"Autumn Feelings"**, fragrant orchids are the last in a series of natural phenomena: "The moon appears, illuminating the northern courtyard, and light resplendent fills the steps beneath. A cool breeze arrives from the west; grasses and trees decay day and night. *T'ung* (tree) and willow diminish their green shade, fragrant orchids reduce their jade nourishment:

Moved by things, I think to myself:
My heart is also like this.
How can I get to extend youthful vigor?
Thriving and decay are pressed by
   Heaven's time.
Man's life is like stone-to-ashes;
to enjoy he is always painfully slow.

Life is but a fleeting moment, concludes the poet, a moment which man fails to enjoy to the fullest. A type of plum blossom becomes one of the poet's concerns; while it is presently numerous and of a beautiful intense blackness, this "one among the flowers with thoughts" quickly decays and falls easily. So the poet pities it and expresses his pity in verse:

Tree small, blossoms fresh and elegant;
perfume clustered, branches soft and weak.
Its height is two or three feet,
layer on layer, calyxes in myriads.
Morning beauty, luxuriously thriving;
evening faded, scattered unknown.
Declining branches, red-powdered fineness,
covering earth with fine red silk.
From the start, fine facial color,
oft-distressed, easily melted fused.
Don't you see the marsh grass blossoms?
The wild wind blows, they (still) don't fall.

The poet, who must have been referring obliquely to people as well as blossoms, thus observed that the beautiful and fine perish while the coarse and ugly last. Alone in the south in 816, away from the capital on official service, he described a new autumn scene:

The west wind whirls a leaf;
before the yard, wind gusts cool.
Wind and pond, bright moon and water,
decayed lotuses lodging white dew.
What to do with the Kiangnan night?
Drawn-drawn out, long from now on.

In 817 he was assisting the Governor in Chiang-chou, also called Hsün-yang. There he left a traveller by the river on a day of autumn rain and conjured up a Chinese painting in verse:

Autumn geese pass, one after another;
plaintive monkeys heard night and morn.
This day a traveller in a lone boat
at this place parts from the mass.
Drizzle-drizzling rain soaks dress,
careless-uncaring sail braves clouds.
If one doesn't get tipsy on Hsün-yang wine,
mist and waves will kill with melancholy.

Encountering an autumn moon during this period, when he was living in demotion away from either capital or native home, reinforced a mood sleepless sad:

Autumn Moon

Night's start—color azured;
night's depth—light unbounded.
Slightly turning beneath west corridor,
gradually filling before south window.
How much more so green wastelands,
here again purely exposed to Heaven.
Falling leaf sounds—pitter-pattering;
startled bird shadows—fluttering-fluttering.
Roosting birds still not settled in;
how can the man of melancholy sleep?

On an autumn evening, alone, he wrote that he and his quarters were unkempt:

Autumn Evening

Leaf sounds fall like rain,
moon color white like frost.
Night's deep, I just lie alone—
who will wipe my dusty bed for me?

The autumn season to the traveller was a saddening time of nature laid waste:

Evening Rain

I have someone I think about,
separated in a distant village;
I have something I'm moved by,
rooted in my innermost self.
The village is distant, I can't go there,
there is no day that I don't longingly gaze.
How much more so this night, the lamp so
   low;
my emotions deep set, I can't resolve them.
There is no night that I don't reflect,
in an empty courtyard sleeping alone.
An autumn day especially, not yet bright,
wind and rain so utterly dark.
If I don't study the ways of release,[3]
how can I forget my full heart of former lives?

The coming of autumn signified wintry days ahead. Autumn clothes had to be washed and winter clothes readied, but in 811 Po's wife was beset by illness and his family was caught unprepared:

Clear Autumn Sky

Gold and fire wait not for each other;
hot and cool change within a rain.
The forest clears, there are remnant cicadas;
nest cold, there are no remaining swallows.
Song-immersed, I roll up the long mat;
pained-sad, I collect the round fan.
By evening it is somewhat unmuddy;
leisurely I stroll to the green moss
   courtyard.
The moon appears. Stone and club (for
   clothes-beating) move;
family after family pound autumn silks.

My oft-ill wife who faces it alone
cannot control needle and thread.
Winter clothes especially not yet made,
summer clothes about to come apart.
How can one therefore welcome early
   autumn?
By relying on a cup for self-encouragement.

In late autumn, he stood by a lake in the south, thinking about his brothers, likewise separated by distance and strange terrain, and contrasted the thoughts of the viewer with the inevitability of the scene:

A Southern Lake in Late Autumn

The eighth month. White dew falls,
the lake water's fragrant (blossoms) age.
Day and night the autumn winds are many,
decaying lotuses half tip and fall.
My hands grasp the green maple tree,
my feet trod the yellow reeds.
Sad and pale—old-looking face;
cold fallen—autumn's cherished embrace.
There's an older brother in Huai-ch'u,
there's a younger brother on Shu Road.
Ten thousand li—when will they come?
Smoke and ripples white vast-vast.

He grieved not only for blood relatives but for distant friends:

North Garden

North Garden—east wind rises,
flowers varied open in sequence.
Heart knowing they'll fall in an instant,
in one day I come three or four times.
Neath the flowers, how without wine?
About to drink, again I hesitate,

thoughts distant a thousand li
who will urge me to the cup?

Autumn in 817 moved him to thoughts of Yüan Chen; it was a year when both were serving in demotion and transfer beyond the capital. The "white seagull" refers to Po, whose surname means "white", flying alongside the rivers and lakes in Chiang-chou, the "green phoenix" to Yüan: "Below the leaves, lakes and also waves—autumn breezes come at this time. Who knows my heart, crying fallen? First I take in the spirit of the soughing wind:

> Expulsion and change—I am moved by the
>   flowing years.
> Floating and drifting—I think of my
>   comrade.
> Formerly associated in (palace) mist-and-
>   clouds,
> now an official on the muddy paths (of
>   demotion).
> The white seagull's skin and feathers are
>   weak,
> the green phoenix's writings differ (from the
>   norm).
> Each is enclosed in a cage;
> at year end each is grief-haggard.

There was a type of hibiscus, the blossoms of which were believed to open and fade on a single autumn day. This remainder of life's transiency and of the human spring's non-return inspired the poet to a sentiment encompassing man and Nature:

Autumn Hibiscus

Wind and dew gusts already cold,
Heaven's color also a dusk yellow.
The central court has a hibiscus blossom,
flourishing and falling on a single morn.
Autumn starts. There is already solitude,
evening deaths so scattering-scattered!
I truly pity its short(-lived) facial color,
sigh again that it does not make its round.

Moved by this, then I think of that.
Feelings! Let me try once to explain:
Men getting aged, wealthy and eminent,
women in their twilight becoming brides.
Hair white, one first gets one's will;
color decaying, then one can serve man.
Time's oncoming cannot be helped;
how can one ever get to be like verdant
   spring?

In 822, when Po was in his fifty-first year, he wrote two poems about his sentiments as he stood one autumn day by the Serpentine. In a preface to the poems, he mentioned his earlier compositions of 806,

807, and 808, similarly called **"Moved by Autumn at the Serpentine"**. He spoke of demotions and transfers, and went on to say that once more he frolicked by the Serpentine; the autumn scene was unchanged, but human events had altered. He said he had been unfortunate in his middle carrer but fortunate afterwards. Once robust, he was now decayed. Life was mostly hindrance, and from one autumn to the next one knew not what to expect. To end-rhyme the first and third lines, the poet used the numbers "thirty-seven" (san-shih ch'i) and "fifty-one" (wu-shih i), but the gap of years between 806 and 822 was sixteen rather than fourteen. Here the discrepancy between actual chronology and the poet's chronology may be attributed to the exigencies of rhyme:

At the Serpentine, Moved by Autumn

The First Poem

The autumn of 806
I was thirty-seven;
the autumn of 822
I am fifty-one.
Of the fourteen years between,
six I lived reprimanded-degraded.
Impoverishment-success and glory-fame
entrust to fate and accord with externals.

"I consequently took as my commander (the monk Wisdom-)Distant of Mount Lu, and consoled (the poet-worthy) of antiquity Ch'u (Yüan) at the Hsiang River. Nights, I listened to the melancholy of bamboo branches; autumn, I saw the submerging of the tributary, blocking (a view of the peaks). Recently I have taken leave of the official seal of Pa Commandery, and again I grasp a Secretariat writing brush:

Late good fortune; how is it worth talking
    about?
My white hair reflects on the red sash—
melted and sunk the former thoughts and spirit,
changed and altered the old looks and
    substance.
There is only autumn at the Serpentine,
wind and mist as in days before.

Here in middle age he showed a resignation to life and career, expressing no wish to return to the mountains:

The Second Poem

Grasses of the weed-scattered southern
    bank,
trees in the soughing-gusting western wind.
Autumn has come; not very long
but cicada sounds already infrequent.
Sedge grasses level, joined by green
    luxuriance;

lotuses fall, their green seeds exposed.
This day when I approach and look,
the moved-by-autumn place of years past.
The water in the pond as of old,
the mountains above the city as before.

Only the hairs among my temple,
formerly black but now suspending white.
Glory fame and robust vigor
shun one another like the day the night.
When timely fate is first about to come,
one's aging looks have already preceded it.
If in facing spring one doesn't enjoy and
    rejoice,
on approaching old age one is merely
    alarmed misinformed.
Therefore, I compose singing-of-emotion
    poems,
inscribing them on the road by the
    Serpentine.

He lamented not only the passing of the seasons but the fact that flowers bloomed but a moment, year after year:

Separated by a river bank, I love the red
    lotus;
yesterday I saw it still there.
Night came; the wind blew it down,
only once could I pluck it.
For flowers to bloom,
though there is next year's time,
I'll grieve again next year
that they are here such a little while.

There was all too little time and, once gone, nowhere for beauty to be found:

Flower-non-Flower

Flower-non-flower
mist-non-mist.
Midnight coming,
daylight leaving,
coming like a spring dream
for how much time?
Leaving like a morning cloud,
nowhere to be sought.

The poet associated autumn with death and desolation:

Late Autumn Evening

Jade-green sky deep full, moon resplendent
    quiet;
within the moon(-glow) a man sad,
mourning his orphaned shadow.
The flowers open, the last chrysanthemums
lean on the distant bamboo fence;

leaves drop off the decaying *t'ung* tree,
falling into the cold well.
Frontier geese fly; of a sudden I realize
  autumn's end.
The neighbor's cock cries late; I know
  nights are long.
Emotions crystallized, I don't speak but
emptily have my thoughts.
The wind blows the white dew,
cold my garments.

Autumn Evening

Chrysanthemums few along the fence,
t'ung leaves fallen along the steps.
Tree shadows separate-apart,
day color thin.
Single-fold coarse hanging screen,
poor and solitary.
Cool winds scattered—fallen,
autumn's lonely desolation.
Light and shade flow about,
suddenly it is late.

My facial color's faded shadow
isn't up to that of yesterday.
Lai's wife[4] lies sick,
the time of moon brightness.
He doesn't pound the cold clothes
but vainly pounds drugs instead.

Po Chü-i communed with Nature and, distressed by decay, took delight in the nourishing of growing things. This was one of the pleasures amidst distress which compensated for his failures in the maze of officialdom. He was partial to the newly planted bamboo!

As a district magistrate, my mind isn't at ease;
closing my gates, the autumn grasses grow.
How can I therefore amuse my rustic
  nature?
By planting more than a hundred bamboo
  stalks.
Seeing this color on the valley
I can recover an in-mountain feeling.
Official affairs at times at rest,
I stroll daylong about the balustrades.
Do not say the roots are still unfirm,
do not say the shade is still unproduced;
I already feel within the garden
somewhat of a lingering breeze.
I love most to lie near the window;
branches in the autumn wind have sounds.

Po felt official work accumulating while he attended to garden chores, and he likened himself to a leaden knife, meaning a man of little talent. The bamboo appealed with its whispered coolness, the moon attracted as a symbol of purity aloof from the strife below:

Forbidden Palace Moon

On the waters, the bright moon appears;
in the palace, the clear night lengthens.
Southeast, terraces and temples (moon-)
  whitened,
little by little it ascends palace walls.
Purified, it falls into the waters of the
  golden dikes,
brightly flowing on the frost of the jade
  tiles.
It can't be compared to sights in the
  mundane realm
(where) dusty earth dirties its purity and
  glow.

In 820, while living in Szechwan, Po wrote the following poem on the occasion of the Double Yang, or Double Nine festival. Celebrating the festival in a distant place reinforced the homesickness and anxiety of the weary traveller: "The sorghum-fragrant wine is first heated, the chrysanthemums warm, blossoms (in the heated wine) opened. Leisurely listening to the "Song of the Bamboo Branches",[5] lightly pouring wine into dogwood cups. (Dogwood supposedly protected one from evil.) Last year on Double Yang I was floating-drifting in a nook of P'en City; this year on Double Yang I am lone-scattered on Pa-tzu Terrace. The traveller's temples whitened, the letters from home long uncome; approaching the goblet, one scratch of my head (in anxiety) and the seated guests also become irresolute (out of sympathy for my homesick plight) . . ."

The poet heard the rain on an autumn evening before he saw it:

Evening Rain

The early cricket cries and then ceases,
the flickering lamp goes out and again
  brightens.
A window apart, I know the night's rain;
the plaintain leaf first had its sounds.

He was sensitive to the life-awakening of early spring, revived by the coming of warmth. Oblivious to food, he viewed the wonders of nature:

Early Spring in the Creek

Southern mountain snows not entirely gone,
shaded peaks leaving a remnant white.
Ice of the western valley stream already
  melted;
spring's water current containing new jade-
  green.

"The coming of the eastern breeze—how many days?
Hibernating insects move, sprouting grasses open.

Secretly I am aware of spring's harmonizing merit, not flinging itself about emptily for (even) a day. I love the warmth of this day's weather, and come to brush off the stones beside the creek. Once I sit, I am about to forget to return; the chirp-chirp sound of night birds. Raspberry and artemisia apart from mulberry and jujube, hidden reflections on a smoky night. Returning home, when I ask about the evening meal the domestic is boiling greens and wheat."

When spring's coolness gave way to summer's heat, Po might find the day somewhat tedious and a noontime nap needed to while away the lengthened hours:

Sleeping at Noon

Sitting and straightening white unlined
    garments,
rising and wearing yellow grass sandals.
Morning meal, basin washing, and rinsing
    completed,
I leisurely go down the stairs and walk
    ahead.
The hot breeze slightly changes time
    periods,
noontime gradually adding to its frequency.
The yard is quiet, the ground shaded,
birds sing on trees with new leaves.

Alone I walk and, returning, alone lie down;
summer's scenes especially have not yet
    dimmed.
If I don't have a noontime nap,
how can I pass the long day?

Po was a great admirer of the pine, which he associated with stateliness and with splendor in nature, aloof and unobserved. The pine symbolized personal control, constancy in adversity, and grandeur.[6] Po presented a short verse to a pine tree seller in Ch'ang-an, explaining why he declined to purchase a tree for transplanting:

A bundle of green, green color;
I know it comes from the valley floor.
How many days since they were dug up?
Leaves and branches fill the world of dust.
In not buying I've no other reason than
    that;
there is no capital land on which to plant.

He wrote two poems about planting a pine:

The First Poem

A small pine, not yet a foot high,
heart-loving, I transplanted with my own
    hands.
Its color the greenness neath the mountain
    stream,

cloud-moistened and light-misted.
To plant and cultivate, my years are late;
to grow and mature, your nature is slow.
How could I have passed forty (before)
planting these few inches of branches?
Will I get to see it produce shade?
Human life rarely (reaches) seventy.

The Second Poem

Beloved—you cherish a late integrity;
pitiful—you contain a straight pattern.
Wishing I could see you morn after morn,
I therefore planted you before the steps.
I know if you die there is no more to be
    said;
but if you don't, you'll aspire to the clouds.

Just as he heard the rain before he saw it, so did he first feel the snow through its glow and effect on nature:

Night Snow

Startled by the cold of coverlet and pillow,
I then note the brightness of the window.
Night-deep, I know the snow is heavy—
I hear the sound of snapping bamboo.

Po, living in lonely officialdom in 820 in Szechwan, an area he thought uncivilized, planted flowers at the eastern slope, the slope east of the city. Su Shih, a Sung poet and admirer of Po Chü-i, was said to have adopted the sobriquet of Tung-p'o[7] ("Eastern Slope") out of admiration for the following two poems:

Planting Flowers at the Eastern Slope

The First Poem

I took money to buy flowers and trees,
planted them on the east-of-city slope;
but the flowers which I bought
were not limited to peach, apricot, and
    plum.
A hundred fruits were mixed-planted,
a thousand branches opened in orderly
    sequence.
By Heaven's time there is early and late,
but Earth's power lacks high and low.
The red were rosy-hued, charming-
    voluptuous,
the white were snow's pure white.
Frolicking bees therefore remained,
and fine birds also came to perch.
In front were long flowing waters,
below was a small level terrace.
I brushed off rocks on the terrace,
raised my cup before the breeze.

Blossoms and branches shaded my head,
flower stamens fell to my bosom.
Drinking alone and singing alone,
before I realized (it) the sun levelled in the
    west.
It is the Szechwan custom not to love
    flowers
and throughout the spring no one comes;
there is only this drunken Governor,
unable to turn away from them.

The Second Poem

At the eastern slope spring faces eve.
What are the flowers and trees like today?
All around, the flowers have fallen.
Everywhere the death of the leaves has
    begun.
Daily, I lead my lads and servants
in carrying hoes to clear the ditches.
We smooth earth and bank up its roots,
draw from streams and irrigate its
    witheredness.
The small trees are a few feet low,
the large trees more than ten feet long.
Heaping earth and planting how many
    times?
The heights even, (plants) spread
    luxuriously.

Nourishing trees is like this,
to nourish people what difference?
If you truly wish
abundant branches and leaves,
first you must save the roots and trunks.
If you say,
"How does one save the roots and
    trunks?",
it is by encouraging farming,
by equalizing levies and taxes.
If you say,
"How does one (make) abundant the
    branches and leaves?",
it is by economizing on things,
by leniently punishing and penalizing.
I have transferred these (principles) to my
    commandery rule
and have almost completely revived the
    inhabitants.

The first of the poems on planting flowers at the eastern slope has been described as one in which the poet, while discussing his interests in planting, quietly looked into the principles of things. To the poet there was the inner meaning of cultivating personal goodness. The second poem enlarges on this theme in a didactic sense, for in governing through adherence to right principles, a stable and prosperous community can be realized. The poems may perhaps also be consid-

ered in the "moved-to-sorrow" category, because Po felt frustrated in his official career and was only able to use a portion of his talents for governing the empire.

In 802 he described the planting of willows near a mountain stream as consolation for having to serve far from the center of the official, intellectual world:

My rustic nature loves to tend and plant,
to plant willows in a water-midst inlet.
Spring profiting, I take an axe to cut,
cut short and then plant them.
Since long and short are not uniform,
they're high or short according to location.

Relying on the bank, I bury great trunks,
overlooking the stream insert small
    branches.
Pines and poplars cannot wait,
assuredly are hard to shift.
It is best to plant these (willow) trees,
for these trees easily flourish and increase.
Rootless, they also can survive;
producing shade, how unslow they are!

Three years I have now left the
    commandery;
I can therefore see them close-cleaving.
Planting finished, I rest by the waterside;
lifting my head, I leisurely think to myself.
Wealth and eminence are basically unhoped
    for,
merit and fame must await the times.
If I didn't plant east stream willows,
I'd sit erect and—what would I wish for?

He sought the sun on a day in 822, to bask in its rays and escape the confines of thought:

Bright-bright the winter's sun appears,
illuminating the south corner of my home.
Seeking its warmth, close-eyed I sit;
harmonious vapors arise on flesh and skin.
At first, it's like drinking heady wine,
like the revival of the hibernating.
It outwardly blends—my every bone is
    pervaded;
It inwardly pleases—(even) one thought is
    lacking.
(In an) expanded state I forget where I am;
my heart joins with the empty and the void.

He bought a house near a group of pines in 822, explaining in verse why he had moved:

Courtyard Pines

What is there below the courtyard? Ten pines
meet me at the stairs. They stand chaotically with

no order in arrangement, heights uneven. High
ones thirty feet long, low ones ten feet low. They
are like field-begotten things, like nothing planted
by man. They make contact (above) through a
green tiled room, receiving (below) at a white
sand terrace. Day and night there is wind and
moon; bubbling over and moist (from the rains),
there is no dust or mud. Remote harmony (of
wind in pines), autumn falling leaves; cool shade,
summer cold-aloof. Spring is deep; a slight
evening rain, filling trees with suspended pearls.
At year end a great snowy day, pressing branches
with jade pure white. The four seasons each have
interest; the myriad trees are not in their category.

Last year I bought this house,
often was laughed at by people;
but one family and twenty mouths
moving-shifting and going to (these) pines,
what was gained from the move?
Merely the unravelling of a troubled heart.
Since these are beneficial friends,
why must I associate with worthy talents?
Look at me: I am just a common person,
official cap and sash trailing in the dust.
Not yet called a Master of Pines,
(from) time to time I feel ashamed.

To the Chinese, the bamboo is associated with peace
and tranquillity.[8] In 822 Po reminisced about the bamboo he had once seen at a temple in Wang-ch'uan,
Shensi, known as the "Temple of the Pure Source."
He concluded the poem with a reference from his
fourth-century predecessor T'ao Yüan-ming (the "man
of ages past") about the pleasures of reclining exceeding pleasures enjoyed by the most famous of the ancient Sages:

The Window of Bamboos

I used to love the temple at Wang-ch'uan,
the window of bamboos in the northeast
  corridor.
Once separated, it has been more than ten
  years,
(but if) I see the bamboos I won't have
  forgotten them.
It is now the start of spring's second
  month;
I'm living at New Glories Ward (in Ch'ang-
  an),
in a dwelling attained through divination.
Not yet free to make stable and storehouse,
I planned first besides to build a courtyard.
Opening the window, I didn't paste paper;
planting bamboos, I didn't rely on a
  pathway.

My intent was to take (the area) under the
  northern eaves

and there position window and bamboos.
Enveloping the room, the sound wind-
  sighed;
pressing against man, the color green-green.
Mist penetrated lovely deep clouds;
moon passed through the elegant openwork
  glow.

The time was the third stage of (summery)
  days,
with Heaven's vapors as hot as boiling
  water.
On returning from court I removed my
  garments.
A light gauze turban of a width (of cloth),
a small mat, six-foot bed.
No guests. Quiet throughout the day,
there was a cool breeze all night.
I then knew the man of ages past
in speaking of things was most
  knowledgeable.
"A clear breeze—lying under the northern
  window,
one can thereby excel (Fu-)hsi the August."[9]

He enjoyed associating with pine and bamboo, the
traditional substitutes for absent friends:

Playing With Pine and Bamboo

The First Poem

Dragons and snakes hide in great swamps,
tailed and tailless deer frolic in luxuriant
  grasses.
The nesting phoenix rests in the *wu* tree,
the concealed fish rejoices in aquatic
  grasses.
I also love my thatched hut,
in its midst rejoicing in my ways.
Pines in front, tall bamboo behind—
sleeping and lying I can end my days.
Each attached to its own tranquil place,
unaware of the good of other things.

The Second Poem

Seated before the beloved front eaves,
lying north of the beloved north window.
The window of bamboos—mostly a fine
  breeze;
the pines of the eaves have excellent
  coloring.
Cherishing solitude, combining with them as
  one,
common thoughts accord with greenness
  and cease.
Though to you they have no feelings,
to me they can be gotten through to.

I then realize that closeness in nature
is not necessarily (only) movement and
planting.

Po Chü-i was more optimistic about the state of nature, which renewed in spring, than about the state of man. To man, spring was not recoverable and life was uncertain and arbitrary. The poet elaborated on the chance nature of things in two poems. In the first, he contrasted historical events and the ways in which worthy officials were mistreated. In conclusion, he alluded to a popular belief about rain falling when the moon was apart from the constellation of Hyades:

Perchance: Two Poems

(Prince) Huai of Ch'u was chaotic and
  perverse,
Ch'u Yüan was straight-forward;
for him to be rejected and abandoned was
  fitting and natural.
Why should one feel pity and
  commiseration?
Han The Cultured (Emperor) was an
  enlightened Sage,
Mr. Chia (I) was virtuous;
(for Chia) to be banished to Ch'ang-sha
(is therefore) worthy of one's sighs.
Human events have many extremes;
how can they be worth marvelling at?
Heaven's patterns are extremely trustworthy,
still they differ (from the expected).

When the moon is apart from the Hyades,
it is fitting for showers,
but there are times when it does not rain.
Who can predict (such things)?

The second of the two poems mentions a popular superstition—which the poet accepted unquestioningly—that a wily dragon lodged in the neck of an ox could cause its death in times of thunder. There are references to integral parts of the divination process, such as milfoil stalks, tortoise bones, hexagrams, and analyses:

Fire starts at the top of the city,
the fish are in the water.
To rescue (all) from the fire,
the pond is exhausted;
the fish lose their water.

A wily dragon is concealed
in an ox's neck.
When thunder beats, the dragon comes,
the ox dies of madness.

People say the milfoil stalks are godly,
the tortoise bones divinely efficacious.

If we try divination,
how do fish and oxen get to (such deaths)?
There are hexagrams sixty-four, analyses
  seventy,
but in the end one can't know the reasons.

Chapter 9

Aging and Death

Po Chü-i, very conscious of aging, inclined towards a belief expressed in the *Chuang-tzu* that one could reach a state of transcendental bliss:[1]

Neither do I dote on this body,
nor do I detest this body.
This body—how is it worth doting on?
Time beyond time the root of trouble
  vexation.
This body—how is it worth detesting?
One collection of the dust of emptiness and
  void.
Not doting on and not detesting—
here first is the man of bliss transcendental.

Fully aware of the lessening of sensation with the onset of age, he lamented his sickness and decay. Explaining that he was of little use to the court, he asked for a simple and non-demanding post somewhere in the mountains:

Decaying-Sick and Devoid of Interest
I Then Sing of my Feelings

Morning meals mostly not eaten to the full,
lying down evenings, often little sleep.
I realize the interval from eating to
  sleeping
lacks entirely the flavor of youth.
Ordinarily I like poetry and wine,
but I am about to forsake and abandon
  them.
Wine I drink only like medicine,
without recovering past joys of tipsiness.
Poetry I mostly listen to others sing,
myself not inscribing a single word.

My sick appearance and decayed looks
day and night in succession arrive.
Now, moreover, I seldom fulfill court duties,
gradually shame at close attending (the
  Throne).
I should finally seek a commandery post,
collecting the few expenses of a fisherman
  or woodcutter.
Assembling the family, I'd return to the
  mountains,
to ask not about things in the realm of man.

He not only pitied his own ill state but also the illnesses of others. In the late autumn of 810, he received a poem while in the capital from the ill official Chang Chi (c. 765-830), and responded in kind. (The reference to "double-south" gold was to a form of southern gold valued at twice the normal rate):[2]

> Your elevated talents are concealed at the
>   Temple of Rites,
> my short feathers hover about the forbidden
>   (palatial) forest.
> Your residence on a western street is far,
> my northern tower is deep with officials.
> You are sick and don't come to visit,
> I am busy and it's hard to go to seek
>   you.
> Uneven all the days of our parting,
> lonely desolate hearts passing the years.
>
> The dew moistens green mossy earth,
> the moon chills the red tree shade.
> Moreover, this night of lone melancholy
> I hear his song of thinking of me.
>
> Above, it sighs at obstruction from our
>   words and laughter;
> below, it grieves at the inroads of the years.
> The form—deteriorating—the dawn
>   window's mirror;
> the thoughts—distressed—the lute of
>   autumn sounds.
>
> It is a piece of silk brocade,
> a beautiful jade sound in eight rhymes.
> How should one reward the precious and
>   esteemed?
> Ashamed am I that I lack double-south
>   gold.

Since to Po white hairs and advancing age were synonymous terms, the sight of a white hair among the black let loose a flood of personal reflection in which we see the poet at his appealing best, sharing his feelings directly with the reader in a one-to-one relationship and talking both to himself and to the men of his own and all generations. He wrote the first poem in his mid-thirties:

On First Seeing A White Hair

> White hairs have grown one strand;
> morning comes and it's in the bright mirror.
> Don't say one strand's few—
> the whole head starts from this.
> Green mountains—just having distantly
>   parted;
> yellow dress—first having gone to serve.
> I never realized that among my locks
> in no time at all it would be like this.

The second poem was written when he was thirty-eight:

> At night I wash, early next morning comb
>   my hair;
> window bright, autumn mirror at dawn.
> Decaying, the hairs I grasp in my hand—
> with one washing I know they have gotten
>   less.
>
> Yearly matters gradually slip and stumble
>   by,
> worldly affinities just wind me about.
> I don't study the way of the Gate of
>   Emptiness;[3]
> old age and illness—how to be
>   comprehended?
> I haven't gotten the non-birth heart;
> white hair is for me an early death.

When he wrote about white hairs at the age of forty, he seemed more resigned to them philosophically and closer to a "non-birth heart" mentality:

White Hairs

> White hairs, knowing their time and season,
> secretly have an appointment with me.
> This morning, under the sun's rays,
> I combed out a few (white) strands.
> My family, not used to seeing them,
> are grieved and silent, pitying me.
>
> I say "Why is it worth marvelling about?
> Of its meaning you're unaware."
> Most men, at the age of thirty
> are strong on the outside
> but already decaying inside.
> They think of food and bed delights,
> already lessened from when they were
>   twenty.
>
> Besides, I am now forty,
> basic shape and form emaciated.
> The book demon has muddled my two eyes,
> the wine sickness immersed my four limbs.
> My loved ones daily scattered and lost,
> those still alive, apart and separated.
>
> Body and heart like this for long,
> white hair production is already late.
> From the start, birth, old age, and death—
> the three sicknesses—lengthily follow one
>   another.
> Unless one has the non-life mentality,
> in the human realm there's no medicine to
>   cure (one).

In a different mood, he complained the mirror made him look older than he really was:

Glistening the bronze mirror,
streaked the white-haired temples.
How can I get to further hide my age?
My true years, you, Sir (Mirror), don't
  believe.

Approaching forty, he sighed gently in three poems about the underniable fact of age. There was a reference in the first poem to Pien Ch'üeh, a famous doctor of antiquity:

Sighs Over Getting Old

The First Poem

In the morning I rise, reflected in a bronze
  mirror,
form and shadow lonely-forlorn.
My youth has taken leave of me,
my white hairs fall out with the comb.
The myriad changes are done with
  gradualness—
gradually decaying, one looks and doesn't
  realize (it).
But I fear that my face in the mirror
is older this morning than yesterday.

Human life seldom fulfills a hundred
and one cannot prolongedly enjoy and
  delight.
Who can understand the heart of Heaven
  and Earth?
A thousand years they give to tortoise and
  crane.
I have heard that one good at curing ills
is called, present and past, a "Pien Ch'Üeh".
The myriad illnesses all can be cured,
lacking only the medicine to cure old age.

The Second Poem

I have got a handful of hairs—
in controlling the comb how dense they are!
They once seemed like the sparkle of black
  clouds,
now they are like the color of white silk.
There is my old mirror in the case;—
about to be reflected in it,
first I deeply sigh.
Ever since the white hairs came,
I don't wish to polish (the mirror) clearly.

The cow's head and the crane's neck
are oft like ink right to old age.
There is only the hair on a man's temples
which won't stay black till the end.

The last poem in the series reminds us that life is fleeting and to be enjoyed:

The Third Poem

Last year I planted peach seeds,
this year they are flowering trees.
Last year's new infant
this year is already learning to walk.

One is only startled by the way things
  grow,
unaware that the body deteriorates and
  ages.
It's gone! Oh, how we wish otherwise;
the years of youth can't be retained.
That's why this day I've written of my
  feelings
to send everywhere to all my friends.
If in the years of vigor
you don't delight and enjoy,
in the declining years
you should repent and apprehend.

Po was a frequenter of the tombs, an intimate of the grave mounds who appreciated that in time the present becomes the past. The year was 813, the next poem written while in mourning at Wei Village:

Climbing to the Old Graves
East of the Village

High and low the graves of olden times;
above them sheep and oxen paths.
Alone I stand at the highest tip;
long-reaching, these feelings I cherish!
Turning my head, I look villagewards
but see only grass of uncultivated fields.
The village people don't love flowers
and plant mostly chestnut and jujube.
Since coming to live in the village,
I'm oblivious to the fineness of wine and
  light.
Flowers few, orioles also rare—
year after year spring ages in secret.

He presented a mirror to someone because it would reflect, not the decay which was the poet's lot in his forty-first year, but the jet-black hair of the recipient's youth:

People say it is like a bright moon;
I say it is better than a bright moon.
The bright moon is always bright,
but in a year it lacks (brightness) twelve
  times.
How is it comparable to (the mirror) in the
  jade box,
like water which is always pure and clear?
When the moon breaks through Heaven's
  darkness,
round and bright, it alone does not rest.

I am ashamed of the ugliness and age of my
   looks,
with streak on streak of snow temple-
   winding:
It is better to present (a mirror) to a youth
who sees reflected in it jet-black hair.
Because you are going away a thousand li,
I've brought this to you just prior to
   departure.

He commented that wine helped release one's encumber-
ing hold on life and noted approvingly the behavior of Liu
Ling and Juan Chi, famed Chin dynasty inebriates:

Facing Wine

Human life—a hundred years;
through calculation—thirty thousand days.
How is it, moreover,
a hundred-year-old
among humans
is not one in a hundred?

Worthy and fool fragmented—fallen
   together;
esteemed and humble buried—lost the same.
Ghosts before and after Sacred East Mount
   (Cemetery),
bones new and old at North Hill (Cemetery).

Further, I hear of those who err through
   herbs,
through a love for the year-extending arts.
Then there are those who worry to death,
because of the greed to write government
   things.
Herb-mistaken, they don't reach old age;
die not from sickness but from worrying.

Who says man is the most spiritual?
He knows how to get but not how to lose.
What's better than to assemble friends and
   relatives
to drink this thing within the cup?
One can pour away troubles and cares,
one can bring out one's true nature.
That is why those in the class of Liu and
   Juan
were steadfastly drunk throughout their
   years.

My black hair daily already whitened,
my white face daily already blackened.
Human life—in the interval before death,
the changes how thorough and final!
It is often said that to oneself
there is nothing (so precious) as one's form
   and color;
one morning, when the changes come

one cannot get them to stop and cease.
How much more so matters beyond the
   body
far distant, throughness and hindrance!

On Bathing

I haven't bathed for over a year—
dust and dirt fill skin and flesh.
This morning, once I bathed clean,
decay and emaciation were excessive.
Aging color, hair on the temples white,
sick frame, limbs devoid of substance.

Clothes spacious, I've a slack girdle;
hairs are few and can't sustain the comb.
I ask myself: "How old this year?
My spring and autumn at forty's start."
At forty I'm already like this—
what will I be like at seventy?

The age of forty to Po symbolized a turning point,
defined in two poems entitled **"Self-Realization"**. In
the first, he noted the psychosomatic influences on
aging, and in the second, he stressed the need for
liberation from mental suffering and the cycle of causation by regarding the body as a floating cloud:

The First Poem

At forty, I am not yet old,
but grief and harm (bring) quick decay and
   evil.
Last year two white hairs produced,
this year one tooth fell out.
Frame and bones daily damaged-
   diminished,
heartfelt matters likewise mournful-isolated.
Night sleep and morning food—
insipid the flavor in those intervals.
Same-aged Official Secretary Ts'ui's[4]
looks sparkle, gleam and gleam.

I first realize that age and looks
decay or flourish according to griefs or
   joys.
Fearing age, age presses round;
worrying over illness, illness fully binds.
To neither worry nor fear,
the medicine to eliminate old age and
   illness.

The Second Poem

Mornings, I weep for what my heart loved;
evenings, I weep for what my heart longed
   for.
Intimate love ends up fragmented-fallen;
of what use is a body existing alone?

How many pleasures in an ordinary life?
limitless the favor from one's flesh and
    bone.
They combine to make for pains inside one,
assemble to produce the distresses of nose
    and head.
Grief comes, the four limbs are slowed;
tears exhausted, the two eyes are muddled.
That is why at the age of forty
my heart is like a seventy-year-old.

I hear the Doctrine of the Buddha[5]
has within it a gate of liberation.
Placing one's heart as stilled water,
seeing one's body as a floating cloud.
One shakes out dirty, unclean garments,
delivered from the wheel of life and death.

Why should one love this distress,
not leave it but still shrink back?
Reflecting, I initiate a great wish,
wishing for this body of the present.
May I merely receive the rewards of the
    past,
not combining (them) with future causations.

I vow to take the waters of wisdom and
    intelligence,
to wash away forever the dust of trouble
    and vexation.
Through the children of favor and love
I'll plant no more the seeds of grief and
    care.

T'ang poets such as Han Yü and Tu Mu[6] referred to a custom of saying farewell to spring (on the thirtieth day of the third lunar month). Po did likewise, as moved by its passing as by the coming or going of autumn:

Seeing Off the Spring

Thirtieth day of the third month,
spring returns and days again darken—
Vexed—provoked, I ask the spring breeze,
"Shouldn't you stay over tomorrow?"

Seeing off the spring above the Serpentine,
tenderly looking back east and west.
What I see are water-fallen flowers,
confusedly, knowing not their numbers.

Human life is like a travelling guest,
with both feet never stopping.
Day after day advancing on the journey
    ahead,
the journey ahead—how many paths?

Soldiers and swords, floods and fires,
can all be avoided as one goes along,

but there's only the coming of old age,
which in the human realm is unavoidable.

Moved by the season, I halt for a good
    while,
resting alone on a tree south of the pond.
Today my heart, in seeing off the spring,
is like the heart of separating from a friend.

During the Cold Food Festival of 800[7], he lamented the occasion with a smile of resignation. For he was ill and his loneliness was incurable. The Cold Food Festival, the only popular festival whose date was fixed according to the solar calendar (fifteen days after the spring equinox), preceded the Festival of the Dead:

Lying Sick During the Cold Food Festival

Sickness encountered on a fine day,
long my sighs.
Spring rain mist-misting,
color of the willows.
Sitting in decay,
totally without
the looks of former days.
Walking with a cane,
half-reliant
on the strength of others.
Shouting hub-hub in lanes and wards,
returning
strollers on the green.
Smiling,
I close my brushwood gates,
pass the Cold Food (Festival)
alone.

One of the poet's favorite pastimes was to drink wine while viewing the flowers. Approaching fifty and governing in a distant commandery, he wrote two poems on the subject of wine and flowers, describing homesickness and sensitive awareness of the swift passage of time. The blossoms in the first poem are euphoniously described as "concubines" and "beauties":

The First Poem

Fresh-fragrant the river vapors' spring;
Nan-pin (County in Chung-chou),
the intercalary first month.
Plum and cherry, peach and apricot
blossom sequentially above the city.
Red concubines, glistening, burst into
    fire,
white beauties, disorderly, spread their
    snow.
Fragrance—regretting it's wind-entrusted,
    blown about;
melancholy—bound up with pressure on
    and breakage of the branches.

In the bower the old Governor,
new white hairs on his head.
Cold and bleak his weary heart feelings;
warm and harmonious the good-time season.
His old home—letters and communication
    broken;
a distant commandery—intimates and guests
    cease.

He wishes to ask the wine cup neath the
    flowers:
on whose behalf were you created?

The Second Poem

Hands drawn forth, I pluck red cherries
and red cherries fall like sleet.
Head raised, I see a bright sun,
a bright sun running like an arrow.
The fragrance of the year,
the scenery of the times,
in a brief instant are like
decadence and change.
How much more so a blood-fleshed body!
How can one be strong and healthy for
    long?
Man's heart is distressed,
blindly grasping illusion,
envying the eminent,
worried about being poor and humble.
Melancholy's color often in his brows,
joyous looks don't reach his countenance.

How much more so with my head half-white!
Taking my mirror,
white hairs are everywhere to be seen;
why must the cup beneath the flowers
await any longer another's urgings?

It was better, concluded the poet, to drink alone than to wait in hopes of a drinking companion and a fellow lover of the flowers. But a most welcome companion was one who visited when the poet was ill and forlorn:

In the Midst of Illness a Friend Visits Me

Long lying down, forgetting the days.
Southern window—muddled and remuddled.
Neath lonely mourning grass eaves,
cold sparrows heard day and night;
I determinedly use a cane to lift myself from
    the bed,
rise and walk towards the courtyard's
    center.

Chancing to meet an old friend arriving,
it then becomes a welcoming encounter.

I move my couch to the slanting sun's rays,
throwing on a fur garment, leaning on a
    pillow.
Quietly chatting is better than taking
    medicine—
I feel I have somewhat (restored) heart
    feelings.

He sang to the sun in a mixed-line style reminiscent of the New Music Bureau odes, interspersing seven- and three-character lines:

Rising, rising, the sun the color of fire,
ascending a path of a thousand li,
descending in an instant.
When it comes out, it's bright day,
when it goes in, it's evening.
Turning round like a pearl,
it can't stay in one place—
it can't stay in one place,
what's to be done?

For you I raise the wine and sing a short
    song;
the song's sounds are bitter,
the words also bitter.
All you youths seated everywhere,
listen to me.
(Before) this night has ended, bright dawn
    urges on.
Autumn's breeze has barely gone
when spring's breeze returns.
Man lacks root and stem, time doesn't halt;
rose faces wither and decay with the bright sun.

I urge you for this once to force a smile,
I urge you to force a drink of the cup.
Man's life can't be pleasure and joy
    prolonged;
his years are few and in an instant old age
    arrives.

Aging was the inescapable theme for Po Chü-i, the theme to which he turned with the advancing years:

Gradually Aging

This day and again the next—
before one realizes, age at its eve.
White hair falls with the comb,
rose face departs with the mirror.
Confronting spring, melancholy and alone;
facing the wine, little pleasure and interest.
Encountered circumstances mostly sadness
    and grief;
meeting people, esteem for old friends
    increases.
Form and substance belong to Heaven and
    Earth,

movement and change never cease.
To be blamed is the heart of youth,
corroding away and falling to nowhere.

At forty-five he noted that he was rapidly balding. He'd washed his hair only once in the past year, but when he did the results were so distressing he was moved to address two poems to a Buddhist monk, admitting his troubled state in one and expressing his desire to attain to the gate of release in the other. (East Temple refers to East Forest Temple at Mount Lu):

The First Poem

> As years advance, one's person changes to
> indolence;
> a hundred things and without desire.
> Coming to the hair on my head,
> a year passes and it's washed just once.
> Washing rarely, I am distressed by falling
> hair—
> one wash and I am half bald.
> My short temple (locks)—
> undergrowth that has gone through frost.
> My old face—
> a tree that has taken leave of spring.
> I am still close to having passed the years
> of strength,
> but how quickly the decay to my looks
> arrives!
> It must be that with troubles and vexations many,
> my heart is scorched and my blood
> insufficient.

The Second Poem

> Gradually scarcer, not even a full handful;
> gradually shorter, not even the desired
> height.
> Moreover, in shortness and scarcity's midst,
> day and night, falling out and white.
>
> Since I lack the arts of an Immortal,
> how can I eliminate
> the register of old age and death?
> There is only the gate of release
> which can cross beyond
> the difficulties of decay and distress.
>
> Covering the mirror,
> I look towards East Temple.
> Submitting my heart,
> I acknowledge the meditating guest.
> Decaying and whitening—
> why talk about these?
> Shave it all off and I'd still not regret.
>
> I also once burned the great (immortality)
> herbs,

> (but) when I rested, the fire perversely
> diminished.
> Coming to the present,
> the remnant cinnabar
> has burned dry and failed to achieve
> results.
>
> Action and concealment failed both times;
> worry and vexation fought together in my
> heart.
> Casting myself into barren rusticity,
> seated and seeing old age and illness press
> close,
> I must get the King of Healers to save me.
> There is only the Gate of Non-Duality,
> between which there is neither early death
> nor longevity.

"The King of Healers" refers to the Buddha, the healer of all sufferings. "The Gate of Non-Duality" embodies a concept of the indivisibility of things; whatever appears to be dualistic actually partakes of the one nature of Buddha.

He summed up his achievements in a poem written in his forty-seventh year, saying that he had been luckier than ancient writers like Yen Hui, the short-lived disciple of Confucius, or Po I, who died of starvation. The burial grounds he alludes to in the poem were in Loyang. Though he had served in important offices, he still felt that Destiny was eluding him:

Refrain of the Great Song

> Heaven is long, earth old,[8]—there is no
> finality or end;
> last night, this morning, and again
> tomorrow.
> Temple and hair spotted white, teeth sparse;
> without realizing it I'm forty-seven years
> old.
> How many years in all before I'm fifty?
> Taking the mirror to illumine my face, heart-
> lost.
> Since I don't have a long rope
> to bind the bright sun
> and also lack immortality herbs
> to arrest my rose face,
> my rose face gradually and day by day
> is not as it was before.
>
> In history, where are the meritorious names?
> I wished to retain the youthful years,
> to await wealth and eminence;
> but wealth and eminence didn't come
> and the youthful years departed.
> Gone and gone again, like a long river
> flowing east to an ocean with no returning
> waves.

Worthy and fool, eminent and humble,
likewise revert to extinction.

North Hill's burial grounds are high and
   rock-encircled.
Since antiquity it has been like this—it's
   not only I.
Not yet dead, there's wine and lofty song.
Yen Hui was short lived, Po I starved.
What I've gotten up to now is already
   much;
meritorious name, wealth, and eminence must
   await destiny.
But if destiny doesn't come, what is to be
   done?

Living in Szechwan (referred to as Pa) in 820, in a remote land which he considered inhabited by barbarians, he wrote about mind and body. His body was feeble but his mind undimmed and entrusted to fate:

My Body

My body—what is it like?
It's like a lone-begotten mugwort.
Autumn frost scissors the root away,
vast-vast it follows the long wind.
I formerly frolicked in the capital's vicinity;
now I have fallen into a land of Pa
   barbarians.
Formerly, I was an official of thought and
   spirit;
now I have become an old man solitary and
   lone.

Though my outer appearance is lone and
   solitary,
inwardly I cherish an extreme of harmonious
   blending.
Heaven-conferred fate is thick or thin;
I entrust my heart whether it be
to impoverishment or success.
Success is as a huge bird
raising wings and brushing azured Heavens.
Impoverishment is as a wren
(so small that) one branch accommodates it.
If there were only those who knew this way,
their bodies might be impoverished
but never their hearts.

In 821, as the year came to a close he remarked that everything returned to its source, everything but the traveller stationed in the south now for the past five years. He counseled himself to accept destiny:

Year's End

Frost descends, water returns to the ravine;
winds fall, trees return to the mountain.

Gradually the year is about to rest,
everything returning to its original source.

Why is it that this south-transferred guest
alone, for five years hasn't yet returned?
Destiny stagnant, my fate's already
   determined.
Days long, my heart has become filled with
   tranquillity.
Once also my heart and mouth
quietly thought, and I said to myself:
"Leaving the nation's (capital) was definitely
   unpleasurable,
returning to my native village won't
   necessarily be joyous.
Why must I beget my own distress
rejecting the easy and seeking the difficult?"

In 822 he advised himself to accept fate, without seeking to change things. He was fifty years old, having completed two-thirds of his lifetime:

When joy goes, then must grief arise;
when prosperity comes, it is at the extreme
   of misfortune.
Who says it is like this?
(If so,) why is my path finally blocked?
I once sought divination from an official
   diviner;
he rubbed the tortoise but was darkly silent.
I also looked up and asked Heaven—
Heaven was merely a blue-blue color.
From here on I'll only entrust to fate,
the profit-riches heart at rest.
Recently, I've shifted to tranquil withdrawal;
my village grounds—setting memories to
   rest.
Turning, I see distress in the world,
distress in seeking but not getting;
I now have nothing which I seek,
have almost left the terrain of worry and grief.

There is another poem of summation written in 822, in which he balanced personal well-being against failure in government service. The reference to a sage in the poem is to the Emperor:

A cool wind arises in the forbidden palace,
a new moon is begotten on the palace
   (pond).
Half through the night autumn comes in
   secret,
the ten-thousand-year willows delicately
   wave.
Hot and cool alternate in time and season,
bells and drums exchange (announcements
   of) dark and dawn.
Encountering a Sage, I regret my year-
   decay;

to reward favor, I grieve my strength is
    little.
Parasitic eating, of no assistance or benefit,
red insignia emptily bound around.
My cap and carriage roosting in the fields
    and clouds,
my rice and millet nourishing the mountain
    birds.

Measuring ability, when I inspect myself
what I've gotten is already considerable.
The fifth rank isn't low,
at fifty I am not an early death.
If I didn't know a heart of satiety
on what day would greed-seeking end?

He cherished an ideal of simple living. In a long poem written in the old five-character style, he described the charms of a village occupied by only two clans, Chu and Ch'en, in which life moved at its own pace, oblivious to outside forces. He contrasted this pristine simplicity with his rootless, wandering existence. At the time of writing he was thirty-six:

The Village of Chu-Ch'en

In Hsü Prefecture, at Ku-feng County (in Kansu), there is a village called Chu-Ch'en. It's over a hundred li from the county (capital); the mulberry and hemp are green and densely abundant. The weaver's shuttle sounding whir-awhir, the oxen and donkeys running to and fro. The women draw water from the valley stream, the men gather firewood on the mountains. The county is distant and official matters few; the mountain is deep and the people's customs unadorned. There are resources (but) one doesn't engage in business; there are full-grown males (but) they don't enter the army. Family on family preserve village enterprise, not leaving their gates (even) when their hairs are white. Alive, they are the people of the village; dead, they are the dust of the village. Within the fields young and old regard one another with such joyfulness. One village—only two surnames forming marriages generation after generation; close and distant relatives—for dwelling there is the clan; for frolicking in youth and maturity, there is the group. Yellow chickens and white wine, pleasurable assemblages less than ten-day periods apart. Those alive are not distantly separated, and in taking brides they give priority to close neighbors. Those dead are not distantly buried, and the graves and mounds mostly encircle the village. Since they are tranquil in life and death, they are not distressed by form and spirit; that's why most are long lived, oft seeing their great-great grandsons.

I was born in a village of rites and duties, in youthful adolescence orphaned and poor. I vainly studied to distinguish right from wrong (but) merely selected (the way of) painful diligence. The way of the world prizes moral teachings; the men of the land esteem capping and marriage. Because of these one distresses oneself, in beliefs becoming a person of great error.

At ten I knew how to read books;
at fifteen I was able to compose.
At twenty I was recommended as a
    Cultivated Talent;
at thirty I became an official Admonitioner.
Below, there was the tie of wife and
    children;
above, there was the favor of Lord and
    parents.
I accepted the family and served the nation,
hoping in these (things) not to be unfilial.

Remembering my yesterdays, at the start of travels and roamings: Coming to the present, it was fifteen springs (ago). My lone boat went three times to Ch'u (in the south); my emaciated horse passed (Ch'ang-an in) Ch'in four times. Proceeding at noon, I had the color of starvation; sleeping at night, there was no tranquillity of spirit.

East or west no place to stay—
coming and going like a floating cloud.
In separation and chaos I lost my old
    village;
my blood-fleshed were mostly scattered and
    divided.
Chiang-nan and Chiang-pei
each had the relations of a lifetime.
A lifetime of partings throughout the day;
the deceased heard of separated by the
    years.
Mourning-grieved, lying down till eve;
nocturnal weeping, sitting unto morn.
A fire of sadness wound the crannies of my
    heart,
a frost of melancholy infiltrated my temple
    roots.
One life distressed like this—
envy do I the people of (Chu-Ch'en) village.

Po Chü-i was moved to sorrow not only by the inevitability of death but by the fact of death when it came to blood relatives and friends. He contrasted the carefree innocence of children with the worries of maturity, and wondered if the child were not father of the man:

Watching Children Play

Milk teeth—shedding seven and eight year
    olds;
fine silk—wearing three and four year olds;
playing with dirt, fighting with grass,

all day joyous and having fun.
The aged guest in the courtyard,
on his temples white hairs anew.
Once he sees the game of (riding) bamboo
    horses
he thinks of his youthful, foolish times.
Youthful foolishness involved play and joy,
getting old has much worry and sadness.
Quietly thinking of the one and the other,
I do not know who is foolish.

His daughter Golden Bells was born when he was nearing forty, and on her first birthday he commemorated the occasion in verse, speaking too soon of there possibly being no worry of her early death:

The First Birthday of Golden Bells

My years are about to be forty;
I've a daughter called Golden Bells.
Since her birth, she is first a full year,
learning to sit but not yet able to talk.
For the nonce I have not yet
the feelings of the all-pervasive ones
and still cannot avoid
the compassion of mundane sentiment.

From now on she will be an additional
    burden,
but I say in vain she is at present a
    comfort.
If there is no worry of early death
then there is the harassment of marriage.
She is causing my return-to-the-mountains plan
to have to be delayed by fifteen years.

But Golden Bells died in her third year. Po Chü-i remembered her in an informal musing way that poignantly revealed his grief:

Remembering Golden Bells
(Who Died at Three)

The First Poem

Decaying and sick, a body of forty;
graceful and foolish, a three-year-old
    daughter.
Not a boy, but still better than nothing—
comforting my emotions, a single comfort at
    the time.
One morning she abandoned me and
    departed,
her spirit shadow without a place.

Oh, remembering the time of her early death,
prattle-noise, first learning to speak.
Then I realize that mortal love
is the wherewithal to worry and grief.

Thinking only that before, this had never been,
I use reason to send away hurt and pain.
Forgotten love—the days already old,
three years have shifted heat and cold.
Today, once having hurt my heart
because I met her old wet nurse.

The Second Poem

You together with your parents
for eighty-six ten day periods.
Of a sudden no longer seen,
already three or four springs.
Form and substance basically unreal;
vapors accumulate, perchance take body
    shape.
Favored love is originally in error,
affinity combines and one is a parent for a
    time.

Remembering this, on the verge of
    enlightenment
I rely on it to send away the sad and bitter.
I temporarily settle down through reason,
but I am not one to forget my feelings.

When Po was living by Wei Village in 813, withdrawn from office and in mourning, he rested one autumn evening at the eastern burial grounds. The "white poplar" mentioned in the poem was planted by the graves. However, from the Han dynasty onward, the pine and cypress were mentioned almost exclusively as the sepulchral trees planted by the Chinese, who believed that they protected the manes of the dead.[9] The "Jade Stream" signifies the place:

A day of cool breeze, cold dew, lonely
    desolation;
field of yellow artesmisia, purple
    chrysanthemums, barren coolness.
Little color have the autumn flowers round
    the graves;
flutter-flutter fly tiny insects and small
    butterflies.

In the midst there is one who nimbly
    moving walks alone,
hand supporting a fishing pole, not riding a
    horse.
Returning late from fishing at the southern
    stream,
I rest in this burial ground beneath a white
    poplar.

My coarse garments are half old, my white
    hair new—
if one met me would he know who I am?
Who would say that the guest living in
    obscurity

by the Wei river bank
once performed as an official
in attendance at the Jade Stream?

He composed elegies for his friends, lamenting their premature deaths and sighing because their talents had been ignored. In 806 he wrote the following elegy for Yang Hung-chen, a fellow scholar. (Yen Hui was a brilliant disciple of Confucius who died young):

Yen Hui of old short lived;
Confucius pitied His Worthiness' (untimely
   end).
Mr. Yang also liked to study;
unluckily, he too reverted to futility (too
   soon).
Who knows the intent of Heaven and
   Earth?
Longevity is given only to tortoises and
   cranes.

Ten years later, in his middle forties, the increasing number of deaths among his acquaintances prompted him to write a poem on death for Yüan Chen and three other friends[10] serving in scattered posts in the provinces. (The prefectures Feng and Feng, which are two names in Chinese, have tonal differences):

Yesterday I heard of *A*'s death,
this morning I hear of *B*'s.
From the threefold division of my friends,
two-thirds have changed to spirits.
The departed ones I don't see again.
How saddened! How prolonged!

The ones alive—now what can I do?
All apart from me ten thousand li.
In a lifetime those who know one's heart,
bend the fingers (to count)—how many can
   there be?

T'ung, Kuo, Feng and Feng Prefectures.
Insignificantly, the four gentlemen
thinking of one another as we age,
the floating life like flowing water.
One must sigh at the old frolics together,
withered and fallen—the days like this.
How fitting would be a cup of wine,
to open my eyes and exchange laughing
   glances.

He dreamed of former Chief Minister P'ei Chi (765-813) long after P'ei had died, and wept with the awareness that it had been but a dream. P'ei Chi had been in close sympathy with Po, especially in supporting his stand in 809 against the eunuchs:[11]

Dreaming of Duke P'ei the Minister,
five years separated by life from death,

one night our spirits communed in dream.
In the dream it was as in days past—
together direct to the Palace of Golden
   Bells.[12]
Like a golden purplish color (the sash you
   wore),
clearly distinguishable your face of jade
   eternal.
Intimate my yearning thoughts of you,
the same as they had been in normal life.

When I awoke, I knew it was a dream,
was grieved with emotions unending.
Pursuing my thoughts to times and events
   of then,
how different from the midst of yesterday
   eve!
Since studying the dharma of heartfulness,
the ten thousand affinities form a single void.
This morning on your behalf
my tears flowed and at once moistened my
   chest.

The death of a villager in 814 elicited an elegy from Po; he had enjoyed the villager's friendship when he had no one to talk with other than the local peasantry:

Sighing Over Mr. Ch'ang

The son of the Ch'ang clan of West Village
had been lying sick for some time.
Till ten days ago he still visited me;
today they suddenly say he has perished.
At the time, often sick and at leisure,
I stayed with him together in the fields.
Our garden forest, green and thriving,
was several li distant from here.

There was no (other) good journeyer among
   village neighbors;
what I encountered were only peasants.
This person—what was he like?
Associating with him was still better than
   nothing.
And now he has already gone;
I should heave a long sigh for him.

In the following year, the death of Li the Third elicited a poem from Po closer in tenor to his poetry of social protest, for he protested to Heaven about the senselessness of snatching away the life of a man of talent with a sick wife and an infant daughter:

Weeping Over Li the Third

Last year, at the bend of the Wei River
in autumn he came to visit me.
This year, at the Ward of Constant Pleasure
   (in Ch'ang-an)

the spring day weeps at your reversion (to
    non-life).
Weeping over you, I look up and ask
    Heaven:
"What indeed is Heaven's intent?
If you had to snatch away his longevity,
wouldn't it have been better not to grant
    him talent?
The fallen state of things after decease—
wife sick and daughter in infancy."

He wrote an elegy in 820 on the death of Wang Chih-
fu, a very close friend from whom he had been separated by official service. Again Po complained about
the arbitrariness of Heaven in rewarding the evil and
punishing the good. It was at the prompting of Wang
Chih-fu fourteen years earlier that Po Chü-i and Ch'en
Hung had collaborated to produce poetry and prose
versions of "Lament Everlasting". The references in
the poem to "T'ao" and "Hsieh" are to famed Chin
dynasty poets T'ao Yüan-ming and Hsieh Ling-yün;
references to "Hsi" and "Juan" are to ancients Hsi
K'ang and Juan Chi:

Weeping Over Wang Chih-fu

We parted in front of the Temple to Which
    Immortals Frolic,
parted more than ten years ago.
Parting in life is still cutting-keen;
to what can a parting through death be
    likened?

A stranger came from Tzu-t'ung (in
    Szechwan)
to say your death was not an empty
    (rumor).
I was startled and suspicious,
not yet believing in my heart,
on the verge of weeping
but again indecisive and irresolute.
Indecisive and irresolute, beside my inner
    gates
sound issued forth and my tears
    accompanied it.

On my garments are today's tears,
in the trunk the previous month's letter.
Pitiable you, with the ways of the ancients,
further, with the manner of the Superior Man.
Your poetry chanted in the style of T'ao
    and Hsieh,
your manner and feelings in the class of Hsi
    and Juan.
As an official you had a bad destiny
and your life was over in an instant.

I know that Heaven is extremely high,
but how could I not once cry out?

Chiang-nan has poisonous snakes,
Chiang-pei has apparitional foxes;
they both enjoy a longevity of a thousand
    years
more than Wang Chih-fu.
I don't know what virtues they have,
I don't know what crimes he had.

Po sent a poem to Yüan Chen in 820, lamenting the
deaths of old friends. He concluded with the hope that
he and Yüan might meet one day in Ch'ang-an, a hope
realized in 821. (Chih-fu refers to Wang Chih-fu):

Crying Over Old Friends, Then Sending (the Poem) to Yüan the Ninth

Yesterday I wept at the inner door,
today I weep at the inner door.
If you ask who I am weeping about,
it is none but my old intimate friends.
Wei-ch'ing has already gone on the long
    (journey),
Chih-fu is also in the gloomy sunkenness.
Counting on my fingers the years they've
    gone,
holding back my tears and thinking of
    myself.

They were both younger than I,
but have gone first as men of the nether
    springs.
Now my head is half-white;
how can my body long survive?
Well do I think of Officer Yüan,
an acquaintance of twenty springs;
formerly I saw you beget a child,
now I hear you enfold a grandson.

The ones alive are grown completely aged,
the ones who have passed are already dust.
Sooner or later, at your home
in (the Ward of) Rising Peacefulness
I'll resolve my melancholy by seeing you.

In 822 he returned late one night after paying a call on
the bereft family of his deceased friend Li Chien. He
had also visited a very sick official, whom I presume
to be Ts'ui Ch'ün, bedridden for three years. Po revealed his feelings in a brief poem. "Yüan" refers to
Yüan Tsung-chien, Yüan Chen's cousin and the poet's
close friend:

Returning Late and Feeling Sad

Morning, I pay a condolence call on the
    bereft of Li family;
evening, I inquire about the illness in the
    Ts'ui family.

Turning my horse, I return alone
with eyebrows lowered, heart depressed-
    despondent.

Those with whom (I was) on good terms in
    life
did not exceed six or seven at the most;
how is it that in a ten-year interval
scattered-fallen, of three there is not one.
Liu previously I saw in dreams,
Yüan earlier I lost before the flowers.
Gradually aging, with whom shall I frolic?
A city of spring, a fine scenic day.

He mourned the death of a friend who died wifeless and childless, and worried about the funeral arrangements:

Weeping at Night Over Li I-tao

The one who passed on has severed
    shadow and echo,
empty courtyard—dawn and again dusk.
The wailing of his family about to end,
at night they lock the gate of the spirit
    chamber.
No wife, no child—who will bury him?
Emptily viewing the inscribed funeral
    standard
fluttering towards the moon.

Po described the singing of a funeral dirge as the coffin was being pulled along. The "solemn city" is Loyang, "North Mang-shan Hill" a tomb site near Loyang:

The Words of a Funeral Dirge

How the cinnabar standard (of the
    deceased) flies aloft!
The white (hearse-pulling) horse further
    sadly neighs.
Dawn's glow illuminates lane and alley,
the hearse-carriage in dignity about to
    proceed.
Soughing wind, a day of the ninth month;
sad dirge(-singers) leave the solemn city.
If one asks who is sending him off,
it is wife-children and elder-younger
    brothers.

Green-green, ascending the ancient field,
high-high, opening the new grave.
Holding in affliction, once moved to cry
different mouths share the wailing sounds.

The old mounds turning to weedy
    inaccessibility,
the new graves daily set in order.
Spring breezes, autumn grasses—North
    Mang-shan Hill;

at this place, year after year, life-death
    partings.

. . . . .

Chapter 13

Po's Influence on Japanese Literature:

Not Dumplings But Flowers[1]

Po Chü-i influenced Japanese literature more than any other Chinese poet. His works were known in Japan while he was still alive; it is a matter of record that Minister Fujiwara no Takamori inspected a T'ang vessel in 838 and secured the collections of Po Chü-i and Yüan Chen. Takamori was given a special investiture when he presented these to the court, and from then on Japanese literati were avid readers of Po's poems. One story alleged that during the lifetime of Emperor Saga (786-842), a part of Po's writings was already kept in the Secretariat. Emperor Saga was said to have been so conversant with the collection that he once changed a word in a poem and showed the change to Ono no Takamura (802-52), prompting Takamura to express deep admiration for the Emperor's poetic talent. This story may be lacking in fact but it is certainly true in spirit, for it symbolizes the enthusiastic response to Po's poetry at court and the profound knowledge of his poems which prevailed throughout the Heian age. Chinese influences were then momentous, for these were the times in which T'ang literature, art, religion, music, calligraphy, and other aspects were first borrowed from and then assimilated into the indigenous culture. Another great Chinese poetic influence was exerted on Heian Japan by the *Wen-hsüan* ("Selections of Literature"), an anthology of third to seventh century poetry and prose selections. But the stimulus provided by Po's Works far excelled it.

Sugawara Michizane (845-903), who has been eulogized in Japan as a virtual God of Literature and Writing, was said to have kept Po's **Works** at his side and not to have let the collection out of his hands. There are certain resemblances between the two lives: Michizane and Po came from families of good lineage and bureaucratic service; learned how to write poetry in early youth; passed a series of official examinations; served in a wide variety of government posts; and were removed from court posts and demoted from the capital. Both men also gained enduring fame as writers rather than as politicians. In 883 Michizane entertained a visitor at court from northeast China named P'ei T'ing, and P'ei was said to have praised his poetry, saying that it was comparable to the poetry of Po Lot'ien. Michizane was almost sent to T'ang China in 894 as ambassador, but he decided not to go because of the unsettled conditions which existed in China towards the close of the T'ang.

Michizane wrote poems in Chinese and adopted the name for one of them from a poem by Po Chü-i called **"Not Leaving The Gates"**. Po actually wrote two poems with this title, but one of them seems to bear a special ideological relationship to Sugawara's composition. Both poems were written by men who, while having been involved through the force of circumstances in court intrigues, preferred cultivation of the ways of quiescence and reflection.

Not Leaving the Gates

Po Chü-i

Since not leaving my gates,
several ten-day periods.
With what do I lock the gates?
With whom am I intimate?
The crane's cage is opened;
I see Gentleman (Crane).
When books and folios are opened,
I meet the ancients.
I self-quiet my heart,
extend my life;
I seek no things,
extend my spirit.
I am able to endure it,
for it's the cultivated way of truth.
Why must one cause evil demons
to submit and be restrained?

Po's concluding line signifies that to him evil is mental, not to be repressed but rather surmounted by achieving a state of quiescence and non-desire.

Not Leaving the Gates

Sugawara Michizane

Once I met with banishment,
was in a house of thorn and brambles.
Ten thousand deaths,
fearful-apprehensive,
in feelings constrained-contracted.
Of the capital towers,
I see only the color of the tiles.
Of the Temple of Mercy,
I hear only the sound of the bells.
What I cherish within well expels
a lone cloud (capital) bound.
Meeting with external objects,
I welcome them with a full heart.
Though on my person here
there's no restriction or encumbrance,
why is it that
I don't step even an inch from my door?

Japanese poets from Sugawara's time onward were generally disinterested in the poems which Po Chü-i had valued the most, the poems through which he criticized social abuses and attacked the corruption of those in power. The literati in Japan weren't attracted by the didactic element in his poetry but were drawn rather to the beauty and simplicity of specific lines and phrases. Po had criticized poetry for poetry's sake, emphasizing the importance of content rather than form, but his was a many-sided talent. While he declared that poetry should serve a didactic purpose, many of his two thousand or so regulated poems conveyed thoughts or contained phrases which were undeniably in the moon-and-flower category. These thoughts and phrases appealed profoundly to the Japanese leisure class, and they were incorporated into poems about aesthetic-aristocratic reflections which were centered about the court and totally removed from the lives of the masses beyond. Po's **Works** came to be considered essential reading for persons of good upbringing. Court Japanese of the Heian era were so familiar with his collection that they referred to it, not as **Po-shih wen-chi**, but simply as **Wen-chi**. Sei Shonagon, the famed authoress who attended an imperial consort late in the tenth century, recorded in *Pillow-Book* (*makura no soshi*) the books which were important to her. She placed Po's **Works** first, followed by the *Collection of Literature* and Ssu-ma Ch'ien's *Chronicle of History* (*shih-chi*).

Sei Shonagon's contemporary, Murasaki Shikibu (died 1016), was another woman writer of extraordinary talent who read Po's poems with such thoroughness that she could draw upon them freely and appropriately for literary sustenance. In *The Tales of Genji,* Murasaki informs us that the men of her age were prejudiced against women who read Chinese, considering them unladylike, but she makes it clear that in private she was an avid reader of Po's verse. She made many references of his writings in *The Tales of Genji.* **"Lament Everlasting"** has proven to be an enduring favorite in Japan, still cited today in high school texts, and Murasaki shows that this poem was popular with the Japanese from much earlier times. In one of the chapters of the book called "The Emperor of Kiritsubo", referring to a beloved imperial favorite, Kiritsubo's circumstances are described as parallel to those of Precious Consort Yang. She too is jealously regarded by other palace ladies and made to suffer indignities by them, but she endures their enmity because of the indebtedness she feels towards her royal lover. In another chapter called "Illusion" (*maboroshi*), the many fireflies fluttering about in the palace are likened to the fireflies described in **"Lament Everlasting"**. And in the chapter about Kiritsubo, the Emperor mourns her death in ways strongly reminiscent of the ways the Illustrious Celestial of the T'ang mourned his deceased consort. He looked over the presents he had given Kiritsubo, immersed in sadness as he noted the hairpins, and felt a desire to locate her spirit. A series of images is then presented which describe Precious Consort Yang: Her painted image could not fully depict her charms; the forlorn T'ang sovereign was reminded of her make-up by the camellias at T'ai-yeh Palace and the willows at Wei-yang Palace; he thought of how lovely she had been, so lovely that even the colors of flowers and birds were not comparable. Her speech mannerisms, the vows they'd made to be like one-winged birds and linked branches—the forlorn ruler was overwhelmed by lament unending. Kiritsubo's sovereign slept alone at the time of the autumn moon, weeping at the sounds of the song "Above The Clouds" and thinking of the night she had entered the palace. He sighed like the T'ang Emperor, and similarly became negligent about rising early to preside at court, lost his appetite for food, and was unable to forget her.

Murasaki once described how, as she was returning home, the mountains were truly three thousand li beyond. As the fifteenth night approached, she revealed how she thought of the amusements being held everywhere at the palace and looked at the face of the moon. She was unable to repress her tears as she chanted of the hearts of the ancients two thousand li beyond. These reflections of Murasaki were probably suggested by the following poetic lines of Po Chü-i. He was writing about the mid-autumn festival, which took place on the fifteenth day of the eighth lunar moon while he was sleeping alone in the Hanlin Academy within palace confines and thinking of his cherished friend Yüan Chen:

> I face the moon,
> remembering Yüan the Ninth.
> Silver Terrace,
> Golden Tower,
> at night deep-darkened.
> Sleeping alone in Hanlin,
> thinking of you.
> On the night of Three Fives,
> the new moon's color;
> two thousand li beyond,
> my old friend's heart.

The last two lines are very well known, being cited in many sources. The poem was popular in Japan during and after the Heian era, and was quoted in *A Collection of Recitable Japanese and Chinese Verse* (*wakan roeishu*, 1013), *The Tales of Heike* (ca. 1240), and *A Record of the Rise and Fall of the Minamoto and Taira Clans* (*Gen Pei seisuiki*, ca. 1338).

In *The Tales of Genji*, Murasaki used a part of Po's theme of the unfairness of the marriage system, namely where Po wrote of the two ways to wed, either in wealth or in poverty—but while extracting an essential phrase she ignored the didacticism. She had an episode in the second chapter about how a group of young nobles gathered together on a rainy night to discuss the merits and shortcomings of the women they knew. One in the group told of his personal experience in the home of a scholar. He heard that the scholar had many daughters, and went there and made an amorous approach to one of them. When the scholar heard about this, he immediately prepared the sake cups used in wedding ceremonies and asked the young man to listen to the song about the two ways of marriage. There is a passing reference in the book to another of Po's poems, in the chapter called "The Festival of Red Leaves". The voice of the lutist is likened to the voice of the lutist that Po Chü-i once described. The point of interest here is that the reference is not to **"Lute Song"**, which next to **"Lament Everlasting"** is probably the best known of Po's poems in present-day Japan. It refers instead to the little-known poem about a lutist playing on a river boat which Po wrote about two years before he wrote **"Lute Song"**.

Kaneko Hikojiro, the foremost authority on the relationship between Po's **Works** and Heian literature, notes that it is relatively easy to uncover citations to Chinese poetry in Japanese literature in which the relevant passages are clearly and unambiguously indicated. That is why he believes such passages have tended to be thoroughly considered and analyzed. Professor Kaneko stated it was much more difficult to trace the influences of Chinese poetry and prose when only an isolated word or phrase was incorporated into what was otherwise a purely Japanese composition, but that this could be done by the properly equipped specialist who painstakingly conducted comparative investigations. Professor Kaneko was able to uncover relationships not noted prior to his researches, and it is some of these original contributions which supply the substance for the subsequent discussion of how the poems by Heian writers and Po Chü-i were interrelated.

Two incidents related by Sei Shonagon in *Pillow-Book* show that she and her court associates were thoroughly familiar with Po's poetry collection, acquainted as well with poems not especially well known or preferred. Heian literati tested one another on their knowledge of such Chinese poems by quoting lines out of context but in appropriate circumstances to see if the recipient could come forth with the proper reaction or response. On one occasion, when the Empress asked her about the snow of Fragrant Hearth Peak, Sei Shonagon responded at once. From where she was seated, with a superlatively graceful move she raised the screen as if to look out at the snow. She was pantomiming a line from the third of five poems by Po Chü-i entitled **"Fragrant Hearth Peak"**:

> The sun is high;
> sleepy-legged,
> I still lazily rise.
> In my room
> the coverlets are piled up,
> I don't fear the cold.

Heard through my pillow
the bell at the Temple of Love Bequeathed;
pushing aside the screen, I see
the snow of Fragrant Hearth Peak.

The lines in this poem about listening to the bell at the temple and pushing aside the screen to see the snow became famous and oft-repeated. But Sei Shonagon was able to respond to a much more difficult test of memory. It was then a common practice for poets to create Japanese poems together in a thirty-one syllable, five-line form. The first poet might contribute the last two lines of seven syllables, while the second poet was expected to compose the first three lines (five-seven-five syllables). *Pillow Book* describes a poetic exchange of this type between the famous scholar-official Fujiwara no Kinto (960-1041) and Sei Shonagon. The time was the last day or so of the second lunar month; the wind was blowing severely, the sky was black, and a light snow was falling. Just then a messenger came to the palace and gave Sei Shonagon a letter from Kinto. She looked at the special writing paper, on which Kinto had the written lines:

There is indeed
a slight spring feeling.

Sei Shonagon comments that the lines were really well attuned to the day's weather and that she was perplexed as how to reply. She asked who was in the palace to assist her with the composition, but everyone was embarrassed and nonplussed as how best to respond to the famous scholar's lines. Sei Shonagon admitted her distress at completing the poem inelegantly. She wanted to let her mistress, the Emperor's second consort, see what Kinto had written, but the mistress was then in the royal bedroom with the Emperor. The messenger urged her to respond and, since she didn't want to be slow as well as inept, she worried no longer but wrote:

In the sky's coldness,
looking like flowers,
the snow is scattering;

(Kinto)

there is indeed
a slight spring feeling.

She wrote out her lines and handed the response to the messenger, worrying about how everyone would regard them. She wanted to find out what the reaction was, but was afraid to for fear her effort was being disparaged. But then she heard that those in authority had praised her composition, saying it was so good they intended to petition the throne to get her promoted.

Kitamura Kigin (1624-1705) commented on this poetic exchange in his famous study of *Pillow-Book,* called *Shunshosho,* completed in 1674, noting that a later poet called Fujiwara Shunzei (1114-1204) was prompted by it to compose a poem on a related theme. Kaneko Hikojiro points out that subsequent Japanese researchers, like Kitamura, regarded the poetic exchange between Kinto and Sei Shonagon as spontaneous, evoked by the natural surroundings. Later generations followed suit, but Professor Kaneko came forward with the thesis that it represented a very skillful adaptation by both poets of a seven-character line, eight-line regulated poem by Po Chü-i called **"The Snow of Southern Ch'in"**:

In former years
I was once
an official in the west,
used to going
from Camel's Mouth
to Southern Ch'in.
At the third hour,
cloud-cold and much flying snow;
in the second month,
mountain-chilly and a slightness of spring.

I think of the old things,
still vexed-depressed.
You're making a first journey,
surely pained-embittered.
I still trust that
the melancholy monkeys
don't cry out in the cold;
if one hears them cry,
it makes man even more melancholy.

Po wrote this poem in response to a poem Yüan Chen had sent him while on his way to Szechwan to serve. Po was used to the road, but commiserated with his friend who had to travel it in the cold, when there was only a slight touch of spring in the air. **"The Snow of Southern Ch'in"** was not highly regarded in Japanese literary circles, being considered mediocre. Fujiwara Kinto may have been prompted to adapt one line midway through the poem because of its relative obscurity and to transform this into the last two lines of a *tanka* poem in order to test the comprehensiveness of Sei Shonagon's knowledge of Chinese verse. It was of course far more difficult for the one being tested to trace the source of a Japanese adaptation of a Chinese poetic line than it would have been if the line had been recited in the original Chinese. But Sei Shonagon responded to the challenge by likewise adapting the appropriate lines in Po's poem to precede what Kinto had written. This is why Kinto was overwhelmed, and why others so admired her astuteness that they spoke of petitioning the throne to have her officially promoted. Other court poets must have realized the connection of Po's poem to the *tanka* written in collaboration, but no record of this was made, and therefore the fact that it was a skillful adaptation from the Chinese escaped the notice of untold generations of students of Heian literature. Professor Kaneko's discovery of the adaptation process in this instance proves conclusively that Heian literati must have known Po's poetry extremely well, for they were able to challenge one another's remembrance of lines in a collection totalling almost three thousand poems.

In still another incident, Sei Shonagon showed her expertise in matters related to Po Chü-i's writings.[2] She was once tested by official Fujiwara no Takanobu (967-1035), who quoted lines from a poem that Po had written in exile and requested that she indicate how the stanza ended. This she did, though in Japanese rather than in the original Chinese characters, perhaps because she felt that her calligraphy was inadequate:

> At the grass hut
> who will pay a call?

She received the nickname of "Grass Hut" as a consequence of this incident, and everyone was said to have written this on their fans. In Fujiwara no Kinto's collected works, he referred to one occasion when he gave the above quotation as the last two lines of a *tanka* and an imperial archives keeper named Takatada completed the poem with these first three lines:

> The Imperial Palace,
> a capital of flowers
> being abandoned:

(Kinto)

> At the grass hut
> who will pay a call?

Kinto edited the well-known *Collection of Japanese and Chinese Recitable Verse (wakan roeishu)*, completing it in 1013. This collection consisted of translations of what he considered superlative lines of Chinese verse written by either Chinese or Japanese, augmented by about two hundred Japanese poems. The collection contained 140 phrases from Po Chü-i, far outnumbering citations from all other Chinese poets. At least two of these selections have preserved their popularity in Japan to the present day and are to be found in current high school texts. The first was written about a pond west of the Honan prefectural office where Po served in later years:

> The willow is spiritless,
> its limbs preceding it in movement.
> The ice has wave crests,
> its ice breaking up throughout.
> Today I was unaware,

but someone contrived a get-together.
> Spring breezes and spring waters
> have come at the same time.

Ki no Tsurayaki (882-945) compressed these thoughts into a thirty-one syllable Japanese verse:

> On the water's surface
> there blows about
> a spring breeze;
> the ice of the pond
> is about to melt.

The second selection from Po's poetry was called **"Confronting The Wine"**. In the opening line, the poet alluded to a phrase from the *Chuang-tzu* about how the two horns of a snail once fought one another in a territorial dispute. In the third line, the "glow from a stone spark" refers to the brevity of life; the concluding thought about laughter is also taken in part from the *Chuang-tzu*, in which it is said that man is so overburdened by illness and grief that he only laughs four or five days a month:

> On the horns of the snail—
> what do they quarrel about?
> To the glow from a stone spark
> do I entrust this body.
> Whether rich or poor
> I take my pleasures.
> One who doesn't
> open his mouth to laugh
> is a fool.

Po Chü-i's theme about life's impermanence inspired an unknown writer to compose a *noh* chant, repeating only the simile of the stone spark:

> Those human faces
> glorious at morn,
> decaying at night.
> The shadow of the glow
> from a lightning flash
> and a stone spark.
> Time is a thatched hut
> which waits for no man.
> From the time he enters
> it darkens quickly,
> and in an instant
> his tears will flow.

The major Heian verse collections contain many Japanese poems in which lines or phrases were adapted from Po Chü-i. Professor Kaneko cites a few examples of these adaptations, noting that the practice of taking words and lines from Chinese writers was initiated by *Manyoshu* poets. One of them, for example, incorporated verbatim a statement in the *Chuang-tzu* about putting one's heart in the village of nothingness.

Heian admirers of Po Chü-i's poetic expression made their adaptations in one of two ways. They either imitated the original content with fidelity or availed themselves of one section in order to express personal reflection or outlook which might or might not coincide with the thought of the Chinese poet. Japanese adaptations tended towards originality rather than towards literal translation. Poets used the Chinese lines and phrases as starting points for amplifying their own ideas.

Po once wrote:

> There's only the coming of old age,
> among men no place to escape it.

Ariwara no Narihira (825-80) expressed a similar but more complex thought, ending on a hopeful note to which was added a touch of whimsy:

> Cherry blossoms
> a profusion of clouds,
> making the road
> on which old age comes
> err (because of the luxuriance of the
>   blossoms).

Po had written:

> There's a departing wild goose,
> turning its back on spring.

This theme was expanded by an early tenth-century poetess of the Fujiwara clan:

> Though spring's haze
> has set in, it's ignored by
> the travelling wild goose.
> Is it used to living
> in a no flower village?

There was this poetic line in Po's **Works** about the willow:

> Slender-delicate willow silk,
> coming forth silkily in the breeze.

Ki no Tsuruyuki (882-945) followed Po's thought closely, in a poem of spring:

> Every spring
> the unseverable things.
> Green willows
> coming forth
> as silk in a breeze.

The Japanese poet placed Chinese poetic phrases in his composition as a sign of erudition, knowing that such usage was well received. Poems which had such phrases were called "poems (based on) topics". In

894 Oe no Chisato collected these poems at imperial order. Professor Kaneko analyzed 109 phrases and concluded that almost three-fourths (seventy-two phrases) were taken from Po Chü-i's poems. Some of his poetic lines must have been extremely popular in Japan and widely used. One of the more famous lines was:

> Neither clear nor unclear,
> the obscure moon.

About fifty years after Po's death, Oe no Chisato made this poetic adaptation:

> Not illuminated,
> not clouded over,
> a springlike
> moon of haze:
> There is nothing better.

Po wrote about the change of seasons:

> Wild goose rapidly flying in the cold—
> I sense the extinction of autumn.

Oe no Chisato followed Po's thought rather closely:

> The travelling wild geese
> are quickly flying.
> From seeing this
> there came to me
> an end-of-autumn feeling.

Po once wrote about the delight of dreams:

> To delight and laugh in dreams
> is to conquer melancholy.

Oshikochi no Mitsune (died 921) viewed joy in dreams as a consolation for the loneliness of the wakeful state:

> If you see happiness
> even in dreams,
> when you're awake
> it's superior
> to feeling lonely.

Po, who repeatedly saw decay and disintegration symbolized in his white hairs, likened them to silken threads:

> In late years my hair seems
> like silken threads before the mirror.

Ki no Tsuruyuki (882-945) adapted the thought but changed the simile:

> The raven-colored
> black hair of mine.
> As years darken,

within the mirror
it's like falling snow.

An anonymous contributor to a mid-tenth century Japanese poetry collection was inspired by these lines from one of Po's poems:

I'll strive to get a great fur garment
a hundred thousand feet in length,
to give you for covering over
all of Loyang City.

But the anonymous poet pitied not the people but the flowers:

May the great heavens
be covered only
by my sleeves.
Flowers that blossom in spring
are not to be wind-entrusted.

Po explained his liking for fire and snow in the opening lines of a poem in which he revealed how he appreciated their existence:

What I ordinarily love at heart:
I love fire and pity snow.
Fire is the spring of a wintry day,
snow is the moon of a darkened night.

In the eleventh century, a Japanese Buddhist priest with the epithet of *Soi* ("Plain Intent") was inspired by Po's theme of fire and snow to expound his own poetic-philosophic thoughts on the subject:

In the banked fire's
vicinity, spring
feelings are evoked,
regarding the falling flakes
truly as flowers.

Po contrasts the splendor of spring with the decay of being, in a poem called **"Sighing Over White Hairs, Neath the Cherry Blossoms"**. These are the opening lines:

Place after place the flowers are fine,
but my looks naturally deteriorate with the years.
The day: red cherries fill my eyes;
the time: white hairs cover half my head.

Ki no Tomonori (845-905) made the same comparison of nature and man:

Both color and fragrance
as in times gone by—
so seem the cherry blossoms.
Only aged persons
are ever changed.

There is conclusive evidence that Japanese poets of the Heian era paid close attention to Po's *Works* and enjoyed making new and unusual poetic adaptations. Po Chü-i's poetry provided intellectual and aesthetic stimuli to Japanese poets, who made skillful and original interpretations, aided by their accurate understanding of the original texts. The Heian poets gradually brought about a change from the poetry of pure emotion of the *Manyoshu* to the more sophisticated compositions of their own age. Qualitatively, the direction was from the simple to the complex; quantitatively, there was a great increase in poetic output. Kaneko Hikojiro concludes that no matter how much the Japanese adapted foreign culture, they were able to make these cultural innovations serve their own needs. In the example provided by Po's *Works,* this certainly seems to be a valid conclusion. His themes provided an initial impetus for the Japanese poet, but subsequent development within Japanese poetic genre conformed to indigenous criteria, so that the borrowing was more imaginative than rote.

The natural lover and poet Saigyo (1118-90) once wrote a poem about the autumn moon:

Saving, be sad!
the moon causes
us to think;
sad-faced,
my tears fall.

This poem expressed the same sentiment as Po Chü-i in a famous poem in which he contrasts the moon's obliviousness to human sufferings:

Autumn Moon

The fine light for ten thousand li can't think.
Added melancholy, increased remorse,
coiling about Heaven's extremes.
Someone beyond the frontiers,
on prolonged subjugation duties;
before a garden somewhere
there's a new separation.
An aged beauty who's lost favor
returns at night to her courtyard;
an old general submerged among barbarians
ascends a tower.
The moon shines on him,
almost causing his heart to break.
This jade rabbit, this silver toad,
is distant and unknowing.

In China the moon was said to assume rabbit and toadlike shapes, and therefore it was also called "Jade Rabbit" and "Silver Toad".

The sixth chapter of The Tales of Heike (ca. 1240) describes a famous incident about red leaves, which came directly from one of Po's poems. The Japanese sovereign had the leaves which had fallen in the wind gathered together and burned, using the fire to warm wine. He felt extremely content and laughingly referred to a poetic line about being, "In the forest burning the red leaves, warming the wine", and asked those assembled if anyone could tell him what the line meant. It was an easy quotation to give, but the courtiers all felt that if the query were answered simply, the person who responded might be praised but the Emperor would become displeased, so nobody answered. The original line was in a poem which Po Chü-i had written to his friend Wang Chih-fu when Wang returned to the mountains:

> I once went in front of Great White Peak,
> several times got inside
> the Temple to Which Immortals Frolic.
> When the black waters were settled,
> the lake's depths appeared.
> White clouds broke through in places,
> the gates of the caves opened.
> In the forest warming wine, burning red
> 　leaves,
> inscribing a poem on a rock, sweeping green
> 　moss.
> Vexed-depressed that the old frolics don't
> 　come again,
> at chrysanthemum blossom season, I envy
> 　your return.

Po Chü-i regretted that he and Wang had been able to frolic together so rarely, and he envied Wang's return to the natural scenic splendors they had enjoyed in the finest season, when the chrysanthemum were in bloom.

Kato Chikage (1735-1808) made a poetic adaptation of the love theme in **"Lament Everlasting"**, with which it is perhaps appropriate to conclude, for this is the poem by Po Chü-i which remains most popular in Japan to the present day.

> Night after night,
> our sleeves enfolded
> just that way,
> to be wing-transformed
> and fly to the Heavens.

Notes

1 Ch'en Yin-k'o, *Yüan Po shih chien-cheng Kao*, p. 284.

2 Ch'en Shou-yi, *Chinese Literature*, p. 310. See Professor Ch'en's ensuing discussion of the rationale behind the New Music Bureau form and its metric patterns.

3 Cf. Takagi, *Haku Kyoi*, Vol. I, pp. 8-9.

4 Takagi, *op. cit.*, Vol. I, p. 10.

5 Ch'en Yin-k'o, *op. cit.*, p. 154, noted that some editions lack the characters for "white-haired". He concluded that the version with the characters is the correct one.

6 For these and other details on annotations for this poem, see Ch'en Yin-k'o, *op. cit.*, pp. 156-58.

7 *Ibid.*, *op. cit.*, p. 158.

8 This is sometimes entitled "Girls of Poor Families".

9 On the connections between this poem and one of Po's later poems in the New Music Bureau style, see Ch'en Yin-k'o, *op. cit.*, p. 259.

10 See Alfred Koehn, "Chinese Flower Symbolism", (*Monumenta Nipponica*, VIII, February, 1952), p. 135.

11 Koehn, "Chinese Flower Symbolism", *op. cit.*, p. 144.

Chapter 4

1 Cf. Ch'en Yu-ch'in, *Po Chü-i chuan*, Introduction, p. 3.

2 Takagi, *op. cit.*, Vol. II, p. 7.

3 *Ibid.*, Vol. II, p. 8.

4 This observation is made by Feifel, *Po Chü-i as a Censor*, p. 6.

5 Itsukai Tomoyoshi, *Tó Enmei* (Tokyo: Iwanami, 1965), p.3. For an English translation of T'ao's verse, cf. Acker, *T'ao the Hermit*, (London, 1952).

6 Itsukai, *op. cit.*, p. 36. This monograph has the original texts of T'ao's preface and the twenty drinking poems, with line-for-line Japanese translations appended below the Chinese lines of each poem.

7 The Duke of Chou and Confucius. (For detailed annotation of the sixteen poems in this series, see *Po Hsiang-shan shih-hsüan* (Hong Kong, 1958), Vol. A, pp. 49-70.

8 Cf. Waley, *The Poetry and Career of Li Po*, p. 25.

9 These identifications are made by Tanaka Katsumi (Tokyo: *Haku Rakuten*, 1964), p. 182. Professor Tanaka, who excels in annotation, has translated the second, fourth, fifth, seventh, eighth, twelfth and fifteenth of the sixteen poems in this series by Po Chü-i.

10 For the specific words and phrases, see Tanaka, *op. cit.*, p. 184.

[11] See Eberhard, *Chinese Festivals*, Vol. III. Professor Eberhard discusses the different origins of the mid-autumn and Double-Nine festivals.

[12] For the details behind each incident alluded to in the poem, mostly dealing with Ch'in or pre-Ch'in in historical episodes, see [Lei Sung-lin,] *Po Chü-i shih hsüan*, I, pp. 59-60.

[13] For the original text, see Itsukai, *op. cit.*, pp. 55-56.

[14] Because he had planted five willows around his home, T'ao styled himself "Mr. Five Willows."

[15] See *Men-shih hsin-yü* (cited in *Haku Rakuten shishü*, Vol. I, p. 478). (The last passage in Chapter 5.)

[16] Haku Rakuten shishü (or *Po Hsiang-shan shih ch'ang-ch'ing chi*), *loc. cit.*

[17] "Mr. Quiet and Chaste" (*Ching-chieh hsien-sheng*), one of the popular appellations of T'ao Yüan-ming.

[18] Noted by Tanaka Katsumi (see *Haku Rakuten*, p. 270).

Chapter 5

[1] Literally a "P'eng (Tsu)", who was said to have lived for seven hundred years (cited in *Shih-chi*).

[2] There was a statement in Mencius about "my immovable heart at forty".

[3] Literally P'eng-tse, referring to T'ao by the name of a district which he governed.

[4] Referring to a priest who built a temple at Ts'ao Rivulet in 502 because the waters there were fragrant.

[5] Hsi Shu-yeh was a literatus (223-62) and one of the seven so-called worthies of the bamboo forest. He tried to conceal himself but failed, and was killed. (Tanaka, *op. cit.*, p. 176.)

[6] See *Chuang-tzu*, the passage called *Ch'i-wu lun* ("a discussion of the sameness of things").

[7] See *Chuang-tzu*, section describing transcendental bliss (*Hsiao-yao yu p'ien*).

[8] For exact references, see Chcn Tsu-lung, *La Vie et les Oeuvres de Wou Tchen*, pp. 86-87.

[9] See the comprehensive monograph by R. H. van Gulik, *The Lore of the Chinese Lute* (Tokyo: Sophia University, 1940), pp. 19-21.

[10] Literally *Lan-jo*, a transliteration of the Sanskrit *Aranya*, literally "forest", by extended meaning used to denote a monastery. (See Soothill and Hodous, *A Dictionary of Chinese Buddhist Terms*, p. 484.)

[11] For the details of this story, see Legge, *The Ch'un Ts'eu, With the Tso Chuen*, Vol. V, Part I, p. 131.

[12] "Mother of the clouds" was a medicinal herb, its origin ascribed to the legendary age of Sage Yao.

[13] The li measurement in the T'ang dynasty was about 1,800 feet; here as elsewhere, the poet simply indicates a great distance.

Chapter 6

[1] Po in 803 was living in Ch'ang-an's Ward of Constant Pleasure (*Ch'ang-lo fang*), in a home formerly belonging to the late Chief Minister Kuan Po (719-97). (See Tanaka, *op. cit.*, p. 26.)

[2] The emperor referred to here was Te-tsung (reigned 780-804).

[3] The reference is to Mencius, who cited a poem by a scholar to the effect that when this river was clear, he could wash his tassels in it, and that when it was turbid he could wash his feet in it. (See Mencius, section called *Li Lou*, A.)

[4] *Yin-ni* ("purplish ink") was an ancient way of sealing letters and memorials, to which reference is made in the *History of Later Han*. *Yin-ni-shu* ("purplish-inked writing") came to connote "memorial".

[5] The "empty boat" as a Taoist metaphor for the enlightened must have been popular at the time, for Po referred to another friend as "Empty Boat Kuo" (cf. Waley, *Po*, p. 127).

[6] Referring to the palace where the Emperor lived.

[7] Wang Chih-fu? (I have been unable to identify this person with certainty.)

[8] See his biography in *Chung-kuo jen-ming ta tzu-tien*, p. 850.

[9] The Star of Fortune (*te-hsing*), was supposed to convey blessings. This belief was already current in Han times.

[10] This phrase was copied, with minor alterations, from a phrase in the *Book of Odes*.

[11] A pond located in Ch'ang-an.

[12] Referring literally to the P'eng-lai Mountains, believed to be one of three mountains of Immortals located in the eastern seas.

[13] See De Groot, *The Religious System of China*, Vol. III, p. 935.

[14] The poem does not give Ch'ü's personal name; he may have been related to Ch'ü Hsin-ling, a noted administrator of the Chen-yüan era (785-804) for whom Po Chü-i was said to have composed the Songs of Ch'in. (See *Chung-kuo jen-ming ta tzu-tien*, 1762.)

[15] The creation of a southern sect, also known as the Bodhidharma School, took place about 700. The difference between north and south in methods of enlightenment came to be expressed in the phrase "southern immediate, northern gradual." (Soothill, *op. cit.*, p. 297-98.) There were ten principal Buddhist sects in late T'ang. (Ch'en Tsu-lung, *La Vie et Les Oeuvres de Wou-Tchen* (816-95), pp. 12-13.)

[16] This is an allusion to a phrase in the *Classic of History* (*Shu-ching, Chün-ya* section), referring to trustworthy ministers as "limbs and arms, heart and back".

[17] Wu referred to the Kiangsu area in the south, not far from where Po was then stationed.

[18] For dating the poem by Po Chü-i, I have relied on the information in *Hakushi monju no hihanteki kenkyū*, 498 seq.

[19] Cf. Waley, *Po*, pp. 127-28.

Chapter 7

[1] Li Fang is one of the best-known of the T'ang portraitists, probably because of Po's poetic references to him. (See *T'ang Sung hua-chia jen-ming tzu-tien*, Peking, 1958, p. 89; Waley, *Po*, p. 49.)

[2] Literally "the double *yang*", nine being considered *yang*, or male element.

[3] For additional details about the site and cottage, see Waley, *Po*, pp. 118-19.

[4] The name of a pavilion established by Emperor T'ai-tsung (reigned 627-50) of the T'ang, in which he had drawn the portraits of meritorious officials.

[5] Cf. *Hsü-ch'i chieh-chi, P'i-p'a chi*.

[6] *Ou-pei shih-hua*, as cited in *Haku Rakuten shishū*, Ch. 6, p. 546.

[7] Original Harmony (*Yüan-ho*) was the name given to Emperor Hsien-tsung's method of reign. This temple was located atop the Wang-shun ("Royal Accord") Mountain, about six or seven miles southeast of Lan-t'ien County. (In translating obscure terms, I usually follow the interpretations in Tanaka, *Haku Rakuten*, pp. 198-212, q.v.)

[8] There were many tombs of Han emperors located north of the Wei River.

[9] Kasyapa Buddha was the name of the sixth of the seven ancient Buddhas said to have preceded Sakyamuni. (Cf. note in Soothill, *op. cit.*, p. 316.)

[10] Kasaya referred to the monk's robe, or cassock, the word meaning "impure in color". The robe was dyed, to distinguish it from secular white dress. (Soothill, *op. cit.*, p. 363.)

[11] The so-called Goddess of Mercy in the Buddhist pantheon, the protector of those in distress.

[12] The seven treasures or precious things, which are variously enumerated.

[13] The name of a park secured from Prince Veta which was Sakyamuni's favorite resort. (Soothill, *op. cit.*, p. 310-11.)

[14] Reference to a local deity, in the temple's vicinity.

[15] Reference to Wang Tzu-ch'iao, a Chou dynasty immortal described in *Leih-hsien chuan*.

[16] The literal reference is to "a volume of Southern Splendors". In 742 Chuang-tzu's writings were ordered by imperial decree to be called "The True Classic of Southern Splendors".

Chapter 8

[1] See J. C. H. Wu's interesting and thought-provoking article entitled "The Four Seasons of T'ang Poetry" (T'ien Hsia Monthly, Vol. VI, Jan.-May, 1938; Vol. VII., Aug.-Dec., 1938), in which he presents translations from Po and other poets, east and west. Professor Wu regarded Po as an autumnal spirit, one to whom Tu Fu's violent searchings of the heart would have seemed excessive; he considered Po the most autumnal of the T'ang poets, in heart as well as head. To him, Po typified Eastern (Buddhist) man, shying away from love for fear of reaping sorrow. Po had a passionate nature, concluded Professor Wu, but was preoccupied by a sense of desolation.

[2] P'an Yüeh, a literatus who lived in the Chin dynasty, was said to have excelled in composing poetry in an elegiac mood.

[3] Dhuta, to be released from life's ties so as attain *nirvana*. There were twelve precepts to be followed, enumerated in Soothill, *op. cit.*, pp. 453-54.

[4] I take this to be an oblique reference to Po's wife being ill. "Lai's wife" refers to a woman praised in *Lieh-tzu* for having spurned a life of officialdom for her husband, willingly sharing poverty with him instead.

[5] Referring to a song which was then very popular in the Szechwan region. (See Waley, *Po,* p. 130.)

[6] Alfred Koehn, *op. cit.,* p. 144.

[7] Lin Yutang, *The Gay Genius,* p. 30, refers to Tung-p'o as Su's poetic name. He says only that it came from part of a title ("The Recluse Tung-p'o") which Su took for himself when he was living in banishment on the eastern slope (*tung-p'o*) of Huang-chou. The allegation that Su Shih took this name from the two poems by Po translated here was made in *Ou-pei shih-hua* (cited in *Haku Rakuten shishū,* Vol. II, p. 126), which states that Su probably adopted this name out of admiration for Po Chü-i's poems. (Po also had a third poem called "Walking the East Slope".)

[8] See Koehn, *op. cit.,* p. 134.

[9] This was a paraphrase by Po of a comment which T'ao Yüan-ming once made to one of his sons. (See Tanaka, *Haku Rakuten,* p. 295.)

Chapter 9

[1] See the *Chuang-tzu,* passage under *Hsiao-yao yu.*

[2] See the references to this term listed in Morohashi, *Dai Kanwa jiten,* under *Shuang-nan* and *Shuang-nan-chin.*

[3] The Buddhist way, the way to which "all things are empty" (*wan-shih chieh-k'ung*).

[4] A reference to Ts'ui Ch'ün (772-832), a talented official and close friend of Po Chü-i. (Cf. Waley, *Po,* pp. 86, 126, 183, 208.)

[5] Literally *fou-t'u,* apparently a transliteration. (Cf. Soothill, *op. cit.,* p. 322.)

[6] The poems are cited in Morohashi, op. cit., under *Sung-ch'un.*

[7] See Gernet, *Daily Life in China* (translated by H. M. Wright, London; 1962), pp. 191-92, for these and other details about the festivals.

[8] The first four characters (*t'ien ch'ang ti-chiu*) are the same as the first four in the next to last line of "Lament Everlasting", composed in 806.

[9] See J. J. M. DeGroot, *The Religious System of China,* Vol. II (*Disposal of the Dead*), pp. 460-473, for a discussion of the appearance and significance of sepulchral trees.

[10] Two of whom I identify as Ts'ui Ch'ün (772-832) and Li Chien (764-821).

[11] Cf. Waley, *Po,* pp. 64-65.

[12] This was a euphonious term for the Hanlin Academy, which was given this name because it was contiguous to the Palace of Golden Bells. Po's calling his daughter "Golden Bells" may have been an oblique reference to his service as a Hanlin Academician.

Chapter 13

[1] The information in this chapter is based primarily on the researches of the foremost Japanese scholar on this subject, Professor Kaneko Hikōjirō. He deals with the question in book form (*Hakushi mōnju to Heian bungaku*), but he also contributed a chapter (*"Hakushi mōnju to Heian jidai no bungaku"*) to a textbook compilation on literature, (*Kokugosan-Sogo* [Tokyo: Ministry of Education, 1964]). Interested specialists should consult this chapter for the original texts of the poems in Chinese and Japanese cited in my essay, unless otherwise indicated. Mizuno Heiji also describes the influences of Po's *Works* on Japanese literature from the early beginnings through the Tokugawa era (*Haku Rakuten to Nihon bungaku,* pp. 108-66.)

[2] For the translation of this section of *Pillow-Book,* see Ivan Morris, "The Captain First Secretary, Tadanobu" (Journal Newsletter of Association of Teachers of Japanese), August, 1966, pp. 37-42.

Bibliography

Ch'en Yin-k'o, *Yüan Po shih chien-cheng kao.* Taipei: privately reprinted, 1956. Detailed consideration of Yüan-Po poetic content, with emphasis on major poems such as "Lament Everlasting" and "Lute Song". The poems in the New Music Bureau style are treated individually and in considerable depth. The direction of the research is primarily historical.

Ch'en Yu-ch'in, *Po Chü-i chuan.* Shanghai: Chung-hua shu-chü, 1965. Introduction to literary criticism of Po's *Works* in China from T'ang to Ch'ing times, followed by over 900 items of criticism in the original texts. Valuable as it is, but it would be priceless if these items were translated into *pai-hua.*

Feifel, Eugene, *Po Chü-i as a Censor.* The Hague: Monton and Co., 1961.

A good introduction to Po's period of service in the court as an imperial critic (808-10), followed by a description of memorials Po wrote in this period and then an annotated translation of the memorials. Despite the lack of an index, this work is informative and useful.

Lei Sung-lin, *Po-Chü-i shih-hsüan i*. Hong Kong: Chien-wen shu-chü, 1965.

Modern colloquial translations of 100 poems, stressing the didactic and pleasure categories. Brief annotation, general but not precise citation of sources.

Mizuno Heiji, *Haku Rakuten to Nihon bungaku*. To-kyo: Meguro shoten, 1930.

The data in the book go far beyond the implications of the title. There is information on the technical changes in Chinese poetry prior to and including the T'ang, an analysis of Po's social status, and biographical details. The poetic forms he used are described, with relevant selections from each. Literary critics of Po's *Works* are mentioned, and one chapter each is devoted to his influence on Chinese and Japanese literature. The second half of the book contains annotated translations of about 200 selected poems and several of his most important prose writings. Annotation of the poems is somewhat skimpy.

Takagi Masakazu, *Haku Kyoi*. 2 vols. in series *Chugoku shijin senshu*. Tokyo: Iwanami, 1964.

The first volume describes the 50 New Music Bureau poems and then translates and annotates them. The second volume describes the pleasure and sorrow poetry and presents about 100 annotated translations, with emphasis on the regulated poems.

Tanaka Katsumi, *Haku Rakuten*. in the series *Kanshi taikei*. Tokyo: Shueisha, 1964.

The texts, line-by-line and overall translations of about 160 of Po's better known poems; thoroughly and accurately annotated, with the results of current research incorporated.

Waley, Arthur, *The Life and Times of Po Chü-i*. London: Allen and Unwin, 1951.

This is a definitive biographical study of the poet-bureaucrat, based on many years of study and a very wide familarity with primary sources. Japanese and Chinese scholars frequently cite it in their own studies, something they rarely do regarding western source materials. The range of consideration is admirable, and much complex research is concealed within the general descriptions and summations of the work.

Benjamin E. Wallacker (essay date 1981)

SOURCE: Benjamin E. Wallacker, "The Poet as Jurist: Po Chü-i and a Case of Conjugal Homicide," in *Harvard*

Journal of Asiatic Studies, Vol. 41, No. 2, 1981, pp. 507-26.

[*In the following essay, Wallacker examines Po Chü-i's written opinion on the case of Yao Wen-hsiu, for which Po had to decide how severe a penalty to impose on a wife-murderer. Chinese characters have been deleted from this essay.*]

Chinese criminal law has for a long time looked not only to the wrongdoer's act, but also to the state of his mind when he committed the act. Various degrees of culpability for the same act were distinguished by the Chinese according to whether the mind of the actor was more or less intent upon achieving the forbidden result. The Chinese forbore from bringing down upon the inadvertent killer, for example, the same weight of punishment laid upon his deliberate and purposeful brother. One who killed through mistake, accident, or carelessness might look to the law for consideration of such factors in mitigation of his punishment. Hulsewé and Bünger have each in fact used the technical term "negligence" in their studies of varying criminal liability in early Chinese law.[1] Niida Noboru lists no fewer than six species of homicide recognized in T'ang times,[2] and it was between two of these six, *tou-sha*, "killing in the course of an affray," and *ku-sha*, "intentional killing," that the poet and civil servant Po Chü-i (772-846) was bid to draw the line of demarcation in 822. Po Chü-i at the time occupied the post of Grand Secretary of the Grand Secretariate, in which capacity he served as advisor to the Emperor on legal as well as governmental matters. For the crime of killing in an affray a convicted defendant was liable to sentence of death by strangulation; for intentional killing, he was decapitated.

"Decapitation," says Wallace Johnson, "was considered to be the more severe of the two death penalties because it damaged the body. According to the tenets of filial piety, the body should be kept whole because it came from one's parents."[3] The difference between the two crimes may, however, have gone further than the contrasting modes of capital punishment prescribed for each of them. Intentional killing was classed with the Ten Abominations, *shih*, at least as regards the penalty of disenrollment, *ch'u ming*, as being beyond the reach of those amnesties so frequently declared by Chinese rulers to invigorate their reigns.[4] Thus, whether a person was convicted of having slain with intent on the one hand, or in the course of a fight on the other, may have determined whether he lived or died for his crime.

The case in which the question was presented to Po Chü-i concerned a certain Yao Wen-hsiu, whose name I have not found elsewhere recorded, who killed his wife A-Wang. That Yao Wen-hsiu had beaten A-Wang to death was conceded, but had he killed in a fight or had he killed with intent? Had an altercation simply got out of control, or had Yao Wen-hsiu carried through a purposeful murder? The case reached Po Chü-i only after it had been considered both by the Supreme Court of Justice (Ta-li ssu) and by the Ministry of Justice (Hsing-pu).[5]

Po Chü-i drafted a lengthy analytical opinion on the case of Yao Wen-hsiu to which we now turn.

> Petition in discussion on [the case of] Yao Wen-hsiu beating and killing his wife. Presented on the tenth day of the fifth month of the second year of Ch'ang-ch'ing.

> According to the decision of the Ministry of Justice as well as the Supreme Court of Justice, "The controlling statute is, 'A killing that does not result from an affray and struggle but with no occasion is termed intentional killing.' [In the case] now [before us], because Yao Wen-hsiu killed with occasion, [the crime] was not intentional killing."[6]

Po Chü-i opens his opinion with a quotation, apparently verbatim, from the decision issued by the legal authorities. The Court, confirmed by the Ministry, had based its decision upon a specific rule of law. The rule cited as controlling the case is referred to here as *lü,* "statute," but it appears in the T'ang Code in a portion of the text headed by the phrase *shu-i,* or Subcommentary.

The area of criminal law within which falls the rule cited as authority by the Court concerns the difference between the penalty meted out for killing committed in the course of an affray or fight and that imposed for killing committed with intent. Article 306 of the T'ang Code provided the penalty of strangulation for killing in a fight. Use of a blade during the fight, however, increased the gravity of the crime and its punishment. That is, one who killed during a fight was punished as though guilty of intentional killing if he had used a knife. Both the person who used a knife in a fight and the person guilty of intentional killing were punished by decapitation.[7]

A second rule of statutory law in Article 306 of the T'ang Code provides a lighter penalty for the crime of inflicting bodily injury during a fight than for the same act done with intent. The rule is evidently quite analogous to the homicide rule just given in that criminal liability was lighter if the defendant inflicted the injury during a fight. This second rule relating to the circumstance of a fight as a factor which lessened criminal liability contains a condition which applies both to wounding and to killing in a fight. Even though the killing or wounding be the result of a fight, the statute declares, if the fight is broken off for a time, then the defendant shall be punished according to the law for intentional killing or wounding. Statutory recognition of an apparent "cooling-off period" indicates that T'ang law regarded a fight as an event necessarily accompanied by hot blood, a point heavily relied upon by Po Chü-i in his argument below.

The Subcommentary, composed by Chang-sun Wu-chi and his colleagues for presentation to Kao-tsung in 653,[8] explains the imposition of a lighter penalty for homicide during a fight under Article 306 as deriving from the absence in the mind of the offender of the will to kill at the beginning of the fatal incident. The Subcommentary continues by giving the very definition of intentional killing which was cited by the Court in its decision on the case of Yao Wen-hsiu.[9]

Having given the finding on the case of Yao Wen-hsiu reached by the Supreme Court of Justice and the Ministry of Justice, Po Chü-i now introduces what may be termed a dissent.

> According to the holding of Judicial Inspector of the Supreme Court of Justice Ts'ui Yüan-shih, "The controlling statute is, 'Mutuality in struggle constitutes an affray; mutuality in blows constitutes an assault.' When such fighting, one with another, results in a death, then only do we designate it killing in the course of an affray. . . ."

Ts'ui Yüan-shih, was one of three younger brothers of Ts'ui Yüan-lüeh, President of the Supreme Court of Justice at some time during the reign of Mu-tsung.[10] His office of Judicial Inspector (Ta-li ssu-chih) is explicitly stated in *T'ung-tien* to have been charged with the "consultative discussion" of "doubtful cases."[11]

The question arises whether it was standard procedure to send along a dissenting view on a case, such as the one here prepared by Ts'ui Yüan-shih. The decision that Yao Wen-hsiu was not guilty of intentional killing was jointly and, it would appear, finally reached by the Supreme Court of Justice and the Ministry of Justice. Yet Po Chü-i had access to the opinion of a single functionary of the Court. Ts'ui Yüan-shih's view of the case of Yao Wen-hsiu had surely been taken into account by the Court and the Ministry before they issued their decision. Ts'ui Yüan-shih's analysis had, that is, been an ingredient in the deliberations which led to the official decision. For Po Chü-i to look at the dissent in reaching his own conclusion was truly to reopen the case. Ts'ui Yüan-shih's dissent had been weighed and rejected by the Court and the Ministry, but now it was being given a second consideration. Certainly Po Chü-i's reopening of the case might well be taken as an attack upon the authority of the Supreme Court of Justice. As we shall see below, it may indeed have been so taken.

The decision of the Supreme Court of Justice and the Ministry of Justice was based, as we have seen, on a specific rule of the T'ang Code. Likewise, the dissenting opinion of Ts'ui Yüan-shih rested on a rule of law, which he cites from the opening portion of the Subcommentary to the first Code section dealing with the penalties for fighting.[12] The Subcommentary here seemed to Ts'ui Yüan-shih to stress the factor of mutuality as a necessary element in an altercation if the word *tou*, "fight, affray," or the word *ou*, "assault, a blow," is to be applied. In point of fact, the word *hsiang* does not demand mutuality or reciprocity of action, merely the presence of two parties to the action. The action may flow wholly in one direction, from one person as actor to the other as one acted upon. The Subcommentary might be construed as defining the word *tou* to mean "one struggling with another" and *ou* as "one striking another." Because of the ambiguity of the word *hsiang* the question is left open whether the violence here described by the law is one-sided or two-sided, an attack or a contest. Ts'ui Yüan-shih's use of the word *chiao*, which is rendered above "one with another," shows, however, that he construed the definitions of the Subcommentary necessarily to include the factor of reciprocity. The word *chiao*, though it does not rule out the possibility of action flowing in one direction, is much stronger than *hsiang* in its implication of interrelatedness between the two parties such that an action by one evokes response from the other. Ts'ui Yüan-shih has placed upon a Subcommentary gloss which is equivocal on the question of reciprocity a construction which makes reciprocity a necessary element.

Only when the death in question has resulted from fighting which is two-sided, says Ts'ui Yüan-shih, does one properly apply the term *tou-sha*, "killing in the course of an affray." The term means, for Ts'ui Yüan-shih, that the death was the outcome of a violent encounter characterized by at least a high likelihood of exchange of injurious violence.

Po Chü-i goes on to quote more of the dissent of Ts'ui Yüan-shih.

> "[In the case] now [before us], A-Wang suffered such a savage beating that she was brought to death. As to Yao Wen-hsiu, at the inquest his person was wholly without bruise or wound; so one may not use the term 'mutuality in blows.'"

Here is confirmation of the fact that Ts'ui Yüan-shih takes *hsiang chi*, "mutuality in blows," to demand two-sidedness. The examination of the body of Yao Wen-hsiu, conducted evidently as part of the official inquiry into A-Wang's death, had revealed no signs of his having been struck. He was unscathed. With no marks of struggle on his body, Ts'ui Yüan-shih argues, Yao Wen-hsiu cannot maintain the claim that he and his wife had engaged in an episode of "mutuality in blows." There had indeed been "one striking another," but husband and wife had not been "striking one another."

Ts'ui Yüan-shih's dissent, as quoted by Po Chü-i, concludes:

> "A-Wang was already dead that very night. Again how can one use the term 'mutuality in struggle'? This was definitely not an affray and struggle. Further, [the defendant] had stored up antipathy and enmity. This then was intentional killing."

Ts'ui Yüan-shih forcefully closes his argument in dissent by observing that A-Wang's having died the night of the beating, while Yao Wen-hsiu emerged unscathed, effectively negates the assertion that there had been a true struggle. And if it be conceded that there had occurred no fight, in the sense of an exchange of blows, then it follows that the defendant must have felt deep resentment of his wife. His ill will may have been adduced in testimonial evidence, but Ts'ui Yüan-shih might have inferred its existence from the coincidence of the savage beating suffered by A-Wang and the fact that Yao Wen-hsiu was unharmed.

If, first, there was clearly no true struggle, and if, second, the beating was so severe as to cause death that same night, then Yao Wen-hsiu must have been motivated by deep malice. Had the beating been instantaneously fatal, as from a chance blow to the temple, then the factor of inadvertence might be introduced. However, the picture that emerges of Yao Wen-hsiu's abuse of his wife is one of methodical administration of blows whose cumulative effect turned out to be, not surprisingly, fatal within hours of the event.

Ts'ui Yüan-shih's dissent ends with the flat declaration that Yao Wen-hsiu's slaying of his wife was in fact intentional killing, this in direct opposition to the decision of the Supreme Court of Justice and the Ministry of Justice that the crime was not intentional killing.

It is to be noted that the single question on which the Court decision and the dissent directly oppose each other is whether or not the crime of Yao Wen-hsiu was intentional killing. In reaching their opposing conclusions neither side addresses the assumptions and arguments made in support of the other's conclusion. That is, the Supreme Court finds that Yao Wen-hsiu had "occasion." Therefore he did not commit an intentional killing. But the Court does not claim that there had been a true fight. Ts'ui Yüan-shih in his dissent does not deny that Yao Wen-hsiu had "occasion," but he does deny that there had been a true fight. And because there had been no fight, Ts'ui Yüan-shih finds the crime to have been intentional killing.

Having quoted the decision of the Supreme Court of Justice and the Ministry of Justice along with the dissent of Ts'ui Yüan-shih, Judicial Inspector of the Supreme Court, Po Chü-i proceeds to make his own analysis.

> Let us take up, to the right (i.e., supra), the statutory Subcommentary which says, "A killing that does not result from a struggle and affray but with no occasion is termed intentional killing."[13] In this talk of "occasion," what is meant is the "occasion" of a struggle and affray. It is not, so to speak, "other occasions."

The word *shih*, Po Chü-i argues, denotes in the context of the rule relied upon by the Court-Ministry decision the specific provocative incident, the immediate spark which sets off a fight. *Shih* is not to be taken in the sense of remote or indirect cause, surely not in the meaning of hidden motivation.[14]

> [In the case] now [before us], it is the holding of the Supreme Court of Justice and the Ministry of Justice that because Yao Wen-hsiu was angry at his wife's having erred, he was therefore not "without occasion." If so, if there was "occasion" and as a result he assaulted her and she died, then this was not intentional killing.

In his paraphrase of the Court-Ministry decision Po Chü-i sets out the argument that because Yao Wen-hsiu had been provoked by the misbehavior of his wife, he was not "without occasion." And, following to the end the logic of the Court-Ministry opinion, Po Chü-i says that if the fatal assault of A-Wang was done pursuant to that "occasion," then Yao Wen-hsiu may not be found guilty of intentional killing.

> If this [be the true reading of the Court-Ministry view], then they have made use only of the pair of words "without occasion" and have not brought in the words preceding, "struggle and affray."

As Po Chü-i sees it, the Court-Ministry opinion has missed the significance of the juxtaposition in the rule of "struggle and affray" with the concept of "occasion." The latter is not to be understood apart from its contextual association with the former. Indeed it appears that there was, for Po Chü-i, a conjunctive, not disjunctive, relation between the two elements. That is, Po Chü-i would see the rule as requiring, for a finding of killing in a fight, both the occasion for that specific fight and the fight itself. To put it the other way round, he would find intentional killing in the absence either of an occasion or of a fight thus occasioned.

Having failed to grasp the linkage between the two elements, the Court-Ministry was without a firm base from which to interpret the term "occasion." Hence they permitted themselves to take it in the broadest possible way, so as to include remote and indirect causation as well as immediate and direct causation. Po Chü-i predicts the consequences of accepting so unrestricted a definition of "occasion":

> To [let the law operate] like this is to bring it about that any person in the empire will be able to kill another person because of an "occasion," and then, having killed him, say, "I had occasion and I killed. It was not intentional killing." Is such a thing permissible? Furthermore, is there any person in the empire who, "without occasion," would kill another person? It is abundantly clear that "occasion" means the "occasion" of a struggle and affray, not "other occasions."

Po Chü-i has now reduced to absurdity the broad and inclusive reading of "occasion" upon which the Court-Ministry opinion rests. If "occasion" is taken simply to denote motivating cause, then it is inconceivable that any voluntary homicide be done "without occasion," because no one kills without reason. There is always a reason, but it may be remote and only tenuously related to events at the actual moment of killing.

> Again, generally when one speaks of death by assault in an affray, one means that the "occasion" [for the affray] was never loathing and rancor. It was by chance that they came to struggle and fight one another: an assault, a striking, and no one having imagined it, a death. When [a killing] is like this, it is not intentional killing because fundamentally at its source the heart to kill was absent.[15]

The emotion which accompanies the commission of killing in the course of an affray, Po Chü-i says, must not be antipathy which has long accumulated and ripened. Indeed, there must be absent any desire to kill at the onset of the conflict. The process which Po Chü-i describes is the familiar escalation of violence which characterizes the true fight. Typically a quarrel of words may move one of the parties to physical action, which action stings the other to retaliate in more than full measure, which retaliation evokes yet stronger response. One who has killed in a fight might in all candor plead that he did not know how it happened and that he was shocked in the aftermath to realize he had killed the other person.

> [In the case] now [before us], Yao Wen-hsiu's enmity towards his wife was deep-seated, and he had long harbored resentment. He assaulted and beat her so savagely that she died that very night. If one examines those facts and circumstances it was not by chance. If this not be intentional killing, then what would be intentional killing?

Even from the physical evidence alone one might infer the existence in Yao Wen-hsiu's mind of long-standing hatred and deep malice for his wife. The facts, as Po Chü-i would have us review them, were these: Yao Wen-hsiu beat his wife with such severity that she died soon after. Unless one presumes otherwise, the cause of death was the beating. Yao Wen-hsiu himself bore no signs of having sustained a violent attack at the hands of his wife. Therefore the beating must have been one-sided. Yao Wen-hsiu beat his wife, as we might say, methodically, even cold-bloodedly. None of his blows could be excused as being snap responses to stinging physical attack by his wife for there were no marks of her blows on his person.

Yet the physical evidence was surely not so strong as to permit Po Chü-i to infer, without stating it to be an inference, that Yao Wen-hsiu's "enmity towards his wife was deep-seated, and he had long harbored resentment." Facts concerning Yao Wen-hsiu's feelings about his wife prior to the beating must have been brought out in course of the initial investigative procedure. Ts'ui Yüan-shih, it will be remembered, closed his dissent with the assertion that Yao Wen-hsiu had "stored up antipathy and enmity." We can only speculate that perhaps Yao Wen-hsiu himself was forced to admit to his festering ill will. Maybe other witnesses were called to attest to the state of their marriage. Possibly the bad feeling between them was common knowledge.

Whatever the source of the nonphysical evidence, when taken by Po Chü-i together with the physical evidence, it firmly establishes the existence of those "other occasions," those remote causes, which he has excluded from the legal scope of the word *shih,* "occasion." Yao Wen-hsiu had, to be sure, "occasion" to kill his wife, but the "occasion" was one of indirect and remote causation. And the very existence of such remote causation makes a showing of adequate immediate causation proportionately difficult.

Po Chü-i continues:

> If [we hold that a killing in which there is] an antecedent causal struggle and scolding is not an intentional killing, then take a case of a plot to kill a person where [the killer] first draws [the victim] into a mutual scolding which then becomes struggling back and forth, and the struggle having begun [the killer] takes an instrument and assaults and kills [the victim]; then he says, "I killed because of an occasion; it was not intentional killing." Again, is such a thing permissible?

To accept as sufficient grounds for a finding of unintentional homicide the mere fact that there had occurred prior to the killing an exchange of verbal abuse is to open the way for a devious plotter of murder to stage such an encounter. He will pick a fight, let the fight escalate into hateful denunciation, push it to physical contact, and then take up an object and with it kill his victim. Afterwards he will plead that the killing had been in pursuit of an "occasion." Clearly an "occasion" thus provoked by the killer is not what Po Chü-i requires to fulfill the legal definition. The "occasion" may not be indirect and remote, much less prearranged. It must be direct, proximate, and spontaneous.

> If the rationale of causal struggle would not be permitted [even if there had been one],[16] then [surely it cannot be permitted in the case of] A-Wang who had already died so that there was no way [the facts of the case] could be distinguished and made clear. Yao Wen-hsiu himself states that there had been a mutual struggle, but what evidence has he?

The fact that a dispute preceded a killing would not, as Po Chü-i understood the rule of law upon which the Court-Ministry relied, in and of itself remove the crime from the category of intentional killing. Therefore, even if it could be proved that a dispute had taken place, that the death was "because of a struggle," it would not suffice to relieve the wrongdoer of liability for the more serious charge. And if it be true, Po Chü-i says, that a presumption of there having been a dispute and struggle would not satisfy the law, then surely Yao Wen-hsiu could not hope to prevail merely on his own testimony that mutual struggle preceded the death of his wife.

Before leaving the problem of the rule of law cited in the Court-Ministry decision and analyzed by Po Chü-i, we may note as confirmation of Po's analysis the interpretation of the rule contained in a memorial of Chou Ting, President of the Supreme Court of Justice, written in the first year of the reign of the Sung emperor Hui-tsung, 1101.[17] Chou Ting opens his memorial with the observation that the statutes provide for strangulation of one guilty of killing committed in the course of an affray and for decapitation of one guilty of intentional killing.[18] Despite the clear-cut distinction between the two species of homicide, Chou Ting goes on to say, many jurists find it difficult to deal with cases which lie along the border. The problem, Chou Ting says, derives from the rule which we have seen cited by the Court-Ministry in their decision on the case of Yao Wen-hsiu.[19]

The question lies in the meaning of the expression *wu shih erh sha,* says Chou Ting. Does it refer to the killing of another person in the absence of an "occasion" for a two-sided (so I take the expression *pi-tz'u*) struggle and affray? Suppose, for the sake of argument, the expression is taken to mean not necessarily the "occasion" for a struggle and affray, but merely a killing in furtherance of some "other occasion," and that on that account the crime is deemed not to be intentional killing. If the presence or absence of "occasion," no matter how broadly defined, is the only factor upon which the rule turns, then how is it that the rule does not read differently?

"Why does it not say, 'Have occasion and kill another, and you will be strangled,' and instead say, 'In an affray kill another, and you will be strangled?' And why does it not say, 'Lack occasion and kill another, and you will be decapitated,' and instead read, 'Intentionally kill another, and you will be decapitated?'"[20]

To return to Po Chü-i, he now shifts his argument:

> Furthermore, as to the cases of assault killings committed by Liu Shih-hsin and Lo Ch'üan-ju cited by the Supreme Court of Justice and accepted as decisions of prior Courts so as not to deem as intentional killing [the case of Yao Wen-hsiu], I fear that the facts and circumstances [of those cases] and the case of Yao Wen-hsiu are not the same.[21]

Liu Shih-hsin and Lo Ch'üan-ju, whose names I have not been able to find elsewhere, were apparently parties to decisions in which assault killings were found not to have been committed with intent. They had evidently been cited in the Court-Ministry decision, but Po Chü-i denies their applicability as precedents in the matter of Yao Wen-hsiu. He says, quite simply, that the facts are different, and then he goes on:

> But supposing they were roughly the same, what harm would there be? A wrong decision will become a precedent, and it will be inadequate as reliable authority.[22]

A faulty decision, Po Chü-i says, becomes a faulty precedent, a wrongful and unreliable authority upon which to base future decisions. The facts and circumstances of the Yao Wen-hsiu case cannot be allowed to serve as a standard against which to measure cases in which it is sought to impose the criminal liability of killing committed in the course of an affray.

> Your servant submits that at trial what we prize is scrutiny of the facts; of law what we require is that it stand the test of time.

Here Po Chü-i has set up, by implication, the eternal contrast between the realm of facts and the realm of law, between the concrete and the ideal, the specific and the general, the evanescent, everchanging parade of real-life occurrences and the law, which by its nature must be lasting, predictable, only gradually to adapt. How is the law to provide justice and yet maintain its stability in the face of the kaleidoscope of fact patterns which it is asked to sort? The solution is found, of course, in the intelligent and sensitive use of the tools of juristic science. Such use requires the closest scrutiny of the facts of each case. In the case at hand the true facts of Yao Wen-hsiu's killing of his

wife must be brought out. Was there a fight? Had there been the occasion for a fight?

As the exact and true facts must be brought out in litigation, so in applying the law we must so design our rules that they will serve as standards across time, reliable and workable patterns of prescribed conduct and sanction. If we make the Yao Wen-hsiu case part of the law of killing committed in the course of an affray, we will have made an abrupt change in the law based upon distortion of the facts of the case, and we will have created law which cannot long stand. We will have made so broad and inclusive the category of killing in an affray as to open the door to willful wrongdoers in the future. To close that door we will have to amend soon what we do here today. And so will we do violence to the law itself by subjecting it to uncertain meandering.

Po Chü-i now gives an ominous picture of the future:

> If Ts'ui Yüan-shih's opinion is not accepted but the Supreme Court of Justice's holding is implemented, then I fear that henceforth those who die by assault will have the wrong done them extended, and from now on those who intentionally kill a man will achieve their design.

Po Chü-i lays out here two distinct wrongs which will flow from adoption of the decision handed up by the Supreme Court of Justice and concurred in by the Ministry of Justice. First, victims of such beatings as the one suffered by A-Wang will have their misery exacerbated and extended by the fact that their murderer will not have received punishment appropriate to his crime. The wrong done to them will have been compounded by not having been redressed. Second, the perpetrator of such a beating will have gleaned a net gain because the punishment he suffers will be less than he deserves. There will be a double wrong in that the victim will be left in a position of loss, and the killer will be left in a position of gain. The scales of justice will remain off balance, unrestored to the middle point.

Thus ends Po Chü-i's opinion on the case of Yao Wen-hsiu. It is followed in the text by an eight-word formal close, which may be given a rough and tentative rendering as follows:

> Respectfully, assimilated to consultative deliberation, in detail filed as preceding.[23]

The two most significant words in the passage are ts'an-cho "consultative deliberation," a clear reference to the ts'an-cho yüan, a formal legal review function instituted and then abolished during the short reign of Mu-tsung. Of the two accounts dealing with the Office of Consultative Deliberation, the earlier is by Li

Chao, whose book *T'ang kuo-shih-pu*, or simply *Kuo-shih-pu*, of three scrolls, includes material from K'ai-yüan (713-41) through the reign of Mu-tsung, Ch'ang-ch'ing (821-24), during which latter era Li Chao himself lived.

The Li Chao account reads as follows:

> At the beginning of Ch'ang-ch'ing, Mu-tsung, who deemed penal law to be a grave matter, would order that each great case which had been decided as to crime and punishment by the [judicial] authorities, be then given to a Grand Secretary of the Department of the Imperial Chancellery [or] a Grand Secretary of the Grand Secretariate for consultative deliberation upon lessening or increasing it. The Hundred Officials called it the Office of Consultative Deliberation.[24]

It is likely that Ou-yang Hsiu, author of a second account of the establishment of the Office of Consultative Deliberation, to which he added the story of its abolition, made use of Li Chao's material for his *Hsin T'ang shu* version, written some two hundred years later.[25] Ou-yang Hsiu adds to Li Chao's account the observation that Mutsung, born in 795 and therefore no mere youth on the throne, was *t'ung hun*, "callow and dim." However, Ou-yang Hsiu continues, Mu-tsung was well enough aware of the importance of the law to give it his sober attention. Of the two offices mentioned in the Li Chao account as providing persons called upon "consultatively to deliberate," Ou-yang Hsiu omits the first. Also he explicitly states that the Emperor was in the habit of ordering one, giving the numeral, of his Grand Secretaries of the Grand Secretariate consultatively to deliberate and to lighten or make more weighty the penalty imposed by the legal authorities. Ou-yang Hsiu says the institution was given the sobriquet Office of Consultative Deliberation.

Opposition to Mu-tsung's practice of soliciting formal review of legal cases from his Grand Secretaries of the Grand Secretariate was given voice by the Vice-President of the Supreme Court of Justice, Ts'ui Ch'i, in a memorial to the throne. Ts'ui Ch'i declared in his memorial that the legal system of the T'ang state had been solidly established by the great founders of the dynasty, Kao-tsu and T'ai-tsung, over two hundred years earlier. From antiquity, he continued, it had been recognized that the state had a duty to make clearly and widely known the provisions of the laws to all the people by posting them in every town and village.

Ts'ui Ch'i has made two points here: The judicial authority of the throne was fixed and delimited by the founders of the dynasty; and it is a cardinal principle of legal administration, observed since Chou times, that the people be informed of the penalties imposed for specific violations of the law. Ts'ui Ch'i goes on:

> When the [judicial] authorities have determined the crime and punishment, [this new office] discusses its lenience or severity. In this way the "giving and taking away" (i.e., the setting of punishments for crimes) being tied to the human factor [of the criminal acts], the law offices will be unable to uphold their duties.

Th'ui Ch'i closes his memorial with the recommendation that the Office of Consultative Deliberation, offensive to the Confucian doctrine of rectification of names, be abolished.[26] Mu-tsung acquiesced. The function was discontinued, at least in its formal aspect. The objection of Ts'ui Ch'i was that the newly established function called "consultative deliberation" had intruded into the chain of legal authority. The office had been placed above the preexisting structure and thereby had rendered the Supreme Court of Justice, whose interests Ts'ui Ch'i represented, unable, as he said, to preserve its assigned role. As we have seen above, the Ministry of Justice traditionally served as reviewing authority of decisions reached by the Supreme Court of Justice. It was empowered to return for appropriate reconsideration such of those decisions as it found wanting. Ts'ui Ch'i did not mention the Ministry of Justice; he refers alone to his own Court as the constitutional conservator of the law. Perhaps he viewed the relation between the Court and the Ministry as coordinate, not hierarchical. And indeed, the Supreme Court may have been empowered, even in the face of dissent by the Ministry, to sustain its decision after due reconsideration.

The Office of Consultative Deliberation, however, had the power to vary the sentences imposed by the court in accord with the results of its own deliberations. Therefore the legal opinions of others had been set above the legal opinions of the highest judicial office. And these others, as we have seen, were high civil officials of the government seconded, as it were, to serve in a judicial function.

The abolition of the Office of Consultative Deliberation meant a return to the traditional mode of palace review. Inasmuch as the Emperor was accustomed traditionally to refer cases to the same high civil officials, the question arises: why was one practice acceptable to the Court and not the other. The answer lies perhaps in the fact that the Emperor in his sovereign role as executor of legal decisions, even when he altered those decisions, was exercising an executive, not a judicial, function. But when Mu-tsung established an office of judicial review within the executive domain, the Court resented the intrusion.

In conclusion, we may observe that the legal reasoning contained in Po Chü-i's piece makes it eminently worthy of attention. As an extended example of cogent juristic argument from so early a date it is a rarity, standing in sharp contrast to the materials preserved and translated in the *T'ang-yin-pi-shih: "Parallel Cases From Under the Pear-tree"* by Robert van Gulik.[27] Despite van Gulik's subtitle, "A 13th Century Manual of Jurisprudence and Detection," there is very little of the former and an overwhelming preponderance of the latter in the gross of court cases there reported. The judge is detective much more than jurist, fact finder more than lawgiver. As Franz Schurmann perceptively observed in his review of van Gulik's translation:

> The point of many—if not most—of the seventy-two double cases in the *TYPS* is that a wise magistrate refuses to judge a case on superficial grounds, but digs into the matter until he comes up with the real solution. . . . The *TYPS* seems to me to be somewhat like the pocket books on "real court cases" that one finds in any book store today. They are not found next to the law books but on the same shelf with the mysteries. We know from Sung popular literature how much in demand crime stories were at the time, and I suppose that these . . . books were compiled more for purposes of entertainment and perhaps general didactic purposes (advice to magistrates) rather than as usable casebooks of law.[28]

Returning to Yao Wen-hsiu, the imperial disposition of his case was published with the text of the Po Chü-i opinion and is translated by Waley (page 141):

> Yao Wên-hsiu killed his wife and is therefore guilty of one of the Ten Major Offences. To treat him with indulgence would be to encourage violence. In cases where the relevant passage in the Code is capable of alternative explanations, judgment should be given in accordance with what is reasonable. Po Chü-i's report is to be accepted. We rule that the defendant is to be thrashed and then executed.

Two points must be made with respect to the imperial order. First, the killing by Yao Wen-hsiu of his wife would not statutorily fall within the Ten Abominations (called by Waley the Ten Major Offences), all of which involve threats to the very substance of the social order, viewed as a hierarchy. A husband killing his wife would of course be seen as a crime committed by a superior against an inferior. It may be that the brutality of the Yao Wen-hsiu case, as presented in the record, and the convincing arguments of Po Chü-i that the killing had been done with intent, combined to move the emperor to include it figuratively among the Ten Abominations. Moreover, as I have mentioned above, intentional killing itself was sometimes classed with the Ten Abominations as being beyond the reach of pardon.

Second, Yao Wen-hsiu may not have suffered capital punishment after all. A reform of 782 provided that only perpetrators of the four most grave of the Ten Abominations were to be punished according to the law demanding execution. All others under sentence of death were to be punished by "one round [of beating] with the heavy stick and put to death." It seems that the offender, provided he survived the prescribed sixty strokes of "one round," was only nominally, not actually, "put to death."[29]

Notes

[1] A. F. P. Hulsewé, *Remnants of Han Law* (Leiden: Brill, 1955), pp. 251-84; Karl Bünger, "The Punishment of Lunatics and Negligents According to Classical Chinese Law," *Studia Serica,* 9.2 (1950), 1-16.

[2] Niida Noboru, *Chūgoku hō seishi kenkyū* (Tokyo: Tokyo Univ. Press, 1959), I, 248, reprint of an article in *TG* (Tokyo), 11.2 (1940).

[3] Wallace S. Johnson, *The T'ang Code* (Princeton: Princeton Univ. Press, 1979), pp. 59-60, n. 74.

[4] *T'ang lü shu-i* (Changsha: Commercial Press, 1939), 2.44-45, translated in Johnson, p. 119, as Article 18.

[5] I employ terms cognate to those used by Robert des Rotours, *Traité des fonctionnaires et traité de l'armee* (Leiden: Brill, 1948), pp. 113-23 and 404-8. Inferences as to the respective roles of the two legal institutions, the Court and the Ministry, can be drawn from an examination of two measures, dating from 809 and 821, intended to expedite judicial process. These are in *Chiu T'ang shu* (*Po-na-pen* ed.), 50.14a and 50.15a, translated in Uchida Tomoo, *Yakuchū zoku Chūgoku rekidai keihōshi* (Tokyo: Sōbunsha, 1970), pp. 229-30 and 237-38, and in Karl Bünger, *Quellen zur Rechtsgeschichte der T'ang-Zeit,* Monumenta Serica Monograph 9 (Peking, 1946), pp. 130, 135. A timetable is set down in the edict of 809 by which the Supreme Court of Justice is given no more than twenty days for the process of investigating and deciding upon a case coming under its jurisdiction. Next, the Ministry of Justice is given ten days in which to conduct a review of the Court's work. Should the review produce discrepancies of opinion sufficient to remand, the case is sent back to the Court for up to fifteen days. Finally, the Ministry has seven days for its second review. Although the reform recommended in 821 does not mention remand by the Ministry to the Court, it does confirm the fact that it was the role of the Ministry to review the work of the Court and then to transmit the results to the throne. According to the T'ang monographs on officialdom, *Chiu T'ang shu,* 44.13a and *Hsin T'ang shu* (*Po-na-pen* ed.), 48.10b (the latter translated in des Rotours, p. 404), it was those cases of grave moment, involving sentences of death or life exile, that underwent review by the Ministry and then by the throne. Palace review was cus-

tomarily delegated by the Emperor to those high-rank-ing officials like Po Chü-i who met in "[la grande salle] du grand secrétariat impérial et de la chancellerie impériale," as des Rotours, p. 13, translates *chung-shu men-hsia.*

6 *Po-shih ch'ang-ch'ing chi* (*SPTK* ed.), 43.14a-16a. Arthur Waley, *The Life and Times of Po Chü-i* (London: George Allen & Unwin, 1949), pp. 140-41, summarizes but does not translate the Po Chü-i opinion on the case of Yao Wen-hsiu. He notes that the opinion is a "document of considerable interest to students of law." Po Chü-i's piece is printed, with certain omissions, in *Wen-hsien t'ung-k'ao,* compiled by Ma Tuanlin, who flourished during the transition from Sung to Yüan, (*Shih-t'ung* ed., Taipei: Hsin-hsing shu-chü, 1959), 170.1473a-b, from which it was taken by Shen Chiapen, 1840-1913, for his study on intentional killing, contained in *Shen Chi-i hsien-sheng i-shu* (rpt. Taipei: Wen-hai ch'u-pan she, 1964), p. 901.

7 *T'ang lü shu-i,* 21.482-83. The same rule appears in the Annamese code, translated by Raymond Deloustal, "La Justice dans l'ancien Annam," *BEFEO,* 12.6 (1912), 3-4: "Ceux qui, dans une rixe, auront tué quelqu'un en lui portant des coups, seront punis de la strangulation. Ceux qui, au cours d'une rixe, auront tué quelqu'un en faisant usage d'une arme aiguë et tranchante, ainsi que les meurtriers volontaires, seront décapités. La faute de ceux qui, bien que les faits se soient produits à l'occasion d'une rixe, auront commis un meurtre en faisant usage d'armes aiguës et tranchantes, sera assimilée au meurtre volontaire."

8 Paul Pelliot, "Notes de bibliographie chinoise: II, Le Droit chinois," *BEFEO,* 9 (1909), 125-26. The surviving T'ang Code is "the text as promulgated in 737, with later interpolations, and not, as had been commonly assumed, the earlier version of 653." This finding we owe to Niida and Makino, as pointed out by Denis Twitchett, "Niida Noboru and Chinese Legal History," *AM,* NS 13 (1967), 219-20.

9 There are minor differences in wording. The Subcommentary version lacks the nominalizer *che;* and while it omits the verb *wei* after *ming,* "name," it has *shih,* "this [is]," preceding it. A variant definition of intentional killing, which omits entirely any mention of the factor of *shih,* "occasion," is found in the Subcommentary to Article 18, cited above in n. 3: "Intentionally to kill a man means an intentional killing, not resulting from an affray."

10 *Chiu T'ang shu,* 163.4b; *Hsin T'ang shu,* 160.6b-7a. Ts'ui Yüan-shih's biography follows that of his older brother, but it does not mention his appointment as Judicial Inspector. Indeed, the earliest date given in the biography is twenty years after the reign of Mu-tsung.

11 *T'ung-tien* (*Shih-t'ung* ed., Taipei: Hsin-hsing shu-chü, 1969), 25.152a.

12 *T'ang lü shu-i,* 21.479.

13 Here again there are slight differences in the wording of the rule both from our existing version of the Subcommentary and from Po Chü-i's earlier citation of the Court decision.

14 I find the English word "occasion" a rendering more satisfactory than its etymological cousin "incident" used by Arthur Waley in his narrative summary. "Occasion" carries with it a stronger sense of causation than "incident."

15 The notion of intent in Chinese law has often, as here, been expressed in terms of *hsin,* "heart, mind," or *i,* "idea, thought." Certain offenders have been described as lacking, "at bottom," *pen,* or "at the source," *yüan,* the thought to do evil.

16 *Wen-hsien t'ung-k'ao,* 170.1473a-b omits, it would appear inadvertently, the words. . . . They are not restored by Shen Chia-pen.

17 The piece is in *Wen-hsien t'ung-k'ao,* 167.1452a, and is quoted therefrom by Shen Chia-pen immediately after the Po Chü-i opinion on the case of Yao Wen-hsiu.

18 Chou Ting then seems to say that when a pair of people are engaged in mutual struggle and strife we call it "intent." As Shen Chia-pen noted, there is something very wrong, in view of Chou Ting's clear contrast between "intent" and "fight" as attributes of homicide. *Ku* must be an error for *tou.*

19 Chou Ting cites as his source for the rule the *Hsing-t'ung* very likely denoting the *Sung hsing-t'ung* (Bureau of Laws edition of T'ien-i Library copy, 1918), 21.5a-b. The possibility cannot be discounted, however, that he was quoting from the first book of law codification designated by the term, the *Ta-chung hsing-lü t'ung-lei* by Chang Lu compiled during the reign of Hsüan-ti (847-60), and apparently no longer extant. It is from the Chang Lu work that the genre takes its name by abbreviation. Sec *Shih-wu chi-yüan* (Taipei: Hsin-hsing shu-chü, 1969), p. 699, and Chang Wejen, *An Annotated Bibliography of Chinese Legal History, Chung-kuo fa-chih-shih shu-mu,* Institute of History and Philology, Academia Sinica, Special Publications, No. 67 (Taipei: 1976), p. 7.

20 Chou Ting's suggestion to the throne is that lower tribunals be required to determine as a matter of fact whether there had been a fight in cases alleging them to have occurred, before sending them up to the higher authorities. He specifically excepted from the category

of qualifying fights those in which the parties had ceased their dispute and parted company only to return later to violence. If a break in time had intervened, the incident could not be reckoned an "angry quarrel." It is a reaffirmation of the "cooling-off period" principle.

[21] I take the word *shih* here as carrying a meaning quite distinct from its legal sense of "occasion." Po Chü-i appears to use it as an informal designation of the "cases" of Liu and Lo.

[22] *Wen-hsien t'ung-k'ao,* and Shen Chia-pen, omit the material on judicial precedent, that is, this paragraph and the one preceding in my translation.

[23] *Wen-hsien t'ung-k'ao,* and Shen Chia-pen, omit the eight-word close.

[24] I have quoted the text as it appears in the *T'ang-tai ts'ung-shu* (1850 ed.), 4.62a, (1911 ed.), 4.11a. A variant tradition is represented by the version in *Pi-chi hsiao-shuo ta-kuan,* in *Ssu-pu chi-yao, Tzu-pu* (Taipei: Hsin-hsing shu-chü, 1960), 1, 89. Omission of *ju* after *ch'u* is an error. The sense of the passage is destroyed if the sentence of the Court is open only to lessening its severity, not to increasing it. It is on the basis of the words *i yüan,* "one member," here, along with similar wording in the second account of the establishment of the Office, that the conclusion may be drawn that the Emperor used to refer each case to a single consultant drawn from among the holders of the title Grand Secretary of the Grand Secretariate. These officers, together with Grand Secretaries of the Imperial Chancellery, mentioned first in the version given in the text but omitted in other versions, were precisely the ones who were accustomed to sit in the *chung-shu men-hsia* (see n. 4). Po Chü-i was a Grand Secretary of the Grand Imperial Secretariate from the tenth month of the first year of Ch'ang-ch'ing (821) until the seventh month of the second year. See *Chiu T'ang shu,* 16.12a and 16.16a. The corresponding sections of *Hsin T'ang shu* do not mention the appointment. The Yao Wen-hsiu case is not discussed in Po Chü-i's biography in the sections covering the period, *Chiu T'ang shu,* 166.5a-b, *Hsin T'ang shu,* 119.5b. Nor is it taken up by Eugen Feifel, "Biography of Po Chü-i," *MS,* 17 (1958), 296-97, or in the same author's *Po Chü-i as a Censor* ('S-Gravenhage: Mouton, 1961), pp. 20-21. The Yao Wen-hsiu piece is chronologically catalogued in Hanabusa Hideki, *Haku Kyoi kenkyü* (Kyoto: Sekai Shish sha, 1971), p. 122. The only other person I have found acting in a "consultative deliberative" function is Yang Ssu-fu, whose biography in *Chiu T'ang shu,* 176.4a, records his occupancy of the office Grand Secretary of the Grand Imperial Secretariate during the reign of Mu-tsung. For the case in which he was involved, see *Ts'e-fu yüan-kuei* (Taipei: Chung-hua shu-chü, 1967), 616.7408.

[25] Ou-yang Hsiu was an admirer of Li Chao's *Kuo-shih-pu,* and he acknowledged his use of it as a model for his own *Kuei-t'ien lu* in a preface to that work, according to *Ssu-k'u ch'üan-shu tsung-mu* (Shanghai: Commercial Press, 1933), p. 2903.

[26] What would seem to have been *pu cheng,* "not rectified," about the term *ts'an-cho yüan* was that the name of the Office gave no hint of its extraordinary authority, superior to that of the Supreme Court of Justice and the Ministry of Justice. Ts'ui Ch'i objects of course not merely to the name but to the function itself.

[27] *Sinica Leidensia,* 10 (Leiden: Brill, 1956).

[28] *JAS,* 17 (1958), 268-69. Another reviewer, John C. H. Wu, himself a lawyer, cites only two of the cases, both from Han times, to illustrate his assessment of the book as "not lacking cases which involved subtle and equitable interpretation and application of the laws," and as containing "cases highly illustrative of good legal reasoning." *MS,* 17 (1948), 474-78.

[29] See Karl Bünger, *Quellen,* pp. 166-67, and Uchida Tomoo, *Yakuchū zoku Chūgoku rekidai keih shi,* pp. 290-91, for translations of *Hsin T'ang shu,* 56.6b. See also *T'ung-tien,* 165.875a, and *T'ang hui-yao* (Taipei: Shih-chieh shu-chü, 1963), 39.711.

Sukehiro Hirakawa (essay date 1983)

SOURCE: Sukehiro Hirakawa, "Chinese Culture and Japanese Identity: Traces of Po Chü-i in a Peripheral Country," in *Tamkang Review,* Vol. XV, Nos. 1-4, Autumn 1984-Summer 1985, pp. 201-19.

[*In this essay, Hirakawa discusses Po Chü-i's influence on Japanese nationalism and the relationship between that nationalism and the assimilation of chinese culture during the T'ang dynasty.*]

The word "nationalism," with its various Japanese equivalents, has been associated in many Japanese minds, as well as in Western minds, with nationalistic wars which Japan fought within the time span of fifty-one years: from 1894 to 1945. Japan fought against China in 1894-95, against Russia in 1904-05, entered World War I in a secondary role, and played an important "villian's" role in World War II. Westerners talk a great deal of the Japanese ultranationalism of the war years. Their knowledge of Japan seems almost exclusively drawn from the World War II experience, so much so that other aspects of the East Asian traditions are often overshadowed. I would like to discuss in this paper then, about earlier expressions of nationalism which were largely in reaction to a Japanese sense of inferiority to China. The discussions about nationalism depend heavily on its definition. But, perhaps it is as well for me to avoid theoretical assumptions and confine myself to a straightforward narrative since Western readers are rather unfamiliar with the problem. First, an overview of cultural relations between China and Japan.

Japan of the 1980s is considered an economic power, however, Japan has always been conscious of her small size geographically: a peripheral country scattered along the continent. Diplomatic relations between Japan and China have not necessarily been equal because Chinese perception of the world order was hierarchical, while the Japanese were not always satisfied with that world view. Shotoku Taishi, Prince Regent of Japan towards the end of the sixth century, sent the following letter to the Emperor of China:

> The Son of Heaven in the land where the sun rises addresses a letter to the Son of Heaven in the land where the sun sets. We hope you are in good health.

Yang-ti, the Emperor of Sui China, was not pleased with this letter and said, "This is an impolite letter from the barbarians. Such a letter should not again be brought to our attention" (This is found in the *Sui History*'s chapter on East Barbarians). The Chinese were accustomed to a Sino-centric view of the world order and conceived of themselves as being on a higher plane than other peoples.

So far as the cultural relationship is concerned, in Japan's history, the first era of assimilating Chinese culture was in the sixth, seventh, and eighth centuries when envoys and students were sent to T'ang China. The second era was around the fourteenth century when ships were sent to Ming China. The third era was from the seventeenth century to the opening of the country in 1868. At that time, Confucianism became the ideological basis of the shogunal government in Japan. The fourth surge in the Sino-Japanese cultural relationship went in the opposite direction, with China's sending several thousand students a year to Japan after Japan's victory over Russia in 1905, at a time when the decadent Ch'ing dynasty abolished the examination system for governmental officials. We might add the fifth period which is just beginning: Den Xiaoping now sends to Japan many Chinese students. This is the general background of Sino-Japanese relations.

All through those years of contact with Chinese culture, the foreign book most widely read and studied in Japan was the *Analects* of Confucius. Indeed, there was a time when the Chinese *Analects* were far easier for many Japanese to understand than the Japanese *Tale of Genji*. Today, there are still quite a number of Japanese men whose names derive from the Chinese sacred book, which is one indication of how deep its

influence has been in Japan. The Japanese Prime Minister of the 1930s, Hirota, who was condemned to death by hanging by the International Military Tribunal for the Far East (by mistake, I believe) as the responsible war criminal for the Japanese aggression against China, had a Confucian name of kōki: ("A gentleman should be open-minded and resolute in his will" of the *Analects*). As Confucian influence in East Asia was so immense, I don't dare touch upon it. It is analogous to Westerner's speaking about the influence of the Bible in the Western world. Instead, I have chosen a literary figure, Po Chü-i, a Chinese poet of the eighth century, known also by his nom de plume Po Lo-t'ien whom Japanese pronounce Haku Rakuten, T'ang poet born in 772 and died in 846. I have chosen Po Chü-i because his case sheds light not only on the problems of literary influence but also on the problems of Japanese cultural nationalism.

Therefore, my discussion consists of two parts: the first part concerns Po Chü-i's influence; the second part details Japanese reaction. On the life and times of Po Chü-i, there is an excellent biography written by Arthur Waley.[1] However, Waley did not deal at any length with the question of the poet's reputation after his death down to the present day. I traced his influence in Japan in one of my books written in Japanese,[2] and I shall try to communicate some of its contents. First, I shall introduce you to one of Po's poems. As a bureaucrat, Po, who was often sent to remote, unhealthy places, wrote:

> The Sun has risen in the sky, but I idly lie
> in bed;
> In my small tower-room the layers of quilts
> protect me from the cold;
> Leaning on my pillow, I want to hear I-ai's
> temple bell,
> Pushing aside the blind, I gaze upon the
> snow of Hsiang-lu peak. . . . [3]

The bureaucrat in a remote province obviously has little to do. He consoles himself by writing poems.

Now let us review the influence of the Chinese poet in the imagery of a Japanese scholar-statesman, Sugawara no Michizane, who was born in 845, one year before Po's death. Michizane went into exile in Kyūshū, where he wrote many poems in Chinese. (It is important to note at this point that despite the proximity of the two empires, the Japanese and Chinese languages had little in common. Therefore, speaking in Japanese and writing in Chinese was a great strain. Yet, the knowledge of written Chinese was indispensible to scholars or government officials in Japan):

Hearing Wild Geese

I am a banished man and you guests;
We are both lonely wayfarers.

Leaning on my pillow, I wonder when I shall
    be allowed to go back;
But you, wild geese, can no doubt go back
    home next spring.

Not Going Out of the Gate

Since I was banished and put in this poor
    hut,
I have always been in horror of death.
I only gaze upon the color of Tofurō's roof
And listen to Kannon's temple bell.

The image of the man leaning on his pillow gazing and wondering derives of course from Chü-i's poem. As the place of Michizane's exile was Dazai-fu in Kyūshū, the temple in the poem was changed from the Chinese I-ai to the Japanese Kannon, and the snow of Hsiang-lu peak to the colour of Tofurō's roof. (Tofuro was a government building whose roof is said to have been built with Chinese tiles). Michizane was an exile who was "always in horror of death," and actually he did die in exile, but he continued to write poems imitating Po Chü-i.

Michizane lived during the Heian period, so named because the capital of Japan was at Heian, present-day Kyōto. This period, from 794 to 1184, was also called the Fujiwara period because Japan was dominated by the Fujiwara family. Institutionally, Japan and China were quite different. Japan was governed by the aristocracy while China was governed by the bureaucracy and Chinese bureaucrates were selected by state examinations. This imported system did not fit the Japanese reality. Michizane was promoted to a high rank in the court for his scholarly merit, but later he was banished by the Fujiwara family and died in exile. Michizane must have been popular, though, among the people who did not owe loyalty to the Fujiwara family. After Michizane's death, many natural disasters and calamities occurred. In order to placate the spirit of Michizane, he was deified and a Shinto shrine was erected in his memory. Michizane was considered to be the symbol of those who by their own scholarly merits attain a very high rank. His Tenjin shrine in Kyōto still has many devotees today, notably mothers who pray for their children's success in university entrance examinations and buy amulets.

Now let us consider the depth of the penetration of Chinese culture into the Japanese courtly life. Sei Shōnagon is a lady-in-waiting who wrote in Japanese *The Pillow Book* around the year 1000, more than a century after Michizane's time. Po Chü-i was known to the Japanese during his lifetime, and by the year 1000, his **Literary Collection** was widely read among the Japanese. Sei Shōnagon herself put the book at the head of her list of important works. *Pillow Book* contains the following episode:

One day, when the snow lay thick on the ground and it was so cold that the lattices had all been closed, I and the other ladies were sitting with Her Majesty, chatting and poking the embers in the brazier.

"Tell me, Shōnagon," said the Empress, "how is the snow on Hsiang-lu peak?"

I told the maid to raise one of the lattices and then rolled up the blind all the way. Her Majesty smiled. . . .[4]

It was because Shōnagon, as well as the Empress, had remembered the phrase in Po's poem quoted above that she instantly took the hint. If a princess of Japan today refers to a phrase from Shakespeare at Court, I do not think any lady-in-waiting would catch the allusion. It is not a question of quality of the ladies-in-waiting; I wish merely to suggest that even a representative of English literature like Shakespeare cannot have as much influence today as Po Chü-i had one thousand years ago. I also doubt whether even at the English Court a princess would convey her thought to a lady-in-waiting in a phrase from Shakespeare, as if they had a code between them.

In the Japan of the tenth century, however, people who memorized famous phrases of Po, like the Empress Sadako and Sei Shōnagon, were not necessarily exceptions. Lady Murasaki, a contemporary of Shōnagon's, wrote in her *Tale of Genji* as follows:

Once when all day long he had sat watching the snow whirling through the dark sky, at dusk the clouds suddenly cleared, and raising the blinds and leaning on his pillow, he looked out on such moonlight as only the glittering nights of late winter can show. Far off the faint chiming of the temple-bell whispered that another day had passed.[5]

It is needless to say that this image also came from the poem by Po quoted earlier, although the passage from the *Tale of Genji* has aesthetically a different mood from Po's poem, in which the poet idly lay in bed in the late morning. There is also an episode in which Lady Murasaki taught Po's **Literary Collection** to the Empress Akiko, to whom she was a lady-in-waiting. Despite the prejudice against women studying Chinese (which was thought to be uniquely a gentlemen's occupation), Murasaki wrote in her diary that

Since the summer before last, very secretly, in odd moments when there happened to be no one about, I have been reading with Her Majesty the two books of ballads (by Po) . . .

It is well known, too, that the authoress made many references to Po's poems, and especially to "The Everlasting Remorse" in the first chapter of the *Tale of Genji*.

In addition, we have material which statistically shows how widely Po Chü-i was read in Japan in that era. The *Tale of Genji* was written about 1000 A.D., and in about 1018, a Sino-Japanese anthology called *Wa-Kan-Rōei-shū* was complied by Fujiwara no Kintō. This Sino-Japanese anthology served as a standard textbook in Japan for more than five hundred years. When the Jesuits came to Japan toward the end of the sixteenth century, an edition was published by the Christian printing press in Nagasaki as a Japanese language text for missionaries. . . .

The anthology indicates something of the tastes of the Japanese in that era, and it continued to influence them. Even the Nō plays written centuries later in the Muromachi era contain many references to Po's verses collected in this anthology.

Po Chü-i knew that his poems were read in Japan, for he said in 845 that copies of his works had been taken to Japan and Korea. As for the relationship between Po and Japan, there is the following episode:

A curious story, connected with Po's cult of the Future Buddha Maitreya, is told in a collection of anecdotes called *I Shih,* which dates from the second half of the ninth century: 'In the first year of Hui Ch'ang (841), when Li Shih-lêng was Inspector General of Ch'ê-tung (the region just south of the Yangtze delta) a merchant met with a hurricane which blew his ship far out of its course. At last, after more than a month, he came to a great mountain, upon which the clouds, the trees, the white cranes were all of strange and magical form unlike any that he had ever seen in the World of Men. Presently someone came down from the mountain-side and having asked how he had got there and heard the merchant's story, told him to tie up his boat and come on shore. "You must present yourself to the heavenly Master," he said. He then led the merchant to a vast building that looked like a Buddhist or Taoist monastery. After his name had been sent in, the merchant was brought into the presence of a venerable Taoist whose hair and eyebrows were completely white. He was seated at the upper end of a large hall, with some twenty or thirty attendants mounting guard over him. "Being a man of the Middle Kingdom," the aged Taoist said, "it must be by some special ordinance of Fate that you succeeded in reaching this place. For this, I would have you know, is the fairy mountain P'êng-lai. But as you are here, I expect you would like to have a look round." And he told one of the attendants to take the merchant round the Palace precincts and show him the sights. He was led on, past jade terraces and trees of halcyon brightness that dazzled him as he passed. They went through courtyard after courtyard, each with its own name, till they came at last to one the gate of which was very tightly locked and barred. But he was allowed to peep in,

and saw borders full of every kind of flower. In a hall that opened on to the garden was a cushioned couch, and on the steps that led up to the hall incense was burning. The merchant asked what courtyard it was. "This," said his guide, "is the courtyard of Po Lo-t'ien. But he is still in the Middle Kingdom and has not yet come to take possession of it." The merchant made note of what he had heard, and when after a voyage of some weeks he arrived back at Yüch-chou, he told the whole story to Li Shih-lêng, who in turn sent a full report to Po Chü-i. Po had always striven for re-birth in the Paradise of Maitreya, and he replied by sending to Li two poems:

A traveller came from across the seas
Telling of strange sights.
'In a deep fold of the sea-hills
I saw a terrace and tower.
In the midst there stood a Fairy Temple
With one niche empty.
They all told me this was waiting
For Lo-t'ien to come.'

Traveller, I have studied the Empty Gate;[6]
I am no disciple of Fairies.
The story you have just told
Is nothing but an idle tale.
The hills of ocean shall never be
Lo-t'ien's home.
When I leave the earth it will be to go
To the Heaven of Bliss Fulfilled.[7]

Arthur Waley imagines the circumstances in which the two poems were written: according to Waley there is not very much doubt as to what actually happened. Po's immense popularity in Japan had already begun, and some Chinese merchant visiting Japan was asked whether Po was still alive and was told that if the poet ever came to Japan a wonderful reception awaited him, or words to that effect. Hearing of this, Li Shih-lêng wrote a story somewhat on the lines of the one just quoted, transposing the merchant's report into a typical Taoist tale in which Japan figures as one of the Islands of the blest (as it often was in poetic language). Li Shih-leng's story was an elegant trifle meant to flatter and amuse Po, of whose illness Li had no doubt heard.

By chance, I found the following anecdote in a Japanese book entitled *Kokon-chomon-jū.* It reveals the psychology of the Japanese who were waiting for Po to come. The title of the anecdote is: "Ōe no Tomotsuna converses with Po Lo-t'ien in his dream." It says:

On the eighteenth of the tenth month of the sixth year of Tenryaku (952), Po Lo-t'ien appeared in Councillor Tomotsuna's dream. Tomotsuna was enchanted to see Po, who was dressed in white and a dark ruddy face. Four men in blue followed him. When Tomotsuna asked him, "Have you come from the Heaven of Bliss Fulfilled?" The poet replied, "Yes." Although Po said he had come to say something to Tomotsuna, he awoke from his dream and felt very sorry.

Tomatsuna might have known the two poems of Po quoted above so he could ask him if he had come from "The Heaven of Bliss Fulfilled," the Paradise of Maitreya.

Po Chü-i was a Buddhist devotee, but in Japan he was once deified in a Shinto shrine near Kyōto. The deification is understandable since Sugawara no Michizane, who was regarded as Po's Japanese counterpart, was deified in the shrine of Kitano Tenjin, it would seem appropriate that Po be worshipped as an incarnation of wisdom and poetry. I don't think that the shrine dedicated to Po Chü-i exists today at Nishi-no-kyō. However there still is in Kyōto a Shinto festival car dedicated to Po Chü-i, which makes a parade together with other cars dedicated to gods and historical heroes of the Japanese people during the gion Metsuri festivals.

If one tries to find a parallel in the West for the relationship between Chinese culture and the surrounding East Asian countries, the relationship between classical Latin culture and the European countries will correspond. As written Chinese had been the cultural language and *lingua franca* of the East Asian countries for more than 1,200 years, so was Latin for European countries. An example of the correlation is the image of the teacher of Chinese classics who often appeared in Japanese novels and who resembles the teachers of Latin in Western novels. He is conservative and severe, wears a moustache, and makes his pupils memorize passages. The pupils do not like this old-fashioned manner of teaching, but later they remember the classes with nostalgia. James Hilton's *Goodbye Mr. Chips* has its counterparts in Japanese literature.

Nevertheless, there are some aspects of the relationship between Chinese culture and the East Asian countries which differ from the relationship between classical Latin culture and the European countries. First, many European languages belong to the same linguistic family as Latin, whereas Japanese and Korean do not belong to the same family as Chinese. The origins are different. Second, some Europeans may regard themselves as the inheritors of classical Latin culture, but it is impossible for the Japanese to think that they are the direct inheritors of Chinese culture. There are eight hundred million or more Chinese living on the Chinese continent. Even if the present-day Chinese of the mainland are rather ignorant of their own past and if perhaps some Chinese classics are much more studied in Japan and in the United States of America, than

they are in China, still the direct inheritors of the Chinese culture are those who speak Chinese in their daily life. Finally, Latin culture now, unlike in the days of the Roman Empire, threatens nobody, while China, with its great population, can still be a threatening presence for the surrounding countries.

Now what I have said in the first half of my paper may appear to have nothing to do with Japanese nationalism. It was a rough sketch of Chinese literary influence on Japan, and particularly of Po Chü-i's immense popularity among the educated Japanese. But I should not talk too much about the cultural borrowings of the Japanese because it confirms the stereotype notion of Japan as a nation of borrowers. Literary historians look for Po Chü-i's influence in the *Tale of Genji,* but what is most important is the fact that the literary genre of psychological novel was a Japanese invention. Chinese began to write novels only in the fourteenth century.

Now I come to the second, and main, part of my discussion of Japanese nationalism. Among Japanese works of literature I very much like Nō plays. In one of them, written probably by Zeami, I think we can recognize early expressions of Japanese cultural nationalism. The title of the Nō play in question is *Haku Rakuten,* which is the Japanese pronunciation of the Chinese poet Po Lo-t'ien (Po Chü-i). As I said earlier, in the ninth century the composition of Chinese verse became fashionable at the Japanese Court. Japanese men like Sugawara no Michizane wrote in Chinese, as Europeans of the Middle Ages tended to write in Latin instead of the vernacular languages. But fortunately, in Japan, thanks to sexual discrimination, women were supposed to be uncultured and therefore continued to write in Japanese. That was one reason why the masterpieces of Japanese literature of that time were written by ladies-in-waiting.

Native forms of poetry disappeared in Korea, where the Chinese influence was overwhelming. In Japan, too, under the strong foreign influences, Japanese had a sort of identity crisis. The Nō play *Haku Rakuten* deals with this literary peril. It was written at the end of the fourteenth century, a time when Japanese art and literature were for the second time becoming subject to strong Chinese influence.

Historically, Po Chü-i (Haku Rakuten) never came to Japan. In Zeami's play, however, Haku Rakuten is sent by the Emperor of China to subdue Japan with his art. On arriving at the coast of Kyūshū, he meets two Japanese fishermen. One of them is in reality the god of Japanese poetry, Sumiyoshi no Kami. In the second act the god's identity is revealed. He summons other gods, and a great dancing scene ensues. Finally, the wind from their dancing sleeves blows the Chinese poet's ship back to his own country. As a drama it is almost nonsensical, but it is interesting because the Nō play sheds light on the ambivalent attitude of the Japanese toward China: the attraction of Chinese culture and the defensiveness of the Japanese.

The play's author, Zeami (1363-1443), lived about six hundred years after Po Chü-i. As Zeami felt the strong, all-pervasive influence of Chinese culture around him, the name of Po, Haku Pakuten, occurred to him as the representative Chinese poet. I imagine Zeami must have had the same state of mind as Dante when Dante let Virgil appear in the *Divine Comedy* as the representative Latin poet. Po Chü-i was, as it were, the symbol of Chinese culture. The Nō play begins with Po Chü-i's self-introduction:[8]

> I am Huku Rakuten, a courtier of the Prince of China. There is a land in the East called Japan. Now at my master's bidding, I am sent to that land to make proof of the wisdom of its people. I must travel over the paths of the sea.

(Bertolt Brecht, incidentally, who was very interested in Nō plays, adopted this style of self-introduction in many of his plays).

Following Po Chü-i's introduction, two Chinese verses are used to describe the voyage across the sea. On arriving, the poet finds two Japanese fishermen, the elder of whom speaks to him:

OLD FISHERMAN

> . . . I am an old fisher of Nihon. And your Honour, I think, is Haku Rakuten of China.

HAKU

> How strange! No sooner am I come to this land than they call me by my name! How can this be?

Then follows a conversation between the two:

HAKU

> Answer me one question. Bring your boat closer and tell me, Fisherman, what is your pastime now in Nippon?

FISHERMAN

> And in the land of China, pray how do your Honours disport yourselves?

HAKU

> In China we play at making poetry.

FISHERMAN

> And in Nihon, may it please you, we feast our hearts on making *uta*-poetry.

When Haku talks about Japan, he calls it Nippon, while the fisherman pronounces it Nihon. This is a theatrical device to emphasize that Haku is a foreigner. *Uta* is a native form of Japanese poetry composed of thirty-one syllables.

It might be because of their different social positions that Haku Rakuten omits the honorific terms of speech while the fisherman speaks deferentially. Haku even composes a Chinese poem about the scene before him, which to Haku's surprise, the fisherman instantly puts into *uta* form:

HAKU

> How strange that a poor fisherman should put my verse into a sweet native measure! Who can he be?

FISHERMAN

> A poor man and unknown. But as for the making of *uta*, it is not only men that make them. "For among things that live there is none that has not the gift of song."

The old fisherman who thus preaches the virtues of Japanese poetry is in reality Sumiyoshi no Kami, the chief of the three gods of *uta*-poetry, and in the second act his identity is revealed. The poetry contest ends in a great dancing scene:

CHORUS

> The God Sumiyoshi whose strength is such
> That he will not let you subdue us, O
>   Rakuten!
> So we bid you return to your home,
> Swiftly over the waves of the shore!
> First the God Sumiyoshi came.
> Now other gods have come—
>
> As they hovered over the void of the sea,
> Moved in the dance, the sleeves of their
>   dancing dress
> Stirred up a wind, a magic wind
> That blew on the Chinese boat
> And filled its sails
> And sent it back again to the land of Han.
> Truly, the God is wondrous;
> The God is wondrous, and thou, our
>   Prince,
> Mayest thou rule for many, many years
> Our Land Inviolate!

In Japan today there are about two million people who take lessons in Nō chanting or dance. Very few of them are interested in the libretto of *Haku Rakuten* because the dramatic quality of the play is not very high. To professional actors, the play is interesting mainly for its dancing scenes. But to cultural historians who are interested in the love-hate relationship between China and Japan, the play is in many ways extremely revealing.

The problem of Chinese culture and Japanese identity is closely related to the problem of the Japanese language. In East Asia, almost all peripheral countries that came under the Chinese influence adopted the Chinese writing system. The Vietnamese spoke Vietnamese but wrote in Chinese, the Koreans spoke in Korean but wrote in Chinese. Neither country developed its own writing system for more than ten centuries. It was rather natural for them to write their histories in Chinese, just as the Venerable Bede wrote the first British history in Latin and St. Gregory of Tours wrote a history of the Franks in Latin. In Japan, however, something different happened. At the beginning of the eighth century, the Japanese compiled their first histories. One is called *Kojiki* or the *Records of Ancient Matters,* and the other is called *Nihonshoki*. The compiler of the *Kojiki* wrote some parts of what a professional reciter of old legends dictated to him in Japanese. At that time the Japanese syllabary had not yet been invented. So the compiler took great pains to devise a method for representing Japanese sounds using Chinese characters phonetically. This must have been much harder for him than simply writing the whole book in classical Chinese. Yet he must have wanted to be true to his conviction that some parts of the national records should not or could not be translated into Chinese. These parts are Japanese poems.

The first anthology of Japanese poems, *Manyōshū,* was compiled around the year 760. In 905, the second anthology of *uta* poems was compiled. This anthology, *Kokinshū,* has a preface in Japanese which begins by insisting on the virtues of Japanese poetry: "Everyone can make an *uta* poem, rich or poor, known or unknown, not only human beings but also nightingales on plum trees; even frogs in ponds can express their poetic emotions. . . ."

In order to compose poems in Chinese you must have some bookish knowledge beforehand, but it is much easier to make poems in the 31-syllable *uta* form. Indeed, the first anthology of the eighth century contained poems composed by people of all walks of life—from emperors and empresses down to soldiers, beggars, and prostitutes. In the Nō play *Haku Rakuten,* the Chinese poet was surprised when a poor Japanese fisherman put his Chinese verse into an *uta* poem. Po Chü-i asked "Who can he be?" and the Fisherman replied:

A poor man and unknown. But so far as the making of *uta,* it is not only men that make them. "For among things that live there is none that has not the gift of song."

The quotation is precisely from the preface of the second national anthology *Kokinshū,* and this needs some more explanation. In the first national anthology there were verses composed by people of all walks of life. In *uta* poetry there was very little discrimination by education.[9] Every one knows it is not easy for all to be equal in the use of a language, as a distinction can be made on the basis of the abundance or poverty of one's vocabulary. As far as verbal richness is concerned, an uneducated person cannot be a match for a learned man, but in the case of *uta* poems, these verses are supposed to consist of exclusively native Japanese words; the use of words of foreign origin is discouraged. Adoption of words of foreign derivation would give rise to a "discrimination by education." As long as the vocabulary permissable for use in Japanese *uta* poems remains restricted to native Japanese words, there is little danger of verbal discrimination. Ki no Tsurayuki may have exaggerated a bit, but rich or poor, educated or uneducated, Japanese are equal before *uta* poems.

From this discussion, which was first advanced by Prof. Watanobe Shōichi of the Sophia University, Tokyo, and which became the topic of controversy between Prof. Roy Miller of the University of Washington, Seattle, and myself in the summer 1981 issue of the *Journal of Japanese Studies,* one definition of what a Japanese is becomes easy. A person can be identified as a Japanese if he writes an *uta* poem. This sense still somewhat remains within us. In 1974, there was an American-born Japanese lady living in Oregon whose *uta* poem was chosen for the traditional *uta* contest held annually before the Emperor. We thought of her as a real Japanese regardless of her citizenship. In fact, she was invited to meet the Emperor. Also among those whose poems were selected was a blind person, and everybody is of the opinion that there is no discrimination by sex or wealth.

In the Nō play *Haku Rakuten,* the *uta*'s superiority is supposed to be proved when the wind from the dancing sleeves of the native gods blows the Chinese ship back to China. The Chorus sings a song in praise of the Emperor which might show that the Emperor and *uta* were the conditions for the self-identification of the Japanese. I quote the final phrase:

The God is wondrous, and thou, our Prince
   (Emperor),
Mayest thou rule for many, many years
   Our Land Inviolate!

This song, as well as the phrase, "And the land of Reeds and Rushes / Ten thousand years our land inviolate!", which the god recites when he begins to dance, is quite similar to the verse of the Japanese national anthem. Although the national anthem was selected in the middle of the nineteenth century, the person who chose it among many old songs, exactly discerned the age-old aspirations of the Japanese nation.

Reading the Nō play *Haku Rakuten* after having seen a series of episodes that show how the Japanese wished Po Chü-i to come, one is tempted to smile wryly, for the play shows so plainly the contradictory psychology of the Japanese intellectual confronting an advanced, great nation—China.

As I have already mentioned, Po himself knew of the existence of Japan and that his poems were read there, but he cannot have had any intention to go abroad. The Japanese, however, desired so earnestly that Po would visit Japan that they once even dreamed of it. However, when the influence of Chinese culture became very strong and the Japanese began to feel uneasy about their cultural independence, they made Po visit Japan, held a contest with him to triumph over him, and eventually drove him back to China with the divine wind—all in their imagination. It is like a weak child who fights with himself and thinks he has won; yet, in spite of such childishness, this play is interesting, for it shows the psychological effects of cultural conflict.

The French Canadians who do not like to use English, the Flemish Belgians who revolt against the French imperialism of the Walloons, and many people of Southeast Asia who are obliged to speak the language of their former colonial masters all must have experienced the same sort of feeling. When we look back in the history of Western Europe, we find many examples of the same nature. The early expression of Italian national self-identification is found in Dante's use of vernacular language; the French began to talk about l'esprit gaulois in the sixteenth century when Joachim du Bellay wrote the defense and illustration of the French language. This was a nationalist movement more than two centuries before the French Revolution. What is interesting about Dante, Joachim du Bellany, and Ki no Tsurayuki is that they were all poets. Scientists, philosophers, and diplomats could express themselves in Latin or written Chinese, but to express the innermost poetic feeling, the most convenient vehicle is the mother tongue. This is a well known fact. We are *not* always aware, though, of the following phenomenon:—in cases of mixed languages such as Japanese, English, or German, some poets tend to use words of native origin. For example, Nietzsche, when he wrote *Thus Spake Zarathustra,* used words of exclusively Germanic origin. That is why the language in *Zarathustra* is as powerful as an orchestra's performance. Anglophone Canadian children learn by heart "In Flanders field the poppies blow" when the

Remembrance Day approaches. While listening to it, I got the impression that John MacCrae's poem contains only one or two words of Latin origin: "cross" is the one. Although originally borrowed, "cross" has been so perfectly assimilated into English that few will doubt its being "native."

This instinctive inclination of the German and the British to use Germanic or Anglo-Saxon words in expressing sentiments while relying on borrowings of Latin-Romance origin when it comes to descriptions of intellectual matters is an exact parallel to the Japanese situation.

The difference is that in Japan there are millions of people who write poetry in *uta* form. I am not very sure of the number, but about 50,000 poems are sent to the Imperial poetry contest every year. Professional poets select them, but selected poems written by housewives, businessmen, farmers, and others are generally far superior to those composed by the professional poets themselves or by the members of the Imperial family. In the art of *uta* or *haiku* poetry, Japanese are very democratic people. Every newspaper has its page of *uta* and *haiku* poetry, even the communist party paper.

Now if we look back at the Nō play *Haku Rakuten,* we see some other expressions which are associated with Japanese nationalism. In the play Japan is protected by Shintō gods and by the divine wind. This is a mythological station of the historical events surrounding abortive Mongol attempts to invade Japan in the thirteenth century. The Japanese withstood the attacks with the help of typhoons. Hence the expression "divine wind" is in Japanese *kamikaze.* These Mongol invasions were the only serious foreign incursions the Japanese experienced before the twentieth century. As is well known, when the situation in World War II became unfavorable in the fall of 1944, the Japanese called on the same imagery in deploying thousands of *kamikaze* attack planes.

Among the world's big nations, Japan was the most isolated and the latest-comer in the society of nations. The physical isolation of Japanese archipelago from its nearest Asian neighbors is a very important factor in the shaping of the Japanese nation. Japan was ideally semi-detached in the sense that it was able to introduce the products of Chinese civilization without being politically dominated. Great Britian's contact with the Eurasian continent has been much more complicated. The Japanese could remain outside power struggles among continental empires, and Japanese governments never tried to divide and rule the continental Chinese, at last not before the twentieth century. Dover strait, which is 23 miles wide, is easy to cross, but Tsushima strait is 120 miles wide and impossible for anyone to swim across. It was quite understandable that many Japanese intellectuals were pro-Chinese in past centuries because the Japanese were practically never threatened by expansions of the Chinese empire. This pro-China sentiment is still very powerful among the Japanese, and Chou En-lai utilized it remarkably well when he tried to normalize the Sino-Japanese relations.

There are scholars who argue that Japan could modernize rather rapidly thanks to her earlier experiences; having already had experiences of borrowing selectively from Chinese civilization, Japan could introduce easily reforms inspired from the West. That explanation seems to be true to a certain extent. I would like to show an example in the field of modern literature. One of the greats of the Meiji literature is Mori Ōgai. He went to study in Germany in the 1880s. After coming back to Tokyo, Ōgai wrote short stories of surprising modernity. In one of them entitled "Fumitsukai" (A Messenger) the action took place in Saxony near Dresden. Ōgai made a remarkable description of a piano concert. Western music was something quite new to the ears of the Japanese. Until the appearance of Ozawa Seiji in the 1960s the Japanese did not believe in their musical talent. In the Meiji period according to a diary left by a German professor Japanese students of the Tokyo Music Academy were not at all enthusiastic about learning Western music. That was the general situation in the latter half of the nineteenth century. However the scene of a piano concert described by Ōgai was so passionately beautiful that everyone believed that the author had described the scene as he had seen it or as he had heard it in Germany. The truth is that Ōgai applied very skillfully some expressions he had found in a poem by Po Chü-i. Those who are familiar with Po Chü-i's poetical works know that one of his masterpieces is not about piano but about lute. Ōgai applied the expressions originally used by the Chinese poet for a lute performance to describe Western music or more exactly the psychological state of a young German girl who passionately played the piano. The episode is somehow indicative. It confirms the impression we have of the Japanese students of the last century: they studied European culture with the same diligence with which they had studied Chinese classics before. The generation of Mori Ōgai and Natsume Sōseki were soundly bi-cultural compared to later generations. After they had passed away, apart from very few exceptions, the Japanese did not pay much attention to Chinese classics as an essential part of their general culture. It is perhaps easier for today's Japanese to read English translations of Po Chü-i than to read original Chinese texts. The situation is rather sad but the tendency is inevitable.

What should not be overlooked, though, is the fact that the Japanese, like many other peoples, have borrowed foreign ideas when it made sense to do so. Moreover, from time to time, Japan became less eager to introduce foreign ideas. There were even nationalistic reactions, as we have seen in the case of the Nō play *Haku Rakutan*. I have to say something about the self-conscious cultural nationalistic movement which occurred in Japan in the eighteenth century. At that time, Confucianism was the official ideology of the shogunal government, and Chinese studies prospered in isolated Japan. At the same time, though, Japanese scholars began to study Japanese mythology and early anthologies of *uta* poems, as well as the *Tale of Genji*. Among the so-called National Scholars, Motoori Norinaga (1730-1801) was the greatest of the philologists. He wrote commentaries on the *Kojiki* compiled one thousand years earlier. Webster's definition of "nationalism" fits Motoori well: it reads in part "loyalty and devotion to a nation, especially an attitude, feeling or belief characterized by a sense of national consciousness, an exaltation of one nation above others, and an emphasis on loyalty to and the promotion of culture and interests of one nation." In 1977 a book was written on Motoori Norinaga by a Japanese critic, Kobayashi Hideo, which got many favorable book reviews and was almost unanimously chosen as the best book of the year. It is symbolic that the book that got such high marks is about the National Scholar Motoori. Japanese are again becoming more and more confident in their traditional values and in their native system of behavior. After the "second opening of Japan" following World War II, Japan is now entering the phase of using imported ideas in a more "Japanese" way, incorporating them into the existing culture.

I should say something about Chinese nationalism. Nationalism was lacking in China. The reason is very simple: China was the world itself. The Chinese for many centuries did not take the "barbarians" outside Chinese influence very seriously. China was a self-sustained world economically, politically, and culturally. There was no psychological reason for the Chinese of pre-modern times to be nationalists, except under Mongol domination.

However, Chinese students became nationalists when they came to Japan around the turn of the century. Thousands of Chinese students who came to Japan wanted to rebuild their country, wanted to modernize China. But the Meiji Japan which they considered as the model of modernized nations turned out to be an imperialistic power. It must have been a very painful experience for the Chinese students in Japan to be despised by the Japanese whom they had considered Eastern barbarians. Japan became a hotbed of Chinese revolutionaries; Chou En-lai was one of those students who came to study in Japan.

Before ending, I would like to relate an episode which deals with the end of Japan's nationalistic venture in World War II. The episode is also about the suggestive power of Po Chu-i's verse.

The Japanese Admiralty building had been burnt down in an air raid in May 1945. Later, Navy Minister Yonai was on duty in a big air raid shelter at the site of the office. In the beginning of June, Admiral Yamanashi visited the Navy Minister. Yamanashi Katsunoshin was senior to Yonai Mitsumasa; he had served as the Vice-Minister of the Navy at the time of the London conference of 1930. (For his efforts to conclude the disarmament treaty, he was later expelled from the Navy). During the war the retired admiral was the principal of the Peers College. When the old Yamanashi said he was anxious about the Navy Minister's high blood pressure, Navy Minister Yonai said: "Well, I can't take care of myself, now that even the Admiralty office is burnt down!" Then Yamanashi suddenly changed the topic: "Have you ever read Po Chü-i's poem? I'm now studying him, and have found a nice poem:

> The prairie fires never burn it up;
> The spring wind blows it into life again.

"No matter how much you worry about, you can do nothing at the moment. The grass in the burnt fields will grow again when the spring wind blows. Yonai, didn't Po say a wonderful thing?" And Yamanashi went off.

Admiral Yamanashi was giving a hint: "Don't hesitate to make peace now. Japan in defeat surely looks like burnt fields, but the grass will grow in the fields," That was Yamanashi's suggestion which Yonai followed.

> Thick, thick the grass grows in the fields;
> Every year it withers, and springs anew.
> The prairie fires never burn it up;
> The spring wind blows it into life again.[10]

When I recite this poem by Po Chü-i, I clearly remember the vast burnt fields of Tokyo in 1945. After the fiasco militaristic adventures of the ultra-nationalistic Japanese Empire of the 1940s, Japanese efforts were shifted to the field of economic recovery. To those Japanese who saw the burnt fields of Tokyo or of Hiroshima, this verse of Po Chü-i still makes a strong impression.

Notes

[1] Arthur Waley: *The Life and Times of Po Chü-i* (London: George Allen & Unwin, 1949.)

[2] The original Japanese version, more detailed, is in Hirakawa: *Yōkyoku no shi to seiyō no shi* (Tokyo: Asahi Shimbun-sha, 1975).

[3] Translation by Ivan Morris in *The Pillow Book of Sei Shōnagon*, 2 vols. (Columbia University Press, 1967).

[4] Translation by Ivan Morris, in *op. cit.*

[5] Translation by Arthur Waley in *The Tale of Genji* (George Allen & Unwin, 1957), p. 889. As the phrase "leaning on his pillow" is lacking in Waley's translation, I added it in the quotation.

[6] The Empty Gate means Buddhism.

[7] The episode and the two poems are translated by Arthur Waley in *The Life and Times of Po Chü-i*, pp. 197-98.

[8] The following excerpts of "Haku Rakuten" are from Arthur Waley's *Nō Plays of Japan*, (London: George Allen & Unwin, 1921). I made a slight modification: instead of "we venture on the sport of making *uta*," I inserted the line "we feast our hearts on making *uta*-poetry," as this is an important difference in attitude toward poetry.

[9] I owe this argument to Professor Watanable Shōichi's article "On the Japanese Language." The English translation of Watanabe's article appeared in *Japan Echo*, 1, No. 2, (1974).

[10] Translation by Arthur Waley in *The Life and Times of Po Chü-i*, p. 13.

FURTHER READING

Biography

Feifel, Eugene. "Biography of Po Chü-i: Annotated Translation from *Chüan* 166 of the *Hsin T'ang-shu*." *Monumenta Serica* 17 (1958): 255-311.
   Translates the *Ssu-pu ts'ung-k'an* edition of *Chiu T'ang-shu*, which explores Po Chü-i's poetry, prose, and political writing, and compares the biographical information of the *Chiu T'ang-shu* with the *Hsin T'ang-shu*.

Waley, Arthur. *The Life and Times of Po Chü-i*. London: George Allen & Unwin Ltd., 1949, 237 p.
   Covers Po Chü-i's historical and political context in addition to the autobiographical elements of his poetry.

Criticism

Feifel, Eugene. *Po Chü-i as a Censor: His Memorials Presented to Emperor Hsien-Tsung during the Years 808-810*. The Hague: Mouton & Co., 1961, 244 p.
   Excerpts and explains Po Chü-i's political opinions written during his time as an imperial censor.

Lattimore, David. "Allusion and T'ang Poetry." In *Perspectives on the T'ang*, edited by Arthur F. Wright and Denis Twitchett, pp. 405-39. New Haven: Yale University Press, 1973.

Explores the political and literary allusions of T'ang poetry, including Po Chü-i's "Everlasting Remorse," in its historical context.

Lin Wen-Yüeh. "*The Collected Work* of Po Chü-i and the Literary Circle of the Heian Period." *Tamkang Review* 2, No. 1 (April 1971): 129-41.

Charts the transmission of Po Chü-i's *Works* into Japan and its influence on the writings of the Heian period, particularly *Senzai Kaku*, *Kudai Waka*, and *The Tale of Genji*.

CLASSICAL
AND MEDIEVAL
LITERATURE
CRITICISM

INDEXES

Literary Criticism Series
Cumulative Author Index

Literary Criticism Series
Cumulative Topic Index

CMLC Cumulative Nationality Index

CMLC Cumulative Title Index

CMLC Cumulative Critic Index

How to Use This Index

The main references

Calvino, Italo
1923-1985.....CLC 5, 8, 11, 22, 33, 39,
73; SSC 3

list all author entries in the following Gale Literary Criticism series:

BLC = *Black Literature Criticism*
CLC = *Contemporary Literary Criticism*
CLR = *Children's Literature Review*
CMLC = *Classical and Medieval Literature Criticism*
DA = *DISCovering Authors*
DC = *Drama Criticism*
HLC = *Hispanic Literature Criticism*
LC = *Literature Criticism from 1400 to 1800*
NCLC = *Nineteenth-Century Literature Criticism*
PC = *Poetry Criticism*
SSC = *Short Story Criticism*
TCLC = *Twentieth-Century Literary Criticism*
WLC = *World Literature Criticism, 1500 to the Present*

The cross-references

See also CANR 23; CA 85-88;
obituary CA 116

list all author entries in the following Gale biographical and literary sources:

AAYA = *Authors & Artists for Young Adults*
AITN = *Authors in the News*
BEST = *Bestsellers*
BW = *Black Writers*
CA = *Contemporary Authors*
CAAS = *Contemporary Authors Autobiography Series*
CABS = *Contemporary Authors Bibliographical Series*
CANR = *Contemporary Authors New Revision Series*
CAP = *Contemporary Authors Permanent Series*
CDALB = *Concise Dictionary of American Literary Biography*
CDBLB = *Concise Dictionary of British Literary Biography*
DLB = *Dictionary of Literary Biography*
DLBD = *Dictionary of Literary Biography Documentary Series*
DLBY = *Dictionary of Literary Biography Yearbook*
HW = *Hispanic Writers*
JRDA = *Junior DISCovering Authors*
MAICYA = *Major Authors and Illustrators for Children and Young Adults*
MTCW = *Major 20th-Century Writers*
NNAL = *Native North American Literature*
SAAS = *Something about the Author Autobiography Series*
SATA = *Something about the Author*
YABC = *Yesterday's Authors of Books for Children*

Literary Criticism Series
Cumulative Author Index

Abasiyanik, Sait Faik 1906-1954
See Sait Faik
See also CA 123

Abbey, Edward 1927-1989 ...... **CLC 36, 59**
See also CA 45-48; 128; CANR 2, 41

Abbott, Lee K(ittredge) 1947- ...... **CLC 48**
See also CA 124; CANR 51; DLB 130

Abe, Kobo
1924-1993 .... **CLC 8, 22, 53, 81;**
DAM NOV
See also CA 65-68; 140; CANR 24, 60;
DLB 182; MTCW

Abelard, Peter c. 1079-c. 1142 ... **CMLC 11**
See also DLB 115

Abell, Kjeld 1901-1961............ **CLC 15**
See also CA 111

Abish, Walter 1931-.............. **CLC 22**
See also CA 101; CANR 37; DLB 130

Abrahams, Peter (Henry) 1919- ..... **CLC 4**
See also BW 1; CA 57-60; CANR 26;
DLB 117; MTCW

Abrams, M(eyer) H(oward) 1912-... **CLC 24**
See also CA 57-60; CANR 13, 33; DLB 67

Abse, Dannie
1923- ... **CLC 7, 29; DAB; DAM POET**
See also CA 53-56; CAAS 1; CANR 4, 46;
DLB 27

Achebe, (Albert) Chinua(lumogu)
1930- ..... **CLC 1, 3, 5, 7, 11, 26, 51, 75;**
BLC; DA; DAB; DAC; DAM MST,
MULT, NOV; WLC
See also AAYA 15; BW 2; CA 1-4R;
CANR 6, 26, 47; CLR 20; DLB 117;
MAICYA; MTCW; SATA 40;
SATA-Brief 38

Acker, Kathy 1948- .... **CLC 45**
See also CA 117; 122; CANR 55

Ackroyd, Peter 1949-.......... **CLC 34, 52**
See also CA 123; 127; CANR 51; DLB 155;
INT 127

Acorn, Milton 1923-......... **CLC 15; DAC**
See also CA 103; DLB 53; INT 103

Adamov, Arthur
1908-1970 .... **CLC 4, 25; DAM DRAM**
See also CA 17-18; 25-28R; CAP 2; MTCW

Adams, Alice (Boyd)
1926- .... **CLC 6, 13, 46; SSC 24**
See also CA 81-84; CANR 26, 53;
DLBY 86; INT CANR-26; MTCW

Adams, Andy 1859-1935.......... **TCLC 56**
See also YABC 1

Adams, Douglas (Noel)
1952- .... **CLC 27, 60; DAM POP**
See also AAYA 4; BEST 89:3; CA 106;
CANR 34; DLBY 83; JRDA

Adams, Francis 1862-1893....... **NCLC 33**

Adams, Henry (Brooks)
1838-1918 ...... **TCLC 4, 52; DA; DAB;**
DAC; DAM MST
See also CA 104; 133; DLB 12, 47

Adams, Richard (George)
1920- .... **CLC 4, 5, 18; DAM NOV**
See also AAYA 16; AITN 1, 2; CA 49-52;
CANR 3, 35; CLR 20; JRDA; MAICYA;
MTCW; SATA 7, 69

Adamson, Joy(-Friederike Victoria)
1910-1980 .... **CLC 17**
See also CA 69-72; 93-96; CANR 22;
MTCW; SATA 11; SATA-Obit 22

Adcock, Fleur 1934-............. **CLC 41**
See also CA 25-28R; CAAS 23; CANR 11,
34; DLB 40

Addams, Charles (Samuel)
1912-1988 .... **CLC 30**
See also CA 61-64; 126; CANR 12

Addison, Joseph 1672-1719 .... **LC 18**
See also CDBLB 1660-1789; DLB 101

Adler, Alfred (F.) 1870-1937 ...... **TCLC 61**
See also CA 119; 159

Adler, C(arole) S(chwerdtfeger)
1932- .... **CLC 35**
See also AAYA 4; CA 89-92; CANR 19,
40; JRDA; MAICYA; SAAS 15;
SATA 26, 63

Adler, Renata 1938-............ **CLC 8, 31**
See also CA 49-52; CANR 5, 22, 52;
MTCW

Ady, Endre 1877-1919 .... **TCLC 11**
See also CA 107

Aeschylus
525B.C.-456B.C........ **CMLC 11; DA;**
DAB; DAC; DAM DRAM, MST; WLCS
See also DLB 176

Africa, Ben
See Bosman, Herman Charles

Afton, Effie
See Harper, Frances Ellen Watkins

Agapida, Fray Antonio
See Irving, Washington

Agee, James (Rufus)
1909-1955 .... **TCLC 1, 19; DAM NOV**
See also AITN 1; CA 108; 148;
CDALB 1941-1968; DLB 2, 26, 152

Aghill, Gordon
See Silverberg, Robert

Agnon, S(hmuel) Y(osef Halevi)
1888-1970 .... **CLC 4, 8, 14; SSC 29**
See also CA 17-18; 25-28R; CANR 60;
CAP 2; MTCW

Agrippa von Nettesheim, Henry Cornelius
1486-1535 .... **LC 27**

Aherne, Owen
See Cassill, R(onald) V(erlin)

Ai 1947-................... **CLC 4, 14, 69**
See also CA 85-88; CAAS 13; DLB 120

Aickman, Robert (Fordyce)
1914-1981 .... **CLC 57**
See also CA 5-8R; CANR 3

Aiken, Conrad (Potter)
1889-1973 .... **CLC 1, 3, 5, 10, 52;**
DAM NOV, POET; SSC 9
See also CA 5-8R; 45-48; CANR 4, 60;
CDALB 1929-1941; DLB 9, 45, 102;
MTCW; SATA 3, 30

Aiken, Joan (Delano) 1924-........ **CLC 35**
See also AAYA 1; CA 9-12R; CANR 4, 23,
34; CLR 1, 19; DLB 161; JRDA;
MAICYA; MTCW; SAAS 1; SATA 2,
30, 73

Ainsworth, William Harrison
1805-1882 .... **NCLC 13**
See also DLB 21; SATA 24

Aitmatov, Chingiz (Torekulovich)
1928- .... **CLC 71**
See also CA 103; CANR 38; MTCW;
SATA 56

Akers, Floyd
See Baum, L(yman) Frank

Akhmadulina, Bella Akhatovna
1937- .... **CLC 53; DAM POET**
See also CA 65-68

Akhmatova, Anna
1888-1966 .... **CLC 11, 25, 64;**
DAM POET; PC 2
See also CA 19-20; 25-28R; CANR 35;
CAP 1; MTCW

Aksakov, Sergei Timofeyvich
1791-1859 .... **NCLC 2**

Aksenov, Vassily
See Aksyonov, Vassily (Pavlovich)

Aksyonov, Vassily (Pavlovich)
1932- .... **CLC 22, 37, 101**
See also CA 53-56; CANR 12, 48

Akutagawa, Ryunosuke
1892-1927 .... **TCLC 16**
See also CA 117; 154

Alain 1868-1951 .... **TCLC 41**

Alain-Fournier.................... **TCLC 6**
See also Fournier, Henri Alban
See also DLB 65

Alarcon, Pedro Antonio de
1833-1891 .... **NCLC 1**

Alas (y Urena), Leopoldo (Enrique Garcia)
1852-1901 .... **TCLC 29**
See also CA 113; 131; HW

Albee, Edward (Franklin III)
1928- . . . . . . CLC 1, 2, 3, 5, 9, 11, 13, 25,
53, 86; DA; DAB; DAC; DAM DRAM,
MST; WLC
See also AITN 1; CA 5-8R; CABS 3;
CANR 8, 54; CDALB 1941-1968; DLB 7;
INT CANR-8; MTCW

Alberti, Rafael 1902- . . . . CLC 7
See also CA 85-88; DLB 108

Albert the Great 1200(?)-1280. . . . CMLC 16
See also DLB 115

Alcala-Galiano, Juan Valera y
See Valera y Alcala-Galiano, Juan

Alcott, Amos Bronson 1799-1888 . . NCLC 1
See also DLB 1

Alcott, Louisa May
1832-1888 . . . . . NCLC 6, 58; DA; DAB;
DAC; DAM MST, NOV; SSC 27; WLC
See also AAYA 20; CDALB 1865-1917;
CLR 1, 38; DLB 1, 42, 79; DLBD 14;
JRDA; MAICYA; YABC 1

Aldanov, M. A.
See Aldanov, Mark (Alexandrovich)

Aldanov, Mark (Alexandrovich)
1886(?)-1957 . . . . TCLC 23
See also CA 118

Aldington, Richard 1892-1962 . . . . . . CLC 49
See also CA 85-88; CANR 45; DLB 20, 36,
100, 149

Aldiss, Brian W(ilson)
1925- . . . . CLC 5, 14, 40; DAM NOV
See also CA 5-8R; CAAS 2; CANR 5, 28;
DLB 14; MTCW; SATA 34

Alegria, Claribel
1924- . . . . CLC 75; DAM MULT
See also CA 131; CAAS 15; DLB 145; HW

Alegria, Fernando 1918- . . . . CLC 57
See also CA 9-12R; CANR 5, 32; HW

Aleichem, Sholom . . . . TCLC 1, 35
See also Rabinovitch, Sholem

Aleixandre, Vicente
1898-1984 . . . . CLC 9, 36; DAM POET;
PC 15
See also CA 85-88; 114; CANR 26;
DLB 108; HW; MTCW

Alepoudelis, Odysseus
See Elytis, Odysseus

Aleshkovsky, Joseph 1929-
See Aleshkovsky, Yuz
See also CA 121; 128

Aleshkovsky, Yuz . . . . CLC 44
See also Aleshkovsky, Joseph

Alexander, Lloyd (Chudley) 1924- . . CLC 35
See also AAYA 1; CA 1-4R; CANR 1, 24,
38, 55; CLR 1, 5; DLB 52; JRDA;
MAICYA; MTCW; SAAS 19; SATA 3,
49, 81

Alexie, Sherman (Joseph, Jr.)
1966- . . . . CLC 96; DAM MULT
See also CA 138; DLB 175; NNAL

Alfau, Felipe 1902- . . . . CLC 66
See also CA 137

Alger, Horatio, Jr. 1832-1899 . . . . . NCLC 8
See also DLB 42; SATA 16

Algren, Nelson 1909-1981 . . . . CLC 4, 10, 33
See also CA 13-16R; 103; CANR 20, 61;
CDALB 1941-1968; DLB 9; DLBY 81,
82; MTCW

Ali, Ahmed 1910- . . . . CLC 69
See also CA 25-28R; CANR 15, 34

Alighieri, Dante
1265-1321 . . . . CMLC 3, 18; WLCS

Allan, John B.
See Westlake, Donald E(dwin)

Allan, Sidney
See Hartmann, Sadakichi

Allan, Sydney
See Hartmann, Sadakichi

Allen, Edward 1948- . . . . CLC 59

Allen, Paula Gunn
1939- . . . . CLC 84; DAM MULT
See also CA 112; 143; DLB 175; NNAL

Allen, Roland
See Ayckbourn, Alan

Allen, Sarah A.
See Hopkins, Pauline Elizabeth

Allen, Sidney H.
See Hartmann, Sadakichi

Allen, Woody
1935- . . . . CLC 16, 52; DAM POP
See also AAYA 10; CA 33-36R; CANR 27,
38; DLB 44; MTCW

Allende, Isabel
1942- . . . . CLC 39, 57, 97; DAM MULT,
NOV; HLC; WLCS
See also AAYA 18; CA 125; 130;
CANR 51; DLB 145; HW; INT 130;
MTCW

Alleyn, Ellen
See Rossetti, Christina (Georgina)

Allingham, Margery (Louise)
1904-1966 . . . . CLC 19
See also CA 5-8R; 25-28R; CANR 4, 58;
DLB 77; MTCW

Allingham, William 1824-1889 . . . NCLC 25
See also DLB 35

Allison, Dorothy E. 1949- . . . . CLC 78
See also CA 140

Allston, Washington 1779-1843. . . . NCLC 2
See also DLB 1

Almedingen, E. M. . . . . CLC 12
See also Almedingen, Martha Edith von
See also SATA 3

Almedingen, Martha Edith von 1898-1971
See Almedingen, E. M.
See also CA 1-4R; CANR 1

Almqvist, Carl Jonas Love
1793-1866 . . . . NCLC 42

Alonso, Damaso 1898-1990 . . . . CLC 14
See also CA 110; 131; 130; DLB 108; HW

Alov
See Gogol, Nikolai (Vasilyevich)

Alta 1942- . . . . CLC 19
See also CA 57-60

Alter, Robert B(ernard) 1935- . . . . . . CLC 34
See also CA 49-52; CANR 1, 47

Alther, Lisa 1944- . . . . CLC 7, 41
See also CA 65-68; CANR 12, 30, 51;
MTCW

Altman, Robert 1925- . . . . CLC 16
See also CA 73-76; CANR 43

Alvarez, A(lfred) 1929- . . . . CLC 5, 13
See also CA 1-4R; CANR 3, 33; DLB 14,
40

Alvarez, Alejandro Rodriguez 1903-1965
See Casona, Alejandro
See also CA 131; 93-96; HW

Alvarez, Julia 1950- . . . . CLC 93
See also CA 147

Alvaro, Corrado 1896-1956 . . . . TCLC 60

Amado, Jorge
1912- . . . . CLC 13, 40; DAM MULT,
NOV; HLC
See also CA 77-80; CANR 35; DLB 113;
MTCW

Ambler, Eric 1909- . . . . CLC 4, 6, 9
See also CA 9-12R; CANR 7, 38; DLB 77;
MTCW

Amichai, Yehuda 1924- . . . . . . CLC 9, 22, 57
See also CA 85-88; CANR 46, 60; MTCW

Amichai, Yehudah
See Amichai, Yehuda

Amiel, Henri Frederic 1821-1881 . . NCLC 4

Amis, Kingsley (William)
1922-1995 . . . . . CLC 1, 2, 3, 5, 8, 13, 40,
44; DA; DAB; DAC; DAM MST, NOV
See also AITN 2; CA 9-12R; 150; CANR 8,
28, 54; CDBLB 1945-1960; DLB 15, 27,
100, 139; DLBY 96; INT CANR-8;
MTCW

Amis, Martin (Louis)
1949- . . . . CLC 4, 9, 38, 62, 101
See also BEST 90:3; CA 65-68; CANR 8,
27, 54; DLB 14; INT CANR-27

Ammons, A(rchie) R(andolph)
1926- . . . . CLC 2, 3, 5, 8, 9, 25, 57;
DAM POET; PC 16
See also AITN 1; CA 9-12R; CANR 6, 36,
51; DLB 5, 165; MTCW

Amo, Tauraatua i
See Adams, Henry (Brooks)

Amr ibn Bahr al-Jahiz
c. 780-c. 869 . . . . CMLC 25

Anand, Mulk Raj
1905- . . . . CLC 23, 93; DAM NOV
See also CA 65-68; CANR 32; MTCW

Anatol
See Schnitzler, Arthur

Anaximander
c. 610B.C.-c. 546B.C. . . . . CMLC 22

Anaya, Rudolfo A(lfonso)
1937- . . . . CLC 23; DAM MULT, NOV;
HLC
See also AAYA 20; CA 45-48; CAAS 4;
CANR 1, 32, 51; DLB 82; HW 1; MTCW

Andersen, Hans Christian
1805-1875 . . . . NCLC 7; DA; DAB;
DAC; DAM MST, POP; SSC 6; WLC
See also CLR 6; MAICYA; YABC 1

Arnold, Matthew
1822-1888 ..... NCLC 6, 29; DA; DAB;
DAC; DAM MST, POET; PC 5; WLC
See also CDBLB 1832-1890; DLB 32, 57

Arnold, Thomas 1795-1842 ...... NCLC 18
See also DLB 55

Arnow, Harriette (Louisa) Simpson
1908-1986 .... CLC 2, 7, 18
See also CA 9-12R; 118; CANR 14; DLB 6;
MTCW; SATA 42; SATA-Obit 47

Arp, Hans
See Arp, Jean

Arp, Jean 1887-1966............... CLC 5
See also CA 81-84; 25-28R; CANR 42

Arrabal
See Arrabal, Fernando

Arrabal, Fernando 1932-... CLC 2, 9, 18, 58
See also CA 9-12R; CANR 15

Arrick, Fran...................... CLC 30
See also Gaberman, Judie Angell

Artaud, Antonin (Marie Joseph)
1896-1948 ... TCLC 3, 36; DAM DRAM
See also CA 104; 149

Arthur, Ruth M(abel) 1905-1979.... CLC 12
See also CA 9-12R; 85-88; CANR 4;
SATA 7, 26

Artsybashev, Mikhail (Petrovich)
1878-1927 .... TCLC 31

Arundel, Honor (Morfydd)
1919-1973 .... CLC 17
See also CA 21-22; 41-44R; CAP 2;
CLR 35; SATA 4; SATA-Obit 24

Arzner, Dorothy 1897-1979........ CLC 98

Asch, Sholem 1880-1957 .... TCLC 3
See also CA 105

Ash, Shalom
See Asch, Sholem

Ashbery, John (Lawrence)
1927- ...... CLC 2, 3, 4, 6, 9, 13, 15, 25,
41, 77; DAM POET
See also CA 5-8R; CANR 9, 37; DLB 5,
165; DLBY 81; INT CANR-9; MTCW

Ashdown, Clifford
See Freeman, R(ichard) Austin

Ashe, Gordon
See Creasey, John

Ashton-Warner, Sylvia (Constance)
1908-1984 .... CLC 19
See also CA 69-72; 112; CANR 29; MTCW

Asimov, Isaac
1920-1992 ...... CLC 1, 3, 9, 19, 26, 76,
92; DAM POP
See also AAYA 13; BEST 90:2; CA 1-4R;
137; CANR 2, 19, 36, 60; CLR 12;
DLB 8; DLBY 92; INT CANR-19;
JRDA; MAICYA; MTCW; SATA 1, 26,
74

Assis, Joaquim Maria Machado de
See Machado de Assis, Joaquim Maria

Astley, Thea (Beatrice May)
1925- .... CLC 41
See also CA 65-68; CANR 11, 43

Aston, James
See White, T(erence) H(anbury)

Asturias, Miguel Angel
1899-1974 .... CLC 3, 8, 13;
DAM MULT, NOV; HLC
See also CA 25-28; 49-52; CANR 32;
CAP 2; DLB 113; HW; MTCW

Atares, Carlos Saura
See Saura (Atares), Carlos

Atheling, William
See Pound, Ezra (Weston Loomis)

Atheling, William, Jr.
See Blish, James (Benjamin)

Atherton, Gertrude (Franklin Horn)
1857-1948 .... TCLC 2
See also CA 104; 155; DLB 9, 78

Atherton, Lucius
See Masters, Edgar Lee

Atkins, Jack
See Harris, Mark

Atkinson, Kate.................. CLC 99

Attaway, William (Alexander)
1911-1986 .... CLC 92; BLC;
DAM MULT
See also BW 2; CA 143; DLB 76

Atticus
See Fleming, Ian (Lancaster)

Atwood, Margaret (Eleanor)
1939- ..... CLC 2, 3, 4, 8, 13, 15, 25, 44,
84; DA; DAB; DAC; DAM MST, NOV,
POET; PC 8; SSC 2; WLC
See also AAYA 12; BEST 89:2; CA 49-52;
CANR 3, 24, 33, 59; DLB 53;
INT CANR-24; MTCW; SATA 50

Aubigny, Pierre d'
See Mencken, H(enry) L(ouis)

Aubin, Penelope 1685-1731(?)........ LC 9
See also DLB 39

Auchincloss, Louis (Stanton)
1917- .... CLC 4, 6, 9, 18, 45;
DAM NOV; SSC 22
See also CA 1-4R; CANR 6, 29, 55; DLB 2;
DLBY 80; INT CANR-29; MTCW

Auden, W(ystan) H(ugh)
1907-1973 ...... CLC 1, 2, 3, 4, 6, 9, 11,
14, 43; DA; DAB; DAC; DAM DRAM,
MST, POET; PC 1; WLC
See also AAYA 18; CA 9-12R; 45-48;
CANR 5, 61; CDBLB 1914-1945;
DLB 10, 20; MTCW

Audiberti, Jacques
1900-1965 ...... CLC 38; DAM DRAM
See also CA 25-28R

Audubon, John James
1785-1851 .... NCLC 47

Auel, Jean M(arie)
1936- .... CLC 31; DAM POP
See also AAYA 7; BEST 90:4; CA 103;
CANR 21; INT CANR-21; SATA 91

Auerbach, Erich 1892-1957 .... TCLC 43
See also CA 118; 155

Augier, Emile 1820-1889 .... NCLC 31

August, John
See De Voto, Bernard (Augustine)

Augustine, St. 354-430 ...... CMLC 6; DAB

Aurelius
See Bourne, Randolph S(illiman)

Aurobindo, Sri 1872-1950 .... TCLC 63

Austen, Jane
1775-1817 ..... NCLC 1, 13, 19, 33, 51;
DA; DAB; DAC; DAM MST, NOV;
WLC
See also AAYA 19; CDBLB 1789-1832;
DLB 116

Auster, Paul 1947- .... CLC 47
See also CA 69-72; CANR 23, 52

Austin, Frank
See Faust, Frederick (Schiller)

Austin, Mary (Hunter)
1868-1934 .... TCLC 25
See also CA 109; DLB 9, 78

Autran Dourado, Waldomiro
See Dourado, (Waldomiro Freitas) Autran

Averroes 1126-1198 .... CMLC 7
See also DLB 115

Avicenna 980-1037 .... CMLC 16
See also DLB 115

Avison, Margaret
1918- .... CLC 2, 4, 97; DAC;
DAM POET
See also CA 17-20R; DLB 53; MTCW

Axton, David
See Koontz, Dean R(ay)

Ayckbourn, Alan
1939- ...... CLC 5, 8, 18, 33, 74; DAB;
DAM DRAM
See also CA 21-24R; CANR 31, 59;
DLB 13; MTCW

Aydy, Catherine
See Tennant, Emma (Christina)

Ayme, Marcel (Andre) 1902-1967... CLC 11
See also CA 89-92; CLR 25; DLB 72;
SATA 91

Ayrton, Michael 1921-1975......... CLC 7
See also CA 5-8R; 61-64; CANR 9, 21

Azorin......................... CLC 11
See also Martinez Ruiz, Jose

Azuela, Mariano
1873-1952 ..... TCLC 3; DAM MULT;
HLC
See also CA 104; 131; HW; MTCW

Baastad, Babbis Friis
See Friis-Baastad, Babbis Ellinor

Bab
See Gilbert, W(illiam) S(chwenck)

Babbis, Eleanor
See Friis-Baastad, Babbis Ellinor

Babel, Isaac
See Babel, Isaak (Emmanuilovich)

Babel, Isaak (Emmanuilovich)
1894-1941(?) ...... TCLC 2, 13; SSC 16
See also CA 104; 155

Babits, Mihaly 1883-1941 .... TCLC 14
See also CA 114

Babur 1483-1530................. LC 18

Bacchelli, Riccardo 1891-1985 ..... CLC 19
See also CA 29-32R; 117

Bach, Richard (David)
1936- ...... CLC 14; DAM NOV, POP
See also AITN 1; BEST 89:2; CA 9-12R;
CANR 18; MTCW; SATA 13

Bachman, Richard
See King, Stephen (Edwin)

Bachmann, Ingeborg 1926-1973..... CLC 69
See also CA 93-96; 45-48; DLB 85

Bacon, Francis 1561-1626 .... LC 18, 32
See also CDBLB Before 1660; DLB 151

Bacon, Roger 1214(?)-1292 ...... CMLC 14
See also DLB 115

Bacovia, George.................. TCLC 24
See also Vasiliu, Gheorghe

Badanes, Jerome 1937-........... CLC 59

Bagehot, Walter 1826-1877 ...... NCLC 10
See also DLB 55

Bagnold, Enid
1889-1981 ...... CLC 25; DAM DRAM
See also CA 5-8R; 103; CANR 5, 40;
DLB 13, 160; MAICYA; SATA 1, 25

Bagritsky, Eduard 1895-1934 ..... TCLC 60

Bagrjana, Elisaveta
See Belcheva, Elisaveta

Bagryana, Elisaveta................ CLC 10
See also Belcheva, Elisaveta
See also DLB 147

Bailey, Paul 1937-................ CLC 45
See also CA 21-24R; CANR 16, 62;
DLB 14

Baillie, Joanna 1762-1851 .... NCLC 2
See also DLB 93

Bainbridge, Beryl (Margaret)
1933-.... CLC 4, 5, 8, 10, 14, 18, 22, 62;
DAM NOV
See also CA 21-24R; CANR 24, 55;
DLB 14; MTCW

Baker, Elliott 1922-................ CLC 8
See also CA 45-48; CANR 2

Baker, Jean H. .... TCLC 3, 10
See also Russell, George William

Baker, Nicholson
1957-............. CLC 61; DAM POP
See also CA 135

Baker, Ray Stannard 1870-1946... TCLC 47
See also CA 118

Baker, Russell (Wayne) 1925-...... CLC 31
See also BEST 89:4; CA 57-60; CANR 11,
41, 59; MTCW

Bakhtin, M.
See Bakhtin, Mikhail Mikhailovich

Bakhtin, M. M.
See Bakhtin, Mikhail Mikhailovich

Bakhtin, Mikhail
See Bakhtin, Mikhail Mikhailovich

Bakhtin, Mikhail Mikhailovich
1895-1975 .... CLC 83
See also CA 128; 113

Bakshi, Ralph 1938(?)-............ CLC 26
See also CA 112; 138

Bakunin, Mikhail (Alexandrovich)
1814-1876 .... NCLC 25, 58

Baldwin, James (Arthur)
1924-1987 ...... CLC 1, 2, 3, 4, 5, 8, 13,
15, 17, 42, 50, 67, 90; BLC; DA; DAB;
DAC; DAM MST, MULT, NOV, POP;
DC 1; SSC 10; WLC
See also AAYA 4; BW 1; CA 1-4R; 124;
CABS 1; CANR 3, 24;
CDALB 1941-1968; DLB 2, 7, 33;
DLBY 87; MTCW; SATA 9;
SATA-Obit 54

Ballard, J(ames) G(raham)
1930-.... CLC 3, 6, 14, 36; DAM NOV,
POP; SSC 1
See also AAYA 3; CA 5-8R; CANR 15, 39;
DLB 14; MTCW; SATA 93

Balmont, Konstantin (Dmitriyevich)
1867-1943 .... TCLC 11
See also CA 109; 155

Balzac, Honore de
1799-1850 .... NCLC 5, 35, 53; DA;
DAB; DAC; DAM MST, NOV; SSC 5;
WLC
See also DLB 119

Bambara, Toni Cade
1939-1995 ...... CLC 19, 88; BLC; DA;
DAC; DAM MST, MULT; WLCS
See also AAYA 5; BW 2; CA 29-32R; 150;
CANR 24, 49; DLB 38; MTCW

Bamdad, A.
See Shamlu, Ahmad

Banat, D. R.
See Bradbury, Ray (Douglas)

Bancroft, Laura
See Baum, L(yman) Frank

Banim, John 1798-1842 .... NCLC 13
See also DLB 116, 158, 159

Banim, Michael 1796-1874 ...... NCLC 13
See also DLB 158, 159

Banjo, The
See Paterson, A(ndrew) B(arton)

Banks, Iain
See Banks, Iain M(enzies)

Banks, Iain M(enzies) 1954-....... CLC 34
See also CA 123; 128; CANR 61; INT 128

Banks, Lynne Reid .... CLC 23
See also Reid Banks, Lynne
See also AAYA 6

Banks, Russell 1940-.......... CLC 37, 72
See also CA 65-68; CAAS 15; CANR 19,
52; DLB 130

Banville, John 1945-.............. CLC 46
See also CA 117; 128; DLB 14; INT 128

Banville, Theodore (Faullain) de
1832-1891 .... NCLC 9

Baraka, Amiri
1934-........ CLC 1, 2, 3, 5, 10, 14, 33;
BLC; DA; DAC; DAM MST, MULT,
POET, POP; DC 6; PC 4; WLCS
See also Jones, LeRoi
See also BW 2; CA 21-24R; CABS 3;
CANR 27, 38, 61; CDALB 1941-1968;
DLB 5, 7, 16, 38; DLBD 8; MTCW

Barbauld, Anna Laetitia
1743-1825 .... NCLC 50
See also DLB 107, 109, 142, 158

Barbellion, W. N. P............... TCLC 24
See also Cummings, Bruce F(rederick)

Barbera, Jack (Vincent) 1945-...... CLC 44
See also CA 110; CANR 45

Barbey d'Aurevilly, Jules Amedee
1808-1889 .... NCLC 1; SSC 17
See also DLB 119

Barbusse, Henri 1873-1935 .... TCLC 5
See also CA 105; 154; DLB 65

Barclay, Bill
See Moorcock, Michael (John)

Barclay, William Ewert
See Moorcock, Michael (John)

Barea, Arturo 1897-1957 .... TCLC 14
See also CA 111

Barfoot, Joan 1946-.............. CLC 18
See also CA 105

Baring, Maurice 1874-1945........ TCLC 8
See also CA 105; DLB 34

Barker, Clive 1952- ... CLC 52; DAM POP
See also AAYA 10; BEST 90:3; CA 121;
129; INT 129; MTCW

Barker, George Granville
1913-1991 ..... CLC 8, 48; DAM POET
See also CA 9-12R; 135; CANR 7, 38;
DLB 20; MTCW

Barker, Harley Granville
See Granville-Barker, Harley
See also DLB 10

Barker, Howard 1946-............ CLC 37
See also CA 102; DLB 13

Barker, Pat(ricia) 1943-........ CLC 32, 94
See also CA 117; 122; CANR 50; INT 122

Barlow, Joel 1754-1812 .... NCLC 23
See also DLB 37

Barnard, Mary (Ethel) 1909-....... CLC 48
See also CA 21-22; CAP 2

Barnes, Djuna
1892-1982 ... CLC 3, 4, 8, 11, 29; SSC 3
See also CA 9-12R; 107; CANR 16, 55;
DLB 4, 9, 45; MTCW

Barnes, Julian (Patrick)
1946-................... CLC 42; DAB
See also CA 102; CANR 19, 54; DLBY 93

Barnes, Peter 1931-............. CLC 5, 56
See also CA 65-68; CAAS 12; CANR 33,
34; DLB 13; MTCW

Baroja (y Nessi), Pio
1872-1956 .... TCLC 8; HLC
See also CA 104

Baron, David
See Pinter, Harold

Baron Corvo
See Rolfe, Frederick (William Serafino
Austin Lewis Mary)

Barondess, Sue K(aufman)
1926-1977 .... CLC 8
See also Kaufman, Sue
See also CA 1-4R; 69-72; CANR 1

Baron de Teive
See Pessoa, Fernando (Antonio Nogueira)

Barres, Maurice 1862-1923 .... TCLC 47
See also DLB 123

Belitt, Ben　1911-................. **CLC 22**
See also CA 13-16R; CAAS 4; CANR 7;
DLB 5

Bell, Gertrude　1868-1926........ **TCLC 67**
See also DLB 174

Bell, James Madison
1826-1902 .... **TCLC 43; BLC;**
DAM MULT
See also BW 1; CA 122; 124; DLB 50

Bell, Madison Smartt　1957-.... **CLC 41, 102**
See also CA 111; CANR 28, 54

Bell, Marvin (Hartley)
1937- .... **CLC 8, 31; DAM POET**
See also CA 21-24R; CAAS 14; CANR 59;
DLB 5; MTCW

Bell, W. L. D.
See Mencken, H(enry) L(ouis)

Bellamy, Atwood C.
See Mencken, H(enry) L(ouis)

Bellamy, Edward　1850-1898 ...... **NCLC 4**
See also DLB 12

Bellin, Edward J.
See Kuttner, Henry

Belloc, (Joseph) Hilaire (Pierre Sebastien
Rene Swanton)
1870-1953 ... **TCLC 7, 18; DAM POET**
See also CA 106; 152; DLB 19, 100, 141,
174; YABC 1

Belloc, Joseph Peter Rene Hilaire
See Belloc, (Joseph) Hilaire (Pierre Sebastien
Rene Swanton)

Belloc, Joseph Pierre Hilaire
See Belloc, (Joseph) Hilaire (Pierre Sebastien
Rene Swanton)

Belloc, M. A.
See Lowndes, Marie Adelaide (Belloc)

Bellow, Saul
1915- .... **CLC 1, 2, 3, 6, 8, 10, 13, 15,**
25, 33, 34, 63, 79; DA; DAB; DAC;
DAM MST, NOV, POP; SSC 14; WLC
See also AITN 2; BEST 89:3; CA 5-8R;
CABS 1; CANR 29, 53;
CDALB 1941-1968; DLB 2, 28; DLBD 3;
DLBY 82; MTCW

Belser, Reimond Karel Maria de　1929-
See Ruyslinck, Ward
See also CA 152

Bely, Andrey .... **TCLC 7; PC 11**
See also Bugayev, Boris Nikolayevich

Benary, Margot
See Benary-Isbert, Margot

Benary-Isbert, Margot　1889-1979... **CLC 12**
See also CA 5-8R; 89-92; CANR 4;
CLR 12; MAICYA; SATA 2;
SATA-Obit 21

Benavente (y Martinez), Jacinto
1866-1954 ..... **TCLC 3; DAM DRAM,**
MULT
See also CA 106; 131; HW; MTCW

Benchley, Peter (Bradford)
1940- ..... **CLC 4, 8; DAM NOV, POP**
See also AAYA 14; AITN 2; CA 17-20R;
CANR 12, 35; MTCW; SATA 3, 89

Benchley, Robert (Charles)
1889-1945 .... **TCLC 1, 55**
See also CA 105; 153; DLB 11

Benda, Julien　1867-1956 .... **TCLC 60**
See also CA 120; 154

Benedict, Ruth (Fulton)
1887-1948 .... **TCLC 60**
See also CA 158

Benedict of Nursia, Saint
c. 480-c. 543 .... **CMLC 25**

Benedikt, Michael　1935- .... **CLC 4, 14**
See also CA 13-16R; CANR 7; DLB 5

Benet, Juan　1927-................. **CLC 28**
See also CA 143

Benet, Stephen Vincent
1898-1943 ...... **TCLC 7; DAM POET;**
SSC 10
See also CA 104; 152; DLB 4, 48, 102;
YABC 1

Benet, William Rose
1886-1950 ...... **TCLC 28; DAM POET**
See also CA 118; 152; DLB 45

Benford, Gregory (Albert)　1941-.... **CLC 52**
See also CA 69-72; CAAS 27; CANR 12,
24, 49; DLBY 82

Bengtsson, Frans (Gunnar)
1894-1954 .... **TCLC 48**

Benjamin, David
See Slavitt, David R(ytman)

Benjamin, Lois
See Gould, Lois

Benjamin, Walter　1892-1940..... **TCLC 39**

Benn, Gottfried　1886-1956........ **TCLC 3**
See also CA 106; 153; DLB 56

Bennett, Alan
1934- ... **CLC 45, 77; DAB; DAM MST**
See also CA 103; CANR 35, 55; MTCW

Bennett, (Enoch) Arnold
1867-1931 .... **TCLC 5, 20**
See also CA 106; 155; CDBLB 1890-1914;
DLB 10, 34, 98, 135

Bennett, Elizabeth
See Mitchell, Margaret (Munnerlyn)

Bennett, George Harold　1930-
See Bennett, Hal
See also BW 1; CA 97-100

Bennett, Hal .... **CLC 5**
See also Bennett, George Harold
See also DLB 33

Bennett, Jay　1912-................ **CLC 35**
See also AAYA 10; CA 69-72; CANR 11,
42; JRDA; SAAS 4; SATA 41, 87;
SATA-Brief 27

Bennett, Louise (Simone)
1919- ..... **CLC 28; BLC; DAM MULT**
See also BW 2; CA 151; DLB 117

Benson, E(dward) F(rederic)
1867-1940 .... **TCLC 27**
See also CA 114; 157; DLB 135, 153

Benson, Jackson J.　1930-......... **CLC 34**
See also CA 25-28R; DLB 111

Benson, Sally　1900-1972 .... **CLC 17**
See also CA 19-20; 37-40R; CAP 1;
SATA 1, 35; SATA-Obit 27

Benson, Stella　1892-1933........ **TCLC 17**
See also CA 117; 155; DLB 36, 162

Bentham, Jeremy　1748-1832 ..... **NCLC 38**
See also DLB 107, 158

Bentley, E(dmund) C(lerihew)
1875-1956 .... **TCLC 12**
See also CA 108; DLB 70

Bentley, Eric (Russell)　1916-....... **CLC 24**
See also CA 5-8R; CANR 6; INT CANR-6

Beranger, Pierre Jean de
1780-1857 .... **NCLC 34**

Berdyaev, Nicolas
See Berdyaev, Nikolai (Aleksandrovich)

Berdyaev, Nikolai (Aleksandrovich)
1874-1948 .... **TCLC 67**
See also CA 120; 157

Berdyayev, Nikolai (Aleksandrovich)
See Berdyaev, Nikolai (Aleksandrovich)

Berendt, John (Lawrence)　1939-.... **CLC 86**
See also CA 146

Berger, Colonel
See Malraux, (Georges-)Andre

Berger, John (Peter)　1926- ...... **CLC 2, 19**
See also CA 81-84; CANR 51; DLB 14

Berger, Melvin H.　1927- .... **CLC 12**
See also CA 5-8R; CANR 4; CLR 32;
SAAS 2; SATA 5, 88

Berger, Thomas (Louis)
1924- .... **CLC 3, 5, 8, 11, 18, 38;**
DAM NOV
See also CA 1-4R; CANR 5, 28, 51; DLB 2;
DLBY 80; INT CANR-28; MTCW

Bergman, (Ernst) Ingmar
1918- .... **CLC 16, 72**
See also CA 81-84; CANR 33

Bergson, Henri　1859-1941........ **TCLC 32**

Bergstein, Eleanor　1938- .... **CLC 4**
See also CA 53-56; CANR 5

Berkoff, Steven　1937-............. **CLC 56**
See also CA 104

Bermant, Chaim (Icyk)　1929- ...... **CLC 40**
See also CA 57-60; CANR 6, 31, 57

Bern, Victoria
See Fisher, M(ary) F(rances) K(ennedy)

Bernanos, (Paul Louis) Georges
1888-1948 .... **TCLC 3**
See also CA 104; 130; DLB 72

Bernard, April　1956- .... **CLC 59**
See also CA 131

Berne, Victoria
See Fisher, M(ary) F(rances) K(ennedy)

Bernhard, Thomas
1931-1989 .... **CLC 3, 32, 61**
See also CA 85-88; 127; CANR 32, 57;
DLB 85, 124; MTCW

Bernhardt, Sarah (Henriette Rosine)
1844-1923 .... **TCLC 75**
See also CA 157

Berriault, Gina　1926-............. **CLC 54**
See also CA 116; 129; DLB 130

Berrigan, Daniel　1921-............. **CLC 4**
See also CA 33-36R; CAAS 1; CANR 11,
43; DLB 5

Blok, Alexander (Alexandrovich)
1880-1921 . . . . TCLC 5
See also CA 104

Blom, Jan
See Breytenbach, Breyten

Bloom, Harold 1930- . . . . CLC 24, 103
See also CA 13-16R; CANR 39; DLB 67

Bloomfield, Aurelius
See Bourne, Randolph S(illiman)

Blount, Roy (Alton), Jr. 1941- . . . . . CLC 38
See also CA 53-56; CANR 10, 28, 61;
INT CANR-28; MTCW

Bloy, Leon 1846-1917. . . . . TCLC 22
See also CA 121; DLB 123

Blume, Judy (Sussman)
1938- . . . CLC 12, 30; DAM NOV, POP
See also AAYA 3; CA 29-32R; CANR 13,
37; CLR 2, 15; DLB 52; JRDA;
MAICYA; MTCW; SATA 2, 31, 79

Blunden, Edmund (Charles)
1896-1974 . . . . CLC 2, 56
See also CA 17-18; 45-48; CANR 54;
CAP 2; DLB 20, 100, 155; MTCW

Bly, Robert (Elwood)
1926- . . . . CLC 1, 2, 5, 10, 15, 38;
DAM POET
See also CA 5-8R; CANR 41; DLB 5;
MTCW

Boas, Franz 1858-1942. . . . . TCLC 56
See also CA 115

Bobette
See Simenon, Georges (Jacques Christian)

Boccaccio, Giovanni
1313-1375 . . . . CMLC 13; SSC 10

Bochco, Steven 1943- . . . . CLC 35
See also AAYA 11; CA 124; 138

Bodenheim, Maxwell 1892-1954 . . . TCLC 44
See also CA 110; DLB 9, 45

Bodker, Cecil 1927- . . . . CLC 21
See also CA 73-76; CANR 13, 44; CLR 23;
MAICYA; SATA 14

Boell, Heinrich (Theodor)
1917-1985 . . . . CLC 2, 3, 6, 9, 11, 15, 27,
32, 72; DA; DAB; DAC; DAM MST,
NOV; SSC 23; WLC
See also CA 21-24R; 116; CANR 24;
DLB 69; DLBY 85; MTCW

Boerne, Alfred
See Doeblin, Alfred

Boethius 480(?)-524(?) . . . . CMLC 15
See also DLB 115

Bogan, Louise
1897-1970 . . . . CLC 4, 39, 46, 93;
DAM POET; PC 12
See also CA 73-76; 25-28R; CANR 33;
DLB 45, 169; MTCW

Bogarde, Dirk . . . . CLC 19
See also Van Den Bogarde, Derek Jules
Gaspard Ulric Niven
See also DLB 14

Bogosian, Eric 1953- . . . . CLC 45
See also CA 138

Bograd, Larry 1953- . . . . CLC 35
See also CA 93-96; CANR 57; SAAS 21;
SATA 33, 89

Boiardo, Matteo Maria 1441-1494 . . . . LC 6

Boileau-Despreaux, Nicolas
1636-1711 . . . . LC 3

Bojer, Johan 1872-1959. . . . . TCLC 64

Boland, Eavan (Aisling)
1944- . . . . CLC 40, 67; DAM POET
See also CA 143; CANR 61; DLB 40

Bolt, Lee
See Faust, Frederick (Schiller)

Bolt, Robert (Oxton)
1924-1995 . . . . . . CLC 14; DAM DRAM
See also CA 17-20R; 147; CANR 35;
DLB 13; MTCW

Bombet, Louis-Alexandre-Cesar
See Stendhal

Bomkauf
See Kaufman, Bob (Garnell)

Bonaventura. . . . . NCLC 35
See also DLB 90

Bond, Edward
1934- . . . CLC 4, 6, 13, 23; DAM DRAM
See also CA 25-28R; CANR 38; DLB 13;
MTCW

Bonham, Frank 1914-1989. . . . . CLC 12
See also AAYA 1; CA 9-12R; CANR 4, 36;
JRDA; MAICYA; SAAS 3; SATA 1, 49;
SATA-Obit 62

Bonnefoy, Yves
1923- . . . . . . CLC 9, 15, 58; DAM MST,
POET
See also CA 85-88; CANR 33; MTCW

Bontemps, Arna(ud Wendell)
1902-1973 . . . . CLC 1, 18; BLC;
DAM MULT, NOV, POET
See also BW 1; CA 1-4R; 41-44R; CANR 4,
35; CLR 6; DLB 48, 51; JRDA;
MAICYA; MTCW; SATA 2, 44;
SATA-Obit 24

Booth, Martin 1944- . . . . CLC 13
See also CA 93-96; CAAS 2

Booth, Philip 1925-. . . . . CLC 23
See also CA 5-8R; CANR 5; DLBY 82

Booth, Wayne C(layson) 1921- . . . . . CLC 24
See also CA 1-4R; CAAS 5; CANR 3, 43;
DLB 67

Borchert, Wolfgang 1921-1947 . . . . . TCLC 5
See also CA 104; DLB 69, 124

Borel, Petrus 1809-1859. . . . . NCLC 41

Borges, Jorge Luis
1899-1986 . . . CLC 1, 2, 3, 4, 6, 8, 9, 10,
13, 19, 44, 48, 83; DA; DAB; DAC;
DAM MST, MULT; HLC; SSC 4; WLC
See also AAYA 19; CA 21-24R; CANR 19,
33; DLB 113; DLBY 86; HW; MTCW

Borowski, Tadeusz 1922-1951 . . . . . . TCLC 9
See also CA 106; 154

Borrow, George (Henry)
1803-1881 . . . . NCLC 9
See also DLB 21, 55, 166

Bosman, Herman Charles
1905-1951 . . . . TCLC 49
See also Malan, Herman
See also CA 160

Bosschere, Jean de 1878(?)-1953. . . TCLC 19
See also CA 115

Boswell, James
1740-1795 . . . . . . LC 4; DA; DAB; DAC;
DAM MST; WLC
See also CDBLB 1660-1789; DLB 104, 142

Bottoms, David 1949-. . . . . CLC 53
See also CA 105; CANR 22; DLB 120;
DLBY 83

Boucicault, Dion 1820-1890. . . . . . NCLC 41

Boucolon, Maryse 1937(?)-
See Conde, Maryse
See also CA 110; CANR 30, 53

Bourget, Paul (Charles Joseph)
1852-1935 . . . . TCLC 12
See also CA 107; DLB 123

Bourjaily, Vance (Nye) 1922- . . . . CLC 8, 62
See also CA 1-4R; CAAS 1; CANR 2;
DLB 2, 143

Bourne, Randolph S(illiman)
1886-1918 . . . . TCLC 16
See also CA 117; 155; DLB 63

Bova, Ben(jamin William) 1932-. . . . CLC 45
See also AAYA 16; CA 5-8R; CAAS 18;
CANR 11, 56; CLR 3; DLBY 81;
INT CANR-11; MAICYA; MTCW;
SATA 6, 68

Bowen, Elizabeth (Dorothea Cole)
1899-1973 . . . . . . CLC 1, 3, 6, 11, 15, 22;
DAM NOV; SSC 3, 28
See also CA 17-18; 41-44R; CANR 35;
CAP 2; CDBLB 1945-1960; DLB 15, 162;
MTCW

Bowering, George 1935-. . . . . CLC 15, 47
See also CA 21-24R; CAAS 16; CANR 10;
DLB 53

Bowering, Marilyn R(uthe) 1949-. . . CLC 32
See also CA 101; CANR 49

Bowers, Edgar 1924- . . . . CLC 9
See also CA 5-8R; CANR 24; DLB 5

Bowie, David . . . . CLC 17
See also Jones, David Robert

Bowles, Jane (Sydney)
1917-1973 . . . . CLC 3, 68
See also CA 19-20; 41-44R; CAP 2

Bowles, Paul (Frederick)
1910- . . . . CLC 1, 2, 19, 53; SSC 3
See also CA 1-4R; CAAS 1; CANR 1, 19,
50; DLB 5, 6; MTCW

Box, Edgar
See Vidal, Gore

Boyd, Nancy
See Millay, Edna St. Vincent

Boyd, William 1952-. . . . . CLC 28, 53, 70
See also CA 114; 120; CANR 51

Boyle, Kay
1902-1992 . . . . . CLC 1, 5, 19, 58; SSC 5
See also CA 13-16R; 140; CAAS 1;
CANR 29, 61; DLB 4, 9, 48, 86;
DLBY 93; MTCW

Boyle, Mark
See Kienzle, William X(avier)

Boyle, Patrick 1905-1982. . . . . CLC 19
See also CA 127

Boyle, T. C. 1948-
See Boyle, T(homas) Coraghessan

Boyle, T(homas) Coraghessan
1948- . . . . . **CLC 36, 55, 90; DAM POP;**
SSC 16
See also BEST 90:4; CA 120; CANR 44;
DLBY 86

Boz
See Dickens, Charles (John Huffam)

Brackenridge, Hugh Henry
1748-1816 . . . . **NCLC 7**
See also DLB 11, 37

Bradbury, Edward P.
See Moorcock, Michael (John)

Bradbury, Malcolm (Stanley)
1932- . . . . **CLC 32, 61; DAM NOV**
See also CA 1-4R; CANR 1, 33; DLB 14;
MTCW

Bradbury, Ray (Douglas)
1920- . . . . . **CLC 1, 3, 10, 15, 42, 98; DA;**
DAB; DAC; DAM MST, NOV, POP;
SSC 29; WLC
See also AAYA 15; AITN 1, 2; CA 1-4R;
CANR 2, 30; CDALB 1968-1988; DLB 2,
8; MTCW; SATA 11, 64

Bradford, Gamaliel 1863-1932. . . . . **TCLC 36**
See also CA 160; DLB 17

Bradley, David (Henry, Jr.)
1950- . . . . . **CLC 23; BLC; DAM MULT**
See also BW 1; CA 104; CANR 26; DLB 33

Bradley, John Ed(mund, Jr.)
1958- . . . . **CLC 55**
See also CA 139

Bradley, Marion Zimmer
1930- . . . . **CLC 30; DAM POP**
See also AAYA 9; CA 57-60; CAAS 10;
CANR 7, 31, 51; DLB 8; MTCW;
SATA 90

Bradstreet, Anne
1612(?)-1672 . . . . . . **LC 4, 30; DA; DAC;**
DAM MST, POET; PC 10
See also CDALB 1640-1865; DLB 24

Brady, Joan 1939- . . . . **CLC 86**
See also CA 141

Bragg, Melvyn 1939- . . . . **CLC 10**
See also BEST 89:3; CA 57-60; CANR 10,
48; DLB 14

Braine, John (Gerard)
1922-1986 . . . . **CLC 1, 3, 41**
See also CA 1-4R; 120; CANR 1, 33;
CDBLB 1945-1960; DLB 15; DLBY 86;
MTCW

Bramah, Ernest 1868-1942. . . . . . . **TCLC 72**
See also CA 156; DLB 70

Brammer, William 1930(?)-1978 . . . . **CLC 31**
See also CA 77-80

Brancati, Vitaliano 1907-1954. . . . . **TCLC 12**
See also CA 109

Brancato, Robin F(idler) 1936- . . . . . **CLC 35**
See also AAYA 9; CA 69-72; CANR 11,
45; CLR 32; JRDA; SAAS 9; SATA 23

Brand, Max
See Faust, Frederick (Schiller)

Brand, Millen 1906-1980. . . . . **CLC 7**
See also CA 21-24R; 97-100

Branden, Barbara . . . . **CLC 44**
See also CA 148

Brandes, Georg (Morris Cohen)
1842-1927 . . . . **TCLC 10**
See also CA 105

Brandys, Kazimierz 1916- . . . . **CLC 62**

Branley, Franklyn M(ansfield)
1915- . . . . **CLC 21**
See also CA 33-36R; CANR 14, 39;
CLR 13; MAICYA; SAAS 16; SATA 4,
68

Brathwaite, Edward Kamau
1930- . . . . **CLC 11; DAM POET**
See also BW 2; CA 25-28R; CANR 11, 26,
47; DLB 125

Brautigan, Richard (Gary)
1935-1984 . . . . **CLC 1, 3, 5, 9, 12, 34, 42;**
DAM NOV
See also CA 53-56; 113; CANR 34; DLB 2,
5; DLBY 80, 84; MTCW; SATA 56

Brave Bird, Mary 1953-
See Crow Dog, Mary (Ellen)
See also NNAL

Braverman, Kate 1950- . . . . **CLC 67**
See also CA 89-92

Brecht, (Eugen) Bertolt (Friedrich)
1898-1956 . . . . . . **TCLC 1, 6, 13, 35; DA;**
DAB; DAC; DAM DRAM, MST; DC 3;
WLC
See also CA 104; 133; CANR 62; DLB 56,
124; MTCW

Brecht, Eugen Berthold Friedrich
See Brecht, (Eugen) Bertolt (Friedrich)

Bremer, Fredrika 1801-1865 . . . . . **NCLC 11**

Brennan, Christopher John
1870-1932 . . . . **TCLC 17**
See also CA 117

Brennan, Maeve 1917- . . . . **CLC 5**
See also CA 81-84

Brentano, Clemens (Maria)
1778-1842 . . . . **NCLC 1**
See also DLB 90

Brent of Bin Bin
See Franklin, (Stella Maraia Sarah) Miles

Brenton, Howard 1942- . . . . **CLC 31**
See also CA 69-72; CANR 33; DLB 13;
MTCW

Breslin, James 1930-
See Breslin, Jimmy
See also CA 73-76; CANR 31; DAM NOV;
MTCW

Breslin, Jimmy . . . . **CLC 4, 43**
See also Breslin, James
See also AITN 1

Bresson, Robert 1901- . . . . **CLC 16**
See also CA 110; CANR 49

Breton, Andre
1896-1966 . . . . . **CLC 2, 9, 15, 54; PC 15**
See also CA 19-20; 25-28R; CANR 40, 60;
CAP 2; DLB 65; MTCW

Breytenbach, Breyten
1939(?)- . . . . . . **CLC 23, 37; DAM POET**
See also CA 113; 129; CANR 61

Bridgers, Sue Ellen 1942- . . . . **CLC 26**
See also AAYA 8; CA 65-68; CANR 11,
36; CLR 18; DLB 52; JRDA; MAICYA;
SAAS 1; SATA 22, 90

Bridges, Robert (Seymour)
1844-1930 . . . . **TCLC 1; DAM POET**
See also CA 104; 152; CDBLB 1890-1914;
DLB 19, 98

Bridie, James. . . . . **TCLC 3**
See also Mavor, Osborne Henry
See also DLB 10

Brin, David 1950- . . . . **CLC 34**
See also AAYA 21; CA 102; CANR 24;
INT CANR-24; SATA 65

Brink, Andre (Philippus)
1935- . . . . **CLC 18, 36**
See also CA 104; CANR 39, 62; INT 103;
MTCW

Brinsmead, H(esba) F(ay) 1922- . . . . **CLC 21**
See also CA 21-24R; CANR 10; CLR 47;
MAICYA; SAAS 5; SATA 18, 78

Brittain, Vera (Mary)
1893(?)-1970 . . . . **CLC 23**
See also CA 13-16; 25-28R; CANR 58;
CAP 1; MTCW

Broch, Hermann 1886-1951. . . . . . . **TCLC 20**
See also CA 117; DLB 85, 124

Brock, Rose
See Hansen, Joseph

Brodkey, Harold (Roy) 1930-1996 . . **CLC 56**
See also CA 111; 151; DLB 130

Brodsky, Iosif Alexandrovich 1940-1996
See Brodsky, Joseph
See also AITN 1; CA 41-44R; 151;
CANR 37; DAM POET; MTCW

Brodsky, Joseph
1940-1996 . . **CLC 4, 6, 13, 36, 100; PC 9**
See also Brodsky, Iosif Alexandrovich

Brodsky, Michael (Mark) 1948- . . . . . **CLC 19**
See also CA 102; CANR 18, 41, 58

Bromell, Henry 1947-. . . . . **CLC 5**
See also CA 53-56; CANR 9

Bromfield, Louis (Brucker)
1896-1956 . . . . **TCLC 11**
See also CA 107; 155; DLB 4, 9, 86

Broner, E(sther) M(asserman)
1930- . . . . **CLC 19**
See also CA 17-20R; CANR 8, 25; DLB 28

Bronk, William 1918-. . . . . **CLC 10**
See also CA 89-92; CANR 23; DLB 165

Bronstein, Lev Davidovich
See Trotsky, Leon

Bronte, Anne 1820-1849. . . . . **NCLC 4**
See also DLB 21

Bronte, Charlotte
1816-1855 . . . . . **NCLC 3, 8, 33, 58; DA;**
DAB; DAC; DAM MST, NOV; WLC
See also AAYA 17; CDBLB 1832-1890;
DLB 21, 159

Bronte, Emily (Jane)
1818-1848 . . . . **NCLC 16, 35; DA; DAB;**
DAC; DAM MST, NOV, POET; PC 8;
WLC
See also AAYA 17; CDBLB 1832-1890;
DLB 21, 32

Brooke, Frances 1724-1789. . . . . **LC 6**
See also DLB 39, 99

Brooke, Henry 1703(?)-1783 . . . . **LC 1**
See also DLB 39

Brooke, Rupert (Chawner)
1887-1915 .... **TCLC 2, 7; DA; DAB;**
DAC; DAM MST, POET; WLC
See also CA 104; 132; CANR 61;
CDBLB 1914-1945; DLB 19; MTCW

Brooke-Haven, P.
See Wodehouse, P(elham) G(renville)

Brooke-Rose, Christine 1926(?)- .... **CLC 40**
See also CA 13-16R; CANR 58; DLB 14

Brookner, Anita
1928- .... **CLC 32, 34, 51; DAB;**
DAM POP
See also CA 114; 120; CANR 37, 56;
DLBY 87; MTCW

Brooks, Cleanth 1906-1994 ..... **CLC 24, 86**
See also CA 17-20R; 145; CANR 33, 35;
DLB 63; DLBY 94; INT CANR-35;
MTCW

Brooks, George
See Baum, L(yman) Frank

Brooks, Gwendolyn
1917- ...... **CLC 1, 2, 4, 5, 15, 49; BLC;**
DA; DAC; DAM MST, MULT, POET;
PC 7; WLC
See also AAYA 20; AITN 1; BW 2;
CA 1-4R; CANR 1, 27, 52;
CDALB 1941-1968; CLR 27; DLB 5, 76,
165; MTCW; SATA 6

Brooks, Mel.............. **CLC 12**
See also Kaminsky, Melvin
See also AAYA 13; DLB 26

Brooks, Peter 1938-.............. **CLC 34**
See also CA 45-48; CANR 1

Brooks, Van Wyck 1886-1963...... **CLC 29**
See also CA 1-4R; CANR 6; DLB 45, 63,
103

Brophy, Brigid (Antonia)
1929-1995 .... **CLC 6, 11, 29**
See also CA 5-8R; 149; CAAS 4; CANR 25,
53; DLB 14; MTCW

Brosman, Catharine Savage 1934-.... **CLC 9**
See also CA 61-64; CANR 21, 46

Brother Antoninus
See Everson, William (Oliver)

Broughton, T(homas) Alan 1936- ... **CLC 19**
See also CA 45-48; CANR 2, 23, 48

Broumas, Olga 1949-.......... **CLC 10, 73**
See also CA 85-88; CANR 20

Brown, Alan 1951-............... **CLC 99**

Brown, Charles Brockden
1771-1810 .... **NCLC 22**
See also CDALB 1640-1865; DLB 37, 59,
73

Brown, Christy 1932-1981......... **CLC 63**
See also CA 105; 104; DLB 14

Brown, Claude
1937- ..... **CLC 30; BLC; DAM MULT**
See also AAYA 7; BW 1; CA 73-76

Brown, Dee (Alexander)
1908- .... **CLC 18, 47; DAM POP**
See also CA 13-16R; CAAS 6; CANR 11,
45, 60; DLBY 80; MTCW; SATA 5

Brown, George
See Wertmueller, Lina

Brown, George Douglas
1869-1902 .... **TCLC 28**

Brown, George Mackay
1921-1996 .... **CLC 5, 48, 100**
See also CA 21-24R; 151; CAAS 6;
CANR 12, 37, 62; DLB 14, 27, 139;
MTCW; SATA 35

Brown, (William) Larry 1951-...... **CLC 73**
See also CA 130; 134; INT 133

Brown, Moses
See Barrett, William (Christopher)

Brown, Rita Mae
1944- ..... **CLC 18, 43, 79; DAM NOV,**
POP
See also CA 45-48; CANR 2, 11, 35, 62;
INT CANR-11; MTCW

Brown, Roderick (Langmere) Haig-
See Haig-Brown, Roderick (Langmere)

Brown, Rosellen 1939-............ **CLC 32**
See also CA 77-80; CAAS 10; CANR 14, 44

Brown, Sterling Allen
1901-1989 .... **CLC 1, 23, 59; BLC;**
DAM MULT, POET
See also BW 1; CA 85-88; 127; CANR 26;
DLB 48, 51, 63; MTCW

Brown, Will
See Ainsworth, William Harrison

Brown, William Wells
1813-1884 .... **NCLC 2; BLC;**
DAM MULT; DC 1
See also DLB 3, 50

Browne, (Clyde) Jackson 1948(?)-... **CLC 21**
See also CA 120

Browning, Elizabeth Barrett
1806-1861 .... **NCLC 1, 16, 61; DA;**
DAB; DAC; DAM MST, POET; PC 6;
WLC
See also CDBLB 1832-1890; DLB 32

Browning, Robert
1812-1889 .... **NCLC 19; DA; DAB;**
DAC; DAM MST, POET; PC 2; WLCS
See also CDBLB 1832-1890; DLB 32, 163;
YABC 1

Browning, Tod 1882-1962 .... **CLC 16**
See also CA 141; 117

Brownson, Orestes (Augustus)
1803-1876 .... **NCLC 50**

Bruccoli, Matthew J(oseph) 1931- .. **CLC 34**
See also CA 9-12R; CANR 7; DLB 103

Bruce, Lenny.................... **CLC 21**
See also Schneider, Leonard Alfred

Bruin, John
See Brutus, Dennis

Brulard, Henri
See Stendhal

Brulls, Christian
See Simenon, Georges (Jacques Christian)

Brunner, John (Kilian Houston)
1934-1995 ...... **CLC 8, 10; DAM POP**
See also CA 1-4R; 149; CAAS 8; CANR 2,
37; MTCW

Bruno, Giordano 1548-1600........ **LC 27**

Brutus, Dennis
1924- ..... **CLC 43; BLC; DAM MULT,**
POET
See also BW 2; CA 49-52; CAAS 14;
CANR 2, 27, 42; DLB 117

Bryan, C(ourtlandt) D(ixon) B(arnes)
1936- .... **CLC 29**
See also CA 73-76; CANR 13;
INT CANR-13

Bryan, Michael
See Moore, Brian

Bryant, William Cullen
1794-1878 ..... **NCLC 6, 46; DA; DAB;**
DAC; DAM MST, POET
See also CDALB 1640-1865; DLB 3, 43, 59

Bryusov, Valery Yakovlevich
1873-1924 .... **TCLC 10**
See also CA 107; 155

Buchan, John
1875-1940 .... **TCLC 41; DAB;**
DAM POP
See also CA 108; 145; DLB 34, 70, 156;
YABC 2

Buchanan, George 1506-1582 .... **LC 4**

Buchheim, Lothar-Guenther 1918- ... **CLC 6**
See also CA 85-88

Buchner, (Karl) Georg
1813-1837 .... **NCLC 26**

Buchwald, Art(hur) 1925-.......... **CLC 33**
See also AITN 1; CA 5-8R; CANR 21;
MTCW; SATA 10

Buck, Pearl S(ydenstricker)
1892-1973 .... **CLC 7, 11, 18; DA; DAB;**
DAC; DAM MST, NOV
See also AITN 1; CA 1-4R; 41-44R;
CANR 1, 34; DLB 9, 102; MTCW;
SATA 1, 25

Buckler, Ernest
1908-1984 .. **CLC 13; DAC; DAM MST**
See also CA 11-12; 114; CAP 1; DLB 68;
SATA 47

Buckley, Vincent (Thomas)
1925-1988 .... **CLC 57**
See also CA 101

Buckley, William F(rank), Jr.
1925- .... **CLC 7, 18, 37; DAM POP**
See also AITN 1; CA 1-4R; CANR 1, 24,
53; DLB 137; DLBY 80; INT CANR-24;
MTCW

Buechner, (Carl) Frederick
1926- ...... **CLC 2, 4, 6, 9; DAM NOV**
See also CA 13-16R; CANR 11, 39;
DLBY 80; INT CANR-11; MTCW

Buell, John (Edward) 1927-........ **CLC 10**
See also CA 1-4R; DLB 53

Buero Vallejo, Antonio 1916- ... **CLC 15, 46**
See also CA 106; CANR 24, 49; HW;
MTCW

Bufalino, Gesualdo 1920(?)-........ **CLC 74**

Bugayev, Boris Nikolayevich 1880-1934
See Bely, Andrey
See also CA 104

Calhoun, John Caldwell
  1782-1850 .... **NCLC 15**
  See also DLB 3

Calisher, Hortense
  1911- ..... **CLC 2, 4, 8, 38; DAM NOV;**
  SSC 15
  See also CA 1-4R; CANR 1, 22; DLB 2;
  INT CANR-22; MTCW

Callaghan, Morley Edward
  1903-1990 ..... **CLC 3, 14, 41, 65; DAC;**
  DAM MST
  See also CA 9-12R; 132; CANR 33;
  DLB 68; MTCW

Callimachus
  c. 305B.C.-c. 240B.C. .... **CMLC 18**
  See also DLB 176

Calvin, John   1509-1564 .... **LC 37**

Calvino, Italo
  1923-1985 ..... **CLC 5, 8, 11, 22, 33, 39,**
  73; DAM NOV; SSC 3
  See also CA 85-88; 116; CANR 23, 61;
  MTCW

Cameron, Carey 1952- .... **CLC 59**
  See also CA 135

Cameron, Peter 1959- .... **CLC 44**
  See also CA 125; CANR 50

Campana, Dino 1885-1932 .... **TCLC 20**
  See also CA 117; DLB 114

Campanella, Tommaso 1568-1639 .... **LC 32**

Campbell, John W(ood, Jr.)
  1910-1971 .... **CLC 32**
  See also CA 21-22; 29-32R; CANR 34;
  CAP 2; DLB 8; MTCW

Campbell, Joseph 1904-1987 .... **CLC 69**
  See also AAYA 3; BEST 89:2; CA 1-4R;
  124; CANR 3, 28, 61; MTCW

Campbell, Maria 1940- .... **CLC 85; DAC**
  See also CA 102; CANR 54; NNAL

Campbell, (John) Ramsey
  1946- .... **CLC 42; SSC 19**
  See also CA 57-60; CANR 7; INT CANR-7

Campbell, (Ignatius) Roy (Dunnachie)
  1901-1957 .... **TCLC 5**
  See also CA 104; 155; DLB 20

Campbell, Thomas 1777-1844 .... **NCLC 19**
  See also DLB 93; 144

Campbell, Wilfred .... **TCLC 9**
  See also Campbell, William

Campbell, William 1858(?)-1918
  See Campbell, Wilfred
  See also CA 106; DLB 92

Campion, Jane .... **CLC 95**
  See also CA 138

Campos, Alvaro de
  See Pessoa, Fernando (Antonio Nogueira)

Camus, Albert
  1913-1960 .... **CLC 1, 2, 4, 9, 11, 14, 32,**
  63, 69; DA; DAB; DAC; DAM DRAM,
  MST, NOV; DC 2; SSC 9; WLC
  See also CA 89-92; DLB 72; MTCW

Canby, Vincent 1924- .... **CLC 13**
  See also CA 81-84

Cancale
  See Desnos, Robert

Canetti, Elias
  1905-1994 .... **CLC 3, 14, 25, 75, 86**
  See also CA 21-24R; 146; CANR 23, 61;
  DLB 85, 124; MTCW

Canin, Ethan 1960- .... **CLC 55**
  See also CA 131; 135

Cannon, Curt
  See Hunter, Evan

Cape, Judith
  See Page, P(atricia) K(athleen)

Capek, Karel
  1890-1938 ...... **TCLC 6, 37; DA; DAB;**
  DAC; DAM DRAM, MST, NOV; DC 1;
  WLC
  See also CA 104; 140

Capote, Truman
  1924-1984 ..... **CLC 1, 3, 8, 13, 19, 34,**
  38, 58; DA; DAB; DAC; DAM MST,
  NOV, POP; SSC 2; WLC
  See also CA 5-8R; 113; CANR 18, 62;
  CDALB 1941-1968; DLB 2; DLBY 80,
  84; MTCW; SATA 91

Capra, Frank 1897-1991 .... **CLC 16**
  See also CA 61-64; 135

Caputo, Philip 1941- .... **CLC 32**
  See also CA 73-76; CANR 40

Card, Orson Scott
  1951- ...... **CLC 44, 47, 50; DAM POP**
  See also AAYA 11; CA 102; CANR 27, 47;
  INT CANR-27; MTCW; SATA 83

Cardenal, Ernesto
  1925- .... **CLC 31; DAM MULT,**
  POET; HLC
  See also CA 49-52; CANR 2, 32; HW;
  MTCW

Cardozo, Benjamin N(athan)
  1870-1938 .... **TCLC 65**
  See also CA 117

Carducci, Giosue 1835-1907 .... **TCLC 32**

Carew, Thomas 1595(?)-1640 .... **LC 13**
  See also DLB 126

Carey, Ernestine Gilbreth 1908- .... **CLC 17**
  See also CA 5-8R; SATA 2

Carey, Peter 1943- .... **CLC 40, 55, 96**
  See also CA 123; 127; CANR 53; INT 127;
  MTCW; SATA 94

Carleton, William 1794-1869 ...... **NCLC 3**
  See also DLB 159

Carlisle, Henry (Coffin) 1926- ...... **CLC 33**
  See also CA 13-16R; CANR 15

Carlsen, Chris
  See Holdstock, Robert P.

Carlson, Ron(ald F.) 1947- .... **CLC 54**
  See also CA 105; CANR 27

Carlyle, Thomas
  1795-1881 .... **NCLC 22; DA; DAB;**
  DAC; DAM MST
  See also CDBLB 1789-1832; DLB 55; 144

Carman, (William) Bliss
  1861-1929 .... **TCLC 7; DAC**
  See also CA 104; 152; DLB 92

Carnegie, Dale 1888-1955 .... **TCLC 53**

Carossa, Hans 1878-1956 .... **TCLC 48**
  See also DLB 66

Carpenter, Don(ald Richard)
  1931-1995 .... **CLC 41**
  See also CA 45-48; 149; CANR 1

Carpentier (y Valmont), Alejo
  1904-1980 .... **CLC 8, 11, 38;**
  DAM MULT; HLC
  See also CA 65-68; 97-100; CANR 11;
  DLB 113; HW

Carr, Caleb 1955(?)- .... **CLC 86**
  See also CA 147

Carr, Emily 1871-1945 .... **TCLC 32**
  See also CA 159; DLB 68

Carr, John Dickson 1906-1977 ...... **CLC 3**
  See also Fairbairn, Roger
  See also CA 49-52; 69-72; CANR 3, 33, 60;
  MTCW

Carr, Philippa
  See Hibbert, Eleanor Alice Burford

Carr, Virginia Spencer 1929- .... **CLC 34**
  See also CA 61-64; DLB 111

Carrere, Emmanuel 1957- .... **CLC 89**

Carrier, Roch
  1937- ... **CLC 13, 78; DAC; DAM MST**
  See also CA 130; CANR 61; DLB 53

Carroll, James P. 1943(?)- .... **CLC 38**
  See also CA 81-84

Carroll, Jim 1951- .... **CLC 35**
  See also AAYA 17; CA 45-48; CANR 42

Carroll, Lewis .... **NCLC 2, 53; PC 18; WLC**
  See also Dodgson, Charles Lutwidge
  See also CDBLB 1832-1890; CLR 2, 18;
  DLB 18, 163, 178; JRDA

Carroll, Paul Vincent 1900-1968 .... **CLC 10**
  See also CA 9-12R; 25-28R; DLB 10

Carruth, Hayden
  1921- ...... **CLC 4, 7, 10, 18, 84; PC 10**
  See also CA 9-12R; CANR 4, 38, 59;
  DLB 5, 165; INT CANR-4; MTCW;
  SATA 47

Carson, Rachel Louise
  1907-1964 .... **CLC 71; DAM POP**
  See also CA 77-80; CANR 35; MTCW;
  SATA 23

Carter, Angela (Olive)
  1940-1992 ...... **CLC 5, 41, 76; SSC 13**
  See also CA 53-56; 136; CANR 12, 36, 61;
  DLB 14; MTCW; SATA 66;
  SATA-Obit 70

Carter, Nick
  See Smith, Martin Cruz

Carver, Raymond
  1938-1988 .... **CLC 22, 36, 53, 55;**
  DAM NOV; SSC 8
  See also CA 33-36R; 126; CANR 17, 34, 61;
  DLB 130; DLBY 84, 88; MTCW

Cary, Elizabeth, Lady Falkland
  1585-1639 .... **LC 30**

Cary, (Arthur) Joyce (Lunel)
  1888-1957 .... **TCLC 1, 29**
  See also CA 104; CDBLB 1914-1945;
  DLB 15, 100

Casanova de Seingalt, Giovanni Jacopo
  1725-1798 .... **LC 13**

Casares, Adolfo Bioy
  See Bioy Casares, Adolfo

Comfort, Alex(ander)
1920- .... **CLC 7; DAM POP**
See also CA 1-4R; CANR 1, 45

Comfort, Montgomery
See Campbell, (John) Ramsey

Compton-Burnett, I(vy)
1884(?)-1969 ...... **CLC 1, 3, 10, 15, 34;
DAM NOV**
See also CA 1-4R; 25-28R; CANR 4;
DLB 36; MTCW

Comstock, Anthony 1844-1915 .... **TCLC 13**
See also CA 110

Comte, Auguste 1798-1857 .... **NCLC 54**

Conan Doyle, Arthur
See Doyle, Arthur Conan

Conde, Maryse
1937- ...... **CLC 52, 92; DAM MULT**
See also Boucolon, Maryse
See also BW 2

Condillac, Etienne Bonnot de
1714-1780 .... **LC 26**

Condon, Richard (Thomas)
1915-1996 ..... **CLC 4, 6, 8, 10, 45, 100;
DAM NOV**
See also BEST 90:3; CA 1-4R; 151;
CAAS 1; CANR 2, 23; INT CANR-23;
MTCW

Confucius
551B.C.-479B.C. .... **CMLC 19; DA;
DAB; DAC; DAM MST; WLCS**

Congreve, William
1670-1729 .... **LC 5, 21; DA; DAB;
DAC; DAM DRAM, MST, POET;
DC 2; WLC**
See also CDBLB 1660-1789; DLB 39, 84

Connell, Evan S(helby), Jr.
1924- ...... **CLC 4, 6, 45; DAM NOV**
See also AAYA 7; CA 1-4R; CAAS 2;
CANR 2, 39; DLB 2; DLBY 81; MTCW

Connelly, Marc(us Cook)
1890-1980 .... **CLC 7**
See also CA 85-88; 102; CANR 30; DLB 7;
DLBY 80; SATA-Obit 25

Connor, Ralph .... **TCLC 31**
See also Gordon, Charles William
See also DLB 92

Conrad, Joseph
1857-1924 .... **TCLC 1, 6, 13, 25, 43, 57;
DA; DAB; DAC; DAM MST, NOV;
SSC 9; WLC**
See also CA 104; 131; CANR 60;
CDBLB 1890-1914; DLB 10, 34, 98, 156;
MTCW; SATA 27

Conrad, Robert Arnold
See Hart, Moss

Conroy, Donald Pat(rick)
1945- ... **CLC 30, 74; DAM NOV, POP**
See also AAYA 8; AITN 1; CA 85-88;
CANR 24, 53; DLB 6; MTCW

Constant (de Rebecque), (Henri) Benjamin
1767-1830 .... **NCLC 6**
See also DLB 119

Conybeare, Charles Augustus
See Eliot, T(homas) S(tearns)

Cook, Michael 1933- .... **CLC 58**
See also CA 93-96; DLB 53

Cook, Robin 1940- .... **CLC 14; DAM POP**
See also BEST 90:2; CA 108; 111;
CANR 41; INT 111

Cook, Roy
See Silverberg, Robert

Cooke, Elizabeth 1948- .... **CLC 55**
See also CA 129

Cooke, John Esten 1830-1886 ..... **NCLC 5**
See also DLB 3

Cooke, John Estes
See Baum, L(yman) Frank

Cooke, M. E.
See Creasey, John

Cooke, Margaret
See Creasey, John

Cook-Lynn, Elizabeth
1930- .... **CLC 93; DAM MULT**
See also CA 133; DLB 175; NNAL

Cooney, Ray .... **CLC 62**

Cooper, Douglas 1960- .... **CLC 86**

Cooper, Henry St. John
See Creasey, John

Cooper, J(oan) California
.... **CLC 56; DAM MULT**
See also AAYA 12; BW 1; CA 125;
CANR 55

Cooper, James Fenimore
1789-1851 .... **NCLC 1, 27, 54**
See also AAYA 22; CDALB 1640-1865;
DLB 3; SATA 19

Coover, Robert (Lowell)
1932- .... **CLC 3, 7, 15, 32, 46, 87;
DAM NOV; SSC 15**
See also CA 45-48; CANR 3, 37, 58;
DLB 2; DLBY 81; MTCW

Copeland, Stewart (Armstrong)
1952- .... **CLC 26**

Coppard, A(lfred) E(dgar)
1878-1957 .... **TCLC 5; SSC 21**
See also CA 114; DLB 162; YABC 1

Coppee, Francois 1842-1908 ...... **TCLC 25**

Coppola, Francis Ford 1939- .... **CLC 16**
See also CA 77-80; CANR 40; DLB 44

Corbiere, Tristan 1845-1875 ..... **NCLC 43**

Corcoran, Barbara 1911- .... **CLC 17**
See also AAYA 14; CA 21-24R; CAAS 2;
CANR 11, 28, 48; DLB 52; JRDA;
SAAS 20; SATA 3, 77

Cordelier, Maurice
See Giraudoux, (Hippolyte) Jean

Corelli, Marie 1855-1924 .... **TCLC 51**
See also Mackay, Mary
See also DLB 34, 156

Corman, Cid .... **CLC 9**
See also Corman, Sidney
See also CAAS 2; DLB 5

Corman, Sidney 1924-
See Corman, Cid
See also CA 85-88; CANR 44; DAM POET

Cormier, Robert (Edmund)
1925- .... **CLC 12, 30; DA; DAB; DAC;
DAM MST, NOV**
See also AAYA 3, 19; CA 1-4R; CANR 5,
23; CDALB 1968-1988; CLR 12; DLB 52;
INT CANR-23; JRDA; MAICYA;
MTCW; SATA 10, 45, 83

Corn, Alfred (DeWitt III) 1943- .... **CLC 33**
See also CA 104; CAAS 25; CANR 44;
DLB 120; DLBY 80

Corneille, Pierre
1606-1684 .... **LC 28; DAB; DAM MST**

Cornwell, David (John Moore)
1931- .... **CLC 9, 15; DAM POP**
See also le Carre, John
See also CA 5-8R; CANR 13, 33, 59;
MTCW

Corso, (Nunzio) Gregory 1930- ... **CLC 1, 11**
See also CA 5-8R; CANR 41; DLB 5, 16;
MTCW

Cortazar, Julio
1914-1984 ...... **CLC 2, 3, 5, 10, 13, 15,
33, 34, 92; DAM MULT, NOV; HLC;
SSC 7**
See also CA 21-24R; CANR 12, 32;
DLB 113; HW; MTCW

CORTES, HERNAN 1484-1547 ..... **LC 31**

Corwin, Cecil
See Kornbluth, C(yril) M.

Cosic, Dobrica 1921- .... **CLC 14**
See also CA 122; 138; DLB 181

Costain, Thomas B(ertram)
1885-1965 .... **CLC 30**
See also CA 5-8R; 25-28R; DLB 9

Costantini, Humberto
1924(?)-1987 .... **CLC 49**
See also CA 131; 122; HW

Costello, Elvis 1955- .... **CLC 21**

Cotes, Cecil V.
See Duncan, Sara Jeannette

Cotter, Joseph Seamon Sr.
1861-1949 .... **TCLC 28; BLC;
DAM MULT**
See also BW 1; CA 124; DLB 50

Couch, Arthur Thomas Quiller
See Quiller-Couch, Arthur Thomas

Coulton, James
See Hansen, Joseph

Couperus, Louis (Marie Anne)
1863-1923 .... **TCLC 15**
See also CA 115

Coupland, Douglas
1961- .... **CLC 85; DAC; DAM POP**
See also CA 142; CANR 57

Court, Wesli
See Turco, Lewis (Putnam)

Courtenay, Bryce 1933- .... **CLC 59**
See also CA 138

Courtney, Robert
See Ellison, Harlan (Jay)

Cousteau, Jacques-Yves
1910-1997 .... **CLC 30**
See also CA 65-68; 159; CANR 15; MTCW;
SATA 38

Curtin, Philip
  See Lowndes, Marie Adelaide (Belloc)

Curtis, Price
  See Ellison, Harlan (Jay)

Cutrate, Joe
  See Spiegelman, Art

Cynewulf c. 770-c. 840 . . . . **CMLC 23**

Czaczkes, Shmuel Yosef
  See Agnon, S(hmuel) Y(osef Halevi)

Dabrowska, Maria (Szumska)
  1889-1965 . . . . **CLC 15**
  See also CA 106

Dabydeen, David 1955- . . . . **CLC 34**
  See also BW 1; CA 125; CANR 56

Dacey, Philip 1939- . . . . **CLC 51**
  See also CA 37-40R; CAAS 17; CANR 14,
    32; DLB 105

Dagerman, Stig (Halvard)
  1923-1954 . . . . **TCLC 17**
  See also CA 117; 155

Dahl, Roald
  1916-1990 . . . . . . **CLC 1, 6, 18, 79; DAB;**
              DAC; DAM MST, NOV, POP
  See also AAYA 15; CA 1-4R; 133;
    CANR 6, 32, 37, 62; CLR 1, 7, 41;
    DLB 139; JRDA; MAICYA; MTCW;
    SATA 1, 26, 73; SATA-Obit 65

Dahlberg, Edward 1900-1977 . . . **CLC 1, 7, 14**
  See also CA 9-12R; 69-72; CANR 31, 62;
    DLB 48; MTCW

Daitch, Susan 1954- . . . . **CLC 103**

Dale, Colin . . . . **TCLC 18**
  See also Lawrence, T(homas) E(dward)

Dale, George E.
  See Asimov, Isaac

Daly, Elizabeth 1878-1967 . . . . **CLC 52**
  See also CA 23-24; 25-28R; CANR 60;
    CAP 2

Daly, Maureen 1921- . . . . **CLC 17**
  See also AAYA 5; CANR 37; JRDA;
    MAICYA; SAAS 1; SATA 2

Damas, Leon-Gontran 1912-1978 . . . **CLC 84**
  See also BW 1; CA 125; 73-76

Dana, Richard Henry Sr.
  1787-1879 . . . . **NCLC 53**

Daniel, Samuel 1562(?)-1619 . . . . **LC 24**
  See also DLB 62

Daniels, Brett
  See Adler, Renata

Dannay, Frederic
  1905-1982 . . . . **CLC 11; DAM POP**
  See also Queen, Ellery
  See also CA 1-4R; 107; CANR 1, 39;
    DLB 137; MTCW

D'Annunzio, Gabriele
  1863-1938 . . . . **TCLC 6, 40**
  See also CA 104; 155

Danois, N. le
  See Gourmont, Remy (-Marie-Charles) de

d'Antibes, Germain
  See Simenon, Georges (Jacques Christian)

Danticat, Edwidge 1969- . . . . **CLC 94**
  See also CA 152

Danvers, Dennis 1947- . . . . **CLC 70**

Danziger, Paula 1944- . . . . **CLC 21**
  See also AAYA 4; CA 112; 115; CANR 37;
    CLR 20; JRDA; MAICYA; SATA 36,
    63; SATA-Brief 30

Da Ponte, Lorenzo 1749-1838 . . . . **NCLC 50**

Dario, Ruben
  1867-1916 . . . . . **TCLC 4; DAM MULT;**
                  HLC; PC 15
  See also CA 131; HW; MTCW

Darley, George 1795-1846 . . . . **NCLC 2**
  See also DLB 96

Darwin, Charles 1809-1882 . . . . . . **NCLC 57**
  See also DLB 57, 166

Daryush, Elizabeth 1887-1977 . . . . **CLC 6, 19**
  See also CA 49-52; CANR 3; DLB 20

Dashwood, Edmee Elizabeth Monica de la
    Pasture 1890-1943
  See Delafield, E. M.
  See also CA 119; 154

Daudet, (Louis Marie) Alphonse
  1840-1897 . . . . **NCLC 1**
  See also DLB 123

Daumal, Rene 1908-1944 . . . . **TCLC 14**
  See also CA 114

Davenport, Guy (Mattison, Jr.)
  1927- . . . . **CLC 6, 14, 38; SSC 16**
  See also CA 33-36R; CANR 23; DLB 130

Davidson, Avram 1923-
  See Queen, Ellery
  See also CA 101; CANR 26; DLB 8

Davidson, Donald (Grady)
  1893-1968 . . . . **CLC 2, 13, 19**
  See also CA 5-8R; 25-28R; CANR 4;
    DLB 45

Davidson, Hugh
  See Hamilton, Edmond

Davidson, John 1857-1909 . . . . **TCLC 24**
  See also CA 118; DLB 19

Davidson, Sara 1943- . . . . **CLC 9**
  See also CA 81-84; CANR 44

Davie, Donald (Alfred)
  1922-1995 . . . . **CLC 5, 8, 10, 31**
  See also CA 1-4R; 149; CAAS 3; CANR 1,
    44; DLB 27; MTCW

Davies, Ray(mond Douglas) 1944- . . **CLC 21**
  See also CA 116; 146

Davies, Rhys 1903-1978 . . . . **CLC 23**
  See also CA 9-12R; 81-84; CANR 4;
    DLB 139

Davies, (William) Robertson
  1913-1995 . . . . . **CLC 2, 7, 13, 25, 42, 75,**
     91; DA; DAB; DAC; DAM MST, NOV,
                       POP; WLC
  See also BEST 89:2; CA 33-36R; 150;
    CANR 17, 42; DLB 68; INT CANR-17;
    MTCW

Davies, W(illiam) H(enry)
  1871-1940 . . . . **TCLC 5**
  See also CA 104; DLB 19, 174

Davies, Walter C.
  See Kornbluth, C(yril) M.

Davis, Angela (Yvonne)
  1944- . . . . **CLC 77; DAM MULT**
  See also BW 2; CA 57-60; CANR 10

Davis, B. Lynch
  See Bioy Casares, Adolfo; Borges, Jorge
    Luis

Davis, Gordon
  See Hunt, E(verette) Howard, (Jr.)

Davis, Harold Lenoir 1896-1960 . . . . **CLC 49**
  See also CA 89-92; DLB 9

Davis, Rebecca (Blaine) Harding
  1831-1910 . . . . **TCLC 6**
  See also CA 104; DLB 74

Davis, Richard Harding
  1864-1916 . . . . **TCLC 24**
  See also CA 114; DLB 12, 23, 78, 79;
    DLBD 13

Davison, Frank Dalby 1893-1970 . . . **CLC 15**
  See also CA 116

Davison, Lawrence H.
  See Lawrence, D(avid) H(erbert Richards)

Davison, Peter (Hubert) 1928- . . . . . **CLC 28**
  See also CA 9-12R; CAAS 4; CANR 3, 43;
    DLB 5

Davys, Mary 1674-1732 . . . . **LC 1**
  See also DLB 39

Dawson, Fielding 1930- . . . . **CLC 6**
  See also CA 85-88; DLB 130

Dawson, Peter
  See Faust, Frederick (Schiller)

Day, Clarence (Shepard, Jr.)
  1874-1935 . . . . **TCLC 25**
  See also CA 108; DLB 11

Day, Thomas 1748-1789 . . . . **LC 1**
  See also DLB 39; YABC 1

Day Lewis, C(ecil)
  1904-1972 . . . . **CLC 1, 6, 10;**
                          DAM POET; PC 11
  See also Blake, Nicholas
  See also CA 13-16; 33-36R; CANR 34;
    CAP 1; DLB 15, 20; MTCW

Dazai, Osamu . . . . **TCLC 11**
  See also Tsushima, Shuji
  See also DLB 182

de Andrade, Carlos Drummond
  See Drummond de Andrade, Carlos

Deane, Norman
  See Creasey, John

de Beauvoir, Simone (Lucie Ernestine Marie
    Bertrand)
  See Beauvoir, Simone (Lucie Ernestine
    Marie Bertrand) de

de Beer, P.
  See Bosman, Herman Charles

de Brissac, Malcolm
  See Dickinson, Peter (Malcolm)

de Chardin, Pierre Teilhard
  See Teilhard de Chardin, (Marie Joseph)
    Pierre

Dee, John 1527-1608 . . . . **LC 20**

Deer, Sandra 1940- . . . . **CLC 45**

De Ferrari, Gabriella 1941- . . . . **CLC 65**
  See also CA 146

Douglas, Leonard
See Bradbury, Ray (Douglas)

Douglas, Michael
See Crichton, (John) Michael

Douglas, Norman 1868-1952 ...... TCLC 68

Douglass, Frederick
1817(?)-1895 .... NCLC 7, 55; BLC; DA;
DAC; DAM MST, MULT; WLC
See also CDALB 1640-1865; DLB 1, 43, 50,
79; SATA 29

Dourado, (Waldomiro Freitas) Autran
1926- .... CLC 23, 60
See also CA 25-28R; CANR 34

Dourado, Waldomiro Autran
See Dourado, (Waldomiro Freitas) Autran

Dove, Rita (Frances)
1952- .... CLC 50, 81; DAM MULT,
POET; PC 6
See also BW 2; CA 109; CAAS 19;
CANR 27, 42; DLB 120

Dowell, Coleman 1925-1985........ CLC 60
See also CA 25-28R; 117; CANR 10;
DLB 130

Dowson, Ernest (Christopher)
1867-1900 .... TCLC 4
See also CA 105; 150; DLB 19, 135

Doyle, A. Conan
See Doyle, Arthur Conan

Doyle, Arthur Conan
1859-1930 .... TCLC 7; DA; DAB;
DAC; DAM MST, NOV; SSC 12; WLC
See also AAYA 14; CA 104; 122;
CDBLB 1890-1914; DLB 18, 70, 156, 178;
MTCW; SATA 24

Doyle, Conan
See Doyle, Arthur Conan

Doyle, John
See Graves, Robert (von Ranke)

Doyle, Roddy 1958(?)- .... CLC 81
See also AAYA 14; CA 143

Doyle, Sir A. Conan
See Doyle, Arthur Conan

Doyle, Sir Arthur Conan
See Doyle, Arthur Conan

Dr. A
See Asimov, Isaac; Silverstein, Alvin

Drabble, Margaret
1939- .... CLC 2, 3, 5, 8, 10, 22, 53;
DAB; DAC; DAM MST, NOV, POP
See also CA 13-16R; CANR 18, 35;
CDBLB 1960 to Present; DLB 14, 155;
MTCW; SATA 48

Drapier, M. B.
See Swift, Jonathan

Drayham, James
See Mencken, H(enry) L(ouis)

Drayton, Michael 1563-1631........ LC 8

Dreadstone, Carl
See Campbell, (John) Ramsey

Dreiser, Theodore (Herman Albert)
1871-1945 .... TCLC 10, 18, 35; DA;
DAC; DAM MST, NOV; WLC
See also CA 106; 132; CDALB 1865-1917;
DLB 9, 12, 102, 137; DLBD 1; MTCW

Drexler, Rosalyn 1926- .... CLC 2, 6
See also CA 81-84

Dreyer, Carl Theodor 1889-1968.... CLC 16
See also CA 116

Drieu la Rochelle, Pierre(-Eugene)
1893-1945 .... TCLC 21
See also CA 117; DLB 72

Drinkwater, John 1882-1937 ...... TCLC 57
See also CA 109; 149; DLB 10, 19, 149

Drop Shot
See Cable, George Washington

Droste-Hulshoff, Annette Freiin von
1797-1848 .... NCLC 3
See also DLB 133

Drummond, Walter
See Silverberg, Robert

Drummond, William Henry
1854-1907 .... TCLC 25
See also CA 160; DLB 92

Drummond de Andrade, Carlos
1902-1987 .... CLC 18
See also Andrade, Carlos Drummond de
See also CA 132; 123

Drury, Allen (Stuart) 1918- .... CLC 37
See also CA 57-60; CANR 18, 52;
INT CANR-18

Dryden, John
1631-1700 .... LC 3, 21; DA; DAB;
DAC; DAM DRAM, MST, POET;
DC 3; WLC
See also CDBLB 1660-1789; DLB 80, 101,
131

Duberman, Martin 1930- .... CLC 8
See also CA 1-4R; CANR 2

Dubie, Norman (Evans) 1945- ...... CLC 36
See also CA 69-72; CANR 12; DLB 120

Du Bois, W(illiam) E(dward) B(urghardt)
1868-1963 .... CLC 1, 2, 13, 64, 96;
BLC; DA; DAC; DAM MST, MULT,
NOV; WLC
See also BW 1; CA 85-88; CANR 34;
CDALB 1865-1917; DLB 47, 50, 91;
MTCW; SATA 42

Dubus, Andre
1936- .... CLC 13, 36, 97; SSC 15
See also CA 21-24R; CANR 17; DLB 130;
INT CANR-17

Duca Minimo
See D'Annunzio, Gabriele

Ducharme, Rejean 1941- .... CLC 74
See also DLB 60

Duclos, Charles Pinot 1704-1772 ..... LC 1

Dudek, Louis 1918- .... CLC 11, 19
See also CA 45-48; CAAS 14; CANR 1;
DLB 88

Duerrenmatt, Friedrich
1921-1990 ...... CLC 1, 4, 8, 11, 15, 43,
102; DAM DRAM
See also CA 17-20R; CANR 33; DLB 69,
124; MTCW

Duffy, Bruce (?)- .... CLC 50

Duffy, Maureen 1933- .... CLC 37
See also CA 25-28R; CANR 33; DLB 14;
MTCW

Dugan, Alan 1923- .... CLC 2, 6
See also CA 81-84; DLB 5

du Gard, Roger Martin
See Martin du Gard, Roger

Duhamel, Georges 1884-1966 .... CLC 8
See also CA 81-84; 25-28R; CANR 35;
DLB 65; MTCW

Dujardin, Edouard (Emile Louis)
1861-1949 .... TCLC 13
See also CA 109; DLB 123

Dulles, John Foster 1888-1959 .... TCLC 72
See also CA 115; 149

Dumas, Alexandre (Davy de la Pailleterie)
1802-1870 .... NCLC 11; DA; DAB;
DAC; DAM MST, NOV; WLC
See also DLB 119; SATA 18

Dumas, Alexandre
1824-1895 .... NCLC 9; DC 1
See also AAYA 22

Dumas, Claudine
See Malzberg, Barry N(athaniel)

Dumas, Henry L. 1934-1968..... CLC 6, 62
See also BW 1; CA 85-88; DLB 41

du Maurier, Daphne
1907-1989 .... CLC 6, 11, 59; DAB;
DAC; DAM MST, POP; SSC 18
See also CA 5-8R; 128; CANR 6, 55;
MTCW; SATA 27; SATA-Obit 60

Dunbar, Paul Laurence
1872-1906 ...... TCLC 2, 12; BLC; DA;
DAC; DAM MST, MULT, POET; PC 5;
SSC 8; WLC
See also BW 1; CA 104; 124;
CDALB 1865-1917; DLB 50, 54, 78;
SATA 34

Dunbar, William 1460(?)-1530(?) .... LC 20
See also DLB 132, 146

Duncan, Dora Angela
See Duncan, Isadora

Duncan, Isadora 1877(?)-1927..... TCLC 68
See also CA 118; 149

Duncan, Lois 1934- .... CLC 26
See also AAYA 4; CA 1-4R; CANR 2, 23,
36; CLR 29; JRDA; MAICYA; SAAS 2;
SATA 1, 36, 75

Duncan, Robert (Edward)
1919-1988 .... CLC 1, 2, 4, 7, 15, 41, 55;
DAM POET; PC 2
See also CA 9-12R; 124; CANR 28, 62;
DLB 5, 16; MTCW

Duncan, Sara Jeannette
1861-1922 .... TCLC 60
See also CA 157; DLB 92

Dunlap, William 1766-1839 .... NCLC 2
See also DLB 30, 37, 59

Dunn, Douglas (Eaglesham)
1942- .... CLC 6, 40
See also CA 45-48; CANR 2, 33; DLB 40;
MTCW

Dunn, Katherine (Karen) 1945- ..... CLC 71
See also CA 33-36R

Dunn, Stephen 1939- .... CLC 36
See also CA 33-36R; CANR 12, 48, 53;
DLB 105

Dunne, Finley Peter 1867-1936.... **TCLC 28**
See also CA 108; DLB 11, 23

Dunne, John Gregory 1932-....... **CLC 28**
See also CA 25-28R; CANR 14, 50;
DLBY 80

Dunsany, Edward John Moreton Drax
Plunkett 1878-1957
See Dunsany, Lord
See also CA 104; 148; DLB 10

Dunsany, Lord................. **TCLC 2, 59**
See also Dunsany, Edward John Moreton
Drax Plunkett
See also DLB 77, 153, 156

du Perry, Jean
See Simenon, Georges (Jacques Christian)

Durang, Christopher (Ferdinand)
1949-.................... **CLC 27, 38**
See also CA 105; CANR 50

Duras, Marguerite
1914-1996 ..... **CLC 3, 6, 11, 20, 34, 40,**
68, 100
See also CA 25-28R; 151; CANR 50;
DLB 83; MTCW

Durban, (Rosa) Pam 1947-......... **CLC 39**
See also CA 123

Durcan, Paul
1944- .... **CLC 43, 70; DAM POET**
See also CA 134

Durkheim, Emile 1858-1917 ...... **TCLC 55**

Durrell, Lawrence (George)
1912-1990 .... **CLC 1, 4, 6, 8, 13, 27, 41;**
DAM NOV
See also CA 9-12R; 132; CANR 40;
CDBLB 1945-1960; DLB 15, 27;
DLBY 90; MTCW

Durrenmatt, Friedrich
See Duerrenmatt, Friedrich

Dutt, Toru 1856-1877.......... **NCLC 29**

Dwight, Timothy 1752-1817...... **NCLC 13**
See also DLB 37

Dworkin, Andrea 1946-........... **CLC 43**
See also CA 77-80; CAAS 21; CANR 16,
39; INT CANR-16; MTCW

Dwyer, Deanna
See Koontz, Dean R(ay)

Dwyer, K. R.
See Koontz, Dean R(ay)

Dye, Richard
See De Voto, Bernard (Augustine)

Dylan, Bob 1941-...... **CLC 3, 4, 6, 12, 77**
See also CA 41-44R; DLB 16

Eagleton, Terence (Francis) 1943-
See Eagleton, Terry
See also CA 57-60; CANR 7, 23; MTCW

Eagleton, Terry.................... **CLC 63**
See also Eagleton, Terence (Francis)

Early, Jack
See Scoppettone, Sandra

East, Michael
See West, Morris L(anglo)

Eastaway, Edward
See Thomas, (Philip) Edward

Eastlake, William (Derry)
1917-1997 .... **CLC 8**
See also CA 5-8R; 158; CAAS 1; CANR 5;
DLB 6; INT CANR-5

Eastman, Charles A(lexander)
1858-1939 ..... **TCLC 55; DAM MULT**
See also DLB 175; NNAL; YABC 1

Eberhart, Richard (Ghormley)
1904- .. **CLC 3, 11, 19, 56; DAM POET**
See also CA 1-4R; CANR 2;
CDALB 1941-1968; DLB 48; MTCW

Eberstadt, Fernanda 1960-......... **CLC 39**
See also CA 136

Echegaray (y Eizaguirre), Jose (Maria Waldo)
1832-1916 .... **TCLC 4**
See also CA 104; CANR 32; HW; MTCW

Echeverria, (Jose) Esteban (Antonino)
1805-1851 .... **NCLC 18**

Echo
See Proust, (Valentin-Louis-George-Eugene-)
Marcel

Eckert, Allan W. 1931-........... **CLC 17**
See also AAYA 18; CA 13-16R; CANR 14,
45; INT CANR-14; SAAS 21; SATA 29,
91; SATA-Brief 27

Eckhart, Meister 1260(?)-1328(?) .. **CMLC 9**
See also DLB 115

Eckmar, F. R.
See de Hartog, Jan

Eco, Umberto
1932- ... **CLC 28, 60; DAM NOV, POP**
See also BEST 90:1; CA 77-80; CANR 12,
33, 55; MTCW

Eddison, E(ric) R(ucker)
1882-1945 .... **TCLC 15**
See also CA 109; 156

Eddy, Mary (Morse) Baker
1821-1910 .... **TCLC 71**
See also CA 113

Edel, (Joseph) Leon 1907-...... **CLC 29, 34**
See also CA 1-4R; CANR 1, 22; DLB 103;
INT CANR-22

Eden, Emily 1797-1869 .... **NCLC 10**

Edgar, David
1948- .... **CLC 42; DAM DRAM**
See also CA 57-60; CANR 12, 61; DLB 13;
MTCW

Edgerton, Clyde (Carlyle) 1944-.... **CLC 39**
See also AAYA 17; CA 118; 134; INT 134

Edgeworth, Maria 1768-1849... **NCLC 1, 51**
See also DLB 116, 159, 163; SATA 21

Edmonds, Paul
See Kuttner, Henry

Edmonds, Walter D(umaux) 1903- .. **CLC 35**
See also CA 5-8R; CANR 2; DLB 9;
MAICYA; SAAS 4; SATA 1, 27

Edmondson, Wallace
See Ellison, Harlan (Jay)

Edson, Russell.................... **CLC 13**
See also CA 33-36R

Edwards, Bronwen Elizabeth
See Rose, Wendy

Edwards, G(erald) B(asil)
1899-1976 .... **CLC 25**
See also CA 110

Edwards, Gus 1939-.............. **CLC 43**
See also CA 108; INT 108

Edwards, Jonathan
1703-1758 .... **LC 7; DA; DAC;**
DAM MST
See also DLB 24

Efron, Marina Ivanovna Tsvetaeva
See Tsvetaeva (Efron), Marina (Ivanovna)

Ehle, John (Marsden, Jr.) 1925-.... **CLC 27**
See also CA 9-12R

Ehrenbourg, Ilya (Grigoryevich)
See Ehrenburg, Ilya (Grigoryevich)

Ehrenburg, Ilya (Grigoryevich)
1891-1967 .... **CLC 18, 34, 62**
See also CA 102; 25-28R

Ehrenburg, Ilyo (Grigoryevich)
See Ehrenburg, Ilya (Grigoryevich)

Eich, Guenter 1907-1972 .... **CLC 15**
See also CA 111; 93-96; DLB 69, 124

Eichendorff, Joseph Freiherr von
1788-1857 .... **NCLC 8**
See also DLB 90

Eigner, Larry..................... **CLC 9**
See also Eigner, Laurence (Joel)
See also CAAS 23; DLB 5

Eigner, Laurence (Joel) 1927-1996
See Eigner, Larry
See also CA 9-12R; 151; CANR 6

Einstein, Albert 1879-1955 .... **TCLC 65**
See also CA 121; 133; MTCW

Eiseley, Loren Corey 1907-1977..... **CLC 7**
See also AAYA 5; CA 1-4R; 73-76;
CANR 6

Eisenstadt, Jill 1963-.............. **CLC 50**
See also CA 140

Eisenstein, Sergei (Mikhailovich)
1898-1948 .... **TCLC 57**
See also CA 114; 149

Eisner, Simon
See Kornbluth, C(yril) M.

Ekeloef, (Bengt) Gunnar
1907-1968 ......:.... **CLC 27; DAM POET**
See also CA 123; 25-28R

Ekelof, (Bengt) Gunnar
See Ekeloef, (Bengt) Gunnar

Ekelund, Vilhelm 1880-1949 ...... **TCLC 75**

Ekwensi, C. O. D.
See Ekwensi, Cyprian (Odiatu Duaka)

Ekwensi, Cyprian (Odiatu Duaka)
1921-...... **CLC 4; BLC; DAM MULT**
See also BW 2; CA 29-32R; CANR 18, 42;
DLB 117; MTCW; SATA 66

Elaine......................... **TCLC 18**
See also Leverson, Ada

El Crummo
See Crumb, R(obert)

Elia
See Lamb, Charles

Eliade, Mircea 1907-1986 .... **CLC 19**
See also CA 65-68; 119; CANR 30, 62;
MTCW

Eliot, A. D.
See Jewett, (Theodora) Sarah Orne

Eliot, Alice
  See Jewett, (Theodora) Sarah Orne

Eliot, Dan
  See Silverberg, Robert

Eliot, George
  1819-1880 ..... NCLC 4, 13, 23, 41, 49;
    DA; DAB; DAC; DAM MST, NOV;
    WLC
  See also CDBLB 1832-1890; DLB 21, 35, 55

Eliot, John 1604-1690 .... LC 5
  See also DLB 24

Eliot, T(homas) S(tearns)
  1888-1965 ..... CLC 1, 2, 3, 6, 9, 10, 13,
    15, 24, 34, 41, 55, 57; DA; DAB; DAC;
    DAM DRAM, MST, POET; PC 5;
    WLC 2
  See also CA 5-8R; 25-28R; CANR 41;
    CDALB 1929-1941; DLB 7, 10, 45, 63;
    DLBY 88; MTCW

Elizabeth 1866-1941 .... TCLC 41

Elkin, Stanley L(awrence)
  1930-1995 ...... CLC 4, 6, 9, 14, 27, 51,
    91; DAM NOV, POP; SSC 12
  See also CA 9-12R; 148; CANR 8, 46;
    DLB 2, 28; DLBY 80; INT CANR-8;
    MTCW

Elledge, Scott. .... CLC 34

Elliot, Don
  See Silverberg, Robert

Elliott, Don
  See Silverberg, Robert

Elliott, George P(aul) 1918-1980 ..... CLC 2
  See also CA 1-4R; 97-100; CANR 2

Elliott, Janice 1931- .... CLC 47
  See also CA 13-16R; CANR 8, 29; DLB 14

Elliott, Sumner Locke 1917-1991 ... CLC 38
  See also CA 5-8R; 134; CANR 2, 21

Elliott, William
  See Bradbury, Ray (Douglas)

Ellis, A. E. .... CLC 7

Ellis, Alice Thomas .... CLC 40
  See also Haycraft, Anna

Ellis, Bret Easton
  1964- .... CLC 39, 71; DAM POP
  See also AAYA 2; CA 118; 123; CANR 51;
    INT 123

Ellis, (Henry) Havelock
  1859-1939 .... TCLC 14
  See also CA 109

Ellis, Landon
  See Ellison, Harlan (Jay)

Ellis, Trey 1962- .... CLC 55
  See also CA 146

Ellison, Harlan (Jay)
  1934- ...... CLC 1, 13, 42; DAM POP;
    SSC 14
  See also CA 5-8R; CANR 5, 46; DLB 8;
    INT CANR-5; MTCW

Ellison, Ralph (Waldo)
  1914-1994 .... CLC 1, 3, 11, 54, 86;
    BLC; DA; DAB; DAC; DAM MST,
    MULT, NOV; SSC 26; WLC
  See also AAYA 19; BW 1; CA 9-12R; 145;
    CANR 24, 53; CDALB 1941-1968;
    DLB 2, 76; DLBY 94; MTCW

Ellmann, Lucy (Elizabeth) 1956- .... CLC 61
  See also CA 128

Ellmann, Richard (David)
  1918-1987 .... CLC 50
  See also BEST 89:2; CA 1-4R; 122;
    CANR 2, 28, 61; DLB 103; DLBY 87;
    MTCW

Elman, Richard 1934- .... CLC 19
  See also CA 17-20R; CAAS 3; CANR 47

Elron
  See Hubbard, L(afayette) Ron(ald)

Eluard, Paul. .... TCLC 7, 41
  See also Grindel, Eugene

Elyot, Sir Thomas 1490(?)-1546 ..... LC 11

Elytis, Odysseus
  1911-1996 .... CLC 15, 49, 100;
    DAM POET
  See also CA 102; 151; MTCW

Emecheta, (Florence Onye) Buchi
  1944- .. CLC 14, 48; BLC; DAM MULT
  See also BW 2; CA 81-84; CANR 27;
    DLB 117; MTCW; SATA 66

Emerson, Ralph Waldo
  1803-1882 ..... NCLC 1, 38; DA; DAB;
    DAC; DAM MST, POET; PC 18; WLC
  See also CDALB 1640-1865; DLB 1, 59, 73

Eminescu, Mihail 1850-1889 ..... NCLC 33

Empson, William
  1906-1984 .... CLC 3, 8, 19, 33, 34
  See also CA 17-20R; 112; CANR 31, 61;
    DLB 20; MTCW

Enchi Fumiko (Ueda) 1905-1986. ... CLC 31
  See also CA 129; 121

Ende, Michael (Andreas Helmuth)
  1929-1995 .... CLC 31
  See also CA 118; 124; 149; CANR 36;
    CLR 14; DLB 75; MAICYA; SATA 61;
    SATA-Brief 42; SATA-Obit 86

Endo, Shusaku
  1923-1996 .... CLC 7, 14, 19, 54, 99;
    DAM NOV
  See also CA 29-32R; 153; CANR 21, 54;
    DLB 182; MTCW

Engel, Marian 1933-1985. .... CLC 36
  See also CA 25-28R; CANR 12; DLB 53;
    INT CANR-12

Engelhardt, Frederick
  See Hubbard, L(afayette) Ron(ald)

Enright, D(ennis) J(oseph)
  1920- .... CLC 4, 8, 31
  See also CA 1-4R; CANR 1, 42; DLB 27;
    SATA 25

Enzensberger, Hans Magnus
  1929- .... CLC 43
  See also CA 116; 119

Ephron, Nora 1941- .... CLC 17, 31
  See also AITN 2; CA 65-68; CANR 12, 39

Epicurus 341B.C.-270B.C. .... CMLC 21
  See also DLB 176

Epsilon
  See Betjeman, John

Epstein, Daniel Mark 1948- .... CLC 7
  See also CA 49-52; CANR 2, 53

Epstein, Jacob 1956- .... CLC 19
  See also CA 114

Epstein, Joseph 1937- .... CLC 39
  See also CA 112; 119; CANR 50

Epstein, Leslie 1938- .... CLC 27
  See also CA 73-76; CAAS 12; CANR 23

Equiano, Olaudah
  1745(?)-1797 .... LC 16; BLC;
    DAM MULT
  See also DLB 37, 50

ER .... TCLC 33
  See also CA 160; DLB 85

Erasmus, Desiderius 1469(?)-1536. ... LC 16

Erdman, Paul E(mil) 1932- .... CLC 25
  See also AITN 1; CA 61-64; CANR 13, 43

Erdrich, Louise
  1954- .... CLC 39, 54; DAM MULT,
    NOV, POP
  See also AAYA 10; BEST 89:1; CA 114;
    CANR 41, 62; DLB 152, 175; MTCW;
    NNAL; SATA 94

Erenburg, Ilya (Grigoryevich)
  See Ehrenburg, Ilya (Grigoryevich)

Erickson, Stephen Michael 1950-
  See Erickson, Steve
  See also CA 129

Erickson, Steve 1950- .... CLC 64
  See also Erickson, Stephen Michael
  See also CANR 60

Ericson, Walter
  See Fast, Howard (Melvin)

Eriksson, Buntel
  See Bergman, (Ernst) Ingmar

Ernaux, Annie 1940- .... CLC 88
  See also CA 147

Eschenbach, Wolfram von
  See Wolfram von Eschenbach

Eseki, Bruno
  See Mphahlele, Ezekiel

Esenin, Sergei (Alexandrovich)
  1895-1925 .... TCLC 4
  See also CA 104

Eshleman, Clayton 1935- .... CLC 7
  See also CA 33-36R; CAAS 6; DLB 5

Espriella, Don Manuel Alvarez
  See Southey, Robert

Espriu, Salvador 1913-1985 .... CLC 9
  See also CA 154; 115; DLB 134

Espronceda, Jose de 1808-1842. .. NCLC 39

Esse, James
  See Stephens, James

Esterbrook, Tom
  See Hubbard, L(afayette) Ron(ald)

Estleman, Loren D.
  1952- ...... CLC 48; DAM NOV, POP
  See also CA 85-88; CANR 27;
    INT CANR-27; MTCW

Euclid 306B.C.-283B.C. .... CMLC 25

Eugenides, Jeffrey 1960(?)- .... CLC 81
  See also CA 144

Euripides
  c. 485B.C.-406B.C. ..... CMLC 23; DA;
    DAB; DAC; DAM DRAM, MST; DC 4;
    WLCS
  See also DLB 176

Evan, Evin
See Faust, Frederick (Schiller)

Evans, Evan
See Faust, Frederick (Schiller)

Evans, Marian
See Eliot, George

Evans, Mary Ann
See Eliot, George

Evarts, Esther
See Benson, Sally

Everett, Percival L. 1956- .... CLC 57
See also BW 2; CA 129

Everson, R(onald) G(ilmour)
1903- .... CLC 27
See also CA 17-20R; DLB 88

Everson, William (Oliver)
1912-1994 .... CLC 1, 5, 14
See also CA 9-12R; 145; CANR 20; DLB 5,
16; MTCW

Evtushenko, Evgenii Aleksandrovich
See Yevtushenko, Yevgeny (Alexandrovich)

Ewart, Gavin (Buchanan)
1916-1995 .... CLC 13, 46
See also CA 89-92; 150; CANR 17, 46;
DLB 40; MTCW

Ewers, Hanns Heinz 1871-1943 ... TCLC 12
See also CA 109; 149

Ewing, Frederick R.
See Sturgeon, Theodore (Hamilton)

Exley, Frederick (Earl)
1929-1992 .... CLC 6, 11
See also AITN 2; CA 81-84; 138; DLB 143;
DLBY 81

Eynhardt, Guillermo
See Quiroga, Horacio (Sylvestre)

Ezekiel, Nissim 1924- .... CLC 61
See also CA 61-64

Ezekiel, Tish O'Dowd 1943- .... CLC 34
See also CA 129

Fadeyev, A.
See Bulgya, Alexander Alexandrovich

Fadeyev, Alexander .... TCLC 53
See also Bulgya, Alexander Alexandrovich

Fagen, Donald 1948- .... CLC 26

Fainzilberg, Ilya Arnoldovich 1897-1937
See Ilf, Ilya
See also CA 120

Fair, Ronald L. 1932- .... CLC 18
See also BW 1; CA 69-72; CANR 25;
DLB 33

Fairbairn, Roger
See Carr, John Dickson

Fairbairns, Zoe (Ann) 1948- .... CLC 32
See also CA 103; CANR 21

Falco, Gian
See Papini, Giovanni

Falconer, James
See Kirkup, James

Falconer, Kenneth
See Kornbluth, C(yril) M.

Falkland, Samuel
See Heijermans, Herman

Fallaci, Oriana 1930- .... CLC 11
See also CA 77-80; CANR 15, 58; MTCW

Faludy, George 1913- .... CLC 42
See also CA 21-24R

Faludy, Gyoergy
See Faludy, George

Fanon, Frantz
1925-1961 .... CLC 74; BLC;
DAM MULT
See also BW 1; CA 116; 89-92

Fanshawe, Ann 1625-1680 .... LC 11

Fante, John (Thomas) 1911-1983 ... CLC 60
See also CA 69-72; 109; CANR 23;
DLB 130; DLBY 83

Farah, Nuruddin
1945- ..... CLC 53; BLC; DAM MULT
See also BW 2; CA 106; DLB 125

Fargue, Leon-Paul 1876(?)-1947 ... TCLC 11
See also CA 109

Farigoule, Louis
See Romains, Jules

Farina, Richard 1936(?)-1966 .... CLC 9
See also CA 81-84; 25-28R

Farley, Walter (Lorimer)
1915-1989 .... CLC 17
See also CA 17-20R; CANR 8, 29; DLB 22;
JRDA; MAICYA; SATA 2, 43

Farmer, Philip Jose 1918- .... CLC 1, 19
See also CA 1-4R; CANR 4, 35; DLB 8;
MTCW; SATA 93

Farquhar, George
1677-1707 .... LC 21; DAM DRAM
See also DLB 84

Farrell, J(ames) G(ordon)
1935-1979 .... CLC 6
See also CA 73-76; 89-92; CANR 36;
DLB 14; MTCW

Farrell, James T(homas)
1904-1979 .. CLC 1, 4, 8, 11, 66; SSC 28
See also CA 5-8R; 89-92; CANR 9, 61;
DLB 4, 9, 86; DLBD 2; MTCW

Farren, Richard J.
See Betjeman, John

Farren, Richard M.
See Betjeman, John

Fassbinder, Rainer Werner
1946-1982 .... CLC 20
See also CA 93-96; 106; CANR 31

Fast, Howard (Melvin)
1914- .... CLC 23; DAM NOV
See also AAYA 16; CA 1-4R; CAAS 18;
CANR 1, 33, 54; DLB 9; INT CANR-33;
SATA 7

Faulcon, Robert
See Holdstock, Robert P.

Faulkner, William (Cuthbert)
1897-1962 ... CLC 1, 3, 6, 8, 9, 11, 14,
18, 28, 52, 68; DA; DAB; DAC;
DAM MST, NOV; SSC 1; WLC
See also AAYA 7; CA 81-84; CANR 33;
CDALB 1929-1941; DLB 9, 11, 44, 102;
DLBD 2; DLBY 86; MTCW

Fauset, Jessie Redmon
1884(?)-1961 .... CLC 19, 54; BLC;
DAM MULT
See also BW 1; CA 109; DLB 51

Faust, Frederick (Schiller)
1892-1944(?) ..... TCLC 49; DAM POP
See also CA 108; 152

Faust, Irvin 1924- .... CLC 8
See also CA 33-36R; CANR 28; DLB 2, 28;
DLBY 80

Fawkes, Guy
See Benchley, Robert (Charles)

Fearing, Kenneth (Flexner)
1902-1961 .... CLC 51
See also CA 93-96; CANR 59; DLB 9

Fecamps, Elise
See Creasey, John

Federman, Raymond 1928- ...... CLC 6, 47
See also CA 17-20R; CAAS 8; CANR 10,
43; DLBY 80

Federspiel, J(uerg) F. 1931- .... CLC 42
See also CA 146

Feiffer, Jules (Ralph)
1929- ...... CLC 2, 8, 64; DAM DRAM
See also AAYA 3; CA 17-20R; CANR 30,
59; DLB 7, 44; INT CANR-30; MTCW;
SATA 8, 61

Feige, Hermann Albert Otto Maximilian
See Traven, B.

Feinberg, David B. 1956-1994 ...... CLC 59
See also CA 135; 147

Feinstein, Elaine 1930- .... CLC 36
See also CA 69-72; CAAS 1; CANR 31;
DLB 14, 40; MTCW

Feldman, Irving (Mordecai) 1928-.... CLC 7
See also CA 1-4R; CANR 1; DLB 169

Felix-Tchicaya, Gerald
See Tchicaya, Gerald Felix

Fellini, Federico 1920-1993 ..... CLC 16, 85
See also CA 65-68; 143; CANR 33

Felsen, Henry Gregor 1916- .... CLC 17
See also CA 1-4R; CANR 1; SAAS 2;
SATA 1

Fenton, James Martin 1949- .... CLC 32
See also CA 102; DLB 40

Ferber, Edna 1887-1968........ CLC 18, 93
See also AITN 1; CA 5-8R; 25-28R; DLB 9,
28, 86; MTCW; SATA 7

Ferguson, Helen
See Kavan, Anna

Ferguson, Samuel 1810-1886..... NCLC 33
See also DLB 32

Fergusson, Robert 1750-1774 .... LC 29
See also DLB 109

Ferling, Lawrence
See Ferlinghetti, Lawrence (Monsanto)

Ferlinghetti, Lawrence (Monsanto)
1919(?)- .... CLC 2, 6, 10, 27;
DAM POET; PC 1
See also CA 5-8R; CANR 3, 41;
CDALB 1941-1968; DLB 5, 16; MTCW

Fernandez, Vicente Garcia Huidobro
See Huidobro Fernandez, Vicente Garcia

Ferrer, Gabriel (Francisco Victor) Miro
  See Miro (Ferrer), Gabriel (Francisco
  Victor)

Ferrier, Susan (Edmonstone)
  1782-1854 .... NCLC 8
  See also DLB 116

Ferrigno, Robert 1948(?)-.......... CLC 65
  See also CA 140

Ferron, Jacques 1921-1985 ... CLC 94; DAC
  See also CA 117; 129; DLB 60

Feuchtwanger, Lion 1884-1958 ..... TCLC 3
  See also CA 104; DLB 66

Feuillet, Octave 1821-1890 ...... NCLC 45

Feydeau, Georges (Leon Jules Marie)
  1862-1921 ..... TCLC 22; DAM DRAM
  See also CA 113; 152

Fichte, Johann Gottlieb
  1762-1814 .... NCLC 62
  See also DLB 90

Ficino, Marsilio 1433-1499 .... LC 12

Fiedeler, Hans
  See Doeblin, Alfred

Fiedler, Leslie A(aron)
  1917- .... CLC 4, 13, 24
  See also CA 9-12R; CANR 7; DLB 28, 67;
  MTCW

Field, Andrew 1938-.............. CLC 44
  See also CA 97-100; CANR 25

Field, Eugene 1850-1895 .... NCLC 3
  See also DLB 23, 42, 140; DLBD 13;
  MAICYA; SATA 16

Field, Gans T.
  See Wellman, Manly Wade

Field, Michael .... TCLC 43

Field, Peter
  See Hobson, Laura Z(ametkin)

Fielding, Henry
  1707-1754 ...... LC 1; DA; DAB; DAC;
  DAM DRAM, MST, NOV; WLC
  See also CDBLB 1660-1789; DLB 39, 84,
  101

Fielding, Sarah 1710-1768 .... LC 1
  See also DLB 39

Fierstein, Harvey (Forbes)
  1954- ..... CLC 33; DAM DRAM, POP
  See also CA 123; 129

Figes, Eva 1932-................ CLC 31
  See also CA 53-56; CANR 4, 44; DLB 14

Finch, Robert (Duer Claydon)
  1900- .... CLC 18
  See also CA 57-60; CANR 9, 24, 49;
  DLB 88

Findley, Timothy
  1930-.. CLC 27, 102; DAC; DAM MST
  See also CA 25-28R; CANR 12, 42;
  DLB 53

Fink, William
  See Mencken, H(enry) L(ouis)

Firbank, Louis 1942-
  See Reed, Lou
  See also CA 117

Firbank, (Arthur Annesley) Ronald
  1886-1926 .... TCLC 1
  See also CA 104; DLB 36

Fisher, M(ary) F(rances) K(ennedy)
  1908-1992 .... CLC 76, 87
  See also CA 77-80; 138; CANR 44

Fisher, Roy 1930-................ CLC 25
  See also CA 81-84; CAAS 10; CANR 16;
  DLB 40

Fisher, Rudolph
  1897-1934 .... TCLC 11; BLC;
  DAM MULT; SSC 25
  See also BW 1; CA 107; 124; DLB 51, 102

Fisher, Vardis (Alvero) 1895-1968.... CLC 7
  See also CA 5-8R; 25-28R; DLB 9

Fiske, Tarleton
  See Bloch, Robert (Albert)

Fitch, Clarke
  See Sinclair, Upton (Beall)

Fitch, John IV
  See Cormier, Robert (Edmund)

Fitzgerald, Captain Hugh
  See Baum, L(yman) Frank

FitzGerald, Edward 1809-1883 .... NCLC 9
  See also DLB 32

Fitzgerald, F(rancis) Scott (Key)
  1896-1940 .... TCLC 1, 6, 14, 28, 55;
  DA; DAB; DAC; DAM MST, NOV;
  SSC 6; WLC
  See also AITN 1; CA 110; 123;
  CDALB 1917-1929; DLB 4, 9, 86;
  DLBD 1, 15, 16; DLBY 81, 96; MTCW

Fitzgerald, Penelope 1916-... CLC 19, 51, 61
  See also CA 85-88; CAAS 10; CANR 56;
  DLB 14

Fitzgerald, Robert (Stuart)
  1910-1985 .... CLC 39
  See also CA 1-4R; 114; CANR 1; DLBY 80

FitzGerald, Robert D(avid)
  1902-1987 .... CLC 19
  See also CA 17-20R

Fitzgerald, Zelda (Sayre)
  1900-1948 .... TCLC 52
  See also CA 117; 126; DLBY 84

Flanagan, Thomas (James Bonner)
  1923- .... CLC 25, 52
  See also CA 108; CANR 55; DLBY 80;
  INT 108; MTCW

Flaubert, Gustave
  1821-1880 .... NCLC 2, 10, 19, 62; DA;
  DAB; DAC; DAM MST, NOV; SSC 11;
  WLC
  See also DLB 119

Flecker, Herman Elroy
  See Flecker, (Herman) James Elroy

Flecker, (Herman) James Elroy
  1884-1915 .... TCLC 43
  See also CA 109; 150; DLB 10, 19

Fleming, Ian (Lancaster)
  1908-1964 ...... CLC 3, 30; DAM POP
  See also CA 5-8R; CANR 59;
  CDBLB 1945-1960; DLB 87; MTCW;
  SATA 9

Fleming, Thomas (James) 1927- .... CLC 37
  See also CA 5-8R; CANR 10;
  INT CANR-10; SATA 8

Fletcher, John 1579-1625..... LC 33; DC 6
  See also CDBLB Before 1660; DLB 58

Fletcher, John Gould 1886-1950... TCLC 35
  See also CA 107; DLB 4, 45

Fleur, Paul
  See Pohl, Frederik

Flooglebuckle, Al
  See Spiegelman, Art

Flying Officer X
  See Bates, H(erbert) E(rnest)

Fo, Dario 1926-..... CLC 32; DAM DRAM
  See also CA 116; 128; MTCW

Fogarty, Jonathan Titulescu Esq.
  See Farrell, James T(homas)

Folke, Will
  See Bloch, Robert (Albert)

Follett, Ken(neth Martin)
  1949- ...... CLC 18; DAM NOV, POP
  See also AAYA 6; BEST 89:4; CA 81-84;
  CANR 13, 33, 54; DLB 87; DLBY 81;
  INT CANR-33; MTCW

Fontane, Theodor 1819-1898 ..... NCLC 26
  See also DLB 129

Foote, Horton
  1916- .... CLC 51, 91; DAM DRAM
  See also CA 73-76; CANR 34, 51; DLB 26;
  INT CANR-34

Foote, Shelby
  1916- ...... CLC 75; DAM NOV, POP
  See also CA 5-8R; CANR 3, 45; DLB 2, 17

Forbes, Esther 1891-1967.......... CLC 12
  See also AAYA 17; CA 13-14; 25-28R;
  CAP 1; CLR 27; DLB 22; JRDA;
  MAICYA; SATA 2

Forche, Carolyn (Louise)
  1950- .... CLC 25, 83, 86; DAM POET;
  PC 10
  See also CA 109; 117; CANR 50; DLB 5;
  INT 117

Ford, Elbur
  See Hibbert, Eleanor Alice Burford

Ford, Ford Madox
  1873-1939 .... TCLC 1, 15, 39, 57;
  DAM NOV
  See also CA 104; 132; CDBLB 1914-1945;
  DLB 162; MTCW

Ford, Henry 1863-1947 .... TCLC 73
  See also CA 115; 148

Ford, John 1895-1973.............. CLC 16
  See also CA 45-48

Ford, Richard .... CLC 99

Ford, Richard 1944-.............. CLC 46
  See also CA 69-72; CANR 11, 47

Ford, Webster
  See Masters, Edgar Lee

Foreman, Richard 1937-........... CLC 50
  See also CA 65-68; CANR 32

Forester, C(ecil) S(cott)
  1899-1966 .... CLC 35
  See also CA 73-76; 25-28R; SATA 13

Forez
  See Mauriac, Francois (Charles)

Forman, James Douglas 1932-...... CLC 21
  See also AAYA 17; CA 9-12R; CANR 4,
  19, 42; JRDA; MAICYA; SATA 8, 70

Fornes, Maria Irene   1930-...... CLC 39, 61
  See also CA 25-28R; CANR 28; DLB 7;
  HW; INT CANR-28; MTCW

Forrest, Leon   1937-.............. CLC 4
  See also BW 2; CA 89-92; CAAS 7;
  CANR 25, 52; DLB 33

Forster, E(dward) M(organ)
  1879-1970 ..... CLC 1, 2, 3, 4, 9, 10, 13,
          15, 22, 45, 77; DA; DAB; DAC;
          DAM MST, NOV; SSC 27; WLC
  See also AAYA 2; CA 13-14; 25-28R;
  CANR 45; CAP 1; CDBLB 1914-1945;
  DLB 34, 98, 162, 178; DLBD 10; MTCW;
  SATA 57

Forster, John   1812-1876 .... NCLC 11
  See also DLB 144, 184

Forsyth, Frederick
  1938-.. CLC 2, 5, 36; DAM NOV, POP
  See also BEST 89:4; CA 85-88; CANR 38,
  62; DLB 87; MTCW

Forten, Charlotte L. .... TCLC 16; BLC
  See also Grimke, Charlotte L(ottie) Forten
  See also DLB 50

Foscolo, Ugo   1778-1827.......... NCLC 8

Fosse, Bob .... CLC 20
  See also Fosse, Robert Louis

Fosse, Robert Louis   1927-1987
  See Fosse, Bob
  See also CA 110; 123

Foster, Stephen Collins
  1826-1864 .... NCLC 26

Foucault, Michel
  1926-1984 .... CLC 31, 34, 69
  See also CA 105; 113; CANR 34; MTCW

Fouque, Friedrich (Heinrich Karl) de la Motte
  1777-1843 .... NCLC 2
  See also DLB 90

Fourier, Charles   1772-1837 ...... NCLC 51

Fournier, Henri Alban   1886-1914
  See Alain-Fournier
  See also CA 104

Fournier, Pierre   1916-............ CLC 11
  See also Gascar, Pierre
  See also CA 89-92; CANR 16, 40

Fowles, John
  1926- ...... CLC 1, 2, 3, 4, 6, 9, 10, 15,
          33, 87; DAB; DAC; DAM MST
  See also CA 5-8R; CANR 25; CDBLB 1960
  to Present; DLB 14, 139; MTCW;
  SATA 22

Fox, Paula   1923-................ CLC 2, 8
  See also AAYA 3; CA 73-76; CANR 20,
  36, 62; CLR 1, 44; DLB 52; JRDA;
  MAICYA; MTCW; SATA 17, 60

Fox, William Price (Jr.)   1926- ..... CLC 22
  See also CA 17-20R; CAAS 19; CANR 11;
  DLB 2; DLBY 81

Foxe, John   1516(?)-1587 .... LC 14

Frame, Janet
  1924-... CLC 2, 3, 6, 22, 66, 96; SSC 29
  See also Clutha, Janet Paterson Frame

France, Anatole .... TCLC 9
  See also Thibault, Jacques Anatole Francois
  See also DLB 123

Francis, Claude   19(?)- .... CLC 50

Francis, Dick
  1920- ... CLC 2, 22, 42, 102; DAM POP
  See also AAYA 5, 21; BEST 89:3; CA 5-8R;
  CANR 9, 42; CDBLB 1960 to Present;
  DLB 87; INT CANR-9; MTCW

Francis, Robert (Churchill)
  1901-1987 .... CLC 15
  See also CA 1-4R; 123; CANR 1

Frank, Anne(lies Marie)
  1929-1945 .... TCLC 17; DA; DAB;
                DAC; DAM MST; WLC
  See also AAYA 12; CA 113; 133; MTCW;
  SATA 87; SATA-Brief 42

Frank, Elizabeth   1945-........... CLC 39
  See also CA 121; 126; INT 126

Frankl, Viktor E(mil)   1905-........ CLC 93
  See also CA 65-68

Franklin, Benjamin
  See Hasek, Jaroslav (Matej Frantisek)

Franklin, Benjamin
  1706-1790 ..... LC 25; DA; DAB; DAC;
                DAM MST; WLCS
  See also CDALB 1640-1865; DLB 24, 43,
  73

Franklin, (Stella Maraia Sarah) Miles
  1879-1954 .... TCLC 7
  See also CA 104

Fraser, (Lady) Antonia (Pakenham)
  1932-...................... CLC 32
  See also CA 85-88; CANR 44; MTCW;
  SATA-Brief 32

Fraser, George MacDonald   1925-.... CLC 7
  See also CA 45-48; CANR 2, 48

Fraser, Sylvia   1935-............. CLC 64
  See also CA 45-48; CANR 1, 16, 60

Frayn, Michael
  1933-............... CLC 3, 7, 31, 47;
                DAM DRAM, NOV
  See also CA 5-8R; CANR 30; DLB 13, 14;
  MTCW

Fraze, Candida (Merrill)   1945-..... CLC 50
  See also CA 126

Frazer, J(ames) G(eorge)
  1854-1941 .... TCLC 32
  See also CA 118

Frazer, Robert Caine
  See Creasey, John

Frazer, Sir James George
  See Frazer, J(ames) G(eorge)

Frazier, Ian   1951-................ CLC 46
  See also CA 130; CANR 54

Frederic, Harold   1856-1898...... NCLC 10
  See also DLB 12, 23; DLBD 13

Frederick, John
  See Faust, Frederick (Schiller)

Frederick the Great   1712-1786 ...... LC 14

Fredro, Aleksander   1793-1876..... NCLC 8

Freeling, Nicolas   1927- .... CLC 38
  See also CA 49-52; CAAS 12; CANR 1, 17,
  50; DLB 87

Freeman, Douglas Southall
  1886-1953 .... TCLC 11
  See also CA 109; DLB 17

Freeman, Judith   1946-............ CLC 55
  See also CA 148

Freeman, Mary Eleanor Wilkins
  1852-1930 .... TCLC 9; SSC 1
  See also CA 106; DLB 12, 78

Freeman, R(ichard) Austin
  1862-1943 .... TCLC 21
  See also CA 113; DLB 70

French, Albert   1943- .... CLC 86

French, Marilyn
  1929-................ CLC 10, 18, 60;
                DAM DRAM, NOV, POP
  See also CA 69-72; CANR 3, 31;
  INT CANR-31; MTCW

French, Paul
  See Asimov, Isaac

Freneau, Philip Morin   1752-1832.. NCLC 1
  See also DLB 37, 43

Freud, Sigmund   1856-1939 .... TCLC 52
  See also CA 115; 133; MTCW

Friedan, Betty (Naomi)   1921-...... CLC 74
  See also CA 65-68; CANR 18, 45; MTCW

Friedlander, Saul   1932-........... CLC 90
  See also CA 117; 130

Friedman, B(ernard) H(arper)
  1926-..................... CLC 7
  See also CA 1-4R; CANR 3, 48

Friedman, Bruce Jay   1930-.... CLC 3, 5, 56
  See also CA 9-12R; CANR 25, 52; DLB 2,
  28; INT CANR-25

Friel, Brian   1929-........... CLC 5, 42, 59
  See also CA 21-24R; CANR 33; DLB 13;
  MTCW

Friis-Baastad, Babbis Ellinor
  1921-1970 .... CLC 12
  See also CA 17-20R; 134; SATA 7

Frisch, Max (Rudolf)
  1911-1991 ..... CLC 3, 9, 14, 18, 32, 44;
                DAM DRAM, NOV
  See also CA 85-88; 134; CANR 32;
  DLB 69, 124; MTCW

Fromentin, Eugene (Samuel Auguste)
  1820-1876 .... NCLC 10
  See also DLB 123

Frost, Frederick
  See Faust, Frederick (Schiller)

Frost, Robert (Lee)
  1874-1963 .... CLC 1, 3, 4, 9, 10, 13, 15,
          26, 34, 44; DA; DAB; DAC; DAM MST,
                POET; PC 1; WLC
  See also AAYA 21; CA 89-92; CANR 33;
  CDALB 1917-1929; DLB 54; DLBD 7;
  MTCW; SATA 14

Froude, James Anthony
  1818-1894 .... NCLC 43
  See also DLB 18, 57, 144

Froy, Herald
  See Waterhouse, Keith (Spencer)

Fry, Christopher
  1907- ..... CLC 2, 10, 14; DAM DRAM
  See also CA 17-20R; CAAS 23; CANR 9,
  30; DLB 13; MTCW; SATA 66

Frye, (Herman) Northrop
  1912-1991 .... CLC 24, 70
  See also CA 5-8R; 133; CANR 8, 37;
  DLB 67, 68; MTCW

Gary, Romain .... CLC 25
See also Kacew, Romain
See also DLB 83

Gascar, Pierre .... CLC 11
See also Fournier, Pierre

Gascoyne, David (Emery) 1916- .... CLC 45
See also CA 65-68; CANR 10, 28, 54;
DLB 20; MTCW

Gaskell, Elizabeth Cleghorn
1810-1865 .... NCLC 5; DAB;
DAM MST; SSC 25
See also CDBLB 1832-1890; DLB 21, 144,
159

Gass, William H(oward)
1924- ... CLC 1, 2, 8, 11, 15, 39; SSC 12
See also CA 17-20R; CANR 30; DLB 2;
MTCW

Gasset, Jose Ortega y
See Ortega y Gasset, Jose

Gates, Henry Louis, Jr.
1950- .... CLC 65; DAM MULT
See also BW 2; CA 109; CANR 25, 53;
DLB 67

Gautier, Theophile
1811-1872 .... NCLC 1, 59;
DAM POET; PC 18; SSC 20
See also DLB 119

Gawsworth, John
See Bates, H(erbert) E(rnest)

Gay, Oliver
See Gogarty, Oliver St. John

Gaye, Marvin (Penze) 1939-1984 ... CLC 26
See also CA 112

Gebler, Carlo (Ernest) 1954- .... CLC 39
See also CA 119; 133

Gee, Maggie (Mary) 1948-......... CLC 57
See also CA 130

Gee, Maurice (Gough) 1931-....... CLC 29
See also CA 97-100; SATA 46

Gelbart, Larry (Simon) 1923- ... CLC 21, 61
See also CA 73-76; CANR 45

Gelber, Jack 1932-........ CLC 1, 6, 14, 79
See also CA 1-4R; CANR 2; DLB 7

Gellhorn, Martha (Ellis) 1908- .. CLC 14, 60
See also CA 77-80; CANR 44; DLBY 82

Genet, Jean
1910-1986 ...... CLC 1, 2, 5, 10, 14, 44,
46; DAM DRAM
See also CA 13-16R; CANR 18; DLB 72;
DLBY 86; MTCW

Gent, Peter 1942-................ CLC 29
See also AITN 1; CA 89-92; DLBY 82

Gentlewoman in New England, A
See Bradstreet, Anne

Gentlewoman in Those Parts, A
See Bradstreet, Anne

George, Jean Craighead 1919-...... CLC 35
See also AAYA 8; CA 5-8R; CANR 25;
CLR 1; DLB 52; JRDA; MAICYA;
SATA 2, 68

George, Stefan (Anton)
1868-1933 .... TCLC 2, 14
See also CA 104

Georges, Georges Martin
See Simenon, Georges (Jacques Christian)

Gerhardi, William Alexander
See Gerhardie, William Alexander

Gerhardie, William Alexander
1895-1977 .... CLC 5
See also CA 25-28R; 73-76; CANR 18;
DLB 36

Gerstler, Amy 1956-.............. CLC 70
See also CA 146

Gertler, T. .... CLC 34
See also CA 116; 121; INT 121

Ghalib........................ NCLC 39
See also Ghalib, Hsadullah Khan

Ghalib, Hsadullah Khan 1797-1869
See Ghalib
See also DAM POET

Ghelderode, Michel de
1898-1962 .... CLC 6, 11; DAM DRAM
See also CA 85-88; CANR 40

Ghiselin, Brewster 1903- .... CLC 23
See also CA 13-16R; CAAS 10; CANR 13

Ghose, Zulfikar 1935-............. CLC 42
See also CA 65-68

Ghosh, Amitav 1956- .... CLC 44
See also CA 147

Giacosa, Giuseppe 1847-1906 ...... TCLC 7
See also CA 104

Gibb, Lee
See Waterhouse, Keith (Spencer)

Gibbon, Lewis Grassic .... TCLC 4
See also Mitchell, James Leslie

Gibbons, Kaye
1960- .... CLC 50, 88; DAM POP
See also CA 151

Gibran, Kahlil
1883-1931 .... TCLC 1, 9; DAM POET,
POP; PC 9
See also CA 104; 150

Gibran, Khalil
See Gibran, Kahlil

Gibson, William
1914- .... CLC 23; DA; DAB; DAC;
DAM DRAM, MST
See also CA 9-12R; CANR 9, 42; DLB 7;
SATA 66

Gibson, William (Ford)
1948- .... CLC 39, 63; DAM POP
See also AAYA 12; CA 126; 133; CANR 52

Gide, Andre (Paul Guillaume)
1869-1951 .... TCLC 5, 12, 36; DA;
DAB; DAC; DAM MST, NOV; SSC 13;
WLC
See also CA 104; 124; DLB 65; MTCW

Gifford, Barry (Colby) 1946-....... CLC 34
See also CA 65-68; CANR 9, 30, 40

Gilbert, Frank
See De Voto, Bernard (Augustine)

Gilbert, W(illiam) S(chwenck)
1836-1911 ..... TCLC 3; DAM DRAM,
POET
See also CA 104; SATA 36

Gilbreth, Frank B., Jr. 1911-....... CLC 17
See also CA 9-12R; SATA 2

Gilchrist, Ellen
1935- .... CLC 34, 48; DAM POP;
SSC 14
See also CA 113; 116; CANR 41, 61;
DLB 130; MTCW

Giles, Molly 1942-................ CLC 39
See also CA 126

Gill, Patrick
See Creasey, John

Gilliam, Terry (Vance) 1940-...... CLC 21
See also Monty Python
See also AAYA 19; CA 108; 113;
CANR 35; INT 113

Gillian, Jerry
See Gilliam, Terry (Vance)

Gilliatt, Penelope (Ann Douglass)
1932-1993 .... CLC 2, 10, 13, 53
See also AITN 2; CA 13-16R; 141;
CANR 49; DLB 14

Gilman, Charlotte (Anna) Perkins (Stetson)
1860-1935 .... TCLC 9, 37; SSC 13
See also CA 106; 150

Gilmour, David 1949-............. CLC 35
See also CA 138; 147

Gilpin, William 1724-1804....... NCLC 30

Gilray, J. D.
See Mencken, H(enry) L(ouis)

Gilroy, Frank D(aniel) 1925-........ CLC 2
See also CA 81-84; CANR 32; DLB 7

Gilstrap, John 1957(?)-............ CLC 99
See also CA 160

Ginsberg, Allen
1926-1997 ..... CLC 1, 2, 3, 4, 6, 13, 36,
69; DA; DAB; DAC; DAM MST, POET;
PC 4; WLC 3
See also AITN 1; CA 1-4R; 157; CANR 2,
41; CDALB 1941-1968; DLB 5, 16, 169;
MTCW

Ginzburg, Natalia
1916-1991 .... CLC 5, 11, 54, 70
See also CA 85-88; 135; CANR 33;
DLB 177; MTCW

Giono, Jean 1895-1970.......... CLC 4, 11
See also CA 45-48; 29-32R; CANR 2, 35;
DLB 72; MTCW

Giovanni, Nikki
1943- ...... CLC 2, 4, 19, 64; BLC; DA;
DAB; DAC; DAM MST, MULT, POET;
PC 19; WLCS
See also AAYA 22; AITN 1; BW 2;
CA 29-32R; CAAS 6; CANR 18, 41, 60;
CLR 6; DLB 5, 41; INT CANR-18;
MAICYA; MTCW; SATA 24

Giovene, Andrea 1904-............. CLC 7
See also CA 85-88

Gippius, Zinaida (Nikolayevna) 1869-1945
See Hippius, Zinaida
See also CA 106

Giraudoux, (Hippolyte) Jean
1882-1944 .... TCLC 2, 7; DAM DRAM
See also CA 104; DLB 65

Gironella, Jose Maria 1917- .... CLC 11
See also CA 101

Gissing, George (Robert)
1857-1903 .... TCLC 3, 24, 47
See also CA 105; DLB 18, 135, 184

Giurlani, Aldo
See Palazzeschi, Aldo

Gladkov, Fyodor (Vasilyevich)
1883-1958 . . . . TCLC 27

Glanville, Brian (Lester)   1931- . . . . . .   CLC 6
See also CA 5-8R; CAAS 9; CANR 3;
DLB 15, 139; SATA 42

Glasgow, Ellen (Anderson Gholson)
1873(?)-1945 . . . . TCLC 2, 7
See also CA 104; DLB 9, 12

Glaspell, Susan   1882(?)-1948 . . . . . .   TCLC 55
See also CA 110; 154; DLB 7, 9, 78;
YABC 2

Glassco, John   1909-1981 . . . .   CLC 9
See also CA 13-16R; 102; CANR 15;
DLB 68

Glasscock, Amnesia
See Steinbeck, John (Ernst)

Glasser, Ronald J.   1940(?)- . . . .   CLC 37

Glassman, Joyce
See Johnson, Joyce

Glendinning, Victoria   1937- . . . .   CLC 50
See also CA 120; 127; CANR 59; DLB 155

Glissant, Edouard
1928- . . . .   CLC 10, 68; DAM MULT
See also CA 153

Gloag, Julian   1930- . . . .   CLC 40
See also AITN 1; CA 65-68; CANR 10

Glowacki, Aleksander
See Prus, Boleslaw

Gluck, Louise (Elisabeth)
1943- . . . .   CLC 7, 22, 44, 81;
DAM POET; PC 16
See also CA 33-36R; CANR 40; DLB 5

Glyn, Elinor   1864-1943 . . . .   TCLC 72
See also DLB 153

Gobineau, Joseph Arthur (Comte) de
1816-1882 . . . .   NCLC 17
See also DLB 123

Godard, Jean-Luc   1930- . . . .   CLC 20
See also CA 93-96

Godden, (Margaret) Rumer   1907- . . .   CLC 53
See also AAYA 6; CA 5-8R; CANR 4, 27,
36, 55; CLR 20; DLB 161; MAICYA;
SAAS 12; SATA 3, 36

Godoy Alcayaga, Lucila   1889-1957
See Mistral, Gabriela
See also BW 2; CA 104; 131; DAM MULT;
HW; MTCW

Godwin, Gail (Kathleen)
1937- . . . .   CLC 5, 8, 22, 31, 69;
DAM POP
See also CA 29-32R; CANR 15, 43; DLB 6;
INT CANR-15; MTCW

Godwin, William   1756-1836 . . . . . .   NCLC 14
See also CDBLB 1789-1832; DLB 39, 104,
142, 158, 163

Goebbels, Josef
See Goebbels, (Paul) Joseph

Goebbels, (Paul) Joseph
1897-1945 . . . .   TCLC 68
See also CA 115; 148

Goebbels, Joseph Paul
See Goebbels, (Paul) Joseph

Goethe, Johann Wolfgang von
1749-1832 . . . .   NCLC 4, 22, 34; DA;
DAB; DAC; DAM DRAM, MST,
POET; PC 5; WLC 3
See also DLB 94

Gogarty, Oliver St. John
1878-1957 . . . .   TCLC 15
See also CA 109; 150; DLB 15, 19

Gogol, Nikolai (Vasilyevich)
1809-1852 . . . .   NCLC 5, 15, 31; DA;
DAB; DAC; DAM DRAM, MST; DC 1;
SSC 4, 29; WLC
See also DLB 94

Goines, Donald
1937(?)-1974 . . . .   CLC 80; BLC;
DAM MULT, POP
See also AITN 1; BW 1; CA 124; 114;
DLB 33

Gold, Herbert   1924- . . . .   CLC 4, 7, 14, 42
See also CA 9-12R; CANR 17, 45; DLB 2;
DLBY 81

Goldbarth, Albert   1948- . . . .   CLC 5, 38
See also CA 53-56; CANR 6, 40; DLB 120

Goldberg, Anatol   1910-1982 . . . .   CLC 34
See also CA 131; 117

Goldemberg, Isaac   1945- . . . .   CLC 52
See also CA 69-72; CAAS 12; CANR 11,
32; HW

Golding, William (Gerald)
1911-1993 . . . .   CLC 1, 2, 3, 8, 10, 17, 27,
58, 81; DA; DAB; DAC; DAM MST,
NOV; WLC
See also AAYA 5; CA 5-8R; 141;
CANR 13, 33, 54; CDBLB 1945-1960;
DLB 15, 100; MTCW

Goldman, Emma   1869-1940 . . . . . .   TCLC 13
See also CA 110; 150

Goldman, Francisco   1955- . . . .   CLC 76

Goldman, William (W.)   1931- . . . .   CLC 1, 48
See also CA 9-12R; CANR 29; DLB 44

Goldmann, Lucien   1913-1970 . . . . . .   CLC 24
See also CA 25-28; CAP 2

Goldoni, Carlo
1707-1793 . . . .   LC 4; DAM DRAM

Goldsberry, Steven   1949- . . . .   CLC 34
See also CA 131

Goldsmith, Oliver
1728-1774 . . . . . .   LC 2; DA; DAB; DAC;
DAM DRAM, MST, NOV, POET;
WLC
See also CDBLB 1660-1789; DLB 39, 89,
104, 109, 142; SATA 26

Goldsmith, Peter
See Priestley, J(ohn) B(oynton)

Gombrowicz, Witold
1904-1969 . . . .   CLC 4, 7, 11, 49;
DAM DRAM
See also CA 19-20; 25-28R; CAP 2

Gomez de la Serna, Ramon
1888-1963 . . . .   CLC 9
See also CA 153; 116; HW

Goncharov, Ivan Alexandrovich
1812-1891 . . . .   NCLC 1, 63

Goncourt, Edmond (Louis Antoine Huot) de
1822-1896 . . . .   NCLC 7
See also DLB 123

Goncourt, Jules (Alfred Huot) de
1830-1870 . . . .   NCLC 7
See also DLB 123

Gontier, Fernande   19(?)- . . . .   CLC 50

Gonzalez Martinez, Enrique
1871-1952 . . . .   TCLC 72
See also HW

Goodman, Paul   1911-1972 . . . .   CLC 1, 2, 4, 7
See also CA 19-20; 37-40R; CANR 34;
CAP 2; DLB 130; MTCW

Gordimer, Nadine
1923- . . . .   CLC 3, 5, 7, 10, 18, 33, 51, 70;
DA; DAB; DAC; DAM MST, NOV;
SSC 17; WLCS
See also CA 5-8R; CANR 3, 28, 56;
INT CANR-28; MTCW

Gordon, Adam Lindsay
1833-1870 . . . .   NCLC 21

Gordon, Caroline
1895-1981 . . .   CLC 6, 13, 29, 83; SSC 15
See also CA 11-12; 103; CANR 36; CAP 1;
DLB 4, 9, 102; DLBY 81; MTCW

Gordon, Charles William   1860-1937
See Connor, Ralph
See also CA 109

Gordon, Mary (Catherine)
1949- . . . .   CLC 13, 22
See also CA 102; CANR 44; DLB 6;
DLBY 81; INT 102; MTCW

Gordon, N. J.
See Bosman, Herman Charles

Gordon, Sol   1923- . . . .   CLC 26
See also CA 53-56; CANR 4; SATA 11

Gordone, Charles
1925-1995 . . . . .   CLC 1, 4; DAM DRAM
See also BW 1; CA 93-96; 150; CANR 55;
DLB 7; INT 93-96; MTCW

Gorenko, Anna Andreevna
See Akhmatova, Anna

Gorky, Maxim
. . . .   TCLC 8; DAB; SSC 28; WLC
See also Peshkov, Alexei Maximovich

Goryan, Sirak
See Saroyan, William

Gosse, Edmund (William)
1849-1928 . . . .   TCLC 28
See also CA 117; DLB 57, 144, 184

Gotlieb, Phyllis Fay (Bloom)
1926- . . . .   CLC 18
See also CA 13-16R; CANR 7; DLB 88

Gottesman, S. D.
See Kornbluth, C(yril) M.; Pohl, Frederik

Gottfried von Strassburg
fl. c. 1210- . . . .   CMLC 10
See also DLB 138

Gould, Lois . . . .   CLC 4, 10
See also CA 77-80; CANR 29; MTCW

Gourmont, Remy (-Marie-Charles) de
1858-1915 . . . .   TCLC 17
See also CA 109; 150

Govier, Katherine   1948- . . . .   CLC 51
See also CA 101; CANR 18, 40

Author Index

Goyen, (Charles) William
1915-1983 . . . . **CLC 5, 8, 14, 40**
See also AITN 2; CA 5-8R; 110; CANR 6;
DLB 2; DLBY 83; INT CANR-6

Goytisolo, Juan
1931- . . . . . **CLC 5, 10, 23; DAM MULT;**
HLC
See also CA 85-88; CANR 32, 61; HW;
MTCW

Gozzano, Guido 1883-1916 . . . . **PC 10**
See also CA 154; DLB 114

Gozzi, (Conte) Carlo 1720-1806 . . **NCLC 23**

Grabbe, Christian Dietrich
1801-1836 . . . . **NCLC 2**
See also DLB 133

Grace, Patricia 1937- . . . . **CLC 56**

Gracian y Morales, Baltasar
1601-1658 . . . . **LC 15**

Gracq, Julien . . . . **CLC 11, 48**
See also Poirier, Louis
See also DLB 83

Grade, Chaim 1910-1982 . . . . **CLC 10**
See also CA 93-96; 107

Graduate of Oxford, A
See Ruskin, John

Grafton, Garth
See Duncan, Sara Jeannette

Graham, John
See Phillips, David Graham

Graham, Jorie 1951- . . . . **CLC 48**
See also CA 111; DLB 120

Graham, R(obert) B(ontine) Cunninghame
See Cunninghame Graham, R(obert)
B(ontine)
See also DLB 98, 135, 174

Graham, Robert
See Haldeman, Joe (William)

Graham, Tom
See Lewis, (Harry) Sinclair

Graham, W(illiam) S(ydney)
1918-1986 . . . . **CLC 29**
See also CA 73-76; 118; DLB 20

Graham, Winston (Mawdsley)
1910- . . . . **CLC 23**
See also CA 49-52; CANR 2, 22, 45;
DLB 77

Grahame, Kenneth
1859-1932 . . . . **TCLC 64; DAB**
See also CA 108; 136; CLR 5; DLB 34, 141,
178; MAICYA; YABC 1

Grant, Skeeter
See Spiegelman, Art

Granville-Barker, Harley
1877-1946 . . . . . . **TCLC 2; DAM DRAM**
See also Barker, Harley Granville
See also CA 104

Grass, Guenter (Wilhelm)
1927- . . . . . **CLC 1, 2, 4, 6, 11, 15, 22, 32,**
49, 88; DA; DAB; DAC; DAM MST,
NOV; WLC
See also CA 13-16R; CANR 20; DLB 75,
124; MTCW

Gratton, Thomas
See Hulme, T(homas) E(rnest)

Grau, Shirley Ann
1929- . . . . **CLC 4, 9; SSC 15**
See also CA 89-92; CANR 22; DLB 2;
INT CANR-22; MTCW

Gravel, Fern
See Hall, James Norman

Graver, Elizabeth 1964- . . . . **CLC 70**
See also CA 135

Graves, Richard Perceval 1945- . . . . **CLC 44**
See also CA 65-68; CANR 9, 26, 51

Graves, Robert (von Ranke)
1895-1985 . . . . . . **CLC 1, 2, 6, 11, 39, 44,**
45; DAB; DAC; DAM MST, POET;
PC 6
See also CA 5-8R; 117; CANR 5, 36;
CDBLB 1914-1945; DLB 20, 100;
DLBY 85; MTCW; SATA 45

Graves, Valerie
See Bradley, Marion Zimmer

Gray, Alasdair (James) 1934- . . . . . . **CLC 41**
See also CA 126; CANR 47; INT 126;
MTCW

Gray, Amlin 1946- . . . . **CLC 29**
See also CA 138

Gray, Francine du Plessix
1930- . . . . **CLC 22; DAM NOV**
See also BEST 90:3; CA 61-64; CAAS 2;
CANR 11, 33; INT CANR-11; MTCW

Gray, John (Henry) 1866-1934 . . . . **TCLC 19**
See also CA 119

Gray, Simon (James Holliday)
1936- . . . . **CLC 9, 14, 36**
See also AITN 1; CA 21-24R; CAAS 3;
CANR 32; DLB 13; MTCW

Gray, Spalding
1941- . . . . . . **CLC 49; DAM POP; DC 7**
See also CA 128

Gray, Thomas
1716-1771 . . . . **LC 4, 40; DA; DAB;**
DAC; DAM MST; PC 2; WLC
See also CDBLB 1660-1789; DLB 109

Grayson, David
See Baker, Ray Stannard

Grayson, Richard (A.) 1951- . . . . **CLC 38**
See also CA 85-88; CANR 14, 31, 57

Greeley, Andrew M(oran)
1928- . . . . **CLC 28; DAM POP**
See also CA 5-8R; CAAS 7; CANR 7, 43;
MTCW

Green, Anna Katharine
1846-1935 . . . . **TCLC 63**
See also CA 112; 159

Green, Brian
See Card, Orson Scott

Green, Hannah
See Greenberg, Joanne (Goldenberg)

Green, Hannah 1927(?)-1996 . . . . **CLC 3**
See also CA 73-76; CANR 59

Green, Henry 1905-1973 . . . . . **CLC 2, 13, 97**
See also Yorke, Henry Vincent
See also DLB 15

Green, Julian (Hartridge) 1900-
See Green, Julien
See also CA 21-24R; CANR 33; DLB 4, 72;
MTCW

Green, Julien . . . . **CLC 3, 11, 77**
See also Green, Julian (Hartridge)

Green, Paul (Eliot)
1894-1981 . . . . . . **CLC 25; DAM DRAM**
See also AITN 1; CA 5-8R; 103; CANR 3;
DLB 7, 9; DLBY 81

Greenberg, Ivan 1908-1973
See Rahv, Philip
See also CA 85-88

Greenberg, Joanne (Goldenberg)
1932- . . . . **CLC 7, 30**
See also AAYA 12; CA 5-8R; CANR 14,
32; SATA 25

Greenberg, Richard 1959(?)- . . . . **CLC 57**
See also CA 138

Greene, Bette 1934- . . . . **CLC 30**
See also AAYA 7; CA 53-56; CANR 4;
CLR 2; JRDA; MAICYA; SAAS 16;
SATA 8

Greene, Gael . . . . **CLC 8**
See also CA 13-16R; CANR 10

Greene, Graham (Henry)
1904-1991 . . . . **CLC 1, 3, 6, 9, 14, 18, 27,**
37, 70, 72; DA; DAB; DAC; DAM MST,
NOV; SSC 29; WLC
See also AITN 2; CA 13-16R; 133;
CANR 35, 61; CDBLB 1945-1960;
DLB 13, 15, 77, 100, 162; DLBY 91;
MTCW; SATA 20

Greer, Richard
See Silverberg, Robert

Gregor, Arthur 1923- . . . . **CLC 9**
See also CA 25-28R; CAAS 10; CANR 11;
SATA 36

Gregor, Lee
See Pohl, Frederik

Gregory, Isabella Augusta (Persse)
1852-1932 . . . . **TCLC 1**
See also CA 104; DLB 10

Gregory, J. Dennis
See Williams, John A(lfred)

Grendon, Stephen
See Derleth, August (William)

Grenville, Kate 1950- . . . . **CLC 61**
See also CA 118; CANR 53

Grenville, Pelham
See Wodehouse, P(elham) G(renville)

Greve, Felix Paul (Berthold Friedrich)
1879-1948
See Grove, Frederick Philip
See also CA 104; 141; DAC; DAM MST

Grey, Zane
1872-1939 . . . . **TCLC 6; DAM POP**
See also CA 104; 132; DLB 9; MTCW

Grieg, (Johan) Nordahl (Brun)
1902-1943 . . . . **TCLC 10**
See also CA 107

Grieve, C(hristopher) M(urray)
1892-1978 . . . . **CLC 11, 19; DAM POET**
See also MacDiarmid, Hugh; Pteleon
See also CA 5-8R; 85-88; CANR 33;
MTCW

Griffin, Gerald 1803-1840 . . . . **NCLC 7**
See also DLB 159

Griffin, John Howard 1920-1980.... **CLC 68**
See also AITN 1; CA 1-4R; 101; CANR 2

Griffin, Peter 1942- .... **CLC 39**
See also CA 136

Griffith, D(avid Lewelyn) W(ark)
1875(?)-1948 .... **TCLC 68**
See also CA 119; 150

Griffith, Lawrence
See Griffith, D(avid Lewelyn) W(ark)

Griffiths, Trevor 1935-........ **CLC 13, 52**
See also CA 97-100; CANR 45; DLB 13

Grigson, Geoffrey (Edward Harvey)
1905-1985 .... **CLC 7, 39**
See also CA 25-28R; 118; CANR 20, 33;
DLB 27; MTCW

Grillparzer, Franz 1791-1872...... **NCLC 1**
See also DLB 133

Grimble, Reverend Charles James
See Eliot, T(homas) S(tearns)

Grimke, Charlotte L(ottie) Forten
1837(?)-1914
See Forten, Charlotte L.
See also BW 1; CA 117; 124; DAM MULT,
POET

Grimm, Jacob Ludwig Karl
1785-1863 .... **NCLC 3**
See also DLB 90; MAICYA; SATA 22

Grimm, Wilhelm Karl 1786-1859 .. **NCLC 3**
See also DLB 90; MAICYA; SATA 22

Grimmelshausen, Johann Jakob Christoffel
von 1621-1676 .... **LC 6**
See also DLB 168

Grindel, Eugene 1895-1952
See Eluard, Paul
See also CA 104

Grisham, John 1955- .. **CLC 84; DAM POP**
See also AAYA 14; CA 138; CANR 47

Grossman, David 1954- .... **CLC 67**
See also CA 138

Grossman, Vasily (Semenovich)
1905-1964 .... **CLC 41**
See also CA 124; 130; MTCW

Grove, Frederick Philip .... **TCLC 4**
See also Greve, Felix Paul (Berthold
Friedrich)
See also DLB 92

Grubb
See Crumb, R(obert)

Grumbach, Doris (Isaac)
1918- .... **CLC 13, 22, 64**
See also CA 5-8R; CAAS 2; CANR 9, 42;
INT CANR-9

Grundtvig, Nicolai Frederik Severin
1783-1872 .... **NCLC 1**

Grunge
See Crumb, R(obert)

Grunwald, Lisa 1959-............. **CLC 44**
See also CA 120

Guare, John
1938- .... **CLC 8, 14, 29, 67;**
　　　　　　　　　　　　　　　　DAM DRAM
See also CA 73-76; CANR 21; DLB 7;
MTCW

Gudjonsson, Halldor Kiljan 1902-
See Laxness, Halldor
See also CA 103

Guenter, Erich
See Eich, Guenter

Guest, Barbara 1920-............. **CLC 34**
See also CA 25-28R; CANR 11, 44; DLB 5

Guest, Judith (Ann)
1936- .... **CLC 8, 30; DAM NOV, POP**
See also AAYA 7; CA 77-80; CANR 15;
INT CANR-15; MTCW

Guevara, Che............... **CLC 87; HLC**
See also Guevara (Serna), Ernesto

Guevara (Serna), Ernesto 1928-1967
See Guevara, Che
See also CA 127; 111; CANR 56;
DAM MULT; HW

Guild, Nicholas M. 1944-.......... **CLC 33**
See also CA 93-96

Guillemin, Jacques
See Sartre, Jean-Paul

Guillen, Jorge
1893-1984 ...... **CLC 11; DAM MULT,**
　　　　　　　　　　　　　　　　　　　POET
See also CA 89-92; 112; DLB 108; HW

Guillen, Nicolas (Cristobal)
1902-1989 .... **CLC 48, 79; BLC;**
　　　　　　DAM MST, MULT, POET; HLC
See also BW 2; CA 116; 125; 129; HW

Guillevic, (Eugene) 1907-.......... **CLC 33**
See also CA 93-96

Guillois
See Desnos, Robert

Guillois, Valentin
See Desnos, Robert

Guiney, Louise Imogen
1861-1920 .... **TCLC 41**
See also CA 160; DLB 54

Guiraldes, Ricardo (Guillermo)
1886-1927 .... **TCLC 39**
See also CA 131; HW; MTCW

Gumilev, Nikolai Stephanovich
1886-1921 .... **TCLC 60**

Gunesekera, Romesh 1954- .... **CLC 91**
See also CA 159

Gunn, Bill .... **CLC 5**
See also Gunn, William Harrison
See also DLB 38

Gunn, Thom(son William)
1929- .... **CLC 3, 6, 18, 32, 81;**
　　　　　　　　　　　　　　　　　　DAM POET
See also CA 17-20R; CANR 9, 33;
CDBLB 1960 to Present; DLB 27;
INT CANR-33; MTCW

Gunn, William Harrison 1934(?)-1989
See Gunn, Bill
See also AITN 1; BW 1; CA 13-16R; 128;
CANR 12, 25

Gunnars, Kristjana 1948-.......... **CLC 69**
See also CA 113; DLB 60

Gurdjieff, G(eorgei) I(vanovich)
1877(?)-1949 .... **TCLC 71**
See also CA 157

Gurganus, Allan
1947- .... **CLC 70; DAM POP**
See also BEST 90:1; CA 135

Gurney, A(lbert) R(amsdell), Jr.
1930- .... **CLC 32, 50, 54; DAM DRAM**
See also CA 77-80; CANR 32

Gurney, Ivor (Bertie) 1890-1937... **TCLC 33**

Gurney, Peter
See Gurney, A(lbert) R(amsdell), Jr.

Guro, Elena 1877-1913........... **TCLC 56**

Gustafson, James M(oody) 1925- .. **CLC 100**
See also CA 25-28R; CANR 37

Gustafson, Ralph (Barker) 1909-.... **CLC 36**
See also CA 21-24R; CANR 8, 45; DLB 88

Gut, Gom
See Simenon, Georges (Jacques Christian)

Guterson, David 1956-............. **CLC 91**
See also CA 132

Guthrie, A(lfred) B(ertram), Jr.
1901-1991 .... **CLC 23**
See also CA 57-60; 134; CANR 24; DLB 6;
SATA 62; SATA-Obit 67

Guthrie, Isobel
See Grieve, C(hristopher) M(urray)

Guthrie, Woodrow Wilson 1912-1967
See Guthrie, Woody
See also CA 113; 93-96

Guthrie, Woody................... **CLC 35**
See also Guthrie, Woodrow Wilson

Guy, Rosa (Cuthbert) 1928-........ **CLC 26**
See also AAYA 4; BW 2; CA 17-20R;
CANR 14, 34; CLR 13; DLB 33; JRDA;
MAICYA; SATA 14, 62

Gwendolyn
See Bennett, (Enoch) Arnold

H. D. .... **CLC 3, 8, 14, 31, 34, 73; PC 5**
See also Doolittle, Hilda

H. de V.
See Buchan, John

Haavikko, Paavo Juhani
1931- .... **CLC 18, 34**
See also CA 106

Habbema, Koos
See Heijermans, Herman

Habermas, Juergen 1929- .... **CLC 104**
See also CA 109

Habermas, Jurgen
See Habermas, Juergen

Hacker, Marilyn
1942- .... **CLC 5, 9, 23, 72, 91;**
　　　　　　　　　　　　　　　　　　DAM POET
See also CA 77-80; DLB 120

Haggard, H(enry) Rider
1856-1925 .... **TCLC 11**
See also CA 108; 148; DLB 70, 156, 174,
178; SATA 16

Hagiosy, L.
See Larbaud, Valery (Nicolas)

Hagiwara Sakutaro
1886-1942 .... **TCLC 60; PC 18**

Haig, Fenil
See Ford, Ford Madox

Haig-Brown, Roderick (Langmere)
　1908-1976 .... **CLC 21**
　See also CA 5-8R; 69-72; CANR 4, 38;
　CLR 31; DLB 88; MAICYA; SATA 12

Hailey, Arthur
　1920- .... **CLC 5; DAM NOV, POP**
　See also AITN 2; BEST 90:3; CA 1-4R;
　CANR 2, 36; DLB 88; DLBY 82; MTCW

Hailey, Elizabeth Forsythe 1938-... **CLC 40**
　See also CA 93-96; CAAS 1; CANR 15, 48;
　INT CANR-15

Haines, John (Meade) 1924-....... **CLC 58**
　See also CA 17-20R; CANR 13, 34; DLB 5

Hakluyt, Richard 1552-1616 .... **LC 31**

Haldeman, Joe (William) 1943-..... **CLC 61**
　See also CA 53-56; CAAS 25; CANR 6;
　DLB 8; INT CANR-6

Haley, Alex(ander Murray Palmer)
　1921-1992 .... **CLC 8, 12, 76; BLC; DA;
　DAB; DAC; DAM MST, MULT, POP**
　See also BW 2; CA 77-80; 136; CANR 61;
　DLB 38; MTCW

Haliburton, Thomas Chandler
　1796-1865 .... **NCLC 15**
　See also DLB 11, 99

Hall, Donald (Andrew, Jr.)
　1928- .. **CLC 1, 13, 37, 59; DAM POET**
　See also CA 5-8R; CAAS 7; CANR 2, 44;
　DLB 5; SATA 23

Hall, Frederic Sauser
　See Sauser-Hall, Frederic

Hall, James
　See Kuttner, Henry

Hall, James Norman 1887-1951 ... **TCLC 23**
　See also CA 123; SATA 21

Hall, (Marguerite) Radclyffe
　1886-1943 .... **TCLC 12**
　See also CA 110; 150

Hall, Rodney 1935- .... **CLC 51**
　See also CA 109

Halleck, Fitz-Greene 1790-1867 .. **NCLC 47**
　See also DLB 3

Halliday, Michael
　See Creasey, John

Halpern, Daniel 1945- .... **CLC 14**
　See also CA 33-36R

Hamburger, Michael (Peter Leopold)
　1924- .... **CLC 5, 14**
　See also CA 5-8R; CAAS 4; CANR 2, 47;
　DLB 27

Hamill, Pete 1935-............... **CLC 10**
　See also CA 25-28R; CANR 18

Hamilton, Alexander
　1755(?)-1804 .... **NCLC 49**
　See also DLB 37

Hamilton, Clive
　See Lewis, C(live) S(taples)

Hamilton, Edmond 1904-1977....... **CLC 1**
　See also CA 1-4R; CANR 3; DLB 8

Hamilton, Eugene (Jacob) Lee
　See Lee-Hamilton, Eugene (Jacob)

Hamilton, Franklin
　See Silverberg, Robert

Hamilton, Gail
　See Corcoran, Barbara

Hamilton, Mollie
　See Kaye, M(ary) M(argaret)

Hamilton, (Anthony Walter) Patrick
　1904-1962 .... **CLC 51**
　See also CA 113; DLB 10

Hamilton, Virginia
　1936- .... **CLC 26; DAM MULT**
　See also AAYA 2, 21; BW 2; CA 25-28R;
　CANR 20, 37; CLR 1, 11, 40; DLB 33,
　52; INT CANR-20; JRDA; MAICYA;
　MTCW; SATA 4, 56, 79

Hammett, (Samuel) Dashiell
　1894-1961 .... **CLC 3, 5, 10, 19, 47;
　SSC 17**
　See also AITN 1; CA 81-84; CANR 42;
　CDALB 1929-1941; DLBD 6; DLBY 96;
　MTCW

Hammon, Jupiter
　1711(?)-1800(?) .... **NCLC 5; BLC;
　DAM MULT, POET; PC 16**
　See also DLB 31, 50

Hammond, Keith
　See Kuttner, Henry

Hamner, Earl (Henry), Jr. 1923-... **CLC 12**
　See also AITN 2; CA 73-76; DLB 6

Hampton, Christopher (James)
　1946-...................... **CLC 4**
　See also CA 25-28R; DLB 13; MTCW

Hamsun, Knut .... **TCLC 2, 14, 49**
　See also Pedersen, Knut

Handke, Peter
　1942- .... **CLC 5, 8, 10, 15, 38;
　DAM DRAM, NOV**
　See also CA 77-80; CANR 33; DLB 85,
　124; MTCW

Hanley, James 1901-1985 ... **CLC 3, 5, 8, 13**
　See also CA 73-76; 117; CANR 36; MTCW

Hannah, Barry 1942-....... **CLC 23, 38, 90**
　See also CA 108; 110; CANR 43; DLB 6;
　INT 110; MTCW

Hannon, Ezra
　See Hunter, Evan

Hansberry, Lorraine (Vivian)
　1930-1965 ...... **CLC 17, 62; BLC; DA;
　DAB; DAC; DAM DRAM, MST,
　MULT; DC 2**
　See also BW 1; CA 109; 25-28R; CABS 3;
　CANR 58; CDALB 1941-1968; DLB 7,
　38; MTCW

Hansen, Joseph 1923-............. **CLC 38**
　See also CA 29-32R; CAAS 17; CANR 16,
　44; INT CANR-16

Hansen, Martin A. 1909-1955..... **TCLC 32**

Hanson, Kenneth O(stlin) 1922-.... **CLC 13**
　See also CA 53-56; CANR 7

Hardwick, Elizabeth
　1916-........... **CLC 13; DAM NOV**
　See also CA 5-8R; CANR 3, 32; DLB 6;
　MTCW

Hardy, Thomas
　1840-1928 ...... **TCLC 4, 10, 18, 32, 48,
　53, 72; DA; DAB; DAC; DAM MST,
　NOV, POET; PC 8; SSC 2; WLC**
　See also CA 104; 123; CDBLB 1890-1914;
　DLB 18, 19, 135; MTCW

Hare, David 1947- .... **CLC 29, 58**
　See also CA 97-100; CANR 39; DLB 13;
　MTCW

Harford, Henry
　See Hudson, W(illiam) H(enry)

Hargrave, Leonie
　See Disch, Thomas M(ichael)

Harjo, Joy 1951- ... **CLC 83; DAM MULT**
　See also CA 114; CANR 35; DLB 120, 175;
　NNAL

Harlan, Louis R(udolph) 1922-..... **CLC 34**
　See also CA 21-24R; CANR 25, 55

Harling, Robert 1951(?)- .... **CLC 53**
　See also CA 147

Harmon, William (Ruth) 1938-..... **CLC 38**
　See also CA 33-36R; CANR 14, 32, 35;
　SATA 65

Harper, F. E. W.
　See Harper, Frances Ellen Watkins

Harper, Frances E. W.
　See Harper, Frances Ellen Watkins

Harper, Frances E. Watkins
　See Harper, Frances Ellen Watkins

Harper, Frances Ellen
　See Harper, Frances Ellen Watkins

Harper, Frances Ellen Watkins
　1825-1911 .... **TCLC 14; BLC;
　DAM MULT, POET**
　See also BW 1; CA 111; 125; DLB 50

Harper, Michael S(teven) 1938- .. **CLC 7, 22**
　See also BW 1; CA 33-36R; CANR 24;
　DLB 41

Harper, Mrs. F. E. W.
　See Harper, Frances Ellen Watkins

Harris, Christie (Lucy) Irwin
　1907- .... **CLC 12**
　See also CA 5-8R; CANR 6; CLR 47;
　DLB 88; JRDA; MAICYA; SAAS 10;
　SATA 6, 74

Harris, Frank 1856-1931........ **TCLC 24**
　See also CA 109; 150; DLB 156

Harris, George Washington
　1814-1869 .... **NCLC 23**
　See also DLB 3, 11

Harris, Joel Chandler
　1848-1908 .... **TCLC 2; SSC 19**
　See also CA 104; 137; DLB 11, 23, 42, 78,
　91; MAICYA; YABC 1

**Harris, John (Wyndham Parkes Lucas)
　Beynon** 1903-1969
　See Wyndham, John
　See also CA 102; 89-92

Harris, MacDonald .... **CLC 9**
　See also Heiney, Donald (William)

Harris, Mark 1922- .... **CLC 19**
　See also CA 5-8R; CAAS 3; CANR 2, 55;
　DLB 2; DLBY 80

Heinlein, Robert A(nson)
1907-1988 ...... CLC **1, 3, 8, 14, 26, 55;**
DAM POP
See also AAYA 17; CA 1-4R; 125;
CANR 1, 20, 53; DLB 8; JRDA;
MAICYA; MTCW; SATA 9, 69;
SATA-Obit 56

Helforth, John
See Doolittle, Hilda

Hellenhofferu, Vojtech Kapristian z
See Hasek, Jaroslav (Matej Frantisek)

Heller, Joseph
1923- .... CLC **1, 3, 5, 8, 11, 36, 63; DA;**
DAB; DAC; DAM MST, NOV, POP;
WLC
See also AITN 1; CA 5-8R; CABS 1;
CANR 8, 42; DLB 2, 28; DLBY 80;
INT CANR-8; MTCW

Hellman, Lillian (Florence)
1906-1984 ...... CLC **2, 4, 8, 14, 18, 34,**
44, 52; DAM DRAM; DC 1
See also AITN 1, 2; CA 13-16R; 112;
CANR 33; DLB 7; DLBY 84; MTCW

Helprin, Mark
1947- .... CLC **7, 10, 22, 32;**
DAM NOV, POP
See also CA 81-84; CANR 47; DLBY 85;
MTCW

Helvetius, Claude-Adrien
1715-1771 .... LC **26**

Helyar, Jane Penelope Josephine 1933-
See Poole, Josephine
See also CA 21-24R; CANR 10, 26;
SATA 82

Hemans, Felicia 1793-1835 ...... NCLC **29**
See also DLB 96

Hemingway, Ernest (Miller)
1899-1961 .... CLC **1, 3, 6, 8, 10, 13, 19,**
30, 34, 39, 41, 44, 50, 61, 80; DA; DAB;
DAC; DAM MST, NOV; SSC 25; WLC
See also AAYA 19; CA 77-80; CANR 34;
CDALB 1917-1929; DLB 4, 9, 102;
DLBD 1, 15, 16; DLBY 81, 87, 96;
MTCW

Hempel, Amy 1951- .... CLC **39**
See also CA 118; 137

Henderson, F. C.
See Mencken, H(enry) L(ouis)

Henderson, Sylvia
See Ashton-Warner, Sylvia (Constance)

Henderson, Zenna (Chlarson)
1917-1983 .... SSC **29**
See also CA 1-4R; 133; CANR 1; DLB 8;
SATA 5

Henley, Beth .... CLC **23; DC 6**
See also Henley, Elizabeth Becker
See also CABS 3; DLBY 86

Henley, Elizabeth Becker 1952-
See Henley, Beth
See also CA 107; CANR 32; DAM DRAM,
MST; MTCW

Henley, William Ernest
1849-1903 .... TCLC **8**
See also CA 105; DLB 19

Hennissart, Martha
See Lathen, Emma
See also CA 85-88

Henry, O. .... TCLC **1, 19; SSC 5; WLC**
See also Porter, William Sydney

Henry, Patrick 1736-1799 .... LC **25**

Henryson, Robert 1430(?)-1506(?).... LC **20**
See also DLB 146

Henry VIII 1491-1547 .... LC **10**

Henschke, Alfred
See Klabund

Hentoff, Nat(han Irving) 1925- ...... CLC **26**
See also AAYA 4; CA 1-4R; CAAS 6;
CANR 5, 25; CLR 1; INT CANR-25;
JRDA; MAICYA; SATA 42, 69;
SATA-Brief 27

Heppenstall, (John) Rayner
1911-1981 .... CLC **10**
See also CA 1-4R; 103; CANR 29

Heraclitus
c. 540B.C.-c. 450B.C. .... CMLC **22**
See also DLB 176

Herbert, Frank (Patrick)
1920-1986 ...... CLC **12, 23, 35, 44, 85;**
DAM POP
See also AAYA 21; CA 53-56; 118;
CANR 5, 43; DLB 8; INT CANR-5;
MTCW; SATA 9, 37; SATA-Obit 47

Herbert, George
1593-1633 .... LC **24; DAB;**
DAM POET; PC 4
See also CDBLB Before 1660; DLB 126

Herbert, Zbigniew
1924- .... CLC **9, 43; DAM POET**
See also CA 89-92; CANR 36; MTCW

Herbst, Josephine (Frey)
1897-1969 .... CLC **34**
See also CA 5-8R; 25-28R; DLB 9

Hergesheimer, Joseph
1880-1954 .... TCLC **11**
See also CA 109; DLB 102, 9

Herlihy, James Leo 1927-1993 ...... CLC **6**
See also CA 1-4R; 143; CANR 2

Hermogenes fl. c. 175- .... CMLC **6**

Hernandez, Jose 1834-1886 ...... NCLC **17**

Herodotus c. 484B.C.-429B.C..... CMLC **17**
See also DLB 176

Herrick, Robert
1591-1674 ..... LC **13; DA; DAB; DAC;**
DAM MST, POP; PC 9
See also DLB 126

Herring, Guilles
See Somerville, Edith

Herriot, James
1916-1995 .... CLC **12; DAM POP**
See also Wight, James Alfred
See also AAYA 1; CA 148; CANR 40;
SATA 86

Herrmann, Dorothy 1941- .... CLC **44**
See also CA 107

Herrmann, Taffy
See Herrmann, Dorothy

Hersey, John (Richard)
1914-1993 .... CLC **1, 2, 7, 9, 40, 81, 97;**
DAM POP
See also CA 17-20R; 140; CANR 33;
DLB 6; MTCW; SATA 25;
SATA-Obit 76

Herzen, Aleksandr Ivanovich
1812-1870 .... NCLC **10, 61**

Herzl, Theodor 1860-1904 .... TCLC **36**

Herzog, Werner 1942- .... CLC **16**
See also CA 89-92

Hesiod c. 8th cent. B.C.- .... CMLC **5**
See also DLB 176

Hesse, Hermann
1877-1962 .... CLC **1, 2, 3, 6, 11, 17, 25,**
69; DA; DAB; DAC; DAM MST, NOV;
SSC 9; WLC
See also CA 17-18; CAP 2; DLB 66;
MTCW; SATA 50

Hewes, Cady
See De Voto, Bernard (Augustine)

Heyen, William 1940- .... CLC **13, 18**
See also CA 33-36R; CAAS 9; DLB 5

Heyerdahl, Thor 1914- .... CLC **26**
See also CA 5-8R; CANR 5, 22; MTCW;
SATA 2, 52

Heym, Georg (Theodor Franz Arthur)
1887-1912 .... TCLC **9**
See also CA 106

Heym, Stefan 1913- .... CLC **41**
See also CA 9-12R; CANR 4; DLB 69

Heyse, Paul (Johann Ludwig von)
1830-1914 .... TCLC **8**
See also CA 104; DLB 129

Heyward, (Edwin) DuBose
1885-1940 .... TCLC **59**
See also CA 108; 157; DLB 7, 9, 45;
SATA 21

Hibbert, Eleanor Alice Burford
1906-1993 .... CLC **7; DAM POP**
See also BEST 90:4; CA 17-20R; 140;
CANR 9, 28, 59; SATA 2; SATA-Obit 74

Hichens, Robert S. 1864-1950 ..... TCLC **64**
See also DLB 153

Higgins, George V(incent)
1939- .... CLC **4, 7, 10, 18**
See also CA 77-80; CAAS 5; CANR 17, 51;
DLB 2; DLBY 81; INT CANR-17;
MTCW

Higginson, Thomas Wentworth
1823-1911 .... TCLC **36**
See also DLB 1, 64

Highet, Helen
See MacInnes, Helen (Clark)

Highsmith, (Mary) Patricia
1921-1995 .... CLC **2, 4, 14, 42, 102;**
DAM NOV, POP
See also CA 1-4R; 147; CANR 1, 20, 48,
62; MTCW

Highwater, Jamake (Mamake)
1942(?)- .... CLC **12**
See also AAYA 7; CA 65-68; CAAS 7;
CANR 10, 34; CLR 17; DLB 52;
DLBY 85; JRDA; MAICYA; SATA 32,
69; SATA-Brief 30

Highway, Tomson
1951- .... CLC **92; DAC; DAM MULT**
See also CA 151; NNAL

Higuchi, Ichiyo 1872-1896....... NCLC **49**

Hijuelos, Oscar
1951- .... **CLC 65; DAM MULT, POP;
HLC**
See also BEST 90:1; CA 123; CANR 50;
DLB 145; HW

Hikmet, Nazim 1902(?)-1963...... **CLC 40**
See also CA 141; 93-96

Hildegard von Bingen
1098-1179 .... **CMLC 20**
See also DLB 148

Hildesheimer, Wolfgang
1916-1991 .... **CLC 49**
See also CA 101; 135; DLB 69, 124

Hill, Geoffrey (William)
1932- ... **CLC 5, 8, 18, 45; DAM POET**
See also CA 81-84; CANR 21;
CDBLB 1960 to Present; DLB 40;
MTCW

Hill, George Roy 1921- .... **CLC 26**
See also CA 110; 122

Hill, John
See Koontz, Dean R(ay)

Hill, Susan (Elizabeth)
1942- .. **CLC 4; DAB; DAM MST, NOV**
See also CA 33-36R; CANR 29; DLB 14,
139; MTCW

Hillerman, Tony
1925- .... **CLC 62; DAM POP**
See also AAYA 6; BEST 89:1; CA 29-32R;
CANR 21, 42; SATA 6

Hillesum, Etty 1914-1943 .... **TCLC 49**
See also CA 137

Hilliard, Noel (Harvey) 1929-...... **CLC 15**
See also CA 9-12R; CANR 7

Hillis, Rick 1956-................ **CLC 66**
See also CA 134

Hilton, James 1900-1954......... **TCLC 21**
See also CA 108; DLB 34, 77; SATA 34

Himes, Chester (Bomar)
1909-1984 .... **CLC 2, 4, 7, 18, 58; BLC;
DAM MULT**
See also BW 2; CA 25-28R; 114; CANR 22;
DLB 2, 76, 143; MTCW

Hinde, Thomas .... **CLC 6, 11**
See also Chitty, Thomas Willes

Hindin, Nathan
See Bloch, Robert (Albert)

Hine, (William) Daryl 1936-....... **CLC 15**
See also CA 1-4R; CAAS 15; CANR 1, 20;
DLB 60

Hinkson, Katharine Tynan
See Tynan, Katharine

Hinton, S(usan) E(loise)
1950- .... **CLC 30; DA; DAB; DAC;
DAM MST, NOV**
See also AAYA 2; CA 81-84; CANR 32,
62; CLR 3, 23; JRDA; MAICYA;
MTCW; SATA 19, 58

Hippius, Zinaida .... **TCLC 9**
See also Gippius, Zinaida (Nikolayevna)

Hiraoka, Kimitake 1925-1970
See Mishima, Yukio
See also CA 97-100; 29-32R; DAM DRAM;
MTCW

Hirsch, E(ric) D(onald), Jr. 1928-... **CLC 79**
See also CA 25-28R; CANR 27, 51;
DLB 67; INT CANR-27; MTCW

Hirsch, Edward 1950- .... **CLC 31, 50**
See also CA 104; CANR 20, 42; DLB 120

Hitchcock, Alfred (Joseph)
1899-1980 .... **CLC 16**
See also AAYA 22; CA 159; 97-100;
SATA 27; SATA-Obit 24

Hitler, Adolf 1889-1945......... **TCLC 53**
See also CA 117; 147

Hoagland, Edward 1932-......... **CLC 28**
See also CA 1-4R; CANR 2, 31, 57; DLB 6;
SATA 51

Hoban, Russell (Conwell)
1925- .... **CLC 7, 25; DAM NOV**
See also CA 5-8R; CANR 23, 37; CLR 3;
DLB 52; MAICYA; MTCW; SATA 1,
40, 78

Hobbes, Thomas 1588-1679........ **LC 36**
See also DLB 151

Hobbs, Perry
See Blackmur, R(ichard) P(almer)

Hobson, Laura Z(ametkin)
1900-1986 .... **CLC 7, 25**
See also CA 17-20R; 118; CANR 55;
DLB 28; SATA 52

Hochhuth, Rolf
1931- ..... **CLC 4, 11, 18; DAM DRAM**
See also CA 5-8R; CANR 33; DLB 124;
MTCW

Hochman, Sandra 1936-.......... **CLC 3, 8**
See also CA 5-8R; DLB 5

Hochwaelder, Fritz
1911-1986 ...... **CLC 36; DAM DRAM**
See also CA 29-32R; 120; CANR 42;
MTCW

Hochwalder, Fritz
See Hochwaelder, Fritz

Hocking, Mary (Eunice) 1921-..... **CLC 13**
See also CA 101; CANR 18, 40

Hodgins, Jack 1938-.............. **CLC 23**
See also CA 93-96; DLB 60

Hodgson, William Hope
1877(?)-1918 .... **TCLC 13**
See also CA 111; DLB 70, 153, 156, 178

Hoeg, Peter 1957-................ **CLC 95**
See also CA 151

Hoffman, Alice
1952- .... **CLC 51; DAM NOV**
See also CA 77-80; CANR 34; MTCW

Hoffman, Daniel (Gerard)
1923- .... **CLC 6, 13, 23**
See also CA 1-4R; CANR 4; DLB 5

Hoffman, Stanley 1944-............ **CLC 5**
See also CA 77-80

Hoffman, William M(oses) 1939- ... **CLC 40**
See also CA 57-60; CANR 11

Hoffmann, E(rnst) T(heodor) A(madeus)
1776-1822 .... **NCLC 2; SSC 13**
See also DLB 90; SATA 27

Hofmann, Gert 1931-............. **CLC 54**
See also CA 128

Hofmannsthal, Hugo von
1874-1929 .... **TCLC 11; DAM DRAM;
DC 4**
See also CA 106; 153; DLB 81, 118

Hogan, Linda
1947- .... **CLC 73; DAM MULT**
See also CA 120; CANR 45; DLB 175;
NNAL

Hogarth, Charles
See Creasey, John

Hogarth, Emmett
See Polonsky, Abraham (Lincoln)

Hogg, James 1770-1835.......... **NCLC 4**
See also DLB 93, 116, 159

Holbach, Paul Henri Thiry Baron
1723-1789 .... **LC 14**

Holberg, Ludvig 1684-1754......... **LC 6**

Holden, Ursula 1921-............. **CLC 18**
See also CA 101; CAAS 8; CANR 22

Holderlin, (Johann Christian) Friedrich
1770-1843 .... **NCLC 16; PC 4**

Holdstock, Robert
See Holdstock, Robert P.

Holdstock, Robert P. 1948-........ **CLC 39**
See also CA 131

Holland, Isabelle 1920- .... **CLC 21**
See also AAYA 11; CA 21-24R; CANR 10,
25, 47; JRDA; MAICYA; SATA 8, 70

Holland, Marcus
See Caldwell, (Janet Miriam) Taylor
(Holland)

Hollander, John 1929-...... **CLC 2, 5, 8, 14**
See also CA 1-4R; CANR 1, 52; DLB 5;
SATA 13

Hollander, Paul
See Silverberg, Robert

Holleran, Andrew 1943(?)-........ **CLC 38**
See also CA 144

Hollinghurst, Alan 1954-....... **CLC 55, 91**
See also CA 114

Hollis, Jim
See Summers, Hollis (Spurgeon, Jr.)

Holly, Buddy 1936-1959 .... **TCLC 65**

Holmes, Gordon
See Shiel, M(atthew) P(hipps)

Holmes, John
See Souster, (Holmes) Raymond

Holmes, John Clellon 1926-1988.... **CLC 56**
See also CA 9-12R; 125; CANR 4; DLB 16

Holmes, Oliver Wendell
1809-1894 .... **NCLC 14**
See also CDALB 1640-1865; DLB 1;
SATA 34

Holmes, Raymond
See Souster, (Holmes) Raymond

Holt, Victoria
See Hibbert, Eleanor Alice Burford

Holub, Miroslav 1923-............. **CLC 4**
See also CA 21-24R; CANR 10

Homer
c. 8th cent. B.C.-..... **CMLC 1, 16; DA;
DAB; DAC; DAM MST, POET; WLCS**
See also DLB 176

Honig, Edwin 1919- .... CLC 33
See also CA 5-8R; CAAS 8; CANR 4, 45;
DLB 5

Hood, Hugh (John Blagdon)
1928- .... CLC 15, 28
See also CA 49-52; CAAS 17; CANR 1, 33;
DLB 53

Hood, Thomas 1799-1845....... NCLC 16
See also DLB 96

Hooker, (Peter) Jeremy 1941-...... CLC 43
See also CA 77-80; CANR 22; DLB 40

hooks, bell .... CLC 94
See also Watkins, Gloria

Hope, A(lec) D(erwent) 1907- .... CLC 3, 51
See also CA 21-24R; CANR 33; MTCW

Hope, Brian
See Creasey, John

Hope, Christopher (David Tully)
1944- .... CLC 52
See also CA 106; CANR 47; SATA 62

Hopkins, Gerard Manley
1844-1889 .... NCLC 17; DA; DAB;
DAC; DAM MST, POET; PC 15; WLC
See also CDBLB 1890-1914; DLB 35, 57

Hopkins, John (Richard) 1931-...... CLC 4
See also CA 85-88

Hopkins, Pauline Elizabeth
1859-1930 .... TCLC 28; BLC;
DAM MULT
See also BW 2; CA 141; DLB 50

Hopkinson, Francis 1737-1791 ...... LC 25
See also DLB 31

Hopley-Woolrich, Cornell George 1903-1968
See Woolrich, Cornell
See also CA 13-14; CANR 58; CAP 1

Horatio
See Proust, (Valentin-Louis-George-Eugene-)
Marcel

Horgan, Paul (George Vincent O'Shaughnessy)
1903-1995 .... CLC 9, 53; DAM NOV
See also CA 13-16R; 147; CANR 9, 35;
DLB 102; DLBY 85; INT CANR-9;
MTCW; SATA 13; SATA-Obit 84

Horn, Peter
See Kuttner, Henry

Hornem, Horace Esq.
See Byron, George Gordon (Noel)

Horney, Karen (Clementine Theodore
Danielsen) 1885-1952....... TCLC 71
See also CA 114

Hornung, E(rnest) W(illiam)
1866-1921 .... TCLC 59
See also CA 108; 160; DLB 70

Horovitz, Israel (Arthur)
1939- .... CLC 56; DAM DRAM
See also CA 33-36R; CANR 46, 59; DLB 7

Horvath, Odon von
See Horvath, Oedoen von
See also DLB 85, 124

Horvath, Oedoen von 1901-1938... TCLC 45
See also Horvath, Odon von
See also CA 118

Horwitz, Julius 1920-1986........ CLC 14
See also CA 9-12R; 119; CANR 12

Hospital, Janette Turner 1942-..... CLC 42
See also CA 108; CANR 48

Hostos, E. M. de
See Hostos (y Bonilla), Eugenio Maria de

Hostos, Eugenio M. de
See Hostos (y Bonilla), Eugenio Maria de

Hostos, Eugenio Maria
See Hostos (y Bonilla), Eugenio Maria de

Hostos (y Bonilla), Eugenio Maria de
1839-1903 .... TCLC 24
See also CA 123; 131; HW

Houdini
See Lovecraft, H(oward) P(hillips)

Hougan, Carolyn 1943- .... CLC 34
See also CA 139

Household, Geoffrey (Edward West)
1900-1988 .... CLC 11
See also CA 77-80; 126; CANR 58;
DLB 87; SATA 14; SATA-Obit 59

Housman, A(lfred) E(dward)
1859-1936 ...... TCLC 1, 10; DA; DAB;
DAC; DAM MST, POET; PC 2; WLCS
See also CA 104; 125; DLB 19; MTCW

Housman, Laurence 1865-1959..... TCLC 7
See also CA 106; 155; DLB 10; SATA 25

Howard, Elizabeth Jane 1923- ... CLC 7, 29
See also CA 5-8R; CANR 8, 62

Howard, Maureen 1930- ..... CLC 5, 14, 46
See also CA 53-56; CANR 31; DLBY 83;
INT CANR-31; MTCW

Howard, Richard 1929- ...... CLC 7, 10, 47
See also AITN 1; CA 85-88; CANR 25;
DLB 5; INT CANR-25

Howard, Robert E(rvin)
1906-1936 .... TCLC 8
See also CA 105; 157

Howard, Warren F.
See Pohl, Frederik

Howe, Fanny 1940- .... CLC 47
See also CA 117; CAAS 27; SATA-Brief 52

Howe, Irving 1920-1993........... CLC 85
See also CA 9-12R; 141; CANR 21, 50;
DLB 67; MTCW

Howe, Julia Ward 1819-1910 ..... TCLC 21
See also CA 117; DLB 1

Howe, Susan 1937-............... CLC 72
See also CA 160; DLB 120

Howe, Tina 1937-................ CLC 48
See also CA 109

Howell, James 1594(?)-1666 .... LC 13
See also DLB 151

Howells, W. D.
See Howells, William Dean

Howells, William D.
See Howells, William Dean

Howells, William Dean
1837-1920 .... TCLC 7, 17, 41
See also CA 104; 134; CDALB 1865-1917;
DLB 12, 64, 74, 79

Howes, Barbara 1914-1996 .... CLC 15
See also CA 9-12R; 151; CAAS 3;
CANR 53; SATA 5

Hrabal, Bohumil 1914-1997..... CLC 13, 67
See also CA 106; 156; CAAS 12; CANR 57

Hsun, Lu
See Lu Hsun

Hubbard, L(afayette) Ron(ald)
1911-1986 .... CLC 43; DAM POP
See also CA 77-80; 118; CANR 52

Huch, Ricarda (Octavia)
1864-1947 .... TCLC 13
See also CA 111; DLB 66

Huddle, David 1942- .... CLC 49
See also CA 57-60; CAAS 20; DLB 130

Hudson, Jeffrey
See Crichton, (John) Michael

Hudson, W(illiam) H(enry)
1841-1922 .... TCLC 29
See also CA 115; DLB 98, 153, 174;
SATA 35

Hueffer, Ford Madox
See Ford, Ford Madox

Hughart, Barry 1934-............. CLC 39
See also CA 137

Hughes, Colin
See Creasey, John

Hughes, David (John) 1930- .... CLC 48
See also CA 116; 129; DLB 14

Hughes, Edward James
See Hughes, Ted
See also DAM MST, POET

Hughes, (James) Langston
1902-1967 ..... CLC 1, 5, 10, 15, 35, 44;
BLC; DA; DAB; DAC; DAM DRAM,
MST, MULT, POET; DC 3; PC 1;
SSC 6; WLC
See also AAYA 12; BW 1; CA 1-4R;
25-28R; CANR 1, 34; CDALB 1929-1941;
CLR 17; DLB 4, 7, 48, 51, 86; JRDA;
MAICYA; MTCW; SATA 4, 33

Hughes, Richard (Arthur Warren)
1900-1976 ...... CLC 1, 11; DAM NOV
See also CA 5-8R; 65-68; CANR 4;
DLB 15, 161; MTCW; SATA 8;
SATA-Obit 25

Hughes, Ted
1930- .... CLC 2, 4, 9, 14, 37; DAB;
DAC; PC 7
See also Hughes, Edward James
See also CA 1-4R; CANR 1, 33; CLR 3;
DLB 40, 161; MAICYA; MTCW;
SATA 49; SATA-Brief 27

Hugo, Richard F(ranklin)
1923-1982 .... CLC 6, 18, 32;
DAM POET
See also CA 49-52; 108; CANR 3; DLB 5

Hugo, Victor (Marie)
1802-1885 .... NCLC 3, 10, 21; DA;
DAB; DAC; DAM DRAM, MST, NOV,
POET; PC 17; WLC
See also DLB 119; SATA 47

Huidobro, Vicente
See Huidobro Fernandez, Vicente Garcia

Huidobro Fernandez, Vicente Garcia
1893-1948 .... TCLC 31
See also CA 131; HW

Hulme, Keri 1947- .... CLC 39
See also CA 125; INT 125

J. R. S.
See Gogarty, Oliver St. John

Jabran, Kahlil
See Gibran, Kahlil

Jabran, Khalil
See Gibran, Kahlil

Jackson, Daniel
See Wingrove, David (John)

Jackson, Jesse 1908-1983 .... **CLC 12**
See also BW 1; CA 25-28R; 109; CANR 27;
CLR 28; MAICYA; SATA 2, 29;
SATA-Obit 48

Jackson, Laura (Riding) 1901-1991
See Riding, Laura
See also CA 65-68; 135; CANR 28; DLB 48

Jackson, Sam
See Trumbo, Dalton

Jackson, Sara
See Wingrove, David (John)

Jackson, Shirley
1919-1965 .... **CLC 11, 60, 87; DA;**
DAC; DAM MST; SSC 9; WLC
See also AAYA 9; CA 1-4R; 25-28R;
CANR 4, 52; CDALB 1941-1968; DLB 6;
SATA 2

Jacob, (Cyprien-)Max 1876-1944 ... **TCLC 6**
See also CA 104

Jacobs, Jim 1942-................. **CLC 12**
See also CA 97-100; INT 97-100

Jacobs, W(illiam) W(ymark)
1863-1943 .... **TCLC 22**
See also CA 121; DLB 135

Jacobsen, Jens Peter 1847-1885 .. **NCLC 34**

Jacobsen, Josephine 1908-..... **CLC 48, 102**
See also CA 33-36R; CAAS 18; CANR 23,
48

Jacobson, Dan 1929- .... **CLC 4, 14**
See also CA 1-4R; CANR 2, 25; DLB 14;
MTCW

Jacqueline
See Carpentier (y Valmont), Alejo

Jagger, Mick 1944-.............. **CLC 17**

Jakes, John (William)
1932- ...... **CLC 29; DAM NOV, POP**
See also BEST 89:4; CA 57-60; CANR 10,
43; DLBY 83; INT CANR-10; MTCW;
SATA 62

James, Andrew
See Kirkup, James

James, C(yril) L(ionel) R(obert)
1901-1989 .... **CLC 33**
See also BW 2; CA 117; 125; 128;
CANR 62; DLB 125; MTCW

James, Daniel (Lewis) 1911-1988
See Santiago, Danny
See also CA 125

James, Dynely
See Mayne, William (James Carter)

James, Henry Sr. 1811-1882..... **NCLC 53**

James, Henry
1843-1916 ...... **TCLC 2, 11, 24, 40, 47,**
64; DA; DAB; DAC; DAM MST, NOV;
SSC 8; WLC
See also CA 104; 132; CDALB 1865-1917;
DLB 12, 71, 74; DLBD 13; MTCW

James, M. R.
See James, Montague (Rhodes)
See also DLB 156

James, Montague (Rhodes)
1862-1936 .... **TCLC 6; SSC 16**
See also CA 104

James, P. D. .... **CLC 18, 46**
See also White, Phyllis Dorothy James
See also BEST 90:2; CDBLB 1960 to
Present; DLB 87

James, Philip
See Moorcock, Michael (John)

James, William 1842-1910..... **TCLC 15, 32**
See also CA 109

James I 1394-1437 .... **LC 20**

Jameson, Anna 1794-1860 ...... **NCLC 43**
See also DLB 99, 166

Jami, Nur al-Din 'Abd al-Rahman
1414-1492 .... **LC 9**

Jammes, Francis 1868-1938...... **TCLC 75**

Jandl, Ernst 1925- .... **CLC 34**

Janowitz, Tama
1957- .... **CLC 43; DAM POP**
See also CA 106; CANR 52

Japrisot, Sebastien 1931-......... **CLC 90**

Jarrell, Randall
1914-1965 .... **CLC 1, 2, 6, 9, 13, 49;**
DAM POET
See also CA 5-8R; 25-28R; CABS 2;
CANR 6, 34; CDALB 1941-1968; CLR 6;
DLB 48, 52; MAICYA; MTCW; SATA 7

Jarry, Alfred
1873-1907 .... **TCLC 2, 14;**
DAM DRAM; SSC 20
See also CA 104; 153

Jarvis, E. K.
See Bloch, Robert (Albert); Ellison, Harlan
(Jay); Silverberg, Robert

Jeake, Samuel, Jr.
See Aiken, Conrad (Potter)

Jean Paul 1763-1825 .... **NCLC 7**

Jefferies, (John) Richard
1848-1887 .... **NCLC 47**
See also DLB 98, 141; SATA 16

Jeffers, (John) Robinson
1887-1962 .... **CLC 2, 3, 11, 15, 54; DA;**
DAC; DAM MST, POET; PC 17; WLC
See also CA 85-88; CANR 35;
CDALB 1917-1929; DLB 45; MTCW

Jefferson, Janet
See Mencken, H(enry) L(ouis)

Jefferson, Thomas 1743-1826 .... **NCLC 11**
See also CDALB 1640-1865; DLB 31

Jeffrey, Francis 1773-1850....... **NCLC 33**
See also DLB 107

Jelakowitch, Ivan
See Heijermans, Herman

Jellicoe, (Patricia) Ann 1927-...... **CLC 27**
See also CA 85-88; DLB 13

Jen, Gish .... **CLC 70**
See also Jen, Lillian

Jen, Lillian 1956(?)-
See Jen, Gish
See also CA 135

Jenkins, (John) Robin 1912-....... **CLC 52**
See also CA 1-4R; CANR 1; DLB 14

Jennings, Elizabeth (Joan)
1926- .... **CLC 5, 14**
See also CA 61-64; CAAS 5; CANR 8, 39;
DLB 27; MTCW; SATA 66

Jennings, Waylon 1937-.......... **CLC 21**

Jensen, Johannes V. 1873-1950.... **TCLC 41**

Jensen, Laura (Linnea) 1948- ...... **CLC 37**
See also CA 103

Jerome, Jerome K(lapka)
1859-1927 ....**TCLC 23**
See also CA 119; DLB 10, 34, 135

Jerrold, Douglas William
1803-1857 .... **NCLC 2**
See also DLB 158, 159

Jewett, (Theodora) Sarah Orne
1849-1909 .... **TCLC 1, 22; SSC 6**
See also CA 108; 127; DLB 12, 74;
SATA 15

Jewsbury, Geraldine (Endsor)
1812-1880 .... **NCLC 22**
See also DLB 21

Jhabvala, Ruth Prawer
1927- .... **CLC 4, 8, 29, 94; DAB;**
DAM NOV
See also CA 1-4R; CANR 2, 29, 51;
DLB 139; INT CANR-29; MTCW

Jibran, Kahlil
See Gibran, Kahlil

Jibran, Khalil
See Gibran, Kahlil

Jiles, Paulette 1943-........... **CLC 13, 58**
See also CA 101

Jimenez (Mantecon), Juan Ramon
1881-1958 ..... **TCLC 4; DAM MULT,**
POET; HLC; PC 7
See also CA 104; 131; DLB 134; HW;
MTCW

Jimenez, Ramon
See Jimenez (Mantecon), Juan Ramon

Jimenez Mantecon, Juan
See Jimenez (Mantecon), Juan Ramon

Joel, Billy .... **CLC 26**
See also Joel, William Martin

Joel, William Martin 1949-
See Joel, Billy
See also CA 108

John of the Cross, St. 1542-1591 .... **LC 18**

Johnson, B(ryan) S(tanley William)
1933-1973 .... **CLC 6, 9**
See also CA 9-12R; 53-56; CANR 9;
DLB 14, 40

Johnson, Benj. F. of Boo
See Riley, James Whitcomb

Johnson, Benjamin F. of Boo
See Riley, James Whitcomb

Johnson, Charles (Richard)
1948- .... **CLC 7, 51, 65; BLC;**
DAM MULT
See also BW 2; CA 116; CAAS 18;
CANR 42; DLB 33

Johnson, Denis 1949-............. **CLC 52**
See also CA 117; 121; DLB 120

Johnson, Diane 1934-........ CLC 5, 13, 48
See also CA 41-44R; CANR 17, 40, 62;
DLBY 80; INT CANR-17; MTCW

Johnson, Eyvind (Olof Verner)
1900-1976 .... CLC 14
See also CA 73-76; 69-72; CANR 34

Johnson, J. R.
See James, C(yril) L(ionel) R(obert)

Johnson, James Weldon
1871-1938 .... TCLC 3, 19; BLC;
DAM MULT, POET
See also BW 1; CA 104; 125;
CDALB 1917-1929; CLR 32; DLB 51;
MTCW; SATA 31

Johnson, Joyce 1935-............ CLC 58
See also CA 125; 129

Johnson, Lionel (Pigot)
1867-1902 .... TCLC 19
See also CA 117; DLB 19

Johnson, Mel
See Malzberg, Barry N(athaniel)

Johnson, Pamela Hansford
1912-1981 .... CLC 1, 7, 27
See also CA 1-4R; 104; CANR 2, 28;
DLB 15; MTCW

Johnson, Robert 1911(?)-1938..... TCLC 69

Johnson, Samuel
1709-1784 ..... LC 15; DA; DAB; DAC;
DAM MST; WLC
See also CDBLB 1660-1789; DLB 39, 95,
104, 142

Johnson, Uwe
1934-1984 .... CLC 5, 10, 15, 40
See also CA 1-4R; 112; CANR 1, 39;
DLB 75; MTCW

Johnston, George (Benson) 1913-... CLC 51
See also CA 1-4R; CANR 5, 20; DLB 88

Johnston, Jennifer 1930-.......... CLC 7
See also CA 85-88; DLB 14

Jolley, (Monica) Elizabeth
1923- .... CLC 46; SSC 19
See also CA 127; CAAS 13; CANR 59

Jones, Arthur Llewellyn 1863-1947
See Machen, Arthur
See also CA 104

Jones, D(ouglas) G(ordon) 1929-.... CLC 10
See also CA 29-32R; CANR 13; DLB 53

Jones, David (Michael)
1895-1974 .... CLC 2, 4, 7, 13, 42
See also CA 9-12R; 53-56; CANR 28;
CDBLB 1945-1960; DLB 20, 100; MTCW

Jones, David Robert 1947-
See Bowie, David
See also CA 103

Jones, Diana Wynne 1934- .... CLC 26
See also AAYA 12; CA 49-52; CANR 4,
26, 56; CLR 23; DLB 161; JRDA;
MAICYA; SAAS 7; SATA 9, 70

Jones, Edward P. 1950-.......... CLC 76
See also BW 2; CA 142

Jones, Gayl
1949- .... CLC 6, 9; BLC; DAM MULT
See also BW 2; CA 77-80; CANR 27;
DLB 33; MTCW

Jones, James 1921-1977.... CLC 1, 3, 10, 39
See also AITN 1, 2; CA 1-4R; 69-72;
CANR 6; DLB 2, 143; MTCW

Jones, John J.
See Lovecraft, H(oward) P(hillips)

Jones, LeRoi .... CLC 1, 2, 3, 5, 10, 14
See also Baraka, Amiri

Jones, Louis B. .... CLC 65
See also CA 141

Jones, Madison (Percy, Jr.) 1925- ... CLC 4
See also CA 13-16R; CAAS 11; CANR 7,
54; DLB 152

Jones, Mervyn 1922- .... CLC 10, 52
See also CA 45-48; CAAS 5; CANR 1;
MTCW

Jones, Mick 1956(?)- .... CLC 30

Jones, Nettie (Pearl) 1941- .... CLC 34
See also BW 2; CA 137; CAAS 20

Jones, Preston 1936-1979 .... CLC 10
See also CA 73-76; 89-92; DLB 7

Jones, Robert F(rancis) 1934-....... CLC 7
See also CA 49-52; CANR 2, 61

Jones, Rod 1953- .... CLC 50
See also CA 128

Jones, Terence Graham Parry
1942- .... CLC 21
See also Jones, Terry; Monty Python
See also CA 112; 116; CANR 35; INT 116

Jones, Terry
See Jones, Terence Graham Parry
See also SATA 67; SATA-Brief 51

Jones, Thom 1945(?)-............. CLC 81
See also CA 157

Jong, Erica
1942- .... CLC 4, 6, 8, 18, 83;
DAM NOV, POP
See also AITN 1; BEST 90:2; CA 73-76;
CANR 26, 52; DLB 2, 5, 28, 152;
INT CANR-26; MTCW

Jonson, Ben(jamin)
1572(?)-1637 ...... LC 6, 33; DA; DAB;
DAC; DAM DRAM, MST, POET;
DC 4; PC 17; WLC
See also CDBLB Before 1660; DLB 62, 121

Jordan, June
1936- ..... CLC 5, 11, 23; DAM MULT,
POET
See also AAYA 2; BW 2; CA 33-36R;
CANR 25; CLR 10; DLB 38; MAICYA;
MTCW; SATA 4

Jordan, Pat(rick M.) 1941- .... CLC 37
See also CA 33-36R

Jorgensen, Ivar
See Ellison, Harlan (Jay)

Jorgenson, Ivar
See Silverberg, Robert

Josephus, Flavius c. 37-100 ...... CMLC 13

Josipovici, Gabriel 1940-........ CLC 6, 43
See also CA 37-40R; CAAS 8; CANR 47;
DLB 14

Joubert, Joseph 1754-1824 .... NCLC 9

Jouve, Pierre Jean 1887-1976...... CLC 47
See also CA 65-68

Joyce, James (Augustine Aloysius)
1882-1941 .... TCLC 3, 8, 16, 35, 52;
DA; DAB; DAC; DAM MST, NOV,
POET; SSC 26; WLC
See also CA 104; 126; CDBLB 1914-1945;
DLB 10, 19, 36, 162; MTCW

Jozsef, Attila 1905-1937......... TCLC 22
See also CA 116

Juana Ines de la Cruz 1651(?)-1695 ... LC 5

Judd, Cyril
See Kornbluth, C(yril) M.; Pohl, Frederik

Julian of Norwich 1342(?)-1416(?) .... LC 6
See also DLB 146

Juniper, Alex
See Hospital, Janette Turner

Junius
See Luxemburg, Rosa

Just, Ward (Swift) 1935-........ CLC 4, 27
See also CA 25-28R; CANR 32;
INT CANR-32

Justice, Donald (Rodney)
1925- ..... CLC 6, 19, 102; DAM POET
See also CA 5-8R; CANR 26, 54;
DLBY 83; INT CANR-26

Juvenal c. 55-c. 127 .... CMLC 8

Juvenis
See Bourne, Randolph S(illiman)

Kacew, Romain 1914-1980
See Gary, Romain
See also CA 108; 102

Kadare, Ismail 1936- .... CLC 52

Kadohata, Cynthia................. CLC 59
See also CA 140

Kafka, Franz
1883-1924 .... TCLC 2, 6, 13, 29, 47, 53;
DA; DAB; DAC; DAM MST, NOV;
SSC 29; WLC
See also CA 105; 126; DLB 81; MTCW

Kahanovitsch, Pinkhes
See Der Nister

Kahn, Roger 1927-.............. CLC 30
See also CA 25-28R; CANR 44; DLB 171;
SATA 37

Kain, Saul
See Sassoon, Siegfried (Lorraine)

Kaiser, Georg 1878-1945 .... TCLC 9
See also CA 106; DLB 124

Kaletski, Alexander 1946-......... CLC 39
See also CA 118; 143

Kalidasa fl. c. 400- .... CMLC 9

Kallman, Chester (Simon)
1921-1975 .... CLC 2
See also CA 45-48; 53-56; CANR 3

Kaminsky, Melvin 1926-
See Brooks, Mel
See also CA 65-68; CANR 16

Kaminsky, Stuart M(elvin) 1934-... CLC 59
See also CA 73-76; CANR 29, 53

Kane, Francis
See Robbins, Harold

Kane, Paul
See Simon, Paul (Frederick)

Kane, Wilson
See Bloch, Robert (Albert)

Kanin, Garson 1912-............. **CLC 22**
See also AITN 1; CA 5-8R; CANR 7;
DLB 7

Kaniuk, Yoram 1930-............ **CLC 19**
See also CA 134

Kant, Immanuel 1724-1804 ...... **NCLC 27**
See also DLB 94

Kantor, MacKinlay 1904-1977 ...... **CLC 7**
See also CA 61-64; 73-76; CANR 60;
DLB 9, 102

Kaplan, David Michael 1946- ...... **CLC 50**

Kaplan, James 1951- .... **CLC 59**
See also CA 135

Karageorge, Michael
See Anderson, Poul (William)

Karamzin, Nikolai Mikhailovich
1766-1826 .... **NCLC 3**
See also DLB 150

Karapanou, Margarita 1946-....... **CLC 13**
See also CA 101

Karinthy, Frigyes 1887-1938...... **TCLC 47**

Karl, Frederick R(obert) 1927- ..... **CLC 34**
See also CA 5-8R; CANR 3, 44

Kastel, Warren
See Silverberg, Robert

Kataev, Evgeny Petrovich 1903-1942
See Petrov, Evgeny
See also CA 120

Kataphusin
See Ruskin, John

Katz, Steve 1935-................ **CLC 47**
See also CA 25-28R; CAAS 14; CANR 12;
DLBY 83

Kauffman, Janet 1945-............ **CLC 42**
See also CA 117; CANR 43; DLBY 86

Kaufman, Bob (Garnell)
1925-1986 .... **CLC 49**
See also BW 1; CA 41-44R; 118; CANR 22;
DLB 16, 41

Kaufman, George S.
1889-1961 ...... **CLC 38; DAM DRAM**
See also CA 108; 93-96; DLB 7; INT 108

Kaufman, Sue .... **CLC 3, 8**
See also Barondess, Sue K(aufman)

Kavafis, Konstantinos Petrou 1863-1933
See Cavafy, C(onstantine) P(eter)
See also CA 104

Kavan, Anna 1901-1968...... **CLC 5, 13, 82**
See also CA 5-8R; CANR 6, 57; MTCW

Kavanagh, Dan
See Barnes, Julian (Patrick)

Kavanagh, Patrick (Joseph)
1904-1967 .... **CLC 22**
See also CA 123; 25-28R; DLB 15, 20;
MTCW

Kawabata, Yasunari
1899-1972 .... **CLC 2, 5, 9, 18;**
DAM MULT; SSC 17
See also CA 93-96; 33-36R; DLB 180

Kaye, M(ary) M(argaret) 1909-..... **CLC 28**
See also CA 89-92; CANR 24, 60; MTCW;
SATA 62

Kaye, Mollie
See Kaye, M(ary) M(argaret)

Kaye-Smith, Sheila 1887-1956..... **TCLC 20**
See also CA 118; DLB 36

Kaymor, Patrice Maguilene
See Senghor, Leopold Sedar

Kazan, Elia 1909-........... **CLC 6, 16, 63**
See also CA 21-24R; CANR 32

Kazantzakis, Nikos
1883(?)-1957 .... **TCLC 2, 5, 33**
See also CA 105; 132; MTCW

Kazin, Alfred 1915- .... **CLC 34, 38**
See also CA 1-4R; CAAS 7; CANR 1, 45;
DLB 67

Keane, Mary Nesta (Skrine) 1904-1996
See Keane, Molly
See also CA 108; 114; 151

Keane, Molly..................... **CLC 31**
See also Keane, Mary Nesta (Skrine)
See also INT 114

Keates, Jonathan 19(?)- .... **CLC 34**

Keaton, Buster 1895-1966 .... **CLC 20**

Keats, John
1795-1821 .... **NCLC 8; DA; DAB;**
DAC; DAM MST, POET; PC 1; WLC
See also CDBLB 1789-1832; DLB 96, 110

Keene, Donald 1922- .... **CLC 34**
See also CA 1-4R; CANR 5

Keillor, Garrison.................. **CLC 40**
See also Keillor, Gary (Edward)
See also AAYA 2; BEST 89:3; DLBY 87;
SATA 58

Keillor, Gary (Edward) 1942-
See Keillor, Garrison
See also CA 111; 117; CANR 36, 59;
DAM POP; MTCW

Keith, Michael
See Hubbard, L(afayette) Ron(ald)

Keller, Gottfried
1819-1890 .... **NCLC 2; SSC 26**
See also DLB 129

Kellerman, Jonathan
1949- .... **CLC 44; DAM POP**
See also BEST 90:1; CA 106; CANR 29, 51;
INT CANR-29

Kelley, William Melvin 1937-...... **CLC 22**
See also BW 1; CA 77-80; CANR 27;
DLB 33

Kellogg, Marjorie 1922-............ **CLC 2**
See also CA 81-84

Kellow, Kathleen
See Hibbert, Eleanor Alice Burford

Kelly, M(ilton) T(erry) 1947-....... **CLC 55**
See also CA 97-100; CAAS 22; CANR 19,
43

Kelman, James 1946-.......... **CLC 58, 86**
See also CA 148

Kemal, Yashar 1923- .... **CLC 14, 29**
See also CA 89-92; CANR 44

Kemble, Fanny 1809-1893 .... **NCLC 18**
See also DLB 32

Kemelman, Harry 1908-1996....... **CLC 2**
See also AITN 1; CA 9-12R; 155; CANR 6;
DLB 28

Kempe, Margery 1373(?)-1440(?) ..... **LC 6**
See also DLB 146

Kempis, Thomas a 1380-1471 .... **LC 11**

Kendall, Henry 1839-1882...... **NCLC 12**

Keneally, Thomas (Michael)
1935- ...... **CLC 5, 8, 10, 14, 19, 27, 43;**
DAM NOV
See also CA 85-88; CANR 10, 50; MTCW

Kennedy, Adrienne (Lita)
1931- ..... **CLC 66; BLC; DAM MULT;**
DC 5
See also BW 2; CA 103; CAAS 20; CABS 3;
CANR 26, 53; DLB 38

Kennedy, John Pendleton
1795-1870 .... **NCLC 2**
See also DLB 3

Kennedy, Joseph Charles 1929-
See Kennedy, X. J.
See also CA 1-4R; CANR 4, 30, 40;
SATA 14, 86

Kennedy, William
1928- ... **CLC 6, 28, 34, 53; DAM NOV**
See also AAYA 1; CA 85-88; CANR 14,
31; DLB 143; DLBY 85; INT CANR-31;
MTCW; SATA 57

Kennedy, X. J................... **CLC 8, 42**
See also Kennedy, Joseph Charles
See also CAAS 9; CLR 27; DLB 5;
SAAS 22

Kenny, Maurice (Francis)
1929- .... **CLC 87; DAM MULT**
See also CA 144; CAAS 22; DLB 175;
NNAL

Kent, Kelvin
See Kuttner, Henry

Kenton, Maxwell
See Southern, Terry

Kenyon, Robert O.
See Kuttner, Henry

Kerouac, Jack ..... **CLC 1, 2, 3, 5, 14, 29, 61**
See also Kerouac, Jean-Louis Lebris de
See also CDALB 1941-1968; DLB 2, 16;
DLBD 3; DLBY 95

Kerouac, Jean-Louis Lebris de 1922-1969
See Kerouac, Jack
See also AITN 1; CA 5-8R; 25-28R;
CANR 26, 54; DA; DAB; DAC;
DAM MST, NOV, POET, POP; MTCW;
WLC

Kerr, Jean 1923-................. **CLC 22**
See also CA 5-8R; CANR 7; INT CANR-7

Kerr, M. E. .... **CLC 12, 35**
See also Meaker, Marijane (Agnes)
See also AAYA 2; CLR 29; SAAS 1

Kerr, Robert .... **CLC 55**

Kerrigan, (Thomas) Anthony
1918- .... **CLC 4, 6**
See also CA 49-52; CAAS 11; CANR 4

Kerry, Lois
See Duncan, Lois

Kesey, Ken (Elton)
1935- ...... **CLC 1, 3, 6, 11, 46, 64; DA;**
DAB; DAC; DAM MST, NOV, POP;
WLC
See also CA 1-4R; CANR 22, 38;
CDALB 1968-1988; DLB 2, 16; MTCW;
SATA 66

Koch, C(hristopher) J(ohn)   1932- ... **CLC 42**
See also CA 127

Koch, Christopher
See Koch, C(hristopher) J(ohn)

Koch, Kenneth
  1925- .... **CLC 5, 8, 44; DAM POET**
See also CA 1-4R; CANR 6, 36, 57; DLB 5;
  INT CANR-36; SATA 65

Kochanowski, Jan   1530-1584....... **LC 10**

Kock, Charles Paul de
  1794-1871 .... **NCLC 16**

Koda Shigeyuki   1867-1947
See Rohan, Koda
See also CA 121

Koestler, Arthur
  1905-1983 .... **CLC 1, 3, 6, 8, 15, 33**
See also CA 1-4R; 109; CANR 1, 33;
  CDBLB 1945-1960; DLBY 83; MTCW

Kogawa, Joy Nozomi
  1935- ...... **CLC 78; DAC; DAM MST,**
                                              MULT
See also CA 101; CANR 19, 62

Kohout, Pavel   1928-.............. **CLC 13**
See also CA 45-48; CANR 3

Koizumi, Yakumo
See Hearn, (Patricio) Lafcadio (Tessima
  Carlos)

Kolmar, Gertrud   1894-1943...... **TCLC 40**

Komunyakaa, Yusef   1947-...... **CLC 86, 94**
See also CA 147; DLB 120

Konrad, George
See Konrad, Gyoergy

Konrad, Gyoergy   1933- ...... **CLC 4, 10, 73**
See also CA 85-88

Konwicki, Tadeusz   1926-..... **CLC 8, 28, 54**
See also CA 101; CAAS 9; CANR 39, 59;
  MTCW

Koontz, Dean R(ay)
  1945- .... **CLC 78; DAM NOV, POP**
See also AAYA 9; BEST 89:3, 90:2;
  CA 108; CANR 19, 36, 52; MTCW;
  SATA 92

Kopit, Arthur (Lee)
  1937- ..... **CLC 1, 18, 33; DAM DRAM**
See also AITN 1; CA 81-84; CABS 3;
  DLB 7; MTCW

Kops, Bernard   1926-.............. **CLC 4**
See also CA 5-8R; DLB 13

Kornbluth, C(yril) M.   1923-1958.... **TCLC 8**
See also CA 105; 160; DLB 8

Korolenko, V. G.
See Korolenko, Vladimir Galaktionovich

Korolenko, Vladimir
See Korolenko, Vladimir Galaktionovich

Korolenko, Vladimir G.
See Korolenko, Vladimir Galaktionovich

Korolenko, Vladimir Galaktionovich
  1853-1921 .... **TCLC 22**
See also CA 121

Korzybski, Alfred (Habdank Skarbek)
  1879-1950 .... **TCLC 61**
See also CA 123; 160

Kosinski, Jerzy (Nikodem)
  1933-1991 .... **CLC 1, 2, 3, 6, 10, 15, 53,**
                                       70; DAM NOV
See also CA 17-20R; 134; CANR 9, 46;
  DLB 2; DLBY 82; MTCW

Kostelanetz, Richard (Cory)   1940- .. **CLC 28**
See also CA 13-16R; CAAS 8; CANR 38

Kostrowitzki, Wilhelm Apollinaris de
  1880-1918
See Apollinaire, Guillaume
See also CA 104

Kotlowitz, Robert   1924-............. **CLC 4**
See also CA 33-36R; CANR 36

Kotzebue, August (Friedrich Ferdinand) von
  1761-1819 .... **NCLC 25**
See also DLB 94

Kotzwinkle, William   1938- ... **CLC 5, 14, 35**
See also CA 45-48; CANR 3, 44; CLR 6;
  DLB 173; MAICYA; SATA 24, 70

Kowna, Stancy
See Szymborska, Wislawa

Kozol, Jonathan   1936-............ **CLC 17**
See also CA 61-64; CANR 16, 45

Kozoll, Michael   1940(?)-.......... **CLC 35**

Kramer, Kathryn   19(?)-........... **CLC 34**

Kramer, Larry   1935- .. **CLC 42; DAM POP**
See also CA 124; 126; CANR 60

Krasicki, Ignacy   1735-1801....... **NCLC 8**

Krasinski, Zygmunt   1812-1859 .... **NCLC 4**

Kraus, Karl   1874-1936........... **TCLC 5**
See also CA 104; DLB 118

Kreve (Mickevicius), Vincas
  1882-1954 .... **TCLC 27**

Kristeva, Julia   1941- .... **CLC 77**
See also CA 154

Kristofferson, Kris   1936-.......... **CLC 26**
See also CA 104

Krizanc, John   1956-.............. **CLC 57**

Krleza, Miroslav   1893-1981........ **CLC 8**
See also CA 97-100; 105; CANR 50;
  DLB 147

Kroetsch, Robert
  1927- .... **CLC 5, 23, 57; DAC;**
                                          DAM POET
See also CA 17-20R; CANR 8, 38; DLB 53;
  MTCW

Kroetz, Franz
See Kroetz, Franz Xaver

Kroetz, Franz Xaver   1946- .... **CLC 41**
See also CA 130

Kroker, Arthur   1945-............. **CLC 77**

Kropotkin, Peter (Aleksieevich)
  1842-1921 .... **TCLC 36**
See also CA 119

Krotkov, Yuri   1917-.............. **CLC 19**
See also CA 102

Krumb
See Crumb, R(obert)

Krumgold, Joseph (Quincy)
  1908-1980 .... **CLC 12**
See also CA 9-12R; 101; CANR 7;
  MAICYA; SATA 1, 48; SATA-Obit 23

Krumwitz
See Crumb, R(obert)

Krutch, Joseph Wood   1893-1970.... **CLC 24**
See also CA 1-4R; 25-28R; CANR 4;
  DLB 63

Krutzch, Gus
See Eliot, T(homas) S(tearns)

Krylov, Ivan Andreevich
  1768(?)-1844 .... **NCLC 1**
See also DLB 150

Kubin, Alfred (Leopold Isidor)
  1877-1959 .... **TCLC 23**
See also CA 112; 149; DLB 81

Kubrick, Stanley   1928-............ **CLC 16**
See also CA 81-84; CANR 33; DLB 26

Kumin, Maxine (Winokur)
  1925- ..... **CLC 5, 13, 28; DAM POET;**
                                              PC 15
See also AITN 2; CA 1-4R; CAAS 8;
  CANR 1, 21; DLB 5; MTCW; SATA 12

Kundera, Milan
  1929- .... **CLC 4, 9, 19, 32, 68;**
                                      DAM NOV; SSC 24
See also AAYA 2; CA 85-88; CANR 19,
  52; MTCW

Kunene, Mazisi (Raymond)   1930-... **CLC 85**
See also BW 1; CA 125; DLB 117

Kunitz, Stanley (Jasspon)
  1905- .... **CLC 6, 11, 14; PC 19**
See also CA 41-44R; CANR 26, 57;
  DLB 48; INT CANR-26; MTCW

Kunze, Reiner   1933-.............. **CLC 10**
See also CA 93-96; DLB 75

Kuprin, Aleksandr Ivanovich
  1870-1938 .... **TCLC 5**
See also CA 104

Kureishi, Hanif   1954(?)-.......... **CLC 64**
See also CA 139

Kurosawa, Akira
  1910- .... **CLC 16; DAM MULT**
See also AAYA 11; CA 101; CANR 46

Kushner, Tony
  1957(?)- .... **CLC 81; DAM DRAM**
See also CA 144

Kuttner, Henry   1915-1958........ **TCLC 10**
See also Vance, Jack
See also CA 107; 157; DLB 8

Kuzma, Greg   1944-.............. **CLC 7**
See also CA 33-36R

Kuzmin, Mikhail   1872(?)-1936 .... **TCLC 40**

Kyd, Thomas
  1558-1594 .... **LC 22; DAM DRAM;**
                                                 DC 3
See also DLB 62

Kyprianos, Iossif
See Samarakis, Antonis

La Bruyere, Jean de   1645-1696...... **LC 17**

Lacan, Jacques (Marie Emile)
  1901-1981 .... **CLC 75**
See also CA 121; 104

Laclos, Pierre Ambroise Francois Choderlos
  de   1741-1803 .... **NCLC 4**

La Colere, Francois
See Aragon, Louis

Lawler, Raymond Evenor　1922- .... **CLC 58**
See also CA 103

Lawrence, D(avid) H(erbert Richards)
1885-1930 .... **TCLC 2, 9, 16, 33, 48, 61;**
DA; DAB; DAC; DAM MST, NOV,
POET; SSC 4, 19; WLC
See also CA 104; 121; CDBLB 1914-1945;
DLB 10, 19, 36, 98, 162; MTCW

Lawrence, T(homas) E(dward)
1888-1935 .... **TCLC 18**
See also Dale, Colin
See also CA 115

Lawrence of Arabia
See Lawrence, T(homas) E(dward)

Lawson, Henry (Archibald Hertzberg)
1867-1922 .... **TCLC 27; SSC 18**
See also CA 120

Lawton, Dennis
See Faust, Frederick (Schiller)

Laxness, Halldor .... **CLC 25**
See also Gudjonsson, Halldor Kiljan

Layamon　fl. c. 1200- .... **CMLC 10**
See also DLB 146

Laye, Camara
1928-1980 .... **CLC 4, 38; BLC;**
DAM MULT
See also BW 1; CA 85-88; 97-100;
CANR 25; MTCW

Layton, Irving (Peter)
1912- .... **CLC 2, 15; DAC; DAM MST,**
POET
See also CA 1-4R; CANR 2, 33, 43;
DLB 88; MTCW

Lazarus, Emma　1849-1887 .... **NCLC 8**

Lazarus, Felix
See Cable, George Washington

Lazarus, Henry
See Slavitt, David R(ytman)

Lea, Joan
See Neufeld, John (Arthur)

Leacock, Stephen (Butler)
1869-1944 .. **TCLC 2; DAC; DAM MST**
See also CA 104; 141; DLB 92

Lear, Edward　1812-1888 .... **NCLC 3**
See also CLR 1; DLB 32, 163, 166;
MAICYA; SATA 18

Lear, Norman (Milton)　1922- ...... **CLC 12**
See also CA 73-76

Leavis, F(rank) R(aymond)
1895-1978 .... **CLC 24**
See also CA 21-24R; 77-80; CANR 44;
MTCW

Leavitt, David　1961-... **CLC 34; DAM POP**
See also CA 116; 122; CANR 50, 62;
DLB 130; INT 122

Leblanc, Maurice (Marie Emile)
1864-1941 .... **TCLC 49**
See also CA 110

Lebowitz, Fran(ces Ann)
1951(?)- .... **CLC 11, 36**
See also CA 81-84; CANR 14, 60;
INT CANR-14; MTCW

Lebrecht, Peter
See Tieck, (Johann) Ludwig

le Carre, John .... **CLC 3, 5, 9, 15, 28**
See also Cornwell, David (John Moore)
See also BEST 89:4; CDBLB 1960 to
Present; DLB 87

Le Clezio, J(ean) M(arie) G(ustave)
1940- .... **CLC 31**
See also CA 116; 128; DLB 83

Leconte de Lisle, Charles-Marie-Rene
1818-1894 .... **NCLC 29**

Le Coq, Monsieur
See Simenon, Georges (Jacques Christian)

Leduc, Violette　1907-1972 .... **CLC 22**
See also CA 13-14; 33-36R; CAP 1

Ledwidge, Francis　1887(?)-1917 ... **TCLC 23**
See also CA 123; DLB 20

Lee, Andrea
1953- ..... **CLC 36; BLC; DAM MULT**
See also BW 1; CA 125

Lee, Andrew
See Auchincloss, Louis (Stanton)

Lee, Chang-rae　1965- .... **CLC 91**
See also CA 148

Lee, Don L. .... **CLC 2**
See also Madhubuti, Haki R.

Lee, George W(ashington)
1894-1976 .... **CLC 52; BLC;**
DAM MULT
See also BW 1; CA 125; DLB 51

Lee, (Nelle) Harper
1926- .... **CLC 12, 60; DA; DAB; DAC;**
DAM MST, NOV; WLC
See also AAYA 13; CA 13-16R; CANR 51;
CDALB 1941-1968; DLB 6; MTCW;
SATA 11

Lee, Helen Elaine　1959(?)- .... **CLC 86**
See also CA 148

Lee, Julian
See Latham, Jean Lee

Lee, Larry
See Lee, Lawrence

Lee, Laurie
1914-1997 ... **CLC 90; DAB; DAM POP**
See also CA 77-80; 158; CANR 33;
DLB 27; MTCW

Lee, Lawrence　1941-1990 .... **CLC 34**
See also CA 131; CANR 43

Lee, Manfred B(ennington)
1905-1971 .... **CLC 11**
See also Queen, Ellery
See also CA 1-4R; 29-32R; CANR 2;
DLB 137

Lee, Stan　1922- .... **CLC 17**
See also AAYA 5; CA 108; 111; INT 111

Lee, Tanith　1947- .... **CLC 46**
See also AAYA 15; CA 37-40R; CANR 53;
SATA 8, 88

Lee, Vernon .... **TCLC 5**
See also Paget, Violet
See also DLB 57, 153, 156, 174, 178

Lee, William
See Burroughs, William S(eward)

Lee, Willy
See Burroughs, William S(eward)

Lee-Hamilton, Eugene (Jacob)
1845-1907 .... **TCLC 22**
See also CA 117

Leet, Judith　1935- .... **CLC 11**

Le Fanu, Joseph Sheridan
1814-1873 .... **NCLC 9, 58; DAM POP;**
SSC 14
See also DLB 21, 70, 159, 178

Leffland, Ella　1931- .... **CLC 19**
See also CA 29-32R; CANR 35; DLBY 84;
INT CANR-35; SATA 65

Leger, Alexis
See Leger, (Marie-Rene Auguste) Alexis
Saint-Leger

Leger, (Marie-Rene Auguste) Alexis
Saint-Leger
1887-1975 .... **CLC 11; DAM POET**
See also Perse, St.-John
See also CA 13-16R; 61-64; CANR 43;
MTCW

Leger, Saintleger
See Leger, (Marie-Rene Auguste) Alexis
Saint-Leger

Le Guin, Ursula K(roeber)
1929- ..... **CLC 8, 13, 22, 45, 71; DAB;**
DAC; DAM MST, POP; SSC 12
See also AAYA 9; AITN 1; CA 21-24R;
CANR 9, 32, 52; CDALB 1968-1988;
CLR 3, 28; DLB 8, 52; INT CANR-32;
JRDA; MAICYA; MTCW; SATA 4, 52

Lehmann, Rosamond (Nina)
1901-1990 .... **CLC 5**
See also CA 77-80; 131; CANR 8; DLB 15

Leiber, Fritz (Reuter, Jr.)
1910-1992 .... **CLC 25**
See also CA 45-48; 139; CANR 2, 40;
DLB 8; MTCW; SATA 45;
SATA-Obit 73

Leibniz, Gottfried Wilhelm von
1646-1716 .... **LC 35**
See also DLB 168

Leimbach, Martha　1963-
See Leimbach, Marti
See also CA 130

Leimbach, Marti .... **CLC 65**
See also Leimbach, Martha

Leino, Eino .... **TCLC 24**
See also Loennbohm, Armas Eino Leopold

Leiris, Michel (Julien)　1901-1990 ... **CLC 61**
See also CA 119; 128; 132

Leithauser, Brad　1953- .... **CLC 27**
See also CA 107; CANR 27; DLB 120

Lelchuk, Alan　1938- .... **CLC 5**
See also CA 45-48; CAAS 20; CANR 1

Lem, Stanislaw　1921- .... **CLC 8, 15, 40**
See also CA 105; CAAS 1; CANR 32;
MTCW

Lemann, Nancy　1956- .... **CLC 39**
See also CA 118; 136

Lemonnier, (Antoine Louis) Camille
1844-1913 .... **TCLC 22**
See also CA 121

Lenau, Nikolaus　1802-1850 ...... **NCLC 16**

L'Engle, Madeleine (Camp Franklin)
   1918- . . . . CLC 12; DAM POP
  See also AAYA 1; AITN 2; CA 1-4R;
   CANR 3, 21, 39; CLR 1, 14; DLB 52;
   JRDA; MAICYA; MTCW; SAAS 15;
   SATA 1, 27, 75

Lengyel, Jozsef 1896-1975. . . . . CLC 7
  See also CA 85-88; 57-60

Lenin 1870-1924
  See Lenin, V. I.
  See also CA 121

Lenin, V. I. . . . . TCLC 67
  See also Lenin

Lennon, John (Ono)
   1940-1980 . . . . CLC 12, 35
  See also CA 102

Lennox, Charlotte Ramsay
   1729(?)-1804 . . . . NCLC 23
  See also DLB 39

Lentricchia, Frank (Jr.) 1940- . . . . . . CLC 34
  See also CA 25-28R; CANR 19

Lenz, Siegfried 1926- . . . . CLC 27
  See also CA 89-92; DLB 75

Leonard, Elmore (John, Jr.)
   1925- . . . . . . CLC 28, 34, 71; DAM POP
  See also AAYA 22; AITN 1; BEST 89:1,
   90:4; CA 81-84; CANR 12, 28, 53;
   DLB 173; INT CANR-28; MTCW

Leonard, Hugh. . . . . CLC 19
  See also Byrne, John Keyes
  See also DLB 13

Leonov, Leonid (Maximovich)
   1899-1994 . . . . CLC 92; DAM NOV
  See also CA 129; MTCW

Leopardi, (Conte) Giacomo
   1798-1837 . . . . NCLC 22

Le Reveler
  See Artaud, Antonin (Marie Joseph)

Lerman, Eleanor 1952- . . . . CLC 9
  See also CA 85-88

Lerman, Rhoda 1936- . . . . CLC 56
  See also CA 49-52

Lermontov, Mikhail Yuryevich
   1814-1841 . . . . NCLC 47; PC 18

Leroux, Gaston 1868-1927. . . . . . . TCLC 25
  See also CA 108; 136; SATA 65

Lesage, Alain-Rene 1668-1747. . . . . . . LC 28

Leskov, Nikolai (Semyonovich)
   1831-1895 . . . . NCLC 25

Lessing, Doris (May)
   1919- . . . . . CLC 1, 2, 3, 6, 10, 15, 22, 40,
   94; DA; DAB; DAC; DAM MST, NOV;
   SSC 6; WLCS
  See also CA 9-12R; CAAS 14; CANR 33,
   54; CDBLB 1960 to Present; DLB 15,
   139; DLBY 85; MTCW

Lessing, Gotthold Ephraim
   1729-1781 . . . . LC 8
  See also DLB 97

Lester, Richard 1932- . . . . CLC 20

Lever, Charles (James)
   1806-1872 . . . . NCLC 23
  See also DLB 21

Leverson, Ada 1865(?)-1936(?) . . . . TCLC 18
  See also Elaine
  See also CA 117; DLB 153

Levertov, Denise
   1923- . . . . . . CLC 1, 2, 3, 5, 8, 15, 28, 66;
   DAM POET; PC 11
  See also CA 1-4R; CAAS 19; CANR 3, 29,
   50; DLB 5, 165; INT CANR-29; MTCW

Levi, Jonathan. . . . . CLC 76

Levi, Peter (Chad Tigar) 1931- . . . . . CLC 41
  See also CA 5-8R; CANR 34; DLB 40

Levi, Primo
   1919-1987 . . . . CLC 37, 50; SSC 12
  See also CA 13-16R; 122; CANR 12, 33, 61;
   DLB 177; MTCW

Levin, Ira 1929- . . . . . CLC 3, 6; DAM POP
  See also CA 21-24R; CANR 17, 44;
   MTCW; SATA 66

Levin, Meyer
   1905-1981 . . . . CLC 7; DAM POP
  See also AITN 1; CA 9-12R; 104;
   CANR 15; DLB 9, 28; DLBY 81;
   SATA 21; SATA-Obit 27

Levine, Norman 1924- . . . . CLC 54
  See also CA 73-76; CAAS 23; CANR 14;
   DLB 88

Levine, Philip
   1928- . . . . CLC 2, 4, 5, 9, 14, 33;
   DAM POET
  See also CA 9-12R; CANR 9, 37, 52;
   DLB 5

Levinson, Deirdre 1931- . . . . CLC 49
  See also CA 73-76

Levi-Strauss, Claude 1908- . . . . CLC 38
  See also CA 1-4R; CANR 6, 32, 57; MTCW

Levitin, Sonia (Wolff) 1934- . . . . CLC 17
  See also AAYA 13; CA 29-32R; CANR 14,
   32; JRDA; MAICYA; SAAS 2; SATA 4,
   68

Levon, O. U.
  See Kesey, Ken (Elton)

Levy, Amy 1861-1889. . . . . NCLC 59
  See also DLB 156

Lewes, George Henry
   1817-1878 . . . . NCLC 25
  See also DLB 55, 144

Lewis, Alun 1915-1944. . . . . TCLC 3
  See also CA 104; DLB 20, 162

Lewis, C. Day
  See Day Lewis, C(ecil)

Lewis, C(live) S(taples)
   1898-1963 . . . . . CLC 1, 3, 6, 14, 27; DA;
   DAB; DAC; DAM MST, NOV, POP;
   WLC
  See also AAYA 3; CA 81-84; CANR 33;
   CDBLB 1945-1960; CLR 3, 27; DLB 15,
   100, 160; JRDA; MAICYA; MTCW;
   SATA 13

Lewis, Janet 1899- . . . . CLC 41
  See also Winters, Janet Lewis
  See also CA 9-12R; CANR 29; CAP 1;
   DLBY 87

Lewis, Matthew Gregory
   1775-1818 . . . . NCLC 11, 62
  See also DLB 39, 158, 178

Lewis, (Harry) Sinclair
   1885-1951 . . . . . TCLC 4, 13, 23, 39; DA;
   DAB; DAC; DAM MST, NOV; WLC
  See also CA 104; 133; CDALB 1917-1929;
   DLB 9, 102; DLBD 1; MTCW

Lewis, (Percy) Wyndham
   1882(?)-1957 . . . . TCLC 2, 9
  See also CA 104; 157; DLB 15

Lewisohn, Ludwig 1883-1955. . . . . . TCLC 19
  See also CA 107; DLB 4, 9, 28, 102

Leyner, Mark 1956- . . . . CLC 92
  See also CA 110; CANR 28, 53

Lezama Lima, Jose
   1910-1976 . . . . CLC 4, 10, 101;
   DAM MULT
  See also CA 77-80; DLB 113; HW

L'Heureux, John (Clarke) 1934- . . . . CLC 52
  See also CA 13-16R; CANR 23, 45

Liddell, C. H.
  See Kuttner, Henry

Lie, Jonas (Lauritz Idemil)
   1833-1908(?) . . . . TCLC 5
  See also CA 115

Lieber, Joel 1937-1971. . . . . CLC 6
  See also CA 73-76; 29-32R

Lieber, Stanley Martin
  See Lee, Stan

Lieberman, Laurence (James)
   1935- . . . . CLC 4, 36
  See also CA 17-20R; CANR 8, 36

Lieh Tzu fl. 500B.C.- . . . . CMLC 25

Lieksman, Anders
  See Haavikko, Paavo Juhani

Li Fei-kan 1904-
  See Pa Chin
  See also CA 105

Lifton, Robert Jay 1926- . . . . CLC 67
  See also CA 17-20R; CANR 27;
   INT CANR-27; SATA 66

Lightfoot, Gordon 1938- . . . . CLC 26
  See also CA 109

Lightman, Alan P. 1948- . . . . CLC 81
  See also CA 141

Ligotti, Thomas (Robert)
   1953- . . . . CLC 44; SSC 16
  See also CA 123; CANR 49

Li Ho 791-817. . . . . PC 13

Liliencron, (Friedrich Adolf Axel) Detlev von
   1844-1909 . . . . TCLC 18
  See also CA 117

Lilly, William 1602-1681. . . . . LC 27

Lima, Jose Lezama
  See Lezama Lima, Jose

Lima Barreto, Afonso Henrique de
   1881-1922 . . . . TCLC 23
  See also CA 117

Limonov, Edward 1944- . . . . CLC 67
  See also CA 137

Lin, Frank
  See Atherton, Gertrude (Franklin Horn)

Lincoln, Abraham 1809-1865. . . . . NCLC 18

Lind, Jakov . . . . CLC 1, 2, 4, 27, 82
  See also Landwirth, Heinz
  See also CAAS 4

MacNeice, (Frederick) Louis
1907-1963 ...... **CLC 1, 4, 10, 53; DAB;**
DAM POET
See also CA 85-88; CANR 61; DLB 10, 20;
MTCW

MacNeill, Dand
See Fraser, George MacDonald

Macpherson, James 1736-1796 ...... **LC 29**
See also DLB 109

Macpherson, (Jean) Jay 1931-..... **CLC 14**
See also CA 5-8R; DLB 53

MacShane, Frank 1927-.......... **CLC 39**
See also CA 9-12R; CANR 3, 33; DLB 111

Macumber, Mari
See Sandoz, Mari(e Susette)

Madach, Imre 1823-1864........ **NCLC 19**

Madden, (Jerry) David 1933- .... **CLC 5, 15**
See also CA 1-4R; CAAS 3; CANR 4, 45;
DLB 6; MTCW

Maddern, Al(an)
See Ellison, Harlan (Jay)

Madhubuti, Haki R.
1942-............... **CLC 6, 73; BLC;**
DAM MULT, POET; PC 5
See also Lee, Don L.
See also BW 2; CA 73-76; CANR 24, 51;
DLB 5, 41; DLBD 8

Maepenn, Hugh
See Kuttner, Henry

Maepenn, K. H.
See Kuttner, Henry

Maeterlinck, Maurice
1862-1949 ...... **TCLC 3; DAM DRAM**
See also CA 104; 136; SATA 66

Maginn, William 1794-1842...... **NCLC 8**
See also DLB 110, 159

Mahapatra, Jayanta
1928-.......... **CLC 33; DAM MULT**
See also CA 73-76; CAAS 9; CANR 15, 33

Mahfouz, Naguib (Abdel Aziz Al-Sabilgi)
1911(?)-
See Mahfuz, Najib
See also BEST 89:2; CA 128; CANR 55;
DAM NOV; MTCW

Mahfuz, Najib................ **CLC 52, 55**
See also Mahfouz, Naguib (Abdel Aziz
Al-Sabilgi)
See also DLBY 88

Mahon, Derek 1941-.............. **CLC 27**
See also CA 113; 128; DLB 40

Mailer, Norman
1923-...... **CLC 1, 2, 3, 4, 5, 8, 11, 14,**
28, 39, 74; DA; DAB; DAC; DAM MST,
NOV, POP
See also AITN 2; CA 9-12R; CABS 1;
CANR 28; CDALB 1968-1988; DLB 2,
16, 28; DLBD 3; DLBY 80, 83; MTCW

Maillet, Antonine 1929-...... **CLC 54; DAC**
See also CA 115; 120; CANR 46; DLB 60;
INT 120

Mais, Roger 1905-1955 .... **TCLC 8**
See also BW 1; CA 105; 124; DLB 125;
MTCW

Maistre, Joseph de 1753-1821.... **NCLC 37**

Maitland, Frederic 1850-1906 ..... **TCLC 65**

Maitland, Sara (Louise) 1950-...... **CLC 49**
See also CA 69-72; CANR 13, 59

Major, Clarence
1936-........... **CLC 3, 19, 48; BLC;**
DAM MULT
See also BW 2; CA 21-24R; CAAS 6;
CANR 13, 25, 53; DLB 33

Major, Kevin (Gerald)
1949-.................. **CLC 26; DAC**
See also AAYA 16; CA 97-100; CANR 21,
38; CLR 11; DLB 60; INT CANR-21;
JRDA; MAICYA; SATA 32, 82

Maki, James
See Ozu, Yasujiro

Malabaila, Damiano
See Levi, Primo

Malamud, Bernard
1914-1986 ...... **CLC 1, 2, 3, 5, 8, 9, 11,**
18, 27, 44, 78, 85; DA; DAB; DAC;
DAM MST, NOV, POP; SSC 15; WLC
See also AAYA 16; CA 5-8R; 118; CABS 1;
CANR 28, 62; CDALB 1941-1968;
DLB 2, 28, 152; DLBY 80, 86; MTCW

Malan, Herman
See Bosman, Herman Charles; Bosman,
Herman Charles

Malaparte, Curzio 1898-1957 ..... **TCLC 52**

Malcolm, Dan
See Silverberg, Robert

Malcolm X.......... **CLC 82; BLC; WLCS**
See also Little, Malcolm

Malherbe, Francois de 1555-1628..... **LC 5**

Mallarme, Stephane
1842-1898 .... **NCLC 4, 41;**
DAM POET; PC 4

Mallet-Joris, Francoise 1930-...... **CLC 11**
See also CA 65-68; CANR 17; DLB 83

Malley, Ern
See McAuley, James Phillip

Mallowan, Agatha Christie
See Christie, Agatha (Mary Clarissa)

Maloff, Saul 1922-................. **CLC 5**
See also CA 33-36R

Malone, Louis
See MacNeice, (Frederick) Louis

Malone, Michael (Christopher)
1942-...................... **CLC 43**
See also CA 77-80; CANR 14, 32, 57

Malory, (Sir) Thomas
1410(?)-1471(?) ...... **LC 11; DA; DAB;**
DAC; DAM MST; WLCS
See also CDBLB Before 1660; DLB 146;
SATA 59; SATA-Brief 33

Malouf, (George Joseph) David
1934-.................... **CLC 28, 86**
See also CA 124; CANR 50

Malraux, (Georges-)Andre
1901-1976 ...... **CLC 1, 4, 9, 13, 15, 57;**
DAM NOV
See also CA 21-22; 69-72; CANR 34, 58;
CAP 2; DLB 72; MTCW

Malzberg, Barry N(athaniel) 1939-... **CLC 7**
See also CA 61-64; CAAS 4; CANR 16;
DLB 8

Mamet, David (Alan)
1947-.......... **CLC 9, 15, 34, 46, 91;**
DAM DRAM; DC 4
See also AAYA 3; CA 81-84; CABS 3;
CANR 15, 41; DLB 7; MTCW

Mamoulian, Rouben (Zachary)
1897-1987 .... **CLC 16**
See also CA 25-28R; 124

Mandelstam, Osip (Emilievich)
1891(?)-1938(?) ...... **TCLC 2, 6; PC 14**
See also CA 104; 150

Mander, (Mary) Jane 1877-1949... **TCLC 31**

Mandeville, John fl. 1350-....... **CMLC 19**
See also DLB 146

Mandiargues, Andre Pieyre de....... CLC 41
See also Pieyre de Mandiargues, Andre
See also DLB 83

Mandrake, Ethel Belle
See Thurman, Wallace (Henry)

Mangan, James Clarence
1803-1849 .... **NCLC 27**

Maniere, J.-E.
See Giraudoux, (Hippolyte) Jean

Manley, (Mary) Delariviere
1672(?)-1724 .... **LC 1**
See also DLB 39, 80

Mann, Abel
See Creasey, John

Mann, Emily 1952-................. **DC 7**
See also CA 130; CANR 55

Mann, (Luiz) Heinrich 1871-1950... **TCLC 9**
See also CA 106; DLB 66

Mann, (Paul) Thomas
1875-1955 .... **TCLC 2, 8, 14, 21, 35, 44,**
60; DA; DAB; DAC; DAM MST, NOV;
SSC 5; WLC
See also CA 104; 128; DLB 66; MTCW

Mannheim, Karl 1893-1947....... **TCLC 65**

Manning, David
See Faust, Frederick (Schiller)

Manning, Frederic 1887(?)-1935... **TCLC 25**
See also CA 124

Manning, Olivia 1915-1980 ...... **CLC 5, 19**
See also CA 5-8R; 101; CANR 29; MTCW

Mano, D. Keith 1942- .... **CLC 2, 10**
See also CA 25-28R; CAAS 6; CANR 26,
57; DLB 6

Mansfield, Katherine
.. **TCLC 2, 8, 39; DAB; SSC 9, 23; WLC**
See also Beauchamp, Kathleen Mansfield
See also DLB 162

Manso, Peter 1940- .... **CLC 39**
See also CA 29-32R; CANR 44

Mantecon, Juan Jimenez
See Jimenez (Mantecon), Juan Ramon

Manton, Peter
See Creasey, John

Man Without a Spleen, A
See Chekhov, Anton (Pavlovich)

Manzoni, Alessandro 1785-1873 .. **NCLC 29**

Mapu, Abraham (ben Jekutiel)
1808-1867 .... **NCLC 18**

Mara, Sally
See Queneau, Raymond

Marat, Jean Paul 1743-1793........ **LC 10**

Marcel, Gabriel Honore
1889-1973 .... **CLC 15**
See also CA 102; 45-48; MTCW

Marchbanks, Samuel
See Davies, (William) Robertson

Marchi, Giacomo
See Bassani, Giorgio

Margulies, Donald................. **CLC 76**

Marie de France c. 12th cent. -.... **CMLC 8**

Marie de l'Incarnation 1599-1672.... **LC 10**

Marier, Captain Victor
See Griffith, D(avid Lewelyn) W(ark)

Mariner, Scott
See Pohl, Frederik

Marinetti, Filippo Tommaso
1876-1944 .... **TCLC 10**
See also CA 107; DLB 114

Marivaux, Pierre Carlet de Chamblain de
1688-1763 .... **LC 4; DC 7**

Markandaya, Kamala .... **CLC 8, 38**
See also Taylor, Kamala (Purnaiya)

Markfield, Wallace 1926-.......... **CLC 8**
See also CA 69-72; CAAS 3; DLB 2, 28

Markham, Edwin 1852-1940 ..... **TCLC 47**
See also CA 160; DLB 54

Markham, Robert
See Amis, Kingsley (William)

Marks, J
See Highwater, Jamake (Mamake)

Marks-Highwater, J
See Highwater, Jamake (Mamake)

Markson, David M(errill) 1927-.... **CLC 67**
See also CA 49-52; CANR 1

Marley, Bob...................... **CLC 17**
See also Marley, Robert Nesta

Marley, Robert Nesta 1945-1981
See Marley, Bob
See also CA 107; 103

Marlowe, Christopher
1564-1593 ..... **LC 22; DA; DAB; DAC;**
DAM DRAM, MST; DC 1; WLC
See also CDBLB Before 1660; DLB 62

Marlowe, Stephen 1928-
See Queen, Ellery
See also CA 13-16R; CANR 6, 55

Marmontel, Jean-Francois
1723-1799 .... **LC 2**

Marquand, John P(hillips)
1893-1960 .... **CLC 2, 10**
See also CA 85-88; DLB 9, 102

Marques, Rene
1919-1979 ...... **CLC 96; DAM MULT;**
HLC
See also CA 97-100; 85-88; DLB 113; HW

Marquez, Gabriel (Jose) Garcia
See Garcia Marquez, Gabriel (Jose)

Marquis, Don(ald Robert Perry)
1878-1937 .... **TCLC 7**
See also CA 104; DLB 11, 25

Marric, J. J.
See Creasey, John

Marrow, Bernard
See Moore, Brian

Marryat, Frederick 1792-1848 .... **NCLC 3**
See also DLB 21, 163

Marsden, James
See Creasey, John

Marsh, (Edith) Ngaio
1899-1982 ...... **CLC 7, 53; DAM POP**
See also CA 9-12R; CANR 6, 58; DLB 77;
MTCW

Marshall, Garry 1934-............ **CLC 17**
See also AAYA 3; CA 111; SATA 60

Marshall, Paule
1929- .... **CLC 27, 72; BLC;**
DAM MULT; SSC 3
See also BW 2; CA 77-80; CANR 25;
DLB 157; MTCW

Marsten, Richard
See Hunter, Evan

Marston, John
1576-1634 .... **LC 33; DAM DRAM**
See also DLB 58, 172

Martha, Henry
See Harris, Mark

Marti, Jose
1853-1895 .... **NCLC 63; DAM MULT;**
HLC

Martial c. 40-c. 104 .... **PC 10**

Martin, Ken
See Hubbard, L(afayette) Ron(ald)

Martin, Richard
See Creasey, John

Martin, Steve 1945-.............. **CLC 30**
See also CA 97-100; CANR 30; MTCW

Martin, Valerie 1948-............ **CLC 89**
See also BEST 90:2; CA 85-88; CANR 49

Martin, Violet Florence
1862-1915 .... **TCLC 51**

Martin, Webber
See Silverberg, Robert

Martindale, Patrick Victor
See White, Patrick (Victor Martindale)

Martin du Gard, Roger
1881-1958 .... **TCLC 24**
See also CA 118; DLB 65

Martineau, Harriet 1802-1876.... **NCLC 26**
See also DLB 21, 55, 159, 163, 166;
YABC 2

Martines, Julia
See O'Faolain, Julia

Martinez, Enrique Gonzalez
See Gonzalez Martinez, Enrique

Martinez, Jacinto Benavente y
See Benavente (y Martinez), Jacinto

Martinez Ruiz, Jose 1873-1967
See Azorin; Ruiz, Jose Martinez
See also CA 93-96; HW

Martinez Sierra, Gregorio
1881-1947 .... **TCLC 6**
See also CA 115

Martinez Sierra, Maria (de la O'LeJarraga)
1874-1974 .... **TCLC 6**
See also CA 115

Martinsen, Martin
See Follett, Ken(neth Martin)

Martinson, Harry (Edmund)
1904-1978 .... **CLC 14**
See also CA 77-80; CANR 34

Marut, Ret
See Traven, B.

Marut, Robert
See Traven, B.

Marvell, Andrew
1621-1678 ...... **LC 4; DA; DAB; DAC;**
DAM MST, POET; PC 10; WLC
See also CDBLB 1660-1789; DLB 131

Marx, Karl (Heinrich)
1818-1883 .... **NCLC 17**
See also DLB 129

Masaoka Shiki.................... **TCLC 18**
See also Masaoka Tsunenori

Masaoka Tsunenori 1867-1902
See Masaoka Shiki
See also CA 117

Masefield, John (Edward)
1878-1967 .... **CLC 11, 47; DAM POET**
See also CA 19-20; 25-28R; CANR 33;
CAP 2; CDBLB 1890-1914; DLB 10, 19,
153, 160; MTCW; SATA 19

Maso, Carole 19(?)- .... **CLC 44**

Mason, Bobbie Ann
1940- .... **CLC 28, 43, 82; SSC 4**
See also AAYA 5; CA 53-56; CANR 11,
31, 58; DLB 173; DLBY 87;
INT CANR-31; MTCW

Mason, Ernst
See Pohl, Frederik

Mason, Lee W.
See Malzberg, Barry N(athaniel)

Mason, Nick 1945-............... **CLC 35**

Mason, Tally
See Derleth, August (William)

Mass, William
See Gibson, William

Masters, Edgar Lee
1868-1950 ...... **TCLC 2, 25; DA; DAC;**
DAM MST, POET; PC 1; WLCS
See also CA 104; 133; CDALB 1865-1917;
DLB 54; MTCW

Masters, Hilary 1928- .... **CLC 48**
See also CA 25-28R; CANR 13, 47

Mastrosimone, William 19(?)-...... **CLC 36**

Mathe, Albert
See Camus, Albert

Mather, Cotton 1663-1728......... **LC 38**
See also CDALB 1640-1865; DLB 24, 30,
140

Mather, Increase 1639-1723 .... **LC 38**
See also DLB 24

Matheson, Richard Burton 1926- ... **CLC 37**
See also CA 97-100; DLB 8, 44; INT 97-100

Mathews, Harry 1930-.......... **CLC 6, 52**
See also CA 21-24R; CAAS 6; CANR 18,
40

Mathews, John Joseph
1894-1979 . . . . . . **CLC 84; DAM MULT**
See also CA 19-20; 142; CANR 45; CAP 2;
DLB 175; NNAL

Mathias, Roland (Glyn) 1915- . . . . . . **CLC 45**
See also CA 97-100; CANR 19, 41; DLB 27

Matsuo Basho 1644-1694 . . . . **PC 3**
See also DAM POET

Mattheson, Rodney
See Creasey, John

Matthews, Greg 1949- . . . . **CLC 45**
See also CA 135

Matthews, William 1942- . . . . **CLC 40**
See also CA 29-32R; CAAS 18; CANR 12,
57; DLB 5

Matthias, John (Edward) 1941- . . . . . . **CLC 9**
See also CA 33-36R; CANR 56

Matthiessen, Peter
1927- . . . . **CLC 5, 7, 11, 32, 64;**
DAM NOV
See also AAYA 6; BEST 90:4; CA 9-12R;
CANR 21, 50; DLB 6, 173; MTCW;
SATA 27

Maturin, Charles Robert
1780(?)-1824 . . . . **NCLC 6**
See also DLB 178

Matute (Ausejo), Ana Maria
1925- . . . . **CLC 11**
See also CA 89-92; MTCW

Maugham, W. S.
See Maugham, W(illiam) Somerset

Maugham, W(illiam) Somerset
1874-1965 . . . . **CLC 1, 11, 15, 67, 93;**
DA; DAB; DAC; DAM DRAM, MST,
NOV; SSC 8; WLC
See also CA 5-8R; 25-28R; CANR 40;
CDBLB 1914-1945; DLB 10, 36, 77, 100,
162; MTCW; SATA 54

Maugham, William Somerset
See Maugham, W(illiam) Somerset

Maupassant, (Henri Rene Albert) Guy de
1850-1893 . . . . . **NCLC 1, 42; DA; DAB;**
DAC; DAM MST; SSC 1; WLC
See also DLB 123

Maupin, Armistead
1944- . . . . **CLC 95; DAM POP**
See also CA 125; 130; CANR 58; INT 130

Maurhut, Richard
See Traven, B.

Mauriac, Claude 1914-1996 . . . . **CLC 9**
See also CA 89-92; 152; DLB 83

Mauriac, Francois (Charles)
1885-1970 . . . . **CLC 4, 9, 56; SSC 24**
See also CA 25-28; CAP 2; DLB 65;
MTCW

Mavor, Osborne Henry 1888-1951
See Bridie, James
See also CA 104

Maxwell, William (Keepers, Jr.)
1908- . . . . **CLC 19**
See also CA 93-96; CANR 54; DLBY 80;
INT 93-96

May, Elaine 1932- . . . . **CLC 16**
See also CA 124; 142; DLB 44

Mayakovski, Vladimir (Vladimirovich)
1893-1930 . . . . **TCLC 4, 18**
See also CA 104; 158

Mayhew, Henry 1812-1887 . . . . . . **NCLC 31**
See also DLB 18, 55

Mayle, Peter 1939(?)- . . . . **CLC 89**
See also CA 139

Maynard, Joyce 1953- . . . . **CLC 23**
See also CA 111; 129

Mayne, William (James Carter)
1928- . . . . **CLC 12**
See also AAYA 20; CA 9-12R; CANR 37;
CLR 25; JRDA; MAICYA; SAAS 11;
SATA 6, 68

Mayo, Jim
See L'Amour, Louis (Dearborn)

Maysles, Albert 1926- . . . . **CLC 16**
See also CA 29-32R

Maysles, David 1932- . . . . **CLC 16**

Mazer, Norma Fox 1931- . . . . **CLC 26**
See also AAYA 5; CA 69-72; CANR 12,
32; CLR 23; JRDA; MAICYA; SAAS 1;
SATA 24, 67

Mazzini, Guiseppe 1805-1872 . . . . **NCLC 34**

McAuley, James Phillip
1917-1976 . . . . **CLC 45**
See also CA 97-100

McBain, Ed
See Hunter, Evan

McBrien, William Augustine
1930- . . . . **CLC 44**
See also CA 107

McCaffrey, Anne (Inez)
1926- . . . . . . **CLC 17; DAM NOV, POP**
See also AAYA 6; AITN 2; BEST 89:2;
CA 25-28R; CANR 15, 35, 55; DLB 8;
JRDA; MAICYA; MTCW; SAAS 11;
SATA 8, 70

McCall, Nathan 1955(?)- . . . . **CLC 86**
See also CA 146

McCann, Arthur
See Campbell, John W(ood, Jr.)

McCann, Edson
See Pohl, Frederik

McCarthy, Charles, Jr. 1933-
See McCarthy, Cormac
See also CANR 42; DAM POP

McCarthy, Cormac
1933- . . . . **CLC 4, 57, 59, 101**
See also McCarthy, Charles, Jr.
See also DLB 6, 143

McCarthy, Mary (Therese)
1912-1989 . . . . . . **CLC 1, 3, 5, 14, 24, 39,**
59; SSC 24
See also CA 5-8R; 129; CANR 16, 50;
DLB 2; DLBY 81; INT CANR-16;
MTCW

McCartney, (James) Paul
1942- . . . . **CLC 12, 35**
See also CA 146

McCauley, Stephen (D.) 1955- . . . . . **CLC 50**
See also CA 141

McClure, Michael (Thomas)
1932- . . . . **CLC 6, 10**
See also CA 21-24R; CANR 17, 46;
DLB 16

McCorkle, Jill (Collins) 1958- . . . . . . **CLC 51**
See also CA 121; DLBY 87

McCourt, James 1941- . . . . **CLC 5**
See also CA 57-60

McCoy, Horace (Stanley)
1897-1955 . . . . **TCLC 28**
See also CA 108; 155; DLB 9

McCrae, John 1872-1918 . . . . **TCLC 12**
See also CA 109; DLB 92

McCreigh, James
See Pohl, Frederik

McCullers, (Lula) Carson (Smith)
1917-1967 . . . . **CLC 1, 4, 10, 12, 48, 100;**
DA; DAB; DAC; DAM MST, NOV;
SSC 9, 24; WLC
See also AAYA 21; CA 5-8R; 25-28R;
CABS 1, 3; CANR 18;
CDALB 1941-1968; DLB 2, 7, 173;
MTCW; SATA 27

McCulloch, John Tyler
See Burroughs, Edgar Rice

McCullough, Colleen
1938(?)- . . . . **CLC 27; DAM NOV, POP**
See also CA 81-84; CANR 17, 46; MTCW

McDermott, Alice 1953- . . . . **CLC 90**
See also CA 109; CANR 40

McElroy, Joseph 1930- . . . . **CLC 5, 47**
See also CA 17-20R

McEwan, Ian (Russell)
1948- . . . . **CLC 13, 66; DAM NOV**
See also BEST 90:4; CA 61-64; CANR 14,
41; DLB 14; MTCW

McFadden, David 1940- . . . . **CLC 48**
See also CA 104; DLB 60; INT 104

McFarland, Dennis 1950- . . . . **CLC 65**

McGahern, John
1934- . . . . **CLC 5, 9, 48; SSC 17**
See also CA 17-20R; CANR 29; DLB 14;
MTCW

McGinley, Patrick (Anthony)
1937- . . . . **CLC 41**
See also CA 120; 127; CANR 56; INT 127

McGinley, Phyllis 1905-1978 . . . . . . **CLC 14**
See also CA 9-12R; 77-80; CANR 19;
DLB 11, 48; SATA 2, 44; SATA-Obit 24

McGinniss, Joe 1942- . . . . **CLC 32**
See also AITN 2; BEST 89:2; CA 25-28R;
CANR 26; INT CANR-26

McGivern, Maureen Daly
See Daly, Maureen

McGrath, Patrick 1950- . . . . **CLC 55**
See also CA 136

McGrath, Thomas (Matthew)
1916-1990 . . . . **CLC 28, 59; DAM POET**
See also CA 9-12R; 132; CANR 6, 33;
MTCW; SATA 41; SATA-Obit 66

McGuane, Thomas (Francis III)
1939- . . . . **CLC 3, 7, 18, 45**
See also AITN 2; CA 49-52; CANR 5, 24,
49; DLB 2; DLBY 80; INT CANR-24;
MTCW

McGuckian, Medbh
1950- .... CLC 48; DAM POET
See also CA 143; DLB 40

McHale, Tom 1942(?)-1982....... CLC 3, 5
See also AITN 1; CA 77-80; 106

McIlvanney, William 1936-........ CLC 42
See also CA 25-28R; CANR 61; DLB 14

McIlwraith, Maureen Mollie Hunter
See Hunter, Mollie
See also SATA 2

McInerney, Jay
1955- .... CLC 34; DAM POP
See also AAYA 18; CA 116; 123;
CANR 45; INT 123

McIntyre, Vonda N(eel) 1948- ..... CLC 18
See also CA 81-84; CANR 17, 34; MTCW

McKay, Claude
.... TCLC 7, 41; BLC; DAB; PC 2
See also McKay, Festus Claudius
See also DLB 4, 45, 51, 117

McKay, Festus Claudius 1889-1948
See McKay, Claude
See also BW 1; CA 104; 124; DA; DAC;
DAM MST, MULT, NOV, POET;
MTCW; WLC

McKuen, Rod 1933-............. CLC 1, 3
See also AITN 1; CA 41-44R; CANR 40

McLoughlin, R. B.
See Mencken, H(enry) L(ouis)

McLuhan, (Herbert) Marshall
1911-1980 .... CLC 37, 83
See also CA 9-12R; 102; CANR 12, 34, 61;
DLB 88; INT CANR-12; MTCW

McMillan, Terry (L.)
1951- .... CLC 50, 61; DAM MULT,
NOV, POP
See also AAYA 21; BW 2; CA 140;
CANR 60

McMurtry, Larry (Jeff)
1936- .... CLC 2, 3, 7, 11, 27, 44;
DAM NOV, POP
See also AAYA 15; AITN 2; BEST 89:2;
CA 5-8R; CANR 19, 43;
CDALB 1968-1988; DLB 2, 143;
DLBY 80, 87; MTCW

McNally, T. M. 1961-............ CLC 82

McNally, Terrence
1939- ... CLC 4, 7, 41, 91; DAM DRAM
See also CA 45-48; CANR 2, 56; DLB 7

McNamer, Deirdre 1950-.......... CLC 70

McNeile, Herman Cyril 1888-1937
See Sapper
See also DLB 77

McNickle, (William) D'Arcy
1904-1977 ...... CLC 89; DAM MULT
See also CA 9-12R; 85-88; CANR 5, 45;
DLB 175; NNAL; SATA-Obit 22

McPhee, John (Angus) 1931- ...... CLC 36
See also BEST 90:1; CA 65-68; CANR 20,
46; MTCW

McPherson, James Alan
1943-.................. CLC 19, 77
See also BW 1; CA 25-28R; CAAS 17;
CANR 24; DLB 38; MTCW

McPherson, William (Alexander)
1933-..................... CLC 34
See also CA 69-72; CANR 28;
INT CANR-28

Mead, Margaret 1901-1978....... CLC 37
See also AITN 1; CA 1-4R; 81-84;
CANR 4; MTCW; SATA-Obit 20

Meaker, Marijane (Agnes) 1927-
See Kerr, M. E.
See also CA 107; CANR 37; INT 107;
JRDA; MAICYA; MTCW; SATA 20, 61

Medoff, Mark (Howard)
1940- .... CLC 6, 23; DAM DRAM
See also AITN 1; CA 53-56; CANR 5;
DLB 7; INT CANR-5

Medvedev, P. N.
See Bakhtin, Mikhail Mikhailovich

Meged, Aharon
See Megged, Aharon

Meged, Aron
See Megged, Aharon

Megged, Aharon 1920-........... CLC 9
See also CA 49-52; CAAS 13; CANR 1

Mehta, Ved (Parkash) 1934-....... CLC 37
See also CA 1-4R; CANR 2, 23; MTCW

Melanter
See Blackmore, R(ichard) D(oddridge)

Melikow, Loris
See Hofmannsthal, Hugo von

Melmoth, Sebastian
See Wilde, Oscar (Fingal O'Flahertie Wills)

Meltzer, Milton 1915-............ CLC 26
See also AAYA 8; CA 13-16R; CANR 38;
CLR 13; DLB 61; JRDA; MAICYA;
SAAS 1; SATA 1, 50, 80

Melville, Herman
1819-1891 ..... NCLC 3, 12, 29, 45, 49;
DA; DAB; DAC; DAM MST, NOV;
SSC 1, 17; WLC
See also CDALB 1640-1865; DLB 3, 74;
SATA 59

Menander
c. 342B.C.-c. 292B.C........ CMLC 9;
DAM DRAM; DC 3
See also DLB 176

Mencken, H(enry) L(ouis)
1880-1956 .... TCLC 13
See also CA 105; 125; CDALB 1917-1929;
DLB 11, 29, 63, 137; MTCW

Mendelsohn, Jane 1965(?)- .... CLC 99
See also CA 154

Mercer, David
1928-1980 .... CLC 5; DAM DRAM
See also CA 9-12R; 102; CANR 23;
DLB 13; MTCW

Merchant, Paul
See Ellison, Harlan (Jay)

Meredith, George
1828-1909 .. TCLC 17, 43; DAM POET
See also CA 117; 153; CDBLB 1832-1890;
DLB 18, 35, 57, 159

Meredith, William (Morris)
1919- .. CLC 4, 13, 22, 55; DAM POET
See also CA 9-12R; CAAS 14; CANR 6, 40;
DLB 5

Merezhkovsky, Dmitry Sergeyevich
1865-1941 .... TCLC 29

Merimee, Prosper
1803-1870 .... NCLC 6; SSC 7
See also DLB 119

Merkin, Daphne 1954-............. CLC 44
See also CA 123

Merlin, Arthur
See Blish, James (Benjamin)

Merrill, James (Ingram)
1926-1995 .... CLC 2, 3, 6, 8, 13, 18, 34,
91; DAM POET
See also CA 13-16R; 147; CANR 10, 49;
DLB 5, 165; DLBY 85; INT CANR-10;
MTCW

Merriman, Alex
See Silverberg, Robert

Merritt, E. B.
See Waddington, Miriam

Merton, Thomas
1915-1968 .. CLC 1, 3, 11, 34, 83; PC 10
See also CA 5-8R; 25-28R; CANR 22, 53;
DLB 48; DLBY 81; MTCW

Merwin, W(illiam) S(tanley)
1927-...... CLC 1, 2, 3, 5, 8, 13, 18, 45,
88; DAM POET
See also CA 13-16R; CANR 15, 51; DLB 5,
169; INT CANR-15; MTCW

Metcalf, John 1938-.............. CLC 37
See also CA 113; DLB 60

Metcalf, Suzanne
See Baum, L(yman) Frank

Mew, Charlotte (Mary)
1870-1928 .... TCLC 8
See also CA 105; DLB 19, 135

Mewshaw, Michael 1943-.......... CLC 9
See also CA 53-56; CANR 7, 47; DLBY 80

Meyer, June
See Jordan, June

Meyer, Lynn
See Slavitt, David R(ytman)

Meyer-Meyrink, Gustav 1868-1932
See Meyrink, Gustav
See also CA 117

Meyers, Jeffrey 1939- .... CLC 39
See also CA 73-76; CANR 54; DLB 111

Meynell, Alice (Christina Gertrude Thompson)
1847-1922 .... TCLC 6
See also CA 104; DLB 19, 98

Meyrink, Gustav .... TCLC 21
See also Meyer-Meyrink, Gustav
See also DLB 81

Michaels, Leonard
1933- .... CLC 6, 25; SSC 16
See also CA 61-64; CANR 21, 62;
DLB 130; MTCW

Michaux, Henri 1899-1984 ...... CLC 8, 19
See also CA 85-88; 114

Michelangelo 1475-1564........... LC 12

Michelet, Jules 1798-1874....... NCLC 31

Michener, James A(lbert)
1907(?)- .... CLC 1, 5, 11, 29, 60;
DAM NOV, POP
See also AITN 1; BEST 90:1; CA 5-8R;
CANR 21, 45; DLB 6; MTCW

Mickiewicz, Adam 1798-1855 . . . . . NCLC 3

Middleton, Christopher 1926- . . . . . . CLC 13
See also CA 13-16R; CANR 29, 54;
DLB 40

Middleton, Richard (Barham)
1882-1911 . . . . TCLC 56
See also DLB 156

Middleton, Stanley 1919- . . . . CLC 7, 38
See also CA 25-28R; CAAS 23; CANR 21,
46; DLB 14

Middleton, Thomas
1580-1627 . . . . LC 33; DAM DRAM,
MST; DC 5
See also DLB 58

Migueis, Jose Rodrigues 1901- . . . . . CLC 10

Mikszath, Kalman 1847-1910 . . . . . TCLC 31

Miles, Jack . . . . CLC 100

Miles, Josephine (Louise)
1911-1985 . . . . CLC 1, 2, 14, 34, 39;
DAM POET
See also CA 1-4R; 116; CANR 2, 55;
DLB 48

Militant
See Sandburg, Carl (August)

Mill, John Stuart 1806-1873 . . NCLC 11, 58
See also CDBLB 1832-1890; DLB 55

Millar, Kenneth
1915-1983 . . . . CLC 14; DAM POP
See also Macdonald, Ross
See also CA 9-12R; 110; CANR 16; DLB 2;
DLBD 6; DLBY 83; MTCW

Millay, E. Vincent
See Millay, Edna St. Vincent

Millay, Edna St. Vincent
1892-1950 . . . . . . TCLC 4, 49; DA; DAB;
DAC; DAM MST, POET; PC 6; WLCS
See also CA 104; 130; CDALB 1917-1929;
DLB 45; MTCW

Miller, Arthur
1915- . . . . CLC 1, 2, 6, 10, 15, 26, 47, 78;
DA; DAB; DAC; DAM DRAM, MST;
DC 1; WLC
See also AAYA 15; AITN 1; CA 1-4R;
CABS 3; CANR 2, 30, 54;
CDALB 1941-1968; DLB 7; MTCW

Miller, Henry (Valentine)
1891-1980 . . . . CLC 1, 2, 4, 9, 14, 43, 84;
DA; DAB; DAC; DAM MST, NOV;
WLC
See also CA 9-12R; 97-100; CANR 33;
CDALB 1929-1941; DLB 4, 9; DLBY 80;
MTCW

Miller, Jason 1939(?)- . . . . CLC 2
See also AITN 1; CA 73-76; DLB 7

Miller, Sue 1943- . . . . . CLC 44; DAM POP
See also BEST 90:3; CA 139; CANR 59;
DLB 143

Miller, Walter M(ichael, Jr.)
1923- . . . . CLC 4, 30
See also CA 85-88; DLB 8

Millett, Kate 1934- . . . . CLC 67
See also AITN 1; CA 73-76; CANR 32, 53;
MTCW

Millhauser, Steven 1943- . . . . CLC 21, 54
See also CA 110; 111; DLB 2; INT 111

Millin, Sarah Gertrude 1889-1968 . . CLC 49
See also CA 102; 93-96

Milne, A(lan) A(lexander)
1882-1956 . . . . TCLC 6; DAB; DAC;
DAM MST
See also CA 104; 133; CLR 1, 26; DLB 10,
77, 100, 160; MAICYA; MTCW;
YABC 1

Milner, Ron(ald)
1938- . . . . . CLC 56; BLC; DAM MULT
See also AITN 1; BW 1; CA 73-76;
CANR 24; DLB 38; MTCW

Milnes, Richard Monckton
1809-1885 . . . . NCLC 61
See also DLB 32, 184

Milosz, Czeslaw
1911- . . . . CLC 5, 11, 22, 31, 56, 82;
DAM MST, POET; PC 8; WLCS
See also CA 81-84; CANR 23, 51; MTCW

Milton, John
1608-1674 . . . . . . LC 9; DA; DAB; DAC;
DAM MST, POET; PC 19; WLC
See also CDBLB 1660-1789; DLB 131, 151

Min, Anchee 1957- . . . . CLC 86
See also CA 146

Minehaha, Cornelius
See Wedekind, (Benjamin) Frank(lin)

Miner, Valerie 1947- . . . . CLC 40
See also CA 97-100; CANR 59

Minimo, Duca
See D'Annunzio, Gabriele

Minot, Susan 1956- . . . . CLC 44
See also CA 134

Minus, Ed 1938- . . . . CLC 39

Miranda, Javier
See Bioy Casares, Adolfo

Mirbeau, Octave 1848-1917 . . . . . . TCLC 55
See also DLB 123

Miro (Ferrer), Gabriel (Francisco Victor)
1879-1930 . . . . TCLC 5
See also CA 104

Mishima, Yukio
1925-1970 . . . . CLC 2, 4, 6, 9, 27; DC 1;
SSC 4
See also Hiraoka, Kimitake
See also DLB 182

Mistral, Frederic 1830-1914 . . . . . . TCLC 51
See also CA 122

Mistral, Gabriela . . . . TCLC 2; HLC
See also Godoy Alcayaga, Lucila

Mistry, Rohinton 1952- . . . . . . CLC 71; DAC
See also CA 141

Mitchell, Clyde
See Ellison, Harlan (Jay); Silverberg, Robert

Mitchell, James Leslie 1901-1935
See Gibbon, Lewis Grassic
See also CA 104; DLB 15

Mitchell, Joni 1943- . . . . CLC 12
See also CA 112

Mitchell, Joseph (Quincy)
1908-1996 . . . . CLC 98
See also CA 77-80; 152; DLBY 96

Mitchell, Margaret (Munnerlyn)
1900-1949 . . . . . . TCLC 11; DAM NOV,
POP
See also CA 109; 125; CANR 55; DLB 9;
MTCW

Mitchell, Peggy
See Mitchell, Margaret (Munnerlyn)

Mitchell, S(ilas) Weir 1829-1914 . . TCLC 36

Mitchell, W(illiam) O(rmond)
1914- . . . . . . CLC 25; DAC; DAM MST
See also CA 77-80; CANR 15, 43; DLB 88

Mitford, Mary Russell 1787-1855. . NCLC 4
See also DLB 110, 116

Mitford, Nancy 1904-1973 . . . . CLC 44
See also CA 9-12R

Miyamoto, Yuriko 1899-1951 . . . . . TCLC 37
See also DLB 180

Mizoguchi, Kenji 1898-1956 . . . . . . TCLC 72

Mo, Timothy (Peter) 1950(?)- . . . . . . CLC 46
See also CA 117; MTCW

Modarressi, Taghi (M.) 1931- . . . . . . CLC 44
See also CA 121; 134; INT 134

Modiano, Patrick (Jean) 1945- . . . . . CLC 18
See also CA 85-88; CANR 17, 40; DLB 83

Moerck, Paal
See Roelvaag, O(le) E(dvart)

Mofolo, Thomas (Mokopu)
1875(?)-1948 . . . . TCLC 22; BLC;
DAM MULT
See also CA 121; 153

Mohr, Nicholasa
1935- . . . . . CLC 12; DAM MULT; HLC
See also AAYA 8; CA 49-52; CANR 1, 32;
CLR 22; DLB 145; HW; JRDA; SAAS 8;
SATA 8

Mojtabai, A(nn) G(race)
1938- . . . . CLC 5, 9, 15, 29
See also CA 85-88

Moliere
1622-1673 . . . . . LC 28; DA; DAB; DAC;
DAM DRAM, MST; WLC

Molin, Charles
See Mayne, William (James Carter)

Molnar, Ferenc
1878-1952 . . . . . TCLC 20; DAM DRAM
See also CA 109; 153

Momaday, N(avarre) Scott
1934- . . . . . CLC 2, 19, 85, 95; DA; DAB;
DAC; DAM MST, MULT, NOV, POP;
WLCS
See also AAYA 11; CA 25-28R; CANR 14,
34; DLB 143, 175; INT CANR-14;
MTCW; NNAL; SATA 48;
SATA-Brief 30

Monette, Paul 1945-1995 . . . . CLC 82
See also CA 139; 147

Monroe, Harriet 1860-1936 . . . . TCLC 12
See also CA 109; DLB 54, 91

Monroe, Lyle
See Heinlein, Robert A(nson)

Montagu, Elizabeth 1917- . . . . NCLC 7
See also CA 9-12R

Montagu, Mary (Pierrepont) Wortley
1689-1762 . . . . LC 9; PC 16
See also DLB 95, 101

Mossgiel, Rab
See Burns, Robert

Motion, Andrew (Peter) 1952-...... **CLC 47**
See also CA 146; DLB 40

Motley, Willard (Francis)
1909-1965 .... **CLC 18**
See also BW 1; CA 117; 106; DLB 76, 143

Motoori, Norinaga 1730-1801 .... **NCLC 45**

Mott, Michael (Charles Alston)
1930-.................... **CLC 15, 34**
See also CA 5-8R; CAAS 7; CANR 7, 29

Mountain Wolf Woman
1884-1960 .... **CLC 92**
See also CA 144; NNAL

Moure, Erin 1955- .... **CLC 88**
See also CA 113; DLB 60

Mowat, Farley (McGill)
1921-...... **CLC 26; DAC; DAM MST**
See also AAYA 1; CA 1-4R; CANR 4, 24,
42; CLR 20; DLB 68; INT CANAR-24;
JRDA; MAICYA; MTCW; SATA 3, 55

Moyers, Bill 1934-.............. **CLC 74**
See also AITN 2; CA 61-64; CANR 31, 52

Mphahlele, Es'kia
See Mphahlele, Ezekiel
See also DLB 125

Mphahlele, Ezekiel
1919-..... **CLC 25; BLC; DAM MULT**
See also Mphahlele, Es'kia
See also BW 2; CA 81-84; CANR 26

Mqhayi, S(amuel) E(dward) K(rune Loliwe)
1875-1945 .... **TCLC 25; BLC;**
DAM MULT
See also CA 153

Mrozek, Slawomir 1930-........ **CLC 3, 13**
See also CA 13-16R; CAAS 10; CANR 29;
MTCW

Mrs. Belloc-Lowndes
See Lowndes, Marie Adelaide (Belloc)

Mtwa, Percy (?)-................. **CLC 47**

Mueller, Lisel 1924-.......... **CLC 13, 51**
See also CA 93-96; DLB 105

Muir, Edwin 1887-1959 .... **TCLC 2**
See also CA 104; DLB 20, 100

Muir, John 1838-1914 .... **TCLC 28**

Mujica Lainez, Manuel
1910-1984 .... **CLC 31**
See also Lainez, Manuel Mujica
See also CA 81-84; 112; CANR 32; HW

Mukherjee, Bharati
1940-............. **CLC 53; DAM NOV**
See also BEST 89:2; CA 107; CANR 45;
DLB 60; MTCW

Muldoon, Paul
1951-........ **CLC 32, 72; DAM POET**
See also CA 113; 129; CANR 52; DLB 40;
INT 129

Mulisch, Harry 1927-............. **CLC 42**
See also CA 9-12R; CANR 6, 26, 56

Mull, Martin 1943-.............. **CLC 17**
See also CA 105

Mulock, Dinah Maria
See Craik, Dinah Maria (Mulock)

Munford, Robert 1737(?)-1783 .... **LC 5**
See also DLB 31

Mungo, Raymond 1946-.......... **CLC 72**
See also CA 49-52; CANR 2

Munro, Alice
1931-...... **CLC 6, 10, 19, 50, 95; DAC;**
DAM MST, NOV; SSC 3; WLCS
See also AITN 2; CA 33-36R; CANR 33,
53; DLB 53; MTCW; SATA 29

Munro, H(ector) H(ugh) 1870-1916
See Saki
See also CA 104; 130; CDBLB 1890-1914;
DA; DAB; DAC; DAM MST, NOV;
DLB 34, 162; MTCW; WLC

Murasaki, Lady................. **CMLC 1**

Murdoch, (Jean) Iris
1919-...... **CLC 1, 2, 3, 4, 6, 8, 11, 15,**
22, 31, 51; DAB; DAC; DAM MST,
NOV
See also CA 13-16R; CANR 8, 43;
CDBLB 1960 to Present; DLB 14;
INT CANR-8; MTCW

Murfree, Mary Noailles
1850-1922 .... **SSC 22**
See also CA 122; DLB 12, 74

Murnau, Friedrich Wilhelm
See Plumpe, Friedrich Wilhelm

Murphy, Richard 1927-........... **CLC 41**
See also CA 29-32R; DLB 40

Murphy, Sylvia 1937-............. **CLC 34**
See also CA 121

Murphy, Thomas (Bernard) 1935-... **CLC 51**
See also CA 101

Murray, Albert L. 1916-.......... **CLC 73**
See also BW 2; CA 49-52; CANR 26, 52;
DLB 38

Murray, Judith Sargent
1751-1820 .... **NCLC 63**
See also DLB 37

Murray, Les(lie) A(llan)
1938-.......... **CLC 40; DAM POET**
See also CA 21-24R; CANR 11, 27, 56

Murry, J. Middleton
See Murry, John Middleton

Murry, John Middleton
1889-1957 .... **TCLC 16**
See also CA 118; DLB 149

Musgrave, Susan 1951- .... **CLC 13, 54**
See also CA 69-72; CANR 45

Musil, Robert (Edler von)
1880-1942 ...... **TCLC 12, 68; SSC 18**
See also CA 109; CANR 55; DLB 81, 124

Muske, Carol 1945- .... **CLC 90**
See also Muske-Dukes, Carol (Anne)

Muske-Dukes, Carol (Anne) 1945-
See Muske, Carol
See also CA 65-68; CANR 32

Musset, (Louis Charles) Alfred de
1810-1857 .... **NCLC 7**

My Brother's Brother
See Chekhov, Anton (Pavlovich)

Myers, L(eopold) H(amilton)
1881-1944 .... **TCLC 59**
See also CA 157; DLB 15

Myers, Walter Dean
1937- ..... **CLC 35; BLC; DAM MULT,**
NOV
See also AAYA 4; BW 2; CA 33-36R;
CANR 20, 42; CLR 4, 16, 35; DLB 33;
INT CANR-20; JRDA; MAICYA;
SAAS 2; SATA 41, 71; SATA-Brief 27

Myers, Walter M.
See Myers, Walter Dean

Myles, Symon
See Follett, Ken(neth Martin)

Nabokov, Vladimir (Vladimirovich)
1899-1977 ..... **CLC 1, 2, 3, 6, 8, 11, 15,**
23, 44, 46, 64; DA; DAB; DAC;
DAM MST, NOV; SSC 11; WLC
See also CA 5-8R; 69-72; CANR 20;
CDALB 1941-1968; DLB 2; DLBD 3;
DLBY 80, 91; MTCW

Nagai Kafu 1879-1959 .... **TCLC 51**
See also Nagai Sokichi
See also DLB 180

Nagai Sokichi 1879-1959
See Nagai Kafu
See also CA 117

Nagy, Laszlo 1925-1978........... **CLC 7**
See also CA 129; 112

Naipaul, Shiva(dhar Srinivasa)
1945-1985 ..... **CLC 32, 39; DAM NOV**
See also CA 110; 112; 116; CANR 33;
DLB 157; DLBY 85; MTCW

Naipaul, V(idiadhar) S(urajprasad)
1932-.... **CLC 4, 7, 9, 13, 18, 37; DAB;**
DAC; DAM MST, NOV
See also CA 1-4R; CANR 1, 33, 51;
CDBLB 1960 to Present; DLB 125;
DLBY 85; MTCW

Nakos, Lilika 1899(?)-............ **CLC 29**

Narayan, R(asipuram) K(rishnaswami)
1906-...... **CLC 7, 28, 47; DAM NOV;**
SSC 25
See also CA 81-84; CANR 33, 61; MTCW;
SATA 62

Nash, (Frediric) Ogden
1902-1971 .... **CLC 23; DAM POET**
See also CA 13-14; 29-32R; CANR 34, 61;
CAP 1; DLB 11; MAICYA; MTCW;
SATA 2, 46

Nathan, Daniel
See Dannay, Frederic

Nathan, George Jean 1882-1958 ... **TCLC 18**
See also Hatteras, Owen
See also CA 114; DLB 137

Natsume, Kinnosuke 1867-1916
See Natsume, Soseki
See also CA 104

Natsume, Soseki 1867-1916..... **TCLC 2, 10**
See also Natsume, Kinnosuke
See also DLB 180

Natti, (Mary) Lee 1919-
See Kingman, Lee
See also CA 5-8R; CANR 2

Naylor, Gloria
1950-..... **CLC 28, 52; BLC; DA; DAC;**
DAM MST, MULT, NOV, POP; WLCS
See also AAYA 6; BW 2; CA 107;
CANR 27, 51; DLB 173; MTCW

Neihardt, John Gneisenau
1881-1973 .... **CLC 32**
See also CA 13-14; CAP 1; DLB 9, 54

Nekrasov, Nikolai Alekseevich
1821-1878 .... **NCLC 11**

Nelligan, Emile 1879-1941 .... **TCLC 14**
See also CA 114; DLB 92

Nelson, Willie 1933- .... **CLC 17**
See also CA 107

Nemerov, Howard (Stanley)
1920-1991 .... **CLC 2, 6, 9, 36;**
DAM POET
See also CA 1-4R; 134; CABS 2; CANR 1,
27, 53; DLB 5, 6; DLBY 83;
INT CANR-27; MTCW

Neruda, Pablo
1904-1973 ..... **CLC 1, 2, 5, 7, 9, 28, 62;**
DA; DAB; DAC; DAM MST, MULT,
POET; HLC; PC 4; WLC
See also CA 19-20; 45-48; CAP 2; HW;
MTCW

Nerval, Gerard de
1808-1855 ..... **NCLC 1; PC 13; SSC 18**

Nervo, (Jose) Amado (Ruiz de)
1870-1919 .... **TCLC 11**
See also CA 109; 131; HW

Nessi, Pio Baroja y
See Baroja (y Nessi), Pio

Nestroy, Johann 1801-1862 ...... **NCLC 42**
See also DLB 133

Netterville, Luke
See O'Grady, Standish (James)

Neufeld, John (Arthur) 1938- ...... **CLC 17**
See also AAYA 11; CA 25-28R; CANR 11,
37, 56; MAICYA; SAAS 3; SATA 6, 81

Neville, Emily Cheney 1919- .... **CLC 12**
See also CA 5-8R; CANR 3, 37; JRDA;
MAICYA; SAAS 2; SATA 1

Newbound, Bernard Slade 1930-
See Slade, Bernard
See also CA 81-84; CANR 49;
DAM DRAM

Newby, P(ercy) H(oward)
1918- .... **CLC 2, 13; DAM NOV**
See also CA 5-8R; CANR 32; DLB 15;
MTCW

Newlove, Donald 1928- .... **CLC 6**
See also CA 29-32R; CANR 25

Newlove, John (Herbert) 1938- ..... **CLC 14**
See also CA 21-24R; CANR 9, 25

Newman, Charles 1938- .... **CLC 2, 8**
See also CA 21-24R

Newman, Edwin (Harold) 1919- .... **CLC 14**
See also AITN 1; CA 69-72; CANR 5

Newman, John Henry
1801-1890 .... **NCLC 38**
See also DLB 18, 32, 55

Newton, Suzanne 1936- .... **CLC 35**
See also CA 41-44R; CANR 14; JRDA;
SATA 5, 77

Nexo, Martin Andersen
1869-1954 .... **TCLC 43**

Nezval, Vitezslav 1900-1958 ...... **TCLC 44**
See also CA 123

Ng, Fae Myenne 1957(?)- .... **CLC 81**
See also CA 146

Ngema, Mbongeni 1955- .... **CLC 57**
See also BW 2; CA 143

Ngugi, James T(hiong'o) .... **CLC 3, 7, 13**
See also Ngugi wa Thiong'o

Ngugi wa Thiong'o
1938- ..... **CLC 36; BLC; DAM MULT,**
NOV
See also Ngugi, James T(hiong'o)
See also BW 2; CA 81-84; CANR 27, 58;
DLB 125; MTCW

Nichol, B(arrie) P(hillip)
1944-1988 .... **CLC 18**
See also CA 53-56; DLB 53; SATA 66

Nichols, John (Treadwell) 1940- .... **CLC 38**
See also CA 9-12R; CAAS 2; CANR 6;
DLBY 82

Nichols, Leigh
See Koontz, Dean R(ay)

Nichols, Peter (Richard)
1927- .... **CLC 5, 36, 65**
See also CA 104; CANR 33; DLB 13;
MTCW

Nicolas, F. R. E.
See Freeling, Nicolas

Niedecker, Lorine
1903-1970 .... **CLC 10, 42; DAM POET**
See also CA 25-28; CAP 2; DLB 48

Nietzsche, Friedrich (Wilhelm)
1844-1900 .... **TCLC 10, 18, 55**
See also CA 107; 121; DLB 129

Nievo, Ippolito 1831-1861 .... **NCLC 22**

Nightingale, Anne Redmon 1943-
See Redmon, Anne
See also CA 103

Nik. T. O.
See Annensky, Innokenty (Fyodorovich)

Nin, Anais
1903-1977 ...... **CLC 1, 4, 8, 11, 14, 60;**
DAM NOV, POP; SSC 10
See also AITN 2; CA 13-16R; 69-72;
CANR 22, 53; DLB 2, 4, 152; MTCW

Nishiwaki, Junzaburo 1894-1982 .... **PC 15**
See also CA 107

Nissenson, Hugh 1933- .... **CLC 4, 9**
See also CA 17-20R; CANR 27; DLB 28

Niven, Larry .... **CLC 8**
See also Niven, Laurence Van Cott
See also DLB 8

Niven, Laurence Van Cott 1938-
See Niven, Larry
See also CA 21-24R; CAAS 12; CANR 14,
44; DAM POP; MTCW; SATA 95

Nixon, Agnes Eckhardt 1927- ...... **CLC 21**
See also CA 110

Nizan, Paul 1905-1940 .... **TCLC 40**
See also DLB 72

Nkosi, Lewis
1936- ..... **CLC 45; BLC; DAM MULT**
See also BW 1; CA 65-68; CANR 27;
DLB 157

Nodier, (Jean) Charles (Emmanuel)
1780-1844 .... **NCLC 19**
See also DLB 119

Nolan, Christopher 1965- .... **CLC 58**
See also CA 111

Noon, Jeff 1957- .... **CLC 91**
See also CA 148

Norden, Charles
See Durrell, Lawrence (George)

Nordhoff, Charles (Bernard)
1887-1947 .... **TCLC 23**
See also CA 108; DLB 9; SATA 23

Norfolk, Lawrence 1963- .... **CLC 76**
See also CA 144

Norman, Marsha
1947- .... **CLC 28; DAM DRAM**
See also CA 105; CABS 3; CANR 41;
DLBY 84

Norris, Frank 1870-1902 .... **SSC 28**
See also Norris, (Benjamin) Frank(lin, Jr.)
See also CDALB 1865-1917; DLB 12, 71

Norris, (Benjamin) Frank(lin, Jr.)
1870-1902 .... **TCLC 24**
See also Norris, Frank
See also CA 110; 160

Norris, Leslie 1921- .... **CLC 14**
See also CA 11-12; CANR 14; CAP 1;
DLB 27

North, Andrew
See Norton, Andre

North, Anthony
See Koontz, Dean R(ay)

North, Captain George
See Stevenson, Robert Louis (Balfour)

North, Milou
See Erdrich, Louise

Northrup, B. A.
See Hubbard, L(afayette) Ron(ald)

North Staffs
See Hulme, T(homas) E(rnest)

Norton, Alice Mary
See Norton, Andre
See also MAICYA; SATA 1, 43

Norton, Andre 1912- .... **CLC 12**
See also Norton, Alice Mary
See also AAYA 14; CA 1-4R; CANR 2, 31;
DLB 8, 52; JRDA; MTCW; SATA 91

Norton, Caroline 1808-1877 ...... **NCLC 47**
See also DLB 21, 159

Norway, Nevil Shute 1899-1960
See Shute, Nevil
See also CA 102; 93-96

Norwid, Cyprian Kamil
1821-1883 .... **NCLC 17**

Nosille, Nabrah
See Ellison, Harlan (Jay)

Nossack, Hans Erich 1901-1978 ..... **CLC 6**
See also CA 93-96; 85-88; DLB 69

Nostradamus 1503-1566 .... **LC 27**

Nosu, Chuji
See Ozu, Yasujiro

Notenburg, Eleanora (Genrikhovna) von
See Guro, Elena

Nova, Craig 1945- .... **CLC 7, 31**
See also CA 45-48; CANR 2, 53

Novak, Joseph
See Kosinski, Jerzy (Nikodem)

Novalis 1772-1801 .... NCLC 13
See also DLB 90

Novis, Emile
See Weil, Simone (Adolphine)

Nowlan, Alden (Albert)
1933-1983 .. CLC 15; DAC; DAM MST
See also CA 9-12R; CANR 5; DLB 53

Noyes, Alfred 1880-1958 .... TCLC 7
See also CA 104; DLB 20

Nunn, Kem .... CLC 34
See also CA 159

Nye, Robert
1939- .... CLC 13, 42; DAM NOV
See also CA 33-36R; CANR 29; DLB 14;
MTCW; SATA 6

Nyro, Laura 1947- .... CLC 17

Oates, Joyce Carol
1938- ...... CLC 1, 2, 3, 6, 9, 11, 15, 19,
33, 52; DA; DAB; DAC; DAM MST,
NOV, POP; SSC 6; WLC
See also AAYA 15; AITN 1; BEST 89:2;
CA 5-8R; CANR 25, 45;
CDALB 1968-1988; DLB 2, 5, 130;
DLBY 81; INT CANR-25; MTCW

O'Brien, Darcy 1939- .... CLC 11
See also CA 21-24R; CANR 8, 59

O'Brien, E. G.
See Clarke, Arthur C(harles)

O'Brien, Edna
1936- .... CLC 3, 5, 8, 13, 36, 65;
DAM NOV; SSC 10
See also CA 1-4R; CANR 6, 41;
CDBLB 1960 to Present; DLB 14;
MTCW

O'Brien, Fitz-James 1828-1862... NCLC 21
See also DLB 74

O'Brien, Flann .... CLC 1, 4, 5, 7, 10, 47
See also O Nuallain, Brian

O'Brien, Richard 1942- .... CLC 17
See also CA 124

O'Brien, (William) Tim(othy)
1946- ... CLC 7, 19, 40, 103; DAM POP
See also AAYA 16; CA 85-88; CANR 40,
58; DLB 152; DLBD 9; DLBY 80

Obstfelder, Sigbjoern 1866-1900... TCLC 23
See also CA 123

O'Casey, Sean
1880-1964 ...... CLC 1, 5, 9, 11, 15, 88;
DAB; DAC; DAM DRAM, MST; WLCS
See also CA 89-92; CANR 62;
CDBLB 1914-1945; DLB 10; MTCW

O'Cathasaigh, Sean
See O'Casey, Sean

Ochs, Phil 1940-1976 .... CLC 17
See also CA 65-68

O'Connor, Edwin (Greene)
1918-1968 .... CLC 14
See also CA 93-96; 25-28R

O'Connor, (Mary) Flannery
1925-1964 ... CLC 1, 2, 3, 6, 10, 13, 15,
21, 66, 104; DA; DAB; DAC;
DAM MST, NOV; SSC 1, 23; WLC
See also AAYA 7; CA 1-4R; CANR 3, 41;
CDALB 1941-1968; DLB 2, 152;
DLBD 12; DLBY 80; MTCW

O'Connor, Frank .... CLC 23; SSC 5
See also O'Donovan, Michael John
See also DLB 162

O'Dell, Scott 1898-1989 .... CLC 30
See also AAYA 3; CA 61-64; 129;
CANR 12, 30; CLR 1, 16; DLB 52;
JRDA; MAICYA; SATA 12, 60

Odets, Clifford
1906-1963 .... CLC 2, 28, 98;
DAM DRAM; DC 6
See also CA 85-88; CANR 62; DLB 7, 26;
MTCW

O'Doherty, Brian 1934- .... CLC 76
See also CA 105

O'Donnell, K. M.
See Malzberg, Barry N(athaniel)

O'Donnell, Lawrence
See Kuttner, Henry

O'Donovan, Michael John
1903-1966 .... CLC 14
See also O'Connor, Frank
See also CA 93-96

Oe, Kenzaburo
1935- ..... CLC 10, 36, 86; DAM NOV;
SSC 20
See also CA 97-100; CANR 36, 50;
DLB 182; DLBY 94; MTCW

O'Faolain, Julia 1932- .... CLC 6, 19, 47
See also CA 81-84; CAAS 2; CANR 12, 61;
DLB 14; MTCW

O'Faolain, Sean
1900-1991 .... CLC 1, 7, 14, 32, 70;
SSC 13
See also CA 61-64; 134; CANR 12;
DLB 15, 162; MTCW

O'Flaherty, Liam
1896-1984 .... CLC 5, 34; SSC 6
See also CA 101; 113; CANR 35; DLB 36,
162; DLBY 84; MTCW

Ogilvy, Gavin
See Barrie, J(ames) M(atthew)

O'Grady, Standish (James)
1846-1928 .... TCLC 5
See also CA 104; 157

O'Grady, Timothy 1951- .... CLC 59
See also CA 138

O'Hara, Frank
1926-1966 .... CLC 2, 5, 13, 78;
DAM POET
See also CA 9-12R; 25-28R; CANR 33;
DLB 5, 16; MTCW

O'Hara, John (Henry)
1905-1970 .... CLC 1, 2, 3, 6, 11, 42;
DAM NOV; SSC 15
See also CA 5-8R; 25-28R; CANR 31, 60;
CDALB 1929-1941; DLB 9, 86; DLBD 2;
MTCW

O Hehir, Diana 1922- .... CLC 41
See also CA 93-96

Okigbo, Christopher (Ifenayichukwu)
1932-1967 .... CLC 25, 84; BLC;
DAM MULT, POET; PC 7
See also BW 1; CA 77-80; DLB 125;
MTCW

Okri, Ben 1959- .... CLC 87
See also BW 2; CA 130; 138; DLB 157;
INT 138

Olds, Sharon
1942- ..... CLC 32, 39, 85; DAM POET
See also CA 101; CANR 18, 41; DLB 120

Oldstyle, Jonathan
See Irving, Washington

Olesha, Yuri (Karlovich)
1899-1960 .... CLC 8
See also CA 85-88

Oliphant, Laurence
1829(?)-1888 .... NCLC 47
See also DLB 18, 166

Oliphant, Margaret (Oliphant Wilson)
1828-1897 .... NCLC 11, 61; SSC 25
See also DLB 18, 159

Oliver, Mary 1935- .... CLC 19, 34, 98
See also CA 21-24R; CANR 9, 43; DLB 5

Olivier, Laurence (Kerr)
1907-1989 .... CLC 20
See also CA 111; 150; 129

Olsen, Tillie
1913- ..... CLC 4, 13; DA; DAB; DAC;
DAM MST; SSC 11
See also CA 1-4R; CANR 1, 43; DLB 28;
DLBY 80; MTCW

Olson, Charles (John)
1910-1970 ..... CLC 1, 2, 5, 6, 9, 11, 29;
DAM POET; PC 19
See also CA 13-16; 25-28R; CABS 2;
CANR 35, 61; CAP 1; DLB 5, 16;
MTCW

Olson, Toby 1937- .... CLC 28
See also CA 65-68; CANR 9, 31

Olyesha, Yuri
See Olesha, Yuri (Karlovich)

Ondaatje, (Philip) Michael
1943- .... CLC 14, 29, 51, 76; DAB;
DAC; DAM MST
See also CA 77-80; CANR 42; DLB 60

Oneal, Elizabeth 1934-
See Oneal, Zibby
See also CA 106; CANR 28; MAICYA;
SATA 30, 82

Oneal, Zibby .... CLC 30
See also Oneal, Elizabeth
See also AAYA 5; CLR 13; JRDA

O'Neill, Eugene (Gladstone)
1888-1953 ...... TCLC 1, 6, 27, 49; DA;
DAB; DAC; DAM DRAM, MST; WLC
See also AITN 1; CA 110; 132;
CDALB 1929-1941; DLB 7; MTCW

Onetti, Juan Carlos
1909-1994 .... CLC 7, 10; DAM MULT,
NOV; SSC 23
See also CA 85-88; 145; CANR 32;
DLB 113; HW; MTCW

O Nuallain, Brian 1911-1966
See O'Brien, Flann
See also CA 21-22; 25-28R; CAP 2

Oppen, George 1908-1984 .... CLC 7, 13, 34
See also CA 13-16R; 113; CANR 8; DLB 5,
165

Oppenheim, E(dward) Phillips
1866-1946 .... **TCLC 45**
See also CA 111; DLB 70

Origen c. 185-c. 254 .... **CMLC 19**

Orlovitz, Gil 1918-1973 .... **CLC 22**
See also CA 77-80; 45-48; DLB 2, 5

Orris
See Ingelow, Jean

Ortega y Gasset, Jose
1883-1955 ..... **TCLC 9; DAM MULT;**
HLC
See also CA 106; 130; HW; MTCW

Ortese, Anna Maria 1914- .... **CLC 89**
See also DLB 177

Ortiz, Simon J(oseph)
1941- .... **CLC 45; DAM MULT,**
POET; PC 17
See also CA 134; DLB 120, 175; NNAL

Orton, Joe .... **CLC 4, 13, 43; DC 3**
See also Orton, John Kingsley
See also CDBLB 1960 to Present; DLB 13

Orton, John Kingsley 1933-1967
See Orton, Joe
See also CA 85-88; CANR 35;
DAM DRAM; MTCW

Orwell, George
..... **TCLC 2, 6, 15, 31, 51; DAB; WLC**
See also Blair, Eric (Arthur)
See also CDBLB 1945-1960; DLB 15, 98

Osborne, David
See Silverberg, Robert

Osborne, George
See Silverberg, Robert

Osborne, John (James)
1929-1994 ..... **CLC 1, 2, 5, 11, 45; DA;**
DAB; DAC; DAM DRAM, MST; WLC
See also CA 13-16R; 147; CANR 21, 56;
CDBLB 1945-1960; DLB 13; MTCW

Osborne, Lawrence 1958- .... **CLC 50**

Oshima, Nagisa 1932- .... **CLC 20**
See also CA 116; 121

Oskison, John Milton
1874-1947 ..... **TCLC 35; DAM MULT**
See also CA 144; DLB 175; NNAL

Ossoli, Sarah Margaret (Fuller marchesa d')
1810-1850
See Fuller, Margaret
See also SATA 25

Ostrovsky, Alexander
1823-1886 .... **NCLC 30, 57**

Otero, Blas de 1916-1979 .... **CLC 11**
See also CA 89-92; DLB 134

Otto, Whitney 1955- .... **CLC 70**
See also CA 140

Ouida .... **TCLC 43**
See also De La Ramee, (Marie) Louise
See also DLB 18, 156

Ousmane, Sembene 1923- .... **CLC 66; BLC**
See also BW 1; CA 117; 125; MTCW

Ovid
43B.C.-18(?) ... **CMLC 7; DAM POET;**
PC 2

Owen, Hugh
See Faust, Frederick (Schiller)

Owen, Wilfred (Edward Salter)
1893-1918 ...... **TCLC 5, 27; DA; DAB;**
DAC; DAM MST, POET; PC 19; WLC
See also CA 104; 141; CDBLB 1914-1945;
DLB 20

Owens, Rochelle 1936- .... **CLC 8**
See also CA 17-20R; CAAS 2; CANR 39

Oz, Amos
1939- .... **CLC 5, 8, 11, 27, 33, 54;**
DAM NOV
See also CA 53-56; CANR 27, 47; MTCW

Ozick, Cynthia
1928- .... **CLC 3, 7, 28, 62; DAM NOV,**
POP; SSC 15
See also BEST 90:1; CA 17-20R; CANR 23,
58; DLB 28, 152; DLBY 82;
INT CANR-23; MTCW

Ozu, Yasujiro 1903-1963 .... **CLC 16**
See also CA 112

Pacheco, C.
See Pessoa, Fernando (Antonio Nogueira)

Pa Chin .... **CLC 18**
See also Li Fei-kan

Pack, Robert 1929- .... **CLC 13**
See also CA 1-4R; CANR 3, 44; DLB 5

Padgett, Lewis
See Kuttner, Henry

Padilla (Lorenzo), Heberto 1932- ... **CLC 38**
See also AITN 1; CA 123; 131; HW

Page, Jimmy 1944- .... **CLC 12**

Page, Louise 1955- .... **CLC 40**
See also CA 140

Page, P(atricia) K(athleen)
1916- .... **CLC 7, 18; DAC; DAM MST;**
PC 12
See also CA 53-56; CANR 4, 22; DLB 68;
MTCW

Page, Thomas Nelson 1853-1922 .... **SSC 23**
See also CA 118; DLB 12, 78; DLBD 13

Pagels, Elaine Hiesey 1943- ...... **CLC 104**
See also CA 45-48; CANR 2, 24, 51

Paget, Violet 1856-1935
See Lee, Vernon
See also CA 104

Paget-Lowe, Henry
See Lovecraft, H(oward) P(hillips)

Paglia, Camille (Anna) 1947- .... **CLC 68**
See also CA 140

Paige, Richard
See Koontz, Dean R(ay)

Paine, Thomas 1737-1809 ...... **NCLC 62**
See also CDALB 1640-1865; DLB 31, 43,
73, 158

Pakenham, Antonia
See Fraser, (Lady) Antonia (Pakenham)

Palamas, Kostes 1859-1943 .... **TCLC 5**
See also CA 105

Palazzeschi, Aldo 1885-1974 .... **CLC 11**
See also CA 89-92; 53-56; DLB 114

Paley, Grace
1922- .... **CLC 4, 6, 37; DAM POP;**
SSC 8
See also CA 25-28R; CANR 13, 46;
DLB 28; INT CANR-13; MTCW

Palin, Michael (Edward) 1943- ..... **CLC 21**
See also Monty Python
See also CA 107; CANR 35; SATA 67

Palliser, Charles 1947- .... **CLC 65**
See also CA 136

Palma, Ricardo 1833-1919 .... **TCLC 29**

Pancake, Breece Dexter 1952-1979
See Pancake, Breece D'J
See also CA 123; 109

Pancake, Breece D'J .... **CLC 29**
See also Pancake, Breece Dexter
See also DLB 130

Panko, Rudy
See Gogol, Nikolai (Vasilyevich)

Papadiamantis, Alexandros
1851-1911 .... **TCLC 29**

Papadiamantopoulos, Johannes 1856-1910
See Moreas, Jean
See also CA 117

Papini, Giovanni 1881-1956 ...... **TCLC 22**
See also CA 121

Paracelsus 1493-1541 .... **LC 14**
See also DLB 179

Parasol, Peter
See Stevens, Wallace

Pareto, Vilfredo 1848-1923 .... **TCLC 69**

Parfenie, Maria
See Codrescu, Andrei

Parini, Jay (Lee) 1948- .... **CLC 54**
See also CA 97-100; CAAS 16; CANR 32

Park, Jordan
See Kornbluth, C(yril) M.; Pohl, Frederik

Park, Robert E(zra) 1864-1944 .... **TCLC 73**
See also CA 122

Parker, Bert
See Ellison, Harlan (Jay)

Parker, Dorothy (Rothschild)
1893-1967 .... **CLC 15, 68;**
DAM POET; SSC 2
See also CA 19-20; 25-28R; CAP 2;
DLB 11, 45, 86; MTCW

Parker, Robert B(rown)
1932- ...... **CLC 27; DAM NOV, POP**
See also BEST 89:4; CA 49-52; CANR 1,
26, 52; INT CANR-26; MTCW

Parkin, Frank 1940- .... **CLC 43**
See also CA 147

Parkman, Francis, Jr.
1823-1893 .... **NCLC 12**
See also DLB 1, 30

Parks, Gordon (Alexander Buchanan)
1912- ... **CLC 1, 16; BLC; DAM MULT**
See also AITN 2; BW 2; CA 41-44R;
CANR 26; DLB 33; SATA 8

Parmenides
c. 515B.C.-c. 450B.C. .... **CMLC 22**
See also DLB 176

Parnell, Thomas 1679-1718 .... **LC 3**
See also DLB 94

Parra, Nicanor
1914- .... **CLC 2, 102; DAM MULT;**
HLC
See also CA 85-88; CANR 32; HW; MTCW

Parrish, Mary Frances
See Fisher, M(ary) F(rances) K(ennedy)

Parson
See Coleridge, Samuel Taylor

Parson Lot
See Kingsley, Charles

Partridge, Anthony
See Oppenheim, E(dward) Phillips

Pascal, Blaise 1623-1662 . . . . **LC 35**

Pascoli, Giovanni 1855-1912 . . . . . . **TCLC 45**

Pasolini, Pier Paolo
1922-1975 . . . . **CLC 20, 37; PC 17**
See also CA 93-96; 61-64; DLB 128, 177;
MTCW

Pasquini
See Silone, Ignazio

Pastan, Linda (Olenik)
1932- . . . . **CLC 27; DAM POET**
See also CA 61-64; CANR 18, 40, 61;
DLB 5

Pasternak, Boris (Leonidovich)
1890-1960 . . . . . . **CLC 7, 10, 18, 63; DA;**
DAB; DAC; DAM MST, NOV, POET;
PC 6; WLC
See also CA 127; 116; MTCW

Patchen, Kenneth
1911-1972 . . . **CLC 1, 2, 18; DAM POET**
See also CA 1-4R; 33-36R; CANR 3, 35;
DLB 16, 48; MTCW

Pater, Walter (Horatio)
1839-1894 . . . . **NCLC 7**
See also CDBLB 1832-1890; DLB 57, 156

Paterson, A(ndrew) B(arton)
1864-1941 . . . . **TCLC 32**
See also CA 155

Paterson, Katherine (Womeldorf)
1932- . . . . **CLC 12, 30**
See also AAYA 1; CA 21-24R; CANR 28,
59; CLR 7; DLB 52; JRDA; MAICYA;
MTCW; SATA 13, 53, 92

Patmore, Coventry Kersey Dighton
1823-1896 . . . . **NCLC 9**
See also DLB 35, 98

Paton, Alan (Stewart)
1903-1988 . . . . . . **CLC 4, 10, 25, 55; DA;**
DAB; DAC; DAM MST, NOV; WLC
See also CA 13-16; 125; CANR 22; CAP 1;
MTCW; SATA 11; SATA-Obit 56

Paton Walsh, Gillian 1937-
See Walsh, Jill Paton
See also CANR 38; JRDA; MAICYA;
SAAS 3; SATA 4, 72

Paulding, James Kirke 1778-1860 . . **NCLC 2**
See also DLB 3, 59, 74

Paulin, Thomas Neilson 1949-
See Paulin, Tom
See also CA 123; 128

Paulin, Tom . . . . **CLC 37**
See also Paulin, Thomas Neilson
See also DLB 40

Paustovsky, Konstantin (Georgievich)
1892-1968 . . . . **CLC 40**
See also CA 93-96; 25-28R

Pavese, Cesare
1908-1950 . . . . . **TCLC 3; PC 13; SSC 19**
See also CA 104; DLB 128, 177

Pavic, Milorad 1929- . . . . **CLC 60**
See also CA 136; DLB 181

Payne, Alan
See Jakes, John (William)

Paz, Gil
See Lugones, Leopoldo

Paz, Octavio
1914- . . . . **CLC 3, 4, 6, 10, 19, 51, 65;**
DA; DAB; DAC; DAM MST, MULT,
POET; HLC; PC 1; WLC
See also CA 73-76; CANR 32; DLBY 90;
HW; MTCW

p'Bitek, Okot
1931-1982 . . . . **CLC 96; BLC;**
DAM MULT
See also BW 2; CA 124; 107; DLB 125;
MTCW

Peacock, Molly 1947- . . . . **CLC 60**
See also CA 103; CAAS 21; CANR 52;
DLB 120

Peacock, Thomas Love
1785-1866 . . . . **NCLC 22**
See also DLB 96, 116

Peake, Mervyn 1911-1968 . . . . **CLC 7, 54**
See also CA 5-8R; 25-28R; CANR 3;
DLB 15, 160; MTCW; SATA 23

Pearce, Philippa . . . . **CLC 21**
See also Christie, (Ann) Philippa
See also CLR 9; DLB 161; MAICYA;
SATA 1, 67

Pearl, Eric
See Elman, Richard

Pearson, T(homas) R(eid) 1956- . . . . **CLC 39**
See also CA 120; 130; INT 130

Peck, Dale 1967- . . . . **CLC 81**
See also CA 146

Peck, John 1941- . . . . **CLC 3**
See also CA 49-52; CANR 3

Peck, Richard (Wayne) 1934- . . . . . . **CLC 21**
See also AAYA 1; CA 85-88; CANR 19,
38; CLR 15; INT CANR-19; JRDA;
MAICYA; SAAS 2; SATA 18, 55

Peck, Robert Newton
1928- . . **CLC 17; DA; DAC; DAM MST**
See also AAYA 3; CA 81-84; CANR 31;
CLR 45; JRDA; MAICYA; SAAS 1;
SATA 21, 62

Peckinpah, (David) Sam(uel)
1925-1984 . . . . **CLC 20**
See also CA 109; 114

Pedersen, Knut 1859-1952
See Hamsun, Knut
See also CA 104; 119; MTCW

Peeslake, Gaffer
See Durrell, Lawrence (George)

Peguy, Charles Pierre
1873-1914 . . . . **TCLC 10**
See also CA 107

Pena, Ramon del Valle y
See Valle-Inclan, Ramon (Maria) del

Pendennis, Arthur Esquir
See Thackeray, William Makepeace

Penn, William 1644-1718 . . . . **LC 25**
See also DLB 24

PEPECE
See Prado (Calvo), Pedro

Pepys, Samuel
1633-1703 . . . . . **LC 11; DA; DAB; DAC;**
DAM MST; WLC
See also CDBLB 1660-1789; DLB 101

Percy, Walker
1916-1990 . . . . **CLC 2, 3, 6, 8, 14, 18, 47,**
65; DAM NOV, POP
See also CA 1-4R; 131; CANR 1, 23;
DLB 2; DLBY 80, 90; MTCW

Perec, Georges 1936-1982 . . . . **CLC 56**
See also CA 141; DLB 83

Pereda (y Sanchez de Porrua), Jose Maria de
1833-1906 . . . . **TCLC 16**
See also CA 117

Pereda y Porrua, Jose Maria de
See Pereda (y Sanchez de Porrua), Jose
Maria de

Peregoy, George Weems
See Mencken, H(enry) L(ouis)

Perelman, S(idney) J(oseph)
1904-1979 . . . . . . **CLC 3, 5, 9, 15, 23, 44,**
49; DAM DRAM
See also AITN 1, 2; CA 73-76; 89-92;
CANR 18; DLB 11, 44; MTCW

Peret, Benjamin 1899-1959 . . . . **TCLC 20**
See also CA 117

Peretz, Isaac Loeb
1851(?)-1915 . . . . **TCLC 16; SSC 26**
See also CA 109

Peretz, Yitzkhok Leibush
See Peretz, Isaac Loeb

Perez Galdos, Benito 1843-1920 . . . **TCLC 27**
See also CA 125; 153; HW

Perrault, Charles 1628-1703 . . . . **LC 2**
See also MAICYA; SATA 25

Perry, Brighton
See Sherwood, Robert E(mmet)

Perse, St.-John . . . . **CLC 4, 11, 46**
See also Leger, (Marie-Rene Auguste) Alexis
Saint-Leger

Perutz, Leo 1882-1957 . . . . **TCLC 60**
See also DLB 81

Peseenz, Tulio F.
See Lopez y Fuentes, Gregorio

Pesetsky, Bette 1932- . . . . **CLC 28**
See also CA 133; DLB 130

Peshkov, Alexei Maximovich 1868-1936
See Gorky, Maxim
See also CA 105; 141; DA; DAC;
DAM DRAM, MST, NOV

Pessoa, Fernando (Antonio Nogueira)
1888-1935 . . . . **TCLC 27; HLC**
See also CA 125

Peterkin, Julia Mood 1880-1961 . . . . **CLC 31**
See also CA 102; DLB 9

Peters, Joan K(aren) 1945- . . . . **CLC 39**
See also CA 158

Peters, Robert L(ouis) 1924- . . . . **CLC 7**
See also CA 13-16R; CAAS 8; DLB 105

Petofi, Sandor 1823-1849 . . . . **NCLC 21**

Petrakis, Harry Mark 1923-........ CLC 3
See also CA 9-12R; CANR 4, 30

Petrarch
1304-1374 .... CMLC 20; DAM POET;
PC 8

Petrov, Evgeny .... TCLC 21
See also Kataev, Evgeny Petrovich

Petry, Ann (Lane) 1908-1997... CLC 1, 7, 18
See also BW 1; CA 5-8R; 157; CAAS 6;
CANR 4, 46; CLR 12; DLB 76; JRDA;
MAICYA; MTCW; SATA 5;
SATA-Obit 94

Petursson, Halligrimur 1614-1674 .... LC 8

Philips, Katherine 1632-1664........ LC 30
See also DLB 131

Philipson, Morris H. 1926-........ CLC 53
See also CA 1-4R; CANR 4

Phillips, Caryl
1958-.......... CLC 96; DAM MULT
See also BW 2; CA 141; DLB 157

Phillips, David Graham
1867-1911 .... TCLC 44
See also CA 108; DLB 9, 12

Phillips, Jack
See Sandburg, Carl (August)

Phillips, Jayne Anne
1952-............ CLC 15, 33; SSC 16
See also CA 101; CANR 24, 50; DLBY 80;
INT CANR-24; MTCW

Phillips, Richard
See Dick, Philip K(indred)

Phillips, Robert (Schaeffer) 1938-... CLC 28
See also CA 17-20R; CAAS 13; CANR 8;
DLB 105

Phillips, Ward
See Lovecraft, H(oward) P(hillips)

Piccolo, Lucio 1901-1969.......... CLC 13
See also CA 97-100; DLB 114

Pickthall, Marjorie L(owry) C(hristie)
1883-1922 .... TCLC 21
See also CA 107; DLB 92

Pico della Mirandola, Giovanni
1463-1494 .... LC 15

Piercy, Marge
1936-.......... CLC 3, 6, 14, 18, 27, 62
See also CA 21-24R; CAAS 1; CANR 13,
43; DLB 120; MTCW

Piers, Robert
See Anthony, Piers

Pieyre de Mandiargues, Andre 1909-1991
See Mandiargues, Andre Pieyre de
See also CA 103; 136; CANR 22

Pilnyak, Boris .... TCLC 23
See also Vogau, Boris Andreyevich

Pincherle, Alberto
1907-1990 ..... CLC 11, 18; DAM NOV
See also Moravia, Alberto
See also CA 25-28R; 132; CANR 33;
MTCW

Pinckney, Darryl 1953-........... CLC 76
See also BW 2; CA 143

Pindar 518B.C.-446B.C.... CMLC 12; PC 19
See also DLB 176

Pineda, Cecile 1942-.............. CLC 39
See also CA 118

Pinero, Arthur Wing
1855-1934 ..... TCLC 32; DAM DRAM
See also CA 110; 153; DLB 10

Pinero, Miguel (Antonio Gomez)
1946-1988 .... CLC 4, 55
See also CA 61-64; 125; CANR 29; HW

Pinget, Robert 1919-1997 .... CLC 7, 13, 37
See also CA 85-88; 160; DLB 83

Pink Floyd
See Barrett, (Roger) Syd; Gilmour, David;
Mason, Nick; Waters, Roger; Wright,
Rick

Pinkney, Edward 1802-1828 ..... NCLC 31

Pinkwater, Daniel Manus 1941-.... CLC 35
See also Pinkwater, Manus
See also AAYA 1; CA 29-32R; CANR 12,
38; CLR 4; JRDA; MAICYA; SAAS 3;
SATA 46, 76

Pinkwater, Manus
See Pinkwater, Daniel Manus
See also SATA 8

Pinsky, Robert
1940- .. CLC 9, 19, 38, 94; DAM POET
See also CA 29-32R; CAAS 4; CANR 58;
DLBY 82

Pinta, Harold
See Pinter, Harold

Pinter, Harold
1930-..... CLC 1, 3, 6, 9, 11, 15, 27, 58,
73; DA; DAB; DAC; DAM DRAM,
MST; WLC
See also CA 5-8R; CANR 33; CDBLB 1960
to Present; DLB 13; MTCW

Piozzi, Hester Lynch (Thrale)
1741-1821 .... NCLC 57
See also DLB 104, 142

Pirandello, Luigi
1867-1936 ...... TCLC 4, 29; DA; DAB;
DAC; DAM DRAM, MST; DC 5;
SSC 22; WLC
See also CA 104; 153

Pirsig, Robert M(aynard)
1928-........ CLC 4, 6, 73; DAM POP
See also CA 53-56; CANR 42; MTCW;
SATA 39

Pisarev, Dmitry Ivanovich
1840-1868 .... NCLC 25

Pix, Mary (Griffith) 1666-1709....... LC 8
See also DLB 80

Pixerecourt, Guilbert de
1773-1844 .... NCLC 39

Plaatje, Sol(omon) T(shekisho)
1876-1932 .... TCLC 73
See also BW 2; CA 141

Plaidy, Jean
See Hibbert, Eleanor Alice Burford

Planche, James Robinson
1796-1880 .... NCLC 42

Plant, Robert 1948-.............. CLC 12

Plante, David (Robert)
1940-........CLC 7, 23, 38; DAM NOV
See also CA 37-40R; CANR 12, 36, 58;
DLBY 83; INT CANR-12; MTCW

Plath, Sylvia
1932-1963 ..... CLC 1, 2, 3, 5, 9, 11, 14,
17, 50, 51, 62; DA; DAB; DAC;
DAM MST, POET; PC 1; WLC
See also AAYA 13; CA 19-20; CANR 34;
CAP 2; CDALB 1941-1968; DLB 5, 6,
152; MTCW

Plato
428(?)B.C.-348(?)B.C..... CMLC 8; DA;
DAB; DAC; DAM MST; WLCS
See also DLB 176

Platonov, Andrei .... TCLC 14
See also Klimentov, Andrei Platonovich

Platt, Kin 1911- .... CLC 26
See also AAYA 11; CA 17-20R; CANR 11;
JRDA; SAAS 17; SATA 21, 86

Plautus c. 251B.C.-184B.C. .... DC 6

Plick et Plock
See Simenon, Georges (Jacques Christian)

Plimpton, George (Ames) 1927-..... CLC 36
See also AITN 1; CA 21-24R; CANR 32;
MTCW; SATA 10

Pliny the Elder c. 23-79........ CMLC 23

Plomer, William Charles Franklin
1903-1973 .... CLC 4, 8
See also CA 21-22; CANR 34; CAP 2;
DLB 20, 162; MTCW; SATA 24

Plowman, Piers
See Kavanagh, Patrick (Joseph)

Plum, J.
See Wodehouse, P(elham) G(renville)

Plumly, Stanley (Ross) 1939- ...... CLC 33
See also CA 108; 110; DLB 5; INT 110

Plumpe, Friedrich Wilhelm
1888-1931 .... TCLC 53
See also CA 112

Poe, Edgar Allan
1809-1849 .... NCLC 1, 16, 55; DA;
DAB; DAC; DAM MST, POET; PC 1;
SSC 1, 22; WLC
See also AAYA 14; CDALB 1640-1865;
DLB 3, 59, 73, 74; SATA 23

Poet of Titchfield Street, The
See Pound, Ezra (Weston Loomis)

Pohl, Frederik 1919- ..... CLC 18; SSC 25
See also CA 61-64; CAAS 1; CANR 11, 37;
DLB 8; INT CANR-11; MTCW;
SATA 24

Poirier, Louis 1910-
See Gracq, Julien
See also CA 122; 126

Poitier, Sidney 1927-.............. CLC 26
See also BW 1; CA 117

Polanski, Roman 1933-........... CLC 16
See also CA 77-80

Poliakoff, Stephen 1952-.......... CLC 38
See also CA 106; DLB 13

Police, The
See Copeland, Stewart (Armstrong);
Summers, Andrew James; Sumner,
Gordon Matthew

Polidori, John William
1795-1821 .... NCLC 51
See also DLB 116

Pollitt, Katha 1949- .... **CLC 28**
　See also CA 120; 122; MTCW

Pollock, (Mary) Sharon
　1936- .... **CLC 50; DAC; DAM DRAM,**
　　　　　　　　　　　　　　　　　　MST
　See also CA 141; DLB 60

Polo, Marco 1254-1324 .... **CMLC 15**

Polonsky, Abraham (Lincoln)
　1910- .... **CLC 92**
　See also CA 104; DLB 26; INT 104

Polybius c. 200B.C.-c. 118B.C. .... **CMLC 17**
　See also DLB 176

Pomerance, Bernard
　1940- .... **CLC 13; DAM DRAM**
　See also CA 101; CANR 49

Ponge, Francis (Jean Gaston Alfred)
　1899-1988 ..... **CLC 6, 18; DAM POET**
　See also CA 85-88; 126; CANR 40

Pontoppidan, Henrik 1857-1943 ... **TCLC 29**

Poole, Josephine .... **CLC 17**
　See also Helyar, Jane Penelope Josephine
　See also SAAS 2; SATA 5

Popa, Vasko 1922-1991 .... **CLC 19**
　See also CA 112; 148; DLB 181

Pope, Alexander
　1688-1744 ...... **LC 3; DA; DAB; DAC;**
　　　　　　　　　DAM MST, POET; WLC
　See also CDBLB 1660-1789; DLB 95, 101

Porter, Connie (Rose) 1959(?)- ..... **CLC 70**
　See also BW 2; CA 142; SATA 81

Porter, Gene(va Grace) Stratton
　1863(?)-1924 .... **TCLC 21**
　See also CA 112

Porter, Katherine Anne
　1890-1980 ...... **CLC 1, 3, 7, 10, 13, 15,**
　　　　27, 101; DA; DAB; DAC; DAM MST,
　　　　　　　　　　　　　NOV; SSC 4
　See also AITN 2; CA 1-4R; 101; CANR 1;
　　DLB 4, 9, 102; DLBD 12; DLBY 80;
　　MTCW; SATA 39; SATA-Obit 23

Porter, Peter (Neville Frederick)
　1929- .... **CLC 5, 13, 33**
　See also CA 85-88; DLB 40

Porter, William Sydney 1862-1910
　See Henry, O.
　See also CA 104; 131; CDALB 1865-1917;
　　DA; DAB; DAC; DAM MST; DLB 12,
　　78, 79; MTCW; YABC 2

Portillo (y Pacheco), Jose Lopez
　See Lopez Portillo (y Pacheco), Jose

Post, Melville Davisson
　1869-1930 .... **TCLC 39**
　See also CA 110

Potok, Chaim
　1929- .... **CLC 2, 7, 14, 26; DAM NOV**
　See also AAYA 15; AITN 1, 2; CA 17-20R;
　　CANR 19, 35; DLB 28, 152;
　　INT CANR-19; MTCW; SATA 33

Potter, (Helen) Beatrix 1866-1943
　See Webb, (Martha) Beatrice (Potter)
　See also MAICYA

Potter, Dennis (Christopher George)
　1935-1994 .... **CLC 58, 86**
　See also CA 107; 145; CANR 33, 61;
　　MTCW

Pound, Ezra (Weston Loomis)
　1885-1972 ...... **CLC 1, 2, 3, 4, 5, 7, 10,**
　　13, 18, 34, 48, 50; DA; DAB; DAC;
　　　　DAM MST, POET; PC 4; WLC
　See also CA 5-8R; 37-40R; CANR 40;
　　CDALB 1917-1929; DLB 4, 45, 63;
　　DLBD 15; MTCW

Povod, Reinaldo 1959-1994 .... **CLC 44**
　See also CA 136; 146

Powell, Adam Clayton, Jr.
　1908-1972 .... **CLC 89; BLC;**
　　　　　　　　　　　　　　　DAM MULT
　See also BW 1; CA 102; 33-36R

Powell, Anthony (Dymoke)
　1905- .... **CLC 1, 3, 7, 9, 10, 31**
　See also CA 1-4R; CANR 1, 32, 62;
　　CDBLB 1945-1960; DLB 15; MTCW

Powell, Dawn 1897-1965 .... **CLC 66**
　See also CA 5-8R

Powell, Padgett 1952- .... **CLC 34**
　See also CA 126

Power, Susan 1961- .... **CLC 91**

Powers, J(ames) F(arl)
　1917- .... **CLC 1, 4, 8, 57; SSC 4**
　See also CA 1-4R; CANR 2, 61; DLB 130;
　　MTCW

Powers, John J(ames) 1945-
　See Powers, John R.
　See also CA 69-72

Powers, John R. .... **CLC 66**
　See also Powers, John J(ames)

Powers, Richard (S.) 1957- .... **CLC 93**
　See also CA 148

Pownall, David 1938- .... **CLC 10**
　See also CA 89-92; CAAS 18; CANR 49;
　　DLB 14

Powys, John Cowper
　1872-1963 .... **CLC 7, 9, 15, 46**
　See also CA 85-88; DLB 15; MTCW

Powys, T(heodore) F(rancis)
　1875-1953 .... **TCLC 9**
　See also CA 106; DLB 36, 162

Prado (Calvo), Pedro 1886-1952 ... **TCLC 75**
　See also CA 131; HW

Prager, Emily 1952- .... **CLC 56**

Pratt, E(dwin) J(ohn)
　1883(?)-1964 .... **CLC 19; DAC;**
　　　　　　　　　　　　　　　DAM POET
　See also CA 141; 93-96; DLB 92

Premchand .... **TCLC 21**
　See also Srivastava, Dhanpat Rai

Preussler, Otfried 1923- .... **CLC 17**
　See also CA 77-80; SATA 24

Prevert, Jacques (Henri Marie)
　1900-1977 .... **CLC 15**
　See also CA 77-80; 69-72; CANR 29, 61;
　　MTCW; SATA-Obit 30

Prevost, Abbe (Antoine Francois)
　1697-1763 .... **LC 1**

Price, (Edward) Reynolds
　1933- .... **CLC 3, 6, 13, 43, 50, 63;**
　　　　　　　　　　　　DAM NOV; SSC 22
　See also CA 1-4R; CANR 1, 37, 57; DLB 2;
　　INT CANR-37

Price, Richard 1949- .... **CLC 6, 12**
　See also CA 49-52; CANR 3; DLBY 81

Prichard, Katharine Susannah
　1883-1969 .... **CLC 46**
　See also CA 11-12; CANR 33; CAP 1;
　　MTCW; SATA 66

Priestley, J(ohn) B(oynton)
　1894-1984 .... **CLC 2, 5, 9, 34;**
　　　　　　　　　　　　DAM DRAM, NOV
　See also CA 9-12R; 113; CANR 33;
　　CDBLB 1914-1945; DLB 10, 34, 77, 100,
　　139; DLBY 84; MTCW

Prince 1958(?)- .... **CLC 35**

Prince, F(rank) T(empleton) 1912- ... **CLC 22**
　See also CA 101; CANR 43; DLB 20

Prince Kropotkin
　See Kropotkin, Peter (Aleksieevich)

Prior, Matthew 1664-1721........... **LC 4**
　See also DLB 95

Prishvin, Mikhail 1873-1954 ...... **TCLC 75**

Pritchard, William H(arrison)
　1932- .... **CLC 34**
　See also CA 65-68; CANR 23; DLB 111

Pritchett, V(ictor) S(awdon)
　1900-1997 .... **CLC 5, 13, 15, 41;**
　　　　　　　　　　　　DAM NOV; SSC 14
　See also CA 61-64; 157; CANR 31;
　　DLB 15, 139; MTCW

Private 19022
　See Manning, Frederic

Probst, Mark 1925- .... **CLC 59**
　See also CA 130

Prokosch, Frederic 1908-1989.... **CLC 4, 48**
　See also CA 73-76; 128; DLB 48

Prophet, The
　See Dreiser, Theodore (Herman Albert)

Prose, Francine 1947- .... **CLC 45**
　See also CA 109; 112; CANR 46

Proudhon
　See Cunha, Euclides (Rodrigues Pimenta) da

Proulx, E. Annie 1935- .... **CLC 81**

Proust, (Valentin-Louis-George-Eugene-)
　Marcel
　1871-1922 .... **TCLC 7, 13, 33; DA;**
　　DAB; DAC; DAM MST, NOV; WLC
　See also CA 104; 120; DLB 65; MTCW

Prowler, Harley
　See Masters, Edgar Lee

Prus, Boleslaw 1845-1912 .... **TCLC 48**

Pryor, Richard (Franklin Lenox Thomas)
　1940- .... **CLC 26**
　See also CA 122

Przybyszewski, Stanislaw
　1868-1927 .... **TCLC 36**
　See also CA 160; DLB 66

Pteleon
　See Grieve, C(hristopher) M(urray)
　See also DAM POET

Puckett, Lute
　See Masters, Edgar Lee

Puig, Manuel
1932-1990 .... **CLC 3, 5, 10, 28, 65; DAM MULT; HLC**
See also CA 45-48; CANR 2, 32; DLB 113; HW; MTCW

Purdy, Al(fred Wellington)
1918- .... **CLC 3, 6, 14, 50; DAC; DAM MST, POET**
See also CA 81-84; CAAS 17; CANR 42; DLB 88

Purdy, James (Amos)
1923- .... **CLC 2, 4, 10, 28, 52**
See also CA 33-36R; CAAS 1; CANR 19, 51; DLB 2; INT CANR-19; MTCW

Pure, Simon
See Swinnerton, Frank Arthur

Pushkin, Alexander (Sergeyevich)
1799-1837 ..... **NCLC 3, 27; DA; DAB; DAC; DAM DRAM, MST, POET; PC 10; SSC 27; WLC**
See also SATA 61

P'u Sung-ling 1640-1715 .... **LC 3**

Putnam, Arthur Lee
See Alger, Horatio, Jr.

Puzo, Mario
1920- ..... **CLC 1, 2, 6, 36; DAM NOV, POP**
See also CA 65-68; CANR 4, 42; DLB 6; MTCW

Pygge, Edward
See Barnes, Julian (Patrick)

Pyle, Ernest Taylor 1900-1945
See Pyle, Ernie
See also CA 115; 160

Pyle, Ernie 1900-1945 .... **TCLC 75**
See also Pyle, Ernest Taylor
See also DLB 29

Pym, Barbara (Mary Crampton)
1913-1980 .... **CLC 13, 19, 37**
See also CA 13-14; 97-100; CANR 13, 34; CAP 1; DLB 14; DLBY 87; MTCW

Pynchon, Thomas (Ruggles, Jr.)
1937- ..... **CLC 2, 3, 6, 9, 11, 18, 33, 62, 72; DA; DAB; DAC; DAM MST, NOV, POP; SSC 14; WLC**
See also BEST 90:2; CA 17-20R; CANR 22, 46; DLB 2, 173; MTCW

Pythagoras
c. 570B.C.-c. 500B.C. .... **CMLC 22**
See also DLB 176

Qian Zhongshu
See Ch'ien Chung-shu

Qroll
See Dagerman, Stig (Halvard)

Quarrington, Paul (Lewis) 1953-.... **CLC 65**
See also CA 129; CANR 62

Quasimodo, Salvatore 1901-1968 ... **CLC 10**
See also CA 13-16; 25-28R; CAP 1; DLB 114; MTCW

Quay, Stephen 1947- .... **CLC 95**

Quay, The Brothers
See Quay, Stephen; Quay, Timothy

Quay, Timothy 1947-............. **CLC 95**

Queen, Ellery................... **CLC 3, 11**
See also Dannay, Frederic; Davidson, Avram; Lee, Manfred B(ennington); Marlowe, Stephen; Sturgeon, Theodore (Hamilton); Vance, John Holbrook

Queen, Ellery, Jr.
See Dannay, Frederic; Lee, Manfred B(ennington)

Queneau, Raymond
1903-1976 .... **CLC 2, 5, 10, 42**
See also CA 77-80; 69-72; CANR 32; DLB 72; MTCW

Quevedo, Francisco de 1580-1645.... **LC 23**

Quiller-Couch, Arthur Thomas
1863-1944 .... **TCLC 53**
See also CA 118; DLB 135, 153

Quin, Ann (Marie) 1936-1973 .... **CLC 6**
See also CA 9-12R; 45-48; DLB 14

Quinn, Martin
See Smith, Martin Cruz

Quinn, Peter 1947-............... **CLC 91**

Quinn, Simon
See Smith, Martin Cruz

Quiroga, Horacio (Sylvestre)
1878-1937 ..... **TCLC 20; DAM MULT; HLC**
See also CA 117; 131; HW; MTCW

Quoirez, Francoise 1935-........... **CLC 9**
See also Sagan, Francoise
See also CA 49-52; CANR 6, 39; MTCW

Raabe, Wilhelm 1831-1910 .... **TCLC 45**
See also DLB 129

Rabe, David (William)
1940- ...... **CLC 4, 8, 33; DAM DRAM**
See also CA 85-88; CABS 3; CANR 59; DLB 7

Rabelais, Francois
1483-1553 ...... **LC 5; DA; DAB; DAC; DAM MST; WLC**

Rabinovitch, Sholem 1859-1916
See Aleichem, Sholom
See also CA 104

Rachilde 1860-1953 .... **TCLC 67**
See also DLB 123

Racine, Jean
1639-1699 .... **LC 28; DAB; DAM MST**

Radcliffe, Ann (Ward)
1764-1823 .... **NCLC 6, 55**
See also DLB 39, 178

Radiguet, Raymond 1903-1923 .... **TCLC 29**
See also DLB 65

Radnoti, Miklos 1909-1944 .... **TCLC 16**
See also CA 118

Rado, James 1939-............... **CLC 17**
See also CA 105

Radvanyi, Netty 1900-1983
See Seghers, Anna
See also CA 85-88; 110

Rae, Ben
See Griffiths, Trevor

Raeburn, John (Hay) 1941-........ **CLC 34**
See also CA 57-60

Ragni, Gerome 1942-1991 .... **CLC 17**
See also CA 105; 134

Rahv, Philip 1908-1973 .... **CLC 24**
See also Greenberg, Ivan
See also DLB 137

Raine, Craig 1944- .... **CLC 32, 103**
See also CA 108; CANR 29, 51; DLB 40

Raine, Kathleen (Jessie) 1908- ... **CLC 7, 45**
See also CA 85-88; CANR 46; DLB 20; MTCW

Rainis, Janis 1865-1929 .... **TCLC 29**

Rakosi, Carl..................... **CLC 47**
See also Rawley, Callman
See also CAAS 5

Raleigh, Richard
See Lovecraft, H(oward) P(hillips)

Raleigh, Sir Walter
1554(?)-1618 .... **LC 31, 39**
See also CDBLB Before 1660; DLB 172

Rallentando, H. P.
See Sayers, Dorothy L(eigh)

Ramal, Walter
See de la Mare, Walter (John)

Ramon, Juan
See Jimenez (Mantecon), Juan Ramon

Ramos, Graciliano 1892-1953 ..... **TCLC 32**

Rampersad, Arnold 1941-......... **CLC 44**
See also BW 2; CA 127; 133; DLB 111; INT 133

Rampling, Anne
See Rice, Anne

Ramsay, Allan 1684(?)-1758 .... **LC 29**
See also DLB 95

Ramuz, Charles-Ferdinand
1878-1947 .... **TCLC 33**

Rand, Ayn
1905-1982 ...... **CLC 3, 30, 44, 79; DA; DAC; DAM MST, NOV, POP; WLC**
See also AAYA 10; CA 13-16R; 105; CANR 27; MTCW

Randall, Dudley (Felker)
1914- ...... **CLC 1; BLC; DAM MULT**
See also BW 1; CA 25-28R; CANR 23; DLB 41

Randall, Robert
See Silverberg, Robert

Ranger, Ken
See Creasey, John

Ransom, John Crowe
1888-1974 .... **CLC 2, 4, 5, 11, 24; DAM POET**
See also CA 5-8R; 49-52; CANR 6, 34; DLB 45, 63; MTCW

Rao, Raja 1909- ... **CLC 25, 56; DAM NOV**
See also CA 73-76; CANR 51; MTCW

Raphael, Frederic (Michael)
1931- .... **CLC 2, 14**
See also CA 1-4R; CANR 1; DLB 14

Ratcliffe, James P.
See Mencken, H(enry) L(ouis)

Rathbone, Julian 1935- .... **CLC 41**
See also CA 101; CANR 34

Rattigan, Terence (Mervyn)
1911-1977 .... **CLC 7; DAM DRAM**
See also CA 85-88; 73-76; CDBLB 1945-1960; DLB 13; MTCW

Ratushinskaya, Irina 1954- .... **CLC 54**
See also CA 129

Raven, Simon (Arthur Noel)
1927- .... **CLC 14**
See also CA 81-84

Rawley, Callman 1903-
See Rakosi, Carl
See also CA 21-24R; CANR 12, 32

Rawlings, Marjorie Kinnan
1896-1953 .... **TCLC 4**
See also AAYA 20; CA 104; 137; DLB 9,
22, 102; JRDA; MAICYA; YABC 1

Ray, Satyajit
1921-1992 ... **CLC 16, 76; DAM MULT**
See also CA 114; 137

Read, Herbert Edward 1893-1968.... **CLC 4**
See also CA 85-88; 25-28R; DLB 20, 149

Read, Piers Paul 1941- ...... **CLC 4, 10, 25**
See also CA 21-24R; CANR 38; DLB 14;
SATA 21

Reade, Charles 1814-1884 .... **NCLC 2**
See also DLB 21

Reade, Hamish
See Gray, Simon (James Holliday)

Reading, Peter 1946- .... **CLC 47**
See also CA 103; CANR 46; DLB 40

Reaney, James
1926- ...... **CLC 13; DAC; DAM MST**
See also CA 41-44R; CAAS 15; CANR 42;
DLB 68; SATA 43

Rebreanu, Liviu 1885-1944 .... **TCLC 28**

Rechy, John (Francisco)
1934- .... **CLC 1, 7, 14, 18;**
DAM MULT; HLC
See also CA 5-8R; CAAS 4; CANR 6, 32;
DLB 122; DLBY 82; HW; INT CANR-6

Redcam, Tom 1870-1933 .... **TCLC 25**

Reddin, Keith.................... **CLC 67**

Redgrove, Peter (William)
1932- .... **CLC 6, 41**
See also CA 1-4R; CANR 3, 39; DLB 40

Redmon, Anne.................... **CLC 22**
See also Nightingale, Anne Redmon
See also DLBY 86

Reed, Eliot
See Ambler, Eric

Reed, Ishmael
1938- .... **CLC 2, 3, 5, 6, 13, 32, 60;**
BLC; DAM MULT
See also BW 2; CA 21-24R; CANR 25, 48;
DLB 2, 5, 33, 169; DLBD 8; MTCW

Reed, John (Silas) 1887-1920 ...... **TCLC 9**
See also CA 106

Reed, Lou........................ **CLC 21**
See also Firbank, Louis

Reeve, Clara 1729-1807 .... **NCLC 19**
See also DLB 39

Reich, Wilhelm 1897-1957........ **TCLC 57**

Reid, Christopher (John) 1949-..... **CLC 33**
See also CA 140; DLB 40

Reid, Desmond
See Moorcock, Michael (John)

Reid Banks, Lynne 1929-
See Banks, Lynne Reid
See also CA 1-4R; CANR 6, 22, 38;
CLR 24; JRDA; MAICYA; SATA 22, 75

Reilly, William K.
See Creasey, John

Reiner, Max
See Caldwell, (Janet Miriam) Taylor
(Holland)

Reis, Ricardo
See Pessoa, Fernando (Antonio Nogueira)

Remarque, Erich Maria
1898-1970 .... **CLC 21; DA; DAB; DAC;**
DAM MST, NOV
See also CA 77-80; 29-32R; DLB 56;
MTCW

Remizov, A.
See Remizov, Aleksei (Mikhailovich)

Remizov, A. M.
See Remizov, Aleksei (Mikhailovich)

Remizov, Aleksei (Mikhailovich)
1877-1957................... **TCLC 27**
See also CA 125; 133

Renan, Joseph Ernest
1823-1892 .... **NCLC 26**

Renard, Jules 1864-1910 .... **TCLC 17**
See also CA 117

Renault, Mary.............. **CLC 3, 11, 17**
See also Challans, Mary
See also DLBY 83

Rendell, Ruth (Barbara)
1930- .... **CLC 28, 48; DAM POP**
See also Vine, Barbara
See also CA 109; CANR 32, 52; DLB 87;
INT CANR-32; MTCW

Renoir, Jean 1894-1979 .... **CLC 20**
See also CA 129; 85-88

Resnais, Alain 1922-.............. **CLC 16**

Reverdy, Pierre 1889-1960 .... **CLC 53**
See also CA 97-100; 89-92

Rexroth, Kenneth
1905-1982 ...... **CLC 1, 2, 6, 11, 22, 49;**
DAM POET
See also CA 5-8R; 107; CANR 14, 34;
CDALB 1941-1968; DLB 16, 48, 165;
DLBY 82; INT CANR-14; MTCW

Reyes, Alfonso 1889-1959 .... **TCLC 33**
See also CA 131; HW

Reyes y Basoalto, Ricardo Eliecer Neftali
See Neruda, Pablo

Reymont, Wladyslaw (Stanislaw)
1868(?)-1925 .... **TCLC 5**
See also CA 104

Reynolds, Jonathan 1942- .... **CLC 6, 38**
See also CA 65-68; CANR 28

Reynolds, Joshua 1723-1792........ **LC 15**
See also DLB 104

Reynolds, Michael Shane 1937- .... **CLC 44**
See also CA 65-68; CANR 9

Reznikoff, Charles 1894-1976 .... **CLC 9**
See also CA 33-36; 61-64; CAP 2; DLB 28,
45

Rezzori (d'Arezzo), Gregor von
1914- .... **CLC 25**
See also CA 122; 136

Rhine, Richard
See Silverstein, Alvin

Rhodes, Eugene Manlove
1869-1934 .... **TCLC 53**

R'hoone
See Balzac, Honore de

Rhys, Jean
1890(?)-1979 .... **CLC 2, 4, 6, 14, 19, 51;**
DAM NOV; SSC 21
See also CA 25-28R; 85-88; CANR 35, 62;
CDBLB 1945-1960; DLB 36, 117, 162;
MTCW

Ribeiro, Darcy 1922-1997 .... **CLC 34**
See also CA 33-36R; 156

Ribeiro, Joao Ubaldo (Osorio Pimentel)
1941- .... **CLC 10, 67**
See also CA 81-84

Ribman, Ronald (Burt) 1932- .... **CLC 7**
See also CA 21-24R; CANR 46

Ricci, Nino 1959-................. **CLC 70**
See also CA 137

Rice, Anne 1941- ..... **CLC 41; DAM POP**
See also AAYA 9; BEST 89:2; CA 65-68;
CANR 12, 36, 53

Rice, Elmer (Leopold)
1892-1967 .... **CLC 7, 49; DAM DRAM**
See also CA 21-22; 25-28R; CAP 2; DLB 4,
7; MTCW

Rice, Tim(othy Miles Bindon)
1944- .... **CLC 21**
See also CA 103; CANR 46

Rich, Adrienne (Cecile)
1929- .... **CLC 3, 6, 7, 11, 18, 36, 73, 76;**
DAM POET; PC 5
See also CA 9-12R; CANR 20, 53; DLB 5,
67; MTCW

Rich, Barbara
See Graves, Robert (von Ranke)

Rich, Robert
See Trumbo, Dalton

Richard, Keith.................... **CLC 17**
See also Richards, Keith

Richards, David Adams
1950- .... **CLC 59; DAC**
See also CA 93-96; CANR 60; DLB 53

Richards, I(vor) A(rmstrong)
1893-1979 .... **CLC 14, 24**
See also CA 41-44R; 89-92; CANR 34;
DLB 27

Richards, Keith 1943-
See Richard, Keith
See also CA 107

Richardson, Anne
See Roiphe, Anne (Richardson)

Richardson, Dorothy Miller
1873-1957 .... **TCLC 3**
See also CA 104; DLB 36

Richardson, Ethel Florence (Lindesay)
1870-1946
See Richardson, Henry Handel
See also CA 105

Richardson, Henry Handel......... **TCLC 4**
See also Richardson, Ethel Florence
(Lindesay)

Richardson, John
   1796-1852 .... **NCLC 55; DAC**
   See also DLB 99

Richardson, Samuel
   1689-1761 ..... **LC 1; DA; DAB; DAC;
      DAM MST, NOV; WLC**
   See also CDBLB 1660-1789; DLB 39

Richler, Mordecai
   1931- .... **CLC 3, 5, 9, 13, 18, 46, 70;
      DAC; DAM MST, NOV**
   See also AITN 1; CA 65-68; CANR 31, 62;
      CLR 17; DLB 53; MAICYA; MTCW;
      SATA 44; SATA-Brief 27

Richter, Conrad (Michael)
   1890-1968 .... **CLC 30**
   See also AAYA 21; CA 5-8R; 25-28R;
      CANR 23; DLB 9; MTCW; SATA 3

Ricostranza, Tom
   See Ellis, Trey

Riddell, J. H. 1832-1906 .... **TCLC 40**

Riding, Laura .... **CLC 3, 7**
   See also Jackson, Laura (Riding)

Riefenstahl, Berta Helene Amalia 1902-
   See Riefenstahl, Leni
   See also CA 108

Riefenstahl, Leni .... **CLC 16**
   See also Riefenstahl, Berta Helene Amalia

Riffe, Ernest
   See Bergman, (Ernst) Ingmar

Riggs, (Rolla) Lynn
   1899-1954 ..... **TCLC 56; DAM MULT**
   See also CA 144; DLB 175; NNAL

Riley, James Whitcomb
   1849-1916 ...... **TCLC 51; DAM POET**
   See also CA 118; 137; MAICYA; SATA 17

Riley, Tex
   See Creasey, John

Rilke, Rainer Maria
   1875-1926 .... **TCLC 1, 6, 19;
      DAM POET; PC 2**
   See also CA 104; 132; CANR 62; DLB 81;
      MTCW

Rimbaud, (Jean Nicolas) Arthur
   1854-1891 ..... **NCLC 4, 35; DA; DAB;
      DAC; DAM MST, POET; PC 3; WLC**

Rinehart, Mary Roberts
   1876-1958 .... **TCLC 52**
   See also CA 108

Ringmaster, The
   See Mencken, H(enry) L(ouis)

Ringwood, Gwen(dolyn Margaret) Pharis
   1910-1984 .... **CLC 48**
   See also CA 148; 112; DLB 88

Rio, Michel 19(?)- .... **CLC 43**

Ritsos, Giannes
   See Ritsos, Yannis

Ritsos, Yannis 1909-1990 ..... **CLC 6, 13, 31**
   See also CA 77-80; 133; CANR 39, 61;
      MTCW

Ritter, Erika 1948(?)- .... **CLC 52**

Rivera, Jose Eustasio 1889-1928 ... **TCLC 35**
   See also HW

Rivers, Conrad Kent 1933-1968 ...... **CLC 1**
   See also BW 1; CA 85-88; DLB 41

Rivers, Elfrida
   See Bradley, Marion Zimmer

Riverside, John
   See Heinlein, Robert A(nson)

Rizal, Jose 1861-1896 .... **NCLC 27**

Roa Bastos, Augusto (Antonio)
   1917- ..... **CLC 45; DAM MULT; HLC**
   See also CA 131; DLB 113; HW

Robbe-Grillet, Alain
   1922- ...... **CLC 1, 2, 4, 6, 8, 10, 14, 43**
   See also CA 9-12R; CANR 33; DLB 83;
      MTCW

Robbins, Harold
   1916- .... **CLC 5; DAM NOV**
   See also CA 73-76; CANR 26, 54; MTCW

Robbins, Thomas Eugene 1936-
   See Robbins, Tom
   See also CA 81-84; CANR 29, 59;
      DAM NOV, POP; MTCW

Robbins, Tom .... **CLC 9, 32, 64**
   See also Robbins, Thomas Eugene
   See also BEST 90:3; DLBY 80

Robbins, Trina 1938- .... **CLC 21**
   See also CA 128

Roberts, Charles G(eorge) D(ouglas)
   1860-1943 .... **TCLC 8**
   See also CA 105; CLR 33; DLB 92;
      SATA 88; SATA-Brief 29

Roberts, Elizabeth Madox
   1886-1941 .... **TCLC 68**
   See also CA 111; DLB 9, 54, 102;
      SATA 33; SATA-Brief 27

Roberts, Kate 1891-1985 .... **CLC 15**
   See also CA 107; 116

Roberts, Keith (John Kingston)
   1935- .... **CLC 14**
   See also CA 25-28R; CANR 46

Roberts, Kenneth (Lewis)
   1885-1957 .... **TCLC 23**
   See also CA 109; DLB 9

Roberts, Michele (B.) 1949- .... **CLC 48**
   See also CA 115; CANR 58

Robertson, Ellis
   See Ellison, Harlan (Jay); Silverberg, Robert

Robertson, Thomas William
   1829-1871 .... **NCLC 35; DAM DRAM**

Robeson, Kenneth
   See Dent, Lester

Robinson, Edwin Arlington
   1869-1935 .... **TCLC 5; DA; DAC;
      DAM MST, POET; PC 1**
   See also CA 104; 133; CDALB 1865-1917;
      DLB 54; MTCW

Robinson, Henry Crabb
   1775-1867 .... **NCLC 15**
   See also DLB 107

Robinson, Jill 1936- .... **CLC 10**
   See also CA 102; INT 102

Robinson, Kim Stanley 1952- ...... **CLC 34**
   See also CA 126

Robinson, Lloyd
   See Silverberg, Robert

Robinson, Marilynne 1944- .... **CLC 25**
   See also CA 116

Robinson, Smokey .... **CLC 21**
   See also Robinson, William, Jr.

Robinson, William, Jr. 1940-
   See Robinson, Smokey
   See also CA 116

Robison, Mary 1949- .... **CLC 42, 98**
   See also CA 113; 116; DLB 130; INT 116

Rod, Edouard 1857-1910 .... **TCLC 52**

Roddenberry, Eugene Wesley 1921-1991
   See Roddenberry, Gene
   See also CA 110; 135; CANR 37; SATA 45;
      SATA-Obit 69

Roddenberry, Gene .... **CLC 17**
   See also Roddenberry, Eugene Wesley
   See also AAYA 5; SATA-Obit 69

Rodgers, Mary 1931- .... **CLC 12**
   See also CA 49-52; CANR 8, 55; CLR 20;
      INT CANR-8; JRDA; MAICYA;
      SATA 8

Rodgers, W(illiam) R(obert)
   1909-1969 .... **CLC 7**
   See also CA 85-88; DLB 20

Rodman, Eric
   See Silverberg, Robert

Rodman, Howard 1920(?)-1985 ..... **CLC 65**
   See also CA 118

Rodman, Maia
   See Wojciechowska, Maia (Teresa)

Rodriguez, Claudio 1934- .... **CLC 10**
   See also DLB 134

Roelvaag, O(le) E(dvart)
   1876-1931 .... **TCLC 17**
   See also CA 117; DLB 9

Roethke, Theodore (Huebner)
   1908-1963 ...... **CLC 1, 3, 8, 11, 19, 46,
      101; DAM POET; PC 15**
   See also CA 81-84; CABS 2;
      CDALB 1941-1968; DLB 5; MTCW

Rogers, Thomas Hunton 1927- ..... **CLC 57**
   See also CA 89-92; INT 89-92

Rogers, Will(iam Penn Adair)
   1879-1935 ... **TCLC 8, 71; DAM MULT**
   See also CA 105; 144; DLB 11; NNAL

Rogin, Gilbert 1929- .... **CLC 18**
   See also CA 65-68; CANR 15

Rohan, Koda .... **TCLC 22**
   See also Koda Shigeyuki

Rohlfs, Anna Katharine Green
   See Green, Anna Katharine

Rohmer, Eric .... **CLC 16**
   See also Scherer, Jean-Marie Maurice

Rohmer, Sax .... **TCLC 28**
   See also Ward, Arthur Henry Sarsfield
   See also DLB 70

Roiphe, Anne (Richardson)
   1935- .... **CLC 3, 9**
   See also CA 89-92; CANR 45; DLBY 80;
      INT 89-92

Rojas, Fernando de 1465-1541 ...... **LC 23**

**Rolfe, Frederick (William Serafino Austin
   Lewis Mary)** 1860-1913 ...... **TCLC 12**
   See also CA 107; DLB 34, 156

Rolland, Romain 1866-1944 .... **TCLC 23**
   See also CA 118; DLB 65

Rolle, Richard   c. 1300-c. 1349 ... **CMLC 21**
See also DLB 146

Rolvaag, O(le) E(dvart)
See Roelvaag, O(le) E(dvart)

Romain Arnaud, Saint
See Aragon, Louis

Romains, Jules   1885-1972 .... **CLC 7**
See also CA 85-88; CANR 34; DLB 65;
MTCW

Romero, Jose Ruben   1890-1952 ... **TCLC 14**
See also CA 114; 131; HW

Ronsard, Pierre de
1524-1585 .... **LC 6; PC 11**

Rooke, Leon
1934- .... **CLC 25, 34; DAM POP**
See also CA 25-28R; CANR 23, 53

Roosevelt, Theodore   1858-1919.... **TCLC 69**
See also CA 115; DLB 47

Roper, William   1498-1578 .... **LC 10**

Roquelaure, A. N.
See Rice, Anne

Rosa, Joao Guimaraes   1908-1967 ... **CLC 23**
See also CA 89-92; DLB 113

Rose, Wendy
1948- .... **CLC 85; DAM MULT; PC 13**
See also CA 53-56; CANR 5, 51; DLB 175;
NNAL; SATA 12

Rosen, R. D.
See Rosen, Richard (Dean)

Rosen, Richard (Dean)   1949-....... **CLC 39**
See also CA 77-80; CANR 62;
INT CANR-30

Rosenberg, Isaac   1890-1918....... **TCLC 12**
See also CA 107; DLB 20

Rosenblatt, Joe .... **CLC 15**
See also Rosenblatt, Joseph

Rosenblatt, Joseph   1933-
See Rosenblatt, Joe
See also CA 89-92; INT 89-92

Rosenfeld, Samuel   1896-1963
See Tzara, Tristan
See also CA 89-92

Rosenstock, Sami
See Tzara, Tristan

Rosenstock, Samuel
See Tzara, Tristan

Rosenthal, M(acha) L(ouis)
1917-1996 .... **CLC 28**
See also CA 1-4R; 152; CAAS 6; CANR 4,
51; DLB 5; SATA 59

Ross, Barnaby
See Dannay, Frederic

Ross, Bernard L.
See Follett, Ken(neth Martin)

Ross, J. H.
See Lawrence, T(homas) E(dward)

Ross, Martin
See Martin, Violet Florence
See also DLB 135

Ross, (James) Sinclair
1908- ...... **CLC 13; DAC; DAM MST;**
SSC 24
See also CA 73-76; DLB 88

Rossetti, Christina (Georgina)
1830-1894 ..... **NCLC 2, 50; DA; DAB;**
DAC; DAM MST, POET; PC 7; WLC
See also DLB 35, 163; MAICYA; SATA 20

Rossetti, Dante Gabriel
1828-1882 .... **NCLC 4; DA; DAB;**
DAC; DAM MST, POET; WLC
See also CDBLB 1832-1890; DLB 35

Rossner, Judith (Perelman)
1935- .... **CLC 6, 9, 29**
See also AITN 2; BEST 90:3; CA 17-20R;
CANR 18, 51; DLB 6; INT CANR-18;
MTCW

Rostand, Edmond (Eugene Alexis)
1868-1918 ...... **TCLC 6, 37; DA; DAB;**
DAC; DAM DRAM, MST
See also CA 104; 126; MTCW

Roth, Henry   1906-1995 ... **CLC 2, 6, 11, 104**
See also CA 11-12; 149; CANR 38; CAP 1;
DLB 28; MTCW

Roth, Philip (Milton)
1933- ...... **CLC 1, 2, 3, 4, 6, 9, 15, 22,**
31, 47, 66, 86; DA; DAB; DAC;
DAM MST, NOV, POP; SSC 26; WLC
See also BEST 90:3; CA 1-4R; CANR 1, 22,
36, 55; CDALB 1968-1988; DLB 2, 28,
173; DLBY 82; MTCW

Rothenberg, Jerome   1931-....... **CLC 6, 57**
See also CA 45-48; CANR 1; DLB 5

Roumain, Jacques (Jean Baptiste)
1907-1944 .... **TCLC 19; BLC;**
DAM MULT
See also BW 1; CA 117; 125

Rourke, Constance (Mayfield)
1885-1941 .... **TCLC 12**
See also CA 107; YABC 1

Rousseau, Jean-Baptiste   1671-1741 ... **LC 9**

Rousseau, Jean-Jacques
1712-1778 .... **LC 14, 36; DA; DAB;**
DAC; DAM MST; WLC

Roussel, Raymond   1877-1933 ..... **TCLC 20**
See also CA 117

Rovit, Earl (Herbert)   1927-......... **CLC 7**
See also CA 5-8R; CANR 12

Rowe, Nicholas   1674-1718 .... **LC 8**
See also DLB 84

Rowley, Ames Dorrance
See Lovecraft, H(oward) P(hillips)

Rowson, Susanna Haswell
1762(?)-1824 .... **NCLC 5**
See also DLB 37

Roy, Gabrielle
1909-1983 .... **CLC 10, 14; DAB; DAC;**
DAM MST
See also CA 53-56; 110; CANR 5, 61;
DLB 68; MTCW

Rozewicz, Tadeusz
1921- .... **CLC 9, 23; DAM POET**
See also CA 108; CANR 36; MTCW

Ruark, Gibbons   1941- .... **CLC 3**
See also CA 33-36R; CAAS 23; CANR 14,
31, 57; DLB 120

Rubens, Bernice (Ruth)   1923-... **CLC 19, 31**
See also CA 25-28R; CANR 33; DLB 14;
MTCW

Rubin, Harold
See Robbins, Harold

Rudkin, (James) David   1936- ...... **CLC 14**
See also CA 89-92; DLB 13

Rudnik, Raphael   1933-............. **CLC 7**
See also CA 29-32R

Ruffian, M.
See Hasek, Jaroslav (Matej Frantisek)

Ruiz, Jose Martinez .... **CLC 11**
See also Martinez Ruiz, Jose

Rukeyser, Muriel
1913-1980 .... **CLC 6, 10, 15, 27;**
DAM POET; PC 12
See also CA 5-8R; 93-96; CANR 26, 60;
DLB 48; MTCW; SATA-Obit 22

Rule, Jane (Vance)   1931-.......... **CLC 27**
See also CA 25-28R; CAAS 18; CANR 12;
DLB 60

Rulfo, Juan
1918-1986 .... **CLC 8, 80; DAM MULT;**
HLC; SSC 25
See also CA 85-88; 118; CANR 26;
DLB 113; HW; MTCW

Rumi, Jalal al-Din   1297-1373 .... **CMLC 20**

Runeberg, Johan   1804-1877...... **NCLC 41**

Runyon, (Alfred) Damon
1884(?)-1946 .... **TCLC 10**
See also CA 107; DLB 11, 86, 171

Rush, Norman   1933-.............. **CLC 44**
See also CA 121; 126; INT 126

Rushdie, (Ahmed) Salman
1947- .... **CLC 23, 31, 55, 100; DAB;**
DAC; DAM MST, NOV, POP; WLCS
See also BEST 89:3; CA 108; 111;
CANR 33, 56; INT 111; MTCW

Rushforth, Peter (Scott)   1945- ..... **CLC 19**
See also CA 101

Ruskin, John   1819-1900.......... **TCLC 63**
See also CA 114; 129; CDBLB 1832-1890;
DLB 55, 163; SATA 24

Russ, Joanna   1937-............... **CLC 15**
See also CA 25-28R; CANR 11, 31; DLB 8;
MTCW

Russell, George William   1867-1935
See Baker, Jean H.
See also CA 104; 153; CDBLB 1890-1914;
DAM POET

Russell, (Henry) Ken(neth Alfred)
1927- .... **CLC 16**
See also CA 105

Russell, Willy   1947-.............. **CLC 60**

Rutherford, Mark .... **TCLC 25**
See also White, William Hale
See also DLB 18

Ruyslinck, Ward   1929-............ **CLC 14**
See also Belser, Reimond Karel Maria de

Ryan, Cornelius (John)   1920-1974 ... **CLC 7**
See also CA 69-72; 53-56; CANR 38

Ryan, Michael   1946- .... **CLC 65**
See also CA 49-52; DLBY 82

Ryan, Tim
See Dent, Lester

Rybakov, Anatoli (Naumovich)
1911- . . . . **CLC 23, 53**
See also CA 126; 135; SATA 79

Ryder, Jonathan
See Ludlum, Robert

Ryga, George
1932-1987 . . **CLC 14; DAC; DAM MST**
See also CA 101; 124; CANR 43; DLB 60

S. H.
See Hartmann, Sadakichi

S. S.
See Sassoon, Siegfried (Lorraine)

Saba, Umberto 1883-1957 . . . . **TCLC 33**
See also CA 144; DLB 114

Sabatini, Rafael 1875-1950 . . . . . . **TCLC 47**

Sabato, Ernesto (R.)
1911- . . . . **CLC 10, 23; DAM MULT;**
HLC
See also CA 97-100; CANR 32; DLB 145;
HW; MTCW

Sacastru, Martin
See Bioy Casares, Adolfo

Sacher-Masoch, Leopold von
1836(?)-1895 . . . . **NCLC 31**

Sachs, Marilyn (Stickle) 1927- . . . . . **CLC 35**
See also AAYA 2; CA 17-20R; CANR 13,
47; CLR 2; JRDA; MAICYA; SAAS 2;
SATA 3, 68

Sachs, Nelly 1891-1970 . . . . **CLC 14, 98**
See also CA 17-18; 25-28R; CAP 2

Sackler, Howard (Oliver)
1929-1982 . . . . **CLC 14**
See also CA 61-64; 108; CANR 30; DLB 7

Sacks, Oliver (Wolf) 1933- . . . . **CLC 67**
See also CA 53-56; CANR 28, 50;
INT CANR-28; MTCW

Sadakichi
See Hartmann, Sadakichi

Sade, Donatien Alphonse Francois Comte
1740-1814 . . . . **NCLC 47**

Sadoff, Ira 1945- . . . . **CLC 9**
See also CA 53-56; CANR 5, 21; DLB 120

Saetone
See Camus, Albert

Safire, William 1929- . . . . **CLC 10**
See also CA 17-20R; CANR 31, 54

Sagan, Carl (Edward) 1934-1996. . . . **CLC 30**
See also AAYA 2; CA 25-28R; 155;
CANR 11, 36; MTCW; SATA 58;
SATA-Obit 94

Sagan, Francoise . . . . **CLC 3, 6, 9, 17, 36**
See also Quoirez, Francoise
See also DLB 83

Sahgal, Nayantara (Pandit) 1927- . . . **CLC 41**
See also CA 9-12R; CANR 11

Saint, H(arry) F. 1941- . . . . **CLC 50**
See also CA 127

St. Aubin de Teran, Lisa 1953-
See Teran, Lisa St. Aubin de
See also CA 118; 126; INT 126

Sainte-Beuve, Charles Augustin
1804-1869 . . . . **NCLC 5**

**Saint-Exupery, Antoine (Jean Baptiste Marie
Roger) de**
1900-1944 . . . . **TCLC 2, 56; DAM NOV;**
WLC
See also CA 108; 132; CLR 10; DLB 72;
MAICYA; MTCW; SATA 20

St. John, David
See Hunt, E(verette) Howard, (Jr.)

Saint-John Perse
See Leger, (Marie-Rene Auguste) Alexis
Saint-Leger

Saintsbury, George (Edward Bateman)
1845-1933 . . . . **TCLC 31**
See also CA 160; DLB 57, 149

Sait Faik . . . . **TCLC 23**
See also Abasiyanik, Sait Faik

Saki . . . . **TCLC 3; SSC 12**
See also Munro, H(ector) H(ugh)

Sala, George Augustus . . . . **NCLC 46**

Salama, Hannu 1936- . . . . **CLC 18**

Salamanca, J(ack) R(ichard)
1922- . . . . **CLC 4, 15**
See also CA 25-28R

Sale, J. Kirkpatrick
See Sale, Kirkpatrick

Sale, Kirkpatrick 1937- . . . . **CLC 68**
See also CA 13-16R; CANR 10

Salinas, Luis Omar
1937- . . . . . **CLC 90; DAM MULT; HLC**
See also CA 131; DLB 82; HW

Salinas (y Serrano), Pedro
1891(?)-1951 . . . . **TCLC 17**
See also CA 117; DLB 134

Salinger, J(erome) D(avid)
1919- . . . . . . **CLC 1, 3, 8, 12, 55, 56; DA;**
DAB; DAC; DAM MST, NOV, POP;
SSC 2, 28; WLC
See also AAYA 2; CA 5-8R; CANR 39;
CDALB 1941-1968; CLR 18; DLB 2, 102,
173; MAICYA; MTCW; SATA 67

Salisbury, John
See Caute, David

Salter, James 1925- . . . . **CLC 7, 52, 59**
See also CA 73-76; DLB 130

Saltus, Edgar (Everton)
1855-1921 . . . . **TCLC 8**
See also CA 105

Saltykov, Mikhail Evgrafovich
1826-1889 . . . . **NCLC 16**

Samarakis, Antonis 1919- . . . . **CLC 5**
See also CA 25-28R; CAAS 16; CANR 36

Sanchez, Florencio 1875-1910 . . . . . **TCLC 37**
See also CA 153; HW

Sanchez, Luis Rafael 1936- . . . . **CLC 23**
See also CA 128; DLB 145; HW

Sanchez, Sonia
1934- . . . . . . **CLC 5; BLC; DAM MULT;**
PC 9
See also BW 2; CA 33-36R; CANR 24, 49;
CLR 18; DLB 41; DLBD 8; MAICYA;
MTCW; SATA 22

Sand, George
1804-1876 . . . . **NCLC 2, 42, 57; DA;**
DAB; DAC; DAM MST, NOV; WLC
See also DLB 119

Sandburg, Carl (August)
1878-1967 . . . . **CLC 1, 4, 10, 15, 35; DA;**
DAB; DAC; DAM MST, POET; PC 2;
WLC
See also CA 5-8R; 25-28R; CANR 35;
CDALB 1865-1917; DLB 17, 54;
MAICYA; MTCW; SATA 8

Sandburg, Charles
See Sandburg, Carl (August)

Sandburg, Charles A.
See Sandburg, Carl (August)

Sanders, (James) Ed(ward) 1939- . . . **CLC 53**
See also CA 13-16R; CAAS 21; CANR 13,
44; DLB 16

Sanders, Lawrence
1920- . . . . **CLC 41; DAM POP**
See also BEST 89:4; CA 81-84; CANR 33,
62; MTCW

Sanders, Noah
See Blount, Roy (Alton), Jr.

Sanders, Winston P.
See Anderson, Poul (William)

Sandoz, Mari(e Susette)
1896-1966 . . . . **CLC 28**
See also CA 1-4R; 25-28R; CANR 17;
DLB 9; MTCW; SATA 5

Saner, Reg(inald Anthony) 1931- . . . . **CLC 9**
See also CA 65-68

Sannazaro, Jacopo 1456(?)-1530 . . . . . . **LC 8**

Sansom, William
1912-1976 . . . . . . **CLC 2, 6; DAM NOV;**
SSC 21
See also CA 5-8R; 65-68; CANR 42;
DLB 139; MTCW

Santayana, George 1863-1952 . . . . . **TCLC 40**
See also CA 115; DLB 54, 71; DLBD 13

Santiago, Danny . . . . **CLC 33**
See also James, Daniel (Lewis)
See also DLB 122

Santmyer, Helen Hoover
1895-1986 . . . . **CLC 33**
See also CA 1-4R; 118; CANR 15, 33;
DLBY 84; MTCW

Santoka, Taneda 1882-1940 . . . . . . **TCLC 72**

Santos, Bienvenido N(uqui)
1911-1996 . . . . . . **CLC 22; DAM MULT**
See also CA 101; 151; CANR 19, 46

Sapper . . . . **TCLC 44**
See also McNeile, Herman Cyril

Sapphire 1950- . . . . **CLC 99**

Sappho
fl. 6th cent. B.C.- . . . . **CMLC 3;**
DAM POET; PC 5
See also DLB 176

Sarduy, Severo 1937-1993 . . . . **CLC 6, 97**
See also CA 89-92; 142; CANR 58;
DLB 113; HW

Sargeson, Frank 1903-1982 . . . . **CLC 31**
See also CA 25-28R; 106; CANR 38

Sarmiento, Felix Ruben Garcia
See Dario, Ruben

Saroyan, William
1908-1981 ..... **CLC 1, 8, 10, 29, 34, 56;**
DA; DAB; DAC; DAM DRAM, MST,
NOV; SSC 21; WLC
See also CA 5-8R; 103; CANR 30; DLB 7,
9, 86; DLBY 81; MTCW; SATA 23;
SATA-Obit 24

Sarraute, Nathalie
1900- .... **CLC 1, 2, 4, 8, 10, 31, 80**
See also CA 9-12R; CANR 23; DLB 83;
MTCW

Sarton, (Eleanor) May
1912-1995 .... **CLC 4, 14, 49, 91;**
DAM POET
See also CA 1-4R; 149; CANR 1, 34, 55;
DLB 48; DLBY 81; INT CANR-34;
MTCW; SATA 36; SATA-Obit 86

Sartre, Jean-Paul
1905-1980 .... **CLC 1, 4, 7, 9, 13, 18, 24,**
44, 50, 52; DA; DAB; DAC;
DAM DRAM, MST, NOV; DC 3; WLC
See also CA 9-12R; 97-100; CANR 21;
DLB 72; MTCW

Sassoon, Siegfried (Lorraine)
1886-1967 .... **CLC 36; DAB;**
DAM MST, NOV, POET; PC 12
See also CA 104; 25-28R; CANR 36;
DLB 20; MTCW

Satterfield, Charles
See Pohl, Frederik

Saul, John (W. III)
1942- ...... **CLC 46; DAM NOV, POP**
See also AAYA 10; BEST 90:4; CA 81-84;
CANR 16, 40

Saunders, Caleb
See Heinlein, Robert A(nson)

Saura (Atares), Carlos 1932-....... **CLC 20**
See also CA 114; 131; HW

Sauser-Hall, Frederic 1887-1961.... **CLC 18**
See also Cendrars, Blaise
See also CA 102; 93-96; CANR 36, 62;
MTCW

Saussure, Ferdinand de
1857-1913 .... **TCLC 49**

Savage, Catharine
See Brosman, Catharine Savage

Savage, Thomas 1915- .... **CLC 40**
See also CA 126; 132; CAAS 15; INT 132

Savan, Glenn 19(?)- .... **CLC 50**

Sayers, Dorothy L(eigh)
1893-1957 ..... **TCLC 2, 15; DAM POP**
See also CA 104; 119; CANR 60;
CDBLB 1914-1945; DLB 10, 36, 77, 100;
MTCW

Sayers, Valerie 1952-............. **CLC 50**
See also CA 134; CANR 61

Sayles, John (Thomas)
1950- .... **CLC 7, 10, 14**
See also CA 57-60; CANR 41; DLB 44

Scammell, Michael 1935-.......... **CLC 34**
See also CA 156

Scannell, Vernon 1922- .... **CLC 49**
See also CA 5-8R; CANR 8, 24, 57;
DLB 27; SATA 59

Scarlett, Susan
See Streatfeild, (Mary) Noel

Schaeffer, Susan Fromberg
1941- .... **CLC 6, 11, 22**
See also CA 49-52; CANR 18; DLB 28;
MTCW; SATA 22

Schary, Jill
See Robinson, Jill

Schell, Jonathan 1943-............ **CLC 35**
See also CA 73-76; CANR 12

Schelling, Friedrich Wilhelm Joseph von
1775-1854 .... **NCLC 30**
See also DLB 90

Schendel, Arthur van 1874-1946... **TCLC 56**

Scherer, Jean-Marie Maurice 1920-
See Rohmer, Eric
See also CA 110

Schevill, James (Erwin) 1920-....... **CLC 7**
See also CA 5-8R; CAAS 12

Schiller, Friedrich
1759-1805 .... **NCLC 39; DAM DRAM**
See also DLB 94

Schisgal, Murray (Joseph) 1926-..... **CLC 6**
See also CA 21-24R; CANR 48

Schlee, Ann 1934-................ **CLC 35**
See also CA 101; CANR 29; SATA 44;
SATA-Brief 36

Schlegel, August Wilhelm von
1767-1845 .... **NCLC 15**
See also DLB 94

Schlegel, Friedrich 1772-1829 .... **NCLC 45**
See also DLB 90

Schlegel, Johann Elias (von)
1719(?)-1749 .... **LC 5**

Schlesinger, Arthur M(eier), Jr.
1917- .... **CLC 84**
See also AITN 1; CA 1-4R; CANR 1, 28,
58; DLB 17; INT CANR-28; MTCW;
SATA 61

Schmidt, Arno (Otto) 1914-1979.... **CLC 56**
See also CA 128; 109; DLB 69

Schmitz, Aron Hector 1861-1928
See Svevo, Italo
See also CA 104; 122; MTCW

Schnackenberg, Gjertrud 1953-..... **CLC 40**
See also CA 116; DLB 120

Schneider, Leonard Alfred 1925-1966
See Bruce, Lenny
See also CA 89-92

Schnitzler, Arthur
1862-1931 .... **TCLC 4; SSC 15**
See also CA 104; DLB 81, 118

Schoenberg, Arnold 1874-1951 .... **TCLC 75**
See also CA 109

Schonberg, Arnold
See Schoenberg, Arnold

Schopenhauer, Arthur
1788-1860 .... **NCLC 51**
See also DLB 90

Schor, Sandra (M.) 1932(?)-1990 ... **CLC 65**
See also CA 132

Schorer, Mark 1908-1977 .... **CLC 9**
See also CA 5-8R; 73-76; CANR 7;
DLB 103

Schrader, Paul (Joseph) 1946-..... **CLC 26**
See also CA 37-40R; CANR 41; DLB 44

Schreiner, Olive (Emilie Albertina)
1855-1920 .... **TCLC 9**
See also CA 105; DLB 18, 156

Schulberg, Budd (Wilson)
1914- .... **CLC 7, 48**
See also CA 25-28R; CANR 19; DLB 6, 26,
28; DLBY 81

Schulz, Bruno
1892-1942 .... **TCLC 5, 51; SSC 13**
See also CA 115; 123

Schulz, Charles M(onroe) 1922- .... **CLC 12**
See also CA 9-12R; CANR 6;
INT CANR-6; SATA 10

Schumacher, E(rnst) F(riedrich)
1911-1977 .... **CLC 80**
See also CA 81-84; 73-76; CANR 34

Schuyler, James Marcus
1923-1991 ..... **CLC 5, 23; DAM POET**
See also CA 101; 134; DLB 5, 169; INT 101

Schwartz, Delmore (David)
1913-1966 ... **CLC 2, 4, 10, 45, 87; PC 8**
See also CA 17-18; 25-28R; CANR 35;
CAP 2; DLB 28, 48; MTCW

Schwartz, Ernst
See Ozu, Yasujiro

Schwartz, John Burnham 1965- .... **CLC 59**
See also CA 132

Schwartz, Lynne Sharon 1939-..... **CLC 31**
See also CA 103; CANR 44

Schwartz, Muriel A.
See Eliot, T(homas) S(tearns)

Schwarz-Bart, Andre 1928-....... **CLC 2, 4**
See also CA 89-92

Schwarz-Bart, Simone 1938-....... **CLC 7**
See also BW 2; CA 97-100

Schwob, (Mayer Andre) Marcel
1867-1905 .... **TCLC 20**
See also CA 117; DLB 123

Sciascia, Leonardo
1921-1989 .... **CLC 8, 9, 41**
See also CA 85-88; 130; CANR 35;
DLB 177; MTCW

Scoppettone, Sandra 1936-.......... **CLC 26**
See also AAYA 11; CA 5-8R; CANR 41;
SATA 9, 92

Scorsese, Martin 1942- .... **CLC 20, 89**
See also CA 110; 114; CANR 46

Scotland, Jay
See Jakes, John (William)

Scott, Duncan Campbell
1862-1947 .... **TCLC 6; DAC**
See also CA 104; 153; DLB 92

Scott, Evelyn 1893-1963........... **CLC 43**
See also CA 104; 112; DLB 9, 48

Scott, F(rancis) R(eginald)
1899-1985 .... **CLC 22**
See also CA 101; 114; DLB 88; INT 101

Scott, Frank
See Scott, F(rancis) R(eginald)

Scott, Joanna 1960-.............. **CLC 50**
See also CA 126; CANR 53

Scott, Paul (Mark) 1920-1978.... **CLC 9, 60**
See also CA 81-84; 77-80; CANR 33;
DLB 14; MTCW

Scott, Walter
  1771-1832 .... **NCLC 15; DA; DAB;
  DAC; DAM MST, NOV, POET; PC 13;
  WLC**
  See also AAYA 22; CDBLB 1789-1832;
  DLB 93, 107, 116, 144, 159; YABC 2

Scribe, (Augustin) Eugene
  1791-1861 .... **NCLC 16; DAM DRAM;
  DC 5**

Scrum, R.
  See Crumb, R(obert)

Scudery, Madeleine de 1607-1701..... **LC 2**

Scum
  See Crumb, R(obert)

Scumbag, Little Bobby
  See Crumb, R(obert)

Seabrook, John
  See Hubbard, L(afayette) Ron(ald)

Sealy, I. Allan 1951- .... **CLC 55**

Search, Alexander
  See Pessoa, Fernando (Antonio Nogueira)

Sebastian, Lee
  See Silverberg, Robert

Sebastian Owl
  See Thompson, Hunter S(tockton)

Sebestyen, Ouida 1924- .... **CLC 30**
  See also AAYA 8; CA 107; CANR 40;
  CLR 17; JRDA; MAICYA; SAAS 10;
  SATA 39

Secundus, H. Scriblerus
  See Fielding, Henry

Sedges, John
  See Buck, Pearl S(ydenstricker)

Sedgwick, Catharine Maria
  1789-1867 .... **NCLC 19**
  See also DLB 1, 74

Seelye, John 1931- .... **CLC 7**

Seferiades, Giorgos Stylianou 1900-1971
  See Seferis, George
  See also CA 5-8R; 33-36R; CANR 5, 36;
  MTCW

Seferis, George .... **CLC 5, 11**
  See also Seferiades, Giorgos Stylianou

Segal, Erich (Wolf)
  1937- .... **CLC 3, 10; DAM POP**
  See also BEST 89:1; CA 25-28R; CANR 20,
  36; DLBY 86; INT CANR-20; MTCW

Seger, Bob 1945-................. **CLC 35**

Seghers, Anna .... **CLC 7**
  See also Radvanyi, Netty
  See also DLB 69

Seidel, Frederick (Lewis) 1936-..... **CLC 18**
  See also CA 13-16R; CANR 8; DLBY 84

Seifert, Jaroslav
  1901-1986 .... **CLC 34, 44, 93**
  See also CA 127; MTCW

Sei Shonagon c. 966-1017(?) ...... **CMLC 6**

Selby, Hubert, Jr.
  1928- .... **CLC 1, 2, 4, 8; SSC 20**
  See also CA 13-16R; CANR 33; DLB 2

Selzer, Richard 1928-............. **CLC 74**
  See also CA 65-68; CANR 14

Sembene, Ousmane
  See Ousmane, Sembene

Senancour, Etienne Pivert de
  1770-1846 .... **NCLC 16**
  See also DLB 119

Sender, Ramon (Jose)
  1902-1982 .. **CLC 8; DAM MULT; HLC**
  See also CA 5-8R; 105; CANR 8; HW;
  MTCW

Seneca, Lucius Annaeus
  4B.C.-65...... **CMLC 6; DAM DRAM;
  DC 5**

Senghor, Leopold Sedar
  1906- ..... **CLC 54; BLC; DAM MULT,
  POET**
  See also BW 2; CA 116; 125; CANR 47;
  MTCW

Serling, (Edward) Rod(man)
  1924-1975 .... **CLC 30**
  See also AAYA 14; AITN 1; CA 65-68;
  57-60; DLB 26

Serna, Ramon Gomez de la
  See Gomez de la Serna, Ramon

Serpieres
  See Guillevic, (Eugene)

Service, Robert
  See Service, Robert W(illiam)
  See also DAB; DLB 92

Service, Robert W(illiam)
  1874(?)-1958 ...... **TCLC 15; DA; DAC;
  DAM MST, POET; WLC**
  See also Service, Robert
  See also CA 115; 140; SATA 20

Seth, Vikram
  1952- .... **CLC 43, 90; DAM MULT**
  See also CA 121; 127; CANR 50; DLB 120;
  INT 127

Seton, Cynthia Propper
  1926-1982 .... **CLC 27**
  See also CA 5-8R; 108; CANR 7

Seton, Ernest (Evan) Thompson
  1860-1946 .... **TCLC 31**
  See also CA 109; DLB 92; DLBD 13;
  JRDA; SATA 18

Seton-Thompson, Ernest
  See Seton, Ernest (Evan) Thompson

Settle, Mary Lee 1918- .... **CLC 19, 61**
  See also CA 89-92; CAAS 1; CANR 44;
  DLB 6; INT 89-92

Seuphor, Michel
  See Arp, Jean

Sevigne, Marie (de Rabutin-Chantal) Marquise
  de 1626-1696 .... **LC 11**

Sewall, Samuel 1652-1730 .... **LC 38**
  See also DLB 24

Sexton, Anne (Harvey)
  1928-1974 .... **CLC 2, 4, 6, 8, 10, 15, 53;
  DA; DAB; DAC; DAM MST, POET;
  PC 2; WLC**
  See also CA 1-4R; 53-56; CABS 2;
  CANR 3, 36; CDALB 1941-1968; DLB 5,
  169; MTCW; SATA 10

Shaara, Michael (Joseph, Jr.)
  1929-1988 .... **CLC 15; DAM POP**
  See also AITN 1; CA 102; 125; CANR 52;
  DLBY 83

Shackleton, C. C.
  See Aldiss, Brian W(ilson)

Shacochis, Bob .... **CLC 39**
  See also Shacochis, Robert G.

Shacochis, Robert G. 1951-
  See Shacochis, Bob
  See also CA 119; 124; INT 124

Shaffer, Anthony (Joshua)
  1926- .... **CLC 19; DAM DRAM**
  See also CA 110; 116; DLB 13

Shaffer, Peter (Levin)
  1926- ...... **CLC 5, 14, 18, 37, 60; DAB;
  DAM DRAM, MST; DC 7**
  See also CA 25-28R; CANR 25, 47;
  CDBLB 1960 to Present; DLB 13;
  MTCW

Shakey, Bernard
  See Young, Neil

Shalamov, Varlam (Tikhonovich)
  1907(?)-1982 .... **CLC 18**
  See also CA 129; 105

Shamlu, Ahmad 1925- .... **CLC 10**

Shammas, Anton 1951-............ **CLC 55**

Shange, Ntozake
  1948- .... **CLC 8, 25, 38, 74; BLC;
  DAM DRAM, MULT; DC 3**
  See also AAYA 9; BW 2; CA 85-88;
  CABS 3; CANR 27, 48; DLB 38; MTCW

Shanley, John Patrick 1950-....... **CLC 75**
  See also CA 128; 133

Shapcott, Thomas W(illiam) 1935- .. **CLC 38**
  See also CA 69-72; CANR 49

Shapiro, Jane..................... **CLC 76**

Shapiro, Karl (Jay) 1913- .. **CLC 4, 8, 15, 53**
  See also CA 1-4R; CAAS 6; CANR 1, 36;
  DLB 48; MTCW

Sharp, William 1855-1905 .... **TCLC 39**
  See also CA 160; DLB 156

Sharpe, Thomas Ridley 1928-
  See Sharpe, Tom
  See also CA 114; 122; INT 122

Sharpe, Tom..................... **CLC 36**
  See also Sharpe, Thomas Ridley
  See also DLB 14

Shaw, Bernard.................... **TCLC 45**
  See also Shaw, George Bernard
  See also BW 1

Shaw, G. Bernard
  See Shaw, George Bernard

Shaw, George Bernard
  1856-1950 ... **TCLC 3, 9, 21; DA; DAB;
  DAC; DAM DRAM, MST; WLC**
  See also Shaw, Bernard
  See also CA 104; 128; CDBLB 1914-1945;
  DLB 10, 57; MTCW

Shaw, Henry Wheeler
  1818-1885 .... **NCLC 15**
  See also DLB 11

Shaw, Irwin
  1913-1984 .... **CLC 7, 23, 34;
  DAM DRAM, POP**
  See also AITN 1; CA 13-16R; 112;
  CANR 21; CDALB 1941-1968; DLB 6,
  102; DLBY 84; MTCW

Shaw, Robert 1927-1978 .... **CLC 5**
  See also AITN 1; CA 1-4R; 81-84;
  CANR 4; DLB 13, 14

Simon, (Marvin) Neil
1927- .... CLC 6, 11, 31, 39, 70;
DAM DRAM
See also AITN 1; CA 21-24R; CANR 26,
54; DLB 7; MTCW

Simon, Paul (Frederick) 1941(?)- ... CLC 17
See also CA 116; 153

Simonon, Paul 1956(?)- .... CLC 30

Simpson, Harriette
See Arnow, Harriette (Louisa) Simpson

Simpson, Louis (Aston Marantz)
1923- .... CLC 4, 7, 9, 32; DAM POET
See also CA 1-4R; CAAS 4; CANR 1, 61;
DLB 5; MTCW

Simpson, Mona (Elizabeth) 1957-... CLC 44
See also CA 122; 135

Simpson, N(orman) F(rederick)
1919- .... CLC 29
See also CA 13-16R; DLB 13

Sinclair, Andrew (Annandale)
1935- .... CLC 2, 14
See also CA 9-12R; CAAS 5; CANR 14, 38;
DLB 14; MTCW

Sinclair, Emil
See Hesse, Hermann

Sinclair, Iain 1943-.............. CLC 76
See also CA 132

Sinclair, Iain MacGregor
See Sinclair, Iain

Sinclair, Irene
See Griffith, D(avid Lewelyn) W(ark)

Sinclair, Mary Amelia St. Clair 1865(?)-1946
See Sinclair, May
See also CA 104

Sinclair, May................TCLC 3, 11
See also Sinclair, Mary Amelia St. Clair
See also DLB 36, 135

Sinclair, Roy
See Griffith, D(avid Lewelyn) W(ark)

Sinclair, Upton (Beall)
1878-1968 ..... CLC 1, 11, 15, 63; DA;
DAB; DAC; DAM MST, NOV; WLC
See also CA 5-8R; 25-28R; CANR 7;
CDALB 1929-1941; DLB 9;
INT CANR-7; MTCW; SATA 9

Singer, Isaac
See Singer, Isaac Bashevis

Singer, Isaac Bashevis
1904-1991 .... CLC 1, 3, 6, 9, 11, 15, 23,
38, 69; DA; DAB; DAC; DAM MST,
NOV; SSC 3; WLC
See also AITN 1, 2; CA 1-4R; 134;
CANR 1, 39; CDALB 1941-1968; CLR 1;
DLB 6, 28, 52; DLBY 91; JRDA;
MAICYA; MTCW; SATA 3, 27;
SATA-Obit 68

Singer, Israel Joshua 1893-1944 ... TCLC 33

Singh, Khushwant 1915-........... CLC 11
See also CA 9-12R; CAAS 9; CANR 6

Singleton, Ann
See Benedict, Ruth (Fulton)

Sinjohn, John
See Galsworthy, John

Sinyavsky, Andrei (Donatevich)
1925-1997 .... CLC 8
See also CA 85-88; 159

Sirin, V.
See Nabokov, Vladimir (Vladimirovich)

Sissman, L(ouis) E(dward)
1928-1976 .... CLC 9, 18
See also CA 21-24R; 65-68; CANR 13;
DLB 5

Sisson, C(harles) H(ubert) 1914-..... CLC 8
See also CA 1-4R; CAAS 3; CANR 3, 48;
DLB 27

Sitwell, Dame Edith
1887-1964 .... CLC 2, 9, 67;
DAM POET; PC 3
See also CA 9-12R; CANR 35;
CDBLB 1945-1960; DLB 20; MTCW

Siwaarmill, H. P.
See Sharp, William

Sjoewall, Maj 1935-.............. CLC 7
See also CA 65-68

Sjowall, Maj
See Sjoewall, Maj

Skelton, Robin 1925-1997 .... CLC 13
See also AITN 2; CA 5-8R; 160; CAAS 5;
CANR 28; DLB 27, 53

Skolimowski, Jerzy 1938-......... CLC 20
See also CA 128

Skram, Amalie (Bertha)
1847-1905 .... TCLC 25

Skvorecky, Josef (Vaclav)
1924- .... CLC 15, 39, 69; DAC;
DAM NOV
See also CA 61-64; CAAS 1; CANR 10, 34;
MTCW

Slade, Bernard................ CLC 11, 46
See also Newbound, Bernard Slade
See also CAAS 9; DLB 53

Slaughter, Carolyn 1946-.......... CLC 56
See also CA 85-88

Slaughter, Frank G(ill) 1908- ...... CLC 29
See also AITN 2; CA 5-8R; CANR 5;
INT CANR-5

Slavitt, David R(ytman) 1935-.... CLC 5, 14
See also CA 21-24R; CAAS 3; CANR 41;
DLB 5, 6

Slesinger, Tess 1905-1945 .... TCLC 10
See also CA 107; DLB 102

Slessor, Kenneth 1901-1971....... CLC 14
See also CA 102; 89-92

Slowacki, Juliusz 1809-1849 ..... NCLC 15

Smart, Christopher
1722-1771 ... LC 3; DAM POET; PC 13
See also DLB 109

Smart, Elizabeth 1913-1986........ CLC 54
See also CA 81-84; 118; DLB 88

Smiley, Jane (Graves)
1949- .... CLC 53, 76; DAM POP
See also CA 104; CANR 30, 50;
INT CANR-30

Smith, A(rthur) J(ames) M(arshall)
1902-1980 .... CLC 15; DAC
See also CA 1-4R; 102; CANR 4; DLB 88

Smith, Adam 1723-1790........... LC 36
See also DLB 104

Smith, Alexander 1829-1867 ..... NCLC 59
See also DLB 32, 55

Smith, Anna Deavere 1950-........ CLC 86
See also CA 133

Smith, Betty (Wehner) 1896-1972... CLC 19
See also CA 5-8R; 33-36R; DLBY 82;
SATA 6

Smith, Charlotte (Turner)
1749-1806 .... NCLC 23
See also DLB 39, 109

Smith, Clark Ashton 1893-1961 .... CLC 43
See also CA 143

Smith, Dave................... CLC 22, 42
See also Smith, David (Jeddie)
See also CAAS 7; DLB 5

Smith, David (Jeddie) 1942-
See Smith, Dave
See also CA 49-52; CANR 1, 59;
DAM POET

Smith, Florence Margaret 1902-1971
See Smith, Stevie
See also CA 17-18; 29-32R; CANR 35;
CAP 2; DAM POET; MTCW

Smith, Iain Crichton 1928- .... CLC 64
See also CA 21-24R; DLB 40, 139

Smith, John 1580(?)-1631 .... LC 9

Smith, Johnston
See Crane, Stephen (Townley)

Smith, Joseph, Jr. 1805-1844 .... NCLC 53

Smith, Lee 1944-.............. CLC 25, 73
See also CA 114; 119; CANR 46; DLB 143;
DLBY 83; INT 119

Smith, Martin
See Smith, Martin Cruz

Smith, Martin Cruz
1942- ..... CLC 25; DAM MULT, POP
See also BEST 89:4; CA 85-88; CANR 6,
23, 43; INT CANR-23; NNAL

Smith, Mary-Ann Tirone 1944-..... CLC 39
See also CA 118; 136

Smith, Patti 1946- .... CLC 12
See also CA 93-96

Smith, Pauline (Urmson)
1882-1959 .... TCLC 25

Smith, Rosamond
See Oates, Joyce Carol

Smith, Sheila Kaye
See Kaye-Smith, Sheila

Smith, Stevie .... CLC 3, 8, 25, 44; PC 12
See also Smith, Florence Margaret
See also DLB 20

Smith, Wilbur (Addison) 1933-..... CLC 33
See also CA 13-16R; CANR 7, 46; MTCW

Smith, William Jay 1918- .... CLC 6
See also CA 5-8R; CANR 44; DLB 5;
MAICYA; SAAS 22; SATA 2, 68

Smith, Woodrow Wilson
See Kuttner, Henry

Smolenskin, Peretz 1842-1885.... NCLC 30

Smollett, Tobias (George) 1721-1771 .. LC 2
See also CDBLB 1660-1789; DLB 39, 104

Snodgrass, W(illiam) D(e Witt)
1926- .... **CLC 2, 6, 10, 18, 68;**
DAM POET
See also CA 1-4R; CANR 6, 36; DLB 5;
MTCW

Snow, C(harles) P(ercy)
1905-1980 ...... **CLC 1, 4, 6, 9, 13, 19;**
DAM NOV
See also CA 5-8R; 101; CANR 28;
CDBLB 1945-1960; DLB 15, 77; MTCW

Snow, Frances Compton
See Adams, Henry (Brooks)

Snyder, Gary (Sherman)
1930- .. **CLC 1, 2, 5, 9, 32; DAM POET**
See also CA 17-20R; CANR 30, 60; DLB 5,
16, 165

Snyder, Zilpha Keatley 1927- ...... **CLC 17**
See also AAYA 15; CA 9-12R; CANR 38;
CLR 31; JRDA; MAICYA; SAAS 2;
SATA 1, 28, 75

Soares, Bernardo
See Pessoa, Fernando (Antonio Nogueira)

Sobh, A.
See Shamlu, Ahmad

Sobol, Joshua .... **CLC 60**

Soderberg, Hjalmar 1869-1941 .... **TCLC 39**

Sodergran, Edith (Irene)
See Soedergran, Edith (Irene)

Soedergran, Edith (Irene)
1892-1923 .... **TCLC 31**

Softly, Edgar
See Lovecraft, H(oward) P(hillips)

Softly, Edward
See Lovecraft, H(oward) P(hillips)

Sokolov, Raymond 1941- .... **CLC 7**
See also CA 85-88

Solo, Jay
See Ellison, Harlan (Jay)

Sologub, Fyodor .... **TCLC 9**
See also Teternikov, Fyodor Kuzmich

Solomons, Ikey Esquir
See Thackeray, William Makepeace

Solomos, Dionysios 1798-1857 ... **NCLC 15**

Solwoska, Mara
See French, Marilyn

Solzhenitsyn, Aleksandr I(sayevich)
1918- ...... **CLC 1, 2, 4, 7, 9, 10, 18, 26,**
34, 78; DA; DAB; DAC; DAM MST,
NOV; WLC
See also AITN 1; CA 69-72; CANR 40;
MTCW

Somers, Jane
See Lessing, Doris (May)

Somerville, Edith 1858-1949 ...... **TCLC 51**
See also DLB 135

Somerville & Ross
See Martin, Violet Florence; Somerville,
Edith

Sommer, Scott 1951- .... **CLC 25**
See also CA 106

Sondheim, Stephen (Joshua)
1930- .... **CLC 30, 39; DAM DRAM**
See also AAYA 11; CA 103; CANR 47

Sontag, Susan
1933- .... **CLC 1, 2, 10, 13, 31;**
DAM POP
See also CA 17-20R; CANR 25, 51; DLB 2,
67; MTCW

Sophocles
496(?)B.C.-406(?)B.C..... **CMLC 2; DA;**
DAB; DAC; DAM DRAM, MST; DC 1;
WLCS
See also DLB 176

Sordello 1189-1269............. **CMLC 15**

Sorel, Julia
See Drexler, Rosalyn

Sorrentino, Gilbert
1929- .... **CLC 3, 7, 14, 22, 40**
See also CA 77-80; CANR 14, 33; DLB 5,
173; DLBY 80; INT CANR-14

Soto, Gary
1952- .... **CLC 32, 80; DAM MULT;**
HLC
See also AAYA 10; CA 119; 125;
CANR 50; CLR 38; DLB 82; HW;
INT 125; JRDA; SATA 80

Soupault, Philippe 1897-1990 ...... **CLC 68**
See also CA 116; 147; 131

Souster, (Holmes) Raymond
1921- ... **CLC 5, 14; DAC; DAM POET**
See also CA 13-16R; CAAS 14; CANR 13,
29, 53; DLB 88; SATA 63

Southern, Terry 1924(?)-1995 .... **CLC 7**
See also CA 1-4R; 150; CANR 1, 55;
DLB 2

Southey, Robert 1774-1843 .... **NCLC 8**
See also DLB 93, 107, 142; SATA 54

Southworth, Emma Dorothy Eliza Nevitte
1819-1899 .... **NCLC 26**

Souza, Ernest
See Scott, Evelyn

Soyinka, Wole
1934- .... **CLC 3, 5, 14, 36, 44; BLC;**
DA; DAB; DAC; DAM DRAM, MST,
MULT; DC 2; WLC
See also BW 2; CA 13-16R; CANR 27, 39;
DLB 125; MTCW

Spackman, W(illiam) M(ode)
1905-1990 .... **CLC 46**
See also CA 81-84; 132

Spacks, Barry (Bernard) 1931- ..... **CLC 14**
See also CA 154; CANR 33; DLB 105

Spanidou, Irini 1946- .... **CLC 44**

Spark, Muriel (Sarah)
1918- ..... **CLC 2, 3, 5, 8, 13, 18, 40, 94;**
DAB; DAC; DAM MST, NOV; SSC 10
See also CA 5-8R; CANR 12, 36;
CDBLB 1945-1960; DLB 15, 139;
INT CANR-12; MTCW

Spaulding, Douglas
See Bradbury, Ray (Douglas)

Spaulding, Leonard
See Bradbury, Ray (Douglas)

Spence, J. A. D.
See Eliot, T(homas) S(tearns)

Spencer, Elizabeth 1921- .... **CLC 22**
See also CA 13-16R; CANR 32; DLB 6;
MTCW; SATA 14

Spencer, Leonard G.
See Silverberg, Robert

Spencer, Scott 1945-.............. **CLC 30**
See also CA 113; CANR 51; DLBY 86

Spender, Stephen (Harold)
1909-1995 ...... **CLC 1, 2, 5, 10, 41, 91;**
DAM POET
See also CA 9-12R; 149; CANR 31, 54;
CDBLB 1945-1960; DLB 20; MTCW

Spengler, Oswald (Arnold Gottfried)
1880-1936 .... **TCLC 25**
See also CA 118

Spenser, Edmund
1552(?)-1599 ...... **LC 5, 39; DA; DAB;**
DAC; DAM MST, POET; PC 8; WLC
See also CDBLB Before 1660; DLB 167

Spicer, Jack
1925-1965 .... **CLC 8, 18, 72;**
DAM POET
See also CA 85-88; DLB 5, 16

Spiegelman, Art 1948- .... **CLC 76**
See also AAYA 10; CA 125; CANR 41, 55

Spielberg, Peter 1929- .... **CLC 6**
See also CA 5-8R; CANR 4, 48; DLBY 81

Spielberg, Steven 1947- .... **CLC 20**
See also AAYA 8; CA 77-80; CANR 32;
SATA 32

Spillane, Frank Morrison 1918-
See Spillane, Mickey
See also CA 25-28R; CANR 28; MTCW;
SATA 66

Spillane, Mickey .... **CLC 3, 13**
See also Spillane, Frank Morrison

Spinoza, Benedictus de 1632-1677 .... **LC 9**

Spinrad, Norman (Richard) 1940-... **CLC 46**
See also CA 37-40R; CAAS 19; CANR 20;
DLB 8; INT CANR-20

Spitteler, Carl (Friedrich Georg)
1845-1924 .... **TCLC 12**
See also CA 109; DLB 129

Spivack, Kathleen (Romola Drucker)
1938- .... **CLC 6**
See also CA 49-52

Spoto, Donald 1941-.............. **CLC 39**
See also CA 65-68; CANR 11, 57

Springsteen, Bruce (F.) 1949- ...... **CLC 17**
See also CA 111

Spurling, Hilary 1940-............. **CLC 34**
See also CA 104; CANR 25, 52

Spyker, John Howland
See Elman, Richard

Squires, (James) Radcliffe
1917-1993 .... **CLC 51**
See also CA 1-4R; 140; CANR 6, 21

Srivastava, Dhanpat Rai 1880(?)-1936
See Premchand
See also CA 118

Stacy, Donald
See Pohl, Frederik

Stael, Germaine de
See Stael-Holstein, Anne Louise Germaine
Necker Baronn
See also DLB 119

Stael-Holstein, Anne Louise Germaine Necker Baronn 1766-1817 . . . . NCLC 3
See also Stael, Germaine de

Stafford, Jean
1915-1979 . . . . CLC 4, 7, 19, 68; SSC 26
See also CA 1-4R; 85-88; CANR 3; DLB 2, 173; MTCW; SATA-Obit 22

Stafford, William (Edgar)
1914-1993 . . . CLC 4, 7, 29; DAM POET
See also CA 5-8R; 142; CAAS 3; CANR 5, 22; DLB 5; INT CANR-22

Stagnelius, Eric Johan
1793-1823 . . . . NCLC 61

Staines, Trevor
See Brunner, John (Kilian Houston)

Stairs, Gordon
See Austin, Mary (Hunter)

Stannard, Martin 1947- . . . . CLC 44
See also CA 142; DLB 155

Stanton, Elizabeth Cady
1815-1902 . . . . TCLC 73
See also DLB 79

Stanton, Maura 1946- . . . . CLC 9
See also CA 89-92; CANR 15; DLB 120

Stanton, Schuyler
See Baum, L(yman) Frank

Stapledon, (William) Olaf
1886-1950 . . . . TCLC 22
See also CA 111; DLB 15

Starbuck, George (Edwin)
1931-1996 . . . . CLC 53; DAM POET
See also CA 21-24R; 153; CANR 23

Stark, Richard
See Westlake, Donald E(dwin)

Staunton, Schuyler
See Baum, L(yman) Frank

Stead, Christina (Ellen)
1902-1983 . . . . CLC 2, 5, 8, 32, 80
See also CA 13-16R; 109; CANR 33, 40; MTCW

Stead, William Thomas
1849-1912 . . . . TCLC 48

Steele, Richard 1672-1729 . . . . LC 18
See also CDBLB 1660-1789; DLB 84, 101

Steele, Timothy (Reid) 1948- . . . . CLC 45
See also CA 93-96; CANR 16, 50; DLB 120

Steffens, (Joseph) Lincoln
1866-1936 . . . . TCLC 20
See also CA 117

Stegner, Wallace (Earle)
1909-1993 . . . . CLC 9, 49, 81;
DAM NOV; SSC 27
See also AITN 1; BEST 90:3; CA 1-4R; 141; CAAS 9; CANR 1, 21, 46; DLB 9; DLBY 93; MTCW

Stein, Gertrude
1874-1946 . . . . . . TCLC 1, 6, 28, 48; DA; DAB; DAC; DAM MST, NOV, POET; PC 18; WLC
See also CA 104; 132; CDALB 1917-1929; DLB 4, 54, 86; DLBD 15; MTCW

Steinbeck, John (Ernst)
1902-1968 . . . . . . CLC 1, 5, 9, 13, 21, 34, 45, 75; DA; DAB; DAC; DAM DRAM, MST, NOV; SSC 11; WLC
See also AAYA 12; CA 1-4R; 25-28R; CANR 1, 35; CDALB 1929-1941; DLB 7, 9; DLBD 2; MTCW; SATA 9

Steinem, Gloria 1934- . . . . CLC 63
See also CA 53-56; CANR 28, 51; MTCW

Steiner, George
1929- . . . . CLC 24; DAM NOV
See also CA 73-76; CANR 31; DLB 67; MTCW; SATA 62

Steiner, K. Leslie
See Delany, Samuel R(ay, Jr.)

Steiner, Rudolf 1861-1925 . . . . TCLC 13
See also CA 107

Stendhal
1783-1842 . . . . NCLC 23, 46; DA; DAB; DAC; DAM MST, NOV; SSC 27; WLC
See also DLB 119

Stephen, Leslie 1832-1904 . . . . TCLC 23
See also CA 123; DLB 57, 144

Stephen, Sir Leslie
See Stephen, Leslie

Stephen, Virginia
See Woolf, (Adeline) Virginia

Stephens, James 1882(?)-1950 . . . . . . TCLC 4
See also CA 104; DLB 19, 153, 162

Stephens, Reed
See Donaldson, Stephen R.

Steptoe, Lydia
See Barnes, Djuna

Sterchi, Beat 1949- . . . . CLC 65

Sterling, Brett
See Bradbury, Ray (Douglas); Hamilton, Edmond

Sterling, Bruce 1954- . . . . CLC 72
See also CA 119; CANR 44

Sterling, George 1869-1926 . . . . TCLC 20
See also CA 117; DLB 54

Stern, Gerald 1925- . . . . CLC 40, 100
See also CA 81-84; CANR 28; DLB 105

Stern, Richard (Gustave) 1928- . . . CLC 4, 39
See also CA 1-4R; CANR 1, 25, 52; DLBY 87; INT CANR-25

Sternberg, Josef von 1894-1969 . . . . . CLC 20
See also CA 81-84

Sterne, Laurence
1713-1768 . . . . . . LC 2; DA; DAB; DAC; DAM MST, NOV; WLC
See also CDBLB 1660-1789; DLB 39

Sternheim, (William Adolf) Carl
1878-1942 . . . . TCLC 8
See also CA 105; DLB 56, 118

Stevens, Mark 1951- . . . . CLC 34
See also CA 122

Stevens, Wallace
1879-1955 . . . . TCLC 3, 12, 45; DA; DAB; DAC; DAM MST, POET; PC 6; WLC
See also CA 104; 124; CDALB 1929-1941; DLB 54; MTCW

Stevenson, Anne (Katharine)
1933- . . . . CLC 7, 33
See also CA 17-20R; CAAS 9; CANR 9, 33; DLB 40; MTCW

Stevenson, Robert Louis (Balfour)
1850-1894 . . . . NCLC 5, 14, 63; DA; DAB; DAC; DAM MST, NOV; SSC 11; WLC
See also CDBLB 1890-1914; CLR 10, 11; DLB 18, 57, 141, 156, 174; DLBD 13; JRDA; MAICYA; YABC 2

Stewart, J(ohn) I(nnes) M(ackintosh)
1906-1994 . . . . CLC 7, 14, 32
See also CA 85-88; 147; CAAS 3; CANR 47; MTCW

Stewart, Mary (Florence Elinor)
1916- . . . . CLC 7, 35; DAB
See also CA 1-4R; CANR 1, 59; SATA 12

Stewart, Mary Rainbow
See Stewart, Mary (Florence Elinor)

Stifle, June
See Campbell, Maria

Stifter, Adalbert
1805-1868 . . . . NCLC 41; SSC 28
See also DLB 133

Still, James 1906- . . . . CLC 49
See also CA 65-68; CAAS 17; CANR 10, 26; DLB 9; SATA 29

Sting
See Sumner, Gordon Matthew

Stirling, Arthur
See Sinclair, Upton (Beall)

Stitt, Milan 1941- . . . . CLC 29
See also CA 69-72

Stockton, Francis Richard 1834-1902
See Stockton, Frank R.
See also CA 108; 137; MAICYA; SATA 44

Stockton, Frank R. . . . . TCLC 47
See also Stockton, Francis Richard
See also DLB 42, 74; DLBD 13; SATA-Brief 32

Stoddard, Charles
See Kuttner, Henry

Stoker, Abraham 1847-1912
See Stoker, Bram
See also CA 105; DA; DAC; DAM MST, NOV; SATA 29

Stoker, Bram
1847-1912 . . . . TCLC 8; DAB; WLC
See also Stoker, Abraham
See also CA 150; CDBLB 1890-1914; DLB 36, 70, 178

Stolz, Mary (Slattery) 1920- . . . . CLC 12
See also AAYA 8; AITN 1; CA 5-8R; CANR 13, 41; JRDA; MAICYA; SAAS 3; SATA 10, 71

Stone, Irving
1903-1989 . . . . CLC 7; DAM POP
See also AITN 1; CA 1-4R; 129; CAAS 3; CANR 1, 23; INT CANR-23; MTCW; SATA 3; SATA-Obit 64

Stone, Oliver (William) 1946- . . . . . . CLC 73
See also AAYA 15; CA 110; CANR 55

Stone, Robert (Anthony)
    1937- . . . . **CLC 5, 23, 42**
    See also CA 85-88; CANR 23; DLB 152;
    INT CANR-23; MTCW

Stone, Zachary
    See Follett, Ken(neth Martin)

Stoppard, Tom
    1937- . . . . . . **CLC 1, 3, 4, 5, 8, 15, 29, 34,**
      63, 91; DA; DAB; DAC; DAM DRAM,
            MST; DC 6; WLC
    See also CA 81-84; CANR 39;
    CDBLB 1960 to Present; DLB 13;
    DLBY 85; MTCW

Storey, David (Malcolm)
    1933- . . . . . **CLC 2, 4, 5, 8; DAM DRAM**
    See also CA 81-84; CANR 36; DLB 13, 14;
    MTCW

Storm, Hyemeyohsts
    1935- . . . . **CLC 3; DAM MULT**
    See also CA 81-84; CANR 45; NNAL

Storm, (Hans) Theodor (Woldsen)
    1817-1888 . . . . **NCLC 1; SSC 27**

Storni, Alfonsina
    1892-1938 . . . . . **TCLC 5; DAM MULT;**
                  HLC
    See also CA 104; 131; HW

Stoughton, William 1631-1701 . . . . . . **LC 38**
    See also DLB 24

Stout, Rex (Todhunter) 1886-1975 . . . **CLC 3**
    See also AITN 2; CA 61-64

Stow, (Julian) Randolph 1935- . . **CLC 23, 48**
    See also CA 13-16R; CANR 33; MTCW

Stowe, Harriet (Elizabeth) Beecher
    1811-1896 . . . . . **NCLC 3, 50; DA; DAB;**
         DAC; DAM MST, NOV; WLC
    See also CDALB 1865-1917; DLB 1, 12, 42,
    74; JRDA; MAICYA; YABC 1

Strachey, (Giles) Lytton
    1880-1932 . . . . **TCLC 12**
    See also CA 110; DLB 149; DLBD 10

Strand, Mark
    1934- . . **CLC 6, 18, 41, 71; DAM POET**
    See also CA 21-24R; CANR 40; DLB 5;
    SATA 41

Straub, Peter (Francis)
    1943- . . . . **CLC 28; DAM POP**
    See also BEST 89:1; CA 85-88; CANR 28;
    DLBY 84; MTCW

Strauss, Botho 1944- . . . . **CLC 22**
    See also CA 157; DLB 124

Streatfeild, (Mary) Noel
    1895(?)-1986 . . . . **CLC 21**
    See also CA 81-84; 120; CANR 31;
    CLR 17; DLB 160; MAICYA; SATA 20;
    SATA-Obit 48

Stribling, T(homas) S(igismund)
    1881-1965 . . . . **CLC 23**
    See also CA 107; DLB 9

Strindberg, (Johan) August
    1849-1912 . . . . . . **TCLC 1, 8, 21, 47; DA;**
      DAB; DAC; DAM DRAM, MST; WLC
    See also CA 104; 135

Stringer, Arthur 1874-1950 . . . . **TCLC 37**
    See also DLB 92

Stringer, David
    See Roberts, Keith (John Kingston)

Stroheim, Erich von 1885-1957 . . . . **TCLC 71**

Strugatskii, Arkadii (Natanovich)
    1925-1991 . . . . **CLC 27**
    See also CA 106; 135

Strugatskii, Boris (Natanovich)
    1933- . . . . **CLC 27**
    See also CA 106

Strummer, Joe 1953(?)- . . . . **CLC 30**

Stuart, Don A.
    See Campbell, John W(ood, Jr.)

Stuart, Ian
    See MacLean, Alistair (Stuart)

Stuart, Jesse (Hilton)
    1906-1984 . . . . **CLC 1, 8, 11, 14, 34**
    See also CA 5-8R; 112; CANR 31; DLB 9,
    48, 102; DLBY 84; SATA 2;
    SATA-Obit 36

Sturgeon, Theodore (Hamilton)
    1918-1985 . . . . **CLC 22, 39**
    See also Queen, Ellery
    See also CA 81-84; 116; CANR 32; DLB 8;
    DLBY 85; MTCW

Sturges, Preston 1898-1959 . . . . . . **TCLC 48**
    See also CA 114; 149; DLB 26

Styron, William
    1925- . . . . **CLC 1, 3, 5, 11, 15, 60;**
            DAM NOV, POP; SSC 25
    See also BEST 90:4; CA 5-8R; CANR 6, 33;
    CDALB 1968-1988; DLB 2, 143;
    DLBY 80; INT CANR-6; MTCW

Suarez Lynch, B.
    See Bioy Casares, Adolfo; Borges, Jorge
    Luis

Su Chien 1884-1918
    See Su Man-shu
    See also CA 123

Suckow, Ruth 1892-1960 . . . . **SSC 18**
    See also CA 113; DLB 9, 102

Sudermann, Hermann 1857-1928 . . **TCLC 15**
    See also CA 107; DLB 118

Sue, Eugene 1804-1857 . . . . **NCLC 1**
    See also DLB 119

Sueskind, Patrick 1949- . . . . **CLC 44**
    See also Suskind, Patrick

Sukenick, Ronald 1932- . . . . . **CLC 3, 4, 6, 48**
    See also CA 25-28R; CAAS 8; CANR 32;
    DLB 173; DLBY 81

Suknaski, Andrew 1942- . . . . **CLC 19**
    See also CA 101; DLB 53

Sullivan, Vernon
    See Vian, Boris

Sully Prudhomme 1839-1907 . . . . . . **TCLC 31**

Su Man-shu . . . . **TCLC 24**
    See also Su Chien

Summerforest, Ivy B.
    See Kirkup, James

Summers, Andrew James 1942- . . . . . **CLC 26**

Summers, Andy
    See Summers, Andrew James

Summers, Hollis (Spurgeon, Jr.)
    1916- . . . . **CLC 10**
    See also CA 5-8R; CANR 3; DLB 6

Summers, (Alphonsus Joseph-Mary Augustus)
    Montague 1880-1948 . . . . **TCLC 16**
    See also CA 118

Sumner, Gordon Matthew 1951- . . . . **CLC 26**

Surtees, Robert Smith
    1803-1864 . . . . **NCLC 14**
    See also DLB 21

Susann, Jacqueline 1921-1974 . . . . **CLC 3**
    See also AITN 1; CA 65-68; 53-56; MTCW

Su Shih 1036-1101 . . . . **CMLC 15**

Suskind, Patrick
    See Sueskind, Patrick
    See also CA 145

Sutcliff, Rosemary
    1920-1992 . . . . **CLC 26; DAB; DAC;**
              DAM MST, POP
    See also AAYA 10; CA 5-8R; 139;
    CANR 37; CLR 1, 37; JRDA; MAICYA;
    SATA 6, 44, 78; SATA-Obit 73

Sutro, Alfred 1863-1933 . . . . **TCLC 6**
    See also CA 105; DLB 10

Sutton, Henry
    See Slavitt, David R(ytman)

Svevo, Italo
    1861-1928 . . . . **TCLC 2, 35; SSC 25**
    See also Schmitz, Aron Hector

Swados, Elizabeth (A.) 1951- . . . . **CLC 12**
    See also CA 97-100; CANR 49; INT 97-100

Swados, Harvey 1920-1972 . . . . **CLC 5**
    See also CA 5-8R; 37-40R; CANR 6;
    DLB 2

Swan, Gladys 1934- . . . . **CLC 69**
    See also CA 101; CANR 17, 39

Swarthout, Glendon (Fred)
    1918-1992 . . . . **CLC 35**
    See also CA 1-4R; 139; CANR 1, 47;
    SATA 26

Sweet, Sarah C.
    See Jewett, (Theodora) Sarah Orne

Swenson, May
    1919-1989 . . . . . **CLC 4, 14, 61; DA; DAB;**
          DAC; DAM MST, POET; PC 14
    See also CA 5-8R; 130; CANR 36, 61;
    DLB 5; MTCW; SATA 15

Swift, Augustus
    See Lovecraft, H(oward) P(hillips)

Swift, Graham (Colin) 1949- . . . . **CLC 41, 88**
    See also CA 117; 122; CANR 46

Swift, Jonathan
    1667-1745 . . . . . . **LC 1; DA; DAB; DAC;**
      ·**DAM MST, NOV, POET; PC 9; WLC**
    See also CDBLB 1660-1789; DLB 39, 95,
    101; SATA 19

Swinburne, Algernon Charles
    1837-1909 . . . . . . **TCLC 8, 36; DA; DAB;**
        DAC; DAM MST, POET; WLC
    See also CA 105; 140; CDBLB 1832-1890;
    DLB 35, 57

Swinfen, Ann . . . . **CLC 34**

Swinnerton, Frank Arthur
    1884-1982 . . . . **CLC 31**
    See also CA 108; DLB 34

Swithen, John
    See King, Stephen (Edwin)

Sylvia
  See Ashton-Warner, Sylvia (Constance)

Symmes, Robert Edward
  See Duncan, Robert (Edward)

Symonds, John Addington
  1840-1893 .... **NCLC 34**
  See also DLB 57, 144

Symons, Arthur 1865-1945 .... **TCLC 11**
  See also CA 107; DLB 19, 57, 149

Symons, Julian (Gustave)
  1912-1994 .... **CLC 2, 14, 32**
  See also CA 49-52; 147; CAAS 3; CANR 3,
  33, 59; DLB 87, 155; DLBY 92; MTCW

Synge, (Edmund) J(ohn) M(illington)
  1871-1909 .... **TCLC 6, 37;**
                            DAM DRAM; DC 2
  See also CA 104; 141; CDBLB 1890-1914;
  DLB 10, 19

Syruc, J.
  See Milosz, Czeslaw

Szirtes, George 1948- .... **CLC 46**
  See also CA 109; CANR 27, 61

Szymborska, Wislawa 1923- .... **CLC 99**
  See also CA 154; DLBY 96

T. O., Nik
  See Annensky, Innokenty (Fyodorovich)

Tabori, George 1914- .... **CLC 19**
  See also CA 49-52; CANR 4

Tagore, Rabindranath
  1861-1941 .... **TCLC 3, 53;**
                         DAM DRAM, POET; PC 8
  See also CA 104; 120; MTCW

Taine, Hippolyte Adolphe
  1828-1893 .... **NCLC 15**

Talese, Gay 1932- .... **CLC 37**
  See also AITN 1; CA 1-4R; CANR 9, 58;
  INT CANR-9; MTCW

Tallent, Elizabeth (Ann) 1954- ..... **CLC 45**
  See also CA 117; DLB 130

Tally, Ted 1952- .... **CLC 42**
  See also CA 120; 124; INT 124

Tamayo y Baus, Manuel
  1829-1898 .... **NCLC 1**

Tammsaare, A(nton) H(ansen)
  1878-1940 .... **TCLC 27**

Tam'si, Tchicaya U
  See Tchicaya, Gerald Felix

Tan, Amy (Ruth)
  1952- .... **CLC 59; DAM MULT, NOV,**
                                      POP
  See also AAYA 9; BEST 89:3; CA 136;
  CANR 54; DLB 173; SATA 75

Tandem, Felix
  See Spitteler, Carl (Friedrich Georg)

Tanizaki, Jun'ichiro
  1886-1965 ...... **CLC 8, 14, 28; SSC 21**
  See also CA 93-96; 25-28R; DLB 180

Tanner, William
  See Amis, Kingsley (William)

Tao Lao
  See Storni, Alfonsina

Tarassoff, Lev
  See Troyat, Henri

Tarbell, Ida M(inerva)
  1857-1944 .... **TCLC 40**
  See also CA 122; DLB 47

Tarkington, (Newton) Booth
  1869-1946 .... **TCLC 9**
  See also CA 110; 143; DLB 9, 102;
  SATA 17

Tarkovsky, Andrei (Arsenyevich)
  1932-1986 .... **CLC 75**
  See also CA 127

Tartt, Donna 1964(?)- .... **CLC 76**
  See also CA 142

Tasso, Torquato 1544-1595 .... **LC 5**

Tate, (John Orley) Allen
  1899-1979 .... **CLC 2, 4, 6, 9, 11, 14, 24**
  See also CA 5-8R; 85-88; CANR 32;
  DLB 4, 45, 63; MTCW

Tate, Ellalice
  See Hibbert, Eleanor Alice Burford

Tate, James (Vincent) 1943- ... **CLC 2, 6, 25**
  See also CA 21-24R; CANR 29, 57; DLB 5,
  169

Tavel, Ronald 1940- .... **CLC 6**
  See also CA 21-24R; CANR 33

Taylor, C(ecil) P(hilip) 1929-1981... **CLC 27**
  See also CA 25-28R; 105; CANR 47

Taylor, Edward
  1642(?)-1729 .... **LC 11; DA; DAB;**
                          DAC; DAM MST, POET
  See also DLB 24

Taylor, Eleanor Ross 1920- .... **CLC 5**
  See also CA 81-84

Taylor, Elizabeth 1912-1975 ... **CLC 2, 4, 29**
  See also CA 13-16R; CANR 9; DLB 139;
  MTCW; SATA 13

Taylor, Henry (Splawn) 1942- ...... **CLC 44**
  See also CA 33-36R; CAAS 7; CANR 31;
  DLB 5

Taylor, Kamala (Purnaiya) 1924-
  See Markandaya, Kamala
  See also CA 77-80

Taylor, Mildred D. .... **CLC 21**
  See also AAYA 10; BW 1; CA 85-88;
  CANR 25; CLR 9; DLB 52; JRDA;
  MAICYA; SAAS 5; SATA 15, 70

Taylor, Peter (Hillsman)
  1917-1994 ..... **CLC 1, 4, 18, 37, 44, 50,**
                                  71; SSC 10
  See also CA 13-16R; 147; CANR 9, 50;
  DLBY 81, 94; INT CANR-9; MTCW

Taylor, Robert Lewis 1912- .... **CLC 14**
  See also CA 1-4R; CANR 3; SATA 10

Tchekhov, Anton
  See Chekhov, Anton (Pavlovich)

Tchicaya, Gerald Felix
  1931-1988 .... **CLC 101**
  See also CA 129; 125

Tchicaya U Tam'si
  See Tchicaya, Gerald Felix

Teasdale, Sara 1884-1933........... **TCLC 4**
  See also CA 104; DLB 45; SATA 32

Tegner, Esaias 1782-1846........ **NCLC 2**

Teilhard de Chardin, (Marie Joseph) Pierre
  1881-1955 .... **TCLC 9**
  See also CA 105

Temple, Ann
  See Mortimer, Penelope (Ruth)

Tennant, Emma (Christina)
  1937- .... **CLC 13, 52**
  See also CA 65-68; CAAS 9; CANR 10, 38,
  59; DLB 14

Tenneshaw, S. M.
  See Silverberg, Robert

Tennyson, Alfred
  1809-1892 ...... **NCLC 30; DA; DAB;**
            DAC; DAM MST, POET; PC 6; WLC
  See also CDBLB 1832-1890; DLB 32

Teran, Lisa St. Aubin de .... **CLC 36**
  See also St. Aubin de Teran, Lisa

Terence
  195(?)B.C.-159B.C..... **CMLC 14; DC 7**

Teresa de Jesus, St. 1515-1582...... **LC 18**

Terkel, Louis 1912-
  See Terkel, Studs
  See also CA 57-60; CANR 18, 45; MTCW

Terkel, Studs .... **CLC 38**
  See also Terkel, Louis
  See also AITN 1

Terry, C. V.
  See Slaughter, Frank G(ill)

Terry, Megan 1932- .... **CLC 19**
  See also CA 77-80; CABS 3; CANR 43;
  DLB 7

Tertz, Abram
  See Sinyavsky, Andrei (Donatevich)

Tesich, Steve 1943(?)-1996...... **CLC 40, 69**
  See also CA 105; 152; DLBY 83

Teternikov, Fyodor Kuzmich 1863-1927
  See Sologub, Fyodor
  See also CA 104

Tevis, Walter 1928-1984 .... **CLC 42**
  See also CA 113

Tey, Josephine................... **TCLC 14**
  See also Mackintosh, Elizabeth
  See also DLB 77

Thackeray, William Makepeace
  1811-1863 .... **NCLC 5, 14, 22, 43; DA;**
              DAB; DAC; DAM MST, NOV; WLC
  See also CDBLB 1832-1890; DLB 21, 55,
  159, 163; SATA 23

Thakura, Ravindranatha
  See Tagore, Rabindranath

Tharoor, Shashi 1956- .... **CLC 70**
  See also CA 141

Thelwell, Michael Miles 1939- ..... **CLC 22**
  See also BW 2; CA 101

Theobald, Lewis, Jr.
  See Lovecraft, H(oward) P(hillips)

Theodorescu, Ion N. 1880-1967
  See Arghezi, Tudor
  See also CA 116

Theriault, Yves
  1915-1983 .. **CLC 79; DAC; DAM MST**
  See also CA 102; DLB 88

Theroux, Alexander (Louis)
  1939- .... **CLC 2, 25**
  See also CA 85-88; CANR 20

Theroux, Paul (Edward)
1941- .... **CLC 5, 8, 11, 15, 28, 46;
DAM POP**
See also BEST 89:4; CA 33-36R; CANR 20,
45; DLB 2; MTCW; SATA 44

Thesen, Sharon 1946-............ **CLC 56**

Thevenin, Denis
See Duhamel, Georges

Thibault, Jacques Anatole Francois
1844-1924
See France, Anatole
See also CA 106; 127; DAM NOV; MTCW

Thiele, Colin (Milton) 1920- .... **CLC 17**
See also CA 29-32R; CANR 12, 28, 53;
CLR 27; MAICYA; SAAS 2; SATA 14,
72

Thomas, Audrey (Callahan)
1935- .... **CLC 7, 13, 37; SSC 20**
See also AITN 2; CA 21-24R; CAAS 19;
CANR 36, 58; DLB 60; MTCW

Thomas, D(onald) M(ichael)
1935- .... **CLC 13, 22, 31**
See also CA 61-64; CAAS 11; CANR 17,
45; CDBLB 1960 to Present; DLB 40;
INT CANR-17; MTCW

Thomas, Dylan (Marlais)
1914-1953 ... **TCLC 1, 8, 45; DA; DAB;
DAC; DAM DRAM, MST, POET;
PC 2; SSC 3; WLC**
See also CA 104; 120; CDBLB 1945-1960;
DLB 13, 20, 139; MTCW; SATA 60

Thomas, (Philip) Edward
1878-1917 ...... **TCLC 10; DAM POET**
See also CA 106; 153; DLB 19

Thomas, Joyce Carol 1938-........ **CLC 35**
See also AAYA 12; BW 2; CA 113; 116;
CANR 48; CLR 19; DLB 33; INT 116;
JRDA; MAICYA; MTCW; SAAS 7;
SATA 40, 78

Thomas, Lewis 1913-1993 .... **CLC 35**
See also CA 85-88; 143; CANR 38, 60;
MTCW

Thomas, Paul
See Mann, (Paul) Thomas

Thomas, Piri 1928-............... **CLC 17**
See also CA 73-76; HW

Thomas, R(onald) S(tuart)
1913- .... **CLC 6, 13, 48; DAB;
DAM POET**
See also CA 89-92; CAAS 4; CANR 30;
CDBLB 1960 to Present; DLB 27;
MTCW

Thomas, Ross (Elmore) 1926-1995 .. **CLC 39**
See also CA 33-36R; 150; CANR 22

Thompson, Francis Clegg
See Mencken, H(enry) L(ouis)

Thompson, Francis Joseph
1859-1907 .... **TCLC 4**
See also CA 104; CDBLB 1890-1914;
DLB 19

Thompson, Hunter S(tockton)
1939- ... **CLC 9, 17, 40, 104; DAM POP**
See also BEST 89:1; CA 17-20R; CANR 23,
46; MTCW

Thompson, James Myers
See Thompson, Jim (Myers)

Thompson, Jim (Myers)
1906-1977(?) .... **CLC 69**
See also CA 140

Thompson, Judith .... **CLC 39**

Thomson, James
1700-1748 .. **LC 16, 29, 40; DAM POET**
See also DLB 95

Thomson, James
1834-1882 ..... **NCLC 18; DAM POET**
See also DLB 35

Thoreau, Henry David
1817-1862 .... **NCLC 7, 21, 61; DA;
DAB; DAC; DAM MST; WLC**
See also CDALB 1640-1865; DLB 1

Thornton, Hall
See Silverberg, Robert

Thucydides c. 455B.C.-399B.C.... **CMLC 17**
See also DLB 176

Thurber, James (Grover)
1894-1961 .... **CLC 5, 11, 25; DA; DAB;
DAC; DAM DRAM, MST, NOV; SSC 1**
See also CA 73-76; CANR 17, 39;
CDALB 1929-1941; DLB 4, 11, 22, 102;
MAICYA; MTCW; SATA 13

Thurman, Wallace (Henry)
1902-1934 .... **TCLC 6; BLC;
DAM MULT**
See also BW 1; CA 104; 124; DLB 51

Ticheburn, Cheviot
See Ainsworth, William Harrison

Tieck, (Johann) Ludwig
1773-1853 .... **NCLC 5, 46**
See also DLB 90

Tiger, Derry
See Ellison, Harlan (Jay)

Tilghman, Christopher 1948(?)-..... **CLC 65**
See also CA 159

Tillinghast, Richard (Williford)
1940- .... **CLC 29**
See also CA 29-32R; CAAS 23; CANR 26,
51

Timrod, Henry 1828-1867 .... **NCLC 25**
See also DLB 3

Tindall, Gillian 1938-............... **CLC 7**
See also CA 21-24R; CANR 11

Tiptree, James, Jr. .... **CLC 48, 50**
See also Sheldon, Alice Hastings Bradley
See also DLB 8

Titmarsh, Michael Angelo
See Thackeray, William Makepeace

**Tocqueville, Alexis (Charles Henri Maurice
Clerel Comte)**
1805-1859 .... **NCLC 7, 63**

Tolkien, J(ohn) R(onald) R(euel)
1892-1973 .... **CLC 1, 2, 3, 8, 12, 38;
DA; DAB; DAC; DAM MST, NOV,
POP; WLC**
See also AAYA 10; AITN 1; CA 17-18;
45-48; CANR 36; CAP 2;
CDBLB 1914-1945; DLB 15, 160; JRDA;
MAICYA; MTCW; SATA 2, 32;
SATA-Obit 24

Toller, Ernst 1893-1939 .... **TCLC 10**
See also CA 107; DLB 124

Tolson, M. B.
See Tolson, Melvin B(eaunorus)

Tolson, Melvin B(eaunorus)
1898(?)-1966 .... **CLC 36; BLC;
DAM MULT, POET**
See also BW 1; CA 124; 89-92; DLB 48, 76

Tolstoi, Aleksei Nikolaevich
See Tolstoy, Alexey Nikolaevich

Tolstoy, Alexey Nikolaevich
1882-1945 .... **TCLC 18**
See also CA 107; 158

Tolstoy, Count Leo
See Tolstoy, Leo (Nikolaevich)

Tolstoy, Leo (Nikolaevich)
1828-1910 ...... **TCLC 4, 11, 17, 28, 44;
DA; DAB; DAC; DAM MST, NOV;
SSC 9; WLC**
See also CA 104; 123; SATA 26

Tomasi di Lampedusa, Giuseppe 1896-1957
See Lampedusa, Giuseppe (Tomasi) di
See also CA 111

Tomlin, Lily...................... **CLC 17**
See also Tomlin, Mary Jean

Tomlin, Mary Jean 1939(?)-
See Tomlin, Lily
See also CA 117

Tomlinson, (Alfred) Charles
1927- .... **CLC 2, 4, 6, 13, 45;
DAM POET; PC 17**
See also CA 5-8R; CANR 33; DLB 40

Tomlinson, H(enry) M(ajor)
1873-1958 .... **TCLC 71**
See also CA 118; DLB 36, 100

Tonson, Jacob
See Bennett, (Enoch) Arnold

Toole, John Kennedy
1937-1969 .... **CLC 19, 64**
See also CA 104; DLBY 81

Toomer, Jean
1894-1967 ...... **CLC 1, 4, 13, 22; BLC;
DAM MULT; PC 7; SSC 1; WLCS**
See also BW 1; CA 85-88;
CDALB 1917-1929; DLB 45, 51; MTCW

Torley, Luke
See Blish, James (Benjamin)

Tornimparte, Alessandra
See Ginzburg, Natalia

Torre, Raoul della
See Mencken, H(enry) L(ouis)

Torrey, E(dwin) Fuller 1937-....... **CLC 34**
See also CA 119

Torsvan, Ben Traven
See Traven, B.

Torsvan, Benno Traven
See Traven, B.

Torsvan, Berick Traven
See Traven, B.

Torsvan, Berwick Traven
See Traven, B.

Torsvan, Bruno Traven
See Traven, B.

Torsvan, Traven
See Traven, B.

Vidal, Gore
1925- ..... CLC 2, 4, 6, 8, 10, 22, 33, 72;
DAM NOV, POP
See also AITN 1; BEST 90:2; CA 5-8R;
CANR 13, 45; DLB 6, 152;
INT CANR-13; MTCW

Viereck, Peter (Robert Edwin)
1916- .... CLC 4
See also CA 1-4R; CANR 1, 47; DLB 5

Vigny, Alfred (Victor) de
1797-1863 ...... NCLC 7; DAM POET
See also DLB 119

Vilakazi, Benedict Wallet
1906-1947 .... TCLC 37

Villiers de l'Isle Adam, Jean Marie Mathias Philippe Auguste Comte
1838-1889 .... NCLC 3; SSC 14
See also DLB 123

Villon, Francois 1431-1463(?) .... PC 13

Vinci, Leonardo da 1452-1519...... LC 12

Vine, Barbara .... CLC 50
See also Rendell, Ruth (Barbara)
See also BEST 90:4

Vinge, Joan D(ennison)
1948- .... CLC 30; SSC 24
See also CA 93-96; SATA 36

Violis, G.
See Simenon, Georges (Jacques Christian)

Visconti, Luchino 1906-1976....... CLC 16
See also CA 81-84; 65-68; CANR 39

Vittorini, Elio 1908-1966...... CLC 6, 9, 14
See also CA 133; 25-28R

Vizenor, Gerald Robert
1934- .... CLC 103; DAM MULT
See also CA 13-16R; CAAS 22; CANR 5,
21, 44; DLB 175; NNAL

Vizinczey, Stephen 1933-.......... CLC 40
See also CA 128; INT 128

Vliet, R(ussell) G(ordon)
1929-1984 .... CLC 22
See also CA 37-40R; 112; CANR 18

Vogau, Boris Andreyevich 1894-1937(?)
See Pilnyak, Boris
See also CA 123

Vogel, Paula A(nne) 1951-......... CLC 76
See also CA 108

Voight, Ellen Bryant 1943-........ CLC 54
See also CA 69-72; CANR 11, 29, 55;
DLB 120

Voigt, Cynthia 1942- .... CLC 30
See also AAYA 3; CA 106; CANR 18, 37,
40; CLR 13; INT CANR-18; JRDA;
MAICYA; SATA 48, 79; SATA-Brief 33

Voinovich, Vladimir (Nikolaevich)
1932- .... CLC 10, 49
See also CA 81-84; CAAS 12; CANR 33;
MTCW

Vollmann, William T.
1959- ...... CLC 89; DAM NOV, POP
See also CA 134

Voloshinov, V. N.
See Bakhtin, Mikhail Mikhailovich

Voltaire
1694-1778 ..... LC 14; DA; DAB; DAC;
DAM DRAM, MST; SSC 12; WLC

von Daeniken, Erich 1935- .... CLC 30
See also AITN 1; CA 37-40R; CANR 17,
44

von Daniken, Erich
See von Daeniken, Erich

von Heidenstam, (Carl Gustaf) Verner
See Heidenstam, (Carl Gustaf) Verner von

von Heyse, Paul (Johann Ludwig)
See Heyse, Paul (Johann Ludwig von)

von Hofmannsthal, Hugo
See Hofmannsthal, Hugo von

von Horvath, Odon
See Horvath, Oedoen von

von Horvath, Oedoen
See Horvath, Oedoen von

von Liliencron, (Friedrich Adolf Axel) Detlev
See Liliencron, (Friedrich Adolf Axel)
Detlev von

Vonnegut, Kurt, Jr.
1922- ...... CLC 1, 2, 3, 4, 5, 8, 12, 22,
40, 60; DA; DAB; DAC; DAM MST,
NOV, POP; SSC 8; WLC
See also AAYA 6; AITN 1; BEST 90:4;
CA 1-4R; CANR 1, 25, 49;
CDALB 1968-1988; DLB 2, 8, 152;
DLBD 3; DLBY 80; MTCW

Von Rachen, Kurt
See Hubbard, L(afayette) Ron(ald)

von Rezzori (d'Arezzo), Gregor
See Rezzori (d'Arezzo), Gregor von

von Sternberg, Josef
See Sternberg, Josef von

Vorster, Gordon 1924-............ CLC 34
See also CA 133

Vosce, Trudie
See Ozick, Cynthia

Voznesensky, Andrei (Andreievich)
1933- ...... CLC 1, 15, 57; DAM POET
See also CA 89-92; CANR 37; MTCW

Waddington, Miriam 1917-........ CLC 28
See also CA 21-24R; CANR 12, 30;
DLB 68

Wagman, Fredrica 1937-........... CLC 7
See also CA 97-100; INT 97-100

Wagner, Linda W.
See Wagner-Martin, Linda (C.)

Wagner, Linda Welshimer
See Wagner-Martin, Linda (C.)

Wagner, Richard 1813-1883....... NCLC 9
See also DLB 129

Wagner-Martin, Linda (C.) 1936-... CLC 50
See also CA 159

Wagoner, David (Russell)
1926- .... CLC 3, 5, 15
See also CA 1-4R; CAAS 3; CANR 2;
DLB 5; SATA 14

Wah, Fred(erick James) 1939-...... CLC 44
See also CA 107; 141; DLB 60

Wahloo, Per 1926-1975 .... CLC 7
See also CA 61-64

Wahloo, Peter
See Wahloo, Per

Wain, John (Barrington)
1925-1994 .... CLC 2, 11, 15, 46
See also CA 5-8R; 145; CAAS 4; CANR 23,
54; CDBLB 1960 to Present; DLB 15, 27,
139, 155; MTCW

Wajda, Andrzej 1926-............. CLC 16
See also CA 102

Wakefield, Dan 1932-.............. CLC 7
See also CA 21-24R; CAAS 7

Wakoski, Diane
1937- .... CLC 2, 4, 7, 9, 11, 40;
DAM POET; PC 15
See also CA 13-16R; CAAS 1; CANR 9, 60;
DLB 5; INT CANR-9

Wakoski-Sherbell, Diane
See Wakoski, Diane

Walcott, Derek (Alton)
1930- .... CLC 2, 4, 9, 14, 25, 42, 67, 76;
BLC; DAB; DAC; DAM MST, MULT,
POET; DC 7
See also BW 2; CA 89-92; CANR 26, 47;
DLB 117; DLBY 81; MTCW

Waldman, Anne 1945- .... CLC 7
See also CA 37-40R; CAAS 17; CANR 34;
DLB 16

Waldo, E. Hunter
See Sturgeon, Theodore (Hamilton)

Waldo, Edward Hamilton
See Sturgeon, Theodore (Hamilton)

Walker, Alice (Malsenior)
1944- .... CLC 5, 6, 9, 19, 27, 46, 58,
103; BLC; DA; DAB; DAC; DAM MST,
MULT, NOV, POET, POP; SSC 5;
WLCS
See also AAYA 3; BEST 89:4; BW 2;
CA 37-40R; CANR 9, 27, 49;
CDALB 1968-1988; DLB 6, 33, 143;
INT CANR-27; MTCW; SATA 31

Walker, David Harry 1911-1992.... CLC 14
See also CA 1-4R; 137; CANR 1; SATA 8;
SATA-Obit 71

Walker, Edward Joseph 1934-
See Walker, Ted
See also CA 21-24R; CANR 12, 28, 53

Walker, George F.
1947- .... CLC 44, 61; DAB; DAC;
DAM MST
See also CA 103; CANR 21, 43, 59;
DLB 60

Walker, Joseph A.
1935- .... CLC 19; DAM DRAM, MST
See also BW 1; CA 89-92; CANR 26;
DLB 38

Walker, Margaret (Abigail)
1915- .... CLC 1, 6; BLC; DAM MULT
See also BW 2; CA 73-76; CANR 26, 54;
DLB 76, 152; MTCW

Walker, Ted...................... CLC 13
See also Walker, Edward Joseph
See also DLB 40

Wallace, David Foster 1962-....... CLC 50
See also CA 132; CANR 59

Wallace, Dexter
See Masters, Edgar Lee

Wallace, (Richard Horatio) Edgar
1875-1932 .... **TCLC 57**
See also CA 115; DLB 70

Wallace, Irving
1916-1990 ..... **CLC 7, 13; DAM NOV,
POP**
See also AITN 1; CA 1-4R; 132; CAAS 1;
CANR 1, 27; INT CANR-27; MTCW

Wallant, Edward Lewis
1926-1962 .... **CLC 5, 10**
See also CA 1-4R; CANR 22; DLB 2, 28,
143; MTCW

Walley, Byron
See Card, Orson Scott

Walpole, Horace 1717-1797 .... **LC 2**
See also DLB 39, 104

Walpole, Hugh (Seymour)
1884-1941 .... **TCLC 5**
See also CA 104; DLB 34

Walser, Martin 1927- .... **CLC 27**
See also CA 57-60; CANR 8, 46; DLB 75,
124

Walser, Robert
1878-1956 .... **TCLC 18; SSC 20**
See also CA 118; DLB 66

Walsh, Jill Paton .... **CLC 35**
See also Paton Walsh, Gillian
See also AAYA 11; CLR 2; DLB 161;
SAAS 3

Walter, Villiam Christian
See Andersen, Hans Christian

Wambaugh, Joseph (Aloysius, Jr.)
1937- .... **CLC 3, 18; DAM NOV, POP**
See also AITN 1; BEST 89:3; CA 33-36R;
CANR 42; DLB 6; DLBY 83; MTCW

Wang Wei 699(?)-761(?) .... **PC 18**

Ward, Arthur Henry Sarsfield 1883-1959
See Rohmer, Sax
See also CA 108

Ward, Douglas Turner 1930- .... **CLC 19**
See also BW 1; CA 81-84; CANR 27;
DLB 7, 38

Ward, Mary Augusta
See Ward, Mrs. Humphry

Ward, Mrs. Humphry
1851-1920 .... **TCLC 55**
See also DLB 18

Ward, Peter
See Faust, Frederick (Schiller)

Warhol, Andy 1928(?)-1987 .... **CLC 20**
See also AAYA 12; BEST 89:4; CA 89-92;
121; CANR 34

Warner, Francis (Robert le Plastrier)
1937- .... **CLC 14**
See also CA 53-56; CANR 11

Warner, Marina 1946- .... **CLC 59**
See also CA 65-68; CANR 21, 55

Warner, Rex (Ernest) 1905-1986.... **CLC 45**
See also CA 89-92; 119; DLB 15

Warner, Susan (Bogert)
1819-1885 .... **NCLC 31**
See also DLB 3, 42

Warner, Sylvia (Constance) Ashton
See Ashton-Warner, Sylvia (Constance)

Warner, Sylvia Townsend
1893-1978 .... **CLC 7, 19; SSC 23**
See also CA 61-64; 77-80; CANR 16, 60;
DLB 34, 139; MTCW

Warren, Mercy Otis 1728-1814... **NCLC 13**
See also DLB 31

Warren, Robert Penn
1905-1989 .... **CLC 1, 4, 6, 8, 10, 13, 18,
39, 53, 59; DA; DAB; DAC; DAM MST,
NOV, POET; SSC 4; WLC**
See also AITN 1; CA 13-16R; 129;
CANR 10, 47; CDALB 1968-1988;
DLB 2, 48, 152; DLBY 80, 89;
INT CANR-10; MTCW; SATA 46;
SATA-Obit 63

Warshofsky, Isaac
See Singer, Isaac Bashevis

Warton, Thomas
1728-1790 .... **LC 15; DAM POET**
See also DLB 104, 109

Waruk, Kona
See Harris, (Theodore) Wilson

Warung, Price 1855-1911........ **TCLC 45**

Warwick, Jarvis
See Garner, Hugh

Washington, Alex
See Harris, Mark

Washington, Booker T(aliaferro)
1856-1915 .... **TCLC 10; BLC;
DAM MULT**
See also BW 1; CA 114; 125; SATA 28

Washington, George 1732-1799 ...... **LC 25**
See also DLB 31

Wassermann, (Karl) Jakob
1873-1934 .... **TCLC 6**
See also CA 104; DLB 66

Wasserstein, Wendy
1950- .... **CLC 32, 59, 90;
DAM DRAM; DC 4**
See also CA 121; 129; CABS 3; CANR 53;
INT 129; SATA 94

Waterhouse, Keith (Spencer)
1929- .... **CLC 47**
See also CA 5-8R; CANR 38; DLB 13, 15;
MTCW

Waters, Frank (Joseph)
1902-1995 .... **CLC 88**
See also CA 5-8R; 149; CAAS 13; CANR 3,
18; DLBY 86

Waters, Roger 1944- .... **CLC 35**

Watkins, Frances Ellen
See Harper, Frances Ellen Watkins

Watkins, Gerrold
See Malzberg, Barry N(athaniel)

Watkins, Gloria 1955(?)-
See hooks, bell
See also BW 2; CA 143

Watkins, Paul 1964- .... **CLC 55**
See also CA 132; CANR 62

Watkins, Vernon Phillips
1906-1967 .... **CLC 43**
See also CA 9-10; 25-28R; CAP 1; DLB 20

Watson, Irving S.
See Mencken, H(enry) L(ouis)

Watson, John H.
See Farmer, Philip Jose

Watson, Richard F.
See Silverberg, Robert

Waugh, Auberon (Alexander) 1939- .. **CLC 7**
See also CA 45-48; CANR 6, 22; DLB 14

Waugh, Evelyn (Arthur St. John)
1903-1966 ...... **CLC 1, 3, 8, 13, 19, 27,
44; DA; DAB; DAC; DAM MST, NOV,
POP; WLC**
See also CA 85-88; 25-28R; CANR 22;
CDBLB 1914-1945; DLB 15, 162; MTCW

Waugh, Harriet 1944- .... **CLC 6**
See also CA 85-88; CANR 22

Ways, C. R.
See Blount, Roy (Alton), Jr.

Waystaff, Simon
See Swift, Jonathan

Webb, (Martha) Beatrice (Potter)
1858-1943 .... **TCLC 22**
See also Potter, (Helen) Beatrix
See also CA 117

Webb, Charles (Richard) 1939- ...... **CLC 7**
See also CA 25-28R

Webb, James H(enry), Jr. 1946- .... **CLC 22**
See also CA 81-84

Webb, Mary (Gladys Meredith)
1881-1927 .... **TCLC 24**
See also CA 123; DLB 34

Webb, Mrs. Sidney
See Webb, (Martha) Beatrice (Potter)

Webb, Phyllis 1927- .... **CLC 18**
See also CA 104; CANR 23; DLB 53

Webb, Sidney (James)
1859-1947 .... **TCLC 22**
See also CA 117

Webber, Andrew Lloyd .... **CLC 21**
See also Lloyd Webber, Andrew

Weber, Lenora Mattingly
1895-1971 .... **CLC 12**
See also CA 19-20; 29-32R; CAP 1;
SATA 2; SATA-Obit 26

Weber, Max 1864-1920 .... **TCLC 69**
See also CA 109

Webster, John
1579(?)-1634(?) ...... **LC 33; DA; DAB;
DAC; DAM DRAM, MST; DC 2; WLC**
See also CDBLB Before 1660; DLB 58

Webster, Noah 1758-1843 .... **NCLC 30**

Wedekind, (Benjamin) Frank(lin)
1864-1918 ...... **TCLC 7; DAM DRAM**
See also CA 104; 153; DLB 118

Weidman, Jerome 1913- .... **CLC 7**
See also AITN 2; CA 1-4R; CANR 1;
DLB 28

Weil, Simone (Adolphine)
1909-1943 .... **TCLC 23**
See also CA 117; 159

Weinstein, Nathan
See West, Nathanael

Weinstein, Nathan von Wallenstein
See West, Nathanael

Weir, Peter (Lindsay) 1944- .... **CLC 20**
See also CA 113; 123

Whittemore, (Edward) Reed (Jr.)
  1919- .... **CLC 4**
  See also CA 9-12R; CAAS 8; CANR 4;
  DLB 5

Whittier, John Greenleaf
  1807-1892 .... **NCLC 8, 59**
  See also DLB 1

Whittlebot, Hernia
  See Coward, Noel (Peirce)

Wicker, Thomas Grey   1926-
  See Wicker, Tom
  See also CA 65-68; CANR 21, 46

Wicker, Tom .... **CLC 7**
  See also Wicker, Thomas Grey

Wideman, John Edgar
  1941- .... **CLC 5, 34, 36, 67; BLC;**
                            DAM MULT
  See also BW 2; CA 85-88; CANR 14, 42;
  DLB 33, 143

Wiebe, Rudy (Henry)
  1934- .... **CLC 6, 11, 14; DAC;**
                            DAM MST
  See also CA 37-40R; CANR 42; DLB 60

Wieland, Christoph Martin
  1733-1813 .... **NCLC 17**
  See also DLB 97

Wiene, Robert   1881-1938........ **TCLC 56**

Wieners, John   1934-.............. **CLC 7**
  See also CA 13-16R; DLB 16

Wiesel, Elie(zer)
  1928- ...... **CLC 3, 5, 11, 37; DA; DAB;**
                    DAC; DAM MST, NOV;
                    WLCS 2:855-57, 854
  See also AAYA 7; AITN 1; CA 5-8R;
  CAAS 4; CANR 8, 40; DLB 83;
  DLBY 87; INT CANR-8; MTCW;
  SATA 56

Wiggins, Marianne   1947-......... **CLC 57**
  See also BEST 89:3; CA 130; CANR 60

Wight, James Alfred   1916-
  See Herriot, James
  See also CA 77-80; SATA 55;
  SATA-Brief 44

Wilbur, Richard (Purdy)
  1921- ... **CLC 3, 6, 9, 14, 53; DA; DAB;**
                    DAC; DAM MST, POET
  See also CA 1-4R; CABS 2; CANR 2, 29;
  DLB 5, 169; INT CANR-29; MTCW;
  SATA 9

Wild, Peter   1940-............... **CLC 14**
  See also CA 37-40R; DLB 5

Wilde, Oscar (Fingal O'Flahertie Wills)
  1854(?)-1900 .... **TCLC 1, 8, 23, 41; DA;**
                    DAB; DAC; DAM DRAM, MST, NOV;
                    SSC 11; WLC
  See also CA 104; 119; CDBLB 1890-1914;
  DLB 10, 19, 34, 57, 141, 156; SATA 24

Wilder, Billy .... **CLC 20**
  See also Wilder, Samuel
  See also DLB 26

Wilder, Samuel   1906-
  See Wilder, Billy
  See also CA 89-92

Wilder, Thornton (Niven)
  1897-1975 ...... **CLC 1, 5, 6, 10, 15, 35,**
                    82; DA; DAB; DAC; DAM DRAM,
                    MST, NOV; DC 1; WLC
  See also AITN 2; CA 13-16R; 61-64;
  CANR 40; DLB 4, 7, 9; MTCW

Wilding, Michael   1942-........... **CLC 73**
  See also CA 104; CANR 24, 49

Wiley, Richard   1944-............. **CLC 44**
  See also CA 121; 129

Wilhelm, Kate .... **CLC 7**
  See also Wilhelm, Katie Gertrude
  See also AAYA 20; CAAS 5; DLB 8;
  INT CANR-17

Wilhelm, Katie Gertrude   1928-
  See Wilhelm, Kate
  See also CA 37-40R; CANR 17, 36, 60;
  MTCW

Wilkins, Mary
  See Freeman, Mary Eleanor Wilkins

Willard, Nancy   1936-........... **CLC 7, 37**
  See also CA 89-92; CANR 10, 39; CLR 5;
  DLB 5, 52; MAICYA; MTCW;
  SATA 37, 71; SATA-Brief 30

Williams, C(harles) K(enneth)
  1936- .... **CLC 33, 56; DAM POET**
  See also CA 37-40R; CAAS 26; CANR 57;
  DLB 5

Williams, Charles
  See Collier, James L(incoln)

Williams, Charles (Walter Stansby)
  1886-1945 .... **TCLC 1, 11**
  See also CA 104; DLB 100, 153

Williams, (George) Emlyn
  1905-1987 ...... **CLC 15; DAM DRAM**
  See also CA 104; 123; CANR 36; DLB 10,
  77; MTCW

Williams, Hugo   1942-............. **CLC 42**
  See also CA 17-20R; CANR 45; DLB 40

Williams, J. Walker
  See Wodehouse, P(elham) G(renville)

Williams, John A(lfred)
  1925- ... **CLC 5, 13; BLC; DAM MULT**
  See also BW 2; CA 53-56; CAAS 3;
  CANR 6, 26, 51; DLB 2, 33;
  INT CANR-6

Williams, Jonathan (Chamberlain)
  1929- .... **CLC 13**
  See also CA 9-12R; CAAS 12; CANR 8;
  DLB 5

Williams, Joy   1944-............. **CLC 31**
  See also CA 41-44R; CANR 22, 48

Williams, Norman   1952-.......... **CLC 39**
  See also CA 118

Williams, Sherley Anne
  1944- ..... **CLC 89; BLC; DAM MULT,**
                                    POET
  See also BW 2; CA 73-76; CANR 25;
  DLB 41; INT CANR-25; SATA 78

Williams, Shirley
  See Williams, Sherley Anne

Williams, Tennessee
  1911-1983 ..... **CLC 1, 2, 5, 7, 8, 11, 15,**
                    19, 30, 39, 45, 71; DA; DAB; DAC;
                    DAM DRAM, MST; DC 4; WLC
  See also AITN 1, 2; CA 5-8R; 108;
  CABS 3; CANR 31; CDALB 1941-1968;
  DLB 7; DLBD 4; DLBY 83; MTCW

Williams, Thomas (Alonzo)
  1926-1990 .... **CLC 14**
  See also CA 1-4R; 132; CANR 2

Williams, William C.
  See Williams, William Carlos

Williams, William Carlos
  1883-1963 .... **CLC 1, 2, 5, 9, 13, 22, 42,**
                    67; DA; DAB; DAC; DAM MST, POET;
                                    PC 7
  See also CA 89-92; CANR 34;
  CDALB 1917-1929; DLB 4, 16, 54, 86;
  MTCW

Williamson, David (Keith)   1942-.... **CLC 56**
  See also CA 103; CANR 41

Williamson, Ellen Douglas   1905-1984
  See Douglas, Ellen
  See also CA 17-20R; 114; CANR 39

Williamson, Jack.................. **CLC 29**
  See also Williamson, John Stewart
  See also CAAS 8; DLB 8

Williamson, John Stewart   1908-
  See Williamson, Jack
  See also CA 17-20R; CANR 23

Willie, Frederick
  See Lovecraft, H(oward) P(hillips)

Willingham, Calder (Baynard, Jr.)
  1922-1995 .... **CLC 5, 51**
  See also CA 5-8R; 147; CANR 3; DLB 2,
  44; MTCW

Willis, Charles
  See Clarke, Arthur C(harles)

Willy
  See Colette, (Sidonie-Gabrielle)

Willy, Colette
  See Colette, (Sidonie-Gabrielle)

Wilson, A(ndrew) N(orman)   1950- .. **CLC 33**
  See also CA 112; 122; DLB 14, 155

Wilson, Angus (Frank Johnstone)
  1913-1991 .. **CLC 2, 3, 5, 25, 34; SSC 21**
  See also CA 5-8R; 134; CANR 21; DLB 15,
  139, 155; MTCW

Wilson, August
  1945- .... **CLC 39, 50, 63; BLC; DA;**
                    DAB; DAC; DAM DRAM, MST,
                    MULT; DC 2; WLCS
  See also AAYA 16; BW 2; CA 115; 122;
  CANR 42, 54; MTCW

Wilson, Brian   1942-.............. **CLC 12**

Wilson, Colin   1931-............. **CLC 3, 14**
  See also CA 1-4R; CAAS 5; CANR 1, 22,
  33; DLB 14; MTCW

Wilson, Dirk
  See Pohl, Frederik

Wilson, Edmund
  1895-1972 .... **CLC 1, 2, 3, 8, 24**
  See also CA 1-4R; 37-40R; CANR 1, 46;
  DLB 63; MTCW

Wilson, Ethel Davis (Bryant)
    1888(?)-1980 .... CLC 13; DAC;
                                    DAM POET
    See also CA 102; DLB 68; MTCW

Wilson, John 1785-1854......... NCLC 5

Wilson, John (Anthony) Burgess 1917-1993
    See Burgess, Anthony
    See also CA 1-4R; 143; CANR 2, 46; DAC;
    DAM NOV; MTCW

Wilson, Lanford
    1937- ..... CLC 7, 14, 36; DAM DRAM
    See also CA 17-20R; CABS 3; CANR 45;
    DLB 7

Wilson, Robert M. 1944-......... CLC 7, 9
    See also CA 49-52; CANR 2, 41; MTCW

Wilson, Robert McLiam 1964- ..... CLC 59
    See also CA 132

Wilson, Sloan 1920-.............. CLC 32
    See also CA 1-4R; CANR 1, 44

Wilson, Snoo 1948-.............. CLC 33
    See also CA 69-72

Wilson, William S(mith) 1932- ..... CLC 49
    See also CA 81-84

Wilson, Woodrow 1856-1924..... TCLC 73
    See also DLB 47

Winchilsea, Anne (Kingsmill) Finch Counte
    1661-1720 .... LC 3

Windham, Basil
    See Wodehouse, P(elham) G(renville)

Wingrove, David (John) 1954-...... CLC 68
    See also CA 133

Wintergreen, Jane
    See Duncan, Sara Jeannette

Winters, Janet Lewis .... CLC 41
    See also Lewis, Janet
    See also DLBY 87

Winters, (Arthur) Yvor
    1900-1968 .... CLC 4, 8, 32
    See also CA 11-12; 25-28R; CAP 1;
    DLB 48; MTCW

Winterson, Jeanette
    1959-............ CLC 64; DAM POP
    See also CA 136; CANR 58

Winthrop, John 1588-1649......... LC 31
    See also DLB 24, 30

Wiseman, Frederick 1930-........ CLC 20
    See also CA 159

Wister, Owen 1860-1938 .... TCLC 21
    See also CA 108; DLB 9, 78; SATA 62

Witkacy
    See Witkiewicz, Stanislaw Ignacy

Witkiewicz, Stanislaw Ignacy
    1885-1939 .... TCLC 8
    See also CA 105

Wittgenstein, Ludwig (Josef Johann)
    1889-1951 .... TCLC 59
    See also CA 113

Wittig, Monique 1935(?)-......... CLC 22
    See also CA 116; 135; DLB 83

Wittlin, Jozef 1896-1976 .... CLC 25
    See also CA 49-52; 65-68; CANR 3

Wodehouse, P(elham) G(renville)
    1881-1975 ... CLC 1, 2, 5, 10, 22; DAB;
                        DAC; DAM NOV; SSC 2
    See also AITN 2; CA 45-48; 57-60;
    CANR 3, 33; CDBLB 1914-1945;
    DLB 34, 162; MTCW; SATA 22

Woiwode, L.
    See Woiwode, Larry (Alfred)

Woiwode, Larry (Alfred) 1941-... CLC 6, 10
    See also CA 73-76; CANR 16; DLB 6;
    INT CANR-16

Wojciechowska, Maia (Teresa)
    1927-...................... CLC 26
    See also AAYA 8; CA 9-12R; CANR 4, 41;
    CLR 1; JRDA; MAICYA; SAAS 1;
    SATA 1, 28, 83

Wolf, Christa 1929- .... CLC 14, 29, 58
    See also CA 85-88; CANR 45; DLB 75;
    MTCW

Wolfe, Gene (Rodman)
    1931-............ CLC 25; DAM POP
    See also CA 57-60; CAAS 9; CANR 6, 32,
    60; DLB 8

Wolfe, George C. 1954-........... CLC 49
    See also CA 149

Wolfe, Thomas (Clayton)
    1900-1938 ..... TCLC 4, 13, 29, 61; DA;
        DAB; DAC; DAM MST, NOV; WLC
    See also CA 104; 132; CDALB 1929-1941;
    DLB 9, 102; DLBD 2, 16; DLBY 85;
    MTCW

Wolfe, Thomas Kennerly, Jr. 1931-
    See Wolfe, Tom
    See also CA 13-16R; CANR 9, 33;
    DAM POP; INT CANR-9; MTCW

Wolfe, Tom .... CLC 1, 2, 9, 15, 35, 51
    See also Wolfe, Thomas Kennerly, Jr.
    See also AAYA 8; AITN 2; BEST 89:1;
    DLB 152

Wolff, Geoffrey (Ansell) 1937- ..... CLC 41
    See also CA 29-32R; CANR 29, 43

Wolff, Sonia
    See Levitin, Sonia (Wolff)

Wolff, Tobias (Jonathan Ansell)
    1945-.................... CLC 39, 64
    See also AAYA 16; BEST 90:2; CA 114;
    117; CAAS 22; CANR 54; DLB 130;
    INT 117

Wolfram von Eschenbach
    c. 1170-c. 1220 .... CMLC 5
    See also DLB 138

Wolitzer, Hilma 1930-............ CLC 17
    See also CA 65-68; CANR 18, 40;
    INT CANR-18; SATA 31

Wollstonecraft, Mary 1759-1797...... LC 5
    See also CDBLB 1789-1832; DLB 39, 104,
    158

Wonder, Stevie .... CLC 12
    See also Morris, Steveland Judkins

Wong, Jade Snow 1922-........... CLC 17
    See also CA 109

Woodberry, George Edward
    1855-1930 .... TCLC 73
    See also DLB 71, 103

Woodcott, Keith
    See Brunner, John (Kilian Houston)

Woodruff, Robert W.
    See Mencken, H(enry) L(ouis)

Woolf, (Adeline) Virginia
    1882-1941 .... TCLC 1, 5, 20, 43, 56;
                DA; DAB; DAC; DAM MST, NOV;
                                    SSC 7; WLC
    See also CA 104; 130; CDBLB 1914-1945;
    DLB 36, 100, 162; DLBD 10; MTCW

Woollcott, Alexander (Humphreys)
    1887-1943 .... TCLC 5
    See also CA 105; DLB 29

Woolrich, Cornell 1903-1968....... CLC 77
    See also Hopley-Woolrich, Cornell George

Wordsworth, Dorothy
    1771-1855 .... NCLC 25
    See also DLB 107

Wordsworth, William
    1770-1850 .... NCLC 12, 38; DA; DAB;
        DAC; DAM MST, POET; PC 4; WLC
    See also CDBLB 1789-1832; DLB 93, 107

Wouk, Herman
    1915- .. CLC 1, 9, 38; DAM NOV, POP
    See also CA 5-8R; CANR 6, 33; DLBY 82;
    INT CANR-6; MTCW

Wright, Charles (Penzel, Jr.)
    1935-.................. CLC 6, 13, 28
    See also CA 29-32R; CAAS 7; CANR 23,
    36, 62; DLB 165; DLBY 82; MTCW

Wright, Charles Stevenson
    1932-................ CLC 49; BLC 3;
                            DAM MULT, POET
    See also BW 1; CA 9-12R; CANR 26;
    DLB 33

Wright, Jack R.
    See Harris, Mark

Wright, James (Arlington)
    1927-1980 .... CLC 3, 5, 10, 28;
                                    DAM POET
    See also AITN 2; CA 49-52; 97-100;
    CANR 4, 34; DLB 5, 169; MTCW

Wright, Judith (Arandell)
    1915-............. CLC 11, 53; PC 14
    See also CA 13-16R; CANR 31; MTCW;
    SATA 14

Wright, L(aurali) R. 1939-........ CLC 44
    See also CA 138

Wright, Richard (Nathaniel)
    1908-1960 .... CLC 1, 3, 4, 9, 14, 21, 48,
        74; BLC; DA; DAB; DAC; DAM MST,
                        MULT, NOV; SSC 2; WLC
    See also AAYA 5; BW 1; CA 108;
    CDALB 1929-1941; DLB 76, 102;
    DLBD 2; MTCW

Wright, Richard B(ruce) 1937- ...... CLC 6
    See also CA 85-88; DLB 53

Wright, Rick 1945-............... CLC 35

Wright, Rowland
    See Wells, Carolyn

Wright, Stephen Caldwell 1946- .... CLC 33
    See also BW 2

Wright, Willard Huntington 1888-1939
    See Van Dine, S. S.
    See also CA 115; DLBD 16

Wright, William 1930-............ CLC 44
    See also CA 53-56; CANR 7, 23

Wroth, LadyMary 1587-1653(?) ..... **LC 30**
See also DLB 121

Wu Ch'eng-en 1500(?)-1582(?) .... **LC 7**

Wu Ching-tzu 1701-1754 .... **LC 2**

Wurlitzer, Rudolph 1938(?)- ... **CLC 2, 4, 15**
See also CA 85-88; DLB 173

Wycherley, William
1641-1715 ..... **LC 8, 21; DAM DRAM**
See also CDBLB 1660-1789; DLB 80

Wylie, Elinor (Morton Hoyt)
1885-1928 .... **TCLC 8**
See also CA 105; DLB 9, 45

Wylie, Philip (Gordon) 1902-1971... **CLC 43**
See also CA 21-22; 33-36R; CAP 2; DLB 9

Wyndham, John. .... **CLC 19**
See also Harris, John (Wyndham Parkes
Lucas) Beynon

Wyss, Johann David Von
1743-1818 .... **NCLC 10**
See also JRDA; MAICYA; SATA 29;
SATA-Brief 27

Xenophon
c. 430B.C.-c. 354B.C. .... **CMLC 17**
See also DLB 176

Yakumo Koizumi
See Hearn, (Patricio) Lafcadio (Tessima
Carlos)

Yanez, Jose Donoso
See Donoso (Yanez), Jose

Yanovsky, Basile S.
See Yanovsky, V(assily) S(emenovich)

Yanovsky, V(assily) S(emenovich)
1906-1989 .... **CLC 2, 18**
See also CA 97-100; 129

Yates, Richard 1926-1992 ..... **CLC 7, 8, 23**
See also CA 5-8R; 139; CANR 10, 43;
DLB 2; DLBY 81, 92; INT CANR-10

Yeats, W. B.
See Yeats, William Butler

Yeats, William Butler
1865-1939 ..... **TCLC 1, 11, 18, 31; DA;
DAB; DAC; DAM DRAM, MST,
POET; WLC**
See also CA 104; 127; CANR 45;
CDBLB 1890-1914; DLB 10, 19, 98, 156;
MTCW

Yehoshua, A(braham) B.
1936- .... **CLC 13, 31**
See also CA 33-36R; CANR 43

Yep, Laurence Michael 1948- ...... **CLC 35**
See also AAYA 5; CA 49-52; CANR 1, 46;
CLR 3, 17; DLB 52; JRDA; MAICYA;
SATA 7, 69

Yerby, Frank G(arvin)
1916-1991 .... **CLC 1, 7, 22; BLC;
DAM MULT**
See also BW 1; CA 9-12R; 136; CANR 16,
52; DLB 76; INT CANR-16; MTCW

Yesenin, Sergei Alexandrovich
See Esenin, Sergei (Alexandrovich)

Yevtushenko, Yevgeny (Alexandrovich)
1933- .... **CLC 1, 3, 13, 26, 51;
DAM POET**
See also CA 81-84; CANR 33, 54; MTCW

Yezierska, Anzia 1885(?)-1970 ..... **CLC 46**
See also CA 126; 89-92; DLB 28; MTCW

Yglesias, Helen 1915-........... **CLC 7, 22**
See also CA 37-40R; CAAS 20; CANR 15;
INT CANR-15; MTCW

Yokomitsu Riichi 1898-1947 ...... **TCLC 47**

Yonge, Charlotte (Mary)
1823-1901 .... **TCLC 48**
See also CA 109; DLB 18, 163; SATA 17

York, Jeremy
See Creasey, John

York, Simon
See Heinlein, Robert A(nson)

Yorke, Henry Vincent 1905-1974 ... **CLC 13**
See also Green, Henry
See also CA 85-88; 49-52

Yosano Akiko 1878-1942 .. **TCLC 59; PC 11**

Yoshimoto, Banana .... **CLC 84**
See also Yoshimoto, Mahoko

Yoshimoto, Mahoko 1964-
See Yoshimoto, Banana
See also CA 144

Young, Al(bert James)
1939- ..... **CLC 19; BLC; DAM MULT**
See also BW 2; CA 29-32R; CANR 26;
DLB 33

Young, Andrew (John) 1885-1971.... **CLC 5**
See also CA 5-8R; CANR 7, 29

Young, Collier
See Bloch, Robert (Albert)

Young, Edward 1683-1765........ **LC 3, 40**
See also DLB 95

Young, Marguerite (Vivian)
1909-1995 .... **CLC 82**
See also CA 13-16; 150; CAP 1

Young, Neil 1945-................ **CLC 17**
See also CA 110

Young Bear, Ray A.
1950- .... **CLC 94; DAM MULT**
See also CA 146; DLB 175; NNAL

Yourcenar, Marguerite
1903-1987 .... **CLC 19, 38, 50, 87;
DAM NOV**
See also CA 69-72; CANR 23, 60; DLB 72;
DLBY 88; MTCW

Yurick, Sol 1925-................ **CLC 6**
See also CA 13-16R; CANR 25

Zabolotskii, Nikolai Alekseevich
1903-1958 .... **TCLC 52**
See also CA 116

Zamiatin, Yevgenii
See Zamyatin, Evgeny Ivanovich

Zamora, Bernice (B. Ortiz)
1938- ..... **CLC 89; DAM MULT; HLC**
See also CA 151; DLB 82; HW

Zamyatin, Evgeny Ivanovich
1884-1937 .... **TCLC 8, 37**
See also CA 105

Zangwill, Israel 1864-1926........ **TCLC 16**
See also CA 109; DLB 10, 135

Zappa, Francis Vincent, Jr. 1940-1993
See Zappa, Frank
See also CA 108; 143; CANR 57

Zappa, Frank .... **CLC 17**
See also Zappa, Francis Vincent, Jr.

Zaturenska, Marya 1902-1982.... **CLC 6, 11**
See also CA 13-16R; 105; CANR 22

Zeami 1363-1443................... **DC 7**

Zelazny, Roger (Joseph)
1937-1995 .... **CLC 21**
See also AAYA 7; CA 21-24R; 148;
CANR 26, 60; DLB 8; MTCW;
SATA 57; SATA-Brief 39

Zhdanov, Andrei A(lexandrovich)
1896-1948 .... **TCLC 18**
See also CA 117

Zhukovsky, Vasily 1783-1852 .... **NCLC 35**

Ziegenhagen, Eric .... **CLC 55**

Zimmer, Jill Schary
See Robinson, Jill

Zimmerman, Robert
See Dylan, Bob

Zindel, Paul
1936- ..... **CLC 6, 26; DA; DAB; DAC;
DAM DRAM, MST, NOV; DC 5**
See also AAYA 2; CA 73-76; CANR 31;
CLR 3, 45; DLB 7, 52; JRDA; MAICYA;
MTCW; SATA 16, 58

Zinov'Ev, A. A.
See Zinoviev, Alexander (Aleksandrovich)

Zinoviev, Alexander (Aleksandrovich)
1922-..................... **CLC 19**
See also CA 116; 133; CAAS 10

Zoilus
See Lovecraft, H(oward) P(hillips)

Zola, Emile (Edouard Charles Antoine)
1840-1902 ...... **TCLC 1, 6, 21, 41; DA;
DAB; DAC; DAM MST, NOV; WLC**
See also CA 104; 138; DLB 123

Zoline, Pamela 1941-............. **CLC 62**

Zorrilla y Moral, Jose 1817-1893 .. **NCLC 6**

Zoshchenko, Mikhail (Mikhailovich)
1895-1958 .... **TCLC 15; SSC 15**
See also CA 115; 160

Zuckmayer, Carl 1896-1977........ **CLC 18**
See also CA 69-72; DLB 56, 124

Zuk, Georges
See Skelton, Robin

Zukofsky, Louis
1904-1978 .... **CLC 1, 2, 4, 7, 11, 18;
DAM POET; PC 11**
See also CA 9-12R; 77-80; CANR 39;
DLB 5, 165; MTCW

Zweig, Paul 1935-1984........ **CLC 34, 42**
See also CA 85-88; 113

Zweig, Stefan 1881-1942 .... **TCLC 17**
See also CA 112; DLB 81, 118

Zwingli, Huldreich 1484-1531....... **LC 37**
See also DLB 179

Literary Criticism Series
Cumulative Topic Index

This index lists all topic entries in Gale's *Classical and Medieval Literature Criticism, Contemporary Literary Criticism, Literature Criticism from 1400 to 1800, Nineteenth-Century Literature Criticism,* and *Twentieth-Century Literary Criticism.*

Topic Index

Topic Index

Topic Index

CMLC Cumulative Nationality Index

CMLC Cumulative Title Index

Title Index

Title Index

Title Index

Title Index

CMLC Cumulative Critic Index

Critic Index

Croce, Benedetto
  Inferno 3:58
  Plato 8:269
  Terence 14:326

Croiset, Maurice
  Aristophanes 4:70

Crombie, A. C.
  Bacon, Roger 14:79

Crump, M. Marjorie
  Ovid 7:314

Cruttwell, Charles Thomas
  Cato, Marcus Porcius 21:22

Cumming, William Patterson
  St. Birgitta 24:89

Cummings, Hubertis M.
  Boccaccio, Giovanni 13:87

Cunliffe, John W.
  Seneca, Lucius Annaeus
    6:339

Cunningham, Stanley B.
  Albert the Great 16:43, 65

Curley III, Thomas F.
  Boethius 15:97

Curtius, Ernst Robert
  Aeneid 9:345, 376
  Augustine, St. 6:56
  Hermogenes 6:158
  Inferno 3:98

Dahlberg, Charles
  Romance of the Rose 8:414

Dall, Caroline H.
  Sordello 15:328

D'Alton, Rev. J. F.
  Cicero, Marcus Tullius
    3:207

Damon, S. Foster
  Marie de France 8:120

Dandekar, R. N.
  Mahabharata 5:227

Dane, Joseph A.
  Mystery of Adam 4:216

Danielou, Jean
  Origen 19:206

Darrow, Clarence
  Khayyam 11:274

Dashti, Ali
  Khayyam 11:280

Davenport, Guy
  Sappho 3:471

Davenport, W. A.
  Sir Gawain and the Green Knight
    2:273

David, E.
  Aristophanes 4:174

Davidson, A. B.
  The Book of Job 14:138

Davidson, Herbert A.
  Avicenna 16:147

Davidson, Thomas
  Sappho 3:388

Davies, James
  Catullus 18:73

Davis, J. Cary
  Poem of the Cid 4:260

Davis, Scott
  Kalevala 6:278

Dawson, Christopher
  Bacon, Roger 14:65

De Boer, T. J.
  Averroes 7:7

De Chasca, Edmund
  Poem of the Cid 4:295

De la Mare, Walter
  Arabian Nights 2:35

De Ley, Margo
  Razon de Amor 16:347

De Quincey, Thomas
  Arabian Nights 2:8
  Herodotus 17:54
  Iliad 1:294
  Odyssey 16:197
  Sophocles 2:309

De Sanctis, Francesco
  Boccaccio, Giovanni 13:
    17
  Inferno 3:23, 31

De Vere, Aubrey
  Poem of the Cid 4:229
  The Song of Roland 1:163

De Vericour, Professor
  Poem of the Cid 4:225

De Vogel, C. J.
  Pythagoras 22:288

Dean, Christopher
  Arthurian Legend 10:65
  Morte Arthure 10:431

Demetillo, Ricaredo
  Murasaki, Lady 1:429

Den Boer, W.
  Thucydides 17:302

DeWitt, Norman Wentworth
  Epicurus 21:144

Deyermond, A. D.
  Poem of the Cid 4:289

Diamond, Robert E.
  The Dream of the Rood
    14:236

Dill, Samuel
  Juvenal 8:26
  Seneca, Lucius Annaeus 6:345

Dimler, G. Richard
  Wolfram von Eschenbach
    5:344

Dinsmore, Charles Allen
  Iliad 1:326

Dionysius of Halicarnassus
  Sappho 3:379
  Thucydides 17:209
  Xenophon 17:329

Disraeli, Issac
  Beowulf 1:56

Dobson, J. F.
  Demosthenes 13:141

Dodds, E. R.
  Augustine, St. 6:21

Dodsley, Robert
  Aesop 24:8

Dole, Nathan Haskell
  Petrarch 20:229

Donner, Morton
  Sir Gawain and the Green Knight
    2:224

Donohoe, Joseph I., Jr.
  The Song of Roland 1:228

Donovan, Mortimer J.
  Marie de France 8:145

Doolittle, Hilda
  Sappho 3:432

Dorfman, Eugene
  Poem of the Cid 4:271

Dover, K. J.
  Aristophanes 4:147, 159
  Demosthenes 13:185

Driberg, J. H.
  Aesop 24:19

Dronke, Peter
  Abelard 11:39
  Hildegard von Bingen
    20:143

Dryden, John
  Aeneid 9:300
  Apuleius 1:7
  Iliad 1:282
  Juvenal 8:5
  Ovid 7:291
  Pindar 12:258

Ducharme, Leonard
  Albert the Great 16:86

Duckett, Eleanor Shipley
  Bede 20:42
  Boethius 15:23

Duckworth, George E.
  Terence 14:337

Duclow, Donald F.
  Meister Eckhart 9:70

Duff, J. Wight
  Cicero, Marcus Tullius 3:197
  Juvenal 8:34
  Livy 11:336
  Terence 14:305

Duff, Mountstuart E. Grant
  Polybius 17:152

Duggan, Joseph J.
  Poem of the Cid 4:312

Dumezil, Georges
  Mahabharata 5:254

Dunlop, John
  Cato, Marcus Porcius 21:17

Dunn, Charles W.
  Romance of the Rose 8;417

Dunne, M.A.
  Sordello 15:339

Durling, Robert M.
  Petrarch 20:270

Earle, John
  Beowulf 1:57

Easton, Stewart C.
  Bacon, Roger 14:73

Eaton, John H.
  The Book of Psalms 4:438

Ebenstein, William
  Cicero, Marcus Tullius 3:251

Echard, Lawrence
  Terence 14:297

Eckermann, Johann Peter
  Longus 7:217
  Sophocles 2:303

Eckhart, Meister
  Meister Eckhart 9:24

Eckstein, A. M.
  Polybius 17:192

Edgerton, Franklin
  Kalidasa 9:113

Edgren, A. Hjalmar
  Kalidasa 9:87

Edmonds, J. M.
  Longus 7:220

Edwards, Bateman
  Aesop 24:20

Critic Index

Critic Index

Critic Index

Critic Index

Critic Index